STRATEGIC MANAGEMENT

—

CONCEPTS AND CASES

STRATEGIC MANAGEMENT

—

CONCEPTS AND CASES

SIXTH EDITION

ARTHUR A. THOMPSON, JR.

A.J. STRICKLAND III

BOTH OF
THE UNIVERSITY OF ALABAMA

IRWIN
HOMEWOOD, IL 60430
BOSTON, MA 02116

Sponsoring editor: Karen Johnson
Developmental editor: Elizabeth Rubenstein
Project editor: Waivah Clement
Production manager: Bette K. Ittersagen
Designer: Tara L. Bazata
Cover designer: Lori Siebert
Art manager: Kim Meriwether
Artist: Arcata Graphics
Compositor: Weimer Typesetting Co., Inc.
Typeface: 10.5/12 Palatino
Printer: Von Hoffmann Press

Library of Congress Cataloging-in-Publication Data
Thompson, Arthur A., 1940-
    Strategic management : concepts and cases / Arthur A. Thompson,
Jr., A. J. Strickland III.—6th ed.
        p.   cm.
    ISBN 0-256-09698-8; 0-256-10808-0 (International student edition);
0-256-10941-9 (STRAT–ANALYST™ IBM® PC version); 0-256-10942-7
(STRAT–ANALYST™ IBM® PS/2® version)
    1. Strategic planning.   2. Strategic planning—Case studies.
I. Strickland. A. J. (Alonzo J.)   II. Title.
    HD32.28.T53   1992
    658.4′012—dc20   91–28614

Printed in the United States of America
1 2 3 4 5 6 7 8 9 0 VH 9 8 7 6 5 4 3 2

To Hasseline and Kitty

Preface

We've left no stone unturned in making the sixth edition better than the fifth and trying to reach the ultimate standard of effectively covering what every student needs to know about strategic management. There are significant enhancements in the chapter presentations, 28 new cases (6 with accompanying videos), new case analysis software, new features in the companion global business simulation game, a comprehensively updated edition of the readings book, and across-the-board improvements in the instructional supplements. We've strived to make every piece of the teaching package—text, cases, simulation game, case analysis software, the readings book, color transparencies and transparency masters, and *Instructor's Manual*—more effective, more appealing, and easier to use.

WHAT'S NEW IN THE TEXT CHAPTERS

Ongoing advances in the strategic management literature mandate important edition-to-edition changes to incorporate new concepts and analytical tools and keep the presentation close to the cutting edge. In this edition, we have (1) expanded and strengthened the discussion of global issues in strategic management, (2) added new sections dealing with best-cost producer strategies, strategic alliances, the concept of strategic intent, core competencies, profit sanctuaries, economies of scope, and several other topics, and (3) created a series of margin inserts for each chapter to draw prominent attention to strategic management principles, basic concepts, and major conclusions. Judicious rewriting to achieve better economy of presentation has allowed us to include all the new material without adding more pages for students to read.

While the organization of the text chapters parallels that of the last edition, we've made some noteworthy refinements in both content and emphasis:

- Chapters 1 and 2 contain new discussions of a company's need for both strategic objectives and financial objectives, the role of each in the strategic management process, and the trade-offs between actions to strengthen long-term competitive position and actions to improve short-term financial performance.

- The strategic role and relevance of a company's *core competences* have been woven into the discussions of company strengths, crafting strategy around what a company does best, and building a capable organization (Chapters 2, 4, and 9).

- To help students tell the difference between good and bad strategies, we've added a section on the tests of a winning strategy (Chapter 2).

- A new section describing how to build sustainable competitive advantage via a strategy of being a *best-cost producer* (as opposed to a low-cost producer) has been added to Chapter 5.

- There are expanded and improved treatments of multicountry (or *multidomestic*) competition versus global competition, the pros and cons of strategic alliances, the ways to achieve competitive advantage with a global strategy, and how global competitors can build profit sanctuaries and use cross-subsidization to outcompete domestic competitors (Chapter 6).

- To draw together the main lessons from the three-chapter module on business strategy, we've added a summary section that presents 13 "commandments" for successful strategy-making in single-business enterprises (Chapter 6).

- How diversified multinational enterprises can rely upon *economies of scope* and cross-subsidization to gain competitive advantage over single-business domestic firms is prominently featured in Chapter 7.

- Chapter 7 also contains new treatments of how to test whether diversification builds shareholder value and of the relationship between strategic fit, economies of scope, and competitive advantage.

- In Chapter 8, we've added more methodological detail in the explanations of how to compare industry attractiveness and business-unit strength in diversified companies.

- There's updated and expanded coverage of how shared values, ethical considerations, and corporate social responsibility enter into the process of crafting and implementing strategy (Chapters 2 and 10).

- There are eight new Illustration Capsules.

The most visible addition to the chapters is the use of "margin notes" high-lighting basic concepts, major conclusions, and "core truths" about strategic behavior in competitive markets. Most of these notes represent an effort to distill the subject matter into a series of concise "principles" expressing what every student should know about strategic management. Our purpose in preparing these margin notes was to bring the text discussion into sharper focus for readers, point them more directly to what is important, and do a better job of helping them learn to think strategically.

All in all, more effort has gone into improving content, clarity, and style than in any previous edition. As a result, we believe you will find the material crisply written, forcefully presented, comfortably mainstream, and as close to the frontiers of theory and practice as a basic textbook should be.

THE COLLECTION OF CASES

Of the 40 cases selected for this edition, 26 are new and 2 of the holdovers (Nucor and Wal-Mart) have been so extensively recast and updated as to turn them into new cases. As before, we have grouped the cases into five sections. In the first section, 6 cases spotlight the role and tasks of the manager as chief strategy-maker and chief strategy-implementer. The second section, consisting of 14 cases, deals with analyzing and crafting business-level strategy. There are 5 cases involving corporate diversification situations. A 10-case grouping covers the ins and outs of implementing strategy. The last section contains 5 cases highlighting the links between strategy, ethics, and social responsibility. Scattered throughout the lineup are 16 cases concerning international companies, globally competitive industries, and cross-cultural situations; these cases, in conjunction with the more globalized content of the text chapters, give this edition a timely international flavor—in keeping with real-world events and new AACSB standards. Six cases have videotape segments for use during the class discussion. Then there are 4 cases involving firms listed in *The 100 Best Companies to Work For in America,* 3 cases about young start-up companies, 12 cases dealing with the strategic problems of family-owned or relatively small entrepreneurial businesses, 3 cases on nonprofit organizations, and 22 cases involving public companies about which students can do further research in the library.

We have continued our traditional practice of choosing cases that feature interesting products and companies and that will provoke lively classroom discussions. At least 22 of the cases involve companies, products, or people that students will have heard of or will know about from personal experience. The case researchers whose work appears in this edition have done a first-rate job of preparing cases that contain valuable teaching points, that illustrate the important kinds of strategic challenges managers face, and that allow students to apply the tools of strategic analysis. We believe you will find the case collection in this edition chock full of interest, effective in the classroom, and tightly linked to the text treatments in Chapters 1 through 10. Quite possibly, this is the most exciting and diverse lineup of cases—from beginning to end—we've ever been able to assemble.

THE BUSINESS STRATEGY GAME OPTION

Version one of *The Business Strategy Game* was very well received and provoked renewed interest in PC-based simulations. The second version, which accompanies this edition, has many new features that make the use of a simulation exercise in the strategy course even more appealing. Based on our experience of having used a simulation game every semester for the past 15 years, we are convinced that simulation games are the *single best exercise* available for helping students pull the pieces of the business puzzle together and giving them an integrated, capstone experience.

The Value a Simulation Adds   First and foremost, the exercise of running a simulated company over a number of decision periods helps develop students' business judgment. They learn about risk taking. They have to react to changing market conditions, study the actions of competitors, and weigh alternative courses of action. They get valuable practice in spotting market opportunities, evaluating threats to their company's well-being, and assessing the long-term consequences of short-term decisions. And by having to live with the decisions they make, they experience what it means to be accountable and responsible for achieving satisfactory results. All of these activities have a positive and meaningful impact on students' business acumen and managerial judgment.

Second, students learn an enormous amount from working with the numbers, exploring options, and trying to unite production, marketing, finance, and human resource decisions into a coherent strategy. The effect is to help students integrate a lot of material, look at decisions from the standpoint of the company as a whole, and see the importance of thinking strategically about a company's competitive position and future prospects. Since a simulation game is, by its very nature, a hands-on exercise, the lessons learned are forcefully planted in students' minds: the impact is far more lasting than what is remembered from lectures. Third, students' entrepreneurial instincts blossom as they get caught up in the competitive spirit of the game. The resulting entertainment value helps maintain an unusually high level of student motivation and emotional involvement in the course throughout the term.

We think you will find *The Business Strategy Game* a welcome course option. It will add a dimension to your course that can't be matched by any other teaching-learning tool. Moreover, with the aid of today's high-speed personal computers and the technical advances in software capability, there's minimal gear-up time on the instructor's part. You'll find that the time and effort required to administer *The Business Strategy Game* is well within tolerable limits.

About the Simulation The product for *The Business Strategy Game* is athletic footwear—chosen because it is a product students personally know about, buy themselves, and wear regularly. The industry setting is global; companies can manufacture and sell their brands in the United States, Europe, or Asia. Competition is head-to-head; each team of students must match its strategic wits against the other company teams. Companies can focus their efforts on one geographic market or two or all three; they can establish a one-country production base or they can manufacture in all three of the geographic markets. Demand conditions, tariffs, and wage rates vary from area to area.

The company that students manage has plants to operate, a work force to compensate, distribution expenses and inventories to control, capital expenditure decisions to make, marketing and sales campaigns to wage, sales forecasts to consider, and changes in exchange rates, interest rates, and the stock market to take into account. Students must evaluate whether to pursue a low-cost producer strategy, a differentiation strategy, or a focus strategy. They have to decide whether to produce "off-shore" in Asia where wage rates are very low or whether to avoid import tariffs and transocean shipping costs by having a producing base in every primary geographic market. And they must endeavor to maximize shareholder wealth via increased dividend payments and stock price appreciation. Each team of students is challenged to use its entrepreneurial and strategic skills to become the next Nike or Reebok and ride the wave of growth to the top of the worldwide athletic footwear industry.

There's a built-in planning and analysis feature that allows students to (1) craft a five-year strategic plan, (2) make five-year financial projections, (3) do all kinds of "what-iffing," (4) assess the revenue-cost-profit consequences of alternative strategic actions, and (5) develop a tentative five-year set of decisions (in effect, a five-year strategic plan) which can easily be revised and updated as the game unfolds. A special "Calc" feature allows all the number-crunching to be done in a matter of seconds.

The Business Strategy Game can be used with any IBM or compatible PC with 640K memory and it is suitable for both senior-level and MBA courses. The game is programmed to accommodate a wide variety of computer setups as concerns disk drives, monitors, and printers.

Features of the Second Edition   This latest version of *The Business Strategy Game* makes things easier and better for both the players and the game administrator:

- No longer is access to Lotus 1-2-3 (or any other spreadsheet software) required as a supporting tool for either players or game administrators. By completely eliminating the need for any kind of outside software supplement, we've cast aside a requirement that complicated the procedures and that proved inconvenient for some and burdensome for others.

- We've enhanced the visual appeal of the screens by using color throughout (something that will be appreciated by those with color monitors).

- The scoring algorithm has been reworked to include a "power rating" for each company's strategy. In addition, the stock price performance measure has been replaced with a stock value measure (stock price × number of shares outstanding) to create a more inclusive measure of how successful the players have been in boosting shareholder value.

- The *Player's Manual* now has an index, and those parts of the manual that students found unclear have been rewritten to improve the explanations of how things work.

- We've recast the treatment of exchange rate fluctuations to impact costs rather than profits. The effect is to make the decision-making implications of exchange rate fluctuations more straightforward and understandable to students.

- A new manufacturing decision variable has been added to give companies another option for increasing the efficiency of existing plants over time. By making expenditures for *production methods improvement*, company managers can reduce production run set-up costs, cut supervision costs, and boost worker productivity.

- The company operations reports provide more extensive cost analysis figures, and the "Footwear Industry Report" provides more complete financial information for each company.

- Based on the experiences and suggestions of users, we've added print options for both dot-matrix and laser printers and reprogrammed several things to reduce the potential for glitches (disk problems and disk errors). We've improved the procedures for processing decisions and done all kinds of behind-the-scenes programming to make things run faster and more trouble-free on almost any kind of IBM or 100 percent-IBM compatible computer setup. Both players and game administrators will find Version 2.0 more user-friendly in virtually every respect.

At the same time, though, we've retained the features that made Version 1.0 so popular:

- Everything is done on disks. Students enter their decisions on disks and, during processing, a complete set of industry and company results is written back on the disks. It takes only a few minutes to collect the disks and return them. A printout of the industry scoreboard and a printout of the instructor's report are automatically generated during processing.

- Decisions can be processed in 40 minutes (less than 25 minutes on a fast PC); simple procedures allow most or all of the processing to be delegated to a student assistant.

- Students will find it convenient and uncomplicated to use the PC to play *The Business Strategy Game* even if they have had no prior exposure to PCs; *no programming of any kind is involved* and full instructions are presented in the *Player's Manual* and on the screens themselves.

- A scoreboard of company performance is automatically calculated each decision period. Instructors determine the weights to be given to each of six performance measures—revenues, after-tax profits, return on stockholders' investment, stock value, bond rating, and strategy rating. The overall performance score can be used to grade team performance.

- An *Instructor's Manual* describes how to integrate the game into your course, provides pointers on how to administer the game, and contains step-by-step processing instructions.

THE STRAT-ANALYST SOFTWARE OPTION

We introduced this optional supplement with the fourth edition as a way of incorporating the calculating power of PCs into the case analysis part of the strategic management course. It proved both popular and effective, and we've instituted another round of enhancements for this edition. The biggest change is eliminating the need for Lotus 1-2-3 to drive the STRAT-ANALYST disks. Everything that students need to use STRAT-ANALYST'S capabilities is now contained on the STRAT-ANALYST disks. This is a big plus, especially for students who have their own personal computers but don't have the Lotus 1-2-3 software package. It also opens the way for STRAT-ANALYST to gain acceptance at universities whose PC labs don't have the Lotus 1-2-3 package available for general use by students. A second change is the introduction of color screens to enhance visual appeal. STRAT-ANALYST works on all IBM or 100 percent-compatible personal computers with 640K memories.

This version of STRAT-ANALYST has three main sections. The first section contains preprogrammed, customized templates for each of 15 cases where substantial number-crunching is called for. With these templates, students can

- Obtain calculations showing financial ratios, profit margins and rates of return, common-size income statements and balance sheets, and annual compound rates of change.

- Calculate Altman's bankruptcy index (a method for predicting when a company may be headed into deep financial trouble).
- Do "What-If" scenarios and compare the projected outcomes for one strategic option versus another.
- Make five-year best-case, expected-case, and worst-case projections of financial performance using the what-if approach.
- Construct line graphs, bar graphs, pie charts, and scatter diagrams using any of the case data or calculations on file.
- Get report-ready printouts of all these calculations and graphs.

Not only is this section of STRAT-ANALYST a big time-saver for students but it also gets them into the habit of always looking at the story the numbers tell about a company's performance and situation. Since students can do a more systematic number-crunching analysis with STRAT-ANALYST than without it, instructors can insist on and expect thorough financial assessments. STRAT-ANALYST's graphing capabilities are particularly valuable to students in preparing written assignments and doing visual aids for oral presentations. The "What-If" features make it easier to quantify the effects of particular strategic actions and to examine the outcomes of alternative scenarios. Five-year projections of performance can be generated in less than 10 minutes.

The second section of STRAT-ANALYST features an easy-to-use, step-by-step generic procedure for using various analytical tools and doing situation analysis. The three-part menu includes:

- Industry and competitive situation analysis (keyed to Table 3–5 in the text).
- Company situation analysis (keyed to Table 4–4 in the text).
- Business portfolio analysis (keyed to Chapter 8's discussion of how to compare industry attractiveness and business strength in diversified firms).

Students can choose to use whatever situation analysis tools are appropriate and, when finished, get a neatly organized, final-copy printout of their analysis in a report format. (This report can then be conveniently graded by the instructor.) Hints for using each situational analysis tool are provided directly on STRAT-ANALYST to guide the student in the right direction. The benefit of these three menu options is that students are prompted to consider the full array of concepts and tools and to do a *systematic* situation analysis rather than trying to get by with spotty analysis and weakly justified opinions.

The third section offers two menu selections for developing action recommendations:

1. Action recommendations pertaining to strategy formulation— development of a basic strategic direction (mission and objectives), proposing an overall business strategy, specifying functional strategies, and recommending specific action steps to develop the strategy and gain competitive advantage.
2. Action recommendations for implementing/executing the chosen strategy and correcting whatever assortment of internal administrative and operating problems may exist.

Both selections walk students step-by-step through areas where actions may need to be taken. A "Hints" screen appears at each step.

The whole intent of the STRAT-ANALYST software package is to give students a major assist in doing higher-caliber strategic analysis and to cut the time that it takes them to do a thorough job of case preparation. It should also build student comfort levels and skills in the use of PCs for managerial analysis purposes. The instructor profits too—from improved student performance and from increased flexibility in varying the nature of case analysis assignments. Start-up instructions for STRAT-ANALYST are included here in the book (see pages 1102-1105); once the disks are booted up, all other directions needed by the user appear right on the screens.

THE READINGS BOOK OPTION

For instructors who want to incorporate samples of the strategic management literature into the course, a companion *Readings in Strategic Management* containing 43 selections is available. Twenty-six of the 43 readings are new to this edition. Over two-thirds have appeared since 1985. All are quite readable, and all are suitable for seniors and MBA students. Most of the selections are articles reprinted from leading journals; they add in-depth treatment to important topic areas covered in the text and put readers at the cutting edge of academic thinking and research on the subject. Some of the articles are drawn from practitioner sources and stress how particular tools and concepts relate directly to actual companies and managerial practices. Nine articles examine the role of the general manager and strategy; 10 articles concern strategic analysis and strategy formation at the business-unit level; 8 articles deal with strategy in diversified companies; 10 articles relate to various aspects of strategy implementation; and 6 articles are about strategy and ethics management. Eight of these articles deal with the international dimensions of strategic management. In tandem, the readings package provides an effective, efficient vehicle for reinforcing and expanding the text-case approach.

THE INSTRUCTOR'S PACKAGE

A full complement of instructional aids is available to assist adopters in using the sixth edition successfully. The *Instructor's Manual* contains suggestions for using the text materials, various approaches to course design and course organization, a sample syllabus, alternative course outlines, a thoroughly revised and expanded set of over 850 multiple-choice and essay questions, a comprehensive teaching note for each case, plus eight "classic" cases from previous editions. There is a computerized test bank for generating examinations, a set of color transparencies depicting the figures and tables in the 10 text chapters, and a package of lecture and transparency masters that thoroughly covers the text (concepts) part of the book and can be used to support the instructor's classroom presentations. To help instructors enrich and vary the pace of class discussions of cases, there are video supplements for use with the Campus Designs, Grand Theatre, Public Service Company of New Mexico, GM Allison-Japan, Utah Jazz, and Kentucky Fried Chicken in China cases.

In concert, the textbook, the three companion supplements, and the comprehensive instructor's package provide a complete, integrated lineup of teaching materials. The package offers wide latitude in course design, full access to the range of computer- assisted instructional techniques, an assortment of visual aids, and plenty of opportunity to keep the nature of student assignments varied and interesting. Our goal has been to give you everything you need to offer a course that is very much in keeping with the strategic management challenges and issues of the 1990s and that is capable of winning enthusiastic student approval.

ACKNOWLEDGMENTS

We have benefited from the help of many people during the evolution of this book. Students, adopters, and reviewers have generously supplied an untold number of insightful comments and helpful suggestions. Our intellectual debt to those academics, writers, and practicing managers who have blazed new trails in the strategy field will be obvious to any reader familiar with the literature of strategic management.

We are particularly indebted to the case researchers whose casewriting efforts appear herein and to the companies whose cooperation made the cases possible. To each one goes a very special thank-you. The importance of timely, carefully researched cases cannot be overestimated in contributing to a substantive study of strategic management issues and practices. From a research standpoint, cases in strategic management are invaluable in exposing the generic kinds of strategic issues which companies face, in forming hypotheses about strategic behavior, and in drawing experienced-based generalizations about the practice of strategic management. Pedagogically, cases about strategic management give students essential practice in diagnosing and evaluating strategic situations, in learning to use the tools and concepts of strategy analysis, in sorting through various strategic options, in crafting strategic action plans, and in figuring out successful ways to implement and execute the chosen strategy. Without a continuing stream of fresh, well-researched, and well-conceived cases, the discipline of strategic management would quickly fall into disrepair, losing much of its energy and excitement. There's no question, therefore, that first-class case research constitutes a valuable scholarly contribution.

The following reviewers made valuable contributions to the sixth edition: Tuck Bounds, Lee Burke, Ralph Catalanello, William Crittenden, Vince Luchsinger, Stan Mendenhall, John Moore, Will Mulvaney, Sandra Richard, Ralph Roberts, Thomas Turk, Gordon VonStroh, and Fred Zimmerman.

We are also indebted to S. A. Billion, Charles Byles, Gerald L. Geisler, Rose Knotts, Joseph Rosenstein, James B. Thurman, Ivan Able, W. Harvey Hegarty, Roger Evered, Charles B. Saunders, Rhae M. Swisher, Claude I. Shell, R. Thomas Lenz, Michael C. White, Dennis Callahan, R. Duane Ireland, William E. Burr, II, C. W. Millard, Richard Mann, Kurt Christensen, Neil W. Jacobs, Louis W. Fry, D. Robley Wood, George J. Gore, and William R. Soukup. These reviewers were of considerable help in directing our efforts at various stages in the evolution of the manuscript through the first five editions.

Naturally, as custom properly dictates, we are responsible for whatever errors of fact, deficiencies in coverage or in exposition, and oversights that remain. As always, we value your recommendations and thoughts about the book. Your comments regarding coverage and content will be most welcome, as will your calling our attention to specific errors. Please write us at P. O. Box 870225, Department of Management and Marketing, The University of Alabama, Tuscaloosa, Alabama 35487-0225.

Arthur A. Thompson, Jr.
A. J. Strickland III

A Special Note to Students

The ground that strategic management covers is challenging, wide-ranging, and exciting. The center of attention is *the total enterprise*—the environment in which it operates, the direction management intends to head, management's strategic plan for getting the enterprise moving in this direction, and the managerial tasks of implementing and executing the chosen strategy successfully. We'll be examining the foremost issue in running a business enterprise: What must managers do, and do well, to make the company a winner rather than a loser in the game of business?

The answer that emerges again and again, and which becomes the theme of the course is that good strategy making and good strategy implementing are always the most reliable signs of good management. The task of this course is to expose you to the reasons why good strategic management nearly always produces good company performance and to instruct you in the methods of crafting a well-conceived strategy and then successfully executing it.

During the course, you can expect to learn what the role and tasks of the strategy-maker are. You will grapple with what strategy means and with all the ramifications of figuring out which strategy is best in light of a company's overall situation. You will get a workout in sizing up a variety of industry and competitive situations, in using the tools of strategic analysis, in considering the pros and cons of strategic alternatives, and in crafting an attractive strategic plan. You will learn about the principal managerial tasks associated with implementing the chosen strategy successfully. You will become more skilled as a strategic thinker and you will develop your powers of business judgment. The excitement comes, believe it or not, from the extra savvy you will pick up about playing the game of business and from the blossoming of your entrepreneurial and competitive instincts.

In the midst of all this, another purpose is accomplished: to help you integrate and apply what you've learned in prior courses. Strategic management is a big picture course. It deals with the grand sweep of how to manage. Unlike your other business courses where the subject matter was narrowly aimed at a particular function or piece of the business—accounting, finance, marketing, production, human resources, or information systems—this course deals with the company's entire makeup and situation from both inside and outside.

Nothing is ignored or assumed away. The task is to arrive at solid judgments about how all the relevant factors add up. This makes strategic management an integrative, capstone course in which you reach back to use concepts and techniques covered in previous courses. For perhaps the first time you'll see how the various pieces of the business puzzle fit together and why the different parts of a business need to be managed in strategic harmony for the organization to operate in winning fashion.

No matter what your major is, the content of this course has all the ingredients to be the best course you've taken—best in the sense of learning a lot about business and holding your interest from beginning to end. Dig in, get involved, and make the most of what the course has to offer. As you tackle the subject matter, ponder Ralph Waldo Emerson's observation, "Commerce is a game of skill which many people play, but which few play well." What we've put between these covers is aimed squarely at helping you become a wiser, shrewder player. Good luck!

A. A. T.
A. J. S.

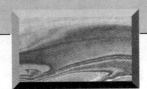

Contents in Brief

Contents

P A R T

II

CASES IN STRATEGIC
MANAGEMENT   277

P A R T

III

Instructions for Using the
STRAT-ANALYST™
Software Package   1101

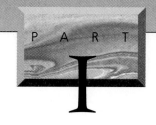

P A R T

I

The Concepts and Techniques of Strategic Management

The Strategic Management Process

"Cheshire Puss," she [Alice] began . . . "would you please tell me which way I ought
to go from here?"
"That depends on where you want to get to," said the cat.
Lewis Carroll

My job is to make sure the company has a strategy and that everybody follows it.
Kenneth H. Olsen
CEO, Digital Equipment Corp.

A strategy is a commitment to undertake one set of actions rather than another.
Sharon M. Oster
Professor, Yale University

This book is about the managerial tasks of crafting and implementing company strategies. *An organization's strategy consists of the moves and approaches devised by management to produce successful organization performance.* Strategy, in effect, is management's game plan for the business. Managers develop strategies to guide *how* an organization conducts its business and *how* it will achieve its target objectives. Without a strategy, there is no established course to follow, no roadmap to manage by, no cohesive action plan to produce the intended results.

Crafting and implementing a strategy for the business are *core* management functions. Among all the things that managers do, few affect organizational performance more lastingly than how well the management team handles the tasks of charting the organization's long-term direction, developing effective strategic moves and approaches, and then executing the strategy in ways that produce the intended results. Indeed, *good strategy and good implementation are the most trustworthy signs of good management.*

There is strong reason to associate "good management" with how well managers develop and execute strategy. Managers cannot be awarded a top grade for designing shrewd strategies but failing to carry them out well—weak implementation opens the door for organizational performance to fall short of full potential. Competent execution of a mediocre strategy scarcely qualifies managers for a gold-star award either. But powerful execution of a powerful strategy is a proven recipe for business success—the instances where a company with a well-conceived, well-executed strategy is unable to build a leading market position are few and far between. The standards for judging whether an organization is well managed, therefore, are grounded in good strategy-making *combined* with good strategy execution. The better conceived an organization's strategy and the more flawless its execution, the greater the chance that the organization will be a peak performer in its industry.

To qualify as excellently-managed, an organization must exhibit excellent execution of an excellent strategy.

However, superior strategy-making and strategy-implementing don't *guarantee superior organizational performance continuously.* Even well-managed organizations can hit the skids for short periods because of adverse conditions beyond management's ability to foresee or react to. But the bad luck of adverse events never excuses weak performance year after year. It is management's responsibility to adjust to negative conditions by undertaking strategic defenses and managerial approaches that can overcome adversity. Indeed, the essence of good strategy-making is to build a position strong and flexible enough to produce successful performance despite unforeseeable and unexpected external factors.

THE FIVE TASKS OF STRATEGIC MANAGEMENT

The strategy-making, strategy-implementing function of managers consists of five interrelated components:

1. *Developing a concept of the business and forming a vision of where the organization needs to be headed*—in effect, infusing the organization with a sense of purpose, providing long-term direction, and establishing a *mission.*
2. *Converting the mission into specific performance objectives.*
3. *Crafting a strategy* to achieve the targeted performance.
4. *Implementing and executing the chosen strategy* efficiently and effectively.
5. *Evaluating performance, reviewing the situation, and initiating corrective adjustments* in mission, objectives, strategy, or implementation in light of actual experience, changing conditions, new ideas, and new opportunities.

Figure 1–1 shows a model of the process. Together, these five components define what we mean by the term *strategic management.* Let's explore this basic conceptual model in more detail to set the stage for the chapters that follow.

Developing a Vision and a Mission

The foremost direction-setting question senior managers of any enterprise need to ask is "What is our business and what will it be?" Developing a carefully reasoned answer to this question pushes managers to consider what the

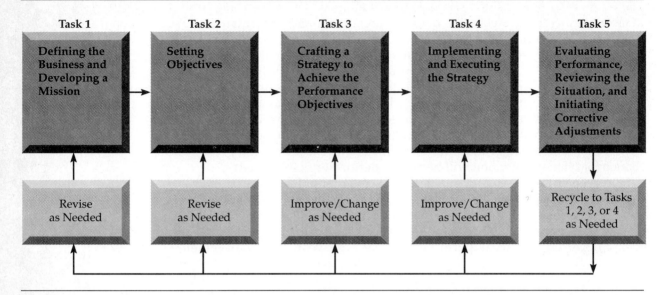

FIGURE 1–1   **The Five Tasks of Strategic Management**

Task 1	Task 2	Task 3	Task 4	Task 5
Defining the Business and Developing a Mission	**Setting Objectives**	**Crafting a Strategy to Achieve the Performance Objectives**	**Implementing and Executing the Strategy**	**Evaluating Performance, Reviewing the Situation, and Initiating Corrective Adjustments**
Revise as Needed	Revise as Needed	Improve/Change as Needed	Improve/Change as Needed	Recycle to Tasks 1, 2, 3, or 4 as Needed

organization's business makeup should be and to develop a clearer vision of where the organization needs to be headed over the next five to ten years. Management's answer to "What is our business and what will it be?" begins the process of carving out a meaningful direction for the organization to take and of establishing a strong organizational identity. Management's vision of what the organization seeks to do and to become is commonly termed the organization's *mission*. A mission statement establishes the organization's future course and outlines "who we are, what we do, and where we're headed." In effect, it sets forth the organization's intent to stake out a particular business position. Some examples of *company mission statements* are presented in Illustration Capsule 1.

Setting Objectives

Objectives serve as yardsticks for tracking an organization's performance and progress.

The purpose of setting objectives is to convert the statement of organizational mission and direction into specific performance targets, something the organization's progress can be measured by. Objective-setting implies challenge, establishing a set of desired outcomes that require stretch and disciplined effort. The challenge of trying to close the gap between actual and desired performance pushes an organization to be more inventive, to exhibit some urgency in improving both its financial performance and its business position, and to be more intentional and focused in its actions. Setting *challenging but achievable* objectives thus helps guard against complacency, drift, internal confusion over what to accomplish, and status quo organizational performance. The set of objectives management establishes should ideally embrace a time horizon that is both near-term and far-term. *Short-range objectives* spell out the immediate improvements and outcomes management desires. *Long-range*

ILLUSTRATION CAPSULE
1

EXAMPLES OF COMPANY MISSION STATEMENTS

Presented below are seven actual company mission statements:

Otis Elevator

Our mission is to provide any customer a means of moving people and things up, down, and sideways over short distances with higher reliability than any similar enterprise in the world.

Deluxe Checks

The mission of Deluxe Checks is to provide all banks, S&L's, and investment firms with error-free financial instruments delivered in a timely fashion.

McCormick & Company

The primary mission of McCormick & Company is to expand our worldwide leadership position in the spice, seasoning, and flavoring markets.

Hewlett-Packard Company

Hewlett-Packard is a major designer and manufacturer of electronic products and systems for measurement and computation. HP's basic business purpose is to provide the capabilities and services needed to help customers worldwide improve their personal and business effectiveness.

The Saturn Division of General Motors

To market vehicles developed and manufactured in the United States that are world leaders in quality, cost, and customer satisfaction through the integration of people, technology, and business systems and to transfer knowledge, technology, and experience throughout General Motors.

Public Service Company of New Mexico

Our mission is to work for the success of the people we serve by providing our CUSTOMERS reliable electric service, energy information, and energy options that best satisfy their needs.

American Red Cross

The mission of the American Red Cross is to improve the quality of human life; to enhance self-reliance and concern for others; and to help people avoid, prepare for, and cope with emergencies.

Source: Company annual reports.

---

objectives prompt managers to consider what they can do *now* to enhance the organization's strength and performance capabilities over the long term.

Objective-setting is required of *all managers*. Every unit in an organization needs concrete, measurable performance targets indicating its contribution to the organization's overall objectives. When organizationwide objectives are broken down into specific targets for each unit and lower-level managers are held accountable for achieving them, a results-oriented climate emerges, with each part of the organization striving to achieve results that will move the whole organization in the intended direction.

Two types of performance yardsticks are called for: *financial objectives* and *strategic objectives*. Financial objectives are needed because acceptable financial performance is critical to preserving an organization's vitality and well-being. Strategic objectives are needed to provide consistent direction in strengthening a company's overall business position. Financial objectives typically focus on such measures as earnings growth, return on investment, and cash flow. Strategic objectives, however, relate more directly to a company's overall competitive situation and involve such performance yardsticks as growing faster than the industry average and making gains in market share, overtaking key competitors on product quality or customer service, achieving lower overall costs than rivals, boosting the company's reputation with customers, winning

Strategic Management Principle

Strategic objectives are, at the very least, coequal in importance to financial objectives.

ILLUSTRATION CAPSULE
2

EXAMPLES OF CORPORATE OBJECTIVES
Nike, La-Z-Boy, Owens-Corning, and McCormick & Company

Nike's Objectives (as stated in 1987)

- Protect and improve NIKE's position as the number one athletic brand in America, with particular attention to the company's existing core businesses in running, basketball, tennis, football, baseball, and kid's shoes and newer businesses with good potential like golf and soccer.
- Build a strong momentum in the growing fitness market, beginning with walking, workout, and cycling.
- Intensify the company's effort to develop products that women need and want.
- Explore the market for products specifically designed for the requirements of maturing Americans.
- Direct and manage the company's international business as it continues to develop.
- Continue the drive for increased margins through proper inventory management and fewer, better products.

La-Z-Boy's Objectives (as stated in 1990)

- To position La-Z-Boy as a full-line furniture manufacturer.
- To strengthen La-Z-Boy's brand name image with American families and businesspeople.
- To improve the quality of the company's distribution network.
- To expand production capacity and make it more efficient.
- To continue to gain financial strength.

Owens-Corning's Objectives (as stated in 1990)

- To anticipate our customers' requirements and provide them with the products which meet their market, quality, and service needs.
- To maintain our number one market positions through continued leadership in technology, manufacturing, and marketing.
- To maximize cash flow for continued debt reduction.
- To focus on operating profit improvements through productivity programs and focused market development.
- To make the most of the talents of our people and provide them with the opportunity and training to reach their full potential.

McCormick & Company's Objectives (as stated in 1990)

- Improve the returns from each of our existing operating groups—consumer, industrial, food service, international, and packaging.
- Dispose of those parts of our business which do not or cannot generate adequate returns or do not fit with our business strategy.
- Make selective acquisitions which complement our current businesses and can enhance our overall returns.
- Achieve a 20% return on equity.
- Achieve a net sales growth rate of 10% per year.
- Maintain an average earnings per share growth rate of 15% per year.
- Maintain total debt to total capital at 40% or less.
- Pay out 25% to 35% of net income in dividends.

Source: Company annual reports.

a stronger foothold in international markets, exercising technological leadership, and developing attractive growth opportunities. Strategic objectives make it explicit that management not only must deliver good financial performance but also must deliver on strengthening the organization's long-term business and competitive position.

Examples of the kinds of strategic and financial objectives companies set are shown in Illustration Capsule 2.

Crafting a Strategy

Strategy-making brings into play the critical managerial issue of *how* to achieve the targeted results in light of the organization's situation and prospects. Objectives are the "ends," and *strategy* is the "means" of achieving them. In effect, strategy is a management tool for achieving strategic targets. The task of forming a strategy starts with hard analysis of the organization's internal and external situation. Armed with an understanding of the "big picture," managers can better devise a strategy to achieve targeted strategic and financial results.

Definitionally, *strategy is the pattern of organizational moves and managerial approaches used to achieve organizational objectives and to pursue the organization's mission*. The pattern of moves and approaches already taken indicates what the prevailing strategy is; the planned moves and approaches signal how the prevailing strategy is to be embellished or changed. Thus, while strategy represents the managerial game plan for running an organization, this plan does not consist of just good intentions and actions yet to be taken. An organization's strategy is nearly always a blend of prior moves, approaches already in place, and new actions being mapped out. Indeed, the biggest part of an organization's strategy usually consists of prior approaches and practices that are working well enough to continue. An organization's strategy that is mostly new most of the time signals erratic decision-making and weak "strategizing" on the part of managers. Quantum changes in strategy can be expected occasionally, especially in crisis situations, but they cannot be made too often without creating undue organizational confusion and disrupting performance.

Strategy and Entrepreneurship   Crafting strategy is an exercise in *entrepreneurship*. Some degree of venturesomeness and risk-taking is inherent in choosing among alternative business directions and devising the next round of moves and approaches. Managers face an ever-present entrepreneurial challenge keeping the organization's strategy fresh, responding to changing conditions, and steering the organization into the right business activities at the right time. Consideration of strategy changes thus cannot and should not be avoided. Often, there is more risk in coasting along with the status quo than there is in assuming the risk of making strategic changes. When managers become reluctant entrepreneurs, they get complacent about current strategy and become overly analytical or hesitant to make strategic decisions that blaze new trails. How boldly or cautiously managers push in new directions and how vigorously they initiate actions for boosting organizational performance are good indicators of their entrepreneurial spirit.

All managers, not just senior executives, need to exercise entrepreneurship in strategy-making. Entrepreneurship is involved when a district customer service manager crafts a strategy to cut the response time on service calls by 25 percent and commits $15,000 to equip all service trucks with mobile telephones. Entrepreneurship is involved when a warehousing manager develops a strategy to reduce the error frequency on filling orders from 1 error per every hundred orders to 1 error per every thousand orders. A sales manager exercises strategic entrepreneurship in deciding to run a special advertising promotion and cut sales prices by 5 percent. A manufacturing manager exercises strategic entrepreneurship in deciding to source an important component from a lower-priced South Korean supplier instead of making it in-house.

An organization's strategy for achieving its performance objectives consists of actions and approaches already in place and scheduled for continuation, supplemented with new actions just underway and additional future moves being mapped out.

Strategy-making is fundamentally an entrepreneurial activity—risk-taking, venturesomeness, business creativity, and an eye for spotting emerging market opportunities are all involved in crafting a strategic action plan.

Strategy-making is not something just top managers do; it is something all managers do—every manager needs an entrepreneurial game plan for the area he/she is in charge of.

A company's strategic action plan is dynamic, undergoing continuous review, refinement, enhancement, and occasional major revision.

Why Strategy Is Constantly Evolving   From the perspective of the whole organization, the task of "strategizing" is always an ongoing exercise.[1] "The whats" of an organization's mission and long-term objectives, once chosen, may remain unaltered for several years. But "the hows" of strategy evolve constantly, partly in response to an everchanging external environment, partly from managers' efforts to create new opportunities, and partly from fresh ideas about how to make the strategy work better. On occasion, quantum changes in strategy emerge when a big strategic move is put to test in the real world or when crisis strikes and managers see that the organization's strategy needs radical reorientation. Refinements and additions, interspersed with periodic quantum leaps, are a normal part of managerial "strategizing."

Because strategic moves and new action approaches are made in an ongoing stream, an organization's strategy forms over a period of time and then reforms, always consisting of a mix of holdover approaches, fresh actions in process, and unrevealed moves being planned. Aside from crisis situations (where many strategic moves are often made quickly to produce a substantially new strategy almost overnight) and new company start-ups (where strategy exists mostly in the form of plans and intended actions), a company's strategy is crafted in bits and pieces as events unfold and as managerial experience accumulates. Everything cannot be planned out in advance, and even the best-laid plans must be responsive to changing conditions and unforeseen events. Strategy-making thus proceeds on two fronts—one proactively thought through in advance, the other conceived in response to new developments, special opportunities, and experiences with the successes and failures of prior strategic moves, approaches, and actions. Figure 1–2 depicts the kinds of actions that form a company's strategy.

Strategy and Strategic Plans   The three tasks of defining the business, setting objectives, and crafting a strategy all involve direction-setting. Together, they specify where the organization is headed and how management intends to achieve the targeted results. Together, they constitute a *strategic plan*. In some companies, especially large corporations committed to regular strategy reviews and formal strategic planning, the strategic plan is explicit and written (although parts of the plan may be omitted if they are too sensitive to reveal before they are actually undertaken). In other companies, the strategic plan is not put on paper but rather exists in the form of understandings among managers about what is to be carried over from the past and what new actions are to be taken. Organizational objectives are the part of the strategic plan that are most often written and circulated among managers and employees.

Illustration Capsule 3 presents an outline of Sara Lee Corporation's mission, objectives, and strategies as an example of how the three direction-setting steps join together.

---

[1]Henry Mintzberg, "Crafting Strategy," *Harvard Business Review* 65, no. 4 (July–August 1987), pp. 66–75; and James B. Quinn, *Strategies for Change: Logical Incrementalism* (Homewood, Ill.: Richard D. Irwin, 1980), chap. 2, especially pp. 58–59.

FIGURE 1–2   The Components of Company Strategy

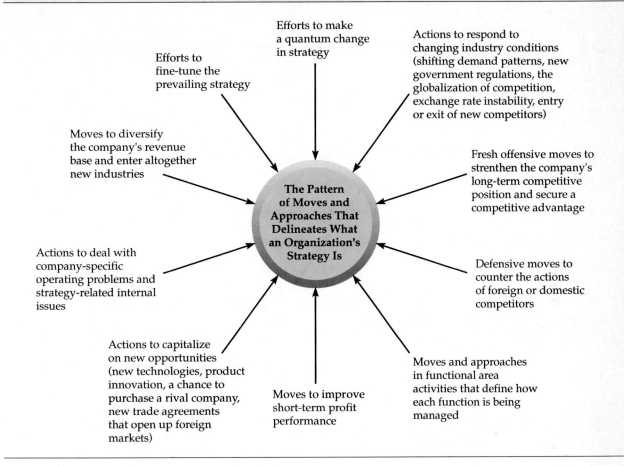

Strategy Implementation and Execution

The strategy-implementing function consists of seeing what it will take to make the strategy work and to reach the targeted performance on schedule—*the skill comes in knowing how to achieve results*. The job of implementing strategy is primarily an action-driven *administrative task* that cuts across many internal matters. The principal administrative aspects associated with putting the strategy into place include:

- Building an organization capable of carrying out the strategy successfully.
- Developing budgets that steer resources into those internal activities critical to strategic success.
- Motivating people in ways that induce them to pursue the target objectives energetically and, if need be, modifying their duties and job behavior to better fit the requirements of successful strategy execution.
- Tying the reward structure tightly to the achievement of the targeted results.

Strategy implementation is fundamentally an administrative activity—organizing, budgeting, motivating, culture-building, supervising, and leading are all part of "making it happen" and achieving the intended strategic and financial outcomes.

ILLUSTRATION CAPSULE

3

SARA LEE CORPORATION: MISSION, OBJECTIVES, AND STRATEGY

In a recent annual report, the management of Sara Lee Corporation set forth the company's mission, objectives, and strategy:

Mission

Sara Lee Corporation's mission is to be the leading brand-name food and consumer packaged goods company with major market share positions in key consumer markets worldwide.

We manufacture and market high-quality, marketing-sensitive products with growth potential. These products, which are sold through common distribution channels, include

- Packaged food products,
- Food products and services for the foodservice industry,
- Consumer personal products, and
- Household and personal care products.

Objectives

Size alone—that is, being the largest by some quantitative measure—does not define leadership. We aspire to be a larger company only to the extent that size and scale contribute to achieving more important measures of pre-eminence.

First, and above all, the leading company must be an outstanding financial performer for its stockholders. We must produce dependable and consistent financial returns which rank high in absolute terms as well as relative to our peer competitors.

Second, our product positions must be very high quality, compete in significant market segments, and command exceptionally strong market shares.

Third, our management people and processes must be of the highest caliber and appropriate to the times.

And fourth, we must be recognized as a corporation with an especially high sense of responsibility to our employees and public constituencies.

Corporate Strategies

1. Invest to accelerate internal growth. Direct and focus investment spending on strategic opportunities to build share and to accelerate unit volume growth in key product positions.

2. Develop the lowest cost position in all product categories. Emphasize and measure operating efficiencies and cost structures in all areas of the corporation to reduce costs consistently and to increase return on sales without sacrificing quality.

3. Make acquisitions. Acquire businesses which fit Sara Lee Corporation's strategic focus and which provide increased opportunity for growth consistent with our mission.

4. Leverage brand names and strategically link businesses for synergy. Generate growth by building and extending brand positions, and improve returns by strategically combining divisions and developing synergies among businesses.

5. Pursue cross-channel distribution for established products, brands and positions. Increase unit volume and return on sales with cross-channel distribution.

Source: 1987 Annual Report.

- Creating a work environment conducive to successful strategy implementation.
- Installing strategy-supportive policies and procedures.
- Developing an information and reporting system to track progress and monitor performance.
- Exerting the internal leadership needed to drive implementation forward and to keep improving on how the strategy is being executed.

The administrative aim is to create "fits" between the way things are done and what it takes for effective strategy execution. The stronger the fits, the better the execution of strategy. The most important fits are between strategy and organizational capabilities, between strategy and the reward structure, between strategy and internal policies and procedures, and between strategy and the organization's culture (the latter emerges from the values and beliefs shared by organizational members and from management's human relations practices). Fitting the ways the organization does things internally to what it takes for effective strategy execution is what unites the organization firmly behind the accomplishment of strategy.

The strategy-implementing task is easily the most complicated and time-consuming part of strategic management. It cuts across virtually all facets of managing and must be initiated from many points inside the organization. The strategy-implementer's agenda for action emerges from careful assessment of what the organization must do differently and better to carry out the strategic plan proficiently. Each manager has to think through the answer to "What has to be done in my area of responsibility to carry out my piece of the overall strategic plan and how can I best get it done?" How much internal change is needed to put the strategy into effect depends on the degree of strategic change, whether internal practices deviate very far from what the strategy requires, and how well strategy and organizational culture already match. As needed changes and actions are identified, management must supervise all the details of implementation and apply enough pressure on the organization to convert objectives into actual results. Depending on the amount of internal change involved, full implementation can take several months to several years.

Evaluating Performance, Reviewing the Situation, and Initiating Corrective Adjustments

None of the previous four tasks are one-time exercises. New circumstances always crop up that make corrective adjustments desirable. Long-term direction may need to be altered, the business redefined, and management's vision of the organization's future course narrowed or broadened. Performance targets may need raising or lowering in light of past experience and future prospects. Strategy may need to be modified because of shifts in long-term direction, because new objectives have been set, or because of changing conditions in the environment.

The search for even better strategy execution is also continuous. Sometimes an aspect of implementation does not go as well as intended and changes have to be made. Progress typically proceeds unevenly—faster in some areas and slower in others. Some tasks get done easily; others prove nettlesome. Implementation occurs through the pooling effect of many administrative decisions about how to do things and how to create stronger fits between strategy and internal operating practices. Budget revisions, policy changes, reorganization, personnel changes, culture-changing actions, and revised compensation practices are typical ways of trying to make the chosen strategy work better.

A company's mission, objectives, strategy, or approach to strategy implementation is never final; evaluating performance, reviewing changes in the surrounding environment, and making adjustments are normal and necessary parts of the strategic management process.

WHY STRATEGIC MANAGEMENT IS AN ONGOING PROCESS

Because each one of the five tasks of strategic management requires constant evaluation and a decision whether to continue with things as they are or to make changes, *the process of managing strategy is ongoing*. Nothing is final—

all prior actions are subject to modification as conditions in the surrounding environment change and ways to improve emerge. Strategic management is a process filled with constant motion. Changes in the organization's situation, either from the inside or outside or both, constantly drive strategic adjustments. This is why, in Figure 1–1, we refer to recycling.

The task of evaluating performance and initiating corrective adjustments is both the end and the beginning of the strategic management cycle. The march of external and internal events guarantees revision in the four previous components will be needed sooner or later. It is always incumbent on management to push for better performance—to find ways to improve the existing strategy and how it is being executed. Changing external conditions add further impetus to the need for periodic revisions in a company's mission, performance objectives, strategy, and approaches to strategy execution. Adjustments usually involve fine-tuning, but occasions for a major strategic reorientation do arise—sometimes prompted by significant external developments and sometimes by sharply sliding financial performance. Strategy managers must stay close enough to the situation to detect when changing conditions require a strategic response and when they don't. It is their job to read the winds of change, recognize significant changes early, and capitalize on events as they unfold.[2]

Characteristics of the Process

Although the tasks of developing a mission, setting objectives, forming a strategy, implementing and executing the strategic plan, and evaluating performance constitute the elements of the strategic management function, actually performing these five tasks is not so cleanly divided and neatly sequenced. There is much interplay among the five tasks. For example, considering what strategic actions to take raises issues about whether and how the strategy can be satisfactorily implemented. Deciding on a company mission shades into setting objectives for the organization to achieve (both involve directional priorities). To establish challenging but achievable objectives, managers must consider both current performance and the strategy options available to improve performance. Deciding on a strategy is entangled with decisions about long-term direction and whether objectives have been set too high or too low.

Second, the five strategic management tasks are not done in isolation. They are carried out in the midst of all other managerial responsibilities—supervising day-to-day operations, dealing with crises, going to meetings, preparing reports, handling people problems, and taking on special assignments and civic duties. Thus, while the job of managing strategy is the most important function management performs insofar as organizational success or failure is concerned, it isn't all managers must do or be concerned about.

Third, strategic management makes erratic demands on a manager's time. An organization's situation does not change in an orderly or predictable way. The events that prompt reconsideration of strategy can build quickly or gradually; they can emerge singly or in rapid-fire succession; and the implications they have for strategic change can be easy or hard to diagnose. Hence strategic

---

[2]Mintzberg, "Crafting Strategy," p. 74.

issues and decisions take up big chunks of management time some months and little or none in other months. As a practical matter, there is as much skill in knowing *when* to institute strategic changes as there is in knowing *what* to do.[3]

Last, the big day-in, day-out time-consuming aspect of strategic management is trying to get the best strategy-supportive performance out of every individual and trying to perfect the current strategy by refining its content and execution. Managing strategy is mostly improving bits and pieces of the strategy in place, not developing and instituting radical strategic changes. Excessive changes in strategy can be disruptive to employees and confusing to customers, and they are usually unnecessary. Most of the time, there's more to be gained from improving execution of the present strategy. Persistence in trying to make a sound strategy work better is often the key to managing the strategy to success.

WHO ARE THE STRATEGY MANAGERS?

An organization's chief executive officer is the most visible and important *strategy manager*. The CEO, as captain of the ship, bears full responsibility for leading the tasks of formulating and implementing the strategic plans of the whole organization, even though many other managers have a hand in the process. The CEO functions as chief direction-setter, chief objective-setter, chief strategy-maker, and chief strategy-implementer for the total enterprise. What the CEO views as important usually moves to the top of every manager's priority list, and the CEO has the final word on big decisions.

Vice presidents for production, marketing, finance, human resources, and other functional departments have important strategy-making and strategy-implementing responsibilities as well. Normally, the production VP oversees production strategy; the marketing VP heads up the marketing strategy effort; the financial VP is in charge of financial strategy; and so on. Usually, functional vice presidents are also involved in proposing and developing key elements of the overall strategy, working closely with the CEO to hammer out a consensus and make certain parts of the strategy more effective. Only rarely does a CEO personally craft all the key pieces of organization strategy.

But managerial positions with strategy-making and strategy-implementing responsibility are by no means restricted to these few senior executives. *Every manager is a strategy-maker and strategy-implementer for the area he/she has authority over and supervises.* Every part of a company—business unit, division, operating department, plant, or district office—has a strategic role to carry out. And the manager in charge of that unit, with guidance from superiors, usually ends up doing some or most of the strategy-making for the unit and implementing whatever strategic choices are made. However, managers farther down in the managerial hierarchy have a narrower, more specific strategy-making/strategy-implementing role than managers closer to the top.

Another reason lower-echelon managers are strategy-makers and strategy-implementers is that the more geographically scattered and diversified an organization's operations are, the more impossible it becomes for a few senior executives to handle all the strategic planning that needs to be done. Managers

All managers are involved in the strategy-making and strategy-implementing process.

---

[3]Ibid., p. 73.

in the corporate office don't know all the situational details in all geographical areas and operating units to be able to prescribe appropriate strategies. Usually, they delegate some of the strategy-making responsibility to the lower-level managers who head the organizational subunits where specific strategic results must be achieved. Delegating a lead strategy-making role to those managers who will be deeply involved in carrying it out in their areas fixes accountability for strategic success or failure. When the managers who implement the strategy are also its architects, it is hard for them to shift the blame or make excuses if they don't achieve the target results.

In diversified companies where the strategies of several different businesses have to be managed, there are usually four distinct levels of strategy managers:

- *The chief executive officer and other senior corporation-level executives* who have primary responsibility and personal authority for big strategic decisions affecting the total enterprise and the collection of individual businesses the enterprise has diversified into.
- *Managers who have profit-and-loss responsibility for one specific business unit* and who are delegated a major leadership role in formulating and implementing strategy for that unit.
- *Functional area managers within a given business unit* who have direct authority over a major piece of the business (manufacturing, marketing and sales, finance, R&D, personnel) and whose role it is to support the business unit's overall strategy with strategic actions in their own areas.
- *Managers of major operating departments and geographic field units* who have front-line responsibility for developing the details of strategic efforts in their areas and for implementing and executing the overall strategic plan at the grassroots level.

Single-business enterprises need no more than three of these levels (business-level strategy managers, functional area strategy managers, and operating-level strategy managers). In a large single-business company, the team of strategy managers consists of the chief executive, who functions as chief strategist with final authority over both strategy and its implementation; the vice presidents in charge of key functions (R&D, production, marketing, finance, human resources, and so on); plus as many operating-unit managers of the various plants, sales offices, distribution centers, and staff support departments as it takes to handle the company's scope of operations. Proprietorships, partnerships, and owner-managed enterprises, however, typically have only one or two strategy managers since in small-scale enterprises the whole strategy-making/strategy-implementing function can be handled by just a few key people.

Managerial jobs involving strategy formulation and implementation abound in not-for-profit organizations as well. For example, a multicampus state university has four strategy-managing levels: (1) the president of the university system is a strategy manager with broad direction-setting responsibility and strategic decision-making authority over all the campuses; (2) the chancellor for each campus customarily has strategy-making/strategy-implementing authority over all academic, student, athletic, and alumni matters, plus budgetary, programmatic, and coordinative responsibilities for that campus; (3) the academic deans have lead responsibility for charting future direction at the college level, steering resources into high-demand programs and out of low-demand programs, and otherwise devising a collegewide plan to fulfill the college's teaching-research-service mission; and (4) the heads of various academic departments are strategy managers with first-line strategy-making/strategy-implementing responsibility for the department's undergraduate and graduate program offerings, faculty research efforts, and all other activities relating to the department's mission, objectives, and future direction. In federal and state government, heads of local, district, and regional offices function as strategy managers in their efforts to respond to the needs and situations of the areas they serve (a district manager in Portland may need a slightly different strategy than a district manager in Orlando). In municipal government, the heads of various departments (fire, police, water and sewer, parks and recreation, health, and so on) are strategy managers because they have line authority for the operations of their departments and thus can influence departmental objectives, the formation of a strategy to achieve these objectives, and how the strategy is implemented.

Managerial jobs with strategy-making/strategy-implementing roles are thus the norm rather than the exception. The job of crafting and implementing strategy touches virtually every managerial job in one way or another, at one time or another. Strategic management is basic to the task of managing; it is not something just top-level managers deal with.[4]

The Role and Tasks of Strategic Planners

If senior and middle managers have the lead roles in strategy-making and strategy-implementing in their areas of responsibility, what should strategic planners do? Is there a legitimate place in big companies for a strategic planning department staffed with specialists in planning and strategic analysis? The answer is yes. But the planning department's role and tasks should consist chiefly of helping to gather and organize information that strategy managers need, establishing and administering an annual strategy review cycle whereby all strategy managers reconsider and refine their strategic plans, and coordinating the process of reviewing and approving the strategic plans developed for all the various parts of the company. Strategic planners are valuable because they help managers at all levels crystallize the strategic issues that ought to be addressed; in addition, they can provide data, help analyze industry and competitive conditions, and distribute information on the company's strategic performance. But strategic planners should *not* make strategic decisions, prepare strategic plans (for someone else to implement), or make strategic action recommendations that usurp the strategy-making responsibilities of managers in charge of major operating units.

When strategic planners are asked to go beyond providing staff assistance and actually prepare a strategic plan for management's consideration, either of two adverse consequences may occur. First, some managers will gladly toss tough strategic problems in their areas onto the desks of strategic planners to

Strategic Management Principle
Strategy-making is not a proper task for strategic planners.

---

[4]Since the scope of a manager's strategy-making/strategy-implementing role varies according to the manager's position in the organizational hierarchy, our use of the word "organization" includes whatever kind of unit the strategy manager is in charge of—an entire company or not-for-profit organization, a business unit within a diversified company, a major geographic division, an important functional area within a business, or an operating department or field unit reporting to the functional area head. It should be clear from the context of the discussion whether the subject applies to the total enterprise or to most or all management levels.

let the planners do their strategic thinking for them. The planners, not knowing as much about the situation as managers do, are in a weaker position to design a workable action plan. And they can't be held responsible for implementing what they recommend. Giving planners responsibility for strategy-making and line managers responsibility for implementation makes it hard to fix accountability for poor results. It also deludes line managers into thinking they don't have to be personally involved in crafting a strategy for their own organizational unit or in finding strategic solutions to strategic problems in their area of responsibility. The hard truth is that strategy-making is not a staff function, nor is it something that can be handed off to an advisory committee of lower-ranking managers. Second, when line managers have no ownership stake in or personal commitment to the strategic agenda proposed by the planners, they give it lip service, make a few token implementation efforts, and quickly get back to "business as usual," knowing that the formal written plan concocted by the planners does not match their own "real" managerial agenda. The written strategic plan, because it lacks credibility and true top-management commitment, soon collects dust on managers' shelves. The result is that few managers take the work product of the strategic planning staff seriously enough to pursue implementation—strategic planning comes to be seen as just another bureaucratic exercise.

Either consequence renders formal strategic planning efforts ineffective and opens the door for a strategy-making vacuum conducive to organizational drift or to fragmented, uncoordinated strategic decisions. The odds are then heightened that the organization will have no strong strategic rudder and insufficient top-down direction. The flaws in having staffers or advisory committees formulate strategies for areas they do not manage are: (1) they can't be held accountable if their recommendations don't produce the desired results since they don't have authority for directing implementation, and (2) what they recommend won't be well accepted or enthusiastically implemented by those who "have to sing the song the planners have written." But when line managers are expected to be the chief strategy-makers and strategy-implementers for the areas they head, it is their own strategy and their own implementation approach that are being put to the test of workability. They are likely to be more committed to making the plan work (their future careers with the organization are at more risk!), and they can be held strictly accountable for achieving the target results in their area.

The Strategic Role of the Board of Directors

Since lead responsibility for crafting and implementing strategy falls to key managers, the chief strategic role of an organization's board of directors is to see that the overall task of managing strategy is adequately done.[5] Boards of directors normally review important strategic moves and officially approve the strategic plans submitted by senior management—a procedure that makes the board ultimately responsible for the strategic actions taken. But directors rarely can or should play a direct role in formulating strategy. The immediate task of directors in ratifying strategy and new direction-setting moves is to ensure that all proposals have been adequately analyzed and

---

[5]Kenneth R. Andrews, *The Concept of Corporate Strategy*, 3rd ed. (Homewood, Illinois: Richard D. Irwin, 1987), p. 123.

considered and that the proposed strategic actions are superior to available alternatives; flawed proposals are customarily withdrawn for revision by management.[6] The longer-range task of directors is to evaluate the caliber of senior executives' strategy-making and strategy-implementing skills. The board must determine whether the current CEO is doing a good job of strategic management (as a basis for awarding salary increases and bonuses and deciding on retention or removal) and evaluate the strategic skills of other senior executives in line to succeed the current CEO.

THE BENEFITS OF A "STRATEGIC APPROACH" TO MANAGING

The message of this book is that doing a good job of managing inherently requires doing a good job of strategic management. Today's managers have to think strategically about their company's position and about the impact of changing conditions. They have to monitor the external situation closely enough to know *when* to institute strategy change. They have to know the business well enough to know *what kind* of strategic changes to initiate. Simply said, the fundamentals of strategic management need to drive the whole approach to managing organizations.[7] The chief executive officer of one successful company put it well when he said:

> In the main, our competitors are acquainted with the same fundamental concepts and techniques and approaches that we follow, and they are as free to pursue them as we are. More often than not, the difference between their level of success and ours lies in the relative thoroughness and self-discipline with which we and they develop and execute our strategies for the future.

The advantages of first-rate strategic thinking and conscious strategy management (as opposed to freewheeling improvisation, gut feel, and drifting along) include (1) providing better guidance to the entire organization on the crucial point of "what it is we are trying to do and to achieve," (2) making managers more alert to the winds of change, new opportunities, and threatening developments, (3) providing managers with a rationale to evaluate competing budget requests for investment capital and new staff—a rationale that argues strongly for steering resources into strategy-supportive, results-producing areas, (4) helping to unify the numerous strategy-related decisions by managers across the organization, and (5) creating a more *proactive* management posture and counteracting tendencies for decisions to be reactive and defensive.[8]

The fifth advantage of being proactive rather than merely reactive is that trail-blazing strategies can be the key to better long-term performance. Business history shows that high-performing enterprises often *initiate* and *lead*, not just *react* and *defend*. They launch strategic *offensives* to secure sustainable competitive advantage and then use their market edge to achieve superior financial

---

[6]Ibid.

[7]For a lucid discussion of the importance of the strategic management function, see V. Ramanujam and N. Venkatraman, "Planning and Performance: A New Look at an Old Question," *Business Horizons* 30, no. 3 (May–June, 1987), pp. 19–25; and Henry Mintzberg, "The Strategy Concept: Another Look at Why Organizations Need Strategies," *California Management Review* 30, no. 1 (Fall 1987), pp. 25–32.

[8]Kenneth R. Andrews, *The Concept of Corporate Strategy*, rev. ed. (Homewood, Ill.: Richard D. Irwin, 1980), pp. 15–16, 46, 123–29; and Seymour Tilles, "How to Evaluate Corporate Strategy," *Harvard Business Review* 41, no. 4 (July–August 1963), p. 116

performance. Aggressive pursuit of a creative, opportunistic strategy can pro-
pel a firm into a leadership position, paving the way for its products/services
to become the industry standard.

A RECAP OF
IMPORTANT
TERMS

We conclude this introductory overview by defining key terms that will be
used again and again in the chapters to come:

Organization mission—management's customized answer to the question
"What is our business and what will it be?" A mission statement broadly
outlines the organization's future direction and serves as a guiding concept
for what the organization is to do and to become.

Performance objectives—the organization's targets for achievement.

Financial objectives—the targets management has established for the
organization's financial performance.

Strategic objectives—the targets management has established for
strengthening the organization's overall position and competitive vitality.

Long-range objectives—the results to be achieved either within the next
three to five years or else on an ongoing basis year after year.

Short-range objectives—the organization's near-term performance
targets; the amount of short-term improvement signals how fast
management is trying to achieve the long-range objectives.

Strategy—the managerial action plan for achieving organizational
objectives; strategy is mirrored in the *pattern* of moves and approaches
devised by management to produce the targeted outcomes. Strategy is the
how of pursuing the organization's mission and achieving the desired
objectives.

Strategic plan—a statement outlining an organization's mission and future
direction, near-term and long-term performance targets, and strategy in
light of the organization's external and internal situation.

Strategy formulation—the entire direction-setting management function
of conceptualizing an organization's mission, setting performance
objectives, and crafting a strategy. The end product of strategy formulation
is a strategic plan.

Strategy implementation—the full range of managerial activities associated with putting the chosen strategy into place, supervising its pursuit,
and achieving the targeted results.

In the chapters to come, we will probe the strategy-related tasks of managers
and the methods of strategic analysis more intensively. When you get to the
end of the book, we think you will see that two factors separate the best-managed organizations from the rest: (1) superior strategy-making and entrepreneurship, and (2) competent implementation and execution of the chosen
strategy. There's no escaping the fact that the quality of managerial strategy-
making and strategy-implementing has a significant impact on organization
performance. A company that lacks clear-cut direction, has vague or unde-
manding objectives, or has a muddled or flawed strategy is a company whose
performance is probably suffering, whose business is at long-term risk, and
whose management is less than capable.

Andrews, Kenneth R. *The Concept of Corporate Strategy.* 3rd ed. Homewood, Ill.: Richard D. Irwin, 1987, chap. 1.

Gluck, Frederick W. "A Fresh Look at Strategic Management." *Journal of Business Strategy* 6, no. 2 (Fall 1985), pp. 4–21.

Hax, Arnoldo C., and Nicolas S. Majluf. *The Strategy Concept and Process: A Pragmatic Approach* (Englewood Cliffs, N.J.: Prentice Hall, 1991), chaps. 1 and 2.

Kelley, C. Aaron. "The Three Planning Questions: A Fable." *Business Horizons* 26, no. 2 (March–April 1983), pp. 46–48.

Kotter, John P. *The General Managers.* New York: Free Press, 1982.

Levinson, Harry, and Stuart Rosenthal. *CEO: Corporate Leadership in Action.* New York: Basic Books, 1987.

Mintzberg, Henry. "The Strategy Concept: Five Ps for Strategy." *California Management Review* 30, no. 1 (Fall 1987), pp. 11–24.

_____. "The Strategy Concept: Another Look at Why Organizations Need Strategies." *California Management Review* 30, no. 1 (Fall 1987), pp. 25–32.

_____. "Crafting Strategy." *Harvard Business Review* 65, no. 4 (July–August 1987), pp. 66–75.

Quinn, James B. *Strategies for Change: Logical Incrementalism.* Homewood, Ill.: Richard D. Irwin, 1980, chaps. 2 and 3.

Ramanujam, V., and N. Venkatraman. "Planning and Performance: A New Look at an Old Question." *Business Horizons* 30, no. 3 (May–June 1987), pp. 19–25.

Yip, George S. "Who Needs Strategic Planning?" *Journal of Business Strategy* 6, no. 2 (Fall 1985), pp. 22–29.

SUGGESTED READINGS

The Three Strategy-Making Tasks
Developing a Mission, Setting Objectives, and Forming a Strategy

———

Management's job is not to see the company as it is . . . but as it can become.
John W. Teets
CEO, Greyhound Corp.

———

Without a strategy the organization is like a ship without a rudder, going around in circles. It's like a tramp; it has no place to go.
Joel Ross and Michael Kami

———

You've got to come up with a plan. You can't wish things will get better.
John F. Welch
CEO, General Electric

———

In this chapter, we provide a more in-depth look at each of the three strategy-making tasks: defining the business and developing a mission, setting performance objectives, and crafting a strategy to produce the desired results. We also examine the nature of strategy-making at each managerial level in the organizational hierarchy and discuss the four basic ways managers perform the strategy-making task.

DEVELOPING A MISSION: THE FIRST DIRECTION-SETTING TASK

Management's vision of what the organization is trying to do and to become over the long term is commonly referred to as the organization's *mission*. A *mission statement* specifies what activities the organization intends to pursue and what course management has charted for the future. It outlines "who *we* are, what *we* do, and where *we* are headed." Mission statements are thus personalized in the sense that they set an organization apart from others in its industry and give it its own special identity, character, and path for development. For example, the mission of a globally active New York bank like Citicorp has little in common with that of a locally owned small town bank even though both are in the banking industry. Without a concept of what the organization should and should not do and a vision of where the organization needs to be going, a manager cannot function effectively as either leader or strategy-maker. There are three distinct aspects to the task of developing a company mission:

Effective strategic leadership starts with a concept of what the organization should and should not do and a vision of where the organization needs to be headed.

- Understanding what business a company is really in.
- Deciding when to change the mission and alter the company's strategic course.
- Communicating the mission in ways that are clear, exciting, and inspiring.

Understanding and Defining the Business

Deciding what business an organization is in is neither obvious nor easy. Is IBM in the computer business (a product-oriented definition) or the information and data processing business (a customer service or customer needs type of definition) or the advanced electronics business (a technology-based definition)? Is Coca-Cola in the soft-drink business (in which case its strategic vision can be trained narrowly on the actions of Pepsi, 7Up, Dr Pepper, Canada Dry, and Schweppes)? Or is it in the beverage industry (in which case management must think strategically about positioning Coca-Cola products in a market that includes fruit juices, alcoholic drinks, milk, bottled water, coffee, and tea)? This is not a trivial question for Coca-Cola. Many young adults get their morning caffeine fix by drinking cola instead of coffee; with a beverage industry perspective as opposed to a soft-drink industry perspective, Coca-Cola management is more likely to perceive a long-term growth opportunity in winning youthful coffee drinkers over to its colas.

Defining what business an organization is in requires taking three factors into account:[1]

A company's business is defined by what needs it is trying to satisfy, by which customer groups it is targeting, and by the technologies it will use and the functions it will perform in serving the target market.

1. Customer needs, or *what* is being satisfied.
2. Customer groups, or *who* is being satisfied.
3. The technologies used and functions performed—*how* customers' needs are satisfied.

Defining a business in terms of what to satisfy, who to satisfy, and how the organization will go about producing the satisfaction adds completeness to the definition. It also directs management to look outward toward customers and markets as well as inward in forming its concept of "who we are and what we

---

[1]Derek F. Abell, *Defining the Business: The Starting Point of Strategic Planning* (Englewood Cliffs, N.J.: Prentice Hall, 1980), p. 169.

ILLUSTRATION CAPSULE
4

CIRCLE K's MISSION STATEMENT

We believe our primary business is not so much retail as it is service oriented.

Certainly, our customers buy merchandise in our stores. But they can buy similar items elsewhere, and perhaps pay lower prices.

But they're willing to buy from Circle K because we give them added value for their money.

That added value is service and convenience.

Our Mission

As a service company, our mission is to:

Satisfy our customers' immediate needs and wants by providing them with a wide variety of goods and services at multiple locations.

Our Customers

We will not place a limit on the conveniences we offer customers.

They buy at Circle K much differently than at a supermarket. They come to our stores for specific purchases, which they make as quickly as possible. They want immediate service and are willing to pay a premium for it.

Our Stores

We will build our stores at locations most accessible to our customers.

We will organize our merchandise to (1) facilitate quick purchases and (2) encourage other purchases.

We will maintain our stores so they will always be brightly lit, colorful, clean, and comfortable places for our customers and our employees.

Our Goods and Services

We will not be one store—but a dozen stores in one.

We are a gas station, a fast-food restaurant, a grocery store, drugstore, liquor store, newsstand, video rental shop, small bank—and more.

Source: 1987 Annual Report.

do."[2] A good example of a business definition that incorporates all three aspects is a paraphrase of Polaroid's business definition during the early 1970s: "perfecting and marketing instant photography to satisfy the needs of more affluent U.S. and West European families for affection, friendship, fond memories, and humor." For years, McDonald's business definition has centered on "serving hot, tasty food quickly in a clean restaurant for a good value" to a broad base of customers worldwide (McDonald's now serves over 25 million customers daily at some 14,000 restaurants in over 40 countries). Illustration Capsule 4 describes how Circle K, the second largest convenience store retailer in the United States, views its mission and business.

The Polaroid, McDonald's, and Circle K examples all adhere closely to the three necessary components of a mission statement: the specific needs served by the company's basic product(s) or service(s), the targeted customer groups, and the technology and functions the company employs in providing its product/service. It takes all three to define what business a company is really in. Just knowing what products or services a firm provides is never enough. Prod-

---

[2]There is a tendency sometimes for companies to view their mission in terms of making a profit. However, profit is more correctly an *objective* and a *result* of what the company does. Missions based on making a profit are incapable of distinguishing one type of profit-seeking enterprise from another—the mission and business of Sears are plainly different from the mission and business of Delta Airlines, even though both endeavor to earn a profit.

ucts or services per se are not important to customers; what turns a product or service into a business is the need or want being satisfied. Without the need or want there is no business. Customer groups are relevant because they indicate the market to be served: the geographic area to be covered and the types of buyers the firm is going after. Technology and functions performed are important because they indicate how the company will satisfy customers' needs and how much of the industry's production chain its own activities will span. For instance, a firm can be *specialized*, participating in one aspect of the whole industry's production chain, or *fully integrated*, operating in all parts of the industry chain. Circle K is a specialized firm operating only in the retail end of the chain; it doesn't manufacture the items it sells. Major international oil companies like Exxon, Mobil, and Chevron, however, are fully integrated; they lease drilling sites, drill wells, pump oil, transport the oil in their own ships and pipelines to their own refineries, and sell gasoline and other refined products through their own distributors and service stations. Because of the disparity in functions performed and technology employed, the business of a retailer like Circle K is much narrower and quite different from a fully integrated enterprise like Exxon. Between these two extremes, firms can stake out *partially integrated* positions, participating only in selected stages of the industry. So one way of distinguishing a firm's business, especially among firms in the same industry, is by looking at which functions it performs in the chain and how far its scope of operation extends across the industry.

A Broad or Narrow Business Definition?   A small Hong Kong printing company that defines its business broadly as "Asian-language communications" gains no practical guidance in making direction-setting decisions; with such a definition the company could pursue limitless courses, most well beyond its scope and capability. To have managerial value, mission statements and business definitions must be narrow enough to pin down the real arena of business interest. Otherwise they cannot serve as boundaries for what to do and not do and as beacons of where managers intend to take the company. Consider the following definitions based on broad-narrow scope:

Broad Definition	Narrow Definition
Beverages	Soft drinks
Footwear	Athletic footwear
Furniture	Wrought iron lawn furniture
Global mail delivery	Overnight package delivery
Travel and tourism	Ship cruises in the Caribbean

Broad-narrow definitions are relative, of course. Being in "the furniture business" is probably too broad a concept for a company intent on being the largest manufacturer of wrought iron lawn furniture in North America. On the other hand, soft drinks has proved too narrow a scope for a growth-oriented company like Coca-Cola, which, with its beverage industry perspective, acquired Minute-Maid and Hi-C (to capitalize on growing consumer interest in fruit juice products) and Taylor Wine Company (using the California Cellars brand to establish a foothold in wines).[3] The U.S. Postal Service operates with a broad definition—providing global mail delivery services to all types of senders. Federal Express, however, operates with a narrow business definition based on handling overnight package delivery for customers who have unplanned emergencies and tight deadlines.

Diversified firms have more expansive business definitions than single-business enterprises. Their mission statements typically use narrow terms to define current customer-market-technology arenas but are open-ended and adaptable enough to incorporate expansion into desirable new businesses. Alcan, Canada's leading aluminum company, used this type of language in its mission statement:

Diversified companies have broader missions and business definitions than single-business enterprises.

> Alcan is determined to be the most innovative diversified aluminum company in the world. To achieve this position, Alcan will be one, global, customer-oriented enterprise committed to excellence and lowest cost in its chosen aluminum businesses, with significant resources devoted to building an array of new businesses with superior growth and profit potential.

Morton-Thiokol, a substantially more diversified enterprise, used simultaneous broad-narrow terms to define its business:

> We are an international, high-technology company serving the diverse needs of government and industry with products and services ranging from massive solid rocket motors to small ordnance devices, from polymers to disc brake pads, from heavy denier yarns to woven carpet backing, from snow-grooming vehicles to trigger sprayers.

John Hancock's mission statement communicates a shift from its long-standing base in insurance to a broader mission in insurance, banking, and diversified financial services:

> At John Hancock, we are determined not just to compete but to advance, building our market share by offering individuals and institutions the broadest possible range of products and services. Apart from insurance, John Hancock encompasses banking products, full brokerage services and institutional investment, to cite only a few of our diversified activities. We believe these new directions constitute the right moves . . . the steps that will drive our growth throughout the remainder of this century.

Where Entrepreneurship Comes In

A member of Maytag's board of directors summed it up well when commenting on why the company acquired a European appliance-maker and shifted its long-term focus to include international markets as well as domestic ones: "Times change, conditions change." The swirl of new events and altered circumstances make it incumbent on managers to continually reassess their company's position and prospects, always checking for *when* it's time to steer a new course and adjust the mission. The key question here is "What new directions should we be moving in *now* to get ready for the changes we see coming in our business?" Repositioning an enterprise in light of emerging developments

---

[3]Coca-Cola's foray into wines evidently was not successful enough; the division was divested about five years after initial acquisition.

lessens the chances of getting caught in a poor market position or being depen-dent on the wrong business at the wrong time. For example, Philip Morris, the leading U.S. manufacturer of cigarettes, in anticipation of long-term deteriora-tion in the demand for tobacco products, positioned itself as a major contender in the food products industry by acquiring two of the largest manufacturers, General Foods and Kraft. Many U.S. companies are broadening their missions geographically and forming joint ventures with European companies to try to capitalize on the dismantling of trade barriers in the European Community in 1992 and the opening of markets in Eastern Europe.

Good entrepreneurs are alert to changing customer wants and needs, cus-tomer dissatisfaction with current products and services, emerging technolo-gies, changing international trade conditions, and other important signs of growing or shrinking business opportunity. Appraising new customer-market-technology developments ultimately leads to entrepreneurial judg-ments about which of several roads to take. A strategy leader must peer down each of the roads, evaluate the risks and prospects of each, and make direction-setting decisions to position the enterprise for success in the years ahead. *A well-chosen mission prepares a company for the future.* Many companies in con-sumer electronics and telecommunications, believing that their future prod-ucts will incorporate microprocessors and other elements of computer technology, are expanding their missions and establishing positions in the computer business to have access to the needed technology. Numerous com-panies in manufacturing, seeing the swing to internationalization and global competition, are broadening their missions from serving domestic markets to serving global markets. Coca-Cola, Kentucky Fried Chicken, and McDonald's are pursuing market opportunities in China, Europe, Japan, and the Soviet Union. Japanese automobile companies are working to establish a bigger pres-ence in the European car market. CNN, Turner Broadcasting's successful all-news cable channel, is pushing hard to become the first global all-news channel. Thus, a company's mission always has a time dimension; it is subject to change whenever top management concludes that the present mission is no longer adequate.

The entrepreneurial challenge in developing a mission is to recognize when emerging opportunities and threats in the surrounding environment make it desirable to revise the organization's long-term direction.

Communicating the Mission

How to phrase the mission statement and communicate it to lower-level man-agers and employees is almost as important as the soundness of the mission itself. A mission statement phrased in words that inspire and challenge can help build committed effort from employees, thus serving as a powerful moti-vational tool.[4] Bland language, platitudes, and motherhood-and-apple-pie-style verbiage should be scrupulously avoided. Companies should communi-cate their mission in words that induce employee buy-in and convey a sense of organizational purpose. In organizations with freshly changed missions, exec-utives need to provide a convincing rationale for the new direction; otherwise a new mission statement does little to change employees' attitudes and behav-ior or to win their commitment—outcomes that make it harder to move the organization down the chosen path.

---

[4]Tom Peters, *Thriving on Chaos* (New York: Harper & Row, 1988), pp. 486–87.

ILLUSTRATION CAPSULE

NOVACARE'S BUSINESS MISSION AND VISION

NovaCare is a fast-growing health care company specializing in providing patient rehabilitation services on a contract basis to nursing homes. Rehabilitation therapy is a $10 billion industry, of which 35% is provided contractually; the contract segment is highly fragmented with over 1,000 competitors. In 1990 NovaCare was a $100 million company, with a goal of being a $275 million business by 1993. The company stated its business mission and vision as follows:

NovaCare is people committed to making a difference . . . enhancing the future of all patients . . . breaking new ground in our professions . . . achieving excellence . . . advancing human capability . . . changing the world in which we live.

We lead the way with our enthusiasm, optimism, patience, drive and commitment.

We work together to enhance the quality of our patients' lives by reshaping lost abilities and teaching new skills. We heighten expectations for the patient and family. We rebuild hope, confidence, self-respect and a desire to continue.

We apply our clinical expertise to benefit our patients through creative and progressive techniques. Our ethical and performance standards require us to expend every effort to achieve the best possible results.

Our customers are national and local health care providers who share our goal of enhancing the patients' quality of life. In each community, our customers consider us a partner in providing the best possible care. Our reputation is based on our responsiveness, high standards and effective systems of quality assurance. Our relationship is open and proactive.

We are advocates of our professions and patients through active participation in the professional, regulatory, educational and research communities at national, state and local levels.

Our approach to health care fulfills our responsibility to provide investors with a high rate of return through consistent growth and profitability.

Our people are our most valuable asset. We are committed to the personal, professional and career development of each individual employee. We are proud of what we do and dedicated to our Company. We foster teamwork and create an environment conducive to productive communication among all disciplines.

NovaCare is a company of people in pursuit of this Vision.

Source: Company annual report.

A well-worded mission statement creates enthusiasm for the future course management has charted; the motivational goal in communicating the mission is to challenge and inspire everyone in the organization.

The best mission statements use simple, concise terminology; they speak loudly and clearly, generate enthusiasm for the firm's future course, and encourage personal effort and dedication from everyone in the organization. They need to be repeated over and over in a challenging, convincing fashion. A short, clear, often-repeated, inspiring mission statement has the power to turn heads in the intended direction and begin a new organizational march. As this occurs, the first step in organizational direction-setting has been completed successfully. Illustration Capsule 5 illustrates an inspiration-oriented mission statement.

A well-conceived, well-said mission statement has real managerial value: (1) it crystallizes top management's own view about the firm's long-term direction and makeup, (2) it helps keep the direction-related actions of lower-level managers on the right path, (3) it conveys an organizational purpose and identity that motivates employees to do their best, (4) it helps managers avoid either visionless or rudderless management, and (5) it helps an organization prepare for the future.

ESTABLISHING OBJECTIVES: THE SECOND DIRECTION-SETTING TASK

Establishing objectives converts the mission and directional course into designated performance outcomes. Objectives represent a managerial commitment to produce specified results in a specified time. They spell out *how much* of *what kind* of performance *by when*. They direct attention and energy to what needs to be accomplished.

The Managerial Value of Establishing Objectives

Unless an organization's mission and direction are translated into *measurable* performance targets, and managers are pressured to show progress in reaching these targets, an organization's mission statement is just window-dressing. Experience tells a powerful story about why objective-setting is a critical task in the strategic management process: *Companies whose managers set objectives for each key result area and then aggressively pursue actions calculated to achieve their performance targets are strong candidates to outperform the companies whose managers operate with hopes, prayers, and good intentions.*

For performance objectives to have value as a management tool, they must be stated in *quantifiable* or measurable terms, and they must contain a *deadline for achievement*. This means avoiding statements like "maximize profits," "reduce costs," "become more efficient," or "increase sales" which specify neither how much or when. Spelling out organization objectives in measurable terms and then holding managers accountable for reaching their assigned targets within a specified time frame (1) substitutes purposeful strategic decision-making for aimless actions and confusion over what to accomplish and (2) provides a set of benchmarks for judging the organization's performance.

> *Objectives are a managerial commitment to achieve specific performance targets by a certain time.*

What Kinds of Objectives to Set

Objectives are needed for each *key result* that managers deem important to success.[5] Two types of key result areas stand out: those relating to *financial performance* and those relating to *strategic performance*. Achieving acceptable financial performance is a must; otherwise the organization's survival ends up at risk. Achieving acceptable strategic performance is essential to sustaining

> **Strategic Management Principle**
> *Every company needs to establish both strategic objectives and financial objectives.*

---

[5]The literature of management is filled with references to *goals* and *objectives*. These terms are used in a variety of ways, many of them conflicting. Some writers use the term *goals* to refer to the long-run results an organization seeks to achieve and the term *objectives* to refer to immediate, short-run performance targets. Some writers reverse the usage. Others use the terms interchangeably. And still others use the term *goals* to refer to broad organizationwide performance targets and the term *objectives* to designate specific targets set by subordinate managers in response to the broader, more inclusive goals of the whole organization. In our view, little is gained from semantic distinctions between *goals* and *objectives*; the important thing is to recognize that the results an enterprise seeks to attain vary both in scope and in time perspective. Nearly always, organizations need to have broad and narrow performance targets for both the near term and long term. It is inconsequential which targets are called "goals" and which are called "objectives." To avoid a semantic jungle, we will use the single term *objectives* to refer to the performance targets and results an organization seeks to attain. We will use the adjectives *long-range* (or long-run) and *short-range* (or short-run) to identify the relevant time frame, and we will try to describe objectives in words that indicate their intended scope and level in the organization.

and improving the company's long-term market position. Specific kinds of
financial and strategic performance objectives are shown below:

Financial Objectives	Strategic Objectives
• Faster revenue growth	• A bigger market share
• Faster earnings growth	• A higher, more secure industry rank
• Higher dividends	• Higher product quality
• Wider profit margins	• Lower costs relative to key competitors
• Higher returns on invested capital	• Broader or more attractive product line
• Stronger bond and credit ratings	• A stronger reputation with customers
• Bigger cash flows	• Superior customer service
• A rising stock price	• Recognition as a leader in technology and/ or product innovation
• Recognition as a "blue chip" company	• Increased ability to compete in international markets
• A more diversified revenue base	• Expanded growth opportunities
• Stable earnings during recessionary periods	

Illustration Capsule 6 provides a sampling of strategic and financial objectives
of some well-known corporations.

Strategic Objectives versus Financial Objectives: Which Take Precedence?
Although both financial and strategic objectives carry top priority because of
their key results character, a dilemma arises when tradeoffs must be made
between actions to boost short-term financial performance and efforts to build
a stronger business position for the long term. Managers with strong financial
instincts often focus on short-term financial performance at the expense of
actions with a longer-term and more uncertain market and competitive payoff.
This is especially true when an organization's financial performance is poor.
Yet, once an organization's financial results are healthy enough to avert crisis,
the objective of building a stronger competitive position for the long term outweighs better financial payoffs in the short term. A company that consistently
passes up opportunities to strengthen its long-term competitive position (opting instead for immediate improvements in its financial performance) risks
diluting its competitiveness, losing momentum in its markets, and impairing
its ability to stave off market challenges from ambitious rivals. The risks are
especially great when a company has growth-minded competitors who place
more value on achieving long-term industry leadership than on current profits. Competitors who will accept lower prices and lower profit margins for long
periods in return for annual gains in market share can in time build a leading
market position at the expense of companies that are preoccupied with their
short-term profitability. One need look no further than the long-range strategic
efforts of Japanese companies to gain market ground on their more profit-
centered American and European rivals to appreciate the pitfall of letting
short-term financial objectives dominate the strategic objective of building
a sustainable competitive position.

The Concept of Strategic Intent   A company's strategic objectives are important for another reason—they delineate its *strategic intent* to stake out a partic-

---

ILLUSTRATION CAPSULE
6

STRATEGIC AND FINANCIAL OBJECTIVES OF WELL-KNOWN CORPORATIONS

Ford Motor Company: To be a low-cost producer of the highest quality products and services that provide the best customer value.

Federal Express: To continue the expansion of Federal Express's global network linking key markets around the world by merging dissimilar networks, providing service to additional countries, increasing the number of flight destinations, expanding our fleet of aircraft, opening new hubs, and adding U.S. gateways for the distribution of packages and freight.

Eastman Kodak: To be the world's best in chemical and electronic imaging.

Alcan Aluminum: To be the lowest cost producer of aluminum and to outperform the average return on equity of the Standard & Poor's Industrial Stock Index.

General Electric: To become the most competitive enterprise in the world by being number one or number two in market share in every business the company is in.

Apple Computer: To offer the best possible personal computing technology, and to put that technology in the hands of as many people as possible.

Atlas Corporation: To become a low-cost, medium-size gold producer, producing in excess of 125,000 ounces of gold a year and building gold reserves of 1,500,000 ounces.

Quaker Oats Company: To achieve return on equity at 20 percent or above, "real" earnings growth averaging 5 percent or better over time, be a leading marketer of strong consumer brands, and improve the profitability of low-return businesses or divest them.

Source: Company annual reports.

ular business position.[6] The strategic intent of a large company may be to exercise industry leadership on a national or global scale. The strategic intent of a small company may be to dominate a market niche and gain recognition as an up-and-coming enterprise. The time horizon underlying the concept of strategic intent is long term. Companies that rise to prominence in their markets almost invariably begin with strategic intents that are out of proportion to their immediate capabilities and market positions. But they set ambitious long-term strategic objectives and then pursue them relentlessly, sometimes even obsessively, over a 10- to 20-year period. In the 1960s, Komatsu, Japan's leading earth-moving equipment company, was less than one-third the size of Caterpillar, had little market presence outside Japan, and depended on its small bulldozers for most of its revenue. Komatsu's strategic intent was to "encircle Caterpillar" with a broader product line and compete globally against Caterpillar. By the late 1980s, Komatsu was the industry's second-ranking company, with a strong sales presence in North America, Europe, and Asia plus a product line that included industrial robots and semiconductors as well as a broad array of earth-moving equipment.

Often, a company's strategic intent takes on a heroic character, serving as a rallying cry for managers and employees alike to go all out and do their very

> **Basic Concept**
> *A company exhibits strategic intent when it relentlessly pursues a long-term strategic objective and concentrates its actions on achieving that objective.*

---

[6]The concept of strategic intent is described in more detail in Gary Hamel and C. K. Pralahad, "Strategic Intent," *Harvard Business Review* 89, no. 3 (May–June 1989), pp. 63–76. This section draws on their pioneering discussion.

best. Canon's strategic intent in copying equipment was to "beat Xerox." The strategic intent of the U.S. government's Apollo space program was to land a person on the moon ahead of the Soviet Union. Wal-Mart's strategic intent has been to "overtake Sears" as the largest U.S. retailer. In such instances, strategic intent signals a deep-seated commitment to winning—unseating the industry leader, remaining the industry leader (and becoming more dominant in the process), or otherwise beating long odds to gain a significantly stronger business position. A capably managed enterprise whose strategic objectives go well beyond its present reach and resources is potentially a more formidable competitor than a company with modest strategic intent.

Long-Range versus Short-Range Objectives An organization needs both long-range and short-range objectives. Long-range objectives serve two purposes. First, setting performance targets five or more years ahead raises the issue of what actions to take *now* in order to achieve the targeted long-range performance *later* (a company can't wait until the end of year 4 of its 5-year strategic plan to begin building the competitive market position it wants to have in year 5!). Second, having explicit long-range objectives pushes managers to weigh the impact of today's decision on longer-range performance. Without the pressure to make progress in meeting long-range performance targets, it is human nature to base decisions on what is most expedient and worry about the future later. The problem with short-sighted decisions, of course, is that they put a company's long-term business position at greater risk.

Short-range objectives spell out the immediate and near-term results to be achieved. They indicate the *speed* at which management wants the organization to progress as well as the *level of performance* being aimed for over the next two or three periods. Short-range objectives can be identical with long-range objectives any time an organization is already performing at the targeted long-term level. For instance, if a company has an ongoing objective of 15 percent profit growth every year and is currently achieving this objective, the company's long-range and short-range profit objectives coincide. The most important situation where short-range objectives differ from long-range objectives occurs when managers are trying to elevate organizational performance and cannot reach the long-range/ongoing target in just one year. Short-range objectives then serve as stairsteps for reaching the ultimate target.

The "Challenging but Achievable" Test

Company performance targets should be challenging but achievable.

Objectives should not represent whatever levels of achievement management decides would be "nice." Wishful thinking has no place in objective-setting. For objectives to serve as a tool for *stretching* an organization to reach its full potential, they must meet the criterion of being *challenging but achievable*. Satisfying this criterion means setting objectives in the light of several important "inside-outside" considerations:

- What performance levels will industry and competitive conditions realistically allow?
- What results will it take for the organization to be a successful performer?
- What performance is the organization capable of *when pushed*?

To set challenging but achievable objectives, managers must judge what performance is possible in light of external conditions and what performance the organization is capable of achieving. The tasks of objective-setting and strategy-making often become intertwined at this point. Strategic choices, for example, cannot be made in a financial vacuum; the money has to be available to execute whatever strategy is chosen. Consequently, decisions about strategy are contingent on setting the organization's financial performance objectives high enough to (1) execute the chosen strategy, (2) fund other needed actions, and (3) please investors and the financial community. Objectives and strategy also intertwine when it comes to matching the means (strategy) with the ends (objectives). If a company can't achieve established objectives by following its current strategy (either because the objectives are unrealistic or because the strategy is), the objectives or the strategy need adjustment to produce a better fit.

The Need for Objectives at All Management Levels

For strategic thinking and strategy-driven decision-making to penetrate the organizational hierarchy, performance targets must be established not only for the organization as a whole but also for each of the organization's separate businesses and product lines down to each functional area and department within the business-unit/product-line structure.[7] Only when every manager, from the chief executive officer to the lowest level manager, is held accountable for achieving specific results in their units is the objective-setting process complete enough to ensure that the whole organization is headed down the chosen path and that each part of the organization knows what it needs to accomplish.

The objective-setting process is more top-down than it is bottom-up. To see why strategic objectives at one managerial level tend to drive objectives and strategies at the next level down, consider the following example. Suppose the senior executives of a diversified corporation establish a corporate profit objective of $5 million for next year. Suppose further, after discussion between corporate management and the general managers of the firm's five different businesses, that each business is given the challenging but achievable profit objective of $1 million by year-end (i.e., if the five business divisions contribute $1 million each in profit, the corporation can reach its $5 million profit objective). A concrete result has thus been agreed on and translated into measurable action commitments at two levels in the managerial hierarchy. Next, suppose the general manager of business unit X, after some analysis and discussion with functional area managers, concludes that reaching the $1 million profit objective will require selling 100,000 units at an average price of $50 and producing them at an average cost of $40 (a $10 profit margin × 100,000 units = $1 million profit). Consequently, the general manager and the manufacturing manager may settle on a production objective of 100,000 units at a unit cost of $40. The general manager and the marketing manager may agree on a sales objective of 100,000 units and a target selling price of $50. In turn, the marketing manager may break the 100,000-unit sales objective into unit sales targets for each sales territory, each item in the product line, and each salesperson.

---

[7]Peter F. Drucker, *Management: Tasks, Responsibilities, Practices* (New York: Harper & Row, 1974), p. 100. See also Charles H. Granger, "The Hierarchy of Objectives," *Harvard Business Review* 42, no. 3 (May–June 1963), pp. 63–74.

Strategic Management Principle
Objective-setting should be more of a top-down than a bottom-up process in order to guide lower-level units toward objectives that support overall business and company objectives.

A top-down approach of establishing performance targets is a logical way to divide organizationwide targets into pieces that lower-level units and managers are responsible for achieving. Such an approach also provides a valuable degree of *unity* and *cohesion* to the objective-setting and strategy-making occurring in different parts of the organization. Generally speaking, organizationwide objectives and strategy need to be established first so they can *guide* objective-setting and strategy-making at lower levels. Top-down objective-setting and strategizing steer lower-level units toward objectives and strategies that take their cues from those of the total enterprise. When objective-setting and strategy-making begin at the bottom levels of an organization and organizationwide objectives and strategies reflect the aggregate of what has bubbled up from below, the resulting strategic action plan won't be consistent, cohesive, or coordinated. Bottom-up objective-setting, with no guidance from above, nearly always signals an absence of strategic leadership on the part of senior executives.

CRAFTING A STRATEGY: THE THIRD DIRECTION-SETTING TASK

Basic Concept
An organization's strategy consists of the combined actions that management has taken and intends to take in achieving strategic and financial objectives and pursuing the organization's mission.

Organizations need strategies to guide *how* to achieve objectives and *how* to pursue the organization's mission. Strategy-making is all about *how*—how to reach performance targets, how to outcompete rivals, how to seek and maintain competitive advantage, how to strengthen the enterprise's long-term business position. An organization's overall strategy and managerial game plan emerge from the *pattern* of actions already initiated and the plans managers have for making fresh moves. In forming a strategy out of many possible options, the strategist forges responses to market change, seeks new opportunities, and synthesizes different approaches taken at various times in various parts of the organization.[8]

An organization's strategy evolves over time. One would be hard pressed to find a company whose strategy was conceived in advance and followed exactly for a sustained time period. As a rule, companies revise their strategies in response to changes inside the company or in the surrounding environment. The unknowable or unpredictable character of competition and market change make it impossible to anticipate and plan for everything in advance. There is always something new to react to and some new strategic window opening up. This is why the task of strategizing is always ongoing, involving continuous review and reconsideration and fresh strategic initiatives to embellish or modify the current strategy.

As we emphasized in the opening chapter, strategy-making is not just a task for senior executives. In large, diversified enterprises, decisions about what approaches to take and what new moves to initiate involve corporate senior executives, heads of business units and product divisions, heads of major functional areas within a business or division (manufacturing, marketing and sales, finance, human resources, and the like), plant managers, product managers,

---

[8]Henry Mintzberg, "The Strategy Concept II: Another Look at Why Organizations Need Strategies," *California Management Review* 30, no. 1 (Fall 1987), pp. 25–32.

2 / The Three Strategy-Making Tasks

T A B L E 2–1 **The Strategy-Making Hierarchy** *(Who has primary responsibility for what kinds of strategy actions)*

Strategy Level	Primary Strategy-Development Responsibility	Strategy-Making Functions and Areas of Focus
Corporate strategy	CEO, other key executives (decisions are typically reviewed/approved by boards of directors)	• Building and managing a high-performing portfolio of business units (making acquisitions, strengthening existing business positions, divesting businesses that no longer fit into management's plans) • Capturing the synergy among related business units and turning it into competitive advantage • Establishing investment priorities and steering corporate resources into businesses with the most attractive opportunities • Reviewing/revising/unifying the major strategic approaches and moves proposed by business-unit managers
Business strategies	General manager/head of business unit (decisions are typically reviewed/approved by a senior executive or a board of directors)	• Devising moves and approaches to compete successfully and to secure a competitive advantage • Forming responses to changing external conditions • Uniting the strategic initiatives of key functional departments • Taking action to address company-specific issues and operating problems
Functional strategies	Functional managers (decisions are typically reviewed/approved by business-unit head)	• Crafting moves and approaches to support business strategy and to achieve functional/departmental performance objectives • Reviewing/revising/unifying strategy-related moves and approaches proposed by lower-level managers
Operating strategies	Field-unit heads/lower-level managers within functional areas (decisions are reviewed/approved by functional area head/department head)	• Crafting still narrower and more specific approaches/moves aimed at supporting functional and business strategies and at achieving operating-unit objectives

district and regional sales managers, and lower-level supervisors. In diversified enterprises, strategies are initiated at four distinct organization levels. There's a strategy for the company and all of its businesses as a whole (*corporate strategy*). There's a strategy for each separate business the company has diversified into (*business strategy*). Then there is a strategy for each specific functional unit within a business (*functional strategy*)—each business usually has a production strategy, a marketing strategy, a finance strategy, and so on. And, finally, there are still narrower strategies for basic operating units—plants, sales districts and regions, and departments within functional areas (*operating strategy*). Single-business enterprises have only three levels of strategy-making (business strategy, functional strategy, and operating strategy) unless diversification into other businesses becomes an active consideration. Table 2–1 highlights which level of management usually has lead responsibility for which level of strategy and indicates the kinds of strategic actions that distinguish each of the four strategy-making levels.

F I G U R E 2–1   **Identifying the Corporate Strategy of a Diversified Company**

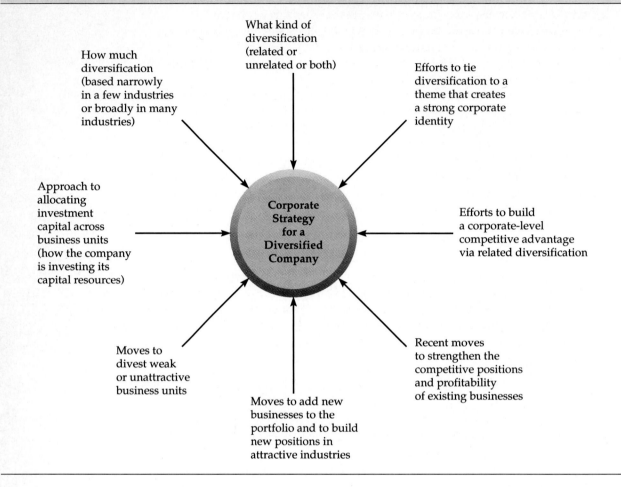

Corporate Strategy

Corporate strategy is the overall managerial game plan for a diversified company. Corporate strategy extends companywide—an umbrella over all businesses that a diversified company is in. It consists of the moves made to establish business positions in different industries and the approaches used to manage the company's group of businesses. Figure 2–1 depicts what to look for in profiling a diversified company's corporate strategy. Crafting corporate strategy for a diversified company involves four kinds of initiatives:

1. *Making the moves to accomplish diversification.* The first concern in diversification is what the portfolio of businesses should consist of—specifically, what industries to diversify into and whether to enter those industries by starting a new business or acquiring a company already in the industry (an established leader, an up-and-coming company, or a troubled company with turnaround potential). This piece of corporate strategy establishes whether diversification is based narrowly in a few industries or broadly in many industries, and it shapes how the company will be positioned in each of the target industries.

2. *Initiating actions to boost the combined performance of the businesses the firm has diversified into.* As positions are created in the chosen industries, corporate strategy-making concentrates on ways to get better performance out of the business-unit portfolio. Decisions must be reached about how to strengthen the long-term competitive positions and profitabilities of the businesses the corporation has invested in. Corporate parents can help their business subsidiaries be more successful by financing additional capacity and efficiency improvements, by supplying missing skills and managerial know-how, by acquiring another company in the same industry and merging the two operations into a stronger business, and/or by acquiring new businesses that strongly complement existing businesses. The overall plan for managing a group of diversified businesses usually involves pursuing rapid-growth strategies in the most promising businesses, keeping the other core businesses healthy, initiating turnaround efforts in weak-performing businesses with potential, and divesting businesses that are no longer attractive or that don't fit into management's long-range plans.

3. *Finding ways to capture the synergy among related business units and turn it into competitive advantage.* When a company diversifies into businesses with related technologies, similar operating characteristics, the same distribution channels, common customers, or some other synergistic relationship, it gains competitive advantage potential not open to a company that has diversified into totally unrelated businesses. With related diversification companies can usually transfer skills, share expertise, or share facilities across businesses, thereby reducing overall costs, strengthening the competitiveness of some of the corporation's products, or enhancing the capabilities of particular business units— any of which can represent a significant source of competitive advantage. The greater the relatedness among the businesses of a diversified company, the greater the opportunities for skills transfer and/or sharing across businesses and the bigger the window for creating competitive advantage. Indeed, what makes related diversification so attractive is the synergistic *strategic fit* across related businesses that allows company resources to be leveraged into a combined performance *greater* than the units could achieve operating independently. The 2 + 2 = 5 aspect of strategic fit makes related diversification a very appealing strategy for boosting corporate performance and shareholder value.

4. *Establishing investment priorities and steering corporate resources into the most attractive business units.* A diversified company's different businesses are usually not equally attractive from the standpoint of investing additional funds. Corporate executives need to rank the attractiveness of investing more capital in each business so they can channel resources into areas where earnings potentials are higher. Corporate strategy may include divesting businesses that are chronically poor performers or those in an unattractive industry. Divestiture frees up unproductive funds for redeployment to promising businesses or for financing attractive new acquisitions.

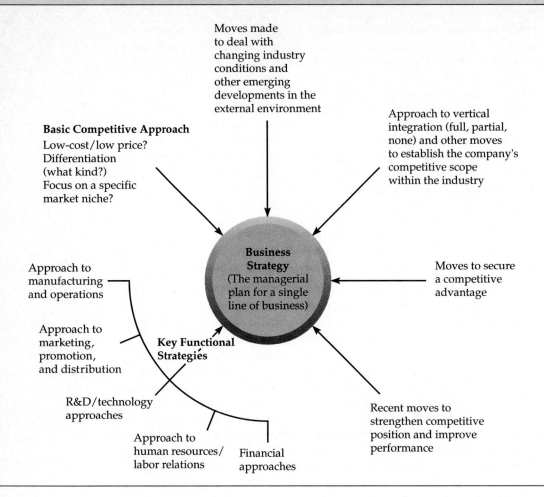

Corporate strategy is crafted at the highest levels of management. Senior corporate executives normally have lead responsibility for devising corporate strategy and for synthesizing whatever recommendations bubble up from lower-level managers. Key business-unit heads may also be influential, especially in strategic decisions affecting the businesses they head. Major strategic decisions are usually reviewed and approved by the company's board of directors.

Business Strategy

The term *business strategy* (or business-level strategy) refers to the managerial game plan for a single business. It is mirrored in the pattern of approaches and moves management devises to produce successful performance in *one specific line of business*. The various elements of business strategy are shown in Figure 2–2. For a stand-alone single-business company, corporate strategy and business strategy are one and the same since there is only one business to form a strategy for; the distinction between corporate strategy and business strategy is relevant only when diversification enters the firm's picture.

The central thrust of business strategy is how to build and strengthen the company's long-term competitive position in the marketplace. Toward this end, business strategy is concerned principally with (1) forming responses to changes underway in the industry, the economy at large, the regulatory and political arena, and other relevant areas, (2) crafting competitive moves and market approaches that can lead to sustainable competitive advantage, (3) uniting the strategic initiatives of functional departments, and (4) addressing specific strategic issues the business faces.

Clearly, business strategy encompasses whatever moves and new approaches managers deem prudent in light of competitive forces, economic trends and market developments, buyer demographics, new legislation and regulatory requirements, and other broad external factors. *A good strategy is well matched to the external situation*; as the external environment changes in significant ways, adjustments in strategy eventually become desirable. Whether a company's response to external change is quick or slow tends to be a function of how long events must unfold before managers can assess any implications for the business and how much longer it takes them to form a strategic response. Some external changes, of course, require little or no response, while others call for significant strategy alterations. On occasions, external factors change in ways that pose a formidable strategic hurdle—for example, cigarette manufacturers face a tough challenge holding their own against the mounting antismoking campaign.

What separates a powerful business strategy from a weak one is the strategist's ability *to forge a series of moves and approaches capable of producing sustainable competitive advantage*. With a competitive advantage, a company has good prospects for above-average profitability and success in the industry. Without competitive advantage, a company risks being outcompeted by stronger rivals and locked into mediocre performance. Crafting a business strategy that yields sustainable competitive advantage has several facets: deciding where a firm has the best chance to win a competitive edge, developing product/service attributes that have strong buyer appeal and set the company apart from rivals, and neutralizing the competitive moves of rival companies. A company's strategy for competing is typically both offensive and defensive—some aggressive actions amount to direct attacks on competitors' market positions; others neutralize fresh moves made by rivals. The three basic competitive approaches are: (1) striving to be the industry's low-cost producer (thereby aiming for a cost-based competitive advantage over rivals); (2) pursuing differentiation based on such advantages as quality, performance, service, styling, technological superiority, or unusually good value; and (3) focusing on a narrow market niche and winning a competitive edge by doing a better job than rivals of serving the special needs and tastes of buyers in the niche.

Internally, business strategy involves taking actions to develop the skills and capabilities needed to achieve competitive advantage. Successful business strategies usually aim at building the company's competence in one or more core activities crucial to strategic success and then using the core competence as a basis for winning a competitive edge over rivals. A *core competence* is something a firm does especially well in comparison to rival companies. It thus

---

Basic Concept
Business strategy concerns the moves and the approaches crafted by management to produce successful performance in one line of business; the central business strategy issue is how to build a stronger long-term competitive position.

Strategic Management Principle
A business strategy is powerful if it produces a sizable and sustainable competitive advantage; it is weak if it produces no advantage or results in competitive disadvantage.

represents a source of competitive strength. Core competences can relate to R&D, mastery of a technological process, manufacturing capability, sales and distribution, customer service, or anything else that is a competitively important aspect of creating, producing, or marketing the company's product or service. *A core competence is a basis for competitive advantage because it represents specialized expertise that rivals don't have and can't readily match.*

On a broader internal front, business strategy must also aim at uniting strategic initiatives in the various functional areas of business (purchasing, production, R&D, finance, human resources, sales and marketing, and distribution). Strategic actions are needed in each functional area to *support* the company's competitive approach and overall business strategy. Strategic unity and coordination across the various functional areas add power to the business strategy.

Business strategy also extends to action plans for addressing any special strategy-related issues unique to the company's competitive position and internal situation (such as whether to add new capacity, replace an obsolete plant, increase R&D funding for a promising technology, or reduce burdensome interest expenses). Such custom-tailoring of strategy is one of the reasons every company in an industry has a different business strategy.

Lead responsibility for business strategy falls in the lap of the manager in charge of the business. Even if the business head does not personally wield a heavy hand in the business strategy-making process, preferring to delegate much of the task to others, he or she is still accountable for the strategy and the results it produces. The business head, as chief strategist for the business, has at least two other responsibilities. The first is seeing that supporting strategies in each of the major functional areas of the business are well-conceived and consistent with each other. The second is getting major strategic moves approved by higher authority (the board of directors and/or corporate-level officers) if needed, and keeping them informed of important new developments, deviations from plan, and potential strategy revisions. In diversified companies, business-unit heads may also have to ensure that business-level objectives and strategy conform to corporate-level objectives and strategy.

Functional Strategy

Functional strategy refers to the set of strategic initiatives taken in one part of a business. A company needs a functional strategy for every major functional activity—an R&D strategy, a production strategy, a marketing strategy, a customer service strategy, a distribution strategy, a finance strategy, a human resources strategy, and so on. Functional strategies add detail to business strategy and govern *how* functional activities will be managed. A company's marketing strategy, for example, represents the managerial game plan for running the marketing part of the business. The primary role of a functional strategy is to *support* the company's overall business strategy and competitive approach. Another role is to create a managerial roadmap for achieving functional area performance objectives. Thus, functional strategy in the production/manufacturing area represents the game plan for *how* manufacturing activities will be managed to support business strategy and achieve manufacturing objectives. Functional strategy in the finance area consists of *how* financial activities will be managed in supporting business strategy and achieving specific financial objectives.

Lead responsibility for strategy-making in functional areas is normally delegated to the functional area heads, unless the business-unit head decides to exert a strong influence. In crafting strategy, a functional department head ideally works closely with key subordinates and often touches base with the heads of other functional areas and the business head. Coordinated and mutually supportive functional strategies are essential for the overall business strategy to have maximum impact. Plainly, a business's marketing strategy, production strategy, finance strategy, and human resource strategy should be working in concert rather than at cross-purposes. Coordination across functional area strategies is best accomplished during the deliberation stage. If inconsistent functional strategies are sent up the line for approval, it is up to the business head to spot the conflicts and get them resolved.

Operating Strategy

Operating strategies concern the even narrower strategic initiatives and approaches for managing key operating units (plants, sales districts, distribution centers) and for handling daily operating tasks with strategic significance (advertising campaigns, materials purchasing, inventory control, maintenance, shipping). Operating strategies, while of lesser scope than the higher levels of strategy-making, add relevant detail and completeness to the overall business plan. Lead responsibility for operating strategies is usually delegated to operating-level managers, subject to review and approval by higher ranking managers.

Even though operating strategy is at the bottom of the strategy-making hierarchy, its importance cannot be minimized. For example, a plant that fails to achieve production volume, unit cost, and quality targets can undercut sales and profit objectives and wreak havoc with the whole company's strategic efforts to build a quality image with customers. One can't always judge the importance of a strategic initiative by the managerial level where it originated.

Operating managers are part of an organization's strategy-making team because numerous operating-level units have strategy-critical performance targets and need to have strategic action plans in place to achieve them. A regional manager needs a strategy customized to the region's particular situation and objectives. A plant manager needs a strategy for accomplishing the plant's objectives, carrying out the plant's part of the company's overall manufacturing game plan, and dealing with any strategy-related problems at the plant. A company's advertising manager needs a strategy for getting maximum audience exposure and sales impact from the ad budget. The following two examples illustrate how operating strategy supports higher-level strategies.

- A company with a low-price, high-volume business strategy and a need to achieve low manufacturing costs launches a companywide effort to boost worker productivity by 10 percent. To contribute to this objective: (1) the manager of employee recruiting develops a strategy for interviewing and testing job applicants that weeds out all but the most highly motivated, best-qualified candidates; (2) the manager of information systems devises a way to use technology to boost the productivity of office workers; (3) the employee benefits manager devises an improved incentive-compensation plan to reward manufacturing

Basic Concept
Operating strategy concerns the game plan for managing key organizational units within a business (plants, sales districts, distribution centers) and for handling strategically significant operating tasks (materials purchasing, inventory control, maintenance, shipping, advertising campaigns).

employees for increased output; (4) the purchasing manager launches a program to obtain new efficiency-increasing equipment faster and easier.

- A distributor of plumbing equipment emphasizes quick delivery and accurate order-filling as keystones of its customer service approach. To support this strategy, the warehouse manager (1) develops an inventory-stocking strategy that allows 99 percent of all orders to be completely filled without back ordering any item and (2) institutes a warehouse staffing strategy that allows any order to be shipped within 24 hours.

Uniting the Strategy-Making Effort

Strategic Management Principle
Companies can't create unified objectives and strategies if each manager has objective-setting and strategy-making autonomy.

The previous discussion underscores that *an organization's strategic plan is a collection of strategies* devised by different managers at different levels in the organizational hierarchy. The larger the enterprise, the more points of strategic initiative it has. Management's direction-setting effort is not complete until managers unify the separate layers of strategy into a coherent, supportive pattern. Ideally the pieces and layers of strategy should fit together like the pieces of a picture puzzle. Unified objectives and strategies don't emerge from an undirected process where managers at each level set objectives and craft strategies *independently*. Indeed, functional and operating-level managers have a duty to set performance targets and invent strategic actions that will help achieve business objectives and make business strategy more effective.

Consistency between business strategy and functional/operating strategies comes from organizationwide allegiance to business objectives.

Harmonizing objectives and strategies piece-by-piece and level-by-level can be tedious and frustrating, requiring numerous consultations and meetings, annual strategy review and approval processes, trial and error, and months (sometimes years) of consensus-building. The politics of gaining strategic consensus and the battle of trying to keep all managers and departments focused on what's best for the total enterprise (as opposed to what's best for their departments or their careers) are often big obstacles in unifying the layers of objectives and strategies.[9] Gaining broad consensus is particularly difficult when there is ample room for opposing views and disagreement. It is not unusual for discussions about the organization's mission and basic direction, what objectives to set, and what strategies to employ to provoke heated debates and strong differences of opinion.

Figure 2–3 portrays the networking of objectives and strategies down through the managerial hierarchy. The two-way arrows indicate that there are simultaneous bottom-up and top-down influences on the objectives and strategies at each level. These vertical linkages, if managed in a way that promotes coordination, can help unify the objective-setting and strategy-making activities of many managers into a mutually reinforcing pattern. The tighter coordination is enforced, the tighter the linkages in the objectives and strategies of the various organizational units. Tight linkages safeguard against organizational units straying from the direction top management has charted.

---

[9]Functional managers can sometimes be more interested in doing what is best for their own areas, in building their own empire, and in consolidating their personal power and influence than they are in cooperating with other functional managers to unify behind the overall business strategy. As a consequence, it's easy for functional area support strategies to conflict, thereby forcing the general manager to spend time and energy refereeing differences and building support for a more unified approach.

FIGURE 2–3   **The Networking of Missions, Objectives, and Strategies through the Managerial Hierarchy**

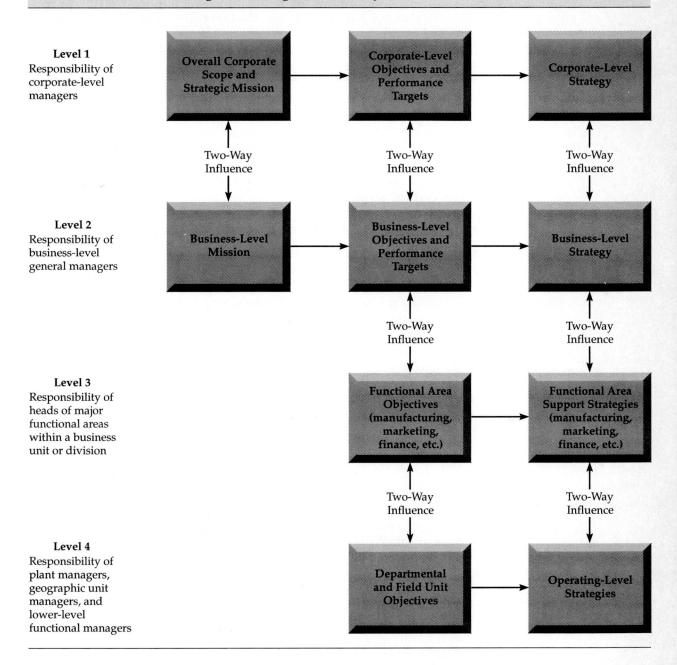

As a practical matter, however, corporate and business missions, objectives, and strategies need to be clearly outlined and communicated down the line before much progress can be made in objective-setting and strategy-making at the functional and operating levels. Direction and guidance needs to flow from the corporate level to the business level and from the business level to the functional and operating levels. The strategic disarray that occurs in an organization when senior managers don't exercise strong top-down direction-setting and strategic leadership is akin to what would happen to a football team's offensive performance if the quarterback decided not to call a play for the team, but instead, gave each player the latitude to pick whatever play he thought would work best at his respective position.

THE FACTORS THAT SHAPE STRATEGY

Many factors enter into the forming of a company's strategy. Figure 2–4 is a simple model of the primary factors that shape the choice of a strategy. The interplay of these factors is frequently complex and always industry- and company-specific. No two strategic choices are made in exactly the same context; the situational factors always differ, if only slightly. This is why managers need to assess all the various situational factors, both external and internal, before they begin crafting strategy.

Societal, Political, Regulatory, and Citizenship Considerations

Societal, political, regulatory, and citizenship factors limit the strategic actions a company can take.

What an enterprise can and cannot do strategywise is always constrained by what is legal, by what is in compliance with government policies and regulations, by what is considered socially acceptable, and by what constitutes community citizenship. Outside pressures also come from other sources—special interest groups, the glare of investigative reporting, a fear of unwanted political action, and the stigma of negative opinion. Societal concerns over health and nutrition, alcohol and drug abuse, hazardous waste disposal, sexual harassment, and the impact of plant closings on local communities have impacted many companies' strategies. American concerns over the growing volume of foreign imports and political debate over whether to impose tariffs and import quotas to help reduce the chronic U.S. trade deficit have been key factors in the strategic decisions of Japanese and European companies to locate plants in the United States. Heightened awareness of the dangers of cholesterol has driven food products companies to substitute low-fat ingredients despite extra costs.

More and more companies now consider societal values and priorities, community concerns, and the potential for onerous legislation and regulatory requirements when analyzing their external situation. Intense public pressure and adverse media coverage have made such a practice prudent. The task of making an organization's strategy "socially responsible" means (1) conducting organizational activities within the bounds of what is considered ethical and in the general public interest; (2) responding positively to emerging societal priorities and expectations; (3) demonstrating a willingness to take action ahead of regulatory confrontation; (4) balancing stockholder interests against the larger interests of society; and (5) being a "good citizen" in the community.

The concept of corporate social responsibility is showing up in company mission statements. John Hancock, for example, concludes its mission statement with the following sentence:

> In pursuit of this mission, we will strive to exemplify the highest standards of business ethics and personal integrity; and shall recognize our corporate obligation to the social and economic well-being of our community.

Factors Shaping the Choice of Company Strategy

External Factors

Societal, political, regulatory, and community citizenship considerations	Industry attractiveness; changing industry and competitive conditions	Company opportunities and threats

A Company's Strategic Situation

Organizational strengths, weaknesses, and competitive market position	Personal ambitions, business philosophies, and ethical principles of key executives	Shared values and company culture

Internal Factors

Conclusions concerning how internal and external factors stack up; their implications for strategy

Identification and evaluation of strategy alternatives

Crafting a strategy that fits the overall situation

Union Electric, a St. Louis–based utility company, includes the following statement in its official corporate policy:

> As a private enterprise entrusted with an essential public service, we recognize our civic responsibility in the communities we serve. We shall strive to advance the growth and welfare of these communities and shall participate in civic activities which fulfill that goal . . . for we believe this is both good citizenship and good business.

Illustration Capsule 7 describes Anheuser-Busch's efforts to be socially responsible.

Industry Attractiveness and Competitive Conditions

Industry attractiveness and competitive conditions are big strategy-determining factors. A company's assessment of the industry and competitive environment directly affects how it should try to position itself in the industry and what its basic competitive strategy approach should be. When a firm concludes its industry environment has grown unattractive, and it is better off investing company resources elsewhere, it may craft a strategy of disinvestment and abandonment. When competitive conditions intensify significantly, a company must respond with strategic actions to protect its position. Fresh moves on the part of rival companies, changes in the industry's price-cost-profit economics, and new technological developments can alter the requirements for competitive success and mandate that a firm reconsider its strategy. A strategist, therefore, has to be a student of industry and competitive conditions.

Specific Company Opportunities and Threats

The particular business opportunities a company has and the threats to its position that it faces are key influences on strategy. Strategy needs to be deliberately crafted to capture some or all of a company's best growth opportunities, especially the ones that can enhance its long-term competitive position and profitability. Likewise, strategy should be geared to providing a defense against external threats to the company's well-being and future performance. For strategy to be successful, it has to be well matched to company opportunities and threats.

Organizational Strengths, Weaknesses, and Competitive Capabilities

Experience shows that in matching strategy to a firm's internal situation, management should build strategy around what the company does well and avoid strategies whose success depends heavily on something the company does poorly or has never done at all. In short, *strategy must be well matched to company strengths, weaknesses, and competitive capabilities.* Pursuing an opportunity without the organizational competences and resources to capture it is foolish. An organization's strengths make some opportunities and strategies attractive; likewise its internal weaknesses and its present competitive market position make certain strategies risky or even out of the question.

ILLUSTRATION CAPSULE

SOCIAL RESPONSIBILITY EFFORTS AT ANHEUSER-BUSCH

In a recent annual report, Anheuser-Busch described three main areas in which it was exercising social responsibility:

Alcohol Issues—Anheuser-Busch has long believed it is in the company's best interest, and in the interest of society as a whole, to play an important role in the fight against the abuse of alcoholic beverages. Although the company's efforts were already the most extensive in the brewing industry, in 1989 Anheuser-Busch created a Department of Consumer Awareness and Education to (1) educate consumers and servers of alcohol about the appropriate use of its products and (2) aggressively defend the right of brewers and beer consumers to make and enjoy beer without the fear of being stigmatized. One of the current activities of this department was an expanded "Know When to Say When" advertising campaign featuring well-known sports celebrities. In addition, Anheuser-Busch supported scientific research into the causes and possible cures of alcoholism and alcohol abuse. More than $15 million was contributed in 1989 to such organizations as the Alcoholic Beverage-Medical Research Foundation in Baltimore, Md., and the Alcohol Research Center at UCLA.

Minority Development—Anheuser-Busch supports minority organizations engaged in economic development, cultural heritage, education and leadership development. As the founder and national sponsor of the Lou Rawls Parade of Stars telethon, Anheuser-Busch commissioned a traveling exhibit to commemorate this television special's 10th anniversary and its success in raising more than $75 million since 1980. The company also contributed $15 million in 1989 to the National Hispanic Scholarship Fund to support its development and scholarship efforts. Anheuser-Busch is the NHSF's largest corporate supporter.

Community Support—Anheuser-Busch tries to enrich the communities in which it operates breweries and other major facilities by supporting local nonprofit organizations such as the United Way, social service agencies, arts and cultural groups, health care institutions, youth groups and colleges and universities. In addition, through the Anheuser-Busch Employee Volunteer Grant Program, the company recognizes its employees who actively volunteer their services to nonprofit organizations by making grants to these organizations. The company also has an employee Matching Gift program for educational institutions.

Source: 1989 Annual Report.

One of the most pivotal strategy-shaping internal considerations is whether a company has or can build the core strengths or competences needed to execute the strategy proficiently. An organization's core strengths—the things it does especially well—are an important strategy-making consideration because of (1) the skills and capabilities they provide in capitalizing on a particular opportunity, (2) the competitive edge they may give in the marketplace, and (3) the potential they have for becoming a cornerstone of strategy. The best path to competitive advantage is found where a firm has core strengths in one or more of the key requirements for market success, where rivals do not have matching or offsetting competences, and where rivals can't develop comparable strengths except at high cost and/or over an extended period of time.[10]

Even if an organization has no outstanding core competences (and many do not), it still must shape its strategy to suit its particular skills and available

[10]David T. Kollat, Roger D. Blackwell, and James F. Robeson, *Strategic Marketing* (New York: Holt, Rinehart & Winston, 1972), p. 24.

resources. It never makes sense to develop a strategic plan that cannot be executed with the skills and resources a firm is able to muster.

The Personal Ambitions, Business Philosophies, and Ethical Beliefs of Managers

Managers' personal ambitions, business philosophies, and ethical beliefs are usually woven into the strategies they craft.

Managers do not dispassionately assess what strategic course to steer. Their decisions are often influenced by their own vision of how to compete and how to position the enterprise and by what image and standing they want the company to have. Both casual observation and formal studies indicate that managers' ambitions, value, business philosophies, attitudes toward risk, and ethical beliefs have important influences on strategy.[11] Sometimes the influence of the manager's personal values and experiences is conscious and deliberate; at other times it is unconscious. As Professor Andrews has noted in explaining the relevance of personal factors to strategy, "People have to have their hearts in it."[12]

Several examples of how business philosophies and personal values enter into strategy-making are particularly noteworthy. Japanese managers are strong proponents of strategies that take a long-term view and that aim at building market share and competitive position. In contrast, some corporate executives and Wall Street financiers have drawn criticism for overemphasizing short-term profits at the expense of long-term competitive positioning and for being more attracted to strategies involving a financial play on assets (leveraged buyouts and stock buybacks) rather than using corporate resources to make long-term strategic investments. Japanese companies also display a different philosophy regarding the role of suppliers. They prefer to establish long-term partnership arrangements with key suppliers to improve the quality and reliability of component parts and to reduce inventory requirements. In the United States and Europe the prevailing managerial philosophy has been to play suppliers off against one another, doing business on a short-term basis with whoever offers the best price and delivery.

Attitudes toward risk also have a big influence on strategy. Risk-avoiders favor "conservative" strategies that minimize downside risk, have a quick payback, and produce sure short-term profits. Risk-takers lean more toward opportunistic strategies where bold moves can produce a big payoff over the long term. Risk-takers prefer innovation to imitation and strategic offensives to defensive conservatism.

Managerial values also shape the ethical quality of a firm's strategy. Managers with strong ethical convictions take pains to see that their companies observe a strict code of ethics in all aspects of the business. They expressly forbid such practices as accepting or giving kickbacks, badmouthing rivals' products, and buying political influence with political contributions. Instances

---

[11]See, for instance, William D. Guth and Renato Tagiuri, "Personal Values and Corporate Strategy," *Harvard Business Review* 43, no. 5 (September–October 1965), pp. 123–32; Kenneth R. Andrews, *The Concept of Corporate Strategy*, 3rd ed. (Homewood Ill.: Richard D. Irwin, 1987), chap. 4; and Richard F. Vancil, "Strategy Formulation in Complex Organizations," *Sloan Management Review* 17, no. 2 (Winter 1986), pp. 4–5.

[12]Andrews, *The Concept of Corporate Strategy*, p. 63.

where a company's strategic actions run counter to high ethical standards include charging excessive interest rates on credit card balances, employing bait-and-switch sales tactics, continuing to market products suspected of having safety problems, and using ingredients that are known health hazards.

The Influence of Shared Values and Company Culture on Strategy

An organization's policies, practices, traditions, philosophical beliefs, and ways of doing things combine to give it a distinctive culture. A company's strategic actions typically reflect its cultural traits and managerial values. In some cases a company's core beliefs and culture even dominate the choice of strategic moves. This is because culture-related values and beliefs become so embedded in management's thinking and actions that they condition how the enterprise responds to external events. Such firms have a culture-driven bias about how to handle strategic issues and what kinds of strategic moves it will consider or reject. Strong cultural influences partly account for why companies gain reputations for such strategic traits as technological leadership, product innovation, dedication to superior craftsmanship, a proclivity for financial wheeling and dealing, growth through acquisitions, a strong people-orientation, or unusual emphasis on customer service and total customer satisfaction.

A company's values and culture sometimes dominate the kinds of strategic moves it will consider or reject.

In recent years, more companies have begun to articulate the core beliefs and values underlying their business approaches. One company expressed its core beliefs and values this way:

> We are market-driven. We believe that functional excellence, combined with teamwork across functions and profit centers, is essential to achieving superb execution. We believe that people are central to everything we will accomplish. We believe that honesty, integrity, and fairness should be the cornerstone of our relationships with consumers, customers, suppliers, stockholders, and employees.

IBM's founder, Thomas Watson, once stated, "We must be prepared to change all the things we are in order to remain competitive in the environment, but we must never change our three basic beliefs: (1) respect for the dignity of the individual, (2) offering the best customer service in the world, and (3) excellence." For nearly a century, AT&T's value system has emphasized (1) universal service, (2) fairness in handling personnel matters, (3) a belief that work should be balanced with commitments to family and community, and (4) relationships (from one part of the organization to another). AT&T's management views these values as essential in a technologically dynamic, highly structured company. Both the IBM and AT&T value systems are deeply ingrained and widely shared by managers and employees. Whenever this happens, values and beliefs become more than an expression of nice platitudes; they become a way of life within the company.[13]

---

[13]For more details, see Richard T. Pascale, "Perspectives on Strategy: The Real Story behind Honda's Success," in Glenn Carroll and David Vogel, *Strategy and Organization: A West Coast Perspective* (Marshfield, Mass.: Pitman Publishing, 1984), p. 60.

LINKING STRATEGY WITH ETHICS

Every strategic action a company takes should be ethically acceptable.

A company has ethical duties to owners, employees, customers, suppliers, and the public.

Strategy ought to be ethical. It should involve rightful actions, not wrongful ones, or it won't pass the test of moral scrutiny. This means more than conforming to what is legal. Ethical and moral standards go beyond the prohibitions of law and the language of "thou shalt not" to the issues of *duty* and the language of "should do and should not do." Ethics concerns human duty and the principles on which these duties rest.[14]

Every business has an ethical duty to each of five constituencies: owners/shareholders, employees, customers, suppliers, and the community at large. Each of these constituencies affects the organization and is affected by it. Each is a stakeholder in the enterprise, with certain expectations as to what the enterprise should do and how it should do it.[15] Owners/shareholders, for instance, expect a return on their investment. Even though individual investors differ in their preferences for profits now versus profits later, their desire to take risks, and their willingness to exercise social responsibility, business executives have a moral duty to profitably manage the owners' investment.

A company's duty to employees arises out of respect for the worth and dignity of individuals who devote their energies to the business and depend on the business for their economic well-being. Principled strategy-making requires that employee-related decisions be made equitably and compassionately, with concern for due process and for the impact that strategic change has on employees' lives. At best, the chosen strategy should promote employee interests in areas such as wage and salary levels, career opportunities, job security, and overall working conditions. At least, the chosen strategy should not disadvantage employees. Even in crisis situations where adverse employee impact cannot be avoided, businesses have an ethical duty to minimize whatever hardships have to be imposed in the form of workforce reductions, plant closings, job transfers, relocations, retraining, and loss of income.

A company's duty to the customer arises out of expectations that attend the purchase of a good or service. Inadequate appreciation of this duty has led to product liability laws and a host of regulatory agencies to protect consumers. All kinds of strategy-related ethical issues still arise here, however. Should a seller inform consumers *fully* about the contents of its product, especially if it contains ingredients that, though officially approved for use, are suspected of having potentially harmful effects? Is it ethical for the makers of alcoholic beverages to sponsor college events, given that many college students are under 21? Is it ethical for cigarette manufacturers to advertise at all (even though it is legal)? Is it ethical for airlines to withhold information about terrorist bomb threats from the public? Is it ethical for manufacturers to produce and sell products they know have faulty parts or defective designs that may not become apparent until after the warranty expires? In submitting bids on a contract, is it unethical to seek access to inside information not available to other bidders? Is it ethical to give some customers special treatment?

A company's ethical duty to its suppliers arises out of the market relationship that exists between them—they are both partners and adversaries. They

---

[14]Harry Downs, "Business Ethics: The Stewardship of Power," forthcoming in *Strategic Management Planning*.
[15]Ibid.

are partners in the sense that the quality of suppliers' parts affects the quality of a firm's own product. They are adversaries in the sense that the supplier wants the highest price and profit it can while the buyer wants a cheaper price, better quality, and speedier service. A business confronts several ethical issues in its supplier relationships. Is it ethical to threaten to cease doing business with a supplier unless the supplier agrees not to do business with key competitors? Is it ethical to reveal one supplier's price quote to a rival supplier? Is it ethical to accept gifts from suppliers? Is it ethical to pay a supplier in cash?

The ethical duty to the community-at-large stems from the business's status as a citizen of the community and as an institution of society. Communities and society are reasonable in expecting businesses to be good citizens—to pay their fair share of taxes for fire and police protection, waste removal, streets and highways, and so on and to exercise care in the impact their activities have on the environment and on the communities in which they operate. The community should be accorded the same recognition and attention as the other four constituencies. Whether a company is a good community citizen is ultimately demonstrated by the way it supports community activities, encourages employees to participate in community activities, handles the health and safety aspects of its operations, accepts responsibility for overcoming environmental pollution, relates to regulatory bodies and employee unions, and exhibits high ethical standards.

NCR Corporation, a $6 billion computer and office equipment company, recently cast its entire mission statement in terms of its duty to stockholders, customers, employees, suppliers, and the community at large. See Illustration Capsule 8.

Carrying Out Ethical Responsibilities   It is management, not constituent groups, who is responsible for managing the enterprise. Thus, it is management's perceptions of its ethical duties and of constituents' claims that determine whether and how strategy is linked to ethical behavior. Ideally, managers weigh strategic decisions from each constituent's viewpoint and, where conflicts arise, strike a rational, objective, and equitable balance among the interests of all five. If any of the five constituencies conclude that management is not doing its duty, they have their own avenues for recourse. Concerned investors can complain at the annual shareholders' meeting, appeal to the board of directors, or sell their stock. Concerned employees can unionize and bargain collectively, or they can seek employment elsewhere. Customers can buy from competitors. Suppliers can find other buyers or pursue other market alternatives. The community and society can do anything from staging protest marches to stimulating political and governmental action.[16]

A company that truly cares about business ethics and corporate social responsibility is proactive rather than reactive in linking strategy and ethics. It steers away from ethically or morally questionable business opportunities. It won't do business with suppliers that engage in activities the company does not condone. Its products are safe for its customers to use. Its workplace environment is safe for employees. It recruits and hires employees whose values and behavior are consistent with the company's principles and

---

[16]Ibid.

ETHICS AND VALUES AT NCR CORPORATION

NCR's corporate mission statement formally recognizes the company's duty to serve the interests of all stakeholders, not just those of stockholders, and represents a blend of ethical principles and values. As management stated in a recent annual report:

NCR is a successful, growing company dedicated to achieving superior results by assuring that its actions are aligned with stakeholder expectations. Stakeholders are all constituencies with a stake in the fortunes of the company. NCR's primary mission is to create value for our stakeholders.

We believe in conducting our business activities with integrity and respect while building mutually beneficial and enduring relationships with all of our stakeholders.

We take customer satisfaction personally: we are committed to providing superior value in our products and services on a continuing basis.

We respect the individuality of each employee and foster an environment in which employees' creativity and productivity are encouraged, recognized, valued and rewarded.

We think of our suppliers as partners who share our goal of achieving the highest quality standards and the most consistent level of service.

We are committed to being caring and supportive corporate citizens within the worldwide communities in which we operate.

We are dedicated to creating value for our shareholders and financial communities by performing in a manner that will enhance returns on investments.

Source: 1987 Annual Report.

ethical standards. It acts to reduce any environmental pollution it causes. It cares about *how* it does business and whether its actions reflect integrity and high ethical standards. Illustration Capsule 9 describes Harris Corporation's ethical commitments to its stakeholders.

Tests of a Winning Strategy

How can a manager judge which strategic option is best for the company? What are the standards for determining whether a strategy is successful or not? Three tests can be used to evaluate the merits of one strategy over another and to gauge how good a strategy is:

The Goodness of Fit Test—A good strategy is well matched to the company's situation—both internal and external factors and its own capabilities and aspirations.

The Competitive Advantage Test—A good strategy leads to sustainable competitive advantage. The bigger the competitive edge that a strategy helps build, the more powerful and effective it is.

The Performance Test—A good strategy boosts company performance. Two kinds of performance improvements are the most telling: gains in profitability and gains in the company's long-term business strength and competitive position.

Strategic options with low potential on one or more of these criteria do not merit strong consideration. The strategic option with the highest potential on all three counts can be regarded as the best or most attractive strategic alternative. Once a strategic commitment has been made and enough time has

ILLUSTRATION CAPSULE
9

HARRIS CORPORATION'S COMMITMENTS TO ITS STAKEHOLDERS

Harris Corp. is a major supplier of information, communication, and semiconductor products, systems, and services to commercial and governmental customers throughout the world. The company utilizes advanced technologies to provide innovative and cost-effective solutions for processing and communicating data, voice, text, and video information. The company's sales exceed $2 billion, and it employs nearly 23,000 people. In a recent annual report, the company set forth its commitment to satisfying the expectations of its stakeholders:

Customers—For customers, our objective is to achieve ever-increasing levels of satisfaction by providing quality products and services with distinctive benefits on a timely and continuing basis worldwide. Our relationships with customers will be forthright and ethical, and will be conducted in a manner to build trust and confidence.

Shareholders—For shareholders, the owners of our company, our objective is to achieve sustained growth in earnings-per-share. The resulting stock-price appreciation combined with dividends should provide our shareholders with a total return on investment that is competitive with similar investment opportunities.

Employees—The people of Harris are our company's most valuable asset, and our objective is for every employee to be personally involved in and share the success of the business. The company is committed to providing an environment which encourages all employees to make full use of their creativity and unique talents; to providing equitable compensation, good working conditions, and the opportunity for personal development and growth which is limited only by individual ability and desire.

Suppliers—Suppliers are a vital part of our resources. Our objective is to develop and maintain mutually beneficial partnerships with suppliers who share our commitment to achieving increasing levels of customer satisfaction through continuing improvements in quality, service, timeliness, and cost. Our relationships with suppliers will be sincere, ethical, and will embrace the highest principles of purchasing practice.

Communities—Our objective is to be a responsible corporate citizen. This includes support of appropriate civic, educational, and business activities, respect for the environment, and the encouragement of Harris employees to practice good citizenship and support community programs. Our greatest contribution to our communities is to be successful so that we can maintain stable employment and create new jobs.

Source: 1988 Annual Report.

elapsed to see results, these same tests can be used to determine how well a company's current strategy is performing. The bigger the margins by which a strategy satisfies all three criteria when put to test in the marketplace, the more it qualifies as a winning strategy.

There are, of course, some additional criteria for judging the merits of a particular strategy: clarity, internal consistency among all the pieces of strategy, timeliness, match to the personal values and ambitions of key executives, the degree of risk involved, and flexibility. These can be used to supplement the three tests posed above whenever it seems appropriate.

APPROACHES TO PERFORMING THE STRATEGY-MAKING TASK

Companies and managers perform the strategy-making task differently. In small, owner-managed companies, strategy-making is developed informally. Often the strategy is never written but exists mainly in the entrepreneur's own mind and in oral understandings with key subordinates. The largest firms, however, tend to develop their plans via an annual strategic planning cycle (complete with prescribed procedures, forms, and timetables) that includes broad management participation, lots of studies, and multiple meetings to probe and question. The larger and more diverse an enterprise, the more managers feel it is better to have a structured annual process with written plans, management scrutiny, and official approval at each level.

Along with variations in the organizational process of formulating strategy are variations in how managers personally participate in analyzing the company's situation and deliberating what strategy to pursue. The four basic strategy-making styles managers use include:[17]

The Master Strategist Approach—Here the manager personally functions as chief strategist and chief entrepreneur, exercising *strong* influence over assessments of the situation, over the strategy alternatives that are explored, and over the details of strategy. This does not mean that the manager personally does all the work; it means the manager personally becomes the chief architect of strategy and wields a proactive hand in shaping some or all of the major pieces of strategy. The manager acts as strategy commander and has a big ownership stake in the chosen strategy.

The Delegate-It-to-Others Approach—Here the manager in charge delegates the exercise of strategy-making to others, perhaps a strategic planning staff or a task force of trusted subordinates. The manager then stays off to the side, keeps in touch via reports and conversations, offers guidance if needed, reacts to informal "trial balloon" recommendations, then puts a stamp of approval on the "strategic plan" after it has been formally presented and discussed and a consensus emerges. But the manager rarely has much ownership in the recommendations and, privately, may not see much urgency in pushing *truly hard* to implement some or much of what has been written down in the company's "official strategic plan." Also, it is generally understood that "of course, we may have to proceed a bit differently if conditions change"—which gives the manager flexibility to go slow or ignore those approaches/moves that "on further reflection may not be the thing to do at this time." This strategy-making style has the advantage of letting the manager pick and choose from the smorgasbord of strategic ideas that bubble up from below, and it allows room for broad participation and input from many managers and areas. The weakness is that a manager can end up so detached from the process of formal strategy-making that he or she exercises no real strategic leadership—indeed, subordinates are likely to conclude that strategic planning isn't important enough to warrant a claim on the boss's personal time and attention. The stage is then set for rudderless direction-setting. Often the strategy-making that does occur is short-run-oriented and reactive; it deals more with today's problems than with positioning the enterprise to capture tomorrow's opportunities.

The Collaborative Approach—This is a middle approach whereby the manager enlists the help of key subordinates in hammering out a

---

[17]This discussion is based on David R. Brodwin and L. J. Bourgeois, "Five Steps to Strategic Action," in Glenn Carroll and David Vogel, *Strategy and Organization: A West Coast Perspective* (Marshfield, Mass.: Pitman Publishing, 1984), pp. 168–78.

consensus strategy that all the key players will back and do their best to implement successfully. The biggest strength of this strategy-making style is that those who are charged with crafting the strategy also have to implement it. Giving subordinate managers such a clear-cut ownership stake in the strategy they subsequently must implement enhances commitment to successful execution. When subordinates have a hand in proposing their part of the overall strategy, they can be held accountable for making it work—the "I told you it was a bad idea" alibi won't fly.

The Champion Approach—In this style, the manager is interested neither in personally crafting the details of strategy nor in the time-consuming task of leading a group to brainstorm a consensus strategy. Rather, the manager encourages subordinate managers to develop, champion, and implement sound strategies. Here strategy moves upward from the "doers" and the "fast-trackers." Executives serve as judges, evaluating the strategy proposals that reach their desks. This approach works best in large diversified corporations where the CEO cannot personally orchestrate strategy-making in each business division. Headquarters executives depend on ambitious and talented entrepreneurs at the business-unit level who can see strategic opportunities that the executives cannot. Corporate executives may articulate general strategic themes as organizationwide guidelines. But the key to strategy-making is stimulating and rewarding new strategic initiatives conceived by champions who believe in the opportunity and badly want the blessing to go after it. With this approach, total "strategy" is shaped by the sum of the championed initiatives that get approved.

These four basic managerial approaches illuminate several aspects about how strategy emerges. In situations where the manager in charge personally functions as the chief architect of strategy, the strategy is a product of his/her own vision, ambitions, values, business philosophies, and sense of what moves to make next. Highly centralized strategy-making works fine when the manager in charge has a powerful, insightful vision of what needs to be done and how to do it. The primary weakness of the master strategist approach is that the caliber of the strategy depends so heavily on one person's strategy-making skills. It also breaks down in large enterprises, where many strategic initiatives are needed and the strategy-making task is too complex for one person to handle.

The group approach to strategy-making has its risks too. Sometimes, the strategy that emerges is a middle-of-the-road compromise that lacks bold, creative initiative. Other times, it represents political consensus, with the outcome shaped by influential subordinates, powerful functional departments, or majority coalitions that have a common interest in promoting their own version of what the strategy ought to be. "Politics" and power plays are most likely in situations where there is no strong consensus on what strategy to adopt. The collaborative approach is especially conducive to political strategy formation, since powerful departments and individuals have ample opportunity to try to build a consensus for their favored strategic approach. However, the big danger of a delegate-it-to-others approach is a serious lack of top-down direction and strategic leadership.

The strength of the champion approach is also its weakness. The value of championing is that it encourages people at lower organizational levels to

Of the four basic approaches managers can use in crafting strategy, none stands out as inherently superior— each has strengths and weaknesses.

propose new strategic initiatives and stay on the lookout for good opportunities to pursue. Individuals with attractive strategic proposals are given the latitude and resources to try them out, thus helping keep strategy fresh and renewing an organization's capacity for innovation. On the other hand, the championed actions, because they come from many parts of the organization, are not likely to form a coherent pattern or promote clear strategic direction. With championing, the chief executive has to work at ensuring that what is championed adds power to the overall organization strategy; otherwise, strategic initiatives may be launched in directions that have no integrating links or overarching rationale.

KEY POINTS

Management's direction-setting task involves developing a mission, setting objectives, and forming a strategy. Early on in the direction-setting process, managers need to form a vision of where to lead the organization and to answer the question, "What is our business and what will it be?" A well-conceived mission statement helps channel organizational efforts along the course management has charted and builds a strong sense of organizational identity. Effective visions are clear, challenging, and inspiring; they prepare a firm for the future, and they make sense in the marketplace. A well-conceived, well-said mission statement serves as a beacon of long-term direction and creates employee "buy-in."

The second direction-setting step is to establish strategic and financial objectives for the organization to achieve. Objectives convert the mission statement into specific performance targets. The agreed-on objectives need to be challenging but achievable, and they need to spell out precisely how much by when. In other words, objectives should be measurable and should involve deadlines for achievement. Objectives are needed at all organizational levels.

The third direction-setting step entails forming strategies to achieve the objectives set in each area of the organization. A corporate strategy is needed to achieve corporate-level objectives; business strategies are needed to achieve business-unit performance objectives; functional strategies are needed to achieve the performance targets set for each functional department; and operating-level strategies are needed to achieve the objectives set in each operating and geographic unit. In effect, an organization's strategic plan is a collection of unified and interlocking strategies. As shown in Table 2–1, different strategic issues are addressed at each level of managerial strategy-making. Typically, the strategy-making task is more top-down than bottom-up. Lower-level strategy supports and complements higher-level strategy and contributes to the achievement of higher-level, companywide objectives.

Strategy is shaped by both outside and inside considerations. The major external considerations are societal, political, regulatory, and community factors; industry attractiveness; and the company's market opportunities and threats. The primary internal considerations are company strengths, weaknesses, and competitive capabilities; managers' personal ambitions, philosophies, and ethics; and the company's culture and shared values. A good strategy must be well matched to all these situational considerations.

There are essentially four basic ways to manage the strategy formation process in an organization: the master strategist approach where the manager in charge personally functions as the chief architect of strategy, the delegate-it-to-others approach, the collaborative approach, and the champion approach. All four have strengths and weaknesses. All four can succeed or fail depending on how well the approach is managed and depending on the strategy-making skills and judgments of the individuals involved.

Andrews, Kenneth R. *The Concept of Corporate Strategy*, 3rd ed. Homewood, Ill.: Dow Jones-Irwin, 1987, chaps. 2, 3, 4, and 5.

Foster, Lawrence W. "From Darwin to Now: The Evolution of Organizational Strategies," *Journal of Business Strategy* 5, no. 4 (Spring 1985), pp. 94–98.

Hamel, Gary, and C. K. Prahalad. "Strategic Intent." *Harvard Business Review* 89, no. 3 (May–June, 1989), pp. 63–76.

McLellan, R., and G. Kelly. "Business Policy Formulation: Understanding the Process." *Journal of General Management* 6, no. 1 (Autumn 1980), pp. 38–47.

Morris, Elinor. "Vision and Strategy: A Focus for the Future." *Journal of Business Strategy* 8, no. 2 (Fall 1987), pp. 51–58.

Mintzberg, Henry. "Crafting Strategy." *Harvard Business Review* 65, no. 4 (July–August 1987), pp. 66–77.

Quinn, James Brian. *Strategies for Change: Logical Incrementalism*. Homewood, Ill.: Richard D. Irwin, 1980, chaps. 2 and 4.

SUGGESTED
READINGS

CHAPTER

3

Industry and Competitive Analysis

—

Analysis is the critical starting point of strategic thinking.
Kenichi Ohmae

—

*Awareness of the environment is not a special project to be undertaken
only when warning of change becomes deafening . . .*
Kenneth R. Andrews

—

Crafting strategy is an analysis-driven exercise, not an activity where managers can succeed by sheer effort and creativity. Judgments about what strategy
to pursue should ideally be grounded in a probing assessment of a company's
external environment and internal situation. Unless a company's strategy is
well-matched to the full range of external and internal situational considerations, its suitability is suspect.

THE ROLE OF SITUATION
ANALYSIS IN STRATEGY-MAKING

While the phrase *situation analysis* tends to conjure up images of collecting
reams of data and developing all sorts of facts and figures, such impressions
don't apply here. From a strategy-making standpoint, *the purpose of situation
analysis is to determine the features in a company's internal/external environment
that will most directly affect its strategic options and opportunities.* The effort concentrates on generating solid answers to a well-defined set of strategic questions, then using these answers first to form an understandable picture of the
company's strategic situation and second to identify what its realistic strategic
options are.

  In studying the methods of strategic situation analysis, it is customary to
begin with single-business companies instead of diversified enterprises. This
is because strategic analysis of diversified companies draws on many of the

concepts and techniques used in evaluating the strategic situations of single-business companies. In single-business strategic analysis, the two biggest situational considerations are (1) industry and competitive conditions (the heart of a single-business company's "external environment") and (2) the company's own internal situation and competitive position. This chapter examines the techniques of *industry and competitive analysis*, the terms used to refer to external situation analysis of a single-business company. Chapter 4 covers the tools of *company situation analysis*. Industry and competitive analysis looks broadly at a company's *macroenvironment*; company situation analysis examines the narrower field of its *microenvironment*.

Figure 3–1 presents the external-internal framework of strategic situation analysis for a single-business company. It indicates both the analytical steps involved and the connection to developing business strategy. Note the logical flow from analysis of the company's external and internal situation to evaluation of alternatives to choice of strategy. Also note that situation analysis is the starting point in the process. Indeed, as we shall see in the rest of this chapter and in Chapter 4, managers must understand a company's macro- and microenvironments to do a good job of establishing a mission, setting objectives, and crafting business strategy. The three criteria for deciding whether a strategy is "good" are whether it fits the situation, whether it helps build competitive advantage, and whether it is likely to boost company performance.

Analysis of industry and competitive conditions is the starting point in evaluating a company's strategic situation and market position.

THE METHODS OF INDUSTRY AND COMPETITIVE ANALYSIS

Industries differ widely in their economic characteristics, competitive situations, and future outlooks. The pace of technological change can range from fast to slow. Capital requirements can be big or small. The market can be worldwide or local. Sellers' products can be standardized or highly differentiated. Competitive forces can be strong or weak and can center on price, quality, service, or other variables. Buyer demand can be rising briskly or declining. Industry conditions differ so much that leading companies in unattractive industries can find it hard to earn respectable profits, while even weak companies in attractive industries can turn in good performances.

Industry and competitive analysis utilizes a toolkit of concepts and techniques to get a clear fix on changing industry conditions and on the nature and strength of competitive forces. It is a way of thinking strategically about an industry's overall situation and drawing conclusions about whether the industry is an attractive investment for company funds. The framework for industry and competitive analysis hangs on developing probing answers to seven questions:

1. What are the chief economic characteristics of the industry?
2. What factors are driving change in the industry, and what impact will they have?
3. What competitive forces are at work in the industry, and how strong are they?
4. Which companies are in the strongest/weakest competitive positions?
5. Who will likely make what competitive moves next?

There are seven questions to ask in thinking strategically about market conditions in a given industry.

INDUSTRY AND COMPETITIVE SITUATION ANALYSIS

Analytical Steps
- Identify the chief economic characteristics of the industry environment
- Identify/assess driving forces
- Evaluate the strength of competition
- Assess the competitive positions of companies in the industry
- Predict who will likely make what competitive moves next
- Pinpoint key success factors
- Draw conclusions about overall industry attractiveness

COMPANY SITUATION ANALYSIS

Analytical Steps
- Determine how well the present strategy is working (is current performance good?)
- Do a SWOT analysis (strengths, weaknesses, opportunities, threats)
- Assess the company's relative competitive strength
- Evaluate the company's relative cost position and cost competitiveness
- Identify the strategic issues and problems the company needs to address (change the mission?/raise or lower objectives?/improve or change strategy?)

IDENTIFY/EVALUATE THE COMPANY STRATEGY OPTIONS

Key Issues
- What realistic choices/ options does the company have?
  - Locked into making improvements in same basic strategy?
  - Room to make major strategy changes?
- How to build a sustainable competitive advantage

CRAFT A STRATEGY

Decision Criteria
- Has good fit with the overall situation
- Helps build competitive advantage
- Contributes to higher company performance

6. What key factors will determine competitive success or failure?
7. How attractive is the industry in terms of its prospects for above-average profitability?

The collective answers to these questions build understanding of a firm's surrounding environment and form the basis for matching strategy to changing industry conditions and to competitive forces. Let's see what each question involves and consider some concepts and techniques that help managers answer them.

Identifying the Industry's Dominant Economic Characteristics

Because industries differ significantly in their basic character and structure, industry and competitive analysis begins with an overview of the industry's dominant economic traits. As a working definition, we use the word *industry* to mean a group of firms whose products have so many of the same attributes that they compete for the same buyers. The factors to consider in profiling an industry's economic features are fairly standard:

- Market size.
- Scope of competitive rivalry (local, regional, national, or global).
- Market growth rate and where the industry is in the growth cycle (early development, rapid growth and takeoff, early maturity, late maturity and saturation, stagnant and aging, decline and decay).
- Number of rivals and their relative sizes—is the industry fragmented with many small companies or concentrated and dominated by a few large companies?
- The number of buyers and their relative sizes.
- The prevalence of backward and forward integration.
- Ease of entry and exit.
- The pace of technological change in both production processes and new product introductions.
- Whether the product(s)/service(s) of rival firms are highly differentiated, weakly differentiated, or essentially identical.
- Whether there are economies of scale in manufacturing, transportation, or mass marketing.
- Whether high rates of capacity utilization are crucial to achieving low-cost production efficiency.
- Whether the industry has a strong learning and experience curve such that average unit cost declines as *cumulative* output (and thus the experience of "learning by doing") builds up.
- Capital requirements.
- Whether industry profitability is above/below par.

Table 3–1 illustrates a profile of an industry's chief economic characteristics.

An industry's economic characteristics are important because of the implications they have for strategy. For example, in capital-intensive industries, where investment in a single plant can run several hundred million dollars, a firm can ease the resulting burden of high fixed costs by pursuing a strategy

An industry's economic characteristics have important implications for crafting an effective strategy.

TABLE 3-1   **A Sample Profile of an Industry's Dominant Economic Characteristics**

Market Size: $400–$500 million annual revenues; 4 million tons, total volume.

Scope of Competitive Rivalry: Primarily regional; producers rarely sell outside a 250-mile radius of plant due to high cost of shipping long distances.

Market Growth Rate: 2–3 percent annually.

Stage in Life Cycle: Mature.

Number of Companies in Industry: About 30 companies with 110 plant locations and capacity of 4.5 million tons. Market shares range from a low of 3 percent to a high of 21 percent.

Customers: About 2,000 buyers; most are industrial chemical firms.

Degree of Vertical Integration: Mixed; 5 of the 10 largest companies are integrated backward into mining operations and also forward in that sister industrial chemical divisions buy over 50 percent of the output of their plants; all other companies are engaged solely in manufacturing.

Ease of Entry/Exit: Moderate entry barriers exist in the form of capital requirements to construct a new plant of minimum efficient size (cost equals $10 million) and ability to build a customer base inside a 250-mile radius of plant.

Technology/Innovation: Production technology is standard and changes have been slow; biggest changes are occurring in products—about 1–2 newly formulated specialty chemicals products are being introduced annually, accounting for nearly all of industry growth.

Product Characteristics: Highly standardized; the brands of different producers are essentially identical (buyers perceive little real difference from seller to seller).

Scale Economies: Moderate; all companies have virtually equal manufacturing costs but scale economies exist in shipping in multiple carloads to same customer and in purchasing large quantities of raw materials.

Experience Curve Effects: Not a factor in this industry.

Capacity Utilization: Manufacturing efficiency is highest between 90–100 percent of rated capacity; below 90 percent utilization, unit costs run significantly higher.

Industry Profitability: Subpar to average; the commodity nature of the industry's product results in intense price-cutting when demand slackens, but prices firm up during periods of strong demand. Profits track the strength of demand for the industry's products.

---

that promotes high utilization of fixed assets and generates more revenue per dollar of fixed-asset investment. Thus commercial airlines employ strategies to boost the revenue productivity of their expensive jet aircraft fleets by cutting ground time at airport gates (to get in more flights per day with the same plane) and by discounting fares to fill up otherwise empty seats on each flight. In industries characterized by one product advance after another, companies are driven to invest enough time and money in R&D to keep their technical skills and innovative capability abreast of competitors—a strategy of continuous product innovation becomes a condition of survival.

Basic Concept

When a strong learning/experience curve effect causes unit costs to decline as production volume builds, a high-volume manufacturer can have the competitive advantage of being the industry's lowest-cost producer.

In industries like semiconductors, the presence of a *learning/experience* curve effect in manufacturing causes unit costs to decline about 20 percent each time *cumulative* production volume doubles. With a 20 percent experience curve effect, if the first 1 million chips cost $1 each, by a production volume of 2 million the unit cost would be $.80 (80 percent of $1); by a production volume of 4 million the unit cost would be $.64 (80 percent of $0.80); and so on. When an industry is characterized by a strong experience curve effect in its manufacturing operations, a company that moves first to initiate production of a new-style product and develops a strategy to capture the largest market share can

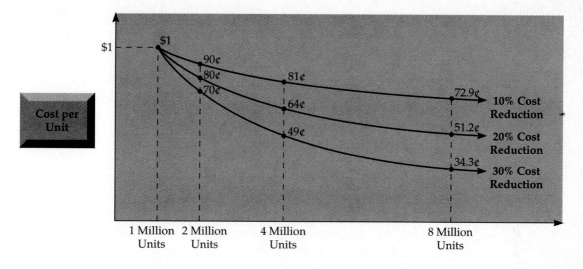

FIGURE 3–2 **Comparison of Experience Curve Effects for 10 Percent, 20 Percent, and 30 Percent Cost Reductions for Each Doubling of Cumulative Production Volume**

Cumulative Production Volume

win the competitive advantage of being the low-cost producer. The bigger the experience curve effect, the bigger the cost advantage of the company with the largest *cumulative* production volume, as shown in Figure 3–2.

Table 3–2 presents some additional examples of how an industry's economic characteristics can be relevant to managerial strategy-making.

The Concept of Driving Forces: Why Industries Change

An industry's economic features say a lot about the basic nature of the industry environment but very little about the ways in which the environment may be changing. All industries are characterized by trends and new developments that, either gradually or speedily, produce changes important enough to require a strategic response from participating firms. The popular hypothesis about industries going through evolutionary growth phases or life-cycle stages helps explain why industry conditions change but is still incomplete.[1] The life-cycle stages are strongly keyed to the overall industry growth rate (which is why stages are described with such terms as rapid growth, early maturity, saturation, and decline). Yet there are more causes of industry and competitive change than moving to a new position on the growth curve.

Basic Concept
Industry conditions change because important forces are driving industry participants (competitors, customers, suppliers) to alter their actions; the driving forces in an industry are the major underlying causes of changing industry and competitive conditions.

---

[1]For a more extended discussion of the problems with the life-cycle hypothesis, see Michael E. Porter, *Competitive Strategy: Techniques for Analyzing Industries and Competitors* (New York: Free Press, 1980), pp. 157–62.

TABLE 3–2   **Examples of the Strategic Importance of an Industry's Key Economic Characteristics**

Factor/Characteristic	Strategic Importance
• Market size	• Small markets don't tend to attract big/new competitors; large markets often draw the interest of corporations looking to acquire companies with established competitive positions in attractive industries.
• Market growth rate	• Fast growth breeds new entry; growth slowdowns spawn increased rivalry and a shakeout of weak competitors.
• Capacity surpluses or shortages	• Surpluses push prices and profit margins down; shortages pull them up.
• Industry profitability	• High-profit industries attract new entrants; depressed conditions encourage exit.
• Entry/exit barriers	• High barriers protect positions and profits of existing firms; low barriers make existing firms vulnerable to entry.
• Product is a big-ticket item for buyers	• More buyers will shop for lowest price.
• Standardized products	• Buyers have more power because it is easier to switch from seller to seller.
• Rapid technological change	• Raises risk factor; investments in technology facilities/equipment may become obsolete before they wear out.
• Capital requirements	• Big requirements make investment decisions critical; timing becomes important; creates a barrier to entry and exit.
• Vertical integration	• Raises capital requirements; often creates competitive differences and cost differences among fully versus partially versus nonintegrated firms.
• Economies of scale	• Increases volume and market share needed to be cost competitive.
• Rapid product innovation	• Shortens product life cycle; increases risk because of opportunities for leapfrogging.

While it is important to judge what growth stage an industry is in, there's more analytical value in identifying the specific factors causing industry change. Industry conditions change *because forces are in motion that create incentives or pressures for change.*[2] The most dominant forces are called *driving forces* because they have the biggest influences on what kinds of changes will take place in the industry's structure and environment. Driving forces analysis has two steps: (1) identifying what the driving forces are and (2) assessing the impact they will have on the industry.

Several different factors can affect an industry powerfully enough to act as driving forces.

The Most Common Driving Forces   Many events affect an industry powerfully enough to qualify as driving forces. Some are one-of-a-kind, but most fall into one of several basic categories. The most common driving forces are shown here.[3]

- **Changes in the Long-Term Industry Growth Rate.** Shifts in industry growth up or down are a force for industry change because they affect the balance between industry supply and buyer demand, entry and exit, and how hard it will be for a firm to capture additional sales. A strong upsurge in long-term demand frequently attracts new firms and encourages

[2]Ibid., p. 162.

[3]What follows draws on the discussion in Porter, *Competitive Strategy*, pp. 164–83.

established ones to invest in additional capacity. In a shrinking market, some firms will exit the industry, and the remaining ones may postpone further capacity investments.

- **Changes in Who Buys the Product and How They Use It.** Shifts in buyer demographics and the emergences of new ways to use the product can force adjustments in customer service offerings (credit, technical assistance, maintenance and repair), open the way to market the industry's product through a different mix of dealers and retail outlets, prompt producers to broaden/narrow their product lines, increase/decrease capital requirements, and change sales and promotion approaches. The computer industry has been transformed by the surge of interest in personal and mid-size computers. Consumer interest in cordless telephones and mobile telephones has opened a major new buyer segment for telephone equipment manufacturers.

- **Product Innovation.** Product innovation can broaden an industry's customer base, rejuvenate industry growth, and widen the degree of product differentiation among rival sellers. Successful new product introductions strengthen a company's position, usually at the expense of companies who stick with their old products or are slow to follow with their own versions of the new product. Industries where product innovation has been a key driving force include copying equipment, cameras and photographic equipment, computers, electronic video games, toys, prescription drugs, frozen foods, and personal computer software.

- **Technological Change.** Advances in technology can dramatically alter an industry's landscape, making it possible to produce new and/or better products at a lower cost and opening up whole new industry frontiers. Technological change can also change in capital requirements, minimum efficient plant sizes, and desirability of vertical integration, and learning or experience curve effects.

- **Marketing Innovation.** When firms are successful in introducing new ways to market their products, they can spark a burst of buyer interest, widen industry demand, increase product differentiation, and/or lower unit costs—any or all of which can alter the competitive positions of rival firms and force strategy revisions.

- **Entry or Exit of Major Firms.** The entry of one or more foreign companies into a market once dominated by domestic firms nearly always produces a big shakeup in industry conditions. Likewise, when an established domestic firm in another industry attempts entry either by acquisition or by launching its own startup venture, it usually intends to apply its skills and resources in some innovative fashion. Entry by a major firm often produces a "new ballgame" not only with new key players but also with new rules for competing. Similarly, exit of a major firm changes industry structure by reducing the number of market leaders (perhaps increasing the dominance of the leaders who remain) and causing a rush to capture the exiting firm's customers.

- **Diffusion of Technical Know-How.** As knowledge about how to perform a particular activity or to execute a particular manufacturing technology spreads, any technically-based competitive advantage held by firms possessing this know-how erodes. Diffusion of technical know-how occurs through scientific journals, trade publications, on-site plant tours, word-of-mouth among suppliers and customers, and the hiring away of knowledgeable employees. It can also occur when the possessors of technological know-how license others to use it for a fee or team up with a company interested in turning the technology into a new business venture. Often companies acquire technical know-how by buying a company with the desired skills, patents, or manufacturing capabilities. In recent years technology transfer across national boundaries has emerged as one of the most important driving forces in globalizing markets and competition. As companies in more countries gain access to technical know-how, they upgrade their manufacturing capabilities to compete with established companies. Technology transfer has turned many domestic industries into global ones (e.g., automobiles, tires, consumer electronics, telecommunications, and computers).

- **Increasing Globalization of the Industry.** Global competition usually changes patterns of competitive advantage among key players. Industries move toward globalization for several reasons. Certain firms may launch aggressive long-term strategies to win a globally dominant market position. Demand for the industry's product may emerge in more countries. Trade barriers may drop. Technology-transfer may open the door for more companies in more countries to enter the industry on a major scale. Significant labor cost differences among countries may create a strong reason to locate plants for labor-intensive products in low-wage countries (wages in South Korea, Taiwan, and Singapore, for example, are about one-fourth those in the United States). Significant cost economies may accrue to firms with world-scale volumes as opposed to national-scale volumes. The growing ability of multinational companies to transfer their production, marketing, and management know-how from country to country at significantly lower cost than companies with a one-country production base may give multinational competitors a significant competitive advantage over domestic-only competitors. Globalization is most likely to be a driving force in industries (a) based on natural resources (supplies of crude oil, copper, and cotton, for example, are geographically scattered all over the globe), (b) where low-cost production is a critical consideration (making it imperative to locate plant facilities in countries where the lowest costs can be achieved), and (c) where one or more growth-oriented, market-seeking companies are pushing hard to gain a significant competitive position in as many attractive country markets as they can.

- **Changes in Cost and Efficiency.** In industries where significant economies of scale are emerging or strong learning curve effects are allowing firms with the most production experience to undercut rivals' prices, large market share becomes such a distinct advantage that all firms are pressured to adopt volume-building strategies—a "race for growth" dominates the industry. Likewise, sharply rising costs for a key input (either raw materials or labor) can cause a scramble to either (a) line up reliable supplies at affordable prices or (b) search out lower-cost substitutes. Any time important changes in cost or efficiency take place, firms' positions can change radically concerning who has how big a cost advantage.

- **Emerging Buyer Preferences for a Differentiated Instead of a Commodity Product (or for a more standardized product instead of strongly differentiated products).** Sometimes growing numbers of buyers decide that a standard product at a bargain price meets their needs as effectively as premium priced brands offering more features and options. These swings in buyer demand can drive industry change by shifting patronage to sellers of cheaper commodity products and creating a price-competitive market environment. Such a development may so dominate the market that industry producers can't do much more than compete hard on price. On the other hand, a shift away from standardized products occurs when sellers are able to win a bigger and more loyal buyer following by introducing new features, making style changes, offering options and accessories, and creating image differences via advertising and packaging. Then the driver of change is the struggle among rivals to out-differentiate one another. Industries evolve differently depending on whether the forces in motion are acting to increase or decrease the emphasis on product differentiation.

- **Regulatory Influences and Government Policy Changes.** Regulatory and governmental actions can often force significant changes in industry practices and strategic approaches. Deregulation has been a major driving force in the airline, banking, natural gas, and telecommunications industries. Drunk driving laws and drinking age legislation recently became driving forces in the alcoholic beverage industry. In international markets, newly-enacted regulations of host governments to open up their domestic markets to foreign participation or to close off foreign participation to protect domestic companies are a major factor in shaping whether the competitive struggle between foreign and domestic companies occurs on a level playing field or whether it is one-sided (owing to government favoritism).

- **Changing Societal Concerns, Attitudes, and Lifestyles.** Emerging social issues and changing attitudes and lifestyles can be powerful instigators of industry change. Consumer concerns about salt, sugar, chemical additives, cholesterol, and nutrition are forcing the food industry to reexamine food processing techniques, redirect R&D efforts, and introduce healthier products. Safety concerns are driving change in the automobile, toy, and outdoor power equipment industries. Increased interest in physical fitness is producing whole new industries to supply exercise equipment, jogging clothes and shoes, and medically supervised diet programs. Social concerns about air and water pollution are affecting industries that discharge waste products. Growing antismoking sentiment is posing a major long-term threat to the cigarette industry.

- **Reductions in Uncertainty and Business Risk.** A young, emerging industry is typically characterized by an unproven cost structure and much uncertainty over potential market size, R&D costs, and distribution channels. Emerging industries tend to attract only the most entrepreneurial companies. Over time, however, if pioneering firms succeed and uncertainty about the industry's viability fades, more conservative firms are usually enticed to enter the industry. Often, the entrants are larger, financially-strong firms hunting for attractive growth industries. In international markets, conservatism is prevalent in the early stages of globalization. Firms tend to minimize their risk by relying initially on exporting, licensing, and joint ventures. Then, as their experience accumulates and as perceived risk levels decline, companies move more quickly and aggressively to form wholly owned subsidiaries and to pursue full-scale, multicountry competitive strategies.

The foregoing list of *potential* driving forces in an industry indicates why it is too simplistic to view industry change only in terms of moving from one growth stage to another and why it is essential to probe for the *causes* underlying the emergence of new industry conditions.

The task of driving forces analysis is to separate the major causes of changing industry conditions from minor ones; usually no more than three or four factors qualify as driving forces.

However, while *many* forces of change may be at work in an industry, no more than three or four are likely to be *driving* forces in the sense that they act as *the major determinants* of how the industry evolves and operates. Strategic analysts must resist the temptation to label everything they see changing as driving forces; the analytical task is to evaluate the forces of industry change carefully enough to separate major factors from minor ones.

Analyzing driving forces has practical strategy-making value. First, the driving forces in an industry indicate to managers what external factors will have the greatest effect on the company's business over the next one to three years. Second, to position the company to deal with these forces, managers must assess the implications and consequences of each driving force—that is, they must project what impact the driving forces will have on the industry. Third, strategy-makers need to craft a strategy that is responsive to the driving forces and their effects on the industry.

Basic Concept
Strategists use environmental scanning to spot budding trends and developments that could emerge as new driving forces.

Environmental Scanning Techniques One way to predict future driving forces is to utilize environmental scanning techniques. *Environmental scanning* involves studying and interpreting social, political, economic, ecological, and technological events in an effort to spot budding trends and conditions that could eventually affect the industry. It attempts to look broadly at "first of its kind" happenings, what kinds of new ideas and approaches are catching on, and extrapolate their possible implications 5 to 20 years into the future. For example, environmental scanning could involve judgments about the demand for energy in the year 2000, uses for computers 20 years from now, or the condition of forests in the 21st century given the growing demand for paper. Environmental scanning raises managers' awareness of potential developments that could have an important impact on industry conditions and pose new opportunities and threats.

Environmental scanning can be accomplished by systematically monitoring and studying current events, constructing scenarios, and employing the Delphi method (a technique for finding consensus among a group of "knowledgeable experts"). Although highly qualitative and subjective, environmental scanning helps managers lengthen their planning horizon, translate vague inklings into clearer strategic issues (for which they can begin to develop a strategic answer), and think strategically about future developments in the surrounding environment.[4] Companies that undertake formal environmental

---

[4]For further discussion of the nature and use of environmental scanning, see Roy Amara and Andrew J. Lipinski, *Business Planning for an Uncertain Future: Scenarios and Strategies* (New York: Pergamon Press, 1983); Harold E. Klein and Robert U. Linneman, "Environmental Assessment: An International Study of Corporate Practice," *Journal of Business Strategy* 5, no. 1 (Summer 1984), pp. 55–75; and Arnoldo C. Hax and Nicolas S. Majluf, *The Strategy Concept and Process* (Englewood Cliffs, N.J.: Prentice Hall, 1991), chaps. 5 and 8.

scanning include General Electric, AT&T, Coca-Cola, Ford, General Motors, Du Pont, and Shell Oil.

Analyzing the Strength of Competitive Forces

One of the big cornerstones of industry and competitive analysis involves carefully studying the industry's competitive process to discover the main sources of competitive pressure and how strong they are. This analytical step is essential because managers cannot devise a successful strategy without understanding the industry's special competitive character.

Even though competitive pressures differ in different industries, competition itself works similarly enough to use a common framework in gauging its nature and intensity. As a rule, *competition in an industry is a composite of five competitive forces*:

1. The rivalry among competing sellers in the industry.
2. The market attempts of companies in other industries to win customers to their own *substitute* products.
3. The potential entry of new competitors.
4. The bargaining power and leverage exercisable by suppliers of key raw materials and components.
5. The bargaining power and leverage exercisable by buyers of the product.

The *five-forces model*, as diagrammed in Figure 3–3, is extremely helpful in systematically diagnosing the principal competitive pressures in a market and assessing how strong and important each one is.[5] Not only is it the most widely used technique of competition analysis, but it is also straightforward to use.

The Rivalry among Competing Sellers
The most powerful of the five competitive forces is *usually* the competitive battle among rival firms.[6] How vigorously sellers use the competitive weapons at their disposal to jockey for a stronger market position and win a competitive edge over rivals shows the strength of this competitive force. *Competitive strategy is the narrower portion of business strategy dealing with a company's competitive approaches for achieving market success, its offensive moves to secure a competitive edge over rival firms, and its defensive moves to protect its competitive position.*[7]

The challenge in crafting a winning competitive strategy, of course, is *how to gain an edge over rivals.* The big complication is that the success of any one firm's strategy hinges on what strategies its rivals employ and the resources rivals

> **Basic Concept**
> *Competitive strategy is the part of business strategy that deals with management's plan for competing successfully— how to build sustainable competitive advantage, how to outmaneuver rivals, how to defend against competitive pressures, and how to strengthen the firm's market position.*

---

[5]For a thorough treatment of the five-forces model by its originator, see Porter, *Competitive Strategy*, chap. 1.

[6]Parts of this section are based on the discussion in Arthur A. Thompson, "Competition as a Strategic Process," *Antitrust Bulletin* 25, no. 4 (Winter 1980), pp. 777–803.

[7]The distinction between *competitive strategy* and *business strategy* is useful here. As we defined it in Chapter 2, business strategy not only addresses the issue of how to compete, it also embraces all of the functional area support strategies, how management plans to respond to changing industry conditions of all kinds (not just those that are competition-related), and how management intends to address the full range of strategic issues. Competitive strategy, however, is narrower in scope. It focuses on the firm's competitive approach, the competitive edge strived for, and specific moves to outmaneuver rival companies.

F I G U R E 3–3   **The "Five-Forces" Model of Competition: A Key Analytical Tool**

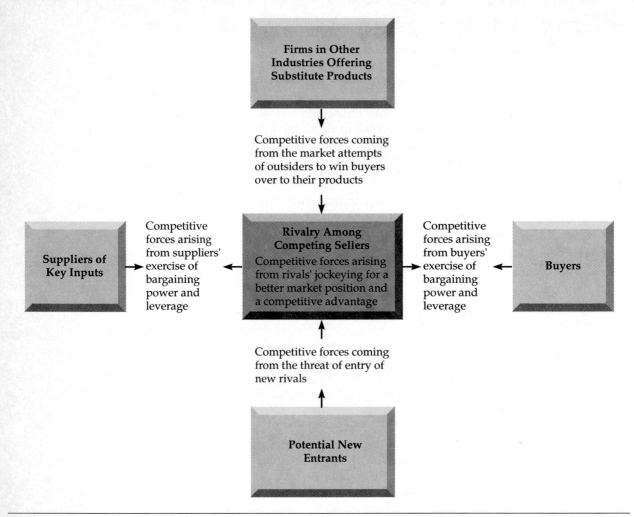

Source: Adapted from Michael E. Porter, "How Competitive Forces Shape Strategy," *Harvard Business Review* 57, no. 2 (March–April 1979), pp.137–45.

are willing and able to put behind their strategies. The "best" strategy for one firm in maneuvering for competitive advantage depends on the competitive strength and strategies of its rivals. Whenever one firm makes a strategic move, rivals often retaliate with offensive or defensive countermoves. Thus, competitive rivalry turns into a game of strategy, of move and countermove, played under "warlike" conditions according to the rules of business competition—in effect, *competitive markets are economic battlefields.*

Competitive battles among rival sellers can assume many forms and degrees of intensity. The weapons used for competing include price, quality, features, services, warranties and guarantees, advertising, better networks of wholesale distributors and retail dealers, innovation, and so on. The relative dependence that competitors place on each of these weapons can change over time, as first one then another is used more extensively to catch buyers' atten-

Principle of Competitive Markets
Competitive jockeying among rivals is ever-changing as firms initiate new offensive and defensive moves and as emphasis swings from one mix of competitive weapons to another.

tion and as competitors initiate fresh offensive and defensive moves. Rivalry is thus dynamic; current conditions are always being modified as companies initiate new moves and countermoves and as the competitive emphasis swings from one weapons mix to another. Two principles of competitive rivalry are particularly important: (1) a powerful competitive strategy used by one company intensifies competitive pressures on the other companies, and (2) the manner in which rivals employ various competitive weapons to try to outmaneuver one another shapes "the rules of competition" in the industry and determines the requirements for competitive success.

Once an industry's rules of competition are understood, then judgments can be made regarding whether competitive rivalry is cutthroat, intense, normal to moderate, or attractively weak. There are several factors that, industry after industry, influence the *strength* of rivalry among competing sellers:[8]

1. *Rivalry tends to intensify as the number of competitors increases and as they become more equal in size and capability.* Up to a point, the greater the number of competitors the greater the probability of fresh, creative strategic initiatives. In addition, when rivals are more equal in size and capability, they compete on a fairly even footing, making it harder for one or two firms to "win" the competitive battle and dominate the market.

2. *Rivalry is usually stronger when demand for the product is growing slowly.* In a rapidly expanding market, there tends to be enough business for everybody to grow. Indeed, it may take all of a firm's financial and managerial resources just to keep pace with buyer demand, much less steal rivals' customers. But when growth slows or when market demand drops unexpectedly, expansion-minded firms and/or firms with excess capacity often cut prices and use other sales-increasing tactics. The ensuing battle for market share can result in a shake out of the weak and less-efficient firms. The industry then "consolidates" into a smaller, but individually stronger, group of sellers.

3. *Rivalry is more intense when industry conditions tempt competitors to use price cuts or other competitive weapons to boost unit volume.* Whenever fixed costs account for a large fraction of total cost, unit costs tend to be lowest at or near full capacity since fixed costs can be spread over more units of production. Unused capacity thus imposes a significant cost-increasing penalty because there are fewer units to carry the fixed cost burden. In such cases, if market demand weakens and capacity utilization begins to fall off, the pressure of rising unit costs pushes firms into secret price concessions, special discounts, rebates, and other sales-increasing tactics, thus heightening competition. Likewise, when a product is perishable, seasonal, or costly to inventory, competitive pressures build quickly anytime one or more competitors decides to dump its excess supplies on the market.

4. *Rivalry is stronger when the costs incurred by customers to switch their purchases from one brand to another are low.* The lower the costs of switching, the easier it is for rival sellers to raid one another's

There are many reasons why the rivalry among competing sellers can grow stronger or weaker.

---

[8]These indicators of what to look for in evaluating the intensity of interfirm rivalry are based on Porter, *Competitive Strategy*, pp. 17–21.

customers. On the other hand, high switching costs give a seller some protection against the efforts of rivals to raid its customers.

5. *Rivalry is stronger when one or more competitors is dissatisfied with its market position and launches moves to bolster its standing at the expense of rivals.* Firms that are losing ground or find themselves in financial trouble often take such aggressive actions as acquiring smaller rivals, introducing new products, increasing advertising, promoting special prices, and so on. Such actions can trigger a new round of competitive maneuvering and a heightened battle for market share.

6. *Rivalry increases in proportion to the size of the payoff from a successful strategic move.* The greater the potential reward, the more likely some firm will aggressively pursue a strategy to capture it. The size of the strategic payoff depends partly on how fast rivals retaliate. When competitors respond slowly (or not at all), the initiator of a fresh competitive strategy can reap benefits in the intervening period and perhaps gain a first-mover advantage that is not easily surmounted. The greater the benefits of moving first, the more likely some firm will accept the risk and try it.

7. *Rivalry tends to be more vigorous when it costs more to get out of a business than to stay in and compete.* The higher the exit barriers (thus the more costly it is to abandon a market), the stronger the incentive for firms to remain and compete as best they can, even though they may be earning low profits or even incurring a loss.

8. *Rivalry becomes more volatile and unpredictable the more diverse competitors are in terms of their strategies, personalities, corporate priorities, resources, and countries of origin.* A diverse group of sellers is more likely to spawn one or more mavericks willing to rock the boat with unconventional moves and approaches, thus generating a more lively and uncertain competitive environment. The added presence of new, lower-cost foreign-based competitors intent on gaining market share is a surefire factor in boosting the intensity of rivalry.

9. *Rivalry increases when strong companies outside the industry acquire weak firms in the industry and launch aggressive, well-funded moves to transform their newly-acquired firms into major market contenders.* For example, Philip Morris, a leading cigarette firm with excellent marketing know-how, shook up the whole beer industry's marketing approach when it acquired stodgy Miller Brewing Company in the late 1960s. In short order, Philip Morris revamped the marketing plan for Miller High Life and pushed it to the number two best-selling brand. PM also pioneered low-calorie beers with the introduction of Miller Lite—a move that made light beer the fastest-growing segment in the beer industry.

Such jockeying for position among competitors unfolds in round after round of moves and countermoves. The strategist has to identify the current competitive weapons, stay on top of how the game is being played, and judge how much pressure competitive rivalry is going to put on profitability. Competitive rivalry is "intense" when competitors' actions are driving down industry profits; rivalry is "moderate" when most companies can earn acceptable profits; and rivalry is "weak" when most companies in the industry can earn above-average returns on investment. Chronic outbreaks of cutthroat competition make an industry brutally competitive.

The Competitive Force of Potential Entry New entrants to a market bring new production capacity, the desire to establish a secure place in the market, and sometimes substantial resources with which to compete.[9] How serious the threat of entry is in a particular market depends on two factors: *barriers to entry* and the *expected reaction of incumbent firms to new entry*. A barrier to entry exists whenever it is hard for a newcomer to break into a market and/or economic factors put a potential entrant at a disadvantage relative to its competitors. There are several types of entry barriers:[10]

- **Economies of scale.** Scale economies deter entry because they force potential entrants either to enter on a large-scale basis (a costly and perhaps risky move) or to accept a cost disadvantage (and consequently lower profitability). Firms that do attempt large-scale entry can cause overcapacity problems in the industry and so threaten the market shares of existing firms that they retaliate aggressively (with price cuts, increased advertising and sales promotion, and similar steps) to maintain their position. Either way, a new entrant can expect to earn lower profits. Entrants may encounter scale-related barriers not just in production, but in advertising, marketing and distribution, financing, after-sale customer service, raw materials purchasing, and R&D as well.

- **Inability to gain access to technology and specialized know-how.** Many industries require technological capability and skills not readily available to a new entrant. Key patents can bar entry as can lack of technically skilled personnel and an inability to execute complicated manufacturing techniques. Existing firms often carefully guard know-how that gives them an edge in technology and manufacturing capability. Unless new entrants can gain access to such knowledge, they will lack the technical capability to compete on an equal footing.

- **Learning and experience curve effects.** When lower unit costs are partly or mostly a result of experience and other learning curve benefits, a new entrant is faced with a cost disadvantage in competing against existing firms with more accumulated know-how.

- **Brand preferences and customer loyalty.** Buyers are often attached to existing brands. European consumers, for example, are fiercely loyal to European brands of major household appliances. High brand loyalty means that a potential entrant must be prepared to spend enough money on advertising and sales promotion to overcome customer loyalties and build its own clientele. Substantial time and money can be involved. In addition, if it is difficult or costly for a customer to switch to a new brand, a new entrant must persuade buyers that its brand is worth the switching costs. To overcome the switching cost barrier, new entrants may have to offer buyers a bigger price cut or extra quality or service. All this can

---

[9]Michael E. Porter, "How Competitive Forces Shape Strategy," *Harvard Business Review* 57, no. 2 (March–April 1979), p. 138.

[10]Porter, *Competitive Strategy*, pp. 7–17.

mean lower profit margins for new entrants—something that increases the risk to startup companies dependent on sizable, early profits to support their new investment.

- **Capital requirements.** The larger the total dollar investment needed to enter the market successfully, the more limited the pool of potential entrants. The most obvious capital requirements are associated with manufacturing plant and equipment, working capital to finance inventories and customer credit, introductory advertising and sales promotion to establish a clientele, and covering startup losses.

- **Cost disadvantages independent of size.** Existing firms may have cost advantages not available to potential entrants regardless of the entrant's size. These advantages can include access to the best and cheapest raw materials, possession of patents and proprietary technological know-how, the benefits of learning and experience curve effects, having built and equipped plants years earlier at lower costs, favorable locations, and lower borrowing costs.

- **Access to distribution channels.** In the case of consumer goods, a potential entrant may face the barrier of gaining adequate access to distribution channels. Wholesale distributors may be reluctant to take on a product that lacks buyer recognition. A network of retail dealers may have to be set up from scratch. Retailers may have to be convinced to give a new brand ample display space and an adequate trial period. The more existing producers have tied up present distribution channels, the tougher entry will be. To overcome this barrier, entrants may have to "buy" distribution access by offering better margins to dealers and distributors or by giving advertising allowances and other promotional incentives. As a consequence, a potential entrant's profits may be squeezed until its product gains such acceptance that distributors and retailers want to carry it.

- **Regulatory policies.** Government agencies can limit or even bar entry by requiring licenses and permits. Regulated industries like banking, insurance, radio and television stations, liquor retailing, and railroads feature government-controlled entry. In international markets, host governments commonly limit foreign entry and must approve all foreign investment applications. Stringent government-mandated safety regulations and environmental pollution standards are entry barriers because they raise entry costs.

- **Tariffs and international trade restrictions.** National governments commonly use tariffs and trade restrictions (antidumping rules, local content requirements, and quotas) to raise entry barriers for foreign firms. In 1988, due to tariffs imposed by the South Korean government, a Ford Taurus cost South Korean car buyers over $40,000. European governments require that certain Asian products, from electronic typewriters to copying machines, contain European-made parts and labor equal to 40 percent of the selling price. And to protect European chipmakers from low-cost Asian competition, European governments instituted a rigid formula to calculate floor prices for computer memory chips.

Even if a potential entrant is willing to tackle the problems of entry barriers, it still faces the issue of how existing firms will react.[11] Will incumbent firms react passively, or will they aggressively defend their market positions with price cuts, increased advertising, product improvements, and whatever else will give a new entrant (as well as other rivals) a hard time? A potential entrant often has second thoughts when incumbents send strong signals that they will stoutly defend their market positions against entry and when they have the financial resources to do so. A potential entrant may also turn away when incumbent firms can use leverage with distributors and customers to keep their business.

The best test of whether potential entry is a strong or weak competitive force is to ask if the industry's growth and profit prospects are attractive enough to induce additional entry. When the answer is no, potential entry is not a source of competitive pressure. When the answer is yes (as in industries where lower-cost foreign competitors are seeking new markets), then potential entry is a strong force. The stronger the threat of entry, the greater the motivation of incumbent firms to fortify their positions against newcomers to make entry more costly or difficult.

One additional point: the threat of entry changes as industry prospects grow brighter or dimmer and as entry barriers rise or fall. For example, the expiration of a key patent can greatly increase the threat of entry. A technological discovery can create an economy of scale and advantage where none existed before. New actions by incumbent firms to increase advertising, strengthen distributor-dealer relations, step up R&D, or improve product quality can erect higher roadblocks to entry. In international markets, entry barriers for foreign-based firms ease when tariffs are lowered; domestic wholesalers and dealers seek out lower-cost foreign-made goods, and domestic buyers become more willing to purchase foreign brands.

The Competitive Force of Substitute Products Firms in one industry are, quite often, in close competition with firms in another industry because their respective products are good substitutes. The producers of eyeglasses compete with the makers of contact lenses. The sugar industry competes with companies that produce artificial sweeteners. The producers of plastic containers confront strong competition from makers of glass bottles and jars, paperboard cartons, and tin and aluminum cans.

Principle of Competitive Markets
The competitive threat posed by substitute products is strong when prices of substitutes are attractive, buyers' switching costs are low, and buyers believe substitutes have equal or better features.

The competitive force of substitute products comes into play in several ways. First, the presence of readily available and competitively priced substitutes places a ceiling on the prices companies in an industry can afford to charge without giving customers an incentive to switch to substitutes and thus eroding their own market position.[12] This price ceiling, at the same time, puts a lid on the profits that industry members can earn unless they find ways to cut costs. When substitutes are cheaper than an industry's product, industry members come under heavy competitive pressure to reduce prices and find ways to absorb the price cuts with cost reductions. Second, the availability of substitutes invites customers to compare quality and performance as well as

[11]Porter, "How Competitive Forces Shape Strategy," p. 140; and Porter, *Competitive Strategy*, pp. 14–15.
[12]Ibid., p. 142; and pp. 23–24.

price. For example, firms that buy glass bottles and jars from glassware manu-facturers monitor whether they can just as effectively package their products in plastic containers, paper cartons, or tin cans. Because of competitive pres-sure from substitute products, industry rivals have to convince customers their product is more advantageous than substitutes. Usually this requires devising a competitive strategy to differentiate the industry's product from substitute products via some combination of lower cost, better quality, better service, and more desirable performance features.

Another determinant of whether substitutes are a strong or weak competi-tive force is whether it is difficult or costly for customers to switch to substi-tutes.[13] Typical switching costs include employee retraining costs, the costs of purchasing additional equipment, costs for technical help needed to make the changeover, the time and cost to test the quality and reliability of the substi-tute, and the psychic costs of severing old supplier relationships and establish-ing new ones. If switching costs are high, sellers of substitutes must offer a major cost or performance benefit to steal the industry's customers. When switching costs are low, it's much easier for the sellers of substitutes to con-vince buyers to change over to their product.

As a rule, then, the lower the price of substitutes, the higher their quality and performance, and the lower the user's switching costs, the more intense are the competitive pressures posed by substitute products. The best indica-tors of the competitive strength of substitute products are the rate at which their sales are growing, the market inroads they are making, the plans the sell-ers of substitutes have for expanding production capacity, and the size of their profits.

Principle of Competitive Markets
The suppliers to an industry are a strong competitive force whenever they have sufficient bargaining power to command a price premium for their materials or components and whenever they can affect the competitive well-being of industry rivals by the reliability of their deliveries or by the quality and performance of the items they supply.

The Power of Suppliers   Whether the suppliers to an industry are a weak or strong competitive force depends on market conditions in the supplier indus-try and the significance of the item they supply.[14] The competitive force of sup-pliers is greatly diminished whenever the item they provide is a standard commodity available on the open market from a large number of suppliers with ample ability to fill orders. Then it is relatively simple to multiple-source whatever is needed, choosing to buy from whichever suppliers offer the best deal. In such cases, suppliers can win concessions only when supplies become tight and users are so anxious to secure what they need that they agree to terms more favorable to suppliers. Suppliers are also in a weak bargaining position whenever there are good substitute inputs and switching is neither costly nor difficult. For example, soft drink bottlers check the power of alumi-num can suppliers by using plastic containers and glass bottles. Suppliers also have less leverage when the industry they are supplying is a *major* customer. In this case, the well-being of suppliers becomes closely tied to the well-being of their major customers. Suppliers then have a big incentive to protect the cus-tomer industry via reasonable prices, improved quality, and new products and services that might enhance their customers' positions, sales, and profits. When industry members form a close working relationship with major sup-pliers, they may gain substantial benefit in the form of better-quality compo-nents, just-in-time deliveries, and reduced inventory costs.

---

[13]Porter, *Competitive Strategy*, p. 10.
[14]Ibid., pp. 27–28.

On the other hand, powerful suppliers can put an industry in a profit squeeze with price increases that can't be fully passed on to the industry's own customers. Suppliers become a strong competitive force when their product makes up a sizable fraction of the costs of an industry's product, is crucial to the industry's production process, and/or significantly affects the quality of the industry's product. Likewise, a supplier (or group of suppliers) gains bargaining leverage the more difficult or costly it is for users to switch suppliers. Big suppliers with good reputations and growing demand for their output are harder to wring concessions from than struggling suppliers striving to broaden their customer base.

Suppliers are also more powerful when they can supply a component cheaper than industry members can make it themselves. For instance, the producers of outdoor power equipment (lawnmowers, rotary tillers, snowblowers, and so on) find it cheaper to buy small engines from outside manufacturers rather than make their own because the quantity they need is too small to justify the investment and master the process. Small-engine manufacturers, by supplying many kinds of engines to the whole power equipment industry, sell enough to capture scale economies, become proficient in the manufacturing techniques, and keep costs well below what power equipment firms would incur on their own. Small engine suppliers can price the item below what it would cost the user to self-manufacture but far enough above their own costs to generate an attractive profit margin. In such situations, suppliers' bargaining position is strong *until* a customer needs enough parts to justify backward integration. Then the balance of power shifts away from the supplier. The more credible the threat of backward integration, the more leverage companies have in negotiating favorable terms with suppliers.

A final instance in which an industry's suppliers play an important competitive role is when suppliers, for one reason or another, do not have the manufacturing capability or a strong enough incentive to provide items of adequate quality. Suppliers who lack the ability or incentive to provide quality parts can seriously damage their customers' business. For example, if auto parts suppliers provide lower-quality components to U.S. automobile manufacturers, they can so increase the warranty and defective goods costs that they seriously impair U.S. auto firms' profits, reputation, and competitive position in world markets.

The Power of Buyers   Just as with suppliers, the competitive strength of buyers can range from strong to weak. Buyers have substantial bargaining leverage in a number of situations.[15] The most obvious is when buyers are large and purchase a sizable percentage of the industry's output. The bigger buyers are and the larger the quantities they purchase, the more clout they have in negotiating with sellers. Often, large buyers successfully leverage their size and volume purchases to obtain price concessions and other favorable terms. Buyers also gain power when the cost of switching to competing brands or substitutes is relatively low. Any time buyers can meet their needs by sourcing from several sellers, they have added room to negotiate. When sellers' products are virtually identical, buyers can switch with little or no cost. However, if sellers'

Principle of
Competitive Markets
Buyers become a stronger competitive force the more they are able to exercise bargaining leverage over price, quality, service, or other terms of conditions of sale.

---

[15]Ibid., pp. 24–27.

products are strongly differentiated, buyers are less able to switch without incurring sizable switching costs.

One last point: all buyers don't have equal bargaining power with sellers; some may be less sensitive than others to price, quality, or service. For example, in the apparel industry, major manufacturers confront significant customer power when they sell to retail chains like Sears or Kmart. But they can get much better prices selling to small owner-managed boutiques.

Strategic Implications of the Five Competitive Forces   The contribution of Figure 3–3 is the assist it provides in exposing the makeup of competitive forces. *To analyze the competitive environment, the strength of each one of the five competitive forces must be assessed.* The collective impact of these forces determines what competition is like in a given market. As a rule, the stronger competitive forces are, the lower the collective profitability of participating firms. The most brutally competitive situation occurs when the five forces are tough enough to cause prolonged subpar profitability or even losses for most or all firms. The competitive structure of an industry is clearly "unattractive" from a profit-making standpoint if rivalry among sellers is very strong, entry barriers are low, competition from substitutes is strong, and both suppliers and customers have considerable bargaining leverage. On the other hand, when an industry offers superior long-term profit prospects, competitive forces are not unduly strong and the competitive structure of the industry is "favorable" and "attractive." The "ideal" competitive environment from a profit-making perspective is one in which both suppliers and customers are in a weak bargaining position, there are no good substitutes, entry barriers are relatively high, and rivalry among present sellers is only moderate. However, even where some of the five competitive forces are strong, an industry can be competitively attractive to those firms whose market position and strategy provide a good enough defense against competitive pressures to preserve their competitive advantage and retain an ability to earn above-average profits.

In coping with competitive forces, successful strategists craft competitive approaches that will (1) insulate the firm as much as possible from the five competitive forces, (2) influence the industry's competitive rules in the company's favor, and (3) provide a strong, secure position of advantage from which to "play the game" of competition as it unfolds in the industry. Strategists cannot do this task well without first perceptively analyzing the whole competitive picture of the industry via the five forces model.

Assessing the Competitive Positions of Rival Companies

The next step in examining the industry's competitive structure is studying the market positions of rival companies. One technique for comparing the competitive positions of industry participants is *strategic group mapping.*[16] This analytical tool bridges the gap between looking at the industry as a whole and considering the standing of each firm separately. It is most useful when an industry has too many competitors to examine each one in depth.

---

[16]Ibid., chap. 7.

A strategic group consists of those rival firms with similar competitive approaches and positions in the market.[17] Companies in the same strategic group can resemble one another in several ways: they may have comparable product lines, be vertically integrated to the same degree, offer buyers similar services and technical assistance, appeal to similar types of buyers with the same product attributes, emphasize the same distribution channels, depend on identical technology, and/or sell in the same price/quality range. An industry has only one strategic group if all sellers use essentially identical strategies. At the other extreme, there are as many strategic groups as there are competitors if each one pursues a distinctively different competitive approach and occupies a substantially different position in the marketplace.

To construct a strategic group map, analysts need to:

1. Identify the competitive characteristics that differentiate firms in the industry—typical variables are price/quality range (high, medium, low), geographic coverage (local, regional, national, global), degree of vertical integration (none, partial, full), product-line breadth (wide, narrow), use of distribution channels (one, some, all), and degree of service offered (no frills, limited, full service).

2. Plot the firms on a two-variable map using pairs of these differentiating characteristics.

3. Assign firms that fall in about the same strategy space to the same strategic group.

4. Draw circles around each strategic group, making the circles proportional to the size of the group's respective share of total industry sales revenues.

This produces a two-dimensional *strategic group map* such as the one for the beer industry shown in Illustration Capsule 10.

To map the positions of strategic groups accurately in the industry's overall "strategy space," several guidelines must be observed.[18] First, the two variables selected as axes for the map should *not* be highly correlated; if they are, the circles on the map will fall along a diagonal and analysts will learn nothing more than they would by considering only one variable. For instance, if companies with broad product lines use multiple distribution channels while companies with narrow lines use a single distribution channel, one of the variables is redundant. Second, the variables chosen as axes for the map should expose big differences in how rivals have positioned themselves to compete in the marketplace. This means that analysts must identify the characteristics that differentiate rival firms and use these differences as variables for the axes and as the basis for deciding which firm belongs in which group. Third, the variables used for the axes don't have to be either quantitative or continuous; they can be discrete variables or defined in terms of distinct classes and combinations. Fourth, the circles on the map should be drawn proportional to the combined sales of the firms in each group so that the map will reflect the relative size of each strategic group. Fifth, if more than two good competitive variables can be used for axes, several maps can be drawn to give different exposures to

---

[17]Ibid., pp. 129–30.
[18]Ibid., pp. 152–54.

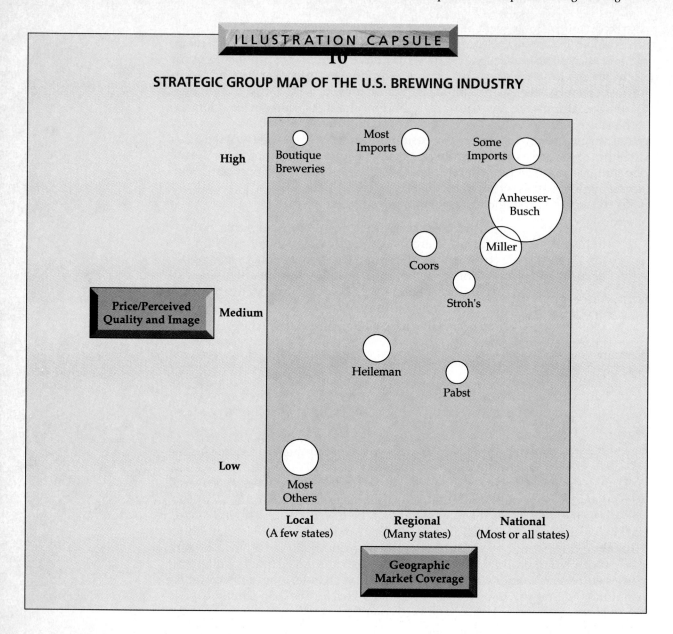

STRATEGIC GROUP MAP OF THE U.S. BREWING INDUSTRY

**Principle of
Competitive Markets**

*Some strategic groups are
usually more favorably
positioned than others
because driving forces and
competitive pressures do
not affect each group
evenly and profit prospects
vary among groups based
on the relative
attractiveness of their
market positions.*

the competitive relationships. Because there is not necessarily one best map, it is advisable to experiment with different pairs of competitive variables.

Strategic group analysis helps deepen understanding of competitive rivalry.[19] To begin with, *driving forces and competitive pressures often favor some strategic groups and hurt others.* Firms in adversely affected strategic groups may try to shift to a more favorably situated group; how hard such a move proves to be depends on whether the entry barriers in the target group are high or low. Attempts by rival firms to enter a new strategic group nearly always increase competitive pressures. If certain firms are known to be changing their

---

[19]Ibid., pp. 130, 132–38, and 154–55.

competitive positions, arrows can be added to the map to show the targeted direction and help clarify the picture of competitive jockeying among rivals.

Second, *the profit potential of different strategic groups may vary due to the strengths and weaknesses in each group's market position*. Differences in profitability can occur because of different bargaining leverage with suppliers or customers and different exposure to competition from substitute products.

Generally speaking, *the closer strategic groups are on the map, the stronger competitive rivalry among member firms tends to be*. Although firms in the same strategic group are the closest rivals, the next closest rivals are in the immediately adjacent groups. Often, firms in strategic groups that are *far apart* on the map hardly compete at all. For instance, Heineken Brewing Co. in Amsterdam and Dixie Brewing Co. in New Orleans both sell beer, but the prices and perceived qualities of their products are much too different to generate any real competition between them. For the same reason, Timex is not a meaningful competitor of Rolex, and Subaru is not a close competitor of Lincoln or Mercedes-Benz.

Competitor Analysis: Predicting What Moves Which Rivals Are Likely to Make Next

Studying the actions and behavior of close competitors is essential. Unless a company pays attention to what competitors are doing, it ends up "flying blind" into battle. A firm can't outmaneuver its rivals without monitoring their actions and anticipating what moves they are likely to make next. The strategies rivals are using and the actions they are likely to take next have direct bearing on what a company's own best strategic moves are—whether it will need to defend against rivals' actions or whether rivals' moves provide an opening for a new offensive thrust.

Competitive Strategy Principle
Successful strategists take great pains in scouting competitors—understanding their strategies, watching their actions, sizing up their strengths and weaknesses, and trying to anticipate what moves they will make next.

Identifying Competitors' Strategies   Strategists can get a quick profile of key competitors by studying where they are in the industry, their strategic objectives (as revealed by their recent actions), and their basic competitive approaches. Table 3–3 provides an easy-to-use scheme for categorizing rivals' objectives and strategies. Such a summary, along with a strategic group map, usually suffices to diagnose the competitive intent of rivals.

Evaluating Who the Industry's Major Players Are Going to Be   It's usually obvious who the *current* major contenders are, but these same firms are not necessarily positioned strongly for the future. Some may be losing ground or be ill-equipped to compete on the industry's future battleground. Smaller companies may be poised for an offensive against larger but vulnerable rivals. In fast-moving, high-technology industries and in globally competitive industries, companies can and do fall from leadership; others end up being acquired. Today's industry leaders don't automatically become tomorrow's.

In deciding whether a competitor is favorably positioned to gain market ground, attention needs to center on *why* there is potential for it to do better or worse than other rivals. Usually, how securely a company holds its present market share is a function of its vulnerability to driving forces and competitive pressures, whether it has a competitive advantage or disadvantage, and whether it is the likely target of offensive attacks from other industry

TABLE 3-3   Categorizing the Objectives and Strategies of Competitors

Competitive Scope	Strategic Intent	Market Share Objective	Competitive Position/Situation	Strategic Posture	Competitive Strategy
• Local	• Be the dominant leader	• Aggressive expansion via both acquisition and internal growth	• Getting stronger; on the move	• Mostly offensive	• Striving for low cost leadership
• Regional	• Overtake the present industry leader	• Expansion via internal growth (boost market share at the expense of rival firms)	• Well-entrenched; able to maintain its present position	• Mostly defensive	• Mostly focusing on a market niche
• National	• Be among the industry leaders (top 5)	• Expansion via acquisition	• Stuck in the middle of the pack	• A combination of offense and defense	–High end
• Multicountry	• Move into the top 10	• Hold onto present share (by growing at a rate equal to the industry average)	• Going after a different market position (trying to move from a weaker to a stronger position)	• Aggressive risk-taker	–Low end
• Global	• Move up a notch or two in the industry rankings	• Give up share if necessary to achieve short-term profit objectives (stress profitability, not volume)	• Struggling; losing ground	• Conservative follower	–Geographic
	• Overtake a particular rival (not necessarily the leader)		• Retrenching to a position that can be defended		–Buyers with special needs
	• Maintain position				–Other
	• Just survive				• Pursuing differentiation based on
					–Quality
					–Service
					–Technological superiority
					–Breadth of product line
					–Image and reputation
					–Other attributes

Note: Since a focus strategy can be aimed at any of several market niches and a differentiation strategy can be keyed to any of several attributes, it is best to be explicit about what kind of focus strategy or differentiation strategy a given firm is pursuing. All focusers do not pursue the same market niche, and all differentiators do not pursue the same differentiating attributes.

participants. Trying to identify which rivals are poised to gain or lose market position helps a strategist figure out what kinds of moves key rivals are likely to make next.

Predicting Competitors' Next Moves Predicting rivals' moves is the hardest yet most useful part of competitor analysis. Good clues about what moves a specific competitor may make next come from finding out how much pressure the rival is under to improve its financial performance. Aggressive rivals usually undertake some type of new strategic initiative. Content rivals are likely to continue their present strategy with only minor fine-tuning. Ailing rivals can be performing so poorly that fresh strategic moves, either offensive or defensive, are virtually certain. Since managers generally operate from assumptions about the industry's future and beliefs about their own firm's situation, strategists can gain insights into the strategic thinking of rival managers by examining their public pronouncements about where the industry is headed and what it will take to be successful, listening to what they are saying about their firm's situation, gathering information about what they are doing, and studying their past actions and leadership styles. Strategists also need to consider whether a rival is flexible enough to make major strategic changes.

To predict a competitor's next moves, an analyst must get a good "feel" for the rival's situation, how its managers think, and what its options are. The detective work can be tedious and time-consuming since the information comes in bits and pieces from many sources. But it is a task worth doing well because the information gives managers more time to prepare countermoves and a chance to beat rivals to the punch by moving first.

Pinpointing the Key Factors for Competitive Success

Key success factors (KSFs) are the major determinants of financial and competitive success in a particular industry. Key success factors highlight the specific outcomes crucial to success in the marketplace and the competences and capabilities with the most bearing on profitability. In the beer industry, the KSFs are full utilization of brewing capacity (to keep manufacturing costs low), a strong network of wholesale distributors (to gain access to as many retail outlets as possible), and clever advertising (to induce beer drinkers to buy a particular brand and thereby pull beer sales through the established wholesale/retail channels). In apparel manufacturing, the KSFs are appealing designs and color combinations (to create buyer interest) and low-cost manufacturing efficiency (to permit attractive retail pricing and ample profit margins). In tin and aluminum cans, where the cost of shipping empty cans is substantial, the KSFs are having plants located close to end-use customers and the ability to market plant output within economical shipping distances (regional market share is far more crucial than national share).

Identifying key success factors is a top-priority strategic consideration. At the very least, management needs to know the industry well enough to conclude what is more important to competitive success and what is less important. At most, KSFs can serve as *the cornerstones* for building a company's strategy. Companies frequently win competitive advantage by concentrating on being distinctively better than rivals in one or more of the industry's key success factors.

Basic Concept
Key success factors spell the difference between profit and loss and, ultimately, between competitive success and failure. A key success factor can be a skill or talent, a competitive capability, or a condition a company must achieve; it can relate to technology, manufacturing, distribution, marketing, or organizational resources.

Key success factors vary from industry to industry, and even over time in the same industry, as driving forces and competitive conditions change. Table 3–4 lists the most common types of key success factors. Only rarely does an industry have more than three or four key success factors at any one time. And even among these three or four, one or two usually outrank the others in importance. Strategic analysts, therefore, have to resist the temptation to include factors that have only minor importance—the purpose of identifying KSFs is to make judgments about what things are more important to competitive success and what things are less important. To compile a list of every factor that matters even a little bit defeats the purpose of training management's eyes on the factors truly crucial to long-term competitive success.

Drawing Conclusions about Overall Industry Attractiveness

The final step of industry and competitive analysis is to review the overall industry situation and develop reasoned conclusions about the relative attractiveness or unattractiveness of the industry, both near-term and long-term. An assessment that the industry is attractive typically calls for some kind of aggressive, expansion-oriented strategic approach. If the industry and competitive situation is judged relatively unattractive, companies are drawn to consider strategies aimed at protecting their profitability. Weaker companies may consider leaving the industry or merging with a rival.

Whether an industry is relatively attractive or unattractive depends on several situational considerations.

Important factors to consider in drawing conclusions about industry attractiveness are:

- The industry's growth potential.
- Whether the industry will be favorably or unfavorably impacted by the prevailing driving forces.
- The potential for the entry/exit of major firms (probable entry reduces attractiveness to existing firms; the exit of a major firm or several weak firms opens up market share growth opportunities for the remaining firms).
- The stability/dependability of demand (as affected by seasonality, the business cycle, the volatility of consumer preferences, inroads by substitutes, and the like).
- Whether competitive forces will become stronger or weaker.
- The severity of problems/issues confronting the industry as a whole.
- The degrees of risk and uncertainty in the industry's future.
- Whether the industry's overall profit prospects are above or below average.

Strategic Management Principle
A company well situated in an unattractive industry can still earn good profits.

However, even if an industry is relatively unattractive overall, it can still be attractive to a company already favorably situated in the industry or to an outsider with the resources and skills to acquire an existing company and turn it into a major contender. Appraising industry attractiveness from the standpoint of a particular company in the industry means looking at the following *additional aspects*:

- The company's competitive position in the industry and whether its position is likely to grow stronger or weaker (a well-entrenched leader in a lackluster industry can still generate good profits).

Technology-Related KSFs
- Scientific research expertise (important in such fields as pharmaceuticals, medicine, space exploration, other "high-tech" industries)
- Production process innovation capability
- Product innovation capability
- Expertise in a given technology

Manufacturing-Related KSFs
- Low-cost production efficiency (achieve scale economies, capture experience curve effects)
- Quality of manufacture (fewer defects, less need for repairs)
- High utilization of fixed assets (important in capital intensive/high fixed-cost industries)
- Low-cost plant locations
- Access to adequate supplies of skilled labor
- High labor productivity (important for items with high labor content)
- Low-cost product design and engineering (reduces manufacturing costs)
- Flexibility to manufacture a range of models and sizes/take care of custom orders

Distribution-Related KSFs
- A strong network of wholesale distributors/dealers
- Gaining ample space on retailer shelves
- Having company-owned retail outlets
- Low distribution costs
- Fast delivery

Marketing-Related KSFs
- A well-trained, effective sales force
- Available, dependable service and technical assistance
- Accurate filling of buyer orders (few back orders or mistakes)
- Breadth of product line and product selection
- Merchandising skills
- Attractive styling/packaging
- Customer guarantees and warranties (important in mail-order retailing, big ticket purchases, new product introductions)

Skills-Related KSFs
- Superior talent (important in professional services)
- Quality control know-how
- Design expertise (important in fashion and apparel industries)
- Expertise in a particular technology
- Ability to come up with clever, catchy ads
- Ability to get newly developed products out of the R&D phase and into the market very quickly

Organizational Capability
- Superior information systems (important in airline travel, car rental, credit card, and lodging industries)
- Ability to respond quickly to shifting market conditions (streamlined decision-making, short lead times to bring new products to market)
- More experience and managerial know-how

Other Types of KSFs
- Favorable image/reputation with buyers
- Overall low cost (not just in manufacturing)
- Convenient locations (important in many retailing businesses)
- Pleasant, courteous employees
- Access to financial capital (important in newly emerging industries with high degrees of business risk and in capital-intensive industries)
- Patent protection
- Overall low cost (not just in manufacturing)

- The company's potential to capitalize on the vulnerabilities of weaker rivals (thereby converting an unattractive *industry* situation into a potentially rewarding *company* opportunity).
- Whether the company is insulated from, or able to defend against, the factors that make the industry unattractive.
- Whether continued participation in the industry adds significantly to the firm's ability to be successful in other industries in which it has business interests.

Conclusions drawn about an industry's attractiveness and competitive situation have a major bearing on a company's strategic options and ultimate choice of strategy.

KEY POINTS

Thinking strategically about a company's external situation involves probing for answers to the following seven questions:

1. What are the chief economic characteristics of the industry?
2. What are the drivers of change in the industry, and what impact will they have?
3. What competitive forces are at work in the industry, and how strong are they?
4. Which companies are in the strongest/weakest competitive positions?
5. Who will likely make what competitive moves next?
6. What key factors will determine competitive success or failure?
7. How attractive is the industry in terms of its prospects for above-average profitability?

To answer these questions, several concepts and techniques are useful—driving forces, the five forces model of competition, strategic groups and strategic group mapping, competitor analysis, key success factors, and industry attractiveness.

Table 3–5 provides a *format* for conducting industry and competitive analysis. It pulls together the relevant concepts and considerations and makes it easier to do a concise, understandable analysis of the industry and competitive environment.

Two final points are worth keeping in mind. First, the task of analyzing a company's external situation is not a mechanical exercise in which analysts plug in data and definitive conclusions come out. There can be several appealing scenarios about how an industry will evolve and what future competitive conditions will be like. For this reason, strategic analysis always leaves room for differences of opinion about how all the factors add up and how industry and competitive conditions will change. However, while no strategic analysis methodology can guarantee a single conclusive diagnosis, it doesn't make sense to shortcut strategic analysis and rely on opinion and casual observation. Managers become better strategists when they know what analytical questions to pose, can use situation analysis techniques to find answers, and have the skills to read clues about industry and competitive change.

Second, in practice, industry and competitive analysis is an incremental and ongoing process, the result of gradually accumulated knowledge and continu-

T A B L E 3–5   **Industry and Competitive Analysis Summary Profile**

1. **DOMINANT ECONOMIC CHARACTERISTICS OF THE INDUSTRY ENVIRONMENT** (market growth, geographic scope, industry structure, scale economies, experience curve effects, capital requirements, and so on)

2. **DRIVING FORCES**

3. **COMPETITION ANALYSIS**
   - Rivalry among competing sellers (a strong, moderate, or weak force/weapons of competition)

   - Threat of potential entry (a strong, moderate, or weak force/assessment of entry barriers)

   - Competition from subsitutes (a strong, moderate, or weak force/why)

   - Power of suppliers (a strong, moderate, or weak force/why)

   - Power of customers (a strong, moderate, or weak force/why)

4. **COMPETITIVE POSITION OF MAJOR COMPANIES/ STRATEGIC GROUPS**
   - Favorably positioned/why

   - Unfavorably positioned/why

5. **COMPETITOR ANALYSIS**
   - Strategic approaches/predicted moves of key competitors

   - Who to watch and why

6. **KEY SUCCESS FACTORS**

7. **INDUSTRY PROSPECTS AND OVERALL ATTRACTIVENESS**
   - Factors making the industry attractive

   - Factors making the industry unattractive

   - Special industry issues/problems

   - Profit outlook (favorable/unfavorable)

ous rethinking and retesting. Sweeping industry and competitive analyses need to be done periodically; in the interim, managers must update and reexamine the picture as events unfold. Important strategic actions usually result from a *gradual* build-up of clues and documentation that important changes in the external environment are occurring, a *gradual* understanding of the implications of these changes, and *gradually* reached conclusions about upcoming conditions in the industry.

Ghemawat, Pankaj. "Building Strategy on the Experience Curve." *Harvard Business Review* 64, no. 2 (March–April 1985), pp. 143–49.

Linneman, Robert E., and Harold E. Klein. "Using Scenarios in Strategic Decision Making." *Business Horizons* 28, no. 1 (January–February 1985), pp. 64–74.

Ohmae, Kenichi. *The Mind of the Strategist.* New York: Penguin Books, 1983, chaps. 3, 6, 7, and 13.

Porter, Michael E. "How Competitive Forces Shape Strategy." *Harvard Business Review* 57, no. 2 (March–April 1979), pp. 137–45.

_____. *Competitive Strategy: Techniques for Analyzing Industries and Competitors.* New York: Free Press, 1980, chap. 1.

_____. *Competitive Advantage.* New York: Free Press, 1985, chap. 2.

SUGGESTED READINGS

Company Situation Analysis

Understand what really makes a company " tick."
Charles R. Scott
CEO, Intermark Corp.

If you think what exists today is permanent and forever true,
you inevitably get your head handed to you.
John Reed
Chairman, Citicorp

The secret of success is to be ready for opportunity when it comes.
Disraeli

In the last chapter, we saw how to use industry and competitive analysis to assess the attractiveness of a company's external environment. In this chapter, we discuss how to evaluate a particular company's strategic situation in that environment. Company situation analysis centers on five questions:

1. How well is the present strategy working?
2. What are the company's strengths, weaknesses, opportunities, and threats?
3. Is the company competitive on cost?
4. How strong is the company's competitive position?
5. What strategic issues does the company face?

There are five questions to answer in analyzing a company's strategic situation.

To explore these questions, strategists use three analytical techniques: SWOT analysis, strategic cost analysis, and competitive strength assessment. These tools are widely used in strategic analysis because they indicate how strongly a company holds its industry position and whether the present strategy is capable of boosting long-term performance.

HOW WELL IS THE PRESENT STRATEGY WORKING?

To evaluate how well a company's present strategy is working, one needs to start with what the strategy is (see Figure 2–2 in Chapter 2 to refresh your recollection of the key components of business strategy). The first thing to understand is the company's competitive approach—whether it is striving for low-cost leadership, trying to differentiate itself from rivals, or focusing narrowly on specific customer groups and market niches. Another important consideration is the firm's competitive scope within the industry—its degree of vertical integration and geographic market coverage. The company's functional area support strategies in production, marketing, finance, human resources, and so on need to be identified and understood as well. In addition, the company may have initiated some recent strategic moves (for instance, a price cut, stepped-up advertising, entry into a new geographic area, or merger with a competitor) that are integral to its strategy and that aim at securing a particular competitive advantage and/or improved competitive position. Examining the rationale for each piece of the strategy—for each competitive move and each functional approach—should clarify what the present strategy is.

While there's merit in evaluating a strategy from a qualitative standpoint (i.e., its completeness, internal consistency, rationale, and suitability), the best evidence of how well a strategy is working comes from the company's recent strategic and financial performance. The most obvious indicators of a firm's strategic and financial performance include: (1) whether the firm's market share is rising or falling, (2) whether the firm's profit margins are increasing or decreasing and how large they are relative to rival firms, (3) trends in the firm's net profits and return on investment, (4) whether the firm's sales are growing faster or slower than the market as a whole, (5) whether the firm enjoys a competitive advantage or is at a disadvantage, and (6) whether its long-term competitive position is becoming stronger or weaker. The better a company's current overall performance, the less likely the need for radical changes in strategy. The weaker a company's strategic and financial performance, the more its current strategy should be questioned.

The stronger a company's strategic and financial performance, the more likely it has a well-conceived, well-executed strategy.

SWOT ANALYSIS

SWOT is an acronym for a company's strengths, weaknesses, opportunities, and threats. A SWOT analysis consists of evaluating a firm's internal strengths and weaknesses and its external opportunities and threats. It is an easy-to-use tool for getting a quick *overview* of a firm's strategic situation. SWOT analysis underscores the basic point that strategy must produce a good fit between a company's internal capability (its strengths and weaknesses) and its external situation (reflected in part by its opportunities and threats).

Basic Concept
A company's internal strengths usually represent competitive assets; its internal weaknesses usually represent competitive liabilities. A company's strengths/assets should outweigh its weaknesses/liabilities by a hefty margin.

Identifying Strengths and Weaknesses

Table 4–1 lists the considerations used to identify a company's internal strengths and weaknesses. A *strength* is something a company is good at doing or a characteristic that gives it an important capability. A strength can be a skill, a competence, a valuable organizational resource or competitive

TABLE 4–1   **SWOT Analysis—What to Look for in Sizing up a Company's Strengths, Weaknesses, Opportunities, and Threats**

Potential Internal Strengths	Potential Internal Weaknesses
• Core competences in key areas	• No clear strategic direction
• Adequate financial resources	• Obsolete facilities
• Well thought of by buyers	• Subpar profitability because . . .
• An acknowledged market leader	• Lack of managerial depth and talent
• Well-conceived functional area strategies	• Missing some key skills or competences
• Access to economies of scale	• Poor track record in implementing strategy
• Insulated (at least somewhat) from strong competitive pressures	• Plagued with internal operating problems
• Proprietary technology	• Falling behind in R & D
• Cost advantages	• Too narrow a product line
• Better advertising campaigns	• Weak market image
• Product innovation skills	• Weak distribution network
• Proven management	• Below-average marketing skills
• Ahead on experience curve	• Unable to finance needed changes in strategy
• Better manufacturing capability	• Higher overall unit costs relative to key competitors
• Superior technological skills	• Other?
• Other?	

Potential External Opportunities	Potential External Threats
• Serve additional customer groups	• Entry of lower-cost foreign competitors
• Enter new markets or segments	• Rising sales of substitute products
• Expand product line to meet broader range of customer needs	• Slower market growth
• Diversify into related products	• Adverse shifts in foreign exchange rates and trade policies of foreign governments
• Vertical integration (forward or backward)	• Costly regulatory requirements
• Falling trade barriers in attractive foreign markets	• Vulnerability to recession and business cycle
• Complacency among rival firms	• Growing bargaining power of customers or suppliers
• Faster market growth	• Changing buyer needs and tastes
• Other?	• Adverse demographic changes
	• Other?

capability, or an achievement that gives the company a market advantage (like having a better product, stronger name recognition, superior technology, or better customer service). A *weakness* is something a company lacks or does poorly (in comparison to others) or a condition that puts it at a disadvantage. A weakness may or may not make a company competitively vulnerable, depending on how much it matters in the competitive battle.

Once a company's internal strengths and weaknesses are identified, the two lists have to be carefully evaluated. Some strengths are more important than others because they count for more in determining performance, in competing successfully, and in forming a powerful strategy. Likewise, some internal weaknesses can prove fatal, while others don't matter much or can be easily remedied. A SWOT analysis is like constructing a *strategic balance sheet—*

strengths are *competitive assets* and weaknesses are *competitive liabilities*. The issue is whether the strengths/assets adequately overcome the weaknesses/liabilities (a 50–50 balance is definitely not desirable!), how to meld strengths into an effective strategy, and whether strategic actions are needed to tilt the strategic balance more toward the asset side and away from the liability side.

From a strategy-making perspective, a company's strengths are significant because they can be used as the cornerstones of strategy and the basis on which to build competitive advantage. If a company doesn't have strong competences and competitive assets around which to craft an attractive strategy, management must move quickly to build capabilities on which a strategy can be grounded. At the same time, a good strategy needs to aim at correcting competitive weaknesses that make the company vulnerable, hurt its performance, or disqualify it from pursuing an attractive opportunity. The point here is simple: *an organization's strategy should be well-suited to company strengths, weaknesses, and competitive capabilities.* As a rule, management should build its strategy around what the company does best and should avoid strategies whose success depends heavily on areas where the company is weak or has unproven ability.

Core Competences   One of the "trade secrets" of first-rate strategic management is consolidating a company's technological, production, and marketing know-how into competences that enhance its competitiveness. *A core competence is something a company does especially well in comparison to its competitors.*[1] In practice, there are many possible types of core competences: manufacturing excellence, exceptional quality control, the ability to provide better service, more know-how in low-cost manufacturing, superior design capability, unique ability to pick out good retail locations, innovativeness in developing new products, better skill in merchandising and product display, mastery of an important technology, a strong understanding of customer needs and tastes, an unusually effective sales force, outstanding skill in working with customers on new applications and uses of the product, and expertise in integrating multiple technologies to create families of new products. *The importance of a core competence to strategy-making rests with (1) the added capability it gives an organization in going after a particular market opportunity, (2) the competitive edge it can yield in the marketplace, and (3) its potential for being a cornerstone of strategy.* It is easier to build competitive advantage when a firm has a core competence in an area important to market success, when rivals do not have offsetting competences, and when it is costly and time-consuming for rivals to match the competence. Core competences are thus valuable competitive assets.

Identifying Opportunities and Threats

Table 4–1 also lists factors that help identify a company's external opportunities and threats. Market opportunity is a big factor in shaping a company's strategy. However, there is an important distinction between *industry opportunities* and *company opportunities*. Not every company in an industry is well

---

[1]For a fuller discussion of the core competence concept, see C. K. Prahalad and Gary Hamel, "The Core Competence of the Corporation," *Harvard Business Review* 90, no. 3 (May–June 1990), pp. 79–93.

positioned to pursue each opportunity that exists in the industry—some companies are always better situated than others and several may be hopelessly out of contention. A company's strengths and weaknesses make it better suited to pursuing some opportunities than others. *The industry opportunities most relevant to a particular company are those that offer important avenues for growth and those where a company has the most potential for competitive advantage.*

Often certain factors in a company's external environment pose *threats* to its well-being. Threats can stem from the emergence of cheaper technologies, rivals' introduction of new or better products, the entry of low-cost foreign competitors into a company's market stronghold, new regulations that are more burdensome to a company than to its competitors, vulnerability to a rise in interest rates, the potential for a hostile takeover, unfavorable demographic shifts, adverse changes in foreign exchange rates, political upheaval at a company's foreign facilities, and the like.

Opportunities and threats not only affect the attractiveness of a company's situation but point to the need for strategic action. To be adequately matched to a company's situation, strategy must (1) be aimed at pursuing opportunities well suited to the company's capabilities and (2) provide a defense against external threats. SWOT analysis is therefore more than an exercise in making four lists. The important part of SWOT analysis involves *evaluating* the strengths, weaknesses, opportunities, and threats and *drawing conclusions* about the attractiveness of the company's situation and the need for strategic action. Some of the pertinent strategy-making questions to consider, once the SWOT listings have been compiled, are:

- Does the company have any internal strengths or core competences an attractive strategy can be built around?
- Do the company's weaknesses make it competitively vulnerable and/or do they disqualify the company from pursuing certain opportunities? Which weaknesses does strategy need to correct?
- Which opportunities does the company have the skills and resources to pursue with a real chance of success? (*Remember*: Opportunity without the means to capture it is an illusion.)
- What threats should managers be worried about most, and what strategic moves should they consider in crafting a good defense?

Strategic Management Principle

Successful strategists aim at capturing a company's best growth opportunities and creating defenses against threats to its competitive position and future performance.

STRATEGIC COST ANALYSIS AND ACTIVITY-COST CHAINS

One of the most telling signs of the strength of a company's strategic position is its cost position relative to competitors. Cost comparisons are especially critical in a commodity-product industry where price competition typically dominates and lower-cost companies have the upper hand. But even in industries where products are differentiated and competition is based on factors other than price, companies have to keep costs *in line with* rivals or risk jeopardizing their competitive position.

Competitors do not necessarily, or even usually, incur the same costs in supplying their products to end-users. Disparities in costs among rival producers can stem from:

- Differences in the prices paid for raw materials, component parts, energy, and other items purchased from suppliers.

Assessing whether a company's costs are competitive with those of its close rivals is a necessary and crucial part of company situation analysis.

- Differences in basic technology and the age of plants and equipment. (Because rivals usually invest in plants and key pieces of equipment at different times, their facilities usually have different technological efficiencies and different fixed costs. Older facilities are typically less efficient, but if they were less expensive to construct or cheaply acquired, they *may* still be reasonably cost competitive with modern facilities.)
- Differences in internal operating costs due to the economies of scale associated with different size plants, learning and experience curve effects, different wage rates, different productivity levels, different administrative overhead expenses, different tax rates, and the like.
- Differences in rivals' exposure to inflation and changes in foreign exchange rates (as can occur in global industries where competitors have plants located in different nations).
- Differences in marketing costs, sales and promotion expenditures, and advertising expenses.
- Differences in inbound transportation costs and outbound shipping costs.
- Differences in forward channel distribution costs (the costs and markups of distributors, wholesalers, and retailers who get the product from the manufacturer to the end-user).

> Cost differences among close rivals can stem from many factors.

For a company to be competitively successful, its costs must be in line with those of rival producers. However, some cost disparity is justified when the products of competing companies are *differentiated*. The need to be cost competitive is not so stringent as to *require* the costs of every firm in the industry to be *equal*, but, as a rule, the higher a firm's costs above low-cost producers, the more vulnerable its market position becomes. Given the numerous opportunities for cost disparities, a company must be aware of how its costs compare with rivals'. This is where *strategic cost analysis* comes in.

> **Strategic Management Principle**
> The higher a company's costs are above those of rivals, the more competitively vulnerable it becomes.

Strategic cost analysis focuses on a firm's cost position relative to its rivals'. The primary analytical tool of strategic cost analysis is an *activity-cost chain* showing the buildup of value from raw materials supply to the price paid by ultimate customers.[2] The activity-cost chain goes beyond a company's own internal cost structure to cover all the stages in the industry chain: raw materials supply, manufacturing, wholesale distribution, and retailing, as shown in Figure 4–1. An activity-cost chain is especially revealing for a manufacturing firm because its ability to supply its product to end-users at a competitive price can easily depend on costs that originate either *backward* in suppliers' portion of the activity-cost chain, or *forward* in the wholesale and retail stages of the chain.

> **Basic Concept**
> Strategic cost analysis involves comparing a company's cost position relative to key competitors, activity by activity, from raw materials purchase to the price paid by ultimate customers.

The data requirements for activity-cost chain analysis are formidable. It requires breaking a firm's own historical cost accounting data out into several principal cost categories and also developing cost estimates for the backward and forward channel portions. To see how the firm's cost position compares with rivals, the same cost elements for each rival must likewise be estimated—an advanced art in competitive intelligence in itself. But despite

---

[2]Strategic cost analysis is described at greater length in Michael E. Porter, *Competitive Advantage* (New York: Free Press, 1985), chap. 2. What follows is a distilled adaptation of the analytical method pioneered by Porter.

	TOTAL INDUSTRY ACTIVITY-COST CHAIN	
SUPPLIER-RELATED ACTIVITIES	MANUFACTURING-RELATED ACTIVITIES	FORWARD CHANNEL ACTIVITIES

Purchased Materials, Components, Inputs, and Inbound Logistics	Production Activities and Operations	Marketing and Sales Activities	Customer Service and Outbound Logistics Activities	In-House Staff Support Activities	General and Administrative Activities	Profit Margin	Wholesale Distributor and Dealer Network Activities	Retailer Activities
Specific activities/costs	Specific activities/costs	Specific activities/costs	Specific activities/costs	Specific activities/costs	Specific activities/costs			

Purchased Materials, Components, Inputs, and Inbound Logistics
- Ingredient raw materials and component parts supplied by outsiders
- Energy
- Inbound shipping
- Inbound materials handling
- Warehousing

Production Activities and Operations
- Facilities and equipment
- Processing
- Assembly and packaging
- Labor and supervision
- Maintenance
- Product design and testing
- Quality and inspection
- Inventory management

Marketing and Sales Activities
- Salesforce operations
- Advertising and promotion
- Market research
- Technical literature
- Travel and entertainment
- Dealer/distributor relations

Customer Service and Outbound Logistics Activities
- Service reps
- Order processing
- Spare parts
- Other outbound logistics costs

In-House Staff Support Activities
- Payroll and benefits
- Recruiting and training
- Internal communications
- Computer services
- Procurement functions
- R&D
- Safety and security
- Union relations

General and Administrative Activities
- Finance and accounting services
- Legal services
- Public relations
- Executive salaries
- Interest on borrowed funds
- Tax-related costs
- Regulatory compliance

Includes all of the activities, associated costs, and markups of distributors, wholesale dealers, retailers, and any other forward channel allies whose efforts are utilized to get the product into the hands of end-users/customers

ACTIVITY-COST CHAINS FOR ANHEUSER-BUSCH AND ADOLPH COORS BEERS

In the table below are average cost estimates for the combined brands of beer produced by Anheuser-Busch and Coors. The example shows raw material costs, other manufacturing costs, and forward channel distribution costs. The data are for 1982.

Activity-Cost Elements	Estimated Average Cost Breakdown for Combined Anheuser-Busch Brands		Estimated Average Cost Breakdown for Combined Adolph Coors Brands	
	Per 6-Pack of 12-oz. Cans	Per Barrel Equivalent	Per 6-Pack of 12-oz. Cans	Per Barrel Equivalent
1. Manufacturing costs:				
Direct production costs:				
Raw material ingredients	$0.1384	$ 7.63	$0.1082	$ 5.96
Direct labor	0.1557	8.58	0.1257	6.93
Salaries for nonunionized personnel	0.0800	4.41	0.0568	3.13
Packaging	0.5055	27.86	0.4663	25.70
Depreciation on plant and equipment	0.0410	2.26	0.0826	4.55
Subtotal	0.9206	50.74	0.8396	46.27
Other expenses:				
Advertising	0.0477	2.63	0.0338	1.86
Other marketing costs and general administrative expenses	0.1096	6.04	0.1989	10.96
Interest	0.0147	0.81	0.0033	0.18
Research and development	0.0277	1.53	0.0195	1.07
Total manufacturing costs	$1.1203	$ 61.75	$1.0951	$ 60.34
2. Manufacturer's operating profit	0.1424	7.85	0.0709	3.91
3. Net selling price	1.2627	69.60	1.1660	64.25
4. Plus federal and state excise taxes paid by brewer	0.1873	10.32	0.1782	9.82
5. Gross manufacturer's selling price to distributor/wholesaler	1.4500	79.92	1.3442	74.07
6. Average margin over manufacturer's cost	0.5500	30.31	0.5158	28.43
7. Average wholesale price charged to retailer (inclusive of taxes in item 4 above but exclusive of other taxes)	$2.00	$110.23	$1.86	$102.50
8. Plus other assorted state and local taxes levied on wholesale and retail sales (this varies from locality to locality)	0.60		0.60	
9. Average 20% retail markup over wholesale cost . .	0.40		0.38	
10. Average price to consumer at retail	$3.00		$2.84	

Note: The difference in the average cost structures for Anheuser-Busch and Adolph Coors is, to a substantial extent, due to A-B's higher proportion of super-premium beer sales. A-B's super-premium brand, Michelob, was the bestseller in its category and somewhat more costly to brew than premium and popular-priced beers.

Source: Compiled by Tom McLean, Elsa Wischkaemper, and Arthur A. Thompson, Jr., from a wide variety of documents and field interviews.

the tediousness of the task and the imprecision of some of the estimates, the payoff in exposing the cost competitiveness of one's position makes it a valuable analytical tool. Illustration Capsule 11 on page 93 shows a simplified activity-cost chain comparison for various brands of beer produced by Anheuser-Busch (the industry leader) and Adolph Coors (the third ranking brewer).

The most important application of the activity-cost technique is to expose how a particular firm's cost position compares with those of its rivals. What is needed is competitor versus competitor cost estimates for a given product. The size of a company's cost advantage/disadvantage can vary from item to item in the product line, from customer group to customer group (if different distribution channels are used), and from geographic market to geographic market (if cost factors vary across geographic regions).

Strategic actions to eliminate a cost disadvantage need to be linked to the location in the activity-cost chain where the cost differences originate.

Looking again at Figure 4–1, observe that there are three main areas in the cost chain where important differences in competitors' *relative* costs can occur: in suppliers' part of the cost chain, in each company's activity segments, or in the forward channel portion. If a firm's lack of cost competitiveness lies either in the backward or forward sections of the chain, the task of re-establishing cost competitiveness may have to extend beyond its own operations. When a firm's cost disadvantage is principally associated with items purchased from suppliers (the backward end of the activity-cost chain), it can pursue any of several strategic actions to correct the problem:

- Negotiate more favorable prices with suppliers.
- Work with suppliers to help them achieve lower costs.
- Integrate backward to gain control over the costs of purchased items.
- Try to use lower-priced substitute inputs.
- Try to save on inbound shipping costs.
- Try to make up the difference by cutting costs elsewhere in the chain.

A company's strategic options for eliminating cost disadvantages in the forward end of the chain include:

- Pushing distributors and other forward channel allies to reduce their costs and markups.
- Changing to a more economical distribution strategy, including forward integration.
- Trying to make up the difference by cutting costs earlier in the chain.

When the source of a firm's cost disadvantage is internal, it can use any of nine strategic approaches to restore cost parity:

- Initiate internal budget-tightening measures.
- Improve production methods and work procedures (to boost the productivity of workers and increase utilization of high-cost equipment).
- Try to eliminate some cost-producing activities altogether.
- Relocate high-cost activities to geographical areas where they can be performed cheaper.
- See if certain activities can be farmed out to contractors cheaper than they can be done internally.

T A B L E 4–2   **The Signs of Strength and Weakness in a Company's Competitive Position**

Signs of Competitive Strength	Signs of Competitive Weakness
• Important core competences	• Confronted with competitive disadvantages
• Strong market share (or a leading market share)	• Losing ground to rival firms
• A pacesetting or distinctive strategy	• Below average growth in revenues
• Growing customer base and customer loyalty	• Short on financial resources
• Above-average market visibility	• A slipping reputation with customers
• In a favorably situated strategic group	• Trailing in product development
• Concentrating on fastest-growing market segments	• In a strategic group destined to lose ground
• Strongly differentiated products	• Weak in areas where there is the most market potential
• Cost advantages	• A higher-cost producer
• Above-average profit margins	• Too small to be a major factor in the marketplace
• Above-average technological and innovational capability	• Not in good position to deal with emerging threats
• A creative, entrepreneurially alert management	• Weak product quality
• In position to capitalize on opportunities	• Lacking skills and capabilities in key areas

- Invest in cost-saving technological improvements (automation, robotics, flexible manufacturing techniques, computerized controls).
- Innovate around the troublesome cost components as new investments are made in plant and equipment.
- Simplify the product design and make it easier to manufacture.
- Try to make up the internal cost disadvantage by cutting costs in the backward and forward portions of the chain.

Activity-cost chains reveal a great deal about a firm's cost competitiveness. Examining the makeup of a company's own activity-cost chain and comparing it to rivals' indicate who has how much of a cost advantage/disadvantage and which cost components are responsible. Such information is vital in crafting strategies to eliminate a cost disadvantage or create a cost advantage.

COMPETITIVE STRENGTH ASSESSMENT

In addition to the cost competitiveness diagnosis that activity-cost chain analysis provides, a more broad-based assessment needs to be made of a company's competitive position and competitive strength. Particular elements to single out for evaluation are: (1) how strongly the firm holds its present competitive position, (2) whether the firm's position can be expected to improve or deteriorate if the present strategy is continued (allowing for fine-tuning), (3) how the firm ranks *relative to key rivals* on each important measure of competitive strength and industry key success factor, (4) whether the firm has a net competitive advantage or disadvantage, and (5) the firm's ability to defend its position in light of industry driving forces, competitive pressures, and the anticipated moves of rivals.

Table 4–2 lists some indicators of whether a firm's competitive position is improving or slipping. But more is needed than just a listing of the signs of improvement or slippage. The important thing is to develop some judgments

Systematic assessment of whether a company's competitive position is strong or weak relative to close rivals is an essential step in company situation analysis.

T A B L E 4–3   **Illustrations of Unweighted and Weighted Competitive Strength Assessments**

A. Sample of an Unweighted Competitive Strength Assessment
Rating scale: 1 = Very weak; 10 = Very strong

Key Success Factor/Strength Measure	ABC Co.	Rival 1	Rival 2	Rival 3	Rival 4
Quality/product performance	8	5	10	1	6
Reputation/image	8	7	10	1	6
Raw material access/cost	2	10	4	5	1
Technological skills	10	1	7	3	8
Advertising effectiveness	9	4	10	5	1
Marketing/distribution	9	4	10	5	1
Financial resource	5	10	7	3	1
Relative cost position	5	10	3	1	4
Ability to compete on price	5	7	10	1	4
Unweighted overall strength rating	61	58	71	25	32

B. Sample of a Weighted Competitive Strength Assessment
Rating scale: 1 = Very weak; 10 = Very strong

Key Success Factor/Strength Measure	Weight	ABC Co.	Rival 1	Rival 2	Rival 3	Rival 4
Quality/product performance	0.10	8/0.80	5/0.50	10/1.00	1/0.10	6/0.60
Reputation/image	0.10	8/0.80	7/0.70	10/1.00	1/0.10	6/0.60
Raw material access/cost	0.10	2/0.20	10/1.00	4/0.40	5/0.50	1/0.10
Technological skills	0.05	10/0.50	1/0.05	7/0.35	3/0.15	8/0.40
Manufacturing capability	0.05	9/0.45	4/0.20	10/0.50	5/0.25	1/0.05
Marketing/distribution	0.05	9/0.45	4/0.20	10/0.50	5/0.25	1/0.05
Financial strength	0.10	5/0.50	10/1.00	7/0.70	3/0.30	1/0.10
Relative cost position	0.35	5/1.75	10/3.50	3/1.05	1/0.35	4/1.40
Ability to compete on price	0.15	5/0.75	7/1.05	10/1.50	1/0.15	4/1.60
Sum of weights	1.00					
Weighted overall strength rating		6.20	8.20	7.00	2.10	2.90

about whether the company's position will improve or deteriorate under the current strategy and to consider what strategic actions are needed to improve the company's market position.

The really telling part of competitive position assessment, however, is the formal appraisal of whether the company is stronger or weaker than close rivals on each key success factor and indicator of competitive strength. Much of the information for competitive position assessment comes from previous analyses. Industry and competitive analysis reveals the key success factors and competitive strength measures that will separate industry winners and losers. Competitor analysis provides a basis for judging the strengths and capabilities of key rivals. Step one is to make a list of the industry's key success factors and measures of competitive strength or weaknesses (6 to 10 measures usually suffice). Step two is to rate the firm and its key rivals on each factor. Rating scales from 1 to 5 or 1 to 10 are straightforward and simple to use although ratings of stronger (+), weaker (–), and about equal (=) may be appropriate when numerical scores are too subjective. Step three is to sum the individual strength ratings to get an overall measure of competitive strength for each competitor. Step four is to draw conclusions about the size and extent of the company's net competitive advantage or disadvantage, noting areas where the company's competitive position is strongest and weakest.

Table 4–3 gives two examples of competitive strength assessments. The first one employs an *unweighted rating scale*; with unweighted ratings each key success factor/competitive strength measure is assumed to be equally important. Whichever company has the highest strength rating on a given measure has implied competitive edge on that factor. The size of its edge is reflected in the margin of difference between its rating and the ratings assigned to rivals. Summing a company's strength ratings on all the measures produces an overall strength rating. The higher a company's overall strength rating, the stronger its competitive position. The bigger the difference between a company's overall rating and a rival's rating, the greater its implied net competitive advantage. Thus, ABC's score of 61 (see the top half of Table 4–3) signals a greater net competitive advantage over Rival 4 (with a score of 32) than Rival 1 (with a score of 58).

High competitive strength ratings signal a strong competitive position and possession of competitive advantage; low ratings signal a weak position and competitive disadvantage.

However, it is conceptually stronger to use a weighted rating system because the different measures of competitive strength are unlikely to be *equally* important. In a commodity-product industry, for instance, low unit costs relative to rivals are the biggest determinant of competitive strength. In an industry with strong product differentiation, the most significant measures of competitive strength may be brand awareness, amount of advertising, reputation for quality, and distribution capability. In a *weighted rating system*, each measure of competitive strength is assigned a weight based on its perceived importance in shaping competitive success. The largest weight could be as high as .75 (or higher) if a variable is overwhelmingly decisive, or as low as .20 when two or three measures are more important than the rest. Lesser indicators can carry weights of .05 or .10. However, *the sum of the weights must add up to 1.0.*

A weighted competitive strength analysis is conceptually stronger than an unweighted analysis because of the inherent weakness in assuming that all the strength measures are equally important.

Weighted strength ratings are calculated by deciding how a company stacks up on each strength measure (using the 1 to 5 or 1 to 10 rating scale) and multiplying the rating by the assigned weight (a rating score of 4 times a weight of .20 gives a weighted rating of .80). Again, the company with the highest rating on a given measure has an implied competitive edge on that measure, with the size of its edge reflected in the difference between its rating and rivals' ratings. Summing a company's weighted strength ratings for all measures yields an overall strength rating. Comparisons of the weighted overall strength scores indicate which competitors are in the strongest and weakest competitive positions and who has how big a net competitive advantage over who.

The bottom half of Table 4–3 shows a sample competitive strength assessment for ABC Company using a weighted rating system. Note that the unweighted and weighted rating schemes produce a different ordering of the companies. In the weighted system, ABC Company dropped from second to third in strength, and Rival 1 jumped from third into first because of its high ratings on the two most important factors. Weighting the importance of the strength measures can thus make a significant difference in the outcome of the assessment.

The foregoing competitive strength assessment procedure yields useful conclusions about a company's competitive situation. The ratings show how a company compares against rivals, factor by factor or measure by measure, thus revealing where it is strongest and weakest. Moreover, the overall competitive strength scores indicate whether the company is at a net competitive advantage or disadvantage against each rival. The firm with the largest overall competitive strength rating has a net competitive advantage over each rival.

Knowing where a company is competitively strong and where it is weak is essential in crafting a strategy to strengthen its long-term competitive position. Generally, a company should try to convert its competitive strengths into sustainable competitive advantage and take strategic actions to protect against its competitive weaknesses. At the same time, competitive strength ratings clearly indicate which rivals may be vulnerable to competitive attack and the areas where they are weakest. When a company has important strengths in areas where one or more rivals are weak, it should consider offensive moves to exploit rivals' weaknesses.

DETERMINING WHAT STRATEGIC ISSUES NEED TO BE ADDRESSED

The final analytical task is to hone in on the strategic issues management needs to address in forming an effective strategic action plan. This step should be taken very seriously because it entails putting the company's overall situation into perspective and getting a lock on exactly where management needs to focus its strategic attention. Without a clear fix on the issues, strategists are ill-prepared for strategy-making.

To pinpoint issues for the company's strategic action agenda, strategists should consider the following:

- Whether the present strategy is adequate in light of driving forces at work in the industry.
- How closely the present strategy matches the industry's *future* key success factors.
- How good a defense the present strategy offers against the five competitive forces—future ones, not necessarily past or present ones.
- In what ways the present strategy may not adequately protect the company against external threats and internal weaknesses.
- Where and how the company may be vulnerable to competitive attack from one or more rivals.
- Whether the company has competitive advantage or must work to offset competitive disadvantage.
- Where the strong spots and weak spots are in the present strategy.
- Whether additional actions are needed to improve the company's cost position, capitalize on emerging opportunities, and strengthen the company's competitive position.

These considerations should indicate whether the company can continue the same basic strategy with minor adjustments or whether it should undertake a major overhaul.

The better matched a company's strategy is to its external environment and internal situation, the less need there is for big shifts in strategy. On the other hand, when the present strategy is not well suited for the future, crafting a new strategy has to take top priority.

There are five steps to conducting a company situation analysis:

1. *Evaluating how well the current strategy is working.* This involves looking at the company's recent strategic performance and determining whether the various pieces of strategy are logically consistent.

2. *Doing a SWOT analysis.* A company's strengths are important because they can serve as major building blocks for strategy; company weaknesses are important because they may represent vulnerabilities that need correction. External opportunities and threats come into play because a good strategy aims at capturing attractive opportunities and defending against threats to the company's well-being.

3. *Evaluating the company's cost position relative to competitors* (using the concepts of strategic cost analysis and activity-cost chains if appropriate). Strategy must always aim at keeping costs sufficiently in line with rivals to preserve the company's ability to compete.

4. *Assessing the company's competitive position and competitive strength.* This step looks at how a company matches rivals on the chief determinants of competitive success. The competitive strength rankings indicate where a company is strong and weak; as a rule, a company's competitive strategy should be built on its competitive strengths and attempt to shore up areas where it is competitively vulnerable. A company has the best potential for offensive attack in areas where it is strong and rivals are weak.

5. *Determining the strategic issues and problems the company needs to address.* The purpose of this analytical step is to develop a complete strategy-making agenda using the results of both company situation analysis and industry and competitive analysis. This step helps management draw conclusions about the strengths and weaknesses of its strategy and pinpoint the issues strategy-makers need to consider.

Table 4–4, on page 100, provides a format for company situation analysis. It incorporates the concepts and analytical techniques discussed in this chapter and makes it easier to perform the analysis in a systematic, concise manner.

Andrews, Kenneth R. *The Concept of Corporate Strategy*, 3rd ed. Homewood, Ill.: Richard D. Irwin, 1987, chap. 3.

Fahey, Liam, and H. Kurt Christensen. "Building Distinctive Competences into Competitive Advantages." Reprinted in Liam Fahey, *The Strategic Planning Management Reader.* Englewood Cliffs, N.J.: Prentice Hall, 1989, pp. 113–18.

Hax, Arnoldo C., and Nicolas S. Majluf. *Strategic Management: An Integrative Perspective.* Englewood Cliffs, N.J.: Prentice Hall, 1984, chap. 15.

Henry, Harold W. "Appraising a Company's Strengths and Weaknesses." *Managerial Planning*, July–August 1980, pp. 31–36.

Company Situation Analysis

1. STRATEGIC PERFORMANCE INDICATORS

Performance Indicator	19__	19__	19__	19__	19__
Market share	____	____	____	____	____
Sales growth	____	____	____	____	____
Net profit margin	____	____	____	____	____
Return on equity investment	____	____	____	____	____
Other?	____	____	____	____	____

2. INTERNAL STRENGTHS

INTERNAL WEAKNESSES

EXTERNAL OPPORTUNITIES

EXTERNAL THREATS

3. COMPETITIVE STRENGTH ASSESSMENT
Rating scale: 1 = Very weak; 10 = Very strong.

Key Success Factor/ Competitive Variable	Weight	Firm A	Firm B	Firm C	Firm D	Firm E
Quality/product performance	____	____	____	____	____	____
Reputation/image	____	____	____	____	____	____
Raw material access/cost	____	____	____	____	____	____
Technological skills	____	____	____	____	____	____
Manufacturing capability	____	____	____	____	____	____
Marketing/distribution	____	____	____	____	____	____
Financial strength	____	____	____	____	____	____
Relative cost position	____	____	____	____	____	____
Other?	____	____	____	____	____	____
Overall strength rating	____	____	____	____	____	____

4. CONCLUSIONS CONCERNING COMPETITIVE POSITION
(Improving/slipping? Competitive advantages/disadvantages?)

5. MAJOR STRATEGIC ISSUES/PROBLEMS THE COMPANY MUST ADDRESS

Paine, Frank T., and Leonard J. Tischler. "Evaluating Your Costs Strategically." Reprinted in Laim Fahey, *The Strategic Planning Management Reader.* Englewood Cliffs, N.J.: Prentice Hall, 1989, pp. 118–23.

Prahalad, C. K., and Gary Hamel. "The Core Competence of the Corporation." *Harvard Business Review* 90, no. 3 (May–June 1990), pp. 79–93.

Stevenson, Howard H. "Defining Corporate Strengths and Weaknesses." *Sloan Management Review* 17, no. 2 (Winter 1976), pp. 1–18.

Strategy and Competitive Advantage

*Competing in the marketplace is like war. You have injuries and casualties,
and the best strategy wins.*
John Collins

*Competitive advantage is at the heart of a firm's performance in
competitive markets.*
Michael E. Porter

Winning business strategies are grounded in sustainable competitive advantage. A company has *competitive advantage* whenever it has an edge over rivals in securing customers and defending against competitive forces. There are many sources of competitive advantage: making the highest-quality product, providing superior customer service, achieving lower costs than rivals, having a more convenient geographic location, designing a product that performs better than competing brands, making a more reliable and longer-lasting product, and providing buyers more value for the money (a combination of good quality, good service, and acceptable price). To succeed in building a competitive advantage, a firm must try to provide what buyers will perceive as "superior value"—either a good product at a low price or a "better" product that is worth paying more for.

> *Competitive Strategy Principle*
> Successful companies invest aggressively in creating sustainable competitive advantage for it is the single most dependable contributor to above-average profitability.

   This chapter focuses on how a company can achieve or defend a competitive advantage.[1] We begin by describing the basic types of competitive strategies and then examine how these approaches rely on offensive moves to build competitive advantage and defensive moves to protect competitive advantage.

---

[1]The definitive work on this subject is Michael E. Porter, *Competitive Advantage* (New York: Free Press, 1985). The treatment in this chapter draws heavily on Porter's pioneering effort.

In the concluding two sections, we survey the pros and cons of a vertical integration strategy and look at the competitive importance of timing strategic moves—when it is advantageous to be a first-mover or a late-mover.

THE THREE GENERIC TYPES OF COMPETITIVE STRATEGY

Competitive strategy consists of all the moves and approaches a firm has taken and is taking to attract buyers, withstand competitive pressures, and improve its market position. In plainer terms, competitive strategy concerns what a firm is doing to try to knock the socks off rival companies and gain competitive advantage. A firm's strategy can be mostly offensive or mostly defensive, shifting from one to the other as market conditions warrant.

Companies the world over have tried every conceivable approach to outcompeting rivals and winning an edge in the marketplace. And because managers tailor strategy to fit the specifics of their own company's situation and market environment, there are countless variations. In this sense, there are as many competitive strategies as there are companies trying to compete. However, beneath all the nuances, the approaches to competitive strategy fall into three categories:

1. Striving to be the overall low-cost producer in the industry (a *low-cost leadership strategy*).
2. Seeking to differentiate one's product offering from rivals' products (a *differentiation strategy*).
3. Focusing on a narrow portion of the market rather than the whole market (a *focus* or *niche strategy*).[2]

Table 5–1 highlights the distinctive features of these three generic competitive strategy approaches.

Striving to Be the Low-Cost Producer

Striving to be the low-cost producer is a powerful competitive approach in markets where many buyers are price-sensitive. The aim is to open up a sustainable cost advantage over competitors and then use lower cost as a basis for either underpricing competitors and gaining market share at their expense or earning a higher profit margin selling at the going price. A cost advantage will generate superior profitability unless it is used up in aggressive price-cutting efforts to win sales from rivals. Firms that achieve low-cost leadership typically make low cost *relative to competitors* the theme of their entire business strategy—though they must be careful not to pursue low cost so zealously that their products end up being too stripped down and cheaply made to generate buyer appeal.

A low-cost leader's basis for competitive advantage is lower overall costs than competitors.

---

[2]The classification scheme follows that presented in Michael E. Porter, *Competitive Strategy: Techniques for Analyzing Industries and Competitors* (New York: Free Press, 1980), chap. 2, especially pp. 35–39 and 44–46.

T A B L E 5–1   **Distinctive Features of the Generic Competitive Strategies**

Type of Feature	Low-Cost Leadership	Differentiation	Focus
Strategic target	• A broad cross-section of the market.	• A broad cross-section of the market.	• A narrow market niche where buyer needs and preferences are distinctively different from the rest of the market.
Basis of competitive advantage	• Lower costs than competitors.	• An ability to offer buyers something different from competitors.	• Lower cost in serving the niche or an ability to offer niche buyers something customized to their requirements and tastes.
Product line	• A good basic product with few frills (acceptable quality and limited selection).	• Many product variations, wide selection, strong emphasis on the chosen differentiating features.	• Customized to fit the specialized needs of the target segment.
Production emphasis	• A continuous search for cost reduction without sacrificing acceptable quality and essential features.	• Invent ways to create value for buyers.	• Tailor-made for the niche.
Marketing emphasis	• Try to make a virtue out of product features that lead to low cost.	• Build in whatever features buyers are willing to pay for. • Charge a premium price to cover the extra costs of differentiating features.	• Communicate the focuser's unique ability to satisfy the buyer's specialized requirements.
Sustaining the strategy	• Economical prices/good value. • All elements of strategy aim at contributing to a sustainable cost advantage—the key is to manage costs down, year after year, in every area of the business.	• Communicate the points of difference in credible ways. • Stress constant improvement and use innovation to stay ahead of imitative competitors. • Concentrate on a few key differentiating features; use them to create a reputation and brand image.	• Remain totally dedicated to serving the niche better than other competitors; don't blunt the firm's image and efforts by entering other segments and adding other product categories to widen market appeal.

ILLUSTRATION CAPSULE
12

WINNING A COST ADVANTAGE:
IOWA BEEF PACKERS AND FEDERAL EXPRESS

Iowa Beef Packers and Federal Express have been able to win strong competitive positions by restructuring the traditional activity-cost chains in their industries. In beef packing, the traditional cost chain involved raising cattle on scattered farms and ranches, shipping them live to labor-intensive, unionized slaughtering plants, and then transporting whole sides of beef to grocery retailers whose butcher departments cut them into smaller pieces and package them for sale to grocery shoppers.

Iowa Beef Packers revamped the traditional chain with a radically different strategy—large automated plants employing nonunion labor were built near economically transportable supplies of cattle, and the meat was partially butchered at the processing plant into smaller high-yield cuts (sometimes sealed in plastic casing ready for purchase), boxed, and shipped to retailers. IBP's inbound cattle transportation expenses, traditionally a major cost item, were cut significantly by avoiding the weight losses that occurred when live animals were shipped long distances; major outbound shipping cost savings were achieved by not having to ship whole sides of beef with their high waste factor. Iowa Beef's strategy was so successful that it was, in 1985, the largest U.S. meatpacker, surpassing the former industry leaders, Swift, Wilson, and Armour.

Federal Express innovatively redefined the activity-cost chain for rapid delivery of small parcels. Traditional firms like Emery and Airborne Express operated by collecting freight packages of varying sizes, shipping them to their destination points via air freight and commercial airlines, and then delivering them to the addressee. Federal Express opted to focus only on the market for overnight delivery of small packages and documents. These were collected at local drop points during the late afternoon hours, flown on company-owned planes during early evening hours to a central hub in Memphis where from 11 P.M. to 3 A.M. each night, all parcels were sorted, then reloaded on company planes, and flown during the early morning hours to their destination points, where they were delivered the next morning by company personnel using company trucks. The cost structure so achieved by Federal Express was low enough to permit it to guarantee overnight delivery of a small parcel anywhere in the United States for a price as low as $11. In 1986, Federal Express had a 58 percent market share of the air-express package delivery market versus a 15 percent share for UPS, 11 percent for Airborne Express, and 10 percent for Emery/Purolator.

Source: Based on information in Michael E. Porter, *Competitive Advantage* (New York: Free Press, 1985), p. 109.

Opening up a Cost Advantage   To achieve a cost advantage, a firm's cumulative costs across its activity-cost chain must be lower than competitors' cumulative costs. There are two ways to accomplish this:

- Do a better job of improving efficiency and controlling costs along the existing activity-cost chain.
- Revamp the firm's activity-cost chain to bypass some cost-producing activities altogether.

Achieving a cost advantage entails (a) outmanaging rivals on efficiency and cost control and/or (b) finding creative ways to cut cost-producing activities out of the activity-cost chain.

Both approaches can be used simultaneously. Successful low-cost producers usually achieve their cost advantages by exhaustively pursuing cost savings throughout the activity-cost chain. No area is overlooked. Normally, low-cost producers have a very cost-conscious organizational culture symbolically reinforced by spartan facilities, limited perks for executives, intolerance of waste, intensive screening of budget requests, and broad employee participation in cost control efforts. But while low-cost producers are champions of frugality, they tend to commit funds aggressively to cost-saving improvements.

A firm intent on being a low-cost producer has to scrutinize each cost-creating activity and identify what drives the cost of the activity. Then it has to use its knowledge about the cost drivers to manage the costs of each activity down further year after year. Where possible, whole activities are eliminated from the activity-cost chain entirely. Companies can achieve dramatic cost advantages from restructuring the cost-chain and eliminating unnecessary cost-producing activities. Illustration Capsule 12 describes how two companies won strong competitive positions by revamping the makeup of their industry's traditional activity-cost chain.

Firms well known for their low-cost leadership strategies include: Lincoln Electric in arc welding equipment, Briggs and Stratton in small horsepower gasoline engines, BIC in ballpoint pens, Black and Decker in tools, Design and Manufacturing in dishwashers (marketed under Sears' Kenmore brand), Beaird-Poulan in chain saws, Ford in heavy-duty trucks, General Electric in major home appliances, Wal-Mart in discount retailing, and Southwest Airlines in commercial airline travel.

The Appeal of Being a Low-Cost Producer   Being the low-cost producer in an industry provides some attractive defenses against the five competitive forces:

- As concerns *rival competitors*, the low-cost company is in the best position to compete offensively on the basis of price, to defend against price war conditions, to use the appeal of a lower price to win sales (and market share) from rivals, and to earn above- average profits (based on bigger profit margins or greater sales volume) in markets where price competition thrives.
- As concerns *buyers*, the low-cost company has partial profit margin protection from powerful customers, since such customers are rarely able to bargain price down past the survival level of the next most cost-efficient seller.
- As concerns *suppliers*, the low-cost producer is more insulated than competitors from powerful suppliers *if* greater internal efficiency is the primary source of its cost advantage.
- As concerns *potential entrants*, the low-cost producer can use price-cutting to make it harder for a new rival to win customers; the pricing power of the low-cost producer acts as a barrier for a new entrant.
- As concerns *substitutes*, a low-cost producer is better positioned than higher-cost rivals to use low price as a defense against substitutes trying to gain market inroads.

A low-cost producer's ability to set the industry's price floor and still earn a profit erects barriers around its market position. Anytime price competition becomes a major market force, less efficient rivals get squeezed the most. Firms in a low-cost position relative to rivals have a significant edge in appealing to buyers who base their purchase decision on low price.

A competitive strategy based on low-cost leadership is particularly powerful when:

1.   Price competition among rival sellers is a dominant competitive force.

2. The industry's product is an essentially standardized, commodity-type item readily available from a variety of sellers (a condition that allows buyers to shop for price).

3. There are few ways to achieve product differentiation that have value to buyers (put another way, the differences from brand to brand don't matter much to buyers).

4. Most buyers use the product in the same ways—with common user requirements, a standardized product can fully satisfy the needs of all buyers, in which case price, not features or quality, becomes the dominant competitive force.

5. Buyers incur low switching costs in changing from one seller to another, thus giving them flexibility to shop for the best price.

6. Buyers are large and have significant power to bargain down prices.

The Risks of a Low-Cost Producer Strategy A low-cost competitive approach has its drawbacks. Technological breakthroughs can open up cost reductions for rivals that nullify a low-cost producer's past investments and hard-won gains in efficiency. Rival firms may find it easy and/or inexpensive to imitate the leader's low-cost methods, thus making any advantage short-lived. A company driving hard to push its costs down can become so fixated on cost reduction that it fails to pick up on such significant market changes as growing buyer preference for added quality or service, subtle shifts in how buyers use the product, or declining buyer sensitivity to price and thus gets left behind as buyer interest swings to quality, performance, service, and other differentiating features. In sum, heavy investments in cost reduction can lock a firm into both its present technology and its present strategy, leaving it vulnerable to new technologies and to growing customer interest in something other than a cheaper price.

Differentiation Strategies

Differentiation strategies come into play whenever buyers' needs and preferences are too diverse to be satisfied by a standardized product. A successful differentiator studies buyers' needs and behavior carefully to learn what they consider important and valuable. Then the differentiator incorporates one or several of those features into its product offering to encourage buyer preferences for its brand over the brands of rivals. Competitive advantage results when enough buyers become strongly attached to the attributes of a differentiator's product offering. Successful differentiation allows a firm to

With a differentiation strategy, the basis for competitive advantage is a product whose attributes differ significantly from the products of rivals.

- command a premium price for its product, and/or
- sell more units (because additional buyers are won over by the differentiating features), and/or
- gain greater buyer loyalty to its brand (because some buyers are strongly attracted to the differentiating features).

Differentiation enhances profitability whenever the extra price the product commands outweighs the added costs of achieving differentiation. Differentiation is unsuccessful when buyers don't value the additional features highly enough to buy the product in profitable quantities. And differentiation is unprofitable when the price premium buyers are willing to pay won't cover the extra costs of achieving brand distinctiveness.

The approaches to differentiating a product take many forms: a different taste (Dr Pepper and Listerine), special features (Jenn Air's indoor cooking tops with a vented built-in grill for barbecuing), superior service (Federal Express in overnight package delivery), spare parts availability (Caterpillar guarantees 48-hour spare parts delivery to any customer anywhere in the world or else the part is furnished free), overall value to the customer (McDonald's), engineering design and performance (Mercedes), prestige and distinctiveness (Rolex), product reliability (Johnson & Johnson baby products), quality manufacture (Honda), technological leadership (3M in bonding and coating products), a full range of services (Merrill Lynch), a complete line of products (Campbell soups), and top-of-the-line image and reputation (Brooks Brothers and Ralph Lauren in menswear, Kitchen Aid in dishwashers, and Cross in writing instruments).

Achieving Differentiation   *Anything a firm can do to create buyer value represents a potential basis for differentiation.* Once a firm finds good sources of buyer value, it must build the value-creating attributes into its product at an acceptable cost. A differentiator can incorporate attributes that raise the product's performance or make it more economical to use. Or a firm can incorporate features that enhance buyer satisfaction in tangible or intangible ways during use. Differentiation possibilities can grow out of activities performed anywhere in the activity-cost chain. McDonald's gets high ratings on its french fries partly because it has very strict specifications on the potatoes it purchases from its supplier. The quality of Japanese cars stems primarily from Japanese automakers' skills in manufacturing and quality control. IBM boosts buyer value by providing its customers with an extensive array of services and technical support. L. L. Bean makes its mail-order customers feel secure by providing an unconditional guarantee with no time limit: "All of our products are guaranteed to give 100 percent satisfaction in every way. Return anything purchased from us at anytime if it proves otherwise. We will replace it, refund your purchase price, or credit your credit card, as you wish." Commercial airlines use their empty seats during off-peak travel periods (i.e., their excess capacity) as the basis for awarding free travel to frequent flyers.

What Makes Differentiation Attractive   Differentiation provides some buffer against rivals' strategies because buyers become loyal to the brand or model they like best and often are willing to pay a little (perhaps a lot!) more for it. In addition, successful differentiation (1) erects entry barriers in the form of customer loyalty and uniqueness that newcomers find hard to overcome, (2) mitigates the bargaining power of large buyers since rivals' products are less attractive to them, and (3) helps a firm fend off threats from substitutes. If differentiation allows a firm to charge a higher price and boost profit margins, it will be in a stronger position to withstand powerful suppliers' efforts to raise their prices. Thus, as with cost leadership, successful differentiation creates lines of defense for dealing with the five competitive forces.

As a rule, differentiation strategies work best in situations where (1) there are many ways to differentiate the product or service and many buyers perceive these differences as valuable, (2) buyer needs and uses of the item

Competitive Strategy Principle
The competitive power of a differentiation strategy is greatest when buyer needs are diverse, there are many ways to differentiate that have value to buyers, few rivals choose the same approach, and the firm's product can't be quickly or cheaply imitated.

are diverse, and (3) few rival firms are following a similar differentiation approach.

The most appealing types of differentiation strategies are those least subject to quick or inexpensive imitation. Here is where having core competences becomes a major competitive asset. When a firm has skills and expertise that competitors cannot match easily, it can use them as a basis for successful differentiation. Differentiation is most likely to produce an attractive, longer-lasting competitive edge if it is based on:

- Technical superiority.
- Quality.
- More customer support services.
- More value for the money.

Such differentiating attributes tend to be harder for rivals to copy quickly and profitably.

Real Value, Perceived Value, and Signals of Value Buyers seldom pay for value they don't perceive, no matter how real the unique features may be.[3] Thus the price premium a differentiation strategy commands reflects *the value actually delivered* to the buyer and *the value the buyer perceives* (even if it is not actually delivered). Actual and perceived value can differ whenever buyers have trouble assessing in advance what their experience with the product will be. Buyers with incomplete knowledge of the product often judge value based on such *signals* as seller's word-of-mouth reputation, attractive packaging, extensive ad campaigns (i.e., how "well known" the product is), ad content and image, brochures and sales presentations, the seller's facilities, the seller's list of customers, the firm's market share, length of time the firm has been in business, price (where price connotes "quality"), and the professionalism, appearance, and personality of the seller's employees. Such signals of value may be as important as actual value (1) when the nature of differentiation is subjective or hard to quantify, (2) when buyers are making a first-time purchase, (3) when repurchase is infrequent, and (4) when buyers are unsophisticated.

Keeping the Cost of Differentiation in Line Attempts to achieve differentiation usually raise costs. The trick to profitable differentiation is either to keep the costs of achieving differentiation below the price premium the differentiating attributes can command in the marketplace (thus increasing the profit margin per unit sold) or to offset thinner profit margins with enough added volume to increase total profits (larger volume can make up for smaller margins provided differentiation adds enough extra sales). In pursuing differentiation, a firm must be careful not to get its overall unit costs so far out of line with competitors that it has to charge a higher price than buyers are willing to pay. There may also be good reason to add extra differentiating features that are not costly but add to buyer satisfaction—fine restaurants typically provide such extras as a slice of lemon in the water glass, valet parking, and complimentary after-dinner mints.

> **Competitive Strategy Principle**
> *A firm whose differentiation strategy delivers only modest extra value but signals that value effectively may command a higher price than a firm that actually delivers higher value but signals it poorly.*

---

[3]This discussion draws from Porter, *Competitive Advantage* pp. 138–42. Porter's insights here are particularly important to formulating differentiating strategies because they highlight the relevance of "intangibles" and "signals."

The Risks of a Differentiation Strategy   There are, of course, no guarantees that differentiation will produce a meaningful competitive advantage. If buyers see little value in uniqueness (i.e., a standard item meets their needs), a low-cost strategy can easily defeat a differentiation strategy. In addition, differentiation can be defeated from the outset if competitors can quickly copy the attempt at differentiating. Rapid imitation means that firms never achieve real differentiation because competing brands keep changing in like ways despite continued efforts to create uniqueness. Thus, to be successful at differentiation, a firm must search out durable sources of uniqueness that cannot be quickly or cheaply imitated. Aside from these considerations, other common pitfalls include:[4]

- Trying to differentiate on the basis of something that does not lower a buyer's cost or enhance a buyer's well-being (as perceived by the buyer).
- Overdifferentiating so that price is too high relative to competitors or product quality or service levels exceed buyers' needs.
- Trying to charge too high a price premium (the bigger the premium, the more buyers can be lured away by lower-priced competitors).
- Ignoring the need to signal value and depending only on tangible product attributes to achieve differentiation.
- Not understanding or identifying what buyers consider as value.

The Strategy of Being a Best-Cost Producer   A differentiation strategy aimed at giving customers *more value for the money* usually means combining an emphasis on low-cost with an emphasis on *more than minimally acceptable* quality, service, features, and performance. The idea is to create superior value by meeting or exceeding buyer expectations on quality-service-features-performance attributes and beating their expectations on price. Strategy-wise, the aim is to be the low-cost producer of a product with *good-to-excellent* product attributes, then use the cost advantage to underprice brands with comparable attributes. Such a competitive approach is termed a *best-cost producer strategy* because the producer has the best (lowest) cost relative to producers whose brands are comparably positioned on the quality-service-features-performance scale. The competitive advantage of a best-cost producer comes from matching close rivals on key attributes and beating them on cost. To become a best-cost producer, a company must match quality at a lower cost than rivals, match features at a lower cost than rivals, match product performance at a lower cost than rivals, and so on. What distinguishes a successful best-cost producer is expertise in incorporating upscale product attributes at a low cost; or, to put it a bit differently, an ability to contain the costs of providing customers with a better product. The most successful best-cost producers have the skills to simultaneously manage unit costs down and product caliber up.

A best-cost producer strategy has great appeal from the standpoint of competitive positioning. It produces superior customer value by balancing strategic emphasis on low cost against strategic emphasis on differentiation. In effect, such a *hybrid* strategy allows a company to combine the competitive advantage appeals of both low-cost and differentiation. In markets where

[4]Ibid., pp. 160–62.

buyer diversity makes product differentiation the norm and buyers are price and value sensitive, a best-cost producer strategy can be more advantageous than either a pure low-cost producer strategy or a pure differentiation strategy keyed to product superiority. This is because a best-cost producer can position itself near the middle of the market with either a medium-quality product at a below-average price or a very good product at a medium price. Many buyers prefer a mid-range product rather than the cheap, basic product of a low-cost producer or the expensive product of a top-of-the-line differentiator.

Focus and Specialization Strategies

Focusing starts by choosing a market niche where buyers have distinctive preferences or requirements. The niche can be defined by geographic uniqueness, by specialized requirements in using the product, or by special product attributes that appeal only to niche members. *A focuser's basis for competitive advantage is either lower costs than competitors in serving the market niche or an ability to offer niche members something different from other competitors.* A focus strategy based on low cost depends on there being a buyer segment whose needs are less costly to satisfy compared to the rest of the market. A focus strategy based on differentiation depends on there being a buyer segment that demands unique product attributes.

What sets a focus strategy apart is concentrated attention on a narrow piece of the total market.

Examples of firms employing a focus strategy include Tandem Computers (a specialist in "nonstop" computers for customers who need a "fail-safe" system), Rolls Royce (in super luxury automobiles), Apple Computer in desktop publishing (Apple computers produce typeset-quality reports and graphics), Fort Howard Paper (specializing in paper products for industrial and commercial enterprises only), commuter airlines like Skywest and Atlantic Southeast (specializing in low-traffic, short-haul flights linking major airports with smaller cities 50 to 250 miles away), and Bandag (a specialist in truck tire recapping that promotes its recaps aggressively at over 1,000 truck stops).

Using a focus strategy to achieve a cost breakthrough is a fairly common technique. Budget-priced motel chains like Days Inn, Motel 6, and LaQuinta have lowered their investment and operating cost per room by using a no-frills approach and catering to price-conscious travelers. Discount stock brokerage houses have lowered costs by focusing on customers mainly interested in buy-sell transactions who are willing to forgo the investment research, investment advice, and financial services offered by full-service firms like Merrill Lynch. Pursuing a cost advantage via focusing works well when a firm can find ways to lower costs by limiting its customer base to a well-defined buyer segment.

When Focusing Is Attractive A focus strategy becomes increasingly attractive as more of the following conditions are met:

- The segment is big enough to be profitable.
- The segment has good growth potential.
- The segment is not crucial to the success of major competitors.
- The focusing firm has the skills and resources to serve the segment effectively.

Competitive Strategy Principle
The competitive power of a focus strategy is greatest when: (a) fast-growing segments are big enough to be profitable but small enough not to interest large competitors, (b) no other rivals are concentrating on the segment, and (c) segment buyers require special expertise or custom products.

- The focuser can defend itself against challengers based on the customer goodwill it has built up and its superior ability to serve buyers in the segment.

A focuser's specialized skills in serving the target market niche provide a basis for defending against the five competitive forces. Multisegment rivals do not have the same competitive capability to serve the target clientele. The focused firm's competence in serving the market niche raises entry barriers, thus making it harder for companies outside the niche to enter. A focuser's unique capabilities in serving the niche also present a hurdle that makers of substitute products must overcome. The bargaining leverage of powerful customers is blunted somewhat by their own unwillingness to shift their business to rival firms less capable of serving their needs.

Focusing works best (1) when it is costly or difficult for multisegment competitors to meet the specialized needs of the niche, (2) when no other rival is attempting to *specialize* in the same target segment; (3) when a firm doesn't have enough resources to pursue a wider part of the total market; and (4) when the industry has many different segments, thereby allowing a focuser to pick an attractive segment suited to its strengths and capabilities.

The Risks of a Focus Strategy   Focusing carries several risks. One is the chance that competitors will find ways to match the focused firm in serving the narrow target market. Second is the potential for the niche buyer's preferences and needs to shift toward the product attributes desired by the market as a whole; such erosion opens the way for rivals with broad market appeal. Third is the chance that the segment will become so attractive that it becomes inundated with competitors, causing profits to be splintered.

USING OFFENSIVE STRATEGIES TO SECURE COMPETITIVE ADVANTAGE

Competitive Strategy Principle
Competitive advantage is usually acquired by employing a creative offensive strategy that can't be easily counteracted by rivals.

An offensive strategy, if successful, can open up a competitive advantage over rivals.[5] How long this process takes depends on the industry's competitive characteristics. The *buildup period*, shown in Figure 5–1, can be short as in service businesses which need little in the way of equipment and distribution support to implement a new offensive move. Or the buildup can take much longer, as in capital intensive and technologically sophisticated industries where firms may need several years to debug a new technology, bring new capacity on line, and win consumer acceptance of a new product. Ideally, an offensive move builds competitive advantage quickly; the longer it takes the more likely rivals will spot the move, see its potential, and begin responding. The size of the advantage (indicated on the vertical scale in Figure 5–1) can be large (as in pharmaceuticals where patents on new drugs produce a substantial advantage) or small (as in apparel where popular new designs can be imitated quickly).

Following a successful competitive offensive, there is a *benefit period* during which the fruits of competitive advantage can be enjoyed. The length of the

[5]Ian C. MacMillan, "How Long Can You Sustain a Competitive Advantage," reprinted in Liam Fahey, *The Strategic Planning Management Reader* (Englewood Cliffs, N.J.: Prentice Hall, 1989), pp. 23–24.

The Building and Eroding of Competitive Advantage

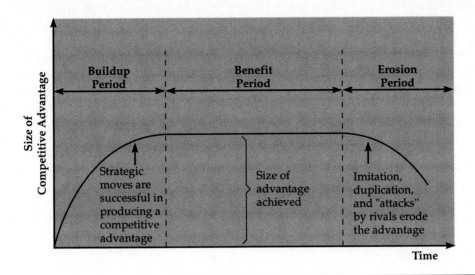

benefit period depends on how much time it takes rivals to launch counter-offensives and begin closing the competitive gap. A lengthy benefit period gives a firm valuable time to earn above-average profits and recoup the investment made in creating the advantage. The best strategic offensives produce big competitive advantages and long benefit periods.

As competitors respond with counteroffensives, the *erosion period* begins. Any competitive advantage a firm currently holds will eventually be eroded by the actions of competent, resourceful competitors.[6] Thus, to sustain its initial advantage, a firm must devise a second strategic offensive. The groundwork for the second offensive needs to be laid during the benefit period so that the firm is ready for launch when competitors respond to the earlier offensive. To successfully sustain a competitive advantage, a firm must stay a step ahead of rivals by mounting one creative strategic offensive after another.

There are six basic ways to mount strategic offensives:[7]

- Attacks on competitor strengths.
- Attacks on competitor weaknesses.
- Simultaneous attack on many fronts.
- End-run offensives.
- Guerrilla offensives.
- Preemptive strikes.

---

[6]Ian C. MacMillan, "Controlling Competitive Dynamics by Taking Strategic Initiative," *The Academy of Management Executive* 2, no. 2 (May 1988), p. 111.

[7]Philip Kotler and Ravi Singh, "Marketing Warfare in the 1980's," *The Journal of Business Strategy* 1, no. 3 (Winter 1981), pp. 30–41; Philip Kotler, *Marketing Management*, 5th ed. (Englewood Cliffs, N.J.: Prentice Hall, 1984), pp. 401–6; and Ian MacMillan, "Preemptive Strategies," *Journal of Business Strategy* 14, no. 2 (Fall 1983), pp. 16–26.

Attacking Competitor Strengths

There are two good reasons to go head-to-head against rivals, pitting one's own strengths against theirs, price for price, model for model, promotion tactic for promotion tactic, and geographic area by geographic area. The first is to try to gain market share by overpowering weaker rivals; challenging weaker rivals where they are strongest is attractive whenever a firm can win a decisive market victory and a commanding edge over struggling competitors. The other reason is to whittle away at a strong rival's competitive advantage; here success is measured by how much the competitive gap is narrowed. The merits of a strength-against-strength offensive challenge, of course, depend on how much the offensive costs compared to its benefits. To succeed, the initiator needs enough competitive strength and resources to take at least some market share from the targeted rivals.

One of the most powerful offensive strategies is to challenge rivals with an equally good or better product and a lower price.

All-out attacks on competitor strengths can involve initiatives on any of several fronts—price-cutting, comparison ads, new features that appeal to a rival's customers, new plant capacity in a rival's backyard, or new models that match rivals'. One of the best ploys is for the aggressor to attack with an equally good product offering and a lower price.[8] This can produce market share gains if the targeted rival has strong reasons for not cutting its prices and if the challenger convinces buyers that its product is just as good. However, such a strategy will increase profits only if volume gains offset the impact of thinner margins per unit sold.

Competitive Strategy Principle

Challenging larger, entrenched competitors with aggressive price-cutting is foolhardy unless the aggressor has either a cost advantage or greater financial strength.

In another type of price-aggressive attack, firms first achieve a cost advantage and then attack competitors with a lower price.[9] Price-cutting supported by a cost advantage is the strongest basis for launching and sustaining a price-aggressive offensive. Without a cost advantage, price-cutting works only if the aggressor has more financial resources and can outlast its rivals in a war of attrition.

Attacking Competitor Weaknesses

In this offensive approach, firms concentrate their competitive attention directly on the weaknesses of rivals. There are a number of weaknesses which can prove fruitful to challenge:

Competitive Strategy Principle

Challenging rivals where they are most vulnerable is more likely to succeed than challenging them where they are strongest, especially if the challenger has advantages in the areas where rivals are weak.

- Attack geographic regions where a rival has a weak market share or is exerting less competitive effort.
- Attack buyer segments that a rival is neglecting or is weakly equipped to serve.
- Attack rivals that lag on quality, features, or product performance; in such cases, a challenger with a better product can often convince the most performance-conscious customers of lagging rivals to switch to its brand.
- Attack rivals that have done a poor job of servicing customers; in such cases, a service-oriented challenger can win a rival's disenchanted customers.

---

[8] Kotler, *Marketing Management*, p. 402.
[9] Ibid., p. 403.

- Attack rivals with weak advertising and brand recognition; a challenger with strong marketing skills and a good image can often move in on lesser-known rivals.
- Attack market leaders that have gaps in their product line; challengers can exploit opportunities to develop these gaps into strong, new market segments.
- Attack market leaders who are ignoring certain buyer needs by introducing product versions that satisfy these needs.

As a rule, attacks on competitor weaknesses have a better chance of succeeding than attacks on competitor strengths, provided the weaknesses represent important vulnerabilities and the rival is caught by surprise with no ready defense.[10]

Simultaneous Attack on Many Fronts

Sometimes aggressors launch a grand competitive offensive involving several major initiatives in an effort to throw a rival off-balance, scatter its attention, and force it into channeling resources to protect all its sides simultaneously. Hunt's tried such an offensive several years ago in an attempt to wrest market share from Heinz ketchup. The attack began when Hunt's introduced two new ketchup flavors to disrupt consumers' taste preferences, try to create new product segments, and capture more shelf space in retail stores. Simultaneously, Hunt's lowered its price to 70 percent of Heinz's; it offered sizable trade allowances to retailers; and it raised its advertising budget to over twice that of Heinz's.[11] The offensive failed because not enough Heinz users tried the Hunt's brands, and many of those who did soon switched back to Heinz. Grand offensives have their best chance of success when a challenger, because of superior resources, can overpower its rivals by outspending them across-the-board long enough to buy its way into a position of market leadership and competitive advantage.

End-Run Offensives

End-run offensives seek to avoid head-on challenges tied to aggressive price-cutting, escalated advertising, or costly efforts to outdifferentiate rivals. Instead the idea is to maneuver *around* competitors and lead the way into unoccupied market territory. Examples of end-run offensives include moving aggressively into geographic areas where close rivals have no market presence, trying to create new segments by introducing products with different attributes and performance features to better meet the needs of selected buyers, and leapfrogging into next-generation technologies to supplant existing products and/or production processes. With an end-run offensive, a firm can gain a significant first-mover advantage in a new arena and force competitors to play catch-up. The most successful end-runs change the rules of the competitive game in the aggressor's favor.

End-run offensives dodge head-to-head confrontations, concentrating instead on innovative product attributes, technological advances, and early entry into less contested geographic markets.

---

[10]For a discussion of the use of surprise, see William E. Rothschild, "Surprise and the Competitive Advantage," *Journal of Business Strategy* 4, no. 3 (Winter 1984), pp. 10–18.

[11]As cited in Kotler, *Marketing Management*, p. 404.

Guerrilla Offensives

Guerrilla offensives are particularly well-suited to small challengers who have neither the resources nor the market visibility to mount a full-fledged attack on industry leaders. A guerrilla offensive uses the hit-and-run principle, selectively attacking where and when an underdog can temporarily exploit the situation to its own advantage. There are several ways to wage a guerrilla offensive:[12]

1. Attack a narrow, well-defined segment that is weakly defended by competitors.

2. Attack areas where rivals are overextended and have spread their resources most thinly (possibilities include going after their customers in less-populated geographic areas, enhancing delivery schedules at times when competitors' deliveries are running behind, adding to quality when rivals have quality control problems, and boosting technical services when buyers are confused by the number of competitors' models and features).

3. Make small, scattered, random raids on leaders with such tactics as occasional lowballing on price (to win a big order or steal a key account), intense bursts of promotional activity, and legal actions charging antitrust violations, patent infringement, and unfair advertising.

Preemptive Strategies

Preemptive strategies create competitive advantage by catapulting the aggressor into a prime competitive position which rivals are prevented or discouraged from matching.

Preemptive strategies involve moving first to secure an advantageous position that rivals are foreclosed or discouraged from duplicating. There are several ways to win a prime strategic position with preemptive moves:[13]

- Expand production capacity ahead of market demand in hopes of discouraging rivals from following suit. When rivals are "bluffed" out of adding capacity by a fear of creating long-term excess supply and underutilized plants, the preemptor can win a bigger market share if market demand grows and its own plant capacity fills.

- Tie up the best (or the most) raw material sources and/or the most reliable, high-quality suppliers via long-term contracts or backward vertical integration. This move can relegate rivals to struggling for second-best supply positions.

- Secure the best geographic locations. An attractive first-mover advantage can often be locked up by moving to obtain the most favorable site along a heavily traveled thoroughfare, at a new interchange or intersection, in a new shopping mall, in a natural beauty spot, close to cheap transportation or raw material supplies or market outlets, and so on.

- Obtain the business of prestigious customers.

---

[12]For more details, see MacMillan, "How Business Strategists Can Use Guerrilla Warfare Tactics," *Journal of Business Statistics* 1, no. 2 (Fall 1980), pp. 63–65; Kathryn R. Harrigan, *Strategic Flexibility* (Lexington, Mass.: Lexington Books, 1985), pp. 30–45; and Liam Fahey, "Guerrilla Strategy: The Hit-and-Run Attack," in Fahey, *The Strategic Planning Management Reader*, pp. 194–97.

[13]The use of preemptive moves is treated comprehensively in Ian C. MacMillan, "Preemptive Strategies," *Journal of Business Strategy*, pp. 16–26. What follows in this section is based on MacMillan's article .

- Build a "psychological" image in the minds of consumers that is unique and hard to copy and that establishes a compelling appeal and rallying cry. Examples include Avis's well-known "We try harder" theme, Frito-Lay's guarantee to retailers of "99.5% service," Holiday Inn's assurance of "no surprises," and Prudential's "piece of the rock" image of safety and permanence.
- Secure exclusive or dominant access to the best distributors in an area.

Preemption has been used successfully by a number of companies. General Mills' Red Lobster restaurant chain has gained a prime position in the restaurant business by establishing strong relationships with very dependable seafood suppliers. DeBeers became the dominant world distributor of diamonds by buying the production of most of the important diamond mines. Du Pont's aggressive capacity expansions in titanium dioxide, while not blocking all competitors from expanding, did discourage enough to give it a leadership position in the titanium dioxide industry.

To be successful, a preemptive move doesn't have to totally block rivals from following or copying; it merely needs to give a firm a "prime" position. A prime position is one that puts rivals at a competitive disadvantage and is not easily circumvented.

Choosing Who to Attack

Aggressor firms need to analyze which of their rivals to attack as well as how to attack them. There are basically three types of firms that can be attacked offensively:[14]

1. *Market leader*(s). Waging an offensive against strong leader(s) risks squandering valuable resources in a futile effort and even precipitating a fierce and profitless industrywide battle for market share. Offensive attacks on a major competitor make the best sense when the leader in terms of size and market share is not the "true leader" in terms of serving the market well. Signs of leader vulnerability include unhappy buyers, sliding profits, strong emotional commitment to a technology the leader has pioneered, outdated plants and equipment, a preoccupation with diversification into other industries, a product line that is clearly not superior to rivals', and a competitive strategy that lacks real strength based on low-cost leadership or differentiation. Attacks on leaders can also succeed when the challenger is able to revamp its activity-cost chain or innovate to gain a fresh cost-based or differentiation-based competitive advantage.[15] Attacks on leaders need not have the objective of making the aggressor the new leader; a challenger may "win" by simply wresting enough sales from the leader to make the aggressor a stronger runner-up.

2. *Runner-up firms*. Offensives against weaker, vulnerable runner-up firms entail relatively low risk. Attacking a runner-up is an especially attractive option when a challenger's competitive strengths match the runner-up's weaknesses.

---

[14]Kotler, *Marketing Management*, p. 400.
[15]Porter, *Competitive Advantage*, p. 518.

3. *Struggling enterprises that are on the verge of going under.* Challenging a hard-pressed rival in ways that further sap its financial strength and competitive position can weaken its resolve enough to prompt its exit from the market.

4. *Small local and regional firms.* Because these firms typically have limited expertise, a challenger with broader capabilities is well-positioned to raid their biggest and best customers—particularly those who are growing rapidly, have increasingly sophisticated needs, and may already be thinking about switching to a supplier with more full-service capability.

As we have said, successful strategies are grounded in competitive advantage. This goes for offensive strategies too. The competitive advantage potentials that offer the strongest basis for a strategic offensive include:[16]

- Developing a lower-cost product design.
- Making changes in production operations that lower costs or enhance differentiation.
- Developing product features that deliver superior performance or lower user costs.
- Giving buyers more responsive after-sale support.
- Escalating the marketing effort in an undermarketed industry.
- Pioneering a new distribution channel.
- Bypassing wholesale distributors and selling direct to the end-user.

A strategic offensive *must* be tied to what a firm does best—its competitive strengths and capabilities. As a rule, these strengths take the form of a *key skill* (cost reduction capabilities, customer service skills, technical expertise) or a uniquely *strong functional competence* (engineering and product design, manufacturing expertise, advertising and promotion, marketing know-how).[17]

USING DEFENSIVE STRATEGIES TO PROTECT COMPETITIVE ADVANTAGE

The foremost purpose of defensive strategy is to protect competitive advantage and fortify the firm's competitive position.

In a competitive market, all firms are subject to attacks from rivals. Offensive attacks can come both from new entrants and from established firms seeking to improve their market positions. The purpose of defensive strategy is to lower the risk of being attacked, weaken the impact of any attack that occurs, and influence challengers to aim their efforts at other rivals. While defensive strategy usually doesn't enhance a firm's competitive advantage, it should help fortify a firm's competitive position and sustain whatever competitive advantage it has.

There are several basic ways for a firm to protect its competitive position. One approach involves trying to block challengers' avenues for mounting an offensive; the options include:[18]

---

[16]Ibid., pp. 520–22.

[17]For more details, see Macmillan, "Controlling Competitive Dynamics," pp. 112–16.

[18]Porter, *Competitive Advantage*, pp. 489–94.

- Broadening the firm's product line to close off vacant niches and gaps to would-be challengers.
- Introducing models or brands that match the characteristics challengers' models already have or might have.
- Keeping prices low on models that most closely match competitors' offerings.
- Signing exclusive agreements with dealers and distributors to keep competitors from using the same ones.
- Granting dealers and distributors sizable volume discounts to discourage them from experimenting with other suppliers.
- Offering free or low-cost training to buyers' personnel in the use of the firm's product.
- Making it harder for competitors to get buyers to try their brands by (1) giving special price discounts to buyers who are considering trial use of rival brands, (2) resorting to high levels of couponing and sample giveaways to buyers most prone to experiment, and (3) making early announcements about impending new products or price changes so buyers postpone switching.
- Raising the amount of financing provided to dealers and/or buyers.
- Reducing delivery times for spare parts.
- Increasing warranty coverages.
- Patenting alternative technologies.
- Protecting proprietary know-how in products, production technologies, and other parts of the activity-cost chain.
- Signing exclusive contracts with the best suppliers to block access of aggressive rivals.
- Purchasing natural resource reserves ahead of present needs to keep them from competitors.
- Avoiding suppliers that also serve competitors.
- Challenging rivals' products or practices in regulatory proceedings.

There are many ways to blunt offensive challenges from rival firms.

Moves such as these not only buttress a firm's present position, they also present competitors with a moving target. It is not enough just to try to protect the status quo. A good defense entails adjusting quickly to changing industry conditions and, on occasion, being a first-mover to block or preempt moves by would-be aggressors. A mobile defense is always preferable to a stationary defense.

A second approach to defensive strategy entails signaling strong retaliation if a challenger attacks. The goal is to dissuade challengers from attacking at all (by raising their expectations that the resulting battle will be more costly than it is worth) or divert challengers to options less threatening to the defender. Would-be challengers can be signaled by:[19]

One of the best defensive strategies is to signal challengers that aggressive actions will be met with strong retaliatory countermeasures.

- Publicly announcing management's commitment to maintain the firm's present market share.

---

[19]Porter, *Competitive Advantage*, pp. 495–97. The listing here is selective; Porter offers a greater number of options.

- Publicly announcing plans to construct adequate production capacity to meet forecast demand growth, and sometimes building ahead of demand.
- Giving out advance information about a new product, technological breakthrough, or the planned introduction of important new brands or models, in hopes that challengers will be induced to delay moves of their own until they see if the signaled actions are true.
- Publicly committing the firm to a policy of matching the prices or terms offered by competitors.
- Maintaining a war chest of cash and marketable securities.
- Making an occasional strong counterresponse to the moves of weak competitors to enhance the firm's image as a tough defender.

Another way to dissuade rivals involves trying to lower the profit inducement for challengers to launch an offensive. When a firm's or industry's profitability is enticingly high, challengers are more willing to tackle high defensive barriers and combat strong retaliation. A defender can deflect attacks, especially from new entrants, by deliberately forgoing some short-run profits and by using accounting methods that obscure profitability.

VERTICAL INTEGRATION STRATEGIES

Vertical integration strategies aim at extending a firm's competitive scope within the same industry. Firms can expand their range of activities backward into sources of supply and/or forward toward end-users. A manufacturer that builds a new plant to make component parts rather than purchase them from suppliers remains in essentially the same industry as before. The only change is that it has business units in two stages of production in the industry's total activity-chain. Similarly, if a personal computer manufacturer elects to integrate forward by opening retail stores to market its brands, it remains in the personal computer business even though its competitive scope extends further forward in the industry chain.

Moves to vertically integrate can aim at *full integration* (participating in all stages of the process of getting products in the hands of final-users) or *partial integration* (building positions in just some stages of the industry's total production-distribution chain). A firm can accomplish vertical integration by starting its own company in other stages of the industry's activity chain or by acquiring a company already positioned in the stage it wishes to integrate.

Competitive Strategy Principle
A vertical integration strategy has appeal only if it significantly strengthens a firm's competitive position.

The Appeal of Vertical Integration

The only good reason for investing company resources in vertical integration is to strengthen the firm's competitive position.[20] Unless vertical integration produces sufficient cost-savings to justify the extra investment or yields a competitive advantage, it has no real profit or strategic payoff.

---

[20]See Kathryn R. Harrigan, "Matching Vertical Integration Strategies to Competitive Conditions," *Strategic Management Journal* 7, no. 6 (November–December 1986), pp. 535–56; for a fuller discussion of the advantages and disadvantages of vertical integration, see Kathryn R. Harrigan, *Strategic Flexibility* (Lexington, Mass.: Lexington Books, 1985), p. 162.

Integrating backward generates cost-savings only when the volume needed is big enough to capture the same scale economies suppliers have and when it can match or exceed suppliers' production efficiency. Backward integration usually generates the largest cost advantage when suppliers have sizable profit margins, when the item being supplied is a major cost component, and when the needed technological skills are easily mastered. Backward vertical integration can produce a differentiation-based competitive advantage when a company, by supplying its own parts, ends up with a better-quality part and thereby significantly enhances the performance of its final product.

Backward integration can also spare a firm the uncertainty of being dependent on suppliers of crucial raw materials or support services, and it can lessen the firm's vulnerability to powerful suppliers intent on raising prices at every opportunity. Stockpiling, fixed-price contracts, or the use of substitute inputs may not be attractive ways for dealing with uncertain supply conditions or economically powerful suppliers. When this is the case, backward integration can be an organization's most profitable and competitively secure option for accessing reliable supplies of essential materials and support services at favorable prices.

The strategic impetus for forward integration has much the same roots. Undependable sales and distribution channels can give rise to costly inventory pileups and frequent underutilization of capacity, thereby undermining the economies of a steady, near-capacity production operation. In such cases, it is often advantageous for a firm to set up its own wholesale-retail distribution network in order to gain dependable channels through which to push its products to end-users. Sometimes even a small percentage increase in the average rate of capacity utilization can boost manufacturing margins enough to make forward integration economical. On other occasions, forward integration into distribution and retailing is cheaper than dealing with independent distributors and retailers, thus providing a source of cost advantage.

Integrating forward into manufacturing may help a raw materials producer achieve greater product differentiation and escape the price-oriented competition of a commodity business. Often, in the early phases of vertical product flow, intermediate goods are "commodities" in the sense that they have essentially identical technical specifications irrespective of producer (as is the case with crude oil, poultry, sheet steel, cement, and textile fibers). Competition in commodity or commodity-like markets is usually fiercely price-competitive, with shifting supply and demand conditions causing volatile profits. However, the closer the production stage to the ultimate consumer, the greater the opportunities for a firm to break out of a commodity-like competitive environment and differentiate its end-product via design, service, quality features, packaging, promotion, and so on. Product differentiation often reduces the importance of price in comparison with other product attributes and allows for improved profit margins.

For a manufacturer, integrating forward may mean building a chain of closely supervised dealer franchises or establishing company-owned and -operated retail outlets. Or it may entail simply establishing a sales force instead of selling through manufacturer's agents or independent distributors.

The Strategic Disadvantages of Vertical Integration

The big disadvantage of vertical integration is that it locks a firm deeper into an industry; unless it builds competitive advantage, it is a questionable strategic move.

Vertical integration has some potential weaknesses, however. First, it boosts a firm's capital investment in the industry, perhaps denying financial resources to more worthwhile pursuits. Second, integration introduces additional risks, since it extends the enterprise's scope of activity across the industry chain. Third, vertical integration increases a firm's interest in protecting its present technology and production facilities even though they are becoming obsolete. Because of the high cost of abandoning such investments before they are worn out, fully integrated firms are more vulnerable to new technologies and new products than partially integrated or nonintegrated firms.

Fourth, vertical integration can pose problems of balancing capacity at each stage in the activity-chain. The most efficient scale of operation at each step in the chain can vary substantially. Exact self-sufficiency at each interface is the exception not the rule. Where internal capacity is deficient to supply the next stage, the difference has to be bought externally. Where internal capacity is excessive, customers need to be found for the surplus. And if by-products are generated, they must be disposed of.

All in all, a strategy of vertical integration can have both strengths and weaknesses. Which direction the scales tip depends on (1) how compatible vertical integration is with the organization's long-term strategic interests and performance objectives, (2) how much it strengthens an organization's position in the overall industry, and (3) the extent to which it creates competitive advantage. Unless these considerations yield solid benefits, vertical integration is unlikely to be an attractive business strategy option.[21]

FIRST-MOVER ADVANTAGES AND DISADVANTAGES

Competitive Strategy Principle
Because of first-mover advantages and disadvantages, when to make a move is often as crucial as what move to make.

When to make a strategic move is often as crucial as *what* move to make. Timing is especially important when *first-mover advantages* or *disadvantages* exist.[22] Being first to initiate a strategic move can have a high payoff when (1) pioneering helps build a firm's image and reputation with buyers, (2) early commitments to supplies of raw materials, new technologies, distribution channels, and so on can produce an absolute cost advantage over rivals, (3) first-time customers remain strongly loyal to pioneering firms in making repeat purchases, and (4) moving first constitutes a preemptive strike, making imitation extra hard or unlikely. The bigger the first-mover advantages, the more attractive that making the first move becomes.

However, a "wait and see" approach doesn't always carry a competitive penalty. Making the first move may carry greater risks than a late move. First-mover disadvantages (or late-mover advantages) arise when: (1) pioneering leadership is much more costly and only negligible experience curve effects accrue to the leader, (2) technological change is so rapid that early investments are soon obsolete (thus allowing following firms to gain the advantages of next-generation newest products and more efficient processes), (3) it is easy for late-

[21]For an extensive, well-researched look at the whole family of approaches to vertical integration, see Kathryn R. Harrigan, "Formulating Vertical Integration Strategies," *Academy of Management Review* 9, no. 4 (October 1984), pp. 638–52.
[22]Porter, *Competitive Strategy*, pp. 232–33.

comers to crack the market because customer loyalty to pioneering firms is weak, and (4) skills and know-how developed by the market leaders can be easily copied or even surpassed by late movers. Good timing, therefore, is an important ingredient in deciding whether to be aggressive or cautious.

The challenge of competitive strategy—low-cost, differentiation, or focus—is to create a competitive advantage for the firm. Competitive advantage comes from positioning a firm in the marketplace so it has an edge in coping with competitive forces and in attracting buyers.

A strategy of trying to be the low-cost producer works well in situations where

- The industry's product is pretty much the same from seller to seller.
- The marketplace is dominated by price competition (buyers are prone to shop for the lowest price).
- There are only a few ways to achieve product differentiation that have much value to buyers.
- Most buyers use the product in the same ways and thus have common user requirements.
- Buyers' costs in switching from one seller or brand to another are low (or even zero).
- Buyers are large and have significant bargaining power.

To achieve a low-cost advantage, a company must become more skilled than rivals in controlling cost drivers and/or it must find innovative cost-saving ways to revamp the activity-cost chain.

Differentiation strategies can produce a competitive edge based on technical superiority, quality, service, or more value for the money. Differentiation strategies work *best* when:

- There are many ways to differentiate the product/service that buyers think have value.
- Buyer needs or uses of the product/service are diverse.
- Not many rivals are following a similar differentiation strategy.

Anything a firm can do to create buyer value represents a potential basis for differentiation. Successful differentiation is usually keyed to lowering the buyer's cost of using the item, raising the performance the buyer gets, giving the buyer more value for the money, or boosting a buyer's psychological satisfaction. A best-cost producer strategy works especially well in market situations where product differentiation is the rule and buyers are price sensitive.

The competitive advantage of focusing comes from achieving lower costs in serving the target market niche or from offering niche buyers something different from rivals—in other words, the advantage a firm gains with a focus strategy is either *cost-based* or *differentiation-based*. Focusing works best when:

- Buyer needs or uses of the item are diverse.
- No other rival is attempting to *specialize* in the same target segment.

- A firm lacks the ability to go after a wider part of the total market.
- Buyer segments differ widely in size, growth rate, profitability, and intensity in the five competitive forces, making some segments more attractive than others.

A variety of offensive strategic moves can be used to secure a competitive advantage. Strategic offensives can be aimed at competitors' strengths or weaknesses; they can involve end-runs or grand offensives; they can be designed as guerrilla actions or as preemptive strikes; and the target of the offensive can be a market leader, a runner-up firm, or the smallest and/or weakest firms in the industry.

To defend its current position, a company can: (1) make moves that fortify its current position, (2) present competitors with a moving target to avoid "out-of-date" vulnerability, and (3) dissuade rivals from even trying to attack.

Vertical integration forward or backward makes strategic sense if it strengthens a company's position via either cost reduction or enhanced product differentiation.

The timing of strategic moves is important. First-movers sometimes gain strategic advantage; at other times, it is cheaper and easier to be a follower than a leader.

SUGGESTED READINGS

Aaker, David A. "Managing Assets and Skills: The Key to a Sustainable Competitive Advantage." *California Management Review* 31, no. 2 (Winter 1989), pp. 91–106.

Cohen, William A. "War in the Marketplace." *Business Horizons* 29, no. 2 (March–April 1986), pp. 10–20.

Coyne, Kevin P. "Sustainable Competitive Advantage—What It Is, What It Isn't." *Business Horizons* 29, no. 1 (January–February 1986), pp. 54–61.

Harrigan, Kathryn R. "Guerrilla Strategies of Underdog Competitors." *Planning Review* 14, no. 16 (November 1986), pp. 4–11.

————. "Formulating Vertical Integration Strategies." *Academy of Management Review* 9, no. 4 (October 1984), pp. 638–52.

Hout, Thomas, Michael E. Porter, and Eileen Rudden. "How Global Companies Win Out." *Harvard Business Review* 60, no. 5 (September–October 1982), pp. 98–108.

MacMillan, Ian C. "Preemptive Strategies." *Journal of Business Strategy* 4, no. 2 (Fall 1983), pp. 16–26.

————. "Controlling Competitive Dynamics by Taking Strategic Initiative." *The Academy of Management Executive* 2, no. 2 (May 1988), pp. 111–18.

Porter, Michael E. *Competitive Advantage* (New York: Free Press, 1985), chaps. 3, 4, 5, 7, 14, and 15.

Rothschild, William E. "Surprise and the Competitive Advantage." *Journal of Business Strategy* 4, no. 3 (Winter 1984), pp. 10–18.

Thompson, Arthur A. "Strategies for Staying Cost Competitive." *Harvard Business Review* 62, no. 1 (January–February 1984) pp. 110–17.

CHAPTER

6

Matching Strategy to the Situation

———

*Strategy isn't something you can nail together in slap-dash fashion
by sitting around a conference table . . .*
Terry Haller

———

*The essence of formulating competitive strategy is relating a company to its
environment . . . the best strategy for a given firm is ultimately a unique
construction reflecting its particular circumstances.*
Michael E. Porter

———

You do not choose to become global. The market chooses for you; it forces your hand.
Alain Gomez
CEO, Thomson, S.A.

———

What kind of strategy best suits a company's business is conditioned partly by
the industry environment in which it competes and partly by the company's
situation. To demonstrate the kinds of considerations involved in matching
strategy to the situation, this chapter examines strategy-making in eight classic
types of industry environments and company situations:

1. Competing in a young, emerging industry.
2. Competing during the transition to industry maturity.
3. Competing in mature or declining industries.
4. Competing in fragmented industries.
5. Competing in international markets.
6. Strategies for industry leaders.
7. Strategies for runner-up firms.
8. Strategies for weak and crisis-ridden firms.

STRATEGIES FOR COMPETING IN EMERGING INDUSTRIES

An emerging industry is one in the early formative stage. Most companies are in a start-up mode, adding people, acquiring or constructing facilities, gearing up production, trying to broaden distribution and gain buyer acceptance. Often, such firms have to work out important product design and technological problems as well. Emerging industries present strategy-makers with some unique challenges:[1]

- Because the market is new and unproven, there are many uncertainties about how it will function, how fast it will grow, and how big it will get; the little historical data available is virtually useless in projecting future trends.

- Much of the technological know-how tends to be proprietary and closely guarded, having been developed in-house by pioneering firms; patent protection is sought for competitive advantage.

- Often, there is no consensus on which production technologies will be most efficient and which product attributes buyers will prefer. The result is industrywide absence of product and technological standardization, wide differences in product quality and performance, and a situation where each firm has to pioneer its own approach to technology, product design, marketing, and distribution.

- Entry barriers tend to be relatively low; additional start-up companies and large outsiders will enter if it becomes more evident that the industry's future is promising.

- Experience curve effects often permit significant cost reductions as volume builds.

- Firms have little hard information about competitors, how fast products are gaining buyer acceptance, and users' experiences with the product; there are no trade associations gathering and distributing information.

- Since all buyers are first-time users, the marketing task is to induce initial purchase and overcome customer concerns about product features, performance reliability, and conflicting claims of rival firms.

- Many buyers expect first-generation products to be rapidly improved, so they wait to buy until technology and product design mature.

- Firms may have trouble securing ample supplies of raw materials and components (until suppliers gear up to meet the industry's needs).

- Many companies find themselves short of funds to support needed R&D and to get through several lean years until the product catches on.

The two critical strategic issues confronting firms in an emerging industry are (1) how to finance the start-up phase and (2) what market segments and competitive advantage to go after to secure a leading industry position.[2] Competitive strategies keyed either to low-cost or differentiation are usually viable. Focusing should be considered when finances are limited and the industry has

---

[1]Michael E. Porter, *Competitive Strategy* (New York: Free Press, 1980), pp. 216–23.
[2]Charles W. Hofer and Dan Schendel, *Strategy Formulation: Analytical Concepts* (St. Paul, Minn.: West Publishing, 1978), pp. 164–65.

too many technological frontiers to pursue at once; one option for financially constrained enterprises is to form a strategic alliance or joint venture with another company to gain access to needed skills and resources. Dealing with all the risks and opportunities of an emerging industry is one of the most challenging business strategy problems. To be successful in an emerging industry, companies need to observe the following guidelines:[3]

1. Try to win the early race for industry leadership by employing a bold, creative entrepreneurial strategy. Because an emerging industry has no established rules of the game and industry participants often try a variety of strategic approaches, a pioneering firm with a powerful strategy can shape the rules and become the industry leader.

2. Push hard to perfect the technology, improve product quality, and develop attractive performance features.

3. Try to capture any first-mover advantages associated with more models, better styling, early commitments to technologies and raw materials suppliers, experience curve effects, and new distribution channels.

4. Search out new customer groups, new geographical areas to enter, and new user applications. Make it easier and cheaper for first-time buyers to try the industry's new product.

5. Gradually shift the advertising emphasis from building product awareness to increasing frequency of use and creating brand loyalty.

6. Move quickly when technological uncertainty clears and a "dominant" technology emerges; try to pioneer the "dominant design" (but be cautious when technology is evolving so rapidly that early investments are likely to become obsolete).

7. Use price cuts to attract price-sensitive buyers into the market.

8. Expect large, established firms looking for growth opportunities to enter the industry as their perceived risk of investing in the industry lessens. Try to prepare for the entry of powerful competitors by forecasting (*a*) who will enter (based on present and future entry barriers) and (*b*) the types of strategies they will employ.

Strategic success in an emerging industry calls for bold entrepreneurship, a willingness to pioneer and take risks, an intuitive feel for what buyers will like and how they will use the product, quick response to new developments, and opportunistic strategy-making.

The short-term value of winning the early race for growth and market share has to be balanced against the longer-range need to build a durable competitive edge and a defendable market position.[4] New entrants, attracted by the growth and profit potential, may crowd the market. Aggressive newcomers, aspiring for industry leadership, can quickly become major players by acquiring and merging the operations of weaker competitors. A young, single-business enterprise in a fast-developing industry can help its cause by selecting knowledgeable members for its board of directors, hiring entrepreneurial managers with experience in guiding young businesses through the development and takeoff, or merging with another firm to gain added expertise and a stronger resource base.

---

[3]Phillip Kotler, *Marketing Management*, 5th ed. (Englewood Cliffs, N.J.: Prentice Hall, 1984), p. 366; and Porter, *Competitive Strategy*, chap. 10.

[4]Hofer and Schendel, *Strategy Formulation*, pp. 164–65.

STRATEGIES FOR COMPETING DURING THE TRANSITION TO INDUSTRY MATURITY

Rapid industry growth doesn't last forever. However, the transition to a slower-growth, maturing environment does not begin on any easily predicted schedule and it can be forestalled by a steady stream of technological advances, product innovations, or other driving forces that keep rejuvenating market demand. Nonetheless, as growth rates slack off, the transition usually produces fundamental changes in the industry's competitive environment:[5]

1. *Slowing growth in buyer demand generates more head-to-head competition for market share.* Firms that want to continue on a rapid-growth track start looking for ways to take customers from competitors. Outbreaks of price-cutting, increased advertising, and other aggressive tactics are common.

2. *Buyers become more sophisticated, often driving a harder bargain on repeat purchases.* Since buyers have experience with the product and are familiar with competing brands, they are better able to evaluate different brands, and will negotiate with sellers to get a better deal.

3. *Competition often produces a greater emphasis on cost and service.* As all sellers begin to offer the product attributes buyers prefer, buyer choices increasingly depend on which seller offers the best combination of price and service.

4. *Firms have a "topping out" problem in adding production capacity.* Slower rates of industry growth mean slowdowns in capacity expansion. Each firm has to monitor rivals' expansion plans and time its own carefully to minimize oversupply conditions in the industry. Adding too much capacity too soon can adversely affect company profits well into the future.

5. *Product innovation and new end-use applications are harder to come by.* Producers find it increasingly difficult to develop new product features, find further uses for the product, and sustain buyer excitement.

6. *International competition increases.* Growth-minded domestic firms start to seek out sales opportunities in foreign markets. Some companies, looking for ways to cut costs, relocate plants to countries with lower wage rates. Greater product standardization and diffusion of technological know-how reduce entry barriers and make it possible for enterprising foreign companies to become serious market contenders in more countries. Industry leadership passes to companies with the biggest global market shares and strong competitive positions in most of the world's major geographic markets.

7. *Industry profitability falls temporarily or permanently.* Slower growth, increased competition, more sophisticated buyers, and occasional periods of overcapacity put pressure on industry profit margins. Weaker, less-efficient firms are usually the hardest hit.

8. *The resulting competitive shakeout induces a number of mergers and acquisitions among former competitors, drives some firms out of the industry, and,*

---

[5]Porter, *Competitive Strategy*, pp. 238–40.

in general, produces industry consolidation. Inefficient firms and firms with weak competitive strategies can survive in a rapid-growth industry. But the much stiffer competition in the industry maturity stage exposes competitive weakness and results in a survival-of-the-fittest market contest.

As market growth slows and competitive pressures build, firms can make several strategic moves to strengthen their competitive positions.[6]

As industry growth slows, strategic emphasis shifts to efficiency-increasing, profit-preserving measures: pruning the product line, improving production methods, reducing costs, expanding internationally, and acquiring distressed rivals.

Pruning the Product Line   A wide selection of models, features, and options has competitive value during the growth stage when buyers' needs are still evolving. But such variety can become too costly as price competition stiffens and profit margins are squeezed. Too many product versions prevent firms from achieving the economies of long production runs. In addition, the prices of slow-selling versions may not cover their true costs. Pruning product lines and concentrating sales efforts on items whose margins are highest and/or where the firm has a competitive advantage reduces costs and helps keep strategy matched to company strengths.

More Emphasis on Process Innovation   Efforts to "re-invent" the manufacturing process can have a twofold payoff: lower costs and better quality control. Process innovation can involve mechanizing high-cost activities, revamping production lines to improve labor efficiency, and increased use of advanced technology (robotics, computerized controls, and automatic guided vehicles). Japanese firms have successfully used manufacturing process innovation to become lower-cost producers of higher-quality products.

A Stronger Focus on Cost Reduction   Stiffening price competition gives firms extra incentive to reduce unit costs. Such efforts can cover a broad front: firms can negotiate with suppliers for better prices, switch to lower-priced components, develop more economical product designs, cut unnecessary tasks out of the activity-cost chain, increase manufacturing and distribution efficiency, and trim administrative overhead.

Increasing Sales to Present Customers   In a mature market, growing by taking customers from rivals may not be as appealing as expanding sales to existing customers. Strategies to increase purchases to existing customers can involve broadening the lines offered to include complementary products and ancillary services, finding more ways for customers to use the product, and performing more functions for the buyers (assembling components prior to shipment). Convenience food stores, for example, have boosted average sales per customer by adding video rentals, automatic bank tellers, and deli counters.

Purchasing Rival Firms at Bargain Prices   Sometimes distressed rivals can be acquired cheaply. Bargain-priced acquisitions can help create a low-cost position if they present opportunities for greater operating efficiency. In addition,

---

[6]The following discussion draws on Porter, *Competitive Strategy,* pp. 241–46.

an acquired firm's customer base can provide expanded market coverage. The most desirable acquisitions are those that will significantly enhance the acquiring firm's competitive strength.

Expanding Internationally   As its domestic market matures, a firm may seek to enter foreign markets where attractive growth potential still exists and competitive pressures are not so strong. Foreign expansion is particularly attractive if equipment no longer suitable for domestic operations is usable for export production or for plants in less developed foreign markets (a condition that lowers entry costs). Such possibilities arise when (1) foreign buyers have less sophisticated needs, (2) end-use applications are much simpler, and (3) foreign competitors are smaller, less formidable, and do not employ the latest production technology. Strategies to expand internationally make particular sense when a domestic firm's skills and reputation are readily transferable to foreign markets.

Strategic Pitfalls

Perhaps the biggest mistake a firm can make during the transition to industry maturity is steering a middle course between low cost, differentiation, and focusing. Such a compromise guarantees that the firm will end up with a fuzzy strategy, no clearly staked out market position, an "average" image with buyers, and no competitive advantage. Other pitfalls include sacrificing long-term competitive position for short-term profit, waiting too long to respond to price-cutting, getting caught with too much capacity as growth slows, overspending on marketing efforts to boost sales growth, and failing to pursue cost reduction soon enough and aggressively enough.

Strategic Management Principle
One of the greatest strategic mistakes a firm can make in a maturing industry is pursuing a compromise between low cost, differentiation, and focusing such that it ends up "stuck in the middle" with little chance of becoming an industry leader.

STRATEGIES FOR FIRMS IN MATURE OR DECLINING INDUSTRIES

Many firms operate in industries where demand is growing slower than the economy average—or even declining. Although cash-flow maximization, selling out, and closing down are obvious strategies for uncommitted competitors with dim long-term prospects, strong competitors can still achieve good performance in a stagnant market environment.[7] Stagnant demand by itself is not enough to make an industry unattractive. Selling out may or may not be practical, and closing down operations is always a last resort.

Businesses competing in slow-growth/declining industries have to accept the difficult realities of continuing stagnancy and they must set performance goals consistent with available market opportunities. Although cash flow and return on investment are more appropriate criteria than growth-oriented performance measures, firms don't have to rule out sales and market share growth. Strong competitors may be able to take sales from weaker rivals, and

---

[7]R. G. Hamermesh and S. B. Silk, "How to Compete in Stagnant Industries," *Harvard Business Review* 57, no. 5 (September–October 1979), p. 161.

the acquisition or exit of weaker firms may help remaining companies capture greater market share.

In general, companies that have succeeded in stagnant industries have relied heavily on one of the following strategic themes:[8]

1. *Pursue a focus strategy by identifying, creating, and exploiting the growth segments within the industry.* Slow-growth or declining markets, like other markets, are composed of numerous segments and subsegments. Frequently, one or more of these segments is growing rapidly, despite a lack of growth in the industry as a whole. An astute competitor who is first to concentrate on the most attractive segments can escape stagnating sales and profits and achieve competitive advantage in the target segments.

2. *Stress differentiation based on quality improvement and product innovation.* Either enhanced quality or innovation can rejuvenate demand by creating important new growth segments or inducing buyers to trade up. Successful product innovation opens up an avenue for competing besides meeting or beating rivals' prices. Differentiation based on innovation has the additional advantage of being difficult and expensive for rivals to imitate.

3. *Work diligently and persistently to drive costs down.* When increases in sales cannot be counted on to generate increased earnings, firms can improve profit margins and return on investment by continuously reducing operating costs and increasing efficiency. They can achieve a lower-cost position by: (1) improving the manufacturing process via automation and increased specialization, (2) consolidating underutilized production facilities, (3) adding more distribution channels to ensure the unit volume needed for low-cost production, (4) closing low-volume, high-cost distribution outlets, and (5) revamping the activity-cost chain to eliminate some cost-producing tasks.

These three themes are not mutually exclusive.[9] Attempts to introduce innovative versions of a product can *create* a fast-growing market segment. Similarly, increased operating efficiencies permit price reductions that create price-conscious growth segments. Note that all three themes are spin-offs of the three generic competitive strategies, adjusted to fit the circumstances of a tough industry environment.

The most attractive declining industries are those in which decline is reasonably slow, there is big built-in demand, and some profitable niches remain. Dangers in a stagnating market include: (1) getting trapped in a profitless war of attrition, (2) diverting too much cash out of a business too quickly (thus accelerating a company's demise), and (3) being overly optimistic about the industry's future and waiting complacently for things to get better.

Illustration Capsule 13 describes the creative approach taken by Yamaha to reverse declining market demand for pianos.

Competitive advantage in industries with stagnant or declining market demand usually involves focusing on growth segments, differentiating on the basis of quality improvement and product innovation, or becoming a lower-cost producer.

---

[8]Ibid., p. 162.
[9]Ibid., p. 165.

YAMAHA'S STRATEGY IN THE PIANO INDUSTRY

For some years now, worldwide demand for pianos has been declining—in the mid-1980s the decline was 10 percent annually. Modern-day parents have not put the same stress on music lessons for their children as prior generations of parents did. In an effort to see if it could revitalize its piano business, Yamaha conducted a market research survey to learn what use was being made of pianos in households that owned one. The survey revealed that the overwhelming majority of the 40 million pianos in American, European, and Japanese households were seldom used. In most cases, the reasons the piano had been purchased no longer applied. Children had either stopped taking piano lessons or were grown and had left the household; adult household members played their pianos sparingly, if at all—only a small percentage were accomplished piano players. Most pianos were serving as a piece of fine furniture and were in good condition despite not being tuned regularly. The survey also confirmed that the income levels of piano owners were well above average.

Yamaha's piano strategists saw the idle pianos in these upscale households as a potential market opportunity. The strategy that emerged entailed marketing an attachment that would convert the piano into an old-fashioned automatic player piano capable of playing a wide number of selections recorded on $3\frac{1}{2}$-inch floppy disks (the same kind used to store computer data). The player piano conversion attachment carried a $2,500 price tag. Concurrently, Yamaha introduced Disklavier, an upright acoustic player piano model that could play *and record* performances up to 90 minutes long; the Disklavier retailed for $8,000. At year-end 1988 Yamaha offered 30 prerecorded disks for $29.95 each. Another 30 selections were scheduled for release in 1989. Yamaha believed that these new high-tech products held potential to reverse the downtrend in piano sales.

STRATEGIES FOR COMPETING IN FRAGMENTED INDUSTRIES

A number of industries are populated with hundreds, even thousands, of small and medium-sized companies, many privately held and none with a substantial share of total industry sales.[10] The outstanding feature of a fragmented industry is the absence of market leaders with king-sized market shares who have the clout and visibility to set the tone of competition. Examples of fragmented industries include book publishing, landscaping and plant nurseries, kitchen cabinets, oil tanker shipping, auto repair, restaurants and fast-food, public accounting, women's dresses, metal foundries, meat packing, paperboard boxes, log homes, hotels and motels, and furniture.

Any of several factors can account for why the supply side of an industry is fragmented.

Many reasons account for why an industry has hundreds or even thousands of small competitors rather than a few large competitors.

- Low entry barriers allow small firms to enter quickly and cheaply.
- An absence of large-scale production economies permit small companies to compete on an equal cost footing with larger firms.
- Buyers require relatively small quantities of customized products (as in business forms, interior design, and advertising); because demand for any particular product version is small, sales volumes can't support producing, distributing, or marketing on a scale that favors a large firm.

---

[10] This section is summarized from Porter, *Competitive Strategy*, chap. 9.

- The market for the industry's product/service is local (dry cleaning, residential construction, medical services, automotive repair), giving competitive advantage to local businesses familiar with local buyers and market conditions.
- Market demand is so large and diverse that it takes large numbers of firms to accommodate buyer requirements (health care, energy, apparel).
- High transportation costs limit the radius a plant can economically service—as in concrete blocks, mobile homes, milk, and gravel.
- Local regulatory requirements make each geographic area unique.
- The industry is so new that no firms have yet developed the skills and resources to command a significant market share.

Some fragmented industries consolidate naturally as they mature. The stiffer competition that accompanies slower growth produces a shake-out of weak, inefficient firms and a greater concentration of larger, more visible sellers. Other industries remain fragmented because it is inherent to the nature of their business. And still others remain "stuck" in a fragmented state because existing firms lack the resources or ingenuity to employ a strategy that might promote industry consolidation.

Firms in fragmented industries usually are in a weak bargaining position with buyers and suppliers. New entrants are an ongoing threat. Competition from substitutes may or may not be a major factor. Rivalry among competitors can vary from moderately strong to fierce. In such an environment, the best a firm can expect is to cultivate a loyal customer base and grow a bit faster than the industry average. Competitive strategies based on low cost, some kind of differentiation theme, or focusing are all viable except when the industry's product is highly standardized; then competitors must rely on low cost or focused specialization. Suitable competitive strategy options in a fragmented industry include:

- **Constructing and operating "formula" facilities**—This is an attractive approach to achieving low cost when firms must operate facilities at multiple locations. Such firms design a standard facility, construct outlets in favorable locations at minimum cost, and then operate them in a super-efficient manner. McDonald's and 7-Eleven have pursued this strategy to perfection, earning excellent profits in their respective industries.
- **Becoming a low-cost operator**—When price competition is intense and profit margins are under constant pressure, firms can pursue no-frills operation featuring low overhead, use of high-productivity/low-cost labor, tight budget control, and total operating efficiency. Successful low-cost producers can play the price-cutting game and still earn profits above the industry average.
- **Increasing customer value through integration**—Backward or forward integration may contain opportunities to lower costs or enhance the value given to customers (like cutting to size, assembling components before shipment to customers, or providing technical advice).
- **Specializing by product type**—When products come in many models and styles, a focus strategy based on specialization in one area of the line can be very effective. Some firms in the furniture industry specialize in only one furniture type such as brass beds, rattan and wicker, lawn and

Competitive advantage in a fragmented industry usually comes from low cost, successful differentiation on well-chosen product attributes, or focusing on a particular market segment.

garden, and early American. In auto repair, firms specialize in transmission repair; body work; and mufflers, brakes, and shocks.

- **Specializing by customer type**—A firm can cope with the intense competition of a fragmented industry by catering to those customers (1) who have the least bargaining leverage (because they are small in size or purchase small amounts), (2) who are the least price sensitive, (3) who are interested in additional services, unique product attributes, or other "extras," (4) who place custom orders, or (5) who have special needs or tastes.

- **Focusing on a limited geographic area**—Even though a firm in a fragmented industry is blocked from winning a big industrywide market share, it can still gain significant internal operating economies by blanketing a local/regional geographic area. Concentrating facilities and marketing activities on a limited territory can produce greater sales force efficiency, speed delivery and customer services, and permit saturation advertising—while avoiding the diseconomies of trying to employ the strategy on a national scale. Convenience food stores, banks, and department store retailers have been successful in operating multiple locations within a limited geographic area.

In fragmented industries, firms have a wide degree of strategic freedom—many different strategic approaches can exist side-by-side.

STRATEGIES FOR COMPETING IN INTERNATIONAL MARKETS

Competing in international markets poses a bigger strategy-making challenge than competing in only the company's home market.

Firms "go international" for any of three basic reasons: a desire to seek out new markets, a competitive need to achieve lower costs, or a desire to access natural resource deposits in other countries. Whatever the reason, an international strategy has to be situation-driven and requires careful analysis of the industry's international aspects. Special attention has to be paid to how national markets differ in buyer needs and habits, distribution channels, long-run growth potential, driving forces, and competitive pressures. In addition to basic market differences from country to country, four other situational considerations are unique to international operations: cost variations among countries, fluctuating exchange rates, host government trade policies, and the pattern of international competition.

Manufacturing Cost Variations   Differences in wage rates, worker productivity, inflation rates, energy costs, tax rates, and the like create sizable variations in manufacturing costs from country to country. Plants in some countries often have major manufacturing cost advantages because of their lower input costs (especially labor) or their unique natural resources. In such cases, the low-cost countries become principal production sites, and most of the output is exported to markets in other parts of the world. Companies with facilities in these locations (or which source their products from contract manufacturers in these countries) typically have a competitive advantage over those that do not. The importance of this consideration is most evident in low-wage countries like Taiwan, South Korea, Mexico, and Brazil, which have become production havens for goods with high labor content.

Another important manufacturing cost consideration in international competition is the concept of *manufacturing share* as distinct from brand share or market share. For example, although less than 40 percent of all the video recorders sold in the United States carry a Japanese brand, Japanese companies do 100 percent of the manufacturing—all sellers source their video recorders from Japanese manufacturers.[11] In microwave ovens, Japanese brands have less than a 50 percent share of the U.S. market, but Japanese companies have a manufacturing share of over 85 percent. *Manufacturing share is significant because it is a better indicator than market share of which competitor is the industry's low-cost producer.* In a globally competitive industry where some competitors are intent on global dominance, being the worldwide low-cost producer is a powerful competitive advantage. Achieving low-cost producer status often requires a company to have the largest worldwide manufacturing share, with production centralized in one or a few super-efficient plants. However, important marketing and distribution economies associated with multinational operations can also yield low-cost leadership.

Fluctuating Exchange Rates   The volatility of exchange rates greatly complicates the issue of locational cost advantages. Exchange rates can fluctuate as much as 20 to 40 percent annually. Changes of this magnitude can totally wipe out a country's low-cost advantage or transform a former high-cost location into a competitive-cost location. A strong U.S. dollar makes it more attractive for U.S. companies to manufacture in foreign countries. A declining dollar can eliminate much of the cost advantage foreign manufacturers have over U.S. manufacturers and can even prompt foreign companies to establish production plants in the United States.

Host Government Trade Policies   National governments have enacted all kinds of measures affecting international trade and the operation of foreign companies in their markets. Host governments may impose import tariffs and quotas, set local content requirements on goods made inside their borders by foreign-based companies, and regulate the prices of imported goods. In addition, firms may face a web of regulations regarding technical standards, product certification, prior approval of capital spending projects, withdrawal of funds from the country, and minority (sometimes majority) ownership by local citizens. Some governments also provide subsidies and low-interest loans to domestic companies to help them compete against foreign-based companies. Other governments, anxious to obtain new plants and jobs, offer foreign companies subsidies, privileged market access, and technical assistance.

Multicountry Competition versus Global Competition

There are important differences in the patterns of international competition from industry to industry.[12] At one extreme, competition can be termed *multicountry* or *multidomestic* because it takes place country-by-country;

Basic Concept
Multicountry (or multidomestic) competition exists when competition in one national market is independent of competition in another national market—there is no "international market," just a collection of self-contained country markets.

---

[11]C. K. Prahalad and Yves L. Doz, *The Multinational Mission* (New York: Free Press, 1987), p. 60.

[12]Michael E. Porter, *The Competitive Advantage of Nations* (New York: Free Press, 1990), pp. 53–54.

competition in each national market is essentially independent of competition in other national markets. For example, there is a banking industry in France, one in Brazil, and one in Japan, but competitive conditions in banking differ markedly in all three countries. Moreover, a bank's reputation, customer base, and competitive position in one nation have little or no bearing on its ability to compete successfully in another. While a company may compete internationally, the power of its strategy in any one nation and any competitive advantage it yields are largely confined to that nation and do not spill over to other countries where it operates. With multicountry competition there is no "international market," just a collection of self-contained country markets. Industries characterized by multicountry competition include many types of food products (coffee, cereals, canned goods, frozen foods), many types of retailing, beer, life insurance, apparel, and metals fabrication.

Basic Concept

Global competition exists when competitive conditions across national markets are linked strongly enough to form a true international market and when leading competitors compete head-to-head in many different countries.

At the other extreme is *global competition* where prices and competitive conditions across country markets are strongly linked and the term *international* or *global market* has true meaning. In a globally competitive industry, a company's competitive position in one country both affects and is affected by its position in other countries. Rival companies compete against each other in many different countries, but especially so in countries where sales volumes are large and where having a competitive presence is strategically important to building a strong global position in the industry. In global competition, a firm's overall competitive advantage grows out of its entire worldwide operations. The competitive advantage it has created at its home base is supplemented by advantages growing out of its foreign operations (plants in low-wage countries, an ability to serve customers with multinational operations of their own, and brand reputation that is transferable from country to country). *A global competitor's strength is directly proportional to its portfolio of country-based competitive advantages.* Global competition exists in automobiles, television sets, tires, telecommunications equipment, copiers, watches, and commercial aircraft.

In multicountry competition, rival firms vie for national market leadership. In globally competitive industries, rival firms vie for worldwide leadership.

An industry can have segments that are globally competitive and segments where competition takes place country-by-country.[13] In the hotel-motel industry, for example, the low- and medium-priced segments are characterized by multicountry competition because competitors mainly serve travelers within the same country. In the business and luxury segments, however, competition is more global; companies like Marriott, Sheraton, and Hilton have hotels in many countries and use worldwide reservation systems and common quality and service standards to service international travelers. In lubricants, the marine engine segment is globally competitive because ships move from port to port and require the same oil everywhere they stop. Brand reputations have a global scope, and successful marine engine lubricant producers (Exxon, British Petroleum, and Shell) operate globally. In automotive motor oil, however, multicountry competition dominates. Countries have different weather conditions and driving patterns, production is subject to limited scale economies and shipping costs are high, and retail distribution channels differ markedly from country to country. Thus domestic firms, like Quaker State and Pennzoil in the United States and Castrol in Great Britain, can be market leaders.

---

[13]Ibid., p. 61.

All these situational considerations, along with the obvious cultural and political differences among countries, shape a company's strategic approach in international markets.

Types of International Strategies

There are six distinct strategic options for a firm participating in international markets. It can:

1. *License foreign firms to use the company's technology or produce and distribute the company's products* (in which case international revenues will equal the royalty income from the licensing agreement).

2. *Maintain a national (one-country) production base and export goods to foreign markets,* using either company-owned or foreign-controlled forward distribution channels.

3. *Follow a multicountry strategy* whereby a company's international strategy is crafted country-by-country to be responsive to buyer needs and competitive conditions in each country where it operates. Strategic moves in one country are made independent of actions taken in another country; strategy coordination across countries is secondary to the need to match company strategy to national conditions.

4. *Follow a global low-cost strategy* where strategy is based on the company being a low-cost supplier to buyers in most or all strategically important markets of the world. The company's strategic efforts are coordinated worldwide to achieve a low-cost position relative to competitors.

5. *Follow a global differentiation strategy* where a firm differentiates its product on the same attributes in all countries to create a consistent image and a consistent competitive theme. The firm's strategic moves are coordinated across countries to achieve consistent worldwide differentiation.

6. *Follow a global focus strategy* where company strategy is aimed at serving the same identifiable niche in each of many strategically important country markets. Strategic actions are coordinated globally to achieve a consistently focused approach in each country market.

Licensing makes sense when a firm with valuable technical know-how or a unique patented product has neither the internal organizational capability nor the resources to compete in foreign markets. By licensing the technology or the production rights to foreign-based firms, it at least realizes income from royalties.

Using domestic plants as a production base for exporting goods to foreign markets is an excellent initial strategy for achieving international sales growth. It minimizes both risk and capital requirements, and it is a conservative way to test the international waters. With an export strategy, a manufacturer can limit its involvement in foreign markets by letting foreign wholesalers experienced in importing assume the entire distribution and marketing function in their countries or regions of the world. If it is more advantageous to maintain control over these functions, a firm can establish its own distribution and sales organizations in some or all of its foreign markets. Either way, a firm minimizes its direct investment in foreign countries because of its home-base production and export strategy. Such strategies are commonly favored by Korean and Italian companies—products are designed and manufactured at home and only marketing activities are performed abroad. Whether such a strategy can be successful over the long run hinges on the relative cost competitiveness of a home-country production base. In some industries, firms gain additional scale economies and experience curve benefits from centralizing production in one or several giant-scale plants whose output capability exceeds demand in any one national market; to capture such economies a company must export to markets in other countries. However, this strategy is competitively vulnerable when manufacturing costs in the home country are substantially higher than in countries where rivals have plants.

The pros and cons of a multicountry versus global strategy are a bit more complex.

A Multicountry Strategy or a Global Strategy?

The logic and appeal of a multicountry strategy derives from the sometimes vast differences in cultural, economic, political, and competitive conditions in different countries. The more diverse national market conditions are, the stronger the case for a *multicountry strategy* where the company tailors its strategic approach to fit each host country's market situation. In such cases, the company's overall international strategy is a collection of its country strategies.

Competitive Strategy Principle

A multicountry strategy is appropriate for industries where multicountry competition dominates; a global strategy works best in markets that are globally competitive or beginning to globalize.

While multicountry strategies are best suited for industries where multicountry competition dominates, global strategies are best suited for globally competitive industries. A *global strategy* is one that is mostly the same in all countries. Although *minor* county-to-country differences do exist to accommodate specific competitive conditions in host countries, the company's fundamental competitive approach (low-cost, differentiation, or focus) remains the same worldwide. Moreover, a global strategy involves (1) integrating and coordinating the company's strategic moves worldwide and (2) selling in many or all nations where there is significant buyer demand. Table 6–1 provides a point-by-point comparison of multicountry versus global strategies. The question of which to pursue is the foremost strategic issue firms face when they compete in international markets.

The strength of a multicountry strategy is that it matches strategy to host-country circumstances. Such a strategy is essential when there are significant national differences in customers' needs and buying habits, when buyers in a country insist on special-order or highly customized products, when buyer demand for the product exists in comparatively few national markets, when host governments enact regulations requiring that products sold locally meet strict manufacturing specifications or performance standards, and when the trade restrictions of host governments are so diverse and complicated they preclude a uniform, coordinated worldwide market approach. However, a multicountry strategy has pitfalls; it entails very little strategic coordination across countries and it is not tightly tied to competitive advantage. Because the primary orientation of a multicountry strategy is responsiveness to local country conditions, it does not help a firm build a multinational-based competitive advantage over other international competitors and the domestic companies of host countries. A global strategy, because it is more uniform from country to country, helps a firm concentrate on securing a sustainable competitive advantage over both international and domestic rivals. Whenever country-to-

T A B L E 6–1   **Differences between Multicountry and Global Strategies**

	Multicountry Strategy	**Global Strategy**
Strategic arena	Selected target countries and trading areas	Most countries which constitute critical markets for the product (at least North America, the European Community, and the Pacific Rim [Australia, Japan, South Korea, and Southeast Asia])
Business strategy	Custom strategies to fit the circumstances of each host country situation; little or no strategy coordination across countries	Same basic strategy worldwide; minor country-by-country variations where essential
Product-line strategy	Adapted to local needs	Mostly standardized products sold worldwide
Production strategy	Plants scattered across many host countries	Plants located on the basis of maximum competitive advantage (in low-cost countries, close to major markets, geographically scattered to minimize shipping costs, or use of a few world-scale plants to maximize economies of scale—as most appropriate)
Source of supply for raw materials and components	Suppliers in host country preferred (local facilities meeting local buyer needs; some local sourcing may be required by host government)	Attractive suppliers from anywhere in the world
Marketing and distribution	Adapted to practices and culture of each host country	Much more worldwide coordination; minor adaption to host country situations if required
Company organization	Form subsidiary companies to handle operations in each host country; each subsidiary operates more or less autonomously to fit host country conditions	All major strategic decisions are closely coordinated at global headquarters; a global organizational structure is used to unify the operations in each country

country differences are small enough to be accommodated within the framework of a global strategy, a global strategy is preferable because of its broader-based competitive advantage potential.

Global Strategy and Competitive Advantage

There are two ways a firm can gain competitive advantage (or offset domestic disadvantages) with a global strategy approach.[14] One involves a global competitor's ability to locate its activities (R&D, parts manufacture, assembly, distribution centers, sales and marketing, customer service centers) among nations in a manner that lowers costs or achieves greater product differentiation. The other concerns a global competitor's ability to coordinate its activities in ways that a domestic-only competitor cannot.

With global strategy a firm can pursue sustainable competitive advantage by locating activities in the most advantageous nations and coordinating strategic actions worldwide; a domestic-only competitor forfeits such opportunities.

Locating Activities   To use location to build competitive advantage, a global firm must consider two issues: (1) whether to concentrate each activity it performs in one or two countries or disperse performance of the activity to many

[14]Ibid., p. 54.

nations and (2) in which countries to locate particular activities. Activities tend to be concentrated in one or two locations when there are significant economies of scale in performing an activity, when there are advantages in locating related activities in the same area to achieve better coordination, and when there is a steep learning or experience curve associated with concentrating performance of an activity in a single location. In some industries, scale economies in parts manufacture or assembly are so great that a company establishes one large plant from which it serves the world market. Where just-in-time inventory practices yield big cost-savings, parts manufacturing plants may be clustered around final assembly plants.

Dispersing activities is more advantageous than concentrating activities in several instances. Buyer-related activities—such as distribution to dealers, sales and advertising, and after-sale service—usually must take place close to buyers. This means physically locating the capability to perform such activities in every country where a global firm has major customers (unless buyers in several adjoining countries can be served quickly from a nearby central location). For example, firms that make mining and oil drilling equipment maintain operations in many international locations to support customers' needs for speedy equipment repair and technical assistance. Large public accounting firms have numerous international offices to service the foreign operations of their multinational corporate clients. A global competitor that effectively disperses its buyer-related activities can gain a service-based competitive edge in world markets over rivals whose buyer-related activities are more concentrated. Dispersing activities to many locations is also competitively advantageous when high transportation costs, diseconomies of large size, and trade barriers make it too expensive to operate from a central location. In addition, firms often disperse activities to hedge against fluctuating exchange rates, supply interruptions (due to strikes, mechanical failures, and transportation delays), and adverse political developments. Such risks are greater when activities are concentrated in a single location.

The classic reason for locating an activity in a particular country is lower costs.[15] Even though a global firm has strong reason to disperse buyer-related activities to many international locations, such activities as materials procurement, parts manufacture, finished goods assembly, technology research, and new product development can frequently be decoupled from buyer locations and performed wherever the best cost advantage lies. Components can be made in Mexico, technology research done in Frankfurt, new products developed and tested in Phoenix, and assembly plants located in Spain, Brazil, Taiwan, and Illinois. Capital can be raised wherever it is available on the best terms. Low cost is not the only locational consideration, however. A research unit may be located in a particular nation because of its pool of technically trained personnel. A customer service center or sales office may be located in a particular country to help develop strong relationships with pivotal customers. An assembly plant may be located in a country in return for the host government allowing freer import of components from centralized parts plants located elsewhere.

---

[15]Ibid., p. 57.

Coordinating Activities and Strategic Moves   By aligning and coordinating company activities in different countries, a firm can build sustainable competitive advantage in several different ways. If a firm learns how to assemble its product more efficiently at its Brazilian plant, the accumulated knowledge and expertise can be transferred to its assembly plant in Spain. Knowledge gained in marketing a company's product in Great Britain can be used to introduce the product in New Zealand and Australia. A company can shift production from one country to another to take advantage of exchange rate fluctuations, to enhance its leverage with host country governments, and to respond to changing wage rates, energy costs, or trade restrictions. A company can enhance its brand reputation by consistently positioning its products with the same differentiating attributes on a worldwide basis. Honda's worldwide reputation for quality, first in motorcycles and then in automobiles, gave it competitive advantage in positioning its lawnmowers at the upper end of the market—the Honda name gave the company instant credibility with buyers. A global competitor can choose where and how to challenge rivals. It may decide to retaliate against aggressive rivals in the country market where the rival has its biggest sales volume or its best profit margins in order to reduce the rival's financial resources for competing in other countries. It may decide to wage a price-cutting offensive against weak rivals in their home markets, capturing greater market share and subsidizing any short-term losses with profits earned in other country markets.

A company that competes only in its home country has access to none of the competitive advantage opportunities associated with multinational location or coordination. By shifting from a domestic to a global strategy, a domestic company that finds itself at a competitive disadvantage to global companies can begin to restore its competitiveness.

Strategic Alliances

Strategic alliances are cooperative agreements between firms that go beyond normal company-to-company dealings but fall short of merger or full partnership.[16] An alliance can involve joint research efforts, technology-sharing, joint use of production facilities, marketing one another's products, or joining forces to manufacture components or assemble finished products. Strategic alliances are a means for firms in the same industry that are based in different countries to compete on a more global scale while still preserving their independence. Historically, export-minded firms in industrialized nations sought alliances with firms in less-developed countries to import and market their products locally—such arrangements were often necessary to gain access to the less-developed country's market. More recently, leading companies from different parts of the world have formed strategic alliances to strengthen their ability to serve whole continental areas and move toward more global market participation. Both Japanese and American companies have formed alliances with European companies in preparation for Europe 1992 and the opening of Eastern European markets.

Strategic alliances are a means for companies in globally competitive industries to strengthen their competitive positions while still preserving their independence.

---

[16]Ibid., p. 65. See, also, Kenichi Ohmae, "The Global Logic of Strategic Alliances," *Harvard Business Review* 89, no. 2 (March–April 1989), pp. 143–54.

Companies enter into alliances for several strategically beneficial reasons.[17] The three most important are to gain economies of scale in production and/or marketing, to fill gaps in their technical and manufacturing expertise, and to acquire market access. By joining forces in producing components, assembling models, and marketing their products, companies can realize cost savings not achievable with their own small volumes. Allies learn much from one another in performing joint research, sharing technological know-how, and studying one another's manufacturing methods. Alliances are often used by outsiders to meet governmental requirements for local ownership, and allies can share distribution facilities and dealer networks, thus mutually strengthening their access to buyers. In addition, alliances affect competition; not only can alliances offset competitive disadvantages but they also can result in the allied companies directing their competitive energies more toward mutual rivals and less toward one another. Many runner-up companies, wanting to preserve their independence, have resorted to alliances rather than merger to try to close the competitive gap on leading companies.

Alliances have their pitfalls, however. Effective coordination between independent companies, each with different motives and perhaps conflicting objectives, is a challenging task requiring numerous meetings of numerous people over a period of time to iron out what is to be shared, what is to remain proprietary, and how the cooperative arrangements will work. Allies may have to overcome language and cultural barriers as well as suspicion and mistrust. After a promising start, relationships may cool, and the hoped-for benefits may never materialize. Most important, though, is the danger of depending on another company for essential expertise and capabilities over the long term. To be a serious contender, a company must ultimately develop its own capabilities in all areas important to strengthening its competitive position and building a sustainable competitive advantage. Where this is not feasible, merger is a better solution than strategic alliance. Strategic alliances are best used as a transitional way to combat competitive disadvantage in international markets; rarely if ever can they be relied on to create competitive advantage.

Strategic Intent, Profit Sanctuaries, and Cross-Subsidization

Competitors in international markets can be distinguished not only by their strategies but also by their long-term strategic objectives or strategic intent. Four types of competitors stand out:[18]

- Firms whose strategic intent is *global dominance* or, at least, high rank among the global market leaders; such firms pursue some form of global strategy.
- Firms whose primary strategic objective is *defending domestic dominance* in their home market, even though they derive some of their sales internationally (usually under 20 percent) and have operations in several or many foreign markets.

---

[17]Porter, *The Competitive Advantage of Nations*, p. 66.
[18]Prahalad and Doz, *The Multinational Mission*, p. 52.

- Firms who aspire to a growing share of worldwide sales and whose primary strategic orientation is *host-country responsiveness*; such firms have a multicountry strategy and may already derive a large portion of their revenues from foreign operations.
- *Domestic-only firms* whose strategic intent does not extend beyond building a strong competitive position in their home country market; such firms base their competitive strategies on domestic market conditions and watch events in the international market only for their impact on domestic conditions.

The four types of firms are *not* equally well positioned to succeed in markets where they compete head-on. Consider the case of a purely domestic U.S. company in competition with a Japanese company operating in many country markets and aspiring to global dominance. The Japanese company can cut its prices in the U.S. market to gain market share at the expense of the U.S. company, subsidizing any losses with profits earned in its home sanctuary and in other foreign markets. The U.S. company has no effective way to retaliate. It is vulnerable even if it is the dominant domestic company. However, if the U.S. company is a multinational competitor and operates in Japan as well as elsewhere, it can counter Japanese pricing in the United States with retaliatory price cuts in its competitor's main profit sanctuary, Japan, and in other countries where it competes against the same Japanese company.

Profit Sanctuaries and Critical Markets   *Profit sanctuaries* are country markets where a company has a strong or protected market position and derives substantial profits. Japan, for example, is a profit sanctuary for most Japanese companies because trade barriers erected by the Japanese government effectively block foreign companies from competing for a large share of Japanese sales. Protected from the threat of foreign competition in their home market, Japanese companies can safely charge somewhat higher prices to their Japanese customers and thus earn attractively large profits at home. In most cases, a company's biggest and most strategically crucial profit sanctuary is its home market, but multinational companies also have profit sanctuaries in those country markets where they have strong competitive positions, big sales volumes, and attractive profit margins.

Profit sanctuaries are valuable competitive assets in global industries. Companies with large, protected profit sanctuaries have a competitive advantage over companies that don't have a dependable sanctuary. Companies with multiple profit sanctuaries are more favorably positioned than companies with a single sanctuary. Normally, a global competitor with multiple profit sanctuaries can successfully attack and beat a domestic competitor whose only profit sanctuary is its home market.

To defend against global competitors, firms don't have to compete in all or even most foreign markets, but they do have to compete in all critical markets; *critical markets* are markets in countries

- That are the profit sanctuaries of key competitors.
- That have big sales volumes.
- That contain prestigious customers whose business it is strategically important to have.

Basic Concept
A nation becomes a company's profit sanctuary when a company, because of its strong competitive position or protective governmental trade policies, derives a substantial portion of its total profits from sales in that nation.

Competitive Strategy Principle
A global competitor with multiple profit sanctuaries can wage and generally win a competitive offensive against a domestic competitor whose only profit sanctuary is its home market.

GLOBAL STRATEGIC ALLIANCES
Successes and Failures

As the chairman of British Aerospace recently observed, a strategic alliance with a foreign company is "one of the quickest and cheapest ways to develop a global strategy." AT&T has formed joint ventures with many of the world's largest telephone and electronics companies. Boeing, the world's premier manufacturer of commercial aircraft, has partnered with Kawasaki, Mitsubishi, and Fuji to produce a long-range, wide-body jet for delivery in 1995. General Electric and Snecma, a French maker of jet engines, have a 50-50 partnership to make jet engines to power aircraft made by Boeing, McDonnell-Douglas, and Airbus Industrie (the leading European maker of commercial aircraft and a company that was formed through an alliance among aerospace companies from Britain, Spain, Germany and France); the GE–Snecma alliance was regarded as a model because not only had it been in existence for 17 years but because it had also produced orders totaling $38 billion for 10,300 engines.

During the past 10 years, hundreds of strategic alliances have been formed in the motor vehicle industry as car and truck manufacturers and automotive parts suppliers moved aggressively to get in stronger position to compete globally. Not only have there been alliances between manufacturers strong in one region of the world and manufacturers strong in another region but there have also been strategic alliances between vehicle-makers and key parts suppliers (especially those with high quality parts and strong technological capabilities).

General Motors and Toyota in 1984 formed a 50-50 partnership called New United Motor Manufacturing, Inc. (NUMMI) to produce cars for both companies at an old GM plant in Fremont, California. The strategic value of the GM–Toyota alliance was that Toyota would learn how to deal with suppliers and workers in the U.S. (as a prelude to building its own plants in the U.S.) while GM would learn about Toyota's approaches to manufacturing and management. Each company sent managers to the NUMMI plant to work for two to three years to learn and absorb all they could, then transferred their NUMMI "graduates" to jobs where they could be instrumental in helping their company apply what had been learned.

Gary Hamel, a professor at the London Business School, regards strategic alliances as a "race to learn" and gain the benefits of the partner's know-how and competitive capabilities. The partner that learns the fastest gains the most and, later, may turn such learning into a competitive edge. From this perspective, alliances become a new form of competition as well as a vehicle for globalizing company strategy. According to Hamel, Japanese managers and companies excel at learning from their allies and then exploiting the benefits. Toyota, for example, had moved quickly to capitalize on its experiences at NUMMI; by 1991 Toyota had opened two plants on its own in North America, was constructing a third plant, and was producing about 50 percent of the vehicles it sold

(continued)

- That offer exceptionally good profit margins due to weak competitive pressures.[19]

The more critical markets a company participates in, the greater its ability to use cross-subsidization as a defense against competitors intent on global dominance.

The Competitive Power of Cross-Subsidization Cross-subsidization is a powerful competitive weapon. It involves using profits earned in one or more country markets to support a competitive offensive against key rivals or to gain

---

[19]Ibid., p. 61.

ILLUSTRATION CAPSULE
14

(concluded)

in North America in its North American plants. While General Motors had incorporated much of its NUMMI learning into the management practices and manufacturing methods it was using at its newly opened Saturn plant in Tennessee, GM had moved more slowly than Toyota. American and European companies were generally regarded as less skilled than the Japanese in transferring the learning from strategic alliances into their own operations.

Consultants and business school professors who have studied company experiences with strategic alliances see four keys to making a strategic alliance work to good advantage:

- Picking a compatible partner, taking the time to build strong bridges of communication and trust, and not expecting immediate payoffs.
- Choosing an ally whose products and market strongholds *complement* rather than compete directly with the company's own products and customer base.
- Learning thoroughly and rapidly about a partner's technology and management.
- Being careful not to divulge competitively sensitive information to a partner.

Many alliances either fail or are terminated when one partner decides to acquire the other. A 1990 survey of 150 companies involved in terminated alliances found that three-fourths of the alliances had been taken over by Japanese partners. A nine-year alliance between Fujitsu and International Computers, Ltd., a British manufacturer, ended when Fujitsu acquired 80 percent of ICL. According to one observer, Fujitsu deliberately maneuvered ICL into a position of having no better choice than to sell out to its partner; Fujitsu began as a supplier of components for ICL's mainframe computers, then expanded its role over the next nine years to the point where it was ICL's only source of new technology. When ICL's parent, a large British electronics firm, saw the mainframe computer business starting to decline and decided to sell, Fujitsu was the only buyer it could find.

There are several reasons why strategic alliances fail. Often, once the bloom is off the initial getting-together period, partners discover they have deep differences of opinion about how to proceed and conflicting objectives and strategies, such that tensions soon build up and cooperative working relationships never emerge. Another is the difficulty of collaborating effectively in competitively sensitive areas, thus raising questions about mutual trust and forthright exchanges of information and expertise. Perhaps the biggest reason is a clash of egos and company cultures—the key people upon whom success or failure depend turn out to be incompatible and incapable of working closely together on a partnership basis. On occasions, partners become suspicious about each other's motives and sometimes they are unwilling to share control and do things on the basis of consensus.

Source: Jeremy Main, "Making Global Alliances Work," *Fortune*, December 17, 1990, pp. 121–26.

increased penetration of a critical market. Typically, a firm may match (or nearly match) rivals on product quality and service, then charge a low enough price to draw customers away from rivals. While price-cutting may entail lower profits (or even losses), the challenger still realizes acceptable overall profits when the above-average earnings from its profit sanctuaries are added in.

Cross-subsidization is most powerful when a global firm with multiple profit sanctuaries is aggressively intent on achieving global market dominance over the long term. A domestic-only competitor and a multicountry competitor with no strategic coordination between its locally responsive country strategies are both vulnerable to competition from rivals intent on global

**Competitive Strategy
Principle**
*To defend against
aggressive international
competitors intent on
global dominance, a
domestic-only competitor
usually has to abandon its
domestic focus, become a
multinational competitor,
and craft a multinational
competitive strategy.*

dominance. A global strategy can defeat a domestic-only strategy because a one-country competitor cannot effectively defend its market share over the long term against a global competitor with cross-subsidization capability. The global company can use lower prices to siphon the domestic company's customers, all the while gaining market share, building market strength, and covering losses with profits earned in its other critical markets. When attacked in this manner, a domestic company's best short-term hope is to seek government protection in the form of tariff barriers, import quotas, and antidumping penalties. In the long term, the domestic company must find ways to compete on a more equal footing—a difficult task when it must charge a price to cover average costs while the global competitor can charge a price only high enough to cover the incremental costs of selling in the domestic company's profit sanctuary. The best long-term strategic defenses for a domestic company are to enter into strategic alliances with foreign firms or adopt a global strategy and compete on an international scale. Competing only domestically is a perilous strategy in an industry populated with global competitors.

While a firm with a multicountry strategy has some cross-subsidy defense against a firm with a global strategy, it lacks competitive advantage and usually faces cost disadvantages. A global competitor with a big manufacturing share and state-of-the-art plants is typically a lower-cost producer than a multicountry strategist with many small plants and short production runs turning out specialized products country-by-country. Companies pursuing a multicountry strategy thus have to develop focusing and differentiation advantages keyed to local responsiveness to defend against a global competitor. Such a defense is adequate in industries with significant enough national differences to impede use of a global strategy. But if an international rival can accommodate necessary local needs within a global strategy and still retain a cost edge, then a global strategy can defeat a multicountry strategy. Illustration Capsule 15, which discusses how Nestlé became the world's number one food company, shows the power of a global strategy in today's markets.

STRATEGIES FOR INDUSTRY LEADERS

The competitive positions of industry leaders normally range from stronger than average to powerful. Leaders typically enjoy a well-known reputation, and strongly entrenched leaders have proven strategies (keyed either to low-cost leadership or differentiation). Some of the best-known industry leaders are Anheuser-Busch (beer), IBM (computers), McDonald's (fast food), Gillette (razor blades), Campbell Soup (canned soups), Gerber (baby food), AT&T (long-distance telephone service), and Levi Strauss (jeans). The main strategic concern for a leader revolves around how to sustain a leadership position, perhaps becoming the dominant leader as opposed to a leader. However, pursuit of industry leadership and large market share per se is primarily important because of the competitive advantage and profitability that accrues to leadership.

Three contrasting strategic postures are open to industry leaders and dominant firms:[20]

---

[20]Kotler, *Marketing Management*, chap. 23; Porter, *Competitive Advantage*, chap. 14; and Ian C. MacMillan, "Seizing Competitive Initiative," *The Journal of Business Strategy* 2, no. 4 (Spring 1982), pp. 43–57.

1. **Stay-on-the-offensive strategy**—This strategy rests on the principle that the best defense is a good offense. Offensive-minded leaders try to be "first-movers" to build a sustainable competitive advantage and a solid reputation as *the* leader. The key to staying on the offensive is relentless pursuit of continuous improvement and innovation. Striving to become *the* source of new products, better performance features, quality enhancements, improved customer services, and ways to cut production costs not only helps a leader avoid complacency but it also keeps rivals on the defensive and scrambling to keep up. The array of offensive options also includes initiatives to expand overall industry demand—discovering new uses for the product, attracting new users, and promoting more frequent use. In addition, a clever offensive leader stays alert for ways to make it easier and less costly for potential customers to switch their purchases from runner-up firms over to its own products. Unless a leader's market share is already so dominant that it presents a threat of antitrust action (a market share under 60 percent is usually "safe"), then a stay-on-the-offensive strategy involves trying to grow *faster* than the industry as a whole and wrest market share from rivals. A leader whose growth does not equal or outpace the industry average is losing ground to competitors.

2. **Fortify and defend strategy**—The essence of "fortify and defend" is to make it harder for new firms to enter and for challengers to gain ground. The goals of a strong defense are to hold onto present market share, strengthen current market position, and protect whatever competitive advantage the firm has. Specific defensive actions can include:

    *   Attempting to raise the competitive ante for challengers and new entrants via increased spending for advertising, customer service, and R&D.
    *   Introducing more of the company's own brands to match the product attributes challenger brands have or could employ.
    *   Figuring out ways to make it harder or more costly for customers to switch to rival products.
    *   Broadening the product line to close off possible vacant niches for competitors to slip into.
    *   Keeping prices reasonable and quality attractive.
    *   Building new capacity ahead of market demand to try to block the market expansion potential of smaller competitors.
    *   Investing enough to remain cost competitive and technologically progressive.
    *   Patenting alternative technologies.
    *   Signing exclusive contracts with the best suppliers and dealer/distributors.

    A fortify-and-defend strategy best suits firms that have already achieved industry dominance and don't wish to risk antitrust action. It is also well-suited to situations where a firm wishes to milk its present position for profits and cash flow because the industry's prospects for growth are low or because further gains in market share do not appear profitable enough to go after. But the fortify-and-defend theme always

Industry leaders can strengthen their long-term competitive positions with strategies keyed to aggressive offense, aggressive defense, or muscling smaller rivals into a follow-the-leader role.

NESTLÉ'S GLOBAL STRATEGY IN FOODS

Once a stodgy Swiss manufacturer of chocolate, Nestlé became one of the first multinational companies and then embarked on a global strategy during the 1980s. The themes of the Nestlé strategy were: acquire a wider lineup of name brands, achieve the economies of worldwide distribution and marketing, accept short-term losses to build a more profitable market share over the long term, and adapt products to local cultures when needed. In 1991 Nestlé ranked as the world's largest food company with over $33 billion in revenues, market penetration on all major continents, and plants in over 60 countries (see table below).

The Nestlé strategy was a response to two driving forces affecting the food industry in more and more nations around the globe: (1) changing consumer demographics, tastes, and cooking habits; and (2) the new cost-volume economics of increasingly "high-tech" food products like gourmet dinners, refrigerated foods, packaged mixes, and even coffee. In both industrialized and developing nations, the 1980s were characterized by growing numbers of relatively affluent single professionals and two-income couples with more cosmopolitan food tastes and less price-sensitive grocery budgets. Moreover, microwave ovens were fast becoming a standard household item, a development that not only affected weeknight and weekend food preparation methods but also changed the kinds of at-home food products people were buying. Products that appealed to this segment had tremendous growth potential. However, bringing such items to market was quickly turned into a high-risk, capital-intensive, R&D-oriented business that required millions of dollars of up-front capital for new product development and market testing, and millions more for advertising and promotional support to win shelf space in grocery chains. To get maximum mileage out of such investments, make up for the cost of product failures, and keep retail prices affordable began to take a larger and larger volume of sales, often more than could be generated from a single national market.

Nestlé management grasped early on that these driving forces would act to globalize the food industry and that companies with worldwide distribution capability, strong brand names, and the flexibility to adapt versions of the basic product to local tastes would gain significant competitive ad-

Continent	1990 Sales	Major Products
Europe	$16.3 billion	Nescafé instant coffee, Vittel mineral water, Chambourcy yogurt, Findus and Lean Cuisine frozen foods, Herta cold cuts, Sundy cereal bars, chocolate candy, Buitoni pasta
North America	$ 8.3 billion	Nescafé instant coffee, Carnation CoffeeMate, Friskies pet foods, Stouffer frozen foods, Nestlé Crunch chocolate bars, Hills Bros. coffee
Asia	$ 3.6 billion	Nescafé instant coffee, Nido powdered milk, Maggi chili powder, infant cereals, and formulas
Latin America	$ 3.6 billion	Nescafé instant coffee, Nido powdered milk, infant cereal, Milo malt-flavored beverages
Africa	$ 1.0 billion	Nescafé instant coffee, Maggi bouillon cubes, Nespray powdered milk, Nestlé chocolates, Milo malt-flavored beverages
Oceania (Australia, New Zealand)	$ 0.9 billion	Nescafé instant coffee, Findus frozen foods, Lean Cuisine frozen foods

(continued)

ILLUSTRATION CAPSULE

(concluded)

product to local tastes would gain significant competitive advantages. A series of acquisitions gave Nestlé a strong lineup of brands, some important new food products to push through its distribution channels, and a bigger presence in some key country markets. In 1985 Nestlé bought Carnation (Pet evaporated milk, Friskies pet foods, and CoffeeMate nondairy creamer) and Hills Bros. coffee (the number three coffee brand in the United States) to strengthen its North American presence. In 1988, Nestlé acquired Rountree, a British chocolate company whose leading candy bar is Kit Kat, and Buitoni, an Italian pastamaker. Shortly after the Rountree acquisition, Nestlé management shifted worldwide responsibility for mapping chocolate strategy and developing new candy products from Nestlé headquarters in Vevey, Switzerland, to Rountree's headquarters in York, England. Nestlé management believed this decentralization put the company's candy business in the hands of people "who think about chocolate 24 hours a day." As of 1989, almost everything Nestlé sold involved food products, and the company was the world's largest producer of coffee, powdered milk, candy, and frozen dinners.

The star performer in Nestlé's lineup was coffee, with 1990 sales of $5.2 billion and operating profits of $600 million. Nestlé's Nescafé brand was the leader in virtually every national market except the United States (Philip Morris's Maxwell House brand was the U.S. leader, but Nescafé was number two and Hills Bros., purchased by Nestlé in 1985, was number three). Nestlé produced 200 types of instant coffee, from lighter blends for the U.S. market to dark espressos for Latin America. Four coffee research labs spent a combined $50 million annually to experiment with new blends in aroma, flavor, and color. Although instant coffee sales were declining worldwide due to the comeback of new-style automatic coffeemakers, they were rising in two tea-drinking countries, Britain and Japan. As the cultural shift from tea to coffee took hold during the

1970s in Britain, Nestlé pushed its Nescafé brand hard, coming out with a market share of about 50 percent. In Japan, Nescafé was considered a luxury item; the company made it available in fancy containers suitable for gift-giving.

Another star performer has been the company's Lean Cuisine line of low-calorie frozen dinners produced by Stouffer, a company Nestlé acquired in the 1970s. Introduced in 1981 in the United States, the Lean Cuisine line has boosted Stouffer's U.S. market share in frozen dinners to 38 percent. To follow up on its U.S. success, Nestlé introduced Lean Cuisine into the British market. At the time, Nestlé products in British supermarkets were mostly low-margin items, from fish sticks to frozen hamburger patties. British managers proposed a bold upgrading to a line of more expensive, high-margin items led by Lean Cuisine. Nestlé headquarters endorsed the plan and indicated a willingness to absorb four years of losses to build market share and make Lean Cuisine a transatlantic hit. The Lean Cuisine line was introduced in Britain in 1985. By 1988 the Lean Cuisine line in Britain included 12 entrées tailored to British tastes, from cod with wine sauce to Kashmiri chicken curry. By 1989 Nestlé had a 33 percent share of the British market for frozen dinners. Sales exceeded $100 million in 1990, putting the Lean Cuisine brand into the black in Britain for the first time since its introduction to the British market. Lean Cuisine has recently been introduced in France.

Western Europe is Nestlé's top target for the early 1990s. The 1992 shift to free trade among the 12 member countries in the European Community will sweep away trade barriers which, according to a recent study, cost food companies over $1 billion in added distribution and marketing costs. With market unification in the 12-country EC, Nestlé sees major opportunities to gain wider distribution of its products, achieve economies, and exploit its skills in transferring products and marketing methods from one country and culture to another.

Source: The information in this capsule was drawn from Shawn Tully, "Nestlé Shows How to Gobble Markets," *Fortune*, January 16, 1989, pp. 74–78 and Nestlé's 1990 annual report.

entails trying to grow as fast as the market as a whole (to stave off market share slippage) and reinvesting enough capital in the business to protect the leader's ability to compete.

3. **Follow-the-leader strategy**—The objective of this strategy is to enforce an unwritten tradition that smaller firms follow the industry leader in adjusting prices up or down and otherwise don't try to rock the boat. Assuming the role of industry policeman gives a leader added strategic flexibility and makes it risky for runner-up firms to mount an offensive attack on the leader's position. In effect, the leader uses its competitive muscle to thwart and discourage would-be challengers. The leader signals smaller rivals that any moves to cut into the leader's business will meet with strong retaliation. Specific "hardball" policing actions include quickly meeting all price cuts (with even larger cuts if necessary), countering with large-scale promotional campaigns when challengers make threatening moves to gain market share, and offering better deals to the major customers of next-in-line or "maverick" firms. Other measures that a leader can use to bully aggressive small rivals into playing follow-the-leader include pressuring distributors not to carry rivals' products, having salespeople bad-mouth the aggressor's products, and trying to hire away the better executives of firms that "get out of line."

STRATEGIES FOR RUNNER-UP FIRMS

Runner-up firms occupy weaker market positions than the industry leader(s). Some runner-ups play the role of *market challengers*, favoring offensive strategies to gain market share and a stronger market position. Others behave as *content followers*, willing to coast along in their current positions because profits are still adequate. Follower firms have no urgent strategic issue to confront beyond that of "What kinds of strategic changes are the leaders initiating and what do we need to do to follow?"

Competitive Strategy Principle

Rarely can a runner-up firm successfully challenge an industry leader with an imitative strategy.

A challenger firm interested in improving its market standing needs a strategy aimed at building a competitive advantage of its own. *Rarely can a runner-up improve its competitive position by imitating the leading firm. A cardinal rule in offensive strategy is to avoid attacking a leader head-on with an imitative strategy, regardless of the resources and staying power an underdog may have.*[21] Moreover, if a challenger has a 5 percent market share and needs a 20 percent share to earn attractive returns, it needs a more creative approach to competing than just "try harder."

In cases where large size yields significantly lower unit costs and gives large-share firms an important cost advantage, small-share firms have only two viable strategic options: increase their market share or withdraw from the business (gradually or quickly). The competitive strategies most used to build market share are based on (1) becoming a lower-cost producer and using lower price to win customers from weak, higher-cost rivals and (2) using differentiation strategies based on quality, technological superiority, better customer service, best-cost, or innovation. Achieving low-cost leadership is usually

---

[21]Porter, *Competitive Advantage*, p. 514.

open to an underdog only when one of the market leaders is not already solidly positioned as the industry's low-cost producer. But a small-share firm may still be able to reduce its cost disadvantage by merging with or acquiring smaller firms; the combined market shares may provide the needed access to size-related economies. Other options include revamping the activity-cost chain to produce cost savings and finding ways to better control cost drivers.

In situations where scale economies or experience curve effects are small and a large market share produces no cost advantage, runner-up companies have more strategic flexibility and can consider any of the following six approaches:[22]

1. **Vacant niche strategy**—This version of a focus strategy involves concentrating on customer or end-use applications that major firms have bypassed or neglected. An "ideal" vacant niche is of sufficient size and scope to be profitable, has some growth potential, is well-suited to a firm's own capabilities and skills, and is outside the interest of leading firms. For example, regional commuter airlines serve cities with too few passengers to attract the interest of major airlines, and health food producers (like Health Valley, Hain, and Tree of Life) supply the growing number of local health food stores—a market segment traditionally ignored by Pillsbury, Kraft General Foods, Heinz, Nabisco, Campbell Soup, and other leading food products firms.

2. **Specialist strategy**—A specialist firm trains its competitive effort on one market segment: a single product, a particular end-use, or a special customer group. The aim is to build competitive advantage through product uniqueness, expertise in special-purpose products, or specialized customer services. Smaller companies that have successfully used a specialist type of focus strategy include Formby's (a specialist in stains and finishes for wood furniture, especially refinishing), Liquid Paper Co. (a leader in correction fluid for typists), Canada Dry (known for its ginger ale, tonic water, and carbonated soda water), and American Tobacco (a leader in chewing tobacco and snuff).

3. **"Ours-is-better-than-theirs strategy"**—This approach uses a combination focus-differentiation strategy keyed to product quality. Sales and marketing efforts focus on quality-conscious and performance-oriented buyers. Fine craftsmanship, prestige quality, frequent product innovations, and/or close contact with customers to develop a better product usually undergird this "superior product" type of approach. Some examples include Beefeater and Tanqueray in gin, Tiffany in diamonds and jewelry, Baccarat in fine crystal, Mazola in cooking oil and margarine, Bally in shoes, and Pennzoil in motor oil.

4. **Content follower strategy**—Follower firms deliberately refrain from initiating trend-setting strategic moves and from aggressive attempts to steal customers away from leaders. Followers prefer approaches that will not provoke competitive retaliation, often opting for focus and

---

[22]For more details, see Kotler, *Marketing Management*, pp. 397-412; R. G. Hamermesh, M. J. Anderson, Jr., and J. E. Harris, "Strategies for Low Market Share Businesses," *Harvard Business Review* 56, no. 3 (May–June 1978), pp. 95–102; and Porter, *Competitive Advantage*, chap. 15.

differentiation strategies that keep them out of the leaders' paths. They react and respond rather than initiate and attack. They prefer defense to offense. And they rarely get out of line with the leaders on price. Burroughs (in computers) and Union Camp (in paper products) have been successful market followers by consciously concentrating on selected product uses and applications for specific customer groups, focused R&D, profits rather than market share, and cautious but efficient management.

5. **Growth via acquisition strategy**—One way to strengthen a company's position is to merge with or acquire weaker rivals to form an enterprise that has more competitive strength and a larger share of the market. Commercial airline companies such as Northwest, US Air, and Delta owe their market share growth during the past decade to acquisition of smaller regional airlines. Likewise, public accounting firms have enhanced their national and international coverage by merging or forming alliances with smaller CPA firms at home and abroad.

6. **Distinctive image strategy**—Some runner-up companies try to stand out from competitors. They use a variety of strategic approaches: creating a reputation for the lowest prices, providing prestige quality at a good price, giving superior customer service, designing unique product attributes, being a leader in new product introduction, or devising unusually creative advertising. Examples include Dr Pepper's strategy of calling attention to its distinctive taste, Apple Computer's approach to making it easier and interesting for people to use a personal computer, and Honda's emphasis on the quality and dependability of its cars.

In industries where big size is definitely a key success factor, firms with low market shares have some obstacles to overcome: (1) less access to economies of scale in manufacturing, distribution, or sales promotion; (2) difficulty in gaining customer recognition; (3) an inability to afford mass media advertising on a grand scale; and (4) difficulty in funding capital requirements.[23] But *it is erroneous to view runner-up firms as inherently less profitable or unable to hold their own against the biggest firms.* Many firms with small market shares earn healthy profits and enjoy good reputations with customers. Often, the handicaps of smaller size can be surmounted and a profitable competitive position established by: (1) focusing on a few market segments where the company's strengths can yield a competitive edge; (2) developing technical expertise that will be highly valued by customers; (3) aggressively pursuing the development of new products for customers in the target market segments; and (4) using innovative, "dare-to-be different," "beat-the-odds" entrepreneurial approaches to outmanage stodgy, slow-to-change market leaders. Runner-up companies have a golden opportunity to gain market share if they make a leapfrog technological breakthrough, if the leaders stumble or become complacent, or if they have patience to nibble away at the leaders and build up their customer base over a long period of time.

---

[23]Hamermesh, Anderson, and Harris, "Strategies for Low Market Share Businesses," p. 102.

STRATEGIES FOR WEAK BUSINESSES

A firm in an also-ran or declining competitive position has four basic strategic options. If it has the financial resources, it can launch a modest *strategic offensive* keyed either to low-cost production or "new" differentiation themes, pouring enough money and talent into the effort to move up a notch or two in the industry rankings. It can pursue *aggressive defense*, using variations of the present strategy and fighting hard to keep sales, market share, profitability, and competitive position at current levels. It can opt for an *immediate abandonment* strategy and get out of the business, either by selling out to another firm or by closing down operations if a buyer cannot be found. Or it can employ a *harvest strategy*, keeping reinvestment to a bare-bones minimum and maximizing short-term cash flows in preparation for an orderly exit. The gist of the first three options is self-explanatory. The fourth merits more discussion.

A *harvest strategy* steers a middle course between preserving the status quo and exiting as soon as possible. Harvesting is a phasing down or endgame strategy where the game plan is to sacrifice market position any time short-term financial benefits can be realized. The overriding financial objective is to reap the greatest possible cash harvest to deploy to other business endeavors.

Harvesting actions are fairly standard. Firms cut their operating budgets to rock-bottom and pursue stringent internal cost control. Capital investment in new equipment is minimal or nonexistent depending on the current condition of fixed assets and whether the harvest is to be fast or slow. Firms may gradually raise prices and cut promotional expenses, reduce quality in not so visible ways, curtail nonessential customer services, decrease equipment maintenance, and the like. They understand that sales will shrink, but if they cut costs proportionately, profits will erode slowly.

Professor Kotler has suggested seven indicators of when a business should be harvested:[24]

1. When the industry's long-term prospects are unattractive.
2. When building up the business would be too costly or not profitable enough.
3. When the firm's market share is becoming increasingly costly to maintain or defend.
4. When reduced levels of competitive effort will not trigger an immediate falloff in sales.
5. When the enterprise can redeploy the freed resources in higher opportunity areas.
6. When the business is *not* a major component in a diversified corporation's portfolio of existing businesses.
7. When the business does not contribute other desired features (sales stability, prestige, a well-rounded product line) to a company's overall business portfolio.

The more of these seven conditions present, the more ideal the business is for harvesting.

> *A competitively weak company can wage a modest offensive to improve its position, defend its present position, be acquired by another company, or employ a harvest strategy.*

---

[24]Phillip Kotler, "Harvesting Strategies for Weak Products," *Business Horizons* 21, no. 5 (August 1978), pp. 17–18.

Harvesting strategies make the most sense for diversified companies that have business units with respectable market shares in unattractive industries. In such situations, cash flows from harvesting unattractive business units can be reallocated to business units with greater profit potential in more attractive industries.

Crisis Turnarounds

Turnaround strategies are used when a business worth rescuing goes into crisis; the objective is to arrest and reverse the sources of competitive and financial weakness as quickly as possible. The first task is to diagnose the problem: What is causing the poor performance? Is it bad competitive strategy or poor implementation and execution of an otherwise workable strategy? Are the causes of distress beyond management control? Can the business be saved? To formulate a turnaround strategy, managers must find the problem and determine how serious it is.

Successful turnaround strategies depend on accurate diagnosis of a distressed company's situation and decisive action to resolve its problems.

Some of the most common causes of business trouble are: overly aggressive efforts to "buy" market share with profit-depressing price-cuts, heavy fixed costs due to underutilized plant capacity, ineffective R&D efforts, reliance on technological long-shots, inability to penetrate new markets, frequent changes in strategy (because the previous strategy didn't work out), and being overpowered by the competitive advantages of more successful rivals. There are five ways to pursue business turnaround:[25]

- Revise the existing strategy.
- Launch efforts to boost revenues.
- Pursue cost reduction.
- Sell off assets to raise cash to save the remaining part of the business.
- Use a combination of these efforts.

Strategy Revision   When weak performance is caused by "bad" strategy, the task of strategy overhaul can proceed along any of several paths: (1) shifting to a new competitive approach to rebuild the firm's market position, (2) overhauling internal operations and functional area strategies to better support the same overall business strategy, (3) merging with another firm in the industry and forging a new strategy keyed to the newly merged firm's strengths, and (4) retrenching into a reduced core of products and customers more closely matched to the firm's strengths. The most appealing path depends on prevailing industry conditions, the firm's particular strengths and weaknesses, and the severity of the crisis. "Situation analysis" of the industry, major competitors, the firm's own competitive position, and its skills and resources are prerequisites to action. As a rule, successful strategy revision must be tied directly to the ailing firm's strengths and near-term competitive capabilities and must focus narrowly on its best market opportunities.

---

[25]For excellent discussions of the ins and outs of rescuing distressed firms, see Charles W. Hofer, "Turnaround Strategies," *Journal of Business Strategy* 1, no. 1 (Summer 1980), pp. 19–31; Donald F. Heany, "Businesses in Profit Trouble," *Journal of Business Strategy* 5, no. 4 (Spring 1985), pp. 4–13; and Eugene F. Finkin, "Company Turnaround," *Journal of Business Strategy* 5, no. 4 (Spring 1985), pp. 14–25.

Boosting Revenues Revenue-increasing turnaround efforts aim at generating increased sales volume. There are a number of revenue-building options: price-cuts, increased promotion, a bigger sales force, added customer services, and quickly achieved product improvements. Attempts to increase revenues and sales volumes are necessary (1) when there is little or no room in the operating budget to cut expenses and still break even and (2) when the key to restoring profitability is increased utilization of existing capacity. In rare situations where buyer demand is not price sensitive, the quickest way to boost short-term revenues may be to raise prices rather than opt for volume-building price cuts.

Cutting Costs Cost-reducing turnaround strategies work best when an ailing firm's cost structure is flexible enough to permit radical surgery, when operating inefficiencies are identifiable and readily correctable, and when the firm is relatively close to its break-even point. To complement a general belt-tightening, firms need to emphasize budgeting and cost control, eliminate jobs and stop hiring, modernize existing plant and equipment to gain greater productivity, and delay nonessential capital expenditures.

Selling Off Assets Asset reduction/retrenchment strategies are essential when cash flow is a critical consideration and when the most practical way to generate cash is (1) through sale of some of the firm's assets (plant and equipment, land, patents, inventories, or profitable subsidiaries) and (2) through retrenchment (pruning marginal products from the product line, closing or selling older plants, reducing the work force, withdrawing from outlying markets, cutting back customer service, and the like). Sometimes firms sell their assets not so much to unload losing operations and stem cash drains as to raise funds to save and strengthen their remaining activities.

Combination Efforts Combination turnaround strategies are usually essential in grim situations that require fast action on a broad front. Likewise, combination actions frequently come into play when a firm brings in new managers and gives them a free hand to make changes. The tougher the problems, the more likely the solutions will involve multiple strategic initiatives.

Turnaround efforts tend to be high-risk undertakings and often fail. A landmark study of 64 companies found no successful turnarounds among the most troubled companies in eight basic industries.[26] Many waited too long to begin a turnaround. Others found themselves short of both cash and entrepreneurial talent to compete in a slow-growth industry characterized by fierce battles for market share; better positioned rivals simply proved too strong to defeat.

THIRTEEN COMMANDMENTS FOR CRAFTING SUCCESSFUL BUSINESS STRATEGIES

Business experiences over the years prove over and over that disastrous courses of action can be avoided by adhering to certain strategy-making principles. The wisdom of these past experiences can be distilled into 13

---

[26]William K. Hall, "Survival Strategies in a Hostile Environment," *Harvard Business Review* 58, no. 5 (September–October 1980), pp. 75–85.

commandments which, if faithfully observed, help strategists craft better strategic action plans.

1. *Always put top priority on crafting and executing strategic moves that enhance the company's competitive position for the long term and that serve to establish it as an industry leader.* In competitive markets, a strongly entrenched leadership position pays off year after year, but the glory of meeting one year's financial targets quickly passes. Shareholders are never well-served by managers who let short-term financial considerations override strategic initiatives that will bolster the company's long-term competitive position and strength.

2. *Understand that a clear, consistent competitive strategy, when well-crafted and well-executed, builds reputation and recognizable industry position; a strategy aimed solely at capturing momentary market opportunities yields fleeting benefits.* The pursuit of short-run financial opportunism without long-term strategic guidance tends to produce the worst kind of profits: one-shot rewards that are unrepeatable. Over the long haul, a company that has a well-conceived competitive strategy aimed at securing a strong market position will outperform and defeat a rival whose strategic decisions are driven by short-term financial expectations. In an ongoing enterprise, the game of competition ought to be played for the long term, not the short term.

3. *Try not to get "stuck back in the pack" with no coherent long-term strategy or distinctive competitive position, an "average" image, and little prospect of climbing into the ranks of the industry leaders.*

4. *Invest in creating a sustainable competitive advantage—it is the single most dependable contributor to above-average profitability.*

5. *Play aggressive offense to build competitive advantage and aggressive defense to protect it.*

6. *Avoid strategies capable of succeeding only in the best of circumstances—* competitors will react with countermeasures and market conditions are not always favorable.

7. *Be cautious in pursuing a rigidly prescribed or inflexible strategy—changing market conditions may render it quickly obsolete.* Any strategy, to perform satisfactorily, must be adaptable to fresh market circumstances. Strategic themes involving "top" quality or "lowest" cost should be interpreted as *relative to competitors* and/or *customer needs* rather than based on arbitrary management standards.

8. *Don't underestimate the reactions and the commitment of rivals—especially* when they are pushed into a corner and their well-being is threatened.

9. *Be wary of attacking strong, resourceful rivals without solid competitive advantage and ample financial strength.*

10. *Consider that attacking competitive weakness is usually more profitable than attacking competitive strength.*

11. *Take care not to cut prices without an established cost advantage—only a low-cost producer can win at price-cutting over the long term.*

12. *Be aware that aggressive moves to wrest market share away from rivals often provoke aggressive retaliation in the form of a marketing "arms race" and/or*

price wars—to the detriment of everyone's profits. Aggressive moves to capture a bigger market share invite cutthroat competition particularly when the market is plagued with high inventories and excess production capacity.

13. *Employ bold strategic moves in pursuing differentiation strategies to open up meaningful gaps in quality, service, or performance features.* Tiny differences between rivals' competitive strategies and product offerings may not be visible or important to buyers.

KEY POINTS

Successful strategies fit a firm's *external* situation (industry and competitive conditions) and *internal* situation (strengths, weaknesses, opportunities, and threats). Table 6–2 provides a summary checklist of the most important situational considerations and strategic options. To match strategy to the situation, analysts must start with an overview of the industry environment and the firm's competitive standing in the industry (columns 1 and 2 in Table 6–2):

1. What type of industry environment does the company operate in (emerging, rapid growth, mature, fragmented, global, commodity product)? What strategic options and strategic postures are best suited for this environment?

2. What position does the firm have in the industry (strong vs. weak vs. crisis-ridden; leader vs. runner-up vs. also-ran)? How does the firm's standing influence its strategic options given the stage of the industry's development—in particular, which options have to be ruled out?

Next, strategists need to factor in the primary external and internal situational consideratons (column 3) and decide how all the factors add up. This should narrow the firm's basic market share and investment options (column 4) and strategic options (column 5).

The final step is to custom-tailor the chosen generic strategic approaches (columns 4 and 5) to fit *both* the industry environment and the firm's standing vis-à-vis competitors. Here it is important to be sure that (1) the customized aspects of the proposed strategy are well-matched to the firm's skills and capabilities and (2) the strategy addresses all strategic issues the firm confronts.

In screening out weak strategies and weighing the pros and cons of the most attractive ones, the answers to the following questions often indicate the way to go:

- What kind of competitive edge can the company realistically hope to have, and what strategic moves/approaches will it take to secure this edge?
- Does the company have the skills and resources to succeed in these moves and approaches—if not, can they be acquired?
- Once built, how can the competitive advantage be protected? What defensive strategies need to be employed? Will rivals counterattack? What will it take to blunt their efforts?
- Are any rivals particularly vulnerable? Should the firm mount an offensive to capitalize on these vulnerabilities? What offensive moves need to be employed?

Matching Strategy to the Situation *(A checklist of optional strategies and generic situations)*

Industry Environments	Company Positions/Situations	Situational Considerations	Market Share and Investment Options	Strategy Options

• Young, emerging industry
• Rapid growth
• Consolidating to a smaller group of competitors
• Mature/slow growth
• Aging/declining
• Fragmented
• International/global
• Commodity product orientation
• High technology/rapid changes
	• Dominant leader
	  – Global
	  – National
	  – Regional
	  – Local
	• Leader
	• Aggressive challenger
	• Content follower
	• Weak/distressed candidate for turn-around or exit
	• "Stuck in the middle"/no clear strategy or market image
		• External
		  – Driving forces
		  – Competitive pressures
		  – Anticipated moves of key rivals
		  – Key success factors
		  – Industry attractiveness
		• Internal
		  – Current company performance
		  – Strengths and weaknesses
		  – Opportunities and threats
		  – Cost position
		  – Competitive strength
		  – Strategic issues and problems
			• Growth and build
			  – Capture a bigger market share by growing faster than industry as a whole
			  – Invest heavily to capture growth potential
			• Fortify and defend
			  – Protect market share; grow at least as fast as whole industry
			  – Invest enough resources to maintain competitive strength and market position
			• Retrench and retreat
			  – Surrender weakly held positions when forced to, but fight hard to defend core markets/customer base
			  – Maximize short-term cash flow
			  – Minimize reinvestment of capital in the business
			• Overhaul and reposition
			  – Try to turn around
			• Abandon/liquidate
			  – Sell out
			  – Close down
				• Competitive approach
				  – Overall low-cost leadership
				  – Differentiation
				  – Focus/specialization
				• Offensive initiatives
				  – Attack
				  – End run
				  – Guerrilla warfare
				  – Preemptive strikes
				• Defensive initiatives
				  – Fortify/protect
				  – Retaliatory
				  – Harvest
				• International initiatives
				  – Licensing
				  – Export
				  – Multicountry
				  – Global
				• Vertical integration initiatives
				  – Forward
				  – Backward

T A B L E 6–3 Sample Format for a Strategic Action Plan

1. Basic long-term direction and mission

2. Key strategic and financial objectives

3. Overall business strategy

4. Specific functional strategies
   • Production
   • Marketing/sales
   • Finance
   • Personnel/human resources
   • Other

5. Recommended actions

- What additional strategic moves are needed to deal with driving forces into the industry, specific threats and weaknesses, and any other issues/problems unique to the firm?

As the choice of strategic initiatives is developed, there are several pitfalls to watch for:

- Designing an overly ambitious strategic plan—one that calls for a lot of different strategic moves and/or that overtaxes the company's resources and capabilities.
- Selecting a strategy that represents a radical departure from or abandonment of the cornerstones of the company's prior success—a radical strategy change need not be rejected automatically, but it should be pursued only after careful risk assessment.
- Choosing a strategy that goes against the grain of the organization's culture or that conflicts with the values and philosophies of senior executives.

Table 6–3 provides a format for presenting a strategic action plan for a single-business enterprise.

SUGGESTED READINGS

Bleeke, Joel A. "Strategic Choices for Newly Opened Markets." *Harvard Business Review* 68, no. 5 (September–October 1990), pp. 158–65.

Bolt, James F. "Global Competitors: Some Criteria for Success." *Business Horizons* 31, no. 1 (January–February 1988), pp. 34–41.

Carroll, Glenn R. "The Specialist Strategy." In *Strategy and Organization: A West Coast Perspective*, ed. Glenn Carroll and David Vogel. Boston: Pitman Publishing, 1984, pp. 117–28.

Feldman, Lawrence P., and Albert L. Page. "Harvesting: The Misunderstood Market Exit Strategy." *Journal of Business Strategy* 5, no. 4 (Spring 1985), pp. 79–85.

Finkin, Eugene F. "Company Turnaround." *Journal of Business Strategy* 5, no. 4 (Spring 1985), pp. 14–25.

Hall, William K. "Survival Strategies in a Hostile Environment." *Harvard Business Review* 58, no. 5 (September–October 1980), pp. 75–85.

Hamermesh, R. G., and S. B. Silk. "How to Compete in Stagnant Industries." *Harvard Business Review* 57, no. 5 (September–October 1979), pp. 161–68.

Harrigan, Kathryn R. *Strategic Flexibility*. Lexington, Mass.: Lexington Books, 1985, chaps. 6 and 8.

Heany, Donald F. "Businesses in Profit Trouble." *Journal of Business Strategy* 5, no. 4 (Spring 1985), pp. 4–13.

Hofer, Charles W. "Turnaround Strategies." *Journal of Business Strategy* 1, no. 1 (Summer 1980), pp. 19–31.

Hout, Thomas, Michael E. Porter, and Eileen Rudden. "How Global Companies Win Out." *Harvard Business Review* 60, no. 5 (September–October 1982), pp. 98–108.

Kotler, Philip. *Marketing Management: Analysis, Planning, Control,* 5th ed. Englewood Cliffs, N.J.: Prentice Hall, 1984, chap. 11.

Lei, David. "Strategies for Global Competition." *Long Range Planning* 22, no. 1 (February 1989), pp. 102–9.

Mayer, Robert J. "Winning Strategies for Manufacturers in Mature Industries." *Journal of Business Strategy* 8, no. 2 (Fall 1987), pp. 23–31.

Ohmae, Kenichi. "The Global Logic of Strategic Alliances." *Harvard Business Review* 67, no. 2 (March–April 1989), pp. 143–54.

Porter, Michael E. *Competitive Strategy: Techniques for Analyzing Industries and Competitors.* New York: Free Press, 1980, chaps. 9–13.

Porter, Michael E. *The Competitive Advantage of Nations.* New York: Free Press, 1990, chap. 2.

Sugiura, Hideo, "How Honda Localizes Its Global Strategy." *Sloan Management Review* 33 (Fall 1990), pp. 77–82.

Thompson, Arthur A. "Strategies for Staying Cost Competitive." *Harvard Business Review* 62, no. 1 (January–February 1984), pp. 110–17.

Corporate Diversification Strategies

. . . to acquire or not to acquire: that is the question.
Robert J. Terry

Strategy is a deliberate search for a plan of action that will develop a business's competitive advantage and compound it.
Bruce D. Henderson

In this chapter and the next, we move up one level in the strategy-making hierarchy. Attention shifts from formulating strategy for a single-business enterprise to formulating strategy for a diversified enterprise. Because a diversified company is a collection of individual businesses, corporate strategy-making is a bigger-picture exercise than crafting strategy for a single-business company. In a single-business enterprise, management only has to contend with one industry environment and how to compete successfully in it. But in a diversified company, corporate managers have to craft a multibusiness, multi-industry strategic action plan for a number of different business divisions competing in diverse industry environments. Managing a group of diverse businesses is usually so time-consuming and complex that corporate-level managers delegate lead responsibility for business-level strategy-making to the head of each business unit.

As explained in Chapter 2, a corporate strategy in a diversified company concentrates on:

1. Making moves to position the company in the industries chosen for diversification (the basic strategy options here are to acquire a company in the target industry, form a joint venture with another company to enter the target industry, or start a new company internally and try to grow it from the ground up).

2. Taking actions to improve the long-term performance of the corporation's portfolio of businesses once diversification has been achieved (helping to strengthen the competitive positions of existing businesses, divesting businesses that no longer fit into management's long-range plans, and adding new businesses to the portfolio).
3. Trying to capture whatever strategic fit benefits exist within the portfolio of businesses and turn them into competitive advantage.
4. Evaluating the profit prospects of each business unit and steering corporate resources into the most attractive strategic opportunities.

In this chapter we survey the generic type of corporate diversification strategies and how competitive advantage can result from a company's diversification approach. In Chapter 8 we will examine how to assess the strategic attractiveness of a diversified company's business portfolio.

FROM SINGLE-BUSINESS CONCENTRATION TO DIVERSIFICATION

Most companies begin as small single-business enterprises serving a local or regional market. During a company's early years, its product line tends to be limited, its capital base thin, and its competitive position vulnerable. Usually, a young company's strategic emphasis is on increasing sales volume, boosting market share, and cultivating a loyal clientele. Profits are reinvested and new debt is taken on to grow the business as fast as conditions permit. Price, quality, service, and promotion are tailored more precisely to customer needs. As soon as practical, the product line is broadened to meet variations in customer wants and end-use applications.

Opportunities for geographical market expansion are normally pursued next. The natural sequence of geographic expansion proceeds from local to regional to national to international markets, though the degree of penetration may be uneven from area to area because of varying profit potentials. Geographic expansion may, of course, stop well short of global or even national proportions because of intense competition, lack of resources, or the unattractiveness of further market coverage.

Somewhere along the way the potential for vertical integration, either backward to sources of supply or forward to the ultimate consumer, may become a strategic consideration. Generally, vertical integration makes strategic sense only if it significantly enhances a company's profitability and competitive strength.

Strategic Management Principle
Diversification doesn't need to become a strategic priority until a company begins to run out of growth opportunities in its core business.

So long as the company has its hands full trying to capitalize on profitable growth opportunities in its present industry, there is no urgency to pursue diversification. But when company growth potential starts to wane, the strategic options are either to become more aggressive in taking market share away from rivals or diversify into other lines of businesses. A decision to diversify raises the question of "what kind and how much diversification?" The strategic possibilities are wide open. A company can diversify into closely related or totally unrelated businesses. It can diversify to a small extent (less than 10 percent of total revenues and profits) or to a large extent (up to 50 percent). It can move into one or two large new businesses or a greater number of small ones. And once it achieves diversification, the time may come when management has to consider divesting or liquidating businesses that are no longer attractive.

Why a Single-Business Strategy Is Attractive

Companies that concentrate on a single business can achieve enviable success over many decades without relying on diversification to sustain their growth. McDonald's, Delta Airlines, Coca-Cola, Domino's Pizza, Apple Computer, Wal-Mart, Federal Express, Timex, Campbell Soup, Anheuser-Busch, Xerox, Gerber, and Polaroid all won their reputations in a single business. In the nonprofit sector, continued emphasis on a single activity has proved beneficial for the Red Cross, Salvation Army, Christian Children's Fund, Girl Scouts, Phi Beta Kappa, and American Civil Liberties Union.

Concentrating on a single line of business (totally or with a small amount of diversification) has some useful organizational and managerial advantages. First, single-business concentration entails less ambiguity about "who we are and what we do." The energies of the *total* organization are directed down *one* business path. There is less chance that senior management's time or organizational resources will be stretched thinly over too many activities. Entrepreneurial efforts can focus exclusively on keeping the firm's business strategy and competitive approach responsive to industry change and fine-tuned to customer needs. All the firm's managers, especially top executives, can have hands-on contact with the core business and in-depth knowledge of operations. (Senior officers usually have risen through the ranks and possess first-hand experience in field operations—something hard to expect of corporate managers in broadly diversified enterprises.) Furthermore, concentrating on a single business carries a heftier built-in incentive for managers to come up with ways to strengthen the firm's long-term competitive position in the industry rather than pursuing the fleeting benefits of higher short-term profits. The company can use all its organizational resources to become better at what it does. Important competencies and competitive skills are more likely to emerge. With management's attention focused exclusively on just one business, the probability is higher that ideas will emerge on how to improve production technology, better meet customer needs with innovative new product features, or enhance efficiencies anywhere in the activity-cost chain. The more successful a single-business enterprise is, the more able it is to parlay its accumulated experience and distinctive expertise into a sustainable competitive advantage and a prominent leadership position in its industry.

There are important organizational and managerial advantages to concentrating on just one business.

The Risk of a Single-Business Strategy

The big risk of single-business concentration is putting all a firm's eggs in one industry basket. If the industry stagnates, declines, or otherwise becomes unattractive, a company's future outlook dims, its growth rate becomes tougher to sustain, and superior profit performance is much harder to achieve. At times, changing customer needs, technological innovation, or new substitute products can undermine or wipe out a single-business firm. Consider, for example, what word processing has done to the electric typewriter business and what compact disc players are doing to the market for cassette tapes and

FIGURE 7–1	**Matching Corporate Strategy Alternatives to Fit an Undiversifed Firm's Situation**

Competitive Position

Weak   Strong

	Weak	Strong
Rapid	**Strategy Options** (in probable order of attractiveness) • Reformulate single-business concentration strategy (to achieve turnaround). • Acquire another firm in the same business (to strengthen competitive position). • Vertical integration (forward or backward if it strengthens competitive position). • Diversification. • Be acquired by/sell out to a stronger rival. • Abandonment (a last resort in the event all else fails).	**Strategy Options** (in probable order of attractiveness) • Continue single-business concentration – International expansion (if market opportunities exist). • Vertical integration (if it strengthens the firm's competitive position). • Related diversification (to transfer skills and expertise built up in the company's core business to adjacent businesses).
Slow	**Strategy Options** (in probable order of attractiveness) • Reformulate single-business concentration strategy (to achieve turnaround). • Merger with a rival firm (to strengthen competitive position). • Vertical integration (only if it strengthens competitive position substantially). • Diversification. • Harvest/divest. • Liquidation (a last resort in the event all else fails).	**Strategy Options** (in probable order of attractiveness) • International expansion (if market opportunities exist). • Related diversification. • Unrelated diversification. • Joint ventures into new areas. • Vertical integration (if it strengthens competitive position). • Continue single-business concentration (achieve growth by taking market share from weaker rivals).

Market Growth Rate

records. For this reason most single-business companies turn their strategic attention to diversification when their business starts to show signs of peaking.

When Diversification Starts to Make Sense

To better understand *when* a single-business company needs to consider diversification, consider Figure 7–1 where the variable of competitive position is plotted against various rates of market growth to create four distinct strategic situations that might be occupied by an undiversified company.[1] Firms that fall into the rapid market growth/strong competitive position box have several logical strategy options, the strongest of which in the near term may be continuing to pursue single-business concentration. Given the industry's high growth rate (and implicit long-term attractiveness), it makes sense for firms in this position to push hard to maintain or increase their market shares, further develop core competences, and make whatever capital investments are necessary to continue in a strong industry position. At some juncture, a company in this box may find it desirable to consider a vertical integration strategy to undergird its competitive strength. Later, when market growth starts to slow, prudence dictates looking into diversification as a means of spreading business risks and transferring the skills or expertise the company has built up into closely *related* businesses.

When to diversify depends partly on the remaining opportunities for further industry growth and partly on the competitive position a company occupies.

Firms in the rapid growth/weak position category should first consider their options for reformulating their present competitive strategy (given the high rate of market growth). Second they need to address the questions of (1) why their current approach has resulted in a weak competitive position and (2) what it will take to become an effective competitor. In a rapidly expanding market, even weak firms should be able to improve their performance and make headway in building a stronger market position. If a firm is young and struggling to develop, it usually has a better chance for survival in a growing market where plenty of new business is up for grabs than in a stable or declining industry. However, if a weakly positioned company in a rapid-growth market lacks the resources and skills to hold its own, its best option is to either merge with another company in the industry or merge with an outsider with the cash and resources to support the firm's development. Vertical integration—either forward, backward, or both—is an option for weakly positioned firms whenever it can materially strengthen the firm's competitive position. A third option is diversification into related or unrelated areas (if adequate financing can be found). If all else fails, abandonment—divestiture for a multibusiness firm or liquidation for a single-business firm—has to become an active strategic option. While abandonment may seem extreme because of the high growth potential, a company unable to make a profit in a booming market probably does not have the ability to make a profit at all—particularly if competition stiffens or industry conditions sour.

Companies with a weak competitive position in a relatively slow-growth market should look at (1) reformulating their present competitive strategy to turn their situation around and create a more attractive competitive position, (2) integrating forward or backward provided good profit improvement and competitive positioning opportunities exist, (3) diversifying into related or unrelated areas, (4) merger with another firm, (5) employing a harvest, then divest strategy, and (6) liquidating their position in the business by either selling out to another firm or closing down operations.

Companies that are strongly positioned in a slow-growth industry should consider using their excess cash to begin diversifying. Diversification into businesses where a firm can leverage its core competences and competitive strengths is usually the best strategy. But diversification into totally unrelated

Companies that have strong competitive positions in slow-growth industries are prime candidates for diversifying into new businesses.

[1]Roland Christensen, Norman A. Berg, and Malcolm S. Salter, *Policy Formulation and Administration*, 7th ed. (Homewood, Ill: Richard D. Irwin, 1976), pp. 16–18.

businesses has to be considered if none of the related business opportunities offer attractive profit prospects. Joint ventures with other organizations into new fields are another logical possibility. Vertical integration should be a last resort (since it provides no escape from the industry's slow-growth condition) and makes strategic sense only if a firm can expect sizable profit gains. A strong company in a slow-growth industry usually needs to curtail new investment in its present facilities (unless it sees important growth *segments* within the industry) to free cash for new endeavors.

The decision on *when to diversify* is therefore partly a function of a firm's competitive position and partly a function of the remaining opportunities in its home-base industry. There really is no well-defined point at which companies in the same industry should diversify. Indeed, companies in the same industry can rationally choose different diversification approaches and launch them at different times.

BUILDING SHAREHOLDER VALUE: THE ULTIMATE JUSTIFICATION FOR DIVERSIFYING

> **Strategic Management Principle**
>
> *To create value for shareholders, a diversifying company must get into businesses that can perform better under common management than they could perform operating as independent enterprises.*

The underlying purpose of corporate diversification is to build shareholder value. For diversification to enhance shareholder value, corporate strategy must do more than simply diversify the company's business risk by investing in more than one industry. Shareholders can achieve the same risk diversification on their own by purchasing stock in companies in different industries. Strictly speaking, *diversification does not create shareholder value unless a group of businesses performs better under a single corporate umbrella than they would perform operating as independent, stand-alone businesses.* For example, if company A diversifies by purchasing company B and if A and B's consolidated profits in the years to come prove no greater than what each would have earned on its own, then A's diversification into business B has failed to provide shareholders with added value. Company A's shareholders could have achieved the same 2 + 2 = 4 result on their own by purchasing stock in company B. Shareholder value is not *created* by diversification unless it produces a 2 + 2 = 5 effect where sister businesses perform better together as part of the same firm than they could perform as independent companies.

Three Tests for Judging a Diversification Move

The problem with such a strict benchmark of whether diversification has enhanced shareholder value is that it requires speculative judgments about how well a diversified company's business would have performed on its own. Comparisons of actual performance against the hypothetical of what performance might have been under other circumstances are never very satisfactory and, besides, they represent after-the-fact assessments. Strategists have to base diversification decisions on future expectations. Attempts to gauge the impact of particular diversification moves on shareholder value do not have to be abandoned, however. Corporate strategists can make before-the-fact assessments of whether a particular diversification move is capable of increasing shareholder value by using three tests:[2]

---

[2]Michael E. Porter, "From Competitive Advantage to Corporate Strategy," *Harvard Business Review* 45, no. 3 (May–June 1987), pp. 46–49.

1. *The Attractiveness Test:* The industry chosen for diversification must be attractive enough to produce consistently good returns on investment. True industry attractiveness is defined by the presence of favorable competitive conditions and a market environment conducive to long-term profitability. Such simple indicators as rapid growth or a sexy product are unreliable proxies of attractiveness.

2. *The Cost of Entry Test:* The cost to enter the target industry must not be so high as to erode the potential for good profitability. A catch-22 situation can prevail here, however. The more attractive the industry, the more expensive it is to get into. Entry barriers for new start-up companies are nearly always high—were barriers low, a rush of new entrants would soon erode the potential for high profitability. And buying a company already in the business typically entails a high acquisition cost because of the industry's strong appeal. Costly entry undermines the potential for enhancing shareholder value.

3. *The Better-Off Test:* The diversifying company must bring some potential for competitive advantage to the new business it enters, or the new business must offer some potential for added competitive advantage to the company's other businesses. The opportunity to *create* sustainable competitive advantage where none existed before means there is also opportunity for added profitability/and share-holder value.

> *To build shareholder value via diversification, the industries and businesses a company targets must be capable of passing the attractiveness, cost-of-entry, and better-off tests.*

Diversification moves that satisfy all three tests have the greatest potential to build shareholder value over the long term. Diversification moves that can pass only one or two tests are highly suspect.

DIVERSIFICATION STRATEGIES

Once the decision is made to pursue diversification, any of several different paths can be taken. There is plenty of room for varied strategic approaches. We can get a better understanding of the strategic issues corporate managers face in creating and managing a diversified group of businesses by looking at six types of diversification strategies:

1. Strategies for entering new industries—acquisition, start-up, and joint ventures.
2. Related diversification strategies.
3. Unrelated diversification strategies.
4. Divestiture and liquidation strategies.
5. Corporate turnaround, retrenchment, and restructuring strategies.
6. Multinational diversification.

The first three involve ways to diversify; the last three involve strategies to strengthen the positions and performance of companies that have already diversified.

Strategies for Entering New Businesses

Entry into new businesses can take any of three forms: acquisition, internal start-up, and joint ventures. *Acquisition of an existing business* is probably the most popular means of diversifying into another industry and has the advantage of much quicker entry into the target market.[3] At the same time, it helps a diversifier overcome such entry barriers as technological inexperience, establishing supplier relationships, being big enough to match rivals' efficiency and unit costs, having to spend large sums on introductory advertising and promotion to gain market visibility and brand recognition, and getting adequate distribution. In many industries, going the internal start-up route and trying to develop the knowledge, resources, scale of operation, and market reputation necessary to become an effective competitor can take years and entails all the problems of getting a brand new company off the ground and operating. However, finding the right kind of company to acquire sometimes presents a challenge.[4] The big dilemma an acquisition-minded firm faces is whether to buy a successful company at a high price or a struggling company at a "bargain" price. If the buying firm has little knowledge of the industry but ample capital, it is often better off purchasing a capable, strongly positioned firm—unless the acquisition price is unreasonably high. On the other hand, when the acquirer sees promising ways to transform a weak firm into a strong one and has the money, know-how, and patience to do it, a struggling company can be the better long-term investment.

One of the big stumbling blocks to entering attractive industries by acquisition is the difficulty of finding a well-positioned company at a price that satisfies the cost-of-entry test.

The cost-of-entry test requires that the expected profit stream of the acquired business provide an attractive return on the total acquisition cost and on any new capital investment needed to sustain or expand its operations. A high acquisition price can make earning an attractive return improbable or difficult. For instance, suppose that the price to purchase a company is $3 million and that the business is earning after-tax profits of $200,000 on an equity investment of $1 million (a 20 percent annual return). Simple arithmetic requires that the acquired busness's profits be tripled for the purchaser to earn the same 20 percent return on its $3 million acquisition price that the previous owners got on their $1 million equity investment. Building the acquired firm's earnings from $200,000 to $600,000 annually could take several years—and require additional investment on which the purchaser would also have to earn a 20 percent return. Since the owners of a successful and growing company usually demand a price that reflects their business's future profit prospects, it's easy for such an acquisition to flunk the cost-of-entry test. It's difficult to find a successful company in an appealing industry at a price that still permits attractive returns on investment.

The big drawbacks to entering an industry by forming a start-up company internally are the costs of overcoming entry barriers and the extra time it takes to build a strong and profitable competitive position.

Diversification through *internal start-up* involves creating a new company under the corporate umbrella to compete in the desired industry. A newly formed organization not only has to overcome entry barriers, it also has to invest in new production capacity, develop sources of supply, hire and train employees, build distribution channels, grow a customer base, and so on. Generally, forming a start-up company to enter a new industry is more attractive when (1) there is ample time to launch the business from the ground up, (2) incumbent firms are likely to be slow or ineffective in responding to a

---

[3]In recent years, takeovers have become an increasingly used approach to acquisition. The term *takeover* refers to the attempt (often sprung as a surprise) of one firm to acquire ownership or control over another firm against the wishes of the latter's management (and perhaps some of its stockholders).

[4]Michael E. Porter, *Competitive Strategy: Techniques for Analyzing Industries and Competitors* (New York: Free Press, 1980), pp. 354–55.

new entrant's efforts to crack the market, (3) internal entry has lower costs than entry via acquisition, (4) the company already has most or all of the skills it needs to compete effectively, (5) adding new production capacity will not adversely impact the supply-demand balance in the industry, and (6) the targeted industry is populated with many relatively small firms so the new start-up does not have to compete head-to-head against larger, more powerful rivals.[5]

Joint ventures are a useful way to gain access to a new business in at least three types of situations.[6] First, a joint venture is a good device for doing something that is uneconomical or risky for an organization to do alone. Second, joint ventures make sense when pooling the resources and competences of two or more independent organizations produces an organization with more of the skills needed to be a strong competitor. In such cases, each partner brings special talents or resources that the other doesn't have and that are important for success. Third, joint ventures with foreign partners are sometimes the only or best way to surmount import quotas, tariffs, nationalistic political interests, and cultural roadblocks. The economic, competitive, and political realities of nationalism often require a foreign company to team up with a domestic partner in order to gain access to the national market in which the domestic partner is located. Domestic partners offer outside companies the benefits of local knowledge, managerial and marketing personnel, and access to distribution channels. However, such joint ventures often pose complicated questions about how to divide efforts among the partners and who has effective control.[7] Conflicts between foreign and domestic partners can arise over local sourcing of components, how much production to export, whether operating procedures should conform to the foreign company's standards or local preferences, and who should control cash flows and the disposition of profits.

RELATED DIVERSIFICATION STRATEGIES

In choosing which industries to diversify into, companies can pick industries either *related* or *unrelated* to the organization's core business. A related diversification strategy involves diversifying into businesses that possess some kind of "strategic fit." *Strategic fit* exists when different businesses have sufficiently related activity-cost chains that there are important opportunities for activity sharing in one business or another.[8] *A diversified firm that exploits these activity-cost chain interrelationships and captures the benefits of strategic fit achieves a consolidated performance greater than the sum of what the businesses can earn pursuing independent strategies.* The presence of strategic fit within a diversified firm's business portfolio, together with corporate management's skill in capturing the benefits of the interrelationships, makes related diversification a 2 + 2 = 5 phenomenon and becomes a basis for competitive advantage. The bigger the strategic fit benefits, the bigger the competitive advantage of related

> ***Basic Concept***
> *Related diversification involves diversifying into businesses whose activity-cost chains are related in ways that satisfy the better-off test.*

---

[5]Ibid., pp. 344–45.

[6]Peter Drucker, *Management, Tasks, Responsibilities, Practices* (New York: Harper & Row, 1974), pp. 720–24.

[7]Porter, *Competitive Strategy*, p. 340.

[8]Michael E. Porter, *Competitive Advantage*, pp. 318–19 and 337–53; Kenichi Ohmae, *The Mind of the Strategist* (New York: Penguin Books, 1983), pp. 121–24; and Porter, "From Competitive Advantage to Corporate Strategy," pp. 53–57.

diversification and the more that related diversification satisfies the better-off test for building shareholder value.

Strategic fit relationships can arise out of technology sharing, common labor skills and requirements, common suppliers and raw material sources, the potential for joint manufacture of parts and components, similar operating methods, similar kinds of managerial know-how, reliance on the same types of marketing and merchandising skills, ability to share a common sales force, ability to use the same wholesale distributors or retail dealers, or potential for combining after-sale service activities. The fit or relatedness can occur anywhere along the businesses' respective activity-cost chains. Strategic fit relationships are important because they represent opportunities for cost-saving efficiencies, technology or skills transfers, or other benefits of activity-sharing, all of which are avenues for gaining competitive advantages over rivals that have not diversified or that have not diversified in ways that give them access to such strategic fit benefits.

Some of the most commonly used approaches to related diversification are:

- Entering businesses where sales force, advertising, and distribution activities can be shared (a bread bakery buying a maker of crackers and salty snack foods).

- Exploiting closely related technologies (a maker of agricultural seeds and fertilizers diversifying into chemicals for insect and plant disease control).

- Transferring know-how and expertise from one business to another (a successful operator of hamburger outlets acquire a chain specializing in Mexican fast foods).

- Transferring the organization's brand name and reputation with consumers to a new product/service (a tire manufacturer diversifying into automotive repair centers).

- Acquiring new businesses that will uniquely help the firm's position in its existing businesses (a cable TV broadcaster purchasing a sports team and a movie production company to provide original programming).

Examples of related diversification abound. BĬC Pen, which pioneered inexpensive disposable ballpoint pens, used its core competences in low-cost manufacturing and mass merchandising as its basis for diversifying into disposable cigarette lighters, disposable razors, and pantyhose—all three businesses required low-cost production know-how and skilled consumer marketing for competitive success. Tandy Corp. practiced related diversification when its chain of Radio Shack outlets, which originally handled mostly radio and stereo equipment, added telephones, intercoms, calculators, clocks, electronic and scientific toys, personal computers, and peripheral computer equipment. The Tandy strategy was to use the marketing access provided by its thousands of Radio Shack locations to become one of the world's leading retailers of electronic technology. Philip Morris, a leading cigarette manufacturer, employed a marketing-related diversification strategy when it purchased Miller Brewing, General Foods, and Kraft and transferred its skills in cigarette marketing to the marketing of beer and food products. Lockheed pursued a customer needs-based diversification strategy in creating business units to supply the Department of Defense with missiles, rocket engines, aircraft, electronic equipment, and ships, and contract R&D for weapons. Procter & Gamble's

---

ILLUSTRATION CAPSULE
16

EXAMPLES OF COMPANIES WITH RELATED BUSINESS PORTFOLIOS

Presented below are the business portfolios of four companies that have pursued some form of related diversification:

Gillette

- Blades and razors
- Toiletries (Right Guard, Silkience, Foamy, Dry Idea, Soft & Dry, Oral-B toothbrushes, White Rain, Toni)
- Writing instruments and stationery products (Paper Mate pens, Liquid Paper correction fluids, Waterman pens)
- Braun shavers, cordless curlers, coffeemakers, alarm clocks, and electric toothbrushes

PepsiCo

- Soft drinks (Pepsi, Mountain Dew, Slice)
- Kentucky Fried Chicken
- Pizza Hut
- Taco Bell
- Frito Lay
- 7 Up International (non-U.S. sales of 7 Up)

Philip Morris Companies

- Cigarettes (Marlboro, Virginia Slims, Benson & Hedges, and Merit)
- Miller Brewing Company
- Kraft General Foods (Maxwell House, Sanka, Oscar Mayer, Kool-Aid, Jell-O, Post cereals, Birds-Eye frozen foods, Kraft cheeses, Sealtest dairy products, Breyer's ice cream)
- Mission Viejo Realty

Johnson & Johnson

- Baby products (powder, shampoo, oil, lotion)
- Disposable diapers
- Bandaids and wound care products
- Stayfree, Carefree, Sure & Natural, and Modess feminine hygiene products
- Tylenol
- Prescription drugs
- Surgical and hospital products
- Dental products
- Oral contraceptives
- Veterinary and animal health products

Source: Company annual reports.

---

lineup of products includes Jif peanut butter, Duncan Hines cake mixes, Folger's coffee, Tide laundry detergent, Crisco vegetable oil, Crest toothpaste, Ivory soap, Charmin toilet tissue, and Head and Shoulders shampoo—all different businesses with different competitors and different production requirements. But P&G's products still represent related diversification because they all move through the same wholesale distribution systems, are sold in common retail settings to the same shoppers, are advertised and promoted in the same ways, and utilize the same marketing and merchandising skills. Illustration Capsule 16 shows the business portfolios of several companies that have pursued a strategy of related diversification.

Strategic Fit, Economies of Scope, and Competitive Advantage

A related diversification strategy has considerable appeal. It allows a firm to preserve a degree of unity in its business activities, reap the competitive advantages of skills transfer or lower costs, and still spread business risks over

Strategic fits among related businesses offer the competitive advantage potential of (a) lower costs or (b) efficient transfer of key skills, technological expertise, or managerial know-how.

a broader base. A company that has developed valuable skills and competences in its original business can employ a related diversification strategy to exploit what it does best and *transfer* its competences and competitive skills to another business. Successful skills or technology transfers can lead to competitive advantage in the new business.

Diversifying into businesses where technology, facilities, functional activities, or distribution channels can also be shared can lead to lower costs because of economies of scope. *Economies of scope* exist whenever it is less costly for two or more businesses to be operated under centralized management than to function as independent businesses. The economies of operating over a wider range of businesses or product lines can arise from cost-saving opportunities anywhere along the respective activity-cost chains of the businesses. The greater the economies of scope associated with the particular businesses a company has diversified into, the greater the potential for creating a competitive advantage based on lower costs.

Both skills transfer and cost-sharing enable the diversifier to earn greater profits from its businesses than the businesses could earn operating independently. The key to cost-sharing and skills transfer opportunities is diversification into businesses with strategic fit. While strategic fit relationships can occur throughout the activity-cost chain, most fall into one of three broad categories.

Market-Related Fits   When the activity-cost chains of different businesses overlap such that the products are used by the same customers, distributed through common dealers and retailers, or marketed and promoted in similar ways, then the businesses exhibit market-related strategic fit. A variety of cost-saving opportunities (or economies of scope) can arise from market-related strategic fit: using a single sales force for all related products rather than separate sales forces for each business, advertising related products in the same ads and brochures, using the same brand names, coordinating delivery and shipping, combining after-sale service and repair organizations, coordinating order processing and billing, using common promotional tie-ins (cents-off couponing, free samples and trial offers, seasonal specials, and the like), and combining dealer networks. Such market-related strategic fits usually allow a firm to economize on its marketing, selling, and distribution costs.

In addition to economies of scope, market-related fit can generate opportunities to transfer selling skills, promotional skills, advertising skills, and product differentiation skills from one business to another. Moreover, a company's brand name and reputation in one product can often be transferred to other products. Honda's name in motorcycles and automobiles gave it instant credibility and recognition in the lawnmower business without spending large sums on advertising. Canon's reputation in photographic equipment was a competitive asset that facilitated the company's diversification into copying equipment. Panasonic's name in consumer electronics (radios, TVs) was readily transferred to microwave ovens, making it easier and cheaper for Panasonic to diversify into the microwave oven market.

Operating Fit   Different businesses have *operating fit* when there is potential for cost-sharing or skills transfer in procuring materials, conducting R&D, developing technology, manufacturing components, assembling finished goods, or performing administrative support functions. Sharing-related operating fits usually present cost-saving opportunities; some derive from the economies of combining activities into a larger-scale operation (*economies of scale*) and some derive from the ability to eliminate costs by doing things together rather than independently (*economies of scope*). The bigger the proportion of cost a shared activity represents, the more significant the shared cost savings become and the bigger the cost advantage that can result. The most important skills-transfer opportunities usually occur in situations where technological or manufacturing expertise in one business has beneficial applications in another.

Management Fit   This type of fit emerges when different business units have comparable types of entrepreneurial, administrative, or operating problems, thereby allowing managerial know-how in one line of business to be transferable to another business. Transfers of managerial expertise can occur anywhere in the activity-cost chain. Ford Motor Co. transferred its automobile financing and credit management know-how to the savings and loan industry when it acquired some failing S&Ls during the bailout of the crisis-ridden S&L industry. Emerson Electric transferred its skills in low-cost manufacture to its newly acquired Beaird-Poulan chain saw business division. The transfer of management know-how drove Beaird-Poulan's new strategy, changed the way its chain saws were designed and manufactured, and paved the way for new pricing and distribution emphasis.

Capturing Strategic Fit Benefits   It is one thing to diversify into industries with strategic fit and another to actually realize the benefits. To capture the benefits of sharing, related activities must be merged into a single functional unit and coordinated; then the cost-savings (or differentiation advantages) must be squeezed out. Merged functions and coordination can entail reorganization costs, and management must determine that the benefit of *some* centralized strategic control is great enough to warrant sacrifice of business-unit autonomy. Likewise, where skills transfer is the cornerstone of strategic fit, management must find a way to make the transfer effective without stripping too many skilled personnel from the business with the expertise. The more a company's diversification strategy is tied to skills transfer, the more it has to build and maintain a sufficient pool of specialized personnel. And it must not only supply new businesses with the skill but also see that they master the skill sufficiently to create competitive advantage.

Strategic Management Principle
Competitive advantage achieved through strategic fits among related businesses adds to the performance potential of the firm's individual businesses; it is this extra source of competitive advantage that allows related diversification to have a 2 + 2 = 5 effect on shareholder value.

Unrelated Diversification Strategies

Despite the strategic fit benefits associated with related diversification, a number of companies opt for unrelated diversification strategies. In unrelated diversification, the corporate strategy is to diversify into *any* industry where top management spots a good profit opportunity. There is no deliberate effort to seek out businesses where strategic fit exists. While firms pursuing unrelated diversification may try to ensure that their strategies meet the industry attractiveness and cost-of-entry tests, the conditions needed for the better-off

Basic Concept
A strategy of unrelated diversification involves diversifying into whatever industries and businesses hold promise for attractive financial gain; pursuing strategic fit relationships assumes a backseat role.

test are either disregarded or relegated to secondary status. Decisions to diversify into one industry versus another are based on an opportunistic search for "good" companies to acquire—*the basic premise of unrelated diversification is that any company that can be acquired on good financial terms represents a good business to diversify into.* Much time and effort goes into finding and screening acquisition candidates. Typically, corporate strategists screen candidate companies using such criteria as:

- Whether the business can meet corporate targets for profitability and return on investment.
- Whether the new business will require substantial infusions of capital to replace fixed assets, fund expansion, and provide working capital.
- Whether the business is in an industry with significant growth potential.
- Whether the business is big enough to contribute significantly to the parent firm's bottom line.
- The potential for union difficulties or adverse government regulations concerning product safety or the environment.
- Industry vulnerability to recession, inflation, high interest rates, or shifts in government policy.

Unrelated diversification is usually accomplished through acquisition; corporate strategists use a variety of criteria to identify suitable companies to acquire.

Sometimes, corporate strategy is directed at identifying companies that offer opportunities for financial gain because of their "special situation"; three types of companies make particularly attractive acquisition targets:

- *Companies whose assets are "undervalued"*—opportunities may exist to acquire such companies for less than full market value and make substantial capital gains by reselling their assets and businesses for more than their acquired costs.
- *Companies that are financially distressed*—such businesses can often be purchased at a bargain price, their operations turned around with the aid of the parent companies' financial resources and managerial know-how, and then either held as a long-term investment (because of their strong earnings potential) or sold at a profit, whichever is more attractive.
- *Companies that have bright growth prospects but are short on investment capital*—capital-poor, opportunity-rich companies are usually coveted diversification candidates for a financially strong firm.

Firms that pursue unrelated diversification nearly always enter new businesses by acquiring an established company rather than by forming a start-up subsidiary within its own corporate structure. Their premise is that growth by acquisition translates into enhanced shareholder value. Suspending application of the better-off test is seen as justifiable so long as unrelated diversification results in sustained growth in corporate revenues and earnings and none of the acquired businesses end up performing badly.

Illustration Capsule 17 shows the business portfolios of several companies that have pursued unrelated diversification. Such companies are frequently described as *conglomerates* because they follow no strategic theme in their diversification and because their business interests range broadly across diverse industries.

ILLUSTRATION CAPSULE
17

DIVERSIFIED COMPANIES WITH UNRELATED BUSINESS PORTFOLIOS

Union Pacific Corporation

- Railroad operations (Union Pacific Railroad Company)
- Oil and gas exploration
- Mining
- Microwave and fiber optic transportation information and control systems
- Hazardous waste management disposal
- Trucking (Overnite Transportation Company)
- Oil refining
- Real estate

United Technologies

- Pratt & Whitney aircraft engines
- Carrier heating and air-conditioning equipment
- Otis elevators
- Sikorsky helicopters
- Essex wire and cable products
- Norden defense systems
- Hamilton Standard controls
- Space transportation systems
- Automotive components

Westinghouse Electric Corp.

- Electric utility power generation equipment
- Nuclear fuel
- Electric transmission and distribution products
- Commercial and residential real estate financing
- Equipment leasing
- Receivables and fixed asset financing
- Radio and television broadcasting
- Longines-Wittnauer Watch Co.
- Beverage bottling
- Elevators and escalators
- Defense electronic systems, missile launch equipment, marine propulsion)
- Commercial furniture
- Community land development

Textron, Inc.

- Bell helicopters
- Paul Revere Insurance
- Missile reentry systems
- Lycoming gas turbine engines and jet propulsion systems
- E-Z-Go golf carts
- Homelite chain saws and lawn and garden equipment
- Davidson automotive parts and trims
- Specialty fasteners
- Avco Financial Services
- Jacobsen turf care equipment
- Tanks and armored vehicles

The Pros and Cons of Unrelated Diversification

Unrelated or conglomerate diversification has appeal from several financial angles:

1. Business risk is scattered over a variety of industries, making the company less dependent on any one business. While the same can be said for related diversification, unrelated diversification places no restraint on how risk is spread. An argument can be made that unrelated diversification is a superior way to diversify financial risk as compared to related diversification.

2. Capital resources can be invested in whatever industries offer the best profit prospects; cash from businesses with lower profit prospects can be diverted to acquiring and expanding businesses with higher growth

With unrelated diversification, a company can spread financial risks broadly, invest in whatever businesses promise financial gain, and try to stabilize earnings by diversifying into businesses with offsetting up-and-down cycles.

and profit potentials. Corporate financial resources are thus employed to maximum advantage.

3. Company profitability is somewhat more stable because hard times in one industry may be partially offset by good times in another— ideally, cyclical downswings in some of the company's businesses are counterbalanced by cyclical upswings in other businesses the company has diversified into.

4. To the extent that corporate managers are astute at spotting bargain-priced companies with big upside profit potential, shareholder wealth can be enhanced.

While entry into an unrelated business can often pass the attractiveness and cost-of-entry tests (and sometimes even the better-off test), unrelated diversification has drawbacks. The real Achilles' heel of conglomerate diversification is the big demand it places on corporate-level management to make sound decisions about fundamentally different businesses operating in fundamentally different industry and competitive environments. The greater the number of businesses a company is in and the more diverse they are, the harder it is for corporate managers to oversee each subsidiary and spot problems early, to become expert at evaluating the attractiveness of each business's industry and competitive environment, and to judge the caliber of strategic actions and plans proposed by business-level managers. As one president of a diversified firm expressed it:

> we've got to make sure that our core businesses are properly managed for solid, long-term earnings. We can't just sit back and watch the numbers. We've got to know what the real issues are out there in the profit centers. Otherwise, we're not even in a position to check out our managers on the big decisions.[9]

The two biggest drawbacks to unrelated diversification are the difficulties of managing broad diversification and the absence of strategic opportunities to turn diversification into competitive advantage.

With broad diversification, corporate managers have to be shrewd and talented enough to: (1) tell a good acquisition from a bad one, (2) select capable managers to run each business, (3) discern sound strategic proposals, and (4) know what to do if a business unit stumbles. Because every business encounters rough sledding, a good way to gauge the risk of diversifying is to ask, "If the new business got into trouble, would we know how to bail it out?" When the answer is no, unrelated diversification can pose significant financial risk, and the business's profit prospects are more chancy.[10] As the former chairman of a Fortune 500 company advised, "Never acquire a business you don't know how to run." It only takes one or two big strategic mistakes (misjudging industry attractiveness, encountering unexpected problems in a newly acquired business, or being too optimistic about the difficulty of turning a struggling subsidiary around) to cause a precipitous drop in corporate earnings and crash the company's stock price.

Second, without some kind of strategic fit and the added measure of competitive advantage it offers, the consolidated performance of a multibusiness portfolio tends to be no better than the sum of what the individual business

---

[9]Carter F. Bales, "Strategic Control: The President's Paradox," *Business Horizons* 20, no. 4 (August 1977), p. 17.

[10]Of course, some firms may be willing to risk that trouble won't strike before management has time to learn the business well enough to bail it out of almost any difficulty. See Peter Drucker, *Management: Tasks, Responsibilities, Practices* (New York: Harper & Row, 1974), p. 709.

units could achieve independently. And, to the extent that corporate managers meddle unwisely in business-unit operations or hamstring them with corporate policies, overall performance can even be worse. Except for the added financial backing from a cash-rich corporate parent, a strategy of unrelated diversification does nothing to enhance the competitive strength of individual business units. Each business is on its own in trying to build a competitive edge—the unrelated nature of sister businesses offers no basis for cost reduction, skills transfer, or technology sharing. In a widely diversified firm, the value added by corporate managers depends primarily on how good they are at deciding what new businesses to add, which ones to get rid of, how to use financial resources to build a higher-performing collection of businesses, and the quality of the decision-making guidance they give to general managers of their business subsidiaries.

Third, although in theory unrelated diversification offers the potential for greater sales-profit stability over the business cycle, in practice attempts at countercyclical diversification fall short of the mark. Few attractive businesses have opposite up- and-down cycles; most are similarly affected by cyclical economic conditions. There's no convincing evidence that the consolidated profits of broadly diversified firms are more stable or less subject to reversal in periods of recession and economic stress than the profits of less diversified firms.[11]

Despite these drawbacks, unrelated diversification can be a desirable corporate strategy. It certainly makes sense when a firm needs to diversify away from an unattractive industry and has no distinctive skills it can transfer to related businesses. Also, some owners prefer to invest in several unrelated businesses instead of a family of related ones. Otherwise, the advantages of unrelated diversification depend on the prospects for financial gain.

A key issue in unrelated diversification is how broad a net to cast in building the business portfolio. In other words, should the corporate portfolio contain few or many unrelated businesses? How much business diversity can corporate executives successfully manage? A reasonable way to resolve the problem is to answer two questions: What is the least diversification the firm needs to achieve acceptable growth and profitability? What is the most diversification the firm can manage given the complexity it adds?[12] The optimal answer usually lies between these two extremes.

Unrelated Diversification and Shareholder Value

Unrelated diversification is fundamentally a finance-driven approach to creating shareholder value whereas related diversification is fundamentally strategy-driven. *Related diversification represents a strategic approach to value creation* because it is predicated on exploiting the links between the activity-cost chains of different businesses to lower costs, transfer skills and technological expertise, and gain benefit of other kinds of strategic fit. The objective is to convert the strategic fits among the firm's businesses into an extra measure of competitive advantage that goes beyond what business subsidiaries are able to

Unrelated diversification represents a financial approach to creating shareholder value; related diversification in contrast, represents a strategic approach.

---

[11]Ibid., p. 767. Research studies in the interval since 1974, when Drucker made his observation, uphold his conclusion—on the whole, broadly diversified firms do not outperform less diversified firms over the course of the business cycle.

[12]Ibid., pp. 692–93.

achieve on their own. The competitive advantage a firm achieves through related diversification is the driver for building greater shareholder value.

In contrast, *unrelated diversification is principally a financial approach to diversification* where shareholder value accrues from astute deployment of corporate financial resources and from executive skill in spotting financially attractive business opportunities. For unrelated diversification to result in enhanced shareholder value (above the 2 + 2 = 4 effect of what the subsidiary businesses could produce through independent operations and what shareholders could obtain by purchasing ownership interests in a variety of businesses to spread investment risk on their own behalf), corporate strategists must exhibit superior skills in creating and managing a portfolio of diversified business interests. This specifically means:

- Doing a superior job of diversifying into new businesses that can produce consistently good returns on investment (satisfying the attractiveness test).
- Doing an excellent job of negotiating favorable acquisition prices (satisfying the cost-of-entry test).
- Making astute moves to sell previously acquired business subsidiaries at their peak and getting premium prices (this requires skills in discerning when a business subsidiary is on the verge of confronting adverse industry and competitive conditions and probable declines in long-term profitability).
- Being shrewd in shifting corporate financial resources out of businesses where profit opportunities are dim and into businesses where rapid earnings growth and high returns on investment are occurring.
- Doing such a good job overseeing the firm's business subsidiaries and contributing to how they are managed (by providing expert problem-solving skills, creative strategy suggestions, and decision-making guidance to business-level managers) that the businesses perform at a higher level than they would otherwise be able to do (a possible way to satisfy the better-off test).

To the extent that corporate executives can craft and execute a strategy of unrelated diversification that produces enough of the above outcomes for the enterprise to consistently outperform other firms in generating dividends and capital gains for stockholders, then a case can be made that shareholder value has truly been enhanced.

DIVESTITURE AND LIQUIDATION STRATEGIES

Even a shrewd corporate diversification strategy can result in the acquisition of business units that, down the road, just do not work out. Misfits or partial fits cannot be completely avoided because it is impossible to predict precisely how getting into a new line of business will actually work out. In addition, long-term industry attractiveness changes with the times; what was once a good diversification move into an attractive industry may later turn sour. Subpar performance by some business units is bound to occur, thereby raising questions of whether to keep them or divest them. Other business units, despite adequate financial performance, may not mesh as well with the rest of the firm as was originally thought.

Sometimes, a business that seems sensible from a strategic fit standpoint turns out to lack the compatibility of values essential to a *cultural fit.*[13] Several pharmaceutical companies had just this experience. When they diversified into cosmetics and perfume, they discovered their personnel had little respect for the "frivolous" nature of such products compared to the far nobler task of developing miracle drugs to cure the ill. The absence of shared values and cultural compatibility between the medical research expertise of the pharmaceutical companies and the fashion-marketing orientation of the cosmetics business was the undoing of what otherwise was diversification into businesses with related chemical compounding expertise and distribution channels.

When a particular line of business loses its appeal, the most attractive solution usually is to sell it. Normally such businesses should be divested as fast as is practical, unless time is needed to get them in better shape to sell. The more business units in a diversified firm's portfolio, the more likely it will have to divest poor performers, "dogs," and misfits. A useful guide to determine if and when to divest a subsidiary is to ask the question, "If we were not in this business today, would we want to get into it now?"[14] When the answer is no or probably not, divestiture must be considered.

Divestiture can take either of two forms. The parent can spin off a business as a financially and managerially independent company in which the parent may or may not retain partial ownership. Or the parent may sell the unit outright, in which case a buyer needs to be found. As a rule, divestiture should not be approached from the angle of "Who can we pawn this business off on and what is the most we can get for it?"[15] Instead, it is wiser to ask "For what sort of organization would this business be a good fit, and under what conditions would it be viewed as a good deal?" Organizations for which the business is a good fit are likely to pay the highest price.

Of all the strategic alternatives, liquidation is the most unpleasant and painful, especially for a single-business enterprise where it means the organization ceases to exist. For a multi-industry, multibusiness firm to liquidate one of its lines of business is less traumatic. The hardships of layoffs, plant closings, and so on, while not to be minimized, still leave an ongoing organization that may be healthier after its pruning. In hopeless situations, an early liquidation usually serves owner-stockholder interests better than bankruptcy. Pursuing a lost cause exhausts an organization's resources and leaves less to liquidate; it can also mar reputations and ruin management careers. Unfortunately, it is seldom simple for management to differentiate between a lost cause and a potential for turnaround. This is particularly true when emotions and pride get mixed with sound managerial judgment—as often they do.

Corporate Turnaround, Retrenchment, and Portfolio Restructuring Strategies

Turnaround, retrenchment, and portfolio restructuring strategies come into play when corporate management has to restore an ailing business portfolio to

---

[13]Ibid., p. 709.
[14]Ibid., p. 94.
[15]Ibid., p. 719.

good health. Poor performance can be caused by large losses in one or more business units that pull the corporation's overall financial performance down, a disproportionate number of businesses in unattractive industries, a bad economy adversely impacting many of the firm's business units, an excessive debt burden, or ill-chosen acquisitions that haven't lived up to expectations.

Corporate turnaround strategies focus on restoring money-losing businesses to profitability rather than divesting them. The intent is to get the whole company back in the black by curing the problems of the subsidiaries most responsible for pulling overall performance down. Turnaround strategies are most appropriate in situations where the reasons for poor performance are short-term, the ailing businesses are in attractive industries, and divesting the money-losers does not make long-term strategic sense.

Corporate retrenchment strategies focus on reducing the scope of diversification to a smaller number of businesses. Retrenchment is usually undertaken when corporate management concludes that the company is in too many businesses and needs to concentrate its efforts on a few core businesses. Sometimes diversified firms retrench because they can't make certain businesses profitable after several years of trying or because they lack funds to support the investment needs of all the businesses in their portfolios. Retrenchment is usually accomplished by divesting businesses that are too small to make a sizable contribution to earnings or that have little or no strategic fit with the company's core businesses. Divesting such businesses frees resources that can be used to reduce debt or support expansion of the corporation's core businesses.

Portfolio restructuring involves bold strategic action to revamp the diversified company's business makeup through divestitures and acquisitions.

Portfolio restructuring strategies involve radical surgery on the mix and percentage makeup of the types of businesses in the portfolio. For instance, one company over a two-year period divested four business units, closed down four others, and added 25 new lines of business to its portfolio—16 through acquisition and 9 through internal start-up. Restructuring can be prompted by any of several conditions: (1) when a strategy review reveals that the firm's long-term performance prospects have become unattractive because the portfolio contains too many slow-growth, declining, or competitively weak businesses, (2) when one or more of the firm's core businesses fall prey to hard times, (3) when a new CEO takes over and decides to redirect where the company is headed, (4) when new technologies or products emerge and the portfolio needs changing to build a position in a potentially big new industry, (5) when the firm has a "unique opportunity" to make an acquisition so big that it has to sell several existing businesses to finance it, or (6) when major businesses in the portfolio have become more and more unattractive, forcing a shakeup in the portfolio in order to produce satisfactory long-term corporate performance.

Portfolio restructuring typically involves both divestitures and new acquisitions. Candidates for divestiture include not only weak or up- and-down performers or those in unattractive industries, but also those that no longer "fit" (even though they may be profitable and in attractive enough industries). Many broadly diversified corporations, disenchanted with how some of their acquisitions perform and unable to make successes out of so many unrelated business units, eventually restructure their portfolios. Business units incompatible with newly established related diversification criteria have been divested and the remaining units regrouped and aligned to capture more strategic fit benefits. Illustration Capsule 18 provides an example of corporate restructuring at Times Mirror Company.

The trend to demerge and deconglomerate has been driven by a growing preference to gear diversification toward creating strong competitive positions in a few, well-selected industries. Indeed, in response to investor disenchantment with the conglomerate approach to diversification (conglomerates often have *lower* price-earnings ratios than companies with related diversification strategies), some conglomerates have undertaken portfolio restructuring and retrenchment in a deliberate effort to escape being regarded as a conglomerate.

MULTINATIONAL DIVERSIFICATION STRATEGIES

The distinguishing characteristic of a multinational diversification strategy is a *diversity of businesses* and a *diversity of national markets*.[16] Here, corporate strategists must conceive and execute a substantial number of strategies—at least one for each industry, with as many multinational variations as is appropriate for the situation. At the same time, managers of diversified multinational corporations (DMNCs) need to be alert for beneficial ways to coordinate the firm's strategic actions across industries and countries. The goal of strategic coordination at the headquarter's level is to bring the full force of corporate resources and capabilities to the task of securing sustainable competitive advantages in each business and national market.[17]

The Emergence of Multinational Diversification

Until the 1960s, multinational companies (MNCs) operated fairly autonomous subsidiaries in each host country, each catering to the special requirements of its own national market.[18] Management tasks at company headquarters primarily involved finance functions, technology transfer, and export coordination. In pursuing a national responsiveness strategy, the primary competitive advantage of an MNC was grounded in its ability to transfer technology, manufacturing know-how, brand name identification, and marketing and management skills from country to country at costs lower than could be achieved by host-country competitors. Standardized administrative procedures helped minimize overhead costs, and once an initial organization for managing foreign subsidiaries was put in place, entry into additional national markets could be accomplished at low incremental costs. Frequently, an MNC's presence and market position in a country was negotiated with the host government rather than driven by international competition.

During the 1970s, however, multicountry strategies based on national responsiveness began to lose their effectiveness. Competition broke out on a global scale in more and more industries as Japanese, European, and U.S. companies expanded internationally in the wake of trade liberalization and the opening of market opportunities in both industrialized and less-developed countries.[19] The relevant market arena in many industries shifted from national to global principally because the strategies of global competitors, most

---

[16]C. K. Prahalad and Yves L. Doz, *The Multinational Mission* (New York: Free Press, 1987), p. 2.

[17]Ibid., p. 15.

[18]Yves L. Doz, *Strategic Management in Multinational Companies* (New York: Pergamon Press, 1985), p. 1.

[19]Ibid., pp. 2–3.

ILLUSTRATION CAPSULE
18

CORPORATE RESTRUCTURING AT TIMES MIRROR COMPANY

Times Mirror is a $3.6 billion media and information company principally engaged in newspaper publishing, broadcast and cable television, and book and magazine publishing. During the 1983–90 period, the company engaged in corporate restructuring activities to revamp the content of its business portfolio. The table below summarizes the company's acquisition and divestiture moves:

		Dispositions	Acquisitions
1983	Dec.	New American Library	
1984	Feb.	Spotlight satellite programming	
	Dec.	Commerce Clearing House stock	*The Morning Call*
1985	June	Art and graphic products companies (3)	Learning International, Inc.
	August		Wolfe Publishing Limited
	Sept.	Hartford, Connecticut, Cable Television	
	Oct.	Long Beach, California, Cable Television	
1986	Feb.	80 percent of Publishers Paper Co.	
	May		*National Journal*
	June	Times Mirror Microwave Communications Co.	
		Television stations in Syracuse and Elmira, New York, and Harrisburg, Pennsylvania	
		Las Vegas, Nevada, Cable Television	
	July		*Bottlang Airfield Manual*
	Sept.	*Dallas Times Herald*	
	Oct.		The *Baltimore Sun* newspapers
	Dec.	Times Mirror Magazines book clubs	*Broadcasting* magazine
		Graphic Controls Corporation	60 percent of Rhode Island CATV (cable)
		The H.M. Goushã Company	CRC Press, Inc.
1987	Feb.		*Government Executive*
	Dec.	*The Denver Post*	*Field & Stream, Home Mechanix, Skiing, Yachting* magazines
	Throughout	Continuing timberland sales	
1988	Jan.	Times Mirror Press	
	Feb.		Richard D. Irwin, Inc.
	Throughout	Continuing timberland sales	

(continued)

notably the Japanese companies, involved gaining a foothold in host-country markets by matching or beating the product quality of local companies and undercutting their prices. To fend off global competitors, traditional MNCs were driven to integrate their operations across national borders in a quest for better efficiencies and lower manufacturing costs. Instead of separately manufacturing a complete product range in each country, the plants of MNCs became more specialized in their production operations to gain the economies

---

(concluded)

	Dispositions	Acquisitions
1989 May		Zenger-Miller
June		Kaset International
1990 Jan.		Sun City Cable TV (California)
		Lewis Publishers
May		B. C. Decker
Oct.		Austen Cornish
Dec.		The Achieve Group
Total	Approximately $1 billion	Approximately $1 billion

This series of moves left Times Mirror with the following business portfolio as of 1991:

Newspaper publishing:
Los Angeles Times, Newsday, the *Baltimore Sun* newspapers, *The Hartford Courant, The Morning Call, The (Stamford) Advocate,* and *Greenwich Time.*

Book publishing:
Abrams art books; Matthew Bender law books; Mosby–Year Book medical books; CRC Press scientific books; Wolfe medical color atlases; Lewis Publishers; B. C. Decker; Austin Cornish nursing texts; and college texts by Richard D. Irwin, Inc.

Broadcast and cable television:
CBS network affiliates KDFW-TV, Dallas, Texas, and KTBC-TV, Austin, Texas; ABC affiliate KTVI, St. Louis, Missouri; NBC affiliate WVTM-TV, Birmingham, Alabama; and cable TV operations in 13 states (Dimension Cable Services).

Magazine publishing:
Popular Science, Outdoor Life, Golf Magazine, Ski Magazine, The Sporting News, The Sporting Goods DEALER, National Journal, Government Executive, Broadcasting, Sports inc., The Sports Business Weekly, Field & Stream, Home Mechanix, Skiing, and *Yachting.*

Other business/properties:
Timberland; Jepperson Sanderson (producer of aeronautical charts and pilot training material); and Learning International, Zenger-Miller, and Kaset International (providers of professional training services).

Source: Company annual reports.

of longer production runs, permit use of faster automated equipment, and capture experience curve effects. Country subsidiaries obtained the rest of the product range they needed from sister plants in other countries. Gains in manufacturing efficiencies from converting to state-of-the- art, world-scale manufacturing plants more than offset increased international shipping costs, especially in light of the other advantages global strategies offered. With a global strategy, an MNC could locate plants in countries with low labor costs—

ILLUSTRATION CAPSULE
19

HONDA'S COMPETITIVE ADVANTAGE
The Technology of Engines

At first blush anyone looking at Honda's lineup of products—cars, motorcycles, lawnmowers, power generators, outboard motors, snowmobiles, snowblowers, and garden tillers—might conclude that Honda has pursued unrelated diversification. But underlying the obvious product diversity is a common core: the technology of engines.

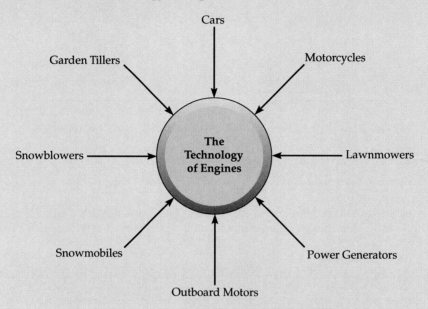

The basic Honda strategy is to exploit the company's expertise in engine technology and manufacturing and to capitalize on its brand recognition. One Honda ad teases consumers with the question, "How do you put six Hondas in a two-car garage?" It then shows a garage containing a Honda car, a Honda motorcycle, a Honda snowmobile, a Honda lawnmower, a Honda power generator, and a Honda outboard motor.

Source: Adapted from C. K. Prahalad and Yves L. Doz, *The Multinational Mission* (New York: Free Press, 1987), p. 62.

> *A multinational corporation can gain competitive advantage by diversifying into global industries with related technologies.*

a key consideration in industries whose products have high labor content. With a global strategy, an MNC could also exploit differences in tax rates, setting transfer prices in its integrated operations to produce higher profits in low-tax countries and lower profits in high-tax countries. Global strategic coordination also gave MNCs increased ability to take advantage of country-to-country differences in interest rates, exchange rates, credit terms, government subsidies, and export guarantees. As a consequence of these advantages, it became increasingly difficult for a company that produced and sold its product in only one country to succeed in an industry populated with aggressive competitors intent on achieving global dominance.

During the 1980s another source of competitive advantage began to emerge: using the strategic fit advantages of related diversification to build stronger competitive positions in several related global industries simultaneously.

Being a diversified MNC (DMNC) became competitively superior to being a single-business MNC in cases where strategic fits existed across global industries. Related diversification is most capable of producing competitive advantage for a multinational company where expertise in a core technology can be applied to different industries (at least one of which is global) and where there are important economies of scope and brand name advantages to being in a family of related businesses.[20] Illustration Capsule 19 explains Honda's ability to exploit the technology of engines and its well-known name via its diversification into a variety of products with engines.

Sources of Competitive Advantage for a DMNC

When a multinational company has expertise in a core technology and has diversified into related products and businesses to exploit that core, a centralized R&D effort coordinated at the headquarters level holds real potential for competitive advantage. By channeling corporate resources into a strategically coordinated R&D/technology effort, as opposed to letting each business unit perform its own R&D function, the DMNC can launch a world-class, global-scale assault to advance the core technology, generate technology-based manufacturing economies within and across product/business lines, make across-the-board product improvements, and develop complementary products—all significant advantages in a globally competitive marketplace. In the absence of centralized coordination, R&D/technology investments are likely to be scaled down to match each business's product-market perspective, setting the stage for the strategic fit benefits of coordinated technology management to slip through the cracks and go uncaptured.[21]

A multinational corporation can also gain competitive advantage by diversifying into related global industries where strategic fits produce economies of scope and the benefits of brand name transfer.

The second source of competitive advantage for a DMNC concerns the distribution and brand name advantages that can accrue from diversifying into related global industries. Consider, for instance, the competitive strength of such Japanese DMNCs as Sanyo and Matsushita. Both have diversified into a range of globally competitive consumer goods industries—TVs, stereo equipment, radios, VCRs, small domestic appliances (microwave ovens, for example), and personal computers. By widening their scope of operations in products marketed through similar distribution channels, Sanyo and Matsushita have not only exploited related technologies but also built stronger distribution capabilities, captured logistical and distribution-related economies, and established greater brand awareness for their products.[22] Such competitive advantages are not available to a domestic-only company pursuing a single business. Moreover, with a well-diversified product line and a multinational market base, a DMNC can enter new country or product markets and gain market share with below-market pricing (and below- average cost pricing if need be), subsidizing the entry with earnings from one or more of its country market profit sanctuaries and/or earnings in other businesses.

Both a one-business multinational company and a one-business domestic company are weakly positioned to defend their market positions against a determined DMNC willing to accept lower short-term profits in order to win a stronger long-term competitive position in a desirable new market. A one-

Principle of Global Competition
A multinational corporation diversified into related global industries is well positioned to out-compete both a one-business domestic company and a one-business multinational company.

---

[20]Prahalad and Doz, *The Multinational Mission*, pp. 62–63.
[21]Ibid.
[22]Ibid., p. 64.

business domestic company has only one profit sanctuary—its home market. A one-business multinational company may have profit sanctuaries in several country markets, but all are in the same business. Both are vulnerable to a DMNC that launches a major strategic offensive in their profit sanctuaries and low-balls its prices to win market share at their expense. A DMNC's ability to keep hammering away at competitors with low-ball prices year after year may reflect either a cost advantage growing out of its related diversification strategy or a willingness to cross-subsidize low profits or even losses with earnings from its profit sanctuaries in other country markets and/or its earnings from other businesses. Sanyo, for example, by pursuing related diversification keyed to product-distribution-technology types of strategic fit and managing its product families on a global scale, can eventually encircle domestic companies like Zenith (TVs and small computer systems) and Maytag (home appliances) and put them under serious competitive pressure. Sanyo can peck away at Zenith's market share in TVs and in the process weaken retailers' loyalty to the Zenith brand. Sanyo can diversify into large home appliances (by acquiring an established appliance maker or manufacturing on its own) and cross-subsidize a low-priced market entry against Maytag and other less-diversified home appliance firms with earnings from its many other business and product lines. If Sanyo chooses, it can keep its prices low for several years to gain market share at the expense of domestic rivals, turning its attention to profits after the battle for market share and competitive position is won.[23]

A DMNC's most potent advantages usually derive from technology-sharing, economies of scope, shared brand names, and its potential to employ cross-subsidization tactics.

The competitive principle is clear: A DMNC has a strategic arsenal capable of defeating both a single-business MNC and a single-business domestic company over the long term. The competitive advantages of a DMNC, however, depend on employing a related diversification strategy in industries that are already globally competitive or are on the verge of becoming so. Then the related businesses have to be managed so as to capture strategic fit benefits. DMNCs have the biggest potential for competitive advantage in industries with technology-sharing and technology-transfer opportunities and in those where there are important economies of scope and brand name benefits associated with competing in related product families.

A DMNC also has important cross-subsidization potential for winning its way into attractive new markets. However, a DMNC's cross-subsidization powers cannot be deployed in the extreme. It is one thing to use a *portion* of the profits and cash flows from existing businesses to cover "reasonable" short-term losses when entering a new business or country market; it is quite another to drain corporate profits indiscriminately (and thus impair overall company performance) to support either deep price discounting and quick market penetration in the short term or continuing losses over the longer term. At some juncture, every business and market entered has to make a profit contribution or become a candidate for abandonment. Moreover, the company has to wrest consistently acceptable performance from the whole business portfolio. So there are limits to cross-subsidization. As a general rule, cross-subsidization is justified only if there is a good chance short-term losses can be amply recouped in some way over the long term.

Illustration Capsule 20 provides examples of the business portfolios and global scope of several DMNCs.

---

[23]Ibid.

ILLUSTRATION CAPSULE 20

THE GLOBAL SCOPE OF PROMINENT DIVERSIFIED MULTINATIONAL CORPORATIONS

Company (headquarters base)	Major Lines of Business	Number of Employees	1990 Global Sales	Global Plant Locations
Unilever (Netherlands, Britain)	Vaseline products, Cutex, Prince Matchabelli products, Ragu sauces, Lipton teas and soups, laundry detergents, soaps, toothpaste and other personal care products, margarine, frozen foods, agribusiness, and chemicals	304,000	$40 billion in 75 different countries • Europe, 61% • North America, 18% • Rest of world, 21%	340 subsidiary companies in 30 different countries
Siemens (West Germany)	Electrical equipment, lighting, power plants, security systems, medical engineering, communications and information systems, telecommunications networks	373,000	$39 billion • Europe, 73% • North America, 10% • Asia and Australia, 9% • Latin America, 4% • Africa, 4%	28 countries
Philips (Netherlands)	Lighting, consumer electronics, domestic appliances, and telecommunications and data systems	273,000	$31 billion • Europe, 53% • North America, 29% • Asia and Australia, 10% • Latin America, 6% • Africa, 2%	60 countries
Nissan Motor Co. (Japan)	Automobiles, trucks, rockets, forklifts, boats, and textile machinery	130,000	$40.2 billion in 150 countries	15 countries
Toyota Motor Corp. (Japan)	Automobiles, trucks, buses, forklifts, power shovels, residential and commercial construction	97,000	$64.5 billion in 150 countries	11 plants in Japan 30 plants in 21 other countries
Hitachi (Japan)	Power plants, turbines, boilers, TV sets, VCRs, kitchen appliances, lighting fixtures, computers, word processors, fax machines, cranes, locomotives, machinery, wire and cable, chemicals, and steel products	291,000	$51 billion in 30 countries	7 countries
Dow Chemical Co. (United States)	Chemicals, plastics, hydrocarbons, pharmaceuticals, consumer products (1,800 different products in all)	62,000	$20 billion • Europe, 31% • U.S., 45% • Rest of world, 24%	120-plus plant locations in 32 countries
CPC International (United States)	Consumer foods (Hellman's, Mazola, Skippy, Knorr soups and sauces, margarine, English muffins, pasta) and corn refining products (corn starches, corn syrups, dextrose, animal feed ingredients)	35,300	$5.8 billion in 50 countries • North America, 46% • Europe, 36% • Latin America, 13% • Asia and Africa, 5%	28 countries

COMBINATION DIVERSIFICATION STRATEGIES

The six corporate diversification approaches described above are not mutually exclusive. They can be pursued in combination and in varying sequences, allowing ample room for companies to customize their diversification strategies to fit their own circumstances. The most common business portfolios created by corporate diversification strategies are:

- A "dominant-business" enterprise with sales concentrated in one major core business but with a modestly diversified portfolio of either related or unrelated businesses (amounting to one third or less of total corporatewide sales).
- A narrowly diversified enterprise having a *few* (two to five) *related core* business units.
- A broadly diversified enterprise made up of *many* mostly *related* business units.
- A narrowly diversified enterprise comprised of a *few* (two to five) *core* business units in *unrelated* industries.
- A broadly diversified enterprise having *many* business units in mostly *unrelated* industries.
- A multibusiness enterprise diversified into unrelated areas but with a portfolio of related businesses within each area—thus giving it *several unrelated groups of related businesses.*

In each case, the geographic markets of individual businesses within the portfolio can be local, regional, national, multinational, or global. Thus, a company can be competing locally in some businesses, nationally in others, and globally in others.

KEY POINTS

Diversification becomes an attractive strategy when a company runs out of profitable growth opportunities in its present business. There are two fundamental approaches to diversification—into related businesses and into unrelated businesses. The rationale for related diversification is *strategic*: diversify into businesses with strategic fit, capitalize on strategic fit relationships to gain competitive advantage, then use competitive advantage to achieve the desired 2 + 2 = 5 impact on shareholder value. The reasons for diversifying into unrelated businesses hinge almost exclusively on opportunities for attractive financial gain—there is nothing *strategic* about unrelated diversification.

Figure 7–2 shows the paths an undiversified company can take on the road to managing a diversified business portfolio. Most companies have their strategic roots in single-business concentration. Vertical integration strategies may or may not be involved depending on the extent to which forward or backward integration strengthens a firm's competitive position or helps it secure a competitive advantage. When diversification becomes a serious strategic option, a company must choose to pursue related diversification, unrelated diversification, or some mix of both. There are advantages and disadvantages to all three options. Once diversification has been accomplished, management's task is to figure out how to manage the existing business portfolio. The six primary post-diversification alternatives are (1) make new acquisitions,

FIGURE 7–2   **Checklist of Major Corporate Strategy Alternatives**

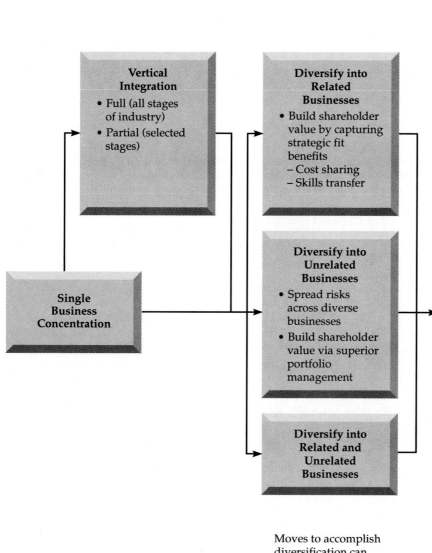

Moves to accomplish diversification can involve one or more of following:

- Acquisition/merger
- Start-up of own new businesses from scratch
- Joint venture partnerships

Vertical Integration
- Full (all stages of industry)
- Partial (selected stages)

Diversify into Related Businesses
- Build shareholder value by capturing strategic fit benefits
  - Cost sharing
  - Skills transfer

Single Business Concentration

Diversify into Unrelated Businesses
- Spread risks across diverse businesses
- Build shareholder value via superior portfolio management

Diversify into Related and Unrelated Businesses

Post-Diversification Strategic Move Alternatives
- Make new acquisitions (or seek merger partnerships)
  - To build positions in new related/unrelated industries
  - To strengthen the position of business units in industries where the firm already has a stake
- Divest some business units
  - To eliminate weak-performing businesses from portfolio
  - To eliminate businesses that no longer fit
- Restructure makeup of whole portfolio if many business units are performing poorly
  - By selling selected business units
  - By using cash from divestitures plus unused debt capacity to make new acquisitions
- Retrench/narrow the diversification base
  - By pruning weak businesses
  - By shedding all noncore businesses
  - By divesting one or more core businesses
- Become a multinational, multi-industry enterprise (DMNC)
  - To succeed in globally competitive core businesses against international rivals
  - To capture strategic fit benefits and win a competitive advantage via multinational diversification
- Liquidate/close down money-losing businesses that cannot be sold

(2) divest weak-performing business units or those that no longer fit, (3) restructure the makeup of the portfolio if overall performance is poor, (4) retrench to a narrower diversification base, (5) pursue multinational diversification, and (6) close down/liquidate money-losing business units that cannot be sold.

SUGGESTED
READINGS

Ansoff, H. Igor. *Corporate Strategy.* New York: McGraw-Hill, 1965, chap. 7.

Bright, William M. "Alternative Strategies for Diversification." *Research Management* 12, no. 4 (July 1969), pp. 247–53.

Buzzell, Robert D. "Is Vertical Integration Profitable?" *Harvard Business Review* 61, no. 1 (January–February 1983), pp. 92–102.

Drucker, Peter. *Management: Tasks, Responsibilities, Practices.* New York: Harper & Row, 1974, chaps. 55, 56, 57, 58, 60, and 61.

Guth, William D. "Corporate Growth Strategies." *Journal of Business Strategy* 1, no. 2 (Fall 1980), pp. 56–62.

Hall, William K. "Survival Strategies in a Hostile Environment." *Harvard Business Review* 58, no. 5 (September–October 1980), pp. 75–85.

Harrigan, Kathryn R. "Matching Vertical Integration Strategies to Competitive Conditions." *Strategic Management Journal* 7, no. 6 (November–December 1986), pp. 535–56.

————. "Formulating Vertical Integration Strategies." *Academy of Management Review* 9, no. 4 (October 1984), pp. 638–52.

————. *Strategic Flexibility.* Lexington, Mass.: Lexington Books, 1985, chap. 4 and Table A-8, p. 162.

Hax, Arnoldo, and Nicolas S. Majluf. *The Strategy Concept and Process.* Englewood Cliffs, N.J.: Prentice Hall, 1991, chaps. 9, 11, and 15.

Hofer, Charles W. "Turnaround Strategies." *Journal of Business Strategy* 1, no. 1 (Summer 1980), pp. 19–31.

Hoffman, Richard C. "Strategies for Corporate Turnarounds: What Do We Know About Them?" *Journal of General Management* 14, no. 3 (Spring 1989), pp. 46–66.

Kumpe, Ted, and Piet T. Bolwijn. "Manufacturing: The New Case for Vertical Integration." *Harvard Business Review* 88, no. 2 (March–April 1988), pp. 75–82.

Lauenstein, Milton, and Wickham Skinner. "Formulating a Strategy of Superior Resources." *Journal of Business Strategy* 1, no. 1 (Summer 1980), pp. 4–10.

Ohmae, Kenichi. *The Mind of the Strategist.* New York: Penguin Books, 1983, chaps. 10 and 12.

Prahalad, C. K., and Yves L. Doz. *The Multinational Mission.* New York: Free Press, 1987, chaps. 1 and 2.

Techniques for Analyzing Diversified Companies

—

If we can know where we are and something about how we got there, we might see where we are trending—and if the outcomes which lie naturally in our course are unacceptable, to make timely change.
Abraham Lincoln

—

No company can afford everything it would like to do. Resources have to be allocated. The essence of strategic planning is to allocate resources to those areas that have the greatest future potential.
Reginald Jones

—

Once a company has diversified, three strategic issues continuously challenge corporate strategy-makers:

- How attractive is the group of businesses the company is in?
- Assuming the company sticks with its present lineup of businesses, how good is its performance outlook in the years ahead?
- If the previous two answers are not satisfactory, what should the company do in the way of getting out of some existing businesses, strengthening the positions of remaining businesses, and getting into new businesses to boost the performance prospects of its business portfolio?

The task of crafting and implementing action plans to improve the attractiveness and competitive strength of a company's business-unit portfolio is the heart of what corporate-level strategic management is all about.

Strategic analysis of diversified companies builds on the concepts and methods used for single-business companies. But there are also new factors to consider and additional analytical approaches to master. The procedure we will use to systematically evaluate the strategy of a diversified company, assess the caliber and potential of its businesses, and decide what strategic actions to take next consists of an eight-step process:

1. Identifying the present corporate strategy.
2. Constructing one or more business portfolio matrixes to reveal the character of the company's business portfolio.
3. Comparing the long-term attractiveness of each industry the company is in.
4. Comparing the competitive strength of the company's business units to see which ones are strong contenders in their respective industries.
5. Rating the business units on the basis of their historical performance and their prospects for the future.
6. Assessing each business unit's compatibility with corporate strategy and determining the value of any strategic fit relationships among existing business units.
7. Ranking the business units in terms of priority for new capital investment and deciding whether the general strategy and direction for each business unit should be aggressive expansion, fortify and defend, overhaul and reposition, or harvest/divest. (The task of initiating *specific* business-unit strategies to improve a subsidiary's competitive position is usually delegated to business-level managers, with corporate-level managers offering suggestions and having authority for final approval.)
8. Crafting new strategic moves to improve overall corporate performance—changing the makeup of the portfolio via acquisitions and divestitures, coordinating the activities of related business units to achieve cost-sharing and skills transfer benefits, and steering corporate resources into the areas of greatest opportunity.

The rest of this chapter describes this eight-step process and introduces the new analytical techniques needed to arrive at sound corporate strategy appraisals.

IDENTIFYING THE PRESENT CORPORATE STRATEGY

Strategic analysis of a diversified company starts by probing the organization's present strategy and business makeup. Recall from Figure 2–2 in Chapter 2 that a good overall perspective of a diversified company's corporate strategy comes from looking at:

- The extent to which the firm is diversified (as measured by the proportion of total sales and operating profits contributed by each business unit and by whether the diversification base is broad or narrow).
- Whether the firm's portfolio is keyed to related or unrelated diversification, or a mixture of both.
- Whether the scope of company operations is mostly domestic, increasingly multinational, or global.
- The nature of recent moves to boost performance of key business units and/or strengthen existing business positions.

- Any moves to add new businesses to the portfolio and build positions in new industries.
- Any moves to divest weak or unattractive business units.
- Corporate management efforts to pursue strategic fit relationships and use diversification to create competitive advantage.
- The proportion of capital expenditures going to each business unit.

Identifying the current corporate strategy lays the foundation for a thorough strategy analysis and, subsequently, for reformulating the strategy as it "should be."

MATRIX TECHNIQUES FOR EVALUATING DIVERSIFIED PORTFOLIOS

The most popular technique for assessing the quality of the businesses a company has diversified into is portfolio matrix analysis. *A business portfolio matrix is a two-dimensional display comparing the strategic positions of every business a diversified company is in.* Matrixes can be constructed using any pair of strategic position indicators. The most revealing indicators are industry growth rate, market share, long-term industry attractiveness, competitive strength, and stage of product/market evolution. Usually one dimension of the matrix relates to the attractiveness of the industry environment and the other to the strength of a business within its industry. Three types of business portfolio matrixes are used most frequently—the growth-share matrix developed by the Boston Consulting Group, the industry attractiveness-business strength matrix pioneered at General Electric, and the Hofer–A. D. Little industry life-cycle matrix.

Basic Concept
A business portfolio matrix is a two-dimensional display comparing the strategic positions of every business a diversified company is in.

The Growth-Share Matrix

The first business portfolio matrix to be widely used was a four-square grid devised by the Boston Consulting Group (BCG), a leading management consulting firm.[1] Figure 8–1 illustrates a BCG-type matrix. The matrix is formed using *industry growth rate* and *relative market share* as the axes. Each business unit appears as a "bubble" on the four-cell matrix, with the size of each bubble or circle scaled to the percent of revenues it represents in the overall corporate portfolio.

Early BCG methodology arbitrarily placed the dividing line between "high" and "low" industry growth rates at around twice the real GNP growth rate plus inflation, but the boundary percentage can be raised or lowered to suit individual preferences. A strong case can be made for placing the line so business units in industries growing faster than the economy as a whole end up in the "high-growth" cells and those in industries growing slower end up in "low-growth" cells ("low-growth" industries are those that can be described as mature, aging, stagnant, or declining).

The BCG portfolio matrix compares a diversified company's businesses on the basis of industry growth rate and relative market share.

---

[1]The original presentation is Bruce D. Henderson, "The Experience Curve—Reviewed. IV. The Growth Share Matrix of the Product Portfolio" (Boston: The Boston Consulting Group, 1973), Perspectives No. 135. For an excellent chapter-length treatment of the use of the BCG growth-share matrix in strategic portfolio analysis, see Arnoldo C. Hax and Nicolas S. Majluf, *Strategic Management: An Integrative Perspective* (Englewood Cliffs, N. J.: Prentice Hall, 1984), chap. 7.

FIGURE 8–1   **The BCG Growth-Share Business Portfolio Matrix**

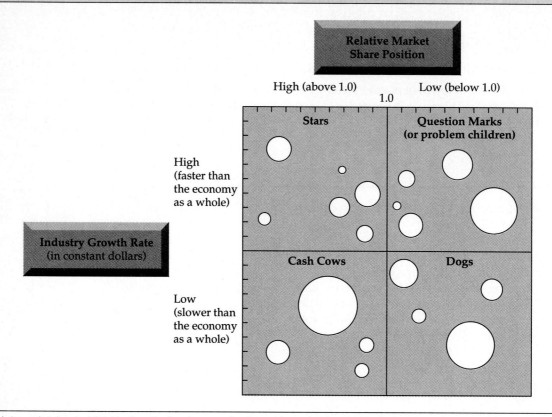

Note: *Relative* market share is defined by the ratio of one's own market share to the market share held by the largest *rival* firm. When the vertical dividing line is set at 1.0, the only way a firm can achieve a star or cash cow position in the growth-share matrix is to have the largest market share in the industry. Since this is a very stringent criterion, it may be "fairer" and more revealing to locate the vertical dividing line in the matrix at about 0.75 or 0.80.

Basic Concept
Relative market share is calculated by dividing a business's percentage share of total industry sales volume by the percentage share held by its largest rival.

Relative market share is the ratio of a business's market share to the market share held by the largest rival firm in the industry, with market share measured in unit volume not dollars. For instance, if business A has a 15 percent share of the industry's total volume and A's largest rival has a 30 percent share, A's relative market share is 0.5. If business B has a market-leading share of 40 percent and its largest rival has 30 percent, B's relative market share is 1.33. Given this definition, only business units that are market-share leaders in their respective industries will have relative market share values greater than 1.0; business units that trail one or more rivals in market share will have ratios below 1.0.

BCG's original standard put the border between "high" and "low" relative market share at 1.0, as shown in Figure 8–1. When the boundary is set at 1.0, circles in the two left-side cells of the matrix represent businesses that are market-share leaders in their industry. Circles in the two right-side cells identify portfolio members that are in runner-up positions in their industry. The degree to which they trail is indicated by the size of the relative market share ratio. A ratio of .10 indicates the business has a market share only $\frac{1}{10}$ that of the largest firm in the market; a ratio of .80 indicates a market share $\frac{4}{5}$ or 80 percent as big as the leading firm's. Many portfolio analysts think that putting the boundary between high and low relative market share at 1.0 is unreasonably stringent because only businesses with the largest market share in their industry qualify for the two left-side cells of the matrix. They advocate putting the boundary at 0.75 or 0.80 so businesses to the left have *strong* or above-average market positions (even though they are not *the* leader) and businesses to the right are clearly in underdog or below- average positions.

Using *relative* market share instead of *actual* market share to construct the growth-share matrix is analytically superior because the former measure is a better indicator of comparative market strength and competitive position. A 10 percent market share is much stronger if the leader's share is 12 percent than if it is 50 percent; the use of relative market share captures this difference. Equally important, relative market share is likely to reflect relative cost based on experience and economies of large-scale production. Large businesses may be able to operate at lower unit costs than smaller ones because of technological and efficiency gains that attach to larger size. But the Boston Consulting Group accumulated evidence that the phenomenon of lower unit costs went beyond just the effects of scale economies; they found that, as the cumulative volume of production increased, the knowledge gained from the firm's growing production experience often led to the discovery of additional efficiencies and ways to reduce costs even further. BCG labeled the relationship between *cumulative production volume* and lower unit costs *the experience curve effect* (for more details, see Figure 3–1 in Chapter 3). A sizable experience curve effect in the industry's activity-cost chain places a strategic premium on market share: the competitor that gains the largest market share tends to realize important cost advantages which, in turn, can be used to lower prices and gain still additional customers, sales, market share, and profit. The stronger the experience curve in a business, the more dominant role in its strategy-making.[2]

With these features of the BCG growth-share matrix in mind, we are ready to explore the portfolio implications for businesses in each cell of the matrix in Figure 8–1.

Relative market share is a better indicator of a business's competitive strength and market position than a simple percentage measure of market share.

Question Marks and Problem Children Business units falling in the upper-right quadrant of the growth-share matrix were labeled by BCG as "question marks" or "problem children." Rapid market growth makes such businesses attractive from an industry standpoint. But their low relative market share (and thus reduced access to experience curve effects) raises a question about whether they can compete successfully against larger, more cost-efficient rivals—hence, the "question mark" or "problem child" designation. Question mark businesses, moreover, are typically "cash hogs"—so labeled because their cash needs are high (owing to the investment requirements of rapid growth and product development) and their internal cash generation is low (owing to low market share, less access to experience curve effects and scale economies, and consequently thinner profit margins). A question mark/cash hog business in a fast-growing industry may require large infusions of cash just to keep up with rapid market growth; it may need even bigger infusions to outgrow the market and become an industry leader. The corporate parent of a cash hog business has to decide if it is worthwhile to fund the perhaps considerable investment requirements of a question mark division.

Basic Concept
A cash hog business is one whose internal cash flows are inadequate to fully fund its needs for working capital and new capital investment.

---

[2]For two recent discussions of the strategic importance of the experience curve, see Pankoy Ghemawat, "Building Strategy on the Experience Curve," *Harvard Business Review* 64, no. 2 (March–April 1985), pp. 143–49 and Bruce D. Henderson, "The Application and Misapplication of the Experience Curve," *Journal of Business Strategy* 4, no. 3 (Winter 1984), pp. 3–9.

BCG has argued that the two best strategic options for a question mark business are: (1) an aggressive invest-and-expand strategy to capitalize on the industry's rapid-growth opportunities or (2) divestiture if the costs of expanding capacity and building market share outweigh the potential payoff and financial risk. Pursuit of a fast-growth strategy is imperative any time an attractive question mark business is in an industry with strong experience curve effects. In such cases, it takes major gains in market share to begin to match the lower costs of firms with greater cumulative production experience and bigger market shares. The stronger the experience curve effect, the more potent the cost advantages of rivals with larger relative market shares. Consequently, so the BCG thesis goes, unless a question mark/problem child business can successfully pursue a fast-growth strategy and win major market-share gains, it cannot hope to ever become cost competitive with large-volume firms that are further down the experience curve. Divestiture then becomes the only other viable long-run alternative. The corporate strategy prescriptions for managing question mark/problem child businesses are straightforward: divest those that are weaker and have less chance to catch the leaders on the experience curve; invest heavily in high-potential question marks and groom them to become tomorrow's "stars."

Stars Businesses with high relative market share positions in high-growth markets rank as "stars" in the BCG grid because they offer excellent profit and growth opportunities. They are the business units an enterprise depends on to boost overall performance of the total portfolio.

Given their dominant market-share position and rapid growth environment, stars typically require large cash investments to expand production facilities and meet working capital needs. But they also tend to generate their own large internal cash flows due to the low-cost advantage of scale economies and cumulative production experience. Star businesses vary as to their cash hog status. Some can cover their investment needs with their own cash flows; others need funds from their corporate parents to stay abreast of rapid industry growth. Normally, strongly-positioned star businesses in industries where growth is beginning to slow tend to be self-sustaining in terms of cash flow and make little claim on the corporate parent's treasury. Young stars, however, typically require substantial investment capital *beyond what they can generate on their own* and are thus cash hogs.

Cash Cows Businesses with a high relative market share in a low-growth market are designated "cash cows" in the BCG scheme. A *cash cow business* generates substantial cash surpluses over what it needs for reinvestment and growth. The reasons why a business in this cell of the matrix tends to be a cash cow are straightforward. Because of the business's high relative market share and industry leadership position, it has the sales volumes and reputation to earn attractive profits. Because it is in a slow-growth industry, it typically generates more cash from current operations than it needs to sustain its market position.

Many of today's cash cows are yesterday's stars, having dropped into the bottom cell as industry demand matured. Cash cows, though less attractive from a growth standpoint, are valuable businesses. Their cash flows can be used to cover dividend payments, finance acquisitions, and provide funds for investing in emerging stars and problem children being groomed as future stars.

Every effort should be made to keep cash cow businesses in healthy condition to preserve their cash-generating capability over the long term. The goal should be to fortify and defend a cash cow's market position while efficiently generating dollars to reallocate to other business investments. Weakening cash cows, however, may become candidates for harvesting and eventual divestiture if industry maturity results in unattractive competitive conditions and dries up the cash flow surpluses.

Dogs Businesses with a low relative market share in a slow-growth industry are called "dogs" because of their dim growth prospects, their trailing market position, and the squeeze that being behind the leaders on the experience curve puts on their profit margins. Weak dog businesses (those positioned in the lower right corner of the dog cell) are often unable to generate attractive cash flows on a long-term basis. Sometimes they cannot produce enough cash to support a rear-guard fortify-and-defend strategy—especially if competition is brutal and profit margins are chronically thin. Consequently, except in unusual cases, BCG prescribes that weaker-performing dog businesses be harvested, divested, or liquidated, depending on which alternative yields the most cash.

Weaker dog businesses should be harvested, divested, or liquidated; stronger dogs can be retained as long as their profits and cash flows remain acceptable.

Implications for Corporate Strategy The chief contribution of the BCG growth-share matrix is the attention it draws to the cash flow and investment characteristics of various types of businesses and how corporate financial resources can be shifted between businesses to optimize the performance of the whole corporate portfolio. According to BCG analysis, a sound, long-term corporate strategy should utilize the excess cash generated by cash cow business units to finance market-share increases for cash hog businesses—the young stars unable to finance their own growth and problem children with the best potential to grow into stars. If successful, cash hogs eventually become self-supporting stars. Then, when stars' markets begin to mature and their growth slows, they become cash cows. The "success sequence" is thus problem child/question mark to young star (but perhaps still a cash hog) to self-supporting star to cash cow.

The BCG growth-share matrix highlights the cash flow, investment, and profitability characteristics of various businesses and the benefits of shifting financial resources between them to optimize the whole portfolio's performance.

Weaker, less-attractive question mark businesses unworthy of a long-term invest-and-expand strategy are often a liability to a diversified company because of the high-cost economics associated with their low relative market share and because they do not generate enough cash to keep pace with market growth. According to BCG prescriptions, these question marks should be prime divestiture candidates *unless* they can be kept profitable and viable with their own internally generated funds. Not every question mark business is a cash hog or a disadvantaged competitor, however. Those in industries with small capital requirements, few scale economies, and weak experience curve effects can often compete satisfactorily against larger industry leaders and contribute enough to corporate earnings to justify retention. Clearly, though, weaker question marks still have a low-priority claim on corporate resources and a dim future in the portfolio. Question mark businesses unable to become stars are destined to drift vertically downward in the matrix, becoming dogs, as their industry growth slows and market demand matures.

Dogs should be retained only as long as they contribute adequately to overall company performance. Strong dogs may produce a positive cash flow and show average profitability. But the further right and down a dog business is positioned in the BCG matrix, the more likely it is tying up assets that could be redeployed more profitably. BCG recommends a harvesting strategy for a weakening or already weak dog business. If a harvesting strategy is no longer attractive, a weak dog should be eliminated from the portfolio.

There are two "disaster sequences" in the BCG scheme of things: (1) when a star's position in the matrix erodes over time to that of a problem child and then is dragged by slowing industry growth down into the dog cell of the matrix and (2) when a cash cow loses market leadership to the point where it becomes a dog on the decline. Other strategic mistakes include overinvesting in a safe cash cow; underinvesting in a question mark so instead of becoming a star it tumbles into the dog category; and shotgunning resources over many question marks rather than concentrating on the best ones to boost their chances of becoming stars.

Strengths and Weaknesses in the Growth-Share Matrix Approach The BCG business portfolio matrix makes a definite contribution to the strategist's tool kit when it comes to evaluating the portfolio's overall attractiveness and reaching broad prescriptions concerning the strategy and direction for each business unit. Viewing a diversified corporation as a collection of cash flows and cash requirements (present and future) is a major step forward in understanding the financial aspects of corporate strategy. The BCG matrix highlights the financial "interaction" within a corporate portfolio, shows the kinds of financial considerations that must be dealt with, and explains why priorities for corporate resource allocation can differ from business to business. It also provides good rationalizations for both invest-and-expand strategies and divestiture. Yet it has several legitimate shortcomings:

Despite the analytical insights it yields, the growth-share matrix has significant shortcomings.

1. A four-cell matrix based on high-low classifications hides the fact that many businesses (the majority?) are in markets with an "average" growth rate and have relative market shares that are neither high nor low but in-between or intermediate. In which cells do these average businesses belong?

2. While labeling businesses as stars, cash cows, dogs, or question marks does have communicative appeal, it is a misleading simplification to pigeonhole all businesses into one of four categories. Some market-share leaders have never really been stars in terms of profitability. All businesses with low relative market shares are not dogs or question marks—in many cases, runner-up firms have proven track records in terms of growth, profitability, and competitive ability, even gaining on the so-called leaders. Hence, a key characteristic to assess is the *trend* in a firm's relative market share. Is it gaining ground or losing ground and why? This weakness can be overcome by placing directional arrows on each of the circles in the matrix—see Figure 8–2.

3. The BCG matrix is not a reliable indicator of relative investment opportunities across business units.[3] For example, investing in a star is not necessarily more attractive than investing in a lucrative cash cow. The matrix doesn't indicate if a question mark is a potential winner or

---

[3]Derek F. Abell and John S. Hammond, *Strategic Market Planning* (Englewood Cliffs, N.J.: Prentice Hall, 1979), p. 212.

FIGURE 8–2   **Present versus Future Positions in the Portfolio Matrix**

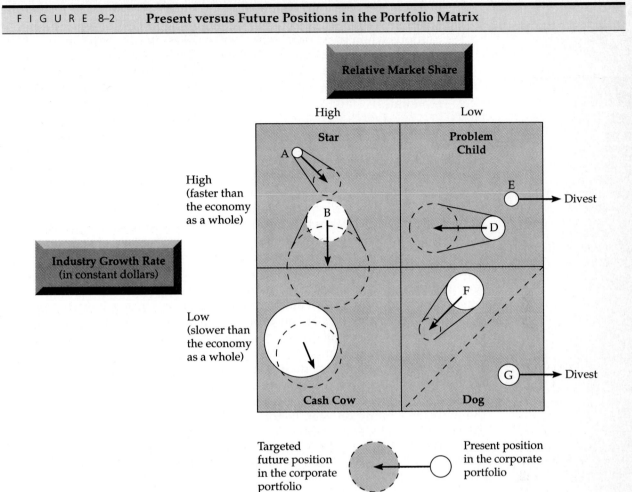

4. a likely loser. It says nothing about whether shrewd investment can turn a strong dog into a cash cow.

4. Being a market leader in a slow-growth industry does not guarantee cash cow status because (*a*) the investment requirements of a fortify-and- defend strategy, given the impact of inflation on the costs of replacing worn-out facilities and equipment, can soak up much or all of the available internal cash flows and (*b*) as markets mature, competitive forces often stiffen, and the ensuing battle for volume and market share can shrink profit margins and wipe out any surplus cash flows.

5. To thoroughly assess the long-term attractiveness of the portfolio's business units, strategists need to examine more than just industry growth and relative market share variables—as we discussed in Chapter 3.

6. The connection between relative market share and profitability is not as tight as the experience curve effect implies. The importance of cumulative production experience in lowering unit costs varies from

industry to industry. Sometimes a larger market share translates into a unit-cost advantage; sometimes it doesn't. Hence, it is wise to be cautious when prescribing strategy based on the assumption that experience curve effects are strong enough and cost differences among competitors big enough to totally drive competitive advantage (there are more sources of competitive advantage than just experience curve economics).

The Industry Attractiveness/Business Strength Matrix

In the attractiveness-strength matrix, each business is plotted using quantitative measures of long-term industry attractiveness and business strength/competitive position.

An alternative approach avoids some of the shortcomings of the BCG growth-share matrix. Pioneered by General Electric as a way to analyze its own diversified portfolio (with help from the consulting firm of McKinsey and Company), this nine-cell matrix is based on the two dimensions of long-term industry attractiveness and business strength/competitive position (see Figure 8–3).[4] Both dimensions of the matrix are a composite of *several* considerations as opposed to a single factor. The criteria for determining long-term industry attractiveness include market size and growth rate; technological requirements; the intensity of competition; entry and exit barriers; seasonality and cyclical influences; capital requirements; emerging industry threats and opportunities; historical and projected industry profitability; and social, environmental, and regulatory influences. To arrive at a formal, quantitative measure of long-term industry attractiveness, the chosen measures are assigned weights based on their importance to corporate management and their role in the diversification strategy. The sum of the weights must add up to 1.0. Weighted attractiveness ratings are calculated by multiplying the industry's rating on each factor (using a 1 to 5 or 1 to 10 rating scale) by the factor's weight. For example, a rating score of 8 times a weight of .25 gives a weighted rating of 2.0. The sum of weighted ratings for all the attractiveness factors yields the industry's long-term attractiveness. The procedure is shown below:

Industry/Attractiveness Factor	Weight	Rating	Weighted Industry Rating
Market size and projected growth	.15	5	0.75
Seasonality and cyclical influences	.10	8	0.80
Technological considerations	.10	1	0.10
Intensity of competition	.25	4	1.00
Emerging opportunities and threats	.15	1	0.15
Capital requirements	.05	2	0.10
Industry profitability	.10	3	0.30
Social, political, regulatory, and environmental factors	.10	7	0.70
	1.00		
Industry attractiveness rating			3.90

---

[4] For an expanded treatment, see Michael G. Allen, "Diagramming G.E.'s Planning for What's WATT," in *Corporate Planning: Techniques and Applications*, ed. Robert J. Allio and Malcolm W. Pennington (New York: AMACOM, 1979); and Hax and Majluf, *Strategic Management: An Integrative Perspective*, chap. 8.

FIGURE 8–3   General Electric's Industry Attractiveness/Business Strength Matrix

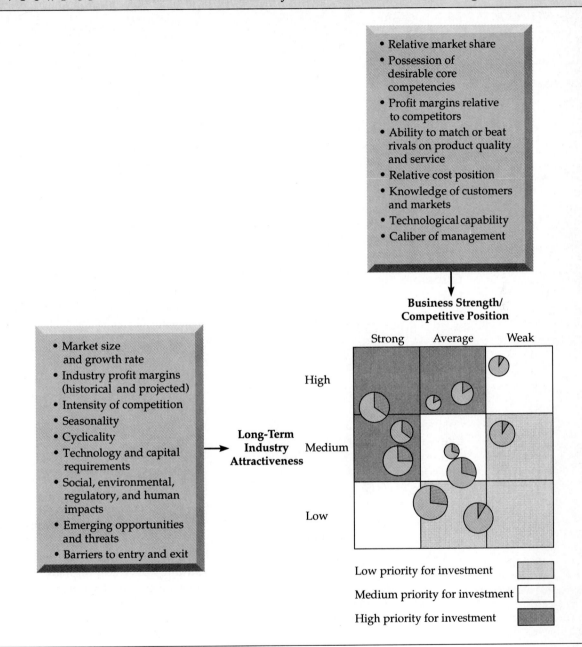

Attractiveness ratings are calculated for each industry represented in the corporate portfolio. Each industry's attractiveness score determines its position on the vertical scale in Figure 8–3.

To arrive at a quantitative measure of business strength/competitive position, each business in the corporate portfolio is rated using the same kind of approach as for industry attractiveness. The factors used to assess business strength/competitive position include such criteria as market share, relative cost position, ability to match rival firms on product quality and service, knowledge of customers and markets, possession of desirable core competences, adequacy of technological know-how, caliber of management, and profitability relative to competitors (as specified in the box in Figure 8–3). The analytical issue is whether to rate each business unit on the same generic factors (which strengthens the basis for interindustry comparisons) or on each unit's strength on the factors most pertinent to its own industry (which gives a sharper measure of competitive position). Each business's strength/position rating determines its position along the horizontal axis of the matrix—that is, whether it merits a strong, average, or weak designation.[5]

The industry attractiveness and business strength scores provide the basis for placing a business in one of the nine cells of the matrix. In the GE attractiveness-strength matrix, the area of the circles is proportional to the size of the industry, and the pie slices within the circle reflect the business's market share.

Corporate Strategy Implications   The most important strategic implications from the attractiveness-strength matrix concern the assignment of investment priorities to each of the company's business units. Businesses in the three cells at the upper left, where long-term industry attractiveness and business strength/competitive position are favorable, are accorded top investment priority. The strategic prescription for businesses falling in these three cells is "grow and build," with businesses in the high-strong cell having the highest claim on investment funds. Next in priority come businesses positioned in the three diagonal cells stretching from the lower left to the upper right. These businesses are usually given medium priority. They merit steady reinvestment to maintain and protect their industry positions; however, if a business in one of these three cells has an unusually attractive opportunity, it can win a higher investment priority and be given the go-ahead to employ a more aggressive strategic approach. The strategy prescription for businesses in the three cells in the lower right corner is typically harvest or divest (in exceptional cases where good turnaround potential exists, it can be "overhaul and reposition" using some type of turnaround approach).[6]

The nine-cell attractiveness-strength approach has three desirable attributes. One, it allows for intermediate rankings between high and low and between strong and weak. Two, it incorporates a much wider variety of strategically relevant variables. The BCG matrix is based totally on two considerations—industry growth rate and relative market share; the nine-cell GE

The nine-cell attractiveness-strength matrix has a stronger conceptual basis than the four-cell growth-share matrix.

---

[5]Essentially the same procedure is used in company situation analysis to do a competitive strength assessment (see Table 4–3 in Chapter 4). The only difference is that in the GE method the same set of competitive strength factors is used for every industry to provide a common benchmark for making comparisons across industries. In strategic analysis at the business level, the strength measures are *always* industry specific, never generic generalizations.

[6]At General Electric, each business actually ended up in one of five categories: (1) *high-growth potential* businesses deserving top investment priority; (2) *stable base* businesses that merit steady reinvestment to maintain position; (3) *support* businesses deserving periodic investment funding; (4) *selective pruning or rejuvenation* businesses deserving reduced investment; and (5) *venture* businesses meriting heavy R&D investment.

matrix takes many factors into account to determine long-term industry attractiveness and business strength/competitive position. Three, and most important, it stresses the channeling of corporate resources to businesses with the greatest probability of achieving competitive advantage and superior performance. It is hard to argue against the logic of concentrating resources in those businesses that enjoy a higher degree of attractiveness and competitive strength, being very selective in making investments in businesses with "intermediate" positions, and withdrawing resources from businesses that are lower in attractiveness and strength unless they offer exceptional turnaround potential.

However, the nine-cell GE matrix, like the four-cell growth-share matrix, provides no real guidance on the *specifics* of business strategy; the most that can be concluded from the GE matrix analysis is what *general* strategic posture to take—aggressive expansion, fortify-and-defend, or harvest-divest. Such prescriptions, though valuable for overall portfolio management, don't address the issue of strategic coordination across related businesses and the specific competitive approaches and strategic actions to take at the business-unit level. Another weakness has been pointed out by Professors Hofer and Schendel: the GE method tends to obscure businesses that are about to become winners because their industries are entering the takeoff stage.[7]

The Life-Cycle Matrix

To better identify a *developing-winner* type of business, Hofer developed a 15-cell matrix. In this matrix businesses are plotted in terms of stage of industry evolution and competitive position, as shown in Figure 8–4.[8] Again, the circles represent the sizes of the industries involved, and pie wedges denote the business's market share. In Figure 8–4, business A could be labeled a *developing winner*; business C a *potential loser*, business E an *established winner*, business F a cash cow, and business G a loser or dog. The power of the life-cycle matrix is the story it tells about the distribution of the firm's businesses across the stages of industry evolution.

The life-cycle matrix highlights whether a firm's businesses are evenly distributed across the stages of the industry life-cycle.

Deciding Which Matrix to Construct

Restricting the analysis to just one type of portfolio matrix is unwise. Each matrix has its pros and cons, and each tells a different story about the portfolio's strengths and weaknesses. Provided adequate data is available, all three matrixes should be constructed since it's best to assess the company's portfolio from different perspectives. The analytical objective is to understand the portfolio's mix of industries, the strategic position each business has in its industry, the portfolio's performance potential, and the kinds of financial and resource allocation considerations that have to be dealt with.

---

[7]Charles W. Hofer and Dan Schendel, *Strategy Formulation: Analytical Concepts* (St. Paul, Minn.: West Publishing, 1978), p. 33.

[8]Ibid., p. 34. This approach to business portfolio analysis was reportedly first used in practice by consultants at Arthur D. Little, Inc. For a full-scale review of this portfolio matrix approach, see Hax and Majluf, *Strategic Management: An Integrative Perspective*, chap. 9.

F I G U R E 8–4   **The Life-Cycle Portfolio Matrix**

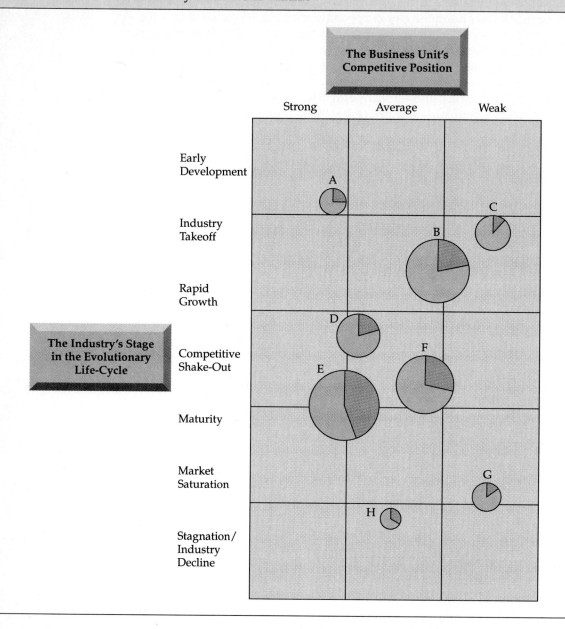

COMPARING INDUSTRY ATTRACTIVENESS

The attractiveness of the industries that a firm has diversified into needs to be evaluated from several angles.

A central issue in evaluating a diversified company's strategy is judging the attractiveness of the industries it is in. Industry attractiveness has to be judged from three perspectives:

1. *The attractiveness of each industry represented in the portfolio.* The relevant question is "Is this a good *industry* for the company to be in?" Ideally, each industry the firm has diversified into can pass the attractiveness test.

2. *Each industry's attractiveness relative to the others.* The question to answer here is "Which industries in the portfolio are the most attractive, and which are the least attractive?" Ranking the industries from most attractive to least attractive is a prerequisite to deciding how to allocate corporate resources.

3. *The attractiveness of all the industries as a group.* The question here is "How appealing is the *mix* of industries?" A company whose revenues and profits come chiefly from businesses in unattractive industries probably needs to consider restructuring its business portfolio.

All the industry attractiveness considerations discussed in Chapter 3 have application in this analytical phase.

An industry attractiveness/business strength portfolio matrix gives a strong, systematic basis for judging which business units are in the most attractive industries. If such a matrix has not been constructed, quantitative rankings of industry attractiveness can be developed using the same procedure described earlier for the nine-cell GE matrix. As a rule, all the industries represented in the business portfolio should, at minimum, be judged on the following attractiveness factors:

- *Market size and projected growth rate*—faster-growing industries tend to be more attractive than slow-growing industries, other things being equal.

- *The intensity of competition*—industries where competitive pressures are relatively weak are more attractive than industries with strong competitive pressures.

- *Technological and production skills required*—industries where the skill requirements are closely matched to company capabilities are more attractive than industries where the company's technical and/or manufacturing know-how is limited.

- *Capital requirements*—industries with low or attainable capital requirements are relatively more attractive than industries where investment requirements could strain corporate resources.

- *Seasonal and cyclical factors*—industries where demand is relatively stable and dependable are more attractive than industries where there are wide swings in buyer demand.

- *Industry profitability*—industries with healthy profit margins and high rates of return on investment are generally more attractive than industries where profits have historically been low or where the business risks are high.

- *Social, political, regulatory, and environmental factors*—industries with significant problems in these areas are less attractive than industries where such problems are no worse than most businesses encounter.

- *Strategic fits with other industries the firm has diversified into*—an industry can be attractive simply because it has valuable strategic fit relationships with other industries in the portfolio.

Strategic Management Principle
The more attractive the industries that a firm has diversified into, the better its performance prospects are likely to be.

Calculation of industry attractiveness ratings for all industries in the corporate portfolio provides a basis for ranking the industries from most to least attractive. If formal industry attractiveness ratings seem too cumbersome or tedious to calculate, analysts can rely on their knowledge of conditions in each industry to classify individual industries as having "high," "medium," or "low" attractiveness. However, the validity of such subjective assessments depends on whether analysts have studied industry conditions enough to make dependable judgments.

For a diversified company to be a strong performer, a substantial portion of its revenues and profits must come from business units in attractive industries. It is particularly important that core businesses be in industries with a good outlook for growth and above-average profitability. Businesses in the least attractive industries may be divestiture candidates, unless they are positioned strongly enough to overcome the adverse industry environment or they are a critical component of the portfolio.

COMPARING BUSINESS-UNIT STRENGTH

Assessments of how a firm's subsidiaries compare in competitive strength should be based on several factors.

Doing an appraisal of each business unit's strength and competitive position in its industry helps corporate managers judge a business unit's chances for success in its industry. The task here is to evaluate whether the business is well-positioned in its industry and the extent to which it already is or can become a strong market contender. The two most revealing techniques for evaluating a business's position in its industry are SWOT analysis and competitive strength assessment. Quantitative rankings of the strength/position of the portfolio's businesses can be calculated using either the attractiveness-strength matrix or the procedure presented in Chapter 4. Assessments of how a diversified company's subsidiaries compare in competitive strength should be based on such factors as:

- *Relative market share*—business units with higher relative market shares have greater competitive strength than business units with lower shares.

- *Ability to compete on price and/or quality*—business units that are cost competitive and/or that have established brand names and a reputation for quality tend to be more strongly positioned than those struggling to establish a name or achieve cost parity with major rivals.

- *Technology and innovation capabilities*—business units recognized for their technological leadership and track record in innovation are usually strong competitors in their industry.

- *How well the business unit's skills and competences match industry key success factors*—the more a business unit's strengths match the industry's key success factors, the stronger its competitive position tends to be.

- *Profitability relative to competitors*—business units that consistently earn above-average returns on investment and have bigger profit margins than their rivals usually have stronger competitive positions than businesses with below-average profitability for their industry. Moreover, above-average profitability signals competitive advantage while below-average profitability usually denotes competitive disadvantage.

Other competitive strength indicators that can be employed include knowledge of customers and markets, production capabilities, marketing skills, reputation and brand name awareness, and the caliber of management.

Calculation of competitive strength ratings for each business unit provides a basis for judging which ones are in strong positions in their industries and which are in weak positions. If calculating competitive strength ratings is complicated by lack of sufficient data, analysts can rely on their knowledge of each business unit's competitive situation to classify each business unit as being in a "strong," "average," or "weak" competitive position. If trustworthy, such subjective judgments can substitute for quantitative measures.

Evaluating which businesses in the portfolio enjoy the strongest competitive positions adds further rationale for corporate resource allocation. A company may earn larger profits over the long term by investing in a business with a strong position in a moderately attractive industry than a weak business in a glamour industry. This is why a diversified company needs to consider *both* industry attractiveness and business strength in deciding where to steer resources.

Many diversified companies concentrate their resources on industries where they can be strong market contenders and divest businesses that are not good candidates for becoming leaders. At General Electric, the whole thrust of corporate strategy and resource allocation is aimed at putting GE's businesses into a number one or two position both in the United States and globally—see Illustration Capsule 21.

Strategic Management Principle
Shareholder interests are generally best served by concentrating corporate resources on businesses that can contend for market leadership in their industry.

COMPARING BUSINESS-UNIT PERFORMANCE

Once each subsidiary has been rated on the basis of industry attractiveness and competitive strength, the next step is to evaluate which businesses have the best performance prospects and which ones have the worst. The most important considerations in judging business-unit performance are sales growth, profit growth, contribution to company earnings, and the return on capital invested in the business; sometimes, cash flow generation is a big consideration, especially for cash cows or businesses with potential for harvesting. Information on a business's past performance can be gleaned from financial records. While past performance doesn't necessarily predict future performance, it does signal which businesses have been strong performers and which have not. Industry attractiveness/business strength evaluations should provide a solid basis for judging future prospects. Normally, strong business units in attractive industries have significantly better prospects than weak businesses in unattractive industries.

The growth and profit outlook for the company's core businesses generally determine whether the portfolio as a whole will turn in a strong or weak performance. Noncore businesses with subpar track records and little expectation for improvement are logical candidates for divestiture. Business subsidiaries with the brightest profit and growth prospects should have priority for having their capital investment requests funded.

Judgments about the expected future performance of each subsidiary indicate whether a firm's outlook for profitable growth with its current business lineup is bright or dim.

STRATEGIC FIT ANALYSIS

The next analytical step is to determine how well each business unit fits into the company's overall business picture. Fit needs to be looked at from two angles: (1) whether a business unit has valuable strategic fit with other

ILLUSTRATION CAPSULE
21

PORTFOLIO MANAGEMENT AT GENERAL ELECTRIC

When Jack Welch became CEO of General Electric in 1981, he launched a corporate strategy effort to reshape the company's diversified business portfolio. Early on he issued a challenge to GE's business-unit managers to become number one or number two in their industry; failing that, the business units either had to capture a decided technological advantage translatable into a competitive edge or face possible divestiture.

By 1989, GE was a different company. Under Welch's prodding, GE divested operations worth $9 billion—TV operations, small appliances, a mining business, and computer chips. It spent a

total of $24 billion acquiring new businesses, most notably RCA, Roper (a maker of major appliances whose biggest customer was Sears), and Kidder Peabody (a Wall Street investment banking firm). Internally, many of the company's smaller business operations were put under the direction of larger "strategic business units." But, most significantly, in 1989, 12 of GE's 14 strategic business units were market leaders in the United States and globally (the company's financial services and communications units served markets too fragmented to rank):

	Market Standing in the United States	Market Standing in the World
Aircraft engines	First	First
Broadcasting (NBC)	First	Not applicable
Circuit breakers	Tied for first with 2 others	Tied for first with 3 others
Defense electronics	Second	Second
Electric motors	First	First
Engineering plastics	First	First
Factory automation	Second	Third
Industrial and power systems	First	First
Lighting	First	Second
Locomotives	First	Tied for first
Major home appliances	First	Tied for second
Medical diagnostic imaging	First	First

In 1989, having divested most of the weak businesses and having built existing businesses into leading contenders, Welch launched a new initiative within GE to dramatically boost productivity and reduce the size of GE's bureaucracy. Welch argued that for GE to continue to be successful in a

global marketplace, the company had to press hard for continuous cost reduction in each of its businesses and cut through bureaucratic procedures to shorten response times to changing market conditions.

Source: Developed from information in Stratford P. Sherman, "Inside the Mind of Jack Welch," *Fortune*, March 27, 1989, pp. 39–50.

Strategic Management Principle

Business subsidiaries that don't fit strategically should be considered for divestiture unless their financial performance is outstanding.

businesses the firm has diversified into (or has an opportunity to diversify into) and (2) whether the business unit meshes well with corporate strategy or adds a beneficial dimension to the corporate portfolio. A business is more attractive *strategically* when it has cost-sharing or skills transfer opportunities that can be translated into stronger competitive advantage and when it fits in with the firm's strategic direction. A business is more valuable *financially* when it can contribute heavily to corporate performance objectives (sales growth, profit growth, above-average return on investment, and so on) and materially enhance the company's overall worth. Just as businesses with poor profit prospects ought to become divestiture candidates so should businesses that don't fit strategically into the company's overall business picture. Firms that emphasize related diversification probably should divest businesses with little or no strategic fit unless such businesses are unusually good financial performers.

RANKING THE BUSINESS UNITS ON INVESTMENT PRIORITY

Using the information and results of the preceding evaluation steps, corporate strategists can rank business units in terms of priority for new capital investment and develop a general strategic direction for each business unit. The task is to decide where the corporation should be investing its financial resources. Which business units should have top priority for new capital investment and financial support? Which business units should carry the lowest priority for new investment? Out of this ranking comes a clearer idea of what the basic strategic approach for each business unit should be—grow and build (aggressive expansion), fortify and defend (protect current position with new investments as needed), overhaul and reposition (try to move the business into a more desirable industry position and a better spot in the business portfolio matrix), or harvest/divest. In deciding whether to divest a business unit, strategists need to use a number of evaluating criteria: industry attractiveness, competitive strength, strategic fit with other businesses, performance potential (profit, return on capital employed, contribution to cash flow), compatibility with corporate priorities, capital requirements, and value to the overall portfolio.

Improving the long-term financial performance of a diversified company entails giving priority to investments in businesses with good to excellent prospects and investing minimally, if at all, in businesses with subpar prospects.

As part of this evaluation step, consideration should be given to whether and how corporate resources and skills can be used to enhance the competitive standing of particular business units.[9] The potential for skills transfer and infusion of new capital become especially important when the firm has business units in less-than-desirable competitive positions and/or where improvement in some key success area could make a big difference to the unit's performance. It is also important when corporate strategy is predicated on strategic fit and the managerial game plan calls for transferring corporate skills and strengths to recently acquired business units in an effort to give them a competitive edge and bolster their market positions.[10]

CRAFTING A CORPORATE STRATEGY

The preceding analysis sets the stage for crafting strategic moves to improve a diversified company's overall performance. The basic issue of "what to do" hinges on the conclusions drawn about the overall *mix* of businesses in the portfolio.[11] Key considerations here are: Does the portfolio contain enough

---

[9]Hofer and Schendel, *Strategy Formulation: Analytical Concepts*, p. 80.

[10]Michael E. Porter, *Competitive Advantage* (New York: Free Press, 1985), chap. 9.

[11]Barry Hedley, "Strategy and the Business Portfolio," *Long Range Planning* 10, no. 1 (February 1977), p. 13; and Hofer and Schendel, *Strategy Formulation*, pp. 82–86.

businesses in very attractive industries? Does the portfolio contain too many marginal businesses or question marks? Is the proportion of mature or declining businesses so great that corporate growth will be sluggish? Does the firm have enough cash cows to finance the stars and emerging winners? Do the company's core businesses generate dependable profits and/or cash flow? Is the portfolio overly vulnerable to seasonal or recessionary influences? Does the portfolio contain businesses that the company really doesn't need to be in? Is the firm burdened with too many businesses in average-to-weak competitive positions? Does the makeup of the business portfolio put the corporation in good position for the future? Answers to these questions indicate whether corporate strategists should consider divesting certain business, acquiring new ones, or restructuring the portfolio.

The Performance Test

Corporate strategists can pursue any of five basic options to avoid a probable shortfall in financial performance.

A good test of the strategic and financial attractiveness of a firm's portfolio is whether the company can attain its performance objectives with its current lineup of businesses. If so, no major corporate strategy changes are indicated. However, if a performance shortfall is probable, corporate strategists can take any of several actions to close the gap:[12]

1. *Alter the strategic plans for some (or all) of the businesses.* This option involves renewed corporate efforts to get better performance out of its present business units. Corporate managers can push business-level managers for better business-unit performance. However, pursuing better short-term performance, if done too zealously, can impair a business's potential to perform better over the long term. Cancelling expenditures that will bolster a business's long-term competitive position in order to squeeze out better short-term financial performance is a perilous strategy. In any case, there are limits as to how much extra performance can be squeezed out.

2. *Add new business units.* Boosting overall performance by making new acquisitions and/or starting new businesses internally raises some new strategy issues. Corporate managers must decide: (*a*) whether to acquire related or unrelated businesses, (*b*) what size acquisition(s) to make, (*c*) how the new units will fit into the present corporate structure, (*d*) what specific features to look for in an acquisition candidate, and (*e*) if acquisitions can be financed without shortchanging present business units in funding their investment requirements. Nonetheless, adding new businesses is a major strategic option, one frequently used by diversified companies to escape sluggish earnings performance.

3. *Divest weak-performing or money-losing businesses.* The most likely candidates for divestiture are businesses in a weak competitive position, in a relatively unattractive industry, or in an industry that does not "fit." Funds from divestitures can, of course, be used to finance new acquisitions, pay down corporate debt, or fund new strategic thrusts in the remaining businesses.

---

[12]Hofer and Schendel, *Strategy Formulation*, pp. 93–100.

4. *Form alliances to try to alter conditions responsible for subpar performance potentials.* In some situations, alliances with domestic or foreign firms, trade associations, suppliers, customers, or special interest groups may help ameliorate adverse performance prospects.[13] Forming or supporting a political action group may be an effective way to lobby for solutions to import-export problems, tax disincentives, and onerous regulatory requirements.

5. *Lower corporate performance objectives.* Adverse market circumstances or declining fortunes in one or more core business units can render companywide performance targets unreachable. So can overly ambitious objective-setting. Closing the gap between actual and desired performance may then require revision of corporate objectives to bring them more in line with reality. Lowering performance objectives is usually a "last-resort" option, used only after other options have come up short.

Finding Additional Diversification Opportunities

One of the major corporate strategy-making concerns in a diversified company is whether to pursue further diversification and, if so, how to identify the "right" kinds of industries and businesses to get into. For firms pursuing unrelated diversification, the issue of where to diversify next is wide open—the search for acquisition candidates is based more on financial criteria than on industry or strategic criteria. Decisions to add unrelated businesses to the firm's portfolio are usually based on such considerations as whether the firm has the financial ability to make another acquisition, whether new acquisitions are needed to boost overall corporate performance, whether one or more acquisition opportunities have to be acted on before they are purchased by other firms, and whether the timing is right for another acquisition (corporate management may have its hands full dealing with the current portfolio of businesses).

In firms with unrelated diversification strategies, the problem of where to diversify next is addressed by hunting for businesses that offer attractive financial returns irrespective of what industry they're in.

With a related diversification strategy, however, the search for new industries needs to be aimed at identifying those that have strategic fits with one or more of the firm's present businesses.[14] This means looking for industries whose activity-cost chains relate to the activity-cost chains of businesses already in the company's portfolio. The interrelationships can concern (1) product or process R&D, (2) opportunities for joint manufacturing and assembly, (3) marketing and distribution channel interrelationships, (4) customer overlaps, (5) opportunities for joint after-sale service, or (6) common managerial know-how requirements—essentially any area where market-related, operating, or management fits can occur.

In firms with related diversification strategies, the problem of where to diversify next is addressed by locating an attractive industry having good strategic fit with one or more of the firm's present businesses.

Once strategic fit opportunities in other industries are identified, corporate strategists have to distinguish between opportunities where important competitive advantage potential exists (through cost-savings, skill transfers, and so on) and those where the strategic fit benefits are really very minor. The size

---

[13]For an excellent discussion of the benefits of alliances among competitors in global industries, see Kenichi Ohmae, "The Global Logic of Strategic Alliances," *Harvard Business Review* 67, no. 2 (March–April 1989), pp. 143–54.

[14]Porter, *Competitive Advantage*, pp. 370–71.

of the competitive advantage potential depends on whether the strategic fit benefits are competitively significant, how much it will cost to capture the benefits, and how difficult it will be to merge and coordinate the business-unit interrelationships.[15] Analysis usually reveals that while there are many actual and potential interrelationships and linkages, only a few have enough strategic importance to generate meaningful competitive advantage.

Deploying Corporate Resources

To get ever-higher levels of performance out of a diversified company's business portfolio, corporate managers must also do an effective job of allocating corporate resources. Their strategy-making task is to steer resources out of low-opportunity areas into high-opportunity areas. Divesting marginal businesses serves this purpose by freeing unproductive assets for redeployment. Surplus funds from cash cows and harvested businesses also add to the corporate treasury. Options for allocating these funds include: (1) investing in the maintenance and expansion of existing businesses, (2) making acquisitions if needed, (3) funding long-range R&D ventures, (4) paying off existing long-term debt, (5) increasing dividends, and (6) repurchasing the company's stock. The first three are *strategic* actions; the last three, *financial* moves. Ideally, funds are available to serve both strategic and financial purposes. If not, strategic uses should take precedence over financial uses except in unusual and compelling circumstances.

GUIDELINES FOR MANAGING THE CORPORATE STRATEGY FORMATION PROCESS

Although formal analysis and entrepreneurial brainstorming are important factors in the corporate strategy-making process, there is more to where corporate strategy comes from and how it evolves. Rarely is there an all-inclusive formulation of the total corporate strategy. Instead, corporate strategy in major enterprises emerges incrementally from the unfolding of many different internal and external events, the result of probing the future, experimenting, gathering more information, sensing problems, building awareness of the various options, developing ad hoc responses to unexpected "crises," communicating partial consensus as it emerges, and acquiring a "feel" for all the strategically relevant factors, their importance, and their interrelationships.[16]

Strategic analysis is not something the executives of diversified companies do all at once in comprehensive fashion. Such big reviews are sometimes scheduled, but studies indicate that major strategic decisions emerge gradually rather than from periodic, full-scale analysis followed by prompt decision. Typically, top executives approach major strategic decisions a step at a time, often starting from broad, intuitive conceptions and then embellishing, fine-tuning, and modifying their original thinking as more information is gathered, as formal analysis confirms or modifies emerging judgments, and as confidence and consensus build for what strategic moves need to be made. Often attention and resources are concentrated on a few critical strategic thrusts that illuminate and integrate corporate direction, objectives, and strategies.

---

[15]Ibid., pp. 371–72.
[16]Ibid., pp. 58 and 196.

Strategic analysis in diversified companies is an eight-step process. Step one is to identify the present corporate strategy. Step two is to construct business portfolio matrixes as needed to examine the overall composition of the present portfolio. Step three is to profile the industry and competitive environment of each business unit and draw conclusions about how attractive each industry in the portfolio is. Step four is to probe the competitive strength of the individual businesses and how well situated each is in its respective industry. Step five is to rank the different business units on the basis of their past performance record and future performance prospects. Step six is to determine how well each business unit fits in with corporate direction and strategy and whether it has important strategic fit relationships with other businesses in the portfolio. Step seven is to rank the business units from highest to lowest in investment priority, drawing conclusions about where the firm should be putting its money and what the general strategic direction of each business unit should be (invest-and-expand, fortify-and-defend, overhaul and reposition, harvest, or divest). Step eight is to use the preceding analysis to craft a series of moves to improve overall corporate performance. The primary corporate strategy moves involve:

- Making acquisitions, starting new businesses from within, and divesting marginal businesses or businesses that no longer match the corporate direction and strategy.
- Devising moves to strengthen the long-term competitive positions of the company's core businesses.
- Acting to create strategic fit opportunities and turn them into long-term competitive advantage.
- Steering corporate resources out of low-opportunity areas into high-opportunity areas.

SUGGESTED READINGS

Bettis, Richard A., and William K. Hall. "Strategic Portfolio Management in the Multibusiness Firm." *California Management Review* 24 (Fall 1981), pp. 23–38.

_____. "The Business Portfolio Approach—Where It Falls Down in Practice." *Long Range Planning* 16, no. 2 (April 1983), pp. 95–104.

Christensen, H. Kurt, Arnold C. Cooper, and Cornelius A. Dekluyuer. "The Dog Business: A Reexamination." *Business Horizons* 25, no. 6 (November–December 1982), pp. 12–18.

Hamermesh, Richard G. *Making Strategy Work* (New York: John Wiley & Sons, 1986), chaps. 1, 4, and 7.

Haspeslagh, Phillippe. "Portfolio Planning: Uses and Limits." *Harvard Business Review* 60, no. 1 (January–February 1982), pp. 58–73.

Hax, Arnoldo, and Nicolas S. Majluf. *Strategic Management: An Integrative Perspective.* Englewood Cliffs, N.J.: Prentice Hall, 1984, chaps. 7–9.

_____. *The Strategy Concept and Process.* Englewood Cliffs, N.J.: Prentice Hall, 1991, chaps. 8–11 and 15.

Henderson, Bruce D. "The Application and Misapplication of the Experience Curve." *Journal of Business Strategy* 4, no. 3 (Winter 1984), pp. 3–9.

Naugle, David G., and Garret A. Davies. "Strategic-Skill Pools and Competitive Advantage." *Business Horizons* 30, no. 6 (November–December 1987), pp. 35–42.

Porter, Michael E. *Competitive Advantage.* New York: Free Press, 1985, chaps. 9–11.

_____. "From Competitive Advantage to Corporate Strategy." *Harvard Business Review* 65, no. 3 (May–June 1987), pp. 43–59.

Implementing Strategy
Organization-Building, Budgets, and Support Systems

We strategize beautifully, we implement pathetically.
An auto-parts firm executive

Just being able to conceive bold new strategies is not enough. The general manager must also be able to translate his or her strategic vision into concrete steps that "get things done."
Richard G. Hamermesh

Organizing is what you do before you do something, so that when you do it, it is not all mixed up.
A. A. Milne

Once the course of strategy has been charted, the manager's priorities swing to converting the strategic plan into actions and good results. Putting the strategy into effect and getting the organization moving in the chosen direction call for a different set of managerial tasks and skills. Whereas crafting strategy is largely an *entrepreneurial* activity, implementing strategy is largely an internal *administrative* activity. Whereas successful strategy formulation depends on business vision, market analysis, and entrepreneurial judgment, successful implementation depends on working through others, organizing, motivating, culture-building, and creating strong fits between strategy and how the organization does things. Ingrained behavior does not change just because a new strategy has been announced.

Implementing strategy is a tougher, more time-consuming challenge than crafting strategy. Practitioners emphatically agree that is is a whole lot easier to develop a sound strategic plan than it is to "make it happen."

THE STRATEGY IMPLEMENTATION FRAMEWORK

Strategy implementation entails *converting the strategic plan into action and then into results.* Implementation is successful if the company achieves its strategic objectives and targeted levels of financial performance. What makes the process so demanding is the wide sweep of managerial activities that have to be attended to, the many ways managers can tackle each activity, the skill it takes to get a variety of initiatives launched and moving, and the resistance to change that has to be overcome. Moreover, each strategy implementation situation is unique enough to require its own specific *action agenda.* Strategy should be implemented in a manner that fits that organization's situation. Managers have to take into account the nature of the strategy (implementing a strategy to become the low-cost producer is different from implementing a differentiation strategy keyed to superior quality and premium prices). And they must consider the amount of strategic change involved (shifting to a bold new strategy poses different implementation problems than making minor changes in an already existing strategy).

The strategy-implementer's task is to convert the strategic plan into action and get on with what needs to be done to achieve the targeted strategic and financial objectives.

The Principal Tasks

While the details of strategy implementation are specific to every situation, certain administrative bases have to be covered no matter what the organization's situation. Figure 9–1 shows the principal administrative tasks that crop up repeatedly in the strategy implementation process. Depending on the organization's circumstances, some of these tasks will prove more significant and time-consuming than others. To devise an action agenda, managers have to determine what internal conditions are necessary to execute the strategy successfully and then create these conditions as rapidly as practical.

The keys to successful implementation are to unite the total organization behind the strategy and to see that every relevant activity and administrative task is done in a manner that tightly matches the requirements for first-rate strategy execution. The motivational and inspirational challenge is to build such determined commitment up and down the ranks that an enthusiastic organizationwide crusade emerges to carry out the strategy and meet performance targets. Along with enthusiasm and strategic commitment, however, must come a concerted managerial effort to create a series of strategy-supportive "fits." The internal organization structure must be matched to the strategy. The necessary organizational skills and capabilities must be developed. Resource and budget allocations must support the strategy, and departments must be given the people and budgets needed to carry out their assigned strategic roles. The company's reward structure, policies, information system, and operating practices all need to reinforce the push for effective strategy execution, as opposed to having a passive role or, even worse, acting as obstacles. Equally important, managers must do things in a manner and style that creates and nurtures a strategy-supportive work environment and corporate culture. The stronger

Successful strategy-implementers generate strong organizationwide commitment to carrying out the strategy.

They also build tight fits between how things are managed internally and what is required for first-rate strategy execution.

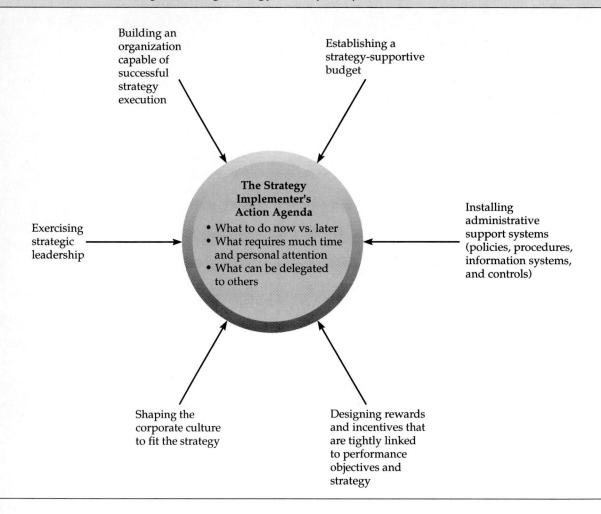

the strategy-supportive fits created internally, the greater the chances of successful implementation.

Who Are the Strategy Implementers?

Every manager has an active role in the process of implementing and executing the firm's strategic plan.

An organization's chief executive officer and the heads of major organizational units are the persons most responsible for seeing that strategy is implemented successfully. However, implementing strategy is not a job just for senior managers; it is a job for the whole management team. Strategy implementation involves every organization unit, from the head office down to each operating department, asking "What do we have to do to implement our part of the strategic plan, and how can we best get it done?" In this sense, all managers become strategy implementers in their areas of authority and responsibility. Although major implementation initiatives have to be orchestrated by the CEO and other senior officers, top-level managers still have to rely on the active support and cooperation of lower-level managers to get things done. Lower-level managers are always active participants in the strategy implementation process. They not only initiate and supervise the implementation process in their areas of responsibility, they also are instrumental in seeing that the desired results and performance targets continue to be met day after day once the strategy is in place.

Leading the Implementation Process

One of the make-or-break determinants of successful strategy implementation is how well management leads the process. Implementers can exercise leadership in many ways. They can play an active, visible role or a low-key, behind-the-scenes one. They can make decisions authoritatively or on the basis of consensus, delegate much or little, be personally involved in the details or stand on the sidelines and coach others, proceed swiftly (launching implementation initiatives on many fronts) or deliberately (working for gradual progress over a long time frame). How managers lead the implementation task tends to be a function of: (1) their experience and accumulated knowledge about the business; (2) whether they are new to the job or seasoned incumbents; (3) their network of personal relationships with others in the organization; (4) their own diagnostic, administrative, interpersonal, and problem-solving skills; (5) the authority they've been given; (6) the leadership style they're comfortable with; and (7) their view of the role they need to play to get things done.

There is no one right way to manage the implementation process; each firm's situation is unique enough to require custom actions and managerial approaches.

Another factor that affects a manager's approach to strategy implementation is the context of the organization's situation: the seriousness of the firm's strategic difficulties, the nature and extent of the strategic change involved, the type of strategy being implemented, the strength of any ingrained behavior that has to be changed, the financial and organizational resources available to work with, the configuration of personal and organization relationships in the firm's history, the pressures for quick results and improvements in near-term financial performance, and other such factors that make up the firm's "culture" and overall work climate. Each company's internal situation is unique enough that managers usually have to custom-tailor their action agenda to fit it. Successful strategy implementers carefully consider all the internal ramifications of implementing a new strategy and carefully diagnose the action priorities and the sequence in which things need to be done; then they get their organization moving and keep pushing it along.

In the remainder of this chapter and in Chapter 10, we survey the ins and outs of the manager's role as chief strategy implementer. For convenience, the discussion will be organized around the six administrative components of the strategy implementation process and the recurring administrative issues associated with each (see Figure 9–2). This chapter explores the management tasks of building an organization, establishing strategy-supportive budgets, and installing administrative support systems. Chapter 10 deals with linking rewards and incentives to performance objectives and strategy, building a strategy-supportive corporate culture, and exercising strategic leadership.

BUILDING A CAPABLE ORGANIZATION

Successful strategy execution depends greatly on good internal organization and competent personnel. Building a capable organization is always a top priority. Three types of organizational actions are paramount:

FIGURE 9–2   **The Administrative Components of Strategy Implementation**

Building an Organization Capable of Executing the Strategy

Specific Tasks
- Creating a strategy-supportive organization structure.
- Developing the skills and core competencies needed to execute the strategy successfully.
- Selecting people for key positions.

Establishing a Strategy-Supportive Budget

Specific Tasks
- Seeing that each organizational unit has a big enough budget to carry out its part of the strategic plan.
- Ensuring that resources are used efficiently to get "the biggest bang for the buck."

Installing Internal Administrative Support Systems

Specific Tasks
- Establishing and administering strategy-facilitating policies and procedures.
- Developing administrative and operating systems to give the organization strategy-critical capabilities.
- Generating the right strategic information on a timely basis.

Devising Rewards and Incentives That Are Tightly Linked to Objectives and Strategy

Specific Tasks
- Motivating organizational units and individuals to do their best to make the strategy work.
- Designing rewards and incentives that induce employees to do the very things needed for successful strategy execution.
- Promoting a results orientation.

Shaping the Corporate Culture to Fit the Strategy

Specific Tasks
- Establishing shared values.
- Setting ethical standards.
- Creating a strategy-supportive work environment.
- Building a spirit of high performance into the culture.

Exercising Strategic Leadership

Specific Tasks
- Leading the process of shaping values, molding culture, and energizing strategy accomplishment.
- Keeping the organization innovative, responsive, and opportunistic.
- Dealing with the politics of strategy, coping with power struggles, and building consensus.
- Enforcing ethical standards and behavior.
- Initiating corrective actions to improve strategy execution.

1. Developing an organizational structure that is conducive to successful strategy execution.
2. Seeing that the organization has the skills, core competencies, managerial talents, technical know-how, and competitive capabilities it needs.
3. Selecting the right people for key positions.

Matching Organization Structure to Strategy

There are very few hard and fast rules for designing a strategy-supportive organization structure. Every firm's internal organization is somewhat idiosyncratic, the result of many organizational decisions and historical circumstances. Moreover, every strategy is grounded in its own set of key success factors and critical tasks. The only real imperative is to design the internal organization structure around the key success factors and critical tasks inherent in the firm's strategy. The following five-sequence procedure is a useful guide for fitting structure to strategy:[1]

1. Pinpoint the key functions and tasks necessary for successful strategy execution.
2. Reflect on how strategy-critical functions and organizational units relate to those that are routine and to those that provide staff support.
3. Make strategy-critical business units and functions the main organizational building blocks.
4. Determine the degrees of authority needed to manage each organizational unit bearing in mind both the benefits and costs of decentralized decision making.
5. Provide for coordination among the various organizational units.

Matching structure to strategy requires making strategy-critical activities and organizational units the main building blocks in the organization structure.

Pinpointing the Strategy-Critical Activities   In any organization, some activities and skills are always more critical to strategic success than others. From a strategy perspective, much of an organization's total work is routine; it involves such administrative housekeeping as handling payrolls, managing cash flows, controlling inventories, processing grievances, warehousing and shipping, processing customer orders, and complying with regulations. Other activities are primarily support functions (data processing, accounting, training, public relations, market research, and purchasing). Yet there are usually certain crucial tasks and functions that have to be done exceedingly well for the strategy to be successful. For instance, tight cost control is essential for a firm trying to be the low-cost producer in a commodity business characterized by low margins and price cutting. For a luxury goods manufacturer, critical skills may be quality craftsmanship, distinctive design, and sophisticated promotional appeal. In high-tech industries, the critical activities tend to be R&D, product innovation, and getting newly-developed products out of the lab and onto the market quickly. Strategy-critical activities vary according to the particulars of a firm's strategy and competitive requirements.

---

[1]LaRue T. Hosmer, *Strategic Management: Text and Cases on Business Policy* (Englewood Cliffs, N.J.: Prentice Hall, 1982), chap. 10; and J. Thomas Cannon, *Business Strategy and Policy* (New York: Harcourt Brace Jovanovich, 1968), p. 316.

Two questions help identify what an organization's strategy-critical activities are: "What functions have to be performed extra well and in timely fashion for the strategy to succeed?" and "In what areas of the organization would malperformance seriously endanger strategic success?"[2] The answers generally show what activities and areas are crucial and where to concentrate organization-building efforts.

Understanding the Relationships among Activities   Before critical, supportive, and routine activities are grouped into organizational units, the strategic relationships among them need to be scrutinized thoughtfully. Activities can be related by the flow of material through the production process, the type of customer served, the distribution channels used, the technical skills and know-how needed to perform them, a strong need for coordination, the sequence in which tasks must be performed, and by geographic location, to mention a few. Such relationships are important because one (or more) of the interrelationships usually become the basis for grouping activities into organizational units. If strategic needs are to drive organization design, then the relationships to look for are those that link one piece of the strategy to another.

Grouping Activities into Organization Units   The chief guideline here is to make strategy-critical activities the main building blocks in the organization structure. The rationale is compelling: if activities crucial to strategic success are to get the attention and visibility they merit, they have to be a prominent part of the organizational scheme. When key business units and strategy-critical functions take a backseat to less important activities, they usually get fewer resources and end up with less clout in the organization's power structure than they deserve. On the other hand, when key units form the core of the whole organization structure, their role and power is highlighted and institutionalized. Senior executives seldom send a stronger signal about what is strategically important than by making key business units and critical functions the most prominent organizational building blocks and, further, giving the managers of these units a visible, influential position in the organization.

Determining the Degree of Authority and Independence to Give Each Unit
Companies must decide how much authority and decision-making latitude to give managers of each organization unit, especially the heads of business subsidiaries. Companies that are extremely centralized retain authority for big strategy and policy decisions at the corporate level and delegate only operating decisions to business-level managers. Those that are extremely decentralized give business units enough autonomy to function independently, with little direct authority exerted by corporate staff.

As a rule, authority to make strategic decisions for an organizational unit should be delegated to the unit's manager.

There are several guidelines for delegating authority to various units. Activities and organizational units with a key role in strategy execution should not be subordinate to routine and nonkey activities. Revenue-producing and results-producing activities should not be subordinate to internal support or staff functions. Decision-making authority should be decentralized (i.e.,

---

[2]Peter F. Drucker, *Management: Tasks, Responsibilities, Practices* (New York: Harper & Row, 1974), pp. 530, 535.

pushed down to managers closest to the scene of the action) whenever lower-level managers are in a position to make better, more informed, and more timely decisions than higher-level managers. However, decision-making authority should be centralized if higher-level managers are in the best decision-making position. With few exceptions, the authority to choose a strategy for an organizational unit and to decide how to implement it should be delegated to the manager in charge of the unit. Corporate-level authority over strategic and operating decisions at the business-unit level and below should be held to a minimum. The best approach is to select strong managers to head each organizational unit and give them enough authority to craft and execute an appropriate strategy; managers that consistently produce unsatisfactory results and have a poor track record in strategy-making and strategy-implementing should be weeded out.

One of the biggest exceptions to decentralizing strategy-related decisions arises in diversified companies with related businesses in their portfolios; in such cases, capturing strategic fit benefits is sometimes best done by centralizing decision-making authority. Suppose, for instance, that businesses with related process and product technologies are performing their own R&D. Merging each business's R&D activities into a single unit under the authority of a corporate officer may be both more cost efficient and more strategically effective.

Centralizing strategic decisions at the corporate level has merit when the related activities of related business units need to be tightly coordinated.

Providing for Coordination among the Units   Coordinating the activities of organizational units is accomplished mainly through positioning them in the hierarchy of authority. Managers higher up in the pecking order generally have authority over more organizational units and thus the clout to coordinate, integrate, and arrange for the cooperation of units under their supervision. The chief executive officer, chief operating officer, and business-level managers are central points of coordination because of their positions of authority over the whole unit. Besides positioning organizational units according to managerial authority, strategic efforts can also be coordinated through project teams, special task forces, standing committees, formal strategy reviews, and annual strategic planning and budgeting cycles. Additionally, the formulation of the strategic plan itself serves a coordinating role. The process of setting objectives and strategies for each organizational unit and making sure related activities mesh helps coordinate operations across units.

On the other hand, when a firm is pursuing a related diversification strategy, coordination may be best accomplished by centralizing authority for a related activity under a corporate-level officer. Also, diversified companies with either related or unrelated diversification strategies commonly centralize such staff support functions as public relations, finance and accounting, employee benefits, and data processing at the corporate level.

The Structure-Follows-Strategy Thesis

The practice of *consciously* matching organization design and structure to the particular needs of strategy is a fairly recent—and research-based—management development. A landmark study by Alfred Chandler found that changes in an organization's strategy bring about new administrative problems which, in turn, require a new or refashioned structure for the new strategy to be successfully implemented.[3] His study of 70 large corporations revealed that structure tends to follow the growth strategy of the firm—but often not until inefficiency and internal operating problems provoke a structural adjustment. The experiences of these firms followed a consistent sequential pattern: new strategy creation, emergence of new administrative problems, decline in profitability and performance, a shift to a more appropriate organizational structure, and recovery to more profitable levels and improved strategy execution. Chandler found this sequence to be oft-repeated as firms grew and modified their corporate strategies. Chandler's research shows that the choice of organization structure *does make a difference* in how an organization performs. A company's internal organization should be reassessed whenever strategy changes.[4] A new strategy is likely to entail new or different skills and key activities; if these go unrecognized, the resulting mismatch between strategy and structure can open the door for implementation and performance problems.

The *structure-follows-strategy* thesis is undergirded with powerful logic: how organizational activities are structured is a means to an end—not an end in itself. Structure is a managerial device for facilitating execution of the organization's strategy and helping to achieve performance targets. An organization's structural design is a tool for "harnessing" individual efforts and coordinating the performance of diverse tasks; a good design helps people do things efficiently and effectively. If activities and responsibilities are *deliberately* organized to link structure and strategy, it is easier to coordinate strategic moves across functional areas. Moreover, efforts to execute strategy on a day-to-day basis are less likely to result in frustration, finger-pointing when foul-ups occur, interdepartmental frictions, and inefficiency.[5]

How Structure Evolves as Strategy Evolves   As firms expand from small, single-business enterprises to more complex strategic phases of vertical integration, geographic expansion, and line-of-business diversification, their organizational structures tend to evolve from one-person management to functional departments to divisions to decentralized business units. Single-business companies almost always have a centralized functional structure. Vertically integrated firms and companies with broad geographic coverage typically are organized into operating divisions. The basic building blocks of a diversified company are its individual businesses; the authority for most decisions is decentralized, and each business operates as an independent, stand-alone unit with corporate headquarters performing only minimal functions for the business.

---

[3]Alfred Chandler, *Strategy and Structure* (Cambridge, Mass.: MIT Press, 1962). Although the stress here is on matching structure to strategy, structure can and does influence the choice of strategy. A "good" strategy must be doable. When an organization's present structure is so far out of line with the requirements of a particular strategy that the organization would have to be turned upside down to implement it, the strategy may not be doable and should not be given further consideration. In such cases, structure shapes the choice of strategy. The point here, however, is that once a strategy is chosen, structure must be modified to fit the strategy if an approximate fit does not already exist. Any influences of structures on strategy should come before the point of strategy selection rather than after it.

[4]For an excellent study documenting how companies have revised their internal organization to accommodate strategic change, see Raymond Corey and Steven H. Star, *Organizational Strategy: A Marketing Approach* (Boston: Harvard Business School, 1971), chap. 3.

[5]Drucker, *Management*, p. 523.

The Strategic Advantages and Disadvantages of Different Organizational Structures

There are five strategy-driven approaches to organization: (1) functional specialization, (2) geographic organization, (3) decentralized business divisions, (4) strategic business units, and (5) matrix structures featuring dual lines of authority and strategic priority. Each form has its own strategic advantages and disadvantages.

The Functional Organization Structure A functional organization structure tends to be effective in single-business firms where key activities revolve around well-defined skills and areas of specialization. In such cases, in-depth specialization and focused concentration on performing functional tasks and activities can enhance both operating efficiency and the development of core competencies. Generally, organizing by functional specialties promotes full utilization of the most up-to-date technical skills and helps a business capitalize on efficiency gains from using specialized manpower, facilities, and equipment. These are strategically important considerations for single-business companies, dominant-product companies, and vertically integrated firms and account for why they usually have some kind of centralized, functionally specialized structure.

However, just what form the functional specialization takes varies according to customer-product-technology considerations. For instance, a technical instruments manufacturer may be departmentalized into research and development, engineering, production, technical services, quality control, marketing, personnel, and finance and accounting. A municipal government, on the other hand, may be departmentalized according to purposeful function—fire, public safety, health services, water and sewer, streets, parks and recreation, and education. A university may divide its organizational units into academic affairs, student services, alumni relations, athletics, buildings and grounds, institutional services, and budget control. Two types of functional organizational approaches are diagrammed in Figure 9–3.

The Achilles heel of a functional structure is the difficulty of getting and keeping tight strategic coordination across functional departments that don't "talk the same language" and that often don't adequately appreciate one another's strategic role and problems. Members of functional departments tend to have strong departmental loyalties and be protective of departmental interests, thus making it hard to achieve strategic and operating coordination across departmental lines. There's a natural tendency for each functional department to push for solutions and decisions that advance its own cause and give it more influence (despite the lip service given to cooperation and "what's best for the company").

Interdepartmental politics, attempts at functional empire-building, and conflicting functional viewpoints can impose a time-consuming administrative burden on the general manager, who is the only person with authority to resolve cross-functional differences and enforce cooperation. In a functional structure, much of a GM's time is spent opening lines of communication across departments, tempering departmental rivalries, and securing cooperation. In addition, a functionally dominated organization, because of strong

Functional departments develop strong functional mindsets and are prone to approach strategic issues more from a functional than a business perspective.

F I G U R E 9–3   **Functional Organizational Structures**

A. The Building Blocks of a "Typical" Functional Organizational Structure

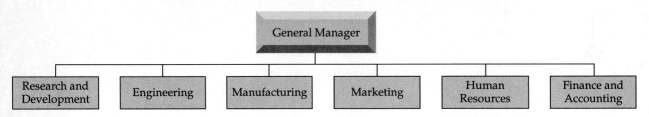

B. The Building Blocks of a Process-Oriented Functional Structure

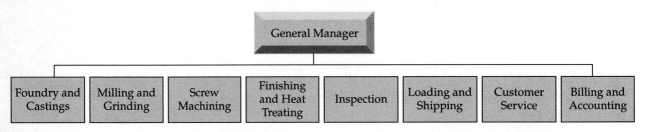

Strategic Advantages	Strategic Disadvantages
• Permits centralized control of strategic results.	• Poses problems of functional coordination.
• Very well suited for structuring a single business.	• Can lead to interfunctional rivalry and conflict, rather than cooperation—GM must referee functional politics.
• Structure is linked tightly to strategy by designating key activities as functional departments.	• May promote overspecialization and narrow management viewpoints.
• Promotes in-depth functional expertise.	• Hinders development of managers with cross-functional experience because the ladder of advancement is up the ranks within the same functional area.
• Well suited to developing a functional-based distinctive competence.	• Forces profit responsibility to the top.
• Conducive to exploiting learning/experience curve effects associated with functional specialization.	• Functional specialists often attach more importance to what's best for the functional area than to what's best for the whole business—can lead to functional empire-building.
• Enhances operating efficiency where tasks are routine and repetitive.	• Functional myopia often works against creative entrepreneurship, adapting to change, and attempts to restructure the activity-cost chain.

preoccupation with developing functional expertise and improving functional performance, tends to have tunnel vision when it comes to promoting entrepreneurial venturesomeness, developing creative responses to major customer-market-technological changes, and pursuing opportunities beyond the industry's conventional boundaries.

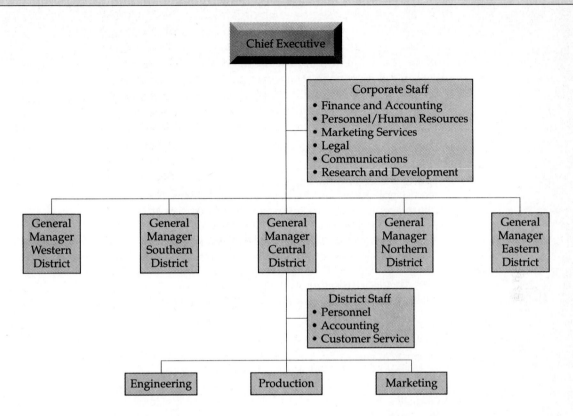

Strategic Advantages

- Allows tailoring of strategy to needs of each geographical market.
- Delegates profit/loss responsibility to lowest strategic level.
- Improves functional coordination within the target market.
- Takes advantage of economies of local operations.
- Area units make an excellent training ground for higher-level general managers.

Strategic Disadvantages

- Poses a problem of how much geographic uniformity headquarters should impose versus how much geographic diversity should be allowed.
- Greater difficulty in maintaining consistent company image/reputation from area to area when area managers exercise much strategic freedom.
- Adds another layer of management to run the geographic units.
- Can result in duplication of staff services at headquarters and district levels, creating a relative-cost disadvantage.

Geographic Forms of Organization   Organizing on the basis of geographic areas or territories is a common structural form for enterprises operating in diverse geographic markets or serving an expansive geographic area. As indicated in Figure 9–4, geographic organization has its advantages and disadvantages, but the chief reason for its popularity is that it promotes improved performance.

A geographic organization structure is well suited for firms pursuing different strategies in different geographic regions.

In the private sector, a territorial structure is typically used by chain stores, power companies, cement firms, restaurant chains, and dairy products enterprises. In the public sector, such organizations as the Internal Revenue Service, the Social Security Administration, the federal courts, the U.S. Postal Service, state troopers, and the Red Cross have adopted territorial structures to be directly accessible to geographically dispersed clienteles. Multinational enterprises use geographic structures to manage the diversity they encounter by operating across national boundaries.

Corey and Star cite Pfizer International as a good example of a company whose strategic requirements made geographic decentralization propitious:

> Pfizer International operated plants in 27 countries and marketed in more than 100 countries. Its product lines included pharmaceuticals (antibiotics and other ethical prescription drugs), agriculture and veterinary products (such as animal feed supplements and vaccines and pesticides), chemicals (fine chemicals, bulk pharmaceuticals, petrochemicals, and plastics), and consumer products (cosmetics and toiletries).
>
> Ten geographic Area Managers reported directly to the President of Pfizer International and exercised line supervision over Country Managers. According to a company position description, it was "the responsibility of each Area Manager to plan, develop, and carry out Pfizer International's business in the assigned foreign area in keeping with company policies and goals."
>
> Country Managers had profit responsibility. In most cases a single Country Manager managed all Pfizer activities in his country. In some of the larger, well-developed countries of Europe there were separate Country Managers for pharmaceutical and agricultural products and for consumer lines.
>
> Except for the fact that New York headquarters exercised control over the to-the-market prices of certain products, especially prices of widely used pharmaceuticals, Area and Country Managers had considerable autonomy in planning and managing the Pfizer International business in their respective geographic areas. This was appropriate because each area, and some countries within areas, provided unique market and regulatory environments. In the case of pharmaceuticals and agriculture and veterinary products (Pfizer International's most important lines), national laws affected formulations, dosages, labeling, distribution, and often price. Trade restrictions affected the flow of bulk pharmaceuticals and chemicals and packaged products, and sometimes required the establishment of manufacturing plants to supply local markets. Competition, too, varied significantly from area to area.[6]

In a diversified firm, the basic organizational building blocks are its business units; each business is operated as a stand-alone profit center.

Decentralized Business Units Grouping activities along business and product lines has been a trend among diversified enterprises for the past half century, beginning with the pioneering efforts of DuPont and General Motors in the 1920s. Separate business/product divisions emerged because diversification made a functionally specialized manager's job incredibly complex. Imagine the problems a manufacturing executive and his/her staff would have if put in charge of, say, 50 different plants using 20 different technologies to produce 30 different products in eight different businesses/industries. In a multibusiness enterprise, the needs of strategy virtually dictate that the organizational sequence be corporate to business to functional area within a business rather than corporate to functional area (aggregated for all businesses).

---

[6]Corey and Star, *Organization Strategy*, pp. 23–24.

Thus while functional departments and geographic divisions are the standard organizational building blocks in a single-business enterprise, in a multibusiness corporation the basic building blocks are the businesses the firm has diversified into. Diversification is generally managed by decentralizing decision-making and delegating authority over each business unit to a business-level manager. The approach, very simply, is to put entrepreneurially oriented general managers in charge of each business unit, give them authority to formulate and implement a business strategy, motivate them with incentives, and hold them accountable for the results they produce. Each business unit then operates as a stand-alone profit center and is organized around whatever functional departments and geographic units suit the business's strategy, key activities, and operating requirements.

Fully independent business units, however, pose a big problem to companies pursuing related diversification: *there is no mechanism for coordinating related activities across business units.* It can be tough to get autonomy-conscious business-unit managers to coordinate and share related activities; they are prone to argue about "turf" and about being held accountable for activities outside their control. To capture strategic fit benefits in a diversified company, corporate headquarters must devise some internal organizational means for achieving strategic coordination across related business-unit activities. One option is to centralize related functions at the corporate level. Examples include having a corporate R&D department if there are technology and product development fits to be managed, creating a corporate sales force to call on customers who purchase from several of the company's businesses, combining dealer networks and sales forces of closely related businesses, merging the order processing and shipping functions of businesses with common customers, and consolidating the production of related components and products into fewer, more efficient plants. Alternatively, corporate officers can develop bonus arrangements that give business-units managers strong incentives to cooperate to achieve the full benefits of strategic fit. If the strategic fit relationships involve skills or technology transfers across businesses, corporate headquarters can set up interbusiness task forces, standing committees, or project teams to work out the specifics of transferring proprietary technology, managerial know-how, and related skills from one business to another.

A typical line-of-business organizational structure is shown in Figure 9–5, along with the strategy-related pros and cons of this type of organizational form.

Strategic Business Units In broadly diversified companies, the number of decentralized business units can be so great that the span of control is too much for a single chief executive. Then it may be useful to group related businesses and to delegate authority over them to a senior executive who reports directly to the chief executive officer. While this imposes a layer of management between business-level managers and the chief executive, it may nonetheless improve strategic planning and top-management coordination of diverse business interests. This explains both the popularity of the group vice president concept among multi-business companies and the recent trend toward the formation of strategic business units.

A *strategic business unit* (SBU) is a grouping of business subsidiaries based on some important strategic elements common to each. The related elements could be an overlapping set of competitors, a closely related strategic mission,

FIGURE 9–5   **A Decentralized Line-of-Business Type of Organization Structure**

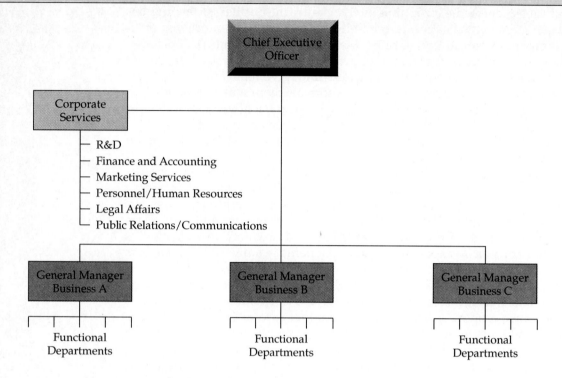

Strategic Advantages

- Offers a logical and workable means of decentralizing responsibility and delegating authority in diversified organizations.
- Puts responsibility for business strategy in closer proximity to each business's unique environment.
- Allows each business unit to organize around its own set of key activities and functional requirements.
- Frees CEO to handle corporate strategy issues.
- Puts clear profit/loss accountability on shoulders of business-unit managers.

Strategic Disadvantages

- May lead to costly duplication of staff functions at corporate and business-unit levels, thus raising administrative overhead costs.
- Poses a problem of what decisions to centralize and what decisions to decentralize (business managers need enough authority to get the job done, but not so much that corporate management loses control of key business-level decisions).
- May lead to excessive division rivalry for corporate resources and attention.
- Business/division autonomy works against achieving coordination of related activities in different business units, thus blocking to some extent the capture of strategic fit benefits.
- Corporate management becomes heavily dependent on business-unit managers.
- Corporate managers can lose touch with business-unit situations, end up surprised when problems arise, and not know much about how to fix such problems.

a common need to compete globally, an ability to accomplish integrated strategic planning, common key success factors, and technologically related growth opportunities. General Electric, a pioneer in the concept of SBUs, grouped 190 units into 43 SBUs and then aggregated them further into six "sectors."[7] At Union Carbide, 15 groups and divisions were decomposed into 150 "strategic planning units" and then regrouped and combined into 9 new "aggregate planning units." General Foods (now a division of Philip Morris) originally defined SBUs on a product-line basis but later redefined them according to menu segments (breakfast foods, beverages, main meal products, desserts, and pet foods).

The SBU concept provides broadly diversified companies with a way to rationalize the organization of many different businesses and a management arrangement for capturing strategic fit benefits and streamlining the strategic planning process. The strategic function of the group vice president is to provide the SBU with some cohesive direction and enforce strategic coordination across related businesses. The group vice president, as strategic coordinator for all businesses in the SBU, is in a position to organize the SBU in ways that facilitate sharing and skills transfers and to centralize "big" strategic decisions at the SBU level. The SBU, in effect, becomes a decision-making unit with broader strategic perspective than a single-business unit. It serves as the organizational mechanism for capturing strategic benefits and helps build competitive advantage for all businesses in the SBU.

SBU structures are a means for managing broad diversification and enforcing strategic coordination across related businesses.

SBUs also help reduce the complexity of dovetailing corporate strategy and business strategy and make it easier to "cross-pollinate" the growth opportunities in different industries. SBUs make headquarters' reviews of the strategies of lower-level units less imposing (there is no practical way for a CEO to review a hundred or more different businesses). A CEO can, however, effectively review the strategic plans of a lesser number of SBUs, leaving strategy reviews and direct supervision of individual businesses to the SBU heads. Figure 9–6 illustrates the SBU form of organization, along with its strategy-related pros and cons.

Matrix Forms of Organization A matrix organization is a structure with two (or more) channels of command, two lines of budget authority, and two sources of performance and reward. The key feature of the matrix is that business (or product, project, or venture) and functional lines of authority are overlaid (to form a matrix or grid), and managerial authority over the activities in each unit/cell of the matrix is shared between the business/project/venture team manager and the functional manager, as shown in Figure 9–7. In a matrix structure, subordinates have a continuing dual assignment: to the business/product/project and to their home-base function.[8] The outcome is a compromise between functional specialization (engineering, R&D, manufacturing,

Matrix structures, although complex to manage and sometimes unwieldy, allow a firm to be organized in two different strategy-supportive ways at the same time.

---

[7]William K. Hall, "SBUs: Hot, New Topic in the Management of Diversification," *Business Horizons* 21, no. 1 (February 1978), p. 19. For an excellent discussion of the problems of implementing the SBU concept at 13 companies, see Richard A. Bettis and William K. Hall, "The Business Portfolio Approach—Where It Falls Down in Practice," *Long Range Planning* 16, no. 2 (April 1983), pp. 95–104.

[8]A more thorough treatment of matrix organizational forms can be found in Jay R. Galbraith, "Matrix Organizational Designs," *Business Horizons* 15, no. 1 (February 1971), pp. 29–40; and Christopher A. Bartlett and Sumantra Ghoshal, "Matrix Management: Not a Structure, a Frame of Mind," *Harvard Business Review* 68, no. 4 (July–August 1990), pp. 138–45.

F I G U R E 9–6   **An SBU Type of Organization Structure**

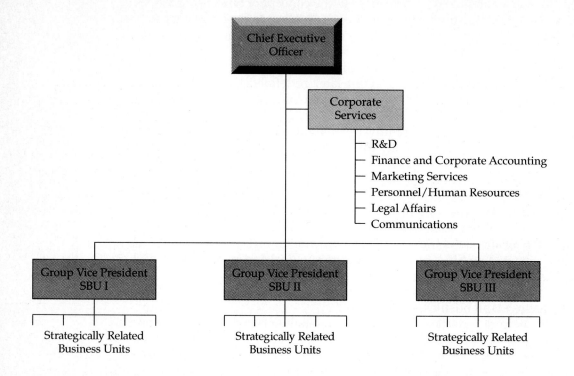

<table>
<tr>
<td>

Strategic Advantages

- Provides a strategically relevant way to organize the business-unit portfolio of a broadly diversified company
- Facilitates the coordination of related activities within an SBU, thus helping to capture the benefits of strategic fits in the SBU.
- Promotes more cohesiveness among the new initiatives of separate but related businesses.
- Allows strategic planning to be done at the most relevant level within the total enterprise.
- Makes the task of strategic review by top executives more objective and more effective.
- Helps allocate corporate resources to areas with greatest growth opportunities.

</td>
<td>

Strategic Disadvantages

- It is easy for the definition and grouping of businesses into SBUs to be so arbitrary that the SBU serves no other purpose than administrative convenience. If the criteria for defining SBUs are rationalizations and have little to do with the nitty-gritty of strategy coordination, then the groupings lose real strategic significance.
- The SBUs can still be myopic in charting their future direction.
- Adds another layer to top management.
- The roles and authority of the CEO, the group vice president, and the business-unit manager have to be carefully worked out or the group vice president gets trapped in the middle with ill-defined authority.
- Unless the SBU head is strong willed, very little strategy coordination is likely to occur across business units in the SBU.
- Performance recognition gets blurred; credit for successful business units tends to go to corporate CEO, then to business-unit head, last to group vice president.

</td>
</tr>
</table>

marketing, finance) and specialization by product line, project, line-of-business, or special venture. All of the specialized talent needed for the product line/project/line-of-business/venture are assigned to the same divisional unit.

FIGURE 9–7   **A Matrix Organization Structure***

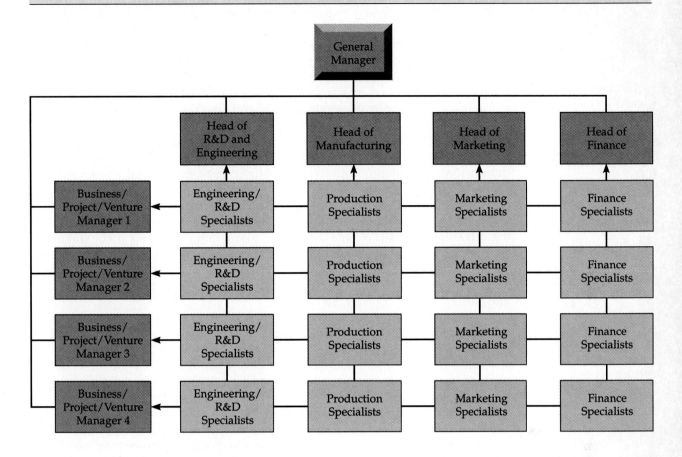

Strategic Advantages

- Gives formal attention to each dimension of strategic priority.
- Creates checks and balances among competing viewpoints.
- Facilitates capture of functionally based strategic fits in diversified companies.
- Promotes making trade-off decisions on the basis of "what's best for the organization as a whole."
- Encourages cooperation, consensus-building, conflict resolution, and coordination of related activities.

Strategic Disadvantages

- Very complex to manage.
- Hard to maintain "balance" between the two lines of authority.
- So much shared authority can result in a transactions logjam and disproportionate amounts of time being spent on communications.
- It is hard to move quickly and decisively without getting clearance from many other people.
- Promotes an organizational bureaucracy and hamstrings creative entrepreneurship.

*Arrows indicate reporting channels

A matrix-type organization is a genuinely different structural form and represents a "new way of life." It breaks the unity-of-command principle; two reporting channels, two bosses, and shared authority create a new kind of organizational climate. In essence, the matrix is a conflict resolution system through which strategic and operating priorities are negotiated, power is shared, and resources are allocated internally on the basis of "strongest case for what is best overall for the unit."[9]

The impetus for matrix organizations stems from growing use of strategies that add new diversity (products, customer groups, technology, lines of business) to a firm's range of activities. Such diversity creates a need for product managers, functional managers, geographic area managers, new venture managers, and business-level managers—all of whom have important strategic responsibilities. When at least two of several variables (product, customer, technology, geography, functional area, and market segment) have roughly equal strategic priorities, a matrix organization can be an effective structural form. A matrix structure promotes internal checks and balances among competing viewpoints and perspectives, with separate managers for different dimensions of strategic initiative. A matrix arrangement thus allows each of several strategic considerations to be managed directly and to be formally represented in the organization structure. In this sense, it helps middle managers make trade-off decisions from an organizationwide perspective.[10] The other big advantage of matrix organization is that it can serve as a mechanism for capturing strategic fit. When the strategic fits in a diversified company are related to a specific functional area (R&D, technology, marketing), matrix organization can be a reasonable structural arrangement for coordinating sharing and skills transfer.

Companies using matrix structures include General Electric, Texas Instruments, Citibank, Shell Oil, TRW, Bechtel, Boeing, and Dow Chemical. Illustration Capsule 22 describes how one broadly diversified corporation with global strategies in each of its businesses has developed a matrix-type structure to manage its operations worldwide. However, most applications of matrix organization are limited to a portion of what the firm does (certain important functions) rather than spanning the whole of a large-scale diversified enterprise.

A number of companies shun matrix organization because of its chief weaknesses.[11] It is a complex structure to manage; people often end up confused over who to report to for what. Moreover, because the matrix signals that everything is important and, further, that everybody needs to communicate with everybody else, a "transactions logjam" can emerge. Action turns into paralysis since, with shared authority, it is hard to move decisively without first considering many points of view and getting clearance from many other people. Sizable transactions costs, communications inefficiency, and delays in responding can result. Even so, in some situations the benefits of conflict resolution and consensus-building outweigh these weaknesses.

Combination and Supplemental Methods of Organization   A single type of structural design is not always sufficient to meet the requirements of strategy. When this occurs, one option is to blend the basic organization forms, match-

---

[9]For two excellent critiques of matrix organizations, see Stanley M. Davis and Paul R. Lawrence, "Problems of Matrix Organizations," *Harvard Business Review* 56, no. 3 (May–June 1978), pp. 131–42; and Erik W. Larson and David H. Gobeli, "Matrix Management: Contradictions and Insights," *California Management Review* 29, no. 4 (Summer 1987), pp. 126–38.

[10]Ibid., p. 132.

[11]Thomas J. Peters and Robert H. Waterman, Jr., *In Search of Excellence* (New York: Harper & Row, 1982), pp. 306–7.

ing structure to strategy requirement by requirement and unit by unit. Another is to supplement a basic organization design with special-situation devices. Three of the most frequently used ones are:

1. The *project team* or *project staff approach*, where a separate, largely self-sufficient work group is created to oversee the completion of a special activity (setting up a new technological process, bringing out a new product, starting up a new venture, consummating a merger with another company, seeing through the completion of a government contract, supervising the construction of a new plant). Project teams are a relatively popular means of handling one-of-a-kind situations with a finite life expectancy when the normal organization is ill-equipped to achieve the same results in addition to regular duties.

2. The *task force approach*, where a number of top-level executives and/or specialists are brought together to work on interdisciplinary assignments requiring specialized expertise from several parts of the organization. Special task forces provide increased opportunity for creativity, open communication across lines of authority, tight integration of specialized talents, expeditious conflict resolution, and common identification for coping with the problem at hand. One study showed that task forces were most effective when they had less than 10 members, membership was voluntary, the seniority of the members was proportional to the importance of the problem, the task force moved swiftly to deal with its assignment, the task force was pulled together only on an as-needed basis, no staff was assigned, and documentation was scant.[12] In these companies, the prevailing philosophy about task forces is to use them to solve real problems, produce some solution efficiently, and then disband them. At the other extreme, Peters and Waterman report one instance where a company had formed 325 task forces, none of which had completed its charge in three years and none of which had been disbanded.

3. The *venture team approach*, whereby a group of individuals is formed for the purpose of bringing a specific product to market or a specific new business into being. Dow, General Mills, Westinghouse, General Electric, and Monsanto have used the venture team approach to regenerate an entrepreneurial spirit. The difficulties with venture teams include deciding who the venture manager should report to; whether funding for ventures should come from corporate, business, or departmental budgets; how to keep the venture clear of bureaucratic and vested interests; and how to coordinate large numbers of different ventures.

Perspectives on the Methods of Organizing

The foregoing discussion brings out two points: (1) there is no perfect or ideal organization design and (2) there are no universally applicable rules for matching strategy and structure. All of the basic organizational forms have their strategy-related strengths and weaknesses. Moreover, two or more can

[12]Peters and Waterman, *In Search of Excellence*, pp. 127–32.

MATRIX ORGANIZATION IN A DIVERSIFIED GLOBAL COMPANY
The Case of Asea Brown Boveri

Asea Brown Boveri (ABB) is a diversified multinational corporation headquartered in Zurich, Switzerland. ABB was formed in 1987 through the merger of Asea, one of Sweden's largest industrial enterprises, and Brown Boveri, a major Swiss company. Both companies manufactured electrical products and equipment. Following the merger, ABB acquired or took minority positions in 60 companies, mostly outside Europe. In 1991 ABB had annual revenues of $25 billion and employed 240,000 people around the world, including 150,000 in Western Europe, 40,000 in North America, 10,000 in South America, and 10,000 in India. The company was a world leader in the global markets for electrical products, electrical installations and service, and power-generation equipment and was the dominant European producer. European sales accounted for 60 percent of revenues, while North America accounted for 30 percent and Asia 15 percent.

To manage its global operations, ABB had devised a matrix organization that leveraged its core competencies in electrical-power technologies and its ability to achieve global economies of scale while, at the same time, maximizing its national market visibility and responsiveness. At the top of ABB's corporate organization structure was an executive committee composed of the CEO, Percy Barnevik, and 12 colleagues; the committee consisted of Swedes, Swiss, Germans, and Americans, several of whom were based outside Switzerland. The group, which met every three weeks at various locations around the world, was responsible for ABB's corporate strategy and performance.

Along one dimension of ABB's global matrix were 50 or so business areas (BAs), each representing a closely related set of products and services. The BAs were grouped into eight "business segments"; each segment was supervised by a different member of the executive committee. Each BA had a leader charged with responsibility for (1) devising and championing a global strategy, (2) setting quality and cost standards for the BA's factories worldwide, (3) deciding which factories would export to which country markets, (4) rotating people across borders to share technical expertise, create mixed-nationality teams to solve BA problems, and build a culture of trust and communication, and (5) pooling expertise and research funds for the benefit of the BA worldwide. BA leaders worked out of whatever world location made the most sense for their BA. For example, the BA leader for power transformers, who had responsibility for 25 factories in 16 countries, was a Swede who worked out of Mannheim, Germany; the BA leader for electric

(continued)

be used simultaneously. Many organizations are large enough and diverse enough to have subunits organized by functional specialty, geographical area, market segment, line of business, SBU, and matrix principles. In a very real sense, *the best organizational arrangement is the one that best fits the firm's situation at the moment.* Judging from the frequency with which firms reorganize, every organizational arrangement outlives its usefulness—either an internal rearrangement becomes desirable or changes in the size and scope of customer-product-technology relationships make the firm's structure strategically obsolete. An organization's structure is dynamic, and changes are inevitable.

There is room to quibble over whether organization design should commence with a strategy-structure framework or with a pragmatic consideration of the situation at hand—the corporate culture, the personalities involved, and the way things have been done before. By and large, agonizing over where to begin is unnecessary; both considerations have to be taken into account. However, strategy-structure factors usually take precedence if structure is to be

ILLUSTRATION CAPSULE
22

(concluded)

metering was an American based in North Carolina.

Along the other dimension of the matrix was a group of national enterprises with presidents, boards of directors, financial statements, and career ladders. The presidents of ABB's national enterprises had responsibility for maximizing the performance and effectiveness of all ABB activities within their country's borders. Country presidents worked closely with the BA leaders to evaluate and improve what was happening in ABB's business areas in his/her country.

Inside the matrix were 1,200 "local" ABB companies with an average of 200 employees, each headed by a president. The local company president reported both to the national president in whose country the local company operated and to the leader of the BA to which its products/ services were assigned. Each local company was a subsidiary of the ABB national enterprise where it was located. Thus, all of ABB's local companies in Norway were subsidiaries of ABB Norway, the national company for Norway; all ABB operations in Portugal were subsidiaries of ABB Portugal, and so on. The 1,200 presidents of ABB's local companies were expected to be excellent profit center managers, able to answer to two bosses effectively. The local president's global boss was the BA manager who established the local company's role in ABB's

global strategy and, also, the rules a local company had to observe in supporting this strategy. The local president's country boss was the national CEO, with whom it was necessary to cooperate on local issues.

ABB believed that its matrix structure allowed it to optimize its pursuit of global business strategies and, at the same time, maximize its performance in every country market where it operated. The matrix was a way of being global and big strategically, yet small and local operationally. Decision-making was decentralized (to BA leaders, country presidents, and local company presidents), but reporting and control was centralized (through the BA leaders, the country presidents, and the executive committee). ABB saw itself as a federation of national companies with a global coordination center.

Only 100 professionals were located in ABB's corporate headquarters in Zurich. A management information system collected data on all profit centers monthly, comparing actual performance against budgets and forecasts. Data was collected in local currencies but translated into U.S. dollars to allow for cross-border analysis. ABB's corporate financial statements were reported in U.S. dollars, and English was ABB's official language. All high-level meetings were conducted in English.

Source: Compiled from information in William Taylor, "The Logic of Global Business: An Interview with ABB's Percy Barnevik," *Harvard Business Review* 69, no. 2 (March–April 1991), pp. 90–105.

built around the organization's strategy-critical tasks, key success factors, and high-priority business units. Adapting structure to the peculiar circumstances of the organization's internal situation and personalities is usually done to modify the strategy-structure match in "minor" ways.

Drucker sums up the intricacies of organization design thusly:

The simplest organization structure that will do the job is the best one. What makes an organization structure "good" are the problems it does not create. The simpler the structure, the less that can go wrong.

Some design principles are more difficult and problematic than others. But none is without difficulties and problems. None is primarily people-focused rather than task-focused; none is more "creative," "free," or "more democratic." Design principles are tools; and tools are neither good nor bad in themselves. They can be used properly or improperly; and that is all. To obtain both the greatest possible simplicity and the greatest "fit," organization design has to start out

ILLUSTRATION CAPSULE
23

ORGANIZATION LESSONS FROM THE "EXCELLENTLY MANAGED" COMPANIES

Peters and Waterman's study of America's best-managed corporations provides some important lessons in building a strategically capable organization:

- The organizational underpinning of most of the excellently managed companies is a fairly stable, unchanging form—usually a decentralized business/product division—that provides the structural building block which everyone in the enterprise understands and that serves as the base for approaching day-to-day issues and complexities.

- Beyond the crystal-clear primacy of this basic and simple organizational building block, the rest of the organization structure is deliberately kept fluid and flexible to permit response to changing environmental conditions. Much use is made of task forces, project teams, and the creation of new, small divisions to address emerging issues and opportunities.

- New divisions are created to pursue budding business opportunities, as opposed to letting them remain a part of the originating division. Often, there are established guidelines when a new product or product line automatically becomes an independent division.

- People and even products and product lines are frequently shifted from one division to another—to improve efficiency, promote shared costs, enhance competitive strength,

and adapt to changing market conditions.

- Many excellently managed companies have comparatively few people at the corporate level, and many of these are out in the field frequently, rather than in the home office all the time. Emerson Electric with 54,000 employees had a headquarters staff of fewer than 100 people. Dana Corporation employed 35,000 people and had a corporate staff numbering about 100. Schlumberger Ltd., a $56 billion diversified oil service company, ran its worldwide organization with a corporate staff of 90 people. At Intel (sales of over $1 billion), all staff assignments were temporary ones given to line officers. Rolm managed a $200 million business with about 15 people in corporate headquarters. In addition, corporate planners were few and far between. Hewlett-Packard Company, Johnson & Johnson, and 3M had no planners at the corporate level; Fluor Corporation ran a $6 billion operation with three corporate planners. At IBM, management rotated staff assignments every three years. Few IBM staff jobs were manned by "career staffers"; most were manned temporarily by managers with line jobs in the divisions who eventually rotate back to line jobs.

- Functional organization forms are efficient and get the basic activities performed well; yet they are not particularly creative or en-

(continued)

with a clear focus on *key activities* needed to produce *key results*. They have to be structured and positioned in the simplest possible design. Above all, the architect of organization needs to keep in mind the purpose of the structure he is designing.[13]

Peters and Waterman, in their study of excellently managed companies, confirm what Drucker says; their organization prescription is "simple form, lean staff." Illustration Capsule 23 explains some of the organizational principles and approaches being used at these companies.

---

[13]Drucker, *Management*, pp. 601–2.

ILLUSTRATION CAPSULE

(concluded)

trepreneurial, they do not adapt quickly, and they are apt to ignore important changes.

- The key to maintaining an entrepreneurial, adaptive organization is *small size*—and the way to keep units small is to spin off new or expanded activities into independent units. Division sizes often run no bigger than $50 to $100 million in sales, with a maximum of 1,000 or so employees. At Emerson Electric, plants rarely employed more than 600 workers, so that management could maintain personal contact with employees. (Emerson, by the way, has a good track record on efficiency; its strategy of being the low-cost producer has worked beautifully in chain saws and several other products.) At Blue Bell, a leading apparel firm, manufacturing units usually employ under 300 people. The lesson seems to be that small units are both more cost-effective and more innovative.

- To prevent "calcification" and stodginess, it helps to rely on such "habitbreaking" techniques as (*a*) reorganizing regularly; (*b*) putting top talent on project teams and giving them a "charter" to move quickly to solve a key problem or execute a central strategic thrust (i.e., the creation of the General Motors Project Center to lead the downsizing effort); (*c*) shifting products or product lines among divisions to take advantage of special management talents or the need for market realignments; (*d*) break-

ing up big, bureaucratic divisions into several new, smaller divisions; and (*e*) being flexible enough to try experimental organization approaches and support the pursuit of new opportunities.

- It is useful to adopt a simultaneous "loose-tight" structure that on the one hand fosters autonomy, entrepreneurship, and innovation from rank-and-file managers yet, on the other hand, allows for strong central direction from the top. Such things as regular reorganization, flexible form (the use of teams and task forces), lots of decentralized autonomy for lower-level general managers, and extensive experimentation all focus on the excitement of trying things out in a slightly "loose" fashion. Yet, regular communication, quick feedback, concise paperwork, strong adherence to a few core values, and self-discipline can impose "tight" central control so that nothing gets far out of line.

Application of these "principles" in the best-managed companies tends to produce an environment that fosters entrepreneurial pursuit of new opportunities and adaptation to change. A fluid, flexible structure is the norm—the basic form is stable, but there is frequent reorganization "around the edges." The aim is to keep structure matched to the changing needs of an evolving strategy and to avoid letting the current organization structure become so ingrained and political that it becomes a major obstacle to be hurdled.

Source: Drawn from Thomas J. Peters and Robert H. Waterman, Jr., *In Search of Excellence* (New York: Harper & Row, 1982), especially chaps. 11 and 12.

Building Core Competencies

A good match between structure and strategy is one key facet of organizational capability. But an equally dominant organization-building concern is that of staffing the structure with the requisite managerial talent, specialized skills, and technical expertise—and, most particularly, staffing in a manner calculated to give the firm a clear edge over rivals in performing one or more critical activities. *When it is difficult or impossible to outstrategize rivals (beat them with a superior strategy), the other main avenue to industry leadership is to outexecute them (beat them with superior strategy implementation).* Superior strategy execution is essential in situations where rivals have very similar strategies and can readily imitate one another's strategic maneuvers. Building core competencies and organizational capabilities that rivals can't match is one of the best ways to outexecute them. This is why one of top management's most important strategy-implementing tasks is to guide the building of core competencies in competitively important ways.[14] Core competencies can relate to any strategically relevant factor: greater proficiency in product development, better manufacturing know-how, the capability to provide customers better after-sale services, an ability to respond quickly to changing customer requirements, superior ability to minimize costs, an ability to re-engineer and redesign products more quickly than rivals, superior inventory management capabilities, better marketing and merchandising skills, or greater effectiveness in promoting union-management cooperation.

However, core competencies don't just appear naturally. They have to be deliberately developed and consciously nurtured. For core competencies to emerge from organization-building actions, strategy implementers have to build a critical mass of technical skills and capabilities in those subunits where superior performance of strategically critical tasks can mean greater strategic success. Usually, this means (1) giving above-average operating budgets to strategy-critical tasks and activities, (2) seeing that these areas are staffed with high-caliber managerial and technical talent, (3) insisting on high standards in performing these tasks/activities, backed up with a policy of rewarding people for outstanding results. In effect, strategy implementers must take actions to see that the organization is staffed with enough of the right kinds of people and that these people have the budgets, the administrative support, and the incentive rewards needed to generate the desired competencies and competitive capabilities.

Distinctive internal skills and capabilities are not easily duplicated by rivals; any competitive advantage that results is likely to be sustainable for some time, thus paving the way for above-average performance. Conscious management attention to building strategically relevant internal skills and strengths into the overall organizational scheme is therefore one of the central tasks of organization-building and effective strategy implementation.

Strategic Management Principle

Building core competencies and organizational capabilities that rivals can't match is a sound basis for sustainable competitive advantage.

Employee Training   Employee training and retraining are important parts of the strategy implementation process when a company shifts to a strategy requiring different skills, managerial approaches, and operating methods. Training is also strategically important in organizational efforts to build skills-based competencies. And it is a key activity in businesses where technical know-how is changing so rapidly that a company loses its ability to compete unless its skilled people are kept updated and maintain their cutting-edge expertise. Successful strategy implementers see that the training function is adequately funded and that effective training programs are in place. Normally, training should be near the top of the action agenda because it needs to be done early in the strategy implementation process.

---

[14]C. K. Prahalad and Gary Hamel, "The Core Competence of the Corporation," *Harvard Business Review* 68 (May–June 1990), pp. 79–93.

Selecting People for Key Positions

Assembling a capable management team is also part of the strategy implementation task. Companies must decide what kind of core management team they need to carry out the strategy and find the right people to fill each slot. Sometimes the existing management team is suitable; sometimes it needs to be strengthened and/or expanded by promoting qualified people from within or by bringing in skilled managers from outside to help infuse fresh ideas and approaches. In turnaround and rapid-growth situations, and in instances where a company doesn't have the necessary type of management skills in-house, recruiting outsiders for key management slots is a fairly standard organization-building approach.

The important skill in assembling a core executive group is discerning what mix of backgrounds, experiences, know-how, values, beliefs, styles of managing, and personalities will contribute to successful strategy execution. As with any kind of team-building, it is important to put together a compatible group of skilled managers. The personal "chemistry" needs to be right, and the talent base needs to be appropriate for the chosen strategy. Molding a solid management team is an essential organization-building function—often the first strategy implementation step to take.[15] Until all the key slots are filled with the right people, it is hard for strategy implementation to proceed at full speed.

> *A strong management team with the right personal chemistry and mix of skills must be put together early in the implementation process.*

LINKING BUDGETS WITH STRATEGY

Keeping an organization on the strategy implementation path thrusts a manager squarely into the budgeting process. Not only must a strategy implementer oversee "who gets how much," but the budget must also be put together with an equal concern for "getting the biggest bang for the buck."

Obviously, organizational units need enough resources to carry out their part of the strategic plan. This includes having enough of the right kinds of people and sufficient operating funds for them to do their work successfully. Moreover, organizational units need to: (1) set up detailed, step-by-step action programs for putting each piece of the strategy into place, (2) establish schedules and deadlines for accomplishment, and (3) designate who is responsible for what by when.

How well a strategy implementer links budget allocations to the needs of strategy can either promote or impede the implementation process. With too little funding, organizational units can't execute their part of the strategic plan proficiently. Too much funding wastes organizational resources and reduces financial performance. Both outcomes argue for the strategy implementer to be deeply involved in the budgeting process, closely reviewing the programs and budget proposals of strategy-critical subunits.

Implementers must also be willing to shift resources when strategy changes. A change in strategy nearly always calls for budget reallocation. Units important in the old strategy may now be oversized and overfunded. Units that now have a bigger and more critical strategic role may need more people,

> *Strategic Management Principle*
> *Depriving strategy-critical organizational units of the funds needed to execute their part of the strategic plan can undermine the implementation process.*

---

[15]For a fuller discussion of the top management team's strategic role, see Donald C. Hambrick, "The Top Management Team: Key to Strategic Success," *California Management Review* 30, no. 1 (Fall 1987), pp. 88–108.

New strategies usually call for significant budget reallocations.

new equipment, additional facilities, and above-average increases in their operating budgets. The strategy implementer must engineer reallocations, downsizing some areas, upsizing others, and steering ample resources into particularly critical activities. *Strategy must drive how budget allocations are made.* Underfunding organizational units essential for strategic success can defeat the whole implementation process.

Successful strategy implementers are good resource reallocators. For example, at Harris Corporation, one element of strategy is to diffuse research ideas into areas that are commercially viable. Top management regularly shifts groups of engineers out of government projects and moves them (as a group) into new commercial venture divisions. Boeing has a similar approach to reallocating ideas and talent; according to one Boeing officer, "We can do it [create a big new unit] in two weeks. We couldn't do it in two years at International Harvester."[16] A fluid, flexible approach to reorganization and reallocation of people and budgets is key to successful implementation of strategic change.

Fine-tuning existing strategy usually involves less reallocation and more extrapolation. Big movements of people and money from one area to another are seldom necessary. Fine-tuning can usually be accomplished by incrementally increasing or decreasing the budgets and staffing of existing organization units. The chief exception occurs where a prime strategy ingredient is to generate fresh, new products and business opportunities from within. Then, as attractive ventures "bubble up" from below, major decisions have to be made regarding budgets and staffing. Companies like 3M, GE, Boeing, IBM, and Digital Equipment shift resources and people from area to area on an "as-needed" basis to support budding ideas and ventures. They empower "product champions" and small groups of would-be entrepreneurs by giving them financial and technical support and by setting up organizational units and programs to help new ventures blossom more quickly.

PUTTING INTERNAL ADMINISTRATIVE SUPPORT SYSTEMS IN PLACE

A third key task of strategy implementation is to install internal administrative support systems that fit the needs of strategy. The specific considerations here are:

1. What kinds of strategy-facilitating policies and procedures to establish.
2. How to enhance organizational capabilities via the installation of new or enhanced administrative and operating systems.
3. How to get the right strategy-critical information on a timely basis.

Creating Strategy-Supportive Policies and Procedures

Successful strategy implementers are good at creating policies and procedures that make the strategy work better.

Changes in strategy generally call for some changes in how internal activities are conducted and administered. The process of changing from old ways to new has to be initiated and managed. Asking people to change their actions always "upsets" the internal order of things. It is normal for pockets of resis-

---

[16]Peters and Waterman, *In Search of Excellence*, p. 125.

tance to emerge and questions to be raised about the *hows* as well as the *whys* of change. The role of new and revised policies is to promulgate "standard operating procedures" that will (1) channel individual and group efforts in the right direction and (2) counteract any tendencies for parts of the organization to resist or reject the actions needed to make the strategy work. Policies and procedures help enforce strategy implementation in several ways:

1. Policy institutionalizes strategy-supportive practices and operating procedures throughout the organization, thus pushing day-to-day activities in the direction of efficient strategy execution.
2. Policy limits independent action and discretionary decisions and behavior. By stating procedures for how things are to be handled, policy communicates what is expected, guides strategy-related activities in particular directions, and restricts unwanted variations.
3. Policy helps align actions and behaviors with strategy, thereby minimizing zigzag decisions and conflicting practices and establishing more regularity, stability, and dependability in how the organization is attempting to make the strategy work.
4. Policy helps to shape the character of the working environment and to translate the corporate philosophy into how things are done, how people are treated, and what corporate beliefs and attitudes mean in terms of everyday activities. Policy operationalizes the corporate philosophy, helping establish a fit between corporate culture and strategy.

Managers need to be inventive in establishing policies to support a strategic plan. McDonald's policy manual, in an attempt to boost quality and service, spells out such detailed procedures as: "Cooks must turn, never flip, hamburgers. If they haven't been purchased, Big Macs must be discarded 10 minutes after being cooked and french fries 7 minutes. Cashiers must make eye contact with and smile at every customer." At Delta Airlines, it is corporate policy to test all applicants for flight attendants' positions for friendliness, cooperativeness, and teamwork. Caterpillar Tractor has a policy of guaranteeing 48-hour parts delivery anywhere in the world; if it fails to fulfill the promise, it supplies the part free. Hewlett-Packard requires R&D people to visit customers to learn about their problems, talk about new-product applications, and, in general, keep the company's R&D programs customer-oriented.

Thus there is a definite role for policies and procedures in the strategy implementation process. Wisely constructed policies and procedures help enforce strategy implementation by channeling actions, behavior, decisions, and practices in directions that promote effective strategy execution. When policies aren't strategy-supportive, they become obstacles and there is risk that people who disagree with the strategy will hide behind outdated policies to thwart the strategic plan. On the other hand, instituting policies that promote strategy-supportive behavior builds organization commitment to the strategic plan and creates a tighter fit between corporate culture and strategy.

None of this is meant to imply, however, that a huge manual full of policies is called for. Too much policy can be as stifling as wrong policy or as chaotic as no policy. Sometimes, the best policy for implementing strategy is a willingness to let subordinates do it any way they want if it makes sense and works. A little "structured chaos" can be a good thing when individual creativity is more essential to strategy than standardization and strict conformity. When Rene McPherson became CEO at Dana Corp., he dramatically threw out 22½ inches of policy manuals and replaced them with a one-page statement of philosophy focusing on "productive people."[17] Creating a strong supportive fit between strategy and policy can mean more policies, fewer policies, or different policies. It can mean policies that require things to be done a certain way or policies that give employees the autonomy to do the job the way they think best.

Installing Support Systems

Effective strategy execution typically involves developing a number of support systems. An airline, for example, cannot function without a computerized reservation system, a baggage handling system at every airport it serves, and a strong aircraft maintenance program. A supermarket that stocks 17,000 different items has to have systems for tracking inventories, maintaining shelf freshness, and allocating shelf space among fast-selling and slow-selling items. A company that manufactures many models and sizes of its product must have a sophisticated cost accounting system to price each item intelligently and know which items generate the biggest profit contribution. In businesses where large number of employees need cutting-edge technical know-how, companies have to install systems to train and retrain employees regularly and keep them supplied with up-to-date information. Fast-growing companies have to develop employee recruiting systems to attract and hire qualified employees in large numbers. Well-conceived, state-of-the-art support systems not only facilitate better strategy execution, they also can strengthen organizational capabilities enough to provide a competitive edge over rivals.

Strategy implementers must be alert to what specific support systems their company needs to execute its strategy successfully. A company with a strategy of superior quality, for example, must develop superior methods for quality control. A company whose strategy is to be a low-cost producer must develop systems to enforce tight cost containment. If the present administrative support and operating systems are inadequate, resources must be allocated to improve them. Illustration Capsule 24 describes the administrative support systems put in place at Mrs. Fields Cookies.

Instituting Formal Reporting of Strategic Information

Accurate information is an essential guide to action. Every organization needs a system for gathering and reporting strategy-critical information. Information is needed *before* actions are completed to steer them to successful conclusion in case the early steps don't produce the intended outcome and need to be modified. Monitoring the outcomes of the first round of implementation actions (1) allows early detection of need to adjust either the strategy or how it is being implemented and (2) provides some assurance that things are moving ahead as planned.[18] Early experiences are sometimes difficult to assess, but

---

[17]Ibid., p. 65.

[18]Boris Yavitz and William H. Newman, *Strategy in Action* (New York: Free Press, 1982), pp. 209–10.

ILLUSTRATION CAPSULE
24

STRATEGY IMPLEMENTATION AT MRS. FIELDS COOKIES, INC.

In 1988 Mrs. Fields Cookies was one of the fastest growing specialty foods companies in the United States. Sales in 1987 were $150 million, up from $87 million in 1986. The company had over 400 Mrs. Fields outlets in operation and over 250 outlets retailing other bakery and cookie products. Debbi Fields, age 31, was the company's founder and CEO. Her business concept for Mrs. Fields Cookies was "to serve absolutely fresh, warm cookies as though you'd stopped by my house and caught me just taking a batch from the oven." Cookies not sold within two hours were removed from the case and given to charity. The company's major form of advertising was sampling; store employees walked around the shopping mall giving away cookie samples. People were hired for store crews on the basis of warmth, friendliness, and the ability to have a good time giving away samples, baking fresh batches, and talking to customers during the course of a sale.

To implement its strategy, the company developed several novel practices and a customized computer support system. One key practice was giving each store an *hourly* sales quota. Another was for Fields to make unannounced visits to her stores, where she masqueraded as a casual shopper to test the enthusiasm and sales techniques of store crews, sample the quality of the cookies they were baking, and observe customer reactions; she visited each outlet once or twice annually.

Debbi's husband Randy developed a software program that kept headquarters and stores in close contact. Via the computer network, each store manager receives a daily sales goal (broken down by the hour) based on the store's recent performance history and on such special factors as special promotions, mall activities, weekdays vs. weekends, holiday shopping patterns, and the weather forecast. With the hourly sales quotas also comes a schedule of the number of cookies to bake and when to bake them. As the day progresses, store managers type in actual hourly sales figures and customer counts. If customer counts are up but sales are lagging, the computer is programmed to recommend more aggressive sampling or more suggestive selling. If it becomes obvious the day is going to be a bust for the store, the computer automatically revises the sales projections for the day, reducing hourly quotas and instructing how much to cut back cookie baking. To facilitate crew scheduling by the store manager, sales projections are also provided for two weeks in advance. All job applicants must sit at the store's terminal and answer a computerized set of questions as part of the interview process.

In addition, the computer software contains a menu giving store staff immediate access to company personnel policies, maintenance schedules for store equipment, and repair instructions. If a store manager has a specific problem, it can be entered on the system and routed to the appropriate person. Messages can be sent directly to Debbi Fields via the computer; even if she is on a store inspection trip, her promise is to respond to all inquiries within 48 hours.

The computerized information support system serves several objectives: (1) it gives store managers more time to work with their crews and achieve sales quotas as opposed to handling administrative chores and (2) it gives headquarters instantaneous information on store performance and a means of controlling store operations. Debbi Fields sees the system as a tool for projecting her influence and enthusiasm into more stores more frequently than she could otherwise reach.

Source: Developed from information in Mike Korologos, "Debbi Fields," *Sky Magazine,* July 1988, pp. 42–50.

they yield the first hard data from the action front and should be closely scrutinized as a basis for corrective action.

Information systems need to be more comprehensive than just monitoring the first signs of progress. All key strategic performance indicators have to be tracked as often as practical. Many retail companies generate daily sales reports for each store and maintain up-to-the-minute inventory and sales records on each item. Manufacturing plants typically generate daily production reports and track labor productivity on every shift. Monthly profit-and-loss statements are common, as are monthly statistical summaries.

In designing formal reports to monitor strategic progress, five guidelines should be observed:[19]

1. Information and reporting systems should involve no more data and reporting than is needed to give a reliable picture of what is going on. The data gathered should emphasize strategically meaningful variables and symptoms of potentially significant developments. Temptations to supplement "what managers need to know" with other "interesting" but marginally useful information should be avoided.

2. Reports and statistical data-gathering have to be timely—not too late to take corrective action or so often as to overburden.

3. The flow of information and statistics should be kept simple. Complicated reports are likely to confound and obscure because of the attention that has to be paid to mechanics, procedures, and interpretive guidelines instead of measuring and reporting the really critical variables.

4. Information and reporting systems should aim at "no surprises" and generating "early-warnings signs" rather than just producing information. Reports don't necessarily need wide distribution, but they should always be provided to managers who are in a position to act when trouble signs appear.

5. Statistical reports should make it easy to flag big or unusual variances from plan, thus directing management attention to significant departures from targeted performance.

Statistical information gives the strategy implementer a feel for the numbers; reports and meetings provide a feel for new developments and problems; and personal contacts add a feel for the people dimension. All are good barometers of overall performance and good indicators of which things are on and off track. Identifying deviations from plan and the problem areas to be addressed are prerequisites for initiating any actions to either improve implementation or fine-tune strategy.

KEY POINTS
The job of strategy implementation is to translate plans into actions and achieve the intended results. The test of successful strategy implementation is whether actual organization performance matches or exceeds the targets spelled out in the strategic plan. Shortfalls in performance signal weak strategy, weak implementation, or both.

In deciding how to implement strategy, managers have to determine what internal conditions are needed to execute the strategic plan successfully. Then

---

[19]Drucker, *Management*, pp. 498–504; Harold Hoontz, "Management Control: A Suggested Formulation of Principles," *California Management Review* 2, no. 2 (Winter 1959), pp. 50–55; and William H. Sihler, "Toward Better Management Control Systems," *California Management Review* 14, no. 2 (Winter 1971), pp. 33–39.

they must create these conditions as rapidly as practical. The process involves creating a series of tight fits:

- Between strategy and organization structure.
- Between strategy and the organization's skills and competencies.
- Between strategy and budget allocations.
- Between strategy and internal policies, procedures, and support systems.
- Between strategy and the reward structure.
- Between strategy and the corporate culture.

The tighter the fits, the more powerful strategy execution becomes and the more likely targeted performance can actually be achieved.

Implementing strategy is not just a top management function; it is a job for the whole management team. All managers function as strategy implementers in their respective areas of authority and responsibility. All managers have to consider what actions to take in their areas to achieve the intended results— they each need an *action agenda*.

The three major components of organization-building are (1) deciding how to organize and what the organization chart should look like, (2) developing the skills and competencies needed to execute the strategy successfully, and (3) filling key positions with the right people. All organization structures have strategic advantages and disadvantages; there is no one best way to organize. In choosing a structure, the guiding principles are to make strategy-critical activities the major building blocks, keep the design simple, and put decision-making authority in the hands of managers closest to the action. Functional and geographic organization structures are well suited to single-business companies. SBU structures are well suited to companies pursuing related diversification. Decentralized business-unit structures are well suited to companies pursuing unrelated diversification. Project teams, task forces, and new venture teams can also be useful organizational mechanisms to handle temporary or one-time strategic initiatives.

The other two aspects of organization-building—skills development and filling key positions—are just as important as matching structure to strategy. Taking action to develop strategy-supportive skills and create a distinctive competence not only strengthens execution but also helps build competitive advantage. Selecting the right people for key positions tends to be one of the earliest strategy implementation steps because it takes a full complement of capable managers to put the strategy into operation and make it work.

Reworking the budget to make it more strategy-supportive is a crucial part of the implementation process because every organization unit needs to have the people, equipment, facilities, and other resources to carry out its part of the strategic plan (but no *more* than what it really needs!). Strategy implementation often entails shifting resources from one area to another—downsizing units that are overstaffed and overfunded and upsizing those more critical to strategic success.

A third key implementation task is to install some necessary support systems—policies and procedures to establish desired types of behavior, information systems to provide strategy-critical information on a timely basis, and whatever inventory, materials management, customer service, cost accounting, and other administrative systems are needed to give the organization important strategy-executing capability.

In the next chapter, we examine the remaining three key tasks of the strategy implementation process: designing the reward system, creating a strategy-supportive corporate culture, and exercising strategic leadership.

SUGGESTED READINGS

Aaker, David A. "Managing Assets and Skills: The Key to a Sustainable Competitive Advantage." *California Management Review* 31 (Winter 1989), pp. 91–106.

Bartlett, Christopher A., and Sumantra Ghoshal. "Matrix Management: Not a Structure, a Frame of Mind." *Harvard Business Review* 68, no. 4 (July–August 1990), pp. 138–45.

Bettis, Richard A., and William K. Hall. "The Business Portfolio Approach—Where It Falls Down in Practice." *Long Range Planning* 16, no. 2 (April 1983), pp. 95–104.

Chandler, Alfred D. *Strategy and Structure.* Cambridge, Mass.: MIT Press, 1962.

Hall, William K. "SBUs: Hot, New Topic in the Management of Diversification." *Business Horizons* 21, no. 1 (February 1978), pp. 17–25.

Hambrick, Donald C. "The Top Management Team: Key to Strategic Success." *California Management Review* 30, no. 1 (Fall 1987), pp. 88–108.

Larson, Erik W., and David H. Gobeli. "Matrix Management: Contradictions and Insights." *California Management Review* 29, no. 4 (Summer 1987), pp. 126–27.

Leontiades, Milton. "Choosing the Right Manager to Fit the Strategy." *Journal of Business Strategy* 3, no. 2 (Fall 1981), pp. 58–69.

Mintzberg, Henry. "Organization Design: Fashion or Fit." *Harvard Business Review* 59, no. 1 (January–February 1981), pp. 103–16.

Paulson, Robert D. "Making It Happen: The Real Strategic Challenge." *The McKinsey Quarterly,* Winter 1982, pp. 58–66.

Peters, Thomas J., and Robert H. Waterman, Jr. *In Search of Excellence.* New York: Harper & Row, 1982.

Powell, Walter W. "Hybrid Organizational Arrangements: New Form or Transitional Development?" *California Management Review* 30, no. 1 (Fall 1987), pp. 67–87.

Prahalad, C. K., and Gary Hamel. "The Core Competence of the Corporation." *Harvard Business Review* 68 (May–June 1990), pp. 79–93.

Waterman, Robert H.; Thomas J. Peters; and Julien R. Phillips. "Structure Is Not Organization." *Business Horizons* 23, no. 3 (June 1980), pp. 14–26.

Implementing Strategy
Commitment, Culture, and Leadership

———

Weak leadership can wreck the soundest strategy; forceful execution of even a poor plan can often bring victory.
Sun Zi

———

Effective leaders do not just reward achievement, they celebrate it.
Shelley A. Kirkpatrick and Edwin A. Locke

———

Ethics is the moral courage to do what we know is right, and not to do what we know is wrong.
C. J. Silas
CEO, Philips Petroleum

———

. . . a leader lives in the field with his troops.
H. Ross Perot

———

In the previous chapter, we examined three of the strategy-implementer's tasks—building a capable organization, steering resources into strategy-critical programs and activities, and creating a series of internal support systems to enable better execution. In this chapter, we explore the three remaining implementation tasks: designing rewards and incentives for carrying out the strategy, creating a strategy-supportive corporate culture, and exercising strategic leadership.

DEVELOPING AN EFFECTIVE REWARD STRUCTURE

It is important for organizational subunits and individuals to be committed to implementing strategy and accomplishing strategic objectives. Companies typically try to solidify organizationwide commitment through motivation, incentives, and rewards for good performance. The range of options includes all the standard reward-punishment techniques—salary raises, bonuses, stock options, fringe benefits, promotions, fear of being "sidelined," praise, recognition, constructive criticism, tension, peer pressure, more (or less) responsibility, increased (or decreased) job control and decision-making autonomy, attractive geographic assignments, group acceptance, and opportunities for personal satisfaction. But rewards have to be used *creatively* and tightly linked to the factors necessary for good strategy execution.

Motivational Practices

Successful strategy-implementers are good at inspiring employees to do their best. They are skilled at getting employees to buy in to the strategy and commit to making it work. They work at devising strategy-supportive motivational approaches and using them effectively. Consider some actual examples:[1]

- At Mars, Inc. (best known for its candy bars), every employee, including the president, gets a weekly 10 percent bonus by coming to work on time each day that week. This on-time incentive is based on minimizing absenteeism and tardiness to boost worker productivity and to produce the greatest number of candy bars during each available minute of machine time.

- In a number of Japanese companies, employees meet regularly to hear inspirational speeches, sing company songs, and chant the corporate litany. In the United States, Tupperware conducts a weekly Monday night rally to honor, applaud, and fire up its salespeople who conduct Tupperware parties. Amway and Mary Kay Cosmetics hold similar inspirational get-togethers for their sales force organizations.

- A San Diego area company assembles its 2,000 employees at its six plants the first thing every workday to listen to a management talk about the state of the company. Then they engage in brisk calisthenics. This company's management believes "that by doing one thing together each day, it reinforces the unity of the company. It's also fun. It gets the blood up." Managers take turns making the presentations. Many of the speeches "are very personal and emotional, not approved beforehand or screened by anybody."

- Texas Instruments and Dana Corp. insist that teams and divisions set their own goals and have regular peer reviews.

- Procter & Gamble's brand managers are asked to compete fiercely against each other; the official policy is "a free-for- all among brands with no holds barred." P&G's system of purposeful internal competition breeds people who love to compete and excel. Those who "win" become corporate "heroes." Around them emerges a folklore of "war stories" of

---

[1]The list that follows is abstracted from Thomas J. Peters and Robert H. Waterman, Jr., *In Search of Excellence* (New York: Harper & Row, 1982), pp. xx, 213–14, 276, and 285.

their valiant uphill struggles against great odds to make a market success out of their assigned brands.

These motivational approaches accentuate the positive; others blend positive and negative features. Consider the way Harold Geneen, former president and chief executive officer of ITT, allegedly combined the use of money, tension, and fear:

> Geneen provides his managers with enough incentives to make them tolerate the system. Salaries all the way through ITT are higher than average—Geneen reckons 10 percent higher—so that few people can leave without taking a drop. As one employee put it: "We're all paid just a bit more than we think we're worth." At the very top, where the demands are greatest, the salaries and stock options are sufficient to compensate for the rigors. As some said, "He's got them by their limousines."
>
> Having bound his men to him with chains of gold, Geneen can induce the tension that drives the machine. "The key to the system," one of his men explains, "is the profit forecast. Once the forecast has been gone over, revised, and agreed on, the managing director has a personal commitment to Geneen to carry it out. That's how he produces the tension on which the success depends." The tension goes through the company, inducing ambition, perhaps exhilaration, but always with some sense of fear: what happens if the target is missed?[2]

If a strategy-implementer's use of rewards and punishments induces too much tension, anxiety, and job insecurity, the results can be counterproductive. Yet implementers should not completely eliminate tension, pressure for performance, and anxiety from the implementation process. There is, for example, no evidence that a no-pressure work environment leads to superior strategy execution. High-performing organizations need a cadre of ambitious people who relish the opportunity to succeed, love a challenge, thrive in a performance-oriented environment, and find some competition and pressure useful to satisfy their own drives for personal recognition, accomplishment, and self-satisfaction. There has to be some meaningful incentive and career consequences associated with implementation or few people will attach much significance to the strategic plan.

Rewards and Incentives

The conventional view is that a manager's plan for strategy implementation should incorporate more positive than negative motivational elements because when cooperation is positively enlisted and rewarded, people tend to respond with more enthusiasm and effort. Nevertheless, how much of which incentives to use depends on how hard the strategy implementation task will be. A manager has to do more than just talk to everyone about how important strategy implementation is to the organization's future well-being. Talk, no matter how inspiring, seldom commands people's best efforts for long. To get employees' sustained, energetic commitment, management almost always has to be resourceful in designing and using incentives. The more a manager understands what motivates subordinates and the more he or she relies on motivational incentives as a tool for implementing strategy, the greater will be employees' commitment to carrying out the strategic plan.

Positive motivational approaches generally work better than negative ones.

---

[2]Anthony Sampson, *The Sovereign State of ITT* (New York: Stein and Day, 1973), p. 132.

Linking Work Assignments to Performance Targets   The first step in creating a strategy-supportive system of rewards and incentives is to define jobs and assignments in terms of the *results to be accomplished*, not the duties and functions to be performed. Training the job holder's attention and energy on what to *achieve* as opposed to what to do improves the chances of reaching the agreed-on objectives. It is flawed thinking to stress duties and activities in job descriptions in hopes that the by-products will be the desired kinds of accomplishment. In any job, performing activities is not equivalent to achieving objectives. Working hard, staying busy, and diligently attending to assigned duties do not guarantee results. As any student knows, just because an instructor teaches doesn't mean students are learning. Teaching and learning are different things—the first is an activity and the second is a result.

Emphasizing what to accomplish—i.e., performance targets for individual jobs, work groups, departments, businesses, and the entire company—makes the whole work environment results-oriented. Without target objectives, people and organizations can become so engrossed in doing their duties and performing assigned functions on schedule that they lose sight of what the tasks are intended to accomplish. By keeping the spotlight on achievement and targeted performance, strategy-implementers take proactive steps to make the right things happen rather than passively hoping they will happen (this, of course, is what "managing by objectives" is all about).

Creating a tight fit between work assignments and accomplishing the strategic plan thus goes straight to the objectives and performance targets spelled out in the strategic plan. If the details of strategy have been fleshed out thoroughly from the corporate level down to the operating level, performance targets exist for the whole company, for each business unit, for each functional department, and for each operating unit. These become the targets that strategy-implementers aim at achieving and the basis for deciding how many jobs and what skills, expertise, funding, and time frame it will take to achieve them.

Usually a number of performance measures are needed at each level; rarely does a single measure suffice. At the corporate and line-of-business levels, typical performance measures include profitability (measured in terms of total profit, return on equity investment, return on total assets, return on sales, operating profit, and so on), market share, growth rates in sales and profits, and hard evidence that competitive position and future prospects have improved. In the manufacturing area, strategy-relevant performance measures may focus on unit manufacturing costs, productivity increases, production and shipping schedules, quality control, the number and extent of work stoppages due to labor disagreements and equipment breakdowns, and so on. In the marketing area, measures may include unit selling costs, increases in dollar sales and unit volume, sales penetration of each target customer group, increases in market share, the success of newly introduced products, the severity of customer complaints, advertising effectiveness, and the number of new accounts acquired. While most performance measures are quantitative, several have elements of subjectivity—labor-management relations, employee morale, customer satisfaction, advertising success, and how far the firm is ahead or behind rivals on quality, service, and technological capability.

Rewarding Performance   The only dependable way to keep people focused on strategic objectives and to make achieving them "a way of life" throughout the organization is to reward individuals who achieve targets and deny rewards to those who don't. For strategy-implementers, "doing a good job" needs to mean "achieving the agreed-on performance targets." Any other standard undermines implementation of the strategic plan and condones the diversion of time and energy into activities that don't matter much (if such activities are really important, they deserve a place in the strategic plan). The pressure to achieve the targeted strategic performance should be unrelenting. A "no excuses" standard has to prevail.[3]

Strategic Management Principle
The strategy-implementer's standard for judging whether individuals and units have done a good job must be whether they achieved their performance targets.

But with pressure to perform must come ample rewards. Without a payoff, the system breaks down, and the strategy-implementer is left with the unworkable options of barking orders or pleading for compliance. Some of the most successful companies—Wal-Mart Stores, Nucor Steel, Lincoln Electric, Electronic Data Systems, Remington Products, and Mary Kay Cosmetics—owe much of their success to incentive and reward systems that induce people to do the very things needed to hit performance targets and execute strategy. Nucor's strategy was (and is) to be *the* low-cost producer of steel products. Because labor costs are a significant portion of total cost in the steel business, successful implementation of such a strategy required Nucor to achieve lower labor costs per ton of steel than competitors. To drive its labor costs per ton below rivals, Nucor management introduced production incentives that gave workers a bonus roughly equal to their regular wages provided their production teams met or exceeded weekly production targets; the regular wage scale was set at levels comparable to other manufacturing jobs in the local areas where Nucor had plants. Bonuses were paid every two weeks based on the prior weeks' actual production levels measured against the target. The results of Nucor's piece-rate incentive plan were impressive. Nucor's labor productivity (in output per worker) was more than double the average of the unionized work forces of the industry's major producers. Nucor enjoyed about a $100 per ton cost advantage over large, integrated steel producers like U.S. Steel and Bethlehem Steel (a substantial part of which came from its labor cost advantage), and Nucor workers were the highest paid workers in the steel industry. At Remington Products, only 65 percent of factory workers' paychecks is salary; the rest is based on piece-work incentives. The company inspects all products and counts rejected items against incentive pay for the responsible worker. Top-level managers earn more from bonuses than from their salaries. During the first four years of Remington's incentive program, productivity rose 17 percent.

These and other experiences demonstrate some important lessons about designing rewards and incentives:

There are some important guidelines to observe in designing rewards and incentives.

1. *The performance payoff must be a major, not minor, piece of the total compensation package*—incentives that amount to 20 percent or more of total compensation are big attention-getters and are capable of driving individual effort.

2. *The incentive plan should extend to all managers and all workers,* not just be restricted to top management (why should all workers and managers work their tails off and hit performance targets so a few senior executives can get lucrative rewards?).

3. *The system must be administered with scrupulous care and fairness*—if performance standards are set unrealistically high or if individual

---

[3]Tom Peters and Nancy Austin, *A Passion for Excellence* (New York: Random House, 1985), p. xix.

performance evaluations are not accurate and well-documented, dissatisfaction and disgruntlement with the system will overcome any positive benefits.

4. *The incentives must be tightly linked to achieving only those performance targets spelled out in the strategic plan*—performance evaluations based on factors not related to the strategy signal that either the strategic plan is incomplete (because important performance targets were left out) or the real managerial action agenda is something other than what was stated in the strategic plan.

5. *The performance targets each individual is expected to achieve should involve outcomes that the individual can personally affect*—the role of incentives is to enhance individual commitment and channel behavior in beneficial directions. This role is not well-served when the performance measures an individual is judged by are outside his/her arena of influence.

Aside from these general guidelines it is hard to prescribe what kinds of incentives and rewards to develop except to say that the payoff must be directly attached to performance measures that indicate the strategy is working and implementation is on track. If the company's strategy is to be a low-cost producer, the incentive system must reward performance that lowers costs. If the company has a differentiation strategy predicated on superior quality and service, the incentive system must reward such outcomes as zero defects, infrequent need for product repair, low numbers of customer complaints, and speedy order processing and delivery. If a company's growth is predicated on a strategy of new-product introduction, incentives should be based on the percentages of revenues and profits coming from new products.

Why the Performance-Reward Link Is Important

Strategic Management Principle
The reward structure is management's most powerful strategy-implementing tool.

The use of incentives and rewards is the single most powerful tool management has to win strong employee commitment to carrying out the strategic plan. Failure to use this tool wisely and powerfully weakens the entire implementation process. *Decisions on salary increases, incentive compensation, promotions, key assignments, and the ways and means of awarding praise and recognition are the strategy-implementer's foremost attention-getting, commitment-generating devices.* How a manager structures incentives and parcels out rewards signals what sort of behavior and performance management wants and who is doing a good job. Such matters seldom escape the scrutiny of every employee. The system of incentives and rewards thus ends up as the vehicle by which strategy is emotionally ratified in the form of real commitment. Incentives make it in employees' self-interest to do what is needed to achieve the performance targets spelled out in the strategic plan.

Using Performance Contracts

Creating a tight fit between strategy and the reward structure is generally best accomplished by agreeing on performance objectives, fixing responsibility and deadlines for achieving them, and treating their achievement as a *contract*. Next, the contracted-for strategic performance has to be the *real* basis for designing incentives, evaluating individual efforts, and handing out rewards. To prevent undermining the "managing-with-objectives" approach to strategy implementation, a manager must insist that actual performance be judged against the contracted-for target objectives. Any deviations must be fully explored to determine whether the causes are poor performance or circumstances beyond the individual's control. And all managers need to understand how their rewards have been calculated. In short, managers at all levels have to be held accountable for carrying out their part of the strategic plan, and they have to know their rewards are based on their strategic accomplishments (allowing for both the favorable and unfavorable impacts of uncontrollable, unforeseeable, and unknowable circumstances).

BUILDING A STRATEGY-SUPPORTIVE CORPORATE CULTURE

Every organization is a unique culture. It has its own history, its own ways of approaching problems and conducting activities, its own mix of managerial personalities and styles, its own patterns of "how we do things around here," its own set of war stories and heroes, its own experiences of how changes have been instituted—in other words, its own atmosphere, folklore, and personality. A company's culture can be weak and fragmented in the sense that most people have no deepfelt sense of company purpose, view their jobs as simply a way to make money, and have divided loyalties—some to their department, some to their colleagues, some to the union, and some to their boss.[4] On the other hand, a company's culture can be strong and cohesive in the sense that most people understand the company's objectives and strategy, know what their individual roles are, and work conscientiously to do their part. A strong culture is a powerful lever for channeling behavior and helping employees do their jobs in a more strategy-supportive manner; this occurs in two ways:[5]

> *Basic Concept*
> Corporate culture refers to a company's inner values, beliefs, rituals, operating style, and political-social atmosphere.

- By knowing exactly what is expected of them, employees in strong-culture firms don't have to waste time figuring out what to do or how to do it—the culture provides a system of informal rules and peer pressures regarding how to behave most of the time. In a weak-culture company, the absence of strong company identity and a purposeful work climate results in substantial employee confusion and wasted effort.

> *Strategic Management Principle*
> A strong culture and a tight strategy-culture fit are powerful levers for influencing people to do their jobs better.

- A strong culture turns a job into a way of life; it provides structure, standards, and a value system in which to operate; and it promotes strong company identification among employees. As a result, employees feel better about what they do, and more often than not, they work harder to help the company become more successful.

This says something important about the leadership task of strategy implementation: *to implement and execute a strategic plan, an organization's culture must be closely aligned with its strategy.* The optimal condition is a work environment

---

[4]Terrence E. Deal and Allen A. Kennedy, *Corporate Culture* (Reading, Mass.: Addison-Wesley, 1982), p. 4.
[5]Ibid., pp. 15–16.

so in tune with strategy that strategy-critical activities are performed in superior fashion. As one observer noted:

> It has not been just strategy that led to big Japanese wins in the American auto market. It is a culture that enspirits workers to excel at fits and finishes, to produce moldings that match and doors that don't sag. It is a culture in which Toyota can use that most sophisticated of management tools, the suggestion box, and in two years increase the number of worker suggestions from under 10,000 to over 1 million with resultant savings of $250 million.[6]

What Is Corporate Culture?

The taproot of corporate culture is the organization's beliefs and philosophy about how its affairs ought to be conducted—the reasons why it does things the way it does. A company's philosophy and beliefs can be hard to pin down, even harder to characterize. In a sense they are intangible. They are manifest in the values and business principles that senior managers espouse, in the ethical standards they demand, in the policies they set, in the style with which things are done, in the traditions the organization maintains, in people's attitudes and feelings and in the stories they tell, in the peer pressures that exist, in the organization's politics, and in the "chemistry" that surrounds the work environment and defines the organization's culture. We are beginning to learn that an organization's culture is an important contributor (or obstacle) to successful strategy execution. A close culture-strategy match is crucial to managing a company's people resources with maximum effectiveness. A culture that energizes people all over the firm to do their jobs in a strategy-supportive manner adds significantly to the power and effectiveness of strategy execution. When a company's culture and strategy are out of sync, the culture has to be changed as rapidly as possible; a sizable and prolonged strategy-culture conflict weakens and may even defeat managerial efforts to make the strategy work.

Illustration Capsule 25 looks at some of the traits and characteristics of strong-culture companies to provide more insight into why the culture-strategy fit makes such a big difference. While the examples help demonstrate the contribution culture can make toward "keeping the herd moving roughly West" (as Professor Terry Deal puts it), the strategy-implementer's concern is with what actions to take to create a culture that facilitates strategy execution.

Creating the Fit between Strategy and Culture

It is the *strategy-maker's* responsibility to select a strategy compatible with the "sacred" or unchangeable parts of prevailing corporate culture. It is the *strategy-implementer's* task, once strategy is chosen, to bring corporate culture into close alignment with the strategy and keep it there.

Aligning culture with strategy presents a strong challenge. The first step is to diagnose which facets of the present culture are strategy-supportive and which are not. Then, there must be some innovative thinking about concrete actions management can take to modify the cultural environment and create a stronger fit with the strategy.

---

[6]Robert H. Waterman, Jr., "The Seven Elements of Strategic Fit," *Journal of Business Strategy* 2, no. 3 (Winter 1982), p. 70.

ILLUSTRATION CAPSULE
25

TRAITS AND CHARACTERISTICS OF STRONG-CULTURE COMPANIES

To better understand what corporate culture is and why it plays a role in successful strategy execution, consider the distinctive traits and themes of companies with strong cultures:

- At Frito-Lay, stories abound about potato chip route salesmen slogging through sleet, mud, hail, snow, and rain to uphold the 99.5 percent service level to customers in which the entire organization takes such great pride. At McDonald's the constant message from management is the overriding importance of quality, service, cleanliness, and value; employees are drilled over and over on the need for attention to detail and perfecting every fundamental of the business. At Delta Airlines, the culture is driven by "Delta's family feeling" that builds a team spirit and nurtures each employee's cooperative attitude toward others, cheerful outlook toward life, and pride in a job well done. At Johnson & Johnson, the credo is that customers come first, employees second, the community third, and shareholders fourth and last. At DuPont, there is a fixation on safety—a report of every accident must be on the chairman's desk within 24 hours (DuPont's safety record is 17 times better than the chemical industry average and 68 times better than the all-manufacturing average).

- Companies with strong cultures are unashamed collectors and tellers of stories, anecdotes, and legends in support of basic beliefs. L. L. Bean tells customer service stories. 3M tells innovation stories. P&G, Johnson & Johnson, Perdue Farms, and Maytag tell quality stories. From an organizational standpoint, such tales are very important because people in the organization take pride in identifying strongly with the stories, and they start to share in the traditions and values which the stories relate.

- The most typical values and beliefs that shape culture include (1) a belief in being the best (or at GE "better than the best"), (2) a belief in superior quality and service, (3) a belief in the importance of people as individuals and a faith in their ability to make a strong, positive contribution, (4) a belief in the importance of the details of execution, the nuts and bolts of doing the job well, (5) a belief that customers should reign supreme, (6) a belief in inspiring people, whatever their ability, (7) a belief in the importance of informality to enhance communication, and (8) a recognition that growth and profits are essential to a company's well-being. While the themes are common, however, every company implements them differently (to fit their particular situations), and every company's values are the articulated handiwork of one or two legendary figures in leadership positions. Accordingly, each company has its own distinct culture which, they believe, no one can copy successfully.

- In companies with strong cultures, managers and workers either "buy in" to the culture and accept its norms or they opt out and leave the company.

- The stronger the corporate culture and the more it is directed toward customers and markets, the less a company uses policy manuals, organization charts, and detailed rules and procedures to enforce discipline and norms. The reason is that the guiding values inherent in the culture convey in crystal-clear fashion what everybody is supposed to do in most situations. Often, poorly performing companies have strong cultures too. The difference is that their cultures are dysfunctional, being focused on internal politics or operating by the numbers as opposed to emphasizing customers and the people who make and sell the product.

Companies with strong cultures are clear on what they stand for, and they are serious about the tasks of establishing company values, winning employees over to these values, and causing employees to observe cultural norms religiously.

Source: Compiled from Thomas J. Peters and Robert H. Waterman, Jr., *In Search of Excellence* (New York: Harper & Row, 1982), pp. xxi, 75–77, and 280–85; and Thomas J. Peters and Nancy Austin, *A Passion for Excellence* (New York: Random House, 1985), pp. 282–83 and 334.

Awards ceremonies, role models, and symbols are a fundamental part of a strategy-implementer's culture-shaping effort.

Symbolic Actions and Substantive Actions   Normally, managerial actions to tighten the culture-strategy fit are both symbolic and substantive. Symbolic actions are valuable for the signals they send about the kinds of behavior and performance strategy-implementers wish to encourage. The most common symbolic actions are events held to honor new kinds of heroes—people whose actions and performance serve as role models. Many universities give outstanding teacher awards each year to symbolize their commitment to and esteem for instructors who display exceptional classroom talents. Numerous businesses have employee-of-the-month awards. The military has a long-standing custom of awarding ribbons and medals for exemplary actions. Some football coaches award emblems to players to wear on their helmets as symbols of their exceptional performance.

Successful strategy-implementers are experts in the use of symbols to build and nurture the culture. They personally conduct ceremonial events, and they go out of their way to personally and publicly congratulate individuals who exhibit the desired traits. Individuals and groups that "get with the program" are singled out for special praise and visibly rewarded. Successful implementers use every ceremonial function and every conversation to implant values, send reinforcing signals, and praise good deeds.

In addition to being out front, personally leading the push for new attitudes and communicating the reasons for new approaches, the manager has to convince all those concerned that the effort is more than cosmetic. Talk and symbols have to be complemented by substance and real movement. The actions taken have to be credible, highly visible, and unmistakably indicative of management's commitment to a new culture and new ways of doing business. There are several ways to accomplish this. One is to engineer some quick successes in reorienting the way some things are done to highlight the value of the new order, thus making enthusiasm for the changes contagious. However, instant results are usually not as important as creating a solid, competent team psychologically committed to carrying out the strategy in a superior fashion. The strongest signs that management is committed to creating a new culture come from actions to replace traditional managers with "new breed" managers, changes in long-standing policies and operating practices, major reorganizational moves, big shifts in how raises and promotions are granted, and reallocations in the budget.

Strategic Management Principle
Senior executives must personally lead efforts to create a strategy-supportive culture.

At the same time, chief strategy-implementers must be careful to *lead by example*. For instance, if the organization's strategy involves a drive to become the industry's low-cost producer, senior managers must be frugal in their own actions and decisions: spartan decorations in the executive suite, conservative expense accounts and entertainment allowances, a lean staff in the corporate office, and so on.

Implanting the needed culture-building values and behavior depends on a sincere, sustained commitment by the chief executive coupled with extraordinary persistence in reinforcing the culture through both word and deed. Neither charisma nor personal magnetism are essential. However, being highly visible around the organization is essential; culture-building cannot be done from an office. Moreover, creating and sustaining a strategy-supportive culture is a job for the whole management team. Senior officers have to keynote the values and shape the organization's philosophy. But for the effort to be successful, strategy-implementers must enlist the support of subordinate

TABLE 10–1   **Topics Generally Covered in Values Statements and Codes of Ethics**

Topics Covered in Values Statements	Topics Covered in Codes of Ethics
• Importance of customers and customer service	• Honesty and observance of the law
• Commitment of quality	• Conflicts of interest
• Commitment to innovation	• Fairness in selling and marketing practices
• Respect for the individual employee and the duty the company has to employees	• Using inside information and securities trading
• Importance of honesty, integrity, and ethical standards	• Supplier relationships and purchasing practices
• Duty to stockholders	• Payments to obtain business/Foreign Corrupt Practices Act
• Duty to suppliers	• Acquiring and using information about others
• Corporate citizenship	• Political activities
• Importance of protecting the environment	• Use of company assets, resources, and property
	• Protection of proprietary information
	• Pricing, contracting, and billing

managers, getting them to instill values and establish culture norms at the lowest levels in the organization. Until a big majority of employees have joined the culture and share an emotional commitment to its basic values and beliefs, there's considerably more work to be done in both installing the culture and tightening the culture-strategy fit.

The task of making culture supportive of strategy is not a short-term exercise. It takes time for a new culture to emerge and prevail. The bigger the organization and the greater the cultural shift needed to produce a culture-strategy fit, the longer it takes. In large companies, changing the corporate culture in significant ways can take three to five years at minimum. In fact, it is usually tougher to reshape a deeply ingrained culture that is not strategy-supportive than it is to instill a strategy-supportive culture from scratch in a brand new organization.

Establishing Ethical Standards and Values

A strong corporate culture founded on ethical principles and sound values is a vital driving force behind continued strategic success. Many executives are convinced that a company must care about *how* it does business; otherwise it puts its reputation at risk and ultimately its performance. Corporate ethics and values programs are not window-dressing; they are undertaken to create an environment of strongly held values and convictions and to make ethical conduct a way of life. Strong values and high ethical standards nurture the corporate culture in a very positive way.

An ethical corporate culture has a positive impact on a company's long-term strategic success; an unethical culture can undermine it.

Companies establish values and ethical standards in a number of different ways.[7] Firms steeped in tradition with a rich folklore to draw on rely on word-of-mouth indoctrination and the power of tradition to instill values and enforce ethical conduct. But many companies today set forth their values and code of ethics in written documents. Table 10–1 shows the kinds of

---

[7]The Business Roundtable, *Corporate Ethics: A Prime Asset*, February 1988, pp. 4–10.

ILLUSTRATION CAPSULE
26

THE JOHNSON & JOHNSON CREDO

—We believe our first responsibility is to the doctors, nurses and patients, to mothers and all others who use our products and services.

—In meeting their needs everything we do must be of high quality.

—We must constantly strive to reduce our costs in order to maintain reasonable prices.

—Customers' orders must be serviced promptly and accurately.

—Our suppliers and distributors must have an opportunity to make a fair profit.

—We are responsible to our employees, the men and women who work with us throughout the world.

—Everyone must be considered as an individual.

—We must respect their dignity and recognize their merit.

—They must have a sense of security in their jobs.

—Compensation must be fair and adequate, and working conditions clean, orderly, and safe.

—Employees must feel free to make suggestions and complaints.

—There must be equal opportunity for employment, development and advancement for those qualified.

—We must provide competent management, and their actions must be just and ethical.

—We are responsible to the communities in which we live and work and to the world community as well.

—We must be good citizens—support good works and charities and bear our fair share of taxes.

—We must encourage civic improvements and better health and education.

—We must maintain in good order the property we are privileged to use, protecting the environment and natural resources.

—Our final responsibility is to our stockholders.

—Business must make a sound profit.

—We must experiment with new ideas.

—Research must be carried on, innovative programs developed and mistakes paid for.

—New equipment must be purchased, new facilities provided and new products launched.

—Reserves must be created to provide for adverse times.

—When we operate according to these principles, the stockholders should realize a fair return.

Source: 1982 Annual Report.

topics such statements cover. Written statements have the advantage of explicitly stating what the company intends and expects; and they serve as benchmarks for judging both company policies and actions and individual conduct. They put a stake in the ground and define the company's position. Value statements serve as a cornerstone for culture-building; a code of ethics serves as a cornerstone for creating a corporate conscience. Illustration Capsule 26 presents the Johnson & Johnson Credo, the most publicized and celebrated code of ethics and values among U.S. companies. J & J's CEO calls the credo "the unifying force for our corporation." Illustration Capsule 27 presents the pledge that Bristol-Myers Squibb makes to all of its stakeholders.

Once values and ethical standards have been formally set forth, they must be institutionalized and ingrained in the company's policies, practices, and actual conduct. Implementing the values and code of ethics entails several actions:

Values and ethical standards not only must be explicitly stated but they also must be deeply ingrained into the corporate culture.

- Incorporating the statement of values and the code of ethics into employee training and educational programs.

ILLUSTRATION CAPSULE
27

THE BRISTOL-MYERS SQUIBB PLEDGE

To those who use our products . . .
We affirm Bristol-Myers Squibb's commitment to the highest standards of excellence, safety and reliability in everything we make. We pledge to offer products of the highest quality and to work diligently to keep improving them.

To our employees and those who may join us . . .
We pledge personal respect, fair compensation and equal treatment. We acknowledge our obligation to provide able and humane leadership throughout the organization, within a clean and safe working environment. To all who qualify for advancement, we will make every effort to provide opportunity.

To our suppliers and customers . . .
We pledge an open door, courteous, efficient and ethical dealing, and appreciation for their right to a fair profit.

To our shareholders . . .
We pledge a companywide dedication to contin-

ued profitable growth, sustained by strong finances, a high level of research and development, and facilities second to none.

To the communities where we have plants and offices . . .
We pledge conscientious citizenship, a helping hand for worthwhile causes, and constructive action in support of civic and environmental progress.

To the countries where we do business . . .
We pledge ourselves to be a good citizen and to show full consideration for the rights of others while reserving the right to stand up for our own.

Above all, to the world we live in . . .
We pledge Bristol-Myers Squibb to policies and practices which fully embody the responsibility, integrity and decency required of free enterprise if it is to merit and maintain the confidence of our society.

Source: 1990 Annual Report.

- Giving explicit attention to values and ethics in recruiting and hiring to screen out applicants who do not exhibit compatible character traits.
- Communicating the values and ethics codes to all employees and explaining compliance procedures.
- Management involvement and oversight, from the CEO to first-line supervisors.
- Strong endorsements by the CEO.
- Word-of-mouth indoctrination.

In the case of codes of ethics, special attention must be given to those sections of the company that are particularly sensitive and vulnerable—purchasing, sales, and political lobbying.[8] Employees who deal with external parties are in ethically sensitive positions and are often drawn into compromising situations. Procedures for enforcing ethical standards and handling potential violations have to be developed.

The implementation effort must permeate the company, extending into every organizational unit. The attitudes, character, and work history of prospective employees must be scrutinized. Every employee must receive adequate training. Line managers at all levels must give serious and continuous attention to the task of explaining how the values and ethical conduct apply

---

[8]Ibid., p. 7.

in their areas. In addition, they must insist that company values and ethical standards become a way of life. In general, instilling values and insisting on ethical conduct must be viewed as a continuous culture-building, culture-nurturing exercise. Whether the effort succeeds or fails depends largely on how well corporate values and ethical standards are visibly integrated into company policies, managerial practices, and actions at all levels.

Building a Spirit of High Performance into the Culture

A results-oriented culture that inspires people to do their best is conducive to superior strategy execution.

An ability to instill strong individual commitment to strategic success and create constructive pressure to perform is one of the most valuable strategy-implementing skills. When an organization performs consistently at or near peak capability, the outcome is not only improved strategic success but also an organizational culture permeated with a spirit of high performance. This should not be confused with whether employees are " happy" or "satisfied," or "get along well together." An organization with a spirit of performance emphasizes achievement and excellence. Its culture is results-oriented, and its management pursues policies and practices that inspire people to do their best.

High-performance cultures make champions out of people who excel.

Companies with a spirit of high performance typically are intensely people-oriented; and they reinforce this orientation at every conceivable occasion in every conceivable way to every employee. They treat employees with dignity and respect, train each employee thoroughly, encourage employees to use their own initiative and creativity in performing their work, set reasonable and clear performance expectations, utilize the full range of rewards and punishment to enforce high performance standards, hold managers at every level responsible for developing the people who report to them, and grant employees enough autonomy to stand out, excel, and contribute. To create a results-oriented organizational culture, a company must make champions out of the people who turn in winning performances:[9]

- At Boeing, IBM, General Electric, and 3M Corporation, top executives deliberately make "champions" out of individuals who believe so strongly in their ideas that they take it on themselves to hurdle the bureaucracy, maneuver their projects through the system, and turn them into improved services, new products, or even new businesses. In these companies, "product champions" are given high visibility, room to push their ideas, and strong executive support. Champions whose ideas prove out are usually handsomely rewarded; those whose ideas don't pan out still have secure jobs and are given chances to try again.

- The manager of a New York area sales office rented the Meadowlands Stadium (home field of the New York Giants) for an evening. After work, the salesmen were all assembled at the stadium and asked to run one at a time through the player's tunnel onto the field. As each one emerged, the electronic scoreboard flashed his name to those gathered in the stands—executives from corporate headquarters, employees from the office, family, and friends. Their role was to cheer loudly in honor of the individual's sales accomplishments. The company involved was IBM. The occasion for this action was to reaffirm IBM's commitment to

---

[9]Peters and Waterman, *In Search of Excellence*, pp. xviii, 240, and 269; and Peters and Austin, *A Passion for Excellence*, pp. 304–7.

satisfy an individual's need to be part of something great and to reiterate IBM's concern for championing individual accomplishment.

- Some companies upgrade the importance and status of individual employees by referring to them as Cast members (Disney), Crew Members (McDonald's), or Associates (Wal-Mart and J. C. Penney). Companies like IBM, Tupperware, and McDonald's actively seek out reasons and opportunities to give pins, buttons, badges, and medals to good showings by average performers—the idea being to express appreciation and help give a boost to the "middle 60 percent" of the work force.

- McDonald's has a contest to determine the best hamburger cooker in its entire chain. It begins with a competition to determine the best hamburger cooker in each store. Store winners go on to compete in regional championships, and regional winners go on to the "All-American" contest. The winners get trophies and an All-American patch to wear on their shirts.

- Milliken & Co. holds Corporate Sharing Rallies once every three months; teams come from all over the company to swap success stories and ideas. A hundred or more teams make five-minute presentations over a two-day period. Each rally has a major theme—quality, cost reduction, and so on. No criticisms and negatives are allowed, and there is no such thing as a big idea or a small one. Quantitative measures of success are used to gauge improvement. All those present vote on the best presentation, and several ascending grades of awards are handed out. Everyone, however, receives a framed certificate for participating.

What makes a spirit of high performance come alive is a complex network of practices, words, symbols, styles, values, and policies pulling together to produce extraordinary results with ordinary people. The drivers of the system are a belief in the worth of the individual, strong company commitments to job security and promotion from within, managerial practices that encourage employees to exercise individual initiative and creativity, and pride in doing the "itty-bitty, teeny-tiny things" right. A company that treats its employees well benefits from increased teamwork, higher morale, and greater employee loyalty.

While emphasizing a spirit of high performance nearly always accentuates the positive, there are negative aspects too. Managers whose units consistently perform poorly have to be removed. Aside from the organizational benefits, weak performing managers should be reassigned for their own good—people who find themselves in a job they cannot handle are usually frustrated, anxiety ridden, harassed, and unhappy.[10] Moreover, subordinates have a right to be managed with competence, dedication, and achievement; unless their boss performs well, they themselves cannot perform well. Weak-performing workers and people who reject the cultural emphasis on dedication and high performance have to be weeded out. Recruitment practices need to aim at selecting highly motivated, ambitious applicants whose attitudes and work habits mesh well with a results-oriented culture.

Illustration Capsule 28 shows how one major company has linked its values and culture with its performance objectives.

---

[10]Peter Drucker, *Management: Tasks, Responsibilities, Practices* (New York: Harper & Row, 1974), p. 457.

ILLUSTRATION CAPSULE

28

SQUARE D COMPANY: VISION, MISSION, PRINCIPLES, OBJECTIVES, PERFORMANCE

Square D Company is a $1.7 billion producer of electrical equipment and electronic products. Below is the company's presentation of its vision, mission, principles, objectives, and actual performance against its long-term financial goals.

Vision

Dedicated to Growth
Committed to Quality

Mission

We are dedicated to growth for our customers, shareholders and employees through quality, innovation and profitable reinvestment.

Principles

As a company responsible to our customers, shareholders and employees, we will:

- Provide our customers with innovative, functional and reliable products and services at a cost and quality level consistent with their needs.
- Concentrate on enhancing long-term shareholder value.
- Actively pursue equal opportunity for all individuals and provide an environment which encourages open communications, personal growth and creativity.
- Expect integrity and professional conduct from our employees in every aspect of our business.
- Conduct our operations ethically and well within the framework of the law.
- Actively contribute to the communities and in-

dustries in which we participate.

Financial Objectives

We are committed to providing our shareholders with an attractive return on their investment, and our specific goals for doing so are to:

- Achieve a minimum after-tax return on capital of 14%.
- Leverage return on shareholders' equity through a capital structure which includes 25 to 35% debt.
- Achieve a minimum return on equity of 18%.
- Pay dividends equal to approximately 40% of earnings.
- Achieve average annual growth in earnings of at least 10%.

Operating Objectives

Market Leadership

- Have a leading market share position in our major markets.
- Be recognized as a leader in the application of technology to meet customer requirements.
- Be a "best-value" supplier throughout the world.
- Expand our international business to a level equaling 20 to 25% of company sales.
- Invest in research and development at a rate of 4% of sales as a means of achieving our market leadership objectives.

(continued)

Bonding the Fits: The Role of Shared Values

As emphasized earlier, "fits" with strategy need to be created internally as concerns structure, organizational skills and distinctive competence, budgets, support systems, rewards and incentives, policies and procedures, and culture. The better the "goodness of fit" among these administrative activities and characteristics, the more powerful strategy execution is likely to be.

McKinsey & Co., a leading consulting firm with wide-ranging experience in strategic analysis, has developed a framework for examining the fits in seven

ILLUSTRATION CAPSULE
28

(concluded)

Employee Development

- Encourage initiative, innovation and productivity by appropriately recognizing and rewarding employee performance.
- Invest in employee training and development at a rate of 2% of payroll.
- Honestly and accurately appraise and evaluate the performance of each employee on at least an annual basis.
- Provide for the orderly succession of management.
- Maintain a positive affirmative action program and provide employees with the opportunity

for advancement commensurate with their abilities.

Social/Community Responsibility

- Maintain a safe, clean and healthy environment for our employees and the communities in which we operate.
- Invest 1.5% of net income in social, cultural, educational and charitable activities.
- Encourage appropriate employee involvement in community activities.

Performance against Financial Goals

Year Ended December 31	Long-Term Financial Goals	1988	1987	1986	1985	1984
After-tax return from continuing operations on average capital	14.0%	14.8%	13.5%	12.5%	13.9%	16.4%
Average total debt as a percentage of average capital	25.0–35.0	28.2	23.7	29.9	30.5	29.5
Return from continuing operations on average equity	18.0	18.1	15.7	15.5	17.7	20.6
Dividend payout percentage	40.0	45.7	48.6	53.9	60.9	49.7
Annual growth in earnings from continuing operations	10.0	8.1	11.2	(3.4)	(6.7)	65.0

Source: 1988 Annual Report.

broad areas: (1) strategy, (2) structure, (3) shared values, attitudes, and philosophy, (4) approach to staffing the organization and its overall "people orientation," (5) administrative systems, practices, and procedures used to run the organization on a day-to-day basis, including the reward structure, formal and informal policies, budgeting and programs, training, cost accounting, and financial controls, (6) the organization's skills, capabilities, and core competencies, and (7) style of top management (how they allocate their time and attention, symbolic actions, their leadership skills, the way the top

The values widely shared by managers and employees are the core of the corporate culture.

F I G U R E   10–1   **Bonding the Administrative Fits**   (*The McKinsey 7-S framework*)

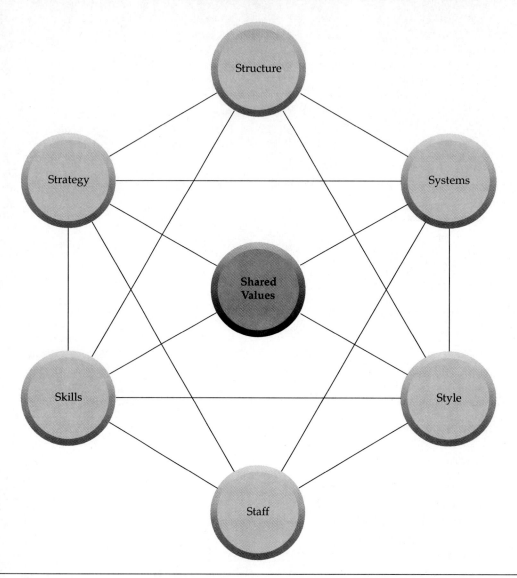

Source: Thomas J. Peters and Robert H. Waterman, Jr., *In Search of Excellence* (New York: Harper & Row, 1982), p. 10.

management team comes across to the rest of the organization).[11] McKinsey has diagrammed these seven elements into what it calls the McKinsey 7-S framework (the seven S's are strategy, structure, shared values, staff, systems, skills, and style—so labeled to promote recall) shown in Figure 10–1.

[11]For a more extended discussion, see Robert H. Waterman, Jr., Thomas J. Peters, and Julien R. Phillips, "Structure Is Not Organization," *Business Horizons* 23, no. 3 (June 1980), pp. 14–26; and Robert H. Waterman, Jr., "The Seven Elements of Strategic Fit," *Journal of Business Strategy* 2, no. 3 (Winter 1982), pp. 68–72.

Shared values are the core of the 7-S framework because they are the heart-and-soul themes around which an organization rallies. They define its main beliefs and aspirations, its guiding concepts of "who we are, what we do, where we are headed, and what principles we will stand for in getting there." They bond the corporate culture and give it energy.

The McKinsey 7-S framework draws attention to some important organizational interconnections and why these interconnections are relevant in trying to effect change. In orchestrating a major shift in strategy and gathering momentum for implementation, the pace of change will be governed by all seven S's. The 7-S framework is a simple way to illustrate that the job of implementing strategy is one of creating fits and harmonizing the seven S's.

EXERTING STRATEGIC LEADERSHIP

The formula for good strategic management is simple enough: develop a sound strategic plan, implement it, execute it to the fullest, win! But it's easier said than done. Exerting take-charge leadership, being a "spark plug," ramrodding things through, and getting things done by coaching others are difficult tasks. Moreover, a strategy manager has many different leadership roles to play: chief entrepreneur and strategist, chief administrator and strategy-implementer, crisis solver, taskmaster, figurehead, spokesperson, resource allocator, negotiator, motivator, adviser, inspirationist, consensus builder, policymaker, mentor, and head cheerleader. Sometimes a strategy manager needs to be authoritarian and hardnosed, sometimes a perceptive listener and compromising decision-maker. And sometimes a participative, collegial approach works best. Many occasions call for a highly visible role and extensive time commitments, while others entail a brief ceremonial performance with the details delegated to subordinates.

Strategic Management Principle
Strong leadership is almost always essential for effective strategy execution.

In general, the problem of strategic leadership is one of diagnosing the situation and choosing from any of several ways to handle it. Six leadership roles dominate the strategy-implementer's action agenda:

1. Staying on top of what is happening and how well things are going.
2. Promoting a culture in which the organization is "energized" to accomplish strategy and perform at a high level.
3. Keeping the organization responsive to changing conditions, alert for new opportunities, and bubbling with innovative ideas.
4. Building consensus, dealing with the politics of strategy formulation and implementation, and containing "power struggles."
5. Enforcing ethical standards.
6. Taking corrective actions to improve strategy execution and overall strategic performance.

Managing By Walking Around (MBWA)

To stay on top of how well the implementation process is going, a manager needs to develop a broad network of contacts and information sources, both formal and informal. The regular channels include talking with key subordinates, reading written reports and the latest operating results, getting feedback from customers, watching the competitive reactions of rivals, tapping into the grapevine, listening to rank-and-file employees, and observing the situation firsthand. However, some information is more reliable than the rest. Written reports can cover up or minimize bad news—or not report it at all. Sometimes subordinates delay reporting failures and problems, hoping that extra time will help them turn things around. As information flows up an organization, it tends to get "censored" and "sterilized" to the point that it may block or obscure strategy-critical information. Strategy managers must guard against surprises by making sure that they have accurate information and a "feel" for the situation. One way to do so is to visit "the field" regularly and talk with many different people at many different levels. The technique of *managing by walking around* (MBWA) is practiced in a variety of styles:[12]

MBWA is one of the techniques effective leaders use.

- At Hewlett-Packard, there are weekly beer busts in each division, attended by both executives and employees, to create a regular opportunity to keep in touch. Tidbits of information flow freely between down-the-line employees and executives—facilitated in part because "the H-P Way" is for people at all ranks to be addressed by their first names. Bill Hewlett, one of HP's co-founders, had a companywide reputation for getting out of his office and "wandering around" the plant greeting people, listening to what was on their minds, and asking questions. He found this so valuable that he made MBWA a standard practice for all HP managers. Furthermore, ad hoc meetings of people from different departments spontaneously arise; they gather in rooms with blackboards and work out solutions informally.

- McDonald's founder Ray Kroc regularly visited store units and did his own personal inspection on Q.S.C.& V. (Quality, Service, Cleanliness, and Value)—the themes he preached regularly. There are stories of him pulling into a unit's parking lot, seeing litter lying on the pavement, getting out of his limousine to pick it up himself, and then lecturing the store staff at length on the subject of cleanliness.

- The CEO of a small manufacturing company spends much of his time riding around the factory in a golf cart, waving and joking with workers, listening to them, and calling all 2,000 employees by their first names. In addition, he spends a lot of time with union officials, inviting them to meetings and keeping them well informed about what is going on.

- Sam Walton, Wal-Mart's founder, insists "The key is to get out into the store and listen to what the associates have to say. Our best ideas come from clerks and stockboys." Walton himself has had a longstanding practice of spending two to three days every week visiting Wal-Mart's stores and talking with store managers and employees. On one occasion he flew the company plane to a Texas town, got out, and instructed the copilot to meet him 100 miles down the road. Then he flagged a Wal-Mart truck and rode the rest of the way to "chat with the driver—it seemed like so much fun." Walton makes a practice of greeting store managers and their spouses by name at annual meetings and has been known to go to the company's distribution centers at 2:00 A.M. (carrying boxes of

---

[12]Ibid., pp. xx, 15, 120–23, 191, 242–43, 246–47, 287–90. For an extensive report on the benefits of MBWA, see Thomas J. Peters and Nancy Austin, *A Passion for Excellence*, (New York: Random House, 1985), chaps. 2, 3, and 19.

doughnuts to share with all those on duty) to have a chance to find out what was on their minds.

- When Ed Carlson became CEO at United Airlines, he traveled some 200,000 miles a year talking with United's employees. He observed, "I wanted these people to identify me and to feel sufficiently comfortable to make suggestions or even argue with me if that's what they felt like doing. . . . Whenever I picked up some information, I would call the senior officer of the division and say that I had just gotten back from visiting Oakland, Reno, and Las Vegas, and here is what I found."

- At Marriott Corp., Bill Marriott not only personally inspects all Marriott hotels at least once a year, but he also invites all Marriott guests to send him their evaluations of Marriott's facilities and services. He personally reads every customer complaint and has been known to telephone hotel managers about them.

Managers at many companies attach great importance to informal communication. They report that it is essential to have a "feel" for situations and to gain quick, easy access to information. When executives stay in their offices, they tend to become isolated and often surround themselves with people who are not likely to offer criticism or different perspectives; the information they get is secondhand, screened and filtered, and sometimes dated.

Fostering a Strategy-Supportive Climate and Culture

Strategy-implementers have to be "out front" in promoting a strategy-supportive organizational climate. When major strategic changes are being implemented, a manager's time is best spent personally leading the changes. When only strategic fine-tuning is being implemented, it takes less time and effort to bring values and culture into alignment with strategy, but there is still a lead role for the manager to play in pushing ahead and prodding for continuous improvements. Successful strategy leaders know it is their responsibility to convince people that the chosen strategy is right and that implementing it to the best of the organization's ability is "top priority."

Both words and deeds play a part. Words inspire people, infuse spirit and drive, define strategy-supportive cultural norms and values, articulate the reasons for strategic and organizational change, legitimize new viewpoints and new priorities, urge and reinforce commitment, and arouse confidence in the new strategy. Deeds add credibility to the words, create strategy-supportive symbols, set examples, give meaning and content to the language, and teach the organization what sort of behavior is needed and expected.

Highly visible symbols and imagery are needed to complement substantive actions. One General Motors manager explained the striking difference in performance between two large plants:[13]

> At the poorly performing plant, the plant manager probably ventured out on the floor once a week, always in a suit. His comments were distant and perfunctory. At South Gate, the better plant, the plant manager was on the floor all the time. He wore a baseball cap and a UAW jacket. By the way, whose plant do you think was spotless? Whose looked like a junkyard?

---

[13]As quoted in Peters and Waterman, *In Search of Excellence*, p. 262.

As a rule, the greater the degree of strategic change being implemented and/or the greater the shift in cultural norms needed to accommodate a new strategy, the more visible the strategy-implementer's words and deeds need to be. Lessons from well-managed companies show that what the strategy-leader says and does has a significant bearing on down-the-line strategy implementation and execution.[14] According to one view, "It is not so much the articulation . . . about what an [organization] should be doing that creates new practice. It's the imagery that creates the understanding, the compelling moral necessity that the new way is right."[15] Moreover, the actions and images, both substantive and symbolic, have to be repeated regularly, not just at ceremonies and special occasions. This is where a high profile and "managing by walking around" comes into play. As a Hewlett-Packard official expresses it in the company publication *The HP Way*:

> Once a division or department has developed a plan of its own—a set of working objectives—it's important for managers and supervisors to keep it in operating condition. This is where observation, measurement, feedback, and guidance come in. It's our "management by wandering around." That's how you find out whether you're ontrack and heading at the right speed and in the right direction. If you don't constantly monitor how people are operating, not only will they tend to wander off track but also they will begin to believe you weren't serious about the plan in the first place. It has the extra benefit of getting you off your chair and moving around your area. By wandering around, I literally mean moving around and talking to people. It's all done on a very informal and spontaneous basis, but it's important in the course of time to cover the whole territory. You start out by being accessible and approachable, but the main thing is to realize you're there to listen. The second reason for MBWA is that it is vital to keep people informed about what's going on in the company, especially those things that are important to them. The third reason for doing this is because it is just plain fun.

Such contacts give the manager a feel for how things are progressing, and they provide opportunities to encourage employees, lift spirits, shift attention from the old to the new priorities, create some excitement, and project an atmosphere of informality and fun—all of which drive implementation in a positive fashion and intensify the organizational energy behind strategy execution. John Welch of General Electric sums up the hands-on role and motivational approach well: "I'm here every day, or out into a factory, smelling it, feeling it, touching it, challenging the people."[16]

Keeping the Internal Organization Responsive and Innovative

While formulating and implementing strategy is a manager's responsibility, the task of generating fresh ideas, identifying new opportunities, and responding to changing conditions cannot be accomplished by a single person. It is an organizationwide task, particularly in large corporations. Strategic leadership must result in a dependable supply of fresh ideas from the rank and file—man-

---

[14]Peters and Waterman, *In Search of Excellence*, chap. 9.

[15]Warren Bennis, *The Unconscious Conspiracy: Why Leaders Can't Lead* (New York: AMACOM, 1987), p. 93.

[16]As quoted in Ann M. Morrison, "Trying to Bring GE to Life," *Fortune*, January 25, 1982, p. 52.

agers and employees alike—and promote an entrepreneurial, opportunistic spirit that permits continuous adaptation to changing conditions. A flexible, responsive, innovative internal environment is critical in fast-moving high-technology industries, in businesses where products have short life cycles and growth depends on new-product innovation, in corporations with widely diversified business portfolios (where opportunities are varied and scattered), in industries where successful product differentiation is key, and in businesses where the strategy of being the low-cost producer hinges on productivity improvement and cost reduction. Managers cannot mandate such an environment by simply exhorting people to be "creative."

One useful leadership approach is to take special pains to foster, nourish, and support people who are willing to champion new ideas, better services, new products and product applications, and who are eager for a chance to turn their ideas into new divisions, new businesses, and even new industries. When Texas Instruments reviewed some 50 or so successful and unsuccessful new-product introductions, one factor marked every failure: "Without exception we found we hadn't had a volunteer champion. There was someone we had cajoled into taking on the task. When we take a look at a product and decide whether to push it or not these days, we've got a new set of criteria. Number one is the presence of a zealous, volunteer champion. After that comes market potential and project economics in a distant second and third."[17] The rule seems to be an idea for something new or something different must either find a champion or die. And the champion needs to be someone who is persistent, competitive, tenacious, committed, and fanatic about the idea and seeing it through to success.

Empowering Champions In order to promote an organizational climate where champions can blossom and thrive, strategy managers need to do several things. First, individuals and groups have to be encouraged to bring their ideas forward, be creative, and exercise initiative. Second, the champion's maverick style has to be tolerated and given room to operate. People's imaginations need to be encouraged to "fly in all directions." Freedom to experiment and informal brainstorming sessions need to become ingrained. Above all, people with creative ideas must not be looked on as disruptive or troublesome. Third, managers have to induce and promote lots of attempts and be willing to tolerate mistakes and failures. Most ideas don't pan out, but people learn from a good attempt even when it fails. Fourth, strategy managers should use all kinds of ad hoc organizational forms to support ideas and experimentation—venture teams, task forces, internal competition among different groups working on the same project (IBM calls the showdown between the competing approaches a "performance shootout"), informal "bootlegged" projects composed of volunteers, and so on. Fifth, strategy managers have to ensure that rewards for a successful champion are large and visible and that people who champion an unsuccessful idea are encouraged to try again rather than punished or shunted aside. In effect, the leadership task here is to devise internal support systems for entrepreneurial innovation.

---

[17]As quoted in Peters and Waterman, *In Search of Excellence*, pp. 203–4.

Dealing with Company Politics

A manager can't formulate and implement strategy effectively without being perceptive about company politics and adept at political maneuvering.[18] Politics virtually always comes into play in formulating the strategic plan. Inevitably, key individuals and groups form coalitions, and each group presses the benefits and potential of its own ideas and vested interests. Politics can influence which objectives take precedence and which businesses in the portfolio have priority in resource allocation. Internal politics is a factor in building a consensus for one strategic option over another.

As a rule, politics has even more influence in strategy implementation. Typically, internal political considerations affect organization structure (whose areas of responsibility need to be reorganized, who reports to who, who has how much authority over subunits), staffing decisions (what individuals should fill key positions and head strategy-critical activities), and budget allocations (which organizational units will get the biggest increases). As a case in point, Quinn cites a situation where three strong managers who fought each other constantly formed a potent coalition to resist a reorganization scheme that would have coordinated the very things that caused their friction.[19]

In short, political considerations and the forming of individual and group alliances are integral parts of building organizationwide support for the strategic plan and gaining consensus on how to implement it. Political skills are a definite, maybe even necessary, asset for managers in orchestrating the whole strategic process.

Company politics presents strategy leaders with the challenge of building consensus for the strategy and how to implement it.

A strategy manager must understand how an organization's power structure works, who wields influence in the executive ranks, which groups and individuals are "activists" and which are "defenders of the status quo," who can be helpful in a showdown on key decisions, and which direction the political winds are blowing on a given issue. When major decisions have to be made, strategy managers need to be especially sensitive to the politics of managing coalitions and reaching consensus. As the chairman of a major British corporation expressed it:

> I've never taken a major decision without consulting my colleagues. It would be unimaginable to me, unimaginable. First, they help me make a better decision in most cases. Second, if they know about it and agree with it, they'll back it. Otherwise, they might challenge it, not openly, but subconsciously.[20]

The politics of strategy centers chiefly around stimulating options, nurturing support for strong proposals and killing weak ones, guiding the formation of coalitions on particular issues, and achieving consensus and commitment. A recent study of strategy management in nine large corporations showed that successful executives used the following political tactics:[21]

---

[18]For further discussion of this point see Abraham Zaleznik, " Power and Politics in Organizational Life," *Harvard Business Review*, 48, no. 3 (May–June 1970), pp. 47–60; R. M. Cyert, H. A. Simon, and D. B. Trow, "Observation of a Business Decision," *Journal of Business*, October 1956, pp. 237–48; and James Brian Quinn, *Strategies for Change: Logical Incrementalism* (Homewood, Ill.: Richard D. Irwin, 1980).

[19]Quinn, *Strategies for Change*, p. 68.

[20]This statement was made by Sir Alastair Pilkington, Chairman, Pilkington Brothers, Ltd.; the quote appears in Quinn, *Strategies for Change*, p. 65.

[21]Quinn, *Strategies for Change*, pp. 128–45.

- Letting weakly supported ideas and proposals die through inaction.
- Establishing additional hurdles or tests for strongly supported ideas that the manager views as unacceptable but that are best not opposed openly.
- Keeping a low political profile on unacceptable proposals by getting subordinate managers to say no.
- Letting most negative decisions come from a group consensus that the manager merely confirms, thereby reserving personal veto for big issues and crucial moments.
- Leading the strategy but not dictating it—giving few orders, announcing few decisions, depending heavily on informal questioning and seeking to probe and clarify until a consensus emerges.
- Staying alert to the symbolic impact of one's actions and statements lest a false signal stimulate proposals and movements in unwanted directions.
- Ensuring that all major power bases within the organization have representation in or access to top management.
- Injecting new faces and new views into considerations of major changes to preclude those involved from coming to see the world the same way and then acting as systematic screens against other views.
- Minimizing political exposure on issues that are highly controversial and in circumstances where opposition from major power centers can trigger a "shootout."

There are several political tactics managers should be adept in using.

The politics of strategy implementation is especially critical when attempting to introduce a new strategy against the support enjoyed by the old strategy. Except for crisis situations where the old strategy is plainly revealed as out-of-date, it is usually bad politics to push the new strategy through attacks on the old one.[22] Bad-mouthing old strategy can easily be interpreted as an attack on those who formulated it and those who supported it. The former strategy and the judgments behind it may have been well-suited to the organization's earlier circumstances, and the people who made these judgments may still be influential.

In addition, the new strategy and/or the plans for implementing it may not have been others' first choices, and lingering doubts may remain. Good arguments may exist for pursuing other actions. Consequently, in trying to surmount resistance, nothing is gained by "knocking" the arguments for alternative approaches. Such attacks often produce alienation instead of cooperation.

In short, to bring the full force of an organization behind a strategic plan, the strategy manager must assess and deal with the most important centers of potential support and opposition to new strategic thrusts.[23] He or she needs to secure the support of key people, co-opt or neutralize serious opposition and resistance, learn where the zones of indifference are, and build as much consensus as possible.

Enforcing Ethical Behavior

For an organization to display consistently high ethical standards, the CEO and those around the CEO must be openly and unequivocally committed to ethical

High ethical standards cannot be enforced without the open and unequivocal commitment of the chief executive.

---

[22]Ibid., pp. 118–19.
[23]Ibid., p. 205.

conduct.[24] In companies that strive hard to make high ethical standards a reality, top management communicates its commitment in a code of ethics, in speeches and company publications, in policies concerning the consequences of unethical behavior, in the deeds of senior executives, and in the actions taken to ensure compliance. Senior management iterates and reiterates to employees that it is not only their *duty* to observe ethical codes but also to report ethical violations. While such companies have provisions for disciplining violators, the main purpose of enforcement is to encourage compliance rather than administer punishment. Although the CEO leads the enforcement process, all managers are expected to contribute by stressing ethical conduct with their subordinates and by monitoring compliance. "Gray areas" must be identified and openly discussed with employees, and mechanisms provided for guidance and resolution. Managers can't assume activities are being conducted ethically or that employees understand they are expected to act with integrity.

There are several things managers can do to exercise ethics leadership.[25] First and foremost, they must set an excellent ethical example in their own behavior and establish a tradition of integrity. Company decisions have to be seen as ethical—"actions speak louder than words." Second, managers and employees have to be educated about what is ethical and what is not; ethics training programs may have to be established and "gray areas" identified and discussed. Everyone must be encouraged to raise ethical issues and discuss them. Third, top management should explicitly refer to the company's ethical code and take a strong stand on ethical issues. Fourth, top management must be prepared to act as the final arbiter on hard calls; this means removing people from a key position or terminating them when they are guilty of a violation. It also means reprimanding those who have been lax in monitoring and enforcing ethical compliance. Failure to act swiftly and decisively in pursuing ethical misconduct is interpreted as a lack of real commitment.

A well-developed program to ensure compliance with ethical standards typically includes: (1) an oversight committee of the board of directors, usually made up of outside directors; (2) a committee of senior managers to direct ongoing training, implementation, and compliance; (3) an annual audit of each manager's efforts and formal reports on managers' actions to remedy deficient conduct, and (4) periodically requiring people to sign documents certifying compliance with ethical standards.[26]

Leading the Process of Making Corrective Adjustments

Corrective adjustments in the company's approach to strategy implementation should be made on an "as-needed" basis.

No strategic plan and no scheme for strategy implementation can foresee all the events and problems that will arise. Making adjustments and "midcourse" corrections is a normal and necessary part of strategic management.

When responding to new conditions involving either the strategy or its implementation, management must first determine if immediate action needs to be taken. In a crisis, the typical approach is to push key subordinates to gather information and formulate recommendations, personally preside over

---

[24]The Business Roundtable, *Corporate Ethics*, pp. 4–10.
[25]Ibid.
[26]Ibid.

extended discussions of the proposed responses, and try to build a quick consensus among members of the executive "inner circle." If no consensus emerges or if several key subordinates remain divided, the burden falls on the strategy manager to choose the response and urge its support.

When time permits a full-fledged evaluation, strategy managers seem to prefer a process of incrementally solidifying commitment to a response.[27] The approach involves:

1. Staying flexible and keeping a number of options open.
2. Asking a lot of questions.
3. Gaining in-depth information from specialists.
4. Encouraging subordinates to participate in developing alternatives and proposing solutions.
5. Getting the reactions of many different people to proposed solutions to test their potential and political acceptability.
6. Seeking to build commitment to a response by gradually moving toward a consensus solution.

The governing principle seems to be to make a final decision as late as possible to: (1) bring as much information to bear as needed, (2) clarify the situation enough to know what to do, and (3) allow the various political constituencies and power bases to move toward a consensus solution. Executives are often wary of committing themselves to a major change too soon because it discourages others from asking questions that need to be raised.

Corrective adjustments to strategy need not be just reactive, however. Proactive adjustments can improve either the strategy or its implementation. The distinctive feature of a proactive adjustment is that it arises from management initiatives rather than forced reactions. Successful strategy managers employ a variety of proactive tactics.[28]

Strategy leaders should be proactive as well as reactive in reshaping strategy and how it is implemented.

1. Commissioning studies to explore and amplify areas where they have a "gut feeling" or sense a need exists.
2. Shopping ideas among trusted colleagues and putting forth trial concepts.
3. Teaming people with different skills, interests, and experiences and letting them push and tug on interesting ideas to expand the variety of approaches considered.
4. Contacting a variety of people inside and outside the organization to sample viewpoints, probe, and listen, thereby trying to get early warning signals of impending problems/issues and deliberating short-circuiting all the careful screens of information flowing up from below.
5. Stimulating proposals for improvement from lower levels, encouraging the development of competing ideas and approaches, and letting the momentum for change come from below, with final choices postponed until it is apparent which option best matches the organization's situation.

---

[27]Quinn, *Strategies for Change*, pp. 20–22.
[28]Ibid., chap. 4.

6. Seeking options and solutions that go beyond extrapolations from the status quo.
7. Accepting and committing to partial steps forward as a way of building comfort levels before going ahead.
8. Managing the politics of change to promote managerial consensus and solidify management's commitment to whatever course of action is chosen.

The process leaders use to decide on adjusting actions is essentially the same for proactive as for reactive changes; they sense needs, gather information, amplify understanding and awareness, put forth trial concepts, develop options, explore the pros and cons, test proposals, generate partial solutions, empower champions, build a managerial consensus, and formally adopt an agreed-on course of action.[29] The ultimate managerial prescription may have been given by Rene McPherson, former CEO at Dana Corporation. In speaking to a class of students at Stanford, he said, " You just keep pushing. You just keep pushing. I made every mistake that could be made. But I just kept pushing."[30]

This points to a key feature of strategic management: the job of formulating and implementing strategy is not one of steering a clear-cut, linear course (i.e., carrying out an original strategy intact according to some preconceived and highly detailed implementation plan). Rather, it is one of creatively (1) adapting and reshaping strategy to unfolding events and (2) applying whatever managerial techniques are needed to align internal activities and attitudes with strategy. The process is iterative, with much looping and recycling to fine-tune and adjust in a continuously evolving process where the conceptually separate acts of strategy formulation and strategy implementation blur and join together.

KEY POINTS   The managerial tasks of designing rewards and incentives, creating a strategy-supportive corporate culture, and exercising strategic leadership are key facets of successful strategy implementation. The use of incentives is management's single most powerful tool in gaining employee buy-in and energetic commitment to carrying out the strategy. For incentives to work well (1) the monetary payoff should be a major percentage of the compensation package, (2) the incentive plan should extend to all managers and workers, (3) the system should be administered with care and fairness, (4) the incentives should be linked to performance targets spelled out in the strategic plan, and (5) each individual's performance targets should involve outcomes the person is able to affect personally.

Building a strategy-supportive corporate culture is important to successful implementation because it produces a work climate and organizational *esprit de corps* that thrives on meeting performance targets and being part of a winning effort. An organization's culture emerges from why and how it does things the way it does, the values and beliefs that senior managers espouse, the

---

[29]Ibid., p. 146.

[30]As quoted in Peters and Waterman, *In Search of Excellence,* p. 319.

ethical standards expected, the tone and philosophy underlying key policies, and the traditions the organization maintains. Culture, thus, concerns the "atmosphere" and "feeling" a company has and the style in which it gets things done. Companies with strong cultures are clear on what they stand for, and they take the process of getting people to "buy-in" to the cultural norms very seriously. The stronger the fit between culture and strategy, the less managers have to depend on policies, rules, procedures, and supervision to enforce what people should and should not do; rather, cultural norms are so well observed that they automatically guide behavior.

Successful strategy-implementers also exercise an important leadership role. They stay on top of how well things are going by spending considerable time outside their offices, wandering around the organization, listening, coaching, cheerleading, picking up important information, and keeping their fingers on the organization's pulse. They take pains to reinforce the corporate culture through the things they say and do. They encourage people to be creative and innovative in order to keep the organization responsive to changing conditions, alert to new opportunities, and anxious to pursue fresh initiatives. They support "champions" who are willing to stick their necks out and try something new. They work hard at building consensus on how to proceed, on what to change and what not to change. They enforce high ethical standards. And they push corrective action to improve strategy execution and overall strategic performance.

The action agenda for strategy implementation is expansive. It involves virtually every aspect of administrative and managerial work. However, each strategy implementation situation is unique to the organization and to its own circumstances. The strategy-implementer's action agenda, therefore, always depends on the current situation. Diagnosing the situation and devising actions to put strategy into place and achieve the desired results are major managerial challenges.

SUGGESTED
READINGS

Bettinger, Cass. "Use Corporate Culture to Trigger High Performance." *Journal of Business Strategy* 10, no. 2 (March–April 1989), pp. 38–42.

Bower, Joseph L., and Martha W. Weinberg. "Statecraft, Strategy, and Corporate Leadership." *California Management Review* 30, no. 2 (Winter 1988), pp. 39–56.

Deal, Terence E., and Allen A. Kennedy. *Corporate Cultures*. Reading, Mass.: Addison-Wesley, 1982, especially chaps. 1 and 2.

Eccles, Robert G. "The Performance Measurement Manifesto." *Harvard Business Review* 69 (January–February 1991), pp. 131–37.

Freeman, R. Edward, and Daniel R. Gilbert, Jr. *Corporate Strategy and the Search for Ethics* (Englewood Cliffs, N.J.: Prentice Hall, 1988).

Gabarro, J. J. "When a New Manager Takes Charge." *Harvard Business Review* 64, no. 3 (May–June 1985), pp. 110–23.

Green, Sebastian. "Strategy, Organizational Culture, and Symbolism." *Long Range Planning* 21, no. 4 (August 1988), pp. 121–29.

Herzberg, Frederick. "One More Time: How Do You Motivate Employees?" *Harvard Business Review* 65, no. 4 (September–October 1987), pp. 109–20.

Kirkpatrick, Shelley A., and Edwin A. Locke. "Leadership: Do Traits Matter?" *Academy of Management Executive* 5, no. 2 (May 1991), pp. 48–60.

Kotter, John P. "What Leaders Really Do." *Harvard Business Review* 68 (May–June 1990), pp. 103–11.

O'Toole, James. "Employee Practices at the Best-Managed Companies." *California Management Review* 28, no. 1 (Fall 1985), pp. 35–66.

Pascale, Richard. "The Paradox of 'Corporate Culture': Reconciling Ourselves to Socialization." *California Management Review* 27, no. 2 (Winter 1985), pp. 26–41.

Peters, Thomas J., and Robert H. Waterman, Jr. *In Search of Excellence.* New York: Harper & Row, 1982, chaps. 4, 5, and 9.

Peters, Thomas J., and Nancy Austin. *A Passion for Excellence.* New York: Random House, 1985, especially chaps. 11, 12, 15–19.

Quinn, James Brian. *Strategies for Change: Logical Incrementalism.* Homewood, Ill.: Richard D. Irwin, 1980, chap. 4.

————. "Managing Innovation: Controlled Chaos." *Harvard Business Review* 64, no. 3 (May–June 1985), pp. 73–84.

Reimann, Bernard C., and Yoash Wiener. "Corporate Culture: Avoiding the Elitest Trap." *Business Horizons* 31, no. 2 (March–April 1988), pp. 36–44.

Scholz, Christian. "Corporate Culture and Strategy—The Problem of Strategic Fit." *Long Range Planning* 20 (August 1987), pp. 78–87.

Vancil, Richard F. *Implementing Strategy: The Role of Top Management.* Boston: Division of Research, Harvard Business School, 1985.

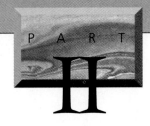
CASES IN STRATEGIC MANAGEMENT

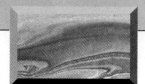

A Guide to Case Analysis

*I keep six honest serving men
(They taught me all I knew);
Their names are What and Why and When;
And How and Where and Who.*
Rudyard Kipling

In most courses in strategic management, students practice at being strategy managers via case analysis. A case sets forth, in a factual manner, the events and organizational circumstances surrounding a particular managerial situation. It puts readers at the scene of the action and familiarizes them with all the relevant circumstances. A case on strategic management can concern a whole industry, a single organization, or some part of an organization; the organization involved can be either profit seeking or not-for-profit. The essence of the student's role in case analysis is to *diagnose* and *size up* the situation described in the case and then to *recommend* appropriate action steps.

WHY USE CASES TO PRACTICE STRATEGIC MANAGEMENT

*A student of business with tact
Absorbed many answers he lacked.
But acquiring a job,
He said with a sob,
"How does one fit answer to fact?"*

The foregoing limerick was used some years ago by Professor Charles Gragg to characterize the plight of business students who had no exposure to cases.[1]

---

[1] Charles I. Gragg, "Because Wisdom Can't Be Told," in *The Case Method at the Harvard Business School*, ed. M. P. McNair (New York: McGraw-Hill, 1954), p. 11.

Gragg observed that the mere act of listening to lectures and sound advice about managing does little for anyone's management skills and that the accumulated managerial wisdom cannot effectively be passed on by lectures and assigned readings alone. Gragg suggested that if anything had been learned about the practice of management, it is that a storehouse of ready-made textbook answers does not exist. Each managerial situation has unique aspects, requiring its own diagnosis, judgment, and tailor-made actions. Cases provide would-be managers with a valuable way to practice wrestling with the actual problems of actual managers in actual companies.

The case approach to strategic analysis is, first and foremost, an exercise in learning by doing. Because cases provide you with detailed information about conditions and problems of different industries and companies, your task of analyzing company after company and situation after situation has the twin benefit of boosting your analytical skills and exposing you to the ways companies and managers actually do things. Most college students have limited managerial backgrounds and only fragmented knowledge about different companies and real-life strategic situations. Cases help substitute for actual on-the-job experience by (1) giving you broader exposure to a variety of industries, organizations, and strategic problems; (2) forcing you to assume a managerial role (as opposed to that of just an onlooker); (3) providing a test of how to apply the tools and techniques of strategic management; and (4) asking you to come up with pragmatic managerial action plans to deal with the issues at hand.

OBJECTIVES OF CASE ANALYSIS

Using cases to learn about the practice of strategic management is a powerful way for you to accomplish five things:[2]

1. Increase your understanding of what managers should and should not do in guiding a business to success.
2. Build your skills in conducting strategic analysis in a variety of industries, competitive situations, and company circumstances.
3. Get valuable practice in diagnosing strategic issues, evaluating strategic alternatives, and formulating workable plans of action.
4. Enhance your sense of business judgment, as opposed to uncritically accepting the authoritative crutch of the professor or "back-of-the-book" answers.
5. Gain in-depth exposure to different industries and companies, thereby gaining something close to actual business experience.

If you understand that these are the objectives of case analysis, you are less likely to be consumed with curiosity about "the answer to the case." Students who have grown comfortable with and accustomed to textbook statements of fact and definitive lecture notes are often frustrated when discussions about a case do not produce concrete answers. Usually, case discussions produce good

---

[2]Ibid., pp. 12–14; and D. R. Schoen and Philip A. Sprague, "What Is the Case Method?" in *The Case Method at the Harvard Business School*, ed. M. P. McNair, pp. 78–79.

arguments for more than one course of action. Differences of opinion nearly always exist. Thus, should a class discussion conclude without a strong, unambiguous consensus on what do to, don't grumble too much when you are *not* told what the answer is or what the company actually did. Just remember that in the business world answers don't come in conclusive black-and-white terms. There are nearly always several feasible courses of action and approaches, each of which may work out satisfactorily. Moreover, in the business world, when one elects a particular course of action, there is no peeking at the back of a book to see if you have chosen the best thing to do and no one to turn to for a provably correct answer. The only valid test of management action is *results*. If the results of an action turn out to be "good," the decision to take it may be presumed "right." If not, then the action chosen was "wrong" in the sense that it didn't work out.

Hence, the important thing for a student to understand in case analysis is that the managerial exercise of identifying, diagnosing, and recommending builds your skills; discovering the right answer or finding out what actually happened is no more than frosting on the cake. Even if you learn what the company did, you can't conclude that it was necessarily right or best. All that can be said is "here is what they did. . . ."

The point is this: *The purpose of giving you a case assignment is not to cause you to run to the library to look up what the company actually did but, rather, to enhance your skills in sizing up situations and developing your managerial judgment about what needs to be done and how to do it*. The aim of case analysis is for *you* to bear the strains of thinking actively, of offering your analysis, of proposing action plans, and of explaining and defending your assessments—this is how cases provide you with meaningful practice at being a manager.

PREPARING A CASE FOR CLASS DISCUSSION

If this is your first experience with the case method, you may have to reorient your study habits. Unlike lecture courses where you can get by without preparing intensively for each class and where you have latitude to work assigned readings and reviews of lecture notes into your schedule, *a case assignment requires conscientious preparation before class*. You will not get much out of hearing the class discuss a case you haven't read, and you certainly won't be able to contribute anything yourself to the discussion. What you have got to do to get ready for class discussion of a case is to study the case, reflect carefully on the situation presented, and develop some reasoned thoughts. Your goal in preparing the case should be to end up with what you think is a sound, well-supported analysis of the situation and a sound, defensible set of recommendations about which managerial actions need to be taken.

To prepare a case for class discussion, we suggest the following approach:

1. *Read the case through rather quickly for familiarity.* The initial reading should give you the general flavor of the situation and indicate which issue or issues are involved. If your instructor has provided you with study questions for the case, now is the time to read them carefully.

2. *Read the case a second time.* On this reading, try to gain full command of the facts. Begin to develop some tentative answers to the study questions your

instructor has provided. If your instructor has elected not to give you assignment questions, then start forming your own picture of the overall situation being described.

3. *Study all the exhibits carefully.* Often, the real story is in the numbers contained in the exhibits. Expect the information in the case exhibits to be crucial enough to materially affect your diagnosis of the situation.

4. *Decide what the strategic issues are.* Until you have identified the strategic issues and problems in the case, you don't know what to analyze, which tools and analytical techniques are called for, or otherwise how to proceed. At times the strategic issues are clear—either being stated in the case or else obvious from reading the case. At other times you will have to dig them out from all the information given.

5. *Start your analysis of the issues with some number crunching.* A big majority of strategy cases call for some kind of number crunching on your part. This means calculating assorted financial ratios to check out the company's financial condition and recent performance, calculating growth rates of sales or profits or unit volume, checking out profit margins and the makeup of the cost structure, and understanding whatever revenue-cost-profit relationships are present. See Table 1 for a summary of key financial ratios, how they are calculated, and what they show.

6. *Use whichever tools and techniques of strategic analysis are called for.* Strategic analysis is not just a collection of opinions; rather, it entails application of a growing number of powerful tools and techniques that cut beneath the surface and produce important insight and understanding of strategic situations. Every case assigned is strategy related and contains an opportunity to usefully apply the weapons of strategic analysis. Your instructor is looking for you to demonstrate that you know *how* and *when* to use the strategic management concepts presented earlier in the course. Furthermore, expect to have to draw regularly on what you have learned in your finance, economics, production, marketing, and human resources management courses.

7. *Check out conflicting opinions and make some judgments about the validity of all the data and information provided.* Many times cases report views and contradictory opinions (after all, people don't always agree on things, and different people see the same things in different ways). Forcing you to evaluate the data and information presented in the case helps you develop your powers of inference and judgment. Asking you to resolve conflicting information "comes with the territory" because a great many managerial situations entail opposing points of view, conflicting trends, and sketchy information.

8. *Support your diagnosis and opinions with reasons and evidence.* The most important things to prepare for are your answers to the question "Why?" For instance, if after studying the case you are of the opinion that the company's managers are doing a poor job, then it is your answer to "Why?" that establishes just how good your analysis of the situation is. If your instructor has provided you with specific study questions for the case, by all means prepare answers that include all the reasons and number-crunching evidence you can muster to support your diagnosis. *Generate at least two pages of notes!*

9. *Develop an appropriate action plan and set of recommendations.* Diagnosis divorced from corrective action is sterile. The test of a manager is always to convert sound analysis into sound actions—actions that will produce the

TABLE 1   A Summary of Key Financial Ratios, How They Are Calculated, and What They Show

Ratio	How Calculated	What It Shows
Profitability Ratios		
1. Gross profit margin	$\dfrac{\text{Sales} - \text{Cost of goods sold}}{\text{Sales}}$	An indication of the total margin available to cover operating expenses and yield a profit.
2. Operating profit margin (or return on sales)	$\dfrac{\text{Profits before taxes and before interest}}{\text{Sales}}$	An indication of the firm's profitability from current operations without regard to the interest charges accruing from the capital structure.
3. Net profit margin (or net return on sales)	$\dfrac{\text{Profits after taxes}}{\text{Sales}}$	Shows aftertax profits per dollar of sales. Subpar-profit margins indicate that the firm's sales prices are relatively low or that its costs are relatively high, or both.
4. Return on total assets	$\dfrac{\text{Profits after taxes}}{\text{Total assets}}$ or $\dfrac{\text{Profits after taxes} + \text{Interest}}{\text{Total assets}}$	A measure of the return on total investment in the enterprise. It is sometimes desirable to add interest to aftertax profits to form the numerator of the ratio since total assets are financed by creditors as well as by stockholders; hence, it is accurate to measure the productivity of assets by the returns provided to both classes of investors.
5. Return on stockholders' equity (or return on net worth)	$\dfrac{\text{Profits after taxes}}{\text{Total stockholders' equity}}$	A measure of the rate of return on stockholders' investment in the enterprise.
6. Return on common equity	$\dfrac{\text{Profits after taxes} - \text{Preferred stock dividends}}{\text{Total stockholders' equity} - \text{Par value of preferred stock}}$	A measure of the rate of return on the investment which the owners of the common stock have made in the enterprise.
7. Earnings per share	$\dfrac{\text{Profits after taxes} - \text{Preferred stock dividends}}{\text{Number of shares of common stock outstanding}}$	Shows the earnings available to the owners of each share of common stock.
Liquidity Ratios		
1. Current ratio	$\dfrac{\text{Current assets}}{\text{Current liabilities}}$	Indicates the extent to which the claims of short-term creditors are covered by assets that are expected to be converted to cash in a period roughly corresponding to the maturity of the liabilities.
2. Quick ratio (or acid-test ratio)	$\dfrac{\text{Current assets} - \text{Inventory}}{\text{Current liabilities}}$	A measure of the firm's ability to pay off short-term obligations without relying on the sale of its inventories.
3. Inventory to net working capital	$\dfrac{\text{Inventory}}{\text{Current assets} - \text{Current liabilities}}$	A measure of the extent to which the firm's working capital is tied up in inventory.
Leverage Ratios		
1. Debt-to-assets ratio	$\dfrac{\text{Total debt}}{\text{Total assets}}$	Measures the extent to which borrowed funds have been used to finance the firm's operations.
2. Debt-to-equity ratio	$\dfrac{\text{Total debt}}{\text{Total stockholders' equity}}$	Provides another measure of the funds provided by creditors versus the funds provided by owners.

desired results. Hence, the final and most telling step in preparing a case is to develop an action agenda for management that lays out a set of specific recommendations on what to do. Bear in mind that proposing realistic, workable solutions is far preferable to casually tossing out off-the-top-of-your-head sug-

Ratio	How Calculated	What It Shows
3. Long-term debt-to-equity ratio	$\dfrac{\text{Long-term debt}}{\text{Total shareholders' equity}}$	A widely used measure of the balance between debt and equity in the firm's long-term capital structure.
4. Times-interest-earned (or coverage) ratio	$\dfrac{\text{Profits before interest and taxes}}{\text{Total interest charges}}$	Measures the extent to which earnings can decline without the firm becoming unable to meet its annual interest costs.
5. Fixed-charge coverage	$\dfrac{\text{Profits before taxes and interest} + \text{Lease obligations}}{\text{Total interest charges} + \text{Lease obligations}}$	A more inclusive indication of the firm's ability to meet all of its fixed-charge obligations.
Activity Ratios		
1. Inventory turnover	$\dfrac{\text{Sales}}{\text{Inventory of finished goods}}$	When compared to industry averages, it provides an indication of whether a company has excessive or perhaps inadequate finished goods inventory.
2. Fixed assets turnover	$\dfrac{\text{Sales}}{\text{Fixed Assets}}$	A measure of the sales productivity and utilization of plant and equipment.
3. Total assets turnover	$\dfrac{\text{Sales}}{\text{Total assets}}$	A measure of the utilization of all the firm's assets; a ratio below the industry average indicates the company is not generating a sufficient volume of business, given the size of its asset investment.
4. Accounts receivable turnover	$\dfrac{\text{Annual credit sales}}{\text{Accounts receivable}}$	A measure of the average length of time it takes the firm to collect the sales made on credit.
5. Average collection period	$\dfrac{\text{Accounts receivable}}{\text{Total sales} \div 365}$ or $\dfrac{\text{Accounts receivable}}{\text{Average daily sales}}$	Indicates the average length of time the firm must wait after making a sale before it receives payment.
Other Ratios		
1. Dividend yield on common stock	$\dfrac{\text{Annual dividends per share}}{\text{Current market price per share}}$	A measure of the return to owners received in the form of dividends.
2. Price-earnings ratio	$\dfrac{\text{Current market price per share}}{\text{Aftertax earnings per share}}$	Faster-growing or less-risky firms tend to have higher price-earnings ratios than slower-growing or more-risky firms.
3. Dividend payout ratio	$\dfrac{\text{Annual dividends per share}}{\text{Aftertax earnings per share}}$	Indicates the percentage of profits paid out as dividends.
4. Cash flow per share	$\dfrac{\text{Aftertax profits} + \text{Depreciation}}{\text{Number of common shares outstanding}}$	A measure of the discretionary funds over and above expenses that are available for use by the firm.

Note: Industry-average ratios against which a particular company's ratios may be judged are available in *Modern Industry* and *Dun's Reviews* published by Dun & Bradstreet (14 ratios for 125 lines of business activities), Robert Morris Associates' *Annual Statement Studies* (11 ratios for 156 lines of business), and the FTC-SEC's *Quarterly Financial Report* for manufacturing corporations.

gestions. Be prepared to argue why your recommendations are more attractive than other courses of action that are open.

As long as you are conscientious in preparing your analysis and recommendations, and as long as you have ample reasons, evidence, and arguments to support your views, you shouldn't fret unduly about whether what you've prepared is the right answer to the case. In case analysis there is rarely just one right approach or one right set of recommendations. Managing companies and devising and implementing strategies are not such exact sciences that there exists a single provably correct analysis and action plan for each strategic situation. Of course, some analyses and action plans are better than others; but, in truth, there's nearly always more than one good way to analyze a situation and more than one good plan of action. So, if you have done a careful and thoughtful job of preparing the case, don't lose confidence in the correctness of your work and judgment.

PARTICIPATING IN CLASS DISCUSSION OF A CASE

Classroom discussions of cases are sharply different from attending a lecture class. In a case class students do most of the talking. The instructor's role is to solicit student participation, keep the discussion on track, ask "Why?" often, offer alternative views, play the devil's advocate (if no students jump in to offer opposing views), and otherwise lead the discussion. The students in the class carry the burden for analyzing the situation and for being prepared to present and defend their diagnoses and recommendations. Expect a classroom environment, therefore, that calls for *your* size up of the situation, *your* analysis, what actions *you* would take, and why *you* would take them. Do not be dismayed if, as the class discussion unfolds, some insightful things are said by your fellow classmates that you did not think of. It is normal for views and analyses to differ and for the comments of others in the class to expand your own thinking about the case. As the old adage goes, "Two heads are better than one." So it is to be expected that the class as a whole will do a more penetrating and searching job of case analysis than will any one person working alone. This is the power of group effort, and its virtues are that it will help you see more analytical applications, let you test your analyses and judgments against those of your peers, and force you to wrestle with differences of opinion and approaches.

To orient you to the classroom environment on the days a case discussion is scheduled, we compiled the following list of things to expect:

1. Expect students to dominate the discussion and do most of the talking. The case method enlists a maximum of individual participation in class discussion. It is not enough to be present as a silent observer; if every student took this approach, there would be no discussion. (Thus, expect a portion of your grade to be based on your participation in case discussions.)

2. Expect the instructor to assume the role of extensive questioner and listener.

3. Be prepared for the instructor to probe for reasons and supporting analysis.

4. Expect and tolerate challenges to the views expressed. All students have to be willing to submit their conclusions for scrutiny and rebuttal. Each student needs to learn to state his or her views without fear of disapproval and to overcome the hesitation of speaking out. Learning respect for the views and approaches of others is an integral part of case analysis exercises. But there are times when it is OK to swim against the tide of majority opinion. In the practice of management, there is always

room for originality and unorthodox approaches. So while discussion of a case is a group process, there is no compulsion for you or anyone else to cave in and conform to group opinions and group consensus.

5. Don't be surprised if you change your mind about some things as the discussion unfolds. Be alert to how these changes affect your analysis and recommendations (in the event you get called on).

6. Expect to learn a lot from each case discussion; use what you learn to be better prepared for the next case discussion.

There are several things you can do on your own to be good and look good as a participant in class discussions:

- Although you should do your own independent work and independent thinking, don't hesitate before (and after) class to discuss the case with other students. In real life, managers often discuss the company's problems and situation with other people to refine their own thinking.

- In participating in the discussion, make a conscious effort to contribute, rather than just talk. There is a big difference between saying something that builds the discussion and offering a long-winded, off-the-cuff remark that leaves the class wondering what the point was.

- Avoid the use of "I think," "I believe," and "I feel"; instead, say, "My analysis shows . . . " and "The company should do . . . because. . . ." Always give supporting reasons and evidence for your views; then your instructor won't have to ask you "Why?" every time you make a comment.

- In making your points, assume that everyone has read the case and knows what it says; avoid reciting and rehashing information in the case—instead, use the data and information to explain your assessment of the situation and to support your position.

- Always prepare good notes (usually two or three pages' worth) for each case and use them extensively when you speak. There's no way you can remember everything off the top of your head—especially the results of your number crunching. To reel off the numbers or to present all five reasons why, instead of one, you will need good notes. When you have prepared good notes to the study questions and use them as the basis for your comments, *everybody* in the room will know you are well prepared, and your contribution to the case discussion will stand out.

PREPARING A WRITTEN CASE ANALYSIS

Preparing a written case analysis is much like preparing a case for class discussion, except that your analysis must be more complete and reduced to writing. Unfortunately, though, *there is no ironclad procedure for doing a written case analysis*. All we can offer are some general guidelines and words of wisdom—this is because company situations and management problems are so diverse that no one mechanical way to approach a written case assignment always works.

Your instructor may assign you a specific topic around which to prepare your written report. Or, alternatively, you may be asked to do a comprehensive written case analysis, where the expectation is that you will (1) *identify* all the pertinent issues that management needs to address, (2) perform whatever *analysis* and *evaluation* is appropriate, and (3) propose an *action plan* and set of *recommendations* addressing the issues you have identified. In going through the exercise of identify, evaluate, and recommend, keep the following pointers in mind.[3]

Identification   It is essential early on in your paper that you provide a sharply focused diagnosis of strategic issues and key problems and that you demonstrate a good grasp of the company's present situation. Make sure you can identify the firm's strategy (use the concepts and tools in Chapters 1–8 as diagnostic aids) and that you can pinpoint whatever strategy implementation issues may exist (again, consult the material in Chapters 9 and 10 for diagnostic help). Consult the key points we have provided at the end of each chapter for further diagnostic suggestions. Consider beginning your paper by sizing up the company's situation, its strategy, and the significant problems and issues that confront management. State problems/issues as clearly and precisely as you can. Unless it is necessary to do so for emphasis, avoid recounting facts and history about the company (assume your professor has read the case and is familiar with the organization).

Analysis and Evaluation   This is usually the hardest part of the report. Analysis is hard work! Check out the firm's financial ratios, its profit margins and rates of return, and its capital structure, and decide how strong the firm is financially. Table 1 contains a summary of various financial ratios and how they are calculated. Use it to assist in your financial diagnosis. Similarly, look at marketing, production, managerial competence, and other factors underlying the organization's strategic successes and failures. Decide whether the firm has core skills and competencies and, if so, whether it is capitalizing on them.

Check to see if the firm's strategy is producing satisfactory results and determine the reasons why or why not. Probe the nature and strength of the competitive forces confronting the company. Decide whether and why the firm's competitive position is getting stronger or weaker. Use the tools and concepts you have learned about to perform whatever analysis and evaluation is appropriate.

In writing your analysis and evaluation, bear in mind four things:

1. You are obliged to offer analysis and evidence to back up your conclusions. Do not rely on unsupported opinions, over-generalizations, and platitudes as a substitute for tight, logical argument backed up with facts and figures.
2. If your analysis involves some important quantitative calculations, use tables and charts to present the calculations clearly and efficiently. Don't just tack the exhibits on at the end of your report and let the reader figure out what they mean and why they were included. Instead,

---

[3]For some additional ideas and viewpoints, you may wish to consult Thomas J. Raymond, "Written Analysis of Cases," in *The Case Method at the Harvard Business School*, ed. M. P. McNair, pp. 139–63. Raymond's article includes an actual case, a sample analysis of the case, and a sample of a student's written report on the case.

in the body of your report cite some of the key numbers, highlight the conclusions to be drawn from the exhibits, and refer the reader to your charts and exhibits for more details.

3. Demonstrate that you have command of the strategic concepts and analytical tools to which you have been exposed. Use them in your report.

4. Your interpretation of the evidence should be reasonable and objective. Be wary of preparing a one-sided argument that omits all aspects not favorable to your conclusions. Likewise, try not to exaggerate or overdramatize. Endeavor to inject balance into your analysis and to avoid emotional rhetoric. Strike phrases such as "I think," "I feel," and "I believe" when you edit your first draft and write in "My analysis shows," instead.

Recommendations   The final section of the written case analysis should consist of a set of definite recommendations and a plan of action. Your set of recommendations should address all of the problems/issues you identified and analyzed. If the recommendations come as a surprise or do not follow logically from the analysis, the effect is to weaken greatly your suggestions of what to do. Obviously, your recommendations for actions should offer a reasonable prospect of success. High-risk, bet-the-company recommendations should be made with caution. State how your recommendations will solve the problems you identified. Be sure the company is financially able to carry out what you recommend; also check to see if your recommendations are workable in terms of acceptance by the persons involved, the organization's competence to implement them, and prevailing market and environmental constraints. Try not to hedge or weasel on the actions you believe should be taken.

By all means state your recommendations in sufficient detail to be meaningful—get down to some definite nitty-gritty specifics. Avoid such unhelpful statements as "the organization should do more planning" or "the company should be more aggressive in marketing its product." For instance, do not simply say "the firm should improve its market position" but state exactly how you think this should be done. Offer a definite agenda for action, stipulating a timetable and sequence for initiating actions, indicating priorities, and suggesting who should be responsible for doing what.

In proposing an action plan, remember there is a great deal of difference between being responsible, on the one hand, for a decision that may be costly if it proves in error and, on the other hand, casually suggesting courses of action that might be taken when you do not have to bear the responsibility for any of the consequences. A good rule to follow in making your recommendations is: *Avoid recommending anything you would not yourself be willing to do if you were in management's shoes.* The importance of learning to develop good judgment in a managerial situation is indicated by the fact that, even though the same information and operating data may be available to every manager or executive in an organization, the quality of the judgments about what the information means and which actions need to be taken does vary from person to person.[4]

---

[4]Gragg, "Because Wisdom Can't Be Told," p. 10.

It goes without saying that your report should be well organized and well written. Great ideas amount to little unless others can be convinced of their merit—this takes tight logic, the presentation of convincing evidence, and persuasively written arguments.

THE TEN COMMANDMENTS OF CASE ANALYSIS

As a way of summarizing our suggestions about how to approach the task of case analysis, we have compiled what we like to call "The Ten Commandments of Case Analysis." They are shown in Table 2. If you observe all or even most of these commandments faithfully as you prepare a case either for class discussion or for a written report, your chances of doing a good job on the assigned cases will be much improved. Hang in there, give it your best shot, and have some fun exploring what the real world of strategic management is all about.

T A B L E   2   **The Ten Commandments of Case Analysis**

To be observed in written reports and oral presentations, and while participating in class discussions.

1. Read the case twice, once for an overview and once to gain full command of the facts; then take care to explore every one of the exhibits.

2. Make a list of the problems and issues that have to be confronted.

3. Do enough number crunching to discover the story told by the data presented in the case. (To help you comply with this commandment, consult Table 1 to guide your probing of a company's financial condition and financial performance.)

4. Look for opportunities to use the concepts and analytical tools you have learned earlier.

5. Be thorough in your diagnosis of the situation and make at least a one- or two-page outline of your assessment.

6. Support any and all opinions with well-reasoned arguments and numerical evidence; don't stop until you can purge "I think" and "I feel" from your assessment and, instead, are able to rely completely on "My analysis shows."

7. Develop charts, tables, and graphs to expose more clearly the main points of your analysis.

8. Prioritize your recommendations and make sure they can be carried out in an acceptable time frame with the available skills and financial resources.

9. Review your recommended action plan to see if it addresses all of the problems and issues you identified.

10. Avoid recommending any course of action that could have disastrous consequences if it doesn't work out as planned; therefore, be as alert to the downside risks of your recommendations as you are to their upside potential and appeal.

SECTION

A

THE MANAGER AS CHIEF STRATEGY-MAKER AND STRATEGY-IMPLEMENTER

CAMPUS DESIGNS, INC.

Barbara J. Allison, MBA graduate, University of Alabama,
Professor A. J. Strickland, University of Alabama

Campus Designs, Inc. (CDI), a small vendor of collegiate licensed products located in Tuscaloosa, Alabama, was started in the spring of 1986 by four University of Alabama fraternity brothers, Seth Chapman, Billy and Tom Pittman, and David Gross, with an investment of $200 apiece. The fourth member, David Gross, was soon bought out by the other three because he was not contributing to the enterprise. Seth Chapman, who grew up in Ridgewood, New Jersey, and graduated from the University of Alabama with a major in marketing, described how Campus Designs got started:

> Noticing that [there were] a lot of T-shirts out on the market, I came up with an idea of my own design and since I have no artistic ability I went to two fraternity brothers who used to do all our fraternity T-shirts . . . and I asked them if it was feasible to do this wraparound design that I had for a shirt. So, they got together, did a design, and we had it printed up.

Billy Pittman, who graduated from the University of Alabama in May 1984 with a double major in graphic design and communications and his younger brother Tom, who planned to graduate in December 1990 with a bachelor of arts in advertising, were responsible for that first design, which featured banner-clad red and white elephants jovially parading around the bottom of a white T-shirt.

In the spring of 1986, Seth and Tom set up a credit account with a Tuscaloosa screen printing company, Promotional Pullovers, and had 25 of these original T-shirts printed up, which they sold out of a bedroom in their fraternity house. According to Seth, the shirts sold "pretty well," and it wasn't long until their fraternity brothers were wanting more shirts. Their fraternity's enthusiasm for the design inspired them to consider taking their imprinted T-shirts to local bookstores. Tom commented that:

> We experienced a great deal of success with local bookstores and that success eventually inspired us to turn the whole thing into a full-time business venture.

By 1989, Campus Designs had grown from a supplier of a single trademarked collegiate design, bearing a trademarked logo and design of the University of Alabama, which was only available in an adult-size T-shirt, to a supplier of (1) two trademarked collegiate designs, bearing the trademarked logos and designs of over 35 colleges and universities around the country, (2) a full line of fraternity and sorority designs, (3) "gameday" designs for the University of Alabama, and (4) custom designs for local organizations, made available in adult T-shirts, sweatshirts, and tank tops.

At the start of 1990, Seth, Billy, and Tom set some objectives that would help them focus better on how to grow their young company to its full potential. These objectives centered around the development of additional trademarked

EXHIBIT 1 **Income Statement for Campus Designs, Inc., 1988 and 1989**

	1989	1988
Sales	$329,548	$225,857
Cost of sales		
Purchases	130,139	102,565
Freight in	2,783	3,891
Printing	54,474	33,480
Total cost of sales	187,396	139,936
Gross profit	142,152	85,921
General and administrative expenses		
Accounting and legal fees	9,085	1,244
Advertising	9,237	4,686
Commissions	20,101	3,119
Depreciation	1,847	882
Dues and subscriptions	1,079	2,528
Insurance—liability	2,661	3,317
Interest	5,731	7,218
Market expense	9,438	3,989
Office supplies	2,808	1,422
Postage and freight	8,303	6,923
Rent	5,883	3,021
Royalties	14,582	9,323
Salaries—officers	27,277	1,891
Supplies	3,420	1,387
Taxes and licenses	4,884	1,141
Telephone	4,907	6,016
Travel and entertainment	5,952	6,328
Utilities	1,934	533
Collection cost	2,815	-0-
Miscellaneous	227	-0-
Total general and administrative expenses	142,171	64,968
Income (Loss) from operations	(19)	20,953
Income taxes	-0-	2,637
Net income (Loss)	$ (19)	$ 18,316

Source: Campus Designs, Inc.

designs for more colleges and universities and the extension of their product line to include a line of children's clothing and additional adult-sized apparel items. At the close of 1989, a review of Campus Designs' financial position revealed a healthy growth in sales for the year (see Exhibits 1 and 2). CDI's sales had increased from $10,000 in 1986 to $329,548 in 1989.

The success of 1989 led the management team at CDI to refer to it as a "springboard" year and one that would bring with it major company changes, including an increased effort to boost company sales in the coming year. In order to facilitate their movement towards successful company growth, the three young men had purchased display space at a large athletic-industry trade show where they could market their company's products to a wide buyer

EXHIBIT 2   **Balance Sheet for Campus Designs, Inc., 1988 and 1989**

	1989	1988
Assets		
Current assets		
Cash	$ 793	$ 6,331
Accounts receivable—net.	50,511	42,292
Inventory	23,809	17,279
Total current assets	75,113	65,902
Property, plant and equipment		
Furniture and fixtures	9,236	6,003
Less: accumulated depreciation	2,730	882
Net property, plant and equipment	6,506	5,121
Total assets.	$81,125	$71,023
Liabilities and Stockholders' Equity		
Current liabilities		
Accounts payable	$15,590	$ 6,382
Accrued interest and taxes	5,708	2,798
Note payable	5,798	2,655
Current portion—long-term debt	10,134	10,134
Total current liabilities	37,230	21,969
Long-term liabilities		
Notes payable	43,043	47,681
Less: current portion	10,134	10,134
Total long-term liabilities	32,909	37,547
Total liabilities	70,139	59,516
Stockholders' equity		
Common stock	840	840
Treasury stock	(2,520)	(2,520)
Retained earnings	12,666	13,187
Total stockholders' equity	10,986	11,507
Total liabilities and stockholders' equity	$81,125	$71,023

Source: Campus Designs, Inc.

audience and also see how their product line stacked up against competitors. The three young co-owners of CDI had attended the trade show for the past three years and had found the vibrant environment, daily industry seminars, and lectures that it offered to be extremely rewarding.

Each February, thousands of manufacturers, distributors, retailers, and curious spectators converged upon the World Congress Center in downtown Atlanta to participate in one of the largest athletic goods conventions in the world. Atlanta's World Congress Center was a fabulous convention facility that lent itself to major trade shows for buyers of all types of products. With several exhibit halls and thousands of square feet of exhibition space, the World Congress Center was capable of bringing several hundred vendors together to create extravagant displays of goods for distributors and retailers to consider carrying in their lines. The athletic goods convention, christened the Super

Show, was a four-day showcase of the wares of nearly 2,000 companies involved in the production of athletic-related products, including exercise equipment, bowling balls, athletic shoes, sports posters, athletic apparel, and an array of objects embellished with sports themes. The Super Show was so large that attendees described it as a comprehensive "show-and-tell" assembly where one could learn a lot about what competitors were doing, gain a perspective of what was happening marketwide, and see what kinds of new products and styles were coming into the marketplace.

THE 1990 SUPER SHOW

Stepping into the Super Show arena, the casewriter was immediately struck by the bustle of activity—suavely dressed businessmen and businesswomen darted past; large groups of adolescent internationals fidgeted in registration lines; and muscle-bound males and Lycra-clad females strolled deliberately through the crowd.

From a nearby exhibit a thunderous roar of rock-and-roll music exploded above the din of the market floor. Simultaneously, clouds of smoke filled the air above a raised platform as a spectrum of stage lights blinked off and on in a continuous, unsynchronized pattern while strobe lights projected their glimmering rays in all directions. Human figures, outfitted in vendor apparel, could be detected sauntering across the elevated stage and the luminous blue letters A-D-I-D-A-S appeared overhead as the blanket of smoke slowly disappeared. The familiar crack of a bat making direct contact with a ball created a startling echo that vibrated through the air as a vendor demonstrated the attributes of his newest batting machine model to curious onlookers. Concurrently, the buzzers and bells of video games sounded in the background, and from the far end of the exhibit hall Converse answered the Adidas extravaganza with a deafening spectacle of its own. The enthusiasm, professionalism, and competitive spirit demonstrated by these sports vendors gave heightened meaning to the popular Nike aphorism "Just do it." Nestled among all this activity was the unpretentious exhibit of Campus Designs.

At one point, Tom Pittman moved along the seemingly endless rows of exhibitors of collegiate licensed products and reflected on the past days' events, especially the seminar he had attended concerning ways in which companies involved in the production of apparel items could integrate forward into screen printing their own designs onto the garments they supplied. CDI had not made a decision to put their own Campus Designs' label in the garments it vended (the company bought garments from Fruit of the Loom) nor to screen print its designs on the garments it sold. As an active step towards greater product control and reduced manufacturing costs, Seth, Billy, and Tom had been seriously considering doing the screen printing for their merchandise. While Tom made his way further along the aisles of competitors, he noticed that many of the vendors had modest exhibits comparable to CDI's. However, some of the larger, better-known suppliers, like Artex, had erected semipermanent two-story structures equipped with wet bars, upholstered seating areas, and elaborate audiovisual displays. The sight of these exhibits roused Tom's imagination and he envisioned the day when CDI might have such an exhibitor display.

| EXHIBIT 3 | **Trademarks of the University of Alabama** |

The University of Alabama restricts the manner in which its official seal can be utilized. Therefore, written consent from the University of Alabama must be obtained prior to the manufacture of any sample or prototype of a product for review by the University of Alabama Licensing Advisory Committee.

WORDING   **GRAPHICS**

University of Alabama ®
U of A ®
ALABAMA ®

BAMA ®
CRIMSON TIDE ®
ROLL TIDE ®

Source: The University of Alabama.

Tom and his co-managers had been contemplating the future direction of CDI and what actions they would have to take in order to prepare their company to compete more effectively with these larger suppliers. Tom felt certain that the marketing ideas learned at the Super Show could be put to good use over the next few months in developing improved production, marketing, and management strategies for CDI.

THE COLLEGIATE LICENSING INDUSTRY

The collegiate licensing industry, an industry that consists of *any* object embellished with the trademarked logos, designs, and emblems of a collegiate institution, flourished in the 1980s (see Exhibit 3 for the trademarks of the University of Alabama). Initially, licensed products consisted mostly of apparel items such as T-shirts, sweats, caps, and jackets, but as the industry grew, so did the types of collegiate products available to consumers. In 1989, for example, diehard alumni of most major universities would have had little difficulty in purchasing a toilet seat with the likeness of the university's mascot adorning it. Other licensed products that became available to consumers over the years

E X H I B I T   4   **Hang-Tags for Officially Licensed Collegiate Products**

Hang-Tag for Officially Licensed Collegiate Products Bearing the Trademarks of CCI/ICE - Represented Institutions

Source: *The Sporting Goods Dealer*, August 1989, front cover.

Hang-Tag for Officially Licensed Collegiate Products Bearing the Trademarks of Independent (Non-CCI/ICE-Represented) Institutions

Source: Pat Battle, CCI/ICE.

were auto accessories, calendars, blankets, fishing lures, license plates, furniture, jewelry, and insulated beverage holders.

Collegiate licensing was a neophyte industry in 1981, when Bill and Pat Battle (father and son) organized a centralized licensing agency, Collegiate Concepts International (CCI). Bill Battle was formerly the head football coach at the University of Tennessee and had won All-American honors playing for Paul "Bear" Bryant's 1961 national championship team at the University of Alabama. Some of the primary reasons the Battles decided to form CCI were, among other things, to relieve university officials from the various formalities associated with licensing, to aid suppliers in obtaining licensing agreements, and to furnish retailers with the names of suppliers of "officially licensed collegiate products." Officially licensed collegiate products could be easily identified by the red, white, and blue hang-tag, or label, which was attached to every item approved by the consortium (see Exhibit 4). Over the next nine years, the market for collegiate licensed products grew from a $1 million a year industry in 1981 to a $1 billion a year industry in 1989, based on retail sales.

The sales of collegiate licensed products had expanded at an average rate of 83 percent per year since 1985.[1]

In August 1983, CCI merged with International Collegiate Enterprises and formed a consortium called CCI/ICE (referred to as either CCI/ICE or CCI). By 1989 the consortium had generated licensing agreements with approximately 1,500 suppliers (200 national and the remaining 1,300 providing regional, state, or local service), and was the exclusive agent for 108 major universities, 10 football bowl games and the Southeastern Conference. In 1989 the retail sales of products bearing the trademarks of CCI/ICE-represented universities topped the $300 million mark (see Exhibit 5). CCI believed it was the agent for 34 percent of the retail sales in the collegiate licensing industry.

CCI was not an agent for transactions involving its licensed suppliers and institutions that preferred to handle their own licensing directly—most notably, Notre Dame, the University of Michigan, and the University of Miami (FL). Officials from these independent universities had recently held an informal meeting at which they developed their own official collegiate licensing hangtag (see Exhibit 4.) It was not unusual for independent universities to require special fees of companies wanting to manufacture or distribute items imprinted with their official trademarks. For instance, licensing agreements with UCLA required the supplier to provide the university with a $1,000 cash advance on sales.[2]

Once a licensing agreement was established between CCI/ICE and a supplier, it was CCI/ICE's responsibility to act as a liaison between that supplier and the consortium's member institutions. The licensing committees for individual universities reserved the right to allow suppliers to produce and sell products bearing the logos and trademarks of their institutions or to refuse suppliers that privilege. At the present time, a supplier had to pay a university a standard royalty fee of 6.5 percent of the net wholesale price of each item sold for the use of its trademarked logos, designs, and emblems. The various suppliers sent the dollar amounts they owed institutions, based on this royalty fee, directly to CCI/ICE for further processing.

According to Dr. Finus Gaston, associate director of business services and purchasing manager at the University of Alabama:

> Traditionally for the past six years universities have charged [suppliers] a 6.5 percent [sometimes 7.5 percent] royalty fee of their net wholesale price [to retailers]. As of January 1990, that's going to change a bit because about 35 to 45 percent of the universities have decided that they need to be more in line with the royalty rates charged by the National Football League, Major League Baseball, the National Hockey League, and the National Basketball Association. Their royalty fees run anywhere from 9 to 11 percent.

Insuring that member institutions received these royalty fees was one of the major services provided by the CCI/ICE consortium. CCI-affiliated suppliers were required to mail the royalty fees they owed member institutions directly to CCI/ICE headquarters. CCI then retained a percentage of the gross royalties owed to its member institutions as compensation for services rendered. The basic fee CCI charged an institution was based on the wholesale dollar amount of licensed products bearing the trademarked logos, designs, and emblems of

---

[1]*The Sporting Goods Dealer*, August 1989, p. L–6.
[2]Interview with Billy Pittman.

E X H I B I T 5   **Retail Sales of Products Bearing the Trademarks of CCI/ICE-Represented Institutions**

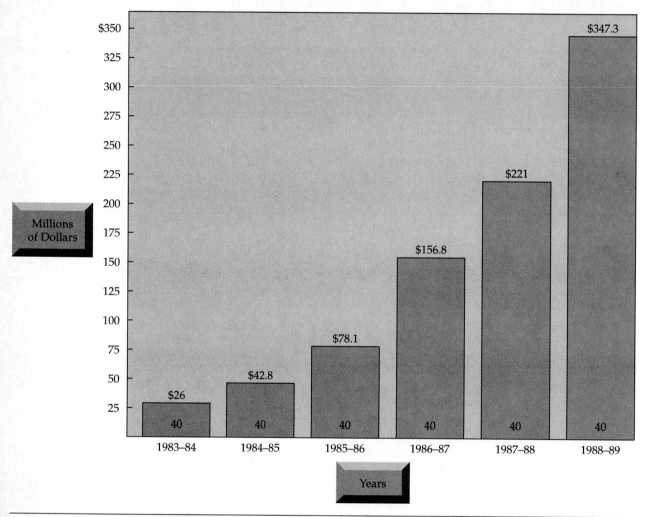

*The remaining $652,700,000 of the $1,000,000,000 is retail sales that CCI/ICE is not involved in.
†Projected sales
Source: *The Sporting Goods Dealer*, August 1989, p. L–2.

that institution that were sold by the various CCI/ICE- affiliated suppliers to retailers. As a rule, the greater the dollar volume, the smaller the percentage fee, but the service was negotiable and could vary based on other factors. According to CCI's Pat Battle:

> The overhead fee charged by CCI is based on the individual relationships we have with any given university and the university always receives a majority of the royalties it has earned.

Without revealing specific fee numbers, Battle indicated that CCI's standard fee schedule was stair-stepped downward as sales volume rose: the highest percentage fee applied to the first $50,000 of licensed products sold by the various CCI/ICE-affiliated suppliers to retailers; the service fee decreased at each of the next three $50,000 intervals of licensed product sold; on all sales over $200,000 the fee became a level fixed percentage.

In 1989 CCI/ICE paid out $8,000,000 in royalty fees. Of the $550,000 in gross royalties generated by the University of Alabama in 1989, $32,000 went to CCI/ICE in the form of a basic overhead fee. University of Alabama officials allocated the university's $518,000 in net royalties to the athletic department budget, a program supporting graduate scholarships, and to the university's internal administrative overhead account. Likewise, Ohio State University set aside $100,000 of its royalties for scholarships.[3]

Approximately 80–85 percent of the royalties received by CCI/ICE member institutions came from suppliers' sales of apparel items; the remainder came from suppliers' sale of hard goods, such as chairs, clocks, glassware, bumper stickers, car tags, pennants, and watches.[4] Of CCI/ICE's 1,500 suppliers, 300 handled only the so-called hard-goods items. The remaining 1,200 supplied only soft goods or both soft and hard goods.

Products/Suppliers

Many licensed suppliers of collegiate products were not only engaged in the production or vending of collegiate apparel items, but the production or vending of other licensed products, such as "huggers," key chains, sunglasses, blankets, and Frisbees. The Game, one of the larger suppliers, for example, offered a wide range of apparel items, including T-shirts, sweatpants, caps, scarves, and gloves, while at the same time providing a host of other products such as team pennants and souvenirs. Many of the smaller suppliers carried only T-shirts, tank tops, and sweatshirts, while larger suppliers, such as Champion Products, Inc., carried larger garment selections consisting of athletic uniforms, recreational and leisure wear, cycling clothes, Lycra workout outfits, and athletic shoes. The various types of suppliers in the collegiate licensing industry are shown in Exhibit 6.

Exhibit 7 contains the names of the top 50 CCI/ICE-affiliated suppliers, based on 1989 sales volume. The sales and market shares of the top 10 CCI/ICE-affiliated suppliers are shown in Exhibit 8.

The major players in this industry had adopted various production methods which they believed to be conducive to the implementation of effective and efficient business operations. Russell Athletic, for example, was a fully integrated national supplier. Its operations spanned the entire manufacturing process: spinning the yarn from cotton and synthetic fibers such as polyester; producing woven and knit fabrics; dying, bleaching, screen printing, and otherwise finishing those fabrics; and manufacturing finished apparel in various cutting and sewing operations. Russell had over 5,000,000 square feet of office, manufacturing, and warehousing space.[5] The company employed a staff of individuals specifically responsible for the development of graphic designs imprinted on apparel items. The majority of these designs were for officially

[3]Candyce Meherani and Rachel Orr, "Be True to Your School," *Nation's Business* 75 (June 1987), pp. 46, 48.
[4]Interview with Pat Battle, CCI/ICE.
[5]Russell Corporation, Annual Report, 1988.

E X H I B I T 6   **Types of Suppliers of Collegiate Licensed Products**

Type of Supplier	Percentage of Suppliers
Fully integrated manufacturer (makes own garments, does own designs, does own screen printing, and may have own in-house sales force)	Less than 1%
Do own designs and own screen printing (or contract screen printing to outsiders) on garments having the supplier's private label	5%
Do own designs and screen printing on garments having the manufacturer's label	75%
Design only; purchase garments from manufacturer and contract out screen printing	Approximately 19%

Source: Pat Battle, CCI/ICE.

E X H I B I T 7   **Top 50 CCI/ICE-Affiliated Suppliers of Collegiate Licensed Products**

1. Champion Products, Inc.
2. Galt Sand
3. Nutmeg Mills
4. Game Sports Novelties
5. Artex
6. Logo 7
7. Russell Athletic
8. H. Wolf & Sons, Inc.
9. Rah-Rah Sales
10. Chalk Line
11. Starter Sportswear
12. Velva Sheen
13. M. J. Soffe Co.
14. Desert Sportswear
15. Jansport/Downers
16. College Concepts
17. Winning Ways/Gear
18. National Screenprint
19. Gulf Coast Sportswear
20. Robby's Sporting Goods
21. Sports Products of America
22. Custom Silk Screen
23. Dodger Manufacturing
24. Swingster
25. Tultex
26. PM Enterprises
27. Ebert Sportswear, Inc.
28. Bike Athletic
29. H. H. Cutler
30. Fieldcrest Cannon
31. Touchdown Sportswear
32. Sports Specialties
33. Hutch Sporting Goods
34. Name Droppers Int.
35. Trau & Loenver, Inc.
36. Gamemaster Athletic
37. Javelin
38. Athletic Distributors
39. Rella Corp.
40. P. & K. Products
41. Custom T's
42. Ram Graphics
43. R. C. Sportswear
44. MVP Corp.
45. Ross Sportswear
46. American Screen Printing Co.
47. J & M Sportswear
48. Imprinted Products Corp.
49. Third Street Sportswear
50. Carolina Connection

Source: *The Sporting Goods Dealer*, August 1989, p. L–14.

EXHIBIT 8   **Top 10 CCI/ICE Suppliers: Market Share, Sales, and Production Method**

Company	Market Share	Sales to Retailers	Type of Supplier
Champion Products, Inc.	8.0%	$13,892,000	Fully integrated manufacturer using own brand in garment
Galt Sand	5.0	8,682,500	Uses own private label in garments supplied by outside manufacturer
Nutmeg Mills	4.7	8,161,550	Uses own private label in garments supplied by outside manufacturer
The Game	3.4	5,904,100	Uses own private label in garments supplied by outside manufacturer
Artex	3.3	5,730,450	Uses own private label in garments supplied by outside manufacturer
Logo 7	3.1	5,383,150	Uses own private label in garments supplied by outside manufacturer
Russell Athletic	2.9	5,035,850	Fully integrated manufacturer using own brand in garment
H. Wolf & Sons, Inc.	2.75	4,775,375	Uses own private label in garments supplied by outside manufacturer
Rah-Rah Sales, Inc.	2.1	3,646,650	Uses garments carrying outside manufacturer's brand
Chalk Line	1.9	3,299,350	Uses own private label in garments supplied by outside manufacturer

Source: Pat Battle, CCI/ICE.

licensed products of universities and professional sports teams. The manufacturing processes that Russell Athletic utilized for its imprinted sportswear were both automated and manual. According to Terrie Lashley, Russell Athletic's Eastern sales manager, manual processes were reserved for smaller or extremely intricate screen printing jobs. Ms. Lashley also stated:

> Russell's direct participation in the entire manufacturing process allows us to maintain greater control over our supply of materials, the fabric content of our products, the quality of our products, basic apparel design and, even more important than these, it allows us to keep production costs down.

Ms. Lashley observed that Russell's relatively low production costs gave the company a competitive advantage over suppliers with less integrated operations who obtained their goods in small lots from sewing contractors or who obtained their garments in bulk lots and farmed out the screen printing function.

Russell was also involved in providing branded and private label apparel items to other suppliers, many of whom it was in direct competition with.

E X H I B I T   9   **Marketing and Distribution Approaches of Champion Products, Inc.**

Distribution Channels	Products	Sales Approach	Commission	Consumer Segments
Athletic/ institutional	Athletic uniforms (custom and standardized)	Company sales force of approximately 90 persons—sell direct to consumer	7%	Coaches, equipment managers, end-users
Bookstore	Imprinted athletic and recreational wear	Same as athletic/ institutional market	7%	Independent and university-affiliated bookstores and leased store operations
Retail	Imprinted athletic and recreational wear, including those bearing the "Champion" and "C" logos; Lycra workout outfits; cycling clothes; athletic shoe line	Company sales force of approximately 50 persons (separate from that of the athletic/ institutional market)	5%	Major department stores, specialty stores, athletic retailers, the military
Special markets	Products centered around corporate premium promotions, sales to theme parks and resorts, specialty catalog sales	Special promotions done by the company		Corporations, theme parks, resorts, and mail-order catalog sales
Factory outlet stores	Discontinued styles, overruns, manufacturing seconds, customer returns	Sold directly through 23 factory outlet stores		General public
International	Champion-branded products	Licensees in foreign countries		Foreign countries including: Austria, Belgium, Canada, England, Finland, Germany, Greece, Italy, Japan, Netherlands, Norway, Spain, Sweden, and Switzerland

*Company hopes that the growth of this market will help them develop a private label business.
Source: Champion Products, Inc. Annual Report, 1988.

Russell's branded apparel items bore the Jerzees™ label, recognized as a sign of quality by both retailers and consumers. Private-label garments provided by Russell contained a label with whatever name and logo the purchaser specified.

Large national suppliers such as The Game and Artex purchased private-label goods from apparel makers and did their own screen printing. Such an arrangement allowed these companies to retain responsibility for graphics and design and the quality of their print work while relying on the services of such apparel manufacturers as Fuentes and Badger for their supply of blank apparel items.

According to Davey Solomon, vice president of finance and materials management, The Game is not involved in the production of "blanks" (the name given to apparel items that have not yet been imprinted) because the production process can be very capital- and labor-intensive. Buying blanks in bulk, imprinted with the Game's private label, allowed the company to achieve brand identity and concentrate all its resources on marketing and distribution

EXHIBIT 10   **Marketing and Distribution Approaches Used by Russell Athletic Corp.**

Distribution Channels	Products	Sales Approach	Consumer Segments
Athletic division	Athletic uniforms—sold under the Russell Athletic label (custom and standardized) and activewear	Company salesmen and six independent sales agents who maintain offices in 12 locations throughout the United States and Canada	Sporting goods dealers, college bookstores, sports specialty shops, department stores
Knit apparel division	Wide variety of knitted apparel under the company's Jerzees™ brand and private labels	Company salesmen out of offices located in New York, Chicago, Atlanta, and Alexander City	Mass merchandisers, whole-salers, discounters, chain stores, screen printers
Fabrics division	Woven fabrics in a wide variety of patterns	Company's own marketing staff from offices located in New York, Atlanta, and Alexander City; sales representatives located in Dallas, Denver, Los Angeles, Miami, Philadelphia, Montreal, and Toronto	Other manufacturers of apparel
Quality mills	Knit products under the Cross Creek label including placket shirts, rugby styled shirts, and turtlenecks	Company-employed sales force with offices in Mt. Airy, Los Angeles, and New York and outside agents	Golf shops, department stores, and specialty shops

Source: Russell Athletic, Annual Report, 1988.

without having to invest scarce dollars in the manufacturing process. The Game, which was not in the collegiate licensing business five years ago, had wholesale sales of $25,000,000 annually (equal to $50 million at retail), much of which came from the sale of collegiate licensed products. Solomon indicated that while The Game had established sound relationships with its private-label suppliers, it did not have a lot of buying leverage insofar as being able to negotiate lower prices on its garment purchases. According to Mr. Solomon, this was true of all companies who bought blanks imprinted with their private labels.

Rah-Rah Sales, Inc., which for the past four years had utilized private-label blanks and done its screen printing in-house, was switching to branded blanks from private-label blanks. The company was also closing a company-operated cut-and-sew facility used to make fleece shorts, shimmel shirts, and T-shirts. The major reason for the company's move away from the use of private-label merchandise was a marked loss of business from major department stores. Many department store shoppers were discerning enough to recognize that they could purchase a shirt, even if it was not of the same design, with a Rah-Rah label in it from a discount store for 20 to 25 percent less than if they purchased it from a leading department store. Rah-Rah Sales felt that switching to apparel items carrying the brands of well-known manufacturers would allow the company to preserve its profitable relationship with department stores. By sourcing garments for its department store customers from suppliers such as

Hanes, Fruit of the Loom, or Russell Athletic and sourcing blanks for its own private-label garments from its present supplier, H. L. Miller, Rah-Rah's management hoped to move the company toward differentiation of its products strictly by design.

DISTRIBUTION/MARKETING

In the early 1980s between 30 and 40 percent of collegiate licensed products were sold at campus bookstores, college athletic events, and off-campus bookstores. By 1990, however, the suppliers of collegiate licensed products had expanded their distribution channels to include J. C. Penney, Wal-Mart, Sears, sporting goods stores, and upscale and specialty apparel stores, driving the market share of campus-related retailers down to under 5 percent. Even so, the volume of collegiate licensed products being sold at campus bookstores, college athletic events, and off-campus bookstores was greater than ever due to mushrooming sales industrywide.[6]

The suppliers of collegiate products used various distribution channels. Exhibits 9 and 10 outline the distribution systems utilized by Champion Products and Russell Athletic, respectively. While both of these companies utilized the services of independent manufacturers' representatives on occasion (both Champion Products and Russell Athletic had their own in-house sales forces as well), they used sales agents that did not represent competing lines.

The Game utilized 70 independent sales representatives geographically scattered across the United States; these sales reps, although handling lines other than collegiate licensed products, were exclusive agents for The Game's line of collegiate products and did not handle competing lines of collegiate items.

For the most part, suppliers with broad geographic coverage and wide product lines had a competitive advantage over narrow-line and local suppliers because of the quality of service they offered retailers, the larger selection of merchandise they carried, and the relatively lower prices they could offer due to scaled economies.

Pat Battle commented that CCI/ICE picked up about 30 new suppliers per month and lost about 10 suppliers per month. The chief reason suppliers withdrew was their poorly developed distribution system and inability to generate a profitable volume of orders from retail outlets. Battle cited instances where mediocre products thrived in the industry because companies had succeeded in convincing retailers to carry their line while potential gold mine products failed miserably because suppliers were unable to secure adequate wholesale or retail distribution. It was common for the larger suppliers to market their collegiate licensed products internationally as well as nationally and several advertised their licensed products in popular men's and women's fashion and sports magazines and trade journals. A few suppliers had developed point-of-sale displays for in-store use by retailers carrying their lines; this was more common for hard-good items than for apparel wear.

---

[6]Interview with Finus Gaston, associate director of business services and purchasing manager, University of Alabama.

INDUSTRY GROWTH

The growth of the collegiate licensing industry was traceable to a number of factors. During the 1980s comfortable, loose-fitting apparel items were seen as the perfect answer for the more active and casual lifestyles that were emerging. Movies such as *Flashdance*, with their sportswear-clad starlets, maneuvered active-wear items out of the gym and into the classroom, grocery store, and the workplace. Apparel items with the trademarks of universities, which previously were worn primarily by university students, gained popularity not only among this initial segment but with other consumer segments as a result.

Also the creative spirit exhibited by suppliers of collegiate licensed products helped fuel industry growth. Imaginative and unique designs began to pour into the marketplace. Garments exhibiting a simple, classic university emblem or traditional mascot design were complemented with all kinds of individualistic, unique, one-of-a-kind, and special-occasion designs. People who wanted something that was different than what the person sitting next to them had on or something that was a reflection of the individual's personality or disposition could find items to their liking. There were items for almost every taste and price range. Designers displayed university mascots and emblems in a variety of ways. Consumers were given an assortment of themes to choose from: happy, sad, and even provocative mascots; designs with hearts, bears, happy faces, and cartoon characters on them; and the names of universities presented in block lettering or script.

Other reasons for the rapid growth in the sales of collegiate licensed products included:

- A rise in the number of televised collegiate athletic events.
- Increased regional fan support for college athletic programs.
- Growing popularity of universities with successful athletic programs.

As one licensing specialist put it, "The ties to alma maters are so strong that people want to wear them (licensed goods) even if you're living in Los Angeles and you went to Bates College in Maine." Rising enrollments and the growing number of alumni a university had also played a vital part in the popularity of its licensed merchandise (see Exhibit 11).

LICENSING ISSUES

The collegiate licensing industry was plagued by the existence of unlicensed collegiate goods in the marketplace. The sale of such goods was illegal. Therefore, CCI/ICE had taken steps to enforce its exclusive right to license the trademarked logos, designs, and emblems of those entities it represented. The consortium's present course of action when dealing with a supplier or retailer of unlicensed goods was to first ask the company to discontinue the unauthorized use of the university's trademarked logos, designs, and emblems; follow the initial request with a cease-and-desist letter, personal visits, and telephone calls; and as a last resort, to proceed with litigation. Litigation required that a university whose trademarked logos, designs, and emblems were being infringed upon initiate legal action. CCI/ICE guided the process, and CCI/ICE attorneys prosecuted the case if the university so desired.

EXHIBIT 11   **Top Royalty Recipients**

Ranked below are the top CCI/ICE member institutions in order of royalty receipts for 1988–89. Large enrollments and total alumni play a major part in the popularity of merchandise with a respective college's license. Success in the athletic arena is another key factor in licensed products demand.

Rank	School	Enrollment	Total Alumni
1.	Michigan	32,432	323,025
2.	North Carolina	20,300	174,000
3.	Indiana	32,550	290,267
4.	Alabama	16,000	150,000
5.	Georgia	26,000	170,000
6.	Kentucky	21,500	76,967
7.	Georgetown	11,967	70,000
8.	Florida State	22,550	140,479
9.	Tennessee	25,842	180,000
10.	Auburn	19,000	115,217
11.	Nebraska	22,730	204,000
12.	Purdue	32,243	235,000
13.	Illinois	34,854	391,652
14.	Arizona State	41,470	115,000
15.	Arizona	23,943	117,778
16.	Clemson	13,062	N.A.
17.	South Carolina	22,685	174,000
18.	North Carolina St.	24,558	N.A.
19.	Kansas	26,500	185,000
20.	Yale	5,151	115,000
21.	Duke	5,100	80,000
22.	Virginia	17,629	110,000
23.	Louisville	21,087	68,000
24.	Maryland	32,528	300,000
25.	Wisconsin	44,584	226,159
26.	UNLV	13,500	17,500
27.	Georgia Tech	11,500	77,805
28.	Hawaii	19,700	N.A.
29.	Oklahoma St.	21,000	N.A.
30.	Mississippi	10,840	56,000
31.	Boston College	14,561	165,000
32.	Connecticut	17,085	85,000
33.	Vanderbilt	8,968	77,000
34.	Kansas St.	19,301	N.A.
35.	Delaware	13,400	N.A.

N.A. Not Available.

Source: *The Sporting Goods Dealer,* August 1989, p. L–4.

CCI/ICE representatives had banned together with various city officials to try and bring a speedy halt to the selling of unlicensed goods. Many cities had implemented infringement ordinances that supplemented existing trademark laws. These ordinances were carried out by enforcement teams, usually consisting of university representatives, CCI/ICE members, and individuals from the city's police department and legal office. These enforcement teams visited stadium vendors who sold their products to sporting fans as they approached sporting events and retailers to check for unlicensed products. If unlicensed products were found, a number of things could happen to the merchant: (1) the merchant could be asked to remove all unlicensed products from sale, (2) the business could be closed down, (3) the merchant could be arrested. In many instances retailers were not even aware of the licensing programs that were in effect. CCI/ICE believed that it was imperative to take aggressive action in stopping the sale of unlicensed products. The consortium saw its best long-run strategy being continued enforcement of the universal use of the "officially licensed collegiate products" hang-tag.

Another issue confronting the collegiate licensing industry was that of copyright infringement. In order to combat the problem of competitors pirating their designs, many suppliers copyrighted their designs. Suppliers who did not have their design copyrighted were at the mercy of suppliers who did "knock-offs" of their designs.

The collegiate licensing industry as a whole did not endorse the selling of products imprinted with offensive language, derogatory messages, inappropriate graphics, or messages that reflected adversely upon a university institution. CCI/ICE, along with university officials had been stepping up measures to insure that knock-offs and offensive products were kept out of the marketplace. This was not an easy task and, according to one licensing official: "The consumer needs to be educated about licensed goods . . . they should be cautioned to only buy those items bearing collegiate markings which have the 'officially licensed collegiate products' hang-tag." The "officially licensed collegiate products" hang-tag did not, however, guarantee a quality product; rather it signified only that a product had been manufactured under legal, university-sanctioned conditions.

Due to the rapid growth of collegiate and sports team licensing, industry observers had speculated that apparel companies such as Fruit of the Loom and Hanes would get in on the action through some form of forward integration. In early 1989, Hanes, a subsidiary of Sara Lee Corp., did so by acquiring Champion Products. Although the acquisition was not solely for the purpose of Champion's extensive licensing business (Champion was in other market segments that were of strategic interest to Sara Lee), Champion's licensing business was seen as both lucrative and having excellent growth potential.

TRENDS

One of the major trends taking place in the collegiate licensing industry was the subtle modification of basic garment designs. Oversized T-shirts were especially popular among adolescent girls and young adult females, doubling as both daywear and sleepwear and, according to their users, being extremely comfortable. Another trend involved cross-licensing of cartoon and animated characters (such as Snoopy, Bugs Bunny, and Elmer Fudd) with collegiate and or professional sports teams; this expanded design possibilities. Several companies, including Nutmeg Mills, Artex, and Chalk Line, had acquired licensing rights to various cartoon and animated characters. David Mitchell, director of retail licensing for NFL Properties, explained the synergism created when cartoon and sport licenses teamed up:

> People who might not think of buying a Snoopy garment by itself would consider buying it if it had the NFL [or college] logo on it. . . . The reverse is also true. Someone who wouldn't buy an NFL [or college] licensed item by itself, like a grandmother buying for a grandchild, would buy it if it had Snoopy on it because of the element of cuteness.

In addition there were growing numbers of hard-goods and soft-goods products embellished with the trademarked logos, designs, and emblems of universities—rear window brake lights in cars, telephones, underwear, towels, beanbag chairs, and jewelry. Suppliers were endeavoring to differentiate their designs through the use of metallic and neon ink and screen printing processes that made their designs resemble newsprint or appear to be three dimensional. A trend, popular among college students, was the "game-day" T-shirt displaying the date, location, and the names of the competing teams in a multicolored design; smaller companies were more likely to provide such specialized products than were larger companies, mainly because of the small production runs and localized markets.

CAMPUS DESIGNS, INC.

> *When we started selling to the bookstores the T-shirts were selling well . . . that's when we kind of had an idea in our head[s] that it might be something a little bit more than making a little extra money to buy beer or whatever on.*
> Seth Chapman
> Cofounder of Campus Designs

When Campus Designs was first getting started, the three cofounders wanted to make sure that the product they were marketing, which was embellished with a trademarked logo and design of the University of Alabama, was legal. This led them to Finus Gaston. By June 1986, a licensing agreement had been signed between the University of Alabama and Campus Designs. Gaston asked the cofounders to get in contact with CCI/ICE for assistance with any licensing opportunities that might become available in the future. Campus Designs signed on with CCI/ICE shortly thereafter, and began marketing its product more aggressively, especially in Alabama. Seth pointed out:

> We then went to a sporting goods store to find out if we could sell through the chain and they were interested and [bookstores] as well as other people [we were selling to] started asking for shirts imprinted with logos and designs for other schools besides Alabama.

With this increased interest in their product, Tom and Billy began developing designs for three other universities in the Southeastern Conference—Auburn, Georgia, and Florida. By the fall of 1986, CDI had severed its ties with its original screen printer, Promotional Pullovers, and was utilizing the services of a newly established screen printing operation—Art Works. Art Works management team consisted of three individuals: Brian Johnson, owner; Mark Gambel, office manager; and Tom LaBee, production manager. All were former employees of Promotional Pullovers.

During the spring and summer of 1986, Campus Designs ran its business out of Tom's bedroom at the fraternity house and a rented house where Seth was living. T-shirt shipments were received at the rented house, while Tom's room functioned as storage space for the T-shirts and the address for important business mail. As sales began to grow, so did the need for a more functional place of business. In the fall of 1986 the cofounders transferred their operations to a rented apartment where Tom and Seth had begun living. This arrangement remained until the spring of 1988. According to Seth:

> We moved into an apartment about a mile away, fairly close to campus and that got really bad because I ended up sleeping with sweatshirts. My apartment, when Tom was living with me, was just covered with sweatshirts and T-shirts and paper. We had salesmen coming in there, so it was really a tight scene. And then we realized that we needed to move our office somewhere where we would just do our office work so we'd have a place to sleep and be able to live comfortably and get away from things.

In early 1988, the company decided to share an office in downtown Tuscaloosa with Art Works; the rent was split 50–50.

By mid-1988, CDI was starting to prosper. Tom and Seth had set up a joint account at Central Bank of Tuscaloosa, through which business operations were handled. As the business continued to grow, so did their need for working capital to finance inventories and accounts receivable. They found it necessary, as Seth put it, to start "hitting our parents up for money." Their parents agreed to cosign a loan. The bank loan gave Campus Designs the financial flexibility needed to foster its growth. The company was able to purchase blanks in greater volume, cover screen printing costs, and expand geographic market coverage to other southeastern universities.

Before long CDI began to outgrow the office space that it shared with Art Works; office space adjacent to Art Works was rented, providing 1,400 square feet of storage, drafting, and office space for Campus Designs to operate in. By early 1990, the business had grown to the point where more space was needed and the owners were looking for a location that would provide them with more room.

Campus Design's Product Line

Products offered by CDI in 1989 consisted of two trademarked lines of apparel, Campus Rapp™ and Circle-M™, a complete line of fraternity and sorority designs, "game-day" shirts, and custom designs for special events sponsored by local organizations. Apparel items were limited to T-shirts, sweatshirts, and tank tops available in adult sizes only. In 1989, Campus Designs experienced a drastic falloff in demand for its tank tops; sales of the once-popular garment type were not expected to rise in the coming year. All production requirements, other than design, were contracted out to other organizations.

Campus Design's Suppliers of Blanks

Originally Promotional Pullovers supplied Campus Designs with all its manufacturing needs, from supplying blank apparel items to performing the screen printing process. Promotional Pullovers charged CDI the normal screen printing price for their services. However, as CDI's sales grew, the owners began to look for ways to lower costs. Their search for lower-cost suppliers was complicated by the fact that the industry was undergoing a cotton shortage—prices were high and supplies of all-cotton garments were limited. The agreements Campus Designs had with its blank suppliers left the company subject to late deliveries and expensive COD charges.

In the summer of 1987, Campus Designs investigated the possibility of establishing an account with Hanes, Inc., to supply blanks, but found the asking prices too high. A few months later the company decided to use Fruit of the Loom as its principal supplier. Accounts with several other wholesalers were maintained as backups in case Fruit of the Loom was unable to fill the company's orders on a timely basis.

In late 1989, Fruit of the Loom announced price increases for the coming year that were substantial enough for CDI to consider changing suppliers. In shopping the market for alternative sources of supply, Campus Designs learned that blank apparel items could be obtained from Hanes at prices comparable to the new prices being charged by Fruit of the Loom. However, the three owners concluded that the business relationship they had established with Fruit of the Loom, considering their dependable service and quality products, justified continuation with the company's present supplier.

The following is a schedule of the prices CDI paid for blank apparel items in 1989:

Item	Price
Tanks	$2.00
T-shirts	2.40
Sweatshirts:	
Raglan	4.42
Set-in	5.04

Screen Printing

The ties the co-owners had established with Promotional Pullovers paid off when Brian Johnson, a former Promotional Pullovers employee, established Art Works. Brian, along with Mark Gambel and Tom LaBee, broke with Promotional Pullovers because of conflicts with its management. CDI began using the screen printing services of Art Works as soon as it was operational early in the fall of 1986.

CDI's relationship with Art Works had evolved over the last few years. Initially, Campus Designs relied on Art Works for the entire screen printing process. Beginning in mid-1988, Campus Designs began supplying film positives to Art Works, significantly reducing screen printing costs. The prices Art Works charged Campus Designs for their services in 1989 were as follows:

Screen charge with film positive provided by Art Works*	$18/per screen
Screen charge with film positive provided by customer	$14/per screen
Screen printing charge per garment—regular design	$0.46 each
Screen printing charge per garment—wraparound design	$0.82 each
10% surcharge on rush jobs.	

*Designs can require up to six or more screens per garment depending on the number of colors in the design.
Source: Campus Designs

Campus Designs became concerned when Art Works announced new screen printing prices starting in 1990. Charges for small orders, the majority of orders placed by CDI, were scheduled to go up more than 30 percent, and in some cases as much as 200 percent, plus the surcharge on rush orders was to be increased from 10 to 20 percent. With this news and on the advice of their accountant, the owners of CDI began actively seeking alternative screen printing options. It was Campus Designs' practice to have a design screen printed as orders for the design were placed. This had resulted in CDI placing small monthly screen printing orders, for the same designs, with Art Works, creating high setup costs for Art Works. The following is a summary of the size of screen printing orders CDI usually placed with Art Works:

Order Size	Approximate Number of Units	As a Percentage of Orders
Small	30–70	75.0%
Medium	71–359	12.5
Large	360–600+	12.5

The Screen Printing Process

Tom LaBee, who oversaw the majority of Art Works' screen printing processes, and Mark Gambel described for the casewriter what is involved in screen printing apparel items. Two distinct processes can be utilized for screen printing materials—a manual process and an automated process. Art Works employed a manual process. Film positives of the design to be screen printed are shot onto screens of clear plastic acetate. Separate film positives are taken for the various parts of the designs that are to appear in different colors.

The individual screens, with their black images, are then exposed to ultraviolet light. The ultraviolet light exposes emulsions on the screen, resulting in a nonporous surface. When the screens have been exposed to the ultraviolet light for the proper amount of time, anywhere from 15 to 20 minutes, they are removed and rinsed down with tap water. The black images on the screens create porous surfaces through which the inks used in screen printing can flow. Next, the screens are clamped securely into place in a manual screen printing apparatus with a revolving base. The apparatus can hold up to six screens at one time. The arms of the apparatus onto which the screens are clamped have an area above them into which colors of ink, corresponding to the design on the screen, are poured. The ink used in screen printing is an ink plastisol, which is the same material, in liquid form, out of which the plastic handles of many pliers and other hardware tools are made.

The individual pieces of clothing to be printed are stretched smooth over a stationary base onto which the various arms of the manual screen printing apparatus are lowered. A squeegee was then pulled across the encasement of ink plastisol, dispersing ink through the porous sections of the individual screens and onto the pieces of clothing. This process is done one screen at a time and one piece of clothing at a time. When the design is complete, the piece of clothing is removed from the stationary base and placed on a conveyor belt which carries it through a large dryer set at 270 degrees Fahrenheit. The drying process utilized by Art Works took two and a half minutes to complete.

In automated processes the articles of clothing are sent along a conveyor belt, which is driven by a hydraulic timing chain. The screens with their various designs and ink colors are hydraulically lowered onto the various pieces of clothing. When the design is complete, the printed items are sent through a dryer. In automated screen printing, the process has to be done under supervision and the changing of screens has to be done manually.

Mark Gambel noted that a major difference between manual and automated screen printing is that machines can work for hours on end, where manual screen printing is strenuous and the workers need to take periodic breaks. He commented further that for a company the size of Art Works, doing relatively small print jobs, a manual process is actually more economical and faster than an automated process would be. Another difference between manual and automated processes is the price of the machinery involved. Automated machinery could cost anywhere from $3,000 to $100,000, while manual equipment ranges from $200 to $2,000. Comparative prices for manual and automatic screen printing equipment in 1989 were as follows:

Equipment	Manual Price	Automated
2–4 arm screen printer	$200–$500	
4–6 arm screen printer	$500–$1,200	$20,000–$40,000
6–8 arm screen printer	$1,200–$2,000	$40,000–$100,000
Very small dryer		$3,000
Small dryer		$6,000–$10,000
Medium dryer		$10,000–$20,000
Large dryer		$20,000–$30,000

Source: Campus Designs, Inc.

Graphic Designs   Billy, who along with his brother Tom, was responsible for most of the company's artwork, explained his start with Campus Designs:

> [I] got started with Campus Designs in a roundabout way. We started out selling the designs locally and to a few other universities, and I was doing the artwork in Huntsville while working a full-time job. It developed into a full-time effort on my part in 1987 and 1988 when we really started getting the business going.

The company's first design was a wraparound front and back print design, which was given the name Campus Rapp. Tom and Billy used their creative talents and came up with a version of this design for 39 colleges and universities. In 1989, they created a second design, trademarked as Circle-M, which Billy explained was

EXHIBIT 12   **Universities Represented in Campus Designs'**
Product Line

CIRCLE–M™ DESIGNS		CAMPUS RAPP™ DESIGNS	
Alabama	Maryland	Alabama	Michigan
Auburn	Miami	Arizona	Michigan State
Duke	Michigan	Auburn	Minnesota
Florida	Michigan State	Baylor	Nebraska
Florida State	North Carolina	Duke	North Carolina
Georgetown	North Carolina State	Florida	North Carolina State
Georgia	Ohio State	Florida State	Ohio State
Georgia Tech	Penn State	Georgia	Oregon State
Indiana	Pittsburgh	Georgetown	Penn State
Kentucky	Syracuse	Georgia Tech	Pittsburgh
LSU	UNC Charlotte	Illinois State	Purdue
Louisville		Indiana	Seton Hall
		Kansas	South Carolina
		Kansas State	Syracuse
		Kentucky	Tennessee
		LSU	Texas
		Louisville	UNLV
		Maryland	Washington
		Miami	West Virginia

*CIRCLE–M™ designs are not available on tank tops.
Source: Campus Designs, Inc.

[an adaptation] of a design that was popular at the University of Alabama, and involves a front pocket area print and a large bold print on the back.

Exhibit 12 shows the colleges and universities for which these two designs were available.

Because of the growth in licensed products, Billy Pittman believed that it was very important for CDI to develop designs which were distinctive enough to set Campus Designs apart from bigger companies. Unique designs were critical because Campus Designs could not compete with large-scale suppliers on price, quantity, and quality.

Apart from design uniqueness, Campus Designs believed it had a competitive edge over many of its competitors, especially larger rivals, because the owners were personally tuned into the university scene. Tom Pittman elaborated:

Because we're so young still, we're not very far removed from the university market itself, especially since we live here in Tuscaloosa. It's kind of hard to become that far removed from it. . . . We can stay in touch with what the students like and I think we can be a little more responsive to the types of designs that the students will like. Likewise we can pick up on what's on students' minds, what's happening on campus, what students like and don't like because we talk to them all the time and we spend a lot of our time on campuses. This puts us in position to respond quicker than some big gigantic company . . . even though we're small.

The owners' personal experiences allowed them to spot opportunities and trends that larger suppliers had not or could not react to. For instance, Campus Designs had the ability to supply the increasingly popular "game-day" shirts for all University of Alabama athletic events, a market niche that larger suppliers such as Russell Athletic found uneconomical to pursue.

In order to stay on the cutting edge of design technology, Campus Designs had begun using computer graphics to enhance the speed, quality, and creativeness of the designs it turned out. The company was monitoring the costs and capabilities of software programs that could perform such tasks as typesetting, a very time-consuming and expensive process if done without the aid of computers. These software programs were expensive and usually required that the user have a special computer system (costing approximately $10,000) in order to utilize the software package effectively. In 1989 Campus Designs had its typesetting done by an outside source at a cost of $20–$30 per design. Billy summed up CDI's design strategy in this way:

> In the future, for the newer lines of designs that we come up with, we're going to have to be very creative . . . use our minds and work on something that not really sets a trend but is in step with what the larger companies are doing—but maybe just half a step beyond what they are doing, so that we can retain our little niche in the marketplace.

Distribution and Marketing

CDI wanted to market its designs to as many schools as possible. It had therefore become a major undertaking to do anything new. Billy expounded, stating:

> Our rep groups, who have done very well for us in the South, in the Northeast . . . , need new things constantly. If we can supply those designs, something that's a little bit different, then we'll remain competitive . . . and be able to increase our volume and that's our goal—to constantly be building the volume and getting the new product out.

A disadvantage that CDI had in gaining wider distribution was its practice of charging buyers the full wholesale price. Larger suppliers generally had three pricing advantages available to them that were unavailable to Campus Designs and other small suppliers: (1) scale economies, (2) purchase discounts, such as 2 percent for payment within 30 days, and (3) price breaks on big volume orders. Although larger companies provided price breaks, Tom believed that CDI's customer service was superior:

> Larger companies can have . . . hundreds of people working in a customer service department. Well, we are the customer service department, so we can be a little more responsive to something. [Since] there are only three of us working, our customers know us all by first name.

Distribution   CDI distributed its products through independent manufacturers' representative groups; the reps called on bookstores, wholesalers, and retailers who stocked collegiate apparel. The various rep groups were generally obtained through contacts made at industry trade shows. The first rep

E X H I B I T 13   **Manufacturers' Representatives Handling Campus Designs' Products, 1990**

Manufacturers' Representatives	Geographic Coverage	Products	Commission
Cole-Harris	Alabama, Mississippi, Georgia, Tennessee, North and South Carolina	Circle-M, Campus Rapp	10 %
Earl Williams	Florida	Circle-M, Campus Rapp	10
Pat and Dan O'Connell	Eastern Pennsylvania, Delaware, Virginia, D.C., Maryland	Circle-M, Campus Rapp	10
Bonnie Ross	Upstate New York, Syracuse	Circle-M, Campus Rapp, Greek Shirts	10
Herman Thompson and Wells	New York City	Circle-M, Campus Rapp	10

Source: Campus Designs, Inc.

group that CDI used was Rupp Bookmeier, who serviced Michigan and Ohio. The relationship between CDI and Rupp Bookmeier had since been dissolved and Campus Designs had begun looking for another rep group to secure orders in those two states. The manufacturers' reps CDI used were independent contractors and handled several lines of apparel. CDI had no guarantee that its reps would push CDI's line harder than any other line they handled. Since reps worked totally on commission, they tended to be loyal to whatever products that were selling the best. See Exhibit 13 for an outline of CDI's system of distribution in 1989.

Tom Pittman believed that CDI's system of distribution needed some improvements. Their distribution force was small in number and many of their current rep groups simply were not as reliable as they needed to be.

CDI "game-day" T-shirts for University of Alabama athletic events were sold exclusively through an account with The Supe Store, the University of Alabama's on-campus bookstore. Campus Designs' fraternity and sorority shirts were sold mostly at industry trade shows and by one independent manufacturers' representative, Jack Kirch. In 1989 Campus Designs was looking for a manufacturers' rep that could give its fraternity and sorority designs wider market exposure.

In addition to the efforts of its independent sales reps, Campus Designs' marketing efforts in 1989 included a direct mail campaign to retailers who had either inquired about the company or who were believed to be potential customers. The company also did limited advertising in trade journals such as *Sports Trends* and *Impressions*.

In 1989, the percentages of Campus Designs' sales accounted for by the various retail outlets were as follows:

Retailers	Spring 1989	Fall 1989
Sporting goods retailers	45%	35%
Campus bookstores	35	45
Department stores	15	15
Specialty/gift stores	5	5

Source: Campus Designs, Inc.

Tom and Billy pointed out that many times retailers would simply say no to their products; the two most significant reasons were that (1) CDI did not offer price breaks on quantity orders as did larger suppliers and (2) CDI supplied branded apparel items as opposed to supplying apparel items with Campus Designs' own private label. A third reason buyers sometimes gave was that they were already stocking a similar design. Billy related an instance where a buyer claimed that CDI's Alabama Campus Rapp design was almost identical to a design she was already carrying. Billy later found out that the existing design she was referring to consisted of the name of the university screen-printed onto the T-shirt in a wraparound pattern. Billy used such episodes as a reminder that CDI must constantly strive to come up with new and creative designs.

It was standard procedure for retailers to mark up collegiate licensed products 100 percent—that is, an item costing the retailer $5 was sold for $10. Parisian, an Alabama-based department store retailer, marked up the collegiate licensed products it merchandised 100 percent plus $2.

CDI's wholesale prices to retailers in 1989 were:

Garment	Wholesale Price	Percentage of 1989 Sales
Tanks	$ 6.00	5%
T-shirts	6.75	75
Sweatshirts:		
Raglan	11.00	20
Set-in	11.50	

Dealing with Knock-Offs of CDI's Designs

"Copying is the highest form of flattery and the lowest form of doing business" noted Billy Pittman following three incidents in which other companies had copied CDI's designs. In one incident in the fall of 1987, Artex, a leading supplier, developed a knock-off of CDI's University of North Carolina Tarheels Campus Rapp design. CDI contacted CCI/ICE, who turned the matter over to university officials. Artex's penalty for copying the CDI design consisted of a small monetary fine and a mandate to destroy their screens of the design.

Other CDI designs that had been copied were its University of Alabama Campus Rapp design and the Syracuse University Circle-M design. These incidents provoked CDI to institute legal action, but as Tom put it:

EXHIBIT 14   **A Sample of CDI's Copyrighted Designs**

. . . as we continue to grow, it's going to continue to happen. Taking legal action against a company that does it is very expensive but it's something we feel we have to do. We can't be seen as a company that lets others get by with knocking off our designs. We're small and we're fresh meat out there for all those sharks.

CDI had trademarked its Campus Rapp and Circle-M designs. Trademarks lasted for 21 years and cost $500 each. It had also copyrighted the individual designs within those product trademarks, such as the specific designs for the University of Tennessee, Florida State University, and Wake Forest. The cost of copyrighting designs was $10 each. See Exhibit 14 for examples of CDI's copyrighted designs.

Company Organization

Campus Designs' owners did not want to become locked into a particular job function. Decisions were made by group consensus. All three were familiar with every aspect of company operations and functioned as coequals. Seth commented on the assignment of job titles and the philosophy behind their rotation of job titles:

The job titles are basically meaningless; they are just assigned for outside business purposes. We rotate jobs so that everyone can get a better feel for the various responsibilities involved in running a company . . . but as I said earlier the titles really don't mean anything to us. Everyone is responsible for any business situation that might come up whether they're the secretary, the vice president, or the president—it doesn't matter.

THE FUTURE

At the beginning of 1990, the three co-owners were in the process of developing a line of children's designs based on the Circle-M design. They planned to test this line in a market consisting of the three major universities in Florida, the two major universities in Alabama, and Syracuse University. They were also in the process of developing another design for a number of schools called "The Big Play." This design was to be an "action sports photo" containing (1) either a basketball player, football player, baseball player, or lacrosse player, (2) the name of the institution, and (3) the institution's key logo (see Exhibit 14). At schools where all four sports were popular, all four designs would be developed; where only three of the four sports were popular, then just those three would be developed. This design was showcased at the Super Show in February 1990.

When the casewriter asked, "Where do you see the company being in five years?" the three men responded in the following ways:

Seth: I see us having top-quality facilities. I also see all aspects of our business, such as production, marketing, and designing being top-notch. I believe that we will be involved in the production of other licensed products like professionally licensed products and maybe even some other fashion type things.

Tom: In five years I see us having our own private label, a better system of distribution, and a larger staff. Hopefully, we will be working fewer hours and not having to pull all-nighters. I also see Campus Designs having better name recognition.

Billy: I see us being more in control of the various facets of the business—not relying so much on outside sources—internalizing more of the aspects of the business. I also see us responding quicker to market opportunities—getting out new designs faster. I also hope to see all three of us become more skilled in the management and training side of the business.

The casewriter also asked whether they were having fun at what they were doing:

Seth: I don't know if you'd call it fun . . . but there is just something here that keeps you going. A business of your own allows you to come and go as you please—I like that. I also like the people I am working with.

Tom: I wouldn't be doing it if it wasn't fun. It is nice to be in a position where you are responsible for everything. The success of Campus Designs depends on us and there is always room for improvement. I find that to be an exciting challenge.

Billy: I'd rather be doing this than anything else.

CARMIKE CINEMAS, INC.*

Marilyn L. Taylor, University of Kansas

In 1982 Fuqua Industries, Inc., sold Martin Theaters for $25 million. The new owners were Carmike, Inc., a private Georgia company owned by the Patrick family and a New York investment company. At the time of the divestiture Martin was the seventh largest U.S. theater circuit and had been a Fuqua subsidiary for over 12 years.

In early 1986 Martin Theaters, now renamed Carmike Cinemas, was headed by Chairman of the Board Carl Patrick and his son Mike Patrick, president. The company faced numerous challenges, including difficult industry conditions and continuing capital requirements. In addition, the Patricks were considering taking the company public.

HISTORY OF THE COMPANY

Originally Carmike Cinemas was the Martin Theaters circuit founded in 1912. C. L. Patrick, the company's chairman of the board, joined Martin Theaters in 1945, and became a director and its general manager in 1948. Martin Theaters was acquired by Fuqua Industries, Inc., in 1969. Patrick served as president of Fuqua from 1970 to 1978 and as vice chairman of the board of directors of Fuqua from 1978 to 1982. The Patrick family and a limited number of investors acquired Martin Theaters in April 1982 in a leveraged buy-out for $20 million in cash and a 10 percent note in the principal amount of $5 million.

In 1986 the company was the fifth largest motion picture exhibitor in the United States and, in the South, the leading exhibitor in the number of theaters and screens operated. The company operated 156 theaters with an aggregate of 436 screens located in 94 cities in 11 southern states with a total seating capacity of 125,758. (See Exhibits 1 and 2.) All but 22 theaters were multiscreen. Most of Carmike's screens were located in smaller communities, typically with populations of 40,000 to 100,000 people, where the company was the sole or leading exhibitor. The company was the sole operator of motion picture theaters in 55 percent of the cities in which it operated, including Montgomery, Alabama; Albany, Georgia; and Longview, Texas. The company's screens constituted a majority of the screens operated in another 22 percent of such cities, including Nashville and Chattanooga in Tennessee and Columbus, Georgia.

Approximately 95 percent of the company's screens were in multiscreen theaters, with over 62 percent in theaters having three or more screens. The company had an average of 2.79 screens per theater. The company's strategy was designed to maximize utilization of theater facilities and enhance operating efficiencies. In the fiscal year ending March 27, 1986, aggregate attendance at the company's theaters was approximately 15.3 million people.

*The research for the case was partially supported by the University of Kansas, School of Business Research Fund provided by the Fourth National Bank and Trust Company, Wichita, Kansas.

EXHIBIT 1   **Theater Locations and Screens per Theater, Carmike Cinemas, Inc., 1986**

	Theater Locations Having						Total Theater Locations	Percent of Total Screens
	1 Screen	**2 Screens**	**3 Screens**	**4 Screens**	**5 Screens**	**6–8 Screens**		
Alabama	1	8	3	3	0	2	17	12.2%
Florida	1	0	1	0	0	0	2	0.9
Georgia	3	6	5	1	2	2	19	13.8
Kentucky	0	1	0	1	1	1	4	3.9
New Mexico	0	1	0	0	0	0	1	0.4
North Carolina	0	14	3	1	0	0	18	9.4
Oklahoma	9	12	1	3	2	3	30	17.4
South Carolina	0	5	2	0	0	0	7	3.7
Tennessee	6	12	4	8	0	3	33	21.1
Texas	2	8	1	7	0	3	21	15.4
Virginia	0	4	0	0	0	0	4	1.8
Total theaters	22	71	20	24	5	14	156	100.0%
Percent of total screens	5.0%	32.6%	13.8%	22.0%	5.7%	20.9%	100.0%	

The company owned 37 of its 156 theaters and leased 78. The land under 30 of its theaters was also leased. In addition, Carmike shared an ownership or leasehold interest in 11 of its theaters with various unrelated third parties.

At the time of Carmike's acquisition of Martin Theaters, the circuit had 265 screens (excluding 26 drive-in theater screens) in 128 theaters. The company acquired or constructed an additional 215 screens and closed or disposed of 44 screens. The following table describes the scope of the company's theater operations at the indicated dates:

Date	Theaters	Screens
March 25, 1982	128	265
March 31, 1983	126	283
March 29, 1984	158	375
March 28, 1985	160	407
March 27, 1986	156	436

The locations of the company's theaters are indicated in Exhibit 2.

THE POSTDIVESTITURE PERIOD

Even though financing arrangements for purchasing Martin Theaters were very favorable, the purchase of the theaters was highly leveraged, as can be seen from the financial statements in Exhibit 3. Early efforts were directed toward improving the company's cash flow to reduce the debt. At the same

EXHIBIT 2   **Carmike's Theater Locations, by State, 1986**

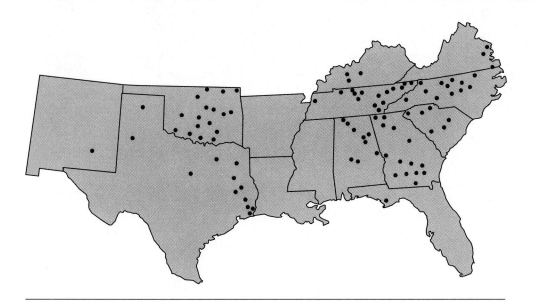

time the company had significant capital improvement requirements. To make
the venture viable, the Patricks undertook a number of changes in operations.
Success was by no means assured, as Mike Patrick explained:

> When we bought Martin, Martin was going downhill. It looked bad. And I want
> you to know that it looked pretty bad for us for a while. I mean it really did. For
> a while there we were asking ourselves, "Why are we in this mess?" Not only
> were we leveraged 100 percent, but we realized that we had to spend somewhere
> in the neighborhood of $25 million more to renew the company.

Streamlining the Organization

Mike Patrick had first worked in Martin Theaters as a high school student in
Columbus, Georgia, and later in Atlanta as a student at Georgia State. Still
later, back in Columbus, he worked at Martin while he finished his studies in
economics at Columbus College. He explained these time periods in his life
and how he became acquainted with the company:

> Movie theaters was the only business in which I really wanted to work . . .
> it's a fun business. If you are in construction, no one cares about your business.
> But if you tell someone that you are in the theater business, then everybody
> has seen a movie. Everyone has something they want to talk about. So it's an
> entertaining industry. Plus when I got into it, I was in the night end of it. I
> wasn't into administrative. So I got captured, as I called it. If you have never
> worked at night, then you don't understand. I really went to work at 8 A.M. and
> got off at 10 A.M. and then went back at 2 P.M. and got off at 11 P.M. at night. So your
> whole group of friends is a total flip-flop. You have nighttime friends. Before you
> know it, you are trapped into this life. All your friends work at night. So your job

EXHIBIT 3   **Financial Statistics, Carmike Cinemas, Inc.**   *(In thousands, except per share data)*

	Fiscal Years Ended				
	March 25, 1982	March 31, 1983	March 29, 1984	March 28, 1985	March 27, 1986
Income Statement Data					
Revenues:					
Admissions.	$33,622	$40,077	$43,778	$49,040	$42,828
Concessions and other	13,595	15,490	16,886	19,917	18,150
	47,217	55,567	60,664	68,957	60,978
Costs and exenses:					
Cost of operations (exclusive of concession merchandise)	36,436	39,981	44,760	50,267	45,902
Cost of concession merchandise . . .	2,695	2,703	3,117	3,566	3,004
General and administrative	2,522	2,878	3,008	2,702	2,760
Depreciation and amortization	2,348	1,964	2,868	3,140	3,385
	44,001	47,526	53,753	59,675	55,051
Operating income	3,216	8,041	6,911	9,282	5,927
Interest expense	380	2,569	2,703	2,337	2,018
Income before income taxes	2,836	5,472	4,208	6,945	3,909
Income taxes.	1,323	2,702	1,615	3,054	1,745
Net income	$ 1,513	$ 2,770	$ 2,593	$ 3,891	$ 2,164
Earnings per common share	—	$ .65	$ .61	$ .92	$ .51
Weighted average common shares outstanding	—	4,200	4,200	4,200	4,200
Balance Sheet Data					
(at end of period)					
Cash and cash equivalents	$(1,317)	$ 433	$ 767	$ 770	$ 786
Total assets	34,742	27,754	35,324	34,953	40,665
Total long-term debt	3,656	18,853	22,125	16,969	18,843
Redeemable preferred stock	—	405	405	405	405
Common shareholders' equity	27,752	2,829	5,382	9,233	11,357

becomes a little more important to you because that's where you spend all your time. Working in a theater . . . is a lot of fun. It really is, especially when you are 19 and you get to handle the cash. A theater is a cash business.

My father was president of Martin. In 1970 he became president of Fuqua and moved to Atlanta. My father wanted to sell the house in Columbus and my mother did not want to. I was very homesick for Columbus. . . . So I said, "I will go to Columbus College and I will live in the house." I moved back here in the summer of 1970 and worked in the accounting department because I wanted to understand the reports, why I filled out all these forms, and where they went. I learned then that the treasurer of the accounting department did not understand the paper flow at all.

The treasurer had been "sort of in the right place at the right time . . . when the previous treasurer, a brilliant man" had a stroke in 1969. When Carl Patrick moved to Atlanta in 1970 as president of the parent company Fuqua, the newly appointed Martin president was "good in real estate but very poor in accounting."

When Carmike purchased Martin Theaters in early 1982, Mike Patrick became president. He explained the advantage of working so long in the company:

> I had done every job in this company except that of Marion Jones, our attorney. But my brother is an attorney, so I have someone in the family to talk to if I have a question. No one can put one over on me . . . I've fired them too, and I want to tell you something—I do my own firing . . . and firing a man who is incompetent when he doesn't know it is hard. He breaks down because he thinks he's good. When I first became president there was a family member who had to go. The other management noticed that.

In considering the purchase of Martin, Mike Patrick had described the firm to his father as "fat." Mike Patrick described what he did after purchase of the firm:

> It appeared that each layer of management got rid of their responsibilities to the next echelon down. For example, I could not figure out what the president, Sam Fowler (Ron Baldwin's successor) did. . . . I kept looking at management trying to figure out what they did. I sort of took an approach like you call zero budgeting. Instead of saying my budget was $40,000 last year and I need 10 percent more this year, I required that an individual had to justify everything he did. For example, there is now only one person in our financial department. The young man in there makes less than the guy that had the job as vice president of finance three years ago and the current guy does not have a subordinate. The advertising department went from a senior vice president level to a clerk. You are talking about the difference between $80,000 and a $19,000 salary.
>
>   When we got hold of the company, we let the president, the financial vice president, and the senior vice president go. At the same time film people retired because they were over 65. All I know is, everyone must answer and be responsible for everything they spend. They can't come to me and say "Well, we've done it every year this way." Since the purchase we have become more and more efficient each year.
>
>   So I have streamlined the organization tremendously. When we got Martin, Martin had 2,100 employees. Since then we bought a circuit called Video out in Oklahoma. They had 900 employees. Today I have 1,600 employees. Let me double check that number. As of October 31, I had 1,687 and the year before I had 1,607. So I actually have 80 more employees than I had last year. But when I got the company, it had 2,100 and the other company had 900.

Approximately 75 percent of the employees were paid minimum wage. About 8 percent of the employees were in a managerial capacity and the company was totally nonunion. Employee relationships were generally good. Initially, however, there were difficulties. Mike Patrick recalled the initial time period:

> Management was not well disciplined when we came into Martin. I had to almost totally clean house: I eliminated all of top management but it took about six months to get second-level management to where it felt secure and had a more aggressive attitude. I call it a predator attitude. But that first year we had some great hits, such as *E.T.* We did so well that first year breaking all previous records so that the management team, even though it was new, became really confident— maybe too confident. Today they don't believe we can lose. Here's a list of the directors and key employees. (See Exhibit 4.)

EXHIBIT 4   **Backgrounds of Directors, Officers, and Key Employees, Carmike Cinemas, 1986**

C. L. Patrick (61) has served as chairman of the board of directors since April 1982. He joined the company in 1945, became its general manager in 1948, and served as president of the company from 1969 to 1970. He served as president of Fuqua from 1970 to 1978, and as vice chairman of the board of directors of Fuqua from 1978 to 1982. Patrick is a director of Columbus (Georgia) Bank & Trust Company and Burnham Service Corporation.

Michael W. Patrick (36) has served as president of the company since October 1981 and as a director of the company since April 1982. He joined the company in 1970 and served in operational, film booking, and buying capacities prior to becoming president.

Carl L. Patrick, Jr. (39) has served as a director of the company since April 1982. He was the director of taxes for the Atlanta, Georgia, office of Arthur Young & Co. from October 1984 to September 1986, and is currently self-employed. Previously, he was a certified public accountant with Arthur Andersen & Co. from 1976 to October 1984.

John W. Jordan II (38) has been a director of the company since April 1982. He is a cofounder and managing partner of The Jordan Company, which was founded in 1982, and a managing partner of Jordan/Zalaznick Capital Company. From 1973 until 1982, he was vice president at Carl Marks & Company, a New York investment banking company. Jordan is a director of Bench Craft, Inc., and Leucadia National Corporation, as well as the companies in which The Jordan Company holds investments. Jordan is a director and executive officer of a privately held company which in November 1985 filed for protection under Chapter 11 of the Federal Bankruptcy Code.

Carl E. Sanders (60) has been a director of the company since April 1982. He is engaged in the private practice of law as chief partner of Troutman, Sanders, Lockerman & Ashmore, an Atlanta, Georgia, law firm. Sanders is a director and chairman of the board of First Georgia Bank, and a director of First Railroad & Banking Company of Georgia, Fuqua Industries, Inc., Advanced Telecommunications, Inc., and Healthdyne, Inc.

David W. Zalaznick (32) has served as a director of the company since April 1982. He is a cofounder and general partner of The Jordan Company, and a managing partner of Jordan/Zalaznick Capital Company. From 1978 to 1980, he worked as an investment banker with Merrill Lynch White Weld Capital Markets Group, and from 1980 until the formation of The Jordan Company in 1982, Zalaznick was a vice president of Carl Marks & Company, a New York investment banking company. Zalaznick is a director of Bench Craft, Inc. as well as the companies in which The Jordan Company holds investments. He is a director and executive officer of a privately held company which in November 1985 filed for protection under Chapter 11 of the Federal Bankruptcy Code.

John O. Barwick III (36) joined the company as controller in July 1977 and was elected treasurer in August 1981. In August 1982 he became vice president–finance of the company. Prior to joining the company, Barwick was an accountant with the accounting firm of Ernst & Whinney from 1973 to 1977.

Anthony J. Rhead (45) joined the company in June 1981 as manager of the film office in Charlotte, North Carolina. Since July 1983, Rhead has been vice president–film of the company. Prior to joining the company he worked as a film booker for Plitt Theatres from 1973 to 1981.

Lloyd E. Reddish (58) has been employed by the company since 1948. He served as a district manager from 1971 to 1982 and as eastern division manager from 1982 to 1984, when he was elected to his present position as vice president–general manager.

Marion Nelson Jones (39) joined the company as its general counsel in December 1984 and was elected secretary of the company in March 1985. Prior to joining the company, Jones was a partner in the law firm of Evert & Jones in Columbus, Georgia, from 1979 to 1984.

The company also implemented improved technology to trim the number of employees. Mike Patrick explained what happened in one city when the firm switched to totally automated projection booths:

> I called our attorney in and I asked him, "What is the recourse?" He said, "You must reinstate them and pay them the back pay." I said, "You mean there is no million dollar fine?" He replied "No, you just got to worry about that." He went on to ask, "Well, why are you going to get rid of them?" I said, "There is equipment for showing movies that will work very similar to an eight-track tape player." And he says, "Well, you can do it."
>
> The city had a code which said to be a projectionist you must take a test from the electrical board to be certified. That law was put in about 1913 because back

in the old days, they didn't have light bulbs. You used two carbon arcs and it was a safety issue because back then film was made out of something that burned. That was before my time that film burned like that and you had a fire in the lamp house. Now we have Zenith bulbs. The projectionists hadn't gone and gotten their cards from the electrical board for years. But the rule was on the books. So I figured the only problem we had was the city. As soon as we fired projectionists, they went to the council and had the police raid my theater. I sued the City of Nashville. . . . In the meantime we sent an engineer from Columbus up and started teaching all our managers how to pass the test. As they began to pass the board's test, it became a moot question.

Martin had already leased and installed all the needed equipment except an automatic lens turn. Its cost of $15,000 per projector was not justified since it took only a few seconds to change the lens. The new equipment made it possible to eliminate the position of projectionist. Patrick explained how he was able to get the theater managers to cooperate:

I told our managers that I would give them a raise consisting of 40 percent of whatever the projectionist had made. So all of a sudden the manager went from being against the program to where I got a flood of letters from managers saying, "I'm now trained. Fire my projectionist."

Improving Theater Profitability

At the time they purchased the Martin Theater circuit, the Patricks were well aware that some of the theaters were losing money and that many of Martin's facilities were quickly being outmoded. A 1981 consulting report on Martin underscored that during the 1970s Martin had not aggressively moved to multiplexing. In addition, one of the previous presidents had put a number of theaters into "B-locations" where there were "great leases . . . but the theaters were off the beaten track." Mike Patrick explained his approach for handling the situation:

I looked at all the markets we were in, the big markets where the money was to be made, and I said, "Here's what we will do. First, let's take the losers and make them profitable." At the time the losing theaters were a $1.2 million deficit on the bottom line. So I decided to experiment . . . Phenix City is a perfect example. I took the admission price from $3.75 to $0.99. Everybody said I was a fool. The first year it made $70,000 which I thought was a great increase over the $26,000 it had been making. The next year what happened was—the people in Phenix City are poor, very poor, blue-collar workers, but the theater is as nice as anything I have over here in Columbus—so as word of mouth got going, it kept getting better and better. Now it almost sells out every Friday, Saturday, and Sunday. And I still charge $0.99. That theater will make over $200,000 this year.

As Patrick put it, the conversion to dollar theaters was "a new concept. No one else is doing that." By 1986 Carmike had 20 99-cent theaters. The company also offered a discount in admission prices on Tuesdays and discount ticket plans to groups. Two facilities called "Flick 'n' Foam" had restaurants and bar services in the theater. Mike Patrick commented on a theater chain he was considering buying and converting to 99-cent theaters with multiplex screens:

I'm looking at a circuit of theaters in a major metropolitan area. Now the owner hasn't told me that it is for sale yet. He wants me to make him an offer and I won't

do it. I want him to make me the first offer. He has no new facilities. All his theaters are twins except one and that's a triple. He's getting killed. A large chain is
coming against him with a 12-plex. He's located all around the metro area and he's
getting killed. He had that town for years and now he's almost knocked out of it.
His circuit is going to be worthless. I've been up there. There are no 99-cent or
dollar theaters anywhere. His locations are good for that.

Facility Upgrading

When Martin Theaters was originally purchased, its facilities were quickly
becoming outmoded. As Mike Patrick put it, "We were basically noncompetitive . . . we were just getting hit left and right in our big markets . . . the biggest thing we had was a twin and we had competitors dropping four and
six-plexes on us." One reason for the earlier reticence was the tendency to put
emphasis on the number of theaters rather than screens. In addition, management of the theater company, although not so required by the parent company,
had managed the circuit for its cash flow. Patrick explained, "Ron [Baldwin]
really never understood working for a $2 billion company. He still managed the
firm as though it were privately owned."

By the early 1980s the lack of capital replacement began to tell on the firm.
Mike Patrick explained:

> Oh, we were just outclassed everywhere you went. Ron Baldwin told me that
> Columbus Square was doomed. I made it an eight-plex. With our nice theater,
> the Peachtree, I added one screen but I didn't have any more room. But I took
> the theater no one liked and made it an eight-plex. It is one of the most profitable
> theaters we have today.

New theaters, either replacements or additions, were undertaken usually
through build, sale, and leaseback arrangements. Carl Patrick explained that
in 1985 the theaters were about 75 percent leased and about 25 percent company owned. Carmike gave close attention to cost control in construction as
Mike Patrick explained:

> Under Fuqua, Martin usually owned the theater. In some instances the land was
> also owned; in others the company had a ground lease. Since theaters were basi-
> cally the same from one site to another, the cost of construction of the building
> was fairly standardized once the site, or pad, was ready.

Mike Patrick built his first theater in 1982 at a cost of $26 per square foot. At the
time the usual price was $31. He explained that even his insurance company
had questioned him when he turned in his replacement cost estimate. To
reduce his costs Mike Patrick had examined every element of cost. Initially the
Patricks worked with the E&W architectural firm as Martin Theaters had done
for years. Mike Patrick explained that their costs were so favorable that other
theater companies began to use E&W. Eventually costs went up. In 1985 Mike
employed a firm of recent University of Alabama graduates to be the architects
on a new theater in Georgia.

Costs were also carefully controlled when a shopping center firm built a
theater for Carmike to lease. The lease specified that if construction costs
exceeded a certain amount, Carmike had the option of building the theater.
Without that specification there was, as Mike Patrick explained, no incentive
for the development firm to contain costs. Carmike's lease payment was based

on a return on investment to the development firm. On a recent theater the estimated costs came in at $39 per square foot versus the $41 per square foot that the lease specified because Mike Patrick convinced the development company to use one of his experienced contractors to hold square foot costs down.

Zone Strategy

Considering total activity in a zone was critical. Mike Patrick explained what happened over a period of two years in one major metropolitan area.[1]

This city has a river which divides it in two. There is only one main bridge and so there are automatically two zones. There is a third zone which is somewhat isolated. When we first bought Martin there were seven theaters and 14 screens. They were as follows:

	Martin	Competition
Singles	1	1
Twins	3	
Triples	1	1

A strong competitor came into Zone 1 and built a six-plex against me. Let me tell you what happened in that zone. I leased land, built a six-plex theater, and did a sale leaseback. I built the six-plex here right off one of the two shopping centers. I leased the equipment and I leased the building. I actually have no investment. Last year that theater made $79,000. Think about the return you have with no investment.

I took one of the single theaters and put a wall down the middle of it. That cost me $30,000. I added an auditorium to a triple. Both of these theaters are near the competitor's six-plex. Now it's six—four here and two here. So that is six against his six. So now I have 12 screens in Zone 1. No one else can come in. My competitor has no advantage over me in negotiations with Warner Brothers and Paramount. In fact, I have an advantage over him. He's only here in one location and I am in three.

In the other zone I took a twin and added three auditoriums. Then I took a triple theater and made it a dollar house, 99-cent discount. . . . It was way off the beaten track, way off. So I had eight screens against the competitor theaters. There was an opposition single screen, but he closed. We basically had 20 screens in the two zones.

If you are playing *Rocky,* you can sell three prints to this town. If you carefully choose your theaters where you show it, you can make a lot more money. That's something the previous president [of Martin] never understood.

EXPANSION

In May 1983 Carmike acquired the outstanding stock of Video Independent Theaters, Inc. The purchase price included $1.1 million cash and $2.7 million in a note. The note was at 11 percent, payable in three equal installments. Mike Patrick talked about the acquisition:

---

[1] A zone was considered a natural geographic division within a city.

During the 1970s Martin had not been aggressive. In our industry if you are not on the attack you are being attacked. Then you are subject to what the industry does. We believe in making things happen.

Video was owned by a company which had bought Video for its cable rights. In the mid 1970s the management was killed in an air crash. I went up and talked to the guy in charge. He told me the parent company wasn't interested in theaters.

The circuit had a lot of singles and a lot of profitable drive-ins. We borrowed $1 million as a down payment and the parent accepted a note for the remainder due in three equal yearly installments.

We immediately looked at all the drive-ins and sold two drive-ins for about $1.5 million. So immediately we paid back the down payment. We planned to use the cash flow to meet the installment payments and the depreciation to rebuild the circuit. Today Video is completely paid for.

In some of the towns we went into a tremendous aggressive buying program for film which was very successful. In another we bought out an independent who was building a five-plex. In others we converted twins into four-plexes. We closed singles and in some instances overbuilt with four, five, or six-plexes. As a result, our revenue per screen is low.

In one town we went in with a new six-plex which cost $620,000. We had used basic cement block construction and furnished the facility beautifully. An independent had put in a four-plex, about the same size facility, which had cost $1.1 million. A large circuit also had a twin. I attacked with a six-plex during a time when the state economy was down. In addition, there were a lot of bad pictures. The two companies really beat each other up during the period bidding up what pictures were available. The independent went under. The circuit was bought by a larger company which wants to concentrate on larger cities. They've offered us their twin. We'll pick up the other theater from the bank.

Control Systems

The company also put considerable emphasis on budgeting and cost control. As Mike Patrick explained, "I was brought up on theater P&L's." The systems he set in place for Carmike theaters were straightforward. Every theater had what Patrick called "a PL . . . I call them a Profit or Loss Statement." Results came across Patrick's desk monthly; results for the theaters were printed out in descending order of amount of profit generated for that month. No overhead was charged to the theaters. As Patrick explained, "if you can charge something to an overhead (account), then no one cares, no one is responsible." Rather, a monthly statement of expenses was generated for each administrative department. Mike Patrick explained his approach:

I used something like zero budgeting on every department. For example, here's the Martin Building. It cost me $18,700 for the month. The report for the Martin Building even has every person's name . . . what they made last year, what they made this year, what they made current month, every expense they have. . . . I know what my dad's office cost me each month and mine also.

Every department head received a recap each week. Charges for business lunches appeared on the statement of the person who signed the bill. Patrick checked the reports and required explanations for anything out of line. Theater expenses also received close scrutiny, as he explained:

Then I go a step beyond that. All district managers have a pet peeve. They all want their facilities to look brand new. You can write them letters, you can swear, you can cuss. It makes no difference. They are in that theater and that's the only thing they see. It's their world. They want new carpet every week. They want a new roof every week. They want a new projector and a new ticket machine every week . . . the government says you have to capitalize (but) I hate to capitalize on expense. If the air conditioning breaks, you capitalize it. Horse feathers. I wrote the check for $18,000. The money is gone. Now I give every district manager a repair report. It shows anything charged to repairs. Yes, I could probably accomplish the same thing with a cash flow statement, but they wouldn't understand it.

Managing the Theaters

The company did not have a policy discouraging nepotism. Indeed, Mike Patrick encouraged the hiring of family. Especially in smaller towns where there might be several family members in visible positions, hiring family was a deterrent to theft. As Mike Patrick explained:

> I will let them hire family for two reasons: One, they don't want to quit me. They're married to me as much as they are the family. Second, you get people who just would not steal. They have more to lose than just the job. None of the family will steal from me because it would have a direct bearing on the father, the uncle, the whole family. I am in a lot of little towns and in a small town a son is either going to work on a farm, a grocery store, a filling station, or a theater, 'cause there is no industry there. The cleanest job in town is the theater manager. Also, in a small town we allow the manager to look like he owns the theater. 'Cause I don't go in and act like "Here's the boss," and all that.
>
> Theater managers are paid straight salary. Under Fuqua ownership the manager's salary was linked to theater performance. But, we changed that. Theater managers don't make the theater profit; the movie does. Theater managers used to select the movies. But now they don't have anything to do with it. I am the only theater chain in the United States in which the booking and buying for the circuit is done by computer from right here. This computer on my desk is hooked to Atlanta and Dallas which are my two booking offices.

Mike Patrick had hired both of the present booking managers after the previous incumbents retired. He explained how one came to work for Carmike:

> Let me tell you how I got Tony Rhead. Tony Rhead was the biggest SOB I went against. He was the booker for Chattanooga. He booked the circuit that was the best in town. He used to give me fits. And I used to spend more time trying to figure out how to get prints away from him than anybody else. So what did I do? I hired him. Rhead made $19,000 a year working for a competitor and he makes $65,000 working for me. That's a lot of difference.

Planning

The orientation under Martin management in the 1970s had been a system-wide operations approach. Mike Patrick's approach to theater location and number of screens was zone by zone and theater by theater.

The planning system for booking films was set up so that past, current, and future bookings could be called up by theater, zone, or film. In addition, competitor's bookings were also available. The system allowed interaction between home office and the two booking offices.

The Outlook in 1986

As the 1985 fiscal year came to a close, Carmike, like much of the industry, faced disappointing year-end results. Part of the problem was attributed to the number of executive turnovers in the movie production companies. Patrick explained:

> A number of production executives changed jobs within a 90-day period. That meant that production stopped. Production is like developing a shopping center. It takes 18 months from the time you decide to do it to the time it opens. This year is off because there were no pictures out there. I believe that it will get better . . . [however] *Rocky IV* has just come out so we will end the year on an upbeat.

The industry faced a number of challenges that affected the company. Lack of films was a negative factor. However, the increase in ancillary markets (movies shown on TV and home VCRs) was viewed as a positive factor; as Patrick explained:

> By 1979–80 the ancillary market became very big. I understand the ancillary market is now about $3 billion and our side is $4 billion . . . [but] I talked to a man in Home Box Office when he first started. He told me that they could not figure a way to sell a movie on its first run at all. If it was a bad movie, he couldn't give it away. If it was a good movie, he had all the attendance watching it he needed. He told me, "Mike, I want you to do better every year. The more blockbusters you get, the more demand I have. And if you get, *Who Shot Mary?* and it dies in your theater, no one will watch it on Home Box Office." The theater is where you go to preview a movie. That establishes the value. I realized then that CBS will pay more for a big movie than they will a lousy one, so anything that comes through the tube is no problem with me. I love it because . . . [the revenues] help create more new movies.

A setback caused by the Justice Department's decision on the right of first sale threatened loss of expected revenue to producers and distributors. In addition, an increase in films might be offset by the unabated increase in the number of screens. However, the Patricks did not, as did others, foresee the demise of the movie theater. Moreover, Mike Patrick especially felt that the difficult times offered opportunities to those who were prepared:

> There is more opportunity in bad times than in good times. The reason is that no one wants to sell when business is good and if they do the multiples are too high. So you want to buy when business is bad [and] . . . you got to plan for those times.
>
> I have to know where my capital is. I run this company through this book. This is every financial thing you want to know about Carmike Cinemas—construction coming up, everything we are going to spend, source of cash, where it's going to go, everything. One of the critical things we are thinking about is how to expand. I know that if business goes bad, within 90 days, three or four more circuits are going to come up for sale. I must be in a position to buy them and I must have the knowledge to do it with. I will not bet the store on any deal.

CINEPLEX ODEON*

Joseph Lampel, New York University
Jamal Shamsie, McGill University

Garth Drabinsky, chairman and CEO of Cineplex Odeon, has never been known to shy away from a fight. On June 30, 1989, he was true to his reputation as he faced a group of unsettled shareholders at the company's annual meeting in a downtown Toronto theater. Drabinsky had burly guards posted at the entrances and exits, instructed his public relations staff to keep their lips sealed, and did not allow reporters to bring in any electronic equipment.

The firm stance reflected a hardball approach to business that had earned Drabinsky the nickname Darth, after the screen super-villain Darth Vader. But this reputation was based on more than just an aura of toughness and a knack for brilliant deals. It was founded on significant accomplishments in the movie industry. Through a combination of innovative theater formats, bold acquisitions, and strong financial alliances, Drabinsky had developed Cineplex Odeon into the second largest theater chain in North America (see Exhibit 1). In the process, Drabinsky had single-handedly changed the face of film exhibition, rejuvenating what had become a stagnant part of the industry.

As long as Drabinsky continued to pile success upon success, his aggressive style and disregard for conventions were tolerated. His dominance over all aspects of Cineplex Odeon had been deemed necessary for the pursuit of his unique and ambitious vision. But now, with doubts being raised about the financial health of Cineplex Odeon (see Exhibits 2 and 3), Drabinsky's reputation as a brilliant strategist was being subjected to increased scrutiny. Drabinsky was also facing strong resistance, and had suffered serious setbacks in his recent attempts to gain a controlling interest in his company. All of these developments had created an unusually high level of anxiety and anticipation among the audience that had gathered for the company's annual meeting.

But the mounting pressure could hardly mute Drabinsky's forceful style. He ruled the meeting with an iron hand, disdainfully rejecting any attacks from the audience, and defiantly reaffirming his faith in the future of Cineplex Odeon. "I am completely sanguine," he remarked, "that the company will continue to grow."[1] As far as Drabinsky was concerned, this was not the first time that he had found himself in a tight corner.

THE EARLY YEARS

A Consuming Passion

Garth Drabinsky's determination to beat the odds began early in life. Struck by polio at the age of three, he spent most of his childhood checking in and out of

---

*The authors wish to acknowledge the assistance of Xavier Gonzalez-Sanfeliu. Copyright 1990, by the authors.
[1]"The Perils of Drabinsky," *Report on Business Magazine*, July 1989.

E X H I B I T   1   **Leading Movie Theatre Chains in North America, 1984–1988**

	1984		1985		1986		1987		1988	
	Screens	Locations	Screens	Locations	Screens	Locations	Screens	Locations	Screens	Locations
United Artists	1,063	344	1,124	329	1,595	437	2,048	485	2,677	686
Cineplex Odeon	439	170	1,117	394	1,510	495	1,644	492	1,832	502
American Multi-Cinema	800	156	956	182	1,336	263	1,528	277	1,614	278
General Cinema	1,083	331	1,163	333	1,275	342	1,358	332	1,400	321
Loews	215	66	232	66	300	85	310	87	822	221
Carmike	432	182	435	168	674	236	669	220	701	213
Hoyts	105	25	103	22	240	52	275	55	550	120
National Amusements	314	84	345	84	393	88	404	77	552	91
Mann	325	98	350	110	456	126	447	110	456	109
Famous Players	466	199	469	196	466	176	427	147	448	148

Source: Variety.

EXHIBIT 2   **Cineplex Odeon's Income Statements, 1984–1988** *(In millions of U.S. dollars for the year ended December)*

	1984	1985	1986	1987	1988
Revenues					
Admissions	$42.7	$ 85.0	$230.3	$322.4	$355.6
Concessions	12.3	24.9	71.4	101.6	114.6
Distribution and other	9.3	7.8	30.8	61.2	156.4§
Sales of properties*	2.8	6.6	24.4	35.0	69.2
	$67.1	$124.3	$356.9	$520.2	$695.8‖
Expenses					
Operating expenses	$48.7	$89.5	$258.3	$371.9	$464.3
Cost of concessions	3.7	6.0	13.7	18.8	21.6
Cost of sold properties	0.9	2.7	11.7	21.6	61.8
General and administrative	3.5	5.7	15.3	18.0	26.6
Depreciation and amortization[†]	2.1	3.7	14.3	24.0	38.1
	$58.9	$107.6	$313.3	$454.3	$612.4
Other income	0.1	0.3	—	—	3.6
Interest expenses[‡]	2.5	4.0	16.2	27.0	42.9
Income taxes	2.2	5.0	6.3	4.3	3.7
Extraordinary items	5.6	2.3	1.4	—	—
Net income	$ 9.2	$ 10.3	$ 22.5	$ 34.6	$ 40.4

[*] Shown as part of operating revenue.
[†] Depreciation schedule changed from 1986 to lower this charge.
[‡] Excludes interest costs that have been capitalized.
[§] Includes proceeds from sale of 49 percent interest in Film House.
[‖] Later changed to $648 million to exclude proceeds from sale of Film House.
Source: Cineplex Odeon annual reports.

hospitals. After a long period of infirmity he was able to walk without a brace, although he has a pronounced limp to this day. The same willpower and concentration that Drabinsky used to confront his illness were later applied to other parts of his life. Although he excelled in a wide variety of activities, it was the silver screen that truly captured his passion.

Beginning with his law studies at the University of Toronto in the early 1970s, Drabinsky began to make movies his life's work. He took a keen interest in the emerging field of entertainment law, and later wrote a textbook on the subject that became a standard reference source. His studies, however, did not prevent him from producing a half-hour TV show starring William Shatner, and launching a movie magazine that was given away free at cinemas.

In 1976, Drabinsky made a foray into movie production. His first film featured Donald Sutherland but it was never completed. The following year, he teamed up with producer Joel Michaels to form a film production company that remained active for several years. Among the movies that the company produced were *The Silent Partner* with Christopher Plummer, *The Changeling* with George C. Scott, and *Tribute* with Jack Lemmon. Although acclaimed critically, none of these films did well at the box office.

EXHIBIT 3   **Cineplex Odeon's Balance Sheets, 1984–1988**   (*In millions of U.S. Dollars for the year ended December*)

	1984	1985	1986	1987	1988
Assets					
Current assets					
Cash and receivables	$ 5.2	$ 10.0	$ 20.1	$ 42.3	$ 151.5
Distribution advances	3.8	5.3	9.0	21.3	36.9
Inventories and prepaid expenses	3.0	4.6	11.0	13.3	13.0
Property investments	—	—	16.6	22.7	25.6
Fixed assets					
Properties and equipment	49.2	53.3	208.9	261.5	296.7
Leaseholds	17.4	26.9	324.1	490.2	594.4
Accumulated depreciation*	4.3	7.2	19.6	40.2	66.3
Other assets					
Long-term investments	2.7	6.2	14.3	50.0	130.3
Goodwill[†]	0.6	0.6	40.9	52.6	54.0
Deferred charges	0.8	1.7	6.6	12.0	27.1
	$78.4	$101.4	$631.9	$925.7	$1,263.2
Liabilities and Equity					
Current liabilities					
Bank loans	—	$ 4.8	$ 0.1	$ 20.7	$ 21.7
Payables and accruals	$10.0	13.5	47.7	74.9	129.5
Income taxes	—	0.4	1.9	4.6	5.7
Matured long-term debt	2.1	1.1	6.3	6.0	10.8
Long-term debt	36.1	40.7	317.6	449.7	663.8
Other liabilities					
Lease obligations	—	—	15.9	14.6	14.9
Deferred income taxes	0.8	4.2	11.1	13.3	10.4
Pension obligations	—	—	3.7	4.0	6.3
Minority interest	—	—	—	—	25.1
Shareholders' equity					
Capital stock	39.5	37.1	212.1	289.2	283.7
Translation adjustment	—	—	(3.6)	1.9	13.4
Retained earnings	(10.1)	(0.4)	19.1	46.8	77.9
	$78.4	$101.4	$631.9	$925.7	$1,263.2

*As of 1986, depreciation rates were reduced to 2.5 percent from 5.0 percent straight-line for buildings and to 6.7 percent from 10.0 percent straight-line for equipment.

[†]As of 1986, goodwill is being amortized over 40 years instead of over 20 years.

Source: Cineplex Odeon annual reports.

A Multiplex Strategy

In 1979, Garth Drabinsky joined forces with Nathan Taylor, an industry veteran who had long believed in the concept of theaters with multiple screens. Drabinsky found the idea appealing, and together the two formed Cineplex. Their first multiplex theater was located in Toronto's Eaton Centre, a newly developed shopping center. It contained 18 screens, with seating capacity ranging from 60 to 150 people per screen.

Cineplex saw itself as a niche player. It countered the trend in the industry that saw exhibitors using their large theaters to get the potentially lucrative releases from the Hollywood distributors (see Appendix). Instead, the newly developed multiplex chain used its small screens to show specialty movies, in particular foreign films and art films that could not be shown profitably in large theaters. As Taylor put it, Cineplex was not out to challenge the major chains, but to complement them:

> We are seeking to develop a market that to some extent doesn't exist. We are taking specialized markets and filling their needs. It's a latent market and a different niche than the major chains go after.[2]

In addition, Cineplex sought to obtain successful U.S. films after they had completed their run with the larger theater chains. It was industry practice for the share of the box office receipts accruing to the distributor to decrease with the run of the movie. Although this allowed exhibitors to keep more of the revenues, the inevitable decline in attendance ordinarily forced large theaters to discontinue exhibition once the number of empty seats exceeded a certain level. It was at this point that Cineplex could pick up the films, and by virtue of its small theaters keep most of the seats full.

The advantages of the multiplex concept were primarily due to a carefully planned use of shared facilities. All the theaters in a location were served by a single box office and a single concession stand. The use of advanced projection technology made it possible for one or two projectionists in a centralized projection booth to handle all screening duties in a multiplex theater. Show times were staggered in order to avoid congestion. Even advertising costs were lowered by using a single ad for all the films playing at a particular location.

The success of the multiplex concept spurred Cineplex to expand its operations across Canada. The company also made an entry into the large U.S. market with the development of a 14-screen theater complex in the Beverly Hills section of Los Angeles. By the end of 1982, the company was operating almost 150 screens in 20 different locations.

A Close Brush with Bankruptcy

The rapid rate of expansion brought Cineplex face to face with financial and market realities that its owners had not anticipated. During its expansion the company had amassed $21 million in debt, mostly in high and floating interest rates. This came in the midst of an economic recession that cut deeply into the company's earnings. To make matters worse, U.S. distributors were increasingly reluctant to supply Cineplex with the hit films for fear of alienating the two large Canadian exhibition chains, Famous Players and Canadian Odeon. Without the revenues of major U.S. releases the company's future was bleak.

To avert imminent bankruptcy, Cineplex took steps throughout 1983 to reduce its debt and improve its cash flow by selling off some of the company's assets, raising funds through the public offering of more shares, and

---

[2]"Cineplex Getting the Big Picture," *Financial Post*, June 14, 1980.

persuading the banks to extend further credit. But these measures did not address the company's blocked access to major releases. To break through the barrier, Drabinsky sought government intervention. Using his legal training, Drabinsky marshaled the evidence and managed to convince the Canadian government that strong grounds existed for launching an investigation into the existence of a conspiracy aimed at depriving Cineplex of access to major releases.

In the face of government investigation, and possible sanctions, the U.S. distributors modified their stand and agreed to a system of competitive bidding that would ensure all had equal access to their films. With this hurdle surmounted Drabinsky was able to secure financial backing from institutional investors. A large investment came from Claridge, a holding company owned by the Bronfmans, one of Canada's most powerful business families.

To Drabinsky, the close brush with bankruptcy had also revealed a basic flaw in his company's position. He became acutely aware that his small theaters generated insufficient revenues to bid for early runs of the most lucrative U.S. films. So when the principal owner of Canadian Odeon passed away, Drabinsky saw an opportunity that was not to be missed. Canadian Odeon had been greatly weakened by the new bidding system that Drabinsky had helped to bring about. Alarmed by Odeon's poor performance, the heirs finally accepted Drabinsky's offer of a little over $22 million for the entire chain.

The acquisition of Canadian Odeon in the spring of 1984, at what many viewed as a bargain-basement price, ended a remarkable turnaround for a company that just two years earlier had faced bankruptcy. Now, with over 450 screens in as many as 170 different locations, Cineplex was a major player in the industry. Drabinsky relished his comeback, and was not above taking a passing shot at his detractors: "A lot of people who were waiting for me to go under were disappointed. Well, they didn't get their jollies."[3]

CINEPLEX ODEON'S STRATEGY

The formation of Cineplex Odeon crowned Drabinsky's comeback from the verge of bankruptcy, but he was not content to rest on his laurels. Now that he controlled one of North America's major theater chains he set out to transform the moviegoing experience itself. With the advent of pay-television channels and prerecorded videocassettes, it was becoming increasingly difficult to lure moviegoers from the comfort of their homes.

Drabinsky aimed to change the public's perceptions by renovating the theaters, beginning with the physical format. Cineplex Odeon discarded the uniformly drab design common in most theater chains in favor of artwork in the lobbies, lush woolen carpets spread over marble floors, and coral and peach color-coordinated walls. The screening auditoriums featured scientifically contoured seats, digital background music, and state-of-the-art projection systems. As a final touch, the company reintroduced real buttered popcorn in the concession stands, and cafes that offered freshly made cappucino.

The metamorphosis was completed with the unveiling of a new company logo in the form of a curved bowl that was reminiscent of a Greek amphitheater. Furthermore, in choosing colors for the logo, Drabinsky decided on a

---

[3]"Upwardly Mogul," *Report on Business Magazine*, December 1985.

combination of imperial purple and fuchsia. For him, the logo was no mere representation; it was intended to make people sit up and take notice. As Drabinsky put it, "I felt that this would be more of a bravado kind of statement. I don't think anyone was ready for that."[4]

Cineplex Odeon's new format differed sharply from the prevailing industry response to the threat posed by pay television and take-home videocassettes. Most theater chains were trying to cut their fixed costs by slicing old movie palaces into tiny cinemas and eliminating many services that were deemed inessential. Drabinsky, on the other hand, believed that the moviegoing experience was not confined to what was shown on the screen. When patrons entered the theater, Drabinsky wanted them to leave behind a mundane existence and gradually move into a different reality. In the words of Drabinsky:

> We are determined to give back to our patrons the rush and excitement and anticipation and curiosity that should be theirs when they leave the techno-regimented world of their daily lives for the fantasy world of escape that is the movies.[5]

Managing Costs

Drabinsky's strategy, however, proved costly. Cineplex Odeon found itself spending almost $3 million on a typical six-screen multiplex, a third more than the average for the industry. But as far as Drabinsky was concerned, the additional investment bore fruit not only at the box office, but at the concession counter as well. The classier upscale atmosphere was meant to entice customers into spending more time in the theaters before and after the movie, resulting in higher sales at the concession counter. Indeed, the concessions at Cineplex Odeon's theaters usually generated almost $2 per moviegoer, an amount close to twice the industry average.

Still, the additional revenues generated by higher concession sales covered only a fraction of the fixed costs of a typical Cineplex Odeon theater. In an effort to reduce costs, Drabinsky had imposed stringent cost controls throughout his organization. Odeon's management was Drabinsky's first target. Upon acquisition, Drabinsky dismissed about two thirds of Odeon's head office staff, and cut the pay of the remaining personnel by 10 percent. He also canceled their company credit cards as an incentive to frugality. As he put it at the time, "When you make people use their own money they think hard about the justification they'll have to provide when filing their expense claims."[6] The cost-cutting campaign did not leave any facet of the company's operations untouched. Even the traditional cardboard containers used to sell popcorn were replaced with bags, a move that saved Cineplex Odeon close to $1 million per year.

In spite of these measures, Drabinsky was forced to search for other sources of revenue. He raised admission fees well above the competition in most markets, and began to show commercials before the screening of the main feature. Both moves were highly unpopular. Irate patrons expressed their anger in a number of cities, sometimes by protesting outside Cineplex Odeon's theaters.

---

[4]"King of the Silver Screen," *Macleans,* September 28, 1987.

[5]"Big Money at the Movies," *Macleans,* July 28, 1986.

[6]"Upwardly Mogul."

The most publicized of these protests occurred in New York City, where Mayor Ed Koch joined picketers in a call for a boycott of the chain because of its price increase.

The criticisms against Drabinsky were tempered by his use of promotional gimmicks. Most significant among these was the tactic of offering lower admission prices on Tuesdays. Attendance at Cineplex theaters had climbed substantially for these Tuesdays, generating additional revenues as well as restoring some measure of goodwill among customers.

A Powerful Competitor

With Drabinsky at the helm, Cineplex Odeon then launched a major expansion into North America's main movie markets. By and large, this expansion was based on a series of acquisitions in the United States (see Exhibit 4). In an industry known for tough negotiators and agile deal makers, Garth Drabinsky gained a reputation as a tenacious and abrasive businessman. He used his stamina and his adversarial style of bargaining to wear opponents down. His biggest acquisition involved the Plitt theater chain, which had almost 600 screens in over 200 locations.

In every market he entered Drabinsky used all the means at his disposal to gain market share, and keep the competition on the defensive. He pursued Famous Players, his long-standing rival in Canada, with special vengeance. In 1986 Drabinsky seized an opportunity to lease part of a building in Toronto that housed the Imperial Theatre, a six-theater complex operated by Famous Players. Since his part of the building contained the main entrance to all of the theaters in the complex, Drabinsky exercised the right to deny Famous Players public access. He used barbed wire and security guards with Doberman pinschers to enforce the blockade. Ultimately, Famous Players was forced to close down and sell this key location to Cineplex Odeon, but not before it extracted a public apology from Drabinsky, and a commitment that the facility would never be used to show motion pictures.

Drabinsky also tried to use the size of his chain to obtain added clout with film studios and distributors. He consistently used Cineplex Odeon's size to bargain hard to obtain potential hits on more favorable terms, but his insistence on having his way created friction in his relationships with suppliers. The tensions erupted into the open in 1987 when Columbia Pictures rejected Drabinsky's demand that Bernardo Bertolucci's oriental epic, *The Last Emperor*, be made available for wide release during the Christmas period. In retaliation, Drabinsky refused to exhibit another of the studio's films that was slated for Christmas release. The episode led to more of Columbia's films being diverted to other chains, such as Famous Players, Drabinsky's major Canadian competitor.

Drabinsky's readiness to challenge industry conventions had upset many who felt that he did not play by the rules. Walter Senior, the president of Famous Players, considered Drabinsky's tactics ultimately destructive. As he put it in the aftermath of the Imperial Theatre affair: "We all learn in school that when you set out to destroy someone, it becomes a weakness."[7] Myron

---

[7]"King of the Silver Screen."

EXHIBIT 4   **Cineplex Odeon's Acquisitions of U.S. Theaters, 1985–1987**

1985	Plitt Theaters	
	Los Angeles, California	
	574 screens / 209 locations	
1986	Septum Cinemas	
	Atlanta, Georgia	
	48 screens / 12 locations	
1986	Essaness Theatres	
	Chicago, Illinois	
	41 screens / 13 locations	
1986	RKO Century Warner Theaters	
	New York, New York	
	97 screens / 42 locations	
1986	Neighborhood Theaters	
	Richmond, Virginia	
	76 screens / 25 locations	
1986	SRO Theaters	
	Seattle, Washington	
	99 screens / 33 locations	
1987	Walter Reade Organization	
	New York, New York	
	11 screens / 8 locations	
1987	Circle Theaters	
	Washington, D.C.	
	80 screens / 22 locations	

Source: Cineplex Odeon.

Gottlieb, Cineplex Odeon's chief administrative officer, believed that much of the harsh treatment meted out to Drabinsky in the press reflected his impact on the industry rather than simply his style:

> There's been a lot of press about Garth, and some of it's been negative up until now. Some of it has been because of his aggressiveness, but more of it is because of the antagonism to the waves he's created in the industry.[8]

Vertical Moves

In 1982, at a time when Cineplex was still a small company screening foreign and art films, Drabinsky moved to consolidate and expand the company's other film-related activities. These consisted mainly of a film-making subsidiary originally started by Nathan Taylor, and a film distribution arm launched by Drabinsky in 1979.

The film-making subsidiary was one of Canada's largest and was located just north of Toronto. Its facilities were rented out to various groups for film and television production. These included two sound stages, dressing and wardrobe rooms, a carpentry mill, a plaster shop, and editing and screening

---

[8]"A Czar Is Born," *Canadian Business*, October 1984.

rooms. The distribution arm had been originally created by Drabinsky to provide foreign and art films to the newly developed Cineplex chain. It quickly
developed into one of the largest distribution companies in Canada, acquiring
the right to distribute films to theaters and on videocassettes, as well as for use
on network and pay television.

In 1986, Drabinsky increased the involvement of his company in film
making through the acquisition of the Film House. The Toronto-based facility
consisted of a large film-processing laboratory, and a fully equipped postpro-
duction sound studio. Following its purchase, Cineplex Odeon increased the
capacity of the film laboratory and constructed new upgraded sound facilities.

Meanwhile, Drabinsky expanded the film production and distribution
activities of his company into the United States. With the move into this larger
market, Cineplex Odeon was able to step up its level of participation in film
making. It began to contribute towards the production of small-budget films
such as Paul Newman's *The Glass Menagerie*, and Prince's rock concert film, *Sign
'O' the Times*.

Finally, Drabinsky entered into a collaborative venture with MCA, a large
U.S. entertainment conglomerate. The two companies agreed to jointly
develop and operate a large film studio and theme park in Orlando, Florida,
that would compete with Disney World. The move reflected Drabinsky's
determination to make Cineplex Odeon into a corporation that spanned every
part of the movie industry. As he had put it:

> It's an amalgamated company with revenue from theatres, distribution, produc-
> tion, the studio, and, down the road, live theatre. People aren't buying a share in
> this company just to have a share in a motion picture. They're getting a share
> in a vertically integrated entertainment corporation.[9]

A One-Man Show

Cineplex Odeon was firmly under the control of Drabinsky, who had concentrated power in his hands over the years. He became president of the company
in 1980, added the title of chief executive officer in 1982, and was confirmed as
chairman of the board in 1986. The titles symbolized Drabinsky's total involvement with the company and it was well known that no one else was allowed
to speak on behalf of the company.

In both deed and word Drabinsky attempted to communicate to his employees the total commitment that was expected of them. The managers who
worked in close proximity to Drabinsky found his driving energy both exhila-
rating and exhausting. Lynda Friendly, vice president of marketing and communications since 1982, sat in on all of Drabinsky's interviews with the press
and was inspired by his stamina and drive:

> Garth is so bloody energetic. I don't know how he does it. It's mind over matter.
> He stretches people to their absolute limit. He is a teacher, a mentor—a leader.[10]

Other officers, however, found Drabinsky's energy difficult to emulate.
They did not appreciate the midnight phone calls they regularly received from

---

[9]"Movie Mogul," *Business Journal*, October 1982.
[10]"King of the Silver Screen."

Drabinsky, nor did they agree that they must be ready to sacrifice all to their work. As a former Cineplex Odeon executive described it, the pressure Drabinsky put on managers was relentless:

> He works seven days a week and doesn't believe in holidays. Holidays are a disloyalty to the corporation and he *is* the corporation. He is tireless and he expects the same amount of dedication and effort from everyone else.[11]

Some of Drabinsky's immediate subordinates found his drive for total control unacceptable. His consolidation of power had been accompanied by a significant turnover among the top executives of the company. Several of the present executive officers had been appointed since 1986 (see Exhibit 5). Those who survived the transition were for the most part people with close personal ties to Drabinsky. Lynda Friendly, for example, had known Drabinsky since they attended synagogue together as teenagers. One of the most important loyalists was Myron Gottlieb, who had financially supported Drabinsky since the starting days of the company. Gottlieb's career in Cineplex Odeon closely dovetailed that of Drabinsky. He became the vice chairman of the board in 1982, and was appointed to the position of chief administrative officer in 1985.

Operating Philosophy

By January 1, 1989, Cineplex Odeon was the second largest motion picture exhibitor in North America with just over 1,800 screens in 500 different locations (Exhibit 1). Almost two thirds of the company's screens were located in the United States and were spread out over 20 different states. The remaining one third of these screens were situated in six different Canadian provinces. Cineplex Odeon theaters could be found in virtually all major population centers, from New York to Los Angeles in the United States, and from Toronto to Vancouver in Canada. Close to 90 percent of the chain's theaters, however, were located in leased premises, with rent calculated as a percentage of box office receipts, subject to a minimum.

As of early 1989, the company had close to 13,000 employees. These include film projectionists, cashiers, concession workers, ushers, and ticket takers. However, the bulk of these employees were hired on a part-time basis during seasons of high demand, and they were paid the minimum wage. Only about 15 percent of the employees were represented by unions. For each theater, the information obtained from its computerized box office terminals was used to schedule the minimal amount of staff for any given show. In addition to staff employed to operate the theater, Cineplex Odeon employed as many as 100 full-time architects, engineers, and draftsmen, all used for the design and renovation of theaters.

The Cineplex Odeon chain of theaters was divided into districts, with each district under the control of a supervisor. The task of a district supervisor was to ensure that all theaters follow guidelines set by the head office. He also regularly inspected theaters and reported the results to the head office. His report was contrasted with information provided by an independent agency whose representatives visited each theater on a random basis. In addition to this

---

[11]"Tough Bosses," *Report on Business Magazine*, December 1987.

E X H I B I T 5   **Profile of Cineplex Odeon's Senior Executives, 1989**

	G. I. Drabinsky	M. I. Gottlieb	J. M. Banks	A. Karp	L. Friendly	C. Bruner	E. Jacob
Title(s)	Chairman of board; president; chief executive officer	Vice chairman of board; chief administrative officer	Senior executive vice president, corporate affairs	Senior executive vice president	Executive vice president, marketing and communications	Senior vice president, treasurer	Senior vice president, chief financial officer
Age	40	45	57	48	39	31	35
Previous positions	Director since 1978	Director since 1980	Director 1983–1986	—	Senior vice president, marketing and communications	Assistant treasurer	Vice president and corporate controller
Year of entry	1980	1985	1987	1986	1982	1985	1987
Previous employment	Law firm	Investment firm	Law firm	Law firm	Not available	Public accounting firm	Electronics firm

Source: Cineplex Odeon, Form 10-K.

information, the head office relied on weekly reports supplied by the theater's manager detailing market conditions, competitors' activities, and audience response to advanced screening.

The centralization of information was matched by a consistent effort to centralize purchasing and accounting. All supplies and services were purchased centrally in order to maximize economies and reduce spoilage and waste. The computerized box office allowed the company to monitor ticket sales, as well as exercise stringent controls on the handling of cash.

Cineplex Odeon put a great deal of emphasis on a set of standards and practices set forth in staff orientation and training manuals. These standards were often drafted by Drabinsky, who went to great length to ensure that they were followed to the letter. He visited theaters regularly, often dropping by unannounced to talk with cashiers or ushers. He also phoned or saw 20 or 25 theater managers a week.

All of this reflected Drabinsky's conviction that he must know everything that goes on in his theaters and be always on the lookout for problems that need correcting. He has been known to deliver a silent but none-too-subtle reprimand to ushers by bending down in front of them to pick up a single piece of spilled popcorn. An employee who has observed Drabinsky in action observed: "Anything that is not absolutely perfect drives him crazy. He leaves people with a lasting impression when they screw up."[12]

Financial Structure

As of January 1, 1989, Cineplex Odeon had 23.9 million common shares and 23.6 subordinate restricted voting shares outstanding. The company made the transition from private to public financing in 1982 when it was listed on the Toronto Stock Exchange. The total value of its equity was estimated at $375 million (Exhibit 3).

A large block of shares, representing just over 30 percent of the company's total equity, was in the hands of Claridge, a holding company. For the most part, Claridge handled the investments of the Bronfman family, owners of the Seagram liquor business. The investment was made in 1983 to help Cineplex out of its early difficulties. Claridge had backed the development of the Eaton Centre, in the basement of which Cineplex had opened its first theaters.

In a subsequent deal Drabinsky sold a large block of shares to MCA, a U.S. entertainment conglomerate that owns Universal Studios. The deal allowed MCA to purchase up to 50 percent of the company's outstanding shares. However, MCA's control of Cineplex Odeon was restricted to 33 percent by Canadian law, which limits voting shares by foreign companies. MCA's total ownership is therefore represented by a specially created subordinate restricted voting shares.

In 1987 Cineplex Odeon consummated its first offering of shares in the United States and was listed on the New York Stock Exchange. In spite of this substantial enlargement of the company's equity base, most of the financing during 1987 and 1988 was through the use of debt. Not surprisingly, the price of Cineplex Odeon's shares has fluctuated. It reached a high around the time

---

[12] "A New Hollywood Legend Called—Garth Drabinsky?" *Business Week*, September 23, 1985.

of the MCA purchase, but has dropped considerably since then. In spite of the decline, Drabinsky continues to defend the company's low gross margins and insists that his chain boasts the highest return on equity among major exhibition chains. The fault, Drabinsky has claimed on one occasion, is to be found in the brokerage industry, and not in the performance of Cineplex Odeon:

> The brokerage industry is just full of people who like to hear themselves speak, but there's not a lot of substance there. This company is complete substance from top to bottom.[13]

FUTURE HORIZONS

Relentless Growth

In spite of growing financial constraints, Cineplex Odeon has not slowed the pace of its expansion. The company continues to construct new theaters, and to refurbish existing ones. At the present rate of expansion Cineplex Odeon will have 2,100 screens in North America alone by 1992. For Drabinsky the expansion has a dual purpose. First, he would like to surge past his competitors and capture an increasing share of the North American market. Second, Drabinsky believes that only a larger Cineplex Odeon can force the major distributors to give the chain the big-budget movies at more favorable terms.

But several other large exhibition chains that compete with Cineplex Odeon are also on the move, building new multiscreen theaters and acquiring smaller chains (see Exhibit 1). Many in the industry fear that the proliferation of screens will not be matched by a corresponding increase in movie attendance. If anything, the strong likelihood of a major recession may aggravate the situation. It will also increase the reliance of exhibitors on the limited supply of major Hollywood releases.

Drabinsky's critics contend that costly acquisitions and expensive theaters are making Cineplex Odeon especially vulnerable to an industry slowdown. For his part, Drabinsky has sought to allay the fears of shareholders by insisting that the growth of Cineplex Odeon is neither haphazard nor reckless:

> I want you to appreciate that everything we do is part of a thoroughly studied, painstakingly thought-out game plan. We're not expanding for the sake of expanding.[14]

Plans for the expansion of theaters are not confined to the North American continent. Drabinsky has recently unveiled plans to spend around $100 million to develop over 100 screens in the United Kingdom by the end of 1990. He believes that better theaters and a faster release of major U.S. films can reverse the decline in attendance and reinvigorate the British market.

In addition to theater expansion, Drabinsky has been getting his company increasingly involved in film production since it has the capacity to both distribute and exhibit movies. During 1988, Cineplex Odeon helped to finance and distribute movies by such noted directors as John Schlesinger and Oliver Stone. The company has also negotiated a joint production agreement with

---

[13]"Drabinsky's Movie Machine," *Financial Times*, August 26, 1985.

[14]"Market Apathy the Real Culprit, Drabinsky Says," *Toronto Globe and Mail*, May 13, 1988.

small production companies headed by Robert Redford and Taylor Hackford. But Drabinsky has frequently stated that Cineplex Odeon will restrict itself to a few low-budget films, and will not become involved in the risky business of producing big-budget movies.

Drabinsky has also extended his production activities to other entertainment areas. Cineplex Odeon had financed the run of some lavish Broadway musicals in Toronto during 1988. At present the company is converting the Toronto theater it wrested from the Famous Players chain into a 2,100-seat center for the performing arts. The theater, a vaudeville palace in its previous incarnation, will be restored to its former glory, and then used to stage the Canadian production of Andrew Lloyd Webber's *The Phantom of the Opera*. The musical is scheduled to open in the fall of 1989, and it is estimated that its initial production cost will total over $6.5 million.

A Performance under Scrutiny

Drabinsky's unrelenting drive for growth had put pressure on the company's finances. During 1988, Cineplex Odeon asked the banks to boost its line of credit by another $175 million to $750 million. More recently, the company sold off 50 percent of the Film House, its film production operation in Toronto, and most of its share in the Florida theme park to a British entertainment firm. The company had also been raising capital by selling off some of its theaters, then leasing them back.

In the opinion of a number of industry observers, the true financial position of Cineplex Odeon was masked by the company's liberal accounting practices (see the footnotes to Exhibits 2 and 3). In 1986, the company extended the period over which it would depreciate its properties and its goodwill, resulting in inflated values of its total assets. The company's operating profits were also believed to be overstated because of the inclusion of one-time sales of assets as part of operating revenue.

The financial uncertainty had created apprehension among the company's stockholders, who still recalled the narrow escape from bankruptcy six years earlier. Drabinsky, however, denied that he was undermining Cineplex Odeon by involving the company in activities it could ill afford. He frequently reiterated his conviction that he must at all times be ready to take advantage of emerging opportunities. When asked in a recent interview to predict the company's future development, he had this to say:

> If you asked me five years ago what Cineplex would look like today, I wouldn't have predicted what we have today. So when you ask me today what Cineplex will look like in five years, I can't tell you exactly.[15]

Publicly, Drabinsky had rebuffed his critics and sought to allay shareholders' fears. In private, he and his close associates had recently sought to gain control of Cineplex Odeon by making an offer to buy the 30 percent stake held by Bronfman's holding company. Taken together with the 8 percent stake that was already owned by Drabinsky and Gottlieb, they would have had enough shares to outvote and outflank MCA, who was restricted to a 33 percent limit on voting rights.

---

[15]"'Darth' Plays Movie Hardball—and Wins," *Financial Times*, December 28, 1987.

But MCA moved swiftly to obtain an injunction preventing the deal from going through, even as Drabinsky and Gottlieb were putting on the finishing touches. A financial analyst attempted to explain the reasons for MCA's reaction:

> No one understands what Drabinsky and Gottlieb are up to. They pulled out of the Florida deal, they sold off Film House, they are taking bigger risks in film production, and now the Bronfmans are getting out. From MCA's point of view there are probably lots of reasons to stop Garth from getting control.[16]

MCA eventually managed to get the court to rule that the offer that had been made by Drabinsky and his associates should be extended to all of Cineplex Odeon's outstanding shareholders. This had forced Drabinsky to scramble for over $1 billion of financing in order to back such an offer. It was widely speculated that if he was not able to raise this required amount, he could be forced out of the company that he had always considered to be his own.

APPENDIX: THE MOVIE INDUSTRY

Supply of Movies

The number of movies available for exhibition had grown significantly over the past few years. Most of this growth in supply resulted from the increased activities of smaller independent distribution companies. The numbers of feature-length films released over the last five years were as follows:

	1984	1985	1986	1987	1988
Major distributors	169	149	142	133	159
Smaller distributors	210	271	296	354	330
Total	379	420	438	487	489

Source: *Variety.*

In spite of the growing number of suppliers, the bulk of the revenues still came from the films distributed by the nine major companies that had dominated the industry for more than 50 years. Based in Hollywood, these companies include Paramount, Warner Brothers, Disney, Universal and Columbia. In 1988, the 159 films that were released by these firms accounted for more than 90 percent of the box office dollars in the United States and Canada.

The relative success of the major distributors stems in large part from their greater supply of capital. The typical Hollywood studio spent, on the average, almost $16 million for each of the films produced during 1988. Another $4 to $6 million was usually spent to market or advertise the movie and up to $2 million can be spent on making sufficient copies of the film so that it can be released to a wide number of theaters.

The movies of the smaller distributors are usually budgeted at under $5 million and frequently lack the major stars or production values that can increase

---

[16]"Clash of the Movie Titans," *Financial Post*, April 22–24, 1989.

their chances of striking it rich at the box office. In fact, an industry publication recently reported that more than half of the movies that are offered by the smaller distributors do not ever play in theaters, but are released directly into the videocassette market.

Although the major distributors continue to dominate the industry, they have long abandoned their practice of binding the most attractive movie directors and stars to long-term employment contracts. Most of the Hollywood movies are now typically made through contractual arrangements with thousands of smaller production outfits. The major distributor may either fund a movie from start to finish or provide a portion of the financing in return for a share of the subsequent box office receipts.

As a result of lackluster financial results, some of the smaller distributors have either folded their operations or merged with other distributors. Even some of the major distributors have merged together, such as the amalgamation of MGM with United Artists. These trends indicate that in the future, fewer major distributors will control the total number of movies available to theaters for exhibition.

Exhibition of Movies

Recent surveys have indicated that a large segment of the population—up to 45 percent in recent years—have stopped going out to see movies. Consequently, there has been a growing emphasis upon improving the quality of theaters to entice more people into visiting them. This has resulted in large-scale renovations of existing theaters as well as the construction of new ones. During this process, hundreds of smaller independent theaters have been forced to sell out to the larger chains that could more easily afford to make the necessary investments.

Industry estimates indicate that there were over 23,000 screens in the United States and Canada by the end of 1988. Almost 50 percent of these were collectively held by the top 10 exhibition chains. Over the past decade, some of the major movie distributors had also begun to buy up theater chains. These distribution companies argued that by owning theaters they could guarantee the public a higher-quality presentation of their movies.

The major distributors had been forced to divest themselves of their theaters at the peak of the growth of the movie industry. In the late 1940s, the U.S. Justice Department ruled that the same companies could not make, as well as show, movies. The legislation was a result of allegations that the movie distributors were restricting their movies to their own theaters and engaging in fixing prices. However, the attitudes towards restrictions on the ownership of movie theaters had become more relaxed in recent years. In part, this had been made possible by clearer and more stringent laws that provided fairer access to movies by all exhibitors.

Revenues from Theaters

There is widespread debate about the effects of recessions on movie attendance. Some financial analysts have recently shown that box office receipts decreased during the early 1930s and during the early 1970s. In fact, ticket sales in 1971 dipped to 820 million admissions before picking up again.

For the most part, however, annual ticket sales had been relatively stable at around one billion admissions per year for almost 30 years. The audience for movies in theaters was heavily dominated by younger individuals, particularly below 30 years of age. But recent evidence suggested that the traditional drop in attendance after the age of 30 had been lessening.

Box office receipts had risen considerably over the years, largely as a result of increases in the prices of tickets. There was considerable variation in ticket sales over the year, with almost half of the sales coming between late May and early September as well as between late November and early January. The box office totals for the United States over the past five years were as follows:

1984	$4.0 billion
1985	$3.8 billion
1986	$3.7 billion
1987	$4.2 billion
1988	$4.4 billion

Source: *Variety.*

The average ticket price had risen to $4.11 in 1988, up from $3.36 in 1984. Theater owners were generally reluctant to raise ticket prices more rapidly than inflation for fear of losing viewers. Increasingly, however, they had come to rely upon the lobby concession stand to make their profits. Once inside the theaters, moviegoers became a captive market for popcorn, soft drinks, and candy sold at inflated prices. Recent surveys indicate that exhibition chains derived as much as 20 percent of their revenues from high-profit items sold at their concessions.

Splitting of Revenues

There was considerable wrangling between the distributors and exhibitors over the distribution of box office revenues. The distributors had tried to use their new sources of revenue from videocassettes and pay TV to reduce their dependence on the theaters.

In spite of the growing availability of these new channels, distribution companies reached more people through exhibiting their movies in theaters. More significantly, the values of their movies on videocassettes and pay TV were heavily dependent upon a respectable theatrical run. A successful movie will create more demand for pay TV as well as for videocassette rentals.

In recent years, the exhibitors had been able to use the increased supply of movies to negotiate a larger share of the box office receipts. But the observed increase in the total number of screens across the continent was expected to allow the distributors to regain the advantage. Several growing exhibition chains may have to compete with each other to get the potential hit movies, which still tend to come from a few large Hollywood studios.

Typically, the distributor and the exhibitor split the box office revenue equally with each other. The distributor eventually passed on to the producers and investors about 20 percent of the revenues of a movie. The remainder was retained by the distributor to cover internal operating and advertising costs.

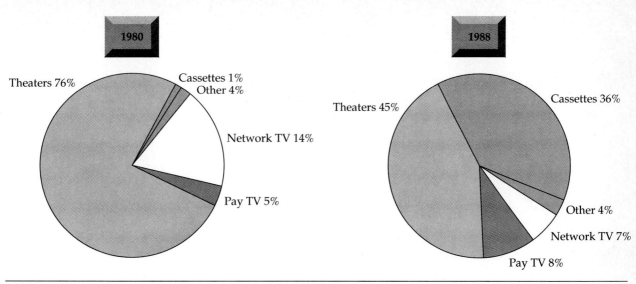

Source: *Variety.*

NCNB CORPORATION*

Frank Barnes, University of North Carolina at Charlotte

While most states restricted banks to one county, North Carolina had allowed statewide banking since 1804. This had important implications on the size and operating style of the banks. In 1960, Commercial National Bank was a medium-sized state bank with assets of $480 million in a southern state, hardly known to the major money-center banks of New York or Chicago. CNB had its hands full competing with its two state rivals, rock-solid Wachovia Bank & Trust and third-place First Union National Bank. In 1960, Hugh McColl was a C student college kid from Bennettsville, South Carolina, who was just free from his hitch in the military. He was ready with his new bride to move into the big city, Charlotte, North Carolina, to see if he could hold onto a job with CNB.

By 1990, CNB was NCNB and the seventh largest bank in the United States with $64 billion in assets. Wachovia was in third place in the state with $24 billion, behind First Union, with $39 billion. NCNB had a worldwide reputation for initiative, ambition, and aggressiveness stemming from such achievements as beating every other bank in the nation into the lucrative Florida market by two years and outwitting the largest U.S. bank, Citicorp of New York, in acquiring failing RepublicBank of Texas in what some called "the deal of the century." The rapid growth of all three North Carolina banks increased the chances they would be among the survivors of the revolution in banking in the deregulated environment.

In 1990, Hugh McColl was NCNB's chief executive and the most famous of a new breed of bankers. His 1989 compensation was $1.5 million and his stock in NCNB was worth $8 million. His reputation for aggressiveness and frankness of speech made him a prime target for newspaper controversy and was reported to make him feared by the managers in acquisition targets. The military jargon he used to describe strategic moves was emphasized by the press and upset the traditional "country club" banker. Numerous writers played up statements by several bankers that they would rather merge with "anyone but NCNB." The press reported that First Atlanta took a $30-per-share offer from Wachovia instead of $33 from NCNB just to avoid McColl. But people in NCNB disagreed and were solidly behind McColl.

NCNB was said to have a corporate culture that emphasized competitiveness and aggressiveness. NCNB was among the most active banks in recruiting talent on college campuses, was an innovator in employee policies such as employee child care, and valued entrepreneurial behavior. Acquisitions were firmly integrated into the NCNB culture.

As the 1990s began, the first great wave of regional bank mergers across state lines was subsiding. The survivors, like NCNB, were working to strengthen their organizations. It wasn't exactly clear who had actually won,

---

*Presented at the North American Case Research Association. All rights are reserved to the author.

though states like Florida and South Carolina, whose banks had been acquired by others, might have lost. In a few years, a larger wave of mergers was expected as the United States would go to full interstate banking and the "super-regional" NCNBs and First Unions would have to go head-to-head with the "money-center" Citicorps. Interstate mergers might eliminate 80 percent of existing banks and many wondered who would survive.

A January 1989 article in *Business—North Carolina* suggested NCNB had the answer: "You make things happen. You don't sit and wait. You lead by example. You go out, you compete, and you do your damnedest to win. This is more than Hugh McColl's approach to banking; it is his approach to life. This is why NCNB is one of the most aggressive, feared competitors in banking today. This is why NCNB succeeds when others don't even try."

Some analysts predicted the entire 1990s would be bearish for banking. Stock prices were off in September 1990; NCNB down 43 percent, First Union down 23 percent, and Wachovia down 14 percent. The savings and loan crisis, the slowing economy with its continuing budget deficit, the increased competition from banks and nonbank financial companies, all created a challenging situation. McColl was concerned about the path NCNB needed to take to succeed.

BACKGROUND

The predecessor to NCNB, Commercial National Bank, was formed in 1874 in Charlotte, N.C. In 1901, American Trust Company opened in Charlotte. In 1957 American Trust, which had become the largest unit bank in the Carolinas and primarily a wholesale (commercial) bank, merged with Commercial National, which had become primarily a retail bank. American Commercial added First National of Raleigh in 1959.

In 1933, Security National Bank had been formed in Greensboro, later adding offices in six cities from Burlington to Wilmington. Security merged with a Durham bank in 1959. Then on July 1, 1960, American Commercial merged with Security to form North Carolina National Bank, NCNB. This created the second largest bank in the state with assets of $480 million and 1,300 employees in 40 offices in 20 North Carolina cities.

During the 1960s, NCNB, headquartered in Charlotte, acquired or opened 51 more offices and doubled deposits as it completed a statewide expansion strategy. The holding company, NCNB Corp., was formed in 1969. In the seventies it added 82 more offices, increased assets to $6 billion, and achieved a 20 percent market share. First Union National Bank (FUNB) and Wachovia Bank had similar market shares.

It was generally agreed that this merger activity by NCNB, and also FUNB, was in response to the competitive dominance of Wachovia. In the 1930s, under the presidency of Robert Hanes of the hosiery family, Wachovia became the largest bank in the state, with a reputation for quality. It was slow to jump on fads, instead seeking growth through conservative management, soundness, and profitability. Wachovia had, over the years, catered more heavily to corporate customers than had the other two banks. Tom Storrs, chairman of NCNB through the seventies, said this history explained the competitiveness of the North Carolina banks.

Government Regulation and Deregulation: 1982

Banking had always been an industry that was closely regulated by government. Until the 1980s, bank regulators set the interest rates that all banks could pay or charge customers. At the same time regulators controlled the price and quantity of money. In this way banks and savings and loans were shielded from most competition and pretty much guaranteed a profit. The activities that banks could undertake were narrowly defined, but were protected from non-bank competitors.

Historically, bank regulation has been aimed at safeguarding depositors' money and minimizing the impact of any bank failures on the economy. In recent years, in addition to the safety issue, regulation has been concerned with the size and distribution of banks (structure issues) and consumer protection issues. Congress periodically enacted new legislation. The process was a political one of treating differences in viewpoints between rich and poor states, large and small banks, North versus South, East versus Midwest and West, and so on. Since 1970, banking had undergone dramatic change. Information technology was speeding and simplifying financial activities and eroding the separation between commercial banks and investment banks.

In 1982 Congress enacted major deregulation, which left banks substantially free to pay what they wanted on interest-bearing accounts and charge what they wished for their services. A profit was no longer guaranteed; instead it had to be achieved, as in any business, by good management. In this environment, fees charged for services began to be a major source of income. There was a movement toward charging for traditionally free services, such as check writing, in addition to the creation of new services, such as credit and financial services. In succeeding years, other new laws and regulations had the effect of eliminating much of the business distinction between the banks and nonbank financial institutions. Banks could move into discount brokerage while stockbrokers could move into checking accounts. All of these changes were having a major impact on the financial landscape of the United States.

HUGH MCCOLL AND NCNB

Hugh McColl was closely associated with the development and style of NCNB. His tenure covered the last 30 years of strategic development. McColl came from a competitive family. He told the story of proudly coming home from school one day to tell his grandmother of coming in second in something. She responded, "You'll do better next time." He was expected to win. His father, Hugh McColl, Sr., told *Business—North Carolina*, "I think he got his fighting spirit from his mother; I give her credit for a lot of Hugh's ability and success." Hugh McColl spoke of her as a talented and "very, very competitive" woman born in the wrong era. All of the men in the family had been small-town bankers, his grandfather, father, and his two brothers. He was the oldest son.

In high school in Bennettsville, S.C., he was active in everything from the Latin Club and Radio Club to almost every sport—though only five feet, seven inches—and was voted Best All-Round. In the graduation yearbook, he was nicknamed "Happy" and recognized with "He who's talented in leadership/ Holds the world's dreams in his grip."

In 1953 he went off to UNC-Chapel Hill, like most of the family had, without much thought. He was cut from the basketball and baseball teams and lost his bid for freshman class president. He worked hard at intramural sports since he was "more interested in athletics than anything else." He wasn't very interested in his business major or in the required ROTC, using "minimum maintenance" to make mostly C's. "It just didn't matter." He figured after graduation he would go home and run the family business.

He went into the military because it was practically required, but chose the Marines for his two years. He thoroughly enjoyed the "maturing" experience and had his eyes opened by living with people from all over the country. It was an important lesson for the young Southerner from a well-off family. "It was a great graduate school, a great management training program, to be an officer and to be responsible for other people." Leadership, he learned, required that he be out with his people all the time.

When he returned home in 1959 from the Marines to join the family business, his father surprised him by telling him to look elsewhere. McColl says, "He did me the greatest favor in the world, sending me off." His father sent him to the bank with which he did his business, American Commercial Bank in Charlotte. He was interviewed by President Addison Reese, but not hired. Hugh, Sr., called another contact in the bank and Hugh had the job. He didn't report until September because, first, he and a friend were headed to Europe for the summer. As the trip started, he met a girl from South Carolina he would end up marrying that fall. In Belgium, he bought her a whole cart of flowers.

His first job was scouring South Carolina for corporate accounts. He left Charlotte in his VW by 6:00 A.M. and returned at night to the office to round up new leads. Spending long hours away from home was the pattern for many years. "It cost me a lot of my family time; my wife had to be both father and mother." But success wasn't guaranteed. In 1983 he remembered for the *Charlotte Observer*, "What drove me was feeling inadequate. I remember telling Jane not to get too comfortable in Charlotte, that I might not make it here."

When Addison Reese became chairman of CNB in 1957, it was still a small wholesale and commercial bank. His aim was to make the bank large enough to compete with Wachovia. Reese hired Tom Storrs in 1960 as an executive vice president to lead the expansion across North Carolina with acquisitions and mergers. Storrs' 25-year career had been split between the Federal Reserve Board in Richmond and wartime Navy duty as an executive officer on a destroyer. He was a professional economist with a master's and doctorate in economics from Harvard. In 1960, Storrs was working with a merger partner in Greensboro and having trouble with bickering between Greensboro and Charlotte. He called McColl with a task and got immediate cooperation: "He stood out, he responded." Storrs became his mentor as McColl took on more responsibilities.

In 1968, NCNB was the third bank in the country to form a one-bank holding company. NCNB was the first to use commercial paper to finance the activities of its nonbank subsidiaries and the first to issue long-term debt securities to raise money for the holding company, setting a pattern that others followed. In 1969 Storrs became president.

In 1973 Storrs succeeded Reese as chairman and named McColl and two other rising stars, Luther Hodges, Jr., and Bill Dougherty, to run the bank. Each expected to succeed Storrs. Hodges, son of a former governor, was seen as an "outside" PR man, while Dougherty, a CPA, was more of a back-office expert.

During the 1974–75 recession, a company with a $28 million loan got into trouble and McColl helped it reorganize without bankruptcy. McColl said, "Losing that $28 million would have taken us out; we only made $16 million the year before." This was one example of McColl's performance, which Storrs said the executive committee viewed as the "best track record of the three."

NCNB's 1979 annual report proposed "an orderly approach to interstate banking" in recognition of the fact that continued rapid growth could only be achieved by crossing state lines, though interstate branching was still not permitted. NCNB began to build equity for out-of-state expansion and looked for opportunities. In December 1980, as Chairman Storrs had completed a stock sale in anticipation of eventual opportunities to go into interstate banking, he stated: "Two things are going to be very important to financial institutions in the 1980s as regulations change and opportunities for expansion arise: the quality of their people and the adequacy of their capital. NCNB has done a good job of attracting and developing competent people. And we are committed to continuing that effort. With the stock sale . . . we have strengthened the capital base that will also be required for future asset expansion."

McColl was president of NCNB bank, the retail operation, and active in carrying out Storrs' statewide acquisitions. In 1981, McColl was named vice chairman, which indicated he would be the one to succeed Storrs. In 1981, Hodges left the chairmanship of the bank to run, unsuccessfully, for governor. Dougherty left his presidency of the holding company in 1982. On September 1, 1973, McColl became chairman and CEO of NCNB Corp.

A Boston securities analyst who monitored NCNB closely noted that McColl had spent his entire career with the bank in the headquarters city and predicted he would be a "hands-on" chief executive: "He is the kind of guy who gets involved in every detail." McColl believed in being in touch with all parts of the organization. He noted that too many executives forgot that information is filtered as it comes up through the organization. He said, "I try to remove some of the filters. I'm an in-the-field manager. There's never a day I'm not out in someone's area. I go and look; it keeps people honest. If I've seen it myself no one's going to say it isn't so."

People at NCNB described McColl as demanding and impatient to get on with decisions. He wanted consensus and was impatient with people who didn't contribute. "He's quick to have an opinion, and he's very perturbed if others involved don't participate," one executive told *Business—North Carolina*. Another added, "He always says what he has to say. He's open, honest, and forthright. You always know where he stands. It's gotten him into trouble outside the bank, but that's how it is." For example, in discussing expansion with reporters, he said NCNB didn't need to have banking offices in "every pig path" in Georgia. When this was reported in the media, a big flap developed.

People inside and outside the bank credited him with creating an entrepreneurial, "can-do" culture. His style had no critics inside the bank. He was described as being very accessible and valuing his associations with employees at all levels. He jogged and entered "fun-runs" with others from the bank, played racquetball with young employees at lunch, and visited sick employees in the hospital. He was energetic and inquisitive. Employees commented it was hard to mention a book he hadn't read. If a trip to a foreign country was ahead, he would be studying the maps and reading several books about it. The bank had been a leader in providing for its employees. In 1990 *Good Housekeeping* magazine praised NCNB as among the best companies for working mothers;

its policies addressed family needs, providing parental leave, day care at or near work, flex-time, and counseling support.

McColl had his style. He told *Business—North Carolina* about being at the beach in the summer of 1988 and going by a newly opened office. He didn't see a sign on the building and the manager said it was being made. It irritated McColl so much that he went to a hardware store and got some letters, board, and paint. Then he returned, where he made and installed a sign. "It's a graphic lesson. You don't wait until things happen. It's part of what leading by example is all about. It would never occur to me to have an office without a sign. I want my managers to feel they can do what it takes to get the job done and not be impeded by bureaucracy and I'll back them up. You are responsible. Be responsible."

EXPANSION INTO FLORIDA: 1981–1984

Even though interstate banking was not allowed until 1985, NCNB was able to expand into Florida in 1981. In 1972, Florida had enacted statutes to prevent acquisition of their banks by out-of-state banks. Just prior to this, NCNB had bought the small Orlando Trust Company. In July 1981, NCNB took the position it was a Florida bank because of the Orlando company and offered to buy First National Bank of Lake City. Banks in Florida and across the country opposed NCNB getting this early start at interstate banking. But by December the Federal Reserve Board had ruled in NCNB's favor and NCNB became the first out-of-state bank to expand into the lucrative Florida market.

NCNB moved quickly in 1982 to buy three Florida banks with 67 branches and over $2 billion in assets. In 1984 it acquired Ellis Banking Corporation with 75 offices and $1.8 billion in assets and in 1985 purchased a $2 billion Miami bank with 51 offices. By 1987 NCNB National Bank of Florida was the fourth largest in the state with assets of $9.9 billion and over 200 offices. The acquisitions were financed by a combination of cash, long-term debt, and issuing more shares of common stock.

In June 1982 McColl had stated, "Our purpose is to build a banking company of a size that can compete more effectively with the money-center banks in providing a range of services to customers here in the southeast, across the nation and in the world markets." Chairman Storrs warned of the dangers of overemphasizing short-run earnings and ignoring long-term needs: "You would leave your successor with the problem of doing the building that you should have been doing. . . . What we are doing is what Addison Reese did twenty years ago—always building on the foundation for the next decade." McColl forecasted, "By 1984, we will have this ship running hot and heavy. Between now and then we will not divert ourselves with casual mergers. We will pay back our debt, and get in good shape to start over when they drop the barriers on interstate banking." Dick Stillinger, a New York banking specialist, told the *Charlotte Observer*, "I think they will have a tough row to hoe for the next couple of years. I am skeptical if NCNB can make it pay off fast enough to offset the dilution of earnings."

Some bankers objected to McColl's style of dealing with newly acquired banks. A former NCNB executive reported to *Business—North Carolina* "a deal in which a Florida banker was ready to sell, only to pull out after listening to

McColl over dinner dictate what changes NCNB would make after the acquisition." In acquisitions, the NCNB name would go on the bank, many services would be centralized, and policies would be set in Charlotte. After NCNB's Florida expansion, it was reported that 41 of 45 top executives left Gulfstream Bank after the 1982 acquisition and that over 150 of Exchange Bancorporation's 300 managers left after their 1983 takeover. Gulfstream's ex-CEO was quoted as saying NCNB's corporate culture was "a snotty-nosed kid aching for a fight." Exchange's ex-CEO complained of NCNB's military style. "Many of our people didn't stay because they didn't like the NCNB culture. There was one way to do things—the NCNB way."

In 1983, when he became CEO, McColl told the *Charlotte Observer* he was working at toning down his image, softening his statements, trying to adopt a posture more appropriate for a CEO. "I have been working on that," McColl said. "But part of our images get to be caricatures. I think people think I'm aggressive. I don't think of myself that way." Yet he was energetic and competitive and admitted to being "downright hostile in competition." "I would probably hurt fewer people's feelings. I might modify my behavior by being less aggressive. But if I tried to be somebody else, I wouldn't do very well at that."

In early 1984, NCNB announced plans to target services for "middle market" firms (sales of $5 million to $250 million) under the direction of 37-year-old Ken Lewis. NCNB already did business with 70 percent of companies in North Carolina with $50 million in sales and had the largest market share of business with southeastern firms that size. Lewis said, "The banks that survive are the ones that pick those market segments they can best compete in."

In the summer of 1984, NCNB announced it would concentrate on increasing shareholder wealth and make no major acquisitions through 1985. Year-end earnings were projected at $3.85 per share, representing about a 4 percent dilution due to acquisitions. Loan offices had been opened in Washington and Memphis. NCNB told the *American Banker*: "We think we need a presence in Atlanta, but don't think it's necessary to have a big branch system in Georgia."

GOVERNMENT REGULATION AND INTERSTATE BANKING

By 1980, it was clear interstate banking was coming. In early 1981, the Southern Growth Policies Board, an important regional study group, recommended that southeastern states let other southeastern banks cross their borders. It was expected that Congress would approve full interstate banking by the end of the decade. In 1982, Massachusetts and Connecticut approved regional interstate banking. When the Supreme Court upheld the legality of regional compacts in 1985, Justice Rehnquist wrote: "One predictable effect of the regionally restrictive statutes will apparently be to allow the growth of regional multi-state bank holding companies which can compete with the established banking giants of New York, California, Illinois, and Texas." In a 1984 meeting Hugh McColl stated: "Our industry is simply not ready for all-out national interstate banking."

The *Charlotte Observer* reported that a senior economist for the Federal Reserve Board had yet to discover any advantages to large banks. His studies showed that maximum economies of scale were achieved at the $100 to $200 million size and that smaller banks tended to be more profitable than larger banks; there was an inverse correlation between size and profitability. Some felt the mergers would concentrate political power and stifle competition. A community banker asked, "Why would bigger be better? Banking is a people business." But others spoke of the access to larger amounts of capital for big projects, participation in the total economy, and the ability to have a role in the direction of change in the banking industry.

REGIONAL BANKING BEGINS

In February 1984, Georgia was about to become the first southeastern state to approve a regional reciprocal interstate banking law. Under these laws, southeastern banks could expand into another southeastern state if the reciprocal was allowed. The entry of other states' banks, primarily major "money-center" banks like the nation's largest, $150 billion Citicorp of New York, was carefully excluded. Some large northern banks were expected to oppose the move in federal courts if provision were not made for eventual full interstate banking. Two of Atlanta's major banks, Citizens and First Atlanta, expressed support for the legislation and took steps to prepare for it. *The Wall Street Journal* reported that NCNB was opposing the legislation; since North Carolina wasn't expected to consider a reciprocal law until 1985, NCNB would not have a chance at the best merger opportunities in Georgia. NCNB was considering using its Florida operation, where there would soon be a reciprocal agreement, to get around this problem. One executive told the *WSJ*: "The way for NCNB to come into Georgia is through its home state of North Carolina. If NCNB managed to get into Georgia through Florida, you can be sure they'll fight claw and nail to defeat regional banking in North Carolina."

In June 1985, the U.S. Supreme Court ruled that state legislatures could set up reciprocal regional agreements allowing banks from states in their region to merge across their borders but excluding out-of-region banks. In July, six southeastern states enacted such laws and there was immediate action by the region's largest banks: NCNB, SunTrust, Wachovia, First Union, and Citizens and Southern. The race for mergers began immediately. By July, C&S of Atlanta had acquired a Florida bank and Wachovia had announced a merger with First Atlanta. An official of C&S of South Carolina told the *WSJ*, after agreeing to be acquired by C&S of Atlanta: "Being part of a large institution gives us the marketing and capital resources to continue being a broad-based bank." NCNB and FUNB appeared not to have succeeded in moving into Atlanta. NCNB commented, "It would be advantageous to have a bank in Atlanta but we don't think a major presence is required. We do an awful lot of business there without a loan production office." Exhibit 1 shows the 10 largest banks in the Southeast as of July 1985.

On October 3, 1985, *The Wall Street Journal* described NCNB as the most aggressive bank in the Southeast; the article went on to say:

> Hugh McColl, Jr., the combative ex-Marine who heads NCNB, often rubs more genteel bankers the wrong way. "He's a little bit more aggressive than the rest of us," says Mr. Poelker [John Poelker, President of Citizens and Southern Georgia Corp.]. The executive has tended to shake up management and insist on the NCNB name on acquired banks. As a result, some banks have taken an anyone-

EXHIBIT 1   The Southeast's 10 Largest Banks as of Mid-1985

Rank	Bank	Pre-Merger Assets*	Mergers/Acquisitions	Acquired Assets*	Post-Merger Total Assets*
1	NCNB Corp. Charlotte, N.C.	$16,900	Bankers Trust (S.C.) Pan American (Fla.) Southern National Bankshares (Ga.)	$2,081 1,658 93	$20,732
2	SunTrust Banks Inc. Atlanta, Ga.	16,293	SunBanks Inc. (Fla.) and Trust Co. of Ga.		16,293
3	First Wachovia Corp. Winston-Salem, N.C. Atlanta, Ga.		Wachovia Corp. (N.C.) First Atlanta Corp. (Ga.)	8,932 7,106	16,038
4	First Union Corp. Charlotte, N.C.	8,250	Northwestern Financial Corp. (N.C.) Atlantic Bancorp (Fla.)	2,983 3,377	15,010
5	Barnett Banks of Florida Inc. Jacksonville, Fla.	13,190			13,190
6	Citizens & Southern Georgia Corp. Atlanta, Ga.	8,480	Landmark Banking Corp. (Fla.)	1,844	12,324
7	Southeast Banking Corp. Miami, Fla.	10,204			10,204
8	Sovran Financial Corp. Norfolk, Va.	8,700	DC National Bancorp (D.C.) Virginia Southern Bank (Va.)	400 50	9,150
9	United Virginia Bankshares Richmond, Va.	6,600	MS&T Bank of Washington, D.C.	900	7,500
10	Florida National Banks Jacksonville, Fla.	5,367			5,367

*Figures in millions as of 6/30/85.
From Jenks Southeastern Business Letter and other sources.

else-but-NCNB stance. First Atlanta rejected a $33.50 a share bid from NCNB in favor of a $30 bid from Wachovia Corp. "Some of NCNB's attitudes came back to haunt it," says a First Atlanta executive.

In response, NCNB's communication chief, Rusty Page, stated the policies on using one name and on centralizing were those of the scholarly, soft-spoken Tom Storrs, not McColl. He believed the approach was sound and that the opportunity to become a part of the South's largest and strongest bank would continue to attract merger partners.

By mid-July, *American Banker* reported: "Wachovia and First Atlanta bent over backwards to try to demonstrate that the transaction is a merger of equals in which there is no clear buyer or seller." Earlier FUNB's Crutchfield and NCNB's McColl had indicated they had no interest in any merger of equals. McColl commented, "I have to say it's like getting married and promising not to sleep with each other."

First Atlanta, with assets of $7 billion, and Wachovia, with assets of $8.7 billion, would be merged into a holding company called First Wachovia. There would be legal addresses in both states and corporate functions would be located wherever they could be performed best. John Medlin, 51, of Wachovia would be president and CEO, while Tom Williams, 56, of First Atlanta would be chairman. Wachovia, with 60 percent of the shares, would name 60 percent of the directors, and First Atlanta would name 40 percent. Board meetings would alternate between the two states.

The *Atlanta Journal* reported on June 23, 1985, that First Atlanta had been eyeing Wachovia for some time. Williams had been educating the directors for months about criteria for merger partners (management compatibility being one of three). "The studies we went through showed us the best combination was unquestionably Wachovia." Earlier in the year, the two banks had discussed a combination, but decided to wait for the Court's decision. On the day of the decision, Medlin called Williams and two days later they met in Greensboro. The *Charlotte Observer* noted that analysts, such as John Maseir in New York, gave the leadership high marks: "I think Tom Williams is one of the most intelligent, statesmanlike individuals I've come across. Medlin is one of the great heroes of the South. It's a combination of two very intelligent men."

In October 1985, *The Wall Street Journal* noted the South was the most active region in mergers because of fear and opportunity:

> The Southeast long has had the smallest banks in the poorest area of the nation. The region's largest bank, NCNB, was only the nation's 25th largest. However, the region now had some of the most attractive retail banking markets in the nation, Atlanta, Nashville, all of Florida. The big, money-center banks, already very active in lending activity in the region, wanted into the retail part of the market. The executive director of the Southern Growth Policies Board told the WSJ: "We don't want our capital resources dominated by money-center banks. The South has a long history of being exploited by corporate interests outside the region."

McColl believed the entry of money-center banks and nationwide banking was inevitable, some said as soon as the early 1990s. He felt his state's big-three banks had ensured their long-term survival by these mergers. Twenty billion dollars in assets was often mentioned as the minimum size to assure continued competitiveness against the large banks and avoid being takeover targets.

The race to acquire the most attractive merger candidates had stretched some banks' resources. McColl said, "There's a limit to what anyone can do in a reasonable time frame." Some dilution of earnings was expected and there were questions of adequate depth of management to run newly acquired operations.

In July 1985, NCNB announced plans to acquire Bankers Trust of South Carolina, the state's third largest with assets of $1.9 billion and 110 branches. NCNB paid 12 to 13 times earnings, which was expected to result in a 2 percent dilution in earnings per share. Bankers Trust was a leader in the industry in profitability, unlike the Florida banks. It was the first in the state to install automatic teller machines and the third in the nation to provide personal cash management accounts. The South Carolina papers stressed the friendly nature of the merger. Bankers Trust Chairman "Hootie" Johnson told *The State* (Columbia, S.C.) he and McColl had been the closest of friends for many years. McColl praised Bankers Trust's leadership in marketing, especially the aggressive marketing of its credit cards. He added: "They are way ahead of a lot of people, including us" in financial services. The bank would operate as an independent subsidiary, NCNB Bankers Trust of South Carolina. He told the *Columbia Record*, "We will be separate banks with the basic same philosophy. All of us will actually be doing business the same way." Johnson, in addition to being chairman of the South Carolina bank, would become chairman of the executive committee of NCNB Corporation, a position held by Tom Storrs; the chief financial officer of Bankers Trust would move to Charlotte to become an executive vice president of NCNB Corporation. Two of Bankers Trust's directors would become directors of NCNB Corporation.

In November 1985, shareholders overwhelmingly (96 percent) approved the merger. The merger would take place after January 1, 1986, when South Carolina's reciprocal banking laws went into effect. NCNB was awaiting approval by regulators of its plan to acquire Southern National Bankshares of Atlanta and Pan American Bank of Miami.

On September 8, 1985, the *Miami Herald*, in an article entitled "North Carolina Banks Take the Lead," noted that while Florida had none of the region's top four banks, North Carolina had three. "Who's going to be around in five, ten years?" asked Hugh McColl. "It's quite clear the North Carolina banks, because they're stronger and better managed, with more capital." *The Herald* noted NCNB tried to be a bank for everyone, while Wachovia was regarded as one of the nation's finest corporate banks. FUNB positioned itself between the two, with a strength in its mortgage operations. FUNB's Ed Crutchfield explained the source of the three banks' strength: "We're at each other's throats on a lot of street corners and that intense competition breeds strength." The rich Florida market bred a group of banks with less drive.

Observers tended to see a race between the three North Carolina banks to see who could be biggest. By 1985, NCNB and FUNB had jumped ahead of Wachovia, the traditional leader. In December, FUNB claimed to be the second biggest behind NCNB. A Wachovia executive referred to "bragging rights" but all disclaimed growth for growth's sake. The pace of expansion in 1985 brought some concern as FUNB faced a 15 percent dilution in earnings, Wachovia 6 percent, and NCNB 4 percent. McColl told analysts, "Instead of concentrating on making money, many banks seem to be concentrating on acquisitions activity. This is certainly not the case at NCNB." He noted the high prices FUNB had paid lately for acquisitions, 2.8 times book compared to NCNB's 1.8. The *Observer* reported Crutchfield's quick response: "If he [McColl] isn't making acquisitions in 1985, I must be reading the wrong papers."

In October 1985, McColl named 45-year-old Francis "Buddy" Kemp, a Davidson College graduate with a Harvard MBA, president and chief operating officer of NCNB Corp.; McColl retained the title of chief executive officer and chairman of the board. McColl indicated that NCNB planned no major acquisition in the coming 18 months, but spoke of an interest in the northern Virginia market. Ken Lewis moved to Tampa as executive vice president of the Florida banking group. As 1985 ended, NCNB reported earnings up 23 percent to $4.60 per share, in line with expectations. Assets reached $19.8 billion and would be $22 billion with the Bankers Trust acquisition. McColl was "very pleased . . . with another year of improved profitability and well-planned growth."

The Texas Coup

In December 1987, NCNB, then the 18th largest U.S. bank with $29 billion in assets, found itself short of opportunities for further acquisitions. Targets above $10 billion were considered too large and those below $1 billion were felt to be too small to have any impact. NCNB's chief strategic planner, Frank Gentry, considered there was a candidate pool of only 20 southeastern banks for NCNB to acquire, some not in good markets. The idea of considering wider options, such as savings and loans or insolvent banks, was discussed.

First RepublicBank, a Texas bank which was the 13th largest in the nation with 171 offices, was on the FDIC's list of troubled banks because of the depressed Texas economy and other problems. In March 1988, the FDIC put $1 billion into First Republic as it sought a solution. A number of large banks became interested, including Citicorp and Wells Fargo. Gentry and John Mack, NCNB treasurer, had McColl's support in examining some role for NCNB, though McColl considered the odds slim. As the smallest bank bidding, they knew their plan must be innovative and kept secret to win. The other potential buyers planned to divide First Republic into a "good" bank and "bad" bank, and buy only the "good" one. This would leave the FDIC the expensive task of liquidating the "bad" one. NCNB offered to acquire the whole bank, 20 percent at once and the rest over five years. A key feature would be NCNB getting tax credits for First Republic's operating losses. This was considered impossible in the legal opinion of the trade journals and New York lawyers. A Charlotte tax lawyer thought it was possible.

In April 1988, Gentry, accompanied by McColl, went on an early negotiating trip to the FDIC in Washington. Gentry noted "the staff guy was shocked when Hugh walked in." A question that would require a decision arose and the staff man said only the FDIC chairman could decide the point. McColl replied, "Well, is he here?" Soon they met face to face discussing their positions. An FDIC official told *Business—North Carolina* in January 1989: "McColl's presence made a difference. I don't think John Reed [Citicorp's chairman] or Wells Fargo's guy ever came by and said, 'We're interested,' at least at that stage of negotiation."

Examination of feasibility went forward in absolute secrecy. Earlier Ross Perot, the Texas billionaire, had been approached by First Republic and briefly considered buying the bank. Lacking banking expertise, he thought of the man he would want for the task, Hugh McColl. He had met and befriended McColl earlier in the year at a dinner in Charlotte. Perot soon dropped the idea but later played an important role by guaranteeing NCNB's $210 million offer.

In June, the IRS ruled in favor of NCNB on the tax credit issue and then only the FDIC's decision remained. One of the three directors of the FDIC who would decide which offer to take was C. C. Hope, retired head of FUNB. He could help or hurt. Ultimately he would vouch for the depth of NCNB's management.

As the time for a decision approached, NCNB prepared to move fast. They wanted to have an NCNB person at all 171 Texas offices on the first day to reassure everyone that they did not plan to make any major changes. After three false starts, on Thursday, July 28, McColl briefed 200 employees in Charlotte for two hours and sent them off to Texas to wait. On Friday, McColl waited nervously at his command center in the Dallas Sheraton. By noon he began to worry that NCNB had lost. At 12:00 the call came: "Your bank has been selected." By 1:30 P.M. all but seven NCNB people were at the branches and all were in place by 3:30 P.M. A few days later, Buddy Kemp, the NCNB executive chosen to head the Texas operation, sent a yellow rose to each First Republic employee.

William Dougherty, who left NCNB in 1982 when McColl won out in the competition to head NCNB, told *Business—North Carolina* in June 1989, "He has put his job on the line. If he pulls it off, he could be the banker of the century, not just the decade." In its May 15, 1989 issue, *U.S. News & World Report* summed it up:

> NCNB's biggest banking coup came last year in acquiring insolvent First RepublicBank of Dallas with the aid of the Federal Deposit Insurance Corporation. Frank Gentry, NCNB's director of corporate planning, calls it the "banking deal of the century." For $210 million, NCNB bought 20 percent of the biggest bank in Texas and received options to buy the rest for another $840 million. For a relative pittance, NCNB has acquired effective control of the bank, all the assets unclouded by bad loans, nearly $2 billion in tax credits and generous incentives to help the FDIC recoup some of the $10 billion in loans that went sour. NCNB's giant foothold in Texas has given it tremendous advantages at just the right time. The state's economy is beginning to recover from its energy-based depression; branch banking, long prohibited in the state, is now allowed, and NCNB Texas has been able to lend aggressively, becoming the biggest lender in the state at a time when other Texas banks have been financially hobbled. If NCNB buys the rest of First Republic, it will become the 10th-largest bank holding company in the country. Its Texas earnings will account for 60 percent of its profits by 1992, estimates Bear Stearns banking analyst Mark Alpert. The deal has already fattened NCNB's bottom line in 1989 and has driven its stock price up by 50 percent to nearly $40 a share.

By 1990 the First RepublicBank acquisition had propelled NCNB into seventh place among the 25 largest U.S. bank holding companies (see Exhibit 2).

INTO A NEW DECADE

In April 1989, NCNB made a try for C&S of Atlanta. McColl reportedly told C&S chairman, Bennett Brown, "You have three hours to answer, or I will launch my missiles." A few hours later couriers delivered letters from NCNB across the Southeast to C&S's 15 directors. McColl insisted the offer was friendly but C&S resisted and refused to negotiate. NCNB's planner, Gentry, said, "We felt it was time to move ahead; if something is worth doing, sooner is better than later." A merger "would be bad for our shareholders, bad for our bank, bad for our community, and bad for the banking industry," C&S's chairman declared. C&S resisted the takeover attempt with the aid of Georgia's antitakeover provisions, including staggered directors' terms, arguing that NCNB shouldn't be able to use its Texas tax breaks to finance the offer and that NCNB's stock was overpriced. However, NCNB's offer represented a 36 percent premium over C&S's current stock value, and C&S executives feared that the institutional investors that held 47 percent of C&S's stock might vote to accept the offer. NCNB's stock fell about 10 percent during the first two weeks of the battle. A C&S employee pointed out that the cultures of the organizations were entirely opposite. Within a few days NCNB gave up trying to overcome C&S's opposition. In McColl's view, "We offered them an exciting and unique opportunity. We are going to make a lot of money here in the Southeast. We're going to make a lot of money in Texas, and we're going to keep it for ourselves."

Business Week saw the pursuit of C&S as evidence of pressure for NCNB to keep up its earnings momentum with whatever acquisitions remained in the

EXHIBIT 2   **Top 25 Bank Holding Companies, 1990**   *(Based on total assets as of March 31, 1990; assets in billions and net income in millions)*

Asset Rank 3/31/90	Asset Rank 12/31/89		Total Assets		Percent Change	First-Quarter Net Income		Percent Change
			3/31/90	12/31/89		1990	1989	
1	1	**Citicorp,** New York	$233.1	$230.6	+1.1	$231.0	$529.0	−56.4
2	2	**Chase Manhattan Corp.,** New York	106.5	107.4	− 0.8	44.0	132.0	−66.7
3	3	**BankAmerica Corp.,** San Francisco	101.1	98.8	+2.3	218.0	208.0	+4.8
4	4	**J. P. Morgan & Co.,** New York	90.8	89.0	+2.0	399.0	179.6	+122.2
5	5	**Security Pacific Corp.,** Los Angeles	86.5	83.9	+3.1	188.4	179.3	+5.1
6	6	**Chemical Banking Corp.,** New York	74.2	71.5	+3.8	151.7	117.9	+28.7
7	7	**NCNB Corp.,** Charlotte, N.C.	63.7	66.2	−3.8	140.1	75.8	+84.8
8	8	**Manufacturers Hanover Corp.,** New York	59.7	60.5	−1.3	96.0	103.0	−6.8
9	10	**Bankers Trust New York Corp.**	59.3	55.7	+6.5	198.0	164.3	+20.5
10	9	**First Interstate Bancorp.,** Los Angeles	57.4	59.1	−2.9	92.1	94.3	−2.3
11	12	**Wells Fargo & Co.,** San Francisco	50.2	48.7	+ 3.1	159.8	141.5	+12.9
12	13	**First Chicago Corp.**	50.0	47.9	+ 4.4	68.5	124.7	−45.0
13	11	**Bank of New York Co., Inc.**	47.8	48.9	−2.2	102.3	101.1	+ 1.2
14	14	**PNC Financial Corp.,** Pittsburgh	46.6	45.7	+ 2.0	74.5	123.6	−39.7
15	17	**First Union Corp.,** Charlotte, N.C.	39.1	32.1	+21.8	77.6	72.2	+ 7.5
16	15	**Bank of Boston Corp.**	37.3	39.2	−4.8	43.6	89.1	−51.1

Source: Earnings releases from the companies. **Net income** is income after taxes and minority interest but before preferred dividends and extraordinary items; income from discontinued operations is excluded. First-quarter net income for 1989 is as reported in 1989. **Total assets** for Dec. 31, 1989, are as originally reported and have not been restated for mergers, changes in accounting practices, etc.

Compiled by American Banker. Copyright 1990.

Southeast. *United States Banker* reported NCNB had captured the imagination of investors worldwide with its aggressive interstate expansion, resulting in its stock price having one of the highest price-earnings multiples of any bank, 12 against an average of 9.6 for the seven largest southeastern banks. They noted employees and directors held 20 percent of NCNB's shares. During 1989 NCNB increased its capital base by $1.65 billion, taking on $880 million in new long-term debt and selling 15 million new shares of common stock for $700 million. Approximately $1 billion was used to complete the purchase of the remaining 80 percent of the Texas banks, giving NCNB $3 billion in tax-loss carryovers.

In NCNB's 1989 annual report, Hugh McColl said, "The 1980s will be remembered as the decade the company built the foundation for a national financial service company" and pointed out with pride that during the 1980s shareholders had received a yearly compound growth rate of 21.1 percent in stock price and 13.5 percent in dividends. But the 1990s promised rigorous

Asset Rank 3/31/90	Asset Rank 12/31/89		Total Assets		Percent Change	First-Quarter Net Income		Percent Change
			3/31/90	12/31/89		1990	1989	
17	16	**Fleet/Norstar Financial Group Inc.,** Providence, R.I.	36.5	33.4	+9.3	(98.1)	92.4	−206.2
18	19	**SunTrust Banks Inc.,** Atlanta	30.9	31.0	−0.3	87.9	84.0	+4.6
19	18	**Mellon Bank Corp.,** Pittsburgh	30.8	31.5	−2.2	65.0	53.0	−22.6
20	20	**First Fidelity Bancorp.,** Newark, N.J.	30.2	30.7	−1.6	21.1	61.9	−65.9
21	23	**Barnett Banks Inc.,** Jacksonville, Fla.	29.3	29.0	+1.0	15.5	62.4	−75.2
22	22	**Continental Bank Corp.,** Chicago	29.0	29.5	−1.7	56.7	75.6	−25.0
23	26	**Banc One Corp.,** Columbus, Ohio	27.2	26.6	+2.3	101.8	87.2	+16.7
24	28	**Republic New York Corp.**	26.2	25.5	+2.7	44.5	41.8	+6.5
25	27	**NBD Bancorp., Inc.,** Detroit	25.7	25.8	−0.4	66.6	63.5	+4.9
		Totals for the top 25	$1,469.1	$1,448.2	+1.4	$2,650.7	$3,057.2	−13.3
Dropping out of the Top 25								
26	25	**Marine Midland Banks Inc.,** Buffalo, N.Y.	25.7	27.1	−5.2	6.0	31.7	−81.1
29	24	**Shawmut National Corp.,** Hartford, Conn.	24.9	27.9	−0.8	32.1*	64.7	−50.4
30	21	**Bank of New England Corp.,** Boston	24.9	29.8	−16.4	(46.6)	42.3	−210.2
Pro Forma Ranking-Merger in Progress								
12	13	**Avantor Financial Corp.**[†]	49.5	44.7	+10.7	128.2	119.7	+7.1

*Excludes an $8.5 million extraordinary credit arising from the utilization of a net operating loss carry-forward.

[†]On 9/25/89, Citizens and Southern Corp., Atlanta, and Sovran Financial Corp., Norfolk, Va., announced a definitive agreement to merge. The deal, expected to be completed at the end of the third quarter, will create Avantor Financial Corp.

challenges in banking. NCNB's Rusty Page predicted the 13,000 U.S. banks would be reduced to 1,500. Kenneth Guenther of the Independent Bankers Association described 1990 to the *Charlotte Observer* as a lull before the storm, "a transitional year looking to cataclysmic banking legislation in 1991." Deregulation had removed the profit protection that banking had enjoyed and bank managers took increasing risks to hold onto profits, sometimes unwisely. Over 1,000 banks had failed in the last 10 years, costing the government over $20 billion. In that time the top-10 U.S. banks wrote off $40 billion in bad loans, while earning less than $30 billion. The cost of the savings and loan debacle was raising questions about the government's role in insuring deposits. Regulators were reviewing banks' portfolios to see that reserves were truly in line with the amount of risk. Most banks were already moving to increase reserves to handle "nonperforming" assets (bad loans). Some analysts saw banking at the start of a multiyear decline.

As 1990 unfolded, NCNB continued to make new acquisitions. In late 1989 NCNB had acquired a $3.5 billion savings and loan in Houston and Austin from the government's Resolution Trust Corporation. In June 1990, it won a bidding battle for nine insolvent banks in the San Antonio area, making NCNB Texas the largest bank in Texas. There was talk that NCNB was preparing to make a private placement of $150 million in preferred stock in anticipation of buying Florida's largest S&L. In addition, a realignment of senior management was completed in which a senior executive was put in charge of each line of business, such as real estate or trusts, instead of a geographical region. Thus Ken Lewis, president of NCNB Texas in Dallas, was responsible for real estate lending wherever it occurred. McColl saw the opportunities for the 1990s to be in fee-income business and nontraditional lines, such as investment banking and trust activity. Against the challenges, McColl saw opportunities. He told stockholders: "Now is not the time to rest. The thing we must guard against is complacency—believing we have arrived. Actually, we still have a long way to go."

Exhibits 3, 4, and 5 present NCNB's financial statements and recent financial performance measures.

EXHIBIT 3   NCNB's Consolidated Statement of Income, 1988–1990
(Dollars in thousands except per-share information)

	Year Ended December 31		
	1988	**1989**	**1990**
Income from earning assets			
Interest and fees on loans	$ 1,851,394	$ 3,776,266	$ 3,845,175
Lease financing income	23,750	31,379	34,408
Interest and dividends on taxable investment securities	352,266	987,623	1,398,573
Interest on investment securities exempt from federal income taxes	78,493	71,088	13,357
Time deposits placed	60,374	200,285	212,532
Federal funds sold	50,784	123,031	73,531
Securities purchased under agreements to resell	31,321	55,808	60,663
Trading account securities	16,069	46,449	89,243
Total income from earning assets	2,464,451	5,291,929	5,727,482
Interest expense			
Deposits	1,039,758	2,830,638	2,963,678
Borrowed funds	472,844	1,074,699	1,096,875
Capital leases and long-term debt	54,165	107,265	154,737
Special Asset Division net funding allocation		(423,553)	(304,019)
Total interest expense	1,566,767	3,589,049	3,911,271
Net interest income	897,684	1,702,880	1,816,211
Provision for credit losses			
Bank provision	121,538	239,123	505,003
Loans transferred to Special Asset Division		216,699	67,474
Assistance from FDIC		(216,699)	(67,474)
Total provision for credit losses	121,538	239,123	505,003
Net credit income	776,146	1,463,757	1,311,208
Noninterest income	369,055	860,517	954,781
Noninterest expense	814,806	1,692,042	1,888,108
Income before taxes and FDIC interest in earnings of NCNB Texas	330,395	632,232	377,881
Special Asset Division			
Net adjustment for asset valuation allowance		(332,390)	(81,023)
Other net costs		(616,445)	(438,076)
Assistance from FDIC		948,835	519,099
Net costs associated with Special Asset Division		—	—
Earnings			
Income before taxes and FDIC interest in earnings of NCNB Texas	330,395	632,232	377,881
Income tax expense	77,924	68,999	12,182
Income before FDIC interest in earnings of NCNB Texas	252,471	563,233	365,699
FDIC interest in earnings of NCNB Texas		(116,164)	
Net income	$ 252,471	$ 447,069	$ 365,699
Net income available to common shareholders	$ 247,371	$ 427,069	$ 345,699
Earnings per common share			
Primary	$ 2.90	$ 4.62	$ 3.40
Fully diluted	$ 2.87	$ 4.44	$ 3.34
Dividends per common share	$ .94	$ 1.10	$ 1.42
Average common shares outstanding			
Primary	85,210,165	92,491,551	101,781,704
Fully diluted	88,269,581	100,791,654	109,694,119

Source: 1990 Annual Report.

EXHIBIT 4 **NCNB's Consolidated Balance Sheet, 1989 and 1990**
(Dollars in thousands)

	December 31	
	1989	1990
Assets		
Cash and cash equivalents	$ 4,111,26	$ 4,044,843
Time deposits placed	2,965,799	789,922
Investment securities, at cost (market value—$16,046,617 and $16,272,532). .	16,169,782	15,894,082
Trading account securities	392,300	112,055
Federal funds sold	46,198	11,950
Securities purchased under agreements to resell	175,434	138,025
Loans, net of unearned income of $370,399 and $310,080	33,998,895	36,714,601
Leases, net	410,247	391,427
Loans and leases, net of unearned income	34,409,142	37,106,028
Less: Allowance for credits losses	(465,469)	(670,388)
Net loans and leases	33,943,673	36,435,640
Premises, equipment and lease rights, net	956,539	1,132,009
Customers' acceptance liability	420,690	500,316
Interest receivable	668,734	596,417
Goodwill	285,377	291,381
Core deposit and other intangibles	305,510	528,266
Other assets	1,049,844	1,169,408
Special Asset Division assets	4,699,615	3,640,201
	$66,190,763	$65,284,515
Liabilities and Shareholders' Equity		
Deposits:		
Demand	$ 8,439,356	$ 8,939,229
Savings	15,938,760	17,860,525
Time.	22,049,163	21,696,051
Foreign	2,149,066	1,726,225
Total deposits	48,576,345	50,222,030
Borrowed funds:		
Federal funds purchased	3,773,095	2,990,735
Securities sold under agreements to repurchase	5,584,375	2,885,327
Commercial paper	174,413	401,659
Other notes payable	2,202,946	2,555,807
Total borrowed funds	11,734,829	8,833,528
Obligations under capital leases	35,424	32,608
Acceptances outstanding	420,690	500,316
Accrued expenses and other liabilities	1,031,862	823,858
Long-term debt	1,430,086	1,664,441
Total liabilities.	63,229,236	62,076,781
Contingent liabilities and other financial commitments		
Shareholders' Equity		
Preferred stock, no par value, $50 liquidation value, $1 designated as stated capital: authorized—15,000,000 shares; issued—5,000,000 shares	250,000	250,000
Common stock, $2.50 par value: authorized—250,000,000 shares; issued— 102,861,169 and 101,225,242 shares	1,383,953	1,425,699
Undivided profits	1,369,526	1,570,696
Other.	(41,952)	(38,661)
Total shareholders' equity	2,961,527	3,207,734
	$66,190,763	$65,284,515

Source: 1990 Annual Report.

EXHIBIT 5   **Financial Performance Statistics for NCNB Corp., 1985–1990**

	1985	1986	1987	1988	1989	1990
Taxable-equivalent yields earned						
Loans and leases, net of unearned income:						
Commercial	11.20%	9.65%	9.40%	10.02%	11.85%	10.37%
Real estate—construction	11.59	9.43	9.21	10.22	11.88	10.61
Real estate—commercial mortgage*					10.80	10.15
Real estate—residential mortgage	11.89	11.56	10.63	10.25	10.70	10.46
Consumer	13.81	12.57	11.29	11.19	11.68	11.70
Bank card	15.97	19.02	17.61	17.67	16.59	15.70
Lease financing	14.56	9.90	8.33	8.53	7.92	9.03
Foreign loans	9.94	9.64	7.74	12.27	11.53	10.75
Total loans and leases, net	11.93	10.75	10.12	10.71	11.77	10.87
Investment securities	11.07	9.79	8.52	8.44	9.10	8.87
Total earning assets	11.39	10.13	9.49	9.97	10.90	10.10
Rates paid						
Savings and interest-bearing demand deposits	6.32	5.45	4.92	5.09	6.08	6.02
Time deposits	9.00	7.56	6.83	7.43	8.71	7.98
Foreign time deposits	9.10	7.73	7.28	7.98	9.78	9.08
Total savings and time deposits	7.87	6.64	6.04	6.53	7.88	7.23
Commercial paper	8.43	6.71	6.55	7.49	9.21	8.01
Long-term debt	11.68	10.99	9.80	9.73	10.31	9.94
Total interest-bearing liabilities	7.98	6.70	6.25	6.81	8.22	7.49
Profit margins						
Domestic spread	3.62	3.64	3.45	3.20	2.83	2.75
Foreign spread	1.37	0.70	0.02	2.08	0.01	(.19)
Consolidated spread	3.41	3.43	3.24	3.16	2.68	2.61
Domestic net interest yield	4.71	4.42	4.15	3.88	3.79	3.38
Foreign net interest yield	1.47	0.83	0.21	2.49	0.50	0.75
Consolidated net interest yield	4.43	4.17	3.91	3.83	3.61	3.25
Year-end data (Dollars in millions)						
Loans and leases, net of unearned income	$12,134	$15,765	$17,087	$18,908	$34,409	$37,106
Investment securities	3,336	5,653	6,826	4,727	16,170	15,894
Time deposits placed	979	1,630	855	963	2,966	790
Total earning assets	17,255	24,065	25,491	26,101	54,159	54,052
Total assets, excluding Special Asset Division	19,754	27,472	28,915	29,848	61,491	61,644
Demand deposits	3,354	4,510	3,862	3,913	8,439	8,939
Domestic savings and time deposits	9,396	12,542	14,383	15,900	37,988	39,557
Foreign time deposits	1,200	1,467	1,305	857	2,149	1,726
Total savings and time deposits	10,596	14,009	15,688	16,757	40,137	41,283
Total deposits	13,950	18,519	19,550	20,670	48,576	50,222
Borrowed funds	3,767	6,596	6,542	5,899	11,735	8,834
Obligations under capital leases	33	36	35	36	35	33
Long-term debt	401	537	533	457	1,430	1,664
Total shareholders' equity	1,039	1,309	1,510	1,942	2,962	3,208

*Commercial mortgage loans were included with commercial loans for 1988 and previous years.

E X H I B I T 5   **(Concluded)**

	1985	1986	1987	1988	1989	1990
Earnings ratios						
Return on average:						
Total assets[†]	0.92%	0.84%	0.62%	0.88%	1.01%	0.57%
Earning asset[‡]	1.06	0.95	0.71	0.99	1.14	0.64
Common shareholders' equity	17.23	16.31	11.70	15.55	20.45	12.01
Net income as a percentage of net interest income	23.98	22.82	18.22	25.78	25.13	19.72
Asset quality						
At year-end:						
Nonperforming assets as a percentage of net loans and leases and foreclosed properties	1.20	1.10	1.67	1.13	1.29	2.54
Nonperforming assets as a percentage of total assets[‡]	0.74	0.63	0.99	0.72	0.73	1.54
Nonperforming assets (in millions)	$146	$173	$286	$215	$446	$948
Capital ratios						
Common shareholders' equity as a percentage of total assets at year-end[‡]	5.26	4.76	5.22	5.67	4.41	4.80
Dividend payout ratio (per common share)	29.78	30.83	42.36	32.41	23.81	41.76
Shareholders' equity per common share:						
Average	$13.35	$15.50	$17.38	$18.67	$22.58	$28.28
Other statistics						
Number of full-time employees (not restated for acquisitions)	9,981	12,107	12,334	12,979	27,002	28,393
Average foreign assets as a percentage of average total assets	9.13	6.78	6.92	4.37	5.70	4.90
Market price of common stock:						
High for the year	$23⅝	$27¾	$29⅛	$29⅛	$55	$47¼
Low for the year	17	20	15½	17½	27	16⅞
Close at the end of the year	22⅝	21½	17¼	27¼	46¼	22⅞
Number of shareholders of record	21,004	28,732	29,789	29,344	29,064	30,824

[†]Includes FDIC's interest in earnings of NCNB Texas for 1989; excludes Special Asset Division assets.
[‡]Excludes Special Asset Division assets.
Source: 1990 Annual Report.

NATIONAL WESTMINSTER BANK USA

Charles Smith, Hofstra University

When Bill Knowles, then an executive vice president at Bankers Trust in New York, was first called by a corporate headhunter in 1981 with an offer to become the chief executive officer (CEO) of National Bank of North America (NBNA), Knowles said he wasn't interested. Two years earlier, NBNA had been acquired by National Westminster Bank Group, a London-based international financial institution with assets of more than $110 billion. NBNA was the result of more than 20 mergers and acquisitions in the 1950s and 60s, structured around Meadow Brook National Bank, a well-run bank that had built a strong presence on Long Island and expanded into New York City and Westchester. However, over a period of many years, NBNA was reputed to have become bureaucratic, depersonalized, and lacking in direction.

Knowles' initial response had no doubt been influenced by the fact that NBNA had been known to be a marginal bank in the very competitive New York marketplace. No doubt his hesitation was reinforced by his strong roots in Bankers Trust, where he was well compensated, recognized as successful, and had as secure a career position as one could ask for. Still, Knowles was intrigued by NBNA's need for strategic planning and cultural redirection, and understood that its new parent bank would be willing to give him a relatively free hand and the space he needed to run things as he saw fit.

Eventually he reconsidered the offer and accepted the job, later confessing that he was also excited by the challenge of a David-and-Goliath situation: NBNA being 11th in size among New York City banks and heading for direct competition in some markets with Chase, Chemical Bank, and Citibank—the industry's giants. He had a hope, which has since become a conviction, that the bank could become a dynamic organization, a good place to work, and outperform its competitors in target markets.

THE EARLY DAYS: SYSTEMS IN PLACE AND INITIAL CHANGES

In his first few months at NBNA, Knowles listened and observed. For one thing, he found himself with a lot of good people and saw some changes already under way. He also found that the bank badly needed a clear mission and a strong corporate culture. Its market needed to be defined more clearly; and from the customer's perspective, working with the bank needed to become simpler and more straightforward. The bank was run through a complex set of checks and balances, and most decisions were made by committees that met almost continuously. Its bureaucratic system allowed for little risk-taking and encouraged political behavior, while control was in the hands of the auditors and staff functionaries. NatWest USA President Bob Wallace recalled some of the early problems:

> Our good officers were frustrated by rules that seemed designed to guard the bank against its own customers. Endless procedural crosschecks made it difficult to put a loan on the books. The emphasis had been on control rather than on

371

service, and line officers couldn't present the bank nor themselves in a positive manner. There were attitude problems. In one instance, a senior officer held up approval of a floor plan for the relocation of his division until he succeeded in adding three feet to his own office. Little kingdoms flourished. There was poor communication between groups, even when it was necessary for the conduct of business. Information was viewed as a source of power and wasn't shared freely.

Clerical employees got no consideration at all. Several of us were shown the site of a processing operation. It was a room without windows, with inadequate lighting, and the paint was peeling off the walls. The officer in charge took pride that it had a low occupancy expense, and was shocked when we told him it would have to be corrected immediately. . . .

Coming in late and leaving early were not causes for reprimand and counseling. Arriving late for meetings had become the standard because they never started on time anyway. There was no sense of urgency. . . .

In some areas, form was more important than substance. The best example was a system purchased to track officer calls on customers. It offered many features, including grouping customers by geographic area, sales size, and the success of the calling effort. However, the bank had only bought the module that accounted for the actual number of calls made, using information from the system for employee performance reviews. It didn't take a genius to realize that what mattered was the number of calls made, rather than the results [of the calls]. The system, needless to say, got an early burial. . . .

All of our contacts with the calling officers convinced us that they did not have a winning mentality. They questioned the value of bringing in new business. They assumed that if we had won the business away from another bank, it had to be tainted. There were no rewards for introducing a new relationship to the bank . . . but there were certainly penalties if something went wrong.

Nevertheless, Knowles did find some positive elements with which to work. The new ownership held to its hands-off policy and provided support and encouragement. Also, there were talented people in the organization who knew how to get things done despite the rules, and who later became valued contributors to the new culture.

Bill Knowles' first task was to describe the values and direction he felt should be operative. He prepared a detailed statement of mission and strategy he hoped would be understandable and relevant at every level in the organization. The statement identified a two-phase transition strategy, intended to first install a solid infrastructure, then build a consistently profitable and competitive bank. In a departure from the past, the bank would concentrate on clearly defined markets, rather than endeavor to be a full-service operation. The bank's Statement of Values and Mission is presented in Exhibit 1.

Knowles also set goals for return on assets (ROA) and return on equity (ROE) at levels that would make NatWest USA's performance comparable to its competitors—Irving Trust, The Bank of New York, Marine Midland, and European American Bank.

In the mission statement, Knowles emphasized the need to gain respect in the financial community; to develop first-class talent; to become more efficient and cost-conscious; to push decision making downward; and to develop group effectiveness, cooperation, and team spirit.

By identifying core businesses and setting financial goals, Knowles created a standard by which success could be measured, and established a time frame within which the goals could be reached. These goals would put NatWest at the high end of New York banks.

EXHIBIT 1   NatWest's Statement of Values and Mission

THE NATWEST WAY:
Our Values, Mission, and Commitment to Quality

The Statement of Values

At National Westminster Bank USA we share values that both support our Mission Statement and commit us to excellence in fulfilling the needs of our customers, the communities we serve, our parent organization, and ourselves.

Customers

Our customers are the foundation of our business. We listen to their needs and respond in a manner that is timely, straightforward, and courteous. We earn our future with them through leadership in quality and service.

Communities

The prosperity and well-being of the communities in which we live and work are fundamental to our long-term success. Therefore, we commit to serve them by providing leadership and support that enrich the overall quality of life.

Parent

The National Westminster Bank Group has entrusted us with capital and its good name. We commit to invest these resources prudently, to earn a superior return, and to work in partnership with our parent to enhance its worldwide stature.

Ourselves

We, the employees, are the strength of the bank and the source of its character. We work together to foster an open environment where trust and caring prevail. Pride and enjoyment come from commitment, leadership by example, and accomplishment. We encourage personal growth and ensure opportunity based on performance.

We recognize our individual responsibility to uphold these values, and in turn, to enhance the bank's reputation rooted in integrity, achievement, and quality.

The Mission Statement

The Mission Statement is the strategic translation of the Statement of Values. It is more specific, converting the value system into goals and programs.

Mission

As the principal banking vehicle of the NatWest Group in the United States, our mission is to serve the overall marketing and operational requirements of the group in this country. In doing so, we achieve profitable growth and an enhanced reputation.

To fulfill this mission we must continue to see ourselves not as a full-service, across-the-board competitor of the largest money-center banks in every market, but rather as a significant competitor in what we regard as our core businesses. In addition, we must continue to develop the considerable potential for synergy that exists with our parent, in international markets as well as in this country.

Customers

We are in four core businesses. In each of these core markets two fundamental precepts apply: our commitment to relationship banking and the essential responsibility of our support units to provide high-quality, low-cost service.

Consumer

In this market, an area of traditional strength, we seek a stable and increasing source of core deposits that can be invested at an acceptable spread. We are relatively well-positioned for this with a sizable branch network, including offices in some key locations in New York City and substantial coverage in the desirable suburban counties surrounding it.

We will compete not by attempting to gain market share through the introduction of product breakthroughs, but by offering superior personal service, coupled with a competitive line of both deposit and consumer credit products introduced in a timely manner.

Commercial lending and deposit responsibility for companies with sales of up to $10 million is an important element of our consumer business. Commercial business adds a significant dimension to what was formerly a purely retail approach, and is aimed at enabling us to use our branch system more efficiently.

Middle Market

The middle market continues to be one of the natural markets for NatWest USA. By our definition, it consists of companies with annual sales ranging between $10 million and $250 million, located primarily within a 100-mile radius of New York City, as well as companies on a selective basis throughout the country wherever we can serve them effectively. We compete by meeting the credit needs of customers in a responsive and flexible manner, and by bringing specialty services—particularly trust, treasury, cash management, and trade finance—to middle-market companies in a more effective way than do other major banks.

Customers (*Continued*)

Corporate

Together with our parent, we have developed a rational and effective way for the group to approach the enormous corporate market on a national basis. NatWest PLC is responsible for multinational companies and for servicing certain specialized-industry customers on behalf of London. Other than these, NatWest USA is responsible for the national market. We address this on a niche basis, both as to industry and geography, through our network of regional offices. Here again, our specialized support services—cash management, trust, treasury, and trade finance—play a key role in our ability to compete effectively against money-center as well as regional banks.

International

Although we will continue to service the well-established and profitable public and quasi-public sectors, our mission in international is to increasingly concentrate on activities that more directly serve the offshore needs of our domestic customer base. These are principally credit and noncredit transactions that facilitate foreign trade.

Further, we will continue to build on our strengths in correspondent banking, and from that base expand selectively into private sector lending if margins are acceptable. Our areas of particular expertise are Latin America and the Far East. In Europe, we utilize the capabilities of our parent to a greater extent. Our international strategy reflects, in a complementary way, our role within the worldwide coverage of the NatWest Group.

Communities

We derive business and our profits from the communities in which we operate. Therefore, we acknowledge a responsibility to invest in those communities to keep them vigorous and attractive. This goes beyond mere compliance with the Community Reinvestment Act. It involves active participation by our staff, as well as direct financial support.

Parent

Because we have been entrusted with our parent's name, we have a responsibility to enhance its reputation in all we do, as well as to achieve a superior financial return.

We expect to achieve this year—two years ahead of schedule—the 60-basis-point return on assets (ROA) goal set forth in the original 1981 Mission Statement. Our new goal is 70 basis points by 1988. In comparing our performance, we continue to regard Bank of New York, Marine Midland, and European American Bank as our peers.

Ourselves

The internal environment we seek, as outlined in the Statement of Values, rests on a set of strategies, policies, and programs that are fundamental in our bank:

- An uncompromising insistence on quality people.
- A pay-for-performance policy which has application bankwide as well as individually.
- A standard of excellence in communications.
- A lean organizational structure, free of redundant staff layers, to encourage individual initiative and decision making.
- A willingness by supervisors and managers to be judged on how well they foster the desired environment in their areas.

Quality Program

The bank's commitment to quality is thoroughgoing and long term. It is how we intend to differentiate ourselves and, at the same time, achieve a cost advantage over our competitors. In addition, customers are willing to pay a premium for high-quality services.

Customers

The everyday things we do to better serve customers are obvious, but they bear repeating. These actions apply to everyone because, even where there is not direct customer contact, everything we do is related to service customers:

- We listen to our customers to determine their needs and then attempt to fill those needs.
- We respond in a thoughtful, professional, and timely manner.
- We deliver our products and services error free and in a consistent manner.
- We price our products and services fairly.
- We are always respectful and courteous.
- We do our work in essential staff areas as cost effectively as possible, because we invest our principal resources in customer-driven activities.

Quality Program (*Concluded*)

Communities

In all our community activities we seek to reflect the bank's commitment to quality and excellence while helping others.

This is a dimension of our job that goes beyond day-to-day duties. It involves community services: giving generously to United Way, donating blood, and taking leadership roles in significant community organizations.

We furnish substantial community support on the corporate level as well. Our contributions budget has grown each year and provides major funding for education, health care, community welfare, and the arts. In addition, we have chosen to direct significant portions of our corporate communications budget to sponsorship of quality arts projects.

Parent

Superior quality in everything we do is the only way to meet the dual responsibility we have to our parent of enhancing its reputation and meeting our financial goals.

High-quality work is key to enhancing the NatWest name. But it is also critical to achieving our new financial goal, because we must do this by improving margins rather than by expanding assets. Quality banking involves several things:

- Wider lending and investing spreads.
- Increased fee and service-charge income, which can be expected if we deliver quality products consistently.
- Expanded demand deposits.
- Higher credit quality, resulting in lower credit costs and fewer nonperforming loans and charge-offs.
- Reduced tax liability.

An additional element that enhances our reputation as a quality institution and ensures that we achieve our goals is consistent prudence both in the extension of credit and in our asset/liability management activities.

Ourselves

The competence, dedication, and hard work of our staff are the essential ingredients in our success. We need quality people. Therefore, we are very selective in hiring, and take training and promotion from within very seriously.

We closely monitor salary and benefit trends and seek to be fully competitive, increasing compensation levels in relation to those of our peers as the performance of the bank improves. On an individual level, we reward according to the contribution.

We have developed a variety of programs to improve communication: an expanded NewsBeam, staff and management bulletins, staff meetings, special surveys, and the like. We constantly seek new ways to increase communication at all levels of the bank.

We encourage leadership by example, creating an environment that is caring, trusting, fair, and enjoyable.

By doing quality work, each of us contributes directly to achieving the bank's goals. In the process, we also foster a stimulating work environment and enhance our individual well-being.

Some thought the new CEO appeared overly optimistic. At a time when the only earnings on the bank's income statement were coming from tax credits, Knowles called for a benchmark ROA of .60 percent by 1987. The targeted ROA was reached in 1985—two years ahead of schedule—and surpassed in 1986. A comparison to 1981 when Knowles accepted the CEO post indicates the extent of the change—return on assets then was .22 percent.[1] A five-year financial summary is presented in Exhibit 2.

With markets well defined and staff functions altered and reduced, the bank set forth strategies to achieve new objectives. The major changes focused on two areas: developing a high-quality management team and developing a customer orientation emphasizing profitability rather than growth.

---

[1]Due to an increase in loan reserves of $295 million in 1987 (against loans to developing countries who were experiencing debt servicing problems) NatWest suffered a loss in 1987 of $212 million. Without the extraordinary item, the 1987 ROA would have been approximately .70 percent.

EXHIBIT 2   **Financial Highlights, National Westminster Bank USA, 1983–1987**
(*In thousands*)

	1983	1984	1985	1986	1987
For the year					
Net interest income	$234,878	$283,699	$336,175	$371,104	$394,125
Provision for loan losses	31,000	44,400	51,500	57,400	349,400
Noninterest income	61,745	81,494	96,187	110,020	130,109
Operating expenses	222,808	255,276	292,978	322,638	352,574
Net income (loss)	25,332	40,062	54,575	67,673	(212,008)
At year-end					
Assets	$7,470,847	$8,726,726	$9,796,328	$11,080,016	$11,539,277
Loans	4,631,661	5,679,582	6,415,038	7,363,751	8,216,356
Deposits:					
Core	3,578,957	4,642,772	5,145,869	6,174,877	6,372,288
Other	2,167,288	2,376,446	2,764,292	2,609,434	3,166,725
Equity capital	498,067	504,534	554,443	621,044	409,036

Source: 1987 Annual Report.

Knowles felt that a complete transformation of NatWest's internal culture was crucial to building a more customer-oriented bank. In his 1981 mission statement, he called for synergy, a less parochial focus on profit-center earnings, and the willingness of management to lead by example.

He communicated a sense of urgency, stressing that changes in corporate culture had to start at the top. Decision making was to be pushed down the line, and pleasing customers, instead of bank examiners, was underscored as paramount.

MANAGEMENT TRANSITIONS

In the 1981 statement, Knowles also tackled the sensitive issue of management personnel changes—changes necessary for more effective functioning and instilling a new culture. He felt senior management needed more qualified people, and recognized the need to go outside to find new managers. He recalls:

> I was very open with the staff about this. I said we were going to have to go outside because we were just too big a bank to be competitive without introducing additional talent. I said I would try to get it over with as quickly as possible, but that I needed a window of about a year to accomplish it. At the end of the year, we were able to limit outside hires to primarily specialists, tax lawyers, and so forth.

The following was part of his public statement, excerpted from the August 1981 Statement of Mission and Strategy:

> The single most important element that will enable us to compete more effectively in the future than we have in the past is people. We have to be uncompro-

mising in insisting on first-class talent, because if we don't have it, or grow it, we cannot move up. Neither our name nor our ownership can compensate for less than top-flight personnel who perform in a superior way. . . .

As a first step, therefore, we are identifying the 50 to 60 key jobs in the organization and determining if the incumbent either is or can operate at a superior performance level. If not, changes will be made. This does not imply a cold or heavy-handed approach to people. On the contrary, we should always conduct ourselves so as to demonstrate respect and compassion in our dealings with our staff. It does mean, however, that we will be rigorous in setting goals and measuring results, and rewarding those who can do the job or making changes where results are not satisfactory. . . .

Once the 50 to 60 key jobs are filled by people who meet high standards of performance as professionals and/or managers, they will serve as role models, and we will then attempt to build the organization by recruiting trainees and advancing people already here. We want to move away from the habit of going outside to fill our senior and even semisenior positions. This will have to be done for a while longer, but our goal is to "grow our own" in time.

Building from the Top Down

The grooming of the management team became the main focus of the transition. Knowles chose to bring in outsiders for two top-level positions: one to be the bank's chief operating officer (COO), the other to be the liaison with the NatWest parent organization. As COO, he brought in Bob Wallace, who had been CEO of an Oregon bank owned by a holding company. John Gale was brought in as the liaison, and the three formed a partnership under the heading Office of the Chairman, that, according to Knowles, "is based on trust, informality and candor. . . . We've developed into a team that represents the values we wanted to see projected throughout the bank."

Knowles, Wallace, and Gale met every Monday before their individual sector meetings and off-site at dinner every few weeks to discuss what was going on in their respective sectors.

The Office of the Chairman saw the selection of people as the key to success. They agreed that all outside hires, as well as internal promotions, had to buy into the new value system, and they held firmly to their standards.

Wallace recalled that, in their internal process, they found outstanding people a couple of levels down in the organization, people who'd gone unrecognized before, but who were able to flourish in the changing environment.

Some jobs did have to be filled from outside, and all three members of the Office of the Chairman interviewed candidates for positions at levels of vice presidents and above. In each case, they looked for people with compatible values. Wallace describes the selection and promotion criteria:

> We want people who are team players who want to work in an atmosphere of openness and caring. We may have made some mistakes with the professional skills of people brought in, but never on their values.
>
> At every opportunity, we promoted people who would be seen by their peers as apolitical. One of the first tasks was to pick four division heads for our United States Group. We reviewed the candidates, their qualifications, and chose the candidates who hadn't run a "campaign" for the job. This and other promotions gave a clear signal that politics were out.

Developing a Customer Orientation

Selection of the management team took place simultaneously with the bank's development of competitive strategies based on customer service. Wallace was instrumental in setting the tone for this aspect of the transition:

First, we had to get a good grip on the bank's strengths and weaknesses. We quickly concluded that the bank's senior officers should get out in the marketplace to sample our customer's attitudes, and evaluate the skill-level of our lending officers. While what follows may seem a litany of what was wrong with the bank, let me assure you that we were encouraged by the good things we found, including some excellent talent among our line officers.

We found product deficiencies that put us at a competitive disadvantage. . . . And we were troubled by the lack of value placed on the contact with customers.

For example, I once asked the head of one division to coordinate his calling with mine. He told me that would be easy, because he didn't call on customers. He viewed himself purely as an administrator, and he added that the bank knew that when he was hired. Unfortunately, while his statement was extreme, it was not inconsistent with the feelings of others. We had to show by example that customer contact was the most important job at the bank.

The three members of the Office of the Chairman emphasized their desire to make calls on customers. At first, we would be taken on safe calls where the customer wouldn't embarrass the officer or the bank by telling stories of inadequate levels of services. But before long, there was less screening of the names we called on. We are still calling on customers wherever it will do the most good in marketing the bank. More to the point, it is [now] recognized throughout the bank that you don't graduate form customer contact. It's the most important thing we do.

When we became serious about developing a customer-oriented atmosphere, changes were dramatic. It was like a dam breaking. We were literally flooded with information on why customers found us a difficult bank to deal with. On some of my early calls, I had found a key symptom of disregard for service. Officers simply did not listen to customers. Therefore, they never found out what customers wanted from the bank. Some of our officers acted as if they'd been sent in on a mission, and the customers better not get in their way. Today, one of the primary thrusts of our sales training is learning to listen. In addition, we have worked hard to change how people think about customer service. We emphasized that everyone in the bank has customers to serve; the support people's customers are the line people, and the line people, in turn, have external customers. It took repeated emphasis, but I think today most people have their priorities in order.

Changes Slow in Coming

Somewhat ironically, a lack of products had forced the bank's officers to develop extraordinary skills in the only area they had available to them: lending. Several parts of the bank were successful, driven by the ability to outperform competitors and to structure difficult credit transactions. In the area of lending, NatWest could function effectively because it was one area where officers did not have to depend on the performance of others in the organization.

In spite of an initial euphoria, some officers thought change was slow to come. Ed McDougal, formerly a line head and now executive vice president for human resources, recalled that his initial enthusiasm was dampened when he saw how attempts at action and decision making were continually swamped in bureaucracy. McDougal recalls:

> I found basically four types of people in the bank at that time. There were the cynics who said, "This, too, shall pass." There were the skeptics who said, "I'm all for it, but it will never work." Both of these groups suffered from a genuine inferiority complex about NBNA. The third group was a small corps of leaders who said, "Believe it." And finally we had a bunch of supporters who said, "Why not?" Many were young, and lacked experience. But they were smart, energetic, and ambitious, and had a real can-do attitude. In my opinion, we needed to convert the skeptics and develop the can-do people.

McDougal also recalled an informal talk with Knowles that kept him from becoming too discouraged. McDougal was then at a midmanager's level, five levels down in the organization. When Knowles would drop in once in a while at NatWest's midtown headquarters, he'd ask how things were going. McDougal would express his frustrations, and Knowles would encourage him and also share his own frustrations. Once he told McDougal, "You keep pushing from the bottom, and I'll keep pushing from the top. Someday, we'll meet in the middle."

When McDougal was finally promoted to department head, he began his push. One particular frustration for him was the lack of credit approval authority at the line level. The charter for his department said that the minimum loan the department could make was $250,000, yet the largest loan anyone could approve, himself included, was $250,000. In effect, despite being solely accountable for growing a loan portfolio, McDougal or his staff couldn't make any loans without someone else's approval.

It was clear the time had come to stop focusing on just the problems and get on with the job at hand. As McDougal said:

> I was tired of hearing about our limited product line and our cumbersome credit approval process. The time had come to do business and to celebrate some victories. It was September [1982]. We were in our budgeting cycle, and we put together a budget for 1983 that showed a 15 percent loan growth despite a three-year history of no growth. Also in September, as a tangible demonstration of our confidence and resolve, we scheduled a party for November, to celebrate the victories we would have over the next two and a half months. There were some skeptics, but we did have our victory party, and we had something to celebrate. In fact, our portfolio grew by over 25 percent in 1983 without sacrificing quality or profitability standards. . . .
>
> My function at that time was to be a teacher of credit and marketing, and we tried to use mistakes as a springboard to learn, and not an excuse to punish. I saw myself as a role model, confidence builder, cheerleader, and facilitator. I learned how to use the bureaucracy to slow down the imposition of new rules, regulations, and controls, and how to avoid it to get the job done.

As slow as the process was, changes were clearly happening. Success stories began to replace complaints and the bank began to openly celebrate these successes. When a deal was completed, a senior person would make a point of saying, "Good job!" Wallace noted that people in the bank responded immediately to the much-needed praise.

A good example that change for the better was manifesting itself was seen in the way NatWest USA handled a new problem. In an effort to build volume, the bank had accepted greater domestic risks than it would have. This, on top

EXHIBIT 3   **Composition of National Westminster Bank's Loan Portfolio, 1983–1987**
             (In thousands)

	December 31				
	1983	**1984**	**1985**	**1986**	**1987**
Domestic					
Commercial, financial, and agricultural	$1,758,653	$2,749,054	$3,630,686	$4,415,500	$5,377,938
Real estate construction	131,689	168,586	164,578	110,102	125,672
Real estate mortgage and warehouse	718,044	715,493	691,940	967,586	816,102
Installment loans to individuals	362,115	446,149	541,440	587,973	696,797
Other loans to individuals	79,793	135,214	205,899	162,174	177,576
Lease financing	4,106	23,561	23,676	21,345	29,581
Other	31,499	96,014	39,424	96,210	114,257
Total domestic	3,085,899	4,334,071	5,297,643	6,360,890	7,337,923
Foreign					
Governments and official institutions	485,695	440,823	435,079	464,163	472,009
Banks and other financial institutions	508,451	438,525	368,934	348,768	284,859
Commercial and industrial	580,391	506,332	358,018	249,645	206,477
Other	1,090	811	1,624	749	436
Total foreign	1,575,627	1,386,491	1,163,655	1,063,325	963,781
Less: Unearned income	29,865	40,980	46,260	60,464	85,348
Total loans, foreign and domestic	$4,631,661	$5,679,582	$6,415,038	$7,363,751	$8,216,356

Source: 1987 Annual Report.

of an emerging international debt crisis, resulted in an overall asset quality in 1983 that was not as good as had been expected. Bob Wallace noted:

> The bank had good enough credit people to deal with the situation quickly. We evaluated the problem loans, devised strategies, and set out to make corrections. The plan worked, and today our asset quality is among the best of the New York banks. Best of all, it was accomplished without enormous write-offs. But solving the asset quality problem had an additional benefit. It demonstrated clearly that we were working as a team. It showed that we were more interested in solutions than in pointing the finger. It proved that we were becoming a different bank.

Exhibits 3, 4, and 5 present changes in the makeup of NWB's loan portfolio.

Flexibility was enhanced at NatWest when the authority for lending was pushed down in the organization, allowing lending departments to make loans of up to $2 million without outside approval. McDougal noted the significance of this event and some of the critical events that followed:

> No one ever believed it could happen. This was the first significant sign to the line units that the bureaucracy was in retreat. The symbolism went well beyond the actual impact. A new core of leaders had made it happen. But the biggest signpost was yet to come. The bank had waited until September 1983—until it was reasonably sure that it would show its third consecutive year of increased earnings—before taking on a name which would identify it with our parent. To celebrate the new name and our success to date, the bank held a party for the entire staff—a party complete with excellent food, music, and a 15-minute sound-and-slide show that actually had people cheering. This was not NBNA, it was

E X H I B I T 4   **Cross-Border Loans Outstanding, National Westminster Bank USA, 1985–1987** *(In thousands)*

	Governments and Official Institutions	Banks and Other Financial Institutions	Commercial and Industrial	Total
December 31, 1987				
Argentina	$ 96,313	$ 23,997	$133,553	$133,863
Brazil	87,579	120,901	250	208,730
Mexico	102,608	9,303	16,858	128,769
December 31, 1986				
Argentina	83,976	30,350	12,823	127,149
Brazil	88,167	115,799	267	204,233
Mexico	93,623	9,280	18,727	121,630
December 31, 1985				
Argentina	69,223	40,936	10,500	120,659
Brazil	73,827	125,706	767	200,300
France		104,771		104,771
Mexico	96,464	4,131	20,466	121,061
South Korea	40,265	63,459	22,730	126,454

The above schedule discloses cross-border outstandings (loans, acceptances, interest bearing deposits with banks, accrued interest receivable, and other interest bearing investments) due from borrowers in each foreign country where such outstandings exceed 1.00 percent of total assets.

At December 31, 1987, 1986, and 1985, countries whose total outstandings were individually between .75 and 1.00 percent of total assets are as follows.
  1987—France and Japan, totaling $197.7 million.
  1986—Chile, France, South Korea, and Venezuela, totaling $362.4 million.
  1985—Canada, Chile, and Venezuela, totaling $267.3 million.
Source: 1987 Annual Report.

E X H I B I T 5   **Loan Maturities, National Westminster Bank USA, 1987**
(In thousands)

	December 31, 1987			
	Total	Due before One Year	Due in One to Five Years	Due after Five Years
Commercial, financial, agricultural and other	$5,492,195	$3,006,427	$1,887,733	$598,035
Real estate construction	125,672	33,931	85,797	5,944
Foreign	963,781	577,506	166,249	220,026
Total	$6,581,648	$3,617,864	$2,139,779	$824,005
Loans with interest-sensitive rates	$6,131,510	$3,518,861	$1,870,741	$741,908
Loans with fixed rates	450,138	99,003	269,038	82,097
Total	$6,581,648	$3,617,864	$2,139,779	$824,005

Excludes real estate mortgage and warehouse loans, loans to individuals, and lease financing loans.
Source: 1987 Annual Report.

NatWest USA. There was a euphoria throughout the whole bank that lasted for weeks. Even when it finally wore away, morale was at a new, higher plateau. The bank has been permanently lifted by this one gala celebration.

Anecdotes about successes increasingly replaced jokes about failure. Stories of teamwork replaced some of the legends about the idiosyncrasies of individuals.

At our victory party, we invited all branch managers to attend. Now, understand, our business customers were primarily medium-sized companies scattered over the five boroughs of New York. They used our branches to make deposits, cash checks, and bring documents. Many saw the local branch manager more often than they saw the account officer. But the branch managers were rarely thanked for their efforts. They felt that they were not appreciated. The only time they ever heard from us was when the customers felt they didn't receive the service they were entitled to. Inviting the managers to our party to thank them for their help in serving our customers seemed like a little thing at the time, but it created a bond which enhanced our ability to serve our customers.

[In addition], my predecessor had started a tradition of a quarterly profit improvement award. We [in middle-market lending] decided to give the award to an assistant branch manager who had referred us a large piece of business. The branch people were ecstatic. It was unheard of that a branch person would receive an award from another group.

The Human Resource Function

Ed McDougal was promoted in 1984 to executive vice president and head of human resources. With the fervor of a crusader, he took responsibility for the staff meetings, audiovisual presentations, and gala celebrations that continue to repeat over and over again the desire for change as stated in the original mission statement. McDougal's recollection of this period indicates the importance of the Human Resources Group and his role in the transition:

My first priority as head of human resources was to have a team. We had many people who were competent from a professional/technical point of view, but effectiveness was hampered by a lack of teamwork. It wasn't a fun place to work. I told the department heads at our first group management meeting that I had never worked in a place for very long where I didn't have a good time, and I didn't expect to start here. That was the only threat I ever issued. From then on we met regularly to discuss all issues.

One of the first major tasks of the group management was to create a strategic plan for human resources. In effect, we needed to create a vision of our future— a vision we all shared, and would work cooperatively to reach. We launched this planning process not through some technical preparation, but rather by spending three days together, off site, learning how to work together. Our next step was to create a statement of values and beliefs for the Human Resources Group. And it was only at this point that we began the process of creating a strategic plan. That plan served as a basis for providing increasingly higher levels of service to our customers, the employees, and managers of the bank.

From the bank's perspective, we went through the process in the spring of 1985 of creating a statement of values for the overall organization. This involved a series of meetings with teams composed of members of the Office of the Chairman, executive vice presidents, all senior vice presidents, and a representative group of eight people, male and female, black and white, vice president to secretary. The final result is a statement of values [see Exhibit 1] which spells out how it is appropriate to act within the bank. This statement of values was presented to all the employees of the organization during a series of 11 breakfasts, conducted in Westchester, New York, and Long Island. The presenters were all the senior and executive officers of the bank.

The final event which stands out in my mind is the bank's second victory celebration. Shortly after I became the head of human resources, Bill Knowles said we needed an occasion to have another employee party. The occasion became the launching of the bank's new quality effort. This, along with our success to date, suggested the name "Just the Beginning" parties throughout the bank. Once again, they were a rousing success and lifted the morale of almost everyone in the organization. But there is one anecdote about the "Just the Beginning" parties which I think is a fitting story to close with.

One of our division heads who managed people on off-shifts asked if we could have one of the parties other than at night when many of her people could not attend. These were employees who often felt ignored. So we held a sit-down luncheon with music and dancing, and concluded with the unveiling of a lavish dessert table. An older woman, whom I had never met before, grabbed my elbow as we walked up to the dessert table and said this reminded her of a wedding reception. Kiddingly I said, "Well, you're really our bride today." She looked at me and said, almost with tears in her eyes, "I feel like royalty." Nothing in my entire time in the bank has ever brought home to me more how people can be made to feel special.

At a conference on organizational development, in the fall of 1986, NatWest USA presented a history of its transformation process since the 1981 changeover. In closing remarks Ed McDougal and Bob Wallace expressed their perceptions of how far the bank had come. McDougal noted:

> We are a successful organization. We have done it by acting in a way that is consistent with values originally outlined in our mission statement, now codified in a statement of values. The challenges ahead of us are greater than the challenges behind. But we are prepared to meet them with a formula for success. There may still be some cynics, but most of the skeptics have been converted, and the core of believers is much larger. The younger people are still mostly here, four years older, and when they see our success to date, still say, "Why not?" I report directly to Bill [Knowles], which says something about the role human resources plays in the organization. Bill and Bob [Wallace] had both talked to me at the time of the change. They said they were looking for someone who was practical, yet sensitive. They wanted the function to have credibility within the bank and to have a customer orientation. I also took it as the ultimate confirmation of a management style.

McDougal's views are consistent with Wallace's:

> We now have an organization whose strengths are apparent. We have a marketing organization based on customer requirements and input from our own officers. Systems and operations areas now work in partnerships with line areas, because of the leadership provided by those who head these groups.
>
> When something we put in place didn't work, it was changed. We were able to prove by example that there was not pride of authorship or a penalty for an innovation that didn't work. And people began to realize that there was more fun in accomplishing an objective than in trying to find out who to blame. We in the Office of the Chairman continue to walk around, to meet with customers and seek information wherever we can. People realize that there is no penalty for speaking their minds.
>
> My own experience . . . [illustrates] the atmosphere. . . . When Bill [Knowles] and I were looking at whether I could make a contribution, he said he was looking for a full partner. I knew he meant that, but I also know that somebody has to run the store. Well, after five years, I can honestly say that the three of us in the Office of the Chairman have a partnership. We trust, respect, and like each other and, maybe more importantly, we feel free to disagree with each other. It's worked for us, and I think it has worked for the whole bank. We are all proud to be part of a winning team.

Candid Observations by the CEO

With changes apparent and financial statements that tell a story of success in many areas, there are still problems and challenges in NatWest's efforts to differentiate itself and to reach its goals. In an interview with the casewriter, Bill Knowles frankly expressed his concerns and hopes:

> We're now finding that we have got to work through, but also around, the system to try to enrich the environment down below, to unleash the energies that are there. There are still supervisors who grew up in the old school, who use knowledge as power, who feel threatened, who will not permit their people to advance their careers by seeking positions elsewhere in the bank.

About bureaucracy:

> What did disappear, fairly quickly, were the committees. There were committees for everything. All the executive vice presidents met to decide the salaries, the computer systems questions, real estate questions, loan questions. It was like the knights would consider everything, whether they had expertise or not in the particular thing.
>
> What didn't go away, and what we had a couple of false starts on, was the clutter in the system. This was because of the mergers, sticking 23 banks together so quickly, and the self-protective mentality that had grown up here. It was very hierarchical.
>
> The clutter was incredibly hard to disassemble. Those vines had grown around all the pipes and wires and furniture, and it was just impossible to pull out. We established a clutter committee to monitor the process. It's like weeding a garden; you cannot do it in 10 minutes. It takes a long time, and you have to pick the weeds out one at a time. We are still doing it, and we still have a six-part-form mentality in some places where we still cannot think simply.
>
> The people in our organization are intelligent and honest. If you catch a dishonest person you deal with that, but you don't set up a whole mechanism to protect yourself from the odd, random event.
>
> We tried to change the whole fundamental philosophical basis of the organization, and say, "Hey, wait a minute, why in God's name do I have to sign a form that I received a report? If I received it, I received it, and if I didn't receive it, I didn't receive it."
>
> There are still vestiges, and they stick out more now, and we can laugh at them a little.

Dealing with the isolation of the CEO:

> I deal with the isolation just by being informal and walking around; I have breakfast with the officers on all levels. We also have an endless series of excuses to get together for meetings and parties here. I mean, I have been to eight events here in the last three weeks with 50 or 60 officers, and it's rare if I don't know who they are. I walk around and try to see everybody in the nonbranch staff at Christmas, to wish them a good holiday. I probably see 2,500 to 3,000, out of the 4,500, and the executive vice presidents do, too.

On basic strategy:

> This has really been the story of trying to make a bank competitive by narrowing its mission, its focus, and trying to achieve superiority in the area of commodity services by working through people. Because all services are the same in the

businesses we are in. It's like insurance companies. If I asked you to identify the differences among them, you can't. Nobody could name the difference between banks either. So what we've got to do is to work very hard to take a representative sample of our society, which is our employees, and somehow to work with them in delivery of faceless services and try to do something special.

What we're doing now is having the "Executive Vice President of the Week." For a week, on a rotating basis, an executive vice president takes all the complaint calls that come into the bank, the "let-me-speak-to-the-president" calls. This means the EVP's are getting calls about their peers and about the organizations of other EVP's, and it saves complainers from being battered around by a dozen or so people before they get an answer.

The CEO's personal philosophy:

In our society, in the business sector of our society and, I'm sure, in other sectors as well, people are driven by the attractiveness, the appeal, of putting their stamp on something, or effecting a change that will be identified with them, putting their imprimatur on something. People go to work to do that—they don't go to work to earn a paycheck. There is a self-pride that says, "I did that, I was associated with that. I was on the team that installed this." Just so that they are a part of something that is significant. I think that's what really motivates me, but I also think it's what motivates others. And for me, putting my stamp on something, not just in profit terms but in human terms as well. I have a feeling that there is a power in the ability of a staff to produce when they are committed to doing something that makes sense to them—if they can see [the mission] is productive in terms of profit and the environment is conducive to letting them put their stamp on something worthwhile.

Then what you do is make it fun. Make it enjoyable to be in that environment. That's part of the compensation and part of the benefits. It's more style.

Work should be fun. . . . If you go out and sample 6 out of 10 people here, they'll tell you work is tough, it's not fun, but 4 will tell you yes, it's fun. There is that slice. If we can make that five next year and six the next year, we're on our way.

Whether it's NatWest or some other organization, it's important to keep in mind what that organization is there for, what you are there to do. An organization left on its own will run off in different directions, because of the natural desire to experiment and grow and change. Unless that is properly channeled all the time, it will grow in a lot of directions; all those energies need to be focused on something that you and they really want. The biggest change around here is not so much what I have done, or anyone has done. The biggest turnaround here is to see what the people are doing translated into something the marketplace values—and that is profit. Can you imagine how disheartening, how debilitating it is to work very hard and end up in a losing enterprise? That is how this organization once was—good people working hard, and it was coming out all wrong.

When most people ask, "What's wrong with this place?" the answer is usually communication, teamwork. But have you ever heard of any place, any organizational system that was perfect? I think we have to work hard to keep on the track we are on now, keep at it all the time.

Exhibits 6 and 7 present NatWest's financial statements. Exhibit 8 profiles NatWest's operations as of 1988. Exhibit 9 presents a summary of recent market research done by NatWest to determine its success in differentiating its customer service and quality of banking operations from competitors'.

EXHIBIT 6   **Consolidated Statement of Operations, National Westminster Bank USA, 1985–1987**   *(In thousands)*

	Year Ended December 31		
	1985	**1986**	**1987**
Interest income			
Loans	$665,170	$680,964	$740,775
Investment securities			
U.S. Treasury and federal agencies	66,339	69,622	71,683
State and municipal	29,426	55,940	52,346
Other	1,100	1,247	4,464
Trading account	4,588	6,220	1,553
Deposits with banks, federal funds sold and securities purchased under agreements to resell	68,177	52,484	53,867
Total interest income	834,800	866,477	924,688
Interest expense			
Deposits.	438,027	399,530	435,424
Borrowed funds	60,131	95,459	94,842
Long-term debt	467	384	297
Total interest expense	498,625	495,373	530,563
Net interest income.	336,175	371,104	394,125
Provision for loan losses.	51,500	57,400	349,400
Net interest income after provision for loan losses	284,675	313,704	44,725
Noninterest income			
Service charges on deposit accounts	30,469	33,027	37,049
Letter of credit and acceptance fees	13,659	16,394	19,583
Credit card fees	14,252	14,933	14,897
Syndication and other loan related fees. . .	2,715	5,481	13,740
Investment securities gains	8,762	7,890	4,926
Other	26,330	32,295	39,914
Total noninterest income	96,187	110,020	130,109
Operating expenses			
Salaries and benefits	173,725	190,390	205,074
Supplies and services	40,833	43,811	48,677
Net occupancy.	26,659	30,618	33,839
Business development	17,154	18,386	24,472
Equipment.	18,816	21,735	24,447
Other	15,791	17,698	16,065
Total operating expenses	292,978	322,638	352,574
Income (loss) before income taxes	87,884	101,086	(177,740)
Provision for income taxes	33,309	33,413	34,268
Net income (loss)	$ 54,575	$ 67,673	$(212,088)

Source: 1987 Annual Report.

EXHIBIT 7   **Consolidated Statement of Condition, National Westminster Bank USA, 1986–1987** *(In thousands)*

	December 31	
	1986	**1987**
Assets		
Cash and due from banks	$ 677,574	$ 582,220
Interest bearing deposits with banks	578,026	646,618
Investment securities		
U.S. Treasury and federal agencies	813,760	919,395
State and municipal.	837,811	734,693
Other	25,867	155,648
Total (approximate market value of $1,787,723 and $1,724,036)	1,677,438	1,809,736
Trading account	95,791	44,560
Federal funds sold and securities purchased under agreements to resell	23,213	6,936
Loans, less unearned income of $85,348 and $60,464 . . .	7,363,751	8,216,356
Allowance for loan losses	(112,299)	(407,790)
Loans–net	7,251,452	7,808,566
Premises and equipment—net	235,276	236,606
Due from customers on acceptances	365,935	249,752
Other assets	175,311	154,283
Total assets	$11,080,016	$11,539,277
Liabilities and Equity Capital		
Deposits		
Demand	$ 2,427,387	$ 2,114,470
Retail savings and time	3,747,490	4,257,818
Other domestic time	983,570	1,335,644
Foreign office	1,625,864	1,831,081
Total	8,784,311	9,539,013
Borrowed funds		
Federal funds purchased	677,957	618,140
Securities sold under agreements to repurchase.	177,103	263,220
Other	313,569	312,740
Total	1,168,629	1,194,100
Acceptances outstanding	372,399	252,668
Accounts payable and accrued liabilities	126,983	139,733
Long-term debt	6,650	4,727
Total liabilities	10,458,972	11,130,241
Equity capital		
Common stock, $5 par value	38,376	38,376
Authorized 7,773,867 shares; issued and outstanding 7,675,138 shares		
Surplus	238,657	238,657
Undivided profits	344,011	132,003
Total equity capital	621,044	409,036
Total liabilities and equity capital	$11,080,016	$11,539,277

Source: 1987 Annual Report.

EXHIBIT 8   **A Profile of NatWest USA in 1988**

In early 1988, once regulatory approvals have been obtained, First Jersey will join the National Westminster Bank Group as an affiliate of a newly formed holding company, to be named National Westminster Bancorp. The other banking subsidiary will be National Westminster Bank USA, headquartered across the Hudson River in New York City.

NatWest USA: In Perspective

National Westminster Bank USA traces its origins to the charter of The First National Bank of Freeport, established in 1905, under which NatWest USA operates today. After a series of mergers, the bank became known as National Bank of North America (NBNA). In 1979 NBNA was acquired by the National Westminster Bank Group. In September 1983 the bank changed its name to National Westminster Bank USA, and in June 1984 dedicated National Westminster Bank Center, the 30-story corporate headquarters at 175 Water Street near Manhattan's South Street Seaport.

Customer Service

These operations include four lending areas (the Community Banking, New York City, Regional, and United States groups), and five support areas (the Technology & Processing, Financial & Planning, Credit Policy & Administration, Human Resources, and Administration groups). The bank's Treasury group supports the line areas and is responsible for asset and liability management, brokerage sales and services, and trading. The bank also has Marketing and Corporate Trust divisions.

NatWest USA serves its retail customers through a 135-branch network and a network of automated teller machines, called Teller Beam, in New York City, Westchester County, and Long Island. Teller Beam is part of the NYCE (New York Cash Exchange) network of automated teller machines and the nationwide CIRRUS network. NatWest USA is a founding member of NYCE, which was established in 1984.

Retail customers are also served by the bank's Consumer Credit division, which offers VISA, MasterCard and Gold Master-Card, as well as a full line of consumer credit products. Individuals whose net worth is $1 million or more may also take advantage of the personalized financial services offered by the bank's private Banking department, through offices in Manhattan and Great Neck, Long Island. This department offers opportunities for cross-selling bank products, an important aspect of doing business at NatWest USA.

NatWest USA's other specialties include lending to middle-market corporate customers in the printing, textile and apparel, diamond and jewelry, publishing and real estate industries, particularly in New York City. Nationwide, NatWest USA specializes in meeting the financial needs of the health services, media, utilities and leasing industries.

The bank also concentrates on geographic niches, lending to middle-market corporate customers in the tristate area outside of New York City. Large corporate and middle-market customers outside the tristate area are served by representative offices and an Edge Act Office in Miami. NatWest USA's international division serves the international needs of the bank's domestic customers.

Two major staff areas provide key support to the bank's lending groups. They are the Administration and Technology & Processing groups. Administration encompasses the Legal, Auditing, Loan Review, Consulting Services, and General Services divisions.

Two separate groups, Systems and Operations, were recently combined to form Technology & Processing. This restructuring was done to open the door to new opportunities and to further enhance customer service.

Community Involvement

NatWest USA encourages voluntarism, is a leading supporter of United Way and has a substantial corporate contributions program. Also, the bank has developed a far-reaching "Arts in the Community" program which, this summer, won a Presidential Citation as part of the White House Program on Private Sector initiatives, and awards in 1985 and 1987 from Business Committee for the Arts.

Major "Arts in the Community" events have included concerts by Luciano Pavarotti and Placido Domingo, and numerous concerts in Carnegie Hall. The bank also sponsors a wide range of arts events in local communities, such as concerts by Long Island Concert Pops, American Concert Band, New Orchestra of Westchester and Brooklyn Philharmonic.

In addition to "Arts in the Community" sponsorships, other community involvement includes employee participation in walk-a-thons and other civic functions, as well as bank sponsorship of events to benefit organizations such as the American Heart Association and Special Olympics. In all, NatWest USA was involved in 107 community events in the past year.

Among the community events sponsored by the bank are several concerned with education. Through its "Outstanding Young Achiever" award program, the bank recognized and gave financial awards to outstanding seniors at 22 New York metropolitan area high schools. And, in connection with its sponsorships of PBS broadcasts, NatWest USA develops and sends teaching kits to music teachers to encourage interest in the arts among students.

During the past four quarters, as part of the NatWest USA "Speakers in Your Community" program, bank representatives have given 102 speeches on financial topics—an average of one every three working days—to business, civic and service organizations important to the bank.

The National Westminster Bank Group, headquartered in London, is among the largest, most profitable financial institutions in the world, with total assets of more than $120 billion and more than 90,000 employees worldwide. Including subsidiary companies, the group has operations in 36 countries.

EXHIBIT 9   **The Results of NatWest's Marketing Research**

The Marketing Department at NatWest USA provided research indicative of the degree to which the firm has been able to achieve its goal of differentiation via quality programs and other strategic and cultural changes. Representatives noted that the true test for NatWest USA is the degree to which any organizational changes translated into changing perceptions by customers. That is, whether customers feel that they are receiving more valuable products and information, and whether they feel confident about the bank and positive about the treatment received from it. It was observed that the types of changes that NatWest USA is seeking are very long term, and the full effects of programs implemented will have to be evaluated over a number of years into the future.

The following summaries describe the conclusions of three major studies:

The Middle Market Study

The Middle Market Study, concluded in March 1986, examined the financial behavior, needs and attitudes of middle-market companies operating nationwide, and also examined NatWest USA's competitive position within the tristate region of New York, New Jersey, and Connecticut. The middle-market study covered firms with sales between $50 and $250 million.

The middle market was dominated by manufacturing (50 percent) and wholesale trade (27 percent) businesses. The manufacturing industry was described as a "huge, attractive market, but also the most competitive market segment." The wholesale trade industry, while less competitive for banking services, also used fewer banks and fewer services. Yet the companies in the wholesale trade had the greatest demand for borrowing, both in the percentage of firms in the industry that borrow as well as the amounts that they seek.

The intense competition in the middle market was evidenced by the fact that most companies used four banks and were, on the average, actively solicited by four new banks as well. The research concluded that the intense competition "underscores the importance of staying actively involved in customer relationships, of having targeted calling programs, and of making effective calls on companies." It was observed that customers are becoming increasingly involved in their bank relationships and that this trend will continue. More companies want to know exactly where they stand with their banks and want the details of their agreements in writing. There were three areas of changes that middle-market customers consistently reported:

1. More calls are being made by bank representatives.
2. More is being asked of the banks.
3. A greater participation of company's treasury staff is present in initiating and maintaining a relationship with a bank.

The study indicated that the vice president of finance was the officer most often responsible for selection of a bank as a service provider. The key selection criterion was described as "the company's overall relationship with the bank," an overall relationship seen as more important than specifics such as loan terms and conditions. For firms dealing internationally, the study indicated that the key criteria for selection of a bank for international services were the presence of an existing domestic relationship and a bank's international service capabilities.

The financial strength of the bank was a very important concern to the middle-market companies. Utilizing annual reports, accounting and financial officers of the middle-market companies evaluate the financial condition of the banks they use and the banks that solicit them.

Banks were found to increase in importance to middle-market companies to the degree they are willing to lend, provide account officer service and have competitive loan pricing. The bank's relationship with the company was found to improve with the introduction of new ideas and new services, the interest of the servicing bank in company information, the improvement of quality, and frequency of the bank's visits. The most serious mistake, from the point of view of the customers, was when the bank was not thoroughly familiar with the company being serviced.

The Middle Market Study concluded that in the tristate region NatWest USA was an important competitor, with a 12 percent market share and positioned similarly to Marine Midland, Bank of New York, and Irving Trust. Most customers consider NatWest USA to be a principal bank (i.e., one of the banks they used most for domestic banking services) and one third used NatWest USA as their overall lead bank.

With regard to customer calling, the study indicated that 78 percent of NatWest USA's prospects were called on more frequently by at least one or more competitors than they were called on by NatWest USA. However, NatWest USA's customer calls were found to be highly effective in gaining new business, and more effective overall when compared to the competition.

The Commercial Banking Study

The Commercial Banking Study was concluded in August 1986 and examined companies with annual sales of between $5 and $50 million.

The Commercial Banking Study focused on the nine-county New York area where NatWest USA's principal commercial market was located (Bronx, Kings, Nassau, New York, Queens, Richmond, Rockland, Suffolk, and Westchester). This study indicated that NatWest USA was a major competitor in the commercial banking market. The bank was tied with Chase Manhattan in market share—in fourth position behind Chemical Bank, Manufacturers Hanover, and Citibank.

EXHIBIT 9   *(Concluded)*

Interviews with the commercial market customers indicated that NatWest USA's account officers and top management were doing an excellent job of visiting and serving the commercial market customers. A high proportion of customers were called on regularly and interactions were perceived as highly effective.

NatWest USA was viewed as a credit provider to the commercial banking market, having a higher proportion of borrowing customers than most of the competition and a credit policy that was viewed more favorably than that of its competition.

The Branch Shopping Study

The Branch Shopping Study, concluded in January 1987, was undertaken to determine how the customer was treated and how the customer perceived a NatWest USA branch when they came in to open an account or inquire about the bank's services.

In this study, a researcher approached the NatWest USA branch representative as a shopper and recorded opinions and experiences resulting from the contact. The shopper either came into a branch to open a checking account or to cash a check and inquire about high-interest-bearing checking accounts.

Approximately 200 account opening and check cashing transactions were evaluated, two thirds of which were with NatWest USA branches and the remaining third with the branches of competitors. The study was completed over a two-month period in late 1986.

The Branch Shopping Study's main conclusions were as follows:

1. Overall, NatWest USA branch personnel are performing equal to, and at times, better than the personnel of competitors in the quality of service they are providing. The study found that 66 percent of the shoppers were either extremely or very satisfied with NatWest USA, while only 59 percent were satisfied with competitor branch personnel.

2. NatWest USA representatives scored at least as high as competitors on courtesy and friendliness and higher on attitude and the initial establishment of rapport.

3. For the personal attributes of tellers and branch representatives, NatWest USA rated equal to or higher than competitors in terms of efficiency, professional appearance, promptness, organization, and businesslike attitudes.

4. Service at NatWest USA branches was found to be slightly better during the busy hours.

5. Concerning branch environments, the study indicated that the interior and exterior environments for both NatWest USA and its competition are in excellent condition. The average waiting time in NatWest USA branches was found to be lower than the average for other banks.

TIMES-WORLD CORPORATION*

Roland E. Kidwell, Jr., Louisiana State University
Gary J. Castrogiovanni, Louisiana State University

In 1978, Landmark Communications, Inc., a privately held media company, hired Walter Rugaber, a career newsman, from the Washington bureau of the *New York Times* as executive editor of its daily newspaper in Greensboro, N.C. Four years later, the retirement of *Roanoke Times & World-News* publisher Barton Morris resulted in Rugaber's promotion to chief executive officer of Times-World Corporation, a Landmark division that publishes the 122,000-circulation Roanoke, Va. newspaper.

THE NEW PUBLISHER

When Walter Rugaber became publisher on August 1, 1982, he needed a quick education. The former reporter and editor had to find out what went on in advertising, circulation, production, and administration, four of the newspaper's five major departments (see Exhibit 1).

As Rugaber began to familiarize himself with the nonnews parts of the operation, which had always been alien to him, he discovered a disturbing fact. His perceptions of the newspaper's goals and the employees' work attitudes were not shared by many of the 564 employees. "I had a pretty high ambition for the paper, and was willing to exert myself a lot to achieve what I thought the goals of the employees would be. I wanted us to be a hard-hitting, aggressive newspaper and a fun place to work. I wanted people to have fun in their jobs." But the employees perceived that the company did not have those objectives, resulting in a breakdown between top-level management and the rank and file.

Landmark, a medium-sized communications company based in Norfolk, Va., gave the new publisher independence to run the newspaper, which it had purchased from the Fishburn family of Roanoke in 1969. At that time, the employees were used to an autocratic, paternalistic organization with a high degree of centralization and little participation in decision making and goal setting from the rank-and-file workers. Even though there had been an 80 percent turnover in the years since the sale (see Exhibits 2 and 3), the pre-1969 values were still generally reflected in the performance of middle managers, front-line supervisors, and employees when Rugaber arrived.

The *Roanoke Times & World-News* (which will be referred to as *Times-World* in this case) was a regional paper publishing one evening and four morning editions in the Roanoke Valley of western Virginia. There were no other daily newspapers within 50 miles and the local television and radio stations provided little competition for the advertising dollar. Advertising rates, therefore,

---

*This case was compiled from interviews with company managers and the review of company documents and other relevant records. Only major citations are noted in the text. The authors wish to thank Times-World publisher Walter Rugaber for his cooperation.

EXHIBIT 1   *Times-World*'s Major Newspaper Departments, 1982

Department	Description
Advertising	Sells space in the newspaper to businesses and individuals wishing to sell products, services, or ideas. Includes sales representatives, artists, copywriters, sales assistants, and sales managers.
Circulation	Distributes the newspaper to homes through a carrier force and to businesses that sell individual copies. Managers coordinate delivery procedures, promotions, sales campaigns, and carriers.
Production	Responsible for the manufacturing processes of the newspaper, from the composing room where type is pasted on a page, to platemaking and engraving where plates are made to put on the press, to the pressroom where the paper is printed.
Administration	Responsible for the fiscal integrity of the newspaper, the making of budgets and cost reports, data processing, payroll, and personnel administration.
News	Plans, prepares, and provides news and other information for all nonadvertising space. Consists of reporters, photographers, and copy editors. The managers are called editors.

EXHIBIT 2   Times-World Corporation, Employment by Department, 1989

Department	Number of Employees
News	145
Advertising	83
Circulation	157
Production	118
Administration*	61

*Administration includes personnel and marketing.
Source: Times-World Corp. personnel department.

EXHIBIT 3   Times-World Corporation, Employee Length of Service, 1989

Length of Service	Number of Employees	Percentage of Employees
20 or more years	118	21%
15–20 years	69	12
10–15 years	60	11
5–10 years	84	15
5 years or less	233	41

Source: Times-World Corp. personnel department.

could be set by the newspaper with little fear of desertion by the valley's major retailers. Based on cost considerations, the circulation department decided the routes where it would deliver either a morning or an evening newspaper. Subscribers had to accept their choices if they wanted newspapers delivered at home. The news department could hold major stories out of the paper as long as the editors deemed necessary to improve them, rather than rushing into print to match a competing daily. The lack of competition sometimes resulted in a laid-back attitude that did not react quickly to changing news conditions. The newspaper's marketing committee met rarely, and there was no department that concentrated on strategic planning.

Shortly after Rugaber arrived, he realized the company was faced with tough times ahead. The Roanoke Valley was barely growing, and the newspaper's revenue increases came almost solely from advertising and circulation rate hikes. Combined with those problems were technological changes, union conflicts, and supervisory difficulties that were most apparent in the circulation and production departments. Rugaber had a growing concern that these conditions could lead to the erosion of the newspaper's profitability in a stagnant market.

HISTORY OF TIMES-WORLD CORP.

Junius Blair Fishburn came to Roanoke in the late 19th century to work in his father's grocery store. By the time he died in 1955 at age 89, he had been president and chairman of the city's largest bank and the founder of Times-World Corporation, publisher of the city's two daily newspapers and owner of a local television and radio station.

The *Roanoke Daily Times*, the first daily newspaper in Roanoke, began publishing on November 30, 1886, four years after the city was incorporated. The *Evening World*—a predecessor to the *World-News*—was started three years later. Fishburn acquired an interest in the morning *Times* in 1909, and in 1913, he bought the *Evening World*. In 1918, he brought about the merger that formed Times-World Corporation.

A strong autocratic/paternalistic attitude permeated the corporation through the Fishburn years. One employee's comment typified life under family control: "If you wanted a new pencil, you had to bring the old one up." Employees expected to be taken care of in hard economic times, and they were willing to put up with low pay. One composing room employee said that when there was not enough work at the newspaper during the Great Depression, Mr. Fishburn would have him come to the house and chop wood. Another employee recalled that you didn't often get a raise in your paycheck, but you were sure to get a ham at Christmas.

Junius Parker Fishburn, son of J. B., was president of the company from 1923 to 1954. After his unexpected death in 1954, the surviving family members appointed M. W. Armistead as president and publisher. Armistead was described as an authoritarian leader over news and editorial operations. For example, he once banished an editorial page editor to an obscure newsroom job for writing an editorial that displeased him. Armistead was less authoritarian regarding business details, delegating much to his chief lieutenant, Shields Johnson.

Shields' Legacy

Shields Johnson began his career at Times-World Corporation in 1931 as a reporter. He became assistant to the general manager in 1941, and rose through the ranks to become general manager five years later. He ran every department except the news operation, and he ran them with an iron hand. "Shields Johnson was probably the smartest man I ever knew. He could do so many different things," recalled one employee.

Johnson could also put the fear of God into almost everyone at the company. Nobody did anything without his permission. "They wouldn't hardly go to the bathroom without checking with Shields," said Cranston Williams, his longtime assistant. Former publisher Barton Morris, who was executive editor during part of Shields' tenure, said Johnson was a "curious mixture of being authoritarian and palsy-walsy with other people." He dominated the meek circulation manager and took fishing trips with the pressroom superintendent.

Decisions about the newspaper's business side were made by Johnson in consultation with Armistead. The company was managed by memo with lower-level managers serving primarily as conduits for the leadership's directions. The operating budget was written by Johnson with little formal planning. In most departments, promotions to foreman, middle manager, and often department head were made on the basis of who had been there the longest and would accept the job. If Johnson found people from other departments walking around in his areas of control, he firmly told them to leave. There was little communication among departments, and cross-training of employees in different departments was virtually unknown.

Despite the horror stories about Johnson, there were indications that he had a heart. One employee told of the time he was at the hospital awaiting the birth of his first child. Johnson showed up there and gave the man some money as the first installment in the baby's savings account. Stories such as these endeared many employees to Johnson and his way of doing things, despite their fear of him.

An apparent contrast to Johnson's normally autocratic nature was his willingness to share some of his power with the unions, which represented the printers and the pressmen. Johnson told the labor leaders that he wanted unions to represent employees in the composing room and the pressroom so he would not have to worry about hiring and scheduling those employees. The union would take care of it for him. Johnson also accepted the fact that many production supervisors kept their union cards after their promotion to management. This attitude toward unions changed when Landmark bought the newspaper.

Acquisition by Landmark

The Fishburn family was ready to sell the business in the late 1960s. The family controlled the daily newspapers, a television station, a radio station, and a shopping center in Roanoke. Knight-Ridder, a respected chain, made an offer for the newspapers, but Armistead had promised Frank Batten, Landmark's owner, a chance to bid. The Landmark bid was accepted, and on November 1, 1969, Times-World Corporation became a division of Landmark. The television station and radio station were sold to other buyers, as was the shopping

EXHIBIT 4   **Times-World Corporation, 1969**

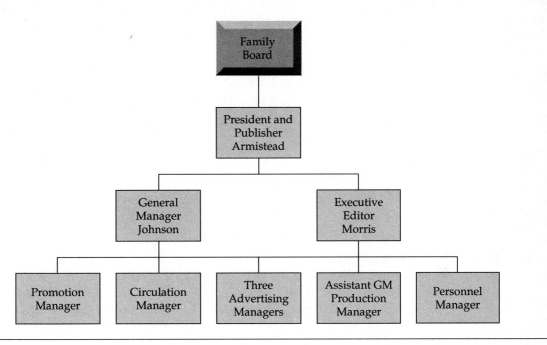

Source: Times-World Corporation.

center. After the purchase, Armistead, Johnson, and other key executives stayed with the firm. The administrative structure, therefore, remained intact (see Exhibit 4).

Old ways of doing things, however, slowly started to change. For example, in a group of 23 southern metropolitan newspapers, Roanoke's advertising rates ranked 20th because the company had favored the low-rate ranking over maximized profits. Applying more "professional" management techniques, Landmark raised the advertising rates. At the same time, salaries were increased for many employees who had been poorly paid for years. The perception in the Roanoke Valley was that a foreign corporation had come in and raised rates, taking more money out of the community. The advertisers and others did not know the additional money was going toward higher salaries and investment in new technology. It was not the Landmark way to tell outsiders this, or even to tell employees. Landmark was also a privately held corporation and closely guarded the release of financial information.

Shortly after the purchase, major technology changes occurred in the production departments. The unions were asked to make concessions for the first time because computers ended the need for large numbers of printers. Those with jobs were guaranteed positions until retirement as the company shifted from linotype operations to computer-driven composition. Video display terminals (VDTs) replaced typewriters and computers replaced linotype operators. (Before the conversion to "cold type," 110 printers worked in the composing room. In 1989, there were 19 printers, 11 photo compositors, and

8 part-timers.) The changes were a reflection of the computerization of the newspaper industry in recent years. From 1969 to 1981, VDT use at U.S. newspapers had grown from zero to 46,217 at 666 newspapers.

It soon became apparent to the owners in Norfolk that the centralized, autocratic style of Shields Johnson did not mesh with corporate goals. His tolerance of unions, lack of participation in decision making, and slipshod budgeting procedures did not fit with professional management as practiced by Landmark. In 1973, Landmark instituted a new rule requiring top officers to retire at age 62. This came to be known within Landmark as the "Shields Johnson rule" because he turned 62 shortly thereafter and was the first officer to be affected.

Shortly before Johnson's retirement, Publisher/President Armistead was promoted to president of Landmark. Frank Batten informed Executive Editor Barton Morris that he would replace Armistead with a different form of executive hierarchy: A president would run the business operations and a publisher would be responsible for news and editorial. This "church-state" separation was standard among the three major Landmark newspapers in the 1970s. Morris opted to become publisher, and a television executive from Norfolk was appointed president.

Between 1973 and 1979, there was a revolving door of presidents (Exhibit 5). The television executive did not do well, and he was replaced by Richard Barry of the Landmark legal staff. Barry started combining the two daily newspapers into one all-day product, and he and Morris established a good working relationship. But Barry was soon promoted back to Norfolk and replaced by another president who was promoted within 19 months to become publisher in Greensboro. In 1978, Batten asked Morris to take the reins as both publisher and president. The separation of powers had not worked very well. There were turf battles if the president and publisher did not get along, and departmental walls did not break down. Departmental communication improved somewhat when Morris took both jobs (see Exhibit 6).

In 1982, Morris told Batten he wanted to step down as publisher and cut back his work activities as he neared retirement age. During his short tenure, there was little time for substantive change in the organization, and the severe recession of 1981–82 occupied much of his attention. To avoid profit deterioration, the company made hard-nosed decisions to cut the work force by hiring fewer people. Not having had a losing month since 1930, the managers had little experience with bad times. But the recession did not do major damage and was ending when Walter Rugaber arrived in Roanoke.

EXTERNAL CONCERNS

In the mid-1980s, the environment for the Roanoke newspaper was slowly changing. On the surface, the situation looked favorable. The recession had bottomed out, profit margins were stable, and the newspaper was strongly in control of its market. There were threats from direct mail, television, and radio advertising, but that had always been the case. The news operation was winning state awards for content. Circulation was growing slightly and advertising revenues were up. The percentage of Roanoke Valley households taking the newspaper had been 85 percent back in the 1970s, but it was down to

EXHIBIT 5   **Times-World Corporation, 1973–1979**

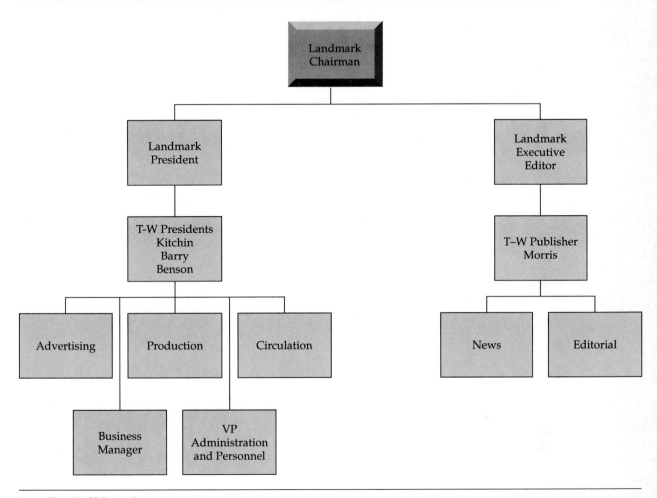

Source: Times-World Corporation.

75 percent in the early 1980s. Circulation managers were not worried because it was still among the top five in the country.

But the Roanoke market was not expanding as quickly as the rest of Virginia. Since 1960, the Roanoke Valley had grown less than any of the 10 largest metropolitan areas in Virginia, the Carolinas, and eastern Tennessee. Many of those areas grew three or four times as much as Roanoke. In the 1980s, Roanoke was growing at one fifth the national average, and compared to the neighboring metropolitan areas, its population growth was poor (see Exhibit 7). In 1940, Roanoke had been roughly the same size as Charlotte, Greensboro, and Winston-Salem, N.C. Forty years later, those other southeastern cities were all much larger. Roanoke, located in a large Blue Ridge Mountain valley in southwest Virginia, still boasted a metropolitan population of 200,000, the headquarters of the Norfolk and Western Railway (4,500 employees in 1982), a center for regional banking and health care,

EXHIBIT 6   **Times-World Corporation, 1982**

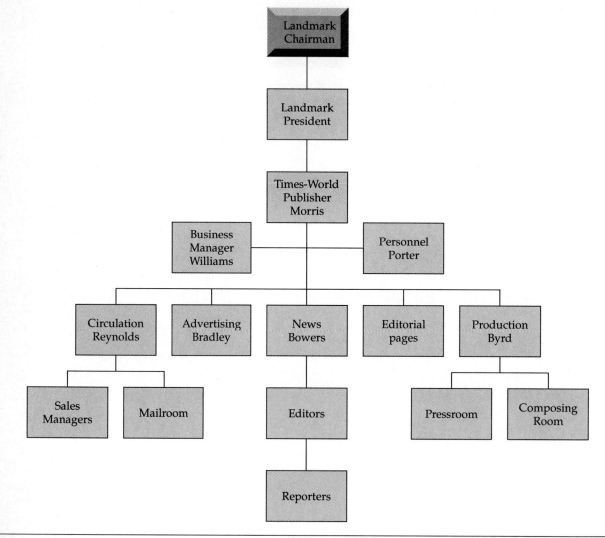

Source: Times-World Corporation.

and the home of a large General Electric Drive Systems plant with 3,350 employees in 1982.

Yet household growth was stagnant. In 1980, there were 84,700 households and in 1988 only 85,800, an annual growth rate of 0.18 percent. The market had a high median age (34.5) and wage levels over time were not increasing significantly. Manufacturing employment was flat as well. In 1982, the NW railway, the city's largest employer, merged with Southern Railway and moved the corporate headquarters of the new railroad holding company to Norfolk. High-paying, white-collar jobs started trickling to other cities, while the railroad moved more blue-collar positions to Roanoke. A couple of years later,

EXHIBIT 7   **1980–1986 Population Growth, Roanoke versus Nearby Metropolitan Areas**

Metro Area	Percent Growth
Raleigh, N.C.	16.0 %
Charleston, S.C.	13.0
Norfolk, Va.	12.9
Charlotte, N.C.	9.7
Washington, D.C.	9.6
Columbia, S.C.	8.5
Greenville, S.C.	6.5
Richmond, Va.	6.4
Greensboro, N.C.	5.6
Knoxville, Tenn.	4.4
Roanoke, Va.	2.0

Source: U.S. Census Bureau.

General Electric Chairman Jack Welch began a campaign to make GE lean, mean, and competitive for the 1990s. This meant fewer employees at General Electric's Roanoke Valley plant.

By 1987, NW/Norfolk Southern's employment level had diminished roughly 30 percent to 3,100, and GE's was down to 2,200, dropping it from second to fourth in the list of Roanoke Valley's top-10 employers. An ominous note sounded when Home Shopping Network, which employs many people at low wages, moved into the top 10. Three of the top-10 employers in 1987 were the city of Roanoke, Roanoke County schools, and Roanoke City schools (Exhibit 8). "Some people in Roanoke have been lulled by the very low unemployment rate [generally between 3 and 4.5 percent] and the very high employment rate," Rugaber said. There have been 12,000–14,000 new jobs created in the valley in the last several years, but many of these were low-paying clerk jobs in catalog sales (Exhibit 9).

These figures formed "the basis of my great anxiety about things." Newspapers are driven by advertising (80 percent of revenues) and advertising is generally driven by retail sales. With a decline in high-paying jobs, retailing could suffer. With no household growth, several heavy advertisers who depended on households—furniture and real estate, for example—might have spent fewer dollars for newspaper advertisements. Direct mail also competed for the big retailers' advertising budget, and some large retailers, such as Sears, were contemplating "everyday low prices," which could ultimately result in less newspaper advertising of discount sales.

"We operate in a slow-growth market, and we're in a business that faces a lot of structural problems even in places where the economy is robust," Rugaber said. Circulation was down in the Roanoke Valley, with any growth coming from bordering counties. The only advertising revenue increases came from raising rates. Another disturbing trend involved demographics: nationally only 30 percent of the important 18–35 age group read a paper regularly, down

EXHIBIT 8   **Roanoke's Top-10 Employers, 1977, 1982, and 1987**

1977	Number of Employees	1982	Number of Employees	1987	Number of Employees
1. Norfolk and Western Railway	5,000	1. Norfolk and Western Railway	4,500	1. Norfolk Southern Corp.	3,10
2. General Electric	3,000	2. General Electric	3,350	2. Roanoke Memorial Hospital	2,71
3. County Schools	2,380	3. County Schools	2,712	3. County Schools	2,37
4. Kroger	1,800	4. City of Roanoke	2,440	4. General Electric	2,20
5. City of Roanoke	1,770	5. Roanoke Memorial Hospital	2,200	5. City of Roanoke	1,84
6. VA Hospital	1,583	6. City Schools	1,716	6. VA Hospital	1,65
7. Roanoke Memorial Hospital	1,550	7. Kroger	1,650	7. City Schools	1,64
8. Halmode	1,300	8. VA Hospital	1,640	8. Kroger	1,60
9. City Schools	1,251	9. Community Hospital	1,060	9. Home Shopping Network	1,60
10. Roanoke Fashions	1,000	10. Appalachian Power	1,000	10. Dominion Bank	1,52

Source: *Roanoke Times & World-News*, 1988 Economy edition.

EXHIBIT 9   **Forecasts of Five Fastest Growing Jobs in Roanoke, 1984–1995**

Position	Number of New Jobs
Sales clerks	902
Janitors	880
Cashiers	869
Nurses	814
Fast-food workers	627

Source: Roanoke Regional Chamber of Commerce.

45 percentage points from 10 years earlier. Future trends looked gloomy for the newspaper, even though the problems had not yet shown up on the income statement. Exhibits 10–12 contain circulation and financial information and Exhibit 13 shows the 1988 company mission statement and business philosophy.

INTERNAL CONCERNS

In 1985, a major change took place in the production department. The newspaper presses were converted from letterpress to offset. This would give better reproduction of stories and photographs and allow the newspaper more color photo opportunities for news content and for advertisers. Most newspapers built new suburban printing plants to house their new presses. The Roanoke paper wanted to stay headquartered downtown and tried to convert half of its units at a time to offset, continuing to publish every day with the other half.

Problems continued for four years after the conversion started, with some major difficulties taking two and a half years to solve. Meanwhile, about 2,000 people quit their subscriptions, and it took four years for the newspaper to

E X H I B I T 10   **Times-World Corporation's Circulation Figures, Selected Years, 1969–1989**
(Based on 12-month averages)

Year	Combined Daily	Percent increase	Saturday	Sunday
1969	112,896	—	112,896	107,486
1979	113,812	0.81	111,137	114,987
1982	117,954	3.64	117,339	120,622
1989	122,476	3.83	123,838	125,553

These figures are for entire newspaper circulation over 20 counties of southwest Virginia. Circulation in the Roanoke Valley, which is especially important to the newspaper because of the retail advertising base, was actually declining in this period.

The percentage of Roanoke Valley households subscribing to the newspaper were 85 percent in 1979 and 75 percent in 1989.

Source: Audit Bureau of Circulation.

E X H I B I T 11   **Average Annual Growth Rates, Times-World Corp., 1969–1989**

Interval	Revenue Growth	Percent Net Profit Growth	Inflation Rate
1969–1974	10.31 %	−10.004 %	7.73 %
1975–1979	13.41	14.890	10.63
1980–1984	9.70	0.004	6.26
1985–1989	6.99	0.017	3.33

Source: Times-World Corporation.

E X H I B I T 12   **Times-World Corporation Profit and Loss Summary, Selected Years, 1969–1989**   *(In millions $)*

	1969	1974	1979	1984	1989
Operating revenue					
Advertising	4.2	6.7	11.9	18.1	24.7
Circulation	1.9	2.7	3.7	5.3	7.0
Other	0.1	0.1	0.3	0.3	0.3
Total	6.2	9.5	15.9	23.7	32.0
Operating expense	5.4	8.2	12.1	17.9	23.5
Operating margin	0.8	1.3	3.8	5.8	8.5
Margin/revenue	14.0 %	13.7 %	23.9 %	24.5 %	26.6 %

Source: Times-World Corporation; all figures have been disguised by factoring.

**Mission Statement and Business Philosophy,
Times-World Corporation, 1988**

Corporate Mission

To serve the western Virginia market with high-quality newspaper and related communications publications and services that meet customer needs as defined by readers and advertisers, provide continued growth, and meet established profit objectives.

Business Philosophy

1. We are a customer-driven organization. Our success depends on our sensitivity to the needs of our customers—both readers and advertisers—and our ability to respond to those needs.

2. Our basic goal is the detection and satisfaction of customer needs, at an acceptable profit.

3. Our primary means for meeting customer needs and achieving profit objectives are through the publishing of a daily and Sunday newspaper, the *Roanoke Times & World-News*.

4. We endeavor to be a high-quality regional newspaper for much of western Virginia, providing the most comprehensive local, regional, state, national, and foreign report possible with the resources available.

5. Our first news priority is to present a faithful and accurate picture of life in our region through detailed coverage of issues, events, and activities within, with particular emphasis on the greater Roanoke metropolitan area of Roanoke, Botetourt, Franklin, Bedford, Montgomery and Pulaski counties and the cities within.

6. Through our editorial and commentary pages, we will serve as a forum to assist readers in forming their own opinions on public issues, clearly stating the newspaper's position, while allowing and encouraging differing opinions as well.

7. We strive to build and maintain a tradition of excellence by producing a newspaper that is consistently thorough, fair, accurate, aggressive, timely, and free of influence from private interests, groups, or individuals.

8. We seek to make our products affordable, accessible, and essential; to make them available to readers when they want them, where they want them, at a price they are willing to pay.

9. The company's primary means of generating operating revenue is through the sale of advertising space or advertising distribution.

10. To serve advertisers' needs, we must provide response potential to their advertising message by supplying access to an audience which they wish to reach. This access is provided via combined news and advertising products, advertising-only products, distribution-only products and any other means deemed appropriate and profitable.

11. We seek to maintain our franchise as the largest volume advertising medium in the markets we serve, by offering advertisers the most effective and cost-efficient vehicles for disseminating advertising messages to their existing and prospective customers.

12. To maintain corporate growth in a low-growth market, we will actively seek new markets, products, and/or services which are related to our business, meet customer needs, and provide acceptable short- and long-term profit potential.

13. We will continually seek and expect increased productivity within the organization.

14. Recognizing that our employees are our most important asset, we shall attempt to create a work environment that will attract and maintain exceptional people and enable them to perform to the upper limits of their abilities.

15. We owe the Roanoke Valley and other communities in which we operate the highest standards of honesty, integrity, ethics, and corporate citizenship.

Source: Times-World Corporation. Used with Permission.

return to its previous circulation level. The defecting subscribers were upset that their newspapers were being delivered late—constantly. Often the newspapers were more than an hour late in delivery to carriers who had to take them to residences. This caused major problems because major carriers had to go to school and could not wait for the late newspapers. Other carriers had full-time jobs and had to go to work before the papers arrived. The evening paper would sometimes be delivered after 9:00 P.M., more than three hours behind schedule. The conversion should have presented problems such as these for six months. But poor supervision and conditions in the pressroom, including faulty machinery, caused difficulties that were not solved until the press superintendent was removed and the assistant to the publisher, Dee Carpenter, was assigned to the pressroom.

To one top manager, the pressroom problems "revealed the fundamental corporate culture crisis around here." Most supervisors were union members and attended union meetings. Two supervisors only took their jobs because no one else wanted to be foreman. On the night shift, if the men had a hard day at home, they would not do as much work, and the foremen—buddies who had been promoted from the ranks—did not press them. Most production supervisors had been in the union for years; until the 1970s, the department head was a member.

The offset presses required a lot more from the pressmen than in the past. In the old days, the workers would arrive, turn on the press, run off a few thousand copies, shut the press down, and go home. It was literally possible to leave during the press run, cut the grass at home, and return to shut the press off at the end of the day. The pressmen were used to the letterpress, which had been operating since 1948. With color availability of the offset press, the pressmen were required to do many more things, such as bring the color into register, decide when the color did not meet quality standards, and make the necessary changes.

Shortly before the press conversion, the company took actions that might have antagonized the pressmen. In the past, all company benefits had been automatically passed on to all employees, even union members. The company did away with this practice shortly after Rugaber arrived, costing the pressmen membership in a new 401K retirement plan and other new benefits. Regardless of the loss of the new benefits, the union had been running the pressroom. Combined with a prototype offset press that had technical difficulties, this led to the problems.

The supervisory problems manifested themselves in web breaks on the press. A press web will break if the web is inadequately prepared before the press is started. Breaks also occur if the press operator is not paying close attention as the press gears up to print thousands of copies. For each eight pages of that day's paper, there is one web. Thus if a "red stop" occurs—stoppage of the press without warning—all eight webs for a 64-page newspaper would break, taking 8–10 minutes per web to fix. This would cause an hour production delay, making the paper an hour late to the subscriber's door. This sometimes happened twice each night.

Supervision problems resulted in many web breaks and thus late newspapers. The pressmen were given a checklist to make sure the press was properly prepared to prevent web breaks. But often their supervisors did not make them fill it out. And when there were press problems, people just threw up their hands and said they could not deal with them. In one instance, some tools that were needed to make a repair had been locked up by one of the day supervisors, who had taken the key home with him and had to be called back to get the tools. At the same time, new equipment in the mailroom was often breaking down, causing red stops and more web breaks.

Carpenter found a mess when he arrived in the pressroom. Several times he was told: "Why don't you go away and leave us alone?" One Sunday morning about 3:00 A.M., he made an inspection and discovered that 18 of the 20 men who were supposed to be on the job—including the foremen—were outside smoking while the press was running. These incidents stopped within months of Carpenter's appointment. Supervisors who could not accept the changes were returned to employee ranks. After several months, the press did not break down as much, and deadline performance improved. Late home deliveries became less frequent, yet there was still resentment lingering among some of the union members.

THE PUBLISHER'S DILEMMA

By 1988, Walter Rugaber had been the publisher in Roanoke for more than five years. The pressroom problems may have turned up the heat, but Rugaber knew that strategic changes were long overdue at the newspaper. Current growth in circulation and advertising was stagnant. Demographic trends and the market's long-term outlook did not look bright. There was no one at the newspaper devoted specifically to strategic planning. There seemed to be a breakdown between top management and the rank and file, and there were internal conflicts with the two remaining unions. Although the problems that troubled the organization had yet to appear on the newspaper's bottom line, the publisher believed that financial difficulties were only a matter of time. Landmark had given Rugaber wide autonomy to run the division, and he had to take steps to address these problems before they started showing up on the profitability reports he sent to corporate headquarters.

STRATEGIC ANALYSIS IN SINGLE BUSINESS COMPANIES

CLUB MED, INC.*
Robert P. Vichas, Florida Atlantic University

Forbes magazine labeled it "Trouble in Paradise"; reporter Richard Phalon wrote in 1988: "Club Med, that once lusty purveyor of packaged sea, sand and sun vacations, is slipping into middle age bearing all the signs of an identity crisis. There are times when an income statement can be more unforgiving than a mirror." Earnings per share had declined 6 percent despite a nearly 10 percent rise in sales; investors had become disenchanted with the stock; political and labor problems had caused temporary closings in Haiti and the Turks and Caicos Islands at the same time the popular Paradise Island (the Bahamas) resort was closed for renovations.

A year later in *Forbes*, Club Med responded with an "I Am Sorry, We Have Changed" advertising campaign. Joshua Levine wrote in 1989: "With a new $12 million advertising campaign, Club Med, Inc., is shedding its old image as an endlessly partying, global singles bar. The playboy-playgirl image that Club Med has projected for the last 21 years is being rejected by much of the crucial U.S. market. An aging, more family-oriented U.S. has outgrown the Club Med of the 1970s." In response to market changes, Club Med by 1990 had restructured organizationally and initiated a strategic shift from an international to a global concept. It refocused its North American marketing strategies. It developed a worldwide growth strategy for the 1990s. Revenues in 1989 rose 12 percent over 1988 and operating profits increased 128 percent. Serge Trigano, chief executive officer (CEO) of Club Med, said "We are beginning 1990, the 40th year of the Club Med concept, with an aggressive strategy for growth. The challenge will be to execute this strategy effectively while rapidly adapting to changes in our markets."

HISTORY

Gerard Blitz, a Belgian, dreamed of providing war-weary continentals a vacation ambience, away from the afflictions and adversities found in a post–World War II Europe, which emphasized sports and love. Gilbert Trigano's family business sold army surplus tents—the ideal guest accommodations for communal bliss. On the Spanish island of Majorca, in Alcudia, Blitz established the first Club Méditerranée village in 1950, where guests helped cook meals and wash dishes before snuggling down into sleeping bags. Despite its "escape from civilization" concept, Club Méditerranée was destined for cascading changes from the day Blitz first approached Trigano, the tent seller, for his ideas.

A French Communist, whose parents were Moroccan Jews, Gilbert Trigano fought in the Communist resistance during World War II, became a reporter with the Communist daily (*L'Humanité*) after the liberation of France, then drifted into the family tent business. Soon after joining Club Med in 1954

*The author acknowledges the contributions of R. Carl Moor and assistance of researchers Phil Breakwell, David Spencer, Mark Deary, and Luis Figuereido.

as managing director (MD), Trigano became the driving force within the company.

The firm nearly ran aground in 1960, but was bailed out of financial distress by Groupe Edmond de Rothschild, a French firm which took controlling interest for a £1.0 million investment; Rothschild subsequently reduced its interest to 2.8 percent and Trigano remained in control. Over the next decade Trigano forged a highly profitable chain of resort villages in France, Italy, Greece, and Africa. Polynesian-style huts and bungalows replaced tents and sleeping bags. Club Med opened its first straw hut village in 1954, its first ski resort in Leysin, Switzerland, in 1965, its first village in the American Zone in 1968, and the first family "Mini-Club" in 1974. In 1976, the company acquired a 45 percent interest in Valtur, an Italian company, which had holiday villages in Italy, Greece, and Tunisia, mainly for an Italian market. Club Med either leased or operated many of its villages under management contract. As an additional corporate activity, Club Med maintained time-sharing apartments and hotels. Although most Club Med vacationers were French in the 1950s, by 1980 the proportion of French visitors had dropped to 45 percent of the total. From global headquarters in Paris, Club Méditerranée marketed its products worldwide.

In late 1981, when the firm again attempted decentralization, Serge Trigano, Gilbert's son, assumed leadership of the American Zone. Club Med also began marketing its Rent-a-Village Program that year to large corporations for meetings and market incentives. In 1984, the firm incorporated its American Zone in the Cayman Islands (B.W.I.) as Club Med, Inc. (CMI), a wholly owned subsidiary of Club Méditerranée S.A. It hoisted a new slogan: "The perfect climate for body and soul." To help Serge Trigano relocate from Paris to New York in 1984, the corporation loaned him $1.4 million, interest free.

With Serge Trigano as its CEO, CMI was chartered to develop markets and operate in the United States, Canada, Mexico, the Bahamas and the rest of the Caribbean, Southeast Asia, the South Pacific, and parts of the Indian Ocean basin; Club Méditerranée, while retaining responsibilities for marketing and operations in the rest of the world (Europe, Africa, and South America), mainly focused on its European market. Worldwide, the organization maintained operations in 35 countries on five continents. CMI went public in September 1984. Its initial public offering in the United States of 3.4 million shares of common stock was oversubscribed at $17 per share. (Club Méditerranée shares traded on the French, Luxembourg, and Belgian exchanges.) In the same month, CMI signed an agreement with the Seibu Saison Group, a Japanese retail and real estate firm, to develop resorts in Japan. A summer mountain resort and winter ski village, Club Med–Sahoro opened on the island of Hokkaido in December 1987.

PRODUCT

The original Trigano formula was to construct villages in exotic places and operate the business as a membership organization.

> What is Club Med? Quite simply, an inimitable style of vacation, based on some very simple ideas:
> The first is to select the most beautiful locations in the world, and there build our leisurely vacation villages.

The next is to offer every activity imaginable to make your vacation ideal.

Then we carefully select a multinational, multilingual team of Gentils Organisateurs (GOs, or congenial hosts).

Finally, we give our villages a sense of complete freedom.

In 1989, the New York office of Club Med circulated a "Club Med Fact Sheet." It stated that the world's largest vacation village organization (actually the 11th largest hotel chain) offered "vacationers unique, all-inclusive escapes from the stresses of daily life in some of the world's most exotic and scenic locations."

Although the original concept remained intact throughout the company's 40 years of operations, product variations abounded. For instance, Club Med entered the corporate meeting and incentive market with its Rent-a-Village program; by the end of 1989, over two dozen corporations had rented parts of or an entire village as sites for company events. Club Med hosted several vacations for Sober Vacations International, a travel firm that specialized in vacations for recovering alcoholics and their families. Some villages added certified scuba diving programs, English-style riding instruction, and lectures. By the 1980s, the organization had gone beyond strictly sun-and-sand vacations and added villages in ski, mountain, and other scenic settings to appeal to a diversity of vacation tastes. June 1989 marked the opening of Club Med Opio, a 1,000-bed, 125-acre luxury village nestled in the hills behind Cannes on the French Riviera with a 360-degree view of the seacoast and mountains. The model for future Club Med villages, Opio offered luxury rooms, Turkish baths, full convention and seminar facilities, plus an 18-hole golf course and a 9-hole executive course designed by Cabell Robinson.

In 1989, the firm promoted a new Mini-Club at St. Lucia for children. The Caribbean resort offered horseback riding for children ages 8 to 12 and flexivacations to encourage visitors to take long weekends at Club Med or combine a village stay with visits to nearby tourist attractions. A new-style village in Huatulco, Mexico boasted five restaurants, larger rooms, and private terraces. Paradise Island (the Bahamas) and The Sandpiper (Florida) were repositioned as prime short-stay villages. Exhibit 1 displays the locations of Club Med vacation sites as of 1990.

In 1990, Club Med introduced luxury packages aboard the Club Med I, the world's largest automated sailing vessel. The 617-foot ship, with five masts and seven passenger decks, was scheduled to cruise the Mediterranean during spring and summer months and the Caribbean in winter. Besides the honeymoon specials and Mediterranean cruise package, Club Med introduced (1) a professional Golf Academy at The Sandpiper, (2) Culinary Week where renowned French chefs might even share culinary secrets with guests, (3) flexi-vacations, and (4) expanded sports programs. CMI also added new amenities in many villages including locks on doors, ice machines, and occasional telephones and televisions. With 110 vacation villages located in 35 countries, Club Med expected to appeal to a wider range of vacationers: singles and couples, retired persons, families with small children, organizations and businesses, middle- and upper-income professionals, and people seeking adventure and excitement. CMI, in 1990, owned, operated, or managed 26 vacation villages throughout its geographical area (see Exhibit 1), plus it had archaeological villas in Mexico, and exclusive rights to sell vacation packages at resorts operated by Club Méditerranée.

E X H I B I T   1   **Location of Club Med Villages and Sales Offices, American Zone
                      and European Zone, 1990**

**Club Med, Inc. Villages,
14,622 beds**

American Zone

United States, 1032 beds
Copper Mountain, Colorado
Sandpiper, Florida

Bermuda, 666 beds
St. George's Cove

Bahamas, 1,196 beds
Paradise Island
Eleuthera

Caribbean, 3,688 beds
Turks and Caicos Islands
Turkoise

Haiti
Magic Isle

Dominican Republic
Punta Cana

Guadeloupe
Caravelle

Martinique
Buccaneer's Creek

Saint Lucia
St. Lucia

Mexico, 3,928 beds
Sonora Bay
Playa Blanca
Ixtapa
Huatulco
Cancun

Archaeological villas
Teotihuacan
Cholula
Uxmal
Chichen Itzá
Coba

Tahiti, 782 beds
Moorea
Bora Bora

Asian Zone
Japan, 200 beds
Sahora

Thailand, 600 beds
Phuket

Malaysia, 600 beds
Cherating

Indonesia, 700 beds
Bali

Republic of Maldives, 250 beds
Farukolufushi

Mauritius, 370 beds
La Pointe aux Cannoniers

New Caledonia, 550 beds
Chateau Roya

Villas

Republic of Maldives, 60 beds
Thulagiri

Reunion, 120 beds
Le Lagon

**Club Med, Inc.
Corporate, Direct Sales, and
Representatives Offices**

North America
Canada
United States
Mexico

Asia
Japan
Taiwan
Hong Kong
Thailand
Malaysia
Singapore
Indonesia

Australia

New Zealand

**Club Méditerranée S.A.
Villages, 50,437 beds**

Europe
Portugal, 1 village, 751 beds
Spain, 4 villages, 3,311 beds
France, 15 villages, 7,486 beds
Italy, 7 villages, 7,883 beds
Switzerland, 10 villages, 4,661 beds
Yugoslavia, 2 villages, 2080 beds
Greece, 6 villages, 5,094 beds
Bulgaria, 1 village, 930 beds
Turkey, 5 villages, 4,164 beds

Africa and the Middle East
Israel, 2 villages, 1,114 beds
Egypt, 2 villages, 620 beds
2 Nile Cruise Ships, 143 beds
Tunisia, 5 villages, 5,000 beds
Morocco, 7 villages, 4,703 beds
Senegal, 2 villages, 960 beds
Ivory Coast, 1 village, 380 beds

South America
Brazil, 2 villages, 1,300 beds

**Club Méditerranée S.A.
Corporate, Direct Sales, and
Representative Offices**

Europe
United Kingdom
Spain
France
Italy
Belgium
The Netherlands
Switzerland
West Germany
Sweden
Turkey

South America
Venezuela
Brazil
Peru
Colombia
Argentina

Source: Company annual report.

MARKETING

Typically, the firm marketed to its membership (called GMs—*Gentils Membres* or Gentle Members) an all-inclusive prepaid vacation package that included transportation, lodging, three meals daily, wine and beer with meals, most sports and leisure activities, and evening entertainment. Additional fees for liquor, golfing, and horseback riding increased total vacation expenditures. Worldwide, there were about 1.2 million GMs. The number of GMs visiting CMI villages rose from 383,600 in 1988 to 425,600 in 1989.

In the 1980s Club Med implemented a carefully orchestrated marketing and ad campaign to convey the message that Club Med was for everyone. The ad budget was raised progressively from $8 million in 1983 to $10 million in 1985, to $12 million in 1989, and to $25 million in 1990. Management said that expanding penetration in the upscale vacation market was the goal of the firm's five new 30-second television ads. These presented vignettes of vacation possibilities available to singles, couples, and families. About three fourths of the ad budget was assigned for television ads, the remainder for newspapers, primarily, and magazines. Hard-copy ads in newspapers and magazines featured testimonials from a variety of vacationers; this represented a new thrust for Club Med. Radio spots were aired during summer 1990. The American Zone promotion budget was about four times the European budget.

In Europe, Club Med positioned itself to appeal to vacationers from all over Europe. Serge Trigano said, "We decided that we had three options: to remain a French company and lose markets elsewhere; to compete in each market; or to become European." The first option was inconsistent with the firm's international perspective. The second option would have led to catastrophic results. Trigano said, "If we had built a village just for, say, the German market, we would have had huge occupancy problems. The German market is at its peak in May and June and falls off in July and August." The third option meant acceptance of Europeanization. "In 1992, 1993, or whenever, we will all be Europe. So why not try to be European before Europe?" asked Trigano. To develop a marketing style appropriate for the 1990s, management decided to be European rather than develop villages and vacation packages on a country by country basis. Seventeen villages were selected for an international flavor, with Club Med guaranteeing customers a welcome in their own language. Instead of a single package, several packages were created during the 1980s to appeal to different customer segments. Forty new villages were planned for 1990–95.

CMI had identified families as a fast-growing market segment. About 40 percent of its members were married, 40 percent had children, and 8 percent of its members were children (see Exhibit 2 for a profile of the North American membership). By late 1989, CMI had opened eight Mini-Clubs and two Baby Clubs, which offered child care and activities up to 12 hours a day and one or two nurses 24 hours each day. The Baby Club, which debuted in April 1985 at Club Med Fort Royal in Guadaloupe, was for infants and toddlers ages 4 to 23 months. Some units provided adjoining rooms for parents and their children. Management estimated that more than 100,000 children worldwide shared vacations with parents each year.

EXHIBIT 2   1989 Survey of North American Club Med Members

Married members	40%
Single, divorced, or widowed	60%
Members with children	40%
Members who are children	8%
Members between ages 25 and 44	71%
Members who are college graduates	72%
Percentage holding postgraduate degrees	28%
Professionals, executives, managers	68%
Median age	35
Median household income (annual)	$60,000
Percent reporting incomes exceeding $75,000	36%
Percent reporting incomes exceeding $100,000	21%

Source: "Club Med Facts," April 1989.

In Asia, the marketing slogan was "Absolutely Paradise." Occupancy in the Asian Zone was less subject to seasonal fluctuations: Australian and New Zealand markets have seasons reversed from Japan and the United States. However, to improve occupancy in Asian Zone villages subject to seasonal fluctuations, Club Med maintained constant reduced off-season rates and raised in-season prices during 1989. It also opened a sales office in Taiwan.

The company's fastest growing Asian market was Japan; between 1984 and 1988 the number of Club Med vacationers from Japan grew 200 percent. Links with Seibu Saison gave Club Med crucial in-store visibility and marketing capability to Seibu Saison's customers. New destinations in Florida and the Bahamas were promoted to the Japanese during 1989. The firm advertised its Mexican villages to the Japanese market in 1990.

Travel agents accounted for about 85 percent of the sales of CMI's vacation packages; typically they earned 10 percent commission on each package sold (in contrast, Club Méditerranée in Paris direct-booked about 70 percent of its business). The U.S. travel agent program embraced four- to five-day training sessions at clubs to acquaint agents with services. Following the on-site visit, agents would then receive a barrage of promotional materials, direct mail flyers, storefront decorations, mailing lists, newsletters, sales manuals, and a priority clearance for the next season. Despite implementation of this program, some travel agents claimed that Club Med's marketing efforts tended to neglect, even offend, them. Club Med had tried to counter the negativism of travel agents by increasing its sales organization from 7 regional managers and a six-person "flying team" of troubleshooters to 23 regional and district sales managers and instituting a plan to double its sales force by the end of 1991.

Two Florida travel agents interviewed in 1990 said that in the past Club Med had been slow to pay commissions. Now, they said, Club Med was increasing commissions (which could reach 18 percent on selected packages), and had improved communications regarding new tour offerings. A New Jersey travel agent, who sold many Club Med vacation packages, believed that the firm had

---

EXHIBIT 3   **One Family's Evaluation of Club Med Vacation Experiences**

Kevin and Karin fit the U.S. member profile in terms of age, income, and professional status. They enjoyed year-round sports: skiing, diving, horseback riding, sailing, swimming. They had frequently visited Club Med villages in Europe, the Caribbean and United States. They like the activities, the security of no surprises, and knowing what to expect from each visit. Besides being a vacationer, Kevin was also a potential investor. Therefore, he carefully observed the care and management of the properties with an eye on potential future growth and competition.

After several visits to the Martinique village in the Caribbean, they witnessed significant deterioration. Kevin said, "When we first started going to Club Martinique, most of the guests were professionals like ourselves. Then Club Med started running vacation specials from New York City. For an $18-an-hour New Yorker who might be a street sweeper, the vacation special was cheap. They were noisy, partying all night. They got off the plane drunk. They were rowdy people who didn't fit with the traditional Club Martinique visitor. We didn't need that kind of environment, so we stopped going there. We now go to Copper Mountain, Colorado [a Club Med ski village]." Kevin interpreted the changing character of Club Martinique as a signal of increasing competitive pressures.

Although Kevin and Karin had visited Copper Mountain twice and planned a return trip in winter 1991, they were unimpressed with the management of that village. "Every village has its local clown," explained Kevin, "but after a day on the slopes, we like to sip our drinks quietly in front of the fireplace and meet new people. This clown is loud, doing nothing anyone really thinks is funny, and it's not the before-dinner environment we prefer. Besides, in American villages, they turn the children loose around six, before dinner, so the kids can eat with their parents. We don't care for the noise or children activity while enjoying a gourmet feast. By contrast, in Europe," Kevin continued, "the villages offer more hours of baby-sitting. Children eat together and join parents after dinner at nine o'clock. It's a more sophisticated atmosphere.

Kevin did not like Club Med as an investment in 1990 any more than he did in 1985. "They seem to be growing for the sake of expansion. There's no quality growth, and I think village managers need more training and experience. Club Med is trying to be all things to all people, and I believe the increased competition, especially in the U.S., has created some corporate panic."

Will Kevin and Karin return to a Club Med village? "We'll probably return to Copper Mountain. And I'm interested in the new sailing ship. We'll go back to Europe; we like it better," he said.

---

difficulty selling itself to older vacationers: "The stories going around about sex and drinking at some Club Med sites really turn off the older, more sophisticated people Club Med is trying to reach." Exhibit 3 presents one couple's evaluation of the vacation experiences at Club Med villages.

PRICING

Club Med offered custom-tailored vacations, honeymoon specials, length-of-stay and transportation flexibility, sailing ship cruises, family villages, singles vacations, and luxury packages in addition to its standard plans at an all-inclusive price. Children, ages two to five, could stay free at selected locations for specified dates. All packages entailed an all-inclusive, prepaid price. Advance booking, when confirmed, required a 25 percent prepayment per person plus membership fees that included an initiation fee of $30 and annual membership dues of $5 per family. Membership fees included illness and medical insurance coverage through a policy issued by Union des Assurances de Paris. Final payment for the balance was due 30 days prior to departure. Although guests could settle accounts for optional beverages, sports equipment, and special rentals when they checked out, not all villages accepted all credit cards for personal expenses, and none accepted personal checks. The inclusive price did not cover costs of entry and exit visas or airport taxes, transfers, beverages after meal periods, snacks, beach towels, optional excursions, equipment rentals, horseback riding, and deep-sea fishing. A strict 44-pound per person luggage allowance necessitated careful packing, because Club Med policy specifically excluded such carry-on items as garment bags and backpacks; extra charges were made for scuba gear and surfboards. Flight times, not guaranteed, were subject to change; other exceptions and caveats suggested careful perusal of the contract. Nevertheless, more than one half of the firm's business derived from repeat customers, some of whom were frequent visitors.

The following samples of prices represent published off-season rates for summer and fall 1990. The Honeymoon Package at Caravelle (Guadaloupe) between May 5 and June 23, for two, was $1,998 from New York City and $1,898 from Miami. Double rooms were basic with shower and 220 voltage (adapters not furnished). The facility featured water sports, golf, tennis, archery, and a fitness center, plus nightly entertainment and dancing, and even a video room with large-screen TV (no television in rooms). The "special honeymoon gift" for newlyweds included:

> . . . a bottle of imported champagne on ice, two exclusive Club Med souvenir T-shirts, a basket of fruit, two complimentary packages of bar beads, [i.e., Club Med money, prepaid with hard currency, used to settle the bar bill, and unused beads were nonrefundable], a private cocktail party for honeymooners only hosted by the village manager. Please ask for the honeymoon gift package at time of booking.

Other off-season rates (usually May 5 to December 15), per week, per person, double occupancy, from major U.S. cities were as follows (rates for children ages 6 to 11, if available, are in parentheses): Bora, Tahiti, $2,100 ($1,315); Opio, French Riviera, $1,625; St. Lucia, Caribbean, $1,200 ($1,100); Eleuthera, the Bahamas, $1,100 ($650); Huatulco ($1,000) or Ixtapa, Mexico, $1,200 ($700).

To compete with popular cruise ship and airline offers, independent tour operators (any person who could put together a group of 20 or more persons) could earn discounts up to 15 percent. Club Med resorts that offered short-term stays charged an average $165 per day.

For more luxurious accommodations, Club Opio, 12 miles from Cannes (France), offered air-conditioned rooms with a telephone, satellite television, a bath with a tub, and a hair dryer. A company brochure describing Club Opio said, "Fashioned after a typical Provincial hamlet, [Club Opio] . . . unfolds on 125 acres of undulating countryside, in the midst of olive trees, pine forests, and flowering gardens, at an altitude of 990 feet. There are five restaurants, an outdoor and a heated indoor pool, piano bar, theatre, bridge room, movie and meeting room, and boutique. Opio welcomes ages 12 and over." Weekly rates during the summer weeks ran $1,850 from Los Angeles or $1,725 from Miami, double occupancy, airfare included.

Club Med offered departures from Pointe-a-Pitre (Cannes) aboard the 14,000-ton Club Med I, a fully automated five-sail (sails could be raised or lowered in 90 seconds) ship; single rates for a 19-day cruise ranged from $3,420 on the Bali (lower) deck to $6,150 for a suite on the Foca deck. Rates for a seven-day "Mediterranean Cruise" depended on the week chosen; low- season rates ranged between $775 and $1,620 for singles whereas high-season rates were $2,490 to $4,620. A seven-day "Caribbean Cruise" aboard the same ship ran between $2,010 and $3,780 for singles during low-season weeks and between $2,490 and $4,620 for singles during high-season weeks. All Club Med I prices above excluded airfare; soft drinks, wine, and liquor on board cost $2 to $4 each.

The 442-passenger Club Med I boasted eight decks of Burmese teak and the latest maritime technology. Created by world-famous designer, Alberto Pinto, its interior consisted of a small casino, 197 guest rooms, two restaurants, four cocktail lounges, a nightclub, a large boutique with a duty-free shop, a health center, a beauty salon, and a multipurpose hall for conferences, movies, shows, and special events. Standard rooms measured about 188 square feet and suites 321 square feet, each with local and closed-circuit television, radio, telephone, mini-bar, and private bathroom with hair dryer and bathrobe, plus 24-hour-a-day room service.

ORGANIZATION

Club Méditerranée began with a very simple and informal organizational structure: Gilbert Trigano appointed some friends, and original vacationers, to manage different vacation spots in Europe. Gradually, a more complex, functional structure evolved and remained in place until 1971. Between 1971 and 1976, the organizational structure was modified. Area managers were named, each responsible for supervising 10 to 15 village managers. Because operationally it seemed as though several Club Meds had been created, management reverted to the pre-1971 structure after 1976. The pre-1971 structure prevailed until the early 1980s, at which time management reorganized to better carry out a five-point corporate strategy:

1. Doubling capacity every five years either by adding new villages or increasing the size of existing ones.
2. Differentiating Club Med from other hotel chains and responding to shifting vacation preferences.
3. Staffing villages with greater numbers of people from outside France because the proportion of Club Med vacationers from France was diminishing.
4. Standardizing procedures to improve productivity and control rising costs.
5. Retaining Club Med's original concept of shielding the village environment from the outside world and having each village take on the atmosphere and mood of the local area as closely as possible.

However, after a few years this new structure began to hinder more than facilitate efficient implementation of the corporate strategy. For instance, reporting to Serge Trigano, managing director of operations, were corporate managing directors, 16 country managers, 100 chiefs of village, and 8 product managers. The structure was too centralized, resulting in information overload and excessive detail for Trigano and leading to bottlenecks in assignments and supervision of personnel. Moreover, the corporation was still recruiting most of its staff members for villages, called GOs*, from France despite the fact that Americans accounted for 20 percent of business. Additionally, poor communications existed between marketing and operations.

To try to correct these deficiencies, Club Med was reorganized along the lines illustrated in Exhibits 4 and 5. Some aspects of the old structure remained the same—for instance, the chief executive officer (CEO) and his managing directors (MDs) of financial affairs and new development. At the next level, however, the titles of functional MDs were changed to joint MDs (JMDs) to help promote greater unity among various functional activities. The MDs of marketing and operations (M&O) were combined into a single job, with the new MD participating in both operations and promotion of vacation programs. Two regional JMDs of M&O assumed responsibility to internationalize these activities. The JMD for the American Zone controlled activities in North and South America, the Caribbean, and Tahiti. The JMD of the European Zone controlled activities in Europe, Australia, and the Far East.

To avoid duplication, Club Med layered product directors between the corporate JMD of M&O and regional JMDs. This facilitated global coordination of products through product directors at an upper-management level, who could examine challenges worldwide instead of the more narrow country focus.

The villages, at the lowest level of the organizational chart in Exhibit 4, are illustrated in greater detail in Exhibit 5. The *chef de village* (chief of village), the key manager in implementing Club Med's M&O strategies, dealt with daily operations, managed the many GOs, coordinated GO activities with the various programs, and was the direct link between customers and upper management. Through regionalization, problems that surfaced at the village level were dealt with at a lower level in the new organizational hierarchy. Further, the *chefs de village* were now selected from many countries to make this element of operations truly multinational.

At the top of the organization, the Triganos remained firmly in charge. Gilbert Trigano, age 69, remained chairman of the board of CMI, and chairman of the board, CEO, and MD of Club Méditerranée S.A. His son, Serge Trigano, born in Paris, May 24, 1946, headed CMI as vice chairman of the board and CEO. Serge had worked as a GO during college breaks from the Faculté de Droit et Science (Paris), where he earned a degree in economics. After serving as *chef de village* in six villages, he was considered executive material. In 1981, following an internal reorganization, Serge assumed leadership of the American Zone and became CEO in 1984 of the newly incorporated CMI. Between 1985 and 1987 he was also Club Méditerranée S.A.'s MD for development and operations of Europe and Africa. In 1987 he became its chief operating officer (COO), dividing time between world headquarters in Paris and offices and villages around the world. Serge concentrated mostly on operational matters, his father on strategic issues. Jean-Luc Oizan-Chapon functioned as president (chief operating officer) and chief financial officer for the American Zone.

One observer described the global organization as too small, too French, with a management system characterized by tight centralized control by a 69-year-old guru and a product that was 40 years old. A company official

---

*GOs, or *"gentils organisateurs,"* specialized by function, had the task of helping people enjoy their Club Med vacations. They both organized and participated in events. Typically there were 80 to 100 GOs per village.

EXHIBIT 4   Club Méditerranée's Organization Structure in the Early 1980s

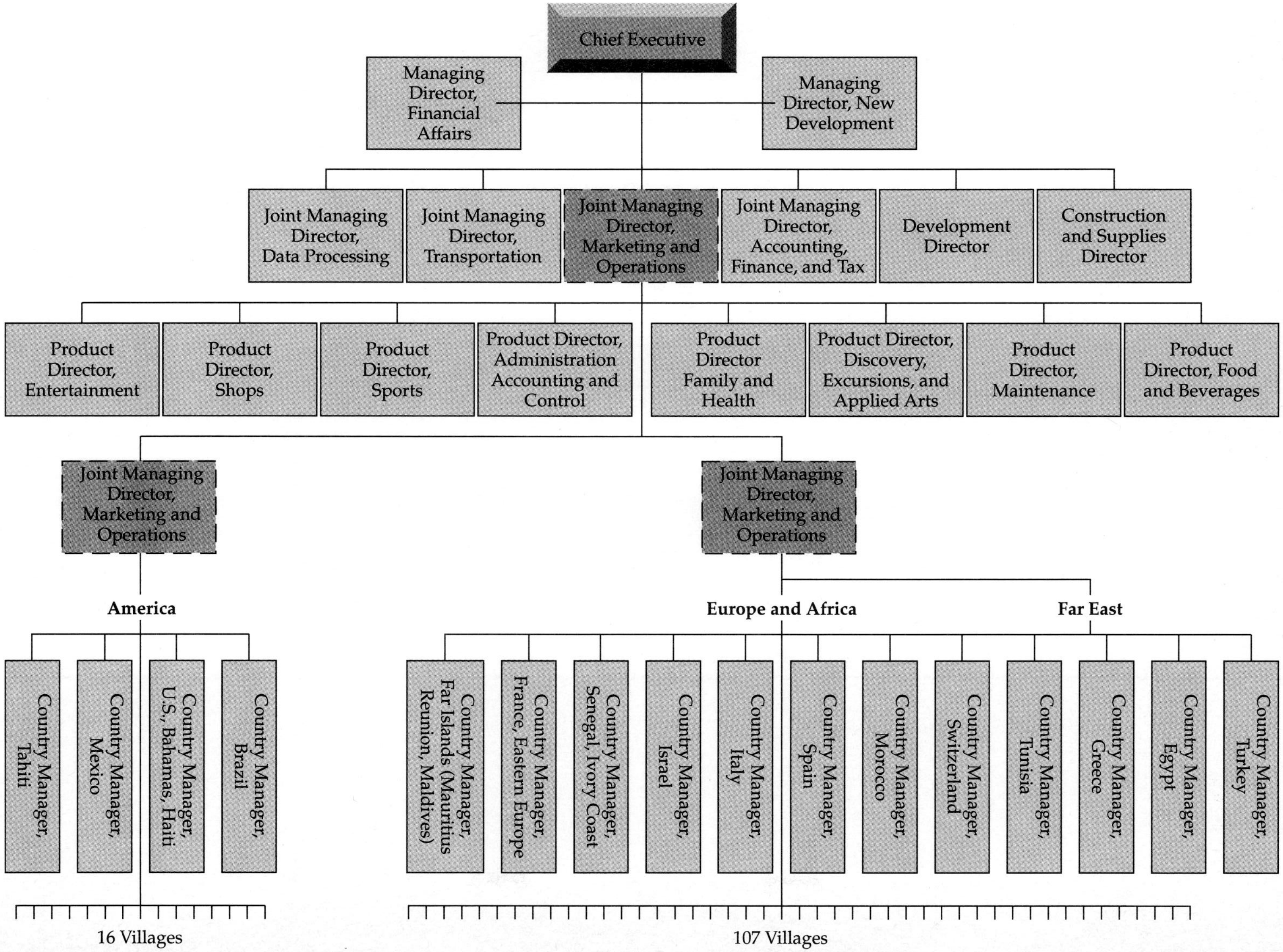

Organization Structure for a Typical Club Med Village

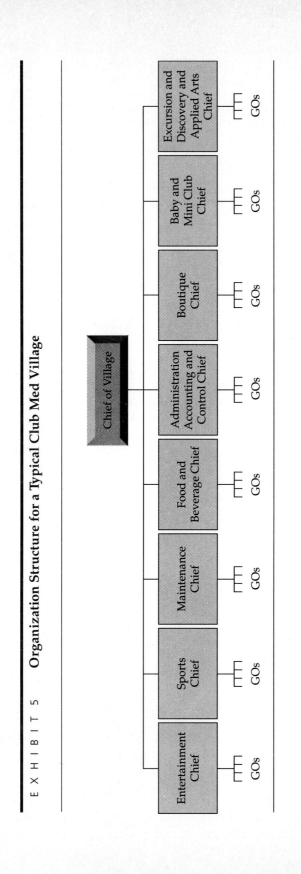

admitted that Club Med's American managers and French managers did not always get along well. Decision making remained highly centralized; according to Stephen Wood:

> Part of the uncertainty about Club Med's future is due to Trigano's dominant position within it. *Le Figaro* described as a "delightful euphemism" the comment by a senior Club Med manager that "the decision making here is relatively centralized." Yet, despite his age, to pose the question of Trigano's succession is, the newspaper noted, "considered as sacrilegious inside the club."

OPERATIONS

The company's basic operating unit, the village, was headed by a *chef de village.* A typical *chef de village* was Janyck Daudet, who in 1983 was the youngest appointed *chef* at age 26. A native of Nimes, France, he began as a ski instructor in Yugoslavia and worked in clubs from Morocco to Thailand as a GO. (Staff members were reassigned to a different village every six months not only to keep them motivated but also because some seasonal villages were closed part of each year.) Typically a GO earned less than the minimum wage paid in most industrialized countries, plus room and board, was under age 30, and unmarried. A U.S. GO earned less than $500 a month in 1990. *Chefs* could earn salaries in the $30,000 to $45,000 range. Daudet worked 18 hours a day but was on call 24 hours, seven days a week; he mingled with guests, performed in after-dinner shows, called midnight staff meetings, and maintained a high level of enthusiasm and energy. "It's impossible to do this job very long," said Daudet. "It's fun, but you can't keep up this much energy forever."

Club Med employed approximately one GO for each five vacationing guests (or "gentils membres"—GMs). Villages had a chief GO for sports, dancing instruction, applied arts, excursions, food, bar, accounting, baby-sitting, etc.— see Exhibit 5. After every season, or every six months, GOs would be moved from one village to another, with the exception of the chief of maintenance and local people hired as service personnel. Having remained firmly intact since inception, the GO concept afforded the firm a competitive advantage, according to management. Worldwide there were more than 8,000 GOs from 32 countries in 1990, 25 percent of whom were employed by CMI. About 3,000 new GOs were selected each year from an applicant pool of 100,000. About one half of the GOs were former GMs.

Toward the end of the 1980s, hiring French GOs was virtually halted as international teams were employed from the United Kingdom, West Germany, and Italy, plus cheaper talent discovered in some less-developed countries. In early 1990 Club Méditerranée employed around 250 British GOs to service 17,000 British GMs in popular villages such as Marbella, Kos, Turkey, and Sardinia. Management also considered opening a London Club Med.

Nevertheless, despite this apparent shift in corporate policy, Shirley Slater and Harry Basch, aboard the newly launched Club Med I, wrote in 1990: "We would hope as more Americans travel aboard this elegantly designed ship, all of the Club Med GO staff, not just a few, will make necessary adjustments in language and attitude to welcome them." Management said Club Med's objective was to achieve a 50–50 mix of American and European GMs on the ship.

The American Zone had suffered its share of setbacks since late 1987. Construction delays at Huatulco (1,000 beds) and Playa Blanca (580 beds) in Mexico resulted in lost revenue. Construction delays in the Bahamas

EXHIBIT 6   Occupancy and Capacity, 1984–1989, CMI

Zone	1989	1988	1987	1986
American Zone				
Number of Beds				
North America	1,032	1,032	1,030	470
Mexico-Caribbean	8,890	8,956	9,068	9,364
Occupancy (%)				
North America	74.6	68.5	56.5	65.4
Mexico-Caribbean	65.6	65.4	65.7	64.4
Asian Zone				
Number of Beds	3,330	3,330	3,250	2,550
Occupancy (%)	73.2	61.5	58.2	47.3
Total American and Asian Zones				
Number of beds	13,252	13,318	13,348	12,384
Occupancy (%)	68.7	65.2	59.6	60.5

Note: Club Med employs a method significantly different from the lodging or hospitality industry, using beds rather than number of rooms. Therefore, data are not comparable with the industry. It reports occupancy in terms of beds, based on two beds per room available for guests. It determines capacity on the basis of the average number of bed days available each year, i.e., the number of beds in each village multiplied by the number of days the village was open annually.
Source: CMI annual reports, 1988, 1989.

postponed reopening of Paradise Island (670 beds) until February 1988. An adverse political environment resulted in the closing of Magic Isle (704 beds) in Haiti. Occupancy rates declined (see Exhibit 6 for data on occupancy rates by geographical areas). Hurricane Gilbert shut down Cancun in September 1988; it reopened in April 1989. Then, in September 1989, Hurricane Hugo caused temporary closings of Caravelle on Guadeloupe and Turkoise in the Turks and Caicos Islands. Eleuthera, closed in May 1989 for renovations, reopened in December 1989. St. George's Cove in Bermuda ceased operations while a sale was negotiated.

On the upside, in 1989 occupancy rates in the American Zone reached a new high of 66.3 percent; hotel days advanced from 2,000,000 in 1988 to 2,099,000 in 1989. The number of GMs from France and other European countries rose nearly 50 percent; and the number of GMs from Mexico, the Caribbean, and South America increased modestly. Inauguration of the newest 700-bed CMI village, under construction on San Salvador (the Bahamas), was anticipated in 1992, in time for the 500th anniversary of Columbus's landing on that island.

Likewise, the Asian Zone in 1989 achieved new records. Occupancy rates attained 73.2 percent, and hotel days increased by 24.4 percent to 857,000. Exhibit 7 breaks down hotel days by zone and origin of business. Japan's market represented the jewel of the Pacific. The Japanese not only visited Sahoro—a winter ski resort and summer mountain resort—in record numbers (70.9 percent occupancy), but traveled in large numbers to locations throughout the Asian and American Zones. The Tahitian villages of Moorea and Bora became more accessible via direct Air France flights between Tokyo and Papeete.

EXHIBIT 7   Hotel Days by Zone, 1986–1989, CMI

Zone and National Origin of GMs	Number of Hotel Days			
	1989	1988	1987	1986
American Zone				
American and Canadian	1,480,000	1,510,000	1,495,000	1,574,000
Mexican and Caribbean	113,000	107,000	70,000	130,000
Asian/Pacific/Indian	78,000	71,000	69,000	48,000
French/Other European	34,000	32,000	28,000	32,000
Total	**2,099,000**	**2,000,000**	**1,891,000**	**1,995,000**
Asian Zone				
American and Canadian	8,000	4,000	4,000	2,000
Asian/Pacific/Indian	607,000	500,000	429,000	306,000
French/Other European	242,000	185,000	183,000	94,000
Total	**857,000**	**689,000**	**616,000**	**402,000**

Source: CMI annual reports, 1988, 1989.

EXHIBIT 8   Number of GMs by National Origin, 1986–1989, CMI

Zone and National Origin	Number of GMs			
	1989	1988	1987	1986
American Zone				
American and Canadian	215,000	218,100	210,800	220,000
Mexican and Caribbean	18,000	10,500	8,400	20,000
Asian/Pacific/Indian	13,200	12,700	12,500	6,100
French/Other European	38,200	25,500	18,900	17,200
South American	5,000	4,500	3,900	4,400
Total	**289,500**	**271,300**	**254,500**	**267,700**
Asian Zone				
American and Canadian	1,200	600	600	300
Asian/Pacific/Indian	113,500	94,300	71,100	55,000
French/Other European	21,400	17,400	24,200	9,500
Total	**136,100**	**112,300**	**95,900**	**64,800**

Source: CMI annual reports, 1988, 1989.

During 1990 CMI expected to increase aggregate bed capacity at several locations: Sahoro (400 beds), Bali in Indonesia (800 beds), Phuket in Thailand (700 beds), and La Pointe aux Canonniers (440 beds). A new village in Vietnam was planned for the early part of the decade. On the other hand, the number of European visitors to Asia actually decreased from 1987 levels. Exhibit 8 summarizes GMs by nationality groups.

COMPETITION

Despite its global coverage, Club Med was still a small company, based on number of clients, compared with such European rivals as Thompson Travel and the German group, TUI. As a tour operator, Club Med fell from third to seventh place between 1984 and 1988. With growth in its home market of less than 3 percent annually and a total of 391,000 French GMs in 1987–88, Club Méditerranée was heavily dependent on patronage from other European countries. When it launched its Europeanization program, the company selected 17 villages for conversion to an international flavor because its biggest competitor, Robinson, had 16 of them. Trigano commented on the changing markets:

> When we started, 99 percent of the people in the Paris region had never seen the Mediterranean. I hadn't. Just to see the sea was a considerable emotional event. And in my first year we had a water-ski boat . . . and you could walk on the water. When the Club offered wonders like that, you didn't worry about the accommodation—in U.S. Army surplus tents. We were all together, sharing these wonderful experiences, so we became friends; and that friendship was a sort of powerful cement.
>
> But the sense of discovery has gone now. People just want the best. Club Med can't be the same because life is not the same.

By the end of the 1980s, CMI had encountered customer price resistance; occupancy rates suffered in the winter 1988 season when it raised prices 13 percent. Political unrest and labor problems, coupled with temporary closings, gave competitors an edge during 1988–1989.

The term "vacation" conjured up different images for different vacationers; in effect, Club Med competed against all types of trips and destinations that people might select. Club Med saw its biggest competitors as being Walt Disney, other lodging chains with destination resorts, cruise-ship operators, and copycat operations with village hideaways similar to Club Med's.

The Walt Disney Corporation, with operations in Florida and California as well as France and Japan, generated revenues approaching $5 billion and net income exceeding $700 million. It had recently opened Disney/MGM Studios at Lake Buena Vista, Florida, to attract adults. The appeal of Disney-related vacations was summarized in an article in *Restaurants and Institutions*:

> You don't have to be a kid to love Disney's new image. You can be a business executive, for instance, booked into one of three new convention hotels opening next year at Disney World. Or you can be a teenager, catching the curl on a boogie board at the new water park. Or a "thirtysomething" baby boomer sitting in a TV kitchen eating a pot roast that would have done Donna Reed proud.

Besides Disney World, Epcot, and Disney/MGM Studios, central Florida had numerous other attractions that made Florida interesting to vacationing families. With two working studios, the area was expected to become the East Coast movie capital. Besides, long-term plans to make Orlando a giant international airline hub, with bullet train service to other Florida cities, could make it a destination city for Asians and Europeans alike. Bargain-basement airfares and tour packages, and a somewhat weaker U.S. dollar, enticed a flood of European travelers to Florida during the winter months of 1989–90.

Additionally, world-class resort hotels catering to an upscale business clientele represented a lucrative segment of the lodging industry. Firms such as

E X H I B I T 9   **Partial Listing of Resorts with Programs for Children**

Year-Round

Marriott Mountain Shadows Resort, Scottsdale, Arizona
Marriott Tan Tar-a, Lake of the Ozarks, Osage Beach, Missouri
South Sea Plantation Resort and Yacht Harbor, Captiva Island, Florida
Sonesta Beach Hotel, Key Biscayne, Florida

Summer

Amelia Island Plantation, Amelia Island, Florida
Case de Campo, La Romana, Dominican Republic
Dunfey Hyannis Resort, Hyannis, Massachusetts
Hyatt Hotel, Hilton Head Island, South Carolina
Hyatt Regency Cerromar Beach, Dorado, Puerto Rico
Mariner's Inn, Hilton Head, South Carolina
Marriott Grand Hotel, Point Clear, Alabama
Marriott Hilton Head Resort, South Carolina
Sagamore Hotel, Lake George, New York

Source: Iris Sanderson Jones, "Traveling with Kids," *Working Woman* (November 1986), p. 232.

Marriott, Hilton, Sheraton, Holiday Inn, and Hyatt, competing on a level with Club Med, had opened luxurious upscale resorts in different environmental settings in Hawaii, Florida, the Caribbean, and Europe. Conference centers, meeting rooms, quarters for executives, and getaway packages were prominently featured by all the major lodging chains. Marriott Corporation, the world's seventh-largest hotel chain, had established resorts in some of the same locations as Club Med. Also, as the larger U.S. lodging and resort chains became more family oriented, they developed children's programs (see Exhibit 9 for resorts with children's programs.)

Other competitors, such as Hedonism II, Club Paradise, and Jack Tar Village, in imitation of Club Med, offered lower-priced vacation packages. Club Med judged these copycat vacation villages to be inconsequential, second-rate competitors. However, Thomas J. Garzelli, vice president of Fly Fare Vacations said, "There's no question that the people who are filling up these resorts are the right demographics to go to Club Med." Most copycats, usually located in the Caribbean, were not global players, but they competed effectively in limited markets.

Similarly, in Japan, competition for the leisure yen was triggered by success of Tokyo Disneyland—15 million people had visited the theme park by March 31, 1990. Japanese companies specializing in leisure and vacation activities were mostly focused on theme and amusement park investments where revenues had jumped from $1.4 billion (U.S. dollar equivalent) in 1982 to $2.5 billion anticipated for 1990. For example, Nippon Steel's $200 million subsidiary, Space World Inc., created a lunar fantasy land, complete with Lucky and Vicky Rabbit, 500 miles southeast of Tokyo. By mid-1990, roughly 100 similar projects were in various stages of planning and construction—many in imitation of U.S. and European successes and some reminiscent of Club Med concepts (a

Mongolian tent village, an indoor wind-surfing pool, a pair of Spanish villas, and Scandinavian towns). However, with increasing competition, Yuji Jemoto, specialist with the Japan Development Bank, believed that some ventures would fail. He said, "After natural selection, the question is which ones will survive."

The newest and fastest-growing wave of Club Med's competitors was the cruise-ship industry, which featured all-inclusive trips and tours, not unlike Club Med's, and frequently traveled to the same exotic destinations. Multinational cruise-ship companies, such as Carnival Cruise Lines, Royal Viking, and Norwegian Caribbean, had vacation packages at various price ranges that appealed to singles, married couples, families, and retirees. Robert H. Dickenson, vice president of sales and marketing for Carnival Cruise Lines said, "Cruising was once the domain of the rich. Now cruising is open to everyone." By the end of 1987, the cruise industry had grown to a $4 billion market in North America alone, and the lines made deep inroads into Club Med's Caribbean domain.

FINANCES

Club Méditerranée, founded as a nonprofit sports organization in 1950, was incorporated as a *societé anonyme* (S.A.) in 1957 in France and went public in 1965. Effective November 1, 1983, via a formation agreement, most of Club Méditerranée's villages, sales activities, related operations, investments, contracts, and commitments in the American Zone were transferred at book value to CMI. Incorporated in the Cayman Islands in 1984, CMI, a majority-owned (74 percent in October 31, 1989) subsidiary of Club Méditerranée S.A., sold 3,400,000 common shares through a public offering in the United States and 300,000 common shares in a private offering to certain club officers, directors, and employees. CMI maintained financial records in U.S. dollars prepared in conformity with generally accepted U.S. accounting principles.

With profits and dividends stagnating during 1987–88, ownership of Club Méditerranée stock changed. For example, the Groupe Depots holding company increased its 2.1 percent interest in 1988 to about 9.0 percent by early 1990. The Japanese conglomerate, Seibu Saison, with its 3.0 percent stake, was joined in 1989 by Nippon Life and its 4.9 interest. Other major stockholders included Warburg Mercury with 4.5 percent and the Agnelli family with 2.9 percent. To make a takeover bid more difficult, Club Méditerranée tried unsuccessfully to negotiate interlocking shareholdings with Nouvelles Frontieres, a tour operator and air charter company; such a joint venture would have made Club Med the third largest tour operator.

Summary financial data appear in Exhibit 10. Less than 5 percent of Club Med's investment in property and equipment represented land value of the villages. Buildings, plus building and leasehold improvements, accounted for the bulk of the value of villages. Most properties had leases ranging from 1 to 27 years, with an average of 15 years. Lease payments could be suspended in case of *force majeure*. Seven leases required rentals based upon occupancy levels. Data in Exhibit 11 highlight the performance of Club Med's common stock.

E X H I B I T 10   **Financial Highlights, 1984–1989, CMI**   *(Millions of U.S. dollars)*

	1989	1988	1987	1986	1985	1984
Income Statement Data						
Revenues	$468.8	$412.4	$370.4	$337.0	$279.7	$235.3
Gross profits	159.4	133.2	125.1	115.3	92.4	81.5
Depreciation	17.9	16.4	13.5	11.5	7.8	6.1
Operating income	25.4	11.2	20.0	19.8	16.0	15.1
Income before extraordinary items	20.4	8.7	16.8	17.4	14.2	11.5
Extraordinary items*	0.7	0.1	0.6	0.7	1.4	0.6
Net income	21.1	8.8	17.4	18.1	15.6	12.0
Balance Sheet Data						
Working capital	$ 27.5	$ 42.5	$ 4.6	$ 30.9	$ 31.9	$ 34.6
Long-term debt	100.1	131.1	89.4	91.2	76.1	39.3
Shareholders' equity	207.6	189.4	184.2	159.0	142.5	129.5
Total assets	415.5	403.2	353.4	313.8	269.1	212.1

*The firm is taxed under many jurisdictions, some of which do not impose an income tax. Resulting from negotiated tax reductions for periods ranging from 1991 to 2005, the firm received incentive concessions from the Dominican Republic, Turks and Caicos Islands, Haiti, Saint Lucia, Mauritius, Thailand, and Indonesia. Also, the firm had net operating losses and various tax credit carryforwards, as well as tax loss carryforwards expiring mostly 1990 through 1994.

Sources: CMI annual reports, 1988, 1989.

E X H I B I T 11   **Common Stock Statistics for CMI, 1984–1990**

	1989	1988	1987	1986	1985	1984
Net Income/Share	$1.50	$0.62	$1.23	$1.32	$1.14	$1.14
Weighted average shares outstanding (in millions)	14.1	14.1	14.1	13.7	13.7	10.6
Dividends per share	$0.20	$0.20	$0.20	$0.20	n/a	n/a

Range of Stock Prices by Quarter, 1987-1989

Quarter Ended	1989 High	1989 Low	1988 High	1988 Low	1987 High	1987 Low
January 31	$16.875	$12.625	$15.000	$ 9.000	$29.250	$21.500
April 30	19.875	15.750	16.250	11.750	29.000	25.000
July 31	21.875	18.250	16.625	12.250	27.000	22.625
October 31	20.625	17.375	15.750	13.250	24.750	12.250

Sources: CMI annual reports, 1988, 1989.

EXHIBIT 12   **Operating Data by Market Segment, 1987–1989, CMI**
                (In millions of U.S. dollars)

Regions	Consolidated Regional Revenues	Operating Income (Loss)	Identifiable Assets
	1989		
North America	$103.4	$ (8.4)	$ 48.1
Mexico–Caribbean	175.4	10.8	264.5
Asia–Pacific	157.9	22.9	102.9
Consolidated	**$468.8**	**$ 25.4**	**$415.5**
	1988		
North America	$133.1	$(11.7)	$ 55.5
Mexico–Caribbean	151.6	8.2	241.6
Asia–Pacific	127.7	14.7	106.2
Consolidated	**$412.4**	**$ 11.2**	**$403.2**
	1987		
North America	$124.6	$ (1.6)	$ 48.1
Mexico–Caribbean	143.6	12.0	223.3
Asia–Pacific	102.2	9.7	82.0
Consolidated	**$370.4**	**$ 20.0**	**$353.4**

Note: Consolidated revenues eliminate revenues between geographic areas and revenues originating in another area. Therefore, although the North American area generated nearly twice the revenues shown above, these were spent in another region. By the same token, about 75 percent of revenues attributed to the Mexico–Caribbean region were generated elsewhere. In the Asia–Pacific area, most revenues generated there were spent in the region.

Source: CMI annual report, 1989.

With international transactions conducted in several currencies, CMI had suffered exchange rate losses. For several years it endured the negative impact from net French franc–based costs and expenses. Despite a 10 percent worsening of the dollar in international markets, these losses stabilized in 1988 partly due to a 35 percent increase in GMs from European countries who paid for visits to American Zone villages with strong currencies. The firm also had experienced adverse effects of Mexico's decision to maintain a fixed-exchange (below market) rate of pesos for dollars.

STRATEGY

Club Méditerranée began as an international firm with headquarters in Paris, operations in the Balearic Islands (about 120 miles southeast of Barcelona, Spain), and customers predominantly, but not exclusively, French. As operations spread across the globe, management largely maintained the original strategies of Trigano with reactive modifications to those strategies as current conditions dictated.

President Oizan-Chapon said, "In business you take the risk; you cannot control everything." He mentioned two major factors that hurt Club Med in 1988: (1) political unrest, which precipitated closing its Magic Isle village in Haiti and negatively impacted occupancy rates in New Caledonia; and (2) construction problems, which delayed opening of a big new village in Huatulco, Mexico, and cost Club Med an extra $7 million. Changing demographics and customer tastes could not be denied, although Oizan-Chapon insisted, "Only part of the market is maturing. Part of it is growing. We are following a life cycle plan."

Product diversification efforts met with limited success. The North American market had encountered problems: West Coast customers were less attuned to French culture than East Coast ones. *Chef de village* Jean-Luc Olivero thought that the problem was even more basic: Americans were puritanical. For instance, when Club Med bought the Sandpiper property in Florida from Hilton Hotels, management ordered removal of TVs and telephones from rooms. Americans preferred them. They were replaced in 1989. (See Exhibit 12 for data on operating results by market segment.)

CMI had a three-pronged growth strategy for the 1990s:

- *Broaden the appeal*—increase market penetration of the core product, the Club Med village vacation.
- *Expand the reach*—introduce the Club Med concept to countries with growing economies and desires for new vacation opportunities.
- *Widen the concept*—develop new vacation products, particularly in the rapidly growing cruise market.

LANCE, INC.

Earl R. Sage, University of North Carolina at Charlotte
Linda E. Swayne, University of North Carolina at Charlotte

In an article in 1982, *Forbes* observed, "The folks at Lance, Inc., the largest independent snack food manufacturer in the U.S., don't cotton much to management tools like debt financing . . . or even advertising. But the company has a remarkable record of performance." The article quoted A. F. "Pete" Sloan, then president of Lance, "Hell, you don't need to go out and get yourself a computer and 14 MBAs to run a successful business." Performance spoke for itself—over the five years through 1982, Lance had one of the best after-tax profit margins in the $11 billion salty snack foods industry, averaging 8.1 percent versus an estimated 4 percent for Nabisco and 7 percent at PepsiCo's Frito-Lay division. From sales of $291 million in 1982 the company has grown to $446 million in 1990. Return on equity had remained close to 20 percent and the company had no long-term debt. Attempts had been made to grow through diversification, but results were disappointing. "Moving beyond our traditional markets is going to make continued growth more challenging," stated Bill Disher, newly appointed CEO of Lance. "We may have to be more aggressive in the supermarket or maybe even consider advertising. . . ."

HISTORY

Lance, Inc., began operations over 75 years ago by accident. Philip L. Lance, a coffee salesman and food broker from Charlotte, North Carolina, purchased 500 pounds of fine Virginia peanuts for a customer. After the customer decided that he could not use the peanuts, Mr. Lance took the peanuts home so as not to disappoint the Virginia peanut farmer. The peanuts were roasted in small quantities in Lance's kitchen and sold in brown paper bags for a nickel. The company was founded in 1913 when Philip Lance formed a partnership with S. A. Van Every, his son-in-law and an associate in the food brokerage business.

The business expanded, outgrowing the Lance home, and with the new space a mechanical roaster was added. The roaster purchase enabled the young company to manufacture peanut butter, which Mr. Lance spread on crackers for his customers to sample. This led to the first packaged peanut butter crackers ever sold. Mr. Lance died in an automobile accident in late 1926, at which point Mr. Van Every took over operations and incorporated the company as Lance, Inc.

Lance added baking operations in 1938 in order to make its own crackers. In 1943, following the death of his father, Phil Van Every became president. Lance had become primarily a candy company prior to World War II but determined that the company could make more extensive use of its wartime sugar allowance by producing snack foods. Phil Van Every automated many operations and reorganized the sales and distribution network; his entrepreneurial and managerial skills helped the company build a recognized position in the snack food industry and paved the way for Lance to succeed even after his death in 1980.

When Phil Van Every retired, he was succeeded by J. B. Meacham and then Glen G. Rhodes. When Rhodes retired, Pete Sloan became chairman. The Van Every family, although no longer directly involved in management, is still represented on the board of directors and continues to control (either directly or in trust) over 44 percent of the outstanding shares of stock. Sloan stepped down as chief executive officer (CEO) in April 1990 after 34 years with Lance (14 years as CEO), but retained the post of chairman of the board. He was succeeded as CEO by J. W. "Bill" Disher, a 25-year veteran of Lance, who had been serving the company as president. A graduate of Wake Forest University, Bill Disher held finance positions prior to becoming president and CEO.

THE SNACK FOOD INDUSTRY

The lines between a snack food and traditional meal food have blurred and a significant portion of the population eats many small meals throughout the day. Because of busy American lifestyles, many consumers have neither the time nor interest to prepare and sit down to eat three complete meals a day. Instead, they eat portable snack foods while on the run. Others enjoy rewarding themselves for all their hard work with an expensive or highly caloric taste treat. Whether called fun foods, finger foods, portable foods, or between-meal foods, snacks are part of the American way of life and represent a $29-billion-dollar industry.[1]

The industry had at least 17 different categories of snack foods, but three major segments were dominant: candy, cookies and crackers, and salty snacks. The candy category had always accounted for the greatest percentage of snack food sales. The salted snack foods category, nearly half of which was potato chips, had traditionally accounted for the smallest share among the three.

The majority of snack food products appeared to have reached the maturity stage of the product life cycle; distribution was pervasive and per capita sales were stable. Growth in unit volume was not expected to exceed population growth, especially considering mounting consumer concerns about eating healthier foods. Snack foods were being increasingly scrutinized and avoided by health-conscious consumers.

New product development centered around line extensions of existing brands: new sizes (more small packages to meet the needs of busy consumers), new flavors of existing products, and new formulations (less salt, oil, or cholesterol). Many of the regional manufacturers followed the lead of the major competitors who spent huge sums on new product research and development as well as marketing research. Regional producers like Lance faced strong competition especially from the large marketing-knowledgeable companies such as Frito-Lay, Borden, and Eagle. Consolidation was expected to continue as the giants bought out regional producers to obtain better distribution. Distribution was critical in the industry because of the high

---

[1] "Industry Sales Top $29 Billion," *Snack Food* 79, no. 6 (June 1990), p. M2.

cost of transportation for products that weighed very little but that were bulky and took up space. The price advantage of shorter distribution routes was a key factor in the success of regional snack manufacturers. All major competitors used a store-to-door delivery system where snack food company–owned trucks deliver and stock product to individual stores rather than to a warehouse.

The bargaining power of raw material suppliers such as potato and corn farmers had become more influential; as weather and crop conditions boosted the costs of agricultural growers, snack food manufacturers found themselves incurring high prices for food ingredients. To some extent, large snack food manufacturers were in a stronger position to try to negotiate quantity discounts on raw material purchases than were smaller producers.

Another issue that snack food manufacturers had to deal with was the bargaining power of their customers, principally supermarkets. Concentration in the food retailing industry was high and supermarket chains accounted for about 70 percent of total snack food sales. "It is risky to depend on a small number of large customers; diversification is important," according to Jack Moore, Lance executive vice president. He continued, "We have 300,000 customers which gives us strength to stand up to any single customer. And we have to balance the various segments. The question is always, is it good for Lance?"

Jerry Swain, vice president of sales for Lance, observed:

> Although snack sales have increased for retailers in recent years and are projected to continue growing in the near future, there is just not enough room on the shelf for the snack food category. The number of products and line extensions being introduced has caused a space crunch. This lack of shelf space has caused a problem with stock-outs and losses in sales and profits. Therefore retailers will use distribution channels, pricing, and manufacturer support programs as critical considerations in the choice among brands.

Another important influence was the differences that prevailed in regional taste preferences. Products such as pork skins, moon pies, and salt and vinegar potato chips were big sellers in some regions (the Southeast) but generated very low sales volumes in others. In order to be competitive, one of the industry leaders, Frito-Lay, implemented a plan in 1987 to regionalize operations, sales, and marketing. The company defined eight regions and allowed managers to tailor product-line strategies to compete head-to-head with local and regional snack manufacturers.

Snack food consumption depended on population growth, the economy (during prosperous times a greater portion of disposable income was spent eating away from home and snack consumption decreased), and consumer concerns about health (use of salt in the diet, cholesterol, and weight concerns). Consumption patterns by age group were also changing as consumers were taking their snack habits with them as they grew older. Maturing baby boomers were continuing as adults to eat many of the snacks they ate as children. Although children were still the biggest group of snackers, adults were a growing portion of the market.

Another consumer trend affecting the industry was that of increased home entertainment. Whether due to the rise in VCR ownership or the increased concern about drunken driving, people were often entertaining their friends at home rather than meeting at a bar. The increasing desire to eat healthfully and conveniently had created opportunities for snack food makers to introduce low-salt, no-salt, low-fat, and no-cholesterol versions of their products. Additionally, companies had introduced smaller sizes of their popular products as a way of helping consumers control the number of calories they consumed.

There was little concern in the industry concerning foreign entry into the market. "We're about to reach zero population growth and flour and snack foods are low tech," according to Bill Disher. He continued, "There are very low barriers to entry—most folks could make our products at home if they wanted to. . . . Demand is static. Most textbooks would say this is a poor industry, but we've been able to set net sales and earnings records for over a decade."

MAJOR COMPETITORS

Jack Moore stated, "Our competition is anything that doesn't have Lance's name on it. Anything that satisfies an appetite—a homemade sandwich, a piece of watermelon, peanuts, anybody else's potato chips, etc., is competition. If it doesn't have Lance on the label, we've lost an opportunity." Lance had a number of direct competitors in the mature snack food industry, however. Some, such as Frito-Lay, were national in scope, but had developed regional strategies and product lines to enhance their competitive capabilities. Borden has amassed a collection of 10 regional snack companies to achieve the advantages of regional customer satisfaction and the efficiencies from operating a larger company. Because of the significant freight charges previously mentioned, most of the competitors maintained regional manufacturing and distribution facilities. On the other hand, some of Lance's rivals were truly regional and operated only in a specific geographic area—Mike Sell's Chips sold only in Tennessee and Ohio, Coors Chips sold in seven western states, and Moore's Chips sold in eight mid-Atlantic states.

Frito-Lay: The Largest Producer of Snack Foods

Frito-Lay was a snack division of PepsiCo and its major profit center. Frito-Lay had 37 manufacturing and processing plants in the United States and 12 foreign countries. Its varied line of snack foods included Fritos brand corn chips, Lay's, Ruffles, and O'Grady's brand potato chips, Munchos brand potato crisps, Cheetos brand cheese-flavored snacks, Doritos and Tostitos brand tortilla chips, Funyun brand onion-flavored snacks, Baken-Ets brand fried pork rinds, Grandma's brand cookies, Frito-Lay brand crackers, and Frito-Lay brand dips and popcorn.

Over 1,600 distribution facilities and 10,000 route sales reps ensured Frito-Lay products arrived fresh and were stocked directly onto supermarket shelves. This store-to-door delivery system allowed Frito-Lay to maintain close inventory control, reduce supermarket labor costs, and provide customers with fresh, uncrushed snack foods.

The company was building on its strength as the largest snack food producer in the United States. It had established brand strength and was seeking to further that strength through successful introduction of line extensions (Doritos Light for example) and reorganization of its marketing effort to create a stronger regional presence. Frito-Lay was rapidly expanding in existing markets as well as entering new markets both in the United States and abroad.

Borden: Snack Foods Division Targeted for Growth

Borden's snack division was one of six company divisions targeted for growth in the 1990s. Acquisitions in 1987 of The Snacktime Company and Laura Scudder's, Inc., increased snack sales by about 40 percent and broadened the company's network of regional companies. Its principal national brands were Wise, La Famous, New York Deli, Borden, and Seyfert. In addition the company had an assortment of purely regional brands such as Laura Scudder's, Geiser's Potato Chips, and Red Seal.

Borden intended to continue its profitable growth in the six designated divisions through carefully focused acquisitions and internal growth. Strong regional companies were prime targets for acquisition as they offered established brands and provided synergy to an already strong regional network of snack companies.

Golden Enterprises: A Major Regional Competitor

The Golden Flake trademark is carried on a full line of snack foods that were distributed in 12 southeastern states. The snack products were manufactured by plants in Alabama, Tennessee, and Florida. Golden Flake's product line included potato chips, tortilla chips, corn chips, fried pork skins, baked and fried cheese curls, peanut butter crackers, cheese crackers, onion rings, and popcorn that were manufactured by the company. Also included in the product line were cakes and cookie items, canned dips, dried meat products, pretzels, and nuts that were manufactured by other companies but packaged under the Golden Flake label. The company's earnings were somewhat depressed for a period of time, primarily due to increased competition and because the level of sales had not been sufficient to offset the higher costs associated with increased production capacity, expanded reach, and higher advertising and promotional expenses.

Similar to Lance, Golden Flake utilized a "follow the leader" strategy. The company did not spend much on developing new products but it did advertise and made profitable use of sales promotion. A tie-in with the Southeastern Conference for football games, where a custom van in each SEC team's colors was given away, had been particularly effective.

Golden Flake dominated in the state of Alabama and was usually second behind Frito-Lay in the other states where the brand was sold. Distribution was primarily through grocery stores, although the Golden Flake brands were sold in vending machines in the company's primary markets of Alabama, Mississippi, Georgia, and Tennessee. With new facilities recently completed and renovation to the Birmingham plant, Golden Flake could increase production 50 percent. Sales in 1990 surpassed $129 million.

LANCE'S CORPORATE CULTURE

Lance was founded as a family business and had worked diligently to maintain that atmosphere despite its growth. Many employees had spent their entire working careers dedicated to serving Lance and its customers. "Stay close to

---

Our Philosophy

We believe we should help develop the people in our organization to their maximum potential in a climate that creates a high degree of employee morale.

We believe in being good citizens—in encouraging our employees to practice thrift—take an active interest in the church of their choice—and in community projects and government.

We believe that the products and services we offer should be of the highest quality that we may merit the respect, confidence and loyalty of our customers and consumers.

We believe we should be a source of strength to our suppliers and that all of our transactions with them should be based on honesty and truth.

We believe all of our activities should be planned and executed so the company can expand its leadership and be regarded as a model in industry.

We believe we should earn a reasonable profit so the company will remain financially strong and may perpetuate this philosophy.

Source: Philip Lance Van Every, *The History of Lance* (New York: The Newcomen Society in North America, 1974).

the customers and the customers are always right." Those company values, along with "quality and value in an honest product from a reputable company," form the core of the Lance culture. The company's business principles and philosophical values are set forth in Exhibit 1.

The family orientation at Lance is encouraged. Everyone at Lance is known on a first-name basis. All executives and employees eat together in a common cafeteria. At 9:00 A.M. each morning a bell rings for silent prayer; it happens again at 5:30 P.M. for the second shift. This custom started during World War II, with prayers for victory. After the war it continued, as a thanksgiving for peace. Jack Moore, executive vice president, says, "Lance believes in basic values of doing what's right . . . in family values. Employees of Lance are the salt of the earth."

Lance promotes from within; outsiders are brought in only when Lance people lack the needed skills and knowledge. Every officer of Lance has worked on a route truck. Food science people with their specialized knowledge are hired early in their career so they can become indoctrinated with the Lance philosophy.

Lance operates by committees or "multiple management," a concept started in the early 1940s shortly after Philip Van Every, Sr., died. His son, Philip Van Every, observed multiple management while visiting McCormick Spices in Philadelphia. Phil Van Every adopted and improved the concept. Although individuals have titles, Lance looks to its board of directors, executive committee, and administrative committee for leadership. The executive committee and the administrative committee are responsible for day-to-day operations. Important decisions with far-reaching implications are taken before the board of directors.

Other committees operate in the functional areas. For example, the products committee (comprising company executives and sales, manufacturing, and technical representatives) approves a new product only when the sales department believes they can sell it, manufacturing believes it can be made, and purchasing believes it can obtain the ingredients. Various tests have to be passed, including the keeping test (length of time that the product could be maintained in inventory and through distribution while still keeping its freshness), profitability test, and the ingredients test (the ingredients have to be in keeping with the management philosophy of quality and good health with low cholesterol and low sodium).

In the spring of the year, "P and R" (planning and review) meetings are held. P and R meetings include all branch managers who operate as route supervisors for up to nine reps. They are in constant contact with the customer as they spend time with the route sales reps in the field. The P and R meetings are followed a few weeks later by a DSM (district sales managers) meeting, which includes the corporate officers (in Lance's culture, "the people from Charlotte"). Early in the summer, the Charlotte people review and critique the minutes of the P and R meetings and the DSM meetings; those minutes become the work sheet for the summer. In the fall, the corporate personnel meet with the district sales managers again to discuss how they have resolved the problems or taken advantage of the opportunities highlighted by the district sales managers. Then the district sales managers meet with all the branch managers in another round of P and R meetings where the problems, solutions, and opportunities are reported to them.

PRODUCTION AND DISTRIBUTION

Lance manufactures, distributes, and sells a wide variety of packaged snack foods and bread basket items (products that would be placed in a basket at restaurants as an addition to or alternate for bread). The principal snack items include: cracker sandwiches filled with either peanut butter or cheese; cookie sandwiches; cheese bits and twists; peanuts; potato, tortilla, and corn chips; fried pork skins; popcorn; fig bars and cookies; cakes, candies, and meat snacks. These products are sold under the Lance label to convenience stores, service stations, drugstores, supermarkets, schools, restaurants, hospitals, and other customers in 35 states and Washington, D.C. The majority of sales are in states east of the Mississippi River. Approximately 15 to 20 percent of the company's net sales volume is generated by products purchased from other manufacturers and distributed under the Lance label.

The company's principal bread basket items are wafers, crackers, bread sticks, and melba toast. These products are individually packaged and sold to restaurants, schools, and similar institutions, along with bulk packaged croutons and cracker meal.

Thirty percent of the company's products are sold through vending machines, which are made available to customers on a rental, sale, or commission basis. These machines are usually situated in noncompetitive locations where Lance does not have to fight for shelf space by offering deep discounts and promotions. Less than 5 percent of sales are made to outside vending distributors. Lance also packages several of its most popular snack and bread basket items in conveniently sized "Home Paks" sold in supermarkets and grocery stores. This product line, first introduced in limited markets in 1982, represents approximately 12 to 13 percent of snack sales. The bulk of Lance's market is an over-the-counter single-serve pack sold in convenience stores, gas stations, and quick stops.

Through a program of continuous expansion, replacement, or renovation of facilities and equipment, and automation of processes, the company seeks to utilize the most advanced technology available. This enables the company to reduce operating costs and increase manufacturing efficiency, allowing Lance to maintain relatively consistent prices, an important advantage in vending sales where step pricing occurs. Lance and others who sell through vending machines have to increase prices in minimum 5 cent increments (steps) because the machines do not accept pennies.

MARKETING

Lance's marketing strategy is anchored on a follow-the-leader strategy for new product development, devotion to a single-serving product size, and no advertising. By waiting for larger companies to develop and market new products and by maintaining its no-advertising policy, Lance has been able to incorporate new products into the line at about half the cost of the industry leaders. In the late 1970s, in an attempt to break out of its follower strategy, Lance introduced honey-coated peanuts. Although the product was unsuccessful, when Anheuser-Busch's Eagle Snacks Honey-Roasted Peanuts caught on with consumers, Lance promptly reintroduced its honey-coated peanuts, and at nearly half the price.

Product Development

Although Lance's main thrust is in the single-serving market, it had $65 million in supermarket sales in 1989. The company has resisted increasing its single-serving product size to capture more supermarket customers, although industry sources estimate 70 percent of all snack food is sold in the supermarket. The decision to enter the competition for supermarket shelf space was carefully considered. Pete Sloan had been reluctant to change the company's marketing mix to include larger-sized packages because, "a supermarket sale takes away a vending machine sale." However, vending machine sales were growing at only about 3 percent a year. The company moved slowly into supermarket sales with its Home Pak product line. Actually, the gas shortages between 1973 and 1975 caused Lance to begin thinking about supermarket sales. "Our route sales reps passed by the supermarkets and we figured they might as well stop in and sell some products," Jack Moore remembered thinking. In addition there were letters from Lance customers who wanted Captain's Wafers (crackers) in a convenient take-home size. Customers had enjoyed the good taste of Captain's Wafers in restaurants and wrote to Lance requesting that they be made available in local grocery stores. In 1982 Lance began supermarket sales with multipacks of Captain's Wafers. The Home Pak consisted of eight of the individual packs combined in one package. This was a cost-effective way to enter the market without changing the product line.

Lance route sales reps knew how to sell the "racks" of product that are used for displaying single-serving product in over-the-counter sales. Because shelf space is always difficult to capture in supermarkets, Lance provided vertical, free-standing racks and a 5 percent discount to win the display space. The racks were totally maintained by Lance's sales force—another benefit to the store. It took Lance about four years to achieve distribution to supermarkets in all the company's territories.

Family-pack potato chips (large size containing six ounces as opposed to the one-ounce snack size) were introduced to the over-the-counter market on July 4, 1988. This expansion of the product mix to include a variety of family-size chip products was made possible by new computerized bagging machinery. Distribution was achieved in about 90 percent of the sales territories by September 1990.

Lance buys some food products from other manufacturers and plans to continue to do so. For example, only two to three companies produce melba toast because of the specialized manufacturing ovens required. Lance purchases melba toast from these companies because it is such a low-volume item. It is not economically feasible for Lance to manufacture melba toast, but it does fill out the line. Lance generates profits from manufacturing *and* distribution for its own products. For private-label items (such as melba toast), there is no manufacturing profit but there is distribution profit achieved by the efficient store-to-door distribution. Companion products are added when the company feels that the items are necessary to be able to offer a full line to their customers. "We're slow to change," according to Jerry Swain, Lance vice president of sales. Recently candy rolls were dropped from Lance's line. The product was private label (manufactured by someone else with Lance's name on it). Candy rolls competed head-to-head with Life Savers. Lance decided that the supplier's manufacturing quality was not up to Lance's standards. Lance always inspects a supplier's facilities, plants, and quality-control practices whenever the Lance name is going on a product. "Customers trust the quality of a product with the Lance label regardless of who makes it," Jerry stated.

New Products

Lance has introduced a new product that combines popcorn with caramel coating and peanuts in a bar. Named Popscotch, it is sold in vending machines and over the counter. However, Lance has found it difficult to introduce a totally new product (such as Popscotch) without advertising. Lance generally uses a copycat strategy (follow the leader), which is compatible with the company's no-advertising philosophy.

Lance is adjusting to market forces by testing chocolate candy sales. Previously, the company had not sold chocolate candy in vending machines because of the problems associated with chocolate melting while on the truck. In November 1990 Lance announced that it would offer customers four Mars Candy Co. candies along with cookie and cracker snacks in about half its 73,000 company-owned vending machines nationwide. The other half will be stocked with Lance brand chocolate candy made by a Georgia-based candy manufacturer. "We've had people tell us: 'We love your products, but one thing you're lacking is chocolate,'" said Bill Disher, Lance president and chief executive officer. "It's a test—to see if that, in fact, is correct." Disher said the goal was to determine whether Lance can increase its vending locations by adding candy to the mix in machines. The Mars products will include Snickers, Milky Way, and peanut and plain M&Ms. "We'll evaluate it in the spring and decide," Disher said.

Robinson Humphrey Co., an Atlanta-based regional brokerage firm that follows Lance, said the candy sold under Lance's label would carry a higher profit margin but probably wouldn't have the sales volume of the popular Mars products. Lance planned to test candy products purchased from Mars for distribution in its company-owned vending machines against private-label chocolate candy manufactured for Lance. The test was scheduled for the month of November so that no problems would be encountered with melting chocolate. If the sales go well, a decision will be made about truck refrigeration—not a minor decision when the company has more than 2,000 trucks on the road.

There is new technology in packaging materials. What used to be a cellophane wrapper is now a layer of film that has a vapor barrier, a moisture barrier, and an odor barrier, plus the logo within the layer of the film. Most of Lance's products have a six-week shelf life. Increased shelf life and fresher products provide cost savings and consumer benefits. Lance is actively pursuing technological improvements in packaging and expects innovations to continue. Any packaging change is quickly copied by competitors, seldom offering a long-term competitive advantage.

Lance Leads with Healthier Snacks

In contrast to its traditional follow-the-leader strategy but in response to growing consumer preferences for health-conscious snacks, Lance gambled and reformulated its traditional recipes in 1988 to make them healthier. The company greatly reduced the saturated fats and cholesterol content for most of its snack foods in order to appeal to customers with health and nutrition concerns. Lance was the first company in the snack food industry to respond to the changing emphasis on nutrition. Pete Sloan, the CEO at the time, was active in regulatory agencies in Washington. Noticing the trends in nutritional labeling and health concerns, Sloan became convinced that Lance should be the leader in providing nutritional snacks.

Lance decided early in the process that taste would have to drive the decision to switch to low-cholesterol ingredients. Taste tests were conducted within Lance until various groups of employees could not tell the difference between the old Lance products that were higher in cholesterol and the new Lance products. It took two years to develop the line of low-cholesterol products. After limited market research but extensive taste testing, Lance instituted changes that resulted in 74 percent of its 69 snack food and bakery items being cholesterol-free, while 97 percent were low in saturated fats. According to Jack Moore:

> The company was particularly sensitive to taste because a granola cake tested awhile back was unsuccessful. For good health, it contained grains and was low in cholesterol, salt, and sugar. It was nutritious, but it didn't taste very good. Sales were disappointing and it was dropped. We concluded that while customers are interested in nutrition, they are more interested in good taste!

The logistics of the changeover to the low-cholesterol products were challenging. The packaging film for the new Lance products contained a low-cholesterol "flag" on the label. Since each product had been changed, each required a new label. Logistically and economically, the old packaging film had to run out at the appropriate time. Lance set a date for every department to be ready to make the changeover. Additionally, all of the old products had to be off the shelf and out of the vending machines before Lance could publicize the new product line. Finally, management had to teach the sales force about saturated and unsaturated fats and cholesterol in order for the reps to be able to illustrate the "value-added" health benefit to the customer. Because the company did no consumer advertising, it was up to the sales force, packaging, and trucks to build awareness.

Six weeks were the normal time to move product through the channel of distribution, but Lance waited three months before announcing the low-cholesterol changeover. In December 1988, the facility was totally manufacturing the low-cholesterol products, but it was not until March 1989 that the announcement was made to the public to ensure that all the old products were out of vending machines and through distribution. As Lance was first to reformulate for better health, the media publicized the change. The company planned for increased sales to offset the cost of using more expensive, healthier oils and did not increase the selling price. It was not until eight months later that there was a price increase and it was not solely because of increased ingredient prices but because of increased costs for other items such as employee health insurance.

Although Lance was the first cookie and cracker manufacturer to reformulate, other companies, notably Keebler, were quick to follow. The reformulation is considered a success by the company and thought to be one of the major contributors to increased revenues in 1989. The publicity following the formulation change has been very favorable. Lance was one of a small number of companies that was recognized by the Washington-based Center for Science in the Public Interest for its move to lower the levels of fats and cholesterol in most of its snacks.

Lance's Strategy of No Advertising

As Pete Sloan said in an interview with *Forbes* magazine, "We have never advertised, and we don't plan to start . . . we get more for our money by putting it into manpower and improving the product line." Lance's strategy of no advertising grew out of its experiences in the 1950s. In 1953 Lance had experienced sluggish sales; management felt that advertising might help. The company engaged an advertising agency from Atlanta. The agency did away with the old logo—Lance in script letters with a charging knight holding a lance— and changed to the logo still used today. It also created some television ads (at a time when only 10 percent of the population had TVs), radio ads, billboard ads, and ads for Sunday supplements. In addition, the agency came up with the slogans, "Don't Go Around Hungry" and "Tasty Snacks in Cellophane Packs." The advertising was continued for four years through 1958. The result was no change in sales. Management concluded, "Lance's products are small purchases for consumers. They won't cross the street to buy something to satisfy their appetite. Availability is much more important than the price or how the product is displayed or promoted. Substitutes are readily available for the customer."

When the company saw no change in sales, it stopped advertising and emphasized what has become known as the "doctrine of availability," which states that "the best advertisement is a snack when you most want it and where you least expect it." During the time that Lance had been advertising, each sales branch had 18 sales reps. Redirecting efforts toward product availability rather than advertising, the company cut all the sales branches in half so that there would be nine sales reps per territory and stipulated in the job description that the branch manager should spend 75 percent of his time working with the sales reps in the field. With greater emphasis on sales reps and with managers spending more time in the field, sales drastically increased.

Sales/Distribution Organization

Lance sells its products through a company-owned sales organization (Exhibit 2). Distribution operations are administered through 24 sales districts, which are divided into 291 sales areas, each under the direction of a branch manager and an assistant branch manager. There are over 2,500 sales territories, each serviced by one sales representative who makes every effort to visit customers at the same time each week. A new trainee spends up to six months learning the territory, the product, and the Lance sales techniques.

The company owns a fleet of trucks and trailers that are used to make weekly deliveries of product to the sales territories. The sales representatives are provided with stockroom space for their inventories, from which they load their trucks for delivery to customers. Because most on the sales force have purchased their own delivery truck, Lance avoids high fleet-maintenance costs. Also, this direct store-delivery system reduces or eliminates many excess retail costs such as warehouse, transportation, and maintenance costs.

An automated route accounting (ARA) system is in the process of being tested and implemented. Two markets are testing the ARA. At night the sales reps in the two test areas hook up to a computer through a modem to the main terminal to report the day's activities. This in turn helps set the baking schedule because it is known what was sold that particular day. Inventory and marketing knowledge are enhanced, and errors are eliminated. Because nearly 300,000 tickets may be written per week, this system was expected to greatly improve communication with the route salesmen.

Local managers have responsibility for recruiting, hiring, and training the route sales reps in their territory. Every Lance employee has worked on a route. Local managers endeavored to hire only good route reps because the performance of the branch affects the pay of the local manager. Because of Lance's reputation as a good company to work for, there are many applicants whenever a route sales rep position becomes available.

DIVERSIFICATION

Lance has attempted to grow through diversification, but the results have generally been "disappointing." The company sold its Hancock's Old Fashioned Hams division to Smithfield Packing Company in 1982. In 1986, the company sold its Tri-Plas division, a manufacturer of injection-molded plastic

Maine

NH
VT
MA
CT
RI
NJ
DE

New York

Pennsylvania

MD

West Virginia

Virginia

North Carolina
* Charlotte

South Carolina

Florida

Ohio

Kentucky

Tennessee

Georgia

Alabama

Lansing

Indiana

Illinois

Mississippi

Wisconsin

Missouri

Arkansas

Louisiana

Minneapolis
St. Paul

Iowa

Minnesota

Oklahoma

Greenville †

Arlington ‡

Texas

North Dakota

South Dakota

Nebraska
Omaha

Kansas

Cheyenne

Denver
Colorado

New Mexico

Wyoming

Montana

Idaho

Utah

Arizona
Phoenix

Tucson

Washington

Oregon

Nevada

California

24 District Sales Offices.
* Charlotte, North Carolina Bakery, Chip Facility
  and General Office.
† Greenville, Texas Bakery.
‡ Arlington, Texas Chip Facility.

containers and Lance's only nonfood subsidiary. Both divestitures resulted in slight losses for Lance. Nutrition Pak Corporation, manufacturer of nutritional food products sold through contracts with distributors, was acquired in 1984. The subsidiary reported an increase in sales in 1987, but it was not enough to make it profitable, and operations ceased in January 1989.

On the other hand, Midwest Biscuit Company, a manufacturer of cookies and crackers acquired in 1979, had continued to grow and made a significant contribution to both sales and profits. Midwest's products were manufactured under both private label and its own "Vista" label. The subsidiary's sales are made through brokers and its own sales force to wholesale grocers, supermarket chains, and distributors throughout the United States, with the majority of its business in the Midwest. Bill Disher commented:

> We're actively searching for acquisitions. We prefer companion items . . . especially those that fit our distribution system. It is our goal in 1991 to get proactive in acquisitions. We haven't been very successful in the past.

FINANCIAL POSITION

Although snack food sales generally have more than doubled in the last five years, Lance's unit volume has been relatively flat with only moderate increases in revenues. Sales growth has averaged about 5 percent over the last five years, with part of that growth being a result of price increases in 1983 and 1986. Earnings, on the other hand, have grown an average of 10 percent over the past decade.

Lance maintains a strong position of liquidity and has the financial strength to meet its regular operating needs, to fund its capital investment program, and to make cash dividend payments, all through funds provided by operations (Exhibits 3–5). Lance has been consistently profitable, with net income rising each year since 1973, dividends rising each year since 1974, and return on equity averaging more than 19 percent since 1974. Since the sale of Tri-Plas in May 1986, the company has had no long-term debt. From 1985 through 1987, new capital investment totaled $75.5 million, all of which was financed out of internal cash flows.

THE FUTURE

Lance tries to do a little "perimeter expansion" each year. Management looks to the boundary of current sales territories to see if there are any major markets that should be included. In 1990 Boston and Chicago became new markets for Lance. The company's strategic objective is consistent growth rather than peaks and valleys. In 1982, Pete Sloan said, "We have no plans to jump over 1,000 miles of jack rabbits to get to the people again." As succinctly stated by Jack Moore, "Lance believes sales without profit is swelling, not growth."

In actuality, the growth of the Sun Belt has brought customers to Lance and made it less important for Lance to go seeking new markets. Sixty percent of the population of the United States is within 600 miles of Charlotte, where Lance's major manufacturing facility is located. A second plant is located in Greenville, Texas. Lance's expansion is restricted primarily by the development of personnel. The company wants to maintain its policy of promotion

EXHIBIT 3 **Statements of Consolidated Income and Retained Earnings, Lance, Inc., 1984–1989**
(In thousands, except per share data)

	1984	1985	1986	1987	1988	1989
Net sales and other operating revenue	$337,420	$355,209	$366,912	$380,020	$407,683	$432,140
Cost of sales and operating expenses:						
Cost of sales	157,340	160,388	157,938	168,585	182,727	188,691
Selling and delivery	109,217	118,233	126,828	132,519	144,407	157,010
General and administrative	11,153	12,714	13,414	12,789	14,117	15,399
Contributions to employees' profit-sharing retirement fund	6,619	7,032	7,328	7,173	7,151	7,764
Total	284,329	298,367	305,508	321,066	348,402	368,864
Profit from operations	53,091	56,842	61,404	58,954	59,281	63,276
Loss from closing subsidiary					(4,270)	
Other income, net	4,929	5,152	4,983	5,634	5,370	6,588
Income before income taxes	58,020	61,994	66,387	64,588	60,381	69,864
Income taxes:						
Current	24,522	26,213	30,661	26,376	21,992	22,245
Deferred (benefit)	2,329	2,487	121	233	(754)	2,756
Total	26,851	28,700	30,782	26,609	21,238	25,001
Net income	31,169	33,294	35,605	37,979	39,143	44,863
Retained earnings at beginning of fiscal year	129,422	146,239	163,975	167,669	186,221	204,048
Total	160,591	179,533	199,580	205,648	225,364	248,911
Less:						
Cash dividends	14,352	15,558	17,270	19,057	20,999	22,774
Stock options exercised			524	370	317	357
Retained earnings at end of fiscal year	$146,239	$163,975	$181,786	$186,221	$204,048	$225,780
Per share amounts: (adjusted for stock split in 1987)						
Net income	$0.93	$1.00	$1.08	$1.17	$1.23	$1.42
Cash dividends	.43	.47	.52	.58	.66	.72

Source: Annual Report.

	1985	1986	1987	1988	1989
Assets					
Current assets:					
Cash (including time deposits)	$ 19,102	$ 20,454	$ 17,382	$ 19,355	$ 27,191
Marketable securities—at amortized cost which approximates market	57,407	66,296	51,628	33,864	37,182
Accounts and notes receivable (less allowance for doubtful accounts)	922	1,518	1,360	1,097	1,133
Refundable income taxes			2,280		
Inventories—finished goods, goods in process, materials, etc.	23,675	20,410	20,255	33,171	33,251
Deferred income tax benefit	3,279	3,747	4,465	6,230	5,988
Total current assets	122,945	130,524	117,213	116,705	130,047
Property, net	100,978	99,741	119,795	135,610	140,339
Other assets:					
Machinery deposits	205	3,091	1,589	189	2,436
Notes receivable, prepayments, etc.	2,921	3,252	3,246	3,116	3,509
Total other assets	3,126	6,343	4,835	3,305	5,945
Total	$227,049	$236,608	$241,843	$255,620	$276,331
Liabilities and Stockholders' Equity					
Current liabilities:					
Accounts payable	$ 6,612	$ 5,694	$ 8,542	$ 7,795	$ 6,655
Accrued compensation	8,938	9,615	9,499	10,306	8,452
Profit-sharing retirement fund	4,623	4,316	3,662	3,643	4,955
Accrued federal and state income taxes	2,177	3,966	1,804	1,573	1,628
Accrual for self insurance	2,005	3,066	3,786	4,294	4,827
Other payables and accrued liabilities	2,798	3,050	3,446	4,345	2,225
Total current liabilities	27,153	29,707	30,739	31,956	28,742
Long-term debt	1,583				
Other liabilities and deferred credits:					
Deferred income taxes	13,822	15,208	17,164	18,982	22,185
Deferred federal income tax investment credits	5,606	4,809	3,804	2,997	2,308
Supplemental retirement benefits	1,962	2,108	2,328	2,598	2,877
Total other liabilities and deferred credits	21,390	22,125	23,296	24,577	27,370
Stockholders' equity:					
Common stock, $0.83 1/3 par value (authorized: 36,000,000 shares; issued: 28,234,000 shares)	14,117	14,117	28,234	28,234	28,234
Additional paid-in capital	19				
Retained earnings	163,975	181,786	186,221	204,048	225,780
Total	178,111	195,903	214,455	232,282	254,014
Less treasury stock at cost	1,188	11,127	26,647	33,195	33,795
Stockholders' equity	176,923	184,776	187,808	199,087	220,219
Total	$227,049	$236,608	$241,843	$255,620	$276,311

EXHIBIT 5 **Statements of Consolidated Cash Flows, Lance, Inc., 1987–1989**
(*In thousands*)

	1987	1988	1989
Operating Activities			
Net income	$ 37,979	$ 39,143	$ 44,863
Adjustments to reconcile net income to cash provided by operating activities:			
Depreciation	16,011	17,197	18,607
Deferred income taxes	233	(754)	2,756
Other, net	484	3,101	7
Changes in operating assets and liabilities:			
Decrease (increase) in accounts receivable	(1,586)	(1,421)	(2,763)
Decrease (increase) in refundable federal income taxes	(2,280)	819	413
Decrease (increase) in inventory	155	(12,916)	(80)
Increase (decrease) in accounts payable	3,319	(357)	(1,140)
Increase (decrease) in accrued income taxes	(2,162)	(231)	55
Increase (decrease) in other payables and accrued liabilities	365	2,196	(2,128)
Net cash flow from operating activities	$ 52,518	$ 46,777	$ 60,590
Investing Activities			
Purchases of property:			
Vending machines	(8,574)	(11,184)	(9,967)
Other property	(21,290)	(20,542)	(12,217)
Deposits	(5,808)	(3,164)	(4,195)
Proceeds from sale of property	264	714	814
Net (increase) decrease in marketable securities with maturities of 3 months or less	10,335	(1,149)	2,554
Purchases of other marketable securities	(28,378)	(12,173)	(26,777)
Sales and maturities of other marketable securities	32,538	30,965	21,175
Other, net	270	(407)	(410)
Net cash used in investing activities	$(20,643)	$(16,940)	$(29,023)
Financing Activities			
Dividends paid	(19,057)	(20,999)	(22,774)
Purchases of treasury stock, net	(15,890)	(6,865)	(957)
Net cash used in financing activities	(34,947)	(27,864)	(23,731)
Increase (decrease) in cash	(3,072)	1,973	7,836
Cash at beginning of fiscal year	20,454	17,382	19,355
Cash at end of fiscal year	$ 17,382	$ 19,355	$ 27,191
Supplemental Information:			
Cash paid for income taxes	$ 30,818	$ 21,404	$ 21,777

Source: Annual Report

from within. Therefore it is growing only as much as its "good quality" and "doing things right" philosophy will allow.

Distribution costs represented an opportunity and a threat for Lance. The company's store-to-door delivery method is expensive in terms of people—labor costs and benefits, and trucks—especially with unstable gasoline prices. If the company can efficiently continue its distribution, Lance can sustain its market position and even expand its customer base.

The company's acquisitions committee looks for and evaluates potential purchases. It is unlikely that Lance would be the target of a takeover attempt because the Van Every family owns approximately 44 percent of the shares of Lance (directly and in trust), and they are not interested in selling. Pete Sloan was quoted in *Forbes* as saying, "Sure, everything has a price—if you're a prostitute. But they can sell it once and they still got it. That ain't the way with companies." *Forbes* then went on to say, "Such conservatism, of course, is what has made Lance so successful. The danger is that changes in the snack food market could leave the company behind—one challenge that more of the same won't overcome."

The company expects to reach the $500 million mark in sales in the near future.

AKRON ZOOLOGICAL PARK, 1990*

F. Bruce Simmons, III, University of Akron

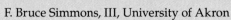

Zoos are perceived as custodians of our cultural wildlife heritage and educators of the skills of conservation. Acting alone, zoos can collectively maintain about 1,500 species of rare and endangered birds and animals. This represents less than one half of 1 percent of the species that are expected to become extinct during the next 10 years. Zoos are strategically placed to inform and to educate the public. More people annually visit zoos than enter all U.S. national parks. Collectively, more people attend North American zoological facilities and programs than the combined number of persons who attend professional football, basketball, baseball, and hockey games. Zoos have remained a strong attraction for the people of the United States.

Collectively, during 1989, member institutions of the American Association of Zoological Parks and Aquariums had 102,187,740 visitors; over $711 million in operating budgets; over 24,000 acres in the parks; and more than 842,000 specimens from among 36,750 species of mammals, birds, reptiles, amphibians, fish, and invertebrates. Zoological parks, aquariums, and botanical gardens come in all sizes; the largest in 1989 had in excess of 4 million visitors and an annual operating budget of $50 million, while the smallest had 3,000 visitors and a $96,000 budget. Approximately 38 percent of AAZPA member institutions had annual operating budgets of less than $1 million. However, 17 percent had budgets in excess of $6 million. The association, at its annual 1989 meeting, awarded membership to the Akron Zoological Park, making it one of the best 150 zoos in North America.

During the late 1970s in Akron, changes in consumer preferences for radial automobile tires, the internationalization of the rubber industry, the economic ravages of rapidly increasing general price levels, and changes in governmental priorities almost resulted in the permanent closing of the Akron Children's Zoo. Sagging attendance and a low level of family memberships did not help matters. Faced with the uncertain prospect of continuing its zoo operations, the city of Akron sought to reduce, or eliminate, its financial commitment. As a response, the Akron Zoological Park was organized as an eleemosynary corporation under Section 501(c)3 of the Internal Revenue Code. The board of trustees contracted with the city to operate the zoo.

Although the zoo made it through these turbulent and difficult times, its president and CEO, Patricia Simmons, remains mindful that yesterday's achievements do not guarantee tomorrow's survival. Under her guidance, the zoo expanded its operations and facilities, increased its annual attendance, and received AAZPA accreditation. In order to keep the zoo open and financially solvent, Simmons believes the zoo needs to develop more animal exhibits, restroom facilities, parking spaces, and community outreach programs. Yet, she must balance the costs of this approach with the flows of operating revenues.

---

*The cooperation and assistance of the Akron Zoological Park is acknowledged and appreciated. All rights are reserved to the author. © 1990.

HISTORY OF AKRON ZOOLOGICAL PARK

Residents of Akron, like people in many other cities, created their zoo by donating animals to their city. Earlier this century, two brown bears were given to the city of Akron. The city fathers constructed an appropriate facility in a neighborhood park. Subsequently, other individuals established a Museum of Natural History near the Perkins Park bears. In 1953, both facilities were combined·to create the Akron Children's Zoo. By the late 1970s, the city's ability and willingness to satisfactorily husband its animals were questioned. The future of the zoo as a community resource and its continuing operation were in grave danger. In response to this turmoil, the trustees of the Akron Zoological Park contracted with the city to manage and operate the zoo.

While contemplating the future direction of the zoo, and mindful of the severe financial constraints, the zoo's trustees decided to restrict their animal husbandry to North, South, and Central America birds, animals, and reptiles. The old Mother Goose exhibits were eliminated. They were replaced by more natural and native animal environments. These animal exhibits contain the zoo's collection of 183 specimens, which represent 66 different species of birds, reptiles, and animals.

During the past six years, the zoo has expanded its operations. Although it continues to follow the western hemisphere exhibits policy, the zoo opened an animal clinic, renovated its "petting zoo" barnyard, and constructed a gift shop, an alpaca exhibit, a concessions area, a reptile building, and a North American river otter exhibit. New maintenance facilities and educational display areas were built. Also, the zoo has completed phase one of its educational signs installation.

Purpose

The Akron Zoological Park saw its mission as one of managing its resources for the recreation and education of the people of Akron and surrounding communities and promoting the conservation of wildlife. To be successful, the Akron Zoological Park tried to maintain its image as a quality place where visitors desired to spend time. It sought to keep animal exhibits clean and neat so that they were easy for all to see and enjoy. Flowers and plants created a pleasant, landscaped environment. It had a balanced program of education, recreation, conservation, and scientific activities. As resources became available for construction and continuing operations, there were plans for new exhibits and new activities. Attendance increased from 63,034 people in 1986 to its record of 133,762 people in 1988.

Operating Season

Due to its northern climate, the zoo conducts its open season from mid-April until mid-October. The zoo is primarily closed for the winter months. It reopens for one week during Halloween, and for the month of December it displays in excess of 150,000 yuletide lights. Its operating season is shorter than many of its local competitors. Also, it is totally dependent on the largess of

EXHIBIT 1   **Attendance and Admission Fees at Akron Zoological Park**

Year	Annual Attendance	Admission Fees		
		Adult	**Child**	**Group**
1990	127,483	$3.00	$2.00	$1.50
1989	108,363	2.50	1.50	1.00
1988	133,762	2.50	1.50	1.00
1987	95,504	2.00	1.00	0.50
1986	63,034	1.50	0.75	0.50
1985	63,853	1.50	0.75	0.50
1984	61,417	1.50	0.75	0.50
1983	53,353	1.50	0.75	0.50

Source: Akron Zoological Park.

nature. For example, in December 1989, local records for the coldest temperature on this date, the lowest windchill factors, and the most snow were broken. Due to this record extreme cold and snow, several evenings of the Holiday Lights were canceled. Attendance at this event in 1988 was over 48,000 patrons. In December 1989, the Holiday Lights' attendance did not exceed 21,000 people. Further, in spring 1989, the Akron area experienced record precipitation. This rainfall served to reduce zoo admissions.

The variations in weather also affect crop yields and the prices of fresh animal foods. A drought in 1988 and too much rain in 1989 had a heavy impact on the costs of feeding the animals. The weather was a major factor in causing the cost of animal feed and paid park admissions to vary. In less extreme circumstances, the zoo believed it could achieve its target goal and attract an annual attendance equal to 40 percent of its community. Its surrounding community has not grown appreciably during the past decade. In recent years, as the zoo became better known as an innovative community resource, the annual attendance had doubled (see Exhibit 1).

Membership

Membership in the Akron Zoological Park is available to all. Becoming a zoo member means one has unlimited, no-charge admission to the zoo grounds during the operating season plus reciprocal admission at over 130 other zoological parks, aquariums, and botanical gardens. Members receive a quarterly newsletter and invitations to members-only events. There exist differing types of memberships. They include: family, grandparents, donor, patron, zookeeper, safari leader, and director's club. Each type of membership reflects different levels of financial support for zoo activities. As indicated in Exhibit 2, during the past several years the number of memberships has increased. This was due partly to concerted efforts to provide extra special attention to the zoo's patrons and to providing exciting and interesting events at the zoo (see Exhibit 3).

EXHIBIT 2   **Annual Memberships at Akron Zoological Park, 1981–1990**

Year	Total
1990	1,307
1989	1,100
1988	1,158
1987	1,200
1986	1,036
1985	1,295
1984	986
1983	492
1982	437
1981	312

Source: Akron Zoological Park.

Edzoocators

An unpaid volunteer group known as the Edzoocators was formed in the 1970s. These volunteers have no responsibility for the direct operations of the zoo. In 1983, the zoo created the position of education curator. One aspect of this position is to coordinate this group's educational activities. As volunteers, members of this group are trained to provide on-site and off-grounds educational programs using the zoo's birds, reptiles, and animals. They provide guided tours of the zoo grounds, give presentations at local schools, provide a speakers' bureau, and appear on radio and television programs. They also receive free admission to the zoo grounds.

Fur, Feathers, and Scales and the Rain Forest Programs

These presentations are two specialized offerings in the zoo's outreach program. For a nominal fee, plus gas mileage if located outside the city, the zoo's educational services are available for citizens groups, day-care centers, schools, and other community organizations. These programs provide the opportunity for people to learn about the zoo and its animals in a personal way. They are taught to respect the animal and to preserve its dignity.

Advertising

Akron and Summit County have a population of nearly 450,000. The area is situated just south of Cleveland, Ohio. Cleveland is a major metropolitan area. It has television stations that are affiliated with all four major networks. It has three independents and one public broadcasting station. By contrast, Akron has one affiliate, one independent, and a public broadcasting station. Since many people view Cleveland television broadcasts, the local residents are as conversant about Cleveland as they are about Akron. To gain media exposure in this market, the zoo had to create media events and develop exciting activities that pass the threshold as newsworthy. Unlike the Cleveland MetroParks Zoo, the Akron Zoo does not have enough funds to advertise on commercial

EXHIBIT 3 **Special Events in 1990 Akron Zoological Park**

Activity	Month
Snow Bowl	January
Appreciation Program	February
Zoo PBS One-Hour Specials	March
Spring Fling and Mrs. Bunny	April
Earth Day	April
Critter Care-A-Thon	May
Super Saturday and Keep Akron Beautiful	May
Mother's Day	May
Adopt an Animal Party	June
National Juggling Day	June
An Evening with Joan Embrey	June
Zoobilation	July
Akron Symphony Concert	July
Reptile Day	July
Teddy Bear Day	August
Ohio Ballet at the Zoo	August
Nocturnal Golf Tournament	August
Recycle with Ohio Zoos	August
The BFGoodrich Conservation Garden	August
Ralston Purina Big Cats Program	August
Galapagos Expedition	August
Members' Night	September
Boo at the Zoo	October
Zoo PBS Half-Hour Special Series	October
Annual Bird Seed Sale	November
Downtown Yule Display	November
Holiday Lights Celebration	December

Source: Akron Zoological Park.

television. Budgetary pressures did not permit advertising expenditures. The zoo is totally dependent on public service announcements, the zoo's public television series, and local press coverage of the activities at the zoo.

Promotional Programs

To create newsworthy activities, the zoo has regular promotions and events designed to attract attention. For example, in the spring when the animals give birth to their young, the zoo conducts a contest to name the new arrivals. In order to create the opportunity for members of the community to learn firsthand about the animals within the zoo's collection, the zoo sponsors an annual expedition. In the past, these expeditions have taken participants to the Amazon of Peru, the forests of Belize, and the Galapagos Islands of Ecuador. The local press has been quite supportive in reporting these globe-trotting activities. The zoo established a highly popular and well-known teen volunteer program. Young adults between the ages of 14 and 18 are trained and permitted to handle the animals while working one or two days per week at the zoo.

Safety

In the event of an animal escape, zoo employees have a written procedure to follow for the recapture of the animal. As a good citizen, the zoo management, through its risk management and safety audit program, aims to ensure a safe environment for the visitor, employee, and the animals that inhabit the zoo. The zoo management remains committed to improving the quality of its exhibits and the habitats of their animals. For example, in conformance with AAZPA's Code of Professional Ethics mandatory standards, exhibit animals are marked with identifying numbers. This animal marking system facilitates the proper care and security of the animal, bird, or reptile. Animal acquisition and disposal, breeding cooperation, and research for the health and preservation of endangered species are coordinated with other zoos. Cooperative research with colleges and universities is performed within written policy guidelines.

ADMINISTRATION

As president and CEO of the zoo, Patricia Simmons believes that her main function is to ensure the fiscal and conservational integrity of the zoo. She strives to maintain and improve the zoo's excellent customer service. A zoo employee for seven years, her contributions have resulted in increases in her operational authority and various promotions. She has a diverse background. Her training and education are in fishery administration, fund-raising, fine arts, and management. She has a graduate degree in arts management. A community organization, Leadership Akron, has honored her contributions by enrolling her in its 1989 class. On April 17, 1989, the trustees adopted the business corporation structure of governance and elected Mrs. Simmons as the president and CEO. Mrs. Simmons holds a seat and a vote on the board of trustees and is a member of the executive committee.

The board of trustees oversees the policies of the zoo and sets the guidelines for membership and promotional activities. The board sees that all financial statements are audited by independent public accountants. Each trustee is elected to serve a three-year term.. There are currently 24 trustees. The executive committee consists of the president and CEO plus the five elected trustee officers and the chairs of three standing board committees. The officers, who are elected annually and have a limit on the number of years in office, are the chairman of the board, two vice chairmen, a secretary, and a treasurer. The three standing committees are planning and finance, promotion and sales, and animal care and education. The board has quarterly and annual meetings.

ORGANIZATION

The director of zoo operations, Pat Barnhardt, is provided through a grant from the city of Akron. He supervises the animal curator and keeping staff as well as the maintenance and security crews. When his father was Akron's

EXHIBIT 4   **Akron Zoological Park's Administrative Organization**

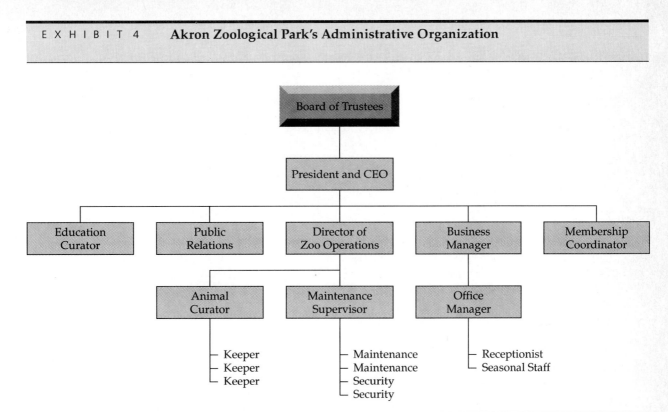

Source: Akron Zoological Park.

parks superintendent, he learned firsthand, as a volunteer, about the daily aspects of zoo operations.

The employees of the zoo are nonunion and non-civil service. As depicted in Exhibit 4, there are 17 full-time zoo employees. The education curator is responsible for ongoing informational activities and coordinates the efforts of the volunteer groups. The public relations person seeks recognition for zoo events in the local media. The business manager supervises the accounting procedures and the daily operations of the office manager and her staff.

It is the zoo's policy that hiring, promotion, and employee transfer are based strictly on individual merit without favoritism or discrimination. An anti-nepotism policy is in place. For example, should an applicant for employment be under the direct supervision or within the same department as a relative, the zoo will not hire the relative of the employee.

OTHER AREA NONPROFIT INSTITUTIONS

With greater competition for private gifts and grants, the decline in the availability of donations due to changes in federal taxation law, and weather-related gate receipts from clientele patronage, the zoo was increasingly concerned about the actions of its competitors. The Akron Zoological Park has to successfully compete for resources within its community. Four other museums currently are in the area: the Historical Society, Hale Farm and Village, the Art Museum, and Stan Hywet Hall and Gardens. A brief description of each

EXHIBIT 5   **Brief Description of Akron Zoological Park's Competitors**

Institution	Description
Historical Society	Consists of the General Simon Perkins Mansion and the abolitionist John Brown's home. Mansion, built in 1837, is 15 rooms of 19th-century items. Located near the zoo.
National Inventors Hall of Fame	Hall of Fame for holders of U.S. patents. Soliciting funds from community to construct a permanent site.
Hale Farm and Village	A living history museum, with authentic renovated buildings with costumed guides, that depicts rural life in mid-19th-century northeast Ohio.
Art Museum	The major exhibition of modern art between New York state and Chicago. It houses the E. C. Shaw collection and contains the finest art from 1850 to the present.
Stan Hywet Hall and Gardens	An English country manor with 65 rooms that once was a self-sufficient estate of 3,000 acres. It is decorated with treasures collected from around the world.

Source: Akron Summit Visitors and Convention Bureau.

institution is provided in Exhibit 5. The most recent addition to the local museums is the National Inventors Hall of Fame. Its organizers have announced an intention to raise $40 million from the community to construct a physical facility. Funds that are raised for this endeavor could reduce the pool available for other community institutions. When coupled with local universities' fund-raising activities, the competition for the community's resources was very intense.

A survey of current admission prices and operating statistics is given in Exhibit 6. The other institutions charge higher fees and have different sources of funding. For example, the historical society receives its funding from the county government. The zoo's admission pricing policy is sensitive to other area attractions.

FINANCIAL STATUS

The zoo's ability to survive depended on its gate receipts, memberships, creative special events, donations, and its many volunteers. Nearly 75 percent of all operating funds are generated from zoo events and activities. During four of the past five years, excluding the grant contracted for with the city, the zoo received an average of $124,000 in donations and grants. During the same period, membership sales increased by a net 144 percent, and ticket and merchandise sales increased by more than 78 percent.

Financing its activities remains an important consideration to zoo management. The zoo has looked into alternate sources of financing. Zoo officials have explored the feasibility of placing a property tax levy before the voters to sustain zoo operations. Also, they have discussed the possibility of a joint tax levy with the other area nonprofit organizations. However, since these institutions receive funding from other sources, it was decided that they should not join with the zoo in a joint effort, as their access to these other funds would be placed in serious jeopardy. The zoo has been left alone in its struggle for fiscal

EXHIBIT 6   1989 Operating Statistics for Summit County Museums and 1990 Admission Fees

Institution	1989 Operating Budget	Visitors	Open Hours	Membership
Historical Society	$ 350,000	10,000	1,200	1,100
Akron Zoological Park	570,000	108,363	1,446	1,063
National Inventors Hall of Fame	600,000	15,000	266	0
Hale Farm and Village	750,500	77,000	1,357	1,120
Art Museum	1,000,000	52,000	2,345	1,300
Stan Hywet Hall and Gardens	1,383,000	109,126	2,070	2,619

Institution	1990 Admission Fees		
	Adult	Child	Group
Historical Society	$ 3.00	$ 2.00	$ 2.00
Akron Zoological Park	2.50	1.50	1.00
National Inventors Hall of Fame (not yet open)			
Hale Farm and Village	6.50	4.00	none
Art Museum	none	none	none
Stan Hywet Hall and Gardens	6.00	3.00	none
Cleveland Zoo	3.50	1.50	1.75
Sea World in Aurora, Ohio	17.50	13.50	17.50

Source: Telephone Survey.

integrity. Zoo trustees want to reduce the uncertainty and to secure a more reliable source of operating revenues.

Audited financial statements are provided in Exhibits 7 and 8. Since nonprofit accounting is somewhat different from conventional business accounting practices, a brief description of the accounts is necessary. The unrestricted fund represents all revenues and expenditures that are not accounted for in other funds. The unrestricted expenditures for each calendar year are financed principally by admissions, donations, memberships, concessions, and a grant from the city of Akron. The restricted fund includes all grants and other revenue that are designated for specific uses by their benefactors. The plant fund accounts for all the acquisition and retirement of building and equipment plus related depreciation. Land is leased from the city of Akron for nominal consideration. Depreciation is straight line over an applicable 5- to 20-year period. Buildings typically represent approximately 80 percent of the amount. Deferred membership income is recognized at the time of receipt but is amortized to operations over the one-year membership period. Deferred restricted contributions are recognized at the time of receipt and are recorded in operations when the expenditure for the specific purpose is made. Inventories are stated at the lower of FIFO cost or market. Contributed utilities and benefits are provided by the city of Akron. The city supplies the utilities to the zoo and provides the salary and benefits of one city worker.

Along with the skyrocketing increases in veterinary and trash disposal costs, the rapid escalation in health and liability insurance is also a major concern. The availability of health care insurance is not guaranteed. Few

EXHIBIT 7   Balance Sheet, Akron Zoological Park, 1989

	Unrestricted Fund	Restricted Fund	Plant Fund	Total
Assets				
Cash.	$138,303	$1,938	$160,739	$300,980
Inventories	26,203	0	0	26,203
Accounts receivable	4,213	0	17,892	22,105
Other assets	824	0	0	824
Total current assets	169,543	1,938	178,631	350,112
Buildings and equipment.	0	0	843,142	843,142
Less accumulated depreciation . . .	0	0	250,167	250,167
Total fixed assets	0	0	592,975	592,975
Total assets	$169,543	$1,938	$771,606	$943,087
Liabilities				
Accounts payable	25,828	0	36,745	62,573
Accrued payroll	2,808	0	0	2,808
Accrued payroll taxes	6,745	0	0	6,745
Deferred membership	14,055	0	0	14,055
Deferred income	8,779	0	0	8,779
Deferred restricted contributions . .	0	1,938	141,886	143,824
Total liabilities	$ 58,215	$1,938	$178,631	$238,784
Fund equities				
Fund balance	54,686	0	592,975	647,661
Board restricted.	56,642	0	0	56,642
Total fund equities	111,328	0	592,975	704,303
Total liabilities and fund equities . . .	$169,543	$1,938	$771,606	$943,087

Source: Akron Zoological Park.

insurance companies are interested in writing a policy for an employer with only 17 employees. The few who are interested want to select only a few employees and leave the others uninsured. Should the zoo have one employee who is deemed to be a high risk by the issuing company, there may be no insurance available for any employee. The dilemma remains how to obtain health insurance for all employees at an affordable rate.

Due to rising costs for fringe benefits, the funds available for increasing employee salary levels were virtually zero. This put the dedicated zoo employee at a distinct financial disadvantage relative to an employee at the city of Akron. The city of Akron wages are among the highest for municipal employees in Ohio. In contrast, the basic wage rate at the zoo is the legally prescribed minimum wage. Recent increases in the minimum wage have raised the wage costs to the zoo by 20 percent. One half of the employees received a pay raise from the enactment of this recent legislation. Without corresponding increases in revenue, the zoo could expect budget difficulty.

Although it has federal nonprofit status, the zoo tries to ensure that its sources of income equal or exceed its operating and physical plant costs. Its continued existence and its promotion of wildlife conservation are totally

EXHIBIT 8   Akron Zoological Park, Statement of Support, Revenue, Expenses, and Changes in Fund Balances, 1986–1989

| | Operating Funds | | | |
	1989	1988	1987	1986
Support and Revenue				
City of Akron grant	$180,000	$175,000	$165,000	$160,000
City services in-kind	55,367	51,160	49,722	50,398
Donations	155,143	227,102	311,263	201,842
Admissions	109,523	113,840	71,725	47,297
Concessions	55,177	54,419	41,054	42,297
Memberships	27,247	24,666	15,891	26,502
Interest	22,291	15,634	13,768	13,901
Total revenue	$604,748	$661,821	$668,423	$542,857
Expenses				
Program				
Animal collections	$127,410	$113,037	$113,897	$118,789
Buildings and grounds	189,763	169,870	161,605	141,914
Cost of concessions	14,267	14,434	13,888	26,336
Education	28,509	22,699	25,169	23,277
Strategic planning	3,838	0	0	0
Total expenses	363,787	320,040	314,559	310,316
Supporting				
Administration	106,217	175,426	131,327	95,629
Promotion	15,795	23,903	23,130	17,534
Legal and accounting	3,522	3,401	2,500	26,073
Total supporting	225,534	202,730	156,957	139,236
Total expenditures	589,427	522,770	471,516	449,552
Excess of support and revenue over expenses	$ 15,427	$139,051	$196,907	$ 93,305
Operating fund balance: Beginning of year	$688,876	$549,825	$352,918	$259,613
Operating fund balance: End of year	704,303	688,876	549,825	352,918

Source: Akron Zoological Park.

dependent on its ability to cover costs and find the monies to sustain its programs.

Admissions Policy

The park is open to all persons who observe the general admission rules printed on the visitor's brochure. All visitors must wear a shirt and shoes. No alcoholic beverages are permitted. The zoo reserves the right to remove visitors who prove to be unruly, harass the animals, feed the animals, enter the exhibit areas, or litter the park.

Master Plan

The zoo is located in Perkins Park. The shade trees serve to keep the grounds relatively free from the harsh effects of the sun. The zoo consists of 25 acres and stretches across two plateaus. Between the upper and lower level there is a comparatively steep natural incline. This incline runs throughout the middle of the zoo. The current master grounds plan, shown in Exhibit 9, was created in 1983. Nationally, zoos are responding to rapid changes in accreditation requirements. Since the Akron Zoo is now an accredited institution, it too had to meet changing standards. The terrain hinders access to the grounds for the handicapped and disabled. Also, to improve zoo access, a higher quality of washroom facilities is necessary.

The zoo has a limited parking area. On days of special events when the crowds number 3,000 or more, the parking space is inadequate. The zoo does have some space within its fenced perimeter in which it can expand parking. However, the zoo is in Perkins Park. By expanding into this park, the zoo could double its size. Yet this presents a dilemma. To expand and to construct new exhibits will increase admissions, but it will require increases in both capital and operating funds. Without additional parking and concession areas, the zoo will not be able to increase its gate receipts. Further, extra exhibits can mean that customers will remain longer in the zoo and are likely to purchase more concessions and souvenirs.

SURVEY REPORT ON THE ZOO

The zoo contracted with the local university to conduct a study of zoo clientele. Telephone surveys were made the last week of September 1989. Interviewers received 757 usable responses. In general, those people who patronize zoos have a positive overall evaluation of the facility. They favorably rate its cleanliness, safety, convenience, and animal displays. Approximately one half of the respondents avail themselves of the opportunity to use the Akron Zoo. The zoo satisfies the current customer in terms of features and facilities.

However, nearly two fifths of the people interviewed report never going to a zoo. The results of this survey are reviewed in Exhibit 10. The basic reasons given for not attending a zoo are a "dislike of zoos," "no time for a visit," "lacking in transportation," "the children are grown," and simply "I do not have an answer."

When asked about the zoo, many people responded that it is too small. Seventy-five percent of its patrons and two thirds of the general public expressed concern at the relative smallness of the facility. The respondents offered suggestions for five additional features: "more exhibits for the children with visitor involvement," "a railroad," "bring back the black bears," and "add more small cats" and "more monkeys."

To better understand the needs of its customers, the survey asked whether the respondents visited any other attractions in the area during 1989. The responses indicated that the zoo's clientele attended five other area institutions. These were the Cleveland Zoo, Sea World, Stan Hywet Hall and Gardens, Hale Farm and Village, and Geauga Lake Park Amusements. Three fifths of those who attend the Akron Zoological Park had visited these competing facilities.

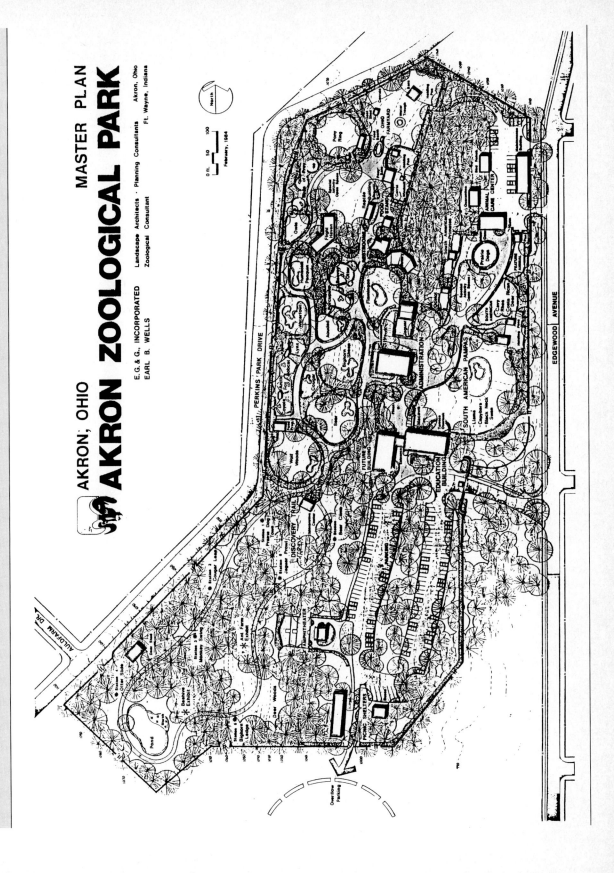

AKRON, OHIO
AKRON ZOOLOGICAL PARK
MASTER PLAN

E. G. & G., INCORPORATED   Landscape Architects · Planning Consultants   Akron, Ohio
EARL B. WELLS   Zoological Consultant   Ft. Wayne, Indiana

EXHIBIT 10   **Survey of Visitors to Akron Zoological Park, September 1989**

Other Attractions Visited in 1989	Percent
Cleveland Zoo	51.8%
Sea World	45.2
Stan Hywet Hall and Gardens	41.2
Hale Farm and Village	32.2
Geauga Lake Park Amusements	31.2

Multiple Reasons Given for Not Visiting Akron Zoological Park	Percent
Do not like zoos	16.3%
Transportation problems	6.1
Not personally able	16.7
Lack of time	27.2
No interest	13.6
Kids are grown	12.2
Unsafe urban neighborhood	2.4
New to area	1.7
Unable to supply an answer	12.0

Suggested New Projects and Additions to Akron Zoological Park	Response Ranking
Build exhibits for children	First (tie)
Addition of a railroad	First (tie)
Bring back the bears	Second
Addition of small cats to collection	Third
More monkeys	Fourth

Source: The University of Akron Survey Research Center Project Report.

THE GRAND THEATRE COMPANY*

Larry M. Agranove, Wilfrid Laurier University

"There is no better director than me. Some may be as good, but none better."
Robin Phillips

In December 1982 the board of directors of Theatre London in London, Ontario, (see Exhibit 1) were considering a proposal to hire Robin Phillips as artistic director to replace Bernard Hopkins. The hiring decision was complicated by Phillips's ambitious plans for the theater, which included a change from a subscription theater to repertory, an increase in budget from $1.9 million to $4.4 million, and even changing the organization's name. The board had to act quickly as plans had to be made, and actors hired, for the next season.

THEATER IN ONTARIO

Theater is big business in Ontario. In Toronto alone (including cabaret, dinner theater, and opera) some 3.5 million people attended 120 productions in 1982, in 28 locations. There are 24 nonprofit professional theaters in Toronto, and 18 in the rest of Ontario.

Virtually all theater organizations in Ontario and the rest of Canada are nonprofit and are subsidized by local, provincial, and federal grants. Thus theaters compete for funds with charities and educational and health care organizations. As shown in Exhibit 2, a third of revenue typically comes from government sources and half of this comes from The Canada Council. Another 10 percent comes from individual and corporate donors, and the balance from the box office. Because of the pressing need for box office revenues, most theater companies sell subscriptions of five or so plays from October to May.

In 1982–83, audience size was 570,000 for the Stratford Festival, the largest art organization in Canada, and 268,000 for The Shaw Festival, the second largest theater company. According to a Stratford audience study, audiences break down into: (1) committed theatergoers (27 percent) who see a number of plays each year, and who tend to be older and more educated and live in Ontario; (2) casual theatergoers (53 percent) who attend a theater every year or two to see plays of particular interest; and (3) first-timers (20 percent). The challenge for these theaters is to develop first-timers to be the audience of the future.

Theater audiences tend to be well educated, with most having university education, and slightly over 50 percent having attended a graduate or professional school. Those aged 36 through 50 make up 35 percent of the Stratford audience, and the 21–to–35 and 51–to–64 age groups each make up 25 percent. Visitors from the United States account for 35 percent of box office receipts at the Stratford Festival; Toronto accounts for 25 percent; and the remaining 40 percent come from elsewhere in Ontario. Twice as many women attend as

*Prepared with the assistance of Dr. J. Peter Killing from published sources and interviews with numerous people in theater, government, and arts organizations. Copyright © 1985, Wilfrid Laurier University. Reprinted with permission.

E X H I B I T   1   **The Grand Theatre Company, Board of Directors, December 1982**

J. Noreen De Shane	President, and president of a stationery firm
Peter J. Ashby	Partner, major consulting firm
W. C. P. Baldwin, Jr.	President, linen supply firm
Bob Beccarea	Alderman and civic representative
Art Ender	Life insurance representative
Ed Escaf	Hotel and restaurant owner
Dr. John Girvin	Surgeon
Stephanie Goble	Representative of London Labour Council
Elaine Hagarty	Former alderman, active in arts community
Barbara Ivey	Active board member of various theater groups
Alan G. Leyland	Entrepreneur
John F. McGarry	Partner, major law firm
C. Agnew Meek	Corporate marketing executive
Robert Mepham	Retired civic leader and businessman
Elizabeth Murray	Board member of theater groups and Ontario Arts Council
John H. Porter	Vice president and partner, major accounting firm
Peter Schwartz	Partner, major law firm
Dr. Tom F. Siess	University professor
Dr. Shiel Warma	Surgeon

men. It is understood that Shaw's market is similar, with slightly fewer coming from the United States.

A recent study showed that while 42 percent of Ontario residents attended live plays and musicals in 1974, this number grew to 55 percent by 1984.[1] Some 24 percent of the Ontario population are "frequent attenders" (at least six times a year). They come from all age groups, but many are "singles," and many are university educated and affluent. In fact, while only 63 percent of Ontarians without a high school education have attended live theater, 94 percent with university degrees have.

There is some price sensitivity: 73 percent said they would attend more often if tickets were less expensive. However, 77 percent (which included young adults and lower-middle income families) said they would accept a tax increase of up to $25 to support the arts.

THE ORGANIZATION OF A THEATER COMPANY

The Board of Directors   The board of directors is fiscally and legally responsible for the theater. They may determine the theater's artistic objectives, then delegate the fulfilling of these objectives to the artistic director. However, any

---

[1]Report to the Honorable Susan Fish, The Minister of Citizenship and Culture, by the Special Committee for the Arts, Spring 1984.

EXHIBIT 2   **The Major Arts Organizations in Canada—Ranked by Size of Total Revenue for 1982–1983**   (*In Canadian dollars*)

Arts Organizations	Total Revenue 1982-1983	Box Office and Earned Revenues	Government Grants	Private Donations	Accumulated Surplus (Deficit), End of 1982–1983
1. Stratford Festival	$12,314,300	$9,678,285	$1,405,939	$1,230,076	$(1,731,492)
2. Toronto Symphony	9,480,503	6,020,112	1,893,100	1,567,291	(149,391)
3. National Ballet	7,271,616	3,233,810	2,943,856	1,093,950	(675,096)
4. Orchestre Symphonique de Montreal	7,071,886	4,048,749	2,164,350	858,787	(857,662)
5. Canadian Opera Company	5,969,077	2,668,698	2,029,100	1,271,279	(290,168)
6. Vancouver Symphony	5,189,041	2,488,690	1,784,315	916,036	(818,951)
7. Shaw Festival	4,801,700	3,848,200	586,000	367,500	(45,167)
8. Royal Winnipeg Ballet	4,021,263	1,884,339	1,611,463	525,461	343,639
9. Centre Stage	3,483,020	1,923,312	1,316,000	243,708	(212,108)
10. Citadel Theatre	3,541,911	2,097,096	1,117,733	327,082	177,821
18. Grand Theatre	1,990,707	1,277,625	390,000	323,082	0*

*Reduced by Wintario Challenge Fund.

Source: Council for Business and the Arts in Canada.

artistic plan has financial objectives, and the board's responsibility is essentially financial. Artistic directors generally demand, and are generally granted, a great deal of autonomy in such matters as programming and casting; to a large extent the board "bets" on the artistic director's ability to put on a season of theater, subject to his accountability in meeting budgets and providing an appropriate level of quality.

Board members are typically expected to assist in fund-raising, and to set an example by contributing generously themselves.

Board members often have business backgrounds. As a result, they may be—and are certainly often perceived to be—insensitive to the unique needs of an artistic organization. Artistic boards often include lawyers and accountants, who are recruited to serve a specific function, but who tend to remain on long enough to achieve positions of power.

Busy businesspeople serve on boards for a number of reasons. They may perceive they are serving as a civic responsibility. Others may see it as an opportunity to wield power at a board level, something they are not allowed to do in their own organizations. Membership on a board allows people to widen their social and business contacts; this can be important to lawyers and accountants, who are limited in their freedom to advertise. One common motivation for businesspeople to join arts boards is the opportunity to mingle with luminaries in the arts. Here is one view of their performance:

It has often been charged that many a hard-headed businessman loses his business sense on entering a meeting of an arts board. Lacking a profit motive to guide the affairs of the organization, businessmen who serve on arts boards sometimes feel unsure of themselves and their expertise. Compounding this problem is the inclination on the part of arts organizations to consider themselves a breed apart, outside the realm of normal business practice. But whether a company manufactures widgets or mounts exhibitions, the basic business concerns remain the same: strategic planning, good marketing, adequate financing, and competent management are essential to any enterprise.[2]

Theater Management   In addition to the artistic director, whose role and relationship with the board were described above, there is usually a general manager who is responsible for the business affairs of the organization. Since artistic directors strive for maximum quality, which is expensive, and since business managers have to find and account for the money to run the theater, conflicts often occur. Not surprisingly, boards often side with the business manager because of their similarities of culture and values. Typically both artistic director and general manager report directly to the board.

MOUNTING A PRODUCTION

The theater company selects "products" to suit its objectives and audiences. For example, a theater might select a playbill of classics or children's plays. A regional theater might select a Canadian play (to satisfy government grant-giving agencies), a classic (to satisfy the artistic aspirations of the artistic director), a resounding hit from Broadway or England (to help sell the series), and one or more plays that have been successful elsewhere.

Each production requires a producer (who may be the artistic director) to act as the "entrepreneur" to put the show together.[3] He acquires the rights to the play, if it is not in the public domain, for a fee of 7 to 10 percent of the box office revenue. He also retains a director, who may be on staff or who may be a free-lance director retained for the run of the play. In the latter case, minimum scale would be $6,174.80 for a run of three weeks of rehearsal and three to four weeks of performance

Casting is done, beginning with the major parts, on the basis of a uniform contract, which sets out fees (minimum of $416.27 per week for a major company), starting date, billing, working time, and "perks" (e.g., dressing room, accommodation).

Finally, a stage manager is contracted, as are designers for sets, costumes, and lighting. It is essential, of course, that all these people work well together.

The above describes the typical stock, or subscription, company. However, Stratford and Shaw operate as repertory companies, hiring a group of actors for one or more seasons, and allocating roles among the members of the company. Repertory companies typically sell tickets for individual plays, while

---

[2]"Developing Effective Arts Boards," undated publication of The Council for Business and the Arts in Canada, pp. 28, 29.

[3]Harry Chartrand, Research Director, "An Economic Impact Assessment of the Canadian Fine Arts," The Canada Council, February 1, 1984, p. 77.

subscription companies sell their series at the beginning of the season, with few single tickets.

Lead times are considerable; in Stratford, for example, plays that open in May are firmly cast by the previous December, and the entire season is planned by March, when rehearsals begin.

THEATRE LONDON

Background

The Grand Opera House was opened in London, Ontario on September 9, 1901, by Ambrose J. Small, a Toronto theatrical entrepreneur and frustrated producer. It quickly became the showcase of Small's theatrical chain, opening with such attractions as the Russian Symphony Orchestra, and later offering such performers as Barry Fitzgerald, Bela Lugosi, Clifton Webb, Sidney Poitier, and Hume Cronyn. Small sold this theater chain in 1919, deposited a million dollars in his bank, and disappeared. There has been no explanation to this day; however, Small's ghost is said to haunt the Grand.

Famous Plays bought the theater in 1924, tore out the second balcony, and converted the theater to a cinema. They sold to The London Little Theatre for a token amount in 1945, and the building housed an amateur community theater until the spring of 1971. The theater employed professional business management and a professional artistic director, but the actors were all amateur. Some of London's leading citizens acted in plays, and some even displayed a high level of competence. The theater was prominent in the social life of the city and attracted one of the largest subscription sales in North America, both as a percentage of available seats and in absolute terms. It also achieved a reputation for a very high level of quality, given that it was essentially an amateur theater. Articles about the theater appeared in such magazines as *Life*. However, there was some concern in the theater that the level of quality was as high as it was going to get as a company of amateurs, and that the community deserved, and was ready to support, a professional theater. Another local organization, the London Symphony, had engaged a conductor with an international reputation and was changing from an amateur to a professional orchestra. An active art gallery association was formed to work toward providing London with a major art gallery. Although strong objections were raised against the proposal for a professional theater, particularly because of the increased financial burden, the risk, and the denial to many of the theater's supporters of an opportunity to participate in their hobby of acting, London Little Theatre changed to Theatre London in 1971 under artistic director Heinar Piller. The progressives were vindicated, as theatergoers in London and the area were treated to a decade of artistically and financially successful theaters.

Piller was succeeded, at the end of the 1975 season, by William Hutt, who had achieved great success as an actor at Stratford and was well known to Londoners. He served from 1976 to 1978. Bernard Hopkins arrived in 1979 and was artistic director until May 1983.

The Grand was attractively and authentically renovated at a cost of $5.5 million, reopening in the fall of 1978, after being closed for a full season.

(The company had a reduced season during that time in small, rented accommodations.) During the renovation, seating capacity was reduced from 1,100 to 845, but the Grand emerged from the renovations as one of the finest theaters in Canada.

Theatre London ran successful stock seasons from 1979 to 1982. The 1981–82 season was particularly successful, operating at 85 percent of capacity. Eighty percent of its tickets were sold through subscription to some 13,431 subscribers. Financial statements are shown in Exhibits 3 and 4.

THE LONDON ENVIRONMENT

London was founded at the forks of the Thames River in 1793 by Governor Simcoe with the intention of making it the capital of Upper Canada. Instead, it became the cultural and commercial center of southwestern Ontario. Located on three railroad lines and on Highway 401, which serves the Quebec-Windsor corridor, London also has a major airport served by two airlines. London is two hours away from Detroit or Toronto; however, it is in a major snow belt. London is a major retail center, with the second highest per capita retail capacity in North America. It serves as a trading area of almost a million people, although its own population is only 259,000—see Exhibit 5. There are four hotels near the core area and motels in outlying areas. Many interesting restaurants had opened with a great deal of excess capacity; a few restaurants closed or changed hands.

There is little heavy industry in London, but there is a major university, a community college, a teacher's college, and two small church-affiliated colleges. Four major hospitals serve a wide area and provide teaching facilities for the university medical school and dental school. In addition to being a retail center, London is the home of major financial institutions and agribusiness firms, as well as a major brewery.

London is also a major cultural center. In addition to Theatre London, London has a professional symphony orchestra and a couple of significant choral groups. The university has an active program of theater and music, and the community is a center for visual artists. There are various commercial art galleries, an art gallery connected with the university, and a major public art gallery located in the city center. There are several museums, including a unique children's museum and a museum of Indian Archaeology. The latter two attract visitors from a wide area.

THE GRAND THEATRE COMPANY

In late 1981, a decade after the company had become professional, concern was again raised in the theater that the level of quality had stagnated, and the theater would have to move in new directions. Bernard Hopkins was a superb actor and a competent artistic director. He had directed a few plays, rather than have to pay for a free-lance director, with some success. However, some members of the board believed that he had taken the theater as far as he was able, and there was no initiative on either side to extend Hopkins' contract beyond its expiration in May 1983.

A planning committee, under one of the board members, addressed the issue of continuing the growth in quality. They conducted a number of retreats

EXHIBIT 3   **Theatre London, Condensed Five-Year Operating Results**

	June 30				
	1979	**1980**	**1981**	**1982**	**1983***
Revenue					
Productions					
Ticket sales	$ 551,650	$ 585,938	$ 620,313	$ 664,058	$1,100,000
Sponsored programs	26,000	25,000	26,500	9,000	9,000
Program advertising	17,283	17,270	19,652	24,241	24,000
	594,933	628,208	666,465	697,299	1,133,000
Grants					
Canada Council	145,000	163,000	173,000	185,000	210,000
Ontario Arts Council	145,000	152,000	160,000	170,000	180,000
Wintario.	89,254	—	—	—	—
City of London.	12,500	—	—	—	—
Cultural Initiative Program	—	—	25,000	—	—
	391,754	315,000	358,000	355,000	390,000
Other					
Operating fund drive	41,222	27,462	182,559	183,188	160,000
Special projects	36,811	36,525	43,881	41,281	65,000
Interest	34,553	50,608	62,128	86,106	80,000
Concessions	33,500	75,073	69,581	62,065	78,000
Theater school	8,720	17,687	19,481	—	—
Box office commissions	3,319	3,721	651	6,142	3,000
Theater rental and miscellaneous . . .	3,170	—	—	4,704	2,000
	161,295	211,076	378,281	383,486	388,000
Total revenue	$1,147,982	$1,154,284	$1,402,946	$1,435,785	$1,911,000
Expenses					
Public relations	$ 179,880	$ 128,502	$ 139,907	$ 177,267	$ 270,000
Administration	91,973	115,798	162,723	167,749	330,000
Production overhead	190,911	237,606	282,270	339,474	350,000
Productions.	466,906	414,644	416,440	421,161	780,000
Front of house, box office, and					
concessions	75,563	123,910	107,617	126,673	140,000
Facility operation	131,445	139,215	152,153	142,061	140,000
Theater school	9,742	20,832	34,804	—	—
Total expenses	1,146,420	1,180,507	1,295,914	1,374,375	2,010,000
Excess of revenue over expense	$ 1,562	$ (26,223)	$ 107,032	$ 61,410	$ (99,000)
Alternate Expense Compilation					
Salaries, fees, and benefits	$ 658,507	$ 754,109	$ 791,954	$ 823,260	$1,100,000†
Supplies and expenses	487,913	426,398	503,960	551,115	910,000
	$1,146,420	$1,180,507	$1,295,914	$1,374,375	$2,010,000

*Estimate.

† In addition, development costs for the establishment of a repertory company in the 1983–84 season could be incurred which could be largely offset by federal and provincial grants.

EXHIBIT 4   **Condensed Balance Sheets, Theatre London, 1979–1982**

	June 30			
	1979	**1980**	**1981**	**1982**
Assets				
Current assets				
Cash and term deposits	$351,010	$372,868	$325,631	$316,939
Accounts receivable	3,908	13,957	35,208	10,916
Inventory	7,463	7,146	6,050	—
Prepaid expenses	20,257	32,788	46,938	72,471
Total assets	$382,638	$426,759	$413,827	$400,326
Liabilities and Surplus				
Current liabilities:				
Bank loan.	—	$ 25,000	—	—
Accounts payable	$ 26,253	24,041	$ 30,112	$ 67,198
Advance ticket sales	280,431	324,524	319,843	302,983
Advance grants	1,060	—	15,201	14,805
Payable to Theatre London Foundation	—	4,523	—	15,340
	307,744	378,088	365,156	400,326
Surplus	74,894	48,671	48,671*	—
Total liabilities and surplus	$382,638	$426,759	$413,827	$400,326

*In addition, there was equity of $453,080 from the Wintario Challenge Fund Program in 1981 and $807,289 in 1982. Under the terms of the program, Wintario will match two dollars for every eligible contributed dollar raised (during the three-year period ending June 30, 1983) in excess of 5.9 percent of the current year's operating expenses. All these matching contributions are placed in a separate investment fund for at least five years, although interest earned on the fund may be used for current operations.

and interviewed experts in professional theater as well as officers of The Canada Council and The Ontario Arts Council. During the course of the investigation, they interviewed Robin Phillips. Phillips had been artistic director at The Stratford Festival and was well known to Barbara Ivey (who served on both the Stratford and Theatre London boards) and to other Theatre London directors. He also had directed, with considerable artistic success, two productions for Theatre London: *The Lady of the Camellias* and *Long Day's Journey into Night*.

Robin Phillips   Robin Phillips was a highly talented artistic director and a person of incredible charm. (In *all* of the interviews conducted by the casewriter, words like *charm, charisma,* and *talent* abounded.) Actress Martha Henry said, "Once you've worked with Robin, it's almost impossible to work for anyone else."

He came to Canada from England in 1974 to plan the 1975 Stratford season, although he would not direct any specific plays until 1976. His tenure at Stratford has been described as successful but stormy. When he was contracting to direct a production for The Canadian Opera Company in 1976, he said he would not renew his Stratford contract unless he had more evidence of support for his ambition to make Stratford the focus of Canadian theater, with film and television productions as well as live theater. He received a five-year

EXHIBIT 5   **Selected Demographic Statistics for Canadian Metropolitan Areas**

	Income Rating		1983 Per Capita Personal Disposable Income	
	Index	**Rank**	**Dollar Amounts**	**Rank**
Toronto	117	6	$12,693	7
Montreal	103	11	11,212	14
Vancouver	118	5	12,793	6
Ottawa-Hull	118	5	12,796	5
Edmonton	126	4	13,668	4
Calgary	132	1	14,324	1
Winnipeg	111	8	11,997	9
Quebec	98	14	10,623	18
Hamilton	112	7	12,114	8
St. Catharines	103	11	11,223	13
Kitchener	101	13	10,974	16
London	106	10	11,462	11
Halifax	101	13	10,923	17
Windsor	107	9	11,602	10
Regina	130	2	14,056	2
Saskatoon	129	3	14,021	3
Oshawa	106	10	11,450	12
Thunder Bay	102	12	11,089	15
Canadian average	100		$10,851	

Note: This list shows all 18 census metropolitan areas in which the principal city had a population of at least 100,000 in the 1981 Census.

London-Centered Seven-County Market Area Data

	Seven Counties	Canada
Population, June 1, 1983	838,500	24,886,600
Ten-year growth rate	5.7%	12.0%
Households (June 1, 1983)	293.7	8,335.0
Wage earner average income (1981)	$14,522	$15,141
Per capita disposable income (1983)	$10,669	$10,851
Per capita retail sales (1983)	$ 4,238	$ 4,153

Source: *Canadian Markets*, 1984, and 1981 income tax returns.

contract to run from November 1, 1976; the contract could be terminated with four months' notice.

There was a series of resignations from, and returns to, Stratford starting in July 1978, until Phillips's departure in 1981. In addition to his Stratford activities, Phillips was involved with theater in Calgary, New York, Toronto's Harbourfront, and Vancouver. He also filmed *The Wars*, a novel by Timothy Findley. It was generally understood that he was seeking a theater in Toronto to serve as a base for his stage, film, and television ambitions. However, none was available.

The Phillips Plan   Robin Phillips had a plan for Theatre London and would only come if he had a budget to fulfill his plan and complete artistic autonomy. His plan called for raising Theatre London from 18th place in Canadian theater to third.

The plan required a budget of $4.7 million, up from $1.9 million. This included $400,000 of capital cost to improve the Grand's facilities. Box office and concessions would provide 73 percent of the budget, 18 percent would come from donations, 5 percent from the Canada Council, and 4 percent from the Ontario Arts Council. Revenue projections were based on playing to 80 percent of capacity; this was considered feasible because Phillips had surpassed that performance at Stratford, and Theatre London had been operating at 85 percent. The theater requested a permanent tax exemption from the city of London; the deputy mayor described this request as "cavalier."

Three of the stage productions would be adapted for television and filmed by Primedia Productions of Toronto. This would provide some $100,000 of additional revenue for each production, as well as audience exposure.

Robin Phillips strongly favored a repertory company over a subscription policy. He believed, and often stated, that subscriptions denied audiences a choice, and audiences must learn to discriminate. A change had to be made to make the theater different, special, and exciting. A repertory company would provide a company of salaried actors who could not be lured away during the season, and who would be attracted by steady employment.

Another advantage of the repertory concept is the flexibility afforded patrons, who may choose the dates they see a play and their seat locations.

In a subscription series, patrons are restricted to the same seat location on the same night for each performance. In repertory theater several productions are typically run simultaneously.

The Playbill   Phillips proposed to offer nine plays from October to May on the main stage (in addition to a children's program in a small, secondary theater):

- *Godspell*, by John-Michael Tebelak—A rousing rock musical with audience appeal, especially for younger audiences.
- *The Doctor's Dilemma*, by George Bernard Shaw—An established, classical hit.
- *Waiting for the Parade*, by John Murrell—A Canadian play, with an all-female cast, showing what women did while their men were fighting World War II.
- *Timon of Athens*, by William Shakespeare—A little-performed, little-known Shakespearean play, ignored by Stratford.
- *The Club*, by Eve Merrian—A musical spoof of men's clubs, with a female cast playing the part of men.
- *Arsenic and Old Lace*, by Joseph Kesselring—A well-known classic comedy of American theater.
- *The Prisoner of Zenda*, adapted by Warren Graves—A comedy of political intrigue and romance, set in a mythical Eastern European kingdom.

- *Hamlet*, by William Shakespeare—One of his best-known plays.
- *Dear Antoine*, by Jean Anouilh—A comedy by a leading contemporary French playwright.

Casting for these plays was not a problem, as leading actors from Canada, the United States, and England were eager to work with Phillips.

Pricing   Since the plan envisioned a box office yield of $3.2 million, up from the $1.2 million planned for the 1982–83 season, revenue would have to be increased in two ways. The number of productions would be increased, with nine productions in the season instead of the previous six. There would be a record 399 performances, instead of the 230 performances in the 1982–83 season. Thus the plan projected an audience of 270,000, compared with the 137,000 planned for the 1982–83 season. In addition, prices would be increased.

A subscriber in the 1982–83 season could see five plays for $55 on weekends or $45 on weekdays. The pricing schedule proposed for the 1983–84 repertory season was:

Seats	Price	
	Weekdays	**Weekends**
178	$20.00	$22.50
245	14.50	15.50
422	10.50	12.50

Promotion   Since the theater would require an expanded audience from a wider area, the plan envisioned a program of investment spending in major area newspapers: *The Toronto Star* and *Globe and Mail*, the *Kitchener-Waterloo Record*, and the *Detroit Free Press*, as well as the *London Free Press*. The advertising would be directed at a first-time audience.

Group sales would be stressed, particularly to schools. Hotel-restaurant-transportation-theater ticket packages were planned to attract theatergoers from neighboring areas.

THE DECISION

The directors were impressed by the charm and the reputation of Robin Phillips. The proposal to hire Phillips—and to accept his plan—was supported by some board members who had sound business backgrounds and who had worked in theater for some years. They had a comfortable, modern theater, with a recently acquired computer to issue tickets. They had a proven record in selling tickets, as did Robin Phillips.

On the other hand, if Phillips were hired, his artistic strengths might not be matched administratively. There was an administrative director who had been there for only two years, and a chief accountant, but no controller. And Stratford, Canada's leading summer theater, was less than an hour's drive down the road.

THE UTAH JAZZ ARENA (A)*

Gary Cornia, Gary McKinnon, Robert Parsons, and Dale Wright,
Brigham Young University

Larry H. Miller, owner of the Utah Jazz NBA franchise, enthusiastically drove back to his office located at his Toyota auto dealership. He had just come from a successful meeting with the heads of various city, county, and state government agencies. The weather was cold but clear in Salt Lake City, typical of a last Friday in January. "It's a breakthrough day," he thought to himself. "It looks as though everything is falling into place for an October 31, 1991, opening of the new Jazz arena." As he parked his car and made his way past the new 1989 Toyotas lining the way to his office building, a thought passed through his mind. "Everything is on target, but I still need to come up with $40–$45 million in the next six months."

As usual, he offered a pleasant greeting to those he passed on his way to his office. As he sat down at his desk, he paused to reflect back on his involvement with the NBA franchise. Three major events of the past year had forced him to rethink his original plans for the Utah Jazz.

THE NBA BOARD OF GOVERNORS MEETING

The NBA board of governors meet officially three times each year: first at the all-star game, next in mid-April in New York City, and finally in September at a designated city.

The major agenda item for the 1988 spring meeting in New York City focused on the contract agreement with the players' association. Two months prior to the 1988 all-star game, the old collective bargaining agreement had expired. The NBA players continued to play without a contract while preliminary negotiations took place. The owners came to New York to discuss several options related to player contracts. Owners could renegotiate, give in to player demands, or "go dark," which meant locking out the players thereby interrupting league play.

It was common knowledge among owners, players, and basketball enthusiasts that the players make their money during the regular season while the owners make their money during the playoffs. Owners were concerned with rumors that the players would continue to play without a contract for a few additional weeks (until they had earned most of their salary), and then strike as the 1988 season ended. This action would place great pressure on the owners for a quick agreement so the playoffs could take place. Without the playoffs, the owner would have to write off the income generated from the playoff games and most teams would end the season with a deficit.

Prior to the meeting, several NBA owners contacted Miller to explain that if the owners were to gain bargaining power they needed to go dark, or lock out

*Kelly Sessions, Stacy Stickler, Jeff Ferguson, and Mick Berry assisted in gathering case materials. Financial support for the case research assistants was provided by the Marriott School of Management Entrepreneurial Founders.

the players and not wait for the players to initiate a strike near the end of the season. Miller didn't like the idea of going dark, but he knew that was about the only way the owners could bargain from a position of strength.

As the dinner meeting began, David Stern, NBA commissioner, surprised the owners with a bombshell when he outlined a new collective bargaining agreement. Commissioner Stern was ready to present the new agreement to the owners for a formal ratification. He described it as "a significant compromise." Larry Flasher, of the NBA Players' Association, later stated he was more than satisfied with what he called "a breakthrough agreement."

Miller listened to what he later called "a triple whammy." The new agreement limited the draft to three rounds the first year and then to two rounds in subsequent years. New free agent rules were introduced that clearly favored the seasoned player, which meant higher salaries for free agents. A more consequential part of the new agreement changed the salary cap and the related revenue-sharing formula. Under the new agreement the players were guaranteed at least 53 percent of the defined gross revenue (revenue from national TV, cable TV, and gate receipts). The salary cap formula was complicated to understand, but it was clear to Miller that under the new salary cap, salaries for the Utah Jazz would go from $4.9 million to $9.8 million in just four years. The change in the salary cap was clearly advantageous to the teams in large metromarkets, to teams with large arenas, and to expansion teams. It clearly had major disadvantages to teams like the Utah Jazz.

As the details of the agreement were being presented, Miller's initial thought was, "I am listening to the death warrant of the Jazz in Utah." He first wondered if the franchise could even survive in the second smallest market in the NBA. (See Exhibit 1.) He then wondered how much time he had before he had to make major changes. Would a larger arena solve his problem? Miller knew he couldn't just give up and sell without meeting the challenge. He had often been the underdog as he built his auto dealerships, and he wasn't about to give up on keeping the Jazz.

Larry H. Miller

The 1989–90 *Utah Jazz Media Guide* provided the following information about Larry H. Miller, owner of the Utah Jazz.

> With a firm personal commitment to professional basketball in Salt Lake, Utah Jazz owner Larry H. Miller has built a successful professional sports franchise in this, the second smallest of major league cities.
>
> Miller's commitment to keeping professional basketball in Utah was first evidenced in the spring of 1985, when he purchased a 50 percent interest in the franchise from then-owner Sam Battistone and his StratAmerican Corporation. Then, a little over a year later, he bought out Battistone's remaining share in the team, assuming full ownership, and saving the team from a possible move to Minnesota at the hands of a Minneapolis-based group of investors interested in buying the team.
>
> In the three years since he assumed full ownership of the team, Miller's unique managing and promoting abilities have been instrumental in building the Jazz into one of the league's most respected and admired teams. And with a new state-of-the-art, 18,000+ seat arena in the works, Miller's commitment to the Jazz's future is as strong and solid as ever.
>
> A native of Salt Lake City, Miller is the owner of the LHM Group, a network of auto dealerships in Murray, Utah; Albuquerque, New Mexico; Denver, Colorado;

EXHIBIT 1   **The NBA Markets**

Team	Metro Population	Home Court Capacity Attendance	Year Home Court Arena Constructed	Number of 1987–88 Games Sold Out
Atlanta Hawks	2,565,000	16.371	1972	4
Boston Celtics	2,841,700	14,890	1928	9
Charlotte Hornets	1,091,000	23,288	1988	1
Chicago Bulls	6,199,000	17,339	1929	3
Cleveland Cavaliers	1,851,000	20,273	1974	2
Dallas Mavericks	3,456,000	17,007	1980	12
Denver Nuggets	1,644,500	17,022	1975	11
Detroit Pistons	4,361,600	21,454	1988	5
Golden State Warriors	1,500,000	15,025	1966	6
Houston Rockets	3,228,100	16,611	1975	14
Indiana Pacers	1,228,000	16,912	1974	3
Los Angeles Clippers	8,504,500	15,310	1959	6
Los Angeles Lakers	8,504,500	17,505	1967	13
Miami Heat	2,954,000	15,008	1988	3
Milwaukee Bucks	1,389,100	18,633	1988	4
Minnesota Timberwolves	2,335,600	25,559	1989	0
New Jersey Nets	1,870,000	20,039	1981	3
New York Knicks	8,528,800	18,351	1968	4
Orlando Magic	934,700	15,500	1989	0
Philadelphia 76ers	4,866,500	18,168	1967	9
Phoenix Suns	1,989,600	14,487	1965	9
Portland Trailblazers	1,167,800	12,880	1982	7
Sacramento Kings	1,336,500	16,517	1986	7
San Antonio Spurs	1,306,700	15,861	1968	10
Seattle Supersonics	1,795,900	14,250	1986	8
Utah Jazz	**1,044,500**	**12,444**	**1969**	**40**
Washington Bullets	3,646,000	18,756	1984	4

and Phoenix, Arizona; as well as several other related businesses. (For example, the Murray Utah dealerships consisted of Chevrolet, Dodge, Geo, Chrysler-Plymouth, Hyundai, Subaru, and Toyota.)

Miller believes in a "hands-on" approach to business, and is actively involved in all aspects of each of his endeavors, from the dealerships to the Jazz. It is not uncommon to see him on the showroom floor or in a service bay at one of his dealerships, or at a Jazz practice session or team meeting. And he is now personally spearheading the effort in all aspects of the new arena project.

Miller's interest in competitive sports is not limited to the basketball court. In fact, for many years prior to his involvement with the Jazz, Miller participated in fast-pitch softball, and was a nationally recognized pitcher. He hung up his glove only recently, as the pressures of his businesses and the team consume an increasing amount of his time, but continues to sponsor several teams.

A devoted family man, Larry and his wife Gail are the parents of five children, four sons and one daughter, and they are very proud grandparents. The Millers reside in Sandy, Utah, a suburb of Salt Lake City.

EXHIBIT 2   Jazz Attendance Figures, 1974–1988

Year	Total Home Attendance	Average Home Attendance	Number of Games Sold Out
1974–75	203,141	4,955	0
1975–76	513,383	12,519	0
1976–77	444,138	10,833	0
1977–78	527,351	12,862	0
1978–79	364,205	8,883	0
1979–80	320,649	7,821	4
1980–81	307,825	7,508	4
1981–82	313,864	7,665	3
1982–83	355,819	8,697	4
1983–84	407,818	9,947	8
1984–85	373,808	9,117	6
1985–86	477,842	11,655	22
1986–87	491,382	11,985	30
1987–88	503,969	12,292	40

Seating capacity for the New Orleans Jazz (Super Dome): approximately 35,000.
Seating capacity for the Utah Jazz (Salt Palace): 12,212 through 1987, then 12,444.

History of the Utah Jazz

In 1974, the New Orleans Jazz became the 18th member of the National Basketball Association when a nine-member group paid $6.15 million for an expansion team. With "Pistol Pete" Maravich leading the expansion players, the Jazz ended the season with a 23–59 record. Total home attendance that first year was 203,141 (see Exhibit 2).

Attendance jumped the following year to 513,000 as the record improved to 38–44, but the attendance fluctuated for the next three years. In the 1978–79 season the win-loss record was 26–56 and attendance fell to 364,205 fans.

In 1979, after five difficult seasons, co-owners Sam Battistone and Larry Hatfield announced plans to move the Jazz from New Orleans to Salt Lake City. They anticipated better fan support in the new location. Games were played at the Salt Palace, and the first sellout (12,015) in Utah Jazz history took place as the Lakers beat the Jazz. Adrian Dantley, obtained in a trade with the Los Angeles Lakers, led the Jazz in scoring. The Jazz finished its first season in Utah with a 24–58 mark.

The management of the Jazz continued to strengthen the club personnel in 1980–81. Darrell Griffith was drafted (named NBA rookie of the year by *Sporting News*), but the season record did not improve much and the Jazz record stood at 28–54.

During the 1981–82 season, Sam Battistone bought out Larry Hatfield and became the sole owner of the Jazz. The record of the Utah Jazz did not improve in the 1981–82 season (25–27) but both Ricky Green and Adrian Dantley were leaders in their respective areas (scoring and assists). Battistone hoped there was a light at the end of the tunnel.

EXHIBIT 3   **Jazz Win-Loss Record, 1974–1988**

Season	Record	Season	Record
1974–75	23–59	1981–82	25–57
1975–76	38–44	1982–83	30–52
1976–77	35–47	1983–84	45–37
1977–78	39–43	1984–85	41–41
1978–79	26–53	1985–86	42–40
1979–80	24–58	1986–87	44–38
1980–81	28–54	1987–88	47–35

Before the 1982–83 season, the Jazz drafted Dominique Wilkins and then traded him to Atlanta for two players and a large cash payment. Battistone was criticized by fans and sportswriters for the trade. Attendance figures were just above 300,000 (see Exhibit 2) during the early years in Utah and the Utah Jazz were rumored to be in financial difficulty. Mark Eaton, a 7-foot, 4-inch center, was drafted in the fourth round. At the end of the season the Jazz requested permission from the NBA board of governors to play selected home games at the Thomas and Mack Center in Las Vegas, Nevada, for 1983–84. Battistone was searching for creative ways to save the Utah Jazz.

In the 1983–84 season, the Utah Jazz improved to a 45–37 mark and the Utah Jazz played their first-ever playoff game against Denver. The Jazz beat Denver in five games and went on to lose to Phoenix in the next round. Season attendance rose to 407,818.

Before the 1984–85 season the Jazz surprised many fans and sportswriters by drafting John Stockton as their first pick. In another major move, the NBA board of governors approved the sale of 50 percent ownership of the Utah Jazz to Larry H. Miller, a relative unknown in NBA circles. With his purchase of 50 percent of the Utah Jazz, the organization seemed solvent. The Utah Jazz then ended the experiment of playing selected home games in Las Vegas.

In the 1985–86 season Karl Malone was drafted. In a gesture of appreciation Jazz jersey number 7 was retired in honor of "Pistol Pete" Maravich. With Dantley, Malone, Stockton, and Eaton the Jazz finished above .500 for only the second time in franchise history and entered into the playoff games for the third straight year.

A Change in Ownership and Business Expansion

In 1986, a major change took place that strengthened the financial health of the Utah Jazz. Larry H. Miller purchased the remaining 50 percent of the Jazz. He was prepared to move forward with plans to make the Utah Jazz a solid NBA franchise so it could remain in Salt Lake City. Miller had learned from his auto dealerships that marketing was a key to success in business. He planned to more effectively market the Jazz and develop associated businesses.

The Jazz Sports Channel was formed with the world's largest cable company (TCI). TCI provided service to about 250,000 subscribers in the Jazz viewing area, but it was estimated that there were an additional 280,000 potential subscribers in Salt Lake Valley itself. In the first year TCI paid $25,000 to broadcast each of 25 games. Advertising revenues from cable television commercials generated another $300,000. Jazz officials estimated that as the number of subscribers increased, multiyear contracts with TCI would eventually approach $1 million per year.

On April 1, 1987, the Utah Jazz purchased four retail stores known as the Pro Image. The product line consisted of official NBA, NFL, NHL, and collegiate athletic merchandise. During the first three months the retail operation resulted in a loss of $150,000 and $130,000 the following year. However, a change in management resulted in a $300,000 profit and a return on investment of over 25 percent in 1989.

For several years the National Basketball Association was a cosponsor of the Youth Basketball Association. When that relationship was severed in 1986, a local YMCA official approached the Jazz management with the idea of forming an independent youth basketball program. A Junior Jazz league was formed with the basic noncompetitive philosophy that all team players would play in each game. By 1988 over 30,000 youths participated in Junior Jazz, the largest program of its kind in the nation. Each Jazz player was contracted to make appearances at Junior Jazz league events. Each youth participant received free Jazz game tickets, certificates of participation, and Jazz team posters.

Revenue from the Junior Jazz program came from selling advertising on game shirts and from fees charged to each participant. Most of the detail of administering league play rests with community recreation personnel resulting in little administrative expense. Net income to the Jazz was approximately $40,000 to $60,000 per year.

An Integrated Product Offering

Player personnel changes were also made after Miller purchased 100 percent of the Jazz. Adrian Dantley, after some disagreements with the likable Jazz coach Frank Layden, was traded. The nucleus of a competitive NBA club was in place and Miller was eager to continue to expand the marketing efforts of the Utah Jazz.

The attendance figures for the 1987–88 season grew to 503,696, and the record was 47–35. Stockton and Malone were each named NBA player of the month (February and March). The Jazz beat Portland in the first round of the playoffs, and the Jazz took the LA Lakers to the seventh game before being eliminated. It was probably the greatest period of Jazz history. As "Hot Rod" Hundley, the voice of the Utah Jazz, stated so well, "You've-got-to-love-it-baby!"

Competition

Four major universities (Brigham Young University, University of Utah, Utah State University, and Weber State University) are located within 75 miles of Salt Lake City. Each sponsors an NCAA basketball team that plays in large and fairly new arenas.

The Golden Eagles Hockey team, a minor league team, plays at the Salt Palace, but Jazz officials do not view them as a major competitive force. They believe NBA games face little direct competition from other athletic events in the Rocky Mountain region.

EXHIBIT 4   **Utah Jazz Ticket Prices, 1979–1990**

Season	Price Selection
1979–80	$9, 7, 5
1980–81	$9, 7, 5
1981–82	$12, 10, 9, 7, 5
1982–83	$30, 20, 12, 10, 7.50, 5
1983–84	$30, 20, 12, 10, 7.50, 5
1984–85	$22.50, 17.50, 12.50, 10, 7.50, 5
1985–86	$22.50, 17.50, 12.50, 10, 7.50, 5
1986–87	$25, 20, 17.50, 15, 10, 5
1987–88	$25, 20, 17.50, 15, 10, 5
1988–89	$30, 25, 20, 17.50, 12.50, 7.50
1989–90	$35, 30, 25, 17.50, 12.50, 7.50

EXHIBIT 5   **Ticket Prices of Selected NBA Teams**

Team	Price Selection
Atlanta Hawks	$75 (VIP), 35 (VIP), 25 (VIP), 20, 15, 10, 5
Boston Celtics	$30, 24, 23, 18, 17, 13, 10
Chicago Bulls	$135, 60, 32.50, 19.50, 14.50, 10.50
Dallas Mavs	$75.60, 29.16, 24,84, 21, 17, 14, 13, 10, 7, 5
Denver Nuggets	$100, 27, 24, 22, 20, 18, 15, 11, 8
LA Lakers	$350 (VIP), 90, 52.50, 32.50, 18.50, 14.50, 11.50, 8.50
New Jersey Nets	$50, 30, 25, 22, 18, 15, 13, 10, 6
Phoenix Suns	$27, 22, 18, 17, 13, 7
San Antonio	$50, 40, 32, 28, 21, 18, 15, 11, 8, 5
Seattle	$25, 20, 18, 15, 12, 9, 5

Ticket prices for the Utah Jazz are shown in Exhibit 4 (does not include VIP tickets). Ticket prices (1989–90) of selected NBA teams are shown in Exhibit 5.

THE SALT LAKE METROPOLITAN AREA

Demographics   As of 1988, population in the Salt Lake/Ogden Metropolitan Statistical Area (MSA) made up 61.8 percent of the entire population of Utah, estimated to be 1,695,000. The population for the Salt Lake MSA is forecasted to grow at a rate of 0.94 percent annually, between the years of 1989 and 1999, reaching 1,150,000 persons.

The 1988 median household family income for the Salt Lake MSA is $30,500. While household income is lower than the national average of $35,400, the cost of living index is also lower, 97.3. The combined personal income for individuals within the Salt Lake MSA is approximately $15 billion. This amount is expected to grow by 7.64 percent per year, reaching $31 billion by 1999.

Economy   In 1989, Utah and Salt Lake experienced impressive economic growth, following six years of economic slowdown. The new job expansion was third in the nation, at 4.4 percent, translating new jobs into greater income and the expansion of sales and services.

Utah's construction industry also started to grow and was at 14.7 percent in the first nine months of 1989. The new-found growth was centered primarily in the commercial community, where construction value was up 32 percent at $277.7 million. Residential construction was $346.5 million, up 7.3 percent over the previous year.

The real estate market rose 1.4 percent in values and 0.4 percent in number compared to the previous year. The selling price of the average home was $80,746.

Work Force   Utah's work force of 305,000 is recognized as hard-working and educated. Projections place the work force at over 1,000,000 by the year 2000.

The overall change in the Utah economy employment picture shows movement away from the state's traditional mining, manufacturing, and government economic base toward services and trade. Industries projected to have the fastest growth rates are machinery and electronic equipment, air transportation, transportation services, hotels and lodging, business services, and health services.

Transportation   Geographically centered in the western United States, Salt Lake City is easily accessible through various modes of travel. The Salt Lake International Airport has 550 daily flights, with 56,000 airline seats and connections with 148 U.S. cities. Salt Lake serves as a major hub for Delta Airlines. The airport is located six miles west of the major hotel district. The Salt Palace is at the center of that district.

Salt Lake is also at the intersection of I-80 and I-15 with access to cities in all directions. Amtrak and the Denver and Rio Grand Western RR provide passenger train service.

Tourism   Tourism and conventions add more than $1 billion to the Salt Lake economy, provide 29,000 jobs, and generate a payroll of over $417 million. Over six million tourists, convention, and business travelers come to the Salt Lake Valley and its mountain resorts annually. There are 12,166 hotel and motel rooms in Salt Lake County.

The Ski Industry   Utah has 15 ski resorts and 7 cross-country touring centers, with 8 of the ski resorts and 5 of the cross-country centers no more than 60 minutes from downtown Salt Lake City. The ski industry accounts for more than $250 million in tourism annually. The average ski tourist spends 3.7 days skiing in Utah and spends $98 per day. Significant media attention on the Utah ski industry and a 1998 Olympic bid for the winter games was forecast to contribute to increased growth in the Utah ski industry.

THE SALT PALACE

Plans for a new civic auditorium in Salt Lake City were first proposed in January 1929, but the idea was shelved with little fanfare until the late 1930s, when arguments for an auditorium again surfaced. With the outbreak of World War II, however, the plans were again put on hold and were not considered for several years after the war in hopes that the cost of building the center would come down. Finally, in 1958, advocates again proposed the idea of building a civic auditorium for Salt Lake City, and in 1961 a committee was appointed to study the feasibility of such a project.

After a year and a half of study, the committee concluded the community needed a two- or three-building complex, and in November 1963, voters approved (by a 59 percent to 41 percent majority) a $17 million bond to fund the project. A downtown site was approved in 1964, ground-breaking commenced in March 1967, and the Salt Palace celebrated its grand opening on July 11, 1969.

In its early days, the Salt Palace was considered to be one of the finest civic auditoriums in the nation. The building consisted of a circular, 13,075-seat sports/show arena and a 70,000-square-foot convention hall with room for an additional 5,266 seats. The sports area featured a portable basketball floor, an NCAA-sanctioned indoor track floor, and an ice hockey rink. With slight modifications, the arena could be used for other events such as rodeos, circuses, and horse shows. The exhibit hall was used to attract events such as car and boat shows, business conventions, and manufacturer's displays.

Six years after the Salt Palace opening, voters approved a general obligation bond to expand the overall facilities to include an adjacent Symphony Hall and Art Center. The bond totaled $8.675 million and the state matched an appropriation of $7.5 million. The entire complex became known as the Salt Palace Center.

The Salt Palace proved itself to be a lucrative investment for Salt Lake County. With the original price tag of $17 million, the Salt Palace by 1979 had brought over $850 million into Salt Lake County.

By the mid-1970s the limited size of the original buildings of the Salt Palace Complex prevented large trade shows and conventions from being booked. Large events were becoming more common at other centers across the nation. A second expansion was needed in order to keep up. In 1980, voters approved $16.5 million of general revenue bonds for construction of two more exhibit halls and to add an additional 200,000 square feet of exhibit space, as well as to expand parking facilities. Ground-breaking began in 1981 and the new center was completed in 1987. Exhibit 6 shows the largest conventions held at the Salt Palace Center in 1987–88.

By 1989 the Salt Palace Center again faced the serious threat of losing out to competition from civic centers in neighboring states. Reports showed that because of inadequate space, the Salt Palace Center had lost 25 major events since 1985, which resulted in a direct loss of an estimated $40 million to the county. The county, therefore, commissioned Coopers & Lybrand, a Minneapolis-based public accounting firm, to do a study of the issue and make recommendations.

Among other things, the Coopers & Lybrand report called for the demolition of the original Salt Palace Arena in order to make room for expanding the existing 200,000 square feet of exhibit space to some 300,000, as well as

EXHIBIT 6   **Twenty Largest Conventions Held in Salt Lake City, 1987–88**

Group	Attendance	Room Nights	$ Impact
Teachers of Math	7,000	15,925	$3,619,116
National Tour Association	3,100	15,580	3,540,711
Presbyterians	6,000	13,728	3,119,825
Sweet Adelines	6,500	10,125	2,301,008
U.S. Figure Skating	3,000	7,272	1,653,317
School Librarians	3,100	6,100	1,386,286
INGRES Users	1,000	5,420	1,231,749
Adult Educators	3,000	5,349	1,215,614
Sports Medicine	3,500	5,305	1,205,614
Mining Engineers	2,500	4,865	1,105,620
Electrical Distributors	3,000	4,593	1,043,805
Professional Secretaries	1,800	4,486	1,019,488
Student Information	1,200	4,050	920,403
State Governments	1,000	3,391	770,639
Outdoor Writers	1,000	3,150	715,000
Equipment Dealers	1,300	3,135	712,460
Nu Skin	1,500	3,101	704,733
Information Association	900	2,765	628,374
Child Abuse Conference	3,000	2,604	591,785
Insurance Commissioners	1,500	2,308	524,516

increasing the available number of meeting rooms from 35 to 50. Additionally, the existing exhibit and assembly halls would need to be renovated in order to lure more out-of-state dollars with a large modern facility that could handle more than what the present facility could: one convention at a time.

One important key to the Coopers & Lybrand report was that it was made under the assumption the Jazz would be playing in their own arena, which would also handle the rodeos, tractor pulls, and concerts and would thus free up the Salt Palace Arena space for other uses. However, even with the full expansion into the Salt Palace Arena space, Salt Lake would still rank 13th out of the 16 western convention centers. Undaunted, county planners considered other city amenities and predicted the new Salt Palace Center would be a "premier" facility and could compete "not only with Denver, Houston, Phoenix, and Albuquerque, but also with the big boys: Los Angeles, Las Vegas, San Francisco, and Anaheim."

Alternative Arena Sites

Soon after acquiring full ownership of the Jazz in 1986, Larry Miller began casually looking at potential sites for a new arena. He knew that someday (probably by the year 2000) he would need additional seating, but he didn't foresee a radical new players' agreement like the one presented by Commissioner Stern. Miller thought there was less than a 20 percent chance he would need a larger arena by 1995.

During his early exploration he was surprised that about eight sites were still available in the Salt Lake Valley which met the criteria for a new arena (see Exhibit 7). A new arena required 54 acres for parking and about 6 acres for the rest of the complex. The eight sites also met the need for easy freeway access and utility hookup. One major developer wanted to enter into a joint venture with Miller, with the Jazz anchoring an industrial park.

During his preliminary site search, Miller contacted NBA owners who had recently built new arenas. These included franchise owners in Milwaukee, Charlotte, Miami, Sacramento, and Detroit. From his discussions with other team owners, he estimated the cost of the new 20,000-seat arena to be between $60 million and $70 million. He thought he could handle about $40 million himself, but he questioned where he would get assistance with the remaining $20–30 million.

A Downtown Site Selection

After Miller returned from the April 1988 New York meetings, he knew he must move rapidly to a larger arena to generate additional revenue for the new salary cap. The other alternative was to sell the Jazz franchise and see the team move to a larger metro-market. The personal challenge of keeping the Jazz in Utah pushed Miller to immediately select one of the preliminary sites he had already identified and to begin construction of a larger arena as soon as possible.

While Miller didn't publicize the search, the word on the street was that Miller was looking for a site for a new arena. Palmer DePaulis, mayor of Salt Lake City, received numerous telephone calls from downtown merchants suggesting the Jazz needed to remain downtown. In late June 1988 Mayor DePaulis telephoned Miller and asked, "Are you looking at any downtown sites for the new arena?" Miller told the mayor the most attractive sites were outside the downtown area, but after some persuasion Miller said he would keep an open mind about the two downtown locations. The mayor suggested Miller would receive much cooperation and support for the city locations.

While Miller had little formal education beyond high school, his ownership and expansion of his auto dealership made him politically astute. He understood a downtown arena was very important to the community and therefore had almost automatic support from all government units and agencies. But Miller's personal set of values were such that he personally felt uncomfortable using power for an unfair advantage. Another dilemma Miller faced was that he had a major aversion to taxpayers subsidizing private enterprise. He had never used political power or pressure and had always avoided government assistance. That personal philosophy made it more difficult as he thought about the financial help he needed in raising $65 million for the new arena.

During those summer months of 1988, Larry Miller did a 180-degree turn from locating outside the city center. He became convinced that downtown Salt Lake City needed the arena to remain a strong capital city. He later stated to a close associate, "I am convinced that the health of a capital city is crucial to the health of the state, especially in a western state. The central city has a special role in Utah; it must remain strong. Downtown Salt Lake City needs the Jazz arena."

EXHIBIT 7   **Possible Arena Site Locations**

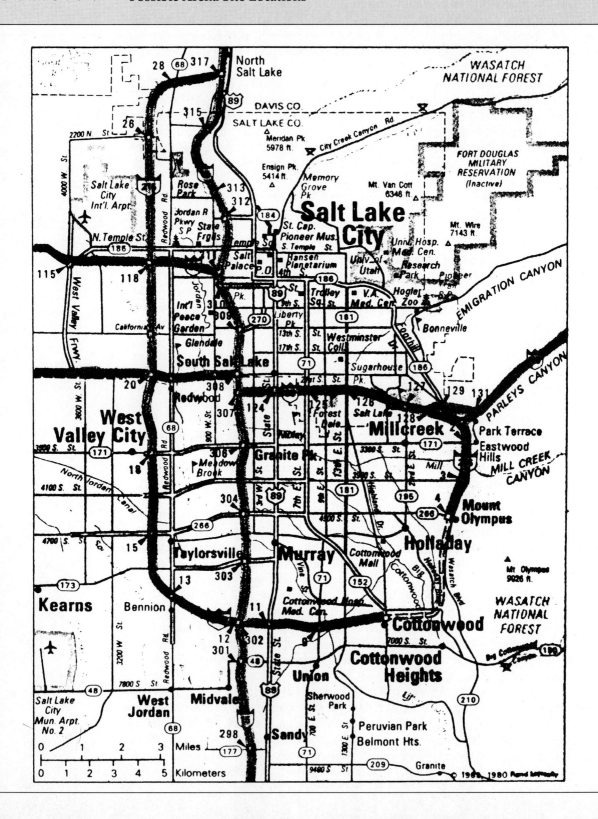

Miller was involved with meetings with many government officials during the late summer. The main players were Palmer DePaulis, mayor of Salt Lake City, and Bill Barker, a senior county commissioner. Miller became frustrated that the various city, county, and state agencies were more concerned about jockeying for power positions rather than offering a downtown site proposal Miller could accept.

While Miller had received support for the arena from Utah Governor Norman Bangerter, he knew the decisions rested at the county and city level. In late September, Miller informed Mayor DePaulis, Commissioner Barker, and other heads of the various governmental agencies that he was running out of time and he needed a decision by October 31. DePaulis balked at the time frame, knowing of the difficulty of assembling all who needed to be in attendance. However, John Rosenthal, Bill Barker's personal assistant, said, "I can do it." In less than a week Rosenthal had 80 "high-profile" government and civic leaders at a meeting where they were organized into committees and subcommittees. They had one month to have a site package ready for Miller.

During October everyone cooperated and loose ends began to come together. Two downtown sites were identified, and public hearings were held about the new arena location. By October 31, most of the details had been worked out and Miller agreed to the downtown location. Miller was impressed with how things worked so well. He later commented, "I wish I had paid better attention to my high school civics class. I really learned how different agencies cooperate with each other when the need is there."

Other Alternatives for the Jazz

As Miller was waiting for all the parts of the arena puzzle to come together, he tried not to think about other alternatives still open to him. Several friends had suggested that the Salt Lake market was too small to support an NBA franchise. Miller was aware that Baltimore and several major cities in Canada were interested in an NBA team. Exhibit 8 presents a financial history for the Utah Jazz for the 1985–89 period.

George Shinn and partners paid $32.5 million for the new franchise in North Carolina. On July 10, 1989, the press reported Bertram M. Lee and Peter C. Bynoe had purchased the Denver Nuggets for $65 million. The health of the NBA was never better, and Miller knew if he sold the club his profit would be substantial.

The January 27, 1989 Meeting

Indeed, January 27, 1989, was a breakthrough day. In an important meeting with various government agencies some important details had been finalized. The Redevelopment Agency (RDA) agreed to provide $20 million of the $65 million for land acquisition, water and utility hookups, plaza development, and on-site parking. It was a complicated arrangement since the RDA needed the cooperation of the school board because of the property tax issues involved with the agreement. At the conclusion of the meeting Miller was pleased that everyone "bought off" on the proposal. The deal had been struck. Only an additional $45 million stood in the way of the October 31, 1991, opening of the new Jazz arena.

E X H I B I T 8   Financial Statistics for Utah Jazz, 1985–1989

	1985-86	Percent of Total Revenue	1986-87	Percent of Total Revenue	1987-88	Percent of Total Revenue	1988-89	Percent of Total Revenue
Division 1 Revenue								
Ticket revenue	$4,604,588	50.18%	$5,334,727	46.30%	$5,372,046	39.96%	$7,107,506	41.50%
NBA revenue	1,857,025	20.24	2,477,069	21.50	3,077,879	22.90	3,262,893	19.05
Exhibition revenue	86,235	0.94	186,041	1.61	399,255	2.97	514,235	3.00
In-arena revenue	164,565	1.79	220,127	1.91	189,341	1.41	202,392	1.18
Other revenue	213,846	2.33	187,631	1.63	163,434	1.22	257,052	1.50
Jazz 100 Club revenue	93,945	1.02	237,185	2.06	311,254	2.32	302,795	1.77
Total division 1 revenue	$7,020,204	76.50%	$8,642,780	75.01%	$9,513,209	70.77%	$11,646,873	68.01%
Division 2 Gross Profit								
Salt Palace	$ 31,180	0.34%	$ 43,333	0.38%	$74,745	0.56%	$ 182,061	1.06%
Fashion Place	0	0.00	9,932	0.09	93,191	0.69	123,623	0.72
ZCMI	0	0.00	9,340	0.08	57,327	0.43	91,516	0.53
University	0	0.00	9,988	0.09	87,909	0.65	123,106	0.72
South Towne	0	0.00	4,328	0.04	42,761	0.32	51,392	0.30
Cottonwood	0	0.00	2,146	0.02	95,523	0.71	124,090	0.72
Valley Fair	0	0.00	0	0.00	95,541	0.71	184,945	1.08
Sandy Mall	0	0.00	0	0.00	0	0.00	8,469	0.05
Total division 2 gross profit	$ 31,180	0.34%	$ 79,067	0.69%	$ 546,997	4.07%	$ 889,202	5.19%
Division 3 Revenue								
TV	$ 839,133	9.14%	$ 706,207	6.13%	$826,194	6.15%	$ 1,307,394	7.63%
Radio	650,906	7.09	461,806	4.01	415,939	3.09	529,027	3.09
Cable	0	0.00	403,022	3.50	637,482	4.74	797,774	4.66
TV production	0	0.00	198,682	1.72	268,600	2.00	274,153	1.60
Promotional	483,724	5.27	783,881	6.80	886,940	6.60	1,150,056	6.72
Other media	0	0.00	46,587	0.40	110,551	0.82	140,754	0.82
Total division 3 revenue	$1,973,763	21.51%	$ 2,600,185	22.57%	$ 3,145,706	23.40%	$ 4,199,158	24.52%
Division 4 Revenue								
Junior Jazz	$ 129,377	1.41%	$ 107,120	0.93%	$224,237	1.67%	$ 378,531	2.21%
Pro Am	22,000	0.24	25,265	0.22	24,733	0.18	12,550	0.07
Other special events	474	0.01	67,861	0.59	(12,704)	−0.09	0	0.00
Total division 4 revenue	$ 151,851	1.65%	$ 200,246	1.74%	$236,266	1.76%	$ 391,081	2.28%
Total revenue	$9,176,998	100.00%	$11,522,278	100.00%	$13,442,178	100.00%	$17,126,314	100.00%

Division 1 Expenses

Player salaries	$2,782,656	30.32%	$3,871,062	33.60%	$ 5,303,227	39.45 %	$ 6,073,672	35.46 %
Other basketball expenses	1,340,075	14.60	1,507,903	13.09	1,994,179	14.84	2,139,148	12.49
Exhibition expenses	113,908	1.24	171,966	1.49	244,005	1.82	372,294	2.17
Same night	787,823	8.58	863,526	7.49	916,723	6.82	1,121,203	6.55
Public relations	75,319	0.82	268,246	2.33	292,234	2.17	362,165	2.11
Marketing	596,917	6.50	520,714	4.52	567,528	4.22	591,681	3.45
In-arena expenses	50,665	0.55	68,437	0.59	73,047	0.54	17,797	0.10
Jazz 100 Club	130,944	1.43	199,012	1.73	216,883	1.61	227,798	1.33
Customer service center	198,598	2.16	192,976	1.67	229,639	1.71	262,948	1.54
General any administrative	2,283,920	24.89	1,896,931	16.46	2,462,364	18.32	2,584,919	15.09
Total division 1 expenses	$8,360,825	91.11%	$9,560,773	82.98%	$12,299,829	91.50%	$13,753,625	80.31%

Division 2 Expenses

Salt Palace	$ 28,075	0.31%	$ 36,825	0.32%	$ 20,660	0.15%	$ 28,922	0.17%
Fashion Place	0	0.00	19,778	0.17	78,908	0.59	102,442	0.60
ZCMI	0	0.00	12,829	0.11	54,889	0.41	68,109	0.40
University	0	0.00	14,445	0.13	69,638	0.52	82,835	0.48
South Towne	0	0.00	11,537	0.10	43,079	0.32	51,296	0.30
Cottonwood	0	0.00	9,140	0.08	83,830	0.62	101,814	0.59
Valley Fair	0	0.00	0	0.00	75,516	0.56	128,696	0.75
Sandy Mall	0	0.00	0	0.00	0	0.00	12,154	0.07
Overhead	0	0.00	69,245	0.60	217,095	1.62	199,772	1.17
Total division 2 expenses	$ 28,075	0.31%	$ 173,799	1.51%	$ 643,615	4.79%	$ 776,040	4.53%

Division 3 Expenses

TV	$ 423,932	4.62%	$ 387,103	3.36%	$ 436,578	3.25%	$ 560,202	3.27%
Radio	152,197	1.66	99,695	0.87	179,968	1.34	282,026	1.65
Cable	0	0.00	248,297	2.15	335,361	2.49	349,422	2.04
TV production	0	0.00	166,369	1.44	198,900	1.48	234,640	1.37
Promotional	340,547	3.71	327,319	2.84	320,685	2.39	515,182	3.01
Other media	70,682	0.77	88,157	0.77	136,009	1.01	126,214	0.74
Sales overhead	23,134	0.25	192,960	1.67	337,064	2.51	466,648	2.72
Broadcasting overhead	285,972	3.12	522,696	4.54	270,919	2.02	233,496	1.36
Total division 3 expenses	$1,296,464	14.13%	$2,032,596	17.64%	$ 2,215,484	16.48%	$ 2,767,830	16.16%

(continued)

	1985–86	Percent of Total Revenue	1986–87	Percent of Total Revenue	1987–88	Percent of Total Revenue	1988–89	Percent of Total Revenue
Division 4 Expenses								
Junior Jazz	$ 105,513	1.15%	$ 163,970	1.42%	$174,240	1.30%	$ 256,468	1.49%
Pro Am	14,953	0.16	25,574	0.22	34,473	0.26	13,117	0.08
Other		0.00	71,784	0.62	5,633	0.04	0	0.00
Total division 4 expenses	$ 120,466	1.31%	$ 261,328	2.27%	$ 214,346	1.59%	$ 268,585	1.57%
Total expenses	$9,805,830	106.85%	$12,028,496	104.39%	$15,373,274	114.37%	$17,566,080	102.57%
Net profit (loss)	$ (628,832)	–6.85%	$ (506,218)	–4.39%	$(1,931,096)	–14.37%	$ (439,766)	–2.57%
Total depreciation	$ 565,563	6.16%	$ 628,546	5.46%	$ 725,338	5.40%	$ 781,166	4.56%
Operating profit (loss)	(63,269)	–0.69	122,328	1.06	(1,205,758)	–8.97	341,400	1.99
Reconciliation of Net Profit or Loss to Audited Statement								
Net profit (loss) from above	$ (628,832)	–6.85%	$ (506,218)	–4.39%	$ (1,931,096)	–14.37%	$ (439,766)	–2.57%
Add back expansion revenue	0	0.00	0	0.00	2,826,087	21.02	2,826,087	16.50
Add back playoff revenue	433,164	4.72	658,814	5.72	1,588,410	11.82	674,377	3.94
Add back playoff expenses	(252,376)	–2.75	(362,570)	–3.15	(784,197)	–5.83	(309,562)	–1.81
Add back Clippers settlement	0	0.00	0	0.00	128,459	0.96	128,459	0.75
Rounding	0	0.00	0	0.00	0	0.00	(11)	0.00
Audited net profit (loss)	$ (448,044)	–4.88%	$ (209,974)	–1.82%	$ 1,827,663	13.60%	$ 2,879,595	16.81%

NUCOR CORPORATION*

Charles Stubbart, University of Massachusetts
Dean Schroeder, Valparaiso University
Arthur A. Thompson, Jr., University of Alabama

It's the closest thing to a perfect company in the steel industry.
Daniel Roling
Analyst for Merrill Lynch

In August 1990, Ken Iverson, Nucor's chief executive officer, believed that the company had the technology and the cost advantage it needed to achieve 15 to 20 percent annual growth in its steel business over the next five years despite a sluggish demand for steel products industrywide. A few years earlier Wall Street analysts had been predicting that Nucor's rapid growth was not sustainable. Iverson had disagreed with the assessment, believing that if Nucor could perfect a promising new technology to cast thin slabs of steel then it could produce steel plate and flat-rolled sheet steel very efficiently and open up sizable expansion opportunities.

Following Iverson's strong convictions about the potential in thin-slab casting, Nucor led all other steel companies during the mid-1980s in investing in R&D efforts to develop thin-slab casting technology. By 1988 Iverson was satisfied the company could make the technology work and Nucor initiated construction of a mill in Crawfordsville, Indiana, to make sheet steel products using the innovative thin-slab casting process. It was the first mill of its kind in the world. Production start-up began in August 1989; over the next 10 months Nucor spent nearly $45 million working out numerous technological bugs in the process and improving the metallurgical quality of the mill's steel output. By June 1990 the Crawfordsville plant reached break-even and was able to turn out prime-quality sheet steel consistently. Nucor's potential in the flat-rolled sheet steel market was vast since the mill was sized to produce only 800,000 to 1,000,000 tons per year in a market where demand was 40 million tons per year and since the efficiency of Nucor's thin-slab casting process gave it a 25 percent cost advantage over both foreign and domestic competitors. Already, Nucor was designing a second mill to come on line in 1992.

Since 1980, Nucor's revenues had grown at a compound annual rate of 11 percent. Annual steel production at Nucor had risen from 1,040,000 tons in 1980 to 2,500,000 tons in 1989; production in 1990 was expected to surpass 3,000,000 tons. Iverson believed that Nucor could become a major player in the steel industry in the United States before the year 2000. Exhibit 1 provides a financial overview of Nucor's recent performance.

THE STEEL INDUSTRY IN THE UNITED STATES

Four types of companies competed in the U.S. market for steel products in 1990: the major domestic integrated producers, minimill companies, specialty

---

*Prepared with the research assistance of University of Alabama Ph.D. candidate Tracy R. Kramer.

EXHIBIT 1   Summary of Nucor's Financial Performance, 1984–1989

	1984	1985	1986	1987	1988	1989
For the Year						
Net sales	$660,259,922	$758,495,374	$755,228 939	$851,022,039	$1,061,364,009	$1,269,007,472
Costs and expenses:						
Cost of products sold	539,731,252	600,797,865	610,378,369	713,346,451	889,140,323	1,105,248,906
Marketing, administrative, and other expenses	45,939,311	59,079,802	65,900,653	55,405,961	62,083,752	66,990,065
Interest expense (income)	(3,959,092)	(7,560,645)	(5,288,971)	(964,823)	2,558,914	11,132,657
	581,711,471	652,317,022	670,990,051	767,787,589	953,782,989	1,183,371,628
Earnings from operations before federal income taxes	78,548,451	106,178,352	84,238,888	83,234,450	107,581,020	85,635,844
Federal income taxes	34,000,000	47,700,000	37,800,000	32,700,000	36,700,000	27,800,000
Earnings from operations	44,548,451	58,478,352	46,438,888	50,534,450	70,881,020	57,835,844
Gain on sale of Research Chemicals	—	—	—	—	38,558,822	—
Net earnings	$ 44,548,451	$ 58,478,352	$ 46,438,888	$ 50,534,450	$ 109,439,842	$ 57,835,844
Earnings per share:						
Earnings per share from operations	$2.10	$2.74	$2.17	$2.39	$3.34	$2.71
Gain per share on sale of Research Chemicals	—	—	—	—	1.82	—
Net earnings per share	2.10	2.74	2.17	2.39	5.16	2.71
Dividends declared per share	.24	.27	.31	.36	.40	.44
Percentage of earnings from operations to sales	6.7%	7.7%	6.1%	5.9%	6.7%	4.6%
Percentage of earnings from operations to average equity	16.0%	17.8%	12.5%	12.5%	15.4%	10.4%
Capital expenditures	$ 26,333,882	$ 28,701,463	$ 86,201,391	$189,990,476	$ 345,632,411	$ 130,200,982
Depreciation	28,899,421	31,105,788	34,931,520	41,793,009	56,264,631	76,571,240
Sales per employee	176,069	197,011	181,983	189,116	218,838	241,716
At Year-End						
Current assets	$253,453,373	$334,769,147	$295,738,255	$234,717,237	$ 247,758,616	$ 280,033,934
Current liabilities	100,533,684	121,255,828	118,440,973	147,473,270	216,107,302	193,560,545
Working capital	152,919,689	213,513,319	177,297,282	87,243,967	31,651,314	86,473,389
Current ratio	2.5	2.8	2.5	1.6	1.1	1.4
Property, plant, and equipment	228,735,092	225,542,041	275,869,389	419,372,902	701,903,094	753,797,578
Total assets	482,188,465	560,311,188	571,607,644	654,090,139	949,661,710	1,033,831,512
Long-term debt	43,232,384	40,233,769	42,147,654	35,462,500	113,248,500	155,981,500
Percentage of debt to capital	12.6%	10.1%	9.9%	7.7%	17.5%	21.1%
Stockholders' equity	299,602,834	357,502,028	383,699,454	428,009,367	532,281,449	584,445,479
Per share	14.10	16.65	18.16	20.19	25.00	27.31
Shares outstanding	21,241,618	21,472,508	21,131,298	21,196,088	21,287,691	21,399,620
Stockholders	22,000	22,000	22,000	27,000	28,000	25,000
Employees	3,800	3,900	4,400	4,600	5,100	5,400

steel producers, and foreign manufacturers. The major domestic integrated producers included the giants of the industry—USX Corp. (formerly U.S. Steel Corp.), Bethlehem Steel, Inland Steel, Armco Steel, LTV Corp., and several others, all of whom operated capital-intensive plant complexes that processed iron ore through a series of production stages into finished steel products of any size and variety. Integrated mills were scaled to turn out several million tons of steel products annually, and the largest integrated producers each had 10–25 million tons of annual capacity. Integrated producers had a combined market share of about 50 percent.

Specialty steel producers manufactured low-volume steel products for specialized markets and applications; about 5 percent of total steel shipments involved specialty steels such as stainless steel. Imported steel, chiefly from Europe, Japan, Korea, Canada, and Latin America, accounted for 20 percent of domestic steel sales, and the percentage had been declining since 1984 when imports accounted for a 26 percent market share.

The minimill companies employed small-scale electric arc furnaces to melt ferrous scrap and recycle it into a relatively limited line of commodity steel items like reinforcing bars, wire rods, roof bolts for underground mines, and light-to-medium structural steel. Minimills ranged in size from a one-plant company with annual capacity as low as 150,000 tons up to multiplant companies with 500,000-ton plants and companywide capacities of 3 million tons per year. The leading minimill producers included North Star Steel, Lukens, Nucor, Oregon Steel Mills, Insteel Industries, Chaparral Steel, Florida Steel, and Birmingham Steel. Exhibit 2 presents comparative statistics for 17 of the leading producers in the United States.

In recent years, minimills had prospered, largely by capturing market share from higher-cost integrated producers. New state-of-the-art minimill plants could be constructed for under $200 per ton of capacity (versus about $2,000 per ton for an integrated mill), and an aging foundry could be modernized and converted to an efficient minimill operation for under $30 million (less than $100 per ton of capacity). Minimills typically were located either near supplies of scrap metal or near product markets to minimize shipping expenses; and they normally enjoyed low labor costs per ton produced. As a consequence, minimills tended to be very cost efficient, able to compete head-to-head against even the most efficient foreign producers. The minimills' share of total steel shipments in 1990 was about 25 percent and trending upward.

Even though steelmaking was a "basic" industry, worldwide demand for steel products was viewed as both stagnant (slow-growth or no-growth) and cyclical. Steel production in the United States had been in a cyclical downtrend since 1972 (see Exhibit 3). Integrated U.S. producers, burdened with aging facilities and high-cost labor contracts, had suffered the most in terms of lost market share, falling production, and unprofitable operations. Since 1979 the U.S. steel industry as a whole had incurred losses in 6 of the past 10 years. However, minimill producers were generally profitable throughout the 1980s; it was the big integrated producers who found themselves forced to close down plants and retreat from markets where their high costs prevented them from competing profitably. LTV Corp., the second largest integrated U.S. producer, had filed for Chapter 11 reorganization and was operating under protection of the courts. Since 1978 closings of inefficient and obsolete plants by the integrated producers had reduced steelmaking capacity in the United

EXHIBIT 2   **Financial and Operating Highlights for Selected Integrated and Minimill Steel Producers, 1980 and 1988**

	Revenues ($ millions)			Net Profits ($ millions)		
	1980	1988	Average Compound Change	1980	1988	Average Compound Change
Integrated Producers						
Bethlehem Steel	$6,743	$5,489	−2.5%	$121	$403	16.2%
LTV Steel	8,010	7,325	−1.1	128	456	17.2
USX Corp. (U.S. Steel Div.)	8,738	5,800	−5.0	58	501	30.8
Armco, Inc.	5,678	3,227	−6.8	265	165	−5.8
Inland Steel	3,256	4,068	2.8	30	249	30.4
National Steel	3,945	2,599	−5.1	84	66	−3.0
Weirton Steel (Formed 1984)	—	1,384	N/A	—	(2)	—
Wheeling-Pittsburgh	1,054	1,103	0.6	15	149	33.5
Minimill Producers						
Bayou Steel (Formed 1988)	—	190	N/A	—	23	N/A
Birmingham Steel (Formed 1985)	—	344	N/A	—	25	N/A
Chaparral Steel	131	376	14.1%	13	61	21.2%
Florida Steel	287	476	6.6	19	20	0.8
Lukens	376	450	2.3	5	63	38.3
New Jersey Steel (Formed 1985)	—	139	N/A	—	16	N/A
Northwestern Steel	426	497	1.9	23	29	3.2
Nucor	482	1,061	10.4	45	71	5.8
Oregon Steel (Formed 1985)	—	190	N/A	—	18	N/A

N/A = not applicable.

Source: Compiled by the casewriters from a variety of sources including company annual reports, company 10-K reports, *Value Line Industry Surveys, Metal Statistics*, and telephone interviews.

States from 158 million tons to 112 million tons, yet capacity utilization rates in the United States were still running below 90 percent.

Steel Types and Steel Products

Steel is made primarily of iron and carbon. Thousands of varieties of steel can be turned out by varying the content of iron, carbon, and alloying elements such as chromium, nickel, manganese, silicon, vanadium, and molybdenum. The most common varieties of steel has carbon contents between 0.25 and 2.0 percent; harder grades of steel have a higher carbon content. The use of alloying elements makes steel more resistant to heat, corrosion, and wear. Stainless

Production of Raw Steel (000 tons)			Shipments of Finished Steel Products (000 tons)			Number of Mills 1988	Principal Products
1980	1988	Average Compound Change	1980	1988	Average Compound Change		
15,000	12,855	−1.9%	11,080	10,303	−0.9%	2	Sheet, strip, bars, rods, structured shapes, plates
9,760	10,461	0.9	7,000	8,963	3.1	4	Hot/cold-rolled sheet, strip, coated goods, tubulars
23,280	15,545	−4.9	17,200	12,175	−4.2	7	Sheet, strip, tin, plates, piling, pipe and tubular, bars
7,300	5,771	−2.9	5,400	4,903	−1.2	3	Carbon flat-rolled and sheet, electrical and stainless, bar, rod, wire
7,049	6,126	−1.7	5,286	5,020	−0.6	1	Sheet, strip, plate, bar, and structural
7,600	5,393	−4.2	6,600	4,970	−3.5	3	Hot/cold-rolled sheet, strip, tin, galvanized
—	3,155	N/A	—	2,729	—	1	Hot/cold flat-rolled sheet
3,119	2,527	2.6	2,210	2,235	0.1	1	Hot/cold-rolled sheet, strip, galvanized, tin, rail
—	540	N/A	—	504	N/A	1	Flats, angles, beams, wide flange, unequal angles
—	1,275	N/A	—	1,031	N/A	6	Rebar, rounds, squares, flats, angles, billets
387	1,360	17.0%	381	1,230	15.8%	1	Rebar, angles, channels, beams, rounds, special bar, quality steel
827	1,374	6.6	736	1,223	6.6	5	Rebar, rounds, flats, angles, rods, merchant
734	741	0.1	—	660	N/A	2	Carbon and alloy steel plates
—	744	N/A	—	433	N/A	1	Rebar, light structurals
1,302	1,754	3.8	1,049	1,455	4.2	2	Beams, angles, channels, flats, rods, coiled rebar, wire
1,150	2,030	7.4	672	1,347	9.1	6	Angles, channels, flats, rounds, billets, beams, rod, rebar
—	420	N/A	—	344	N/A	3	Plate and pipe

steel is the most popular of the alloy steels; it contains 8 percent nickel and 18 percent chromium.

Steel is produced in a broad variety of shapes, thicknesses, and lengths—there are round bars, flat bars, thick plates, coiled sheets, steel rails, I beams, steel pipes and tubing, and wire and cable of all dimensions, alloys, and grades. Container companies use tin sheets to make tin cans and flat-rolled sheet steel for oil drums and pails. The automobile companies use flat-rolled thin sheet steel in automobile bodies, structural steel in the frames and chassis, and iron castings for the engine block and other parts. Construction companies use steel beams, reinforcing rods, steel siding, and steel decking. Electrical equipment companies are big buyers of wire and cable. Drilling companies use steel pipes and tubing in drilling oil and gas wells. Major steel users typically buy their supplies directly from the producing mill. Small users and occasional users purchase from local steel service centers and distributors that make their

E X H I B I T   3   Selected Statistical Highlights for the U.S. Steel Industry, 1978–1989

Year	Production Capacity (Million tons)	Raw Steel Production (Million tons)	Operating Rate (Percent)	Shipments of Steel Products (Million tons)	Exports (Million tons)	U.S. Imports (Million tons)	Apparent Supply (Million tons)	Imports as a Percent of Supply	Average Number of Employees	Employment Cost per Hour (All employees)
1989	115.9	97.9	84.5	84.1	4.6	17.3	96.8	17.9%	169,000	$25.35
1988	112.0	99.3	88.7	84.0	2.1	20.9	102.8	20.3	168,898	25.30
1987	112.2	89.2	79.5	76.6	0.9	20.4	96.1	21.2	163,338	24.23
1986	127.9	81.6	63.8	70.3	0.9	20.7	90.0	23.0	174,783	23.56
1985	133.6	88.3	66.1	73.0	0.9	24.3	96.4	25.2	208,168	23.26
1984	135.3	92.5	68.4	73.7	0.9	26.2	98.9	26.4	236,002	21.82
1983	150.6	84.6	56.2	67.6	1.2	17.1	83.5	20.5	242,745	22.49
1982	154.0	74.6	48.4	61.6	1.8	16.7	76.4	21.8	289,437	23.60
1981	154.3	120.8	78.3	88.4	2.9	19.9	105.4	18.9	390,914	20.70
1980	153.7	111.8	72.8	83.9	4.1	15.5	95.2	16.3	398,829	18.79
1979	155.3	136.0	87.8	100.3	2.8	17.5	115.0	15.2	453,181	16.38
1978	157.9	137.0	86.8	97.9	2.4	21.1	116.6	18.1	—	—

Source: American Iron and Steel Institute.

business from stocking a variety of shapes and grades and being able to deliver them on short notice. About 20 percent of total steel production is marketed through area service centers and distributors. Exhibit 4 shows steel shipments by major product category. Exhibit 5 shows the markets for steel products by major end-user category.

Some steel products, like reinforcing bars, are commodities and have essentially the same metallurgical properties no matter which plant or company produces them. Other products, however, are made to the customer's specifications and have to meet sometimes stringent metallurgical requirements so that the steel will perform properly in the intended application. Automakers, for instance, require prime-quality sheet steel with no surface defects that can be bent and shaped without cracking and that withstands rust corrosion. Customers with rigid specifications require a mill to produce samples for testing and scrutinize the quality of its output for several months before deciding to include a mill on their list of acceptable steel suppliers. As one steel buyer for Ford Motor Co. put it, "We like to buy from people with an established record . . . our first sourcing criterion is quality, not price."

Substitute Products

A portion of the stagnant demand for steel industry products was attributable to the challenge from substitute products. The substitution of aluminum for steel in beverage cans had cut steel's share of the can market from 87 percent in 1972 to 26 percent in 1988. In 1977 the typical U.S.-made passenger car contained 2,535 pounds of iron and steel; by 1988, the average passenger car contained 1,897 pounds. Some users of plastics, aluminum, and steel had flexible enough production systems to switch from one material to another within a short time frame whenever prices changed enough to make switching advantageous. Within the past few years, switching away from steel had slowed considerably, since many of the most attractive substitution possibilities had run their course.

Assembled and finished plastic parts were generally less expensive than steel parts because of cheaper tooling costs and because one plastic part could take the place of several steel parts that had to be welded or bolted, thus allowing labor savings in assembly. Plastics were also lighter and more corrosion resistant. On the other hand, steel had several advantages over plastics—superior surface finish, better paintability, and more adaptability to faster production speeds. The auto industry expected that steel would remain the material of choice for body skins well into the 1990s; so far, plastic body panels had not gained great acceptance among vehicle owners.

Steelmaking Technology

Although the pace had quickened recently, steelmaking technology had evolved slowly over several centuries. The first blast furnace in the United States was built in the 1600s; until the 1900s the principal improvements involved increased size, better design, and speedier operation. Blast furnaces made molten iron from iron-ore pellets, crushed limestone, and coke. In the early 1900s the open hearth furnace (OHF) came into use; OHFs involved

Steel Shipments in the U.S. by Major Product Category, 1982–1989
(In thousands of net tons)

Products	1982	1983	1984	1985	1986	1987	1988	1989
Semifinished steel	3,693	3,861	4,407	4,345	4,954	5,456	5,978	6,236
Shapes and piling	3,563	3,622	4,156	4,699	4,528	5,120	5,209	5,355
Plates	4,146	3,816	4,339	4,327	3,565	4,048	7,328	7,384
Rails	517	634	965	704	461	366	497	458
Other railroad products	265	250	274	228	179	149	118	104
Bars and tool steel	10,812	11,700	13,232	12,668	12,171	13,575	14,489	14,171
Pipe and tubing	5,026	3,242	4,276	4,096	2,836	3,570	4,443	4,011
Wire products	1,308	1,359	1,222	1,136	1,080	1,105	1,073	1,002
Tin mill products	4,321	4,308	4,062	3,773	3,802	3,988	4,069	4,126
Sheets—hot rolled	9,052	11,619	13,133	12,952	12,167	13,048	12,589	13,281
Sheets—cold rolled	1,132	13,781	13,664	13,574	13,250	13,859	13,871	13,854
Sheets—galvanized	6,063	7,380	7,867	8,669	9,299	12,320	11,511	12,071
Electrical sheets and strip	445	458	490	413	416	465	524	484
Hot- and cold-rolled strip	1,222	1,554	1,652	1,462	1,555	1,587	2,144	1,572
Net total steel products	61,567	67,584	73,739	73,043	70,263	76,654	83,840	84,109

Source: American Iron and Steel Institute.

E X H I B I T   5   **Purchase of Steel Mill Products by Major End-User or Customer Category, 1984–1989**   *(In millions of net tons)*

End-Use/Customer Category	1984	1985	1986	1987	1988	1989	Average Annual Compound Change, 1984–1989
Appliances	1,635	1,466	1,648	1,633	1,638	1,623	−0.15%
Automotive	12,882	12,950	11,889	11,343	12,555	12,000	−1.41
Construction	10,153	11,230	10,614	11,018	12,101	12,464	4.19
Containers	4,352	4,089	4,113	4,371	4,421	4,465	0.51
Converting and processing	5,136	5,484	5,635	7,195	8,492	7,982	9.22
Electrical equipment	2,365	1,869	2,113	2,373	2,459	2,533	1.38
Machinery	2,886	2,271	2,076	2,277	2,798	2,630	−1.84
Oil and gas	2,003	2,044	1,023	1,489	1,477	1,107	−11.18
Steel service centers	18,364	18,439	17,478	19,840	21,037	19,564	1.27
Other domestic and commercial equipment	1,339	1,215	1,173	1,149	1,199	1,187	−2.38
Other	4,389	3,725	3,121	3,252	4,071	3,867	−2.50
Nonclassified	7,807	7,767	8,885	10,199	10,359	10,773	6.65
Exports	428	494	495	514	1,233	1,700	31.76
Total	72,739	73,043	70,263	76,654	83,840	81,895	2.12%

Source: American Iron and Steel Institute.

loading molten iron from the blast furnace, scrap steel, and limestone into a shallow steelmaking hearth open to flames from both ends. The process resulted in higher-quality steels needed in automobiles and certain other applications. The percentage of steel made in OHFs peaked in 1968 and fell to under 5 percent by 1990.

The technological replacement was the basic oxygen furnace (BOF), developed in Austria following World War II. The BOF utilized molten iron ore (pig iron) from a blast furnace, scrap steel, and oxygen fed into the vessel to produce a vigorous chemical reaction that accelerated the steelmaking process. Whereas the open hearth process consumed several hours, a basic oxygen furnace did the job in 45 minutes. In 1990 about 60 percent of domestic steel output was produced using BOFs.

The third steelmaking approach involved electric arc furnaces (EAFs). EAF technology bypassed the need for iron-ore preparation, coke ovens, and blast furnaces required in OHF and BOF technology (see Exhibit 6). The only raw material needed was scrap iron and steel. In EAFs an electric current arcs from one electrode to another inside the furnace to melt ferrous scrap; the molten steel is then formed into the desired shapes or poured into slabs for further processing. As of 1990, about 35 percent of the total raw steel production in the United States was produced in EAFs, up from 20 percent in 1975.

Integrated steel mills employed OHF and BOF technology. Electric arc furnaces were the mainstay of the minimills. Minimills producers were particularly cost efficient when a company could source its electric power economically and when scrap steel prices were relatively low. Moreover, minimills were designed in a manner that made technical updating and rebuilding a fairly simple, economical undertaking; this was in sharp contrast to integrated mills, where changing the production scheme called for major investments. The primary drawback to EAFs was the limited range of steel products that could be produced. Whereas the use of OHFs and BOFs gave integrated producers the ability to make all grades and shapes of steel products, minimills with EAFs were restricted to low-grade commodity steel products.

Continuous Casting Continuous casting is a relatively new production approach that greatly increases the efficiency of steelmaking by converting molten steel directly into solid shapes ready for rolling and finishing. Without continuous-casting equipment, the steel ingot produced by the furnace (be it OHF, BOF, or EAF), has to go through additional time-consuming production steps, including costly reheating, before it is converted to semifinished steel shapes. In mills with continuous-casting equipment, molten steel coming out of the furnace is transferred quickly into a ladle and poured into a container at the top of the caster where it is fed continuously into the caster. The molten steel then flows downward through the caster in a continuous ribbon. As it moves through a series of water-cooled molds in the caster, it is sprayed with water, cooled, and turned into a more solidified state. Guided by rollers and channels, the solidifying steel is gradually directed onto a horizontal plane where, now solid, it is cut into 8- to 10-inch slabs of predetermined lengths. Exhibit 6 provides a simplified overview of the production steps in integrated mills as compared to minimills.

Continuous casting reduces operating costs about $30 per ton compared with the older ingot/slab process and, also, results in higher-quality steel.

EXHIBIT 6   Comparative Steelmaking Methods

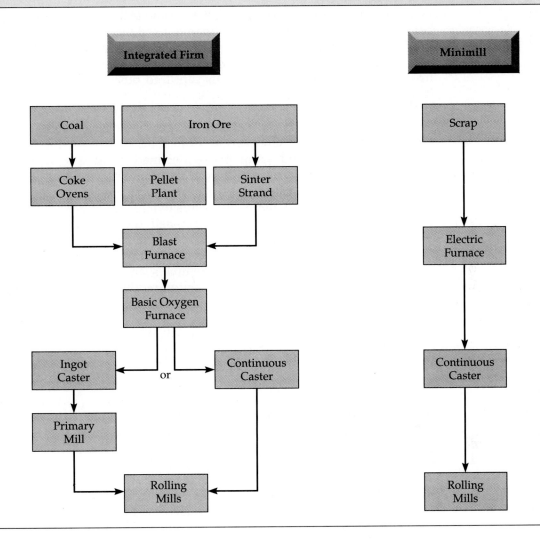

In the mid-1970s only about 15 percent of the steel produced in the United States was continuously cast; by 1990, however, U.S. steelmakers had installed additional continuous-casting capability and boosted the percentage of continuously cast products to 70 percent—versus over 90 percent in Japan and over 80 percent in Europe. Over 95 percent of U.S. minimills used continuous casting.

The Rising Stature of Minimills

Minimill companies first began to be a force in the steel industry in the 1970s. The strategy of early minimills was to locate plants some distance away from integrated mills but relatively close to customer markets and scrap metal sources. Each plant was dedicated to the production of just one or two products. Product specialization boosted operating efficiency and simplified the marketing task. Most minimills operated with nonunion work forces to avoid union work rule restrictions and gain the flexibility to organize work in the most efficient manner. Workers were usually paid an hourly wage below the union scale but many companies used incentive pay schemes linked to worker output that pushed the compensation of minimill workers close to what union workers earned. Using their substantial cost advantage (anywhere from $25 to $200 per ton), minimills captured business by underpricing the integrated producers.

During the late 1970s and the 1980s, minimills in the United States prospered. A number of new minimill companies were formed and existing minimill firms opened new plants. Scrap remained in plentiful supply and for much of the period scrap prices declined relative to iron-ore prices. Output per worker at minimills ran about double the worker output at integrated mills; since the wages of minimill workers were comparable to workers' earnings in the unionized plants of large integrated producers, labor costs per ton at minimills were about half the labor costs of integrated companies. The market success of minimills was limited, however, to lower-grade commodity steel products like reinforcing bars (rebar) used in construction—angle steel, flats, rounds, channels, and I beams. By the mid-1980s minimills dominated the U.S. market for commodity steel (about 25 percent of total domestic steel shipments); no integrated producer had a significant market share in commodity steel and most had ceased production of such items entirely. In 1988, for the first time, the biggest minimill producer outshipped the ninth largest integrated producer. Going into 1990 minimills supplied 100 percent of the rebar market, 75 percent of the wire rod market, 60 percent of the hot-rolled bar market, and 30 percent of the light-to-medium structural steel market.

Because the minimills were running out of market share to take away from the integrated producers in commodity steel products, most were searching for opportunities to penetrate the markets for large structural steel products and flat-rolled sheet steels—segments traditionally dominated by domestic and foreign integrated producers. Chaparral Steel, a Texas-based minimill, had announced a 300,000-ton capacity expansion to increase its structural size capability from 18 inches to 24 inches. Nucor had formed a joint venture with a Japanese firm, Yamato, to produce 10-inch- to 24-inch-wide flange steel beams at a new 650,000-ton plant in Arkansas; the plant design could accommodate another 300,000 tons with improvements. Another minimill was considering opening a 700,000-ton plant to produce structurals in Texas. Such significant capacity additions would put additional competitive pressure on USX Corp. and Bethlehem Steel, the two biggest U.S. integrated producers in the medium and heavy structural steel market. The market for heavy structurals ranged from 4.8 to 6.3 million tons, with imports capturing up to 33 percent of shipments.

Innovations in Thin-Slab Casting

However, the most significant market opportunity for minimills was in adapting the continuous-casting process to produce thin slabs rather than the customary thick slabs. With thin-slab casting, minimills could compete in the market for sheet- and strip-mill products (45–50 percent of total industry shipments) that had come to be the heart of the integrated producers' business. Without thin-slab casting, minimills were effectively precluded from making flat-rolled steel products because of the prohibitively high cost of building a hot strip mill to roll thick steel slabs into thin sheet and strip-steel products; conventional rolling equipment cost about $600 million to install and required a volume of 3 million tons annually for efficient operation. Thin-slab casting gave minimills entry access because thinner slabs, coming directly from the continuous caster, greatly reduced the capital costs for the necessary equipment and cut the volume needed to operate efficiently. Nucor's new mill at Crawfordsville was the first attempt by a U.S. minimill company to use newly developed thin-slab casting techniques to produce flat-rolled steel products. Most modern integrated mills used casting equipment that turned out slabs 8 inches to 10 inches thick; a few mills in the world could turn out 6-inch-thick slabs. Nucor's Crawfordsville plant utilized a novel machine that produced a 2-inch-thick slab that could be rolled, hot, into sheets with thicknesses of 0.1 to 0.5 inches, as specified by customers. Three other minimill companies had announced plans to follow Nucor's lead in building new plants to turn out flat-rolled steel products, though none as yet had commenced construction.

So far, competitors had not moved aggressively to embrace thin-slab casting technology, perhaps waiting for Nucor's pioneering effort to prove successful. Most recently, USX Corp., the largest integrated producer, had opted for a conventional slab casting machine for one of its plants. Birmingham Steel had canceled plans for a thin-slab plant using different equipment from that at Crawfordsville. The conventional industry view was that the metallurgical qualities of a thin cast would be poor. Integrated producers were said to be hesitant to take on the risks of an unproven technology, given the difficulty of realizing all the potential labor savings with a unionized work force; they also had the additional problem of how to engineer the technology into the configuration of an existing integrated mill at an acceptable cost.

Competitive Conditions

The demand for steel products varied up and down with overall industrial production and economic activity. Steel prices generally rose during periods of strong demand. Price discounting was prevalent in slack times as mills tried to maintain production efficiency by operating as close to full capacity as possible. Once buyers were satisfied that the metallurgical properties and quality of a mill's products were satisfactory, purchase decisions hinged upon price and ability to meet delivery schedules. Steel users were price sensitive and nearly always shopped among the acceptable suppliers for the best price. Unless market demand was especially strong and mills were struggling to meet delivery schedules, price was usually decisive in choosing which mill to purchase from.

In 1989 and early 1990 market demand was soft, with shipments running about 5 percent under 1988 levels. The prices of many steel products had dropped as much as $50 per ton, shaving producers' profit margins significantly and reflecting active price competition and price discounting. Public spending for construction was off by 7 percent and industrial/commercial construction had been in a downtrend since 1987. Automakers were not expecting 1990 to be a strong year for automobile and truck sales. Increased scrap prices since late 1987 had eroded much of the raw material cost advantage that minimills previously had over integrated producers.

The Potential for Competitive Change

A number of factors had the potential to alter the competitive structure of the steel industry, especially as concerned the position of the minimill producers. To begin with, entry barriers were low into the minimill segment; new minimills could be constructed and existing steel facilities could be converted into a cost-efficient minimill option for under $50 million. A number of entrepreneurial companies and investor groups, both inside and outside the minimill segment, were known to be looking at new start-up or conversion opportunities to make steel products for specialized market niches.

Second, the cost gap between minimills and fully integrated producers was narrowing in several respects. Integrated producers had cut their costs by downsizing their white-collar and blue-collar work forces, modernizing their plants, and gaining wage and work rule concessions in newly negotiated labor contracts. Meanwhile, minimills were confronted with rising prices and tighter supplies for high-quality scrap metal (see Exhibit 7). Widening use of continuous casting had reduced the supply of scrap generated in-house at fully integrated mills and prompted integrated producers to become bigger buyers of scrap on the open market. At the same time, with more and more flat-rolled sheet steel being zinc-coated to meet auto industry requirements for rustproofing, minimills were confronted with bigger dust disposal and heavy-metal pollution problems associated with recycling auto bodies. Industry observers believed that the quality of the available scrap supplies would progressively deteriorate, not only driving scrap prices higher but also forcing minimills to incur higher transportation costs as they had to go farther and farther out from millsites to obtain quality scrap supplies. Further complicating the scrap problem was the fragmented nature of the scrap metal junkyard business, a factor that forced scrap users to seek out needed supplies from a comparatively large number of dealers under highly competitive conditions.

A third force for competitive change was the fact that there were strong signs of overcapacity in certain commodity steel products, promoting the outbreak of frequent price discounting and the narrowing of profit margins during periods of weak demand. And last, the emergence of new steelmaking technologies having relative low capital costs to implement—like Nucor's innovative efforts in thin-slab casting—was opening up new product markets to small-scale production methods. Among the products being studied or already in production by at least one minimill were sheet steels, medium and heavy structural steels, seamless tubing, and special-quality bar steels. To the extent that technological changes opened more and more product doors to economic small-scale production and entailed low attendant capital costs, it was likely that an industry once dominated by a few integrated giants would gradually fragment into more and more small production units specializing in niche markets. Product specialization reduced downtime for product changeovers and equipment adjustments, required fewer operating

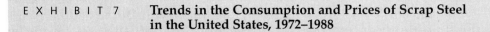

EXHIBIT 7   **Trends in the Consumption and Prices of Scrap Steel in the United States, 1972–1988**

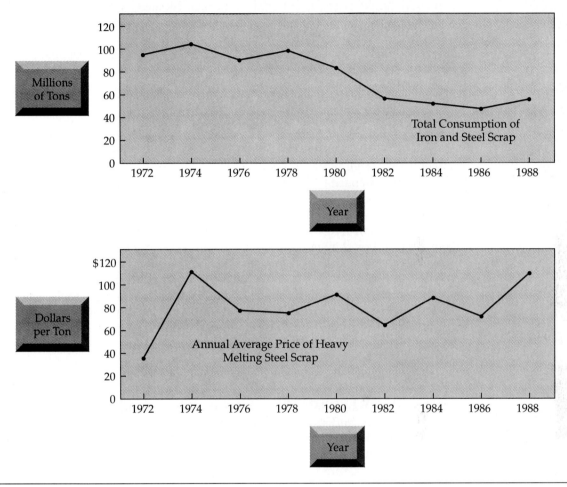

Source: *1989 Metal Statistics.*

skills, and economized on sales and engineering staffs—all of which translated into cost advantages for a minimill producer as compared to a fully integrated producer. Minimill companies led the steel industry in the United States in worker productivity, the use of state-of-the-art manufacturing technologies, guaranteed quality programs, new product development, and innovative marketing practices.

NUCOR CORPORATION

Although Nucor was the third largest minimill company in the United States, it was widely recognized as *the* leader of the minimill industry and one of the best-run steel companies in the world. The company built its first minimill in 1968 in Darlington, South Carolina; the mill had annual capacity of 120,000 tons. By 1990 the company was operating six minimills with combined capacity close to 3,600,000 tons. In addition, the company produced and marketed steel joists, girders, and steel deck through its Vulcraft Division. Five other small divisions produced steel bars, steel grinding balls, bolts, steel bearings and machined parts, and metal buildings. Management believed that Nucor was among the lowest-cost steel producers in the world. For a number of years, the prices charged by Nucor had been competitive with the prices of imported steel products. Nucor had operated profitably every quarter of every year that it had been in the minimill business.

Nucor's Steel Division

Nucor's steel division consisted of four mills—one each in South Carolina, Nebraska, Texas, and Utah—which produced steel reinforcing bars and light structural carbon and alloy steels. At all four mills steel scrap was melted in electric arc furnaces and poured directly into continuous-casting systems that produced steel billets (thick, long slabs of steel). Highly sophisticated rolling mills converted the billets into a wide range of chemistries and sizes of steel angles, straight-length and coiled round reinforcing rods, channel steel, flat bars, and other shapes. The mills were major suppliers of steel angles. Nucor Steel Division customers were primarily steel service centers, building construction firms, and the manufacturers of farm equipment, oil and gas equipment, mobile homes, bed frames, transmission towers, hand tools, automotive parts, highway signs, machinery, and industrial equipment.

Nucor's Darlington mill had been expanded and extensively modernized since its construction in 1968. The other three mills were constructed between 1973 and 1981. A new continuous caster, a new reheat furnace, and a new high-speed rolling mill had recently been installed at the Nebraska mill at a cost of $35 million. All four Nucor plants were among the most modern and efficient mills in the United States. The total cost of all four mills, including expansions, improvements, and modernizations, averaged less than $175 per ton of current annual capacity.

Productivity was quite high at all four mills; the average Nucor worker produced 700 to 800 tons of steel per year versus 450 tons per employee at the mills of unionized integrated companies; labor costs at Nucor's mills ran about 15 percent of revenues, compared to 25–35 percent at integrated companies. All employees had a significant part of their compensation based on their productivity. Employee turnover in all mills was extremely low.

Scrap steel was the most significant cost item for Nucor, running $60 to $120 per ton depending on scrap prices and averaging 25 to 35 percent of selling price per ton. Energy costs amounted to about $45 per ton; Nucor management bargained aggressively with its power company suppliers to obtain the lowest possible rates on electric power. Exhibit 8 presents selected operating statistics for Nucor's four steel minimills.

Nucor used a far simpler pricing system than most other steel companies: All customers were charged the same announced price, regardless of quantity ordered. Management believed this allowed customers to maintain the lowest practical inventory. In contrast, other steel suppliers commonly granted quantity discounts and many made special price concessions to win a particular order. Nucor's steel prices were very competitive, generally being equal to or

EXHIBIT 8   Actual and Projected Performance of Nucor's Steel Division, 1984–1993

	1984	1985	1986	1987	1988	1989E	1990E	1991E	1992E	1993E
Capacity (000s of tons)										
Darlington, S.C.	500	500	500	500	500	513	525	538	552	566
Norfolk, Neb.	600	600	615	615	621	559	573	587	602	617
Jewett, Texas	600	600	615	630	646	650	666	683	700	717
Plymouth, Utah	400	400	410	550	594	609	624	640	656	672
Total	2,100	2,100	2,140	2,296	2,361	2,330	2,389	2,448	2,510	2,572
Raw steel production (000s of tons)										
Darlington	393	465	416	400	500	475	475	525	525	525
Norfolk	393	402	412	460	500	485	475	550	575	575
Jewett	465	451	443	446	550	480	500	625	650	650
Plymouth	291	375	435	474	545	560	600	575	600	600
Total	1,542	1,693	1,706	1,790	2,095	2,000	2,050	2,275	2,350	2,350
Operating rate										
Darlington	79%	93%	83%	80%	100%	93%	90%	98%	95%	93%
Norfolk	66	67	67	75	80	87	83	94	96	93
Jewett	78	75	72	72	85	74	75	92	93	91
Plymouth	73	94	106	86	92	92	96	90	92	89
Average	73	81	80	78	89	86	86	93	94	91
Shipments of steel products (000s of tons)	990	1,152	1,140	1,313	1,437	1,450	1,460	1,677	1,744	1,735
Average price/ton	$ 282	$ 273	$ 278	$ 288	$ 340	$ 340	$ 320	$ 323	$ 326	$ 330
Operating cost/ton										
Scrap	$ 88	$ 79	$ 77	$ 76	$ 117	$ 112	$ 100	$ 102	$ 104	$ 106
Energy	43	44	44	45	44	44	44	45	45	46
Labor	55	52	52	51	50	52	52	52	52	52
Other direct production costs	54	54	50	51	50	55	53	53	53	53
Total	$ 240	$ 228	$ 223	$ 223	$ 261	$ 263	$ 249	$ 251	$ 254	$ 256
Divisional revenue-cost-profit performance (in millions of $)										
Revenues	$398.32	$439.35	$442.94	$501.12	$712.30	$680.00	$656.00	$735.28	$767.12	$774.79
Operating costs	338.89	367.45	355.25	387.39	547.20	529.01	510.47	572.05	596.75	602.71
Depreciation and administration	19.75	20.74	21.77	23.30	24.93	25.93	29.82	31.90	34.14	36.53
Division cost	358.64	388.18	377.03	410.69	572.13	554.94	540.28	603.95	630.89	639.23
Division profit	$ 39.68	$ 51.16	$ 65.91	$ 90.43	$140.17	$125.06	$115.72	$131.33	$136.23	$135.56

Source: R. Douglas Moffat, Robinson-Humphrey Equities Research, February 21, 1990.

below the prices of imported steel. In years past a big portion of Nucor's sales growth had come at the expense of integrated and foreign producers. However, now that minimills had used their low-cost advantage to force integrated companies and imports out of the market for commodity steel products, Nucor was increasingly competing with other low-cost minimills for the available business in commodity steel products. Kenneth Iverson, Nucor's CEO, observed:

> We are now head-to-head against much tougher competition in the market for commodity steel products. It was no contest when we were up against the integrated companies. Now we are facing minimills who have the same scrap prices, the same electrical costs, and who use the same technologies.

It was this lack of further growth opportunity for low-end commodity steel products that prompted Iverson to push the development of thin-casting technology at Nucor and to form a joint venture with a Japanese partner to enter into the production of structural steel beams—two altogether new product markets for Nucor.

The New Crawfordsville Mill   In 1989 Nucor completed construction of a $270 million steel mill to produce 800,000 tons per year of hot- and cold-rolled sheet steel products near Crawfordsville, Indiana. This mill was the largest single project Nucor had ever undertaken and represented a capital intensity ($335 per ton of annual capacity) that was much larger than usual for a minimill operation. It used a new process for casting a thin slab 2 inches thick by 52 inches wide. Without reheating, the slab was cut to length and processed immediately on rolling equipment into sheets 0.096 to 0.500 inches thick, then coiled for shipment or further processing. The plant was equipped with state-of-the-art electric arc furnaces and rolling mill equipment, plus it enjoyed a substantial labor cost advantage arising from labor productivity of 0.75 to 1.0 man-hours/ton compared with 2.5 man-hours/ton at the most efficient integrated steel plants. Nucor was operating the plant with its customary incentive-compensated, nonunion labor force. The plant was in the heart of the sheet steel–consuming section of the United States, had an unusually attractive 10-year contract for electric power that yielded the lowest electric energy costs per ton of any Nucor plant, had ample supplies of high-quality scrap steel available locally, and was served by two railroads. Overall, Nucor management estimated that its production costs at Crawfordsville would run about $100 per ton lower than the costs incurred by integrated producers. Exhibit 9 presents actual and projected operating performances for the mill.

   Despite high start-up and debugging costs (about $45 million), the new thin-slab process at Crawfordsville had turned out quality steel during its first 10 months of operation, with some 90 percent of the latest months' output being of prime quality metallurgically. A variety of superficial surface defects, however, were holding back production and delaying the qualification process with potential purchasers. Several sections of the plant had to be redesigned and reequipped to eliminate some of the trouble spots; this had lengthened the time frame to break in the plant and increased start-up costs. As of August 1990, weekly production had not exceeded 10,000 tons, versus a planned capacity of about 16,000 tons weekly. Nucor management was confident that the problems it was having mastering the technology would be

EXHIBIT 9   **Actual and Projected Performance of Nucor's Crawfordsville Mill, 1989–1993**

	1988	1989E	1990E	1991E	1992E	1993E
Production (000s of tons)						
Hot rolled		40	170	450	500	600
Cold rolled		0	300	350	400	400
Total		40	470	800	900	1000
Price/ton						
Hot		$320	$345	$400	$425	$450
Cold		475	450	500	525	550
Average	$450	$320	$412	$444	$469	$490
Production costs/ton						
Scrap	$142	$112	$110	$122	$129	$131
Labor	50	60	48	40	35	35
Energy	44	44	30	30	30	30
Hot rolling	135	115	111	95	95	95
Cold rolling	60	54	55	35	33	32
Total	$431	$385	$354	$322	$322	$323
Overall revenues-costs-profits (in millions of $)						
Revenues	$ 0.00	$ 12.80	$193.65	$355.00	$422.50	$490.00
Operating costs	0.00	15.41	166.15	257.60	290.06	322.71
Operating profit	0.00	(2.61)	27.51	97.40	132.44	167.29
Depreciation and administration	0.00	12.00	21.00	24.00	24.00	24.00
Start-up cost	12.00	33.40	0.00			
Division profit	$(12.00)	$(48.01)	$ 6.50	$ 73.40	$108.44	$143.29

Source: R. Douglas Moffat, Robinson-Humphrey Equities Research, February 21, 1990.

worked out and that the plant would be close to capacity production by the end of 1990.

Nucor had spent $5 million on engineering for a second plant; the second plant design incorporated numerous improvements based on experiences at Crawfordsville, and management was anticipating that the second plant could be brought up to capacity production in perhaps half the time needed at Crawfordsville and with less expense. Air-quality monitoring at several potential sites was already in progress in order to fast-track the construction of additional plants. Nucor was also working on ways to expand the width of the sheets its new flat-rolled process could turn out. At 52 inches wide, Crawfordsville's steel was too narrow for hoods, doors, and other body parts that accounted for 60 to 70 percent of the steel consumption of the motor vehicle industry.

Nucor-Yamato's Structural Beam Mill

Nucor and Yamato Kogyo, one of Japan's major producers of wide-flange steel beams, were partners in a new 650,000-ton minimill in Blytheville, Arkansas, that produced wide-flange steel beams and heavy structural steel products.

The plant cost $220 million. Nucor had 51 percent ownership in the joint venture. For more than 10 years Yamato Kogyo had used a special continuous-casting method that turned out a semifinished beam closer in shape to a finished beam than traditional methods; Yamato's technology was being used in the Arkansas mill. Operations started in the second half of 1988; within six months the mill was operating profitably. By early 1990 the mill was at capacity production and had orders for all of its output. Virtually all of the sales came at the expense of integrated producers; approximately 100,000 tons were exported to Japan, Indonesia, Norway, and several other countries.

Nucor employed 406 people at the Blytheville plant. It took approximately 1 man-hour of labor to produce a ton of steel, compared with 1.7–2.0 man-hours per ton typical at Japanese plants. The mill enjoyed very favorable electric rates, a factor that was critical in selecting the Blytheville location. Melting capacity was between 900,000 and 1,000,000 tons annually, but the capacity of the rolling mill was 750,000 tons. Nucor planned to continue exporting as long as it could price competitively and as long as melting capacity for producing semifinished beams and blooms (slabs suitable for forming semifinished shapes) exceeded the mill's capacity to roll finished shapes. Studies were underway to expand this mill's capacity. The mill was laid out for an easy expansion to 1 million tons per year at an incremental capital investment of $25 million; very few additional workers would be needed.

Direct production costs averaged just over $300 per ton in 1989 but had dropped to $275 per ton in early 1990 as additional operating experience produced internal efficiency gains. Further efficiencies, driving costs down to the $250–$265-per-ton range, were expected. Nucor's costs allowed it to be competitive in Japan at current exchange rates. Margins were attractive, despite the fact that market prices had dropped from $400 to $355 per ton during 1989, as Nucor took the industry lead in cutting prices to win orders for the new mill's output. Exhibit 10 provides estimates of the mill's costs and profit contribution.

The wide-flange beam market was an estimated 4 million tons in 1990, with imports accounting for a 27 percent market share. Domestic producers had 3 million tons of capacity in place. Chaparral Steel was bringing a new 500,000-ton plant on-line in 1991, and Northwestern Steel and Wire was planning to reopen a 500,000-ton mill in Houston obtained from Armco Steel. Chaparral's plant had a novel thin-casting feature that produced a semifinished beam even closer to final shape than Blytheville's product, but its output was thought to be aimed more at the lighter structural segment, whereas the beams at Blytheville were for heavy structural uses.

The Vulcraft Division

Nucor's Vulcraft Division was the largest U.S. producer of steel joists and joist girders; these products formed support systems for warehouses, retail stores, shopping centers, manufacturing buildings, schools, churches, and, to a lesser extent, multistory buildings and apartments. The division also produced steel deck for floor and roof systems; steel deck was specified in 90 percent of the buildings using steel joists and joist girders. Vulcraft was Nucor's original steel business and it was management's desire to supply Vulcraft's basic steel needs internally that prompted the company to integrate backward into minimills

EXHIBIT 10 **Actual and Projected Performance of Nucor-Yamato's Structural Beam Mill, 1988–1993**

	1988	1989E	1990E	1991E	1992E	1993E
Production (000s of tons)	65	625	650	750	850	1,000
Average price/ton	$ 400	$ 380	$ 350	$ 390	$ 395	$ 400
Costs/ton						
Scrap	$ 117	$ 112	$ 100	$ 102	$ 104	$ 106
Energy	30	25	20	20	20	20
Labor	80	33	20	28	28	28
Rolling	140	125	100	100	100	100
Other	25	10	10	10	10	10
Total	$ 392	$ 305	$ 250	$ 260	$ 262	$ 264
Overall revenues-costs-profits (in millions of $)						
Revenues	$ 26.00	$237.50	$227.50	$292.50	$335.75	$400.00
Operating costs	25.48	190.63	162.50	195.00	222.73	264.12
Operating profit	0.52	46.88	65.00	97.50	113.02	135.88
Depreciation	2.93	23.13	24.05	27.75	31.45	37.00
Start-up costs	36.60	0	0	0	0	0
Division profit	$(33.01)	$ 23.75	$ 40.95	$ 69.75	$ 81.57	$ 98.88

Source: R. Douglas Moffat, Robinson-Humphrey Equities Research, February 21, 1990.

and steelmaking. Material costs, primarily steel, represented about 50 percent of Vulcraft's sales dollar; about 95 percent of Vulcraft's steel requirements were obtained from Nucor's steel plants. Vulcraft's strategy was to be the low-cost supplier of joists. The division competed with a large number of other joist manufacturers. Competition centered around timely delivery and price.

Vulcraft's products were produced and marketed nationally from six plants. Joists were manufactured on assembly lines. The steel moved on rolling conveyors from station to station. Teams of workers at each station cut and bent the steel to shape, welded joists together, drilled holes in them, and painted the finished joists. Almost all Vulcraft production employees worked under a group incentive system that offered weekly bonuses for above-standard performance. The division had a fleet of 150 trucks to insure on-time delivery.

Joist and joist girder sales were obtained by competitive bidding. Vulcraft provided price quotes on 80 to 90 percent of the domestic buildings using joists and joist girders; in 1989 Vulcraft's market share was about 35 percent of total domestic sales. Vulcraft's joist sales had been in the 445,000-ton-per-year range for the past three years; current joist production capacity was just over 600,000 tons. Vulcraft's sales of steel deck were in the 140,000-ton range, with increases to the 260,000-ton range expected by 1993; operating profits from deck sales in 1989 were about $7 million, and increases to about $14 million by 1993 were being anticipated. Exhibit 11 provides data on the costs and profitability of Vulcraft's joist and deck products.

EXHIBIT 11   Actual and Projected Performance of Nucor's Vulcraft Division, 1984–1993

Joist Products	1984	1985	1986	1987	1988	1989E	1990E	1991E	1992E	1993E
Production (000s of tons)	424	471	453	444	446	446	430	430	430	430
Percent change	21.93%	9.98%	(3.97)%	(2.03)%	0.00%	(3.26)%	0.00%	0.00%	0.00%	0.00%
Average price/ton	$ 590	$ 595	$ 575	$ 559	$ 595	$ 608	$ 590	$ 613	$ 636	$ 655
Cost/ton										
Steel	$ 275	$ 263	$ 268	$ 278	$ 330	$ 330	$ 310	$ 313	$ 316	$ 320
Conversion	163	158	152	152	152	152	152	156	161	166
Freight	50	23	45	45	45	45	45	45	45	45
Total	$ 488	$ 444	$ 464	$ 475	$ 527	$ 527	$ 507	$ 515	$ 522	$ 531
Overall joist revenues-costs-profits (in millions of $)										
Revenues	$250.16	$280.15	$260.48	$248.20	$264.14	$261.40	$253.66	$263.42	$273.47	$281.67
Operating costs	206.91	208.99	210.39	210.82	233.91	226.53	217.93	221.27	224.67	228.15
Depreciation and administration	8.50	9.35	10.00	10.70	11.45	12.26	13.11	14.03	15.01	16.07
Division profit	$ 34.75	$ 61.90	$ 40.08	$ 26.67	$ 18.77	$ 22.61	$ 22.61	$ 28.12	$ 33.78	$ 37.45

Deck Products	1984	1985	1986	1987	1988	1989E	1990E	1991E	1992E	1993E
Production (000s of tons)	118	169	176	154	147	135	149	201	231	266
Price/ton	$ 600	$ 600	$ 600	$ 575	$ 670	$ 670	$ 620	$ 670	$ 690	$ 711
Cost/ton										
Steel	455	457	456	447	520	515	450	500	525	500
Conversion	45	45	45	47	45	45	47	47	47	47
Freight	35	35	34	35	35	35	37	39	41	43
Total	$ 535	$ 537	$ 536	$ 529	$ 600	$ 595	$ 534	$ 586	$ 613	$ 640
Overall deck revenues-costs-profits (in millions of $)										
Revenues	$ 70.80	$101.40	$105.60	$ 88.55	$ 98.49	$ 90.61	$ 92.23	$134.56	$159.38	$188.79
Operating cost	63.13	90.76	94.27	81.53	88.23	80.50	79.47	117.70	141.58	170.00
Depreciation and administration	2.49	2.74	2.88	3.02	3.17	3.33	3.50	3.67	3.85	4.05
Division profit	$ 5.18	$ 7.90	$ 8.45	$ 4.00	$ 7.09	$ 6.78	$ 9.26	$ 13.18	$ 13.95	$ 14.74

Nucor Cold Finish Bar Division

Nucor had three facilities that produced turned, ground, and polished steel bars in round, hexagon, square, and flat rectangular shapes; such cold-finished steel products were used extensively in making machine shafts and precision parts. All three facilities were among the most modern in the world and used in-line electronic testing to insure outstanding quality. The division obtained its steel from nearby Nucor minimills. Costs were low enough to permit competitive pricing. Nucor's current share of this segment was 16 percent. Total market segment size was about 1,000,000 tons. Total capacity at Nucor's three facilities was close to 200,000 tons. Nucor management expected sales and earnings of this division to increase over the next several years (see Exhibit 12).

Other Divisions

Nucor had four other small divisions with combined sales of about $90 million in 1989. Nucor Grinding Balls produced steel grinding balls in Utah for the mining industry; the division was a low-cost producer and was able to charge very competitive sales prices. Nucor Fastener operated a state-of-the-art bolt-making facility having annual capacity of 45,000 tons; the plant was highly automated and had fewer employees than comparable facilities. Nucor Fastener competed in a highly competitive market dominated by foreign suppliers; the plant ran close to capacity in 1989, with the division capturing a 12 percent market share. Nucor Machined Products, acquired in 1986, produced high-quality steel parts and bearings for a variety of large industrial users; a portion of its steel came from Nucor Cold Finish. Nucor Building Products commenced operations in 1988 to produce metal buildings and metal framing; much of its steel was supplied by Nucor's minimills. By 1993 these divisions were expected to be generating combined revenues of about $135 million and combined operating profits of about $13 million. A fifth division, Research Chemicals, was sold in 1988 at a profit of $38.6 million. In 1989 Nucor's minimills supplied about 525,000 tons of steel (about 20 percent of total production) to the company's Vulcraft, Cold Finish, Grinding Balls, and other divisions.

KEN IVERSON AND THE NUCOR CULTURE

Kenneth Iverson took over the reins of Nucor in 1965 before Nucor's entry into minimills. He had previously been general manager of Vulcraft, then the only profitable part of Nucor. It was Iverson who decided that Nucor ought to be making steel to supply Vulcraft. Iverson's goal was to be able to match the prices of imported steel: "We had some vision that if we were successful, we could expand and create another business by selling steel in the general marketplace."

During his tenure as CEO, Iverson had consciously modeled Nucor on certain bedrock values: productivity, simplicity, thrift, and innovation.

Productivity   Iverson liked to contrast Nucor to integrated companies. He recounted a field trip he took to an integrated steel plant when he was a

E X H I B I T 12   **Actual and Projected Performance of Nucor's Cold Finish Bar Division, 1984–1993**

	1984	1985	1986	1987	1988	1989E	1990E	1991E	1992E	1993E
Production (000s of tons)	90	87	108	133	155	160	160	168	176	185
Price/ton	$450	$440	$462	$456	$515	$515	$505	$505	$505	$505
Costs/ton	$378	$368	$449	$421	$451	$460	$450	$450	$450	$450
Division performance (in millions of $)										
Revenues	$40.60	$38.38	$49.90	$60.65	$79.83	$82.48	$80.80	$84.82	$89.06	$93.51
Operating cost	34.00	32.00	48.50	55.95	69.91	73.54	71.91	75.53	79.31	83.28
Division profit	$ 6.50	$ 6.36	$ 1.41	$ 4.79	$ 9.97	$ 8.94	$ 8.91	$ 9.39	$ 9.75	$10.24

Source: R. Douglas Moffat, Robinson-Humphrey Equities Research, February 21, 1990.

student at Purdue: "This was the late afternoon. We were touring through the plant, and we actually had to step over workers who were sleeping there. I decided right then that I didn't want to work for a big steel plant." As Nucor's CEO, Iverson saw to it that workers had a strong incentive to be as productive as possible. Work teams had production standards and were paid bonuses proportional to the amount their output exceeded the standard—production 25 percent above the standard resulted in a 25 percent wage bonus, paid the following week.

Simplicity and Thrift   Iverson and other managers at Nucor had developed practices and symbols that conveyed simplicity and reinforced the company's low-cost producer strategy. One of their notable achievements was lean staffing and a streamlined organizational structure. Only four levels separated the official hierarchy: workers, department managers, division managers, corporate. Iverson said:

> You can tell a lot about a company by looking at its organization charts. . . . If you see a lot of staff, you can bet that it is not a very efficient organization. . . . Secondly, don't have assistants. We do not have that title and prohibit it in our company. . . . And one of the most important things is to restrict as much as possible the number of management layers. . . . It is probably the most important single factor in business.

Nucor's spartan values were most evident at its corporate headquarters. Instead of having a handsome, expensive showcase building sited on landscaped grounds, Nucor rented a few thousand square feet of the fourth floor of a nondescript office building with an insurance company's name on it. The only clue that Nucor was there was its name (listed in ordinary size letters) in the building directory. The office decor was spartan, simple, and functional. Under 30 people worked in the headquarters as of 1990, up from 16 in 1985. The latest additions were attributable to Nucor's growth and planned expansions. The company assiduously avoided the normal paraphernalia of bureaucracy. No one had a formal job description. The company had no written mission statement, no written strategic plan, and no MBO system. There was little paperwork, few regular reports, and fewer meetings. Iverson commented on his staff and how it functioned:

> They are all very sharp people. We don't centralize anything. We have a financial vice president, a president, a manager of personnel, a planner, internal auditing, and accounting. . . . With such a small staff there are opportunities you miss and things you don't do well because you don't have time. . . . But the advantages so far outweigh the disadvantages. . . . We focus on what can really benefit the business. . . . We don't have job descriptions, we just kind of divide up the work.

Innovation   Nucor was a leading innovator among steel minimills and also in the joist business. The company aggressively searched for ways to improve its production methods and was noted for its experimentation with new technologies. Internally, much emphasis was placed on improving efficiency and achieving lower costs. Cost-saving opportunities were pursued relentlessly and all plant managers were quick to install cutting-edge technologies and improve production practices to boost efficiency and drive costs down. As a consequence, Nucor plants tended to be kept in state-of-the-art condition despite their having been constructed years earlier. The new Crawfordsville mill was the result of over five years of research and engineering study into pioneering thin-slab casting; Nucor had invested almost $25 million of its own money to develop the technology and had monitored experimental efforts worldwide. Iverson and other Nucor executives had kept pushing R&D to make thin-slab casting commercially feasible despite widespread skepticism across the industry that such an effort would pay off.

Ken Iverson: Public Figure

Nucor's success had made Iverson a public figure. He had been interviewed by newspapers, magazines, radio, and TV; he spoke to industry groups and business schools; and he had been called to testify before Congress. He explained why he was willing to devote his time to these extracurricular activities:

> Generally, our policy is to stay as far away as we can from government . . . except that I felt so strongly about protectionism that I thought I should make my views known—especially because our view is so different from the other steel mills. . . . Talking to investors is an important part of the company's relationship with the marketplace. . . . The company gets a direct benefit and it makes good sense. . . . I do some talks at business schools just from the standpoint that I get pleasure out of that. . . . We do occasionally hire MBAs, but we haven't had much success with them.

Iverson had a casual, informal, and unaffected style. His office was neither large nor furnished with expensive decorations. For lunch he took visitors across the street to a delicatessen—their "executive dining room"—for a quick sandwich. Nucor had no executive parking spaces, no executive restrooms, no company cars. Everyone, including Iverson, flew coach class. When Iverson went to New York he rode the subway instead of taking a limousine or taxi. Other Nucor managers followed Iverson's example, shunning ostentation, luxury, and status symbols common among other successful companies.

Organization

Following Iverson's "lean management" philosophy, only four levels of management separated Iverson from the hourly employees. At corporate headquarters they joked that with four promotions, a janitor could become CEO! Exhibit 13 depicts Nucor's organization chart. Below the corporate level the company was organized into divisions. These divisions roughly corresponded to plant locations.

In 1984, under the pressure of the growing size of the company and Iverson's busy public role, the jobs of president and CEO were separated. By trying to be "everything to everyone," Iverson was spreading himself a little thin. Dave Aycock was promoted from a plant manager's job to president, responsible for day-to-day operations of Nucor. Aycock talked about his role:

> I worked at Vulcraft when it was acquired by Nucor in 1955. . . . I've been in this new job for about a year. . . . It's very exciting. . . . If I had actually known roughly half of what I thought I knew, I would probably have been more valuable. . . . Most of my time has been spent learning the personalities, the reactions, and philosophies of the operating personnel. . . . Many of them were glad to see the change because they thought Ken was overworked.

EXHIBIT 13   **Nucor's Organization Structure, 1990**

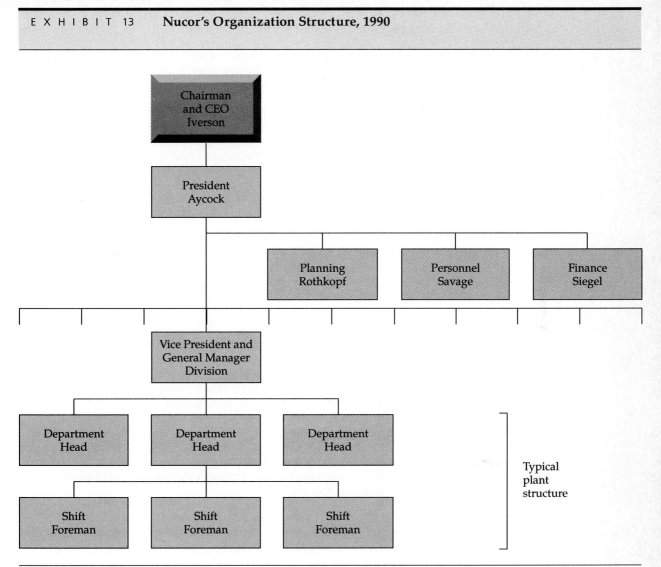

*Note: Nucor's six steel mills (divisions), six joist plants, fastener division, and machined products division were each headed by a vice president and general manager.

Division Management   Because Nucor had a very small headquarters staff (about 30 people in 1990) and because of top management's great confidence in operating personnel, division managers played a key role in decision making. Iverson said of the division managers: "They are all vice presidents, and they are behind our success. They make the policies of this company. Most of them have been with Nucor at least 10 years. But their pay is based on how this company does—not on how well their division does—it's the group concept again."

Corporate-Division Interaction   Contact between divisions and corporate headquarters was limited to a report of production volume, costs, sales, and margin—the "Monthly Operations Analysis." Each month every division received the "smiling face" report, comparing all the divisions across about a dozen categories of efficiency and performance. One division manager described how Iverson delegated and supervised:

> Mr. Iverson's style of management is to allow the manager all the latitude in the world. His involvement with managers is quite limited. As we have grown, he no longer has the time to visit with division managers more than once or twice a year. . . . In a way I feel like I run my own company because I don't get marching orders from Mr. Iverson. He lets you run the division the way you see fit, and the only way he will step in is if he sees something he doesn't like, particularly bad profits, high costs, or whatever. But in the four years I've worked with him I don't recall a single instance where he issued an instruction to me to do something differently.

The casewriters asked a division manager how the corporate officers would handle a division that wasn't performing as it should:

> I imagine Dave Aycock would call first and come out later, but it would be appropriate to the situation. Ken and Dave are great psychologists. Right now, for instance, the steel business is showing a lower return on assets, but I don't feel any pressure on me because the market is not there. I do feel pressure to keep my costs down, and that is appropriate. If something went wrong Dave would know.

How does Nucor respond to problems in management performance?

> We had a situation where we were concerned about the performance of a particular employee . . . a department manager. Ken, Dave, and I sat down with the general manager to let him know where we were coming from. So now the ball is in his court. We will offer support and help that the general manager wants. Later I spent a long evening with the general manager and the department manager. Now the department manager understands the corporate concern. Ken will allow the general manager to resolve this issue. To do otherwise would take the trust out of the system. . . . We are not going to just call someone in and say "We're not satisfied. You're gone." . . . But eventually, the string may run out. Ken will terminate people. He takes a long time to do it. I respect that. Ken would rather give people too much time than too little.

Important issues merited a phone call or perhaps a visit from a corporate officer. A division manager told the casewriters that he talked to headquarters about once a week. Divisions made their own decisions about hiring, purchasing, processes, and equipment. There was no formal limit on a division manager's spending authority. Sales policy and personnel policy were set at the corporate level. Divisions didn't produce a plan, but: "People in this company have real firm ideas about what is going on and what will be happening . . . mostly by word of mouth." Relationships between the divisions were close. They shared ideas and information; the steel mills worked closely to meet the steel needs of the steel products divisions.

Decision Making   Division managers met formally in a group with corporate management three times a year at the "Roundtable." Sessions began at 7 A.M. and ended at 8 P.M. At these meetings, budgets, capital expenditures, and changes in wages or benefits were agreed on, and department managers were reviewed. Iverson waited for a consensus to emerge about an alternative before going ahead with a decision. He did not impose decisions. Corporate officers described Nucor's decision-making processes:

Over a long period of time, decisions in this company have been made at the lowest level that they can—subject to staying within the philosophy of the company. We get a lot of work done without too many managers. Ken has the business courage to stay out of the small things. It takes a lot of courage for general managers to resist the temptation to control every event.

I can walk into Ken's office anytime and talk about anything I want to talk about. Agree or disagree with anything he has done. I don't agree with every decision that is made. I have the right to disagree. Sometimes I disagree strongly. Ken hears me out. Ken listens to other people. He does not feel that he is always right. Sometimes he will change his mind.

I remember when I first started to work for Nucor and I was sitting down with Ken Iverson. He told me, "John, you are going to make at least three mistakes with this company in the first few years that you are with us. Each one of these mistakes will cost us $50,000. I want you to be aggressive, and I want you to make decisions. One word of caution. We don't mind you making the mistakes, but please don't make them all in one year."

Ken defers a decision when the executives are strongly divided to give people a chance to consider it more. Ken is a superb negotiator. He might look at the various positions and say "I have a compromise," and lay that out. Many times he can see a compromise that everyone is comfortable with.

Finance and Capital Budgeting

The theme of simplicity also extended to financial matters. Sam Siegel, Nucor's vice president of finance, did not use a computer. He told the casewriters:

> When you make too many calculations they get in the way of business. Each of the divisions uses computers for many purposes, including financial analysis. You could make an economic case for centralizing some of that here at corporate headquarters. We could save money and create all kinds of information, but then we would have to hire more people to study that information.

No financial analysts worked at corporate headquarters. Nucor did not use sophisticated models of discounted cash flow or complicated formulas to govern capital expenditures, preferring an eclectic capital investment policy. Iverson commented: "Priority? No. We don't even do that with capital expenditures. Sometimes we'll say . . . we won't put up any buildings this year. . . . But in recent years we've been able to fund anything we felt we needed. We don't do it by priorities." During the 1987–89 period, capital expenditures had totaled $665 million, versus $141 million over the preceding three years; the majority of the spending had gone for the Crawfordsville plant ($270 million) and for the new plant at Blytheville to build steel beams ($220 million). These projects were the two largest ever undertaken by the company; funds had been provided from operations and new long-term debt. In 1989, Nucor's ratio of long-term debt to total capital (long-term debt plus stockholders' equity) was 0.21; the company's objective was to keep the ratio below 0.3. Management believed the company had the financial ability to borrow significant additional funds without going above its leverage target. Capital expenditures for 1990 were projected to be in the range of $75 million, and the percentage of long-term debt to total capital was projected to fall below 20 percent by year-end 1990.

> We look at it from the standpoint of whether it's replacement and if it's modernization, what the payback period is, or if it is a new facility. In many cases the

payback on a new steel mill is longer than you would like, but you can't afford not to do it. I think maybe that is where other manufacturing companies go wrong—where they have these rigid ideas about investments. If you don't put some of these investments in, after four or five years you are behind. . . . You can't afford to fall behind, even if you don't get the payback. That's why the integrated steel companies didn't put in continuous casters, because they couldn't get the payback they wanted. . . . Now they have got to do it. . . . From an economics point of view they didn't do anything wrong, they didn't make a mistake.

Financial Reporting Each division had a controller who reported directly to the division manager and indirectly to Siegel. Siegel saw the role of his controllers as being broad: "Controllers who merely do financial work are not doing a good job. A controller should become involved with key plant operations . . . should learn the whole operation." Siegel spent only about one half of his own time on strictly financial matters, contributing the other half toward "problems, issues, and projects" of importance to the company.

Human Resources

Nucor was known for its human resources practices. The casewriters visited a Vulcraft plant and talked with a department manager who had worked at Vulcraft for 16 years about what made Nucor different:

> Our plants are located strategically. The company puts them in rural areas, where we can find a good supply of quality labor—people who believe in hard work. We have beaten back three unionizing campaigns in the last 10 years. These employees are very loyal. In fact, we had to hire a guard to protect the union organizers from some of our workers. We see about 3 percent turnover and very little absenteeism. They are proud of working with us. It's fun when they come to you and ask for work.

Why did Nucor do so well with employees?

> Most companies want to take their profits out of their employees. We treat employees right. They are the ones who make the profits. Other companies aren't willing to offer what is needed to allow people to work. They can't see the dollar down the road for the nickel in their hand. Nucor's people make it strong.

Nucor's incentive systems had been a subject of much discussion and comment. *Fortune* estimated in 1981 that Nucor's workers earned an average of $5,000 more than union steelworkers. Nucor workers were among the highest paid manufacturing, blue-collar employees in the United States.

> **Casewriter:** But aren't Nucor's wages high—how can a low-cost producer afford to pay top dollars for labor?
> **Iverson:** They earn every bit of it! Sure, it's generous. . . . There's a reason for it. It's hot, hard, dirty, dangerous, skilled work. We have melters who earn more than $40,000, and I'm glad they earn it. It's not what a person earns in an absolute sense, it's what he earns in relation to what he produces that matters.

The incentive system at Nucor had several key elements. John Savage, manager of personnel services, explained the company's personnel philosophy:

Our employee relations philosophy has four primary components. . . . Management's first and foremost obligation to employees is to provide them the opportunity to earn according to their productivity. . . . Next, we are obligated to manage the company in such a way that employees can feel that if they are doing their job properly, they will have a job tomorrow. . . . Third, employees must believe that they are treated fairly. . . . Lastly, employees must have an avenue of appeal if they believe they are being treated unfairly, to Mr. Iverson himself if necessary.

Everyone at Nucor participated in incentive plans. These incentives took several different forms depending on the type of work involved.

Production Incentives   Production groups of 25 to 30 employees were assigned clearly measurable production tasks and the time needed to perform each task was based on historical time standards. If, for example, a group produced a joist in 50 percent less than standard time, they got a 50 percent bonus. Bonuses were paid at the end of the following week. When equipment sat idle, no bonus accrued. If an employee was absent for a day, he or she lost a week's bonus—a difference amounting to as much as $7 per hour. Although workers often earned wages far above the average for manufacturing, the system was very tough:

> If you work real hard and you get performance, the payment is there next week. . . . You worked like a dog and here is the money. . . . There are lots of people who don't like to work that hard, and they don't last for long. We have had groups get so mad at a guy who wasn't carrying his weight that they chased him around a joist plant with a piece of angle iron and were gonna kill him. . . . Don't get the idea that we're paternalistic. If you are late even five minutes you lose your bonus for the day. If you are late by more than 30 minutes because of sickness or anything else, you lose your bonus for the week. We do grant four "forgiveness" days a year. We have a melter, Phil Johnson, down in Darlington. One day a worker arrived at the plant and said that Phil had been in an auto accident and was sitting by his car on Route 52 holding his head. The foreman asked, "Why didn't you stop to help him?" The guy said, "And lose my bonus?"

Many Nucor workers earned between $30,000 and $50,000 per year. Nucor's monetary incentives made the company attractive to job seekers (see Exhibit 14). Iverson told a story about hiring new workers:

> We needed a couple new employees for Darlington, so we put out a sign and put a small ad in the local paper. The ads told people to show up Saturday morning at the employment office at the plant. When Saturday rolled around, the first person to arrive at the personnel office was greeted by 1,200 anxious job seekers. There were so many of them that the size of the crowd began to interfere with access into and out of the plant. So the plant manager called the state police to send some officers over to control the crowd. But, the sergeant at the state police barracks told the plant manager that he couldn't spare any officers. You see, he was shorthanded himself because three of his officers were at the plant applying for jobs!

Managerial Compensation   Department managers received a bonus based on a percentage of their division's contribution to corporate earnings. In an operating division such bonuses could run as high as 50 percent of a person's base pay. In the corporate office the bonus could reach 30 percent of base pay. Plant

EXHIBIT 14   **Excerpts of Interviews with Hourly Employees at Nucor**

Jim

(Jim is 32 years old, did not finish school, and has worked at Vulcraft for 10 years. He works at a job that requires heavy lifting. Last year he earned about $38,500.)

This is hard physical work. Getting used to it is tough, too. After I started working as a spliceman my upper body was sore for about a month. . . . Before I came to work here I worked as a farmer and cut timber. . . . I got this job through a friend who was already working here. . . . I reckon I was very nervous when I started here, but people showed me how to work. . . . The bonuses and the benefits are mighty good here. . . . and I have never been laid off. . . . I enjoy this work. . . . This company is good to you. They might let employees go if they had problems, but first they'd give him a chance to straighten out. . . . In 1981 things were slow and we only worked three or four days a week. Sometimes we would spend a day doing maintenance, painting, sweeping. . . . and there wasn't no incentive. I was glad I was working. . . . I was against the union.

Kerry

(Kerry is 31 years old, married, and expecting a child. He has worked on the production line for about three years.)

I was laid off from my last job after working there five years. I went without work for three months. I got this job through a friend. My brother works as a supervisor for Nucor in Texas. . . . This is good, hard work. You get dirty, too hot in the summer and too cold in the winter. They should air-condition the entire plant (laughs). On this joist line we have to work fast. Right now I'm working $8\frac{1}{2}$ hours a day, six days a week. . . . I get good pay and benefits. Vulcraft is one of the better companies in Florence (South Carolina). . . . Everyone does not always get along, but we work as a team. Our supervisor has his off days. . . . I want to get ahead in life, but I don't see openings for promotion here. Most of the foremen have had their jobs for a long time, and most people are senior to me in line. . . . This place is very efficient. If I see a way to improve the work, I tell somebody. They will listen to you.

Other comments from hourly workers

I am running all day long. It gets hot and you get tired. My wife doesn't like it because sometimes I come home and fall asleep right away.

When something goes down, people ask how they can help. Nobody sits around. Every minute you are down, it's like dollars out of your pocket. So everybody really hustles.

employees who didn't work on the production line got a bonus based on either their division's profit contribution or corporate return on assets.

Senior officers had no employment contracts or company-paid pension plan. More than half of their compensation was based on company earnings. Their base salaries were set at about 70 percent of market rates for similar jobs. Ten percent of pretax earnings were set aside and allocated to senior officers according to their base salary. The base level was tied to a 12 percent return on shareholders' equity. Half the bonus was paid in cash, and half was deferred in the form of Nucor stock. In a profitable year officers could earn as much as 190 percent of their base salary as bonus and 115 percent on top of that in stock.

Other Compensation Incentives   Nucor also operated a profit sharing trust. The plan called for 10 percent of pretax earnings to be assigned to profit sharing each year. Of that amount, 20 percent was paid to employees in the following year, and the remainder was held to fund the worker retirement program. Vesting in the trust was 20 percent after one year and 10 percent each following year. The arrangement had the effect of making the retirement income of Nucor employees depend on the company's success. Additionally, Nucor paid 10 percent of whatever amount an employee was willing to invest in Nucor stock, gave employees five shares of stock for each five years of employment, and occasionally paid extraordinary bonuses.

Lastly, Nucor ran a scholarship program for children of full-time employees. In 1985 over 300 children were enrolled in universities, colleges, and vocational schools. One family had educated eight children on Nucor's plan.

No Layoffs   Nucor had never laid off or fired an employee for lack of work. Iverson explained how the company handled the need to make production cutbacks:

> When we have a difficult period, we don't lay anybody off. . . . We call it our "share the pain program." . . . The bonus system remains in place, but it's based on four days' production instead of five. The production workers' compensation drops about 25 percent, the department managers' drops 35 to 40 percent, and the division managers' can drop as much as 60 to 80 percent. Nobody complains. They understand. And they still push to get that bonus on the days they work.

The Downside   Nucor's flat structure and steep incentives also had certain negative side effects. First, the incentive system was oriented toward the short term. If a general manager was thinking about a major capital investment project, he was also thinking about reducing his short-term income. Iverson described how the ups and downs of the incentive plans affected officers: "If the company can hit about 24 percent return on equity, an officer's salary can reach 300 percent of the base amount. It maxed out in 1979 and 1980. In 1981 total officers' compensation dropped way off. In 1980 I earned about $400,000, but in 1981 I earned $108,000. So officers have to watch their life-style!" Iverson's 1981 pay made him, according to *Fortune* the lowest paid CEO in the *Fortune* 500 industrial ranking. Iverson commented that it was "Something I was really a little proud of." In 1989 Iverson's salary was $220,000 and he earned an additional $107,750 in cash and stock incentive compensation. The company's 16 most senior officers earned a combined $2.7 million in salary and incentives in 1989.

Second, promotions came very slowly. Many managers had occupied their current jobs for a very long time. Nucor had experienced some problems in developing the skills of its first-line supervisors.

Many other companies studied Nucor's compensation plans. The casewriters asked John Savage about the visits other companies made to study Nucor's system:

> Many companies visit us. We had managers and union people from General Motors' Saturn project come in and spend a couple of days. They were oriented toward a bureaucratic style. . . . You could tell it from their questions. I was more impressed with the union people than with the management people. The union people wanted to talk dirty, nitty-gritty issues. But the management people thought it was too simple, they didn't think it would work. Maybe their business is too complex for our system. . . . We never hear from these visitors after they leave. . . . I believe it would take five to seven years of working at this system before you could detect a measurable change.

High wages and employment stability got Nucor listed in the book, *The 100 Best Companies to Work for in America*. A division manager summed up the Nucor human relations philosophy this way: "It's amazing what people can do if you let them. Nucor gives people responsibility and then stands behind them." Exhibit 14 presents selected excerpts from interviews with hourly employees about their jobs at Nucor.

Strategic Planning and Nucor's Future

Nucor followed no written strategic plan, had no written objectives (except those stated in the incentive programs), and had no mission statement. Divisions were not asked to do formal strategic plans. We asked Sam Siegel about long-range strategic planning. He confided: "You can't predict the future. . . . No matter how great you may think your decisions are, the future is unknown. You don't know what will happen. . . . Nucor concentrates on the here- and-now. We do make five-year projections, and they are good about three months. Five to 10 years out is philosophy." We also asked Bob Rothkopf (planning director) about planning at Nucor:

> I work on the strategic plan with Ken twice a year. It's formulated out of the projects we are looking at. He and I talk about the direction we feel the company is going. . . . The elements of the most recent plan are that we take the basic level of the company today and project it out for five years. We look at net sales, net income, under different likely scenarios. We add new products or projects to that baseline.

Rothkopf had responsibility for generating most of the information he used in his forecasts. He often used consultants or other companies to get the information he needed. None of the other senior executives or division managers got deeply involved in developing long-term projections. Rothkopf described how decisions to pursue new projects were reached:

> Projects come from all over. Some come from our general managers, or from our suppliers, our customers . . . or come walking in the door here. Iverson is like a magnet for ideas, because of who he is and what Nucor is. . . . We evaluate each project on its own, as it comes up. As each opportunity arises, we go in and investigate it. Some investigations are short; we throw out quite a few of them. We don't make any systematic search for these ideas.

Rothkopf compared Nucor's strategic decision-making approach to formal strategic planning done by other companies:

> Our businesses are all related and easy to keep track of. When a big decision comes up we discuss it. That's easy because of the simple structure of the company. . . . Planning has disadvantages . . . time-consuming . . . expensive . . . hard to get the information for it . . . tends to get bureaucratic.

Nucor's Future

Nucor's top strategic priority for the 1990s seemed straightforward and clear-cut: Assuming all went well in perfecting the thin-slab casting technology at Crawfordsville, then proceed to build additional mills for flat-rolled sheet steel products as fast as circumstances allowed. But Iverson wondered whether it was really that simple. What was there to worry about? How could the expansion opportunities best be financed? What threats were there to Nucor's strategy and how could these be defended against? Was Nucor's cost advantage sustainable?

NORTHERN TELECOM, INC.

Lew G. Brown, University of North Carolina at Greensboro
Richard Sharpe, The University of Tennessee

Hall Miller, vice president of marketing for the Central Office Switching Division of Northern Telecom, Inc., looked up from the reports on his desk to a picture on the wall of his office that reminded him of his childhood in British Columbia. It was of a single snow-covered log cabin, with stately mountains rising in the background. His eyes moved from the picture to the window, where he could see traffic already starting to pile up on Interstate 40 running through Research Triangle Park, North Carolina, between Durham, Chapel Hill, and Raleigh. It was midafternoon in March 1988, and the traffic would be bumper-to-bumper in another hour.

Miller had been reviewing the results of a survey conducted by *Communications Week* in the fourth quarter of 1987. The purpose of the study was to identify purchase trends and priorities in the selection of central office telephone switching equipment and manufacturers. The respondents were primarily telephone company planners, and as such they were directly involved with selecting the purchasing central office switches. It was obvious that Miller was extremely interested in the results.

While Miller had also been reviewing the company's 1987 performance, his thoughts were on the future—if and how the telecommunications market was changing and how to best position the division in response to these changes. Miller smiled as he realized that the picture on the wall represented his perception of Northern's performance in the United States to this point, while the impending traffic jam reminded him of the changing market conditions he felt the company would soon be facing.

HISTORY

Northern Telecom, Inc. (NTI), the U.S. subsidiary of Canadian-based Northern Telecom, Ltd. (NTL), was originally part of the Bell System. Bell Canada, the parent company of NTL, was a subsidiary of AT&T until the late 1950s when AT&T was ordered to divest its foreign subsidiaries. Prior to divestiture, Northern Telecom was known as Northern Electric, serving as the Canadian counterpart to Western Electric, the U.S. manufacturing arm of AT&T.

Northern Telecom established its presence in the United States in the 1960s and 1970s as a private branch exchange supplier (customer-owned telephone switches that reside at customer sites) and a vendor of terminals (telephone sets). (A switch is a device that routes individual calls from the calling party [point of origin] to the telephone network. Once in the network, the call is routed from switch to switch until reaching the party being called.) Manufacturing and support facilities were established in West Palm Beach, Florida; Atlanta, Georgia; Richardson, Texas; Minnetonka, Minnesota; San Ramon, California; and Nashville, Tennessee, the U.S. headquarters of NTI. Northern's first facility in North Carolina opened in the early 1970s in Creedmoor, a small community north of Durham. It still amazed Miller to think that Northern had grown from 300 people at Creedmoor to 10,000 employees in the Raleigh area in less than a decade.

DEVELOPMENT OF THE DIGITAL SWITCH

Throughout the 1970s, Northern Telecom, in conjunction with Bell-Northern Research (BNR), Northern's R&D equivalent to Bell Labs, developed a process known as *digital* switching. Unlike *analog* signals—continuous electrical signals varying in amplitude and frequency in response to changes in sound— *digital* signals involve sampling the human voice at a rate of 8,000 times per second, breaking it into a stream of thousands of bits of electrical impulses in a binary code. As calls are routed through the network, they are multiplexed, which involves coding and sending the digital bits together in streams, allowing transmission of multiple conversations simultaneously on the same line. At the next switching office, the bits are either routed to another destination or are multiplexed back into voice signals and sent to the appropriate terminating parties for the cells. Digital technology offers a number of advantages over analog switching, including faster and cleaner transmission, lower costs per line, and decreased floor space requirements for switching equipment (a digital switch required less than 50 percent the space of an analog switch.)

THE BREAKUP OF AT&T AND EQUAL ACCESS

Northern installed its first digital central office switch in 1979. AT&T still had a monopoly in the U.S. telephone market at the time, providing local and long-distance telephone service through the Bell System to more than 85 percent of the United States with Western Electric as the only supplier of the telecommunications equipment. The remaining 15 percent of the U.S. market was served by 1,200 independent telephone companies. Northern, along with other vendors, sold its products only to the independents until the early 1980s.

In 1982 through the provisions of the Modification of Final Judgment which ordered the breakup of AT&T, AT&T divested the 22 local operating companies comprising the Bell System. Although the new AT&T retained the long-distance portion of the business (called AT&T Communications), the newly formed Bell operating companies providing local service became distinct entities and were no longer tied to AT&T. As such, the Bell operating companies were free to buy telecommunications equipment from suppliers other than Western Electric (renamed AT&T Technologies). For Northern Telecom and other vendors, divestiture was the end of a monopoly and the beginning of a highly competitive marketplace. Exhibit 1 shows the territories of the new regional Bell operating companies.

The Modification of Final Judgment also included the provision that the local telephone companies must provide exchange access to all long-distance carriers (such as MCI and US Sprint) "equal in type, quality, and price to that provided to AT&T and its affiliates." To provide equal access many telephone exchanges (central office switches) had to be replaced with digital technology switches. Northern Telecom was well positioned for success in the U.S. central office switching market, having a product lead in digital switching and now being able to compete in an open market driven by equal access. Thus began

E X H I B I T   1   Regional Bell Operating Companies

NYNEX
- New England Telephone (ME, NH, MA, VT, CT, RI)
- New York Telephone (NY)

BELL ATLANTIC
- New Jersey Bell (NJ)
- Bell of Pennsylvania (PA)
- Diamond State Telephone (DE)
- C&P Telephone Companies (MD, VA, WV)

BELL SOUTH
- Southern Bell (NC, SC, GA, FL)
- South Central Bell (KY, TN, AL, MS, LA)

AMERITECH
- Wisconsin Telephone (WI)
- Michigan Bell (MI)
- Ohio Bell (OH)
- Indiana Bell (IN)
- Illinois Bell (IL)

US WEST
- Northwestern Bell (MN, ND, SD, NE, IA)
- Mountain Bell (MT, WY, CO, NM, UT, ID, AZ)
- Pacific Northwest Bell (WA, OR)

SOUTHWESTERN BELL
- Southwestern Bell Corporation (MO, KS, OK, AR, TX)

PACIFIC TELESIS
- Nevada Bell (NV)
- Pacific Telephone (CA)

an era for Northern known to some observers in the industry as "one of the great marketing successes of recent times."

NORTHERN'S PRODUCTS

Hardware

Northern Telecom's digital central office switching components fell into four categories: systems, remotes, extensions, and lines. Systems equated to digital central-office switches. Northern had three versions collectively known as the DMS-100 Family—the DMS (Digital Multiplex System)-100, the DMS-100/200, and the DMS-200. The DMS-100 handled local lines only, the DMS-100/200 handled both local lines and toll trunks (trunks were lines between offices carrying long-distance traffic), and the DMS-200 handled toll trunks only. Each DMS system had a maximum capacity of 100,000 lines. Exhibits 2 and 3 show Northern Telecom's U.S. installed equipment base by customer type, by service type, and sales by year.

Remotes were digital switching units that extended central office features to remote areas. Northern's remotes ranged in size from 600 to 5,000 lines. Unlike central office systems, which were housed in buildings, remotes were usually constructed in environmentally controlled cabinets and placed outside on concrete platforms in areas away from central offices. In addition to extending central office features and services, most remotes had some stand-alone capability (i.e., if the host central office switch went out of service for some reason, calls could still be made between customers being served by the same remote). Remotes also provided a cost savings in lines by performing a line concentrating function since all the subscribers who were served by a remote in a particular location were wired to the remote rather than to the central office. All the customers on the remote were served by a single pair of wires extending from the remote to the central office. Remotes could be located up to 150 miles away from their hosts.

Extensions represented hardware additions and software upgrades to existing Northern switches. Lines are reported in thousands; thus, as of year-end 1987, NTI had over 15.5 million lines in service.

Software

In addition to hardware, an important portion of Northern Telcom's product line was software. Northern Telecom's DMS switches were driven by both operating software (similar to DOS in a PC environment) and applications software performing specific functions. Originally an AT&T brand name, centrex had become a generic term describing any central-office-based applications software package combining business-oriented voice, data networking, and control features bundled with intercom calling and offered to end-users as a package. As a shared central-office-based service, centrex was designed to replace applications served by equipment located at the customer's premises, such as key telephone systems and private branch exchanges. As opposed to investing in telephone switching equipment, the customer simply paid the telephone company a monthly fee per centrex line for access to a multitude of sophisticated business voice and high-speed data features. Call Forwarding and Call Waiting are examples of centrex basic voice features that have been

EXHIBIT 2   **Northern Telecom's DMS-100 Family Installed Base by Customer Type as of Year-End 1987**

Customer	Systems	Remotes	Extension	Lines (Thousands)
Bell operating companies	658	248	1,106	9,841
Independent operating companies	434	1,303	1,120	5,686
Total United States	1,092	1,551	2,226	15,527

EXHIBIT 3   **DMS-100 Family U.S. Sales by Year**

Year	Systems	Remotes	Extensions	Lines (Thousands)
1979	5			2
1980	13			75
1981	69	31	19	453
1982	51	86	41	492
1983	83	130	58	798
1984	116	210	152	1,379
1985	266	304	332	3,665
1986	235	359	604	3,962
1987	254	431	1,015	4,701
Total	1,092	1,551	2,226	15,527

Source: Northern Telecom Data.

offered to the residential market. Centrex (as an AT&T brand offering) was widespread throughout the 22 local Bell System telephone companies prior to divestiture; as a generic product, centrex was a major source of revenue for the telephone operating companies.

In the late 1970s AT&T began what was known as a migration strategy, urging business customers to switch over to a private branch exchange (on-site) solution as opposed to a central-office-based solution for business service features. Implementation of this strategy, which was designed to bypass the local telephone companies, intensified during and following divestiture. Telephone companies were directly affected by this strategy, for end-users began purchasing their own private branch exchanges directly from AT&T and other vendors, rather than paying the telephone company's monthly per-line fees for central-office-based business service features. The telephone companies did not like this migration strategy.

Northern Telecom introduced its digital centrex applications software and was able to capitalize on the resentment telephone companies felt toward AT&T. Meridian Digital Centrex (MDC), Northern's centrex software offering, was introduced in 1982, and sales grew significantly from 1985 to 1987. Exhibit 4 shows NTI's MDC statistics by customer type.

EXHIBIT 4   **Meridian Digital Centrex Use in the United States as of March 26, 1988**

	In Service		Shipped and in Service		In Service, Shipped, and Firm Orders		
	Systems	Lines	Systems	Lines	Systems	Lines	SRs*
Bell operating companies	594	1,610,166	696	1,956,973	757	2,087,921	44
Independent operating companies	265	292,633	280	387,810	288	401,299	6
Total United States	859	1,902,799	976	2,344,783	1,045	2,489,220	50

*Schedule requests are jobs that are not yet firm orders.
Source: Northern Telecom data.

EXHIBIT 5   **Major End-Users of NTI's Meridian Digital Centrex**

Vertical Markets	Major MDC End-Users	Example
Universities	35	Indiana University
Government offices		
Municipal	30	City of Las Vegas
State	20	Suncom (Florida)
Federal	11	Senate/White House
Major businesses	50	Ford Motor Company
Airports	15	Los Angeles (LAX)
Banks	27	Citicorp
Hospitals	16	Marquette Hospital
Telephone companies	11	NYNEX headquarters

Source: Northern Telecom data.

Telephone companies purchased MDC software for their DMS switches from NTI for the purpose of reselling to end-users the business service features the applications software provided. They often renamed the service for the purpose of developing brand identity and loyalty (much as in the same way Sears bought appliances made by Whirlpool and sold them under the Kenmore label). Bell South, for example, used John Naismith to advertise centrex as ESSX service. Exhibit 5 provides a profile of some of the major Meridian Digital Centrex end-users by vertical markets served; Exhibit 6 provides a breakdown by line size of the Northern Telecom DMS systems that have Meridian Digital Centrex software.

FINANCIAL PERFORMANCE

Exhibit 7 is a consolidated review of the financial performance of Northern Telecom Limited and its subsidiaries during the period 1979–87. As indicated, revenues for 1987 were $4.8 billion, up 11 percent from 1986. Net earnings for 1987 rose 15 percent to $329 million; up from $287 million in 1986. Central

EXHIBIT 6   **Meridian Digital Centrex Line Size Distribution**

MDC lines	Systems
1–1,999	658
2,000–9,999	241
10,000 +	71
MDC software, no lines	75
Total in service, shipped, and on order through 1Q88	1,045

Source: Northern Telecom data.

office switching accounted for $2.6 billion or 53 percent of total revenues in 1987. NTL had 48,778 employees as of year-end 1987, and 1987 earnings per share were $1.39.

Miller felt that Northern's success through the 1980s had been driven by five major factors:

- A sustained product development lead in digital central office switching technology (AT&T did not introduce a digital central office switch until 1983).
- Access to a huge market that had previously been restricted due to monopolistic constraints.
- A willingness by the regional Bell operating companies to be served by a vendor other than AT&T (AT&T had moved from the position of supplier and parent organization to that of a competitor).
- Equal access legislation requiring product replacement of old technology exchanges with new digital switches.
- The ability to dilute the effect of AT&T's migration strategy on the Bell operating companies by providing them with revenue-generating features in MDC applications software for the DMS.

AT&T's 5ESS

Hall Miller believed that the marketplace was changing in a number of ways, in spite of Northern's continued success. Demand for digital switches had exceeded supply in the early 1980s. AT&T did not enter the digital switching marketplace until 1983 with the 5ESS switch; as a result, Northern Telecom had a substantial competitive lead in both product and feature development and in marketing its products to the telephone companies. AT&T found itself in the unusual position of being an industry technology follower rather than the industry leader. Moreover, AT&T had not been concerned previously with having to market its products.

Exhibit 8 compares Northern's DMS and AT&T's 5ESS shipments in half-year increments starting in 1985. Although only 13 of AT&T's 5ESSs were in service by the end of 1983, with an additional 72 being placed in service in 1984, pent-up demand in the telephone companies for additional products and suppliers to help satisfy equal access requirements helped sales of the 5ESS to

E X H I B I T 7   Consolidated 11-Year Statistical Review, Northern Telecom, Inc., 1977–1987   *(Dollars in millions, except per share figures)*

	1977	1979	1981	1983	1984	1985	1986	1987
Earnings and Related Data								
Revenues	$1,149.7	$1,625.5	$2,146.1	$2,680.2	$3,374.0	$4,262.9	$4,383.6	$4,853.5
Cost of revenues	821.4	1,117.0	1,542.5	1,713.3	2,074.1	2,495.6	2,730.5	2,895.8
Selling, general, and administrative expense	149.1	234.9	300.1	454.8	603.2	701.9	764.6	917.8
Research and development expense	64.2	117.6	151.8	263.2	333.1	430.0	474.5	587.5
Depreciation on plant and equipment	29.1	77.9	100.8	126.6	162.8	203.3	247.3	264.1
Provision for income taxes	45.5	30.3	29.8	79.3	120.3	132.8	127.9	141.5
Earnings before extraordinary items	76.3	97.4	92.1	183.2	255.8	299.2	313.2	347.2
Net earnings applicable to common shares	80.2	97.4	105.4	216.7	243.2	273.8	286.6	328.8
Earnings per revenue dollar (cents)	7.0	6.0	4.9	8.1	7.2	6.4	6.5	6.8
Earnings per common share (dollars)								
Before extraordinary items	0.48	0.53	0.45	0.83	1.06	1.18	1.23	1.39
After extraordinary items	0.51	0.53	0.50	0.98	1.06	1.18	1.23	1.39
Dividends per share (dollars)	0.11	0.12	0.14	0.16	0.16	0.18	0.20	0.23
Financial Position at December 31								
Working capital	$ 307.3	$ 477.4	$ 421.6	$ 563.4	$1,570.7	$ 859.0	$ 933.9	$1,188.7
Plant and equipment (at cost)	356.9	602.4	829.8	1,152.2	1,458.0	1,737.5	1,975.2	2,345.6
Accumulated depreciation	184.3	237.8	355.0	506.4	591.5	672.4	877.3	1,084.2
Total assets	698.8	1,620.8	1,809.4	2,309.4	3,072.9	3,490.0	3,961.1	4,869.0
Long-term debt	48.0	165.0	207.5	102.3	100.2	107.6	101.1	224.8
Redeemable retractable preferred shares	—	—	—	—	293.6	277.5	281.0	153.9
Redeemable preferred shares	—	—	—	—	—	73.3	73.3	73.3
Common shareholders' equity	431.0	793.5	719.5	1,178.3	1,379.8	1,614.6	1,894.9	2,333.3
Return on common shareholders' equity	19.4%	14.6%	15.7%	21.7%	19.0%	18.3%	16.3%	15.6%
Capital expenditures	42.1	148.4	174.9	305.7	437.3	457.3	303.8	416.7
Employees at December 31	24,962	33,301	35,444	39,318	46,993	46,549	46,202	48,778

Quarterly Financial Data (Unaudited)

	1st Quarter		2nd Quarter		3rd Quarter		4th Quarter	
	1986	1987	1986	1987	1986	1987	1986	1987
Revenues	$ 969.6	$1,143.3	$1,067.4	$1,253.0	$1,032.2	$1,158.1	$1,314.4	$1,299.1
Gross profit	323.1	403.8	389.4	489.9	404.5	479.1	536.1	584.9
Net earnings	50.1	60.1	64.9	77.6	66.0	69.5	132.2	140.0
Net earnings applicable to common shares	43.3	53.7	58.0	72.9	59.4	66.2	125.9	136.0
Earnings per common share	0.19	0.23	0.25	0.31	0.25	0.38	0.54	0.57
Weighted average number of common shares outstanding (thousands)	233,154	235,237	223,650	235,573	234,199	236,024	234,767	236,444

Revenues by Principal Product Lines

	1983	1984	1985	1986	1987
Central office switching	$ 981.9	$1,452.9	$2,141.3	$2,230.9	$2,577.2
Integrated business systems and terminals	985.8	1,162.9	1,256.6	1,284.7	1,302.0
Transmission	376.3	385.1	431.2	468.1	498.6
Cable and outside plant	275.5	314.9	373.4	348.4	408.2
Other telecommunications	60.7	58.9	60.4	51.5	67.5
Total	$2,680.2	$3,374.0	$4,262.9	$4,383.6	$4,853.5

EXHIBIT 8   **Northern Telecom DMS and AT&T 5ESS System Shipments by Half Year**

	Northern Telecom	AT&T
1985		
First half	144	169
Second half	145	141
1986		
First half	108	152
Second half	139	144
1987		
First half	128	135
Second half	127	130

Sources: Northern Telecom data; AT&T estimates.

grow. Moreover, Northern experienced delivery problems in 1985 with its Remote Switching Center (RSC), one if its remote products, as well as performance issues with a particular release of operating system software. Combined with the strong market demand for digital technology, these events helped to assure that AT&T's 5ESS would be a successful product. The U.S. telephone digital switching market became a two-supplier arena. AT&T claimed to have 800 5ESS systems, 660 remotes, and 15 million lines in service as of September 1987.

PRICING

Due to equal access, demand for digital switches exceeded supply from 1982 to 1986. During this period, delivery time determined which vendor a telephone company would choose to buy digital switches from. Volume sales agreements negotiated with each regional or local telephone company for multiple changeouts of old technology switches were the norm rather than the exception; price was not a key selection criterion. However, with supply exceeding the demand for digital switches from 1986 onward, the situation had become one of competitive bidding for each switch replacement, with bidding parties offering aggressive discounts. The objective was to win the initial system even at the expense of short-term profits, for winning the switch meant additional opportunities for revenue through software and hardware upgrades and extensions.

As in many companies, Northern Telecom's marketing organization had a competitive intelligence group. A major emphasis of this group was tracking competitive positioning in the marketplace. Hall Miller had developed a great deal of confidence in the reliability of the models used by this group to support the competitive bidding process. Pricing had become an extremely sensitive issue. Miller had concerns that the discounts the vendors were offering often resulted in the winner leaving large sums of money on the table (e.g., coming in with a bid at $500,000 less than the next lowest competitor, when all that would have been necessary to win the switch was a $100,000 discount). Moreover, Miller did not want bids to be so low that the telephone companies would refuse to accept higher bids.

In addition to increased competition and pricing pressures from AT&T, other factors were affecting the market. With the completion of the equal access process, telephone company construction budgets were declining 3–4 percent annually. Along with the decline in capital budgets was a corresponding increase in the expense budgets. As a result of this shift, telephone companies were expected to allocate more budget dollars toward upgrading equipment and less toward the purchase of new switches.

THE ANALOG SWITCH REPLACEMENT MARKET

Following equal access, the next major determinant of growth in the U. S. telecommunications market was replacement of analog switches. These switches were analog-stored program control (software driven) AT&T switches that were installed throughout the late 1960s and the 1970s. Exhibit 9 shows historical information and projections of the central office switch market by technology through 1991. As indicated in Exhibit 9, the analog switches accounted for 57 million lines of the total installed base, or 46 percent of the market, compared to a total of 36 million digital lines. The analog replacement market was said to be a $30 billion market for switch manufacturers over the next 20 years.

Numerous factors were involved in analog replacement. Unlike other switches that had to be replaced, analog switches had been upgraded to support equal access requirements because they were software driven. With depreciation service lives of 15–20 years, they would remain in the network until the early 1990s, assuming that the depreciation rates and regulatory positions continued (switch replacement required approval from the appropriate Public Utility Commission). The latest versions of these switches offered a comprehensive set of centrex features, and they traditionally were large in terms of line size (30,000–55,000 lines). As such, a digital replacement switch would require both sufficient capacity and an equivalent set of centrex features.

These analog switches were traditionally located in wire centers, which were simply buildings that housed more than one type of central office switch. Northern had a number of strategies to establish a presence in these wire centers (which were typically located in high-growth metropolitan areas) in the hope that this initial presence would provide a competitive advantage when an analog switch became available for digital replacement. Other vendors were marketing adjuncts for the analog switches, which were enhancements designed to prolong their lives, while these same vendors worked to develop competitive replacement digital switches. As such, adjuncts were basically stopgap measures designed to meet a particular need and to buy additional R&D switch development time.

INTEGRATED SERVICES DIGITAL NETWORKS

Beyond the replacement of analog switches, the next phase of telecommunications technology was called ISDN (Integrated Services Digital Network). ISDN would allow standard interfaces between different pieces of equipment, such as computers, and it would free end-users from concerns as to whether

EXHIBIT 9   **Central Office Equipment Market by Technology**   *(Lines in thousands)*

	1986	1987	1988	1989	1990	1991
Total Market						
Installed base:						
Digital	27,048	36,560	45,230	54,072	62,693	72,057
Analog	56,143	57,022	57,426	57,854	56,750	54,800
Other	38,175	31,322	25,613	19,826	15,933	12,293
Total	121,366	124,904	128,269	131,752	135,376	139,150
Percent:						
Digital	22.3%	29.3%	35.3%	41.0%	46.3%	51.8%
Analog	46.3	45.6	44.8	43.9	41.9	39.4
Other	31.4	25.1	19.9	15.1	11.8	8.8
Demand:						
Digital	10,066	9,508	8,670	8,844	8,620	9,365
Analog	1,591	881	417	429	36	0
Total	11,657	10,389	9,087	9,273	8,656	9,365
Regional Bell Operating Companies						
Installed base:						
Digital	14,509	21,341	27,389	33,553	39,997	46,966
Analog	53,899	54,729	55,114	55,451	54,317	52,379
Other	25,246	20,114	15,998	11,891	9,077	6,648
Total	93,654	96,184	98,501	100,895	103,391	105,993
Percent:						
Digital	15.5%	22.2%	27.8%	33.3%	38.7%	44.3%
Analog	57.6	56.9	56.0	55.0	52.5	49.4
Other	27.0	20.9	17.2	11.8	8.8	6.2
Demand:						
Digital	6,904	6,832	6,048	6,165	6,443	6,969
Analog	1,530	830	385	338	0	0
Total	8,434	7,662	6,432	6,502	6,443	6,969
Independent Operating Companies						
Installed base:						
Digital	12,539	15,219	17,841	20,519	22,696	25,091
Analog	2,244	2,293	2,312	2,403	2,433	2,421
Other	12,929	11,208	9,615	7,935	6,856	5,645
Total	27,712	28,720	29,768	30,857	31,895	33,157
Percent:						
Digital	45.2%	53.0%	59.9%	66.5%	71.0%	75.7%
Analog	8.1	7.9	7.8	7.8	7.6	7.3
Other	46.7	39.1	32.3	25.7	21.4	17.0
Demand:						
Digital	3,162	2,676	2,622	2,679	2,177	2,396
Analog	61	51	32	91	36	0
Total	3,223	2,727	2,654	2,770	2,213	2,396

Source: Northern Business Information, *Central Office Equipment Market*: 1987 Edition.

new equipment from one vendor would interface with existing equipment made by another vendor that an end-user might already own. ISDN would also allow the transmission of voice, data, and video simultaneously over the same facilities (with existing technology, voice, high-speed data, and video must be transmitted separately or over separate lines).

Although universal standards for ISDN had yet to be resolved, useful applications were already apparent. Since ISDN phones were designed to display the calling number and the name assigned to the number on a small screen simultaneous with ringing, the party being called would be able to know where the call was coming from prior to answering. This call screening ability would severely limit the ability of prank callers to remain anonymous, and could provide opportunities to greatly enhance 911 services (police, fire department, and rescue squad) by immediately identifying the calling party's location and other useful information (such as a known medical condition or the location of the nearest fire hydrant) and efficiently routing both the call and the information to all parties involved.

Northern was positioning ISDN as its premier Meridian Digital Centrex offering, as it offered both business voice features and high-speed data capabilities over a single line. Northern's strategy was to move end-users from MDC to ISDN, stressing that existing MDC feature capabilities could serve customer needs today while ISDN standards and applications were being developed by industry regulatory organizations and other telecommunications equipment and computer vendors. In addition, MDC was fully integrated with ISDN, with ISDN combining existing voice and data services while adding additional new features and sophisticated applications.

AT&T, on the other hand, had been advertising ISDN heavily to end-users and was attempting to position it as a technologically superior *replacement* to centrex, rather than as a centrex enhancement. AT&T was pursuing this strategy since BRCS, its digital centrex offering, was perceived as being much less "feature-rich" than its analog centrex systems or Northern's Meridian Digital Centrex.

Northern Telecom placed the first successful ISDN phone call in the United States in November 1987, and had a number of DMS sites in service offering ISDN capabilities. In addition, both Northern Telecom and AT&T had numerous ISDN field trials and commercial applications scheduled with telephone companies and business end-users throughout the country at specific sites during the 1988–1990 time frame.

OTHER COMPETITORS

Replacement of analog switches and ISDN were two potential markets attracting other companies into the U.S. digital central office telecommunications market. Another potential opportunity/threat for Northern was that the seven regional Bell operating companies (RBOCs) had petitioned Judge Green to lift the restrictions barring them from providing information services, going into the long-distance business, and manufacturing terminals and central office switches through direct subsidiaries and/or joint ventures. Most of the telephone companies were interested in having a third supplier in addition to AT&T and Northern Telecom to ensure that pricing and product development remained highly competitive. Following is a discussion of some of these potential competitors and the inroads each had made into the RBOCs.

Siemens

Siemens, a West German conglomerate, had sales of DM 8 billion for its telecommunications segment in 1987 (sales for the entire company in 1987 were $20 billion). Seventy-three percent of Siemens's total sales for the year were from Germany and Europe, with 10 percent from North America.

The headquarters for Siemens's U.S. telecommunications division was in Boca Raton, Florida. Also located at Boca Raton was an R&D facility, while manufacturing sites were located at Cherry Hill, New Jersey, and Hauppauge, New York. Siemens had 25,000 employees in the United States.

Siemens's digital central office offering was available in three versions: DE3, with a maximum capacity of 7,500 lines; DE4, with a maximum capacity of 30,000 lines; and DE5, with a maximum capacity of 100,000 lines.

Siemens had announced ambitious feature rollout plans for its offerings, promising both centrex and ISDN feature parity with both AT&T and Northern Telecom. However, whether it could effectively leapfrog the software development intervals incurred by the industry leaders remained to be seen.

Siemens had made inroads with five of the seven RBOCs: Ameritech, Bell South, Bell Atlantic, NYNEX, and Southwestern Bell. Siemens's progress to this point had been based primarily on both competitive pricing and the desire of the Bell Operating Companies to increase competition in the central office switch market.

In spite of Siemens's recent success, industry consultants cited operational and maintenance problems with the company's digital products regarding system reliability, architecture, and compliance to Bellcore standards. (Bell Communications Research, or "Bellcore," was a standards organization jointly owned by the seven RBOCs.) However, heavy R&D efforts were underway to resolve these issues at Boca Raton, and Siemens was fully committed to adapting its products to U.S. market specifications.

Siemens had a $2.1 million contract with West Virginia University to develop computer-based training courses in operating its digital central office equipment. To strengthen its international position in telecommunications, the company purchased 80 percent of GTE's foreign transmissions operations in 1986.

Ericsson

Ericsson, a Swedish-based telecommunications company, had consolidated international sales of $5.5 billion in 1987. Europe and Sweden accounted for 84 percent of the geographic distribution of total sales for the year, with the United States and Canada contributing 7 percent. Like Siemens, Ericsson was attempting to crack the hold that Northern Telecom and AT&T shared on the U.S. central office switch market. Ericsson had targeted BellSouth, NYNEX, Southwestern Bell, and US West as key accounts it wanted to go after.

Ericsson's digital central office offering was the AXE 10. Ericsson had already installed the AXE in 64 countries and had a worldwide installed base of over 11 million lines. Like Siemens, Ericsson had announced aggressive feature rollout plans (bypassing years of software development by AT&T Technologies and Bell-Northern Research) which it might not be able to deliver.

The AXE was manufactured in 16 countries and was being made available by Ericsson's Network Systems Division in Richardson, Texas. No plans were underway to construct manufacturing facilities for the AXE in the United States.

Ericsson had made a number of recent strategic moves intended to strengthen its position in the U.S. marketplace. The company had reorganized by regions to serve more effectively the RBOC markets; moreover, it had reorganized marketing for the division into the functional areas of market development, marketing communications, systems engineering, and marketing systems. Plans had been announced for a technical training center at the company's U.S. headquarters in Richardson, Texas. In addition, Ericsson had announced that it would be working with IBM to develop private networking capabilities.

NEC

NEC had $13 billion in worldwide sales for 1987, $4 billion of which was from its communications segment. NEC was the leading telecommunications company in Japan; 67 percent of sales were to Japanese customers and 33 percent were in overseas markets.

NEC's digital central office offering was the NEAX61E. The switch was primarily an ISDN adjunct that interfaced analog systems and grew into a full central office. As such, it was basically an interim offering designed to extend the life of analog switches while buying time to improve the product in the hopes of having a competitive offering ready when analog replacement began.

NEC claimed that the NEAX61E was serving 4.8 million lines in over 250 sites in 40 countries. The U.S. headquarters was located in Irving, Texas, where production of the system was scheduled to begin by mid-1988. NEC had made inroads with four of the seven RBOCs—Bell Atlantic, NYNEX, Pacific Telesis, and US West.

The company had recently announced plans for a switching technology center in Irving, Texas, dedicated to developing software for central office switches and customer premises equipment. A second facility in San Jose, California, would develop software for intelligent transport networks, transmission systems, data communications, and network management systems. NEC claimed that it was moving its software development closer to its customers.

A major problem that NEC had to overcome was one of perception. NEC's first attempt to enter the U.S. market with the NEAX61E in the early 1980s met with little success. The product was highly touted, launched, and subsequently withdrawn due to numerous performance issues. Many industry experts felt that NEC was again entering the U.S. market prematurely with a product that was not powerful enough to provide advanced business features or large capacities.

Stromberg-Carlson

Stromberg-Carlson was a division of Plessy, a British telecommunications corporation. Reliable data on Plessy and Stromberg's 1987 financial performance were not available. Stromberg-Carlson's offering, the DCO (Digital Central

Office), was available in three versions: the DCO-CS, which was a toll version of the DCO (7,000 trunks maximum); the DCO-SE (a 1,080 line switch designed to serve as a rural central office); and the DCO (32,000 lines maximum). In addition, Stromberg-Carlson offered a full line of remotes, ranging in size from 90 lines to 10,000 lines.

Unlike Siemens, Ericsson, and NEC, Stromberg-Carlson had been a player in the U.S. telecommunications marketplace for a number of years. Stromberg was a primary supplier to the independent operating companies; however, it was now trying to crack the RBOC market as well.

Although owned by Britain's Plessy Telecommunications, Stromberg-Carlson's U.S. headquarters and DCO manufacturing were located in Lake Mary, Florida, a suburb of Orlando. Stromberg's manufacturing capacity was 1 million lines per year at the Lake Mary facility; however, less than half of this capability was being used.

Stromberg-Carlson was committed to maintaining strong ties with its independent operating company customers. In addition, the company had made inroads with BellSouth and Pacific Telesis. Stromberg had recently signed a volume supply agreement with South Central Bell over the 1989–1990 time frame.

Stromberg's strategy was to target small-to-mid-size central offices (5,000–12,000 lines), focusing on rural applications. Stromberg's lack of a large switch limited the market it could address; however, its niche strategy had served it well over the years in that it could economically provide digital central office capabilities in small line sizes.

In response to its agreement with South Central Bell, Stromberg-Carlson had recently opened a sales office in Birmingham, Alabama. The company had a small installation force and was negotiating with AT&T to arrange to install some of its switches in South Central Bell.

Stromberg-Carlson shipped its 1,000th remote in December 1987 and placed its 2 millionth line in service in January 1988; 200 switches, 400 remotes, and 400,000 lines were shipped by Stromberg-Carlson to the U.S. market in 1987.

HALL MILLER'S STRATEGIC PROBLEM

Musing over the status of Northern's potential competitors, Hall Miller's gaze returned to the report on his desk. Overall, the *Communications Week* study had given Northern high marks relative to most of the competitors. However, there were shortcomings in particular areas he wanted to address (Exhibits 10 and 11 contain the results of the study, segmented by Bell and independent operating company respondents).

In terms of the changing market and increased competition, Miller felt Northern had a competitive advantage in that the company had the largest installed base of digital switches of any vendor. This would help generate revenue through hardware and software extensions and new features prior to the replacement of analog switches. However, Hall had seen AT&T's 5ESS shipments reach parity in a relatively short period of time, and it seemed that competitors were popping up everywhere. In addition, 1988 MDC sales had been sluggish; Hall felt this was largely due to customer misperception resulting from AT&T's hype of ISDN.

E X H I B I T   10   **Summary of Vendor Performance Rankings by Bell Operating Company Respondents**   *(n = 497; scale of 1 to 5, where 1 = Poor and 5 = Excellent)*

	AT&T	Ericsson	NEC	Northern Telecom	Siemens	Stromberg-Carlson
Initial cost	3.12	3.37	3.42	3.83	3.51	3.76
Life cycle cost	3.55	3.26	3.29	3.53	3.48	3.26
Strength of financial backing	4.66	3.48	3.74	4.24	4.05	3.05
Availability	3.90	3.36	3.29	4.17	3.40	3.56
Service/support	4.07	3.21	2.97	3.39	3.22	3.50
Reliability	4.06	3.31	3.08	3.52	3.47	3.24
Delivery	3.76	3.18	2.80	3.71	3.21	3.39
Experience in industry	4.88	3.97	3.34	4.29	3.78	3.91
High technology company	4.63	3.77	3.69	4.28	4.08	3.23
Sound technical documentation	4.32	3.24	2.67	3.50	3.37	3.10
Breadth of product line	4.07	3.24	3.14	3.90	3.33	2.80
International experience	3.19	4.08	3.83	3.58	4.20	2.64
Long-term commitment to R&D	4.44	3.81	3.83	3.99	3.91	3.04

Source: *Communications Week.*

E X H I B I T   11   **Summary of Vendor Performance Rankings by Independent Operating Company Respondents**   *(n = 1,047; scale of 1 to 5, where 1 = Poor and 5 = Excellent)*

	AT&T	Ericsson	NEC	Northern Telecom	Siemens	Stromberg-Carlson
Initial cost	2.40	2.67	3.70	3.67	3.12	3.96
Life cycle cost	3.24	2.74	3.17	3.71	3.04	3.61
Strength of financial backing	4.65	3.31	3.69	4.34	3.65	3.50
Availability	3.56	2.61	3.22	4.06	2.93	4.03
Service/support	3.79	2.81	2.98	3.81	3.02	3.75
Reliability	4.23	2.80	3.41	4.06	3.25	3.63
Delivery	3.46	2.61	3.16	3.83	2.91	3.80
Experience in industry	4.74	3.27	3.55	4.58	3.62	4.19
High technology company	4.72	3.35	3.93	4.45	3.84	3.72
Sound technical documentation	4.47	2.78	2.95	4.08	3.32	3.63
Breadth of product line	4.16	2.83	3.43	4.12	3.27	3.47
International experience	3.84	3.48	4.04	3.84	4.03	3.27
Long-term commitment to R&D	4.67	3.21	3.80	4.29	3.69	3.57

Source: *Communications Week.*

Miller glanced out the window toward the Raleigh-Durham Airport. It was 5:20 P.M., and the highway was packed with traffic. He knew that he faced a number of strategic decisions if Northern Telecom were to maintain its leadership position in the digital central office switch market.

STM TECHNOLOGY, INC.*

Ray M. Kinnunen, Northeastern University
John A. Seeger, Bentley College
James F. Molloy, Jr., Northeastern University

It was May 1990, and Jerry Budinoff—founder, president, and 80 percent owner of STM Technology, Inc.—sat in his office, looking at the large framed print on the wall. It showed a C-130 military transport plane, the kind Jerry had navigated for two years in Vietnam. "That's what I want this company to be," he said. "A vehicle, capable of supporting large-scale projects in systems development. A rugged vehicle. The C-130 is exciting to fly and tough to shoot down."

Jerry grinned as he contrasted that vision for the future with the short-run plans facing his nine-person firm. "First, we have to develop the expanded system features demanded by our present customers. Then, I have to rewrite the business plan in order to attract $900,000 in new capital. Then I'll switch back to my salesman role, to bring in the new business." He mused about the change in his thinking about the company's growth:

> Originally, I thought if you developed good software and supported it well, you would be successful. That was all you had to worry about. That got us up to this point, but we really won't go any further until I worry about the business stuff.
>
> We're at three quarters of a million dollars a year in revenue now, but it isn't going to get any bigger without marketing, distribution, people, money—all of them. Just doing good software doesn't get it any bigger than this.
>
> I just figured that out. It hit me like a club. It's that simple. We never had a business plan. We never had *any* long-range plan. The company just grew.

STM Technology, Inc., located near Boston in Acton, Massachusetts, was founded in 1983 to exploit Jerry Budinoff's skills in systems design and application. The first commercial customer was a small mental health center; STM had gone on to specialize in microcomputer-based management information systems for smaller health care providers and nonprofit human service agencies. The product STM offered was more than just software. The company sold total systems: its customer support department provided training, software support, and consulting services, while its hardware and network department provided hardware, multiuser local area networks, and on-site maintenance services.

Since its founding STM had installed some 129 systems in a wide variety of outpatient health care facilities. Revenues had grown steadily since 1983 and the company had been consistently profitable. By 1989 the company had developed a hospital management system based on personal computers—the first to run on PCs, according to Budinoff. This new product development prompted

---

*This case has accompanying videotapes of Jerry Budinoff in a question-and-answer session in front of an Executive MBA class. The tapes may be purchased from Northeastern University, College of Business Administration, Boston, MA 02115.

The case was presented at the North American Case Research Association. Copyright © 1990 by Ray M. Kinnunen, John A. Seeger, and the North American Case Research Association.

EXHIBIT 1　　STM Technology's Income Statement, 1985–1989　(In thousands of dollars)

	1985	1986	1987	1988	1989
Sales and service	$93	$331	$555	$680	$700
Cost of sales and service	64	174	404	353	380
Gross profit	28	157	151	327	320
General and administrative costs . .	NA	NA	78	144	184
Product development costs	NA	NA	NA	148	133
Total operating expenses	28	133	78	292	317
Income from operations	0	24	73	35	3
Interest income	1	1	4	3	3
Interest expense	0	0	3	5	5
Miscellaneous income	0	0	0	3	1
Miscellaneous expenses	0	1	0	0	0
Income before taxes	1	25	73	37	3
Provision for income taxes	0	4	23	7	1
Net income	$ 1	$ 21	$ 51	$ 30	$ 2

EXHIBIT 2　　Breakdown of STM Technology's Expenses, 1988 and 1989
(In thousands of dollars)

	Cost of Sales and Service		Product Development Expenses		Selling, General, and Administrative Expenses	
	1988	1989	1988	1989	1988	1989
Purchases	$189	$174				
Salaries	118	141	$113	$96	$90	$113
Auto expenses and travel	17	21			11	14
Payroll taxes	10	12	10	8	6	7
Consultants	3	9	—	2		3
Employee benefits	1	8	4	7	4	5
Telephone	5	4	—	1	5	7
Depreciation	3	4	10	7	—	3
User meetings	1	2				
Insurance	3	2				
Equipment repair	1	1				
Printing	1	1			1	1
Recruiting expenses			9	13		1
Development supplies			1	—		
Rent					2	13
Accounting and legal services . . .					8	5
Commissions					5	3
Office expense					1	3
Sales exhibits					3	2
Sales expense					1	1
Miscellaneous expenses					3	3
Advertising					1	—
Seminar costs					2	—
Bad debt expense					1	—
Total*	$353	$380	$148	$133	$144	$184

*Totals may not add due to rounding.

EXHIBIT 3   **Comparative Balance Sheets for STM Technology, 1985–1989**
(In thousands of dollars)

	1985	1986	1987	1988	1989
Assets					
Current assets:					
Cash	$ 0	$55	$ 89	$ 83	$ 79
Accounts receivable	0	0	73	90	127
Supplies	0	0	1	2	7
Prepaid income taxes		0	0	15	3
Total current assets	0	55	163	190	216
Property and equipment (at cost):					
Equipment	21	26	35	47	59
Motor vehicles	14	14	14	40	40
	34	39	48	86	98
Less accumulated depreciation	14	22	32	45	59
Net property and equipment	20	17	16	41	40
Miscellaneous costs	0	0	0	0	0
Organization costs	3	2	2	1	0
Total assets	$23	$74	$180	$232	$256
Liabilities and Stockholders' Equity					
Current liabilities					
Accounts payable	$ 4	$ 5	$ 10	$ 12	$ 25
Accrued taxes	0	27	13	0	0
Deferred taxes	0	0	4	4	7
Deferred revenue	0	0	63	70	76
Total current liabilities	4	33	90	86	108
Notes payable—stockholders	22	24	22	48	48
Total liabilities	26	57	112	134	156
Stockholders' equity					
Common stock, no par value;					
1,250 shares issued and outstanding	4	4	4	4	4
Retained earnings	–7	14	64	94	96
Total stockholders' equity	–3	18	68	98	100
Total liabilities and stockholders' equity	$23	$74	$180	$232	$256

Note: Totals may not add due to rounding.

him to seek outside financing for STM, which had until this point financed its growth internally. Budinoff had concluded that proper exploitation of this new product and other systems required financial backing. Exhibits 1 through 4 present recent financial data for the company.

THE MICROCOMPUTER SOFTWARE INDUSTRY

In the early 1980s, following the introduction of IBM's personal computer and wide market acceptance of microcomputers, demand for application software skyrocketed. Hundreds—then thousands—of individual entrepreneurs

EXHIBIT 4　　**STM's Restated Sales by Business Line**　*(In thousands of dollars)*

Item	Actual			Estimated			
	1987	1988	1989	1990	1991	1992	1993
Hospitals and clinics							
Software sales							
New clients	$412	$248	$350				
Old clients*	19	137[§]	20				
Subtotal	431	385	370				
Hardware							
Contracts	61	85	101				
Equipment/labor[ǁ]	66	103	110				
Subtotal	127	188	211				
Total hospitals and clinics	558	573	581	$1,125	$3,160	$5,305	$ 8,030
Support-software							
Contracts[†]	36	70	94				
Training[‡]	10	16	22				
Consulting	8	19	21				
Total support	54	105	137	286	760	1,196	1,748
Tracking	–	–	–	45	200	300	400
Total revenues	$612	$678	$718	$1,456	$4,120	$6,081	$10,178

*Additional software sales to existing clients.
[†]Extended service contracts.
[‡]Special training programs not associated with sales.
[ǁ]Labor for installation.
[§]Includes one special contract for $80,000.
Source: Estimated by Jerry Budinoff.

founded businesses as designers, programmers, distributors, or retailers of computer software. By 1988 there were approximately 30,000 microcomputer software manufacturers in the United States, producing more than 70,000 products, according to the CIRR Index, 1989. In the Boston area alone, the "Business to Business" telephone directory listed 906 computer software and service firms, and 555 computer systems designers and consultants.

This proliferation of entrants in the industry required firms to do more than just produce technologically sound products if they wished to grow. By 1990, success in the industry called for brand development and firm name recognition, marketing and support, and product development and enhancement. Business expertise in marketing, sales, and support became increasingly more significant as prerequisites for success. Jerry Budinoff commented on the importance of providing service:

> Hardware and software require a lot of support. Technology changes quickly and if you're not supporting the changes they just run by you. We're small, but we try to provide all of the services. That's what really sells our products. It's not just the system; it's all of the training and support. A system is not just software. It's the whole human element and you have to concentrate on the people side with your service organization. Without that we'd be out of business.

THE HEALTH CARE INDUSTRY

For several decades, expenditures on health care had represented the fastest-growing sector of the American economy. The adoption of government payment programs (medicare and medicaid) in the mid-1960s and growth in private insurance (such as Blue Cross/Blue Shield) encouraged the use of health care, since most people could pass their medical costs on to third-party payers. Estimated total U.S. health care expenditures for 1990 were 2.6 times the level of 1980, at $647 billion (see Exhibit 5).

As medical costs rose, governments and employers who were paying the bills came under increasing budget pressure. Repeated efforts to control costs had little effect. In October 1983, the federal government changed its medicare payment policy from full reimbursement for hospital charges to reimbursement at predetermined rates for specific treatments. The government set rates for hospital services according to "Diagnostic Related Groups" (DRGs), resulting in standard reimbursements for medical treatments, regardless of how long the patient remained in the hospital. This new fixed-fee payment system provided strong incentives for health care facilities to control costs, since payment rates were non-negotiable. Hospitals immediately began to send patients home to complete their recuperation.

Employers also responded to the ever-rising costs of employee health benefits. Some companies raised their employees' portion of health insurance premiums; some increased efforts to promote overall healthy living; still others encouraged employees to elect lower-cost plans like health maintenance organizations (HMOs).

These changes in health care payment did not, however, curtail national health care spending. Health care's portion of the gross national product grew steadily from 5.2 percent in 1960 to 11.5 percent in 1988. The increase, due partly to the aging population and partly to costly advances in medical technology, was expected to continue. In 1989, the S&P industry surveys, *Health Care*, showed that 11 percent of the total national population was over 65 years of age and generated 35 percent of the country's total health care bill. Older patients required more attention, thus increasing the labor costs of most health care facilities. Additionally, the number of diagnostic tests, medical treatments, and prescribed pharmaceuticals billed by hospitals to their patients increased greatly, even as hospital stays dropped under the pressure of the DRG payment system.

Except for outpatient services, hospital utilization declined steadily after 1983. Hospitals faced tighter margins, due to lower admissions and inadequate reimbursement. DRG rate increases lagged behind actual cost increases for health services, and under the Bush administration this condition was expected to continue: Medicare's fiscal 1990 budget was cut by more than $2 billion. Additionally, hospitals had to contend with the high cost of preventing in-hospital contraction of infectious diseases such as AIDS along with increasing liability insurance.

Declining usage and tightening margins hit small public and rural hospitals (those having fewer than 100 beds) especially hard. Many public and rural hospitals faced the threat of bankruptcy or closure. In addition to inadequate DRG rates, these hospitals were adversely affected by demographic changes and the distribution of federal health care funds. Increasing numbers of young

EXHIBIT 5   U.S. Health Expenditures, by Type, 1980–1990   (*In billions of dollars*)

Type of Expenditure	1980	1981	1982	1983	1984	1985	1986	1987	1988	1990E
Health service and supplies	$237.1	$273.5	$308.3	$341.8	$375.4	$407.8	$443.0	$485.4	$535.7	$626.5
Personal health care	219.4	254.6	286.9	314.8	341.9	373.4	406.0	447.0	494.8	573.5
Hospital care	100.4	118.0	135.5	148.8	156.3	168.6	180.4	196.9	216.2	250.4
Physician's services	46.8	54.8	61.8	68.4	75.4	79.3	89.2	100.1	112.9	132.6
Dentist's services	15.4	17.3	19.5	21.7	24.6	27.5	29.9	33.2	37.0	41.8
Other professional services	5.6	6.4	7.1	9.3	10.9	15.7	18.0	20.8	24.1	22.9
Drugs and medical sundries	19.3	21.3	22.4	24.5	26.5	32.1	34.1	36.5	39.0	42.1
Eyeglasses and appliances	5.1	5.7	5.7	6.2	7.0	7.7	8.5	9.4	10.5	11.2
Nursing home care	20.6	24.2	27.3	29.4	31.7	34.1	36.8	40.0	43.8	54.5
Other health services	6.0	6.9	7.6	8.4	9.4	8.3	9.1	10.1	11.3	18.0
Prepayment and administration	10.7	11.1	12.7	17.1	22.6	22.1	23.5	24.0	25.0	34.6
Government public health activities	7.0	7.7	8.6	10.0	11.0	12.3	13.5	14.4	15.9	18.5
Medical facilities	11.8	13.1	14.1	15.4	15.6	19.1	20.4	21.6	23.0	20.7
Research	5.3	5.7	5.9	6.2	6.8	11.0	12.3	13.4	14.6	11.5
Construction	8.5	7.5	8.2	9.2	8.9	8.1	8.0	8.3	8.4	9.3
Total health expenditures, exclusive of health service and supplies	$249.0	$286.6	$322.4	$357.2	$391.1	$426.9	$463.4	$507.0	$558.7	$647.3

E—Estimated.

Source: Standard & Poor's Industry Surveys, *Health Care*, July 13, 1989, p. H15. Taken from data supplied by Health Care Financing Administration.

EXHIBIT 6   **Growth of Health Maintenance Organizations, 1980–1988**

Date	Prepaid Plans	Enrollment (Millions)	Percent Population
June 1980	236	9.1	4.0%
June 1981	243	10.2	4.4
June 1982	265	10.8	4.7
June 1983	280	12.5	5.3
June 1984	306	15.1	6.4
December 1984	337	16.7	7.1
December 1985	480	21.0	8.8
December 1986	593	25.0	10.4
December 1987	650	30.0	12.2
June 1988	643	NA	NA

Source: Adapted from Standard & Poor's Industry Surveys, *Health Care*, July 13, 1989, p. H32.

rural residents moved away, reducing the tax base that supported community health care and shifting the balance of patients to an older, more medicare-dependent base. Rural hospitals generally received 40 percent less in medicare reimbursement per case than did urban hospitals, because government audits showed that rural hospitals had lower operating costs. A study by the University of Illinois Center for Health Services Research, quoted by S&P, found that 161 rural hospitals closed between 1980 and 1987, with 70 percent of those remaining losing money in 1987. And 600 more rural hospitals were expected to close before 1990.

Many hospitals attempted to compensate for declining revenues by shifting the weight of costs to private patients. Private and corporate consumers, however, reacted by seeking alternate means of health care. Outpatient services grew substantially in usage. In 1980 18 percent of all surgical procedures were performed on an outpatient or ambulatory basis. This increased to 28 percent in 1985 and was expected to be at 59 percent by 1990, according to Joyce Keithly, writing in *Nursing Economics* in 1989.

Health maintenance organizations first became a key component of health care in 1973 with a law requiring many corporations to include HMO coverage in their health care benefit menus. HMOs operate on fixed cost contracts with health care providers, eliminating any fee for service. Although there was some concern that HMOs' protection might be discontinued, a Duff & Phelps HMO industry analysis expected annual membership growth to continue (see Exhibit 6) and revenue growth to remain near 20 percent.

In summary, health care providers felt intense pressure in 1990 to control costs. A prime area for their attention was administrative systems, where hospitals had automated many of their processes but smaller institutions had been unable to afford the high costs of modernizing systems to improve their efficiency.

STM's Competitive Situation

A number of large competitors and a multitude of small ones served the medical market with computer systems, said Budinoff:

> Meditech, IDX, and Baxter are big in the hospital systems market, for example, but they don't bother with outpatient clinics. Baxter is huge. But their product sells for $250,000 to $300,000 to get the whole system in, including hardware. Baxter and IDX will both lease their systems at $75,000 per year. Clinics can't even look at that kind of money, and even a hospital of 100 to 125 beds can't afford it. They may pay it, but they're real unhappy.

Baxter International, a major supplier to large hospitals, was a manufacturer and distributor of health care products whose 1988 sales reached $6.8 billion. Baxter's products included intravenous solutions, dialysis and blood collection equipment, drugs, urological and diagnostic products, cardiovascular devices, and information systems. Additionally, Baxter operated 120 of its own outpatient health care facilities.

> The big guys have had their systems out there for several years, and they're all based on minicomputers. We want to go in with a PC-based system that sells in the neighborhood of $75,000 to $90,000. We're the first ones to do it on PCs, and we have to get the financing so we can develop it properly and grow it before the others copy us. It's not easy to downsize a system from minis to micros, and the big guys have a minicomputer mindset. We have maybe a year's lead.

STM did not offer a lease plan to its customers. "I have no training in business," said Jerry, "and that kind of arrangement requires a lot of expertise."

Small hospitals and clinics, Jerry said, were "an everywhere market." Some 60 percent of hospitals tabulated in the 1989 American Hospital Association's data were below 200 beds in size (see Exhibit 7), and there was evidence that the smaller hospitals were having difficulty finding the systems they wanted. A survey of 3,000 hospitals with more than 100 beds, conducted by *Modern Healthcare* (see Exhibit 8), indicated a large number of small shoppers for systems, with many purchase plans canceled or delayed for years.

The small institutions were served by a few small companies—Practice Management Systems, at about $5 million annual sales, was the largest—and by a legion of independent operators. Many of these, Jerry thought, were amateurs or programmers who had built a system for their own employers and were trying to peddle it to others. As "basement operators," they often quoted unrealistically low prices. Wise buyers in the market had come to demand evidence of a supplier's financial stability.

Every successful installation, Budinoff felt, would generate new sales through word-of-mouth contact from satisfied customers. Already, STM's development work in five hospitals was generating inquiries beyond the firm's capacity to service them. Jerry had just decided against pursuing a California hospital inquiry; the distance made installation and support unfeasible. Still, many hospital and clinic administrators desperately wanted economical systems. Budinoff had firsthand knowledge of their problem:

> I've had directors of facilities get a little annoyed with me because they wanted something like our system but didn't know we existed, so they bought something else. When they found out about us they'd call and say, "Where the hell were you when I needed you?"

EXHIBIT 7   **1989 Health Facilities in Target Areas**

| | Hospitals* | | | | | | |
	Total	<50 Beds	<100 Beds	<200 Beds	HMOs	Psychiatric Facilities	Substance Abuse Facilities	Total Facilities†
New England								
Connecticut	65	7	23	34	12	8	32	117
Maine	46	11	29	34	4	0	9	59
Massachusetts	173	12	52	98	26	4	34	237
New Hampshire	41	9	24	34	5	6	14	66
Rhode Island	19	2	11	15	4	1	6	30
Vermont	86	0	18	37	3	0	4	93
Total‡	430	41	157	252	54	19	99	602
Mid-Atlantic								
New Jersey	125	4	14	37	22	8	43	198
New York	322	25	72	138	30	23	119	494
Pennsylvania	302	19	72	160	26	5	90	423
Total	749	48	158	335	78	36	252	1,115
South Atlantic								
Florida	276	27	82	164	39	25	100	440
Washington, D.C.	18	0	2	4	8	0	7	33
Georgia	204	39	98	147	11	5	49	269
South Carolina	90	14	41	67	5	1	12	108
North Carolina	159	24	71	115	9	3	25	196
Maryland	85	8	18	40	22	6	51	164
Virginia	136	9	40	87	19	2	43	200
West Virginia	70	19	39	48	4	1	14	89
Delaware	13	1	4	8	7	1	4	25
Total	1,051	141	395	680	124	44	305	1,524
Miscellaneous								
Texas	553	184	313	437	47	31	139	770
California	566	91	233	386	119	21	163	869
Total	1,119	275	546	823	166	52	302	1,639

*Hospitals are grouped by bed number. Each category includes previous category's number. Total refers to all hospitals with unlimited bed size.
†Total facilities equal sum of total hospitals, HMOs, and psychiatric and substance abuse facilities.
‡Total refers to sum of geographic groups column.
Source: "1989 AHA Guide to the Health Care Field," American Hospital Association, Chicago, IL.

STM TECHNOLOGY, INC.: CURRENT PRODUCTS

The success to date of STM was attributed to the sales of its Outpatient Billing and Administration System, with an installed base of 129 systems in the fall of 1989. Jerry estimated the market to be approximately 2,500 clinics in New England; he was targeting an additional 335 installations over the next four years. This estimate was based on a significant upgrade to the present system, automating nearly the entire billing process. The new STM "Robotic" version

E X H I B I T   8   **Buying Plans for Patient Care Systems and Patient Accounting Systems**

A. Buying Plans for Patient Care Systems

Outcome of 1987 Plans, as of End of 1988

| | | | Still Pending | | | |
| | | | --- | --- | | |
Bed Size	Implemented Plans	Canceled Plans	From 1986	From 1987	New Plans in 1988	Total
100–199	58	19	79	37	117	233
200–299	47	23	46	13	71	130
300–399	24	13	29	18	37	84
400–499	10	5	14	0	13	27
500 and over	21	5	33	10	27	68
Total	160	65	201	76	265	542

B. Buying Plans for Patient Accounting Systems

Outcome of 1987 Plans, as of End of 1988

| | | | Still Pending | | | |
| | | | --- | --- | | |
Bed Size	Implemented Plans	Canceled Plans	From 1986	From 1987	New Plans in 1988	Total
100–199	53	14	32	30	112	174
200–299	58	12	20	16	54	90
300–399	34	2	29	12	29	70
400–499	14	4	13	1	13	27
500 and over	25	2	13	10	28	51
Total	184	34	107	69	136	412

Source: *Modern Healthcare*, July 1989, p. 58.

would incorporate automatic scanning of services at the front end and electronic transmission and posting of receipts at the back end. Little or no hand data entry would be required. This new version could be marketable in four months with additional R&D funding, Jerry said.

Two additional products had been developed: a microcomputer Inpatient Billing and Administrative system targeted at small hospitals (under 150 beds), clinics, and HMOs; and a Patient Database, which provided a Medical Tracking and Analysis system linked with either the hospital or the clinic systems. These programs formed an interrelated family of products that met the need for affordable, integrated medical systems. STM continued its market research in order to add to this family of products further through the development of new and follow-up software.

The Medical Tracking and Analysis System was a system to track the health care data of patients throughout their lifetimes. It could be integrated into the Billing and Accounting System, but could also be available as a stand-alone product. The product needed six to nine months to complete, after funding came in. Jerry viewed the market as nationwide and potentially worldwide. He had targeted 245 sales within four years to employee assistance program providers, employers, government agencies, and health care practices.

E X H I B I T   9   **Jerold E. Budinoff's Educational Background and Career Experiences**

Summary of Qualifications

Six years president software development company.
Seventeen years system development experience.
Designed and implemented systems in health care billing and administration, order processing, production control, bill of materials, MRP, receivables and general ledger.

Education

Purdue University: M.S. Astronautical Engineering, 1965.
U.S. Air Force Academy: B.S. Engineering Science (Distinguished Graduate), 1964.

Job History

1983 to Present: President, STM Technology, Inc.
1981 to 1983: Senior Analyst, Raytheon Computer Services
1975 to 1981: Manufacturing/MIS Manager, Digital Equipment Corporation
1972 to 1975: Systems Analyst, Keydata Corporation
1971 to 1972: Partner, Plast-Alum Manufacturing Company
1970 to 1971: Production Manager, Procter & Gamble
1964 to 1970: Officer, U.S. Air Force

8/83 **to** **Present**	**STM Technology, Inc.—Acton, MA** **President** Founded company which develops and installs a wide variety of software for the health care industry. STM's Health Care Office Management Systems are the most advanced patient registration, billing, and accounts receivable systems available today in Massachusetts. Serves as STM's primary systems developer. All STM systems have been designed by Mr. Budinoff working with agency executive directors, business managers, and administrative personnel throughout Massachusetts. Also serves as STM's only salesman. Responsible for all sales and marketing of STM's products. STM employs eight people.
12/81 **to** **8/83**	**Raytheon Computer Services—Wellesley, MA** **Senior Analyst** Developed systems for Raytheon commercial customers. Responsibilities included client interface and project management, specification, design, test, and implementation. Produced systems in medical insurance and retail sales. IBM mainframes.
10/75 **to** **7/81**	**Digital Equipment Corporation—Maynard, MA** **Group MIS Functional Manager**—Headquarters 4/80 to 7/81 Responsible for program management of all common systems in the areas of manufacturing engineering and quality. Established strategies, business plans, and staffing. Coordinated system development between plants. **Systems Development Manager**—Westminster Plant 2/78 to 4/80 Managed 15 analysts and programmers developing systems in materials, BOMs, quality assurance, and purchasing. Responsibilities included planning, budgeting, staffing, and project management. Successfully developed and implemented the first common material requirements planning and BOM system in the Systems Manufacturing Group. DEC hardware. **Manufacturing Planning Manager**—Westminster Plant 2/77 to 2/78 Managed a group that accomplished long-range planning and developed tools for management analysis.

(continued)

EXHIBIT 9   (*Concluded*)

Systems Analysis Manager—Product Line Systems
10/75 to 2/77

Built and managed a team of analysts working in the Product Line Order Processing Group. Accomplished feasibility studies and functional specifications for order processing systems.

6/72
to
10/75

Keydata Corporation—Watertown, MA
Manager of Communications—Headquarters
1/75 to 10/75

Managed 35 people responsible for Keydata's nationwide 1,000-terminal teleprocessing network. Department included communication customer services, line troubleshooting, contracts, and evaluation of new equipment.

Systems Analyst/Customer Rep—National Accounts
Region—6/72 to 1/75

Developed systems for Keydata's major national accounts. Worked closely with salesmen and customers in the sales phase and assumed full account responsibility after contract was signed. Designed and implemented systems in manufacturing, order processing, accounting, and electronic mail.

9/71
to
5/72

Plast-Alum Manufacturing Company—North Hollywood, CA
Partner

Managed the entire operation of a small (20 people) manufacturing business including manufacturing operations, budgeting, inventory, and inside sales.

6/70
to
9/71

Procter & Gamble Corporation—Cape Girardeau, MO
Production Manager

Managed a 22-person crew operating four Pampers production lines. Responsibilities included personnel supervision, training, production, maintenance, and packaging.

6/64
to
6/70

United States Air Force
Officer

Was primarily a flyer with over 3,000 hours flying time. Two years Vietnam. Was also an instructor at the U.S. Air Force Academy in the department of engineering mechanics.

STM Technology, Inc.: History

Jerry Budinoff was an electrical and astronautical engineer by training (see Exhibit 9). He began working with computer systems shortly after leaving active duty with the Air Force, and joined Procter & Gamble as a production manager. While working with computer professionals there, Budinoff discovered that he really enjoyed systems design. This would be his new profession.

After P&G, Budinoff worked for DEC and Raytheon to gain management experience. Budinoff says, "I had a friend who thought you couldn't really run your own company unless you could be an executive in a large corporation. So I got to where I worked for a vice president. Then I said, "Okay, I can do this," and started this company.

In 1982, Budinoff left Raytheon to develop systems and start STM. He describes his entry into the health care market:

It was an accident. The first person I found who wanted a system developed happened to own a mental health center. That was it. There was no formal market research. It could have been a gas station. It didn't make a difference to me. I was a techie, and I just wanted to develop software.

After Budinoff incorporated the company in 1983 he brought in Evelyn Mittler (a Raytheon programming consultant) as a 10 percent stockholder, and Richard Kelley (a software development administrator from Honeywell). It was with this limited staff that STM developed software products to enter the health care market, focusing on systems for nonphysician outpatient facilities. Budinoff saw STM's ability to serve a wide variety of outpatient clinics as his competitive advantage. He commented on this and the derivation of the company's name:

Mental health facilities, rehabilitation facilities, substance abuse facilities . . . there are no other general-purpose systems out there that are right for all of them. Maybe 50 to 60 percent of them are nonprofit, and systems for them are much more difficult to do than for physicians. So there is much less competition for systems work for these facilities: Everyone sees physicians as the big market, and these other things are much smaller.

There is no one who competes in all the different kinds of places we're in. We run into one set of competitors in mental health facilities, and another set in substance abuse companies. We're the only one with a generic product—one that serves all kinds of clinics. That is an advantage because when one of these guys gets aggressive and starts doing very well in some market, we can turn to another market. We're always going one direction or another within health care, while our competition is tied to one market and they go up and down as that market moves.

One thing all our customers have in common: They all want to save time and money. That's what STM stands for—"Save Time and Money." When I first went out to the market, I asked what people wanted. They said, "anything that saves me time and money," so I put that right into the name. A panel at Harvard said it was a "harsh and nondescriptive" name for a company, where you want a name that's warm and friendly. But I want to tell you our customers and prospects remember it and identify with it. It always gets a smile. They greet me, "Here's the guy who'll save us time and money." Maybe that's why I haven't gone to Harvard.

In its first six years of operation, STM did not have an office facility; all employees operated out of their homes. In July 1989, Jerry leased a 1,400-square-foot, ranch-style building. A classroom for weekly training sessions and tastefully decorated offices for all the staff occupied the first floor. An equal-size basement, vacant but subject to rental, would provide expansion space when funding permitted the increased staff. STM at the time employed nine people, who provided administration, hardware maintenance, customer support, training, and programming. Budinoff did most of the systems design work and was also the company's only salesperson. Evelyn Mittler, whose 24 years of systems and programming experience included extensive service with Raytheon, Varian, and Wang, assisted with design and was in charge of coding. All STM programs were written in COBOL. "It may not be the newest language, but it is much easier to find customer support people who understand COBOL," Mittler said.

STM had no affiliation or official status with the computer manufacturers whose hardware they selected for customer systems. Some years earlier, an IBM Value Added Reseller had offered Jerry a System 36 minicomputer, hoping he could program the outpatient management system for their machine. "Even then, we thought the minis were dinosaurs, so we didn't do it," Jerry said. IBM itself was now showing interest—this time with the thought of selling STM's software along with their PCs and the new "6000 series" machines. Budinoff was hesitant, however: "I don't understand that kind of intercompany dealing," he said, "and it would take an immense amount of time to learn it."

As it became apparent during 1989 that the year would be profitable—so profitable that substantial taxes would be due—Jerry Budinoff decided to invest in additional marketing. He employed a salesperson for six months. Budinoff described him as "not having an in-depth knowledge of the product and the market. He tried to sell on personality and didn't get anywhere. This isn't like selling a car. And he didn't want to *get* the knowledge. We parted company." In 1990 STM's marketing still relied only on Budinoff's efforts, word-of-mouth between health care organizations, a couple of ads in the yellow pages, and past attendance at a few trade shows.

THE STM BUSINESS PLAN

In January 1990, in order to solicit investments from venture capitalists, Jerry developed a business plan that aimed to take advantage of STM's innovative PC-based systems for small hospitals. The plan sought $900,000 in new capital (two thirds in debt, one third in equity), which would support the hiring of

> ... a director of operations, who will relieve Mr. Budinoff's time for concentration on the key skill of systems design ... immediate expansion of the programming and system analyst staff ... a director of sales and marketing, who will hire the telemarketing and sales support staff ... and a chief financial officer. ...

The new funds would be used, the plan said, in approximately the following amounts:

Research and development	$350,000
Extra marketing expenses in 1990–91	440,000
Hiring of new professional staffs	110,000

STM's business plan projected growth to 74 employees by the end of 1993, with sales just over $10 million (see Exhibits 10–12). Jerry Budinoff commented on the opportunity:

> I never wanted to get financing before. I never understood the business side, or the huge need for capital. But we've been in the health care market for six years now, and I do know what that market needs and how to design for it. We've got a real lock on it. I am positive that if we get the financing this thing is going to go through the roof like a rocket ship. There is just no doubt in my mind. So I'm not worried about the financing; it will be paid back. We just need the $900,000; that's the difference between total expenses and total income in the first year of the plan.
>
> But we have to take the new inpatient hospital system into the market the right way, not just dribble it in. Because as soon as we get visibility and prove to the

EXHIBIT 10   **STM Technology's Estimated Profit and Loss Statement, 1990–1993**
(In thousands of dollars)

	1990	1991	1992	1993
Revenues				
Hospitals	$ 675	$2,425	$4,345	$ 7,100
Clinics	450	735	960	930
Tracking	45	200	300	400
Support	286	760	1,196	1,748
Total revenues	1,456	4,120	6,801	10,178
Less cost of sales/service	562	1,315	2,057	2,906
Gross profit	894	2,805	4,744	7,272
Operating expenses				
Product development	346	659	931	1,377
Marketing/sales	665	1,169	1,874	2,455
General and administrative	311	452	768	1,025
Total expenses	1,322	2,280	3,573	4,857
Operating profit	(428)	525	1,171	2,415
Nonoperating expense	27	63	66	45
Profit before tax	(455)	462	1,105	2,370
Taxes	0	0	400	950
Profit after tax	$ (455)	$ 462	$ 705	$ 1,420

Source: STM Technology, Inc., Corporate Business Plan, January 1990.

market that 386s and 286s can do the job, then one of the big companies will come in. When we break the idea barrier, they'll get going with their resources, and go right by us with marketing. We have maybe a year's lead, but if we don't get going we'll lose our real window.

Of the five hospitals with installed systems in 1990, two were in Massachusetts; one each was in Connecticut (at Yale University's infirmary), New Hampshire, and Maine. The business plan estimated the market as 3,000 small hospitals nationwide and 450 in New England. It targeted 235 installations in the next four years, representing a 12 percent market share nationwide.

The plan envisioned growth in STM's outpatient systems as well, based on selling the new "Robotic" integrated system to clinics throughout New England. Nineteen new sales in 1990 to Massachusetts facilities would bring that state's total to 143, representing 13 percent of its potential market. Twenty-six new sales were targeted for the six other New England states. For the first time in its history, a marketing campaign of mailings, trade journal advertising, and telemarketing would supplement the word-of-mouth networking that had so far carried STM.

The proposed marketing program began with direct sales by STM's own staff, expanding to branch offices in New York City and Tampa in 1991. California, Texas, Chicago, Denver, and St. Louis would follow in 1992. These remote sites would cultivate local vendors to provide hardware and

EXHIBIT 11   **STM Technology's Pro Forma Balance Sheet, 1990–1993**
(In thousands of dollars)

	December 31			
	1990	**1991**	**1992**	**1993**
Assets				
Current assets				
Cash	$140	$ 254	$ 325	$1,114
Accounts receivable—net	260	517	830	1,213
Inventory	11	29	41	53
Prepaid deposits	3	6	11	21
Total current assets	414	806	1,197	2,401
Fixed assets				
Equipment at cost	199	299	499	699
Reserve for depreciation	89	141	201	261
Net	110	158	298	438
Other assets				
Research and development	150	280	390	350
Miscellaneous	10	40	90	160
Total other assets	160	320	480	510
Total assets	$684	$1,284	$1,975	$3,349
Liabilities and Equity				
Current liabilities				
Accounts payable/accruals	$58	$96	$132	$186
Deferred taxes	7	7	57	157
Deferred revenues	126	226	326	426
Notes payable—current	0	100	100	—
Total current liabilities	191	429	615	769
Long-term notes				
New	500	400	200	0
Stockholders	48	48	48	48
Total liabilities	739	877	863	817
Equity				
Common stocks	304	304	304	304
Earned surplus	(359)	103	808	2,228
Total equity	(55)	407	1,112	2,532
Total liabilities and equity	$684	$1,284	$1,975	$3,349

Source: STM Technology, Inc., Corporate Business Plan, January 1990.

maintenance, and eventually distribution of STM software. New products—including some for diagnostics—would be sold through mail order and off-the-shelf through computer stores. By 1993, the plan called for marketing outside the continental United States. To support these efforts, a variety of new promotional tools had to be developed, including new product packaging, advertisements, news releases, brochures, an exhibit booth for trade shows, a sales kit, sales training materials, professional videotapes, and

EXHIBIT 12   **STM Technology's Estimated Cash Flow, 1990–1993**
(In thousands of dollars)

| | December | | | |
	1990	**1991**	**1992**	**1993**
Beginning balance	$ 79	$170	$254	$ 325
Cash in				
Profit and (loss)	(455)	462	705	1,420
Depreciation	30	52	60	60
Amortization	0	70	190	340
Accounts receivable decrease (increase)	(133)	(257)	(303)	(393)
Inventory decrease (increase)	(4)	(18)	(12)	(12)
Prepaid decrease (increase)	0	(3)	(5)	(10)
Research and development decrease (increase)	(150)	(200)	(300)	(300)
Loans/notes	500	100	0	0
Equity	300	0	0	0
Miscellaneous assets decrease (increase)	0	10	10	10
Total in	88	216	345	1,115
Total cash available	167	356	599	1,440
Cash outgo				
Accounts payable decrease (increase)	(33)	(38)	(36)	(54)
Taxes decrease (increase)	0	0	(50)	(100)
Deferred revenue decrease (increase)	(50)	(100)	(100)	(100)
Equipment purchases	100	100	200	200
Note repayment	0	100	200	300
Miscellaneous purchases . . .	10	40	60	80
Total out	27	102	274	326
Ending balance	$140	$254	$325	$1,114

Source: STM Technology, Inc., Corporate Business Plan, January 1990.

telemarketing scripts. The business plan put the cost of these marketing and sales tools at $260,000.

STM AND THE FUTURE

To Jerry, the new financing was absolutely critical. Without it, he saw little point in continuing development work on the hospital system at all. In May 1990 no new sales of the existing inpatient system were contemplated. The development work had to come first. Jerry commented:

I deeply believe in the philosophy I learned at DEC: don't try to force a product onto an unwilling market—let the market pull you in. Well, we were pulled into the hospital market, without knowing better. It is a very difficult system, and we might not have done it if we'd analyzed it first. We successfully automated what the hospitals were doing already. In the process, we have learned what the market really *wants*, and that would be a product that opens up the entire market.

But we ought to do it right. Without financial backing, we can't even begin to cope with that market. We would just make a little dent in it. I know how to "piecemeal" into these markets, and that's exactly what I *don't* want to do.

Budinoff and STM's two other equityholders were willing to relinquish 33 percent of the ownership for the $900,000 they sought. STM had already refused a $500,000 offer from one of its customers for 48 percent of the company. Jerry talked of his ideal investor:

Health care is a very parochial, localized market. And we've got an image problem because we're the little guy in the market and people worry about us going out of business. My criterion for capital is credibility. I want someone who can give us credibility and who can give us second and third rounds. Ideally I would like a large computer-based company such as an insurance company to back us. That way they would have an interest in us. They could turn to us for consulting help. I'd be more comfortable with that.

I suppose one of our options, though, if the financing didn't come through, would be to shift into "retirement mode"—stay small, and make a pile of money.

Evelyn Mittler, who had been quiet through much of the conversation, winced at this last suggestion. "Oh, no," she said. Jerry continued:

Yeah, we *could* stay at about $750,000 a year, with a gross profit of maybe $300K. There are lots of other people who need systems work done, outside of the business. It's a never-ending market. I get calls all the time; it's hilarious. I was down in Washington [Jerry served one week per month as reserve assistant division chief for the Air Force Arms Control and International Negotiations Division, designing computer systems to comply with the Strategic Arms Reduction Treaty], and they wanted to know how to automate a whole Pentagon division of operations. I'm no expert in that, but it doesn't matter to them. I've got the reputation, and that's it. So we *could* turn away from growth in the medical systems.

"But none of us wants to," said Evelyn.

We *could* cut back on the R&D, and reap profits for the business. But we're not interested in just going along at a steady size.

"That would be boring," said Evelyn.
Jerry Budinoff concluded:

I view the company as a vehicle—a resource base for the fabulous systems we'll develop next year and the year after that. That's what my core group of people like doing and we're very good at that. Now I have to get the company big enough to support what we come up with. I want to move it out of health care and into other markets too, eventually. In six years I would like us to be a $20–30 million company.

REFERENCES

American Hospital Association. "1989 AHA Guide to the Health Care Field." Chicago, Ill.

Eberstadt Fleming, Inc. "The PC Software Industry." August 3, 1988, p. 5. (Found in CIRR Index, 1989.)

Fuller, Jerry E. "The HMO Industry." Duff & Phelps, Inc., December, 1987.

Keithly, Joyce, et al. "The Cost Effectiveness of Same-Day Admission Surgery." *Nursing Economics* 7, no. 2 (March–April 1989),

Standard & Poor's Industry Surveys, *Health Care*, July 13, 1989.

COMPETITION IN OUTDOOR POWER EQUIPMENT: BRIGGS & STRATTON VERSUS HONDA*

Richard C. Hoffman, University of Delaware

In early 1984 Briggs & Stratton President and Chief Executive Officer Frederick P. Stratton told the company's shareholders:

> The most significant development in our industry in recent years has been the increased activity of Japanese manufacturers. The strength of the U.S. dollar . . . combined with the perennial artificial weakness of the Japanese yen has given Japanese manufacturers an unearned price advantage. Their [Japanese] stated interest in engine-powered equipment and the continued strengths of the dollar and weakness of the yen make them a continuing threat.

Briggs & Stratton had long been the industry leader in manufacturing small gasoline engines for such outdoor power equipment as lawn mowers, rotary tillers, snow throwers, and lawn vacuums (see Exhibit 1). Now Honda, the largest Japanese manufacturer of small engines, was in the process of challenging Briggs & Stratton's leadership position in the U.S. market.

COMPANY HISTORY

Briggs & Stratton (B&S) began conducting business in Milwaukee in 1908. The company's first product was a six-cylinder, two-cycle engine that Stephen F. Briggs had developed during his engineering courses at South Dakota State College. After he graduated in 1907 he was eager to produce his engine and enter the rapidly expanding automobile industry. Through a mutual friend, Briggs, the inventor, met Harold M. Stratton, the successful businessman. With that introduction, the Briggs & Stratton Corporation was born. Unfortunately, the engine cost too much to produce as did their second product, an automobile called the Superior. The partners were soon out of money and out of the automobile assembly business.

However, they were not out of the automobile industry. In 1909 Briggs filed a patent for a gas engine igniter to replace the existing magneto ignition system in automobiles. This product set the stage for the company to later become the largest U.S. producer of switch and lock apparatuses used in automobiles. By 1920 the company was widely recognized as a major producer of electrical specialties.

In 1920 Briggs & Stratton acquired the patents and manufacturing rights to the Smith motor wheel and the Flyer, a buckboard-like motor vehicle powered by the Smith motor wheel. The Smith motor wheel was a wheel with a small engine attached for propulsion. It could also be used on bicycles. The price for the two-passenger Flyer was $150, but it still could not compete with Ford's

---

*Prepared with the assistance of graduate researchers John Couch and David Monti, School of Business Administration, College of William and Mary.

EXHIBIT 1   **Outdoor Power Equipment Products**

Lawn mowers	Lawn edger-trimmers
Garden tractors	Shredder-grinders
Rotary tillers	Lawn vacuums
Snow throwers	Leaf blowers

Source: "Facts about OPEI."

Model T. The Model T was higher priced but was technologically more advanced.

As sales of the motor wheel slowed, the company found that a stationary version, the model PB, provided a good power source for washing machines, garden tractors, and lawn mowers. By 1936 engines were being mass-produced at the rate of 120 units per hour. During World War II, Briggs & Stratton produced bomb fuses and aircraft ignitions.

After the war, Briggs & Stratton set out to capture a larger share of the growing lawn and garden equipment market. Recognizing the lawn mower market as a potential growth area, the company set out to make a lighter weight, low-cost engine. Briggs developed and introduced the aluminum alloy engine in 1953, which achieved both a 40 percent weight and price reduction. The aluminum engine was a huge success, with initial demand outstripping supply. In response to demand, the company opened a new engine plant in Wauwatosa, Wisconsin, on an 85-acre site.

In November 1975, some 56 years after the motor wheel opened the way into the small engine business, the 100 millionth Briggs & Stratton engine came off the assembly line. In 1983 B&S ranked 392nd in sales and 75th in ROI on the *Fortune* 500 list of the largest U.S. industrial corporations. Over 90 percent of the company's revenues came from the sale of small gasoline-powered engines.

OUTDOOR POWER EQUIPMENT INDUSTRY

In 1984 the outdoor power equipment (OPE) industry was a divergent group of various-sized manufacturers of finished goods, attachments, and components. Composed of 87 major manufacturers located in 31 states, the industry produced over 8 million pieces of equipment having an annual retail value of over $3 billion. Seven companies produced some 65 percent of the output of four key products: rotary lawn mowers, riding mowers, lawn tractors, and tillers. Six companies produced 70 percent of the walk-behind power mowers.

Approximately 75 percent of lawn mower purchases were for replacement demand, and 25 percent were first-time purchases. First-time purchases closely tracked the number of new single-family housing starts. In 1983 1.61 million new single and multiple dwellings were constructed; forecasts called for new housing starts in 1984 and 1985 of 1.74 million and 1.59 million, respectively. The number of housing starts was highly dependent on interest rates. Most lawn mowers had a life of six to eight years, making replacement demand dependent on housing starts and related demographics.

Industry Trends

The power equipment industry had been consolidating since 1974. The number of manufacturers had declined from 145 competitors in 1974 (about half of which were power mower manufacturers) to under 90 in 1984. The 10 largest companies in 1984 accounted for nearly 70 percent of total production.

In 1983 power equipment manufacturers employed 13,000 people, with component manufacturing affiliates adding some 22,000–27,000 more jobs. An additional 45,000 people worked for distributors and suppliers. More than 50 percent of the industry's workers were union members. A total of 33 manufacturing plants existed nationwide. In recent years most new plant openings had been in the South and Southwest where unions were not as strong.

Outdoor power equipment manufacturing was not vertically integrated to any significant extent. Industry members manufactured components, attachments, or finished goods (see Exhibit 2). Component manufacturers comprised 30 percent of the industry and produced one or more of the following: engines, transmissions, gear assemblies, and other parts for use in fully assembled outdoor power equipment. Attachment manufacturers produced optional equipment that could be used with the power equipment to supplement its basic operation or to add new capabilities such as lawn dethatching, leaf or snow blowing, and garden tilling. The finished goods manufacturers produced consumer end-use products such as lawn mowers, tillers, and tractors. Lawn-Boy was the only finished goods manufacturer that had vertically integrated backward into the manufacture of major components, particularly engines, in producing its outdoor power equipment. All other domestic power equipment manufacturers had chosen not to integrate backward to any significant degree, opting instead to assemble their products from parts supplied by the components and attachments manufacturers. The assemblers of power equipment did do some of their own metal fabrication such as producing the frame and housing for lawn mowers.

Largely because the power equipment manufacturers had not engaged in much backward integration, the industry was a big purchaser of basic raw materials (see Exhibit 3). In 1974 purchases of both materials and components were $720 million, with raw materials amounting to $200 million; engines, $360 million; and components, $160 million. By 1983 purchases were $712 million, equal to 54 percent of total finished goods sales.

Distribution in the industry was fragmented among independent, factory-direct, and company-owned distributors. Independent distributors handled 48 percent of total manufacturing output, with factory-direct sales accounting for 35 percent of manufacturers' sales. At the retail level, sales through national department stores comprised 22 percent of total sales, whereas hardware stores, farm equipment dealers, and home improvement and building suppliers handled 35 percent of total retail sales. The remaining sales were through lawn mower stores (17 percent), discount department stores (8 percent), and other types of retail outlets (18 percent).

In 1983 outdoor power equipment manufacturers spent $60 million on advertising and promotion, $35 million on R&D, $11 million on new product development, and $67 million for new facilities and equipment. During the 1970s sales in the industry had grown rapidly, and many companies prospered. Shipments of walk-behind rotary lawn mowers had peaked at 5.7

EXHIBIT 2   **Selected U.S. Outdoor Power Equipment Manufacturers**
              (Sales in millions of dollars)

Company	1983 Sales	Main Product(s)
Ariens Corp.	N/A	Finished goods*
Auburn Consolidated Industries	$ 4	Attachments
Bolens Corp.	55	Finished goods
Briggs & Stratton Corp.	572	Engines
Brinly-Hardy Co.	20	Attachments
Engineering Products Co.	12	Attachments
Excel Industries, Inc.	20	Attachments
J. B. Foote Foundry Co.	14	Finished goods
Jacobsen/Homelite (division of Textron)	372	Finished goods
John Deere & Co.	400[†]	Finished goods
Kohler Co.	N/A	Engines
Lawn-Boy (division of Outdoor Marine)	129	Finished goods
Magna American Corp.	$ 9	Finished goods
MTD Products Co.	400[†]	Finished goods
Murray Ohio Mfg. Co.	386	Finished goods
Roper Corporation	256	Finished goods
Snapper (division of Fuqua Industries)	190	Finished goods
Southland Mower Co., Inc.	26	Finished goods
Tecumseh Products Co.	232	Engines
Teledyne Wisconsin Motor Co.	N/A	Engines
Toro Company, Inc.	241	Finished goods
Wheel Horse Products, Inc.	78[†]	Finished goods
Yazoo Mfg. Co., Inc.	19	Finished goods

N/A = not available (usually because firm was privately held).

* Mowers, tractors, tillers, and so forth.

[†] Estimate.

EXHIBIT 3   **Raw Materials Purchased from Suppliers by the Outdoor
              Power Equipment Industry**   *(In millions)*

Material	1983 Amount	1983 Percent of Total	1974 Amount	1974 Percent of Total
Steel	$186	52%	$123	61%
Cartons	18	5	31	15
Aluminum	39	11	16	8
Plastics	72	21	8	4
Magnesium	2	1	10	5
Paint	8	2	6	3
Other	26	8	6	4
Total	$351	100%	$200	100%

Source: *Profile of the Consumer Outdoor Power Equipment Industry,* 1984.

EXHIBIT 4 Shipments of Outdoor Power Equipment, 1980–1983, with Forecasts for 1984–1989 *(Units in thousands and dollars in millions)*

| Year | Walk-Behind | | | Riding | | |
	Rotary Mowers	Rotary Tillers	Snow Throwers	Rear-Engine Mowers	Front-Engine Mowers	Garden Tractors
1980:						
Units	5,700	667	1,577	314	494	220
Dollar value*	$701	$159	$397	$185	$345	$351
1981:						
Units	4,600	501	345	250	370	151
Dollar value*	$606	$138	$98	$162	$291	$266
1982:						
Units	4,600	497	95	261	393	146
Dollar value*	$674	$143	$27	$190	$359	$280
1983:						
Units	4,400	408	264	276	415	129
Dollar value*	$695	$132	$91	$205	$395	$275
Near-term forecasts:						
1984:						
Units	5,000	416	340	314	467	151
Dollar value*	$750	$205	$120	$246	$448	$309
1985:						
Units	5,015	430	258	322	479	153
Dollar value*	$617	$215	$88	$260	$467	$315

Extended Forecasts (Units only)	Walk-Behind Mowers and Tillers	Riding Units
1986	5,700	945
1987	5,500	900
1988	5,700	920
1989	5,900	1,000

* F.O.B. factory shipment value. Not available for extended forecast.

million units in 1980 and then tumbled to 4.4 million by 1983. Much of this decline in sales was caused by a recession and a drop-off in housing starts. Industry shipments are presented in Exhibit 4.

Foreign Exports and Imports

In 1974 U.S. exports amounted to $85 million, with imports amounting to a meager $2 million. By 1983 exports were $52 million, and imports into the United States were $30 million. In 1981 exports accounted for 8 percent of total shipments. This number was expected to decline to 3 percent by 1985. Industry experts believed that exports and imports were closely tied to exchange

EXHIBIT 5   **Exchange Rates for Canadian Dollars and Japanese Yen per U.S. Dollar, 1979–1983**

	1979	1980	1981	1982	1983
Canadian dollars per $	1.16	1.17	1.19	1.23	1.23
Japanese yen per $	219	227	221	249	237

Source: "International Statistics," *Federal Reserve Bulletin*, August 1985.

rates. Exports went mainly to Canada, while Japan accounted for over 70 percent of the imports to the United States in 1983. Exchange rates from 1979 to 1983 are displayed in Exhibit 5.

Industry Regulation

Prior to 1982 manufacturers of OPE were not regulated by the Consumer Product Safety Commission (CPSC); compliance was voluntary. Voluntary standards were promulgated by the American National Standards Institute and had been supported by the industry trade association since the mid-1950s. The standards were primarily concerned with improved product performance and safety. Safety standards involved both the protection from thrown objects and noise level. About 90 percent of the industry's products were in compliance with these voluntary standards. Products complying with the standards were affixed with a triangular seal.

Since 1973 the industry had been working with the CPSC for mandatory power mower safety standards. At that time, mowers ranked third on the commission's most hazardous products list. Improvements in voluntary standards had reduced mowers to 20th place on the hazardous products list by the end of the decade.

However, in 1982 a number of new CPSC regulations were put into effect calling for increased safety restrictions for walk-behind power mowers, including performance and labeling requirements. The standards included the use of shields to protect people from thrown objects, deflectors and drain holes to prevent fuel ignition, and the deadman blade control system. Mowers built after July 1, 1982, had to have blades that stopped within 3 seconds after the operator released a deadman control at the handle of the mower. Meeting this standard involved either installing a blade brake or the addition of a rechargeable, battery-powered electric starter. Both of these alternatives were very expensive. The CPSC estimated that the cost of compliance would be approximately $35 per unit.

By 1981 many companies, including Briggs & Stratton, had successfully developed the technology to make manual starting of engines much easier. The lawn mower industry asked Congress to amend the safety standard to allow engine stop with manual restart as a third method of compliance with the blade control requirement. President Reagan signed the amendment despite the CPSC's strong opposition.

The industry also had to comply with the Magnuson-Moss Act of 1975 requiring that all products with a written warranty, and costing the consumer $15 or more, come with either a statement concerning the duration of the warranty or a limited warranty. The industry also had to comply with an assortment of state and local regulations concerning noise and pollution levels for outdoor power equipment. In 1983 OPE product liability expenses amounted to $21 million ($18 million on warranty claims plus $3 million on insurance premiums).

The Outdoor Power Equipment Institute (OPEI)

The trade association for outdoor power equipment was the Outdoor Power Equipment Institute (OPEI). OPEI's membership represented over 90 percent of the industry's annual volume. Founded in 1952 as a nonprofit organization, the OPEI represented the outdoor power equipment industry before governmental bodies on the state and national level. OPEI compiled industry statistics for its members and was active in promoting safety of equipment through voluntary industry activities and in conjunction with the federal government. The institute also monitored tariff and freight rates to reduce shipping costs for the industry's products.

In recent years OPEI had worked closely to help develop international safety standards for power mowers. Recently, OPEI had confronted whether foreign importers should be allowed membership. Foreign manufacturers with plants in the United States were automatically admitted. Several U.S. manufacturers did not want to admit foreign importers, but OPEI's executive director felt that one good way of learning what foreign competitors were doing was by admitting them as members.

Competition: Domestic

Competition within the industry occurred mainly within two broad strategic groups—finished goods producers and components producers. The finished goods manufacturers, which represented the largest group of competitors, could be further subdivided by market segment. The major producers of premium-priced lawn mowers included Lawn-Boy, Toro, Snapper, Jacobsen, and Deere and Co. MTD Products, Murray, and Roper Corporation were the chief producers of outdoor power equipment for the medium-priced and discount markets; they were also the major suppliers of equipment for the private-label segment of the market.

Lawn-Boy, a subsidiary of Outboard Marine Corporation, achieved sales of $128.9 million and earnings of $11.1 million in 1983. By designing and making all the components needed to assemble its final products, Lawn-Boy was able to give its products a distinctive integrated look (that is, its engines didn't look bolted on). This was appealing to some consumers in the premium-priced segment. Lawn-Boy was the only leading U.S. brand-name manufacturer to produce its own engines. All of its engines were of two-cycle design (meaning that they ran on a mixture of gasoline and oil) while the other major engine manufacturers in the industry produced four-cycle engines (engines running on gasoline only).

The largest assembler of finished goods for the premium-priced segment was the Toro Company, Inc., headquartered in Minneapolis. Toro sold $241 million of OPE in 1983. Toro was also the leading manufacturer of snow-throwing equipment.

The Snapper Division of Fuqua Industries was also a major producer of OPE in 1983 and competed in the premium-priced market. Snapper marketed a full line of lawn mowers, tillers, and snow blowers. The division sold $190 million of OPE in 1983 and accounted for 26 percent of Fuqua's total sales.

The Jacobsen/Homelite Division of Textron, Inc., also produced high-quality lawn mowers, power appliances, and chain saws. In 1983 this division had sales totaling $372 million, a significant portion of which involved chain saws (which used two-cycle engines).

Deere and Company was the remaining leading producer of premium-priced OPE products. Its OPE sales in 1983 amounted to $400 million, but a significant portion of this figure was for farm and industrial equipment. In recent years, Deere, Toro, and Snapper had chosen B&S engines to power their mowers.

MTD Products, Inc., of Valley City, Ohio, was closely held and had estimated annual sales of about $400 million. MTD bought its engines from Briggs & Stratton, manufactured its own OPE frames and bodies, and assembled the units for sale. MTD sold to private-label distributors and marketed nationally under the brand name Yardman. MTD was the nation's largest producer of walk-behind lawn mowers and competed in the lower-priced end of the market.

Roper Corporation was the nation's second largest producer of lawn mowers with total OPE sales in 1983 of $256 million. Seventy-three percent of Roper's 1983 output was purchased by Sears and sold under the Sears Craftsman label. Roper was also a private-label supplier to other discount chains. Roper primarily used Tecumseh engines on its equipment.

The Murray Ohio Manufacturing Co., located in Brentwood, Tennessee, was a major producer of both OPE and bicycles for the medium-priced and discount segments. Total corporate sales amounted to $386 million in 1983. The company sold mowers under its own Murray brand and also supplied a variety of private-label retailers.

The major cost component of lawn mowers was the engine. The four largest producers of mower engines were Briggs & Stratton, Tecumseh Products, Kohler, and Teledyne Wisconsin. Tecumseh posed the only real domestic competitive threat to Briggs & Stratton; its strongest product category was air-cooled aluminum alloy engines ranging from 2 to 18 horsepower. Tecumseh Products was the largest U.S. producer of refrigerator compressors and the second largest producer of small, gasoline-powered engines. The company also produced gear assemblies and related transmission parts. In 1983 Tecumseh's net income from engine sales was $41 million. Eleven percent of its total sales and 39 percent of its engine output went to Sears or suppliers to Sears such as Roper. Tecumseh's next three engine customers bought only 6.3 percent, 5.7 percent, and 5.6 percent of the company's total volume, respectively. Exhibit 2 lists some of the key industry competitors and their sales.

Competition: Foreign

Japan was the primary source of imported OPE products into the United States, and in 1983 Japanese products made up 76 percent of the total value of OPE goods imported into the United States. Most foreign imports of OPE products into the United States were garden tractors and rotary walk-behind lawn mowers. Garden tractors were imported as agricultural machinery and were exempted from paying U.S. tariffs. The three leading import brands of garden tractors were all Japanese: Kubota, Yanmar, and Satoh. The leading Japanese importers of riding and walk-behind lawn mowers were Honda, Kawasaki, Suzuki, and Yamaha, all of whom also produced motorcycles for the U.S. market.

In lawn mowers, Honda was the only foreign brand considered to be a factor in the U.S. market. Japanese competition was not a new problem for the industry, but it had become much more severe since the early 1980s. Japanese firms manufactured both engines and finished products. The value of Japanese imports of lawn mowers and parts increased from less than $3 million in 1978 to $22.7 million in 1983. This increase in Japanese competition was attributed to the extraordinary strength of the dollar against the yen and the worldwide weakness of the motorcycle business.

Global recession in general and the softening of the motorcycle business in particular had forced Japanese motorcycle manufacturers to look to other product markets in order to maintain full use of their production facilities. All four Japanese motorcycle manufacturers (Honda, Kawasaki, Suzuki, and Yamaha) had identified power products as appropriate new business opportunities. Honda had stated publicly that it intended to become a leader in the powered products field and had transferred resources from its motorcycle division to its powered products division. Honda had achieved the greatest penetration in the United States. Its small engine production was about 1.3 million units in 1982. Honda also expanded capacity in that year, giving the firm a combined capacity of over 4 million units per year. The company sold its mowers through established OPE distributors and not its own auto or motorcycle dealers.

Although Honda sold small gasoline-powered engines, it preferred to sell finished goods. The company marketed a broad line of outdoor power equipment including garden tillers, snow throwers, walk-behind power mowers, and lawn tractors. This product line represented approximately 6 percent of total sales. Honda and other Japanese manufacturers were also strong OPE competitors in other parts of the world.

Honda's strategy in the OPE industry focused on the high-priced segment as a manufacturer of finished goods for the consumer market. Similar to Lawn-Boy, it manufactured both the lawn mower engine and body, which resulted in equipment having an integrated look. Honda engines were noted for being lightweight and dependable. Professional users of OPE had casually dubbed Honda's engines "Briggs-Hondas" because of their dependability. They often replaced worn-out Briggs & Stratton engines with new Honda engines on still-serviceable used equipment. Honda's product strength was based on heavy R&D expenditures. Honda marketed its products by making extensive use of advertising and promotion. It also priced its products competitively, setting prices below rivals in order to gain market share. Honda had been

E X H I B I T 6   **Selected Financial and Statistical Data for Honda Motor Co.**
(*In thousands*)

	For Years Ended February 28			
	1983	**1982**	**1981**	**1980**
Sales	$8,771,902	$8,254,192	$7,545,423	$5,703,204
Net income	289,215	292,297	422,151	122,986
Assets	5,558,243	4,940,944	4,655,544	3,546,191
Stockholders' equity	2,020,151	1,607,435	1,608,444	894,576
Number of employees	46,238	42,415	38,481	33,405

Compiled from: "The International 500," *Fortune.*

extremely successful in both the U.S. motorcycle and automobile markets using similar strategies and possessed extensive resources to support its strategy in the OPE market (see Exhibit 6). The company had considerable expertise in gasoline engine technology and produced a wide line of products incorporating gasoline engines: automobiles and trucks, motorcycles, power generators, snowmobiles, outboard motors, garden tillers, pumps, snow throwers, and lawn tractors, as well as lawn mowers.

In 1983 Honda sold approximately 10,000 high-priced lawn mowers in the United States. Honda also sold replacement engines compatible with many makes of mowers. Until 1983 Honda lawn mowers bound for the United States had been manufactured in Japan. Apparently satisfied that it could gain significant market share, Honda decided, in August 1983, to build a manufacturing plant for lawn mowers in Alamance County, North Carolina. Honda planned to produce 10,000 units in the first year and employ 80 workers. The engines would still be produced at the Hamamatsu plant in Japan. Labor costs in Japan were, on average, 30 percent lower than in the United States and 50 percent lower than at Briggs & Stratton. Labor costs were typically around 40 percent of the total cost of outdoor power equipment.

Honda's products had been well received in the United States, getting excellent ratings from consumer magazines. Comparisons with domestic models revealed that there were no disadvantages associated with Honda mowers themselves. The few disadvantages had to do with distribution, parts, and service. Honda mowers received high marks for convenience, performance, and safety. The starting controls were simple, easy to reach, and had an automatic choke that eliminated the need for a choke control on the throttle. The cutting performance of Honda mowers was usually rated excellent; they provided a level cut, even in tall heavy grass, and efficiently bagged clippings. Honda's mowers met or exceeded safety standards including a deadman clutch that stopped the blade one second after the control was released, well within the three-second requirement. In 1983 Honda had an estimated 1 percent of the U.S. walk-behind lawn mower market.

Other Japanese manufacturers were actively calling on B&S's OEM customers. By the end of 1983 Toro and John Deere had switched from B&S to Suzuki and Kawasaki engines, respectively, for their consumer walk-behind lawn mowers.

EXHIBIT 7   **Briggs & Stratton Sales of OEM and Air-Cooled Engines by End Use, 1978-1983**

End Uses	Engine Sales as a Percent of Total B&S Revenues					
	1978	1979	1980	1981	1982	1983
Lawn and garden equipment	77%	80%	84%	83%	85%	88%
Industrial, agricultural	23	20	16	17	15	12
All exports	20	23	26	23	21	16
Total engine sales as a % of total B&S revenues	91%	91%	94%	93%	94%	93%

Source: Company annual reports.

In February 1983 Frederick Stratton said in an interview with *Business Week*, "The real battle over the next five years is with the Japanese. I hate to admit it, but Japan has set a new standard of quality."

THE BRIGGS & STRATTON CORPORATION

Briggs & Stratton (B&S), headquartered in Wauwatosa, Wisconsin, was the world's largest producer of small, gas-powered engines used primarily for outdoor power equipment. The company operated in a mature market with growth averaging 2 percent per year. B&S had an estimated 70 to 80 percent share of the small engine market in the United States and over 50 percent of the worldwide market in 1983. Engines and parts accounted for 93 percent of Briggs's total revenues in 1983 (see Exhibit 7). The other 7 percent was from the sale of automotive lock and key sets. B&S was the largest producer of automobile ignition systems and door and trunk locks in the United States with over a 90 percent market share. B&S sales are summarized in Exhibit 7.

Briggs's number one customer for small engines was MTD, which bought about 10 percent of B&S's total output in 1983. Toro also used B&S engines on some of its mowers. Kendrik B. Melrose, president of Toro, referred to B&S as "The General Motors of the small lawn mower engine business." Snapper was another heavy user of B&S engines.

In 1980 export sales were a record 26 percent of Briggs & Stratton's engine sales; in June close to half of the company's engine shipments were to customers outside of North America. Foreign customers received longer payment terms than domestic customers in recognition of longer shipping times. In addition, many of B&S's domestic customers exported products powered by B&S engines. B&S estimated that 30 percent of its total engine business was derived from markets outside the United States. Frederick P. Stratton, the company's CEO, observed:

> The markets for products powered by our engines is increasingly international. The flow of material around the world is truly amazing. For example, we know of cases where engines we ship to customers in Australia are mounted on equipment destined for Europe, and engines we ship to customers in Europe are mounted on equipment destined for the United States.

In 1981 B&S's engine sales declined 31 percent, the largest year-to-year percentage decline since 1932. Because of the slow demand and dry weather, B&S customers' inventories were at a high level. By late December, when the prime rate reached 21 percent, most B&S customers had made inventory reduction a major objective.

In March 1982 B&S made its first shipments from a new distribution center in Lambertheim, West Germany. This new facility was the stocking point for service parts and replacement engines bound for central service distributors in Europe. Later the same year B&S opened a sales office in Manila, Philippines, to promote sales and service to lesser-developed nations in the Pacific Basin. These nations primarily used larger cast-iron engines for agriculture, marine, and industrial use. During 1983 B&S again expanded its sales network to developed countries having markets for lawn and garden equipment by opening sales offices in Oslo, Norway, and Auckland, New Zealand.

Economic conditions in export markets remained depressed in 1983, and the continued strength of the dollar made B&S prices less competitive in those markets. Export sales fell to the lowest level in 10 years.

Products

B&S made a wide line of engines. All were 4-cycle engines that ran on straight gas (not mixed with oil). More than 95 percent of the engines sold by B&S were air-cooled, aluminum alloy gasoline engines ranging from 2 to 18 horsepower. Less than 5 percent of the engines were the air-cooled, cast-iron variety ranging from 9 to 16 horsepower. B&S also produced air- and water-cooled diesel engines ranging from 3 to 28.5 horsepower. Walk-behind power mowers generally had a 3 to 4 horsepower engine. B&S engines were of high quality and had many innovative features. Some of B&S's successful innovations are listed in Exhibit 8.

B&S emphasized continuing product improvements. In addition to the introduction of electronic ignition in 1982 (see Exhibit 8), the company had, in recent years, designed new features to reduce noise levels such as better mufflers and synchro-balanced engines. In 1983 the company introduced a small electric engine for use on lawn and garden equipment. The new 120 volt, 1,000 watt motor was quiet, light (11 pounds), had a 10-year life, and met the government's standards for deadman blade control.

B&S's major form of distribution was through contractual arrangements with finished goods manufacturers, which were generally negotiated on a yearly basis. Contracts with finished goods manufacturers of lawn mowers accounted for 75 percent of B&S's sales.

Marketing and Promotion

Traditionally B&S sold engines directly to finished goods manufacturers. B&S engines were functional and did not have fancy decals or paint jobs. B&S relied heavily on its quality image and reputation to gain sales. B&S was well known among older consumers, many of whom were accustomed to seeing B&S engines on their equipment. Younger consumers, many of whom were starting to buy their first homes, were not as familiar with the Briggs & Stratton name.

E X H I B I T 8   **Small-Engine Innovations Developed by Briggs & Stratton**

1953:	Aluminum alloy gasoline engine: Reduced weight and cost of small engines.
1961:	Easy spin starting: Engine starting effort cut in half by a simple cam-controlled, fault-proof compression release.
1962:	Oil foam air cleaner: Dirt banned from the engine for its life by an easy-to-clean polyurethane foam filter.
1966:	Synchro balance design: Engine and riding equipment vibrations smoothed out by a synchronized counterweight system.
1968:	Automatic vacuum controlled choke: Replaced manual choke, providing extra power when needed for heavy loads.
1971:	12-volt gear-type starter with dual circuit alternator: Provided for quick starting at low temperatures. Alternator provided both D/C battery charging and A/C for lights or external loads.
1977:	Quiet power: The 16 HP twin-cylinder engine prompted by the noise abatement guidelines provided quiet running and low vibration levels.
1982:	Magnetron ignition: A self-contained transistor with no moving parts. Provided more consistent spark for dependable starting. Could be installed on existing engines.
1983:	The electric engine was introduced for power mowers.

Source: Compiled from company pamphlets.

B&S had recently put together a six-member marketing staff. One of its roles was to market engines to end-use consumers and retailers. B&S wanted consumers to ask for their engines by name when buying a lawn mower. In 1983 the company began a television advertising campaign for the first time. The campaign slogan was "Briggs & Stratton: the power in power equipment." The commercial employed trick photography to show B&S engines floating above invisible tillers and lawn mowers, emphasizing the fact that B&S engines were responsible for providing the power. The company quadrupled its 1982 advertising expenditures, spending $4 million in 1983. Company engineers had also taken steps to improve the appearance of B&S engines.

B&S assured service for its engines (even though they became components of other manufacturer's products) via a network of over 25,000 authorized service centers worldwide. To shore up relations with its OEM customers, B&S assured them that it would not enter the end-use product market and compete with them. No customer enjoyed a special price.

Production

Briggs & Stratton manufactured almost all of the components used in assembling its engines except for piston rings, spark plugs, and valves. All gasoline engine manufacturing facilities were located in the Milwaukee area; diesel engines were manufactured in the company-owned plant in West Germany. During 1983, 20 percent of each revenue dollar went for direct materials, 48 percent for wages and benefits, 5 percent for taxes, 8 percent for new machinery, and 8 percent for all other expenses; profit margins on sales were 5 percent. The compounded growth rate in net plant investment over the last 10 years was 13 percent. Production was highly seasonal and was heaviest from

December to March. B&S manufactured engines to individual customer specifications and, as a result, did not build finished goods for its own inventory. To try to even out seasonal demand, B&S offered incentive discounts to customers who would accept delivery in the off season; however, payment terms on these orders were very short. Growth in year-end order backlogs had averaged 13 percent over the last five years.

Labor costs represented the largest proportion of the total cost of a B&S mower engine in 1983. Company wages and benefits in Wisconsin averaged $17.70 per hour, higher than both domestic and foreign competitors. Growth in the number of employees had been nearly zero for the past 10 years. In an effort to hold down labor costs, the company in 1983 proposed a three-year wage freeze and work rule concessions in return for a profit-sharing plan and an improved pension. Local 232 of the Allied Industrial Workers' Union (AIW) rejected the proposal, and over 7,000 employees went on strike when their labor contract expired on August 1, 1983. The strike occurred during the slowest point in the production season but, nonetheless, caused concern from customers about the dependability of their supplies. The AIW agreed three months later to a new contract that did not reduce labor costs for B&S but did reduce the rate of increase of such costs in the future.

The ready acceptance of Japanese products by American consumers had created new production challenges for B&S. The company had committed large capital expenditures to new technologies such as robotics. Over $20 million was scheduled to be spent on cost-reducing machinery in 1984. This figure was expected to double in 1985.

Improved production management techniques were implemented in 1983 and included installation of materials requirement planning (MRP), an inventory reduction program (EOQ), and statistical process control. The purpose of the MRP system was to provide the correct parts in the right quantities when they were needed in the manufacturing process. This system took advantage of information stored in a computer for timely response and scheduling. The goal of the new inventory reduction program was to cut inventory in half with no loss of response to customer needs. Quality centers were being created to ensure a constant flow of ideas from the bottom up on how to improve inventory and other production management activities.

The statistical process control system was intended to provide detection of any trend toward making bad parts before such parts were even produced. On a regular basis, sample parts were taken from inventory and measured in terms of allowable tolerances, and the average measure for each sample was plotted on a chart. Should the measures fall outside of accepted limits, corrective action would be taken immediately. Management believed the system would produce two benefits: (1) the elimination of shipments of poorly made products and (2) a reduction in safety stock held by the firm.

Finance

Briggs & Stratton reported declining earnings and sales in fiscal 1983. Growth in sales for the last five years was almost zero (0.9 percent). Sales of most types of OPE in 1983 were flat or declining. However, the market for automobile locks was quite strong; B&S was gaining a larger share of the market by becoming the exclusive supplier to GM. Despite the poor sales and earnings, the company raised the yearly dividend to $1.58 from $1.54; B&S tried to maintain a constant dividend payout ratio of 50 percent of earnings to shareholders. However, in low-profit years, dividends were not reduced to meet the 50 percent payout target.

B&S was continuing its long-standing policy of financing capital expenditures entirely out of retained earnings. The company had no long-term debt. The *Value Line* survey gave B&S its highest rating of A+ for its financial strength. B&S's financial statements are presented in Exhibits 9–11.

Outlook

Frederick Stratton commented on the challenge from Honda: "We are determined to build customer awareness of our product and maintain our leadership position. We are not going to let the Japanese take this market from us." Some skeptics doubted that a component manufacturer could effectively advertise directly to a consumer. But Stratton argued that the company's advertising, combined with its clean balance sheet, modern plant, and new product commitment, would carry the day.

EXHIBIT 9 **Briggs & Stratton's Performance by Business Segment, 1980–1983** *(In thousands)*

	Year Ending June 30			
	1983	**1982**	**1981**	**1980**
Sales:				
Engines and parts	$571,736	$597,669	$527,954	$669,305
Locks	42,071	37,997	41,032	39,257
Total	$613,807	$635,666	$568,986	$708,562
Operating income:				
Engines and parts	$ 52,447	$ 66,566	$ 38,623	$85,375
Locks	1,875	574	646	1,903
Total	$ 54,233	$ 67,140	$ 39,269	$ 87,278
Assets:				
Engines and parts	$298,463	$271,454	$253,835	$281,491
Locks	33,445	24,518	25,798	30,007
Unallocated	55,872	70,684	53,534	29,986
Total	$387,780	$366,656	$333,167	$341,484
Depreciation expense:				
Engines and parts	$ 14,537	$ 13,074	$ 11,645	$ 9,866
Locks	1,189	964	896	818
Total	$ 15,726	$ 14,038	$ 12,541	$ 10,684
Expenditures for plant and equipment:				
Engines and parts	$ 31,037	$ 20,089	$ 26,094	$ 52,443
Locks	1,073	1,186	2,478	2,672
Total	$ 32,110	$ 21,275	$ 28,572	$ 55,115

Source: Company annual reports.

EXHIBIT 10   **Briggs & Stratton's Sales, Earnings, and Statistical Data, 1974–1983**   *(In thousands of dollars except per share data)*

For the Years Ended June 30

	1983	1982	1981	1980	1979	1978	1977	1976	1975	1974
Summary of operations:										
Net sales	$613,807	$635,666	$568,986	$708,562	$590,964	$456,960	$388,852	$326,959	$316,286	$317,852
Gross profit on sales*	97,491	105,295	77,533	126,771	118,838	96,501	86,389	72,024	51,439	65,801
Provision for income taxes	27,020	34,250	19,470	42,370	44,770	36,570	32,140	26,690	17,050	26,630
Net income*	31,762	39,353	23,495	49,098	48,455	37,466	33,360	27,572	18,269	25,873
Average number of shares of common stock outstanding (in thousands)†	14,464	14,464	14,464	14,464	14,464	14,464	14,464	14,464	14,464	14,464
Per share of common stock:†										
Net income	$ 2.20	$ 2.70	$ 1.62	3.39	3.35	2.59	2.31	$ 1.91	1.26	$ 1.79
Cash dividends	1.58	1.54	1.52	1.46	1.35	1.22	1.12	.93	.80	.88
Shareholders' investment	18.05	17.44	16.31	16.17	14.24	12.24	10.87	9.68	8.70	8.24
Other data:										
Shareholders' investment	$261,054	$252,240	$235,923	$233,915	$205,934	$177,005	$157,185	$140,025	$125,832	$119,134
Total assets	$387,780	$366,656	$333,167	$341,484	$290,047	$241,922	$213,303	$191,524	$153,183	$155,830
Plant and equipment	$310,449	$283,147	$265,644	$240,435	$190,277	$168,320	$150,839	$137,508	$127,359	$107,609
Plant and equipment, net of reserves	$179,436	$165,689	$160,902	$148,303	$107,659	$ 93,862	$ 83,803	$ 77,218	$ 72,911	$ 59,219
Provision for depreciation	$ 15,726	$ 14,038	$ 12,541	$ 10,684	$ 8,901	$ 8,092	$ 7,585	$ 6,708	$ 5,856	$ 4,999
Expenditures for plant and equipment	$ 32,110	$ 21,275	$ 28,572	$ 55,115	$ 24,782	$ 19,300	$ 15,252	$ 12,302	$ 20,760	$ 24,771
Working capital	$108,836	$111,008	$ 95,476	$102,082	$111,206	$ 94,010	$ 82,410	$ 69,379	$ 57,148	$ 62,026
Current ratio	2.1 to 1	2.2 to 1	2.2 to 1	2.1 to 1	2.6 to 1	2.7 to 1	2.8 to 1	2.5 to 1	3.5 to 1	2.8 to 1
Number of employees at year-end	9,254	8,138	8,179	10,873	10,605	8,931	7,936	6,950	6,378	8,601
Number of shareholders at year-end	10,006	11,140	11,865	12,893	13,185	13,368	12,973	12,634	13,037	13,535
Quoted market price:										
High	$ 37¼	$ 26⅝	$ 28¼	29⅛	31¼	30⅜	33⅜	32¾	25	31¼
Low	23⅞	22	22	20¾	25	23½	25⅛	20⅞	14¾	17½

* Years prior to 1977 reflect the first-in, first-out (FIFO) method for pricing inventory while 1977 and years after reflect the last-in, first-out (LIFO) method.
† Number of shares of common stock and per share data have been adjusted for the 2-for-1 stock split in 1976.
Source: Company annual reports.

EXHIBIT 11 **Consolidated Balance Sheets, Briggs & Stratton, 1980–1983** *(In thousands)*

	Fiscal Year Ending June 30			
	1983	**1982**	**1981**	**1980**
Assets				
Current assets:				
Cash	$ 4,255	$ 3,666	$ 3,081	$ 4,099
Certificates of deposit	41,223	52,428	35,224	11,626
U.S. government securities	0	1,990	4,062	2,046
Receivables, net	59,273	53,064	44,484	75,241
Inventories:				
Finished products	60,359	39,968	33,351	34,444
Work in process	23,224	27,683	31,674	37,824
Raw materials	8,015	8,965	7,814	15,285
Total inventories	91,598	76,616	72,839	87,553
Future income tax benefits	5,878	8,294	7,751	7,797
Prepaid expense	6,117	4,909	4,854	4,819
Total current assets	208,344	200,967	172,295	193,181
Plant and equipment:				
Land and land improvements	8,779	8,757	8,599	6,255
Buildings	83,275	82,473	79,249	56,523
Machinery and equipment	193,342	175,593	159,245	136,953
Construction in progress	25,053	16,324	18,551	40,704
	310,449	283,147	265,644	240,435
Less accumulated depreciation and unamortized investment tax credit	131,013	117,458	104,736	92,132
Total plant and equipment, net	179,436	165,689	160,908	148,303
Total assets	$387,780	$366,656	$333,167	$341,484
Liabilities and Shareholders' Equity				
Current liabilities:				
Accounts payable	$ 23,925	$ 16,069	$ 16,486	$ 29,065
Foreign loans	9,987	8,229	9,891	
Accrued liabilities:				
Wages and salaries	14,245	14,502	12,675	12,048
Retirement plan	17,879	18,186	18,779	18,756
Taxes, nonincome	3,973	3,201	2,498	2,345
Other	21,189	20,268	16,608	17,461
Total accrued liabilities	57,286	56,157	50,560	50,610
Federal and state income taxes	8,310	9,504	1,882	11,424
Total current liabilities	99,508	89,959	78,819	91,099
Deferred income taxes	18,202	16,145	10,373	8,702
Accrued employment benefits	9,016	8,312	8,052	7,768
Shareholders' equity:				
Common stock:				
Authorized 15,000,000 shares, $3.00 par value; issued and outstanding, 14,463,500 shares in 1983 and 1982	43,391	43,391	43,391	43,391
Retained earnings	218,021	209,111	192,032	190,524
Cumulative translation adjustments	(358)	(262)	500	
Total shareholders' equity	261,054	252,240	235,923	233,925
Total liabilities and shareholders' equity	$387,780	$366,656	$333,167	$341,484

Source: Company annual reports.

THE WORLD AUTOMOTIVE INDUSTRY*

Arthur A. Thompson, Jr., University of Alabama

When the world automotive industry entered the 1990s, there were 150-plus motor vehicle companies producing nearly 50 million passenger cars, vans, light trucks, heavy-duty trucks, buses, and assorted other commercial vehicles annually. Motor vehicle production was the world's biggest industrial activity, accounting for 2 percent of world GNP and $600–$650 billion in revenues. Motor vehicle producers ranged from obscure Third World companies making less than 50,000 vehicles for their own home country market to well-known global competitors like General Motors, Toyota, Ford, Honda, and Volkswagen-Audi that produced millions of vehicles and that had a presence in most of the world's major geographic markets. The 25 largest manufacturers (Exhibit 1) accounted for over 90 percent of total production in 1989. A global battle for market share was shaping up among the United States, European, and Japanese producers, with the three Korean companies trying hard to position themselves to join the fray. Comparative production volumes for the various company groups as of 1988 were as follows:

	Passenger Cars	Commercial Vehicles	Total
U.S. companies (General Motors, Ford, Chrysler, Navistar, and PACCAR)	11,106,600	5,320,300	16,426,900
Japanese companies (Honda, Mazda, Mitsubishi, Suzuki, Daihatsu, Fuji-Subaru, Toyota, Nissan, Isuzu, and Hino)	9,174,500	4,706,300	13,880,300
Western European companies (Volkswagen, Peugeot-Citroen, Renault, Fiat, Daimler-Benz, Rover Group, Volvo, BMW, and several others)	10,814,000	1,392,000	12,206,000
Eastern European companies (Vaz Lada, Zastava, Skoda, and others)	1,913,700	11,400	1,925,100
Korean companies (Hyundai, Kia, Daewoo)	865,700	194,000	1,059,700

THE INDUSTRY CLIMATE

Over the past 20 years, Japanese automakers had earned worldwide prominence as the masters of high-quality, low-cost manufacture. The core of the Japanese automakers' strategy revolved around building world-scale production facilities in Japan, capturing 97 percent of their own growing home market at very profitable prices (Japanese trade restrictions eliminated any worry that the Japanese automakers might have about losing sales to foreign imports), and then aggressively exporting the balance of their production to world markets

---

*Prepared with the research assistance of Ph.D. candidate Jana Kuzmicki. Copyright © 1990 by Arthur A. Thompson, Jr.

World's 25 Largest Motor Vehicle Producers, 1989   *(All monetary data in millions of U.S. dollars)*

Rank	Company	Country	World Market Share (Units)	Automotive Revenues	Total Revenues	Worldwide Unit Production Total (Thousands)	Auto (Percent)	Truck (Percent)	Net Earnings	Capital Expenditures	R&D
1	General Motors	United States	17.7	$99.7	$126.9	7,946	74	26	$3,831	$7,386	$5,248
2	Ford	United States	14.6	76.8	96.1	6,336	70	30	4,259	6,695	3,100
3	Toyota	Japan	9.4	53.8	63.3	4,115	76	24	2,836	3,273	3,709
4	Volkswagen	West Germany	6.6	34.4	34.4	2,948	93	7	921	2,434	1,111
5	Nissan	Japan	6.4	36.4	37.8	2,930	77	23	945	1,222	1,564
6	Chrysler	United States	5.4	30.8	34.9	2,382	48	52	629	1,531	954
7	Fiat	Italy	5.4	26.4	37.9	2,436	90	10	2,453	2,612	1,306
8	Peugeot	France	4.6	22.8	23.9	2,216	88	12	1,518	1,872	546
9	Renault	France	4.2	26.4	27.2	2,053	80	20	1,451	1,616	468
10	Honda	Japan	4.0	25.2	26.5	1,960	86	14	945	1,222	1,564
11	Mazda	Japan	2.8	14.5	17.1	1,460	74	26	189	655	545
12	Mitsubishi Motors	Japan	2.7	16.7	16.7	1,335	55	45	167	873	836
13	Hyundai	South Korea	1.9	3.9	5.6	819	89	11	67	NA	NA
14	Suzuki	Japan	1.7	7.3	7.3	875	33	67	73	436	218
15	Daimler-Benz	West Germany	1.7	29.8	40.5	803	67	33	1,317	2,910	2,646
16	Daihatsu	Japan	1.4	5.1	5.5	600	38	62	49	305	182
17	Fuji-Subaru	Japan	1.2	5.0	5.4	530	65	35	44	393	218
18	BMW	West Germany	1.2	14.0	14.0	523	100	0	460	1,058	661
19	Rover Group	Britain	1.1	5.6	5.6	535	90	10	105	328	NA
20	Volvo	Sweden	1.0	11.0	14.1	465	87	13	793	971	955
21	Isuzu	Japan	0.8	9.6	9.6	590	19	81	124	313	291
22	Kia Motors	South Korea	0.7	1.1	2.7	412	67	33	41	NA	NA
23	Daewoo Motors	South Korea	0.4	NA	NA	NA	NA	NA	NA	NA	NA
24	Lada	Soviet Union	0.3	NA	NA	NA	NA	NA	NA	NA	NA
25	Saab-Scania	Sweden	0.3	6.0	6.9	138	74	26	495	575	493

Source: UBS Phillips & Drew Global Research Group, as reported in *Business Week*, May 7, 1990, pp. 54–55.

at prices calculated to gain market share over the long term. Most recently, the Japanese companies had expanded their strategy to include building production bases in both the United States and Europe and entering into the production of luxury and sports cars. Led by Toyota, Nissan, and Honda, Japanese producers were endeavoring to gain strong competitive positions in all major geographic markets and globally dominate the industry. Worldwide, Japanese automakers had a combined market share approaching 30 percent and had their sights set on increasing it to 35–40 percent by the late 1990s. Exhibit 2 depicts the success of Japanese producers in boosting their sales volumes at home and abroad.

While the Japanese producers were busy forging their long-term global strategic offensive, U.S. producers were busy struggling to ward off rising sales of foreign imports in their strategically important U.S. home market. Five major factors had kept General Motors, Ford, and Chrysler on the defensive for well over a decade:

- When U.S. gasoline prices spiraled past $1.00 per gallon in the late 1970s, making drivers more conscious of the costs of a fill-up, new-car buyers began to exhibit a stronger preference for smaller, fuel-efficient cars. Sales of foreign-made compacts getting over 25 miles per gallon rose. Sales of U.S.-made models—long, roomy, six-passenger cars with heavy bodies and powerful V-8 engines that delivered only 10–14 miles per gallon—fell. The shift in buyer preferences forced General Motors, Ford, and Chrysler into crash programs to downsize their lineup of big-car models, introduce a host of compact and subcompact models to compete in the fast growing small-car end of the market, and play catch-up to the Japanese producers in building low-priced, high-quality small cars. But the strategic responses fashioned by the U.S. producers put them on the horns of a short-term profit dilemma: There were no foreseeable prospects of earning the same big profit margins on small cars that they had historically earned on large cars. To counteract the profit erosion entailed by upping their small car production, all three U.S. producers continued their long-standing practice of not putting the same look and feel of quality and the same caliber of technological features into their low-priced small cars as they put into their middle and upper-end models. Until GM introduced its Saturn models in fall 1990, no U.S. producer exhibited a long-term commitment to build a truly high-quality "import-fighter" that could be produced and marketed at a profit.

- A 32 percent falloff in the demand for new vehicles in the United States between 1979 and 1983 sent profits skidding just as U.S. companies were spending heavily to redesign their product lines, retool assembly lines, and try to meet the market challenge from foreign imports. The profit declines prompted U.S. auto executives to cut corners on quality-enhancing features in order to help restore short-term profitability.

- Rapidly escalating labor and materials costs pushed the average price of a U.S.-made car up from $6,000 in 1977 to $15,000 in 1989, prompting buyers to stretch out their car payments and buy a new vehicle less frequently.

- Stricter government regulations regarding fuel economy, safety, and pollution emissions forced U.S. companies to make further costly design changes in all their models, contributed to higher sticker prices, and kept

EXHIBIT 2   **The Success of Japanese Producers in Penetrating World Markets for Motor Vehicles, 1960–1988**

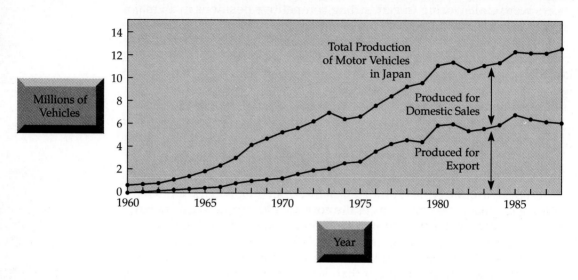

Sources: *Automotive News*, 1989 Market Data Book Issue, p. 3; *1989 Ward's Automotive Yearbook*, p. 109; and Motor Vehicle Manufacturers Association, *World Motor Vehicle Data*, 1983 Edition, p. 79.

Japanese Passenger Car Import Penetration—Selected Countries, 1978–1988
(As a percent of domestic new car registrations)

	1978	1980	1982	1984	1986	1988
Australia	33.3%	35.2%	47.2%	47.4%	44.9%	46.5%
Austria	7.0	19.2	26.4	27.0	26.9	33.0
Belgium	17.9	24.7	21.5	20.1	20.8	21.3
Denmark	13.7	30.9	25.3	32.7	35.1	32.8
Finland	20.4	36.3	35.3	37.9	40.4	41.4
France	1.8	2.9	2.9	3.0	2.9	2.9
Germany, West	3.7	10.4	9.8	12.0	15.0	15.2
Greece	13.8	49.2	45.8	30.9	28.6	38.9
Ireland	23.9	30.5	26.9	27.4	43.4	44.0
Italy	0.1	0.1	0.1	0.2	0.5	1.0
The Netherlands	19.0	25.7	22.4	22.0	24.4	27.7
New Zealand	33.5	58.4	64.3	65.2	60.2	58.2
Norway	20.4	39.1	36.8	33.5	35.0	39.3
Portugal	17.6	7.5	8.5	8.5	9.8	7.8
Spain	0.0	0.0	1.4	0.6	0.8	0.9
Sweden	9.7	12.1	15.2	15.0	20.9	25.5
Switzerland	12.6	23.2	26.7	24.5	26.7	31.1
United Kingdom	11.0	11.9	11.0	11.1	11.1	9.4
United States	12.0	21.3	22.6	18.3	20.8	19.9

Source: Motor Vehicle Manufacturers Association, *World Motor Vehicle Data*, 1990 Edition, p. 29.

> Detroit auto executives busy wrangling with politicians and regulators over what the new standards should be and when they should take effect.

- Preoccupied with their scramble to comply with tougher government regulations, revamp their product lines, and protect short-term profits, U.S. manufacturers paid insufficient attention to assembly-line "fits and finishes" and to quality control in parts manufacture during the late 1970s and early 1980s. Buyers of U.S. makes complained of an inordinately large number of new-car defects. Even though U.S. manufacturers had made major progress since 1985 in narrowing the quality gap, in 1990 they were still trying to overcome widespread buyer perception that American vehicles were not as well made as Japanese vehicles.

Going into 1990 all three U.S. producers were striving to boost the quality and attractiveness of their models in order to meet the competitive challenges posed by the Japanese producers.

European vehicle producers had recently consolidated into a smaller number of stronger companies and were bracing for renewed Japanese attempts to penetrate the European market. Japanese success in Europe had been restricted by protectionist trade practices—as of 1988, Japanese imports were limited to 11 percent of the market in Britain, 3 percent in France, 1 percent in Spain, and to 2,500 vehicles in Italy. In West Germany, the Japanese had been given freer market access and had won an 18 percent market share. It was unclear how soon European trade barriers would be lowered on Japanese imports when the 12-member European Community started functioning as a unified market in 1992, although the EC was committed in principle to abolishing all national automotive quotas eventually.[1] The stakes in Europe were big because of its size and growth prospects; Europe's Big Six—Volkswagen-Audi, Fiat, Peugeot-Citroen, Renault, and the European subsidiaries of General Motors and Ford—were not all expected to survive in their present form. In general, the European companies lagged behind both Japanese and American companies in competitive capabilities and only a few competed globally.

MOTOR VEHICLE PRODUCTION

Motor vehicles, with their 10,000 to 15,000 parts, were one of the most complex products to manufacture and were a telling measure of an industrial society's production skills. Going into the 1990s, two thirds of all motor vehicles were produced in four countries—Japan, the United States, West Germany, and France. In the years immediately following World War II, U.S.-based companies produced 75 percent of the world's motor vehicles, but the percentage eroded steadily as auto companies in other countries gained the technical skills needed for vehicle manufacture and geared up production to meet growing demand in their geographic areas. By 1988, motor vehicle production in the U.S. accounted for less than 25 percent of world output. In 1980 Japan surpassed the United States as the largest producer of motor vehicles. Since 1978, when U.S. production hit an all-time peak of 12.8 million vehicles, U.S. output had fluctuated between 6.9 million and 11.3 million vehicles annually. While

---

[1]The 12 member nations of the European Community were Great Britain, France, Germany, the Netherlands, Italy, Portugal, Greece, Luxembourg, Spain, Belgium, Turkey, and Ireland.

**Trends in World Motor Vehicle Production by
Geographic Location, 1960–1989**

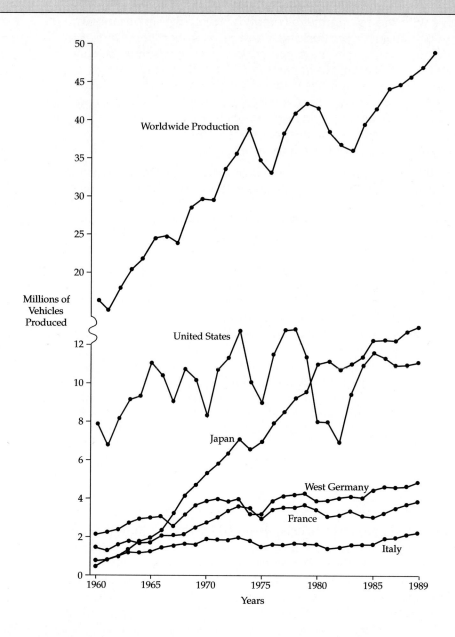

	Continental Production and Assembly						Continental Production and Assembly			
	North America	**Europe**	**Asia**	**South America**			**North America**	**Europe**	**Asia**	**South America**
1989	13,690,005	19,356,455	15,335,322	1,139,917		1984	13,145,741	15,215,560	11,759,738	977,419
1988	13,295,254	18,164,984	14,975,852	1,234,838		1983	11,015,273	15,682,826	11,486,316	1,055,457
1987	12,934,502	17,635,428	14,563,129	1,251,647		1982	8,734,684	14,787,194	11,047,858	992,708
1986	13,461,068	16,706,054	13,835,201	1,231,098		1981	9,862,814	14,412,000	11,462,754	952,190
1985	14,006,178	15,901,217	12,880,368	1,104,300		1980	9,874,206	15,412,225	11,279,345	1,454,124

Definitions: North America—Canada, Mexico, U.S.; Europe—Western Europe and Eastern Bloc including USSR; Asia—India, Japan, Korea; South America—Argentina, Brazil. Source: *Automotive News*, 1990 Market Data Book Issue, pp. 3 and 6.

EXHIBIT 4   **Where Motor Vehicles Are Produced**

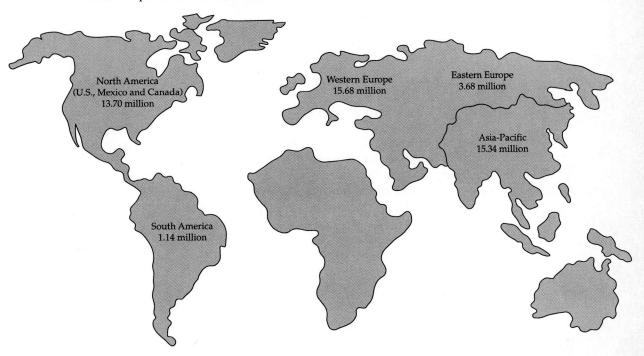

1989 World Vehicle Production by Continent

Total 1989 production and assemblies were about 49.0 million vs. 47.67 million in calendar 1988.

North America
(U.S., Mexico and Canada)
13.70 million

South America
1.14 million

Western Europe
15.68 million

Eastern Europe
3.68 million

Asia-Pacific
15.34 million

Major Motor Vehicle Producing Countries, 1989

Country	Passenger Cars	Trucks and Buses	Total	Country	Passenger Cars	Trucks and Buses	Total
Japan	9,052,406	3,973,272	13,025,679	China	21,568	467,907	489,475
United States	6,823,097	4,029,958	10,852,055	Sweden	384,206	81,670	465,876
Germany, West	4,563,673	287,974	4,851,647	Belgium	304,055	84,524	388,579
France	3,409,017	510,759	3,919,776	Australia	330,492	27,772	358,264
Italy	1,971,969	248,805	2,220,774	Yugoslavia	302,985	39,949	342,934
USSR	1,200,000	900,000	2,100,000	Poland	285,600	53,000	339,600
Spain	1,638,615	406,942	2,045,657	India	177,190	155,325	332,515
Canada	1,001,588	937,914	1,939,502	Germany, East	215,000	42,000	257,000
United Kingdom	1,299,082	326,590	1,625,672	Czechoslovakia	188,611	50,570	239,181
Korea, South	871,898	257,572	1,129,470	The Netherlands	130,000	33,330	163,330
Brazil	731,013	280,970	1,011,983	Argentina	107,597	20,227	127,824
Mexico	439,538	202,241	641,779	World Total	35,455,838	13,435,227	48,891,065

Source: *Automotive News*, 1990 Market Data Book Issue, p. 3 and Motor Vehicle Manufacturers Association, *World Motor Vehicle Data*, 1990 Edition, p. 30.

U.S. production stalled, production in Japan and Western Europe was on the upswing throughout much of the 1980s—see the trends in Exhibits 3 and 4. Total production in South America had been stuck in the 1.0–1.4 million range since 1975.

The Japanese automakers' aggressive export strategy had made Japan the world's leading exporter of motor vehicles (Exhibit 5). In the 1950s Japanese producers began pursuing export sales as a way of escaping the economy-of-scale limitations of a small home country market; by the mid-1980s Japanese companies were exporting over 6 million vehicles annually, chiefly to the United States and Europe.

Most of the vehicles exported by West Germany and France were to other European countries, although about 10 percent of West Germany's exports were for the U.S. market. Virtually all of Canada's motor vehicle exports were to the United States. None of the U.S. automakers competed in foreign markets via the export route; vehicles made in North American plants were designed expressly for North American buyers and less than 2 percent were exported overseas. Instead, U.S. producers had established production bases overseas. General Motors and Ford had big subsidiary operations in Europe, and each had captured about 12 percent of the European market with their European-produced makes. Worldwide, GM had facilities in 32 countries and Ford operated in 25 countries. Chrysler was a factor only in North America—the United States, Canada, and Mexico. Virtually all of the world's leading manufacturers were exploring ways to increase their global reach, through exports or by establishing foreign production bases or by forming strategic alliances with a foreign producer.

THE WORLD MARKET FOR MOTOR VEHICLES

In 1990 there were about 525 million motor vehicles in operation worldwide—about 400 million passenger cars and 125 million pickup trucks and commercial vehicles—and the total was growing 2 to 3 percent annually. The U.S. was far and away the biggest consumer of motor vehicles from a country standpoint with 139.2 million passenger cars and 50.2 million trucks in operation, equal to 36 percent of the world total. Relative to population size, there was one vehicle in operation for every 1.4 persons in the United States, one for every 2.5 persons in Western Europe, one for every 2.6 persons in Japan, one for every 11 persons in Mexico, and one for every 13 persons in Brazil; in less developed nations, the ratios ranged all the way up to 1 vehicle for every 500 persons.

New vehicle demand ran 8–10% of the number of vehicles in operation; over 92% of new vehicle sales represented replacement in one form or another. The average life of a motor vehicle ranged from about 8 years in the United States to about 15 years in countries where travel by vehicle was much less prevalent. Comparative sizes of the various major markets (based on new car and truck registrations) were as shown in the table at the bottom of the following page.

EXHIBIT 5

World Motor Vehicle Exports (Cars and Trucks)

Year	World Total*	Japan	South Korea	France	West Germany	Italy	Sweden	United Kingdom	Canada[†]	United States[†]
					Vehicle Exports by Country of Origin (In Thousands)					
1988	19,322.6	6,104.2	576.1	2,279.2	2,676.9	827.3	214.6	331.9	1,643.3	1,016.7
1987	18,653.3	6,304.9	546.3	2,103.0	2,607.3	766.0	245.6	299.6	1,364.8	860.4
1986	18,338.0	6,604.9	299.0	1,994.1	2,693.7	718.4	273.9	245.6	1,578.4	881.6
1985	17,810.5	6,730.5	119.0	1,892.8	2,745.9	565.7	257.8	291.8	1,612.1	890.6
1984	16,351.1	6,109.2	—	1,886.0	2,388.7	583.6	270.2	295.7	1,568.7	772.2
1980	15,161.7	5,967.0	—	2,219.0	2,084.3	591.6	195.0	481.0	938.5	807.2
1975	10,807.2	2,677.6	—	1,938.3	1,653.5	710.5	196.6	695.9	1,005.6	864.1
1970	8,660.5	1,086.8	—	1,525.4	2,103.9	671.0	210.3	862.7	928.8	379.1
					Percent of World Vehicle Exports					
1988	100.0	31.6	3.0	11.8	13.9	4.3	1.1	1.7	8.5	5.3
1987	100.0	33.8	2.9	11.3	14.0	4.1	1.3	1.6	7.3	4.6
1986	100.0	36.0	1.6	10.9	14.7	3.9	1.5	1.3	8.6	4.8
1985	100.0	37.8	0.7	10.6	15.4	3.2	1.4	1.6	9.1	5.0
1984	100.0	37.4	—	11.5	14.6	3.6	1.7	1.8	9.6	4.7
1980	100.0	39.4	—	14.6	13.7	3.9	1.3	3.2	6.2	5.3
1975	100.0	24.8	—	18.0	15.3	6.6	1.8	6.4	9.3	8.0
1970	100.0	12.5	—	17.6	24.3	7.8	2.4	10.0	10.7	4.4

(continued)

*World Total includes countries with a small number of vehicle exports not shown separately. In 1988, identifiable vehicle exports from these countries totaled 3,039,784 units, 15.7 percent of world vehicle exports.
[†]Includes shipments from the United States to Canada and vice versa.

	1988 New Car and Truck Registrations	Percent of World Market
United States	15.7 million	32.3%
Western Europe	14.4	29.6
Japan	6.7	13.8
USSR	1.6	3.3
Canada	1.5	3.1
Brazil	.7	1.4
Australia	.5	1.0
South Korea	.5	1.0
Argentina	.2	.4
Taiwan	.2	.4
South Africa	.2	.4
All other country markets	6.4	13.2
Total	48.6 million	100.0%

In terms of just passenger cars, Western Europe was the largest market, with new car sales of 13 million units versus 10 million in the United States and nearly 4 million in Japan. The United States was the world's biggest market for trucks and commercial vehicles with annual sales of about 5.2 million vehicles;

EXHIBIT 5   (*Concluded*)

Passenger Car Imports (Based on new car registrations)

			New Passenger Car Import Registrations by Selected Countries (In Thousands)				
Year	Japan	France	West Germany	Italy	Sweden	United Kingdom	United States
1988	133.5	846.8	816.9	858.9	251.8	1,249.7	3,708.9
1987	97.7	760.0	852.1	780.4	226.5	1,040.7	3,654.1
1986	68.4	695.6	840.6	701.6	185.9	1,053.6	3,444.2
1985	50.2	648.2	647.9	698.8	175.8	1,064.4	3,011.1
1984	41.9	630.3	638.9	603.3	150.4	1,006.5	2,523.9
1983	35.3	658.8	591.6	579.9	136.3	1,019.7	2,457.4
1982	35.5	629.5	520.2	685.4	141.4	897.5	2,295.8
1981	38.1	514.9	589.9	711.8	122.3	826.5	2,431.7
1980	44.8	428.5	638.7	617.5	126.8	858.3	2,469.2
1975	42.9	301.5	524.5	330.3	183.1	396.8	1,500.9
1970	16.8	257.2	474.1	378.1	114.7	153.8	1,230.9
			Percent of Domestic Car Market Held by Imports				
1988	3.6	36.8	29.1	39.3	73.2	56.4	35.4
1987	3.0	36.1	29.2	39.5	71.7	51.7	35.9
1986	2.2	36.4	29.7	38.4	68.8	56.0	30.9
1985	1.6	36.6	27.2	40.0	66.8	58.1	27.6
1984	1.4	35.9	26.7	36.9	65.1	57.5	24.9
1983	1.1	32.7	24.4	36.6	62.8	56.9	27.5
1982	1.2	30.6	24.1	40.7	64.7	57.7	29.6
1981	1.3	28.1	25.3	40.9	64.9	55.7	28.8
1980	1.5	22.9	26.3	41.5	65.8	56.7	28.2
1975	1.6	20.3	24.9	31.4	64.2	33.2	18.2
1970	0.7	19.8	22.5	27.7	56.4	14.3	14.7

Source: Motor Vehicle Manufacturers Association, *World Motor Vehicle Data*, 1990 Edition, p. 27 and MVMA, *Motor Vehicle Facts and Figures*, p. 34.

Japan was second with 3 million units annually; and Western Europe was third with annual sales just under 2 million trucks. The Japanese truck market, like the Japanese car market, was effectively closed to foreign companies; imports of foreign-made trucks into Japan amounted to less than 3,400 units in 1989 out of a market volume of 2.3 million units (1989 sales of all foreign-made cars in Japan totaled only 151,000 units out of a market volume of 4.1 million units). Exhibit 6 shows the market shares of the major car and truck producers in the world's three largest geographic markets.

Market Growth   Demand for motor vehicles was quite cyclical (see Exhibit 3). Since 1978 worldwide demand had grown at a 1.3 percent compound rate. Sales tended to be strongest during periods of economic prosperity and weakest during recessionary periods. Forecasters expected slim annual growth rates of 1 to 1.5 percent worldwide during the 1990s, with annual demand approaching 55 million units by the year 2000. The fastest rates of growth were expected to come in newly developing and Third World countries where there were substantially fewer vehicles in operation relative to total populations. The vehicle markets in North America, Western Europe, and Japan were the most mature—annual demand in these three largest markets of the world was pro-

EXHIBIT 6   **Market Share Leaders in Passenger Cars and Light Trucks, Three Largest Geographic Markets, 1989**

Passenger Car Market Shares, 1989

Western Europe		United States		Japan	
Fiat-Lancia	14.9%	General Motors	34.8%	Toyota	43.9%
Peugeot	12.9	Ford	22.1	Nissan	23.2
VW-Audi	14.8	Chrysler	10.3	Honda	10.8
Ford	11.9	Honda	7.9	Mazda	5.9
GM-Opel	10.4	Toyota	7.3	Mitsubishi	4.9
Renault	10.1	Nissan	5.2	Daihatsu	2.4
Rover Group	3.4	Mazda	2.7	Subaru	2.1
Mercedes-Benz	3.4	Hyundai	1.8	Suzuki	1.7
Nissan	2.9	Volkswagen	1.6	Isuzu	1.5
BMW	2.7	Subaru	1.4	All imports	3.6
Toyota	2.1	Volvo	1.0		
Volvo	2.1	All other imports	3.9		
		All Japanese imports	26.0		
		All European imports	4.9		

Light Truck Market Shares, 1989

Western Europe	United States		Japan	
	General Motors	35.7%	Toyota	16.2%
Not	Ford	30.0	Suzuki	15.4
Available	Chrysler	21.0	Mitsubishi	14.6
	Toyota	4.7	Daihatsu	14.5
	Nissan	3.3	Nissan	11.0
	Isuzu	2.2	Fuji	8.3
	All other imports	3.1	Honda	7.1
	All Japanese imports	13.3	Mazda	6.3
	All European imports	0.1	Isuzu	4.9
			Imports	0.04

Sources: *Automotive News*, *Business Japan*, and *Ward's Automotive Yearbook*.

jected to increase over 1988 levels by no more than 2 million units throughout the entire decade of the 1990s. Producers regarded Europe as the most attractive of the three major markets in the 1990s because of the opening up of Eastern Europe, the formation of the European Community as a unified trade area of 320 million consumers, and the potential for further growth in vehicle usage across Europe. The Asian market was also expected to boom, jumping from 4.7 percent of global unit sales in 1987 to 8.7 percent by the mid-1990s.

Some analysts predicted that producers in Asia, South America, and Eastern Europe could be making 18–20 percent of the world's cars and trucks by the year 2000, up from 12.5 percent in 1986. But most producers in developing countries were small and lacked the technology to match the sophistication of vehicles made by the major producers in the United States, Japan, and Western

Europe; moreover, the technology gap was widening. In 1990 Japan was the main exporter of vehicles to developing and Third World nations, followed by France and then the United States.

The Truck Segment   Worldwide, light- and heavy-duty trucks, buses, taxis, vans, and assorted types of other commercial vehicles accounted for 25 percent of total motor vehicle sales. However, the division between passenger car sales and truck-bus-commercial vehicle sales varied significantly from market to market. In Western Europe, eight passenger cars were sold for every one truck-bus-commercial vehicle. In the United States the breakdown was 63 percent passenger cars and 37 percent trucks, vans, and buses; in Japan the composition was 57 percent passenger cars and 43 percent trucks, buses, and commercial vehicles.

Truck sales grew a bit faster than passenger car sales worldwide during the 1980s, partly because they provided a cheaper form of transportation. In the United States, where truck demand had grown the most, light-truck sales (mostly pickups and 4-wheel-drive utility vehicles) grew from 2.2 million in 1980 to 4.8 million in 1989, equal to a 9.1 percent compound growth rate; sales of light trucks in the United States were expected to reach 6 million vehicles annually by the mid-1990s. Worldwide, most producers saw the market for light pickup trucks, vans, and sport utility vehicles (like the Jeep Cherokee) continuing to grow 1 or 2 percentage points faster than the passenger car market. The base demand for heavy trucks was about 150,000 vehicles annually in the United States and about 250,000 vehicles worldwide.

Japanese and U.S. producers controlled 70 percent of the world's truck sales. General Motors and Ford were the coleaders in the overall truck-bus-van-commercial vehicle segment with worldwide sales of close to 1.9 million vehicles each. Toyota was the third leading truck producer with sales of 1 million vehicles; 8 of the world's 12 largest truck producers in 1990 were Japanese companies:

Company (Country Base)	Estimated 1990 Sales
General Motors (U.S.)	1.9 million
Ford (U.S.)	1.9
Toyota (Japan)	1.0
Chrysler (U.S.)	0.8
Nissan (Japan)	0.7
Mitsubishi (Japan)	0.6
Suzuki (Japan)	0.6
Daihatsu (Japan)	0.5
Mazda (Japan)	0.4
Isuzu (Japan)	0.4
Fuji (Japan)	0.4
Renault (France)	0.3

In Europe, the leaders in heavy trucks were Renault, Daimler-Benz (Mercedes), and Volvo; in Japan, the heavy truck leaders were Hino and Nissan Diesel; and in the United States, the leaders were Navistar (the maker of International

EXHIBIT 7   Size of U.S. Passenger Car and Light-Truck Market Segments, 1990

Passenger Car Segments	Percent of Total Market	Light Truck Segments	Percent of Total Market
Subcompacts	24.4%	Compact pickup	26.7%
Compacts	33.8	Regular size pickup	27.2
Intermediates	23.8	Compact van	16.8
Full-size	8.9	Regular size van	10.7
Luxury	9.2	Compact utility vehicle	15.5
		Regular size utility vehicle	4.2
	100.1%		100.1%

Source: *Automotive News*, 1989 Market Data Book Issue, p. 129.

trucks), PACCAR (the maker of Peterbuilt and Kenworth brands), Mack, Daimler-Benz (Mercedes and Freightliner brands), and GM Volvo. Truck exports from Europe and the United States had declined in recent years whereas Japanese truck exports had increased.

MAKES AND MODELS

Automakers produced a variety of models and styles—subcompacts, compacts, full-size sedans, hatchbacks, station wagons, vans, pickup trucks, sports cars, and convertibles—to cater to differing driver tastes and user needs. Exhibit 7 shows the percentage composition of the various segments. While every vehicle was factory-equipped with certain "standard" features (included in the base price), it was common practice to equip each vehicle with desirable add-on "options" such as air conditioning, power windows and door locks, AM-FM radios, stereo sound systems, compact disk players, leather or vinyl upholstery, whitewall or high-performance tires, deluxe wheel covers, sunroofs, antilock brakes, bucket seats and gearshift consoles, airbags, and trim packages; these, along with a choice of interior and exterior colors, permitted the vehicle to be "customized" to a buyer's tastes and pocketbook. Optional equipment could boost the base price by $1,000 to $4,000 per vehicle.

In recent years, the number of models on the market had proliferated in response to increasingly diverse buyer needs and preferences. Whereas in the 1970s, car owners across the United States opted for much the same type vehicles (full-size family sedans), by the 1990s buyer preferences had splintered into varying market niches—subcompacts, compacts, mid-size, family-size, personal luxury models, two-doors, four-doors, pickup trucks, vans, sports cars, 4-wheel drives, and so on. In 1990, for example, U.S. car buyers could choose from 600 models offered by 3 American makers, 19 European makers, 9 Japanese makers, and a Korean maker. The fragmenting of homogeneous mass markets into differentiated niche markets greatly reduced the sales volume any one model achieved. Whereas in the 1970s sales volumes of popular-selling models could amount to 400,000–700,000 units annually, by 1990 annual sales volumes of 350,000 units per model was "large" and annual volumes of only 25,000 units per model were not uncommon. Automakers believed that the diversity of buyer needs mandated offering a variety of models and price ranges for buyers to choose from. Shifting buyer preferences had also made it important for manufacturers to read market trends accurately and be able to put freshly designed models with sales appeal into showrooms within a short time frame.

The most profitable models were full-size sedans, luxury cars, pickup trucks, vans, and 2-wheel- or 4-wheel-drive utility vehicles. Light trucks and utility vehicles were profitable because they were less costly to produce than cars. Luxury and full-size cars were high-margin items because the extra prices they commanded far exceeded their incremental production costs. For instance, it cost General Motors only about $4,000 more to produce a $32,000 Cadillac Eldorado as compared to a $14,000 Pontiac Grand AM. Exhibit 8 shows the 10 best-selling passenger car models in selected countries.

Japanese producers were at a disadvantage in competing for the light-truck and sports-utility segments of the U.S. market. Japanese companies did not produce full-size pickup trucks because Japanese streets were too narrow to accommodate them. Moreover, the United States imposed a 25 percent import tax on all 2-door trucks—pickups, minivans, and sports-utility vehicles. To detour the import tax, the Japanese had introduced 4-door model vans and utility vehicles; several Japanese companies were considering entering the full-size pickup truck market.

BUYER PREFERENCES AND PURCHASING HABITS

In selecting the make and model to purchase, buyers typically took many considerations into account: vehicle size, the number of passengers that could be transported, comfort and roominess, styling appeal, drivability and handling, price, the manufacturer's reputation for quality, fuel economy, the length of warranty periods, word-of-mouth reports from acquaintances, and ratings of independent consumerist groups. Older buyers tended to be more brand loyal than younger and better-educated buyers; older buyers also favored domestic brands over imports. First-time buyers were disposed towards economically priced small cars and tended to shop the market more thoroughly, looking at several brands and models. In metropolitan areas buyers often preferred compact, fuel-efficient vehicles for commuting to work in rush-hour traffic. Outdoor enthusiasts and rural residents frequently were owners of a pickup truck or a 4-wheel-drive vehicle. In areas where snow conditions were often severe, 4-wheel-drive utility vehicles were also quite popular. Households with more than one vehicle normally opted for different models to better accommodate the needs of individual family members.

On the whole, buyers were viewed as increasingly prone to brand-switching and model-switching, especially as their transportation needs changed due to the number and ages of family members, commuting requirements, place of residence, and adjustments in life-style. Growing numbers of buyers were switching to an altogether different model like a van or a 4-wheel-drive sports-utility vehicle or a pickup truck or a two-passenger sports car. In the

EXHIBIT 8   **Best-Selling Passenger Cars in Selected Countries, 1988**

Australia

1.	Ford Falcon/Fairmont	69,382
2.	Holden Commodore/Calais	57,648
3.	Mitsubishi Magna	40,518
4.	Toyota Camry	31,103
5.	Ford Laser	28,031
6.	Toyota Corolla	23,586
7.	Nissan Pulsar	16,039
8.	Holden Camira	14,702
9.	Nissan Pintara	11,615
10.	Nissan Skyline	10,778

Brazil

1.	VW Golf	100,177
2.	GM Monza	70,575
3.	Ford Escort	69,291
4.	GM Chevette	49,270
5.	VW Voyage	38,597
6.	Fiat Uno	37,606
7.	VW Santana	32,985
8.	VW Parati	27,678
9.	Ford Del Ray	23,000
10.	GM Opala	22,638

Canada

1.	Ford Tempo	50,806
2.	Chevrolet Cavalier	48,736
3.	Mercury Topaz	35,828
4.	Honda Civic	31,014
5.	Chevrolet Corsica/Beretta	29,920
6.	Pontiac 6000	29,319
7.	Honda Accord	29,186
8.	Pontiac Sunbird	27,114
9.	Chevrolet Celebrity	26,514
10.	Hyundai Excel	26,203

France

1.	Renault R5	241,849
2.	Peugeot 205	230,617
3.	Renault R21	155,171
4.	Peugeot 405	138,700
5.	Citroen AX	129,315
6.	Citroen BX	109,353
7.	Peugeot 309	98,228
8.	VW Golf/Jetta	87,105
9.	Renault R9/R11	75,166
10.	Fiat Uno	66,863

Italy

1.	Fiat Uno	374,850
2.	Fiat Tipo	217,410
3.	Fiat Panda	212,640
4.	Lancia Y10	110,990
5.	VW Golf/Jetta	104,760
6.	Renault R5	84,050
7.	Peugeot 205	65,000
8.	Opel Kadett	44,500
9.	Audi 80/90	43,570
10.	Seat Ibiza	42,670

Japan

1.	Toyota Corolla	281,768
2.	Toyota Mark II	183,199
3.	Toyota Crown	174,554
4.	Toyota Carina	168,763
5.	Nissan Sunny	158,152
6.	Toyota Corona	149,676
7.	Nissan Bluebird	134,574
8.	Honda Civic	134,019
9.	Toyota Sprinter	120,485
10.	Toyota Starlet	86,636

Mexico

1.	Nissan Tsuru	60,247
2.	VW Beetle	19,348
3.	Ford Topaz	19,116
4.	VW Golf	16,988
5.	Chrysler Shadow	15,005
6.	Chrysler Dart	14,406
7.	Chrysler Volare	13,159
8.	VW Jetta	12,293
9.	Chevrolet Cutlass	9,152
10.	Ford Taurus	6,855

Netherlands

1.	Opel Kadett	38,530
2.	VW Golf/Jetta	26,728
3.	Ford Escort	19,920
4.	Peugeot 205	15,846
5.	Ford Sierra	15,117
6.	Citroen BX	14,950
7.	Nissan Sunny	13,760
8.	Toyota Corolla	13,698
9.	Audi 80/90	11,261
10.	Opel Corsa	10,907

Spain

1.	Opel Kadett	79,240
2.	Renault R9/R11	68,865
3.	Seat Ibiza	66,933
4.	Renault R5	65,341
5.	Opel Corsa	59,744
6.	Renault R21	54,504
7.	Peugeot 205	53,588
8.	Citroen AX	53,114
9.	Ford Orion	44,251
10.	Peugeot 309	43,870

Switzerland

1.	VW Golf/Jetta	22,894
2.	Opel Kadett	15,032
3.	Toyota Corolla	14,503
4.	Peugeot 205	8,365
5.	Fiat Uno	7,998
6.	BMW 3-Series	7,912
7.	Ford Sierra	7,841
8.	Audi 80/90	7,323
9.	Ford Escort	7,030
10.	Opel Ascona	6,419

United Kingdom

1.	Ford Escort	172,706
2.	Ford Sierra	162,684
3.	Ford Fiesta	144,991
4.	Rover Metro	116,811
5.	Opel Ascona	113,283
6.	Opel Kadett	96,086
7.	Ford Orion	67,713
8.	VW Golf/Jetta	58,996
9.	Opel Corsa	56,937
10.	Peugeot	54,147

United States

1.	Ford Escort	387,815
2.	Chevrolet Corsica/Beretta	380,301
3.	Ford Taurus	374,627
4.	Honda Accord	362,663
5.	Chevrolet Cavalier	306,267
6.	Ford Tempo	285,141
7.	Hyundai	264,282
8.	Chevrolet Celebrity	252,861
9.	Nissan Sentra	249,523
10.	Oldsmobile Cutlass Ciera	237,386

West Germany

1.	Opel Kadett	226,487
2.	Mercedes W124	171,276
3.	Audi 80/90	136,500
4.	VW Passat	121,485
5.	Mercedes 190	96,667
6.	Ford Escort	84,862
7.	Ford Sierra	80,427
8.	VW Polo	77,347
9.	Ford Fiesta	71,396
10.	Opel Ascona	51,508

Source: *Automotive News,* 1989 Market Data Book Issue, p. 34.

EXHIBIT 9   **Results of Recent J. D. Power Surveys of Customer Satisfaction with Product Quality and Dealer Service**

1989 Customer Satisfaction Index Top 10 Nameplates		
1.	Acura	147
2.	Mercedes-Benz	138
3.	Honda	137
4.	Toyota	134
5.	Cadillac	131
6.	Nissan	128
7.	Subaru	126
8.	Mazda	125
8.	BMW	125
10.	Buick	123

1989 Customer Satisfaction Index Top 10 Models			
1.	Acura	INTEGRA	149
2.	Toyota	Cressida	148
3.	Honda	ACCORD	146
4.	Acura	LEGEND	145
5.	Cadillac	Seville	144
6.	Toyota	Camry	143
6.	Mercedes-Benz	E-Class	143
8.	Mercedes-Benz	S-Class	141
9.	Cadillac	Eldorado	140
9.	Subaru	Sedan	140
9.	Mazda	929	140

Customer Satisfaction, Top Five Nameplates, 1985–1989

	1985	1986	1987	1988	1989
1.	Mercedes-Benz	Honda	Acura	Acura	Acura
2.	Subaru	Mercedes-Benz	Honda	Mercedes-Benz	Mercedes-Benz
3.	Toyota	Toyota	Mercedes-Benz	Honda	Honda
4.	Honda	Mazda/Lincoln (tie)	Toyota	Cadillac	Toyota
5.	Jaguar	BMW	Mazda	Toyota	Cadillac

United States an estimated 1 million car buyers had crossed over to buy pickup trucks, vans, and sports-utility vehicles. It was common for buyers to trade up to more luxurious or sporty expensive vehicles as their incomes rose. Some buyers switched models and brands with each purchase for the sake of variety or because they found the styling and design of certain new models particularly appealing. Others were trend-conscious and opted for whatever new models were "in." Prestige-conscious buyers purchased brands and models best suited to the image they wanted to project—the rich and famous bought Rolls-Royces and expensive sports cars; upscale professionals preferred a Mercedes sedan; older, well-to-do couples bought Cadillacs and Lincolns; young professionals liked BMWs. In the United States, repurchase of the same make of car ranged from about 30 percent for buyers above age 65 down to 13 percent for buyers under age 25.

The biggest buyer segment consisted of those whose top priority was practical, dependable transportation at an economical price; all the major manufacturers offered low-priced subcompacts and compacts for buyers who considered function and price more important than styling, luxury, and image. Because of rising vehicle prices, greater use of 48-month financing plans, and improving vehicle quality, many drivers were making a new-vehicle purchase over a longer life cycle and the average age of vehicles in operation was rising.

In the world's major motor vehicle markets, buyers were relatively sophisticated about the features they wanted their vehicles to have and about the

E X H I B I T   10   *Consumer Reports'* **Overall Quality Ratings of 1989 Cars and Trucks Marketed in the United States**

Manufacturer	Number of 1989 Car and Truck Models with Repair Frequencies Rated				
	Much Better than Average	Better than Average	Average	Worse than Average	Much Worse than Average
General Motors	0	1	9	9	21
Ford Motor Company	0	1	10	7	8
Chrysler	0	2	13	7	8
Toyota	6	5	2	0	0
Nissan	1	2	2	0	0
Honda	5	1	0	0	0
Mazda	6	1	0	0	0
Mitsubishi	1	1	1	0	0
BMW	0	0	2	0	0
Volkswagen-Audi	0	0	2	0	0
Mercedes-Benz	0	0	1	0	0
Jaguar	0	0	0	0	1
Volvo	0	0	2	0	0

Note: Data provided by survey respondents did not permit statistically reliable ratings to be developed for all of the models produced by each manufacturer.

Source: *Consumer Reports*, April 1990, pp. 259–78.

driving performance they expected. Buyers placed a high value on mechanical reliability, quality manufacture, and trouble-free operation. High-tech gadgetry tended to be a plus, serving as a sign of cutting-edge automotive know-how on the manufacturer's part. Vehicles with squeaks and rattles and vehicles that frequently had to be taken in for repairs irritated owners and were the most frequently cited reasons for brand-switching. Manufacturers' recalls to repair defective mechanical designs and consumer satisfaction surveys identifying the "best" and "worst" models were well covered by the news media.

The two most widely reported surveys were done by J. D. Power & Associates and *Consumer Reports* magazine. The J. D. Power survey reported customer satisfaction levels and repair problems of a statistically representative sample of buyers during the first 90 days of new-car ownership; Japanese cars had topped the quality ratings for the past five years and 6 of the top 10 models in the most recent survey were Japanese-made (see Exhibit 9). *Consumer Reports* based its quality ratings on reader responses to its questionnaire survey about their repair experiences during the whole time they had owned their present vehicle. In its latest survey, *Consumer Reports* found that all of the best-rated models for quality were Japanese; 37 of the 38 worst-rated models were made by General Motors, Ford, and Chrysler. For more details see Exhibit 10.

VEHICLE DESIGN

Typically, the task of designing a new model began with a concept based on extensive market research, assessment of buyer tastes and needs, a feel for the market, and manufacturing capability. Once preliminary sketches won approval, designers developed full-size mock-ups, drawings, and specifications. Very large investments could be involved in introducing a new model—development and tooling for Ford's Escort approached $3 billion. Redesigning existing models was a less expensive proposition, but modification of a single component could so affect the interface with related parts and components that entire systems would have to be redesigned and parts production lines retooled at considerable expense.

The length of a vehicle-maker's design cycle was competitively significant. Compressing the time it took to design, engineer, and manufacture new models enabled an automaker to respond more quickly to sales trends and changing buyer preferences, as well as shrinking the time it took to incorporate new product features and manufacturing improvements. In 1990 Japanese automakers could design, engineer, and manufacture completely new models in 42 months; the design-to-production cycle ran five years for U.S. automakers and eight years for European companies. The shorter product cycles allowed the Japanese to make technological improvements faster and to introduce new designs more often.

As of 1990, Japanese automakers were redesigning 80 percent of their models every five years compared to U.S. companies' practice of changing just 40 percent in a five-year span. For instance, the Ford Taurus, introduced in 1985, was reportedly not scheduled for revamping until 1995. Honda had launched two new Accords since 1985 and had plans for a third redesign in 1994. When stodgy designs caused a downturn in Nissan's sales in the mid-1980s, it accelerated redesign of practically its entire lineup of models. In contrast, when General Motors downsized its lineup of personal luxury cars (Cadillac Eldorado, Buick Riviera, and Oldsmobile Toronado) in 1985 and sales plummeted, GM stuck with the same basic styling until the regularly scheduled redesign in 1992.

Japanese automakers were said to have product introduction costs and model redesign costs well below those of rival U.S. and European producers. When Toyota decided to introduce its luxury car line, it spent $700 million to develop the all-new Lexus LS 400, added a second Lexus model for about $350 million, and introduced design and production technologies for the Lexus program that could be adapted for the company's lesser-priced car lines. GM invested $3–$4 billion to bring out its Saturn line and there were no meaningful design synergies between its U.S. and European models. When Ford decided it wanted another luxury brand, it bought British-based Jaguar for $2.5 billion in 1989 and was investing another $1 billion or so to modernize Jaguar's factories and to rejuvenate Jaguar's faltering product line. In years past, U.S. and European automakers had sought to recover their higher model redesign costs by stretching out redesign cycles and thereby spreading the costs over a bigger overall volume.

Analysts predicted that by the year 2000, the lead time to develop a completely new model would shrink to 32 months for Japanese manufacturers and to about 40 months for U.S. manufacturers. To restyle the appearance of an existing model, the Japanese lead time advantage over U.S. manufacturers was expected to drop from 13 months to 5 months. While European manufacturers had recently shortened their design cycles, observers believed they would continue to lag behind Japanese and American companies.

RESEARCH AND DEVELOPMENT

Automotive R&D covered a broad front, ranging from manufacturing technology to cost reduction to improved features and quality to high-tech frontiers. As automakers entered the 1990s, R&D efforts were aimed at reducing engine pollution emissions, boosting fuel economy, developing robots to replace assembly workers, improving powertrain efficiency, exploring the use of ceramics in engine components, enhancing corrosion protection, improving crashworthiness and occupant safety, expanding onboard self-service/diagnostic systems, and using more electronic components (graphic displays, electronic key systems, and computerized control of engine operation and suspension systems). Whereas typical vehicles contained $900 worth of electronics in 1990, the amount was expected to reach $2,000 by the late 1990s. Engines and transmissions were expected to utilize fully integrated electronic controls to help meet tougher fuel-economy and environmental regulations. Japanese companies were working on electronically controlled suspension systems and were stressing the development of better-performing, high-tech 4-cylinder engines. Ford was developing a revolutionary modular engine that could be assembled three different ways to create 4-, 6-, and 8-cylinder variations. GM was developing designs for four new engine families and was working on an electric-powered car. Japanese and U.S. carmakers were racing to develop a new generation two-stroke engine that would be lighter, cheaper, more powerful, and less polluting than present-day four-stroke engines.

In general, Japanese and European manufacturers spent 4–6 percent of company revenues on R&D as compared to 3 percent for U.S. companies—see Exhibit 1 for 1989 R&D expenditures of the various companies. The Japanese government encouraged joint R&D efforts and cost sharing among the Japanese automakers to boost both R&D efficiency and R&D effectiveness. An MIT study showed that in 1985 Honda spent $670 million on R&D and General Motors spent $3.7 billion; each company ended up with about 300 patents. Some European manufacturers cooperated on basic research in such areas as fuel economy and materials usage. Virtually all automakers relied on the research efforts of parts suppliers for improved parts performance, advances in components design, development of new materials such as ceramics, and new applications for electronic components and computerized controls.

PARTS AND COMPONENTS SUPPLIERS

Motor vehicles had between 10,000 and 15,000 parts. Some were made in-house and some were sourced outside. Reliance on outside suppliers varied greatly from manufacturer to manufacturer. The two extremes were GM, which sourced about 40 percent of its components externally, and Honda which sourced 80 percent externally; Ford sourced about 50 percent of its parts externally, Toyota about 73 percent, and Chrysler about 75 percent. Make-or-buy decisions were normally driven solely by cost and investment considerations. External sourcing dominated when component manufacture required large investments, highly specialized know-how or equipment, big experience-curve effects, or scale economies such that the volume of components a manufacturer needed was too small to permit low-cost production in-house. Even where in-house components manufacture was cost-justified, automakers sometimes produced only 60 to 80 percent of their requirements for a particular component internally so that ups and downs in the volume needed could be accommodated by ordering more or less from outside suppliers.

Worldwide, there were over 100,000 suppliers providing original equipment parts and accessories for new vehicles and replacement parts for the "aftermarket." Most were small enterprises employing fewer than 100 people, but the number also included major companies with sales of $1 billion or more. Original equipment parts were the backbone of the business, accounting for 75–90 percent of total parts sales, but aftermarket parts sales were more lucrative. Because vehicle-makers demanded low-cost parts meeting precise specifications and delivery schedules, suppliers were under great pressure to be both efficient and reliable as to quality and delivery. Many parts companies were nonunionized. To keep costs down, they ran plants continuously with three shifts and overtime, kept the sizes of their engineering and administrative overhead to an acceptable minimum, watched overhead expenses like hawks, and substituted less-expensive materials where possible. However, suppliers were pressured to accept responsibility for increased R&D efforts to improve their products, and they were under strong mandates to provide better and better quality assurance. Vehicle-makers often preferred to let suppliers do the engineering on new-model parts to accelerate the introduction of new car lines and to divide the heavy development expense.

Parts Supply Strategies of U.S. Vehicle-Makers

About 40,000 suppliers were engaged in furnishing parts to U.S. vehicle-makers in the United States. GM, Ford, and Chrysler usually divided supply contracts for a part among several suppliers, both to insure uninterrupted deliveries in case one particular supplier had difficulties and to foster strong price competition among rival suppliers. It was common practice to switch suppliers to gain lower prices or better quality or more reliable delivery. Vehicle-makers purchased primarily on the basis of low price, but they also looked for consistent quality from suppliers and a track record of reliability. A supplier who forced two assembly-line shutdowns because of inability to deliver on schedule was generally dropped by the vehicle-maker involved; to reduce the risk of assembly-line stoppages, the U.S. auto companies maintained sizable parts inventories and stressed deliveries in advance of scheduled assembly-line usage. All arriving parts were inspected. It was not uncommon for a supplier to lose a contract it had held for several years when a U.S. automaker's volume needs or cost economics allowed it to bring manufacture in-house at fractionally lower costs. U.S. auto companies were reluctant to source a complete system from outside suppliers if it was a high-volume item or if the component was considered critical (engines, transmissions, axles). Typically, a higher percentage of newly introduced components was purchased from outside suppliers than was the case for components used for many years running. Recently, U.S. companies had begun sourcing parts from fewer, more technologically capable suppliers and granting contracts for 3–5 years in return for price concessions; this contrasted with the past practices of buying most outside parts under annual contracts covering the model year.

There was ferocious competition between candidate material suppliers in a host of applications: plastic versus steel in body panels, aluminum versus copper in radiators, rubber versus plastic versus chrome in interior and exterior trim. Gaining a vehicle-maker's acceptance for a new material or innovative component could be an arduous process; it was not uncommon for U.S. companies to insist on several years of testing for reliability, and in situations where the incumbent component was made in-house they were loathe to incur early write-offs on their existing parts-making investments. Even if an outside supplier developed a patented position on a desirable new part, U.S. vehicle-makers seldom accepted a sole source arrangement past the early stage of the innovation's acceptance.

General Motors, Ford, and Chrysler had goals of standardizing more parts and systems across their car and truck models to capture the economies of longer production runs and to cut back on the number of parts they had to be concerned with. Parts standardization yielded cost and quality benefits in design, engineering, and manufacturing, as well as making it cheaper and simpler to supply replacement parts for after-the-sale repairs. Although many parts suppliers had plants in the industrial Midwest where vehicle assembly plants were concentrated, it was not unusual for parts suppliers to be located far enough away from the final assembly point that shipping costs were significant.

Parts Supply Strategies of Japan Vehicle-Makers

There were some 400 Japanese parts makers, plus another 10,000 parts-making enterprises that operated as subcontractors to the major parts companies. Over 96 percent of Japanese parts production was controlled by companies with 500 or more employees. Most Japanese parts suppliers belonged to a major automaker "family" (or *keiretsu*) and located their plants relatively close to the associated automaker's final assembly plant.[2] The smallest subcontractors in the family tended to be responsible for one simple item. Their production was shipped to a minor components family member who assembled their assigned component from the several parts it received plus those made in-house; these minor components assemblers channeled their output on up the line to a bigger systems or major components assembler who delivered it "just-in-time" (*kanban*) to the automaker. Japanese automakers, except for Honda, sourced most of their parts from within their families, but in special cases purchased from suppliers in other families. Honda had no family of suppliers, relying instead on internal sourcing, independent suppliers, and modest purchases from competitors' families. Japanese vehicle-makers were reluctant to source parts from other than Japanese suppliers (even when they assembled vehicles in foreign locations) and they encouraged their Japan-based suppliers to develop export markets and to be capable of supplying their foreign assembly plants.

---

[2]The *keiretsu* system, common to many Japanese industries, involved intricate alliances, interlocking company structures, and ownership of each other's stock such that separate companies in the same *keiretsu* often cooperated closely on matters of mutual business interest. Competition and arm's-length business transactions tended to be more intense across *keiretsu*s than within them.

Suppliers were expected to meet rigorous just-in-time delivery schedules and to be scrupulous about quality—Japanese automakers maintained no mechanisms for inspecting arriving parts. Automakers guaranteed their suppliers long-term contracts, extended them credit, and often had a minority ownership stake. Vehicle manufacturers held extensive discussions with their suppliers about their production plans, volume requirements, impending technological changes, potential new specifications, and ways for making improvements. When gearing up to make a new part, it was standard practice for suppliers to work closely with automakers in phasing parts production *gradually* up to full capacity so that parts quality would be high all along the way to maximum line speeds.

Japanese automakers provided technical assistance to their suppliers in modifying equipment or the parts-making process when needed, but suppliers were pressured hard to stay abreast of advanced components technology, to pay special attention to parts design and engineering, and to pursue continuous improvement in their parts manufacturing and parts quality. Automakers expected that the prices they paid for parts should normally be declining over time and they exerted continual downward pressure on suppliers' prices. Many Japanese parts suppliers, as a consequence, were less profitable than the Japanese automakers, paid their employees lower wages, did not guarantee lifetime employment, and occasionally laid off workers if business slackened.

Parts Supply in Europe

Most European vehicle-makers sourced 60–80 percent of their components externally, chiefly from suppliers within their own national boundaries. U.S. parts suppliers operating in Europe typically sold to vehicle manufacturers all over Europe, however, as well as to the European assembly plants of Ford and GM.

The German supplier industry was dominated by large, technologically advanced firms that produced well-engineered, high-quality components. They maintained sizable research and engineering staffs and participated broadly in joint R&D efforts with automakers and related suppliers. Exports were often substantial.

Fiat dominated the Italian supplier industry, producing key components in-house and purchasing the balance from hundreds of small, family-owned suppliers. Fiat was the most integrated European manufacturer.

French auto parts suppliers were mostly small and medium-sized firms lacking in resources to invest in modern facilities and advanced research. Many had problems keeping quality up and unit costs down and nearly all were heavily dependent on orders from Renault and Peugeot.

MANUFACTURING AND ASSEMBLY

Motor vehicle assembly was an intricate process requiring the coordination of outside suppliers, in-house parts manufacture, skilled craftsmen, semiskilled assembly-line workers, and mechanized techniques. Assembly plants were typically huge complexes, requiring anywhere from $200 million to $2 billion in capital investment and employing thousands of workers. Often, suppliers' plants were clustered nearby. In years past when producers could sell 500,000 or more units of the same model, efficient, low-cost production depended on capturing scale economies and experience-curve benefits. More recently, though, as demand fragmented and model sales under 100,000 units became commonplace, efficient assembly depended on flexible manufacturing techniques that allowed the same plant to turn out several models with minimal changeover costs. The new keys to overall low costs were achieving economical parts production, utilizing plant layouts and equipment that permitted assembly of different models, maintaining a high level of capacity utilization (to spread high fixed costs out over more units), making use of state-of-the-art automated equipment, minimizing down-time for model changeovers when parallel assembly lines were unfeasible, continually pursuing ways to improve work methods and boost assembly-line productivity, and using people-management skills to gain full worker cooperation in performing tasks more efficiently. Minimum efficient plant sizes for passenger car assembly were in the neighborhood of 100,000–200,000 units annually. Even with automated techniques, the labor content of assembly-line production methods made wage rates and union work rules a big cost determinant. Union rules traditionally put narrow bounds on the tasks a worker in a particular job classification could be assigned; this was tolerable in a mass production situation where tasks were repetitive, but such restrictions were a major obstacle to high labor productivity on assembly lines where worker flexibility was needed in assembling different models and accomplishing efficient changeovers. Flexible assembly methods, to be low-cost, demanded far more of plant management in the way of manufacturing know-how and people-management skills than did routinized mass production of a single model.

High-quality manufacture and assembly had become a pervasive concern at all auto companies. Nothing irritated buyers more than a rash of problems with a newly purchased vehicle; there was always much publicity surrounding models with defects and high repair frequencies, and it could take a producer years to overcome the stigma of turning out problem-causing vehicles.

Japanese companies were widely regarded as the most adept at high-quality manufacture and assembly. They started their quality control effort at the design stage and Japanese design engineers took pains to ensure that their designs were "manufacturable"; painstaking engineering effort went into the whole assembly process. Attention to detail, pride of workmanship, and a strong quality consciousness pervaded the work forces at Japanese assembly plants. Continuous striving to improve manufacturing techniques and assembly-line technology was the norm among both workers and managers. The Japanese had only one or two job classifications for assembly-line workers so that workers could perform multiple tasks as needed. When problems were identified, they were attacked aggressively and corrected. Strict quality-control procedures were in place everywhere.

Exhibit 11 presents data on the number of new-car defects for Japanese companies as compared to American and European companies. The most common auto defects were faulty electrical accessories, blemishes in paint and trim, engine trouble, and squeaks and rattles.

EXHIBIT 11   **Comparisons of Quality of Japanese, American, and European Cars,
1980 and 1989**

| | Number of Defects per Car | |
Car Manufacturer	1980	1989
Chrysler	8.1	1.8
General Motors	7.4	1.7
Ford	6.7	1.5
Japanese average	2.0	1.2
European average	2.8	2.1

Source: Harbour & Associates.

EXHIBIT 12   **Manufacturing Comparisons for the World's Three Largest
Automotive Producers, 1986**

	General Motors	Ford	Toyota
Passenger vehicles produced per employee, 1986	11.7	16.1	57.7
Labor cost per vehicle, 1986	$4,148	$2,379	$630
Percentage of parts and components made in-house	70%	50%	27%
Earnings per vehicle, 1986	$343	$555	$466

Source: *Fortune*, February 15, 1988, p. 35.

PRODUCTION COSTS

Production costs of similar type vehicles varied widely from manufacturer to manufacturer owing to differences in the geographic locations of plants, the age of plant equipment, plant sizes, whether the work force was unionized, local wage rates, labor productivity, the ease/difficulty with which a vehicle's design could be manufactured and assembled, the costs of raw materials and components, the extent of automation, and the manufacturing approaches and practices employed by management.

Japanese companies were very cost-efficient as well as being adept at high-quality manufacture. A recent MIT study of 40 assembly plants in 13 countries revealed that the average assembly plant in Japan used 20.3 hours of labor to produce a car versus 24.4 hours for the average facility in North America and 32.9 hours for European carmakers. The difference between the Japanese and the North American averages was mostly attributable to superior management and greater worker involvement rather than simpler cars and greater automation. Following Toyota's pioneering efforts, Japanese automakers had

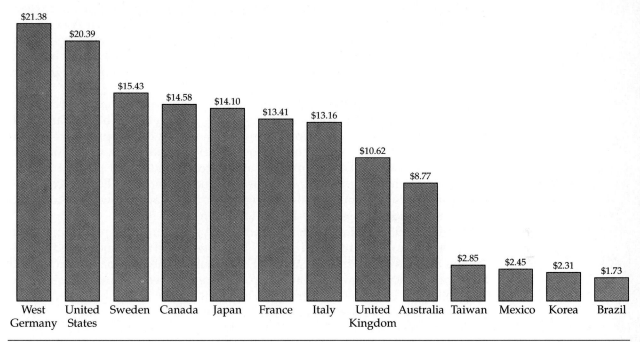

EXHIBIT 13   **Average Hourly Compensation Rates in the Motor Vehicle Industry, Selected Countries, 1987**

Note: This tabulation is based on average earnings, including benefits and bonuses.

Source: U.S. Bureau of Labor Statistics, as reported in *1989 Ward's Automotive Yearbook*, p. 79.

put in place a lean production system that required less manufacturing space, less investment in tools, fewer engineering hours, and fewer workers than the mass production systems of U.S. and European automakers. The production goals of Japanese companies were continually declining costs, zero defects, zero inventories, and superior quality fits and finishes. Exhibit 12 provides some additional cost comparisons.

Since the mid-1980s, the once-big Japanese cost advantage over U.S. producers (about $1,500 to $2,500 per car) and European producers (about $500 to $700 per car) had narrowed significantly, owing to both the dollar and European currencies declining against the yen. As of 1990, Japanese manufacturers had just a $300 cost advantage over U.S. producers on cars made in Japan and a $600–$750 edge on cars built at newly constructed Japanese assembly plants in the United States. One reason for the cost advantage was the low interest rates available to Japan automakers from Japanese banks. Since 1986 Toyota had borrowed $6.2 billion at interest rates of 1.2 to 4 percent; GM and Ford had paid 9 percent and more on their borrowings during the same time frame. Wages and fringe benefits paid out by Detroit's Big Three ranged up to $30 per hour for some skilled classifications as compared to a top of $24 at Toyota's Japanese plants—see Exhibit 13 for wage rate averages in selected countries. Chrysler officials estimated that health care alone cost Chrysler $300 to $500 more per car than Japanese manufacturers (in Japan a high fraction of medical care costs were handled by government programs). However, because American manufacturers had closed down their most inefficient plants and introduced lean production techniques in their newer facilities, the best car plants of U.S. manufacturers were in 1990 more productive than the average Japanese auto plant. Labor productivity at two Ford assembly plants in the United States surpassed the Japanese average, and Ford's Taurus-Sable assembly plant in Atlanta was the most labor efficient plant in the United States. Another study done from publicly available 1989 data showed that it took an average of 39 labor hours to build a vehicle at GM's plants versus 37 hours at Chrysler's plants and 26 hours at Ford's plants.

Toyota was the low-cost producer among Japanese automakers. Ford was the low-cost producer among U.S. automakers, followed by Chrysler and then General Motors. General Motors' standing as the high-cost producer was in sharp contrast to its position throughout the 1950s and 1960s, when long production runs of fewer basic models and a commanding 50 percent market share had made it the world's low-cost producer. Fiat was the low-cost producer among European carmakers despite the fact that Volkswagen-Audi was the world's leader in assembly-line automation.

When the 1980s began, GM, Ford, and Chrysler were each producing small car lines they called "import-fighters." But none of the three succeeded in producing these low-end models at a cost that enabled them to make a profit, and none of the models except Ford's Escort were a hit with buyers. Going into 1990, all three U.S. makers were sourcing their low-priced subcompacts from more cost-efficient Asian competitors. However, GM's state-of-the-art Saturn project represented an all-out effort to learn to make small cars profitably; even so, assuming that the Saturn models were well received in the market and sales climbed to 500,000 vehicles annually, GM was not expecting profits on its Saturn investment before 1995.

CAR RETAILING AND DEALERSHIPS

Worldwide, most new motor vehicles were retailed to buyers through independent franchised dealers. The one big exception to the use of retail dealerships was in Japan, where vehicles were marketed through both large distributors and manufacturers' direct sales forces. Toyota had over 30,000 salespeople and Nissan employed over 25,000. Distributors in Japan sold an average of 5,000-plus vehicles annually. Each distributor marketed only one producer's models—dual or multiple franchises were prohibited. Sales staffers were organized into teams of seven or eight people who were trained in all aspects of the job. Every day started and ended with a team meeting. Team members drew up profiles of every household within the geographic area around the distributorship; after calling for an appointment, sales agents made house calls. During a visit, the profile would be updated and, based on the new answers, the agent would suggest the most appropriate specifications for a new vehicle. Should the household actually be in the market for a new car, detailed discussions would ensue regarding optional equipment, colors, trade-in price, a financing package, insurance, and delivery date. Since the vast majority of new cars sold were manufactured to order and delivered to the buyer within five days or less, dealers kept only three or four demonstrator models on hand.

When sales lagged, the sales team put in extra hours (the team was paid on a group commission), and if sales lagged to the point where the factory did not have enough orders to sustain full output, production workers were transferred over to sales. Dealers fixed all defects the owner encountered with the cars at no cost to the owner (even after the end of the formal warranty); however, the owner was responsible for normal maintenance and for repairs needed to pass Ministry of Transportation inspections. The first inspection had to be passed when the car was three years old; thereafter, inspections became more frequent and more demanding. Dealers' service areas were primarily used for handling the inspection process.

The prime objective of Japanese dealers was to build brand loyalty by creating a long-term relationship with their customers, making them feel part of the manufacturer's "family," treating them well, and charging a fair price. Sales agents called their customers regularly, stayed up-to-date on when sons and daughters might be needing their first car, and sent owners birthday cards. Car sales agents in Japan were so attentive and persistent that, so the saying went, the only way to escape them was to leave the country.

Outside Japan, retail automobile dealers handled the vast majority of new-vehicle sales (the big exceptions were fleet sales to rental car companies and to large corporations that utilized many vehicles in day-to-day operations). Dealers also handled final inspection and preparation of vehicles for delivery, warranty claims, repairs and service, trade-ins, and financing. Manufacturers supported their dealerships by conducting nationally advertised sales campaigns, developing sales literature, sponsoring training programs for repair mechanics, cooperating in local sales promotions, providing new-car financing, and offering incentives to stimulate sales when showroom traffic slacked off. About 30 to 35 percent of the retail price of a vehicle represented dealers' markups and the marketing and distribution costs incurred by manufacturers. With the gap in perceived product quality narrowing, industry observers were predicting that the competitive edge in automotive retailing would swing to dealers with the widest choice, best on-the-spot delivery capabilities, and best price.

In the United States dual or multiple franchises were common. In smaller towns dealers had long been franchised to carry two brands of the same domestic manufacturer (Oldsmobile-Cadillac, Lincoln-Mercury, Dodge-Plymouth). More recently, though, long-time domestic dealers had added one or more import brands to supplement sales of their original domestic brand and to spread their economic risk and large overhead costs. Most foreign manufacturers had built their dealer networks by getting domestic dealers with lagging sales to take on an import brand. The popularity of import brands in the United States, coupled with fewer numbers of import dealers, had resulted in many import brands having substantially bigger unit sales volumes per dealer than was the case for domestic brands—for instance, the 1,100 Toyota dealers in the United States average 850 new cars per year whereas the 4,900 Chevrolet dealers averaged only 570 cars annually. The average U.S. car dealership sold 1,200 new and used vehicles annually and had sales totaling $12 million. Large "super-dealers," with multiple branches and multiple locations in metro areas, had sales of $100 to $800 million on volumes of 20,000 to 70,000 vehicles.

In 1990, there were 17,000 car dealers in the United States who had 51,400 franchises (an average of three brands per dealer) and who operated 25,000 new-car sales outlets; by 2000 it was anticipated that there would be just 8,000 dealer principals operating 18,000 retail sales outlets. In trucks, there were 9,150 dealers and 26,400 new truck franchises, an average of 2.9 brands per dealer. Several of the largest and most successful U.S. dealerships also operated outlets in foreign countries, and the numbers were expected to increase during the 1990s. Consolidation among retail dealers was occurring because of growing popularity of multiple-franchise dealerships and thinner dealer profit margins. To offset the decline in profits from new-vehicle sales, dealers were relying on income from car financing, extended warranty contracts, paint protectors, rustproofing and undercoating, and installation of optional deluxe trim packages.

European producers generally had their strongest dealer networks in their own countries. However, the leading companies all had dealer outlets scattered across Europe and several (Mercedes-Benz, Volvo, BMW, Volkswagen-Audi, Peugeot, and Porsche) had 200 or more dealers in the United States, plus distribution capabilities in selected other countries. Dual or multiple franchising was restricted in most European nations, particularly in Britain.

JAPAN'S CLIMB TO INDUSTRY PROMINENCE

Since World War II, Japanese companies had boosted annual production from 10,000 vehicles to nearly 13 million vehicles at Japan-based plants and to 14 million vehicles worldwide. Despite the cyclical nature of the industry, Japanese automakers had achieved sales gains in 37 of the past 41 years. By way of comparison, over the same time frame U.S. manufacturers had increased production less than threefold, fallen behind Japan in total production, and been able to boost sales in only 23 of the past 41 years.

In taking over leadership of the world automotive industry, Japan's automakers had progressed through four distinct phases. The first phase entailed importing the technology needed for manufacturing (mostly from the United States), building the requisite labor and managerial skills, and developing a larger home market for Japanese-made vehicles. Japan's initial success reflected (1) low-cost skilled labor and cheap steel, (2) home demand conditions (narrow roads and streets, short driving distances, and high gasoline prices) that led manufacturers to focus on small car production, (3) an emphasis on quality ("fit and finish") to satisfy appearance-conscious Japanese buyers, and (4) strong competitive rivalry among Japanese producers that honed their manufacturing skills and marketing savvy.

The second phase was marked by a strong emphasis on exports and development of a world market for Japanese-made vehicles. The first Japanese cars introduced in the United States in the late 1950s were very small, slow, and underpowered, rendering them unsatisfactory on American highways. But Japanese engineers learned from their mistakes and designed the next generation of Japanese vehicles to be suitable for both Japanese and American driving conditions. In 1968 Toyota introduced its Corolla line and Nissan introduced the Datsun 510, helping push all Japanese car and truck exports to the United States past the 100,000 mark for the first time. By 1971 Toyota was the second largest foreign seller in the U.S. market, behind Volkswagen, and Japanese-made vehicles passed European-made vehicles in sales in the American market. Japanese automakers succeeded in penetrating the markets in many other countries as well, and Japan became the world's leading exporter of vehicles by the end of the 1970s.

Much of the Japanese success during this second phase stemmed from their automakers' ability to achieve large gains in labor productivity via manufacturing process improvements, thereby keeping the costs of their cars under U.S. and European makes. Meanwhile, Japanese companies invested aggressively in large modern plants to capture scale economies. Between 1965 and 1975, Japanese car output rose 300 percent, yet the number of workers grew by just 50 percent. To secure worker cooperation in the productivity-enhancing effort, Japanese automakers guaranteed their employees lifetime employment and often provided such other benefits as promotion by seniority, corporate recreational facilities, subsidized housing, semiannual bonuses based on productivity gains and company profitability, and retirement plans. Japanese unions welcomed productivity-enhancing technological change as a means of preserving long-term employment guarantees. Unions maintained a cooperative relationship with manufacturers, and manufacturers went to great lengths to cultivate worker loyalty and keep enthusiasm at a high pitch. Employee turnover was low and unexcused absenteeism averaged less than 1 percent. The culture in Japanese plants encouraged assembly-line workers to maintain their equipment, take pride in the quality of their work, and suggest ways to improve their work methods.

At the same time that the Japanese were making an all-out effort to reduce the labor-cost content in their cars and capture scale economies, they pursued quality improvement. In effect, Japanese automakers patterned their strategy after the example set by West Germany's Volkswagen—make small, fuel-efficient, reliable, and affordable cars (during the 1960s and early 1970s, the VW Beetle was the most popular imported car in the United States and was regarded as the world's best high-quality, inexpensive small car).

The third phase in Japan's climb to prominence came during the early and mid-1980s. Prodded by rises in the value of the Japanese yen (which tended to boost the prices of Japanese cars sold in foreign markets), Japanese automakers put new meaning into the term efficient manufacturing. They developed their now-famous just-in-time supply procedures, redesigned parts to allow greater production efficiency, made use of robots during assembly, and instituted a host of other quality control and productivity practices. They relentlessly pursued a strategy of continuous improvement, leaving no stones unturned in their ongoing efforts to ferret out innovative ways to cut costs and boost quality. And they invested heavily in flexible manufacturing systems and in shortening their design cycles. The outcomes were better vehicle quality, better repair records, and better customer satisfaction ratings than their foreign competitors had. Steps were also taken to establish a production base in the United States to circumvent the continuing rise in the yen against the dollar and to deflect the protests of American labor unions about the rising tide of Japanese car imports and U.S. politicians' concerns over the worsening trade deficit between the United States and Japan. Going into 1990 Hondas were being made in Ohio, Toyotas in Kentucky, Nissans in Tennessee, Mazdas in Michigan, Mitsubishis in Illinois, and Subarus and Isuzus in Indiana. Suzuki was making utility vehicles in Ontario, Canada. Nissan was in the process of doubling its assembly capability in Mexico from 100,000 vehicles to 200,000

EXHIBIT 14   **Comparative Sales Volumes of Top-Selling Luxury Cars in the United States, 1988**

Nameplate	Vehicles Sold
Cadillac	266,548
Lincoln	191,624
Acura	128,238
Volvo	98,497
Mercedes-Benz	83,727
BMW	73,359
Saab	38,490
Chevrolet Corvette	23,281
Audi	22,943
Jaguar	20,727

vehicles; it already had a Mexican plant that assembled engines, transaxles, and some stamped parts. Honda and Toyota also had assembly plants in Canada. Daihatsu was the only one of nine Japanese producers without North American assembly capability. Japanese automakers had installed capacity to make 1.7 million vehicles at eight wholly or partly owned U.S. assembly plants, and they had plans in place to expand U.S. production capability to nearly 3.0 million units by 1995. Japanese production capability in Canada and Mexico was moving toward 500,000 vehicles annually. In addition, three Japanese producers had built or were constructing large assembly facilities in Great Britain to provide onshore access to European markets and to buffer the effects of any European restrictions on foreign car imports when the 12-country European Community began to function as a unified trade area in 1992.

Most recently, Japanese strategy to dominate the world automotive industry had entered a fourth phase: the introduction of premium-priced luxury cars to compete head-on against the most prestigious names in passenger cars—Cadillac, Lincoln, Mercedes-Benz, BMW, Volvo, Porsche, and Jaguar. Honda was the first Japanese maker to enter the luxury car field, introducing the Acura Legend (sticker prices of about $30,000) in 1986; the company sold 71,000 Legends in the United States in 1987 and 128,000 in 1988, making Acura the third best-selling luxury car in the United States (see Exhibit 14). In fall 1989 Toyota introduced its 1990 Lexus models and Nissan introduced the Infiniti; both were priced in the $35,000–$45,000 range. Mazda and Mitsubishi had announced plans to introduce upscale vehicles in 1992 and 1993. The addition of luxury cars meant that the leading Japanese companies now had product entries ranging from low-priced subcompacts and compacts to top-of-the-line cars equipped with a variety of advanced engineering and technology features. Luxury car sales accounted for almost 10 percent of total passenger car volume in the United States and Europe; the $50 billion luxury segment was attractive to both manufacturers and dealers because of the wider profit margins built into the prices of luxury models. As of 1990, three German automakers (Mercedes, Porsche, and BMW) sold 80 percent of the world's cars priced over $40,000.

STRATEGIC ALLIANCES AND JOINT VENTURES

During the 1980s, automakers formed dozens of joint ventures to conduct automotive research, produce components and engines, and assemble new car and truck models. Such alliances not only allowed investment risks and operating costs to be shared but they also gave the partners attractive new avenues for accessing technology, manufacturing methods, management practices, and global markets. Japanese–American, Japanese–European, and European–European ventures were the most common. General Motors and Toyota were 50–50 partners in an assembly plant in Fremont, California, which turned out GM's Geo Prism models as well as 100,000 Toyota Corollas; GM and Toyota had also teamed up in Australia. GM owned a 39 percent stake in Isuzu Motors and a portion of the production from the new Subaru-Isuzu plant in Indiana was GM-related. Chrysler and Mitsubishi were partners in an assembly operation in Illinois which turned out Plymouth Lasers and Mitsubishi Eclipses. Sweden's Volvo and France's state-owned Renault had bought minority ownerships in each other (perhaps as a prelude to a full merger) and were planning to combine their design facilities, parts production, and engine manufacture; Renault was studying the potential for using Volvo's U.S. dealerships to make a third attempt at selling Renaults in the U.S. market. Ford, which owned a 25 percent stake in Mazda, had arranged for up to 120,000 Ford Probes a year to be produced at Mazda's new Flat Rock, Michigan, assembly plant where Mazda was producing two of its own models for the U.S. market. Nissan was handling the imports of Volkswagen in Japan and Volkswagen was marketing Nissan's 4-wheel-drive vehicle in West Germany. Volkswagen had ties with 11 other companies including Volvo, Daimler-Benz (the maker of Mercedes cars and trucks), Nissan, and Porsche. Chrysler, which had no production base outside North America, was rumored to be looking for ways it could develop sales in foreign markets by linking up with European and/or Japanese companies. Daimler-Benz, West Germany's largest company, was exploring intensive cooperation with the Mitsubishi Group, Japan's biggest trading and manufacturing conglomerate with sales of $200 billion and 28 separate core businesses; the two companies were talking about cooperating in aerospace and microelectronics, as well as motor vehicles.

The economic integration of the 12-country European Community in 1992 was driving many of the cross-border alliances with European companies; the political upheaval in the Eastern European bloc further increased the potential size of this new market. Ford estimated that sales across all of Eastern and Western Europe could total 24 million vehicles annually by the year 2008. Japanese companies, anxious to get a much bigger foothold in Europe, had formed several alliances with European firms. However, the Japanese saw alliances as more than a way to gain stronger access to attractive markets; they went into deals as student rather than teacher, with the objective of learning all they could about the skills and practices of their partners. Japanese automakers were said to keep as many of their own "secrets" under wraps as possible, and since many of their alliances were for a limited time frame, when their confidence and market experience grew, they could strike out on their own.

One of the most far-reaching alliances was the collaboration between Ford and Mazda to design and engineer a 1990s-style version of Ford's best-selling Escort and market it as the world's first "global car." Ford designed the styling inside and out while Mazda (1) engineered the mechanical parts, engine, and drivetrain, (2) designed the assembly plant layout, and (3) trained Ford workers to build the car. Production of the first models commenced in February 1990; plans called for the assembly of 900,000 units in 12 locations for sale in 90 markets either as the Ford Escort or as one of various Mazda models (the 323, Protege, or Familia). Ford did not mention its partnership with Mazda in advertising the new Escort.

The concept of a world car sold in multiple markets had intrigued manufacturers since the 1970s because of the potential for dramatically reducing development and production costs by spreading R&D, tooling, and engineering expenses across worldwide operations and economizing on the number of models. Scale economies were generally greater in component manufacture than in assembly operations. Components for a world car could be produced in large, modern plants located in low-wage countries and shipped to smaller assembly plants located in or near regional and large-country markets. Designs for the world car would be similar in most countries and would incorporate as many of the same components as feasible; limited modifications would be made to accommodate differing consumer tastes and regulatory requirements across country markets. So far, however, automakers had met with only moderate success in manufacturing and marketing a world car because buyer demand had historically been fairly divergent across national markets due to different styling preferences, uneven buyer sophistication regarding options and driving performance, disparate income levels and buying power, dissimilar gasoline prices, and widely varying road systems. Additionally, there had been problems regarding local content rules, transcontinental shipping costs, political instability in key low-wage countries, differing pollution emission standards, and the logistical complexity of integrating production, distribution, and marketing across such a wide geographic expanse. Truckmakers faced much the same obstacles in trying to market a global truck.

Prior to the Ford-Mazda effort, which was yet to prove out in the world marketplace, Toyota had come closest to executing a world car concept; Toyota essentially built one version of each model at its huge assembly complex in Japan, making only minor country-specific modifications when needed. However, Toyota engineers were careful to design cars that were suitable for multiple markets. Honda made the same car at its U.S. plants that were made at its Japanese plants and was beginning to export cars made at its Marysville, Ohio, plant back to Japan.

COMPETITIVE CONDITIONS IN 1990

Both American and European automakers viewed the Japanese companies as their strongest competitive threats. Even though the U.S. government, urged on by U.S. automakers and the influential United Automobile Workers union, had pressured the Japanese into accepting voluntary quotas on Japanese car exports to the United States and even though the Japanese yen had risen strongly against the U.S. dollar (thus pushing up the prices of Japanese cars exported to the United States to levels equal to or above comparable U.S.-made cars), more and more U.S. consumers were buying Japanese-made vehicles. Japanese companies had captured 40 percent of passenger car sales in California, 26 percent of the total U.S. passenger car market, and 14 percent of the U.S. truck market. In California, where about 12 percent of all new cars in the United States were sold, Hondas and Toyotas were outselling Fords and also every GM brand but Chevrolets; Nissan was outselling all Chrysler brands combined. Japanese brands were almost as popular in population-heavy East Coast metropolitan areas as they were in California. Likewise, Japanese automakers were making bigger inroads into the European market, though their success so far had been tempered by restrictions placed on Japanese imports.

Since 1982 Japanese companies had invested $5.5 billion to construct seven assembly plants in the United States, three in Canada, and two in Mexico. Although Japanese car and truck imports into the United States had peaked at 3.4 million vehicles in 1986, the newly constructed North American capacity had boosted Japanese capacity to serve the U.S., Canadian, and Mexican markets. Analysts were predicting that Japanese carmakers could draw upon their North American production capability and continued vehicle exports to the United States to capture 30–35 percent of the U.S. passenger car market by the mid-1990s.

While Japanese companies were adding U.S.-based production capacity, U.S. automakers were closing plants and permanently laying off workers. During the 1987–90 period alone, General Motors closed 16 plants, Chrysler closed 13 plants, and Ford closed 3 plants. Since 1980, the United Automobile Workers union had lost 500,000 members to job cutbacks in the U.S. automotive industry, an amount equal to one third of the UAW's membership. Despite the plant closings, an overcapacity situation still prevailed in North America, and it was widely expected that Detroit's Big Three would soon initiate more plant shutdowns since it was they who had older, less-efficient, and less-adaptable facilities. By one calculation, the Japanese expansion of their North American facilities could push excess capacity to over 4 million units and force the closing of 10 or more domestic plants.

The Japanese automakers' U.S. plants had five features that yielded advantages over typical assembly plants of U.S. manufacturers: (1) equipment that allowed for faster die changes and expedient troubleshooting, (2) computerized delivery systems that avoided line shutdowns when suppliers stumbled and that eliminated the need for so much plant warehouse space, (3) stamping and parts-making that was done on or near the assembly site, (4) only a few levels of factory job classifications (to detour costly union work rules and promote higher productivity), and (5) the flexibility to produce several models and vehicle configurations on either the same assembly line or within the same plant. Moreover, these plants were primarily located in rural areas where job applicants had little history with either the automotive industry or manufacturing in general. Job applicants went through long screening sessions and skills assessments to determine if they had the desired temperament and work attitudes. The result was work forces that were younger on average than those at Big Three plants, that were slightly better educated, that were not strongly disposed to unionism, that were more willing to accept job rotation practices and accountability for production-line quality, and that exhibited high levels of morale and job commitment. Managers of these plants worked closely with employees to master the art of making gradual, minute, incremental labor-saving changes in production operations (the concept of *kaizen*). According to an official at Honda's Marysville, Ohio, plant:

We don't set out to double the output of our number two stamping line. We look for only the next step. We shorten the time it takes to stamp our largest body panel by two seconds. And when we accomplish that, we shorten the time on the next largest panel, and then all the panels. And then we do the same thing on the next stamping line. When we've gone through the whole process, perhaps we've made the entire stamping plant 20 percent more efficient.

It was standard Japanese management practice to pursue continuous improvement, year after year, concerning work force methods, process technology, and use of more efficient equipment. Employees who put forth good suggestions for improvement were rewarded. Managers concentrated on creating a gung ho work environment. The efficiency of Japanese automaking plants in the United States was on a par with comparable plants in Japan.

To counter European trade restrictions on Japanese car imports and to hedge against adverse currency exchange fluctuations, Japanese automakers were establishing a production base in Europe. Nissan had just opened up an assembly plant facility in Great Britain, and both Toyota and Honda had new plants under construction in Britain. At least three more Japanese assembly plants were scheduled for the Continent. Mazda and Mitsubishi were in the final stages of selecting European plant sites. Japanese production in Europe was projected to reach 1 million vehicles by 1997. Observers believed the Japanese companies would increase their global market share from 28 percent in 1989 to 40 percent by the year 2000.

To support the Japanese assembly plants in the United States, Japanese parts suppliers had established 300-plus parts-making operations in the United States; Japanese parts suppliers were likewise arranging for European locations to supply the Toyota, Honda, and Nissan plants in Great Britain and to solicit business from other European-based vehicle producers. In many instances, the Japanese parts suppliers had entered into joint ventures with host-country partners to help them become comfortable in dealing with government officials, construction companies, labor unions, and other organizations that had to be dealt with in starting up new plant operations outside Japan. Virtually all of the Japanese parts suppliers were eagerly seeking customers other than the Japanese assembly plants and were stressing the engineering support they would provide to customers. At the same time, Japanese automakers and Japanese auto parts suppliers were opening up automotive-related engineering research centers, seeking partnerships with small automotive technology firms needing funds for expansion, and establishing liaisons and making grants to engineering research programs at U.S. universities to gain early access to American developments in automotive technology.

Meanwhile, Korean vehicle producers were actively investing in new production capacity. Korean manufacturers (chiefly Hyundai, Daewoo Motors, and Kia Motors) planned to expand their Korean-based capacity from the present 1 million units annually to 5 million units annually by 1995. Kia Motors, partly owned by Ford, was supplying Ford with its low-end Ford Fiesta models. Daewoo, 50 percent-owned by GM, was making the Pontiac LeMans. The Korean companies were highly desirous of duplicating the Japanese success and were pushing hard to boost their production know-how, manufacturing efficiency, and vehicle quality. The aggressive capacity expansion efforts of the Koreans were expected to cause even greater excess capacity problems worldwide, since global demand was growing 1–2 percent annually and was not expected to reach 55 million units annually until 2000. More than enough near-term capacity was already in place with more coming on line. The United States alone had 2.5 million units of unused capacity in 1990; worldwide, the total in 1990 was close to 6 million units of unused capacity.

PROFILE OF SELECTED JAPANESE AUTOMAKERS

Exhibit 15 shows the assembly plant locations for cars and trucks made by the leading Japanese motor vehicle manufacturers as of 1988.

Honda Motor Company

Founded in 1948, Honda was a maverick among Japanese carmakers. It did not belong to any of Japan's powerful trading groups and it was not prone to coordinate its actions with Japan's Ministry of International Trade and Industry that guided the long-term strategic thrusts of Japanese companies. Rather, Honda's success had been engineered by the entrepreneurial instincts of its founder, Soichiro Honda. First in motorcycles and later in automobiles, Soichiro Honda came up with state-of-the-art products that surpassed, in one way or another, the models previously on the market. Honda first made a name for itself in the 1950s and 1960s when it emerged as the world's leading producer of motorcycles, scooters, and mopeds. The company did not start making automobiles until the 1960s.

Honda Motor was the most multinational of all the Japanese automakers. It had over 50 plants in 31 countries and its product line included cars, trucks, motorcycles, portable power generators, garden tillers, lawn mowers, and several other power equipment items—all of which used gasoline engines of one type or another. Over 60 percent of sales were outside Japan. Honda products were designed to appeal to a global target market—Honda's strategic intent was to conquer world markets rather than just Japanese markets.

Honda was the first Japanese company to build abroad after World War II, starting with a moped plant in Belgium in 1962. It was the first Japanese automaker to open an assembly plant in the United States (1982) and Honda was the top-selling Japanese nameplate in the American market. The Marysville, Ohio, plant had generated numerous stories in the media concerning its immaculate appearance, the workers clad in white uniforms, the $30,000 average wage, the division of line workers into only two job classifications—production associate and maintenance associate—the on-site sports complex, the one cafeteria where everyone ate, and the prolific employee suggestion system. Honda managers believed that the expert on any task was the person who did it every day on the assembly line. Honda made sure that employees who made the best suggestions for improvement were visibly recognized.

Honda's reputation for manufacturing quality and customer satisfaction was a big factor in the company's success. In the latest J. D. Power report on consumer satisfaction with automobile quality and dealer service, Honda's Acura Legend model ranked first in the luxury car segment, the Acura Integra model was tops in the sporty sedan segment, and the Honda Accord was first in the lower-middle price-range segment. Honda's Acura brand was

EXHIBIT 15 **Assembly Locations and Production Volumes of Japanese Motor Vehicle Manufacturers, 1988**

Assembly Locations	1988 Production Volume		
	Total	**Passenger Cars**	**Commercial Vehicles**
Toyota			
Toyota—Japan	3,968,697	2,982,922	985,775
Toyota—U.S.A.	55,480	55,480	0
Toyota—Australia	55,080	55,080	0
Toyota—Brazil	5,007	210	4,797
Total, all locations	4,084,264	3,093,692	990,572
(Outside parent country)	(115,567)	(110,770)	(4,797)
Nissan			
Nissan—Japan	2,164,218	1,730,948	433,270
Nissan Diesel—Japan	49,288	0	49,288
Nissan—Mexico	101,140	72,395	28,745
Nissan—Australia	46,845	46,845	0
Nissan Motor Iberica—Spain	75,902	0	75,902
Nissan—U.K.	56,541	56,541	0
Nissan—U.S.A.	205,816	109,897	95,919
Total, all locations	2,699,750	2,016,626	683,124
(Outside parent country)	(486,244)	(285,678)	(200,566)
Honda			
Honda—Japan	1,293,416	1,072,773	220,643
Honda—Canada	50,058	50,058	0
Honda—U.S.A.	366,354	366,354	0
Total, all locations	1,709,828	1,489,185	220,643
(Outside parent country)	(416,412)	(416,412)	0
Mazda			
Mazda—Japan	1,220,664	880,131	340,533
Mazda—U.S.A.	163,289	163,289	0
Total, all locations	1,383,953	1,043,420	340,533
(Outside parent country)	(163,289)	(163,289)	0
Mitsubishi—Japan	1,261,409	639,890	621,519
Suzuki—Japan	845,923	296,413	549,510
Daihatsu—Japan	643,485	160,125	483,360
Fuji-Subaru—Japan	595,286	276,448	318,838
Isuzu—Japan	575,978	158,750	417,228

Source: Motor Vehicle Manufacturers Association, *World Motor Vehicle Data*, 1990 Edition, pp. 18–20.

the top-rated nameplate in 1987, 1988, and 1989. The Honda nameplate (Accord, Prelude, Civic, and CRX) had achieved top-five rankings in each of the last five J. D. Power surveys. In the eight years that *Car and Driver* magazine had named its "Ten Best" cars, only the Honda Accord had made the list every year.

Although Honda shunned alliances with other automotive companies, it had collaborated with Britain's Rover Group (the last remaining British automotive company) on a variety of projects since 1979. In 1989 Honda and Rover Group initiated a joint project to construct a 100,000-vehicle-per-year assembly plant next to an existing Honda engine plant in Swindon, England; plans called for the plant to reach capacity production for the European market by mid-1993.

Honda had recently begun to equip some of its models with a small, newly developed four-cylinder engine that delivered 10–15 percent more power than six-cylinder engines made by GM, Ford, and Chrysler and that had much improved fuel economy over its existing engines. Honda's newest assembly line at its main factory in Suzuka, Japan, permitted doors, dashboards, tires, seats, bumpers, engines, and batteries to be installed automatically, without the aid of human hands. Company executives in 1987 had declared an aim to triple Honda's already high productivity.

Nissan Motor Company

As early as 1983 Nissan was making cars and trucks in eight countries outside Japan: the United States, Mexico, Peru, Australia, Spain, Italy, Thailand, and the Philippines. In addition, Nissan had affiliates in a dozen other countries where its vehicles were being assembled or made under license and had formed a number of strategic alliances to strengthen its access to foreign markets. In 1986 Nissan became the first Japanese producer to open an assembly plant in Britain. Nissan was strongly committed to establishing fully integrated operations in Europe, from vehicle design and development to manufacturing to sales and service.

In the late 1980s Nissan had introduced a number of new models that won praise and acclaim from customers. Nissan's philosophy of vehicle development was based on three principles: (1) creating cars that fulfilled buyer expectations and that met continually diversifying marketplace preferences, (2) developing cars backed by superior technology, and (3) engineering cars to provide driving pleasure as well as transportation. The company focused its efforts on the trendsetting target segments and tried to create distinctive vehicles that enabled it to cultivate new markets.

Nissan differed from other Japanese producers in two respects. Throughout Nissan's history, decisions had come to be made in a highly charged political atmosphere, with fierce factional struggles and power politics being commonplace; fear and turmoil were an integral part of Nissan's heritage and culture. Second, stories had appeared in the media describing assembly-line speedups at Nissan plants and how strict conformity with managerial policies was achieved by subjecting dissenting workers to wage discrimination, ostracism, and harassment. At its Yokohama facilities, Nissan maintained low-rent bachelor dormitories for 12,500 people and provided subsidized meals. Virtually all workers were required to be members of the All Nissan Motor Workers' Union.

Toyota Motor Company

Toyota was Japan's largest industrial enterprise, the world's third largest automaker, and the largest of 14 interlocking companies known as the Toyota Group. Included in the Toyota Group were Hino Motors, Japan's biggest maker of heavy trucks, and Daihatsu, Japan's eighth largest automaker; Toyota owned 11 percent of Hino Motors and 14 percent of Daihatsu.

Toyota made 90 percent of its vehicles at a rural location called Toyota City, 150 miles outside Tokyo. Toyota City had all the trappings of a company town—company housing, a company hospital that provided free health care to workers, and a huge recreational center. The production facilities at Toyota City were the most efficient in the world, making Toyota the world's low-cost vehicle producer. Toyota produced 45 percent as many vehicles as GM with a work force one tenth the size of GM's. Other than its facilities at Toyota City, the company had a 200,000-car assembly plant in Georgetown, Kentucky, which was being expanded to a capacity of 500,000 cars. Next to the Georgetown plant, Toyota was building a $300 million facility to supply pistons, valves, cylinder heads, and 4-cylinder engines for the cars produced in Georgetown. Toyota's 50–50 venture with GM at the New United Motor Manufacturing, Inc. (NUMMI) plant in Fremont, California, provided Toyota with 100,000 Corollas a year. Toyota was expected to gain full control of the output of the NUMMI plant (200,000 vehicles per year) when its joint production agreement with General Motors ended in 1996. Independently of GM, Toyota planned to open a second assembly line at NUMMI in 1991 to produce 100,000 Toyota trucks annually. In Britain, Toyota was constructing a 200,000-vehicle plant for 1992 startup and was moving to develop plans for expanding and integrating its operations throughout Europe.

In 1990 Toyota planned to produce 4 million vehicles, 2.3 million for markets outside Japan. Toyota's production mix was 75 percent passenger cars and 25 percent trucks. Indications were that Toyota's foray into the luxury car segment with its Lexus models would be successful. Early sales figures showed 18 percent of the Lexus buyers were Cadillac and Lincoln owners, while 28 percent were Mercedes and BMW owners. Some rivals believed Toyota had lowballed the introductory prices set on the Lexus, given its advanced multivalve V-8 engine and other sophisticated technical features. Overall, Toyota's profit margins on vehicles sold in Japan were three to four times its margin on vehicles sold in foreign markets.

Mitsubishi Motors

Mitsubishi Motors was one of 28 companies comprising the Mitsubishi Group, a confederation of Japanese companies that included Mitsubishi Bank, Mitsubishi Electric, Asahi Glass, Kirin Brewery, Mitsubishi Heavy Industries, Tokio Marine and Fire Insurance (Japan's largest property and casualty insurer), and Nippon Kogaku (the maker of Nikon cameras). Although the various Mitsubishi companies were separately listed on the Tokyo Stock exchange, each tended to own stock in the others; the heads of all the Mitsubishi companies attended a joint meeting on the second Friday of every month.

Mitsubishi Motors was the fifth largest Japanese auto producer; 12 percent of its stock was owned by Chrysler. In a 50–50 joint venture with Chrysler called Diamond-Star Motor Manufacturing, Mitsubishi and Chrysler were producing 120,000 Mitsubishi Eclipses and Plymouth Lasers at a new assembly plant in Illinois. In 1989, Mitsubishi sold 150,000 cars and trucks in the United States. Mitsubishi was actively looking for production sites in Europe.

The Smaller Japanese Makers

The makers of the four lowest-volume Japanese nameplates—Subaru, Daihatsu, Isuzu, and Suzuki—were struggling to remain competitive. Tax changes in Japan, a tougher export outlook, and heavy capital-spending requirements to turn out a full line of appealing new models and build manufacturing bases in Europe and the United States had increased the prospects of industry consolidation via merger and closer alliances. Subaru, a division of Fuji Heavy Industries, was forging closer cooperative ventures with Nissan (Fuji and Nissan were both members of the same Japanese trading conglomerate and Nissan owned 5.9 percent of Fuji's stock). Daihatsu had asked Toyota to increase the 14 percent ownership stake that Toyota already had in Daihatsu. Suzuki had been hurt when *Consumer Reports* in June 1988 called its Samurai 4-wheel-drive model unsafe and urged a model recall; in 1989 Suzuki's sales in the United States dropped from 81,349 to 30,181 vehicles, despite the introduction of two new models.

PROFILES OF THE AMERICAN AUTOMAKERS

Exhibit 16 shows the geographic locations of the assembly operations of GM, Ford, and Chrysler.

General Motors

Not only was GM the longtime leader in the automotive industry, it was also the world's largest industrial corporation with 1989 revenues of $127 billion and after-tax profits of $4.2 billion. GM had 775,000 employees, 15,000 dealers, 35,000 suppliers in 26 countries, and more than 200 plants and facilities spread across 34 countries. The company for years had sold five brands of cars in the United States (Chevrolet, Pontiac, Buick, Oldsmobile, and Cadillac). In 1989 it introduced the Geo line sold through Chevrolet dealers and a seventh brand was launched by the company's all-new, showcase Saturn division in fall 1990. Both Geo and Saturn were small cars intended to compete head-on against low-end Japanese models. The Geo line models were produced for GM by Toyota, Isuzu, and Suzuki. Since 1987 the company had introduced more redesigned models than Ford and Chrysler combined; in 1987 the company produced 175 car models for the North American market but was reducing its line to a planned 132 models in 1992. Trucks were sold under the GMC and Chevrolet names; GM was tied with Ford for the world lead in the truck segment. In Europe GM's Opel and Vauxhall models had won a 10.5 percent market share, following a big turnaround in sales that started in 1986. To further strengthen its European operations, GM in 1989 purchased 50 percent of the auto division of Saab-Scania, Sweden's second largest auto company.

In 1989, the company's overseas car operations (mainly in Europe) earned $2.6 billion. Earnings from truck sales were just over $1 billion. The company's GMAC financing unit contributed $1.1 billion to 1989 earnings while the flagship North American car division lost $1 billion.

During the 1980s GM invested $50 billion to refurbish its factories, install new equipment, and improve labor productivity—the most massive modernization and rebuilding ever undertaken by any corporation. Another $2 billion was spent on employee training and education. So far, the productivity gains

EXHIBIT 16   **Assembly Locations and Production Volumes of U.S.-Based Motor Vehicle Manufacturers, 1988**

Assembly Locations	1988 Production Volumes		
	Total	Passenger Cars	Commercial Vehicles
General Motors			
G.M.—U.S.A.	5,147,300	3,501,124	1,646,176
G.M.—Canada	722,713	409,951	312,762
Opel—W. Germany	904,421	895,504	8,917
Lotus—U.K.	1,336	1,336	0
Vauxhall—U.K.	206,700	176,489	30,211
G.M.—Spain	361,291	361,291	0
G.M.—Brazil	242,785	192,854	49,931
G.M.—Mexico	84,055	51,477	32,578
G.M.-Holden—Australia	72,817	72,817	0
Total, all locations	7,743,418	5,662,843	2,080,575
(Outside parent country)	(2,596,118)	(2,161,719)	(434,399)
Ford			
Ford—U.S.A.	3,329,096	1,805,741	1,523,355
Ford—Canada	653,113	499,616	153,497
Ford—W. Germany	608,890	608,890	0
Ford—Belgium	397,532	324,708	72,824
Ford—U.K.	508,375	375,542	132,833
Ford—Spain	281,666	281,666	0
Ford—Brazil	176,302	124,683	51,619
Ford—Mexico	128,753	98,815	29,938
Ford—Australia	111,899	95,318	16,581
Ford—Argentina	31,197	19,604	11,593
Total, all locations	6,226,823	4,234,583	1,992,240
(Outside parent country)	(2,897,727)	(2,428,842)	(468,885)
Chrysler			
Chrysler—U.S.A.	1,718,279	1,072,845	645,434
Chrysler—Canada	488,825	59,016	429,809
Chrysler—Mexico	130,476	77,295	53,181
Total, all locations	2,337,580	1,209,156	1,128,424
(Outside parent country)	(619,301)	(136,311)	(482,990)

Source: Motor Vehicle Manufacturers Association, *World Motor Vehicle Data*, 1990 Edition, pp. 18–20.

had been a disappointingly small 5 percent over the 1980–88 period (versus 17 percent at Chrysler and 40 percent at Ford), leaving GM still stuck as the high-cost U.S. producer.

On average, GM's costs were $100 to $200 per vehicle above Ford's and $750 above the Japanese models made at U.S.-based plants. Even though GM had cut 40,000 people from its white-collar work force since 1985, it still had 100,000 white-collar employees and, in the words of one knowledge-able observer, "overhead coming out its ears." Critics claimed GM was mired in bureaucracy and moving painfully slow to rejuvenate its manufacturing approaches and plant working environments. However, its research and technical skills were said to be as good or better than any of its rivals.

From 1979 through 1989, GM's market share dropped 11.6 percentage points (from 46.3 percent to 34.7 percent) and the combined shares of Japanese brands went up 10.4 percentage points. GM sold 1.1 million fewer cars in 1989 than in 1979, an outcome that had prompted plant closings and forced other plants to operate well below capacity. A number of GM's new models had not sold as well as expected, and losses on these models were running $1,000 to $2,000 per car. GM had high hopes for its new Saturn models; internally, Saturn's success was seen as a crucial demonstration of whether GM could compete profitably in the small car segment—subcompacts and compacts accounted for 30 percent of North American sales volume. One of GM's near-term strategic goals was to get its share of the North American market back up to 40 percent.

Some 80 percent of GM's Buick, Oldsmobile, and Pontiac models varied only slightly in price and mechanical design. Their styling and image, though different, was not sufficiently distinctive to preclude widespread criticism of look-alike models. Except for Cadillac, all models were designed by GM's central design staff; each car division had to negotiate with the design staff on styling for its models. Since GM had reorganized the design function into a centralized unit, none of GM's new models had been a smash hit in the market. GM executives, however, were confident that the new models scheduled for 1991–93 would be well received and very successful. The strategy was to achieve greater differentiation through design and extra features while cutting costs in nonvisible areas by using more common mechanical parts. Company executives were convinced that the investments made in the 1980s would pay off in the 1990s as freshly designed models were introduced.

Ford Motor Company

Ford was the most successful U.S. automaker of the 1980s. It began the decade by losing $3 billion. It ended the decade more profitable than GM in three of the last four years, leading U.S. manufacturers in productivity gains, cost reductions, quality improvements, and fuel-efficient aerodynamic styling. At least two of Ford's plants were the equal of Japanese plants in labor efficiency. Several of Ford's new models had been market successes, and Ford's car and truck market share had risen 6 percentage points during the 1980s to 24.6 percent.

Ford was investing heavily in plant modernization and Japanese-style production methods to further improve its cost competitiveness. Ford had learned much from its partnership with Mazda Motors and was deeply involved in changing the ways it built vehicles to mimic Japanese approaches. For example, at Ford's new stamping and assembly plant in Wayne, Michigan, Ford had installed giant Japanese-made presses that allowed workers to change dies in as little as two minutes—compared to 6 to 12 hours in a traditional Ford stamping plant. Plant managers wore the same uniforms as hourly workers and pocket patches emphasized first names; the plant contract with the UAW called for one job classification for nonskilled workers, allowing workers to swap responsibilities, instead of the usual 12 job classifications that spelled out precisely what a worker could and could not do. Workers ate beside managers in the cafeteria and parked in the same lots. Many of Ford's plant had Japanese-style production teams. As of 1990, labor efficiency at Ford's assembly plants matched that of the average Japanese plant in Japan. In Europe, Ford had announced it would stop buying parts from any plant that failed to meet defect standards and delivery requirements by 1993; about 250 out of 1,600 suppliers weren't expected to make the grade.

Ford was committed to maintaining its position as a leader in the truck segment. Plans called for tripling capital expenditures in its heavy-duty truck business in North America. Ford's F-series trucks and Rangers had outsold all competitors for several years.

In addition to its truck products, Ford's competitive strengths were its high rates of capacity utilization, its strong design capability, its solid cash position to cushion downturns and finance the development of new models, and its strong overseas operations. Ford's long product cycle times were one of its biggest weaknesses. The first major redesign of the Taurus/Sable models was scheduled for 1995, 9 years after the original models debuted; the Tempo/Topaz model redesigns were scheduled for 1994, 10 years after their launch. To develop new big-volume models with multinational sales potential, Ford had created "Centers of Responsibility" whereby Mazda was leading Ford's development of small cars, Ford of Europe was in charge of mid-sized cars, and Ford's North American Automotive Operations unit was spearheading the designs for large cars and trucks. Ford had recently introduced a program to cut material costs and product development costs. The company was gearing up a new flexible manufacturing plant to build more than a dozen engine sizes and configurations on a single assembly line; the engines would share 350 parts and the modular engine designs would give Ford unprecedented freedom to shift production from one engine type to another to meet changing sales patterns. (Previously, Ford had dedicated each of its engine plants to building a single engine type.)

In Europe Ford was putting plans in place to double the size and sales of its newly acquired Jaguar facilities in Britain. Ford had 8,000 dealers across Europe, the most of any competitor in Europe. It held the biggest market share of any seller in Britain and was in the top three in Germany, Sweden, and Ireland. In 1989 Ford had boosted its overall market share in Europe from 11.4 percent to 11.9 percent. Ford was more globally integrated than any other non-Japanese automaker and for 25 years in a row Ford led all U.S. producers in overseas automotive sales. Ford marketed its vehicles in more than 180 countries.

Chrysler Corporation

Even though Lee Iacocca had brought Chrysler back from the brink of bankruptcy in the early 1980s, the company faced major challenges in the 1990s. Its models were dated, its costs were not competitive with the Japanese producers, and it had only a North American production base. Its best-selling models were minivans and Jeep Cherokees. All of Chrysler's small car models were Japanese-built. New models to revitalize Chrysler's car lines were scheduled for 1992. The company was exporting 50,000 Jeeps and minivans to Europe and hoped to increase the number to the 200,000 range.

Chrysler had worked hard to boost assembly plant efficiency. Its best factory in Sterling Heights, Michigan, was nearly as efficient as the newest Japanese plants and matched the average Japanese plant in quality. Recently, the company had formed ventures with Fiat, Mitsubishi, and Hyundai. According to Iacocca, "If we want to be a full-line car and truck producer, we'll need a partner."

PROFILES OF SELECTED EUROPEAN AUTOMAKERS

Exhibit 17 shows the car-truck assembly plant locations of the leading European motor vehicle manufacturers as of 1988. Exhibit 18 shows market share trends for all the major producers active in the European market for passenger cars.

Daimler-Benz

Daimler-Benz was a $48 billion manufacturer of Mercedes-Benz cars and trucks (68 percent of sales), aerospace and defense products (17 percent of sales), and electronics and technology systems (15 percent of sales). The company was the world's largest producer of heavy trucks (over six tons), the largest bus manufacturer in Europe, the world's 14th largest carmaker, and the world's largest maker of diesel engine cars. Its Mercedes line of luxury cars was world renowned for engineering excellence and had surpassed Cadillac as the world's top-selling luxury car in the early 1970s. Mercedes cars were coveted around the world and symbolized wealth, prestige, and quality. The least expensive Mercedes cost about $30,000 and the most expensive model was about $85,000. Mercedes was regarded as the premier brand in the automotive industry, even though other models like the famed Rolls-Royce and Italy's Lamborghini commanded bigger price tags. Year-in and year-out, Mercedes outpaced all other European models in customer satisfaction and quality, usually ranking in the top three in the J. D. Power surveys.

Underlying the Mercedes mystique was a deep-rooted philosophy of building vehicles that excelled in engineering design, handling, braking, quality manufacture, and road performance at high speeds. Major model changes were made every seven to eight years. It was deliberate company policy to let supply lag behind demand in order to add to the mystique and to help ensure Mercedes owners a high resale value. The company insisted that it made the cars its engineers wanted to build instead of following sales trends or polling consumers to find out what they wanted. Owner loyalty was extremely high; in Germany 90 percent of Mercedes owners bought another Mercedes and in the United States the number approached 75 percent.

Daimler-Benz produced about 600,000 passenger cars, about 2 percent of the worldwide total; all of its cars were made in German plants and about half were exported. The company had about a 12 percent market share in West Germany. One out of three cars had a diesel engine. The company produced about 225,000 trucks, about one third of which were produced in foreign plants scattered across 10 countries.

Ford, General Motors, and the Japanese were all moving to test Mercedes' supremacy in the European luxury-car market. Toyota was shipping Lexus

EXHIBIT 17   **Assembly Locations and Production Volumes of Major European Motor Vehicle Manufacturers, 1988**

Assembly Locations	1988 Production Volumes		
	Total	Passenger Cars	Commercial Vehicles
Volkswagen			
V.W.—West Germany	1,453,286	1,372,035	81,251
V.W. Audi—West Germany	426,462	426,462	0
V.W.—Argentina	16,511	16,051	460
V.W.—Brazil	371,600	332,492	39,108
V.W.—Mexico	59,164	52,798	6,366
V.W.—U.S.A.	35,998	35,998	0
SEAT—Spain	512,316	512,316	0
Total, all locations	2,875,337	2,748,152	127,185
(Outside parent country)	(995,589)	(949,655)	(45,934)
Peugeot			
Peugeot—France	1,244,408	1,157,695	86,713
Citroen—France	773,162	681,333	91,829
Sevel Peugeot—Italy	59,197	0	59,107
Peugeot Talbot—Spain	107,553	107,553	0
Citroen—Spain	198,621	198,621	0
Peugeot/Talbot—U.K.	82,326	82,326	0
Total, all locations	2,465,267	2,227,528	237,739
(Outside parent country)	(447,697)	(388,500)	(59,197)
Renault			
Renault—France	1,680,636	1,384,959	295,677
Renault—Argentina	45,886	42,969	2,917
Renault FASA—Spain	339,588	339,588	0
Renault RVI—Spain	3,907	0	3,907
Renault—U.K.	4,585	0	4,585
Mack—U.S.A.	22,668	0	22,668
Mack—Canada	4,580	0	4,580
Total, all locations	2,101,850	1,767,516	334,33
(Outside parent country)	(421,214)	(382,557)	(38,657)

Source: Motor Vehicle Manufacturers Association, *World Motor Vehicle Data*, 1990 Edition, pp. 18–20.

models to Europe; Honda had come out with a $50,000 sports car model; Ford had acquired Jaguar in an effort to penetrate the luxury market in Europe; and General Motors had gone into a joint venture with Sweden's Saab-Scania to produce upscale models for the European market. To defend its position, Mercedes was introducing a lower-priced version of its 190 model to appeal to younger buyers and was bringing out a completely new top-of-the-line S-Class model priced at $70,000-plus—over 1 million drivers had purchased S-Class models during the 1980s. It was also redesigning its diesel models to curtail pollution emission problems and moving rapidly into "smart" cars equipped with devices that enhanced vision and warned about road hazards.

Assembly Locations	1988 Production Volumes		
	Total	Passenger Cars	Commercial Vehicles
Fiat			
Fiat—Italy	1,378,994	1,371,014	7,980
Lancia—Italy	132,626	132,626	0
Autobianchi—Italy	132,151	132,151	0
Iveco—Italy	92,368	0	92,368
Sevel Fiat—Italy	62,183	0	62,183
Ferrari—Italy	3,996	3,996	0
Fiat Vehiculos—Argentina	1,155	0	1,155
Fiat—Brazil	213,649	150,844	62,805
Iveco Unic—France	61	0	61
Iveco-Magirus—West Germany	15,945	0	15,945
Iveco Ford—U.K.	16,519	0	16,519
Total, all locations	2,049,647	1,790,631	259,016
(Outside parent country)	(247,329)	(150,844)	(96,485)
Daimler-Benz			
Mercedes-Benz—West Germany	698,600	553,772	144,828
Mercedes-Benz—Argentina	4,193	0	4,193
Mercedes-Benz—Brazil	45,791	0	45,791
Mercedes-Benz—Spain	23,140	0	23,140
Mercedes-Benz—U.S.A.	3,221	0	3,221
Freightliner—U.S.A.	23,688	0	23,688
Freightliner—Canada	3,238	0	3,238
Total, all locations	801,871	553,772	248,099
(Outside parent country)	(103,271)	0	(103,271)
Volvo			
Volvo—Sweden	331,218	286,555	44,663
Volvo—The Netherlands	119,786	119,786	0
Volvo—Brazil	4,588	0	4,588
Volvo—Canada	6,166	6,166	0
Volvo—U.S.A.	19,837	0	19,837
Total, all locations	481,595	412,507	69,088
(Outside parent country)	(150,377)	(125,952)	(24,425)

To accomplish these changes more quickly, Mercedes was planning to bring out one new model or major variant every year during the 1990s.

Volkswagen-Audi

Volkswagen-Audi was West Germany's second largest company and the largest European exporter of cars to the United States. In English, Volkswagen translated into "the people's car." The company had made a name for itself

EXHIBIT 18   European Market Shares of Major Automakers, Passenger Car Segment, 1985–1988

| | 1985 | | 1986 | | 1987 | | 1988 | |
	Units	Percent Share	Units	Percent Share	Units	Percent Share	Units	Percent Share
VW Group	1,529,415	14.4%	1,715,956	14.7%	1,857,600	15.0%	1,930,026	14.9%
VW	1,113,124	10.5	1,247,838	10.7	1,260,560	10.2	1,282,343	9.9
Audi	260,840	2.5	276,436	2.4	352,332	2.8	371,939	2.9
SEAT	155,451	1.5	191,682	1.6	244,708	2.0	275,744	2.1
Fiat Group	1,304,494	12.3	1,634,385	14.0	1,761,678	14.2	1,916,091	14.8
Ford total	1,267,830	11.9	1,366,023	11.7	1,483,869	12.0	1,465,665	11.3
Ford Europe	1,266,970	11.9	1,363,466	11.7	1,481,143	11.9	1,461,783	11.3
Ford other	—		2,557	0.0	2,726	0.0	3,882	0.0
Peugeot Group	1,226,179	11.5	1,327,183	11.4	1,503,776	12.1	1,672,142	12.9
Peugeot	661,258	6.2	802,366	6.9	920,787	7.4	1,051,143	8.1
Citroen	476,322	4.5	500,391	4.3	581,175	4.7	620,646	4.8
Talbot	88,599	0.8	24,426	0.2	1,814	0.0	353	0.0
GM total	1,212,339	11.4	1,286,536	11.0	1,326,216	10.7	1,375,312	10.6
Opel/Vauxhall	1,205,915	11.3	1,277,268	10.9	1,311,637	10.6	1,352,177	10.4
Isuzu	5,469	0.1	7,607	0.1	10,250	0.1	15,328	0.1
GM-US/Canada	955	0.0	1,661	0.0	4,329	0.0	7,807	0.1
Renault	1,139,305	10.7	1,242,340	10.6	1,320,966	10.6	1,325,543	10.2
Mercedes	394,015	3.7	437,354	3.7	434,856	3.5	444,981	3.4
Austin Rover	420,052	3.9	409,444	3.5	416,755	3.4	447,902	3.5
Nissan	306,614	2.9	349,578	3.0	363,804	2.9	378,008	2.9
Toyota	247,580	2.6	337,139	2.9	349,538	2.8	348,635	2.7
BMW	290,565	2.7	298,727	2.6	296,237	2.4	355,255	2.7
Volvo	254,697	2.4	267,924	2.3	267,504	2.2	265,226	2.0
Mazda	203,477	1.9	238,192	2.0	234,037	1.9	245,446	1.9
Alfa Romeo	161,330	1.5	172,862	1.5	186,995	1.5	212,762	1.6
Mitsubishi	116,345	1.1	141,486	1.2	151,010	1.2	156,491	1.2
Honda	—		136,850	1.2	129,639	1.0	139,703	1.1
Total passenger car market	10,074,237	100.0%	11,673,919	100.0%	12,413,359	100.0%	12,977,778	100.0%
Japanese makes	1,140,401	10.7	1,359,866	11.6	1,404,059	11.3	1,445,748	11.1

Source: 1989 *Ward's Automotive Yearbook*, p. 87.

worldwide with its VW Beetle, the most successful model of any car ever produced. More than 21 million Beetles were produced at plants in West Germany, Brazil, and Mexico. More than 5 million Beetles were sold in the United States and the Beetle had been the best-selling model in Brazil. Volkswagen's share of the U.S. market peaked in 1970 at 7.2 percent when 570,000 vehicles, mostly Beetles, were sold. When the Beetle met its market demise in the late 1970s, Volkswagen elected to erase its reputation as a builder of small, inexpensive cars and move instead to selling "classless" vehicles. The strategy worked well in Europe and the VW Golf became the best-selling car in Europe. But the Golf never caught on with U.S. buyers, some of whom were burned by the high price and poor quality of the Volkswagen Rabbit, the first successor to the Beetle. In 1975 Volkswagen lost its import leadership to the Japanese in the U.S. market, and it had never been able to stage a comeback. In 1989, VW's share of the U.S. car market was 1.5 percent. Even so, Volkswagen-Audi was the most multinational of the European auto companies, engaging in overseas manufacture, joint ventures and acquisitions, as well as exporting, to build its global visibility. In Japan, Nissan made VW's Santana model under license. In Germany, VW and Toyota had teamed up to make pickup trucks. In Latin America, Ford and VW had merged their operations in Argentina and Brazil into a new company called Autolatina, which had 15 plants and annual capacity of 900,000 vehicles. VW acquired the biggest auto company in Spain, SEAT, in 1986.

Volkswagen was the market leader in West Germany, Belgium, Austria, and Switzerland. It had recently redesigned the cars produced by SEAT and had an attractive lineup, ranging from the subcompact Golf to the sleek, high-priced Audi 100. Volkswagen had suffered from low profitability during much of the 1980s.

Fiat

Fiat was the largest company in Italy's private sector and the world's sixth biggest automaker. About 40 percent of Fiat's stock was owned by the Agnelli family, which founded Fiat; the Agnellis had major shareholdings in a host of other Italian enterprises. According to London's *Financial Times,* companies in which the Agnellis had ownership interests accounted for one third of the total capitalization of all stocks traded on the Milan Bourse (the Italian stock exchange); an article in the *Financial Times* said, "Fiat is to the Italian state what the Duke of Burgundy was to medieval kings of France—technically part of the kingdom, but barely less powerful than they were." Giovanni Agnelli, grandson of the founder of Fiat and currently Fiat's chief executive, had superstar recognition in Italy.

Fiat was a world leader in the use of robots and computers; the automated technology was provided by Fiat's machine tool subsidiary, Comau, which was a world leader in the development of automated production lines. GM, Ford, Chrysler, Daimler-Benz, BMW, and Volvo were all users of Comau robots. One of Comau's most impressive installations was a $300 million engine plant that had five parallel assembly lines, each equipped with 148 robots controlled by 600 personal computers, which in turn were coordinated by 103 larger computers; the plant turned out 2,600 engines per day with a work force of 950 people. On the whole, Fiat's plants were the most highly automated of any company.

The company's main production facilities were in Italy, Portugal, and Brazil, with additional operations in Yugoslavia, Poland, Spain, Turkey, Indonesia, Thailand, Argentina, Zambia, Morocco, Egypt, and South Africa.

Fiat enjoyed a 55 percent market share in Italy. Ford and GM were barred from building auto plants in Italy, and Japanese imports were restricted to 2,500 cars per year. The company's product line was broad, ranging from mini-cars at the bottom to Ferrari sports cars at the top. Fiat's efforts to penetrate the U.S. market had been disastrous, and the company withdrew in 1983. Fiat incurred $19 billion in losses from 1981 to 1986, but in 1989 the company earned $3 billion on sales of $41 billion. In 1986 Ford and Fiat joined forces and merged their heavy-truck operations in Europe; talks between the two companies to merge their European car operations had fallen through in 1985. As Europe's low-cost producer, Fiat was jockeying with Volkswagen-Audi, Ford, and Peugeot for leadership in the European market.

Peugeot

Peugeot was the second-oldest automobile manufacturer in the world and the largest company in France *not* owned by the French government. In the 1970s, Peugeot had embarked on a strategy to become "the General Motors of Europe," a move loudly applauded by the French government. Peugeot executives reasoned that to compete against the Americans and the Japanese Peugeot would have to be big and have an international reach. Peugeot proceeded to merge with Citroen, the third largest French auto company, in 1976. In 1978 Peugeot purchased all of Chrysler's European operations, which included plants in Britain, France, and Spain. These acquisitions catapulted Peugeot into the ranks of the world's largest automotive companies and made it the biggest European producer. Peugeot planned to use Chrysler's dealer network in the United States to establish a strong base in the American market, a feat no French carmaker had ever accomplished. It turned out to be a nightmare. The Chrysler factories in Europe were antiquated and turned out unappealing cars; even though Peugeot changed the name of Chrysler's products to Talbot (giving Peugeot three nameplates—Peugeot, Citroen, and Talbot), the face-lift didn't work. Peugeot lost money for five straight years. Between 1978 and 1987 Peugeot retrenched, closing plants, consolidating operations, and cutting its work force by 100,000 (abandoning its 170-year-old policy of never laying off its workers). Production dropped from 2.2 million cars at the time of the mergers to 1.6 million in 1985, and Peugeot fell to fourth place in Europe behind Volkswagen, Ford, and Fiat.

A new chief executive and two new small cars that were market successes helped get Peugeot back in contention by 1988. Factories were modernized, robots installed, the size of the work force cut by 20 percent, and parts production for Peugeot and Citroen models merged into common plants. Sales in 1989 were back up to 2.2 million vehicles and the company was profitable. Peugeot held about a 35 percent market share in France, just ahead of Renault's 30 percent share. Peugeot was also strong in Spain, Portugal, and Belgium-Luxembourg. Peugeot's new CEO aspired to overtake Volkswagen-Audi as the European leader by 1993. His plan was to produce two full lines of cars—four models each of Peugeot and Citroen, ranging in size from subcompacts to luxury sedans.

Renault

Despite record profits of $1.5 billion in 1989, Renault was financially and competitively vulnerable. It was both owned and heavily subsidized by the French government, often serving over the years as a laboratory of socialist ideas for the government. The company had $10 billion in debt and a debt-to-equity ratio of 2 to 1. About 90 percent of its cars were sold in France, Italy, and Spain, all highly protected markets. Quality had improved in recent years, but labor productivity was low. Its cars were less appealing than those made by Peugeot. The recent alliance with Volvo promised several strategic benefits. Volvo was strong in luxury cars; Renault had strength in small cars. Volvo turned out heavy trucks; Renault made small and medium commercial vehicles. Together, the two companies would have a 26 percent market share in heavy-duty trucks. By standardizing gearshifts, subassembly units, and other parts, the two companies could achieve substantial savings on design, product development, and components production.

GENERAL MOTORS CORPORATION*

Arthur A. Thompson, Jr., University of Alabama

When Roger B. Smith retired in July 1990 after serving for nearly a decade as chairman and CEO of General Motors (GM), admirers hailed him as a visionary and innovative leader who had prepared the company for the 21st century. Smith's years as CEO were marked by unprecedented efforts to fight off a mounting competitive challenge from Japanese automakers and to bolster the company's sagging position as worldwide leader of the motor vehicle industry. Early in his administration, Smith stated the vision he had for GM:

> I want General Motors to be number one and not just in sales. I want us to be number one in quality. I want us to be number one in employee relations. I want us to be number one in profitability. And I want us to be a diversified, growing corporation with new products like robotics and new products like electronics.

In pursuit of these goals, Smith initiated some sweeping strategic moves at GM during the 1980s:

- Over $50 billion was invested in plant modernization and high-tech equipment, including the construction of 8 new plants and the renovation of 19 others.
- More than two dozen outmoded or inefficient parts and assembly facilities were closed.
- Strategic alliances were forged with three Japanese producers (Toyota, Isuzu, and Suzuki) and a Korean maker (Daewoo Motors) to supply GM with small car models that filled gaps in GM's product lineup.
- A new car division, Saturn Corp., was created to pioneer radically new manufacturing approaches inside GM, to establish GM's ability to make high-quality small cars at a profit, and to challenge Japanese competitors in the low-priced end of the market.
- GM's overseas operations were restructured, including the divestiture of some unprofitable subsidiaries and the formation of joint ventures to revive others.
- U.S. operations were reorganized into two car groups and a truck group, eliminating in the process two of GM's long-standing manufacturing units, the Fisher Body Division and the General Motors Assembly Division.
- Electronic Data Systems was acquired to revolutionize GM's revenue-profit stream.
- Hughes Aircraft Corp. was acquired to provide GM with access to valuable electronics technology.
- A joint venture with a Japanese robot maker was formed to get GM more deeply involved in advanced automation techniques, and a number of other small high-tech firms were purchased to give GM technological capabilities unmatched by competitors.

---

*Prepared with the assistance of graduate researcher Jana Kuzmicki. Copyright © 1990 by Arthur A. Thompson, Jr.

The heart of Smith's strategy was to transform GM into a low-cost producer using the most technologically sophisticated automaking techniques in the world (robotics, automatic guided vehicles, high-speed equipment, and computerized controls) and, at the same time, to begin a long-term effort to incorporate quality-enhancing, high-technology features into GM cars and trucks.

Yet, on the day Roger Smith retired, GM had more characteristics of a still-struggling giant than it did of a resurgent industry leader using its trailblazing technology to overwhelm competitors and dominate world markets. Throughout Smith's nearly 10 years as CEO, GM's global and domestic market shares had both continued to erode (Exhibit 1), with the lion's share of GM's lost share going to the Japanese producers. Although Smith had orchestrated the largest facilities modernization program ever undertaken by any company in the history of business, in 1990 GM remained a high-cost producer—all of the new capital investments Smith had made in high technology had paid off only in the sense of having narrowed the cost advantage of the more efficient Japanese producers down from the $1,500–$2,000 per car range to an estimated $300–$700 per car. None of GM's assembly plants stood out among the world's most efficient from a labor productivity standpoint. A majority of GM cars and trucks continued to receive comparatively low quality ratings in virtually all of the consumer surveys, and none of GM's new models and styling designs had stirred the enthusiasm of car buyers enough to make a real splash in the market. Roger Smith's legacy, said a legion of critics, was transforming the world's largest industrial corporation into a vulnerable giant and failing to concentrate GM's efforts on building exciting, high-quality cars and trucks that made customers happy. As H. Ross Perot, a former GM director, put it:

> GM has more talent, more money, more research capability, and more manufacturing facilities than any other carmaker. Logically it should be first and best in building the finest cars in the world. It is not. GM has failed to tap the full potential of its resources, especially its people.

It remained to be seen whether Roger Smith's successor, Robert Stempel, could reverse the slide in GM's market share and get GM in shape to outcompete the Japanese producers.

Exhibits 2 and 3 provide additional highlights of GM's financial and strategic performance during Smith's years as CEO.

COMPANY HISTORY AND BACKGROUND

In 1908, the same year Henry Ford announced the development of the Model T, William C. Durant formed the General Motors Company. Durant, a self-made man and super salesman, had made a name for himself creating the largest carriage manufacturing company in the United States and then turning the faltering Buick Motor Company into the largest seller of motor cars in America. His vision was to become a car baron. Within two years, using Buick as a base, Durant purchased Oldsmobile Motor Vehicle Company, Cadillac Automobile Company, Oakland Motor Car Company (later renamed Pontiac Motor Division), 7 other automobile companies, 2 electrical-lamp companies, and 12 auto parts and accessory companies. Unable to buy the Champion Spark Plug Company, Durant persuaded Albert Champion to join GM and start the AC

E X H I B I T 1   **General Motors' Market Share Trends, 1960–1989**

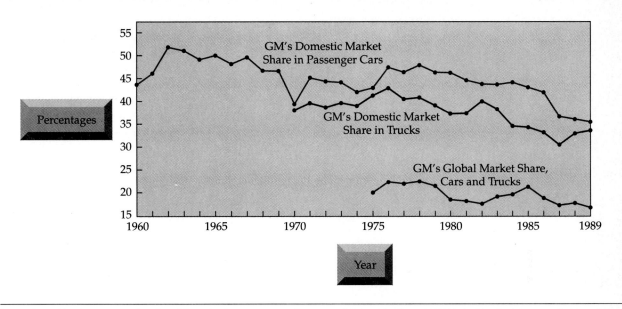

Source: Derived by the case researchers from information in company annual reports and *Automotive News*, 1990 Market Data Book Issue, pp. 3, 40, and 46.

E X H I B I T 2   **Worldwide Factory Sales of GM Cars and Trucks, 1975–1989**
(Units in thousands)

	1975	1980	1985	1986	1987	1988	1989
Cars							
United States	3,680	4,072	4,882	4,302	3,592	3,516	3,238
Canada	406	512	562	545	344	411	414
All other countries	1,114	1,196	1,762	1,783	1,857	1,955	2,083
Total	5,200	5,780	7,206	6,630	5,793	5,882	5,735
Trucks and buses							
United States	978	699	1,537	1,520	1,520	1,661	1,599
Canada	189	257	280	192	238	327	323
All other countries	262	365	282	234	214	238	289
Total	1,429	1,321	2,099	1,936	1,972	2,226	2,211
Total							
United States	4,658	4,771	6,419	5,822	5,112	5,177	4,837
Canada	595	769	842	737	582	738	737
All other countries	1,376	1,561	2,044	2,017	2,071	2,193	2,372
Total	6,629	7,101	9,305	8,576	7,765	8,108	7,946

Note: Figures include units that are made either overseas or in the United States by other manufacturers, but marketed by General Motors under one of its brands.
Source: Company annual reports.

EXHIBIT 3   **Financial Performance Summary, General Motors Corporation, 1980–1989**
               (In billions of dollars)

	1980	1981	1982	1983	1984	1985	1986	1987	1988	1989
Total sales and revenues	$62.7	$69.2	$67.7	$82.5	$93.1	$106.7	$115.6	$114.9	$123.6	$126.9
Net income	(0.8)	0.3	0.9	3.7	4.5	4.0	2.9	3.5	4.9	4.2
Total stockholders' equity	17.8	17.7	18.3	20.8	24.2	29.5	30.7	33.2	35.7	35.0
Cash and marketable securities	5.2	3.0	4.8	8.2	10.7	7.9	7.4	7.8	10.2	10.2
Working capital	3.2	1.2	1.7	5.9	6.3	2.0	3.9	13.0	17.7	17.2
Total assets	64.5	76.8	81.2	89.5	98.4	130.0	150.2	162.3	164.1	173.3
Long-term debt and capitalized leases	2.1	4.0	4.7	3.5	2.8	2.9	4.3	4.3	4.5	4.6

Source: Company annual reports.

General Motors' Capital Expenditures, 1975–1989

Year	Expenditures for Real Estate, Plants, and Equipment (In billions)	Expenditures for Special Tools (In billions)	Total Capital Expenditures (In billions)
1989	$4.58	$2.93	$ 7.51
1988	3.43	2.19	5.62
1987	4.80	2.35	7.15
1986	8.16	3.63	11.79
1985	8.07	3.08	11.15
1984	3.61	2.45	6.06
1983	1.93	2.08	4.01
1982	3.62	2.60	6.22
1981	6.57	3.18	9.75
1980	5.17	2.60	7.77
1979	3.35	2.02	5.37
1978	2.70	1.83	4.53
1977	1.87	1.78	3.65
1976	1.00	1.31	2.31
1975	1.20	1.04	2.24

Source: Company annual reports.

Spark Plug Division. Trying to integrate all these companies and oversee all the day-to-day affairs associated with such rapid expansion overtaxed Durant's administrative skills and led to a financial crisis in 1910 that resulted in Durant's ouster as president. A group of eastern investment bankers gained control of the company, installed Charles Nash as president, and put Walter Chrysler in charge of production operations (both men later established their own car companies); the company returned to profitability and began to repay its bank loans ahead of schedule.

Meanwhile, the entrepreneurial and charismatic Durant put together a new group of automobile companies that included the Chevrolet Motor Company; Chevrolet's success allowed Durant to purchase enough GM stock to regain control of the company in 1916, Durant's takeover was assisted financially by Pierre du Pont, whose own Du Pont Company had become the leader of the chemical industry and a leading supplier of automotive paint to GM. Durant fired Charles Nash, reorganized the company, renamed it General Motors Corporation, and then proceeded to make another series of acquisitions that included Dayton Engineering Laboratories (later to become the Delco Division), the Fisher Body Company, Frigidaire Refrigerator Company, a tractor company, and several other car companies. Durant also created General Motors Acceptance Corporation (GMAC), the industry's first company formed to provide loans for car buyers, car dealers, and prospective dealership owners. However, Durant's informal management style and loose approach to financial controls resulted in almost total lack of coordination among the divisions and companies he had acquired; this, combined with a recession, produced another financial crisis and forced Durant to resign in 1920.

Pierre du Pont took charge and brought in Donaldson Brown as chief financial officer; Brown set about instilling a strong financial philosophy at GM and developed GM's famed "standard volume" approach to pricing whereby prices were calculated in a manner intended to produce a 20 percent return on investment in spite of the state of the economy. Uninterested in automaking, Pierre du Pont in 1923 backed out of running GM on a daily basis. Alfred P. Sloan, Jr., an engineer and former executive of a supplier company Durant had acquired, replaced Du Pont as president and CEO.

The Sloan Years

When Sloan took over in 1923, he was confronted with a sprawling company that had 75 factories in 40 cities, a disorganized product line, and a lack of cohesive direction. Over the next several years, Sloan instituted strategic moves and administrative actions that laid the foundation for GM's climb to the top of the industry and that established Sloan as "the George Washington of General Motors" and the company's dominant cultural hero. Five carmaking divisions (Chevrolet, Pontiac, Oldsmobile, Buick, and Cadillac) were formed to serve as the core of the GM organization.

GM's Strategies Under Sloan In the product area, Sloan's strategy called for each division to produce a line of cars in each of five price categories, starting with the lowest price and stairstepping up to the price level of a luxury-grade car that was still inexpensive enough to be produced and sold in sizable quantities. Sloan's objective was for GM to produce and market a diverse lineup of cars covering a broad price-quality spectrum (the phrase Sloan used was "a car for every purse and purpose"). Ideally, as a family's income rose over time, it could trade up progressively from a low-priced Chevrolet to a bit higher-priced Pontiac to a medium-priced and more luxurious Oldsmobile model to a pricier and still-fancier Buick, and finally to a top-of-the-line Cadillac if the family prospered financially. The product line strategy envisioned by Sloan was to keep the price steps small enough to preclude wide gaps in the company's car lines, yet large enough to avoid undue production duplication and price overlapping. Sloan stressed keeping the number of models and lines within reason so that most scale economies could be fully captured. From a competitive standpoint, Sloan's concept was for each division to position its models at the top of its customary price range and make them of such a quality that customers who might be willing to pay a little more for additional quality would be attracted away from the lower-priced models of competitors, and that customers who might see the price advantage in a GM car of nearly equal quality would be drawn away from the higher-priced models of competitors. Sloan's strategy amounted to quality competition against rival cars below a given GM car's price tag, and price competition against rival cars selling just above a GM car's price.

Sloan did not see that GM's multiple car-line strategy presented any real problem in distinguishing one line from another; as he put it:

> It is perfectly possible from an engineering and manufacturing standpoint to make two cars to not a great difference in price and weight but considerably different in appearance.

Sloan made a point of emphasizing how extremely important it was to GM's success for each division's cars to be "so distinctive that you can tell one division's cars from another at a glance."

Annual model changes were another Sloan innovation. He felt changing models each year would cause cars to become outdated more quickly, thus creating a bigger market for repeat sales. The annual changes not only boosted new car sales but also made it hard for small companies, unable to afford the expenses for constant product development and retooling, to survive. Sloan also pushed the concept of used-car trade-ins and greatly refined the practice of selling automobiles via monthly installment payments.

Early in his presidency, Sloan asserted that GM's future depended on its ability to design cars of maximum utility value and to produce them in quantity at minimum cost. To Sloan this meant doing several things: limiting the number of models, avoiding duplication among the models and lines, designing cars that were at least equal in design to the best of its competitors in a given price grade, achieving greater companywide efficiency than competitors via coordinated operation of GM plants and extensive cooperation among GM's divisions, and having quality standards that would allow GM to become as good as rivals in whatever they were good at and better at what they were not good at. Sloan wanted GM cars to equal the best, in any respect, that competitor's cars in any grade had to offer and then to exceed the quality of rivals' cars in some respects.

Sloan's Administrative Contributions   To instill cohesiveness and cooperation among GM's many operations, Sloan instituted decentralized decision making subject to established corporate policy. An Executive Committee formulated policy and set the tone for how the corporation would operate. An Administration Committee, chaired by the president, oversaw implementation and set guidelines for cooperation and coordination among the divisions. Specific decisions relating to design, production, and marketing of particular models were delegated to division-level managers, but all division-level managers were expected to observe established corporate policy and guidelines for interdivisional cooperation. Divisions functioned as self-contained profit centers headed by a manager and had their own plants, suppliers, engineers, sales staff, and research projects. The main exception to decentralization was the

Fisher Body Division, which built the bodies (or "skins") for all of the car divisions and which had a say in exterior styling so as to promote some degree of common appearance in GM-made vehicles. A series of committees was established to achieve interdivisional cooperation; each relevant division had a member on each committee.

The career progression of managers was another component that Sloan infused into GM's organization and culture. Two career paths to top management positions evolved under Sloan. To track toward jobs with high-level operating responsibility and perhaps become chief operating officer, individuals would hold various assignments in the areas of engineering, manufacturing, or marketing and would likely graduate from General Motors Institute (the company's training ground in automotive technology). To move up toward chief executive officer, individuals would typically possess a graduate degree in business and advance principally through the financial ranks; however, to gain some hands-on experience in the operations side of the business, finance people with top leadership potential might spend a few years as executive assistant to key operating managers and later on be put in charge of a manufacturing division. Sloan felt that the two-track approach to developing GM's future leaders would strike a healthy balance between decisions that made good financial sense for GM and decisions that made good production and sales sense at the divisional level. The rationale was that the perspective of GM's financial staff would help make up for the limitations of a president and other executives with engineering backgrounds who simply were not as skilled in evaluating the corporatewide financial impact of decisions. As one observer said, "The concept was simplicity itself—an engineer or a product man would oversee manufacturing, and a financial guy would watch the money to make sure the engineer didn't give away the store."

To help harmonize the efforts of the several divisions and promote more of a companywide point of view, Sloan created a management bonus plan based on the principle that the interests of GM and its stockholders were best served by making key employees partners in the corporation's prosperity and that key managers should be rewarded in proportion to their contributions to the profits of the corporation as a whole. (At the time, GM's package of performance-based management bonuses was considered revolutionary, but the basic system devised under Sloan was still in effect in 1990.) Prior to Sloan, incentives for division-level managers had been based on divisional profits; Sloan put bonus determination on corporate profitability to cut back on efforts he perceived were exaggerating divisional interests at the expense of corporatewide interests. A Bonus and Salary Committee oversaw the amount of the bonus pool, procedures for determining eligibility, and the sizes of bonus awards.

Sloan's Leadership Style While Alfred Sloan lacked Durant's charisma and entrepreneurial flair, he excelled in finding ways to structure GM's wide-ranging operations so the company could function smoothly and cohesively. He had an intuitive grasp of the marketplace and made a conscious effort not to isolate himself from daily operations. He held frequent meetings with employees, visited the proving grounds regularly, and stayed in close touch with what went on at the division level. Sloan surrounded himself with high-quality people and solicited their advice.

When Sloan assumed the reins at GM in 1923, the company trailed Ford by a huge margin in both sales volume and market share. By the end of the 1920s GM was in position to take the industry lead. From 1928 onward GM sold more cars every year than any other company in the world. Sloan served as president and CEO until 1946. In 1946 at the age of 71 he relinquished the presidency and CEO title, but remained on as chairman of the board until 1956 when he was 81. When he left the post of chairman, GM was the undisputed world leader of the automotive industry and ranked as the largest manufacturing company in the world based on annual sales revenues.

The Post–Sloan Years, 1956–1981

Throughout the 1950s, GM's competitive position in the U.S. automotive market was unchallenged. Its market share in cars ranged between 42 percent and 51 percent, versus 25–30 percent for Ford, and 11–20 percent for Chrysler. The only foreign import to make a splash in the U.S. market was the Volkswagen Beetle, which near its high point in the late 1950s captured about a 5 percent market share; prior to 1958 the market share of all import brands combined never exceeded 5 percent. Fierce price competition among the Big Three (GM, Ford, and Chrysler) in the mid-1950s forced mergers among the other U.S. automakers: Packard with Studebaker, Hudson with Nash, and Kaiser-Frazer with Willys-Overland (Jeep). Except for the Hudson-Nash merger, which led to the creation of American Motors, none survived. American Motors acquired Jeep and then limped along for another 20 years with a market share under 4 percent until being acquired by Chrysler in 1987. In 1955 GM became the first corporation in the world to earn more than $1 billion in a single year.

As GM entered the decade of the 1960s, it dominated the marketplace—its domestic market share consistently approached 50 percent and its world market share was about 33 percent. GM's profits set a record every year from 1962 to 1965, and 25 new plants in the United States and abroad were opened during the decade. GM was the world's low-cost producer of vehicles, due primarily to its size, which enabled it to achieve scale economies in design, engineering, and production. It was also viewed as an innovative leader, especially in the areas of engineering and styling. GM introduced the first completely automatic shift transmission on 1940 Oldsmobile models. High-compression V-8 engines were a GM innovation in 1948. Power steering, power brakes, and power windows were introduced in the 1950s. GM's tailfin look for the 1948 Cadillac fostered a whole series of styling designs that carried over into the early 1960s. The styling of GM cars set appearance standards for the whole industry.

Nonetheless, the 1960s and 1970s presented major new challenges for GM management. Commenting on this period in the company's history, a former GM chairman observed:

> Practically every value of our society was being challenged, and business, especially "big" business, was on the top of many lists for change. GM, because of its size, type of products and number of employees and dealers, was a visible and

easily accusable target. Popular subjects were the environment and safety, minority discrimination, so-called consumerism, inflation, and government interest in and government regulation of business.

Auto Safety, New-Car Defects, and Pollution Regulations

In the early 1960s, a struggling law school graduate named Ralph Nader launched a public crusade against built-in car defects and the automotive industry's lack of commitment to vehicle safety. He singled out GM's new "import fighter," the Chevrolet Corvair, as a principal target. Nader's book, *Unsafe at Any Speed*, alleged that the Corvair was unstable on turns, that the cooling system leaked carbon monoxide fumes into the car, and that drivers could be lanced by the steering column in a front-end crash. He laid the blame for the Corvair's safety defects on Ed Cole, chief engineer and general manager of Chevrolet (who later would become GM's president); Nader said of Cole, "No man in the last twenty years had the authority and the knowledge to make safe cars, and didn't use it, like Ed Cole." A Senate committee investigation on auto safety and defects, featuring Ralph Nader's testimony, not only led to GM being embarrassed and confronted with a rash of lawsuits relating to the Corvair's safety but also resulted in the National Traffic and Motor Vehicle Safety Act of 1966, which mandated seat belts, energy-absorbing instrument panels and steering columns, more protective bumpers, and additional lights. By the late 1960s, one out of three cars sold in the United States was being recalled to repair safety defects, and manufacturers' expenses for new-car warranties became a substantial cost factor. GM discontinued the production of Corvairs in 1969.

Congress's first effort to regulate engine emissions came in the Clean Air Act of 1963; subsequent amendments required 90 percent reduction in pollution emissions by 1976. Protests by GM executives and officials at other auto companies that the standards were too costly and could not be met in the time frames specified went unheeded. Research by GM indicated the catalytic converter was the most appropriate option; an added bonus of the converter was an improvement in fuel economy. The rest of the industry followed GM's lead in using catalytic converters to meet emission standards. The total costs to GM of complying with pollution and safety regulations exceeded $600 billion in 1971; GM, along with other auto manufacturers, passed the added costs on to consumers in the form of higher sticker prices.

The 1965 Organizational Change

As far back as the 1950s, GM's size had generated talk about an antitrust breakup. Partly out of concern over possible antitrust action and partly out of a motivation to obtain more efficiency in the assembly process, Fred Donner, GM's CEO from 1958 to 1967, created the General Motors Assembly Division (GMAD) in 1965, the first major reorganization of GM since the early Sloan era. The establishment of GMAD took control of the assembly plants away from the car divisions and consolidated their operation under GMAD management—a move that was intended to make it harder to break GM into freestanding companies since its main purpose was to begin assembling different brands of

GM cars in the same assembly plant. The creation of GMAD was a cost-efficient move aimed at achieving greater utilization of GM's many assembly plants, allowing similar models of the different car divisions to be "mass-produced" in the same plant with the same equipment by the same workers, and potentially reducing the number of different components and parts used in GM cars. Like GM's other divisions, GMAD was set up to operate on a decentralized basis with its own division management staff. GMAD's creation had an unintended side effect, however: It forced the car divisions to spend more time in meetings with both Fisher Body and GMAD (as well as the relevant coordinating committees) on all the details associated with getting their new car models designed, produced, and into showrooms.

The Energy Shocks and Rising Gasoline Prices

The Saudi Arabian oil embargo in October 1973 and the subsequent emergence of the OPEC oil cartel hit General Motors, the biggest producer of gas-guzzling models, very hard. Thousands of U.S. car buyers, confronted with long waiting lines at service stations and faced with paying twice as much for gasoline, began purchasing fuel-efficient compact cars that got two to three times the mileage of GM cars. The bottom dropped out of the market of big expensive cars; by January 1974, small-car sales, both domestic and foreign, represented nearly 50 percent of the market. At the time, most GM executives expected the demand shift to economical small cars to be short-lived, believing that traditional GM car buyers were wedded to large, powerful "family cars." Time and events proved GM executives wrong. As automobile industry analyst Maryann Keller later observed:

> On a fundamental level, GM missed the point of what was happening around them. And they were locked into narrow concepts about what customers found desirable in their cars. They defined small as cheap, uncomfortable, underpowered, and spartan. In fact, when GM tried to build small cars they were just that. They were afraid of making good, desirable small cars for fear it would cut into their big-car business. What they failed to appreciate was that the Japanese were prepared to design small cars with big-car quality and features—and good mileage to boot.
>
> The energy crisis merely pushed an already emerging trend over the edge. Even as General Motors complacently continued to design its "family" cars, the shape of the American family was changing. Women were returning to the workplace in droves, creating the demand for a second, more economical family car. The first generation of suburban youth were coming of age; they got driver's licenses and needed to have cars to get around, and parents were discovering that it was cheaper to buy their teenagers and college-age children new gas-efficient imports like the Volkswagen than to spring for larger, used cars that would cost more to run. The energy crisis merely deepened an already existing consumer sensitivity to car economy—both in purchase price and operating costs. The GM leadership could not grasp the very simple fact that the small car was here to stay—with or without an energy crisis.[1]

---

[1]Maryann Keller, *Rude Awakening: The Rise, Fall, and Struggle for Recovery of General Motors* (New York: William Morrow and Company, 1989), p. 53.

Other company critics said the corporate culture at GM isolated GM executives from events in the real world and that they led a "cloistered life" inside their executive suite.

When the oil crisis struck, Richard Gerstenberg, GM's CEO and chairman, decided to bypass GM's slow-functioning committee system and to ram through a plan reducing the vehicle weight of most GM cars by 800 to 1,000 pounds (thus boosting fuel economy three miles per gallon), downsizing the entire fleet by 1977, and allowing each division, including Cadillac, to have its own small car. GM's new product line message became "smaller is better" and "the more you pay, the more you get."

When federal fuel economy standards were enacted in 1978 and a second jump in gasoline prices occurred in 1979, then GM chairman and CEO Thomas Murphy put in place a second program to downsize every GM car even more by 1985. Murphy's program, announced in 1979, called for GM to spend $40 billion over a five-year period on "the most comprehensive, ambitious, far-reaching, and costly product and facilities improvement program ever undertaken by any corporation anywhere in the world at any time in history." The strategy included redesigning the entire product line, replacing selected factories, modernizing other plants to enable the company to achieve world technological leadership, and increasing capacity to take advantage of longer production runs. Murphy said GM's objective was to halt the invasion of the imports and gain a three-year lead in product innovation over Ford and Chrysler.

The Challenge from Foreign Imports

In 1959, imports, led by the Volkswagen "Bug" and Renault, captured 10 percent of the U.S. market, up from 1.7 percent in 1956. GM officials announced it would soon introduce small-car models. The introduction of the first American-made small cars (GM's Corvair, Ford's Falcon, and Chrysler's Valiant) in 1959–61, coupled with the fact that import manufacturers had quality and service problems and weak dealer networks, resulted in the market share of imports dropping below 5 percent in 1962. Thinking the imports were beaten and believing that U.S. consumers preferred performance, comfort, and utility in excess of what foreign import models offered, GM began upgrading its small-car lines, making them bigger, heavier, loaded with options, and more expensive. They did not see why any buyer would find an austere, small car appealing; GM executives believed that small foreign cars were bought mostly by misfits and people who had a snobbish appeal for foreign products. From a practical perspective, GM executives viewed low-priced small cars with anxiety because of their thin profit margins. Due to the labor intensity of auto manufacturing, GM's costs for producing a small car were not significantly lower than they were for a large car, and two subcompacts did not yield as much profit as one full-size car. In addition, the chance a customer would buy optional equipment was less because what attracted compact-car buyers in the first place was the low price and low operating costs. Thus, GM's management was reluctant to pursue the small-car buyer on a grand scale because of the likelihood that smaller, less profitable models would cannibalize sales of GM's larger, higher-profit-margin models.

EXHIBIT 4   **Registration of New Foreign-Brand Motor Vehicles in the United States, 1969–1989**

Year	Passenger Cars		Trucks and Commercial Vehicles	
	Units	Percent of Total	Units	Percent of Total
1960	499,000	7.6%	37,000	0.4%
1965	569,000	6.1	14,000	0.9
1970	1,231,000	14.7	73,000	4.1
1975	1,501,000	18.2	237,000	9.9
1980	2,469,000	28.2	523,000	21.1
1985	3,011,000	27.6	953,000	20.4
1986	3,444,000	30.9	1,042,000	21.7
1987	3,654,000	35.9	1,057,000	21.2
1988	3,709,000	35.4	852,000	16.4
1989	3,131,000	31.8	803,000	15.7

Source: R. L. Polk & Co., as reported in *Automotive News*, 1990 Market Data Book Issue, pp. 36–46 and in Motor Vehicle Manufacturers Association, *World Motor Vehicle Data*, 1990 Edition, p. 350.

Foreign automakers, particularly the Japanese, used the 1960s to study U.S. preferences, design more appropriate and better cars, and strengthen their dealer networks. By the early 1970s, imports were gaining greater buyer acceptance with their advances in quality, improved marketing techniques, and stronger dealer networks. Whereas full-sized cars amounted to over 95 percent of the market in 1949, by 1970 full-sized cars were only 46.5 percent of total volume and compact models had a 40 percent market share. GM ranked second to Ford in U.S. sales of small cars.

The import-fighting strategy that evolved at GM during the mid-1970s entailed building two new families of small-car models. The first was the "X-car" with front-wheel drive and engine refinements designed to deliver lower emissions and higher gas mileage. Front-wheel drive allowed for a lighter car, better handling, and a roomier interior. GM's X-car models (Chevrolet Citation, Pontiac Phoenix, Oldsmobile Omega, and Buick Skylark) hit the market right in the middle of the second oil shock when gasoline prices jumped to $1.25–$1.75 per gallon. Initially the X-car models sold well, but quality problems soon led to declining sales. X-car production was halted in 1985, a year earlier than planned.

The second small-car design was the "J-car," introduced in 1981 as the Chevrolet Cavalier, Pontiac 2000, Oldsmobile Firenza, Buick Skylark, and Cadillac Cimarron. The expected sales volumes never materialized; GM's share of small car sales was over 4 percentage points lower in 1983 than it had been in 1980, the year before the new J-cars were introduced. The J-car designs generated further complaints about GM's look-alike models.

Neither of GM's efforts stemmed the growing sales of foreign imports in the U.S. market—see Exhibits 4, 5, and 6. Meanwhile, the Japanese producers launched a long-term strategy of designing compact-size cars with big-car

E X H I B I T   5   **Comparative Retail Sales of Passenger Cars in the United States, 1984–1989**

	1984	1985	1986	1987	1988	1989
American Motors Corporation*	190,255	123,449	72,853	—	—	—
Chrysler Corporation						
Plymouth	289,244	329,731	362,798	289,112	291,059	271,645
Dodge	369,255	434,325	456,777	348,294	455,787	410,995
Chrysler	327,499	375,880	353,888	295,125	269,254	188,175
Eagle	—	—	—	29,526	46,682	46,691
Total Chrysler	986,998	1,139,936	1,173,463	932,531	1,062,782	917,506
Ford Motor Company						
Ford	1,300,644	1,386,195	1,397,141	1,389,886	1,527,504	1,433,550
Mercury	527,198	519,059	491,782	463,860	486,208	465,908
Lincoln	151,475	165,138	177,584	166,037	191,624	200,315
Total Ford	1,979,317	2,070,392	2,066,507	2,019,783	2,205,336	2,099,773
General Motors Corporation						
Chevrolet	1,565,143	1,600,200	1,558,476	1,363,187	1,363,181	1,232,761
Pontiac	704,684	796,795	841,441	659,262	715,119	634,327
Oldsmobile	1,056,053	1,066,122	1,059,390	714,394	715,270	600,037
Buick	941,611	845,579	769,434	557,411	581,424	542,917
Cadillac	320,017	298,762	304,057	261,284	266,548	266,899
Total GM	4,587,508	4,607,458	4,532,798	3,555,538	3,641,542	3,276,941
Honda Motor Company						
U.S.-built	133,601	145,976	235,247	316,618	375,625	389,472
Imported	374,819	406,413	458,268	421,688	393,360	393,630
Total Honda	508,420	552,389	693,515	738,306	768,985	783,102
Toyota Motor Company						
U.S.-built	—	—	7,281	44,853	72,354	212,388
Imported	557,982	620,043	632,904	583,809	616,529	511,271
Total Toyota	557,982	620,043	640,185	628,662	688,883	723,659
Nissan Motor Corporation						
U.S.-built	—	39,794	52,602	119,678	112,125	103,134
Imported	485,292	535,372	501,247	456,985	360,745	406,870
Total Nissan	485,292	575,166	553,849	576,663	472,870	510,004
Mazda Motor Company						
U.S.-built	—	—	—	1,671	31,331	41,584
Imported	N/A	211,093	222,716	206,354	224,719	221,794
Total Mazda	N/A	211,093	222,716	208,025	256,050	263,378
Volkswagen-Audi	177,322	214,560	203,115	191,705	191,741	154,933
Mercedes-Benz	N/A	89,098	99,314	89,918	83,627	75,714
BMW	N/A	87,832	96,759	87,839	73,359	64,881
Volvo	N/A	104,267	113,269	106,539	98,497	102,620
All others	917,271	646,432	991,166	1,135,035	1,047,435	894,903
Total retail passenger car sales	10,390,365	11,042,115	11,459,509	10,270,544	10,591,107	9,867,414

N/A = not available.

*Acquired by Chrysler in 1987.

Source: *Automotive News*, 1990 Market Data Book Issue, p. 27, and Motor Vehicle Manufacturers Association, *1990 Facts and Figures*, pp. 14 and 15.

EXHIBIT 6   **Comparative Sales of Trucks in the United States, Selected Manufacturers, 1984–1989**

	1984	1985	1986	1987	1988	1989
Light-Truck Manufacturers (Includes pickups, vans, and sports vehicles)						
General Motors Corporation						
Chevrolet	1,090,178	1,256,964	1,245,768	1,166,155	1,331,291	1,340,666
GMC	305,206	347,577	340,877	337,034	386,864	373,254
Total GM	1,395,384	1,604,541	1,586,645	1,503,189	1,718,155	1,713,920
Ford Motor Company	1,162,834	1,245,805	1,348,988	1,433,910	1,517,356	1,466,929
Chrysler Corporation						
Jeep	148,292	182,210	195,973	205,106	245,603	248,981
Dodge-Plymouth	355,789	418,741	379,598	700,999	757,786	735,796
Total Chrysler	504,081	600,951	575,571	906,105	1,003,389	984,777
Nissan Motor Company	203,724	255,601	223,406	216,514	169,591	153,412
Toyota Motor Company	264,183	329,930	384,150	303,783	247,077	221,694
Mazda Motor Company	119,127	115,464	157,127	123,699	93,287	78,539
Isuzu Motor Company	45,379	78,149	88,720	86,990	90,405	103,373
Heavy-Duty Truck Manufacturers						
Daimler-Benz						
Freightliner	N/A	N/A	N/A	23,482	24,009	25,123
Mercedes-Benz	N/A	N/A	N/A	3,987	3,080	2,055
Total Daimler-Benz	18,889	23,310	21,073	27,469	27,089	27,178
Mack	25,617	29,514	21,829	22,666	24,928	25,228
Navistar (International)	66,713	73,463	68,522	70,481	84,915	77,959
PACCAR Corporation						
Kenworth	N/A	N/A	N/A	14,572	17,284	19,477
Peterbilt	N/A	N/A	N/A	12,551	17,019	18,603
Total PACCAR	26,732	24,286	21,110	27,123	34,303	38,080
All Other Manufacturers (Light and heavy-duty)	216,335	294,178	303,880	241,959	200,605	209,106
Total	4,048,998	4,675,192	4,801,021	4,963,888	5,211,100	5,100,195

N/A = not applicable.
Source: *Automotive News*, 1990 Market Book Issue, pp. 37 and 46.

features and performance and they progressively improved their manufacturing skills to where their models had fewer defects, nicer "fits and finishes," and superior repair records than GM's top-of-the-line models, much less its import-fighting models.

Labor Problems

GM's labor costs became a source of increasing concern during the 1960s and 1970s as the UAW won record wage settlements and pioneered numerous contractual benefits for its members. In 1970 the UAW went on strike to force GM to remove the limit on the automatic wage increases that GM workers would

EXHIBIT 7   **Average Transaction Price per New Car in the United States, 1970–1989**

Year	Domestic	Import
1989	$14,939	$16,563
1988	14,019	15,620
1987	13,210	14,515
1986	12,526	13,815
1985	11,733	12,875
1984	11,172	12,354
1983	10,559	10,873
1982	9,865	9,957
1981	8,912	8,896
1980	7,609	7,482
1979	6,889	6,704
1978	6,478	5,934
1977	5,985	5,072
1976	5,506	4,923
1975	5,084	4,384
1970	3,708	2,648

Source: U.S. Bureau of Labor Statistics.

get as the consumer price index rose; GM finally capitulated after a 67-day strike. Double-digit inflation during the 1970s then drove up GM's labor costs sharply and put GM management under increased pressure to improve labor productivity. The 1970 contract was viewed as the main reason why GM's labor costs rose from 29.5 percent of sales in 1962 to over 33 percent by 1972. Nonetheless, GM looked to areas other than labor to find cost savings; its main efforts went into reducing the number of car models; standardizing more of the parts used in models across the five car divisions; developing cheaper materials, such as plastics, to be used in car parts and interiors; stretching the intervals between model changes to reduce the need for designers, engineers, and testing staffs; and further consolidating its auto-assembly operations, placing all but four assembly plants under GMAD's jurisdiction in order to increase GM's flexibility in utilizing the same assembly plant to turn out models for several divisions.

During the latter 1970s, car prices rose tremendously (Exhibit 7). Sticker shock became a new phenomenon for new-car buyers. In 1975, the price of a Buick Regal was $4,257; in January 1981, the price was $7,787, an increase of 82.9 percent. Labor costs were partially responsible; by the late 1970s, compensation of UAW employees was approximately 65 percent above the average for other American manufacturing employees.

Changes in GM's Corporate Culture

Between the time Alfred Sloan retired and Roger Smith assumed the reins, the corporate culture at General Motors became more and more dominated by the financial staff. Whereas Sloan had been careful to preserve a balance between the influence of the financial staff and the operating autonomy of the general managers of the divisions, after his retirement several events tipped the scales toward progressively greater financial dominance. One was the concern about an antitrust breakup. By the mid-1950s concern over GM's size was such that any effort on GM's part to aggressively increase its market share would invite strong antitrust action; as a consequence, GM's priorities shifted away from the strategic objectives of making more and better cars to the financial objectives of increasing profits and return on investment from a relatively stable volume of sales. The added emphasis on short-term profitability translated into more influence for the corporate financial staff. Another incident in the mid-1950s, said to have been a factor, was related by Albert Lee, a one-time speechwriter for Roger Smith:

> Old-timers tell me the shift in power came about because of Harlow Curtice, the dynamic and universally popular leader who was the last chief-executive president. As the story goes, Curtice visited GM's European operations and approved several product and capital expenditures without checking back with the bean counters in New York. The financial people decided that the only way to prevent that from happening again was to assume the reins.[2]

In 1958, Frederick Donner, a financial executive, was made chairman and chief executive officer; Donner's appointment began a trend for GM's CEO to come from the financial ranks and for the president (chief operating officer) to come from the engineering and production ranks.

The presence of a financially trained executive at the helm of GM for all but four years between 1958 and 1990 was symbolic of the growing impact that GM's financial staff had on internal decision making. A former GM executive vice president claimed that Chevrolet's engineers knew that the Corvair had problems and proposed how to cure them but that GM's financial staff rejected them as too expensive; according to him, it was not until three years after the Corvair's problems were aired in public that the financial staff agreed to requests from the Chevrolet division's managers to equip the Corvair with a stabilizer bar costing $15 per car. The chief engineer at Cadillac from 1973 to 1984 said:

> I was always impressed with the fact that I was being pushed to reduce engineering costs by ten dollars a car, when the sales incentives and warranty costs totaled something like a couple of thousand dollars a car, and that we must have the pressure on the wrong thing.[3]

In the late 1970s, it was decided that the executive assistants to high-level operating executives not only should come from the ranks of the corporate financial staff (already traditional practice) but also that they should report to the corporate treasurer's office rather than the executives they served under. It was common for the sharpest "fast-trackers" on the financial staff who were being groomed for leadership positions to be given the executive assistant assignments (Roger Smith and his predecessor, Thomas Murphy, both served in this capacity on their climb through the ranks). Symbolic of the corporate

---

[2]Albert Lee, *Call Me Roger* (Chicago: Contemporary Books, 1987) p. 46.
[3]As quoted in Maryann Keller, *Rude Awakening*, p. 28.

finance staff's power at GM was the fact that their offices were directly below the CEO's office, connected by a back stairway that gave them the only way to get to the CEO's office without going through the elaborate double-door security system to the executive office suite.

By the time Roger Smith became chairman and CEO in 1981, the management culture at GM held two role models in the highest esteem: people who had proven expertise in corporate finance matters and people who had championed the design and development of important new models (product engineers). According to industry analyst Maryann Keller:

> The company has always been run by two distinct types. The first is the real power, the finance people. It is from their ranks that the chairmen have been selected since Fred Donner in 1958, with the single exception of James Roche, who became chairman in 1968. The second type is the product engineers. They are the real "car guys"—they know a lot about cars and they know that remaining as engineers precludes their ever getting the big money rewards at the top.
>
> The finance staff is the circulatory system of the company, recruited from the best schools and compensated on a salary scale that is more lucrative than the rest of the corporation. They are responsible for coordinating decision making and bringing information to the attention of top management. But they're not always sensitive to life in the real world of the factory or showroom. Finance people don't rise from the ranks of the product or production engineers, so they've never had hands-on experience in the making of cars. They are accused of having little sensitivity to the common problems that are encountered in production or design or engineering. They only know how things are supposed to look on paper. Since they work for GM, where company cars are a common executive perk, they don't even have to have the experience of shopping for, buying, driving, and maintaining a car.
>
> Product engineers usually have never worked anywhere but in the automotive industry, and their status increases with seniority—the more years they put in at the company, the higher they rise within the ranks. Car guys have big garages that, for the true loyalists, often house at least one classic car. Their offices are filled with car memorabilia. They are fully conversant in areas like acceleration, horsepower, and valves-per-cylinder. . . . Many of them have graduated from the General Motors Institute (GMI), a good school that pioneered sound technical training but offered limited exposure to liberal arts.
>
> Missing from the power equation are the production engineers, who perform critical functions in the plant, and set out the manufacturing systems by which parts and cars are made . . . the very people who are responsible for the hands-on creation of the product. Nor has there been status given to the marketing people, a possible factor in GM's failure to understand and address the needs of the changing marketplace.[4]

Managers with experience and expertise in manufacturing, production engineering, and marketing tended to be viewed by GM's financial people as philosophically allied with product engineers and more a part of the "car guy" segment of the culture. GM's critics argued that the company's finance-dominated "manage by the numbers" culture explained why there had been frequent decisions to pinch pennies at the expense of design, production quality, and technical features. According to the critics, the biggest reason so many of GM's new models lacked innovative designs and exciting

[4]Maryann Keller, *Rude Awakening*, pp. 23–24.

features was that the financial staff had intervened and forced the original designs to be altered to save money. A similar reason was said to explain some, though not all, of the defects that had plagued GM cars: The finance staff would not approve expenditures needed to eliminate the defect until the next design cycle or model year unless forced by federal regulators into making a product recall.

THE ROGER SMITH ERA, JANUARY 1981–JULY 1990

Roger Smith grew up in Detroit. After receiving his MBA from the University of Michigan, he joined GM in 1949 as a general accounting clerk. Within nine years, he became director of the general accounting section. Over the next several years Smith moved up through a series of financial positions: director of financial analysis, assistant treasurer, general assistant comptroller, and treasurer. In 1971 he was promoted to vice president in charge of the financial staff. Later that same year Smith was named vice president and group executive in charge of the nonautomotive and defense group. In 1974 he was promoted to executive vice president and elected to GM's board of directors; he was given responsibility for finance, public relations, and industry and government relations. In 1978 six more staff departments were brought in under his reporting line: consumer relations, marketing, personnel administration, and development and materials management. While in this job, he argued that GM should divest its Frigidaire appliance business and its TEREX earthmoving operations; his efforts resulted in the sale of both divisions during 1979 and 1980. In September 1980 GM announced that Roger Smith would succeed Thomas Murphy as chairman and CEO, effective January 1, 1981. At the time of his appointment as CEO, he was regarded as a dedicated company man who would quietly and capably carry forward the programs his predecessor had set in motion. He was not expected to do anything unusual. When his appointment was first announced, Smith himself said, "I do not expect to make any significant changes."

GM's Strategy under Roger Smith

Weeks after Smith took over, GM reported a $762 million loss for 1980, the company's first money-losing year since 1921. Ford and Chrysler seemed to pose no immediate competitive threat. Chrysler was struggling to survive and avoided bankruptcy only by the grace of a last-minute bailout with government guaranteed loans, while Ford was in the midst of three years of losses totaling $3.3 billion. GM accounted for 46 percent of U.S. car sales (only slightly less than in 1979), whereas Ford and Chrysler had lost share to foreign models. Imports, however, were an obvious and growing long-term threat, having captured 28.2 percent of the U.S. car market in 1980, up from 17.8 percent in 1978 and 14.7 percent in 1970. Worldwide, GM's market share in 1980 was 18.3 percent, compared with 21.4 percent in 1979.

Smith saw his first task as restoring GM to profitability. He launched cost-cutting moves that resulted in layoffs for 27,000 white-collar workers and 172,000 blue-collar workers and in the sale of the General Motors Building in New York City. A total of $3 billion was cut from GM's budget, producing a profit of $333 million in 1981.

Shortly thereafter, Smith came to the conclusion that he would have to institute major changes at GM if the company was going to cope with swiftly changing customer preferences, fragmentation of buyer demand into more models with wide-ranging styles and features, and globalized competition keyed to low-cost production efficiency and the use of advanced technology. Over the next few years a five-point strategic agenda began to emerge:

- Improve product quality to the point where GM models set industry standards for quality, performance, styling, safety, and customer value.
- Replace older, less-efficient manufacturing facilities with new modernized plants and equipment.
- Reduce costs to a level that would reestablish GM's cost competitiveness.
- Ensure GM's leadership in all phases of automotive and manufacturing technology on into the 21st century.
- Build a more effective relationship with employees.

Transforming GM into a creative, innovative, high-technology corporation ranked near the top of Smith's goals. To lead GM into the 21st century and to narrow the productivity advantage of the Japanese, Smith felt it was imperative to invest in high technology:

> Technological leadership is what will keep us ahead in world competition, and it's also one of the things that is going to make the difference between high and low profit margins.

Smith's plans called for heavy capital investment in three major areas: (1) computer-controlled equipment and machines, (2) robotics, and (3) flexible automation (assembly methods that were flexible enough to permit similar models to be assembled simultaneously on the same product line).

Exhibit 8 provides a detailed chronology of the major strategic actions and organizational changes made at GM during the Roger Smith era. The following sections describe the most significant initiatives Smith undertook.

The 1984 Reorganization

GM's leadership became alerted to the need for reorganization because of a myriad of internal problems that were being encountered in getting new models from the design stage to the showroom in timely fashion, at acceptable cost, and with fewer quality defects. GM's president, James McDonald, who had risen up through the production engineering ranks and who had considerable manufacturing experience, began to see that GM's organization wasn't functioning well during the X-car years. The fundamental cause, concluded McDonald, was that it took three separate divisions—a car division, Fisher Body, and GMAD—to get a car designed, produced, and into the marketplace. Each operated autonomously and jealously protected its turf. A car division would approve a new design and turn it over to Fisher Body. Fisher engineered the body to conform to the design. GMAD planned the necessary tooling and equipment modifications and handled final assembly. All divisions reported ultimately to the president, who was responsible for arbitrating disputes and enforcing cooperation. A study by outside consultants concluded that GMAD and Fisher Body had become entrenched, powerful bureaucracies that impeded GM's need to get new models to market faster and at lower cost.

EXHIBIT 8   **A Chronology of Major Strategic Actions and Organizational Changes at GM during Roger Smith's Tenure (1981–1990)**

1981
- Reorganized truck and bus operations into a single worldwide group.
- Acquired a 5.3 percent equity interest in Suzuki Motor of Japan for $38 million; Suzuki began developing a subcompact car (the Sprint) for sale by GM in the United States.
- Led all competitors in new model introductions (a total of 29).
- Folded operations of the Diesel Equipment Division into the Rochester Products Division to eliminate overlapping efforts of the two divisions in the field of advanced fuel systems.
- Merged operations of the Delco Air Conditioning division into the Harrison Radiator Division to consolidate company efforts in the development and manufacture of heating, ventilation, and air-conditioning systems.
- Merged the AC Delco Division and the GM Parts Division into a new Warehousing and Distribution Division that provided service and replacement parts worldwide to all GM sales units.

1982
- Invested $5 million and its own robotics expertise in a 50–50 joint venture with Fanuc Ltd. of Japan (a leading robot and computer controls manufacturer) to design, manufacture, and sell robotics systems.
- Opened a new European assembly plant in Spain and new engine/transmission plant in Austria and announced construction of five other European facilities.
- Announced that Isuzu would make a small car called the Spectrum to be sold by GM in the United States.

1983
- Formed a 50–50 joint venture with Toyota called the New United Motor Manufacturing, Inc. (NUMMI) to build a version of the Toyota Corolla to be sold as the Chevrolet Nova at an unused GM plant in Fremont, California.
- Opened two all-new assembly plants in the United States.
- Announced the Buick City concept where Buick suppliers would locate near Buick's core manufacturing cluster in Flint, Michigan, to permit maximum benefits from "just-in-time" inventory practices.
- Introduced two major new models in Europe—the Opel Corsa and the Vauxhall Nova.
- Announced that GM would develop an all-new, top-quality small car to be called the Saturn—GM's first new nameplate since Pontiac in 1926.

1984
- Reorganized the company's North American passenger car operations into two self-contained business units.
- Acquired a 10 percent interest in Philip Crosby Associates, a recognized firm in quality training and consulting; together GM and Crosby created the General Motors Quality Institute to train GM managers in how to implement statistical process control techniques.
- Initiated a quality program for suppliers.
- Announced a $52 million Factory of the Future project to test and develop highly flexible, automated production equipment, fully integrated as a system using computer controls.
- Invested another $100 million in a 50–50 joint venture with South Korea's Daewoo Motors to build small cars (including the Pontiac LeMans) for GM.
- Announced the acquisition of Electronic Data Systems, Inc. (EDS) for $2.55 billion.

1985
- Reorganized the Saturn Project as Saturn Corporation, forming a separate car division with an all-new dealer network.
- Made several acquisitions to establish GMAC as one of the largest mortgage banking companies in the United States.
- Agreed to acquire the Hughes Aircraft Company for $2.7 billion in cash plus $2.3 billion in common stock.

(continued)

EXHIBIT 8   *(Concluded)*

1986
- Established a program to reduce the salaried work force by 40,000 in two years, reduce corporate staff expenses by $200 million by 1990, phase out obsolete plant and component-manufacturing operations, divest unprofitable subsidiaries, and improve assembly plant efficiency. These efforts were expected to produce annual cost savings of $10 billion annually by 1990.
- Acquired Group Lotus, a British company specializing in engineering consulting, performance car manufacturing, and advanced automotive technologies.
- Sold GM's South African operations to local management.
- GM of Canada and Suzuki Motor of Japan announced a joint venture to manufacture small cars and sport vehicles in Canada, with production to begin in 1989.

1987
- Sold the company's transit bus operations to Greyhound.
- Sold the company's heavy-truck operations in Europe; formed a joint venture with Volvo to develop, produce, and market heavy-duty trucks for sale in the United States and Canada— Volvo had majority ownership and management control.
- Formed the Allison Transmission Division to serve the worldwide medium-and heavy-duty truck and military markets.
- Established a Quality Network throughout GM with the cooperation of the United Automobile Workers Union in an effort to unite all GM employees in becoming a high-quality, low-cost producer.
- Introduced a new generation of engines, the Quad 4, having lower emissions, more power, and better fuel economy.
- Entered into a joint venture with Isuzu for commercial vehicles in Europe.
- Entered into a joint venture with Penske Corporation relating to diesel engines.

1988
- Formed a joint venture with Toyota to merge the two companies' operations in Australia.
- Established a trial program in the Pontiac and Oldsmobile divisions whereby any car buyer who became dissatisfied could return their cars within 30 days or 3,000 miles for any reason, receiving a credit equal to the purchase price toward the purchase of another model.
- Launched the new Geo model line, sold through Chevrolet dealerships.
- Established a more comprehensive "Bumper to Bumper Plus" warranty coverage program.

1989
- Upped the $10 billion cost-reduction targets established in 1987 to $13 billion by year-end 1990.

1990
- Introduced as many new car and truck models as Ford, Chrysler, Toyota, and Honda combined.
- Introduced the new Saturn line of cars.

By 1982 both Roger Smith and Jim McDonald were evaluating preliminary reorganization plans and a task force on reorganization was formed. The problems the task force found were described thusly:

> The bureaucracy was a virtual quicksand bog of procedures. One consultant reported an incident where a simple design solution was found to fix a clutch problem. Finding the solution was the easy part. Getting it implemented was another story entirely. It might take years. In a well-organized environment, the engineer on the project should have been empowered to contact the supplier and

order the change. But not at General Motors. "You have to produce *fifty thousand* studies to show that it's a better solution," the consultant said. "Then you have to go through *ten* different committees to get it approved."

The complaints rolled in. Too much oversight by top management. Too many people assigned to the same programs. Too little accountability. Too much resistance to letting middle managers run with the ball.

Many of the problems were tangled up in GM's no-risk management environment, where individuals were not held accountable for the decisions they made. Since the high-potential managers were frequently rotated from one assignment to another, there was little continuity. This was devastating to the company and to the staffers, who were constantly subjected to new personalities whose private agendas included making themselves look good so they could move up the next rung on the ladder.[5]

One of the major intents of reorganization was to fix accountability and responsibility for the total vehicle and eliminate finger pointing at problems allegedly caused by work done or not done in another division.

In January 1984, Roger Smith announced the reorganization that had been rumored for over a year. The personnel and facilities of both the Fisher Body and GMAD divisions were reassigned to one of two new car groups. One group consisted of the Chevrolet-Pontiac-GM of Canada divisions and became known as CPC. The second group was composed of the Buick-Oldsmobile-Cadillac car divisions and was dubbed BOC. While the 1983 annual report stated that CPC would design and produce small cars and that BOC would focus on regular-size and large cars, each group ended up with responsibility for both small and large cars. Robert Stempel, who would later be Roger Smith's successor, was named vice president and group executive in charge of BOC. Although top executives at GM strongly supported the reorganization effort, considerable employee resistance built up against the announced changes. This was partly because the purposes of the reorganization were not sufficiently explained, partly because of heightened employee fears about their job and career prospects in the new organizational arrangement, and partly because divisional employees felt strong loyalties for their divisions. A Buick worker from Flint, Michigan (a Buick town) expressed the feelings of many of the affected workers:

> My granddaddy was a Buick guy, my daddy was a Buick guy, and I was a Buick guy. So now, when I go to a party or I go on vacation and somebody asks me where I work, what do I say? They know what a Buick is, I know what a Buick is. There's a sense of identity we've lost here.[6]

Another problem that had to be overcome was the rebuilding of the informal communications network people used to cut through the bureaucratic management layers and committees. Over the years, people had learned who to call to get something done. It took time for people to forge new working relationships and for an efficient informal network to emerge. The CPC car group came together faster than BOC because it consisted mainly of Chevrolet (the Pontiac and GM of Canada units were comparatively small) and because the bulk of the CPC organization was in Detroit.

---

[5]Maryann Keller, *Rude Awakening*, pp. 23–24.

[6]As quoted in Maryann Keller, *Rude Awakening*, p. 117.

While the reorganization process at BOC was lengthier, Stempel's participatory management approach, together with his stress on being product-oriented and developing teams that could make changes fast, moved BOC further along in the process of instilling a more product-oriented, market-driven culture. Early on in the process of implementing the announced reorganization, Stempel and his key executives became concerned that the new structure held too much potential for making BOC a mini-GM with too little interdepartmental communications and an overload of bureaucratic procedures. They proposed organizational revisions to create three groups within BOC, each with the capability of engineering and building a car of specified size (compact, mid-size, or large). Each group in turn would be divided into product teams that would be fully responsible and accountable for a given model; a product team leader would have authority over everything related to the model. At first, headquarters executives objected to Stempel's proposed structural changes, but Stempel persisted with persuasive arguments and finally prevailed.

Labor–Management Relations at GM during the 1980s

The relationship between General Motors management and the company's UAW-represented work force tended to be highly adversarial, characterized by mistrust and suspicion on both sides. The discord began several decades prior to the Roger Smith era. Many of the problems were traceable to a standard paragraph contained in GM-UAW contracts since the 1930s:

> The right to hire, promote, discipline for cause, and to maintain discipline and efficiency of employees; . . . [and] the products to be manufactured, the location of the plants, the schedules of production, the methods, processes and means of manufacturing are solely and exclusively the responsibility of the Corporation.

Management's insistence on its contractual right to run the company as it saw fit had, over the years, produced an atmosphere of almost constant confrontation with the UAW. Thousands of grievances challenging management's authority under this clause were filed annually.

A large percentage of GM's work force were "old-guard unionists" who had been through bitter strikes in the past, who zealously guarded their rights under the union contract, and who resisted attempts to boost their workloads as a management guise to cut out jobs. The cyclical nature of car sales produced periodic plant layoffs, making job security a paramount concern among workers. At each round of contract negotiations, the UAW succeeded in bargaining for bigger supplemental unemployment benefits (to provide added job security) and additional work rules limiting management's authority to define worker duties and workloads (to block any management efforts to speed up production, push employees to work harder, and thereby reduce the number of union jobs). Between 1950 and 1980, the number of job classifications at GM plants multiplied. Many of the jobs were defined so narrowly as to make the work monotonous and mindless. Meanwhile, wage rates and fringe benefits had escalated swiftly. Abuses crept into the system: At one GM plant, the rules required six different job classifications just to move parts from a delivery truck to the work station; at another, a forklift driver, by working overtime and skipping vacations, earned $59,000 hauling crates of car seat

EXHIBIT 9   **Employment and Payroll Costs at General Motors, 1975–1989**

	1975	1980	1985	1987	1988	1989
Average worldwide employment						
GM (automotive)	—	—	762,000	673,000	624,000	628,500
GMAC and related subsidiaries	—	—	14,000	18,200	18,500	18,400
Electronic Data Systems	—	—	35,000	44,600	47,500	55,000
Hughes Electronics	—	—	—	77,500	75,700	73,200
Company total	681,000	746,000	811,000	813,400	765,700	775,100
Worldwide payroll (in billions)	$10.0	$17.8	$25.6	$27.1	$27.5	$28.3
Average labor cost per hour worked, U.S. hourly employees (excluding GMAC, EDS, and Hughes)	N/A	$18.45	$23.40	$25.90	$27.90	$29.50
Payments for benefit plans (In billions)	N/A	N/A	$5.7	$6.1	$5.7	$4.7
North American employment at December 31 (excluding GMAC, EDS, and Hughes)						
Salaried	N/A	N/A	127,100	106,500	99,900	100,700
Hourly	N/A	N/A	441,800	366,000	343,600	328,500
Total			568,900	472,500	443,500	429,200

N/A = not applicable.
Source: Company annual reports.

cushions and boxes of seat covers from the receiving dock to the assembly line. Generous health-care benefits added about $600 to the average cost of each vehicle produced. Absenteeism ran as high as 20–25 percent a day during Michigan's deer-hunting season and during holiday periods.

Ford and Chrysler were plagued by the same problems. During the 1970s there was a running series of confrontation between the UAW and all three automakers over wage rates, fringe benefits, work rules, and job security. Because of its prominence in the industry, GM was typically singled out by the UAW as the target company for negotiating a pattern-setting contract.

When Roger Smith took over in 1981, one of his first actions to restore GM's profitability involved laying off 142,000 hourly workers. In its 1982 contract negotiations with the UAW, GM pushed for and won concessions relating to work rules and wages. On the eve of signing the new labor pact, GM announced bigger bonus payments for its top 6,000 managers. The union leadership and GM's workers were livid. Employee outrage continued to mount as Smith and GM implemented numerous plant closings and automated production processes. During the 1980s the size of GM's hourly work force shrunk from 468,000 to 300,000 (nationwide, membership in the UAW dropped from 1.5 million to 1.0 million). In speeches to workers and in his public appearances Smith often described the wages GM paid its workers as excessive, and he left no doubts that he believed hourly workers were overpaid and underworked. At several plant appearances he was booed by workers; workers openly made derogatory remarks about him, organized anti-Smith protests, and called for his resignation. Exhibit 9 presents statistics regarding employment and payroll costs at General Motors.

In 1987, GM management began in earnest to try to establish more of a partnership with its employees. Despite resistance from supervisory workers who saw a loss of authority, leeway was being made in setting up production teams at most GM plants. Yet, success was mixed. In a gesture of trust at a Flint plant, GM managers gave workers permission to clock out early with no pay penalty as soon as the established production quota was met. Productivity swiftly skyrocketed; employees, many on the job for more than 20 years, suddenly found ways to reach the daily quota before lunch. Management, dismayed at paying a full-day's wage for a half-day's work, unilaterally raised the quotas to where workers had to put in a full eight hours at the higher productivity levels to reach the quota. Workers felt they had been tricked into a speedup and the UAW local threatened a strike.

A clause in GM's 1987 labor contract called for a plant-closing moratorium on GM's part. Later, when management determined production from certain plants was no longer needed, it announced "indefinite idling" of such plants and proceeded to lay off workers "temporarily." Between May 1987 and June 1989, GM shut down 16 plants involving 36,000 jobs. In all, GM eliminated one in 10 UAW jobs from 1987 until mid-1990. The UAW sought arbitration over what it considered infraction of GM's no-closings pledge; on one occasion, a strike was sanctioned that rippled over to force GM to temporarily shut down all or part of 6 assembly plants and 10 parts factories. Again in 1989, Roger Smith outraged GM workers and UAW leaders by announcing one week that workers would receive only $50 in profit sharing bonuses and the next week granting bonuses to top management averaging $44,800 a person. Smith justified such actions on grounds that GM's management compensation program entailed relatively low salaries and relatively high performance bonuses. During the 1987–89 period the average GM worker received a total of $304 in profit sharing whereas Ford workers received $7,900. In spring 1990 Smith led a successful effort to nearly double the pensions of top executives; under the plan, Smith was to draw an annual pension of $1.1 million when he retired in July 1990. News of the plan hit just as top UAW leaders were trying to convince the rank and file that it would be too costly to demand cost-of-living adjustments to worker pensions in the upcoming 1990 contract negotiations.

Despite the antagonism that Roger Smith's actions aroused among workers, labor–management relations at GM were in overall better shape in 1990 than they had been in 1980. The mounting threat to union jobs posed by growing sales of Japanese cars served to promote a more cooperative and conciliatory posture on both sides. Since 1984, the UAW and GM had jointly committed more than $1.6 billion to educate, train, and retrain GM employees.

The NUMMI Venture with Toyota

Roger Smith saw the New United Motor Manufacturing, Inc. (NUMMI) joint venture with Toyota as an opportunity for GM to get invaluable hands-on experience in Japanese small-car assembly and management techniques, thus helping GM find ways to produce small cars domestically at costs competitive with the Japanese. Toyota's approach to car-building stressed worker initiative, teamwork between production employees and managers, accountability for quality, and a work environment where employees felt personally connected to an important effort. GM's idle Fremont plant, chosen as the project site, was notorious as having one of GM's most unmanageable work forces. Before the plant was closed and the 5,000 employees laid off, daily absenteeism was regularly over 20 percent, the parking lot was normally littered, and grievances were filed at a fast pace. In negotiating with the UAW, Toyota granted the union a strong job-security clause and a greater say in plant operations. The union, in return, agreed to eliminate unproductive job classifications and let Toyota management have virtually complete freedom in designing production techniques and supervising the assembly process. The UAW and NUMMI management collaborated in selectively hiring from the ranks of the laid-off workers; the evaluation process for each candidate took about 35 hours. Known "troublemakers" were rejected.

Toyota management spent much time on setting up the plant layout. Very little brand-new technology was introduced; the philosophy was that good product design, quality components, and a labor-efficient assembly system were the keys to cost-effectiveness. High labor productivity was seen as dependent on how people were organized and managed rather than on providing assembly workers with the most sophisticated tools and equipment; advanced technology was employed only when and where it enhanced quality. NUMMI's Japanese managers implemented a manufacturing approach that stressed seven points:

1. Searching for continuous improvement (the concept of *kaizen*).
2. Reducing costs through just-in-time techniques (the concept of *kanban*).
3. Developing human potential to the fullest.
4. Building mutual trust between managers and workers.
5. Developing team performance.
6. Treating every employee as a manager.
7. Providing a stable livelihood for all employees.

The plant utilized only 4 job classifications (versus over 150 at some GM plants). Employees were placed on five-person teams headed by fellow hourly workers trained in Japan. The team leader functioned as mediator and instructor, rather than as boss. Each member of the team was trained to do the leader's job when called upon. Workers were rewarded for finding ways to improve the assembly process, boost quality, and eliminate waste. In 1989, about 10,000 suggestions for improvement were offered from workers.

After production got under way, GM's surveys showed that the Chevrolet Nova models being turned out ranked among GM's top three models in quality. Absenteeism rates averaged 2 percent, versus 9 percent at other GM plants. Studies by outside experts concluded NUMMI's team approach was a main reason the plant made about the same number of vehicles with a work force about half the size GM had formerly used. By 1987 GM had begun efforts to institute the team approach at many other GM plants; however, resistance from mistrustful UAW hardliners slowed efforts to transfer the NUMMI experience. Exhibit 10 presents efficiency comparisons for the NUMMI plant versus representative GM and Toyota plants as of 1987.

Since the GM–Toyota agreement at NUMMI expressly prohibited the exchange of competitively sensitive information (a requirement imposed by the Federal Trade Commission), it was not readily apparent how the relatively

EXHIBIT 10   **Comparative Operating Efficiency of a GM Assembly Plant versus NUMMI Plant versus a Toyota Plant, 1987**

Efficiency Measure	GM's Framingham Assembly Plant (Closed in July 1989)	GM–Toyota NUMMI Plant	Toyota's Takaota Plant
Assembly hours per car	31	19	16
Square feet of assembly space per car produced	8.1	7.0	4.8
Assembly defects per hundred cars	135	45	45
Average inventory of parts maintained in assembly plant	2 weeks	2 days	2 hours

Source: James P. Womack and Daniel T. Jones, *The Machine That Changed the World* (New York: Macmillan, 1990), as reported in *The New York Times Magazine*, September 23, 1990, p. 23.

low-tech nature of the Fremont plant operation actually matched up against Toyota's use of technology in its Toyota City operations in Japan. While the NUMMI venture gave GM a close-up view of the productivity levels that could be achieved with UAW workers using Japanese production techniques, the plant also provided Toyota with a production base in California. Toyota had the right to produce up to 100,000 Toyota Corollas a year; GM's production quota was a matching 100,000 vehicles. When the Chevrolet Nova was phased out of GM's line, the NUMMI plant in Fremont became the production site for GM's new Geo Prism models. The NUMMI venture had a legal cutoff date of 1996; industry analysts expected Toyota to then acquire GM's ownership share and operate the facility as a Toyota plant.

GM's Detroit–Hamtramck Plant

In the mid-1980s, GM opened its first high-tech showcase plant in the Hamtramck section of Detroit. Roger Smith and other GM executives saw the plant as a demonstration of what could be done with state-of-the-art technology—it was where Cadillacs of the future were to be built with automated techniques of the future and it was to be a pilot for the new Saturn manufacturing complex. The Hamtramck plant had 260 robots for welding, parts assembly, and painting; 50 automated guided vehicles for moving parts from inventory to the assembly line; and a battery of cameras and computers that used laser beams to inspect and control the manufacturing process. When an underbody started down the assembly line, there was equipment that read a computerized specification sheet detailing the car's make and model (Eldorado or Seville or Buick Riviera or Oldsmobile Toronado), scheduled optional equipment, and color scheme. Along the line, scanners read the specs and converted them into customized instructions for the automated machines on how to build that particular underbody. Display monitors provided instructions to the workers.

Instead of a showcase "factory of the future" achievement, however, the Hamtramck plant became a nightmare of bugs and glitches:[7]

_____
[7]Maryann Keller, *Rude Awakening*, pp. 207–08.

- Robots designed to spray-paint cars sometimes painted each other instead.
- A robot designed to install windshields was found systematically smashing them.
- Robots went haywire and smashed into cars, demolishing both the vehicle and the robot.
- Computer systems sent erroneous instructions, leading to body parts being installed on the wrong cars.
- Factory lines were halted for hours while technicians scrambled to debug the software and get robots working properly.

A common scenario, as outlined in a *Ward's Auto World* magazine report, would be a robot abruptly shutting down and no one in the plant knowing the cause of the problem. An electrician familiar with one brand of robot hurries to the scene, only to find that this is a robot manufactured by a different company, and he doesn't understand how it operates. As the entire plant slowly grinds to a halt, and the electrician begins to plow through a complicated manual, the robot's manufacturer is called for advice. A company-trained expert is flown to the scene to analyze the situation and solve the problem. He looks at the robot for a minute, then hits a reset button (the modern equivalent of checking to see if the thing is plugged in). The machine springs to life. Everyone goes back to work.

Downtime at the Hamtramck plant was estimated to cost $200 per second. After a year of operation, the production rate was 30 to 35 cars per hour, well below the design rate of 60. A 1988 study by MIT researchers concluded that labor productivity and production efficiency at GM's Hamtramck plant was (1) no better than at Ford's Wixcom plant, which produced luxury cars with much less capital investment and technological sophistication and (2) only about 50 percent as efficient as comparable Japanese plants.

Despite GM's troubles at Hamtramck, Roger Smith remained committed to making GM the technological leader. He continued the investments in high-tech state-of-the-art equipment, regardless of the initial cost, although there were some scalebacks in assembly-line automation and use of robotics. The company's financial analysis indicated that the added fixed costs associated with the $50 billion effort to modernize GM's plants would pay off over the long term by allowing GM to eliminate the variable cost excesses GM suffered from UAW-imposed overcompensation of hourly workers and overmanning of assembly lines. Smith argued that once GM worked the bugs out of its technological investments, productivity would rise dramatically and GM would match or beat the production costs of Japanese producers.

The EDS Acquisition

In 1984 General Motors acquired Electronic Data Systems (EDS), the second largest provider of data processing services for client companies in the United States. EDS had a reputation for designing and operating large-scale data processing systems on a lower-cost basis than customers could achieve with their own personnel and equipment. The company was formed in 1962 by H. Ross

Perot, a creative and charismatic Texas entrepreneur. Perot had a competitive spirit that bordered on the fanatical; he loved to take on causes and was a hard-driving taskmaster. Prospective EDS employees were carefully screened; only people who were highly intelligent, ambitious, and willing to work long hours were hired. All EDS employees had to sign an agreement to abide by a strict code of conduct concerning drug abuse, consuming alcohol during working hours, and not discussing one's salary with fellow employees. Employees could not leave the company without forfeiting their stock bonus awards. Employees were trained from the day they joined the company to spend all their work effort on serving the customer, getting results, and being effective. Perot pushed employees to their limits, expecting them to go all out to meet challenging deadlines. "Can't" was a forbidden word at EDS. Dedicated high performers were well rewarded. Perot ran the company in true "lean and mean" fashion, mixing the discipline of a military boot camp with the esprit de corps of a young, aggressive company on the move. One outsider observed, "I've never seen a company with such tremendous discipline, tremendous loyalty, and tremendous respect for the quality of the work."[8] The company motto was, "Eagles don't flock, they fly alone."

Perot was a highly visible and inspirational leader; he spent much of his time with employees, urging them to strive for heroic individual achievements and instilling personal and company values. He considered EDS employees as "family" and always made himself accessible. An EDS staffer remarked, "I'd go to hell on a pair of roller skates if he asked me to, and he'd do the same for me." In 1979, Perot's leadership heroics gained national attention when he put together a commando team of 15 EDS employees and went to Iran to rescue two EDS employees who were being held hostage.

EDS had revenues approaching $800 million and profits of $80 million at the time of acquisition. The company had multiyear contracts with a diverse range of domestic and international clients in health care, financial services, insurance, and government. Major clients included AT&T, Blue Cross/Blue Shield organizations in 13 states, Unilever, Aetna, and an array of state and federal agencies.

When the idea of acquiring EDS was first presented to Roger Smith by a New York investment banker, he immediately became intrigued with the potential EDS had for eliminating the considerable inefficiency GM had in its computer operations and the contribution EDS could make to computerizing GM's plant operations and to injecting a much-needed entrepreneurial spirit into GM's culture. GM was the single largest user of computers outside the U.S. government and employed 10,000 people in its computer operations; however, GM's computer operations were not centrally linked and the company lacked the technical skills to develop advanced computer systems for manufacturing process control and for order entry from dealers and to suppliers.

Roger Smith personally spearheaded the negotiations to convince Ross Perot to sell EDS to GM. In their early negotiations, a strong rapport emerged between the two men. Perot was attracted by Smith's plan to use the unique

---

[8]Quoted in *Newsweek*, June 17, 1985, p. 69.

EDS culture as a major vehicle for changing GM and by the chance to be a part of the greatest industrial rescue mission of the century. Perot later told GM's board of directors, "The only reason we at EDS decided to sell our company to GM was to become involved in the challenge of building the best cars in the world at competitive prices." Smith and Perot agreed that EDS would operate as an independent entity, taking over the management of GM's entire computer operations and also continuing to grow its computer services business on the outside as rapidly as possible. Perot envisioned that as GM's ally EDS could become the greatest computer services organization in the world. Perot continued as head of EDS, reporting directly to Roger Smith, and was immediately made a member of GM's board of directors. To preserve EDS's economic identity, GM created a new class of GM common stock, known as Class E, that traded on the NYSE and reflected EDS's revenue and profit contribution. Perot received 11.3 million shares of Class E stock in the acquisition deal, making him GM's largest single shareholder.

The first problem Smith and Perot faced was how to merge the two alien cultures. As one wit said, "EDS merging with GM is like a Green Beret outfit joining forces with the Social Security Administration." One writer described the outcome:

> From the first, confusion reigned. Perot insisted on independence for EDS; Smith demanded fealty to GM bureaucracy. The opposing styles quickly created dissension among the rank and file. It didn't help that GM workers knew little about the merger in advance. Virtually overnight, EDS employees became GM employees, while GM's computer technicians found themselves suddenly reporting to EDS managers. Tempers flared.
>
> Before long, Perot and Smith were clashing over basic elements of their agreement, such as employees' pay. Perot thought he should decide EDS salaries, but Smith claimed the amounts were too high compared with General Motors' payment structure. In one case, he complained, a senior EDS executive was drawing a higher salary than he was as chairman of GM.
>
> Throughout, Smith attempted to keep a veil over the conflict, maintaining that he and Perot had only minor differences.[9]

Meanwhile Perot, acting in his capacity as a GM board member, proceeded to educate himself about GM. He had a series of informal meetings with GM's computer technicians, who had become EDS employees under the acquisition agreement. He made impromptu visits to GM plants, talking with both managers and union workers. He conversed with GM car dealers, with new-car buyers, and with suppliers. He learned as much as he could about competitors. And, much to the irritation of Roger Smith, he began to comment candidly on what he thought was wrong with General Motors and he openly criticized some of Roger Smith's actions. He made a number of comments to reporters that appeared in the business press:

> What it takes to be successful [at GM] has nothing to do with better products . . . it has to do with following the procedures, understanding the politics . . . understanding the power structure.

*****

---

[9]Doron P. Levin, "Breaking Up Is Hard to Do," *The New York Times Magazine*, March 26, 1989, p. 37.

The first EDSer to see a snake kills it. At GM, first thing you do is organize a committee on snakes. Then you bring in a consultant who knows a lot about snakes. Third thing you do is talk about it for a year.

*****

Let's say there's a problem with the brakes. . . . They will send some bright, highly motivated staff person, probably a financial type, out to check on the brake problem. He talks with an accountant who talks to someone in long-range planning, and finally they form a committee to talk to some poor devil working on brakes who knows what the hell to do.

*****

This place cries out for engineers with greasy hands who know how to make cars to be making the policy and motivating every member of the GM team.

*****

Just a trip to the 14th floor [the executive suite in the headquarters building] is depressing. . . . I'd get rid of the 14th floor. I'd get rid of the private dining rooms and chauffeured limos and heated [parking] garages. I would urge the senior executives to locate their offices where real people are doing real work—live with them, listen to them, spend time with them, find out what it would take to win, and do it.

Perot's comments made him a folk hero to many GM employees, dealers, and suppliers because he was saying publicly what knowledgeable insiders were telling each other privately. In 1985 Perot sent Smith a letter that in part said:

The only issue is the success of GM. Our compatibility is not the issue. . . . I am one of the few people who can and will disagree with you. . . . I will tell you anything that will build and strengthen GM, whether you want to hear it or not. . . . I will support you when I believe you are right. I will tell you candidly when I believe you are wrong. If you continue your present autocratic style, I will be your adversary on critical issues. . . . Your style intimidates people. . . . GMers at all levels use terms like bully and ruthless in describing you. There is a widespread feeling throughout GM that you don't care about people. . . . I do not believe GM can become world class and cost competitive by throwing technology and money at its problem. The Japanese are not beating us with technology or money. They use old equipment, and build better, less-expensive cars by better management, both in Japan and with UAW workers in the U.S. We are not closing the quality and price gaps in spite of huge expenditures on automating plants. The fact that we have not set a date to have competitive prices indicates the prevalent attitudes about our will to win. . . .[10]

The relationship between Perot and Smith continued to deteriorate in the ensuing months. Perot, however, reiterated his overall support for Smith, describing him as "one of the smartest, creative businessmen I've ever known and a prodigious worker." In late 1986 Smith got GM's board of directors to approve a $743 million cash buyout of Perot's stake in GM and EDS; Perot resigned as a GM director.

As of 1990 EDS was the world's largest supplier of computer services. The company handled most of the computing needs for some 7,000 clients

---

[10]Excerpted from Maryann Keller, *Rude Awakening*, pp. 171–72.

E X H I B I T   11   **Summary Financial Data for Electronic Data Systems (EDS) Operations, 1985–1989**   *(Dollars in millions, except per share amounts)*

	1989	1988	1987	1986	1985
Revenues:					
Systems and other contracts:					
GM and affiliates	$2,988.9	$2,837.0	$2,883.3	$3,195.1	$2,428.1
Outside customers	2,384.6	1,907.6	1,444.8	1,125.9	978.3
Interest and other income	93.3	99.5	99.6	58.4	38.3
Total revenues	5,466.8	4,844.1	4,427.7	4,379.4	3,444.7
Costs and expenses	4,786.5	4,254.7	3,903.4	3,916.3	3,082.2
Income taxes	245.0	205.3	201.2	202.2	172.7
Separate consolidated net income	$ 435.3	$ 384.1	$ 323.1	$ 260.9	$ 189.9
Available separate consolidated net income*	$ 171.0	$ 160.3	$ 139.1	$ 136.2	$ 103.8
Average number of shares of Class E common stock outstanding (in millions)[†]	94.5	101.8	105.2	127.6	133.0
Earnings attributable to Class E common stock on a per share basis[†]	$1.81	$1.57	$1.33	$1.07	$0.78
Cash dividends per share of Class E common stock[†]	$0.48	$0.34	$0.26	$0.20	$0.10

*Separate consolidated net income of EDS multiplied by a fraction, the numerator of which is the weighted average number of shares of Class E common stock outstanding and the denominator of which is currently 238.7 million shares (post-split). The denominator during 1988 and 1987 was 243.8 million shares (post-split). Available separate consolidated net income is determined quarterly.

[†]Adjusted to reflect the two-for-one stock split in the form of a 100% stock dividend declared February 5, 1990, payable to Class E common stockholders on March 10, 1990.

Source: General Motors' 1987 and 1989 annual reports.

worldwide. By 1993, outsourcing of computer services was expected to be a $43 billion industry, up from $25 billion in 1989. EDS believed its revenues could reach $20 billion by the year 2000. Exhibit 11 summarizes EDS's financial performance in the years since the 1984 acquisition.

The Acquisition of Hughes Aircraft

In 1985 General Motors outbid Ford and Boeing to acquire Hughes Aircraft Company for $2.7 billion in cash plus 50 million shares of GM Class H common stock valued at $46 per share. Hughes was considered one of the premier high-technology companies in the United States; nearly 40 percent of Hughes' 75,000-plus employees had college degrees, (mostly in sciences and engineering), and over 1,400 had doctorates. Roger Smith touted the acquisition as a key part of his long-range strategy to boost GM's technological capabilities. The company's 1985 annual report stated:

> Hughes, a world leader in electronic control systems and components, brings to GM advanced technologies and scientific expertise essential for its products and factories of the future.
>
> GM will benefit from Hughes' position as a leader in systems engineering, communications, integrated circuits, microelectronics, integrated and real-time software, instrumentation and displays, radar, and electro-optical sensors.

With the help of Hughes technology, GM will develop new cars and trucks that will outperform today's vehicles in terms of driveability, fuel economy, safety, comfort, and emissions, and at the same time, provide superior information, communication, and entertainment systems. Hughes engineering skills also will assist GM in taking a total systems approach to its production and assembly operations, creating a computer-integrated manufacturing and management information process. Such a system will speed decision making, cut costs, improve product quality, and enable GM to react more quickly in the marketplace.

An area of immediate technology transfer potential is in communications. Hughes is the world leader in the design, development and deployment of commercial satellite communications systems. Electronic Data Systems (EDS), also a GM subsidiary, is a world leader in data processing and industrial communications. Together, Hughes and EDS will develop a new, advanced global satellite communications system for the transmission of management and technical data among GM's plants and operations worldwide.

These strategic uses of advanced electronics and systems engineering will enable GM to maintain its position as the leader in the worldwide automotive industry, and enable it to develop totally new business ventures.

Ross Perot actively opposed the Hughes Aircraft acquisition because he saw Hughes' technical skills as being peripheral to GM's car business. He was the only GM director to vote against the acquisition.

The new Class H common stock created by GM as part of the Hughes acquisition was linked to the performance of a newly created subsidiary called GM Hughes Electronic Corporation (GMHE). This subsidiary included Hughes Aircraft and Delco Electronics Corp., the latter being a newly formed consolidation of (1) the Delco Electronics Division, which supplied chips, sensors, and computers for GM cars; (2) the instrumentation and display systems wing of the AC Spark Plug Division; (3) a military products unit, Delco Systems Operations; and (4) several related foreign operating units. Hughes Aircraft and Delco Electronics both operated as independent companies, with Delco Electronics serving as the technology transfer conduit between Hughes and GM. By 1990 GMHE was working with GM on approximately 150 projects to adapt aerospace technology to automotive products and operations. GM plants were using Hughes-developed infrared scanning equipment to check assembly-line quality. Several of GM's 1991 models were equipped with Hughes-developed "head-up displays" that allowed drivers to view the data on dashboard gauges without taking their eyes off the road. Exhibit 12 shows the financial performance of GMHE for the 1986–89 period.

GM's International Operations

In 1989 over 60 percent of GM's profits came from its overseas car operations, mostly from GM Europe (see Exhibit 13). As recently as 1986, GM Europe was losing money. But a vigorous cost-cutting effort, a plant automation program, and the introduction of models that proved popular had turned things around. GM's share of the European car market was about 11 percent, roughly equal to the market shares of five other producers.

GM operated in 17 Western European countries and had plans to invest in several Eastern European countries. The company's European operations

EXHIBIT 12   **Summary Financial Data for GM Hughes Electronics Operations, 1986–1989** *(Dollars in millions, except per share amounts)*

	1989	1988	1987	1986
Revenues				
Net sales:				
Outside customers	$ 7,647.7	$ 7,518.2	$ 7,273.2	$ 7,212.8
GM and affiliates	3,521.8	3,482.8	3,134.4	3,158.7
Other income—net	189.5	242.6	73.4	68.5
Total revenues	11,359.0	11,243.6	10,481.0	10,440.0
Costs and expenses	10,371.3	10,259.7	9,581.8	9,628.8
Income taxes	355.3	349.3	378.1	366.1
Income before cumulative effect of accounting change	632.4	634.6	521.1	445.1
Cumulative effect of accounting change	—	18.7*	—	—
Separate consolidated net income	632.4	653.3	521.1	445.1
Available separate consolidated net income:				
Adjustments to exclude the effect of purchase accounting[†]	148.8	148.8	148.8	148.8
Earnings of GMHE, excluding purchase accounting adjustments	$781.2	$802.1	$669.9	$593.9
Available separate consolidated net income[‡]	$188.1	$256.9	$219.2	$190.0
Average number of shares of Class H common stock outstanding (in millions)	95.7	127.9	130.8	127.8
Earnings attributable to Class H common stock on a per share basis:				
Before cumulative effect of accounting change	$1.94	$1.96	$1.67	$1.48
Cumulative effect of accounting change	—	0.05	—	—
Net earnings attributable to Class H common stock	$1.94	$2.01	$1.67	$1.48
Cash dividends per share of Class H common stock	$0.72	$0.44	$0.36	$0.30

*Effective January 1, 1988, accounting procedures at Delco Electronics were changed to include in inventory certain manufacturing overhead costs previously charged directly to expense.

[†]Amortization of intangible assets arising from the acquisition of Hughes Aircraft Company.

[‡]Earnings of GMHE, excluding purchase accounting adjustments, multiplied by a fraction, the numerator of which is the weighted average number of shares of Class H common stock outstanding and the denominator of which is currently 400 million shares. Available separate consolidated net income is determined quarterly.

Source: General Motors' 1987 and 1989 annual reports.

consisted mainly of Adam Opel in Germany and Vauxhall Motors in the U.K.; together the two subsidiaries were the fastest-growing of the "Big Six" European automakers. In Europe, GM passenger-car sales had risen from 1.3 million units in 1987 to a record 1.5 million units in 1989. The Opel Kadett was GM's best-selling car worldwide. Many of GM's European components and assembly plants were operating at or near full capacity, as compared to about an 80 percent average in North America. Plans were underway to increase production capacity in Europe from 1.5 million units to 2 million units by the mid-1990s.

Productivity levels at GM's European assembly plants were the second best in Europe:

Company	Cars Produced Annually per Employee			
	1982	**1984**	**1986**	**1987**
Peugeot Group	10.54	11.69	14.30	17.36
GM	11.64	12.37	15.31	15.82
Fiat	9.86	13.44	14.74	15.16
Ford	10.12	11.65	13.80	14.52
Renault	12.19	10.12	12.75	13.96
Rover	4.89	5.54	7.63	13.09
Volvo	10.74	11.53	11.47	11.41
VW-Audi	8.94	9.66	10.26	11.06
Saab	7.93	8.27	8.62	8.53
BMW	8.90	9.23	8.52	8.07
Daimler-Benz	4.41	4.35	5.10	5.05
Jaguar	2.25	3.50	3.61	3.84
Average	9.27	9.88	11.35	12.30

Source: Euromotor Group, as reported in *Automotive News*, August 13, 1990.

In general, productivity at the plants of European automakers lagged well behind that of Japanese producers; in 1988 Japanese plants turned out an average of 16.27 vehicles annually per employee. The annual average output of European auto plants was 230,000 vehicles. Both Peugeot and GM Europe had embarked on a productivity enhancement strategy that included:

- Rehabilitating existing plants.
- Eliminating production line bottlenecks.
- Selective use of three-shift scheduling instead of building new plants.

GM Europe was less vertically integrated than the North American car groups, giving it more flexibility to buy parts from low-cost, high-quality suppliers. Managers in GM Europe operated with more autonomy and less bureaucracy than their North American peers.

International Operations outside Europe Looking to the year 2000 and beyond, GM saw the largest potential growth in sales occurring in the Asia/ Pacific region. The company had made progress in Taiwan, moving from essentially no market presence in 1986 to a passenger-car market share of 10 percent in 1989. To take advantage of the appeal of European products in Japan, GM had begun marketing four Opel models in that country. In Korea, Daewoo Motors, 50 percent–owned by GM, had doubled sales between 1986 and 1989. Over the longer term, GM was looking at entry into China, India, Thailand, and Indonesia.

GM's Latin American operations had been profitable for the past six years. The Brazilian subsidiary had a 30 percent share of the passenger-car market. In Mexico, GM had a 29 percent share of the light-truck market. Just over 100,000 U.S.-made vehicles were exported to overseas dealers.

E X H I B I T 13 **Selected Financial and Operating Statistics for General Motors, by Geographic Region, 1985–1989** *(Dollar figures are in millions; the data do not include operations of the Hughes and EDS subsidiaries)*

	1985	1986	1987	1988	1989
Net revenues					
United States	$59,668.7	$80,204.7	$77,690.6	$93,878.4	$ 93,163.6
Canada	3,866.4	5,283.7	5,791.3	7,260.5	7,821.4
Europe	7,761.7	7,671.6	14,476.6	17,359.0	19,344.9
Latin America	1,742.7	1,841.9	1,904.0	2,863.8	3,715.3
All other areas	1,542.1	1,369.8	1,919.4	2,279.9	2,886.7
Net income (loss)					
United States	$3,469.0	$3,624.3	$1,702.2	$1,813.2	$1,279.0
Canada	592.3	473.7	42.9	387.2	288.5
Europe	(228.3)	(372.1)	1,255.4	1,781.4	1,830.0
Latin America	(15.0)	308.3	445.0	539.6	488.4
All other areas	(91.1)	9.1	175.9	300.6	345.3
Average number of employees (in thousands)					
United States	463	561	583	538	531
Canada	39	44	41	39	42
Europe	123	125	118	112	118
Latin America	41	59	57	62	71
All other areas	25	22	14	15	13
Retail sales of GM cars and trucks					
United States	6,419,000	5,822,000	5,112,000	5,177,000	4,837,000
Canada	842,000	737,000	582,000	738,000	737,000
Europe	—	1,370,000	1,397,000	1,450,000	1,595,000
West Germany	—	424,000	463,000	441,000	472,000
United Kingdom	—	329,000	308,000	348,000	395,000
GM market share, Europe	—	10.4%	9.9%	10.0%	10.5%
Latin America	—	343,000	288,000	342,000	361,000
Brazil	—	205,000	149,000	195,000	212,000
Mexico	—	32,000	41,000	48,000	72,000
Venezuela	—	54,000	38,000	36,000	7,000
Africa	—	45,000	33,000	37,000	29,000
Middle East	—	46,000	46,000	65,000	52,000
Asia/Pacific	—	176,000	209,000	249,000	287,000
Australia	—	96,000	82,000	92,000	98,000

Source: Company annual reports.

Exhibit 13 shows trends in GM's foreign sales of cars and trucks and presents selected financial and operating statistics by geographic market region. In 1979 GM averaged $215 profit per vehicle sold overseas; by 1989 profits per vehicle sold outside North America were up to $1,150.

GMAC

General Motors Acceptance Corp. (GMAC) was the largest finance company in the United States; in 1989 it had gross revenues of $14.5 billion, assets of $89.9 billion, and earnings of $1.1 billion. In 1987 GMAC had earned a record $1.5 billion. The division's primary role was to arrange financing for purchasing and leasing GM products, mostly motor vehicles. In 1985 GMAC acquired a group of seven mortgage banking and mortgage servicing companies and the rights to service another mortgage company's $11 billion loan portfolio; these acquisitions made GMAC one of the nation's largest mortgage servicing companies.

The Saturn Project

In 1983 Roger Smith announced that GM would introduce a new nameplate, the Saturn, as a top-quality small car to compete in the low-priced end of the market. Saturn became his pet project and a centerpiece in GM's strategy to counter the success that Japanese companies were enjoying in small cars—he termed the Saturn effort "a project of cosmic proportions." To come up with its "import-buster," GM opted for a "cleansheet" approach, gleaning the best technology and labor–management approaches from around the world. A group of 99 Saturn workers visited 160 companies collecting ideas and studying innovative manufacturing approaches; the conclusions were that successful companies provided employees with a sense of ownership, had few and flexible guidelines, and imposed no confining work rules or job descriptions. The plan that emerged at Saturn was to build an all-new car in an all-new plant featuring an all-new production system operated by all-new workers, with the models to be sold and serviced in all-new dealer franchises.

It took GM seven years to launch production and sale of the first Saturn models—longer than Honda took to first build and then expand its new U.S. facility in Marysville, Ohio. But the achievements were encouraging. The Saturn division's entire manufacturing complex, located in Spring Hill, Tennessee, represented the most highly integrated and automated car operation in the United States. The 4.4-million-square-foot facility, containing over 100 acres under one roof, included an assembly plant, stamping plant, engine and transaxle plant, forging operations for the powertrain, assorted other component manufacturing operations, and Saturn's administrative offices. Fully 65 percent of the parts and 90 percent of the car's bulk were built on site. Most outside suppliers had their facilities within a 100-mile radius. The complex's $3.5 billion cost made it GM's most expensive facility.

The plant employed some 3,300 workers and managers. More than 16,000 experienced autoworkers at UAW locals and 38 states applied for jobs, many of whom were attracted by the challenge of trying to outcompete the Japanese. One worker said, "The thing that interested me most was the idea we could beat the Japanese. That's why I came here." Some 1,600 Saturn workers were UAW members. GM and the UAW negotiated a wholly separate contract for Saturn; absent from the agreement were restrictive job classifications and the customary myriad of work rules. The contract stipulated that workers could be laid off only in the instance of "unforeseen or catastrophic events or severe economic conditions" and it established 165 work teams (average size: 10 members) that gave Saturn workers unprecedented involvement in decision making. Not only were the work teams involved in developing assembly-line procedures (as was increasingly the case at many other U.S. auto plants) but they were also represented on teams to help pick dealers, to interview and choose co-workers, to choose an ad agency, and to select tools and equipment. The philosophy was that all teams had to be committed to decisions affecting them before actions were taken. Symbolic of the power sharing and team-work between Saturn managers and union leaders was the fact that the executive suite in Spring Hill was shared by Saturn's president and the UAW coordinator.

New workers went through an initial five-day training course learning how to work in teams and build consensus. After that, workers got from 100 to 750 hours of training, including data concerning how much their tasks added to the cost of the car. Plans called for 5 percent of each employee's time to be spent in training on an ongoing basis.

All employees were paid a salary (about 20 percent below what their counterparts at other GM plants earned); there were no hourly jobs. However, all Saturn employees were eligible for bonuses of 20 percent or more (to bring average compensation up to about $34,000 annually) if Saturn met goals relating to quality, productivity, and profit. The bonuses of production workers were tied to their team's achievement of its quality targets. Employees were dedicated to producing cars with no defects. There were pull cords in every team area so that, if a defect was spotted, the assembly line could be stopped. Any such stoppage triggered blaring music and caused a master computer to light up in a kind of digital fireworks display—finding a defect was considered something to celebrate and correct. Morale throughout the whole Saturn organization was described as gung ho and "like a cult." A local union official at Saturn said, "You're not going to find one Saturn team member who won't tell you this car is not going to be the best thing on the road." There were one half the number of white-collar supervisors at Saturn as at most other GM plants.

Much effort had gone into plant layout. Incoming parts arrived at multiple docks scattered around the site close to where the parts were used. No workers had to walk more than five minutes from their parked car to their job on the line. Materials and parts flowed smoothly from one plant operation to the next. The production setup was flexible enough to produce four or five models simultaneously. The assembly-line process was designed to facilitate quality production and to promote worker comfort and efficiency. At full production, Saturn was expected to assemble a car in less than 20 worker-hours, two hours less than any other U.S. plant. Unit leaders in Saturn's powertrain plant were predicting that uptime (the time machinery was in production) would hit 95 percent, 20 percent above Ford's best transmission plant. The Saturn organization believed it had the capability to bring newly designed models to market every three years.

Saturn dealers were handpicked from a pool of applicants already having a GM dealer franchise. The chief criteria were having high scores on customer-satisfaction surveys and willingness to invest $2 million in showroom and service facilities. Saturn asked dealers to give their facilities a uniform look and insisted that dealer personnel be trained in customer-satisfaction techniques.

Dealers who had test-driven Saturn models praised performance of the multivalve 4-cylinder engine, the smooth-shifting transmission, interior features, appealing looks, and good handling. Saturn personnel described the cars as "sports touring sedans and coupes" with "systems that will make the customer feel very loved by the vehicle." When Saturn models first went on sale, the media reported that many of those people who came to look and to buy were there because they wanted to buy a top-quality small car made by a U.S. company rather than one made by a Japanese company.

From a competitive standpoint, GM wanted Saturn to get 80 percent of its sales from non-GM brands. One marketing strategy under consideration was to have dealers place a Honda Civic, Toyota Corolla, and Acura Integra on the showroom floor so shoppers could make on-the-spot comparisons. Initial plans called for building 120,000 cars annually on a single shift, then scaling up to 240,000 cars a year on two shifts. To be profitable over the long term, Saturn would have to expand its physical facilities and double production capacity to about 500,000 vehicles annually. Roger Smith believed that the test of Saturn's success hinged not on its bottom-line contribution but rather on its impact on GM's approach to building vehicles:

> Saturn will give us the entree to go back and Saturnize the rest of the company. That, to me, is 90 percent of the goal. Saturn, the car, is 10 percent.

On the day before he retired, Roger Smith drove the first Saturn off the end of the production line. His successor, Robert Stempel, drove off the second Saturn produced.

A CHANGE OF LEADERSHIP

When Robert Stempel took charge as CEO in August 1990, GM's competitive strength was on the upswing in several key areas: better quality, reduced costs, modernized plant facilities, a growing ability to apply advanced technology, and an improving labor–management partnership. Roger Smith could rightfully point to several strategic accomplishments:

- The average number of defects per vehicle assembled at GM had dropped from 7.4 in 1980 to 1.7 in 1989. (However, GM still lagged behind Ford at 1.5 assembly defects per car and the Japanese manufacturers which had an average of 1.2.)
- As of 1986, nearly 7 percent of the parts and components GM produced were defective or deficient in some respect; by 1990, the figure was under 2 percent.
- More than 50 joint venture and partial ownership arrangements had been established worldwide to gain GM more flexible and efficient production capabilities and to develop new technologies. GM owned 50 percent of Daewoo Motors in Korea, 38 percent of Isuzu Motors, and 4.9 percent of Suzuki.
- GMFanuc Robotics was the North American sales leader in factory-floor robotics.
- The Chevrolet Corsica/Beretta models introduced in 1987, the first all-new vehicles designed by the new CPC unit, had become the best-selling

compact series in the United States—domestic or import. Exciting, restyled models with futuristic looks and features were scheduled for introduction in 1992 and 1993, following on the heels of the all-new 1991 Saturn models and three other restyled models.

- Through product simplification, GM had consolidated engine offerings, reduced the total number of parts used in its model lineup, and cut the number of "build combinations." The total number of models marketed had been cut from 175 in 1986 to 150 in 1990, with a planned reduction to 130 by 1992. These moves were producing scale economies and significant gains in manufacturing efficiency.

- To improve component quality, GM was involving suppliers earlier in the design process and developing longer-term relationships with fewer suppliers. The average number of suppliers to a GM assembly plant had dropped from 800 in 1986 to 425 in 1990. With the aid of EDS, a sophisticated "just-in-time" inventory management system had been put in place.

- Labor productivity was up companywide (dramatically in some areas, albeit below expectations in others) and major cost savings had been achieved via workforce reduction.

- GM's technical and research skills were unmatched by any other company in the industry.

Financially GM was in excellent shape. Profits in 1988 set an all-time record high; in 1989 GM earned the third largest annual profit in history (behind 1984) and more than any other manufacturing company in the world. The company had $10.2 billion in cash and marketable securities and long-term debt under $5 billion (see Exhibit 3).

Yet, troubling problems persisted. GM's market share in the United States was continuing to erode. According to the *Ward's Automotive Reports*, the industry's most authoritative statistical source, GM's market share slid from 46.3 percent in 1979 to 34.7 percent in 1989. During the first 10 months of 1990, GM's share was running in the 32–35 percent range. GM had unused factory capacity equal to at least 1 million vehicles plus additional plants that had been "indefinitely idled." The company's drive to promote the Japanese-inspired team concept at its plants had been resisted by old-line UAW workers who believed their interests were best served by the union taking an adversarial position against GM and bargaining for strict seniority provisions, narrow job classifications, and rigid work rules. As a result, GM's plants—despite the modernization effort—remained a patchwork of different production systems, manufacturing approaches, and degrees of labor–management cooperation. Some plants were light-years ahead of others in labor productivity and implementation of the teamwork concept.

Although truck operations in North America were profitable (earnings of about $1 billion in 1989), car operations in North America had only broken even for the past three years. GM's profitability per vehicle sold in North America reached a high of $584 in 1984 and had been headed downhill since then, reaching about $12 in 1989. Losses were running about $1 billion on the GM-10 line—Buick Regal, Pontiac Grand AM, and Oldsmobile Calais; four GM-10 plants were running at about 60 percent capacity. Unused plant capacity (due to weak sales) at the troubled Hamtramck plant was also producing losses of about \$1,250 per vehicle on Cadillac Eldorado, Buick Riviera, and Oldsmobile Toronado models even though the incremental costs of building a \$30,000 Eldorado ran only \$4,000 more than a \$14,000 Pontiac Firebird. The company's white-collar bureaucracy was still sizable and slow-moving despite a 40,000-person reduction in the past four years; an outside management consultant said in 1990, "More time is spent on meetings than anyplace I've ever seen, but less is accomplished." There were 21 layers of management between a production line worker and the chief executive officer (as compared to 17 at Ford and 7 at Toyota). Exhibit 14 presents a company organization chart as of 1990.

Perhaps the most troubling problem GM had was its image among consumers. As GM's president candidly admitted to a *Time* magazine reporter:

> In the early and mid-1980s, we let a lot of people down. We disappointed customers with some of our products' quality, reliabilitiy, and durability. And as we were going through the change from rear-wheel drive to front-wheel drive, we had too many cars that looked alike.[11]

Robert Stempel

Robert Stempel was only the second engineer to hold the rank of CEO since Alfred Sloan. He got his engineering degree from Worcester Polytechnic Institute in Massachusetts, where he played football. He went to night school at Michigan State to get his MBA degree. He moved up through the management ranks at GM rapidly, getting 11 promotions during one 18-year stretch. None of his assignments were in GM's finance department. As head of Opel in Europe during the early 1980s, he began the reorganization and restructuring that turned GM Europe into a major profit producer by the end of the decade. He had been head of the BOC car group for several years and he had served as president and chief operating officer under Roger Smith for three years. He was popular among both managers and workers, and his appointment as CEO was greeted with enthusiasm by Wall Street and many of Roger Smith's critics (including Ross Perot). During his career Stempel had shown an aversion to "the big-bang approach to change." His style was more subtle and more participatory; he had the reputation of being a strong believer in teamwork. He was a "product guy."

Stempel, within days of his appointment, put top priority on two strategic objectives: achieving a 40 percent market share in the United States and operating at 100 percent of full capacity by 1992. Stempel commented:

> We've been through enough mergers, diversifications, and acquisitions for a while. I look for this team to focus on cars and trucks. . . . There's a definite effort to reduce layers of management . . . a definite effort to move decisions down. . . . [But] we aren't going to take GM apart and put it back together again.

Even so, speculation centered on which of Roger Smith's programs and strategic initiatives he would support and execute, which he might abandon, and what strategic moves and organizational changes of his own he would institute.

---

[11]As quoted in *Time*, October 29, 1990, p. 81.

E X H I B I T 14 **General Motors Organization Chart, as of August 1990**

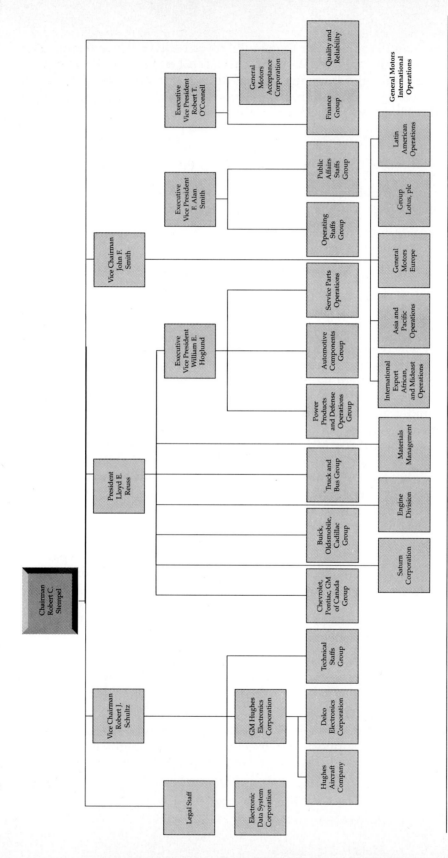

Source: *Ward's Auto World*, September 1990, p. 83.

Many car industry analysts saw signs of a dramatic resurgence at GM. The company's 1991 models had some impressive features: multivalve engines, antilock braking systems, all-wheel drive, traction control, and new electronic transmissions that were winning rave reviews from the automotive press. In fall 1990 the Cadillac Division won the coveted Malcolm Baldridge National Quality Award for its efforts in improving the quality of its Cadillac models. One auto industry consultant said:

> General Motors is about to kick butt from one end of this country to the other. They're renewing products faster, they're continually reducing the cost of renewing those products, and you're starting to see a real distinctiveness between cars.[12]

However, the day after Stempel took over as CEO, Iraq invaded Kuwait, sending the price of unleaded regular gasoline soaring from 90 cents per gallon to $1.40 per gallon. By fall 1990, recessionary conditions were widespread in the U.S. economy and sales of new vehicles were slumping badly. As of fall 1991, the new-car market was still depressed.

---

[12]*Time*, October 29, 1990, p. 81.

TOYOTA MOTOR CORPORATION

Jana F. Kuzmicki, The University of Alabama

One of the dreams I have is to see our automobiles being driven in every corner of the world, allowing people to lead fuller lives. I intend to undertake every effort so that Toyota will be able to meet whatever challenges may emerge and continue to build attractive products.

Shoichiro Toyoda, President
Toyota Motor Corporation

Toyota Motor Corporation, the third-largest automaker in the world, was acknowledged by both industry observers and its competitors as the " best carmaker in the world." Headquartered in Toyota City, approximately 150 miles west of Tokyo in central Japan, Toyota was not only the largest industrial enterprise in Japan, but also the most profitable. In fiscal 1990, Toyota had sales of $64.5 billion, a net profit of about $3 billion, and $22 billion in cash—enough to buy both Ford and Chrysler at current stock prices, with nearly $5 billion to spare—which had earned it the nickname as the "Bank of Toyota." Under the leadership of current President Shoichiro Toyoda, Toyota Motor's accomplishments included:

- Developing a fundamentally new approach to manufacturing, admired and emulated by competitors, that was predicted to eventually transform the way things were made in virtually every industry.

- Maintaining its status as the most efficient automaker in the world, having achieved this feat in 1965.

- Being the undisputed quality leader in automotive manufacturing (three of the four car models with the fewest defects sold in the United States in 1990 were Toyota-made).

- Introducing a new luxury-style automobile, the Lexus, which achieved the distinction of being ranked No. 1 in quality in less than a year of being on the market.

- Having outstanding labor relations.

As the 1990s began, Toyota held 43 percent of the Japanese auto market, about 9 percent of the global market, and 7.6 percent of the U.S. vehicle market. Toyota was predicted to sell nearly 5 million vehicles worldwide in 1990 (versus about 8 million for General Motors and 6 million for Ford). At the end of the 1990 model year, Toyota's sales of autos and trucks in the United States exceeded 1 million for the first time. One of the company's top-priority goals was to produce 6 million vehicles by 1995. Articulated as early as 1969 by then-President Taizo Ishida, Toyota's long-term ambition was to become worldwide what it already was in Japan—*Ichiban*, or No. 1—thus guaranteeing a battle with GM, the current global leader, for the world's top spot by the turn of the century. Exhibit 1 presents the global market shares of the companies vying for world leadership of the auto industry.

E X H I B I T   1   **Global Market Shares of the Top 10 Motor Vehicle Producers, 1987–1989***

Company	1989	1988	1987
General Motors	16.9%	17.0%	16.7%
Ford	13.7	13.7	13.2
Toyota	9.5	8.1	7.9
Nissan	6.4	5.7	4.9
Volkswagen	6.2	5.9	5.9
Fiat Group	5.2	4.5	4.2
Chrysler Corp.	5.1	5.4	4.8
Peugeot-Citroen	4.7	4.4	4.2
Renault	4.4	4.1	3.9
Honda	4.0	3.7	3.4

*Based on total production of all vehicles, including cars, trucks, and buses.

Sources: *Automotive News*, 1990 Market Data Book Issue, pp. 3, 6; and *Automotive News*, 1989 Market Data Book Issue, p. 6.

COMPANY HISTORY AND BACKGROUND

Toyota's beginnings could be traced to Sakichi Toyoda, an inveterate tinkerer, who received a total of 84 patents for his inventions. The automatic loom, his most famous invention, resulted in the establishment of Toyoda Automatic Loom Works in 1926. Early in his career (1910), Sakichi Toyoda became discouraged with his work and decided to visit the United States, where he spent six months inspecting factories. Several years after his return, Sakichi Toyoda stated to a group of engineers:

> To tell you the truth, I felt that my eyes had been opened. As I viewed the plants in cities all across the United States, and felt the tremendous energy of the Americans, I got angry at myself for being so blind. I was ashamed for having been ready to throw everything away after only a few failures.[1]

Kiichiro Toyoda (Sakichi Toyoda's son) inherited his father's inquisitive nature, but his interest lay in the fledgling auto industry. Like his father, Kiichiro Toyoda visited the United States in 1930 to study the art of automaking. Armed with $500,000 from the sale of the automatic loom patent to a British company in 1929, Kiichiro Toyoda pursued the development of a small passenger car. Initially, he concentrated on learning the technique of mass production. For inspiration, Kiichiro Toyoda often turned to Henry Ford's book, *My Life and Work*, urging others in the company to read it. By the mid-1920s, both Ford and GM had built assembly plants in Japan, turning out 18,000 vehicles a year. The auto quickly caught on in Japan, resulting in early dominance of the Japanese auto market by American automakers.

Kiichiro Toyoda was handicapped in his endeavors by the underdeveloped Japanese parts and machinery industries. Typically, these firms were family enterprises, and their products were either unreliable or high priced.

---

[1]Milton Moskowitz, *The Global Marketplace: And 101 Other Global Corporate Players* (New York: Macmillan, 1987), p. 601.

Undaunted, Kiichiro Toyoda focused on what kind and how many automobiles to build to develop a successful enterprise. He decided it was essential to mass produce a passenger car of the size most in demand in Japan; according to Kiichiro Toyoda:

> Instead of avoiding competition with Ford and Chevrolet, we will develop and mass produce a car that incorporates the strong points of both and that can rival foreign cars in performance and price. Although we will base our method of production on the American mass production system, it will not be an exact imitation but will reflect the particular conditions in Japan.[2]

Kiichiro Toyoda's persistent efforts culminated in the production of Toyota's first passenger car prototype in 1935.

Meanwhile, the government took steps to stimulate domestic auto production. In 1936, the Law Concerning the Manufacture of Motor Vehicles was passed to promote the establishment of the Japanese auto industry and to curb vehicle imports from abroad; the law required that companies manufacturing more than 3,000 units annually within Japan be licensed by the government, that a majority of the stockholders in such companies be Japanese, and that 100 percent domestic production of all vehicle parts be a goal. Ford and GM were never granted licenses, resulting in the eventual end to their Japanese auto operations.

Toyoda Automatic Loom Works was granted a license, officially designating it as a company eligible to make motor vehicles. Aware of the importance of a brand name, Kiichiro Toyoda held a public contest, which drew 27,000 entries, for a new Toyoda logo. "Toyota" was the winning entry; as a design, it imparted a sense of speed, was considered aesthetically superior, and required eight (considered a lucky number in Japan) strokes to write it. The automotive department was separated out as a new company in August 1937, resulting in the formation of the Toyota Motor Company. The Toyoda Precepts, embodying the philosophy and convictions of Sakichi Toyoda, were to serve as guidelines for the operations of the companies in the Toyota group (see Exhibit 2). In the following year, Toyota completed construction of its first major plant located in Koromo (today's Toyota City).

In designing the Koromo plant, Kiichiro Toyoda's ideas provided the foundation for what was to become known as the Toyota Production System. Kiichiro Toyoda's approach to vehicle manufacturing, codified into a manual four inches thick, described in meticulous detail the flow-production system, or "just-in-time" (JIT) concept. By this he meant: "Just make what is needed in time, but don't make too much." The manufacturing system Kiichiro Toyoda designed was predicated on four principles:

- Have the 30 or more factory buildings of various sizes laid out so that their proximities to one another will be conducive to the smooth production of complete automobiles.
- Locate machinery in the plant so the layout will facilitate work flow from one machine to the other.
- Build machines that will be flexible enough in function to meet any requirement, bearing in mind that they are to be used for 20 or 30 years.

---

[2]*Toyota: A History of the First 50 Years* (1 Toyota-cho, Toyota City, Aichi Prefecture, Japan: Toyota Motor Corporation, 1988), p. 45.

E X H I B I T 2   **The Toyota Precepts**

1. Be contributive to the development and welfare of the country by working together, regardless of position, in faithfully fulfilling your duties.
2. Be at the vanguard of the times through endless creativity, inquisitiveness, and pursuit of improvement.
3. Be practical and avoid frivolity.
4. Be kind and generous; strive to create a warm, homelike atmosphere.
5. Be reverent, and show gratitude for things great and small in thought and deed.

Source: *Toyota: A History of the First 50 Years* (1 Toyota-cho, Toyota City, Aichi Prefecture, Japan: Toyota Motor Corporation, 1988), pp. 37–38.

- Forget the commonly held notion that warehouses are essential in a plant.[3]

Creating product quality within the process was another idea of Kiichiro Toyoda. The goal was not to just differentiate between good and bad products, but to find a way to correct whatever needed fixing, be it machinery, equipment, or tools, to prevent defects from happening in the first place. Implementing the system involved thorough training of the employees and getting them to abandon their old ways of doing things.

The advent of WWII disrupted Kiichiro Toyoda's vision of producing passenger cars and utilizing his innovative concepts. Automakers were obliged to concentrate on producing trucks for the military due to governmental limitations on the building of small vehicles. Scarce raw materials, such as iron and steel, were a major problem, and Toyota spent more energy scavenging for materials than building vehicles. Wartime production of trucks and buses peaked in 1941 with 42,813 units built by all the Japanese automakers; in that same year, Toyota produced only 208 passenger cars. In 1945, Toyota produced 3,275 trucks and buses and no passenger cars.

Post–WWII Operations

Following WWII, the Japanese auto industry had to begin anew. Determined to enter car and truck production on a full-scale basis, Toyota executives faced several obstacles: producing a variety of vehicles appropriate for a small domestic market, coping with obsolete production equipment and facilities in disrepair, dealing with a native Japanese work force no longer content to be treated as an expendable factor of production, being unable to purchase the latest U.S. and European technology due to a lack of capital, and growing interest of expansion-minded foreign motor vehicle producers in building plants in Japan or, at least, serving the Japanese market with vehicles exported from their own domestic plants.

Kiichiro Toyoda firmly believed the era of the small passenger car had arrived; research on a small car became Toyota's top priority:

---

[3]*Toyota: A History*, p. 70.

The passenger car that will be appropriate for Japan will be not an American-style large car, but rather a small car. In Japan, there is some experience accumulated in the area of small cars, yet when it comes to development on the basis of the functions which are peculiar to a small car, the record is quite short. As a result, existing small cars suffer from many problems, such as cramped interiors, excessive weight, low horsepower and excessive vibration. If these problems could be solved, then naturally people would come to evaluate the utility of small cars on the same level as that of large ones. And undoubtedly, along with such advantageous characteristics would come the possibility of exporting small cars.[4]

When permission was received to produce a limited number of small vehicles in mid-1947, Toyota launched a small passenger car, named the Toyopet.

Adverse economic conditions at the end of 1949 resulted in a financial crisis at Toyota. A consortium of banks agreed to provide aid to Toyota if the sales department was incorporated as an independent company—Toyota Motor Sales (TMS)—and substantial personnel cuts were made. By the end of 1950, after 13 years in business, Toyota had produced 2,685 automobiles, compared with the 7,000 that Ford's River Rouge plant was producing in a single day.

In the spring of 1950, Eiji Toyoda (Kiichiro Toyoda's cousin) visited the Ford facilities in the United States to study the U.S. approach to automaking. Upon his return, when asked how long it would take to catch up to Ford, Eiji Toyoda responded: "Ford's not doing anything we don't already know." If a difference existed, it was due to a large gap in production scale, not in technological know-how.

Eiji Toyoda's reports provided the basis for a five-year modernization plan, affecting all aspects of Toyota's operations. The ultimate goal was to increase production capacity to 3,000 units per month. The Toyota Creative Ideas and Suggestions System, based on the suggestion system used by Ford, was implemented to support companywide improvements in production methods and efficiency. One outcome of this program was the company slogan, "Good thinking, good products," adopted in 1953. By 1951, Toyota's financial development had improved, enabling it to direct profits into research and development and to expand its capital base.

Role of the Government

Rapid growth in the development of the Japanese auto industry was aided by government policies. Targeted as one of the high-priority industries in the government's economic reconstruction program after WWII, the government pursued two major initiatives to promote automobile self-sufficiency in the quasi-closed economy. First, the Ministry of International Trade and Industry (MITI) limited imports to about 1 percent of the Japanese market. Second, a plan was proposed to "rationalize" the auto industry through mergers and specialization. Although the plan never materialized, it resulted in heavy investment by the auto companies, enabling them to become more competitive.

Additional government measures to strengthen and protect the ability of the industry to compete included protective tariffs, restrictions on foreign capital participation and loans, accelerated depreciation, special import

---

[4]*Toyota: A History,* p. 101.

arrangements for machinery and technology, and long-term, low-interest loans for the auto parts industry. Unprecedented economic growth in Japan in the 1960s (average annual rate of 15 percent), combined with the spread of private car ownership, caused the Japanese auto industry to boom.

The Crown Line of Toyota cars, with a top speed of 65 mph, debuted on January 1, 1955, to an enthusiastic reception by the Japanese public. Barely able to keep up with the orders due to brisk demand for the Crown, Toyota decided to construct the Motomachi Plant, which could produce 5,000 units per month. According to Eiji Toyoda, the plant was viewed as a big gamble, but enabled Toyota to:

> [rise] head and shoulders above its domestic competitors. . . . So we gained a decisive edge right from the start. Ever since then, we've continually pressed on for fear of being overtaken, rapidly putting up one new factory after another . . . to keep pace with the wave of motorization that hit Japan in the 1960s. By that time, we had won the confidence of the banks and no longer had difficulty raising capital or securing loans for new construction.[5]

THE TOYOTA PRODUCTION SYSTEM

In the late 1940s, top Toyota executives determined that traditional mass-production systems used in Europe and the United States were inappropriate for building autos suitable for the Japanese market. That decision, followed by four decades of experimenting with and improving on Kiichiro Toyoda's flow-production system, steered Toyota on a course that resulted in the Toyota Production System (TPS), a customer-focused, lean production approach to motor vehicle manufacturing—a system so novel and efficient that it represented a reinvention of modern manufacturing techniques. The total system began with and was totally geared to the needs of dealers and customers. In contrast, with traditional mass production the needs of the factory came first, and dealers and customers were expected to make any necessary accommodations.

Lean production combined the best features of both craft and mass production, while avoiding the high cost of the former and the rigidity of the latter. Emphasis on teamwork, communication, efficient use of resources, elimination of waste, and continuous improvement guided the development of the TPS. The system focused on excellence—continually declining costs, zero defects, zero inventories, and growing ability to expand product variety. The TPS melded the activities of everyone from top management to line workers, suppliers, and dealers into a tightly integrated process, capable of responding almost instantly to customer demand. The Toyota Production System had six components:

- A motivated and extremely productive work force.
- Low-cost, high-quality factory operations guided by just-in-time deliveries of parts and flow-production techniques.
- Long-term partnerships with suppliers.
- Careful market research and short design-to-showroom cycles so as to keep models closely aligned with market demand.
- Custom-order production and superior customer service.

---

[5]Eiji Toyoda, *Toyota: Fifty Years in Motion* (New York: Harper & Row, 1985), p. 127.

- A management approach focused on continuous improvement, teamwork, and decentralized decision-making.

The following sections describe each of these in more detail.

Work Force Practices

With prodding from the Japanese government, Toyota (and many other Japanese companies) agreed to guarantee lifetime employment for employees. Toyota consented to provide a pay scale based on seniority and not job classification, with bonus payments tied to company profitability. In return, employees agreed to be flexible in their work assignments and to commit to initiating improvements rather than merely responding to problems.

A major implication was that the work force was a significant, long-term fixed cost much like the company's plants and machinery. Toyota needed to get the most out of its human resources over their working lifetime. Thus, it was only logical to continuously enhance employees' skills and to gain the benefit of their knowledge and experience as well as their physical strength.

Mutual trust, communication, and continuous training characterized the employment relationship. A Labor–Management Declaration, signed in 1962, symbolized the mutual trust relationship. Eiji Toyoda believed that maintaining a relationship of mutual trust with the employees was largely responsible for improvements in labor–management relations.

> Mutual trust is the basis of labor relations. Labor relations at Toyota were initially marked by doubts and disbelief, but with time differences were ironed out. The labor–management declaration we signed was simply a written statement of this rapprochement. The purpose of this document was to uphold and sustain the trust that had been built up between management and labor, and to prevent backsliding by either side from this position. It also was intended as a reminder to those who came after to guard the fruits won through the sacrifices made by both sides. The spirit of this declaration still lives on at Toyota.[6]

Management consistently worked hard at maintaining good relations with labor. Establishing quality circles was integral to the overall relationship. The goal of these employee groups was not just to look for ways to improve product quality, but to improve all facets of production—unit cost, speed of assembly, and delivery schedules. Additionally, management initiated elaborate orientation programs and actively promoted informal contact among employees at all levels of the company. The result was enthusiastic, devoted, conscientious employees who often hung around the assembly line after hours, offering suggestions on improvements in work methods. In 1985, Toyota received 45.6 suggestions per employee and 96 percent of them (2.4 million) were adopted.

Factory Operations

Toyota management regarded final assembly of a vehicle in a typical mass-production plant as extremely inefficient. Mass production involved wasted materials, effort, and time. For example, during the late 1940s and early 1950s, an assembly plant might operate normally for only 10 days, while remaining

---

[6]Eiji Toyoda, *Toyota: Fifty Years in Motion*, p. 128.

idle for 20 days due to a lack of parts. Toyota's goal was to manufacture only what was needed, when it was needed, and in the quantity needed.

Technologically advanced machinery, teams of workers, a high level of work standardization, and small inventories and repair areas typified the factory system. Toyota implemented several innovations to improve production efficiency:

1. Multiskilled assembly workers: Workers were organized into teams and each team was given responsibility for determining the necessary operations associated with building a vehicle. Each employee was responsible for operating more than one machine (multimachine handling). Employees operated an average of five machines each without difficulty, and productivity continued to increase. Gradually, the teams assumed additional responsibilities, such as housekeeping, minor tool repair, and quality checking, thus reducing the need for engineering and production specialists to perform these functions.

2. *Andon* boards (electrical signs): These were installed at visible locations in a plant to track daily production, signal overtime requirements, and identify trouble spots along the line. Individual workers had smaller versions to tell them, for example, whether a bolt was attached tightly enough.

3. Just-in-time or "flow" production: The objective here was to smooth the flow between the processes supervised by various employees and to drastically reduce the inventories of parts and components. The *kanban* system, using the exchange of various sized cards, was developed to transfer information between processes. Each card showed the number of parts, and parts numbers of items, needing replacement. This system was called the "supermarket method," since it imitated the practice in U.S. supermarkets where customers went to stores to buy what they wanted when they wanted it (rather than store goods at home) while the supermarket restocked items as they were sold. Thus a "pull" system evolved—each employee went back to the previous station on the assembly line to retrieve work-in-process, just at the necessary time, getting only the amount needed for immediate processing.

4. Zero defects or built-in quality: Implementation of a problem-solving system, "the five why's," involved a worker being trained to systematically trace every error back to its ultimate cause (by asking "why" as each layer of the problem was uncovered) and then devising a fix so it would not occur again. Cords were installed above the production line to be pulled by any employee at any time to stop the line if complications or problems arose. Each worker served as the customer for the output of the immediately preceding workstep and in essence became a quality-control inspector.

Implementation proceeded gradually as employees learned the system. Adjusting production speed, improving production layouts, and gaining experience in error detection and correction resulted in fewer errors occurring.

A tour of the Takaoka assembly plant in Toyota City by an MIT research team, when contrasted with a tour of a comparable GM plant in Framingham, Massachusetts, vividly illustrated the results of Toyota's innovations:

> The armies of indirect workers so visible at GM were missing, and practically every worker in sight was actually adding value to the car. This fact was even more apparent because Takaoka's aisles are so narrow.
>
> Toyota's philosophy about the amount of plant space needed for a given production volume is just the opposite of GM's at Framingham: Toyota believes in having as little space as possible so that face-to-face communication among

EXHIBIT 3   **Comparative Operating Efficiency of a GM Assembly Plant versus a Toyota Plant, 1986**

	GM's Framingham Plant	Toyota's Takaoka Plant
Gross assembly hours per car	40.7	18.0
Adjusted assembly hours per car	31.0	16.0
Assembly defects per 100 cars	130.0	45.0
Assembly space per car	8.1	4.8
Inventories of parts (average)	2 weeks	2 hours

Notes: Gross assembly hours per car are calculated by dividing total hours of effort in the plant by the total number of cars produced. Defects per car were estimated from the J. D. Power Initial Quality Survey for 1987. Assembly space per car is square feet per vehicle per year, corrected for vehicle size. Inventories are a rough average for major parts.

Source: James P. Womack, Daniel T. Jones, and Daniel Roos, *The Machine That Changed the World* (New York: Macmillan, 1990), p. 81.

workers is easier, and there is no room to store inventories. GM, by contrast, has believed that extra space is necessary to work on vehicles needing repairs and to store the large inventories needed to ensure smooth production.

The final assembly line revealed further differences. Less than an hour's worth of inventory was next to each worker at Takaoka. The parts went on more smoothly and the work tasks were better balanced, so that every worker worked at about the same pace. When a worker found a defective part, he—there are no women working in Toyota plants in Japan—carefully tagged it and sent it to the quality-control area in order to obtain a replacement part.

At the end of the line, the difference between [the TPS] and mass production was even more striking. At Takaoka, [there was] almost no rework area at all. Almost every car was driven directly from the line to the boat or the trucks taking cars to the buyer.

. . . [At Takaoka], there were practically no buffers between the welding shop and paint booth and between paint and final assembly. And there were no parts warehouses at all. Instead parts were delivered directly to the line at hourly intervals from the supplier plants where they had just been made. (Indeed, [the] initial plant survey form asked how many days of inventory were in the plant. A Toyota manager politely asked whether there was an error in translation. Surely, minutes of inventory [were meant].)

A final and striking difference with Framingham was the morale of the work force. The work pace was clearly harder at Takaoka, and yet there was a sense of purposefulness, not simply of workers going through the motions with their minds elsewhere under the watchful eye of the foreman.[7]

Differences in operations between the GM Framingham and Toyota Takaok assembly plants are displayed in Exhibit 3.

Supplier Relationships

Auto assembly plants accounted for approximately 15 percent of Toyota's total manufacturing process, with the rest being attributed to the 10,000 or so discrete parts going into a single car. Toyota divided its suppliers into separate

---

[7]James P. Womack, Daniel T. Jones, and Daniel Roos, *The Machine That Changed the World* (New York: Macmillan, 1990), pp. ⁷⁰ ⁰⁰

tiers, each having different responsibilities. Toyota dealt only with its first-tier suppliers, numbering less than 300, on a development project. These suppliers were each assigned a whole component, such as car seats or the electrical system. The suppliers would then contact second-tier suppliers to provide individual parts or subsystem components.

First-tier suppliers were treated as an integral part of Toyota's product development team and were given performance rather than engineering specifications for their assigned component parts. For example, a supplier was told to design a set of brakes that would stop a 2,200 pound car going 60 miles per hour in the space of 200 feet, and do it 10 times in succession without fading. Both the space within which the brakes had to fit and the price ($40) were specified. A prototype had to be delivered to Toyota for testing, and if it worked, a production order was awarded. When production of the new model began, suppliers delivered the component parts directly to Toyota's assembly lines, typically several times per day (occasionally every hour or two) and with no inspection of incoming deliveries.

Other aspects of Toyota's approach to its supplier relationships included:

- Becoming completely familiar with every first-tier supplier's operations, including having Toyota design engineers stationed at supplier plants.
- Making equity investments in suppliers' businesses (often, Toyota and its suppliers had substantial holdings of each other's stock).
- Establishing supplier associations that met regularly to share new findings on better ways of making parts.
- Reaching agreements with suppliers that allowed Toyota representatives access to the supplier's costs and profit margins and that provided these representatives opportunities to suggest to the supplier how cost-savings might be achieved.
- Providing loans to suppliers, if needed, to purchase cost-saving or quality-enhancing equipment.
- Fostering cooperative, stable, long-term business relationships with suppliers.

Product Design and Development

Leadership, teamwork, communication, and simultaneous development formed the basis of Toyota's approach to designing and engineering a new model. Customer needs and attitudes were carefully analyzed and teams of functional specialists, under the guidance of a *shusa* (chief engineer), were responsible for all activities related to the development of a new product— design, engineering, selection of all suppliers, and marketing strategies. Although ties were maintained with their functional departments, the specialists were committed to the project until their phase of the project was completed. At the inception of the project, team members signed formal pledges to do exactly what everyone agreed upon as a group. If conflicts about resources and priorities occurred, it was at the beginning rather than the end of the process. At the outset of a project, all relevant functional specialties were represented, resulting in the most people being involved at the initial stages. The job of the *shusa* was to force the group to face all the difficult trade-offs they would have to make to reach consensus.

Simultaneous development involved product and manufacturing engineers working closely together under the *shusa* so factory machinery was developed in tandem with prototype testing. Typically, prototype testing led to changes in the car that required alterations in the assembly line; since design and production processes proceeded simultaneously, last-minute changes infrequently stalled production plans.

Fewer tools, lower inventories, a higher proportion of projects going into production on time, no productivity penalty, higher quality, and less human effort resulted in the lowest development time per new car when compared with non-Japanese automakers—less than 4 years for Toyota versus more than 5 years for U.S. automakers and 7 years for Mercedes-Benz. According to one study, Toyota employed slightly more than half as many engineers in designing a new model when compared to U.S. companies. As a consequence, Toyota offered a wider variety of models, introducing them to the marketplace quicker and cheaper than traditional mass producers. By the latter 1980s, for example, Toyota made 59 passenger car models from 22 basic designs; in contrast, Ford, which sold about a third more cars, produced only 46 passenger car models.

Customer and Dealer Relations

Cooperative links between Toyota, its dealers, and customers were seen as integral to long-term success. In Japan, Toyota had five nationwide dealer channels (Toyota, Toyopet, Auto, Vista, and Corolla), each of which marketed a portion of the Toyota line. For example, one channel sold less-expensive models while another sold sportier models. The five dealer channels had different labels and model names for their cars, but the main distinction among them was their focus on different types of customers. The major purpose of the channel was to develop a direct link between the manufacturing system and the customer or car owner.

A description of the Corolla channel illustrates how Toyota's distribution system in Japan functioned. Established in 1961, the channel sold the Corolla, Camry, Supra, Celica, and several truck models. The channel consisted of 78 dealer firms, operating from approximately 17 different sites. Corolla owned 20 percent of the dealerships outright and had a partial ownership in others, but most dealerships were financially independent. Corolla provided training to the approximately 30,000 people who made up the sales staffs at the 78 dealerships, and also offered a full range of services and sales assistance to the dealerships it did not own. In 1989, the Corolla dealer channel, with a staff of some 30,400 people, sold about 635,000 cars and trucks (an average of just over 21 vehicles per staff member). With the exception of the showroom, few similarities existed between a Japanese and a U.S. dealership. A typical Corolla channel dealership in Japan had only three or four demonstrator models and no parking lots of unsold vehicles for prospective buyers to look at. Nor was there a battle over the walk-in customer by the sales staff, since the sales team was paid on a group commission rather than on an individual commission basis.

The salespeople at each Corolla dealership were multiskilled, having been trained in all aspects of sales—product information, order-taking, financing, insurance, and data collection—and were divided into teams of seven or eight members. A team meeting began and ended each work day. After developing a profile of all households in the dealership's geographic area and calling for an appointment, members of the sales team made door-to-door sales calls. Updating the household profile was one objective; if the family was ready to purchase a car, a custom order—every Toyota sold in Japan was tailor-made to customer specifications—was placed with the factory via an on-line computer. Haggling over price was almost nonexistent, and the deal was not concluded until arrangements regarding financing, trade-in of the old car, and insurance were made. The sales representative delivered the new car directly to the owner's house.

Additional services provided were registration, arrangements for regular maintenance, taking care of rigorous government inspections, fixing any problems encountered by the owner even after the formal warranty expired, providing a substitute while the car was being repaired, sending birthday cards, and sending condolence cards in the event of a death in the family. The principal objective was not just a one-time sale; rather, it was to make the customer feel a part of the Toyota "family," to establish a long-term relationship with the customer, and to build strong brand loyalty. The success of the sales system Toyota (and other Japanese automakers) employed was reflected by the fact that brand switching was much less common in Japan than in other countries.

The door-to-door sales system was gradually being phased out. Younger buyers, more interested than older buyers in shopping around, wanted to purchase their cars directly from a dealership. Toyota, along with other Japanese automakers, was also having difficulty recruiting salespeople willing to sell cars door-to-door.

Toyota was exploring the use of information technology to cut the high costs associated with the sales system, particularly door-to-door sales. This involved installing an extensive computer system in the dealerships. A current Corolla owner entering a Corolla dealership inserted his or her membership card into the system, which displayed all the pertinent information on the owner's household. The owner made relevant changes in the information, and the system then suggested the most appropriate models for the owner's needs, with prices included. The owner also had access to databases dealing with such things as financing, car insurance, and parking permits. If seriously interested in buying, the owner approached the sales team to discuss specific details. Cars sold in this way were steadily increasing in Japan, and Toyota hoped to deal with most existing owners using this method. The sales force could then concentrate on "conquest" sales—those to owners currently purchasing other brands.

Customer Relations Outside of Japan   Toyota's sales approach to customers in the United States and Europe currently resembled the dealer networks used by American and European producers. Customized orders were not accepted due to the distance involved in supply. Instead, Toyota sold through a network of franchised dealers; to make sure its models were equipped to buyer preferences, Toyota focused on adding a variety of options as standard equipment on their exports, resulting in customers having more choices. As Toyota established independent production facilities in countries outside of Japan, the company planned to investigate the feasibility of building cars to customer order and delivering them almost immediately, imitating the approach used in Japan.

Toyota's Approach to Managing Its Production System

Management of Toyota's production system required different career paths when compared with mass production. In mass production, career progression was virtually nonexistent for production employees, and specialists in engineering, marketing, and finance were promoted on the basis of technical expertise while general managers progressed through the numerous layers in the corporate hierarchy.

At Toyota, however, union members had an opportunity to move into the company's management structure. Each employee's first assignment at Toyota entailed working on the production line. Decentralized decision-making was reflected in the career opportunities of all employees, regardless of their career path. For employees remaining in the factory, the reward system consisted of performance bonuses and pay increases based on seniority. Since fewer layers of management existed, resulting in less opportunity for promotions, the ability to solve increasingly difficult problems was emphasized as the most important aspect of the job, even if job titles did not change. Technical specialists and engineers were assigned to product development teams; often they had to learn new skills as they progressed through their careers. The goal was to expose these specialists to the day-to-day activities of the company and have them study intensively the changing moods, tastes, and driving habits of ve-hicle buyers. Responsibilities of general managers consisted of tying supplier organizations to the assembly operations and tying geographically dispersed units of the company together. Often, managers were rotated among the company's various operations, including foreign operations, or they might be assigned to management positions in the supplier organizations.

Overall, the TPS was an exercise in trying to achieve perfection—it focused each employee on anticipating problems and finding preventive solutions. Implementation of the TPS had been a long, gradual process. Begun in the early 1950s and only after much trial and error, it was in place in all Toyota plants by 1963; subsequently, TPS was introduced to parts and materials suppliers. By the 1970s, the entire system was firmly ingrained in Toyota's operations and was formally named the Toyota Production System.

Guided by the philosophy of *kaizen* (continuous improvement), Toyota management constantly pushed for improvements to the TPS and for better and better execution. TPS and *kaizen* became an integral part of the Toyota culture. From time to time, Toyota launched bold efforts to make TPS work even better. For instance, after years of leaving technological innovation to Nissan and Honda, Toyota tripled its research and development (R&D) spending from about $750 million to $2.2 billion between 1984 and 1989. Toyota moved anew to emphasize the fundamentals of the TPS and to tackle the problem of building a system that responded flexibly to increased proliferation in car models and to changes in the kinds of cars that people bought. Enhancements to the system included construction of new integrated facilities, incorporating the most advanced production technology; increased emphasis on maintenance of machinery and equipment; and expansion of automation. Automation involved the introduction of on-line computers for production control; increased use of robots to perform such jobs as spot welding, painting, arc welding, and attaching nuts; and computerization of Toyota's entire operation through the installation of a CAD/CAM (computer-aided design/computer-aided manufacturing) system.

Toyota's overriding objective was to produce only the product demanded in the volumes required. To avoid extreme fluctuations in production volumes associated with changes in customer preferences, Toyota produced the same model simultaneously at more than one plant and produced a number of different models at each plant. Toyota gradually introduced "flexible body lines" (assembly of a number of distinct models on the same product line without decreasing productivity or quality) at its plants, beginning in 1985. Since each line handled mixed production, the time needed to switch to new models was considerably shortened.

According to an MIT study conducted in the 1980s, the TPS used less of everything—"half the human effort in the factory, half the manufacturing space, half the investment in tools, half the engineering hours to develop a new product"—when compared with the traditional mass-production methods relied on by American and European manufacturers.[8] Toyota's reinvention of the manufacturing process resulted in a high-quality car or truck built to customer specifications and delivered within 10 days to 3 weeks.

DOMESTIC OPERATIONS

Nagoya, Japan, home of Toyota City, was the hub of Toyota's worldwide operations network. Toyota City had all the trappings of a "company" town—12 manufacturing plants (4 were dedicated to assembly), factories for nearly 140 of its parts suppliers, company housing (dormitories, apartments, and houses), a huge Toyota Sports Center (with an Olympic-size pool, two football fields, four baseball diamonds, and two gymnasiums), a Toyota Hospital (free medical care was provided), and clubs of all kinds. Top executives worked out of a flat-roofed, three-story structure smaller than a typical U.S. high school.

In 1969, Toyota became fifth-largest automaker in the world, surpassing Fiat. In 1970, Toyota passed Chrysler, advancing to fourth place; in 1971, it jumped ahead of Volkswagen to become the third largest. In 1985, Toyota was producing 40 percent as many cars as GM with a work force slightly more than one tenth the size of GM's (part—but only part—of the difference was due to Toyota's greater use of subcontractors). In 1990, Toyota had 91,790 employees and produced nearly 5 million vehicles. Toyota's share of the passenger car market in Japan consistently topped 40 percent (43.4 percent as of 1990); Toyota's closest rival, Nissan, had a 25 percent market share (see Exhibit 4).

The competitive environment of the 1970s and 1980s introduced several factors (some unique to Japanese automakers) that affected the ability to compete both domestically and internationally:

- Rising gasoline prices triggered by decisions of the OPEC oil cartel to hike crude oil prices substantially (1973 and 1978–79).
- Declining economic growth on a global scale.
- Continuing trade frictions due to trade imbalances between Japan and other countries and the lack of openness of the Japanese market to imports.

---

[8]Ibid., p. 13.

EXHIBIT 4   **Domestic Market Shares of Five Largest Japanese Automakers, 1970-1988***

Year	Toyota	Nissan	Honda	Mazda	Mitsubishi	All Others
1970	29.8%	24.7%	10.6%	6.6%	8.9%	19.4%
1975	39.2	31.3	5.9	6.5	6.2	10.9
1978	37.9	29.2	6.0	6.0	9.1	11.8
1980	37.3	29.0	5.9	6.9	8.8	12.1
1981	38.3	28.1	6.5	7.7	8.2	11.2
1982	38.6	27.1	7.9	8.1	7.4	10.9
1983	39.8	26.6	7.8	7.8	6.0	12.0
1984	41.2	26.0	7.9	6.9	6.4	11.6
1985	42.6	25.2	9.6	6.1	5.4	11.1
1986	43.9	24.3	9.7	6.2	4.6	11.3
1987	44.4	23.4	10.3	6.1	4.8	11.1
1988	43.9	23.2	10.8	5.9	4.9	11.3

* Total new passenger car registrations.
Source: Motor Vehicle Manufacturer's Association, *World Motor Vehicle Data*, 1989 Edition, pp. 69–71.

- Declining exports due to import restrictions in the United States and Europe and strict domestic content laws in other countries.
- Continuing appreciation of the yen (whereas it took 260 yen to equal a dollar in early 1985, by early 1988 it took only 129 yen to equal a dollar).
- Expanding demand in the Japanese auto market.
- Escalating competition in the low-priced car market marked by the entrance of several newly industrialized countries (abundant low-cost labor and rising levels of technology placed them on the heels of the Japanese auto industry).
- Increasing sales of imports in the Japanese market (from a level of about 1%, imports had increased to 3% in 1988).

To build a stronger position in the highly competitive, global auto market, Toyota recognized it not only had to strengthen its corporate foundation but it also needed a certain degree of excess production capacity to respond to unexpected spurts in demand in various country markets. In 1976, Toyota re-evaluated its production system, with the goal of establishing a plan to support annual production of 3 million vehicles. In 1981, Shoichiro Toyoda, then-president of Toyota Motor Sales, outlined three management goals: (1) to identify market needs accurately and have those needs reflected in attractive products, (2) to establish a domestic sales organization capable of selling 2 million units per year, and (3) to pursue an energetic overseas strategy based on a long-term perspective.

Toyota moved to achieve greater efficiency in its management operations by merging Toyota Motor Company and Toyota Motor Sales in 1982. According to a joint statement by the new chairman, Eiji Toyoda, and Shoichiro Toyoda, the new president of Toyota Motor, the major reason for the merger was to develop Toyota's international operations and to make decisions more quickly:

To cope with the turbulent 1980s and to progress further along the path we have taken thus far, a need has emerged to integrate our production and sales functions, which are in fact two sides of the same coin, so that they can augment each other more comprehensively and organically.[9]

Toyota launched the "T-50 Operation" in June 1986, to commemorate the 50th anniversary of its first passenger car. Competitors interpreted the intent of the "Operation" as meaning that Toyota aspired to a 50 percent share of the Japanese passenger car market. According to a manager of a mid-level automaker, "It is a shame for the auto industry to permit Toyota to grab a share of 50 percent. Toyota, as the leader of Japan's auto industry, should behave in a more adult-like manner."[10] Redoubled sales efforts by the other automakers succeeded in keeping Toyota's share at 49.2 percent (its highest in history) of all new cars registered in June. This compared with the respective shares of Nissan at 22.8 percent, Honda at 11 percent, and Mazda at 5.6 percent. Typical comments by rival automakers and dealers, who requested anonymity, regarding Toyota's performance included:

> "Toyota is formidable. There is a qualitative difference in its sales system."

> "To be honest, we have received a tremendous jolt. We cannot but ask Toyota to relent a little more."

> "Dealers down to the periphery are exhorted to adhere to orderly sales practices. But such developments may inevitably lead to drastic price-cutting tactics."

> "To be frank, we have no other course but defense. We cannot understand why Toyota cars sell so well. Our parent company (Nissan) insists on fair play and discipline, but we can no longer stick to all our scruples. It is a miracle that Toyota has not adopted the incentive system."[11]

According to rivals, Toyota's strength lay in technical development, enabling it to supply cars exactly matched to customer needs; a powerful distribution system; and near-perfect user services. It was also being rumored among Toyota insiders that the target of capturing 10 percent of the global vehicle market ("Global 10" strategy) had been upped to 12 percent.

By the end of the 1980s, Toyota's success was, according to industry observers, beginning to breed complacency due to *dai-kigyo-byo* (big company disease) and lagging corporate morale. Shoichiro Toyoda commented: ". . . things have changed. The days when every employee committed himself completely—and with utter satisfaction—to his job and his company are gone. People are much more varied in their expectations today."[12] During the first four months of 1989, Toyota's market share in Japan fell, partly due to a strong effort by Nissan to recapture market share.

Since declines in market share figured even more prominently in the Japanese psyche than the bottom line, Shoichiro Toyoda implemented a "put the customer first" campaign aimed at challenging the company's total approach to making cars and recertifying that customer satisfaction was the first priority. The committee responsible for this "customer satisfaction" drive was

---

[9]*Toyota: A History*, p. 314.

[10]As quoted in *Business Japan*, October 1986, p. 44.

[11]As quoted in *Business Japan*, October 1986, pp. 44–45.

[12]As quoted in *Tokyo Business Today*, August 1989, p. 17.

given three years—one thousand days—to get Toyota on the move again and institute *kaizen* on a corporate scale. Additional actions by President Shoichiro Toyoda included eliminating two layers of middle management, stripping 1,000 executives of their staffs, and reorganizing product development, putting himself in charge.

Toyota indicated to its foreign competitors that it was willing to restrain its growth in the name of peaceful coexistence and coprosperity. According to Shoichiro Toyoda:

> We manufacturers realize that we must reexamine and redefine Japan's role in the world, provide positive support and, taking into account the necessity of contributing to the economies of our trade partners, never forget "coexistence and coprosperity" [the need for *kyozon-kyoei*, or both competition and cooperation].
>
> In other words, the world is changing. The time has come for the industry, taken as a global unit, to learn to live together. In the past, competition was the rule, and some firms went to the wall as a consequence. We cannot have a repeat of this today. The new goal of the car industry must be collective prosperity, not cut-throat competition.[13]

Complicating Toyota's predicament was the fact that, although the growth of Japan's auto industry was brisk, competition among Japan's 11 car and truck makers had intensified to the point that some consolidation seemed imminent.

Financial Operations

Toyota Motor Corporation was the largest entity in an affiliation of 14 interlocking companies known as the Toyota Group (see Exhibit 5). Combined, the Toyota Group accounted for 3 percent of Japan's GNP, with total sales exceeding $50 billion. Although members of the Toyoda family were at the helm of 11 of these companies, their total stake in the Toyota Group was estimated at less than 2 percent, with banks and insurance companies holding the majority.

The Toyota Group was affiliated with the Mitsui *keiretsu*. A Japanese *keiretsu* typically consisted of about 20 major companies, one in each industrial sector, but there was no holding company at the top of the organization. Key companies in a *keiretsu* were a bank, an insurance company, and a trading company. The companies were not legally part of a common corporate structure but were held together by cross-locking equity structures—each company owning a portion of every other company's equity—and a sense of reciprocal obligation. Although a key purpose was to help each other raise investment funds, members were also provided protection against hostile takeovers. Another advantage was the ability of group members to obtain low-cost financing from the bank in their *keiretsu*.

Toyota was regarded as conservative, a trait that was reflected in its cash hoard and strong balance sheet. One estimate indicated the company held $13.7 billion in cash reserves. Successful utilization of *zaiteku* (financial management of surplus cash) resulted in Toyota earning more profits on its financial investments than its annual car operations. Toyota allocated its investment funds to financial institutions offering the best interest rates, regardless of the

---

[13]As quoted in *Business Japan*, September 1985, p. 18; and *Tokyo Business Today*, p. 16.

EXHIBIT 5   The Toyota Group Companies, 1985

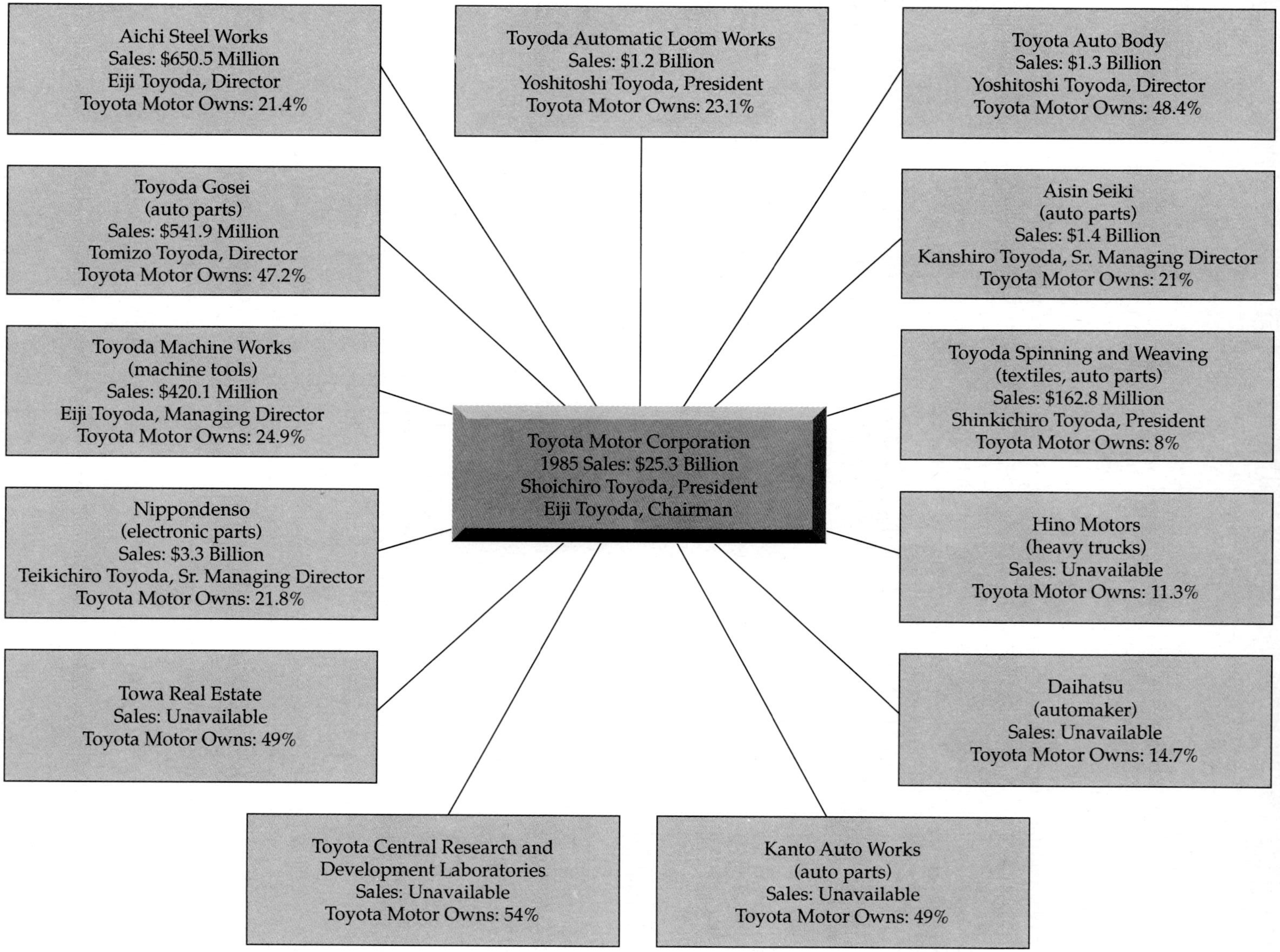

Toyota Auto Body
Sales: $1.3 Billion
Yoshitoshi Toyoda, Director
Toyota Motor Owns: 48.4%

Aisin Seiki
(auto parts)
Sales: $1.4 Billion
Kanshiro Toyoda, Sr. Managing Director
Toyota Motor Owns: 21%

Toyoda Spinning and Weaving
(textiles, auto parts)
Sales: $162.8 Million
Shinkichiro Toyoda, President
Toyota Motor Owns: 8%

Hino Motors
(heavy trucks)
Sales: Unavailable
Toyota Motor Owns: 11.3%

Daihatsu
(automaker)
Sales: Unavailable
Toyota Motor Owns: 14.7%

Toyoda Automatic Loom Works
Sales: $1.2 Billion
Yoshitoshi Toyoda, President
Toyota Motor Owns: 23.1%

Toyota Motor Corporation
1985 Sales: $25.3 Billion
Shoichiro Toyoda, President
Eiji Toyoda, Chairman

Kanto Auto Works
(auto parts)
Sales: Unavailable
Toyota Motor Owns: 49%

Aichi Steel Works
Sales: $650.5 Million
Eiji Toyoda, Director
Toyota Motor Owns: 21.4%

Toyoda Gosei
(auto parts)
Sales: $541.9 Million
Tomizo Toyoda, Director
Toyota Motor Owns: 47.2%

Toyoda Machine Works
(machine tools)
Sales: $420.1 Million
Eiji Toyoda, Managing Director
Toyota Motor Owns: 24.9%

Nippondenso
(electronic parts)
Sales: $3.3 Billion
Teikichiro Toyoda, Sr. Managing Director
Toyota Motor Owns: 21.8%

Towa Real Estate
Sales: Unavailable
Toyota Motor Owns: 49%

Toyota Central Research and
Development Laboratories
Sales: Unavailable
Toyota Motor Owns: 54%

Sources: *Business Week*, November 4, 1985, p. 45; and *1989 International Directory of Corporate Affiliations* (Illinois: National Register Publishing), p. 475.

E X H I B I T   6   **Selected Financial Statistics, Toyota Motor Corporation, 1940–1989** *(In thousands of yen)*

Period	Net Sales	Net Income	Capital
1940	¥ 67,261	¥ 2,375	¥ 30,000
1945	100,416	8,707	91,500
1950	4,199,801	(76,524)	418,000
1955	16,960,486	1,439,622	3,344,000
1960	102,680,798	9,579,376	16,000,000
1965	247,520,977	12,228,722	38,250,000
1970	837,561,198	38,807,877	40,600,000
1975/76	1,995,742,392	99,558,792	53,210,000
1979/80	3,310,181,153	143,576,563	83,808,900
1984/85	6,064,420,350	308,309,633	133,297,664
1985/86	6,304,858,970	255,185,609	N/A
1986/87	6,024,909,943	200,208,459	N/A
1987/88	6,691,299,157	238,006,711	134,537,653
1988/89	7,190,590,000	305,863,000	N/A

Notes: Figures for periods 1940 to 1960 are for pre-tax income. Financial statistics for Toyota Motor Sales, an independent entity from 1950 to 1982, are not included.

N/A = not available.

Source: *Toyota: A History of the First 50 Years* (1 Toyota-cho, Toyota City, Aichi Prefecture, Japan: Toyota Motor Corporation, 1988) pp. 455–56, 459.

type of product, via its competitive bidding system. Thus, Toyota commanded the highest possible interest rates on its cash balances, referred to as the "Toyota Rate" in Japanese financial circles, and its interest income had risen over the last several years. Toyota was considered as one of Japan's most powerful financial institutions. Toyota's cash management system closely resembled its *kanban* production system and was typical of its efforts to reduce inefficiencies. According to one account, Toyota limited employees to one pencil at a time and a sign over the towel dispenser in the restroom at headquarters read: "Visitors Only."

Toyota's potential plans for its excess cash included building new factories around the world; diversifying through acquisitions in electronics, telecommunications, factory automation, financial, and aerospace; and buying or creating joint ventures with other automakers, most likely in Europe. According to one high-ranking Toyota executive:

> If an acquisition looks right, we'll look at the candidates positively. We wouldn't like to refuse some food without even tasting it. Such an acquisition would be for the purpose of winning the survival race in the world automotive business, which is getting more and more heated. It's not that we want to beat General Motors, it's that we want to make sure they won't beat us.[14]

Exhibit 6 presents selected financial statistics of Toyota Motor Corporation.

---

[14]As quoted in *Fortune*, November 21, 1988, p. 198.

Product Strategy

By the latter 1960s, Toyota's strategy resembled GM's—blanketing the market with a variety of nameplates, each one a step above the other in size and cost. Initial emphasis was on cars for the family market, rather than specialized models. The Publica, the least expensive model, was intended for buyers moving up from motorcycles or minicars. Then, in ascending order, were the Corolla (similar in size and price to the VW Beetle), the best-selling Corona, the Corona Mark II (Cressida), and the six-cylinder Crown (about the size of an American compact). Additional limited-production prestige models built but not exported were the eight-cylinder, luxurious Century and the 2000GT, a two-seater similar to the Jaguar XKE. A full range of trucks complemented Toyota's autos.

Although new, sportier models (Celica) aimed at the youth market were subsequently introduced, Toyota lagged behind other Japanese automakers in introducing new models due to its concentrated efforts to meet the emission control standards of the 1970s. Additionally, the oil crises of the 1970s dictated a new approach to developing passenger cars appropriate to the international market—small, fuel-efficient, front-wheel-drive passenger cars. Toyota's first products in this area were the Tercel and Camry. When the Camry debuted in 1982, it was hailed by auto enthusiasts as the first in a new generation of front-wheel-drive cars; however, some critics thought it lacked elegance due to its functional styling and plain interior. Toyota entered the high-performance, specialty car market with the MR2 and the Supra, introduced in the 1980s. One impartial indicator of the attractiveness of Toyota's car was their price in the used-car market. According to one study, Toyota's vehicles retained more than 70 percent of their value five years after being purchased. Only three other brands were in this category. Exhibit 7 displays Toyota's overall motor vehicle production. Exhibits 8 and 9 display Toyota's passenger car and commercial vehicle production.

EXPORT ACTIVITIES

Toyota established an Export Department in 1950 to explore the feasibility of overseas exports. Toyota's early export efforts were characterized by trial and error since the company was generally unfamiliar with the competitive conditions and import restrictions in foreign countries. Toyota targeted Southeast Asia, Latin America, and the Caribbean as its first export channels due to their proximity and interest. With an increase in local content laws prohibiting the export of completely built autos to several countries (such as Brazil and Mexico), Toyota experimented with a knockdown (KD) system, beginning in the latter 1950s. A KD set was one whose shipment price was less than 60 percent of the total cost of component parts making up a whole car. Problems, such as unavailability of local parts or assembly with incorrect or missing parts, hampered the early exports of KD sets. Toyota revamped the KD system and resumed knockdown exports to several countries beginning in 1962. Toyota continued to export KD sets to several countries, including Africa and Southeast Asia, as part of its export strategy. Toyota's KD exports and exports by geographic region are displayed in Exhibits 10 and 11.

EXHIBIT 7   Motor Vehicle Production, Toyota Motor Corporation, 1935–1989

Year	Cars	Trucks & Buses	Total
1935	0	20	20
1940	268	14,519	14,787
1945	0	3,275	3,275
1950	463	11,243	11,706
1955	7,403	15,383	22,786
1960	42,118	112,652	154,770
1965	236,151	241,492	477,643
1970	1,068,321	540,869	1,609,190
1975	1,714,836	621,217	2,336,053
1980	2,303,284	990,060	3,293,344
1981	2,248,171	972,247	3,220,418
1982	2,258,253	886,304	3,144,557
1983	2,380,753	891,582	3,272,335
1984	2,413,133	1,061,116	3,429,249
1985	2,569,284	1,096,338	3,665,622
1986	2,684,024	976,143	3,660,167
1987	2,708,069	930,210	3,638,279
1988	2,982,922	985,775	3,968,697
1989	3,055,101	920,801	3,975,902

Sources: *Toyota: A History of the First 50 Years* (1 Toyota-cho, Toyota City, Aichi Prefecture, Japan: Toyota Motor Corporation, 1988), p. 461; and *1990 Ward's Automotive Yearbook*, p. 285.

United States

Toyota's top management initially opposed exporting to the United States. Numerous doubts existed regarding the suitability of the Toyota car in terms of performance, reliability, and price. Several factors influenced Toyota to begin exporting to the United States: growth of the small car market (European competitors, primarily Volkswagen, had captured almost 10 percent of this market by the late 1950s); U.S. automakers were not building small cars; and it was probable the United States would adopt import restrictions. According to a Toyota executive, "If the U.S. goes ahead and restricts imports, Toyota will be cut out of the American market for good. We've got to get in there now or never."

Toyota shipped two Crown Toyopets to the United States in 1957. The Crown was a flop. Lacking power to travel on high-speed roads, it vibrated badly at speeds over 70 mph and overheated when driven over mountains and on desert roads. It was unable to traverse a California hill to the dealer showroom where it was to debut. Shoichiro Toyoda labeled it a "junk" car, unsuitable for American roads.

In late 1960, Toyota halted passenger car exports to the United States. Determined to make a comeback, it vigorously set about designing and building the right cars for the U.S. market. When Toyota introduced the Corona to the United States in 1965, it was a hit with American consumers. Toyota's strategy

EXHIBIT 8   Passenger Vehicle Production by Model, Toyota Motor Corporation, 1961–1988

	Century	Crown	Mark II (Cressida)	Chaser	Cresta	Soarer	Corona	Carina	Camry
Before 1961	0	144,435	0	0	0	0	41,216	0	0
1961	0	55,475	0	0	0	0	46,972	0	0
1962	0	47,483	0	0	0	0	49,739	0	0
1963	0	80,266	0	0	0	0	66,195	0	0
1964	0	95,012	0	0	0	0	98,503	0	0
1965	0	81,188	0	0	0	0	179,447	0	0
1966	0	86,843	0	0	0	0	252,492	0	0
1967	174	92,092	0	0	0	0	320,250	0	0
1968	1,063	130,854	69,451	0	0	0	308,644	0	0
1969	883	134,747	297,378	0	0	0	231,683	0	0
1970	775	135,321	248,334	0	0	0	284,485	12,592	0
1971	853	106,223	251,967	0	0	0	311,614	95,854	0
1972	1,143	90,096	219,842	0	0	0	297,306	130,807	0
1973	1,332	117,814	205,960	0	0	0	295,237	180,499	0
1974	1,253	85,199	108,173	0	0	0	356,420	121,770	0
1975	748	134,697	108,405	0	0	0	366,527	152,008	0
1976	985	105,605	92,134	0	0	0	326,244	167,122	0
1977	1,138	112,205	233,442	25,555	0	0	266,129	165,616	0
1978	1,014	131,410	213,293	38,784	0	0	257,881	206,561	0
1979	1,267	143,761	189,047	33,814	0	0	267,580	212,314	0
1980	712	150,616	167,954	21,834	29,875	0	219,614	171,427	59,546
1981	738	150,528	222,031	22,531	43,409	30,728	183,382	167,056	65,469
1982	664	136,005	222,901	28,209	54,772	22,185	191,570	179,189	36,202
1983	1,419	130,630	206,162	27,359	65,368	28,060	190,077	150,749	150,323
1984	977	158,555	210,214	32,865	68,277	25,777	237,454	140,358	191,727
1985	1,043	166,474	255,685	47,595	76,004	23,016	201,661	156,141	225,116
1986	1,344	129,832	248,145	58,414	86,121	40,009	188,482	186,347	251,994
1987	1,534	143,345	230,306	48,214	78,944	30,322	173,521	178,418	349,814
1988	1,895	196,019	238,159	51,988	86,483	32,187	255,988	187,198	326,096

Year	Celica	Vista	Corolla	Sprinter	Tercel	Corsa	Starlet	Tercel 4-WD	Corolla II	Toyota MR2	Supra
1966	0	0	12,180	0	0	0	0	0	0	0	0
1967	0	0	162,555	0	0	0	0	0	0	0	0
1968	0	0	242,749	43,058	0	0	0	0	0	0	0
1989	0	0	354,518	87,796	0	0	0	0	0	0	0
1970	5,602	0	460,319	76,737	0	0	0	0	0	0	0
1971	111,204	0	596,863	73,312	0	0	0	0	0	0	0
1972	150,162	0	647,700	86,432	0	0	0	0	0	0	0
1973	177,174	0	669,402	87,353	0	0	48,762	0	0	0	0
1974	148,751	0	677,455	95,650	0	0	45,688	0	0	0	0
1975	139,193	0	757,265	136,367	0	0	46,003	0	0	0	0
1976	223,831	0	816,897	114,273	0	0	31,160	0	0	0	0
1977	254,234	0	817,732	101,202	0	0	17,858	0	0	0	0
1978	293,917	0	735,603	103,441	26,424	21,586	128,561	0	0	0	0
1979	245,468	0	727,419	116,849	104,914	28,827	143,281	0	0	0	0
1980	208,523	0	856,623	96,620	183,908	36,523	173,235	0	0	0	0
1981	180,444	0	722,599	96,681	204,298	25,863	197,914	0	0	0	0
1982	218,934	15,800	655,316	87,462	215,310	36,787	154,538	31,979	47,811	0	0
1983	183,502	26,762	625,833	119,737	183,904	42,210	118,808	86,558	95,942	0	0
1984	155,713	24,648	813,695	95,484	108,986	35,926	114,787	93,230	82,900	14,877	0
1985	135,484	27,834	666,260	82,182	98,013	38,998	163,774	82,182	65,400	51,271	0
1986	151,469	30,003	636,815	70,384	96,425	45,895	191,080	86,139	63,503	42,508	59,534
1987	118,000	53,500	874,215	108,223	150,573	43,888	138,755	36,768	56,325	26,368	47,013
1988	93,725	56,307	784,521	125,987	187,851	44,832	135,996	50,879	56,487	18,129	37,220

Source: Motor Vehicle Manufacturer's Association, *World Motor Vehicle Data*, 1989 Edition, pp. 58–60.

EXHIBIT 9   Commercial Vehicle Production by Model, Toyota Motor Corporation, 1971–1988

	Dyna	Toyoace	Hiace	TownAce	Liteace	Stout	Master Ace	Hilux	Publica Pickup	Coaster	Land Cruiser	Blizzard	Toyota Truck
1971	41,454	32,014	55,386	0	27,343	10.630	0	77,865	36,896	4,549	39,193	0	N/A
1972	46,440	45,793	58,183	0	42,036	7,955	0	79,523	37,365	5,238	38,811	0	N/A
1973	50,813	54,981	78,471	0	63,203	7,707	0	100,050	37,913	7,278	38,846	0	N/A
1974	45,158	42,042	73,578	0	49,015	10,395	0	120,866	28,355	6,403	52,893	0	8,746
1975	41,058	35,356	68,610	0	61,115	12,495	0	129,782	26,570	6,073	68,943	0	8,731
1976	49,894	38,900	79,219	13,195	70,850	17,645	0	179,952	29,480	8,174	84,249	0	9,903
1977	55,067	25,613	90,919	57,356	52,642	19,328	0	236,863	25,951	8,417	109,050	0	10,396
1978	67,790	32,527	101,767	67,560	45,526	15,632	0	241,144	20,987	9,182	133,376	0	6,817
1979	63,426	33,700	118,997	89,233	52,582	12,239	0	251,888	9,541	10,041	115,592	0	7,211
1980	67,029	30,345	165,503	31,826	60,412	15,665	0	334,481	9,918	12,395	116,223	1,806	9,143
1981	60,101	25,811	163,432	60,304	95,108	11,881	0	326,593	7,162	14,270	127,798	2,104	9,649
1982	45,841	22,185	127,036	49,599	78,807	10,065	0	324,627	4,135	11,116	129,620	1,274	5,148
1983	46,890	23,565	120,733	90,309	77,707	10,324	0	349,816	3,424	7,052	124,297	391	4,378
1984	51,664	35,094	138,628	144,217	81,084	6,445	0	434,786	3,301	9,619	115,048	1,383	2,709
1985	55,874	39,872	145,593	135,568	76,120	4,822	13,694	480,560	3,075	11,888	135,694	1,220	2,346
1986	45,742	19,094	116,017	138,947	78,984	3,026	16,930	490,248	2,794	5,893	95,206	1,049	1,747
1987	53,458	21,065	136,460	115,734	81,715	2,530	20,726	419,989	2,190	6,391	94,274	962	1,605
1988	59,434	24,491	150,883	119,112	90,355	2,433	24,234	448,003	1,586	7,577	100,895	1,004	1,008

Note: N/A = Not available.

Source: Motor Vehicle Manufacturer's Association, *World Motor Vehicle Data*, 1989 Edition, pp. 58–60.

E X H I B I T 10 **Knockdown (KD) Exports by Geographic Region, Toyota Motor Corporation, 1980–1987**

Year	North America	Europe	Southeast Asia and Oceania	Africa	Total
1980			59,950	27,960	87,910
1982			57,800	72,560	130,360
1984	157		68,120	83,990	152,267
1985	78,240	40	68,680	55,060	202,020
1986	211,680	720	67,320	63,520	343,240
1987	180,870	904	74,620	71,800	328,230

Notes: A KD set is one whose shipment price is less than 60 percent of the total cost of component parts making up a whole car.

Regional categorization of countries follows Toyota's internal administrative conventions and may therefore differ from generally accepted categorizations.

Source: *Toyota: A History of the First 50 Years* (1 Toyota-cho, Toyota City, Aichi Prefecture, Japan: Toyota Motor Corporation, 1988), p. 463.

involved offering a comparatively luxurious, well-built, small car with acceleration superior to other economy imports. Outfitted with a 90-horsepower engine, it was nearly twice as powerful as a VW Beetle. With a larger engine, it was possible to offer options, such as automatic transmission and air conditioning. Toyota also strengthened its dealer network, after-sales service, and advertising promotions, and concentrated its initial sales efforts in Los Angeles. In 1968, Toyota introduced the smaller Corolla, which conformed to its policy at that time of avoiding direct competition with the U.S. automakers. Toyota sold 6,388 vehicles in the United States in 1965; by 1969, volume exceeded 100,000. By 1975, the United States was Toyota's largest export market, and Toyota had usurped Volkswagen as the best-selling foreign import. Aided by the growth in the small-car market (from 43 percent in 1973 to about 60 percent in 1980) Toyota's exports climbed rapidly until the early 1980s, when the combination of several events conspired to contain the invasion of Japanese vehicle imports.

Allegations of dumping surfaced when a Volkswagen executive stated that Volkswagen was selling its models in the United States at losses ranging from $250 to $600 each. A dumping investigation, directed at automakers in eight countries, was conducted. Although Toyota was included in this investigation, it was officially cleared of these charges; however, skepticism that dumping was a common practice among certain automakers persisted. In 1980, based on a change in "definition," the United States increased its customs duty on trucks from 4 percent to 25 percent. In the same year, the United Auto Workers and Ford argued that Japanese vehicle imports had resulted in increasing unemployment among U.S. auto workers and was harming the domestic auto industry. They petitioned the U.S. International Trade Commission to require Japanese automakers to build plants in the United States and to apply volume restrictions on their exports. Although the ITC ruled that there was no direct causal relation between the increase in auto imports and the difficulties experienced by the U.S. auto industry, voluntary restraints on exports were

E X H I B I T   11   **Exports by Geographic Region, Toyota Motor Corporation, 1955–1987**

Year	North America	Latin America and Caribbean	Europe	Southeast Asia and Oceania	Middle East	Africa	Total
1955		57	1	193	30		281
1960	534	2,102	13	2,898	467	87	6,397
1965	13,224	4,983	5,916	28,697	3,188	7,464	63,474
1970	245,062	28,470	59,019	86,644	18,977	43,720	481,892
1975	318,684	43,803	185,699	149,823	102,820	67,523	868,352
1980	762,829	106,238	318,714	223,592	279,493	94,579	1,785,445
1982	735,397	80,956	271,932	196,565	323,907	57,036	1,665,793
1984	900,900	77,888	302,554	253,529	229,930	36,122	1,800,923
1985	1,017,289	79,432	347,743	281,392	221,207	32,892	1,979,955
1986	1,115,062	81,595	415,047	139,573	91,391	33,095	1,875,763
1987	992,901	67,971	422,627	127,476	118,943	41,019	1,770,937

Notes: Regional categorization of countries follows Toyota's internal administrative conventions and may therefore differ from generally accepted categorizations.
Source: *Toyota: A History of the First 50 Years* (1 Toyota-cho, Toyota City, Aichi Prefecture, Japan: Toyota Motor Corporation, 1988), p. 463.

established by the Japanese government, beginning on May 1, 1981. Under the VRA (voluntary restraint agreement), the nine Japanese automakers were limited to a U.S. market share equal to their level of imports during 1974–1975. Initially slated to last three years, the voluntary restraints were extended, with the "quotas" increasing gradually:

1981–1983	1,680,000 passenger cars
1984	1,850,000 passenger cars
1985–1986	2,300,000 passenger cars

The quotas actually benefited Toyota. Forced to limit exports, Toyota not only increased prices, it also began to replace its small, inexpensive export cars with larger, more expensive ones loaded with options. Toyota was able to sell all of its allotted quota and often found itself without enough vehicles to sell. Toyota's sales in the United States declined in the mid-1980s, but by the latter 1980s, Toyota's market share rebounded as several new models were introduced and U.S. production facilities were established. Exhibit 12 shows the U.S. market share of the major automakers.

Lexus   Having mastered the formula for producing and selling low- and mid-priced cars, Toyota hoped to repeat this success in the luxury car market. A dream of chairman Eiji Toyoda, who felt that Toyota did not get the respect it deserved, was to "develop the best car in the world." In 1983, he challenged the Toyota engineers, using Mercedes and BMW as the benchmarks, to pursue this dream and to do what no other automaker had achieved: design a sedan

EXHIBIT 12   **U.S. Market Share of the Major Automakers, 1973–1989***

Year	General Motors	Ford	Chrysler	Toyota	Honda	Nissan	All Imports
1973	44.96%	24.37%	13.72%	2.53%	.34%	2.02%	15.15%
1974	42.41	25.88	14.08	2.69	.47	2.09	15.74
1975	43.83	23.61	12.25	3.33	1.19	3.01	18.17
1976	47.61	22.62	13.67	3.43	1.49	2.67	14.84
1977	46.31	23.40	12.00	4.41	2.00	3.47	18.26
1978	47.79	23.54	11.05	3.91	2.43	3.00	17.78
1979	46.26	20.81	10.13	4.77	3.31	4.43	22.70
1980	45.86	17.20	8.77	6.49	4.18	5.76	28.18
1981	44.49	16.56	9.85	6.76	4.35	5.45	28.80
1982	44.06	16.87	9.95	6.65	4.58	5.89	29.57
1983	44.15	17.11	10.36	6.05	4.37	5.68	27.54
1984	44.33	19.07	10.39	5.37	4.90	4.68	24.93
1985	42.49	18.83	11.28	5.61	5.00	5.21	25.90
1986	40.95	18.16	11.42	5.58	6.05	4.84	28.18
1987	36.30	20.06	10.68	6.12	7.19	5.61	32.23
1988	35.94	21.53	11.20	6.48	7.23	4.83	31.17
1989	35.15	22.27	10.43	6.92	8.01	5.22	31.77

*U.S. passenger car sales.
Sources: *1990 Ward's Automotive Yearbook*, p. 208; and *1984 Ward's Automotive Yearbook*, p. 101.

that would travel 150 mph while carrying four passengers in relative quiet, comfort, and safety—without incurring the American gas-guzzler tax. The overall strategy involved marketing a high-performance car equal in quality to Mercedes and BMW, but priced below them and above the U.S. luxury models, Cadillac and Lincoln.

The first step involved the purchase of the competitors' cars—four Mercedes, a Jaguar XJ6, and two BMWs—which were subjected to grueling test drives and then taken apart for further study. Next, 11 performance goals, relating to such characteristics as aerodynamics, weight, noise levels, and fuel efficiency, were established. Overall, the extensive development process involved six years, an investment of over $500 million, creation of a flexible organizational structure to oversee the project, development of a new engine, and establishment of separate marketing and advertising entities, involving a separate dealership organization to sell the car. In contrast to European automakers, which utilized extensive hand labor to achieve quality, Toyota installed the most elaborate automation that was feasible, believing that only mechanized processes could meet the stringent assembly standards it had established for its new Lexus models.

Incorporating such advanced features as hydraulic active suspension, a two-stroke engine, and traction control, the Lexus was faster, more fuel efficient, and less expensive than its German competitors:

	Lexus	**BMW**	**Mercedes**
Acceleration speed (0–60 mph)	8.6 seconds	10.3 seconds	9.3 seconds
Official highway gas mileage	23.5 mpg	19.0 mpg	18.0 mpg
Price	$35,000	$54,000	$61,210

The Lexus 400 was analyzed by the engineers of all of Toyota's rivals; reputedly, no evidence of technical shortcuts were found. Some industry observers suggested that Toyota had low-balled the prices of its Lexus models; Toyota claimed it was earning its usual profit on the car.

According to Shoichiro Toyoda, the success of Lexus depended on how well it was made. "Our biggest challenge will be to have no defects and to build a reliable car that won't break down."[15] The size of the luxury segment (1 million units annually in the latter 1980s) was projected to grow annually by about 10 percent, reaching about 1.5 million units by the mid-1990s. Growth, combined with gross margins of 20 percent versus 12 percent to 16 percent on less expensive models), were additional incentives for Toyota to enter this market. And at the lower end of the Lexus line was a $20,000-plus V-6 model that was predicted to be even more significant than the bigger Lexus; it represented Toyota's entry into the profitable segment of intermediate-priced family sedans and mid-size coupes.

The Lexus was launched in the United States in September 1989; three months after its introduction, three minor glitches, including one that could cause the cruise-control system to remain on after the driver attempted to turn it off, were found in the LS 400s, resulting in Toyota recalling about 8,500 units. Toyota responded by personally calling each owner with two options:

> Bring the car in yourself to be fixed on the spot, or have Lexus pick it up at night and return it ready-to-go the next morning. Either way, Lexus not only fixed the defect but also washed the car, cleaned the inside and filled it with gasoline. Some dealers even placed a small gift, such as an ice scraper, on the front seat. Owners were mollified, and many were impressed.[16]

After-sales service was also a top priority:

> A customer who had just purchased an LS 400 rushed back to the dealer, saying he was furious that a new car should break down so fast. When we looked for the problem, we found that the emergency brake was on. When the "faulty car" was replaced at no cost, the customer was so thrilled with the unexpected service that he bought another car.[17]

According to one industry analyst: "When the Lexus LS 400 first came out, people said it was a better value than a comparable Mercedes or BMW. Now they are saying flat out that it is a better car than a Mercedes or BMW."[18] After being on the market less than one year, the Lexus brand ranked No. 1 in the J. D. Power's Initial Quality Survey of new cars. Lexus was outselling its

[15]As quoted in *Fortune*, August 14, 1989, p. 65.
[16]As quoted in *The Wall Street Journal*, July 20, 1990, p. A8.
[17]As quoted in *Tokyo Business Today*, February 1990, p. 28.
[18]As quoted in *Fortune*, July 2, 1990, pp. 60 and 64.

competitors' models in the United States after only 14 months. In Japan, there was a one-year waiting list.

Export Activities Outside the United States

Strict import restrictions, idiosyncratic tastes of European consumers in their choice of autos, intense competition in countries having their own automakers, and the great diversity among the European countries hindered Toyota's ability to penetrate the European auto market. By the latter 1970s, several countries had established import restrictions. Toyota's maximum share of the British market was set at 2 percent (later increased to 11 percent) of the total market, and France set the maximum share for all Japanese vehicles at 3 percent of the total market. Quotas in Italy and Spain limited Japan's share to less than 1 percent. In 1981, the EEC placed passenger cars on the list of import items from Japan to be monitored.

The main attraction of early Toyota vehicles to Europeans were their novelty and simplicity of mechanical structure, making them relatively trouble-free. By the early 1980s, virtually all new European cars were front-wheel drive models. They displayed excellent driving performance, had luxury-class specifications, and offered numerous options. European automakers were discounting their prices in bold competitive moves. Thus, Toyota's exports to Europe were negatively affected. Shoichiro Toyoda outlined Toyota's market strategy at a European dealers' meeting in late 1982:

> The European market holds much potential for Toyota, and it demands only the finest products. . . . We feel strongly that Toyota must be a leader with vision in Europe and elsewhere, and the first step in becoming a leader is to regain the number one position among Japanese automakers as early as possible, and after that to widen the gap between ourselves and others. . . . In short, Toyota's success in Europe becomes possible only when your thinking and our thinking are the same, when we share the same goal.[19]

In 1986, Western Europe overtook the United States as the largest market for new-car sales in the world, and Toyota was battling Nissan for the role of No. 1 Japanese importer. Toyota was already the overall top-selling maker in several European countries—Finland, Denmark, Ireland, and Norway. While current plans called for the Common Market nations to lower their intercountry trade barriers in 1992, it was being hotly debated about what to do regarding Japanese autos. If trade barriers were eased, projections indicated the Japanese share of the market could increase from its current 11 percent to between 20 and 25 percent by the end of the 1990s. In countries without quotas, the Japanese had obtained 40 percent of the market in Ireland, 25 percent in Sweden, and 15 percent in West Germany.

To combat the Japanese, European carmakers were exploring possible new relationships with each other to become more competitive. However, with the European carmakers experiencing some of the same problems (inefficiency, quality problems, and slowness of bringing new cars to market) as the U.S. carmakers, the Japanese threat was viewed as formidable by European automakers. Toyota had recently begun exporting its luxury and sports cars to

---

[19]*Toyota: A History*, p. 351.

E X H I B I T   13   **European Market Shares of the Major Automakers, 1982–1990***

Company	1990	1989	1988	1987	1986	1985	1984	1983	1982
VW Group	15.4%	15.0%	14.9%	15.0%	14.7%	14.4%	12.0%	11.8%	12.0%
Fiat Group	14.2	13.1	14.8	14.2	14.0	12.3	12.7	12.0	12.3
Peugeot Group	12.9	12.6	12.9	12.1	11.4	11.5	11.5	11.8	12.3
Ford	11.6	11.6	11.3	12.0	11.7	11.9	12.8	12.5	12.3
General Motors	11.8	11.0	10.6	10.7	11.0	11.4	11.1	11.1	9.6
Renault	9.9	10.4	10.2	10.6	10.6	10.7	10.9	12.6	14.4
Mercedes	3.3	3.2	3.4	3.5	3.7	3.7	3.2	3.2	3.2
Austin Rover	2.9	3.1	3.5	3.4	3.5	3.9	3.9	4.0	3.9
Nissan	2.8	2.9	2.9	2.9	3.0	2.9	2.8	2.8	2.9
Toyota	2.7	2.5	2.7	2.8	2.9	2.6	2.2	2.2	2.3
BMW	2.8	2.8	2.7	2.4	2.6	2.7	3.0	2.9	2.7
Volvo	1.8	2.0	2.0	2.2	2.3	2.4	2.3	2.2	2.0
Mazda	2.1	1.8	1.9	1.9	2.0	1.9	2.0	2.0	—
Alfa Romeo	1.7	1.7	1.6	1.5	1.5	1.5	1.8	1.7	—
Mitsubishi	1.3	1.2	1.2	1.2	1.2	1.1	—	—	—
Honda	1.2	1.0	1.1	1.0	1.2	—	—	—	—

*Total new passenger car registrations.

Sources: *1990 Ward's Automotive Yearbook*. p. 269; *1986 Ward's Automotive Yearbook*, p. 65; and *1984 Ward's Automotive Yearbook*, p. 54.

Europe, such as the Cressida and Lexus (late 1990), and plans for European production of its mass-market models were under way. Exhibit 13 shows the European market shares of the major automakers.

Toyota gradually expanded its markets in other countries during the 1960s and 1970s. Distinctive factors associated with some of these countries, including worsening economic conditions, a harsh business environment, political instability, high foreign debt, and stringent domestic content laws, resulted in declining exports to an overwhelming majority of them in the 1980s. However, Toyota had been able to lay solid foundations in several countries, such as Indonesia and Australia, through cooperative relationships with joint-venture partners or companies with which it had business ties.

OVERSEAS PRODUCTION OPERATIONS

The necessity for establishing local production bases outside Japan became evident to Toyota in the early 1980s. Prior to 1982, Toyota had not engaged in any major strategic alliances or independent overseas production, but the rapidly changing competitive situation prompted the company to reevaluate its posture. Prominent concerns of Toyota executives included the nature of labor relations practices, the degree to which various components of the TPS could be transferred to facilities in other countries, and the ability to manage an operation on another continent.

United States

Lagging behind the other leading Japanese automakers, Honda and Nissan, in establishing production facilities in the United States, it was inevitable that Toyota would establish an alliance with a U.S. automaker. Talks of a tie-in with Ford had occurred on four occasions, beginning in 1939, with the last discussion of building a plant together (this time in the United States and not Japan) to develop and produce small cars occurring in 1980. According to Eiji Toyoda, the roles were reversed:

> As before, Toyota did the proposing, but the nature of the proposal was different. In 1960, we had asked Ford to teach us everything they could about small cars, but in 1980 the situation had changed. This time, we were offering to jointly produce our vehicle at Ford. The student had traded places with the teacher. This only goes to show how much the world can change in the short space of twenty years.[20]

Like prior discussions, this one did not culminate in an agreement.

Toyota linked up with GM in 1984 to establish NUMMI, its first base of operations in the United States. The 50–50 joint venture initially produced Chevy Novas and Toyota Corollas at a closed GM plant in Fremont, California. In the latter 1980s, the Nova was replaced by the Geo Prism model line, and production of a new Toyota small pickup truck was slated to begin in the early 1990s. GM contributed the manufacturing plant and was responsible for marketing and selling the Geo. Toyota managed NUMMI, and former UAW workers were rehired for the production jobs. From Toyota's perspective, the venture would enable it to reduce the risk and allow it to gain valuable experience associated with local production. Specifically, Toyota wanted to evaluate the competency of U.S. suppliers, the adequacy of the transportation systems, and options for dealing with unionized labor in the U.S.

To implement certain components of the TPS, Toyota's top priority was to establish stable labor relations with the UAW. Mutual trust and respect between management and labor was emphasized in the negotiated contract that provided affirmative action before laying off any employee, allowed any employee to stop the production line to fix a problem, eliminated multiple job classifications to encourage flexible workers, and arranged workers into teams. Team leaders were carefully selected, with on-site training provided in Toyota City. Indoctrination included courses on Toyota's history, corporate policies, production philosophy, quality-control circle activities, and the concept of teamwork. Hands-on training involved exposure to production activities and worksite management at the Takaoka plant for two weeks. Nine groups of 257 trainees participated in this training. American production employees were not typically promoted to management-level jobs. In contrast, NUMMI established a contract with the UAW to introduce a foreman-promotion system. As of 1990, 110 employees had been promoted.

The Fremont facility was extensively remodeled with simplicity guiding the process. Renovation entailed (1) replacing old equipment; (2) restructuring the body, painting, and assembly lines into a series of short parallel lines that were less complex and less robotic-intensive than the long, complex, and highly

---

[20]Eiji Toyoda, *Toyota: Fifty Years in Motion*, p. 130.

automated assembly lines typical of most GM plants; (3) installing line-stop switches; and (4) establishing the *kanban* system of production control.

The philosophy in selecting suppliers was to abandon the traditional adversarial nature of supplier-buyer relationships. NUMMI established a practice of almost never switching vendors and used only one or two suppliers for each purchased part. Vendors were carefully selected, were expected to utilize the practices of *kanban* or just-in-time inventory control, and had little chance of losing their contract if they fulfilled the agreed-upon terms. There was no competitive bidding in awarding contracts, and suppliers were expected to meet rigid standards in return for security.

At the opening ceremony in April 1985, NUMMI's president commented:

> Principally as a result of the efforts of the team members of NUMMI and the people in so many related companies who have cooperated in this project, we have built here in Fremont a first-class assembly plant. Thanks to our cooperative parts suppliers and our 1,200 employees, we are now producing cars of world-class quality. Our slogan at NUMMI this year is "Quality assurance through teamwork." People working together means teamwork, and I believe it is teamwork that will be the key to our success.[21]

The following practices were implemented at NUMMI—an "open office" floor plan, a single cafeteria, common parking facilities, announcement of managerial decisions to the union before implementation, personal announcements of company policy by the president, and a suggestion system focusing on work improvements for use by all employees. Employee attendance reached 97 percent during the first year of operation. By 1989, productivity levels were 40 percent higher than typical GM plants, and NUMMI had the highest quality levels GM had ever known.

At about the time NUMMI was launched, Toyota announced plans to begin independent production in North America with the construction of plants in the United States and Canada. Toyota's decision to locate the Toyota Motor Manufacturing (TMM) plant in Georgetown, Kentucky, was based on several factors: parts procurement, transportation convenience, land prices, electricity supplies, labor resources, and tax and other preferential treatment (a $125 million financial incentive package was offered by Kentucky officials). Commenting on the selection decision in late 1985, Shoichiro Toyoda stated:

> We view today's official announcement of our plant site selection as one of the highlights in our company's history. . . . In fact, choosing the site for our American plant was one of the most difficult decisions we've ever had to make at Toyota. After considering all of the factors involved, however, we decided that Kentucky is the best location for our American plant. At the same time, we wish to thank all the other states that presented site proposals. More than 25 years have passed since we started our exports to the United States, and since then we have moved steadily forward toward realizing our dream of building a perfect partnership with our American friends. As we continue to move into the future, we intend not only to contribute toward creating more job opportunities and promoting economic growth, but also to try and build a new relationship that will serve everyone's needs.[22]

---

[21]*Toyota: A History,* p. 336.

[22]*Toyota: A History,* p. 338.

Toyota opened the Georgetown plant in 1988. It involved an investment of $1.1 billion to construct an assembly plant and related facilities to produce 200,000 annual units of the Camry model, in addition to engines, axles, and steering components. By 1990, the four-door Camry was being built at a rate of one every 75 seconds, or about 170 per day on a single shift. Domestic content of the vehicle was at 60 percent but was projected to reach about 75 percent when the powertrain plant under construction reached full production in 1991.

While quality was high at Georgetown, productivity was about 10 percent below Toyota's plants in Japan. According to a Toyota executive, U.S. suppliers were the problem. Although Toyota preferred to purchase major parts from the 250 Japanese suppliers who had established plants in the United States, political concerns prompted Toyota to purchase American-made parts. However, Toyota purchased engine blocks, cylinder heads, and other vital parts for four-cylinder engines from suppliers in Japan for assembly at Georgetown and kept emergency inventories of Japanese-made parts as insurance against defective American parts.

Flooded with over 50,000 applicants for the 3,000 factory jobs, Toyota devised an extensive selection system, which focused on employee potential, rather than on education and work experience. The process consumed about 18 hours per applicant and involved tests and simulations that assessed technical, interpersonal, and leadership skills. One new employee (a former hairdresser) likened getting a job at Toyota to winning a lottery, "The odds were tremendous, but I would have swept floors."

In late 1990, Toyota announced plans to build a second assembly plant at Georgetown, doubling the capacity to approximately 400,000. When completed, the Georgetown complex would increase jobs to more than 5,000 and place Toyota's total investment at more than $2 billion. Industry observers speculated that the additional capacity would be used to build either a mid-sized family car or a big pickup truck.

By 1990, Toyota was on its way to becoming an almost stand-alone U.S. producer, able to research and engineer, as well as to design and assemble, its cars in the United States. In addition to its NUMMI and Georgetown production facilities, Toyota had established the Calty Design Center in California in the early 1970s. Several models, including the Celica and the new Previa minivan, were developed at the Center, specifically to suit the tastes of U.S. consumers. Thus, Toyota maintained separate U.S. subsidiaries for sales, manufacturing, engineering, and R&D, each reporting individually to Toyota City. By 1995, Toyota anticipated selling 1.5 million vehicles in the United States, 50 percent of them made in the United States.

Toyota was gaining the ability to execute its lean distribution approach of built-to-order cars, but this critical component of the TPS had yet to be achieved. Toyota had expanded its distribution network during the 1980s in the United States—in 1983, it had 1,093 new-car franchises, and by 1990, the number had increased to 1,248. In contrast, the total number of U.S. car dealerships had steadily declined—from 30,800 in 1970 to 25,100 in 1989. Implementing the lean approach to distribution appeared to be part of the plan. According to one Japanese auto executive, "The system makes no sense unless cars are built to order and delivered almost immediately. We can do this only as we develop a complete top-to-bottom manufacturing system in North

America and Europe by the end of the 1990s."[23] According to one authority, Toyota had not reached its full potential in the United States since the TPS worked best when "the entire complement of car-production activities are performed as close as possible to the point of final production."[24]

Overseas Operations Outside the United States

Calls for protectionism echoed loudest on the European continent. Strict import restrictions had limited the Japanese share to a consistent 11 percent of the market. In mid-1989, Toyota announced plans to construct a passenger car plant to produce the Corona in Great Britain beginning in late 1992. Facilities were to be built for stamping, body welding, paint, plastics, and assembly operations. Plans called for eventual employment of 3,000 employees and production of 200,000 cars annually by 1997. Commenting on the plant, Shoichiro Toyoda stated:

> All of us at Toyota will do everything possible to earn acceptance for this plant as a truly British venture and as a genuinely European operation. We will pursue active exchange of technology. And we will do our utmost to integrate production locally. In short, we will become a cooperative and contributing member of the European automobile industry. What we most want to do is expand and integrate our activities throughout Europe as a valued member of the community in each nation.[25]

Toyota's earliest moves toward local production had begun in countries outside the United States and Europe. Restricted by rigorous domestic content laws in several countries, Toyota (along with other Japanese automakers) had a virtual monopoly in Asia where the presence of U.S. and European automakers was almost unknown. Auto sales in Asia were projected to grow from 4.7 percent of global sales in 1987 to 8.7 percent by 1995. Billions of dollars of investment, combined with long-term thinking, persistence, and flexibility, had aided in Toyota's securing a leadership role.

In countries that banned auto imports, such as South Korea, Toyota had taken minority stakes in Korean auto companies and provided technology or parts supplies. In countries affected by political instability or uncertain economic prospects, such as the Philippines, Toyota had signed on with local partners, cautiously expanding its presence. Toyota had assisted in building local auto industries in some East Asian countries to alleviate concerns over Japanese domination. Overall, the Japanese automakers had been surprisingly successful at establishing a regional auto production base. Although major profits had not yet been achieved from the Asian strategy, the pieces were in place, and the region was poised for sustained economic growth. Exhibit 14 displays the location and production capacity of Toyota's overseas production facilities as of 1987.

---

[23]Womack, Jones, and Roos, *The Machine That Changed the World*, p. 188.
[24]As quoted in *Fortune*, September 10, 1990, p. 80.
[25]As quoted in *Business Japan*, July 1989, p. 15.

EXHIBIT 14   **Overseas Production Companies and Production Capacity, Toyota Motor Corporation, 1987**

Geographic Region	Production Capacity in the Region	Countries Where Facilities Are Located	Local Name of Toyota's Subsidiary
North America	500,000	United States	Toyota Motor Manufacturing, U.S.A., Inc. New United Motor Manufacturing, Inc. TABC, Inc.
		Canada	Toyota Motor Manufacturing Canada, Inc. Canadian Autoparts Toyota, Inc.
South America and the Caribbean	25,000	Brazil	Toyota do Brasil S.A., Industria e Comercio
		Peru	Toyota del Peru S.A.
		Venezuela	Servicios de Ensamblaje, C.A.
		Trinidad and Tobago	Amar Assembly Plant '85 Ltd.
		Uruguay	Ayax S.A.
		Ecuador	Mare S.A.
Europe	13,000	Portugal	Salvador Caetano I.M.V.T., S.A.
Southeast Asia and Oceania	127,000	Australia	Toyota Motor Corporation Australia Ltd. AMI Toyota Ltd.
		New Zealand	Toyota New Zealand (Thames) Ltd. Toyota New Zealand (Christchurch) Ltd.
		Indonesia	P.T. Multi-Astra P.T. Toyota-Mobilindo P.T. Toyota Engine Indonesia
		Thailand	Toyota Motor Thailand Co., Ltd. Thai Hino Industry Co., Ltd. Toyota Auto Body Thailand Co., Ltd. Siam Toyota Manufacturing Co., Ltd.
		Malaysia	Assembly Services Sdn. Bhd.
		Taiwan	Kuozui Motors, Ltd. Fung Yong Co., Ltd.
		Philippines	Toyota Motor Philippines Corporation
Middle East	3,500	India	DCM Toyota Ltd.
		Bangladesh	Aftab Automobiles Ltd.
Africa	n.a.	South Africa	Toyota South Africa Manufacturing Ltd.
		Kenya	Associated Vehicle Assemblers Ltd.
		Zambia	Rover (Zambia) Ltd.
		Zimbabwe	Willowvale Motor Industries (Pvt.) Ltd.

Source: Toyota: *A History of the First 50 Years* (1 Toyota-cho, Toyota City, Aichi Prefecture, Japan: Toyota Motor Corporation, 1988), pp. 464–65.

COMPANY OUTLOOK

Toyota's efforts to improve its image resulted in impressive outcomes by the end of 1990. By introducing six all-new vehicles within 14 months, Toyota had captured a 43 percent share of car sales in Japan. With the Camry and the Corolla among the 10 best-selling cars in the United States, Toyota was selling more cars in the United States than every GM division except Chevrolet and was on the brink of passing Chrysler in total units sold. Another half-dozen new Toyota models were scheduled to debut in the United States during 1991. Toyota was beginning to be viewed as a fashion leader, putting to rest its reputation for fuddy-duddy design, as evidenced by several of its latest new vehicles: the Sera, a glass-topped minicoupe with gull-wing doors being sold only in Japan; the jellybean-shaped Previa, designed in California and a hit with U.S. buyers; and the Lexus, which was outselling its competitors in the United States. Toyota enjoyed the highest operating margin in the world auto industry—in Japan it earned a 9 percent profit in fiscal 1989, versus 8.4 percent for Nissan and 6.5 percent for Honda. According to one projection, Toyota planned on selling 2 million vehicles in the United States by 2000, hoping to surpass Ford. Industry observers predicted that Toyota could surpass Ford in production of cars in the world market by 1993.

Toyota's plan for the 1990s included:

Japan

- A 580 billion yen ($4.47 billion) plant and capital expenditure program for 1991.
- Constructing two new production plants to eliminate overtime and meet domestic demand.
- Selling and servicing German-made Volkswagen and Audi vehicles in Japan (the Toyota-VW alliance aimed for initial sales of 7,000 to 8,000 vehicles, increasing to 30,000 by 1995).
- Investing $770 million by 1995 to improve employee housing, add dining halls, and build new recreational facilities.

United States

- Spending $400 million on a 12,000-acre test track in Arizona and on new engineering and design studios in Michigan and California.
- Increasing its U.S. factory capacity to almost 700,000 cars and trucks over the next three years. (This included expansion of NUMMI to produce approximately 100,000 small pickup trucks annually, expansion of Georgetown operations to double capacity, and production of a big pickup truck to compete against full-size trucks made by automakers.)

Europe

- Expanding Toyota's presence in Western Europe (one rumored target was the purchase of Porsche; another possibility being considered was an equity or production deal with a carmaker in Spain or Turkey).

- Constructing factories in Turkey and Pakistan to push production into areas where Toyota had little presence.

East Asia/Pacific Rim

- Doubling car and truck capacity in Thailand to about 150,000 within three years.
- Operating one or two assembly plants in the region and selling 1 million vehicles annually in a 3.5 million vehicle market by 2000.

GM ALLISON JAPAN LTD.*

Richard T. Dailey, University of Montana

The decision by the Allison Division of General Motors Corporation (GM) to name James D. Swaim as president of GM Allison Japan Ltd. (GMAJ) in June 1987 was a significant departure from the way Allison had been dealing with its Japanese joint venture. Mr. Swaim, who came to work at GMAJ in October 1984, was not only the first American selected to run the company, but also the first employee sent to GMAJ from Allison on a long-term assignment.

Even though GMAJ had been in operation since 1972, the business had not performed up to Allison's expectations. By the early 1980s the problems had become serious, and Allison's management realized that something had to be changed.

Upon his arrival in Tokyo, Mr. Swaim said his first goal was "to help try to fix the problems at GMAJ and learn if we had product problems that were aggravating those problems too." After his appointment as GMAJ's president, he reflected on the need to change the way the Japanese company had been doing business. One of his primary concerns, he commented, "was how to make sure that Allison's Japanese customers understood that Allison was indeed committed to the Japanese market for the long term."

ALLISON DIVISION

In the early 1970s, the Allison Division of General Motors Corporation and Isuzu Motors established GM Allison Japan Ltd. as a joint venture company for the purpose of selling heavy-duty transmissions to Japanese truck manufacturers. Although General Motors Corporation had established a marketing organization to sell automobiles in Japan in the late 1920s, this was its first effort at selling components to Japanese original equipment manufacturers (OEMs).

Allison was a well-known U.S. manufacturer of gas turbine engines for fixed-wing aircraft and helicopters, and of heavy-duty transmissions for trucks and buses, mining and construction equipment, and industrial applications. In 1970, a major change took place in the transmission side of the business when the company began manufacturing a family of new automatic transmissions for trucks, buses, and certain types of off-highway construction and mining equipment. The initial members of this family of transmissions were designed primarily for use in highway vehicles equipped with gasoline engines.

The company manufactured transmissions in a variety of sizes for a variety of vehicle types—from school buses to the largest intercity buses, and from small city delivery trucks to the largest over-the-road trailer trucks. This new line of transmissions represented a major shift in both product line and

*Copyright © 1990 by Richard T. Dailey. The generous cooperation of GM Allison Japan Ltd. is gratefully acknowledged.

EXHIBIT 1   **Isuzu's Truck Sales in Japan, 1984–1988**

	Model Year				
	1984	**1985**	**1986**	**1987**	**1988**
Heavy Duty					
Industry total	116,326	111,374	109,243	126,925	165,419
Isuzu's share	30,214	28,492	28,215	33,055	42,460
10 Ton					
Industry total	39,647	37,227	36,958	44,624	58,375
Isuzu's share	9,768	8,471	8,487	10,641	13,644
4 Ton					
Industry total	65,237	63,767	62,749	72,256	93,729
Isuzu's share	17,965	17,781	17,514	20,278	26,193
Light Duty					
Industry total	701,783	706,683	728,097	784,682	927,786
Isuzu's share	87,617	88,451	82,171	84,813	102,408
2–3 Ton					
Industry total	154,876	158,869	160,835	170,112	207,551
Isuzu's share	49,120	50,798	48,576	53,310	65,260
1–1 ½ Ton					
Industry total	206,077	209,825	208,602	228,103	272,053
Isuzu's share	32,761	33,004	29,585	27,727	30,286

Source: Company records.

product development for the company and entailed extensive marketing efforts to gain acceptance by end-users.

In September 1970, General Motors merged its Detroit Diesel and Allison Divisions, giving Allison full access to Detroit Diesel's worldwide distribution system. This new division, called the Detroit Diesel Allison Division, permitted a smoother integration of the new line of transmissions into GM's Detroit Diesel products.

ESTABLISHING THE JOINT VENTURE COMPANY

In early 1970, General Motors Corporation began discussions with Isuzu Motors, a Japanese maker of automobiles, trucks, and buses, regarding the feasibility of GM assuming an equity position in Isuzu. While Isuzu was not a major producer of passenger cars in Japan (its market share was about three percent), it was a major manufacturer of commercial vehicles (see Exhibits 1 and 2).

The idea of an automatic transmission for trucks intrigued Isuzu's management. The Japanese partners envisioned local manufacture when sales volume reached sustainable levels. An equity position in Isuzu, GM executives reasoned, would provide GM with a foothold in the growing Japanese motor vehicle market, a market which GM, as well as other U.S. manufacturers, had been unsuccessful in entering. Other U.S. motor vehicle manufacturers were also

---

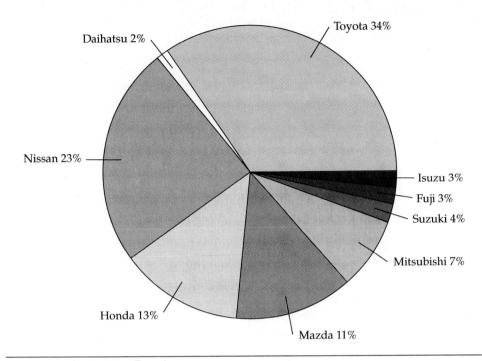

*1987 Auto Production = 7.9 million units.
Source: Japan Automobile Manufacturer Association.

developing relationships with Japanese auto and truck manufacturers. Of necessity, the talks between Isuzu and GM were kept very quiet, because if word leaked out that a corporation the size of GM was negotiating with a company of Isuzu's size, the rumor would have a major impact on the price of Isuzu shares on the Tokyo stock exchange.

In order to smooth the development and operation of the new joint venture, GM needed to link up with one of Japan's industrial groups, known in Japan as a *keiretsu*. A *keiretsu* consists of about 20 major companies, one in each industrial sector. The typical *keiretsu* contains a bank, a trading company, an insurance company, and a company in each of several basic industries, such as steel or motor vehicle manufacturing. Nearly all of the equity of the individual companies in the group is held by other members of the *keiretsu*, one of the characteristics of Japanese business culture that makes it difficult for outsiders to obtain a controlling ownership in a Japanese firm. A major purpose of the *keiretsu* is to help members of the group raise investment funds. General Motors looked with favor on the *keiretsu* headed by Dai-Ichi Kangyo Bank (DKB) because it had worked with DKB on previous occasions. Isuzu was part of the DKB *keiretsu*.

To ease any problems that GM might encounter in importing components to Japan, the company followed a suggestion that a Japanese trading company become a partner in the joint venture. C. Itoh, one of Japan's largest trading companies and also a member of the DKB *keiretsu*, was the logical choice. Kawasaki Heavy Industries (KHI), another member of the DKB group, also became part of the joint venture because it manufactured manual transmissions for Isuzu and was interested in the vehicular gas turbine engine Allison was developing. Kawasaki Heavy Industry executives thought the engine might have applications in Japanese heavy-duty trucks and construction equipment.

By 1972, the negotiations were completed and General Motors Allison Japan Ltd. became a reality. It was formed as a joint venture company with General Motors having 50 percent of the shares, Isuzu 20 percent, Kawasaki 20 percent, and C. Itoh the remaining 10 percent. The new company was capitalized at ¥90 million. General Motors Corporation, meanwhile, had purchased a 38 percent equity position in Isuzu Motors, providing new equity capital for Isuzu. As a result of the new joint venture, Detroit Diesel Allison's distributor in Japan, who had been buying transmissions from Allison and selling them to Japanese truck manufacturers, lost its marketing rights as an Allison transmission distributor.

STAFFING THE NEW COMPANY

The agreement for staffing the new organization called for the president of the company to represent the Japanese partners of the joint venture and for the vice president to represent the GM side of the business. GMAJ's first president came from Kawasaki Heavy Industries. The vice president chosen to represent GM's interests was an American who was also vice president of GM Overseas Corporation—Japan Branch; his office, while in Tokyo, was some distance from GMAJ's offices. All other managers of the joint venture company, including the president, were Japanese.

Source of Employees for GMAJ

Some employees of GMAJ were "seconded" employees from other companies participating in the joint venture. It was common practice among the Japanese *keiretsu* for one company in the group, especially one of the lead companies, to provide employees to another company in the group. Sometimes employees were loaned on a short-term basis to work on technical problems, and sometimes they were sent to the company for an indefinite period of time. Employees seconded to a company for the long term were typically near retirement age with no possibility of advancing any further in their organization. Often, they were loaned to make room for younger employees or selected as a favor to some manager of one of the participating companies. Several employees seconded to GMAJ were in these latter two categories.

Isuzu, on the other hand, had high hopes for the success of the joint venture and seconded some of its best people to the new company. For example, an engineer who was seconded was considered one of Isuzu's best transmission designers for manual transmissions. Allison executives in Indianapolis reasoned that since the Japanese knew the truck market in Japan better than they did, it would not take long for GMAJ to become a profitable company.

In 1974, GMAJ's first president returned to Kawasaki Heavy Industries and Toshihiko Tamura of Isuzu Motors became GMAJ's second president. He remained in that position until 1987. Mr. Tamura was trained as an electrical engineer and had extensive experience in the marine engine business, but none in the transmission business.

Staff Training and Support

GMAJ's product engineers and certain technical support people were sent to Allison's manufacturing headquarters in Indianapolis for two- to four-week training sessions. They were provided with the latest technical information about Allison's automatic transmissions and had sessions on trouble shooting, the types of vehicles that were best suited for an automatic transmission, and the associated manuals and documentation that would assist them in answering their questions after they had returned to Japan. All technical manuals and other documentation provided to the GMAJ engineers were in English.

Periodically engineers would visit GMAJ from Indianapolis to provide on-site technical support and service. Typically, these people visited Japan three or four times each year and stayed for two to three weeks each trip.

A final support mechanism was provided by the Detroit Diesel Allison regional marketing organization headquartered in Singapore. Every four to six weeks, a Singapore-based sales representative (not necessarily an engineer) would visit GMAJ and spend one or two days providing whatever assistance he could to solve problems that could not be handled by the Japanese staff.

PRODUCT MARKETING

GM Allison Japan was established as a Japanese company to sell truck and bus transmissions initially to Isuzu Motors and subsequently to other Japanese vehicle manufacturers. Although a U.S. firm owned 50 percent of GMAJ, it conducted business as a Japanese firm. Mr. Swaim pointed out that:

> as a "child" company or captive firm, it serves as the pleasure of its owners, all of whom are represented on the board of directors. Japanese tradition for component suppliers required them to work only with the OEMs and leave all end user contact to the OEMs. Most U.S. component manufacturers and distributors work with the end users of their products, encouraging them to specify their equipment from the vehicle manufacturers. In this kind of relationship the component manufacturers quite often become complementary engineering organizations to the end users, as well as marketing partners to the OEMs.
>
> In Japan, however, the situation is much different. Sales representatives of the component manufacturers do not call on the end users. Rather they work primarily with the OEMs and, to a limited extent, the dealers, when selling their products. Thus, the executives of GMAJ never established the type of relationships with the end users that would result in their specifying Allison transmissions.

The Japanese Truck Market

The Japanese truck market was unique in that over 95 percent of all trucks were equipped with diesel engines because they were more fuel efficient than gasoline engines. By comparison, approximately 45 percent of the U.S. trucks in the medium-duty class had diesel engines in 1984. However, dieselization was expected to approach 90 percent of the trucks in this category by 1990.

E X H I B I T 3   **Annual Average Exchange Rate between Japanese Yen and U.S. Dollars, 1971–1989**

Year	Number of Japanese Yen per U.S. Dollar
1971	¥347.48
1972	303.08
1973	270.89
1974	291.53
1975	296.69
1976	296.38
1977	267.80
1978	208.42
1979	218.18
1980	226.63
1981	220.63
1982	249.06
1983	237.55
1984	237.45
1985	238.47
1986	168.35
1987	144.60
1988	128.17
1989	138.07

Source: Federal Reserve Bulletin.

Another aspect of the Japanese market that made it different from its U.S. counterpart was that Japanese trucks were much smaller on average than those in the United States.

Marketing Strategy

The marketing strategy Isuzu implemented was traditional for a Japanese company. It offered low option prices, special deals for fleet operators, and special programs to get the Allison product into the marketplace as a replacement for worn-out transmissions in Japanese trucks. Because of the relatively weak yen at that time (see Exhibit 3), import prices for GMAJ's replacement transmissions were rather high. Isuzu, however, absorbed the higher costs internally in order to price the Allison product competitively. Exhibit 4 shows the number of transmission units sold by GMAJ between 1973 and 1988.

Price Increases

Captive suppliers, such as GMAJ, were constrained from raising the product prices they charged their parent firms solely on the basis of higher costs they incurred for labor, raw materials, energy, and the like. Instead, they were

EXHIBIT 4   **GMAJ Sales of Allison Automatic Transmissions to Japanese Buyers, 1973–1988**

Fiscal Year	Units
1973	10
1974	26
1975	114
1976	81
1977	299
1978	724
1979	1,138
1980	977
1981	643
1982	481
1983	378
1984	445
1985	476
1986	600
1987	1,034
1988	1,050

Source: Company records.

expected to improve productivity and manufacturing efficiency at least enough to hold the line on prices. Japanese automakers expected component suppliers to improve their production methods enough to reduce prices. If the supplier firms were unable to develop programs that reduced their costs and prices, Japanese automakers would usually provide assistance by lending personnel, granting loans for new technology, or whatever else it took to achieve productivity improvements. Price increases were considered a last resort.

Allison's costs of manufacturing the transmissions at its U.S.-based plant were escalating due to a high rate of inflation. Plant managers wanted to pass these costs on to GMAJ in the form of higher prices. In spite of these cost increases, however, GMAJ was expected to do business in the Japanese manner. That meant minimal price increases to its customers, even if it incurred losses for a few years. Exhibits 5 and 6 present GMAJ's financial statements for the period prior to Mr. Swaim's appointment as GMAJ president.

Product

Isuzu was so anxious to get Allison automatic transmissions into the marketplace that it sold one to anybody willing to try it. This led to some technical difficulties because dealers often failed to select the proper options necessary for the GMAJ transmission to deliver good performance, given the type of vehicle and the conditions of use. Isuzu worked hard to overcome these initial growing pains and eventually was able to surmount most of the technical problems.

EXHIBIT 5   **Income Statement for GMAJ, Fiscal Years 1986 and 1987**
                (All figures in Japanese yen)

	April 1, 1985 to March 31, 1986	April 1, 1986 to March 31, 1987
Sales	¥632,687,169	¥318,832,286
Cost of sales	499,902,770	277,039,435
Selling profit	132,784,399	41,792,851
Selling, general, and administrative expenses		
Salaries and bonus	45,635,054	61,913,065
Legal welfare expenses	8,106,522	16,986,979
Rent	13,338,798	18,421,354
Advertisement	727,249	5,680,796
Claim expenses	4,676,082	5,906,500
Travel expenses	2,185,202	1,349,040
Depreciation	2,465,829	7,525,619
Other expenses	16,123,811	19,261,665
Total expenses	93,258,547	137,045,018
Operating profit (loss)	39,525,852	(95,252,167)
Nonoperating Income		
Interest income	2,719,680	2,177,422
Miscellaneous income*	12,951,823	123,085,022
Total nonoperating income	15,671,503	125,262,444
Gross profit (loss) for the term	55,197,355	30,010,277
Nonoperating Expenses		
Interest paid	9,202,363	8,474,853
Tax for interest on deposit	465,311	403,635
Miscellaneous	15,239,486	15,210,587
Total nonoperating expenses	24,907,160	24,089,075
Pre-tax profit (loss)	30,290,195	5,921,202
Income tax	10,915,660	5,700,000
Net profit (loss) after taxes	19,374,535	221,202
Profit (loss) brought forward	(16,730,732)	2,643,803
Unappropriated profit	2,643,803	2,865,005
Remarks		
Corporate income tax	4,540,000	
Municipal inhabitant tax	1,160,000	
Total	5,700,000	

Disposition of Profit

Unappropriated profit	¥2,865,005
(Including the profit for the term)	¥ 221,202
We would like to dispose the above amount as follows:	
Profit carried forward	¥2,865,005

*Includes payments by Isuzu for marketing assistance.

EXHIBIT 6 **Balance Sheets for GMAJ, Fiscal Years 1986 and 1987**
(All figures in Japanese yen)

	March 31, 1986	March 31, 1987
Assets		
Current		
Cash, banks	¥ 94,982,382	¥ 81,304,533
Notes receivable	92,145,502	65,110,802
Accounts receivable	99,182,586	56,476,327
Inventory	89,034,191	94,361,413
Other current	84,701,978	*112,277,592
Allowance for doubtful accounts	(2,900,000)	(2,750,000)
Total current assets	457,146,639	406,780,667
Fixed		
Buildings/structures	6,173,000	8,729,390
Machinery and equipment	11,124,742	11,274,742
Vehicles	5,874,450	8,320,000
Tools and office equipment	13,518,655	28,697,833
Telephone right	399,793	618,913
Telex right	25,938	0
Guarantee money	12,912,360	22,376,640
Accumulated depreciation	(28,655,767)	(32,428,476)
Total fixed assets	21,373,171	47,588,322
Total assets	¥478,519,810	¥454,368,989
Liabilities and Equity		
Current		
Short-term borrowings	¥155,000,000	¥155,000,000
Notes payable	120,738,452	124,857,421
Accounts payable trade	74,284,562	39,920,661
Accounts payable others, Due within one year	3,741,888	2,549,810
Tax payable for business tax	3,120,000	150,000
Other current	780,136	7,170,129
Total current liabilities	357,665,038	329,648,021
Reserve		
Reserve for corporation tax	11,021,960	0
Reserve for bonus	1,930,000	4,670,105
Reserve for retirement allowances	13,799,009	25,725,858
Total reserve	26,750,969	30,395,963
Total liabilities and reserve	384,416,007	360,043,984
Equity of shareholders		
Common stock, ¥10,000 par value; authorized 36,000 shares, issues 9,000 shares	90,000,000	90,000,000
Profit (loss) brought forward	(16,730,732)	2,643,803
Profit (loss) for term	19,374,535	221,202
General contingency	1,460,000	1,460,000
Total shareholders' equity	94,103,803	94,325,005
Total liabilities and shareholders' equity	¥478,519,810	¥454,368,989

*Includes amounts owed by Isuzu for marketing assistance.

By the end of 1973, the first transmissions were being installed in Isuzu trucks and being tested under actual highway and other working conditions. The program was about ready to launch on a commercial scale, and with growing confidence in the product, Isuzu began an active marketing campaign.

RISING GASOLINE PRICES AND CONCERNS FOR FUEL EFFICIENCY

Just about the time the market for the GMAJ's automatic transmission began to show significant growth (see Exhibit 4), the Organization for Petroleum Exporting Countries (OPEC) announced sharply higher prices for its crude oil supplies. Crude oil prices topped $30 per barrel and prices for gasoline soared worldwide. Rising prices for energy in Japan helped trigger a significant recession and an annual rate of inflation that reached 18 percent. Commercial vehicle sales, as a result, declined to low levels for the next several years, and fuel efficiency became of paramount importance (see Exhibit 7). In spite of rapidly rising prices for raw materials and energy products, it was impossible for GMAJ to raise transmission prices; pressure mounted for GMAJ to find ways to reduce costs rather than to raise prices. GMAJ's president, Mr. Tamura, was forced to implement a cost-cutting drive that included greatly reduced funds for travel and telephone expenses. The budget was so tight GMAJ salespeople could not respond to requests from customers who needed on-site assistance.

The drop in truck and bus sales in Japan led to lower sales for automatic transmissions. Another factor discouraging automatic transmission sales at this time was the perception among some end-users that automatics were less fuel efficient than manual transmissions.

TECHNICAL PROBLEMS

As a Japanese company, GMAJ was obliged to provide after-sales service to its end-user customers on a continuing basis. Allison provided the same warranty for its products to the Japanese original equipment manufacturers as it did for its U.S. customers, a two-year warranty on parts and labor. The OEMs, in turn, provided a one-year warranty as their standard vehicle warranty. However, Japanese vehicle manufacturers were accustomed to providing generous coverage on power train components to their customers regardless of the published warranty provisions.

In 1979, Allison began experiencing serious technical problems with its automatic transmissions, nearly all of which had been installed in on-highway trucks and buses. The problems, and in many cases complete failure of the unit, resulted in escalating warranty costs for the company. These problems were also experienced by GMAJ, and were far more serious in the Japanese market than in the United States. Starting in 1979 and continuing until 1984, GMAJ's sales of transmissions dropped off sharply (see Exhibit 4).

GM Allison Japan was also caught in the position of receiving a product with a fixed set of technical specifications and requirements from Allison in the United States, and then representing those specifications to a third party, an OEM. There were several instances where Japanese truck manufacturers wanted changes made in the transmission specifications to meet what they

E X H I B I T 7   **Motor Vehicle Sales in Japan, 1974–1988**

	Cars					Trucks					Buses			Grand Total
	Large	Small	Mini	Total	Large	Small	Mini	Total	Large	Small	Mini			
1974	9,064	1,652,855	713,170	2,379,137	164,086	986,672	538,743	1,693,502	10,256	17,572	27,828			4,100,467
1975	45,125	2,531,396	157,320	2,737,641	121,118	999,155	431,181	1,551,454	8,818	11,018	19,836			4,308,931
1976	46,592	2,224,783	178,054	2,449,429	128,501	1,043,467	459,395	1,631,363	9,415	13,044	23,259			4,104,051
1977	53,069	2,277,934	165,072	2,500,095	132,041	1,031,804	587,393	1,671,238	9,327	13,509	22,916			4,194,249
1978	64,428	2,620,069	172,213	2,056,710	156,764	1,094,590	549,022	1,800,376	10,496	14,281	24,777			4,681,063
1979	84,721	2,781,889	170,263	3,036,873	185,732	1,220,668	686,494	2,092,894	9,589	14,396	23,985			5,153,752
1980	74,931	2,608,215	174,038	2,854,176	154,472	1,144,167	839,308	2,137,947	9,414	13,973	23,381			5,015,518
1981	78,221	2,522,936	165,538	2,866,695	126,731	1,045,420	1,064,253	2,237,404	9,358	13,539	22,897			5,126,996
1982	63,697	2,794,789	179,786	3,038,272	113,136	933,321	1,154,909	2,201,366	8,705	13,088	21,793			5,261,431
1983	80,210	2,857,490	197,911	3,135,611	111,314	910,529	1,204,553	2,226,396	7,947	12,363	20,310			5,382,317
1984	82,068	2,019,540	193,546	3,095,554	120,717	935,031	1,265,190	2,320,938	7,688	12,579	20,267			5,436,759
1985	73,539	2,069,527	161,013	3,104,083	110,009	945,484	1,367,685	2,431,172	8,798	12,775	21,513			5,556,834
1986	81,178	2,926,590	138,255	3,146,823	109,676	954,918	1,475,580	2,540,174	8,826	12,791	21,617			5,793,014
1987	111,415	3,036,517	126,868	3,274,880	132,114	1,042,219	1,547,247	2,721,581	8,786	13,232	22,018			6,010,399
1988	166,054	3,397,628	153,677	3,717,359	169,036	1,214,847	1,596,220	2,900,103	9,177	14,365	23,542			6,721,004

Source: Japan Automobile Manufacturers' Association.

considered special Japanese operating conditions. Allison, however, was unwilling to agree to any changes in the technical specifications that GMAJ's engineers suggested or requested. Allison's marketing department took the position that since its transmissions were sold without design changes in several other countries, none were necessary for Japan. Furthermore, in the opinion of Allison's management, the Japanese market was not big enough to justify costly design alterations. As a result of the technical problems Allison was experiencing at this time, the Japanese OEMs were forced to deal with both application problems and product problems without recourse to technical improvements in the product. This left the Japanese manufacturers with the impression that Allison, a nonresident company attempting to sell automatic transmissions in Japan, was not interested in them—in short, that the Japanese market was not important to Allison.

Although GMAJ had sales volume in its early years that pointed toward a successful joint venture, recent events had placed the company in an unprofitable position. Managers at Allison's headquarters in Indiana, meanwhile, were paying little attention to what was taking place in Japan. They recognized that sales in the Japanese market had become sluggish, but they were preoccupied with quality problems and escalating warranty costs in their much larger, core U.S. market.

INCREASING COMPETITION

In early 1984, Allison noted a developing shift occurring in the U.S. market for medium-duty trucks—U.S. truck manufacturers had fallen behind their Japanese and European counterparts in the development and design of low-cab-forward or stub-nose trucks (vehicles with the engine behind or underneath the cab). Trucks of this type formed the backbone of many inner-city delivery systems. Companies needing trucks that were fuel-efficient and maneuverable in congested central cities were turning to Japanese and European models because of their superior designs and advanced dieselization.

Allison's Response

The Japanese entry into the U.S. medium-duty truck market was of primary importance. Allison had a 25 percent penetration in this market segment and broad availability of Allison transmissions in Japanese imports was seen as a way to maintain its market share. It was this realization that prompted Allison's senior management to conclude that to protect the home market, Allison—through GMAJ—must battle the Japanese on their home turf.

THE EARLY-1980s SITUATION

The technical problems Allison was experiencing with its automatic transmissions in the United States had an additional ramification in the Japanese market. There, GMAJ's engineers discovered, the automatic transmission was still not technically correct for vehicles equipped with diesel engines. Additionally, Mr. Tamura's cost-cutting drive only added to GMAJ's problems, because its salespeople could not provide adequate customer service.

In 1981 Allison's management, recognizing the need to solve the company's continuing warranty problems, formed a special interdisciplinary team to address those issues. Team members were relieved of their current responsibilities and given a six-month assignment to study and provide solutions for the whole range of problems Allison was having with its transmissions. Among the disciplines represented were engineering, service, marketing, warranty, manufacturing, finance, and reliability. The team was headed by the director of quality control at Allison's aircraft engine operation, while Mr. Swaim represented the sales and service side of the business.

Mr. Swaim's Background

After earning a degree in engineering from the General Motors Institute, Mr. Swaim joined Allison's aircraft service department. From there he moved through several other departments at Allison, including an assignment as a field service representative in Okinawa from 1964 to 1966. As a manager in the transmission service department, Mr. Swaim created an after-sales service infrastructure that permitted a smooth integration of the transmission line into the Detroit Diesel Allison distribution system. From that position he was named manager of the service operations organization in the transmission service department. Here his responsibilities included technical support for the field organization and manufacturers, customer contact, product liability, and product liability litigation. In addition, he was worldwide technical coordinator for Allison's transmission products, a position that required him to interface with all of the various disciplines in the transmission operation.

Allison's Decision to Assign an Engineer to GMAJ

By the early part of 1984, Allison's senior executives had reached the conclusion that the problems facing GMAJ required someone from the United States to be in Tokyo on a permanent basis. Considerable thought went into Allison's decision regarding the type of individual who should be sent to Japan. Mr. Swaim was selected on the basis of his previous experience in Okinawa, knowledge of Allison's product line, the wide range of positions he had held with the company, and the fact that he and his wife could adapt to the Japanese culture.

Arrival in Japan

When Mr. Swaim arrived in Tokyo in October 1984, his assignment was to provide technical and engineering support to the GMAJ staff. His reporting line was to Allison's headquarters in Indianapolis rather than to anyone in Japan.

One of the first things Mr. Swaim learned after his arrival in Tokyo was that because GMAJ acted as a traditional Japanese company, no one from GMAJ was contacting the end-user customers—in the Japanese culture only the manufacturers and dealers have direct customer contact. Although Allison managers had been urging GMAJ's president to make direct customer contact in order to convince them of the advantages of automatic transmissions, Mr. Tamura did not feel that that was his responsibility. It was unusual for a Japanese component manufacturer to deal directly with end-users, unless technical questions were involved.

THE SITUATION IN 1984

Allison's managers in Indianapolis did not fully appreciate the rigidity of these Japanese business practices. Thus, they were unable to fully understand the extent of the problems at their joint venture operation in Tokyo. Likewise, the managers at GMAJ had very little knowledge of how to work with U.S. vendors or suppliers.

Mr. Swaim also learned that some of GMAJ's salespeople who were attempting to sell Allison's products had little technical understanding of the products. Furthermore, OEM engineering groups that were part of the joint venture were often operating with insufficient technical data, and on some occasions data that were obsolete. GMAJ management had decided to forgo supplying comprehensive technical data to some of its non-Isuzu Japanese manufacturers. Since GMAJ considered the data to be proprietary in nature, there was concern about it falling into the hands of the "Isuzu competitors." In the vendor-subservient role required of Japanese component suppliers, GMAJ found it difficult to enforce the new technical requirements developed by the task force in Indianapolis to correct the product problems.

Building Relationships

Mr. Swaim considered it of primary importance "to convince the Japanese that he would indeed be in Japan for an extended period of time." Until his arrival, no American from Allison had stayed at GMAJ longer than six weeks. Mr. Swaim set out to reassure the Japanese that he was an Allison employee, his company was committed to the Japanese market, and he was now a resident in Japan and there to help GMAJ and its OEM customers solve their technical problems.

Transmission Service Network

GMAJ sold Allison transmissions directly to the OEMs and thus acted as both wholesaler and distributor. It did not, however, provide company-owned, after-sales service to either the manufacturers or the motor vehicle buyers. Instead GMAJ, by contracting with an Isuzu dealer and an Isuzu dealer-related organization, developed a service support network for Allison transmissions. Since the owner of a Nissan Diesel, for example, would be unwilling to take his or her truck to an Isuzu dealer for service, GMAJ arranged for an independent diesel repair shop to service Allison transmissions for truck owners who did not have Isuzu trucks.

Pricing

GMAJ purchased Allison transmissions at a special discounted price from the Allison factory, for resale to the four Japanese OEMs that were its customers. In wholesaling the transmissions, GMAJ charged the OEMs prices ranging from ¥500,000 to ¥600,000 with no fixed, recognizable pricing policy. Because of the special relationships between GMAJ and Isuzu, however, GMAJ was able to charge Isuzu slightly higher prices than it charged the other three OEMs. To increase the sales volume of its subsidiary company, Isuzu elected to sell Allison transmissions in the marketplace as an option for ¥200,000 and absorb the cost difference. The other OEMs' option prices were ¥800,000. Because of this large disparity, the other OEMs concluded that GMAJ, with its close Isuzu relationship, was preferentially pricing to Isuzu.

The GMAJ Staff in 1984

When Mr. Swaim arrived in Tokyo, the staff at GMAJ consisted of two engineers, a bookkeeper, a sales manager, and three salespeople, all of whom were seconded employees from Isuzu. One of the engineers was an engineering manager who, although a competent engineer, had little management experience. The sales manager had been in the sales promotion side of the business at Isuzu, was without technical ability, and had no experience in selling trucks or truck components. There was also an employee who had been seconded from C. Itoh. Most of these people were near retirement age and came to GMAJ with the expectation of being there for three or four years. In addition, there were two young employees who had been hired from outside any of the companies participating in the joint venture. None of the employees at GMAJ in 1984 had been there when the company was started in 1972.

A New President

Although Mr. Swaim had been in Japan for nearly three years when he was named president of GMAJ in 1987, he quickly realized that he now had the responsibility to move the company in a new direction. He understood the need to develop a strategy that would expand Allison's share of the Japanese transmission market. He also was aware of the importance of developing the Japanese market in order to help protect Allison's market share in the United States.

YUGO AMERICA, INC.*

Carolyn Silliman, Clemson University
Jeffrey S. Harrison, Clemson University

The five years that I invested in the Yugo project were rewarding and maturing for me, although I had a modest financial equity and a large amount of sweat equity invested in the company. In hindsight, there were areas where we failed, but I feel as though it all made a significant impact on the product and pricing aspect of the automobile industry.
William E. Prior
June 1989

William Prior, cofounder and former chief executive and president of Yugo America, Inc., collected his thoughts and reflected on the past five years as he glanced across a crowded airport. It was June 1989, only five months after his company had filed for Chapter 11 reorganization. Looking back, he noted that the privately held company had traveled a rocky road, yet had made a significant impact on the automobile industry in the 1980s.

It was 1983 when Prior and his two partners, Malcolm Bricklin and Ira Edelson, decided to form a company featuring a low-priced imported car. Bricklin, who was probably best known for the flashy sports car prototype that bears his name, was heading up the project as its main financial backer. William Prior was the former president and general manager of Automobile Importers from Subaru, the nation's second-largest Subaru distributor, a company Bricklin had founded after the collapse of his sports car project. Ira Edelson was Bricklin's accountant and financial advisor. The three men had been researching the automobile industry, looking for a niche in the already-crowded new-car market. From their research, the men came to the conclusion that there was no "entry-level car"; that is, there was not a new automobile inexpensive enough for the average first-time buyer. Bricklin, Prior, and Edelson concluded that they had discovered "a market in search of a product."

Pursuing the concept for their business venture, the three entrepreneurs began a search for a low-priced, no-frills mode of basic transportation. They determined that production costs would be too high in the United States, so they began evaluating the possibility of importing. In selecting a foreign manufacturer whose car models could satisfy their business concept, they wanted to meet three requirements:

1. The foreign company should not be presently exporting to the United States, but should be desirous of gaining access to the U.S. market.
2. The overall quality of the car, even if inferior to American and Japanese cars, had to meet U.S. standards and consumer requirements.
3. The foreign company had to be able to supply the cars at a price low enough for their new company and the dealers they recruited to make money retailing the car at a rock-bottom market price.

Bricklin, Prior, and Edelson spent four months investigating and traveling to foreign countries in pursuit of the right country and product that

*Distributed by the North American Case Research Association. All rights reserved to the authors and the North American Case Research Association.

met the three requirements. They researched manufacturing plants in Brazil, Japan, Mexico, Poland, France, Rumania, Czechoslovakia, England, and the Soviet Union before they discovered the Zastava car factory in Yugoslavia. Zavodi Crvena Zastava, Yugoslavia's leading automobile manufacturer, had been producing the Yugo GV model for five years and was quite receptive to Bricklin's proposal. Bricklin, Prior, and Edelson toured the Yugoslavian plant in May 1984 and began discussing the terms of a contract that same month.

Yugoslavian officials were eager to hear of the Yugo America venture. The country's economy was weak, and it owed (in 1985) approximately $19 billion to the Western world. In order to purchase goods from the West, such as oil, steel, and electronics, Yugoslavia had to have "hard" currency (a universal currency of choice). The dinar, Yugoslavia's monetary unit, was generally not acceptable payment for firms shipping goods to Yugoslavia, so the country had to earn dollars by exporting. Yugoslavia's modest exports, including jewelry, tourism, furniture, leather, and sporting guns, did not contribute a significant sum toward reduction of the $19 billion foreign debt. Since car exports would generate lots of U.S. dollars (because the price of the car was so great in relation to other exported goods), Yugoslavian officials saw the venture as one of the biggest and best ways it could increase the supply of hard currency to finance imports into Yugoslavia.

Bricklin and Zastava agreed that 500 Yugos should be shipped to a Baltimore port in early August 1985, so that the cars would be in showrooms and ready to sell later that month. In addition, technicians would be trained at Zastava's plant prior to the launch in America, in order to guarantee customer satisfaction when the cars were sold and serviced. Bricklin and his partners returned to the United States in late May 1984 and began setting up operations.

COMPETITIVE STRATEGY

Competitive maneuvering among car manufacturers revolves around such factors as innovative options and styles, pricing, and brand name/reputation. Innovative options and styles were not considered important to the Yugo, since they would increase the price of the car. Also, the company could not rely on reputation, since the Yugo did not have an established name in the United States. Therefore, Yugo's strategy focused on pricing.

Yugo America took advantage of a pricing scheme that set it apart from other automobile manufacturers. At $3,990, it was the lowest-priced car in America. Because price is important to most car buyers, Yugo felt that its low-price strategy gave the company an advantage over other small cars. Major price competitors included the Chevrolet Sprint, Subaru hatchback, and Toyota Tercel; however, the Yugo GV was priced below all of these competitors (see Exhibit 1). Instead of targeting families or status-conscious individuals, Yugo America made its car appealing to the first-time buyer looking for an economical subcompact.

OPERATIONS BEGIN

Four strategic decisions were made at the onset of operations:

1. The cars would be sold through dual dealerships; that is, Yugo would be taken on as a second brand by established auto dealers looking for a

EXHIBIT 1   **Low-Priced Small Cars Available in the United States in 1986**

	Price	Destination Charge	Engine Size*	Fuel Economy†	Predicted Reliability
Chevrolet Chevette	$5,645	$290	1.6	19 (32)	Below average
Chevrolet Sprint	5,380	190	1.0	37 (59)	Average
Dodge Colt	5,633	210	1.5	23 (45)	Above average
Ford Escort	6,052	308	1.9	21 (41)	Average
Honda Civic	5,649	189	1.5	22 (39)	Above average
Mazda 323	5,645	205	1.6	22 (42)	N/A
Mitsubishi Mirage	5,659	210	N/A	N/A	N/A
Nissan Sentra	5,649	210	1.6	24 (45)	Above average
Renault Alliance	5,999	358	1.4	21 (45)	Below average
Subaru Hatchback	4,989	N/A	1.8	21 (45)	Above average
Toyota Tercel	5,598	210	1.5	23 (46)	Above average
Yugo GV	3,990	299	1.1	24 (42)	N/A

Note: N/A = not available.
*Engine size is in liters.
†Miles per gallon in city; highway miles per gallon in parentheses.
Source: *Consumer Reports*, April 1986, pp. 230–34.

low-priced model that could boost sales volume. In this manner, Yugo America's executives hoped the public would associate its name with another successful manufacturer's name and reputation.

2. Prior, Bricklin, and Edelson decided that the company would market the Yugo regionally rather than nationally. Yugo America, based in Upper Saddle River, New Jersey, decided to focus on Northeastern dealers first. Approximately 23 percent of all import cars were sold in this region. Also, the Northeastern coast, being closest to Yugoslavia, would allow the company to minimize shipping costs.

3. There would be a small number of dealers selling a large number of Yugos. The idea behind this decision was that the dealers would be making a substantial profit from the large number of cars, which would motivate them and encourage them to sell more.

4. The price of the car would be low, but the company would stress the fact that the car was of acceptable quality.

The first task to accomplish before announcing the introduction of the Yugo GV in America was to set up a management hierarchy. As mentioned previously, Malcolm Bricklin was Yugo America's chief financial backer. As chairman, he owned 75 percent of the company. William Prior, who would act as president and head of operations, owned 1 percent. Ira Edelson owned 2 percent of the company and held the title of financial administrator. The remaining 22 percent was held by investors who were not involved in the management of the company.

In February 1985, the company began recruiting automobile dealers. (The company's founders had been reviewing dealers for over four months, but the actual signing did not take place until February.) Tony Cappadona was hired as dealer development manager and given the responsibility of locating established dealers who were interested in selling the Yugo. In addition, extensive surveys helped Mr. Cappadona determine the best area placement of Yugo franchises. By the end of July, the first 50 dealers were contracted in Pennsylvania, Massachusetts, New York, New Jersey, Connecticut, Rhode Island, Delaware, Maryland, and Washington, D.C.

Some dealers were hesitant to sign because of the financial commitment involved. Pressure from Manufacturers Hanover Trust Company required that Yugo America produce 50 letters of credit by December 1985. By the terms of agreement, all dealers had to produce a $400,000 standby letter of credit to cover at least two months of vehicle shipments. Each dealer also had to pay $37,000 to cover initial start-up costs and arrange financing for a floor plan. A floor plan is an agreement between a financial institution and an auto dealership to finance vehicles that are on the lot. The financial institution retains title to the automobiles until they are sold. A typical floor plan entailed a $600,000 line of credit. Dealers were reluctant to take on such debt and incur $37,000 in up-front costs to take on an unknown, unproven car model. Yugo executives countered such arguments with assurances that the Yugo GV would sell itself.

Bricklin contacted Leonard Sirowitz, a New York advertiser, to write and launch a $10 million media campaign to introduce the Yugo GV. Sirowitz, who helped to create the Volkswagen Beetle advertisements during the 1960s, expected the Yugo advertisements to reach a potential one million buyers via newspapers, magazines, and television. He hoped to convince Americans that, despite their views of communist Yugoslavia, the $3,990 car was of sound quality.[1] Yugo's first slogan intended to catch the consumer's eye by asking, "The Road Back to Sanity: Why Pay Higher Prices?"

In addition to trained technicians, Yugo's support system of quality parts and service was comprehensive. The company received 180 tons of spare parts to distribute among dealers during the summer of 1985. The company implemented the industry's first Universal Product Code inventory system, which enhanced the accuracy and efficiency of inventory processing. In addition, service schools were developed so that technicians would have no problems or questions when repairing the cars. For do-it-yourself consumers, Yugo America published its own repair manuals and included a toll-free telephone number for assistance.

THE YUGO ARRIVES IN AMERICA

The first shipment of 500 cars from the Zastava plant arrived in mid-August 1985 (Yugo features are listed in Exhibit 2). Ten cars were sent to each of the 50 dealers in the Northeast. Each dealer was asked to reserve two cars as demonstration vehicles and then to keep two demonstrators on hand at all times as further shipments and sales occurred.

Yugo's official entry into the automobile industry was announced on August 26, 1985. Consumers responded with enthusiasm. The Yugo frenzy spread so quickly that 33 dealerships were added and 3,000 orders were taken for cars by September 9. Customers paid deposits in order to reserve their cars, and by the

---

[1]J. Fierman, "Can A Beetle Brain Stir a Yearning for Yugos?" *Fortune*, May 13, 1985, p. 73.

EXHIBIT 2   **Yugo GV Standard Features**

Vehicle Type
Front-engine, front-wheel drive,
    4-passenger, 3-door hatchback

Dimensions and Capacities
Wheelbase: 84.6 inches
Overall length: 139.0 inches
Overall height: 54.7 inches
Overall width: 60.7 inches
Headroom: Front: 37.0 inches
            Rear: 36.0 inches
Legroom: Front: 39.0 inches
            Rear: 39.0 inches
Ground clearance: 4.8 inches
Luggage capacity: 18.5 + 9.0 cubic feet
Fuel capacity: 8.4 gallons
Curb weight: 1,832 pounds

Engine
Type: Single overhead cam, 1.1 liter
        4-cylinder with aluminum cylinder
        head; dual-barrel carburetor
Bore and stroke: 80 × 55.5 mm.
Displacement: 1116 cc.
Compression ratio: 9.2:1
Horsepower: 54hp at 5,000 rpm
Torque: 52 lbs. at 4,000 rpm.

Drive Train
Transmission: 4-speed manual
Final drive ratio: 3.7
Gear ratios: 1st—3.5, 2nd—2.2, 3rd—1.4,
            4th—1.0, reverse—3.7

Suspension
Front: Independent, MacPherson struts,
        anti-sway bar.
Rear: Independent, transverse leaf
        spring with lower control arms

Brakes
Front: 8.0″ disc, power-assisted
Rear: 7.2″ drum, power-assisted
Rear brake proportioning valve

Wheels and Tires
Wheels: Steel
Tires: Tigar 145SR-13,
        steel-belted radials
        with all-weather tread design

Electrical
Bosch electronic ignition
Alternator: 55 amp
Battery: 12 volt, 45 amp

Fuel Economy
City: 28 mpg
Highway: 31 mpg

Standard Equipment
1.1 liter 4-cylinder overhead cam engine
Front-wheel drive
4-wheel independent suspension
Power-assisted brakes, disc front,
    drum rear
Front anti-sway bar
Rack and pinion steering
Color-coordinated fabric upholstery
Full carpeting, including carpeted
    luggage compartment
Reclining front seats
Folding rear seats—
    27.5 cu. ft. luggage space
3 grab handles
2 dome lights
Visor vanity mirror
Analog instrument gauges
Low-fuel warning light
Steel-belted radial tires
Lexan bumpers
Plastic inner-front fender shields
Bosch electronic ignition
Rear brake proportioning valve
Full-size spare tire
Front spoiler
Hood scoop
Hub caps
PVC undercoating
Opening rear-quarter windows
Rear-window electric defroster
Quartz halogen headlights
Body side molding
Special owner's tool kit
Cigarette lighter
Locking gas cap
Dual storage pockets
Concealed radio antenna
Spare fuse and bulb kit
Night/day rear-view mirror
Electric cooling fan
Console

Source: Yugo America, Inc. promotional materials.

EXHIBIT 3   **Yugo GV Sales in the United States, by Calendar Year**

Year	Unit Sales
1985	3,895
1986	35,959
1987	48,812
1988	31,545
1989	10,576
1990	6,359

Source: *Automotive News*, last January issue, 1986–1991.

end of 1985, a six-month waiting list was tallied. Indeed, Yugo America's founders had discovered "a market in search of a product."[2]

During its first year of operations, which ended July 31, 1986, Yugo America, Inc. grossed $122 million from the sale of 27,000 automobiles and parts and accessories (Exhibit 3 contains a sales breakdown by calendar year). The Yugo was hailed as "the fastest selling import car in the history of the U.S."[3] By mid-1986 Yugo had 220 dealers throughout the Southeast and East Coast. It was estimated that the consumer credit divisions of Chrysler, Ford, and General Motors financed one third of the Yugo retail sales.[4] At the end of July, Prior announced the expansion of the New Jersey home office to include a corporate planning department. He also informed reporters of Yugo's new slogan, "Everybody Needs a Yugo Sometime."[5]

PROBLEMS BEGIN

In February 1986, *Consumer Reports* published the first of several articles criticizing the Yugo GV. Reporters criticized Malcolm Bricklin for his other car ventures (the Subaru 360 and the Fiat Spider) that had recently failed, and pointed out that, after adding destination charges, dealer preparation fees, and a stereo, the price of the Yugo GV exceeded $4,600. The magazine's personal test evaluation was also published. It stated that the transmission was "sloppy," the steering was "heavy," the ride was "jerky," and the heating system was "weak and obtrusive."[6]

The writers continued by denigrating almost every aspect of the car, from seat coverings to the "not-so-spacious" trunk. The safety of the car was questioned, but could not be verified by government crash tests. It was noted, however, that the impact of collisions at 3 and 5 miles per hour severely twisted and crushed the bumpers. It was estimated that repairing the damage to the

---

[2]"The Price Is Right," *Time*, September 9, 1985, p. 58.
[3]J. L. Kovach, "We Don't Overpromise," *Industry Week*, October 13, 1986, p. 73.
[4]Ibid.
[5]J. A. Russell, "Yugo Grosses $122 Million in First Year," *Automotive News*, September 1, 1986, p. 42.
[6]"How Much Car for $3990?" *Consumer Reports*, February 1986, pp. 84–86.

front and rear bumpers was $620 and $461, respectively.[7] Twenty-one other defects were discovered, ranging from oil leaks to squealing brakes. A survey by J. D. Power and Associates (included in the article) concerning customer satisfaction revealed that over 80 percent of Yugo buyers had reported problems. In short, *Consumer Reports* did not recommend the Yugo GV at *any* price.

The Yugo was facing increasing competition as well. Hyundai Motor America, a subsidiary of the giant South Korean industrial company, introduced the Hyundai Excel for $4,995. The Excel was a hatchback model that included standard features comparable to those of the Yugo GV. It posed a direct threat to the Yugo GV in the lower-priced automobile market.

By mid-October 1986, Yugo America responded to the *Consumer Reports* article and increasing consumer complaints by making 176 improvements to the car without raising its price.[8] William Prior stated that Yugo America spent between $2.5 and $3 million to improve its image through advertisements and national incentives. Independent dealers offered additional rebates as well in an effort to boost sagging sales.

Looking ahead, Yugo America planned to introduce some new models, all within the lower price range. For 1987, the Yugo GV would be given a "face-lift" to take on an aerodynamic look, and a convertible GV was planned for later in the year. In order to meet the needs of couples and small families, Yugo anticipated the 1988 debut of a five-door hatchback, which would compete with the Honda Accord. A four-door sedan would be added to the line between 1989 and 1990, and a two-seater sports car named TCX would be the highlight of 1990.[9]

During 1986, Yugo America contemplated a move to go public by issuing common stock. The idea was abandoned for two reasons. First, Bricklin did not want to surrender any of his equity (75 percent). Second, the company was starting to feel the effects of negative publicity, and financial consultants felt that the stock would not bring a fair price.

MORE TROUBLE

In April 1987, *Consumer Reports* released its annual survey of the 1987 domestic and foreign car models and, once again, Yugo's image was tainted. The writers criticized the Yugo GV from bumper to bumper, stating that "the manual transmission was very imprecise . . . the worst we've tried in years." As for comfort, "small, insufficiently contoured front seats" contributed to an "awkward driving position." In addition, the ride of the car was described as "noisy" and "harsh."[10]

Besides the negative description of the car's driving performance, the article published the results of an independent crash test. This test, which was not mandated by law, disclosed the results of a crash at 35 miles per hour among domestic and foreign automobiles. (The National Highway Traffic Safety Administration requires that all cars pass the national standard impact at 30

---

[7]Ibid.
[8]Kovach, p. 73.
[9]J. A. Russell, "Zastava to Construct Plant for U.S. Yugos," *Automotive News*, May 20, 1985, p. 2.
[10]"The 1987 Cars," *Consumer Reports*, April 1987, pp. 200–15.

miles per hour.) The Yugo GV was among the 40 percent that did not pass the test. In fact, it received the lowest possible ranking with respect to driver and passenger protection. The report indicated that the steering column "moved up and back into the path of the driver's head," and the seats "moved forward during the crash, increasing the load on occupants."[11]

Consumer Reports also reported that damage to the front and rear bumpers when hit at impacts of 3 and 5 miles per hour was $1,081, the highest in its class. This was particularly embarrassing to Yugo America because many of its foreign competitors (including Toyota, Mazda, and Saab) escaped the collisions without a scratch.[12]

Before the second *Consumer Reports* article, Yugo America sold every car coming into its ports every month. Sales in 1987 were the highest to date in number, but this proved to be the sales peak. The negative press the Yugo received made car shoppers wary, and dealers were forced to offer $500–$750 rebates as an incentive to buy. In addition, several new programs and extended warranties were offered to entice customers. Monthly sales levels started to decline, and waiting lists became virtually nonexistent.

Through all of these problems, William Prior remained enthusiastic, upbeat, and positive about the Yugo, thus providing a source of motivation for all of the employees. As Tony Cappadona stated, "Bill added a lot of charisma and dedication to the company. He let the employees know that everyone was working to achieve a mission. They (the employees) didn't mind working 10 or 12 hours a day, because they saw Bill putting in twice as much."

CHANGES IN OWNERSHIP

In 1987, Yugo America, Inc. was acquired by Global Motors, Inc., a company founded by Malcolm Bricklin. Bricklin established Global Motors as an umbrella corporation for importing cars worldwide. Gaining 91 percent of Yugo America, Global became its parent, distributor, and holding company, and it helped with the coordination and distribution of Yugos as they arrived at the Baltimore port.

By 1988, Yugo America and Global Motors began contemplating the sale of a substantial portion of the company in an effort to avoid bankruptcy. In April, Mabon Nugent and Company, a New York investment firm, purchased Global Motors for $40 million.[13] Bricklin sold 70 percent of his equity for $20 million, and a debenture was purchased from Global for an additional $20 million. A management group headed by Prior and Edelson agreed to contribute $2.1 million to obtain 5.5 percent of the company. The management group would be awarded stock options periodically over the following three years, bringing the group's total ownership to 22 percent. Prior was named chief executive officer during the acquisition.[14]

---

[11]Ibid., p. 200.

[12]Ibid., p. 208.

[13]J. A. Russell, "Bricklin's Import Firm Sold in $40 Million Deal," *Automotive News*, April 18, 1988, pp. 1, 56.

[14]Ibid.

THE FINAL YEAR

By April 1988, the company's operating problems had also increased. Not only had a third *Consumer Reports* article on the 1988 models thrashed the Yugo GV again, but dealers were beginning to push potential Yugo buyers to consider their other models. To make things worse, buyers could only get 36-month financing toward the purchase of a Yugo, whereas they could get 48- and 60-month financing on many American models. The thought of lower monthly payments was incentive enough for many prospective Yugo buyers to change their decision in favor of an American-made automobile. If the former tactic did not persuade the buyer, salespeople would criticize the Yugo directly and accentuate the features of the other line the dealer carried. Higher commissions on more costly brands increased the motivation of salespeople to move away from the Yugo.

Even after deciding to buy a Yugo, many consumers ran into additional difficulties when they tried to obtain financing. Because the typical Yugo customer was a young, low-income, first-time buyer, lending institutions were hesitant to make high-risk loans to persons in this segment of the market. It was estimated that as many as 70 percent of all Yugo customers were turned down for credit, since the majority had no previous credit history and a debt–income ratio of over 50 percent. This common scenario was discouraging for both the customers and dealers. Enticing advertisements lured customers in, and yet many could not obtain financing. The dealers became frustrated because of the amount of time and effort it took to put the deal together. Mr. Prior described the situation as "an inefficiency in the market."

In an effort to hurdle these financing roadblocks, Yugo America announced in June 1988 that it would design its own program for financing. The first-time buyer plan was administered through Imperial Savings Association, a $10-billion institution based in San Diego. Yugo and Imperial intended to protect themselves by charging a higher annual percentage rate—as much as four percentage points higher than those of other finance companies. In doing so, Yugo America could establish a higher-than-average reserve for loan defaults. Though the annual percentage rate was higher, buyers could finance the loan over 60 months so that monthly payments remained low.[15]

Approximately 50 dealers were enrolled in the program. Imperial was hesitant to allow all of the dealers to take advantage of Yugo Credit, since there were still some bugs in the system. Also, each state required separate licensing, and Yugo did not have the time to wait for acceptance in each state.

The financing program was terminated after 90 days. One of the provisions of the plan required Yugo America to be in good standing financially. Unpaid bills were accumulating at Yugo America so fast that the company's debt was becoming unmanageable. Imperial Savings pulled out.

In November 1988, William Prior and 71 other employees were dismissed from the company, leaving a skeleton crew of 71 remaining. Mabon Nugent's intentions were to cut costs in an effort to relieve cash-flow pressures and generate additional funds for product development. Marcel Kole, senior

---

[15]J. Henry, "Low Finance: Yugo Offers Loans to Spur Buyers," *Automotive News*, August 1, 1988, pp. 1, 51.

EXHIBIT 4   **Global Motors' Unaudited Balance Sheet, 1988**   *(In thousands of dollars)*

Assets	
Cash.	$ 0
Due from subsidiaries	27,145
Due from manufacturer	15
Inventories	0
Prepaid and other current assets	48
	27,208
Property, plant, and equipment (at cost)	8
Less: Accumulated depreciation	(1)
	7
Investment in subsidiaries	223
Total assets	$27,438
Liabilities and Shareholders' Equity	
Accounts payable and accrued expenses	$ 1,429
Notes payable	11,825
	13,254
Long-term debt.	11,000
Shareholders' equity	3,184
Total liabilities and equity	$27,438

Source: Bankruptcy Docket Number 89 00680, filed January 30, 1989, United States Bankruptcy Court, District of New Jersey.

vice president and chief financial officer of Global Motors, temporarily replaced Prior as president and chief executive of Yugo America. Turnover within the company was high, and national advertising was brought to a halt.[16] Norauto LP of Ohio agreed to finance two shipments of Yugos backed by letters of credit. Norauto, a firm that aids bankrupt, terminated, or distressed companies, took possession of the cars until Yugo America could repay the $14.3 million letter of credit.[17]

Mabon Nugent and Company had written off $10.5 million as a loss in Global Motors by January 30, 1989. It was estimated that Global would need $10 million to get back on its feet, but Mabon Nugent did not feel that contributing more money to a dying company was a worthy investment. The firm's partners considered selling the company to Zastava or private investors, but neither of the ideas were pursued.[18] Global officially filed for Chapter 11 protection under the bankruptcy laws on January 30, 1989.[19] This provided Global with temporary protection from its creditors and some time to work out a plan of reorganization. Global's unaudited balance sheet reported in the petition for bankruptcy is contained in Exhibit 4.

---

[16]C. Thomas, "Prior Ousted: Shaky Global Trims Ranks," *Automotive News*, November 14, 1988, pp. 1, 58.

[17]J. Henry, "Yugo, Liquidator in Accord," *Automotive News*, March 27, 1989, p. 1.

[18]J. Henry, "Global Struggles to Remain Afloat," *Automotive News*, January 30, 1989, pp. 1, 257.

[19]Henry, "Yugo, Liquidator," p. 1.

A Hazy Future For Yugo America

After filing for Chapter 11 reorganization in January 1989, parent company Global Motors, Inc. discharged most of the remaining Yugo America employees. Zastava, honoring the warranty of the cars, began seeking financial backing so that the company could remain afloat. By February 1989, three lawsuits had been filed against Global Motors and Mabon Nugent and Company. William Prior sued the companies for breach of contract, and Turner Broadcasting System in Atlanta filed suit demanding $182,000 for unpaid bills. A third lawsuit, by Imperial Savings, alleged that Mabon Nugent was "involved in the day-to-day operations of the company (Global)" before it (Mabon Nugent) actually took control of Yugo-Global in 1988. Mabon Nugent denied the charge.[20]

On March 14, 1989, John A. Spiech became Yugo's new president and chief executive, succeeding Marcel Kole. Spiech, a veteran of the automobile industry, had full confidence in the company and its product, stating, "whatever happened wasn't the car's fault. It is still good, low-cost, reliable transportation."[21] Mr. Spiech intended to develop a strategy to revitalize the company and get sales of Yugos headed upward as soon as possible. As starters, Yugo America had plans to add a better warranty and extensive rust protection to its automobiles. Several new models were also under consideration. But Spiech knew that much more would have to go into making Yugo America's comeback strategy a success.

---

[20]J. Henry, "More Yugo Grief—Maker Plans Termination," *Automotive News*, February 20, 1989, pp. 1, 51.
[21]D. Cuff, "A Car Industry Veteran Will Try to Revive Yugo," *New York Times*, March 17, 1989, pp. D4.

STRATEGIC ANALYSIS IN DIVERSIFIED COMPANIES

WALSH PETROLEUM

George Overstreet, Jr., The University of Virginia
Stewart Malone, The University of Virginia
Bernard Morin, The University of Virginia

John Walsh sighed as he looked again at the financial statements his accountant had delivered that morning (see Exhibits 1 and 2). When John's father died two years ago, his accountant had advised against selling the business. "It's a good business, John," he said, "and I think you could do a lot to improve it."

While Walsh Petroleum, Inc., had increased profits in 1985, John still considered them unacceptably low. Company sales had declined for the third straight year, and, while John realized that other oil distributors faced the same problems, he had to wonder what type of future he could expect if he stayed with the family business. Now 31 years old and just married, maybe he should consider selling the business and starting another career before he got too old.

COMPANY HISTORY

Walsh Petroleum was founded in 1957 by John's mother and father as commission agents in the oil business. By 1976 the senior Walsh had converted the company to a conventional oil distributorship. Both the family and the company were well respected in the local community, and the company grew steadily. The 1970s and early 1980s were a period of relative prosperity for Walsh Petroleum. Dollar sales in 1982 were four times higher than sales in 1977 (although most of this increase was a result of increased unit sales prices). Nonetheless, profits were at their highest level in 1982. A year later, sales gallonage started a decline that had continued unabated. In 1984, John's father died, leaving John's mother and John to manage the firm.

COMPANY OPERATIONS

Walsh Petroleum distributed oil products throughout a seven-county area of the southeastern United States. The marketing area was semi-rural, but contained two county seats with populations of 15,000 and 25,000. The area's proximity to a growing, major city was expected to result in higher-than-average population growth over the next 10 years, but in no way was the area likely to become a suburb of the city. The firm represented a major branded oil company and carried a full line of petroleum products. There were three basic classes of customers for Walsh:

Reseller Accounts   Walsh served as a distributor of oil products to 10 reseller locations, most of which were local gas stations. Gaining new reseller customers depended more on financial considerations than marketing techniques because gasoline and oil products were generally considered commodities, and most distributors offered similar types of services. When a new gas station was about to be constructed (an event that had been occurring with decreasing frequency over the past 20 years), the operator would contact

E X H I B I T 1   **Walsh Petroleum's Income Statements, 1981–1985**

	1981	1982	1983	1984	1985
Gallons sold					
Premium	386,144	687,087	584,076	617,420	593,777
Unleaded	1,193,536	1,236,757	830,002	898,065	841,184
Regular	1,930,719	2,656,736	1,660,004	1,290,969	1,039,110
Lube	24,847	17,793	18,184	16,660	15,725
Heating oil	491,583	409,267	327,845	373,609	335,054
Diesel	375,478	373,704	338,249	348,420	327,098
Kerosene	79,769	96,215	99,733	138,555	125,182
Other products	1,810	414	713	5,301	10,682
Total gallons sold	4,483,886	5,477,973	3,858,806	3,688,999	3,287,812
Sales revenues					
Premium	$ 322,225	$ 533,091	$ 551,540	$ 517,510	$ 533,998
Unleaded	1,195,855	1,493,304	1,020,024	1,019,856	881,903
Regular	2,385,763	2,967,718	1,633,912	1,187,458	854,324
Lube	84,438	64,681	66,005	60,491	58,988
Heating oil	533,368	478,842	368,498	411,344	364,539
Diesel	397,663	410,090	332,637	345,317	310,858
Kerosene	92,252	119,845	117,952	162,359	147,066
Other products	53,960	10,757	48,261	140,259	177,768
Total sales revenues	5,065,524	6,078,328	4,138,829	3,844,594	3,329,444
Cost of sales					
Beginning inventory	77,420	84,927	84,804	136,862	131,592
Purchases net of discounts	4,725,693	5,691,682	3,885,557	3,528,264	2,942,582
	4,803,113	5,776,609	3,970,381	3,665,126	3,074,174
Ending inventory	84,927	84,804	136,862	131,592	149,007
Cost of sales	4,718,186	5,691,805	3,833,519	3,533,534	2,925,167
Gross profit	347,338	386,523	305,310	311,060	404,277
Selling, general, and administrative expenses					
Licenses and nonincome taxes	22,447	22,462	18,472	22,604	8,917
Vehicle expense	23,362	41,510	36,837	43,950	32,583
Officers' salaries	68,248	63,370	53,970	52,952	50,780
Other salaries and wages	78,763	92,138	121,160	135,692	140,623
Other expenses	132,880	135,589	136,903	127,892	150,957
Depreciation	46,524	68,676	72,842	73,404	69,441
Interest on borrowing needs	6,457	7,410	11,232	11,999	9,299
Operating income (loss)	(31,343)	(44,632)	(146,106)	(157,433)	(58,323)
Earnings on marketable securities	4,456	2,853	3,009	2,943	3,739
Other income (for hauling)	83,587	112,425	103,109	144,878	85,038
Earnings before taxes	56,700	70,646	(39,988)	(9,612)	30,454
Provision for federal income taxes	6,590	11,870	(15,294)	(2,229)	2,485
Net income	$ 50,110	$ 58,776	$ (24,694)	$ (7,383)	$ 27,969

Note: Inventory is recorded on a LIFO basis.

EXHIBIT 2   **Walsh Petroleum's Balance Sheets, 1981–1985**

	1981	1982	1983	1984	1985
Assets					
Current assets					
Cash	$ 36,305	$ 7,704	$ 38,510	$ 55,652	$ 14,003
Marketable securities	0	0	0	0	0
Accounts receivable	262,047	254,809	190,673	143,802	155,839
Inventories	84,927	84,804	136,862	131,592	149,007
Refundable taxes	3,964	0	27,194	2,665	200
Prepaid expenses	5,756	7,121	13,698	8,625	9,609
Notes receivable	0	0	0	0	9,368
Other current assets	0	0	0	0	116,607
Total current assets	392,999	354,438	406,937	342,336	454,633
Property, plant, and equipment					
Land	25,201	28,134	25,489	34,893	30,544
Equipment	154,029	140,493	163,011	130,797	144,965
Vehicles	51,930	60,678	42,367	37,032	24,604
Furniture and fixtures	5,544	3,730	3,449	4,102	3,425
Total	236,704	233,035	234,316	206,824	203,538
Long-term investments	677	1,202	1,202	1,202	1,202
Cash surrender value—officers' life	30,970	35,117	690	3,116	0
Loan fees—net	370	277	195	0	0
Total other assets	32,017	36,596	2,087	4,318	1,202
Total assets	$661,720	$624,069	$643,340	$553,478	$659,373
Liabilities and Stockholders' Equity					
Current liabilities					
Accounts payable	$264,812	$155,012	$157,254	$ 80,624	$ 98,505
Notes payable	0	0	50,000	30,000	0
Current portion of long-term debt	18,163	18,315	18,204	17,900	50,675
Income taxes payable	334	4,506	0	235	2,485
Accrued expenses	42,834	45,944	55,125	44,424	40,724
Other current liabilities	0	0	522	846	0
Total current liabilities	326,143	223,777	281,105	174,029	192,389
Long-term debt	19,849	10,305	0	0	0
Other long-term	14,572	30,054	26,992	51,592	0
Total liabilities	360,564	264,136	308,097	225,621	192,389
Owners' equity	301,157	359,933	335,240	327,856	466,984
Total liabilities and owners' equity	$661,721	$624,069	$643,337	$553,477	$659,373

Note: Walsh has limited underground tank liability due to placing tanks in reseller's name and having installed double-walled tanks at the bulk plant over the past five years.

EXHIBIT 3   Sales Trends at Walsh's Reseller Locations, 1984–1986

| | | Average Gallonage per Month (000s) | | |
Unit	Description of Reseller Location	1984	1985	1986 (est.)
1	4,000-square-foot rural grocery, owner change in 1984	6.0	10.5	10.8
2	Village two-bay, financial problems, cash only, pool hall	11.7	16.8	14.3
3	5,000-square-foot rural grocery in low-growth area	—	—	8.2
4	C-store in growing rural area	—	6.7	18.1
5	Two-bay station with marina service, new C-store competition	20.3	17.9	20.7
6	Rehab two-bay on front of bulk plant property, owned by mother and leased to corporation, good location on four-lane with crossover access, growth area	28.4	35.3	37.5
7	Three-bay station in low-growth rural area, father and son	9.9	9.9	10.1
8	1,500-square-foot rural grocery with new owner, business recovery	14.0	9.1	11.6
9	3,000-square-foot rural C-store with interceptor location, sell on consignment with Walsh controlling price, considering canopy to be leased by Walsh from owner	17.6	18.8	20.0
10	3,000-square-foot rural C-store with interceptor location	21.9	22.4	22.7

several distributors such as Walsh. The distributor would formulate a proposal based on expected sales gallonage. In return for an exclusive, long-term contract to supply the location with gasoline and oil products, the distributor provided the station with fuel storage tanks, pumps, remote consoles, and a canopy. Walsh's profit margin per gallon declined as the reseller's volume climbed based on a sliding scale. If up to 50,000 gallons a month were delivered, he received 4.5 cents over delivered cost (including freight). If 50,000 to 65,000 gallons per month were delivered, he received 4.0 cents per gallon. For 65,000 to 75,000 gallons he received 3.65 cents, and for over 75,000 gallons he received 3.5 cents per gallon. Over the course of the contract, the station operator could switch suppliers if he or she was willing to make a settlement on the equipment provided by the original distributor.

John had recently audited the profitability of his reseller accounts and found that many of the accounts yielded over a 20 percent after-tax internal rate of return. New reseller contracts also tended to be very lucrative, but there were relatively few high-gallonage locations left in Walsh's trading area, and only two or three new reseller accounts were out for bid each year. The capital requirements for such investments had grown over the years and ranged from $60,000 to $100,000. Exhibit 3 presents sales trends at the 10 contract locations.

In addition to the 10 contract locations, Walsh operated a reseller location on which it had constructed a convenience store (C-store). This diversification move was initiated by Mr. Walsh, Sr., in 1983. The C-store facility was located on 3 acres with 300 feet of road frontage on a four-lane U.S. highway. The property had been appraised at $356,000 and included not only the convenience store but also the bulk storage facilities (144,000 gallons). Mrs. Walsh owned the site and leased it to Walsh Petroleum at $4,000 per month ($2,500 for the bulk storage plant and $1,500 for the C-store). The property had a $100,000 note payable over five years at 9 percent.

Home Heating Oil   Active accounts numbered 624, of which 325 were classified as automatic (with refills scheduled by the distributor). While the home heating oil business was relatively profitable, it was also highly seasonal, and, thus, efficient utilization of equipment and personnel was viewed as a problem. Some other distributors had taken on equipment sales and service, as well as related businesses such as air conditioning, in order to balance the seasonality of fuel oil sales. John had concluded that heating oil sales would have to double in order to justify the equipment investment and personnel training for an in-house sales/service department.

Commercial/Agricultural Accounts   Approximately 120 businesses and/or farms maintained their own tanks and pumps for which Walsh supplied oil products. While these accounts had generally shown some loyalty to their petroleum supplier, there was no contractual relationship that would prevent them from changing suppliers.

Within Walsh Petroleum's trading area, there were three other gasoline and oil distributors. Competitive pressures were moderate for existing gasoline reseller and home heating oil accounts, but John had recently noticed an increased level of competition for the one or two new reseller locations constructed each year. None of the four distributors possessed a large competitive advantage over the others. Each competitor had about the same level of sales, and all possessed a similar amount of financial resources. Since gasoline and oil products have a significant freight-cost-to-value ratio, distributors of these products generally had a trading radius of approximately 75 miles around their terminal or distribution point. While the local competitors did not really worry John, some of the distributors that served the nearby metropolitan area were significantly larger than Walsh, and a move by one of these larger competitors into Walsh's trading area could well upset the competitive equilibrium that had evolved over the years.

FAMILY AND MANAGEMENT

Mrs. Walsh assumed the chairmanship of the company following the death of her husband, and she held 52 percent of the voting stock of the corporation (the remaining 48 percent being held equally by John and his two younger brothers). Having worked with her husband for several years, she was very knowledgeable about the firm's operations. While she held the title of chairman, Mrs. Walsh's duties consisted of supervising the convenience store adjacent to the distributorship and maintaining relationships with the fuel oil customers. A prominent citizen of the local community, Mrs. Walsh also served on the town council.

John Walsh had been employed as a geologist with an energy consulting firm in Denver before 1982. When he was visiting at home one weekend, he mentioned to his father that he was concerned his career would be hurt by the recent recession in the oil drilling business. Later that weekend, while having coffee together in the local doughnut shop, John, Sr., said, "John, our business here is changing rapidly, too. If you have any interest in joining the family business, you better make up your mind soon, because I may just sell the business rather than put up with all the changes that are occurring."

John returned to Denver, but after several months he decided the opportunity at Walsh Petroleum might offer a better future than his current job. John returned home in late 1982 and began to learn the business from his father. Not only did John assume many of the administrative duties, but he also managed the marketing relationships with the major accounts.

John's two younger brothers were not active in the management of the business at the time, although each held 16 percent of the corporate stock. Richard was 26 years old and was employed in another city. Daniel was a sophomore in college.

Aside from John and his mother, Walsh Petroleum employed three clerks and four drivers/maintenance workers. The three clerks handled much of the administrative paperwork for both the oil distributorship and convenience store. Convenience stores have a multitude of vendors, all of which expect payment within 10 days. Managing the payables took a great deal of time, and Walsh's bookkeeping clerk had complained that she couldn't keep up with the work load. All the accounting was done manually, and John planned to install a computer system in the near future.

In addition, the convenience store employed two full-time and three part-time workers. Salaries and benefits for these workers corresponded to industry averages, and all employees were nonunionized. During the first quarter of 1986, John purchased a new tractor/trailer for $60,000 (9,000-gallon capacity). In addition, Walsh had three older "bobtail" trucks for short deliveries (2,000-gallon capacity) and two used service delivery vans.

THE OIL DISTRIBUTION INDUSTRY

Few industries had experienced the volatility and changes connected with the oil business in the past 15 years. In 1973 the Arab oil embargo resulted in a 119 percent increase in the price of crude oil during a 12-month period. While demand fell slightly from 1973 to 1981, prices were expected to continue climbing. Spurred by higher prices, oil exploration and refinery construction continued to increase. In 1981 President Reagan decontrolled gasoline and crude oil prices. The acquisition price of crude oil began to drop, and demand also fell as the world economy entered a recession.

The changes that occurred upstream in the oil production industry had a large impact on the independent petroleum market:

1. Between 1974 and 1985, American auto manufacturers doubled the miles per gallon of new cars, from 13.2 to 26.4.
2. During the same period, gasoline consumption of passenger cars declined from approximately 75 billion gallons to 65 billion.
3. The number of service stations (defined as outlets with 50 percent or more dollar volume from the sale of petroleum products) fell from 226,459 in 1972 to 121,000 in 1985.

In addition to these changes, oil distributors also faced declining margins, increased real estate costs, and a proliferation of environmental regulations.

News for distributors had not been all bad. The past two years had seen firmer gross profit margins and increased gallonage pumped. Although the market had not recovered to the volume levels of the late 1970s and early 1980s, gasoline gallonage used by motorists increased 1.5 percent in 1983, 1.5 percent

TABLE 1   Gallonage Volumes of Wholesale Oil Distributorships

Millions of Gallons Sold	1984	1982
Less than 1.0	13.8%	18.0%
1.0–2.49	23.8	26.3
2.5–4.99	21.9	20.8
5.0–7.49	12.2	9.7
7.5–9.99	6.6	6.7
10.0–14.99	9.3	7.1
15.0–19.99	3.8	2.8
20.0–24.99	2.2	1.8
25.0–29.99	1.7	1.4
30.0–39.99	1.8	1.5
40.0–49.99	1.1	1.2
50.00 and above	1.8	2.7
Average annual volume	7.80	7.12
Median annual volume	3.91	3.18

Source: *1985 Petroleum Marketing Databook* (Alexandria, Va.: Petroleum Marketing Education Foundation, 1985), p. 12.

in 1984, and 3.4 percent in 1985.[1] A significant portion of the increased demand had to be attributed to the oversupply of world crude and, hence, to lower prices during each of the last three years (down 3.3 percent for 1983, 1.6 percent for 1984, and 1.6 percent for 1985).

Independent petroleum marketers are entrepreneurs involved in the sale and distribution of refined petroleum and ancillary products. While the exact number of the companies was unknown, one trade association report estimated their number between 11,000 and 12,000 in 1985.[2] The trade association membership is broken down in terms of size in Table 1.

Independent petroleum marketers have responded to the pressures in their industry in one of two ways: diversification or consolidation (mergers and acquisition). Table 2 shows how many oil distributors were engaged in various types of diversified activities.

Aside from diversifying into other areas, the number of acquisitions had increased in the past few years, spurred by industry decontrol. Independent marketers, particularly larger ones with the capital available to make acquisitions, had acquired other distributors to take advantage of economies of scale in storage, distribution, and other areas such as billing and general administrative services. A 1984 study found that 56 of 135 marketers had purchased one or more marketing companies within the last five years, and 24 of the 56 had purchased more than one.[3] Most of the acquisition activity occurred

---

[1] *1986 State of the Convenience Store Industry* (Alexandria, Va.: National Association of Convenience Stores, Inc.), p. 7.

[2] *1985 Petroleum Marketing Databook* (Alexandria, Va.: Petroleum Marketing Education Foundation, 1985), p. 12.

[3] *1984 Petroleum Marketing Databook* (Alexandria, Va.: Petroleum Marketing Education Foundation, 1984), p. 19.

TABLE 2   **Types of Diversified Activities Engaged in
                 by Wholesale Oil Distributors**

Types of Diversified Activities	Number of Distributors
Auto repair maintenance center	7,081
Auto/truck/trailer rentals	638
Beverage only stores	228
Car washes	2,961
Convenience stores	14,235
Fast-food operations	1,002
Heating/air-conditioning service	3,189
Kerosene heater sales	1,275
Lube centers	1,549
Plumbing service	501
Tires/tires, battery, and accessory stores	3,507
Truck stops	1,734
Towing service	911
Coal sales	164
Other	1,000

Source: *1985 Petroleum Marketing Databook* (Alexandria, Va.: Petroleum Marketing Education Foundation, 1985), p. 15.

among marketers with assets greater than $1 million. Of the 90 firms in this category in the sample, 46 had acquired one or more businesses during the period.

As a result of increasing profit pressure, a number of operating changes had occurred on the distribution level.[4] First, the total number of distributor-owned transportation vehicles had declined dramatically from 106,868 in 1982 to 96,972 in 1984. Second, distributors had decreased the amount of their storage facilities from a 2.3 billion-gallon capacity in 1982 to 1.7 billion in 1984. Finally, credit terms to distributors had tightened. In 1982, net 30-day payment terms were reported by 21 percent of trade association members, while in 1984 this percentage had dropped to 8.2 percent. These changes and others had led gasoline and oil distributors to redefine the term *good customer*. Whereas in the 1960s and 1970s, distributors were willing to inventory product and deliver relatively small amounts of gasoline on small bobtail trucks, the new market realities made these practices less attractive. Instead of inventorying product, successful distributors would now send a large transport truck (9,000-gallon capacity) to the terminal or distribution point and transport the gasoline directly to one service station. Since it was inefficient to have the large truck tied up making multiple deliveries, customer emphasis was on the volume gas station with tank capacity large enough to handle one large delivery. The "mom-and-pop" gasoline retailer was now considered undesirable. John Walsh stated, "In 1980 we considered a good account one that pumped 20,000 to 25,000 gallons per month, while in 1986 we consider a good account to be in the range of 40,000 to 50,000 gallons per month."

---

[4]*1985 Petroleum Marketing Databook*, pp. 15–16.

In addition to the deregulation of gasoline and crude oil prices in 1981, another regulatory development that affected oil distributors was the issuance of Environmental Protection Agency (EPA) regulations regarding leakage of gasoline from underground steel storage tanks. According to one authority, as many as 30 percent of steel tanks currently in the ground might be leaking.[5] Since both past and present owners of property with underground tanks could be held legally liable for leakage pollution, many companies were completely removing older tanks (more than 10 to 15 years old) at a cost of approximately $1,000 for a 1,000- to 3,000-gallon tank. The cost of removing and then reinstalling a similar size tank cost approximately $6,000. If there was a minor leak, clean-up costs would be approximately $5,000 extra. Liability insurance for tank leakage had become exceedingly expensive and difficult to obtain, especially for older, single-wall steel tanks.

The Current Situation

From his study of trade journals and attendance at industry conferences, John Walsh concluded basic industry trends portended a bleak future for Walsh Petroleum unless the company's strategy was changed substantially. It seemed apparent to John that his company had to do something different or get out of the business. Being relatively young, John was confident he could start a career elsewhere, but he enjoyed living in his hometown of Lancaster and like the idea of being his own boss. Furthermore, his mother was currently receiving an annual salary of $50,000 in addition to rent she received on the C-store. If they sold the company, would the proceeds generate sufficient income to replace his mother's current income?

If they decided not to sell the business, John wondered how the business could be changed. He had received an offer to purchase a competitor, Valley Oil, only weeks before.

THE VALLEY OIL ALTERNATIVE

In many respects, it seemed as though Valley Oil faced the same problems as Walsh. The two companies sold basically the same product lines, although Valley's percentage of heating fuel sales was higher than Walsh's. This aspect of Valley was attractive to John because heating fuel commanded higher margins than gasoline (25 cents per gallon versus 8 to 10 cents per gallon), and customers were a little less sensitive to price than gasoline resellers. Overall, though, Valley's unit sales were declining and unit profit margins were being squeezed. Many of Valley's contract resellers were low-volume accounts and had experienced declining sales volumes. Furthermore, their underground tanks were old.

The owner of Valley had died recently, and Valley's current 55-year-old CEO wanted to get out of the business. Valley's CEO had sent along a copy of the company's recent financial statements—see Exhibits 4 and 5. Valley's CEO said that, while the company wasn't for sale on the open market yet, he believed an $800,000 offer would buy the company.

---

[5]Steffen W. Plenn, *Underground Tankage: The Liability of Leaks* (Alexandria, Va.: Petroleum Marketing Education Foundation, 1986), pp. 9–12.

EXHIBIT 4   **Valley Oil Company's Income Statements, 1981–1985**

	1981	1982	1983	1984	1985
Gallons sold					
Premium	NA	NA	NA	NA	382,869
Unleaded	NA	NA	NA	NA	1,152,730
Regular	3,956,353	3,316,151	4,004,842	3,101,595	1,418,560
Lube	NA	NA	NA	NA	NA
Heating oil	978,113	1,004,000	1,057,131	1,137,072	1,267,011
Diesel	NA	NA	NA	NA	NA
Kerosene	286,870	286,430	262,802	310,066	315,739
Other products	NA	NA	NA	NA	NA
Total gallons sold	5,221,336	4,606,581	5,324,775	4,548,733	4,536,909
Sales revenues					
Premium	NA	NA	NA	NA	$ 298,068
Unleaded	NA	NA	NA	NA	1,038,871
Regular	NA	NA	NA	$2,831,323	1,222,758
Lube	NA	NA	NA	95,781	100,922
Heating oil	NA	NA	NA	942,600	871,031
Diesel	NA	NA	NA	NA	295,955
Kerosene	NA	NA	NA	364,573	359,583
Other products	NA	NA	NA	NA	92,493
Total sales revenues	$4,734,881	$4,332,049	$4,657,833	4,234,277	4,279,681
Cost of sales					
Beginning inventory	211,832	210,000	192,449	153,639	160,344
Purchases net of discounts	4,292,934	3,873,798	4,138,784	3,752,969	3,714,003
	4,504,766	4,083,798	4,331,233	3,906,608	3,874,347
Ending inventory	210,000	192,449	153,639	160,344	153,135
Cost of sales	4,294,766	3,891,349	4,177,594	3,746,264	3,721,212
Gross profit	440,115	440,700	480,239	488,013	558,469
Selling, general, and administrative expenses					
Licenses and nonincome taxes	23,584	24,450	25,943	25,810	22,252
Vehicle expense	100,471	61,397	85,365	74,066	81,748
Officers' salaries	45,500	49,414	48,700	51,000	53,100
Other salaries and wages	155,843	142,087	154,104	148,434	162,161
Other expenses	145,081	168,015	168,076	186,921	224,159
Depreciation	44,428	38,032	36,920	54,639	61,015
Interest on borrowing needs	10,025	3,496	5,272	7,144	11,203
Operating income (loss)	(84,817)	(46,191)	(44,141)	(60,001)	(57,169)
Earnings on marketable securities	8,746	14,493	5,134	6,426	8,103
Other income (for hauling)	72,552	74,672	90,703	96,501	95,066
Earnings before taxes	(3,519)	42,974	51,696	42,926	46,000
Provision for federal income taxes	(1,983)	4,942	10,776	707	9,049
Net income	$ (1,536)	$ 38,032	$ 40,920	$ 42,219	$ 36,951

Note: From 1981 to 1984, gallonage data are available only as aggregate gasoline sales—these are entered as regular. Likewise, during the entire five-year period, heating oil and diesel are combined under heating oil. During the same time period, dollar values are often unavailable. N/A = not available.

EXHIBIT 5   **Valley Oil Company's Balance Sheets, 1981–1985**

	1981	1982	1983	1984	1985
	Assets				
Current assets					
Cash	$ 64,468	$ 31,922	$ 24,076	$ 10,000	$ 26,558
Accounts receivable	656,187	579,313	471,803	470,120	421,308
Inventories	210,000	192,449	153,639	160,344	153,135
Refundable taxes	33,054	0	0	9,920	3,888
Prepaid expenses	2,636	1,535	1,526	1,766	25,883
Notes receivable	1,804	40,277	14,481	59,342	5,099
Total current assets	968,149	845,496	665,525	711,492	635,871
Property, plant, and equipment					
Land	79,942	79,942	79,942	79,942	79,942
Buildings	0	0	0	0	0
Equipment	207,463	216,139	208,116	207,873	227,444
Vehicles	247,339	274,634	253,153	279,634	255,355
Furniture and fixtures	5,032	21,588	22,393	24,388	30,464
Total	539,776	592,303	563,604	591,837	593,205
Less accumulated depreciation	392,800	430,332	427,310	392,465	422,781
Net property plant and equipment	146,976	161,971	136,294	199,372	170,424
Other assets					
Long-term investments	0	0	0	0	0
Deposits and licenses	0	0	0	0	0
Cash surrender value—officers' life insurance	0	0	0	0	0
Loan fees—net	0	0	0	0	0
Advances to affiliated companies	0	0	0	0	0
Total other assets	0	0	0	0	0
Total assets	$1,115,125	$1,007,467	$801,819	$910,864	$806,295
	Liabilities and Stockholders' Equity				
Current liabilities					
Accounts payable	$ 670,524	$ 474,892	$272,434	$295,092	$196,670
Notes payable	0	45,000	0	50,000	0
Income taxes payable	0	4,942	5,832	0	6,899
Total current liabilities	670,524	524,834	278,266	345,092	203,569
Long-term debt	0	0	0	0	0
Total liabilities	670,524	524,834	278,266	345,092	203,569
Owners' equity	444,601	482,633	523,553	565,772	602,726
Total liabilities and owners' equity	$1,115,125	$1,007,467	$801,819	$910,864	$806,295

John thought that acquiring Valley Oil could offer some unique advantages—advantages that many other potential acquirers could not realize. First, many of the selling and administrative expenses that Valley incurred could be performed by Walsh's personnel. A potential buyer from outside the industry would probably have substantially higher operating costs than John would have.

EXHIBIT 6   **Gallons Pumped at Valley Oil's 18 Station Locations, 1985**

Stations*	1985 Gallonages
1	346,279
2	160,316
3	128,620
4	111,702
5	105,036
6	116,286
7	37,894
8	19,746
9	121,440
10[†]	244,802
11	304,772
12	189,422
13	196,152
14	148,226
15	47,118
16	130,472
17	100,106
18	220,440
Total	2,728,829

*Reseller locations with contracts ranging from two to five years.
†Wholly owned by Valley Oil with appraised value of $100,000 (good potential, four-lane interceptor, C-store location).

Rather than beginning his analysis with what employees he would be able to eliminate from Valley's payroll, John decided to examine how many people he would have to add to Walsh Petroleum to serve Valley's customers. He figured that initially he would need at least two additional clerks to handle the scheduling and the billing for Valley accounts. Two additional full-time drivers would be needed for deliveries and two seasonal drivers for fuel oil. Salaries for clerks and drivers were estimated at $9,000 and $18,000 a year, respectively, and fringe benefits would probably add about 35 percent. John thought he could get someone to manage the new business at $30,000 (benefits included). John also felt that if he could get his computerized account system running within a year for approximately $40,000 he might be able to eventually eliminate one of the clerks. John was also pleased with the thought that the Valley acquisition would allow him to spread the significant upfront investment in hardware and software over a greater number of accounts, and by adding a delivery scheduling module to the computer system, he should be able to schedule his deliveries more efficiently. In addition, John's accountant recommended that he use a conservative tax rate of 30 percent in his analysis of Valley. Exhibit 6 shows the gallonages at Valley Oil's 18 locations. Exhibit 7 shows the age, capacity, and other characteristics of the underground tanks at various Valley Oil locations.

Even with the operating savings John might be able to utilize, Valley would probably be an attractive acquisition to some of the large distributors in the

EXHIBIT 7   **Characteristics of Underground Tanks at Valley Oil Sites**

Sites*	Capacity	Age	Type	Product
1	4,000 gallons	12 years	Steel	Gasoline
	4,000	12	Steel	Gasoline
	3,000	25	Steel	Gasoline
	4,000	25	Steel	Gasoline
	3,000	25	Steel	Gasoline
2	2,000	7	Steel	Gasoline
	2,000	7	Steel	Gasoline
	1,000	2	Steel	Gasoline
3	1,000	8	Steel	Gasoline
	1,000	8	Steel	Gasoline
4	1,000	10	Steel	Gasoline
	1,000	10	Steel	Gasoline
	1,000	10	Steel	Gasoline
5	2,000	20	Steel	Gasoline
	1,000	20	Steel	Gasoline
	1,000	20	Steel	Gasoline
6	1,000	12	Steel	Gasoline
	1,000	10	Steel	Diesel
	1,000	10	Steel	Diesel
7	1,000	15	Steel	Gasoline
	1,000	15	Steel	Gasoline
	2,000	10	Steel	Gasoline
	1,000	1	Steel	Gasoline
	1,000	1	Steel	Gasoline
8	1,000	25	Steel	Gasoline
	2,000	3	Steel	Gasoline
	2,000	3	Steel	Gasoline
	2,000	3	Steel	Gasoline
9	2,000	10	Steel	Gasoline
	4,000	11	Steel	Gasoline
	3,000	11	Steel	Gasoline
	3,000	11	Steel	Gasoline
	1,000	11	Steel	Gasoline
10	1,000	12	Steel	Gasoline
	1,000	5	Steel	Gasoline
11	1,000	15	Steel	Diesel
	1,000	15	Steel	Gasoline
12	10,000	15	Steel	Gasoline
	4,000	15	Steel	Gasoline
	4,000	15	Steel	Gasoline
	1,000	15	Steel	Kerosene
13	1,000	12	Steel	Gasoline
	1,000	12	Steel	Gasoline
	1,000	12	Steel	Gasoline

*Sites include reseller locations, large individual users, and bulk plant (number 21).

Sites*	Capacity	Age	Type	Product
14	2,000	14	Steel	Gasoline
	1,000	14	Steel	Gasoline
15	1,000	12	Steel	Gasoline
	1,000	12	Steel	Diesel
	2,000	12	Steel	Fuel oil
16	10,000	10	Steel	Gasoline
	2,000	10	Steel	Gasoline
17	2,000	10	Steel	Gasoline
18	1,000	5	Steel	Gasoline
	1,000	5	Steel	Gasoline
19	1,000	9	Steel	Gasoline
	1,000	9	Steel	Gasoline
	1,000	9	Steel	Gasoline
20	10,000	35	Steel	Diesel
21	20,000	15	Steel	Fuel oil
	20,000	15	Steel	Fuel oil
	20,000	15	Steel	Fuel oil
	20,000	15	Steel	Fuel oil
	20,000	15	Steel	Gasoline
	20,000	15	Steel	Gasoline
	20,000	15	Steel	Gasoline
	20,000	15	Steel	Gasoline
	10,000	15	Steel	Gasoline
	6,266	35	Steel	Kerosene
	6,266	35	Steel	Kerosene
	5,631	35	Steel	Kerosene
	6,266	35	Steel	Kerosene
	6,266	35	Steel	Kerosene
	6,266	35	Steel	Kerosene
	6,769	35	Steel	Kerosene
22	4,000	10	Steel	Gasoline
	4,000	10	Steel	Gasoline
	3,000	10	Steel	Gasoline
	3,000	25	Steel	Gasoline
	3,000	25	Steel	Gasoline
23	1,000	20	Steel	Gasoline
	1,000	20	Steel	Gasoline
24	2,000	7	Steel	Gasoline
	1,000	7	Steel	Gasoline
	1,000	7	Steel	Gasoline
	1,000	7	Steel	Kerosene
25	2,000	11	Steel	Gasoline
	2,000	11	Steel	Gasoline

nearby city. Compared to the fierce competition in that city, John's trading area would probably look very attractive to them. While John's knowledge of the local market gave him an advantage, the larger city-based distributors could achieve many of the operating cost savings John was contemplating. By purchasing Valley, John believed his gross profit margin would improve due to a reduced level of competition.

The more John thought about the possibility of combining Walsh and Valley, the more likely it seemed he wouldn't need most of Valley's physical assets to service the accounts he would be acquiring. John had scheduled a lunch with Valley's CEO to discuss the possible acquisition. John's hopes of acquiring Valley's customers only were quickly dashed. Valley's CEO stated that if he was getting out of the business, he was going to sell the whole business as a unit, not hold a "rummage sale." Moreover, he seemed firm about the price of $800,000. The rise in Valley's gross profit margin in 1985 had continued through the first half of 1986 because of the unprecedented drop in oil prices and "sticky" retail prices. However, John knew Valley's CEO would want to sell the business this year before long-term capital gains rates expired.

A big issue in John's mind was how to finance the acquisition. Neither he nor his mother had enough liquid funds outside the business to acquire Valley. Valley's owners indicated they might be willing to hold a note, but they would require certain covenants regarding Walsh Petroleum's financial condition in order to protect their position. Also, personal guarantees from John, his mother, and his brothers would be required. John decided to try to get Valley's owners to finance 75 percent of the acquisition price over 10 years. While he would have to pay a premium over the prime rate, in his opinion it might still be a good investment.

To help him in his deliberations about the Valley Oil acquisition, John employed an independent consultant to Valley Oil. Excerpts from the consultant's report are shown in Exhibit 8. John was somewhat skeptical about the consultant's conclusions, however, because the consultant did not have experience in the petroleum business.

THE C-STORE ALTERNATIVE

One of the relative bright spots in Walsh Petroleum's operation had been the C-store. C-stores originated as a convenient alternative to the traditional grocery store, and the premise that consumers would pay higher than grocery store prices in exchange for convenience proved correct. Since customers typically bought only a few items, checkout lines were very short. C-stores carried a relatively limited product line of items generally regarded as necessities. Milk, bread, snack foods, cigarettes, beer, and soft drinks made up a substantial percentage of C-store sales. Although a majority of C-stores carried a very similar product mix, opportunities did exist for C-store operators to differentiate themselves. A number of operators offered video rentals, hot food service (hot dogs, pizza, and so on), and other amenities. Geographic location was also a critical success factor. Customers selected a C-store based on its proximity to their home or their daily route of travel.

Many motor fuel operators had taken the traditional gas station, closed the maintenance bays, and remodeled them into small convenience stores

EXHIBIT 8   **Excerpts from Consultant's Report on the Value of Valley Oil Company**

Income-Based Value

In any discounted, income-based valuation, two factors must be determined: the discount rate and the earnings base. Theoretically, the discount rate can be assumed to be the rate of return an investor could earn on a portfolio of similar risk assets. As a starting point, one can consider that for the week of August 1, the Standard and Poor's 10-bond utility average yielded 9.03 percent. This range of 9 percent is consistent with performance over recent months and actually is low for the past decade. Working from this starting point, one can logically assume that there would have to be some risk premium; therefore, a minimum capitalization rate would be 10 percent. As an earnings base, one can use a weighted average of the last five years. This both eliminates any unusual blip in the last year and takes into account the overall trend.

Year	Weight Factor	Income	W × I
1981	1	$ (1,536)	$ (1,536)
1982	2	38,032	76,064
1983	3	40,920	122,760
1984	4	42,219	168,876
1985	5	36,951	184,755
	15		$550,919

Weighted average earnings = $36,728

When this average earnings figure is capitalized at 10 percent, an income-based valuation of $367,280 emerges. Using a more reasonable discount rate of 12 percent yields a value of $306,067.

Adjusted Asset Value

Another step that must be taken in any valuation is an assessment of the asset value of the company. If the market-related asset value is higher than the income-based value, then the business has negative operating value and is worth more liquidated.

When this step is taken with Valley, the analysis is fairly simple. All of the current assets can be liquidated at their book value except for accounts receivables. These must be carried across to market less a 10 percent bad debt adjustment. This brings the value of total current assets to $620,557.

Adjustments for the fixed assets are a bit more complex. First, the land/buildings account must be adjusted to $100,000 market value. Equipment, with the exception of tanks, is valued at about $20,000 (79 pumps @ $250). The vehicles have an appraised market value of $156,500. The market value for furniture and fixtures is $7,050, giving a total market value to long-term assets of $283,550. The next step to be followed is to deduct any liabilities. These are deducted at book value of $203,569.

The final step in the adjusted asset valuation is to consider any hidden assets or liabilities. These can take several forms:

• Undervalued real estate which would actually bring much more than its book value.

• Exclusive distribution contracts or other market-related, hidden assets.

• Contingent liabilities such as pending lawsuits or potential lawsuits from sources such as leaking underground tanks.

The first of these is ruled out by the fact that Valley owns only one piece of real estate, which was recently appraised and is included in the valuation at its appraised value of $100,000. Neither does the second factor enter into the value—Valley has no unique market-related advantages.

The question of contingent liabilities is important; the possibility that one or more of the approximately 90 tanks could develop or already possess a leak is far from remote. According to Steffen Plenn, author of *Underground Tankage: The Liability of Leaks*, as many as 30 percent of the steel tanks currently in the ground may be leaking. What's worse, that number is expected to rise. The volatile nature of this problem is most clearly seen in its propensity to wind up in court. Plenn explains that these leaks, when discovered, are disasters of a magnitude that will not avoid court.* The most serious

EXHIBIT 8   *(Concluded)*

implication, however, is that the liability has historically extended to all owners of the tanks, both past and present, vis-a-vis the concept of joint and several liability. Thus, in the process of any rationally executed liquidation, the seller would have to remove each of the older tanks. In the case of Valley, this cost would amount to approximately $90,000. Deducting this contingent tank liability (cost of removal) from the previously computed values yields a liquidation value of $610,538.

Conclusion

This now presents us with two different values for consideration:

1. The income-based value of $367,280.
2. The adjusted asset liquidation basis of $610,538.

Realizing that

- The liquidation value exceeds the income-based value;
- There is a trend toward decreasing blue-sky premiums;
- Goodwill is usually paid for growing or unusually profitable gallons, of which Valley has none;
- There is a significant contingent liability attached to the tanks, all of which cannot be eliminated by tank removal (due to potential for previous leaks);
- Valley is a declining firm in a mature industry.

We recommend use of the adjusted asset liquidation value of $610,538 as our best estimate of market value.

*Steffen W. Plenn, *Underground Tankage: The Liability of Leaks* (Alexandria, Va.: Petroleum Marketing Education Foundation, 1986), pp. 9–12.

(800 to 1,200 square feet) with gasoline pumps out front. Likewise, convenience store operators, such as Southland (7-Eleven), added self-service gas pumps. According to the National Association of Convenience Stores, gasoline margins averaged 7.3 percent, while nongasoline margins averaged 32.2 percent.[6]

In early 1982 the Walshes had commissioned a marketing consulting group to conduct a feasibility study of a C-store location adjacent to the fuel oil distributorship. The location had approximately 300 feet of frontage on a major highway, and the traffic count looked as though it would make the operation feasible. Mr. Walsh, Sr., had remodeled an existing two-bay station, and within two years the unit was meeting and then exceeding the marketing consultants' projections.

Walsh Petroleum currently owned an unoccupied two-bay service station on a corner lot with good access from all directions and a stable traffic flow in a growing nearby community. In the past the Walshes had leased the property to a number of service station operators. None of them had made a success of the operation, and it was John's opinion that the day of the traditional two-bay station was past its prime. Customers wanted either the pricing and convenience of a self-service station or a super-premium station that provided clearly superior maintenance and service. The turnover of operators was consuming much of Walsh's time, and the station would often sit empty.

[6]"Why the C-Store Image Race Could Lead to a Shakeout," *National Petroleum News*, September 1987, p. 40.

T A B L E 3   **C-Store Estimated Costs**

Appraised value of lot	$100,000
Building ($\approx$ $60 per square foot for 2,400 sq.ft. of C-store)	144,400
Market research	1,000
Equipment costs	
Gas equipment	150,000
Food equipment	60,000
Canopy	17,500
Capitalized site plan (consultant)	20,000
Inventory	
Food	40,000
Fuel	14,500
Net operating capital	20,000
Total	$567,400
Salvage value	
Gas equipment	$ 13,500
Food equipment	6,000
Canopy	1,750
Capitalized site plan	0
Asset lives	
Gas equipment	5 years
Food equipment	7 years
Canopy	10 years
Site plan and building	31.5 years
Depreciation method	
Gas, food, and canopy equipment	Double declining balance
Site plan and building	Straight line

John believed it might be possible to demolish the station and erect a C-store with self-serve gasoline pumps on the site. To investigate this possibility, John commissioned the same market research firm that had provided the feasibility study for the original C-store to analyze the new location. This firm had developed a forecasting model that would generate fairly accurate sales estimates for both gasoline and in-store sales for a C-store. Among the many variables included in the model were highway traffic flow, store size and layout, distance to the nearest existing C-store, as well as a variety of demographic data on the area. John's corner lot had a traffic count of 14,000 vehicles per day on the main road and 4,000 vehicles a day on the side street. The resulting sales forecast for gasoline was 915,000 gallons a year, reached by the end of year 2, and first year sales of 410,000 gallons. Kerosene sales were forecast at 7,500 gallons in year 1 and 10,000 gallons per annum thereafter. Inside sales items totaled $213,000 (year 1), $428,000 (year 2), maturing at $530,000 in year 3. Expected margins were 50 cents a gallon for kerosene, 8 cents a gallon for gasoline, and 32 percent for inside sales.

John also retained an architectural firm as a design consultant. Table 3 shows the costs that had been estimated under John's close supervision. Another option John had was to build a C-store using his major oil supplier's generic C-store design plan. The generic design included a smaller C-store (40 by 50 feet) under a 90 by 40 feet canopy with pumps on either side of the store (35 feet from pump to entrance). The advantage to this design was that the major oil company would refund Walsh 2 cents per gallon on all gallons sold (up to 150,000 gallons per month) for 36 months and provide a detailed site plan without charge. John felt he would lose some inside sales with the oil supplier's fatter margins and he wouldn't get to build his own C-store identity and goodwill. The overall cost would be approximately the same for the two options, and John was uncertain which choice was best from a marketing point of view.

Based on those of his other store, John estimated the operating expenses per annum for the new store as follows: salaries and benefits for a 126-hour week at $80,000, utilities at $14,000, property taxes at $2,000, and other miscellaneous expenses at $20,000.

While the research pertaining to the original C-store had been highly accurate, John wondered how reliable the model could be in forecasting future sales for the proposed C-store. Because even the major highways were relatively undeveloped in his rural market, there were desirable road frontage locations near his site. A one-acre site directly across the street could be used for a C-store location. While he had considered buying the property as a defensive move, he felt he really couldn't afford to buy it at $150,000.

John felt that the threat of new C-store competitors was very real. Even though a half-million-dollar investment for a C-store was a substantial investment to John, this sum might look like a bargain to the major C-store chains that had been paying up to $1 million for prime suburban locations. Surely, John reasoned, a competing C-store within a mile or two of his location would hurt the validity of his financial projections. The design consultant had added a drive-in window at a cost of approximately $25,000 to differentiate the store and build customer loyalty. John felt a drive-in window would add 15 percent annually to projected inside sales.

At a recent petroleum distributors conference, John discussed his C-store plans with several fellow distributors. Most felt that the generic C-store designs offered by the major oil companies were too small to provide the maximum level of in-store sales, particularly in a rural market. They questioned the wisdom of the drive-in window, suggesting a car-wash operation instead.

While John believed the C-store alternative had potential, he also was aware that the move had its risks. Nationally, the number of C-stores had increased rapidly. At the end of 1981 there were 38,000 C-stores, and only 16,416 of these sold gasoline. Just four years later, the C-store population had reached 61,000, with 33,500 selling gasoline.[7]

There was general agreement in the industry that the danger of C-store saturation was greatest in suburban areas, but substantial opportunities remained in both urban and rural markets. One rural operator, who competed successfully in towns with as few as 1,000 residents, said, "For the rest of the industry, the mark-up on gas is 6 to 8 cents a gallon, while we get 8 to 10 cents. Often we are the only gas station in town."[8] While gas margins would be higher in rural areas, C-stores often increased margins on other products as

[7]Ibid., p. 41.
[8]"Rural versus Urban: A Site Selection Dilemma," *Convenience Store News*, July 13–August 2, 1987, p. 54.

well. Fast foods and video rentals were extremely profitable in the absence of strong competitors. Pizza, for example, carried a 70 percent profit margin. One C-store/pizza vendor said the pizza concept probably wouldn't work in cities where people could go to a Pizza Hut, "but out in the rural areas, there's no place else to get a good pizza."[9]

Until recently, most of the competitors in the C-store industry were convenience store chains, such as Southland, and locations operated by independent oil distributors. There were increasing indications that the big oil refiners were entering the industry in force. Eight refiner/supplier oil companies, such as Texaco, Mobil, and Exxon, were ranked in the top 50 C-store operators. Many industry observers expected that the entry of the big-oil-owned C-stores would touch off a price war in the industry, particularly in the in-store segment. The rationale behind this expectation was that oil companies would lower in-store merchandise mark-ups in order to increase pump gallonage. However, the major oil companies had tended to concentrate on the urban areas, leaving the rural markets to the distributors.

THE FUTURE OF WALSH OIL

During one of the recent executive education programs John had attended, a few sessions had been devoted to evaluating investment opportunities. He knew he should try to determine an appropriate hurdle rate to use. There were some discussions at these sessions about calculating a cost of capital, but that seemed too academic and complicated. Instead, he went to the library and looked up various interest rates and decided to add a couple of percentage points to them. He figured a small company like his would have to pay somewhere between 2 and 5 percent over the going rate. The interest rates as of August 1986 are listed in Table 4.

As he reviewed his notes from the training session, John found that real estate investments were evaluated differently from other types of investments. Rather than using the total acquisition price as a measure of investment, real estate investments were analyzed on the basis of equity cash investment to determine the payback. One of John's friends in the real estate business told him that, rather than using the purchase price of the acquisition as a measure of its cost, he should use the down payment, or the immediate cash investment, as the cost measure and calculate a levered rate of return on investment.

John scheduled an initial meeting with his banker to see what type of financing he might be able to obtain. While the banker expressed interest in the C-store, he didn't believe the bank would be willing to lend funds for the acquisition of Valley Oil. "John, it's just too risky for us," he said. "Valley's assets just aren't liquid enough to qualify as high-quality collateral. With those old tanks and trucks, we would never get our money out. Now, the C-store is something I could sell to the loan committee. It's my guess that we could finance 80 percent of the land and building at 11.5 percent for 15 years.[10] In addition, we would finance 80 percent of the equipment including the site plan over 7 years at a 9.75 percent fixed rate."

---

[9]Ibid.

[10]It should be noted that the bank is refinancing land that Walsh currently owns.

T A B L E   4   **Selected Interest Rates, August 1986**

Prime rate charged by banks	7.75%
U.S. Treasury bonds—10 years	7.17%
Corporate bonds—Aaa seasoned	8.72%
Home mortgages—FHLBB	10.26%

The banker paused, as if unsure how to proceed. "You know, John, what I'm about to bring up is somewhat sensitive," he said, "so just tell me to stop if I'm out of line. I've watched you work like a dog over the past year to turn your business around, but at some point you have to start thinking about yourself. You can work like hell for 30 years and still only be a minority stockholder. If your mother and two brothers wanted to sell out at some point in the future, all your efforts, not to mention your career, are down the drain.

"Here's an alternative you might just think about," said the banker. "Walsh Petroleum owns the C-store site you are talking about developing. Why don't you buy the land personally and construct the C-store on it? We here at the bank would lend you the money, although we would probably have to have Walsh Petroleum guarantee the loan. You could then lease the C-store back to Walsh Petroleum and start building up some personal equity for yourself through the real estate investment."

As John Walsh pondered his alternatives, one thing seemed certain to him— he would have to act soon. Many of his friends he met at the trade association meetings seemed to be complacent about the pressure on their industry, but as John glanced at the financial statements again, he knew that a few more years like these past two would threaten not only his family's financial security, but his own as well. After all, he was really the only member of the family whose income was directly related to the future of Walsh Petroleum. He remembered the discussion of these issues at a recent dinner with his mother and brothers.

"John, I agree with the idea of expanding the business, and I think it would have pleased your dad," said Mrs. Walsh, "but you have to remember that Walsh Petroleum is really all I have. If we take on too much debt, and get into trouble, I don't know what I'll do in my old age."

"I see your point, Mom," said John, "but the fact is that I'm the only one in the family who is devoting the rest of my life to running the business. You already own C-store 1, and Richard and Daniel either don't want to be in the business or aren't sure yet. I don't want to sound selfish, but my interest in the business is only 16 percent. I don't want to wake up when I'm 50 and find that I've spent my whole life running this business for the rest of the family and have relatively little to show for it."

Richard puffed on his pipe and said, "John, I'm not sure the C-store alternative is a good idea for the family business. Sure, it's a good deal for you personally, but the rest of us have to guarantee your loan at the bank. I think Walsh Petroleum should give serious consideration to the Valley Oil deal."

"And why do you think that Valley is better than the C-store?" asked John.

"The main reason," Richard replied, "is that Walsh Petroleum is primarily a gasoline distributor. The original C-store was a great idea of Dad's, but the oil business is this family's cash cow. This is an opportunity to take out a competitor. We all agree there aren't a whole lot of new people going into this business, but if a big gasoline distributor in the region buys Valley, then Walsh Petroleum has got some major problems on its hands. The increased competition could certainly lower our gross margin 1 to 2 cents a gallon, and we all know that there are two large distributors that are interested in Valley."

"But, Richard, can't you see that we're in a declining industry?" said John. "If you looked at those financials I sent you, it should be obvious that our gallonage has been declining for several years."

"What do you think, Daniel?" asked Mrs. Walsh. "After all, it's as much your business as it is John's or Richard's."

"I think that John and Richard both have good points," said Daniel. "While John is the only one of us three in the business now, I may want to join the company when I finish school, and I really don't care to be a clerk in a convenience store. And while John certainly has a right to try to accumulate some wealth, I don't know that using the family business's credit rating to guarantee his personal investments is really fair to the rest of us. After all, John is at least getting a decent salary, and Richard and I don't even receive any dividends."

"Wait a second, Dan," said John, somewhat resentfully. "I'm not riding a gravy train here. My $30,000 salary at Walsh is no higher than what my market worth is, and especially the way things are going, my upside potential is much lower than I could get working for someone else. Even more importantly, the family couldn't find anyone else to do this job for any less than what I'm getting."

The family discussion had ended without resolving anything, but John was certain the business would be worth substantially less if he was unable to turn the operation around. Aside from the purely financial considerations, John knew that the major oil companies were now evaluating their distributors on sales levels and sales growth. A distributor in an attractive market who wasn't showing the appropriate level of sales or sales growth might soon find itself without a supply contract.

Further, while John was eager to stop the decline in the company's financial performance, he also felt strongly that the business plan he developed now should lay the foundation for the business growth for the next 5 to 10 years. The questions in his mind were, "How do we do it, and is it worth the trouble?"

BOMBARDIER LTD.*

Joseph Lampel, New York University
Jamal Shamsie, McGill University

I want a company with a continuous flow that is not subject to the drastic fluctuations of being in just one business.

These were the words of Laurent Beaudoin, chairman of Bombardier, as he contemplated his company's dramatic rise to prominence during the 1960s and 1970s.[1] The Canadian company's name had been at one point synonymous with snowmobiles. Its pioneering efforts in the development and the launching of the Ski-Doo had been handsomely rewarded. By the late 1960s, Bombardier controlled close to 50 percent of the snowmobile market, about three times as much as its closest competitor (see Exhibit 1).

Laurent Beaudoin had long believed that the fortunes of this company were too closely tied to a single product. Thus, even before the demand for snowmobiles began to slow, Bombardier took steps to insulate itself from the uncertainties of the recreational market. Throughout the 1970s, Beaudoin led the company on an aggressive strategy of diversification into other areas of leisure and transportation. As the company moved into the 1980s, its revenues had grown considerably beyond the $165 million it had generated from snowmobiles at the start of the previous decade. But while Bombardier's revenues grew dramatically, it continued to experience wide swings in profits. In 1981 and 1982 Bombardier lost money (see Exhibit 2); the 1982 loss was the biggest in company history.

GROWING WITH SNOWMOBILES

Work on the snowmobile started in the mid-1920s by Joseph-Armand Bombardier in his father's garage at Valcourt, Quebec. But it took until 1935 before Joseph-Armand had built the first snowmobile. It consisted of a large plywood body set on caterpillar tracks and driven by a heavy, conventional internal combustion engine.

These early snowmobiles were hand-assembled in versions intended to accommodate from 5 to 25 passengers. In each case, the machine was individually adapted for a specific use according to the wishes of different customers. By 1942, Joseph-Armand had incorporated his garage to form Bombardier Snowmobile Limited and was producing snowmobiles to serve doctors, missionaries, woodcutters, foresters, trappers, and farmers in outlying districts of Quebec.

With the advent of World War II, the basic snowmobile design was adapted to produce an amphitrack armored carrier called the "Penguin" for use by

---

*Copyright © 1988, by Joseph Lampel and Jamal Shamsie.

[1]"Bombardier: Making a Second Leap from Snowmobiles to Mass Transit," *Business Week*, February 23, 1981.

EXHIBIT 1   **Bombardier's Snowmobile Sales, 1963–1986**

Season	Industry	Bombardier	Bombardier's Market Share
1963–64	17,000	8,000	47%
1964–65	30,000	14,000	47
1965–66	60,000	26,000	43
1966–67	120,000	48,000	40
1967–68	170,000	78,000	46
1968–69	250,000	120,000	48
1969–70	415,000	170,000	41
1970–71	540,000	195,000	36
1971–72	530,000	190,000	36
1972–73	515,000	150,000	29
1973–74	400,000	110,000	28
1974–75	330,000	84,000	25
1975–76	245,000	67,000	27
1976–77	195,000	62,000	32
1977–78	225,000	68,000	30
1978–79	270,000	72,000	27
1979–80	200,000	55,000	28
1980–81	180,000	60,000	33
1981–82	145,000	55,000	38
1982–83	105,000	37,000	35
1983–84	115,000	38,000	33
1984–85	100,000	34,000	34
1985–86	110,000	39,000	35

Source: Bombardier annual reports.

Canadian troops. Subsequently, the demonstrated durability and ruggedness of the snowmobile also led to the development and production of various forms of specialized industrial equipment. These consisted of machines that were especially suited for use in forestry, logging, oil exploration, and snow removal.

Eventually, Joseph-Armand and his son Germain tackled the challenge of developing and producing a smaller and lighter version of the basic snowmobile design intended to carry one or two persons. The key to the new design was the coupling of a recently introduced two-cycle motor-scooter engine with an all-rubber track that had internal steel rods built in for added strength. By 1959, the first snowmobile directed at the individual user was introduced. Initially, Joseph-Armand thought of calling his invention the Ski-Dog, but he decided in favor of a more bilingual name, the Ski-Doo.

Development of the Snowmobile

When he died in 1964, Joseph-Armand left behind a company that had 700 employees and a product that was enjoying increasing popularity. Some 16,500

EXHIBIT 2   **Bombardier's Consolidated Income Statements, 1981–1986**
(In millions of Canadian dollars)

| | For the Year Ended January 31 | | | | | |
	1981	1982	1983	1984	1985	1986
Net sales	$394.4	$448.8	$551.1	$491.0	$515.5	$656.6
Cost of sales	310.8	368.1	452.6	418.9	428.8	557.5
Selling and administrative	72.2	85.4	62.1	50.0	58.7	56.2
Depreciation and amortization	8.1	9.9	11.3	10.8	15.6	21.5
Other income	(1.0)	(0.5)	(2.7)	(7.5)	(11.2)	(12.2)
Interest on long-term debt	3.1	8.3	7.5	5.6	6.7	5.2
Other interest	9.4	11.5	10.1	2.8	0.1	1.6
Income taxes	(2.4)	(15.4)	4.1	4.1	6.7	10.7
Net income (loss)	$ (5.8)	$ (18.5)	$ 6.1	$ 6.3	$ 10.1	$ 16.1

Source: Bombardier annual reports.

Ski-Doos had been sold, and demand was clearly on the rise. Germain took over as president but shortly after relinquished his post for health reasons. The company passed into the hands of son-in-law Laurent Beaudoin, a chartered accountant and one of the first management graduates of the University of Sherbrooke. Beaudoin realized certain factors were standing in the way of the development of the full potential of the snowmobile.

> There were two fundamental problems arising from the nature of the company's beginnings. First, there was no research and development department because it had all taken place in the mind of Joseph-Armand Bombardier. Second, the company which he created was, very naturally, a production-oriented company. It produced machines to fill a market need, which was mainly for large machines to do practical jobs, rather than creating and seeking out new markets.[2]

Beaudoin introduced an R&D section, set up an integrated marketing system, and geared up facilities for efficient mass production. Extensive research confirmed that an untapped snowmobile market existed not only for transport, but also for recreation and sport. Bombardier invested heavily in the development of this potential market. Over the next several years, massive advertising, combined with the establishment of a dealership network, culminated in the creation of 18 regional sales groups covering Canada, the United States, and Europe. These efforts resulted in making Bombardier a leader in the snowmobile market and turned the Ski-Doo trademark into a generic term for snowmobiles.

But the success of Bombardier also brought about the entry of new producers of snowmobiles. Most of the new competition came from U.S. companies that had been closely watching the development of the snowmobile business. Beaudoin, however, was not fazed at the prospect of more competition. He was confident about the capabilities of his company to maintain its leadership:

---

[2]"Bombardier Skids to Success," *International Management*, January 1972.

It's an industry that looks very simple. Everybody looks and says, "Gee, we can get in tomorrow morning and grab everything." But it's not that simple. The advantage we have over all those companies is that we eat snow, we know snow, and are snowmobilers ourselves.[3]

In order to ensure that it could meet this growing competition, Beaudoin also decided to start acquiring all of his suppliers, most of which were situated within the province of Quebec. These acquisitions led to the development of a series of subsidiaries and affiliates that manufactured parts or accessories related to snowmobile production. This push for acquisitions eventually climaxed in the $30 million purchase of Rotax-Werk A. G. Located in Austria, Rotax-Werk manufactured the two-stroke engines used in the Ski-Doos. By 1970, Bombardier's own production facilities or those of its subsidiaries and affiliates were supplying over 90 percent of the 1,400 parts that went into the manufacturing of the Ski-Doo. Beaudoin saw these moves as a necessary precaution against an eventual intensification of competition, in particular the likely outbreak of price wars: "If there is any price war, we will be in a position to face it. This has been our first idea."[4]

Shortly after, Bombardier moved to buy out its largest competitor. In 1971, it finalized the acquisition of Moto-Ski from its U.S. parent, Giffin Industries. This acquisition consolidated Bombardier's domination of the snowmobile market. By this time, the achievements and stature of Bombardier were acclaimed as a product of Canadian imagination and entrepreneurial vigor. An article, published at the beginning of 1972, bestowed praise upon the company:

> Not many companies can claim to have started an entirely new industry—fewer still to have done so and stayed ahead of the pack. Bombardier Ltd. has done just that.... It is a company owned and managed by Canadians, which several foreign companies would dearly love to own. It is the largest Quebec-owned company operating in the province, and is one of the 200 most profitable public companies in Canada.[5]

The Crunch for Snowmobiles

The early 1970s saw an increasing number of companies competing in the snowmobile market. In addition to new American and Canadian firms, Bombardier saw the entry of Swedish, Italian, and Japanese manufacturers. Yet while the number of competitors was increasing, market growth in snowmobiles was slowing.

Several reasons were advanced for the softening of snowmobile sales. The main blame was put on the stagnant economy, which was seen as the principal cause of the decline in demand. Snowmobiles constituted a type of purchase that was often postponed by consumers during a downturn in the economy. Other reasons were more peculiar to the snowmobile market. Poor winters, with late snow and unusually low precipitation, reduced the recreational use of snowmobiles. At the same time, newspaper stories of crashes and decapitated riders led to a mounting concern over the safety of snowmobiles.

---

[3]"Snow Job?" *Forbes*, February 1, 1970.
[4]Ibid.
[5]"Bombardier Skids to Success."

Finally, environmentalists were vocal in their criticism of the high noise levels generated by snowmobiles, particularly in wilderness areas.

There was growing awareness that stricter legislation covering the design and use of snowmobiles was likely to be forthcoming. For its part, Bombardier attempted to meet these concerns by trying to design better safety features and special mufflers for their upcoming snowmobile models. It also produced films, slides, and brochures on safety measures and the proper use of the snowmobile. Furthermore, a newly created public relations department tried to involve the various levels of government and different types of businesses in the creation of a system comparable to the one found in the ski industry. This was to include the development of snowmobile trails, snowmobile weekends, and snowmobile resorts.

Early in 1973 it looked like demand would increase again; but the sudden fuel crisis dampened the hopes of Bombardier. Its sales of snowmobiles continued to decline sharply, down from the high of 195,000 units sold during the winter of 1970–71 (see Exhibit 1). This was accompanied by consecutive losses of $5.8 million in 1973 and $7.3 million in 1974.

Beaudoin attributed the poor performance of Bombardier to the general state of the snowmobile industry. But eventually he acknowledged that Bombardier's position in the depressed snowmobile market had also been slipping. From a 40 percent share in 1970, based on the Ski-Doo alone, the company's share had declined to about 25 percent for the combined Ski-Doo and Motor-Ski brands. The competition had been closing in on Bombardier's leadership, causing it to have second thoughts about the merits of the industry it had pioneered.

MOVING AWAY FROM SNOWMOBILES

In 1974 Bombardier seized an opportunity to bid on a four-year $118 million contract to build 423 new cars for the proposed extension of the Montreal subway system. The bid represented a major departure from the core business of the company. It was not, however, the first time Bombardier had ventured away from snowmobiles.

Early Moves

Even before the snowmobile market was developed, Bombardier had been producing all-terrain tracked and wheeled vehicles for different kinds of industrial use. The company had continuously developed and marketed many basic types or sizes of vehicles for work in swamps, forests, and snow. The earliest of these were the Muskeg series of carriers, tractors, and brush cutters that were used in logging, construction, petroleum, and mining. Later developments included the SW series for urban snow removal, the Skidozer line for grooming snowmobile trails and ski slopes, and the Bombi carrier for transporting people over snowy or marshy terrain.

A further departure from snowmobiles came as a result of Bombardier's acquisition of suppliers. Originally, the acquisitions were undertaken to consolidate the company's position in the snowmobile market. Once made, they presented attractive opportunities. For example, Rotax-Werk was acquired in 1970 because it supplied the engines that were used on Ski-Doos, but it also manufactured engines for boats and motorcycles. Another acquired subsidiary proceeded to develop and introduce a new type of fiberglass sail-boat, followed by a canoe and a catamaran.

In addition, the success of the snowmobile created other ancillary markets. For instance, traveling on snowmobiles at 40 miles per hour in subfreezing temperatures required specialized clothing. Beaudoin saw this new type of market as a promising opportunity:

> Someone was going to have to supply wet-proof clothing that was warm enough to prevent our customers from freezing to death on our machines. We decided it might as well be us.[6]

Consequently, Bombardier acquired an apparel manufacturer in order to introduce snowmobile clothing. This led the company into the sportswear market because the acquired manufacturer was already engaged in the production and marketing of several other types of sportswear. Said Beaudoin: "We are in the leisure business."[7]

In other instances, Bombardier sought to enter markets not directly related to its core snowmobile business. In 1970 the company introduced a new product called the Sea-Doo, which was a kind of snowmobile on water. This was marketed most heavily in Florida and California. Unfortunately, the Sea-Doo was found to rust in salt water, and production was suspended after a couple of years. A more technically successful product was the Can-Am motorcycle, which was test marketed by Bombardier in 1973. The idea for the motorcycle originated with the development of a new engine by Bombardier's new Rotax subsidiary in Austria. The result was a light, high-performance motorcycle that quickly gained recognition after it won several races in Canada, the United States, and Europe.

New Thrusts

It was around this time that Bombardier began to see mass transit as a potentially lucrative market. As Beaudoin put it some time later, the company had already entered into this line of business when it had purchased Rotax-Werk in 1970:

> We acquired Rotax-Werk . . . and its parent company, Lohnerwerke, which made tramways for the city of Vienna, came along with it. We didn't intend to stay in the mass transit business, but at first sign of the energy crisis, that changed.[8]

But the move was facilitated by overtures to Bombardier from the French-based Compagnie Industrielle de Matériel de Transport (CIMT). CIMT had been involved in a partnership with Canadian Vickers Limited on a previous subway car order. Charles Leblanc, who was vice president of administration for Bombardier at the time, stated:

> CIMT came to us. They said don't be afraid of it. They pointed out that the same manufacturing steps were needed for subway cars as for snowmobiles. So we went ahead and bid.[9]

---

[6]Ibid.

[7]Ibid.

[8]"Snowmobiles to Subways: Bombardier Maps Out Its Route," *Financial Post*, September 13, 1980.

[9]"Why Bombardier Is Trying Out Mass Transit," *Business Week*, March 10, 1975.

Although Vickers had underbid it by $140,000, Bombardier won the contract. It was stated that Vickers had been disqualified because its bid did not include a specified Swedish coupling device.

The award of this substantial contract represented Bombardier's entry into the mass-transit market. The company moved to convert the Moto-Ski plant at La Pocatiere to handle production of subway cars. There were strong doubts about whether Bombardier had the necessary capabilities to complete the order. Up to this point, the company's involvement in mass-transit products had been limited to trams and streetcars produced by its Austrian subsidiary. But trams and streetcars are classified as light-rail vehicles and are substantially different in design from subway cars.

Bombardier did experience some problems in production, due in part to a labor strike in its newly converted plant. Nevertheless, the company began to make deliveries of subway cars to the city of Montreal late in 1976. By this time, Bombardier had also received its first order from outside Canada. This was for 36 electric-powered double-decker commuter cars that were to be built at a cost of $27 million for the South Chicago Transit Authority.

In the following years, Bombardier began to receive larger orders from all parts of North America (see Exhibit 3). It received an order for 117 push-pull commuter cars from the New Jersey Transit Corporation. This was followed by an even larger order for 180 subway cars for Mexico City. A senior marketing official subsequently described the manner in which Bombardier had been developing its mass-transit business:

> We progress in terms of both regional expansion and product expansion in a logical, structured fashion. It's more a question of corporate policy or strategy. We started off in Canada in Montreal, then we went to the United States. Now, we've broadened it into Mexico. There are no wild leaps into blue sky and the glorious beyond because that's the way companies go out of business.[10]

Spreading Out

Shortly after its entry into mass transit, Bombardier was trying to find new acquisitions that would help it to become a significant competitor in the transportation business. In 1976, Bombardier eventually succeeded in purchasing the Montreal Locomotive Works (MLW) from its U.S. parent for a cash payment of $16.8 million. Bombardier was given much-needed financial help from the Quebec government in finalizing this deal. The province's holding company, Société Générale de Financement, contributed about 40 percent of the purchase price of MLW in exchange for a block of Bombardier's shares.

MLW had previously made subway cars for Toronto, but its main products were diesel-electric locomotives and diesel engines for locomotives, ships, and power plants. The locomotives produced by the MLW plant were mostly in the lighter category, ranging from 1,000 to 2,000 horsepower. Because of this, their appeal was largely restricted to railways in developing countries. Bombardier was subsequently able to generate sales of diesel-engine locomotives to customers in several of these countries, including Venezuela, Jamaica, Cuba, Mexico, Guatemala, Pakistan, Bangladesh, Cameroon, Tanzania, and Malawi.

---

[10]"Firm Looks to Commuter Vehicles as Gravy Train to Large Profits," *Financial Post*, December 12, 1981.

EXHIBIT 3   Mass Transit Orders, 1974–1985

Year	Type of Vehicle	Quantity	Customer	Delivery
1974	Rubber-tired subway cars	423	Montreal Urban Community	1976–1979
1976	Self-propelled commuter cars	36	Chicago South Suburban Transit	1978–1979
1978	LRC coaches	50	Via Rail Canada	1981–1982
1980	Push-pull commuter cars	117	New Jersey Transit	1982–1983
1981	Rubber-tired subway cars	180	Mexico City	1982–1983
1981	Light-rail vehicles	26	Portland, Oregon	1984–1985
1981	Push-pull commuter cars	9	Metropolitan Authority of New York	1983
1982	LRC coaches	50	Via Rail Canada	1984
1982	Steel-wheeled subway cars	825	Metropolitan Authority of New York	1984–1987
1983	Push-pull commuter cars	19	Metro-North Commuter of New York	1985
1984	Push-pull commuter cars	20	Connecticut Department of Transportation	1986
1985	Push-pull commuter cars	15	Metro-North Commuter of New York	1987

Source: Fred Schilling, Nesbitt Research, 1986.

However, Bombardier's purchase of MLW had been largely motivated by its growing interest in the design and development of a light, rapid, and comfortable (LRC) passenger train. Its partners in this project were Alcan and Dofasco. The Canadian government also contributed development grants through its program for the advancement of industrial technology. The new train was meant to run at constant high speeds on existing North American tracks. Bombardier Vice President Henry Valle, who had previously headed MLW, talked about the distinctive features of the LRC:

> We think the LRC is as good or better than anything comparable on the market anywhere. And we don't think anyone anywhere knows any more about high-speed trains than we do.[11]

One of the first LRC contracts Bombardier managed to obtain was a $10 million lease-purchase contract with Amtrak for two trains. The Amtrak contract

---

[11]"Bombardier Looks to Amtrak to Open Doors to U.S. Inter-City Market," *Globe & Mail*, November 16, 1977.

was followed shortly thereafter by a $70 million order for 21 locomotives and 50 coaches for Via Rail in Canada (see Exhibit 3). The locomotives went into production at the MLW facility in Montreal, while the cars were slated for assembly at the La Pocatiere plant for mass-transit products. Upon obtaining the contract from Via Rail, a senior marketing official at Bombardier declared: "Now that we have a home base, we can really begin to sell actively internationally."[12]

Thus far, according to Beaudoin, Bombardier's move into mass transit and rail products had done much to ameliorate the company's dependence on recreational products such as the snowmobile. He summed up his company's goals in the following terms:

> Our goal is to develop some equilibrium between transportation and recreation. The transportation and recreation cycles are different. Recreational products are strong when the economy is strong. It's the reverse for transportation because of energy problems.[13]

CURRENT SITUATION

The change in Bombardier during the 1970s was seen by Beaudoin as more than merely a shift in the company's products and markets—it represented a strong desire for an expansion of the company's scope of activities that would allow it to better spread out its risk. During the 1980s Bombardier was trying to push for the further development of its several different types of business. In addition to the original line of recreational and utility products, the company was now engaged in new lines of mass-transit and rail and diesel products. Exhibits 4 through 7 present financial data for each of the company's primary business segments. Exhibit 8 presents Bombardier's balance sheets.

Recreational Products

The bulk of sales in recreational products continued to come from snowmobiles. Bombardier offered about 15 models of snowmobiles that were geared toward different uses. These included family models developed for better comfort and more safety as well as sporty models designed for higher speed and better performance.

The market for snowmobiles had picked up in the late 1970s, but declined again in the early 1980s. This resulted in lower profits for Bombardier from its lines of snowmobiles. Beaudoin, however, believed good snowfalls and an improving economy would bring about a growth in sales as well as greater profits. As he saw it, snowmobiles still had an important role to play in the future of Bombardier:

> We see it as a cash cow. The shakeout has taken place and, with around 40 percent of the market, it could be a very profitable business for us in the future even on lower volume.[14]

---

[12]"LRC Sale Considered Key to Foreign Market," *Globe & Mail*, November 4, 1977.
[13]"Snowmobiles to Subways."
[14]"Making the 'A' Train," *Forbes*, September 27, 1982.

E X H I B I T 4   **Bombardier's Sales by Class of Business, 1981–1986**
                      (In millions of Canadian dollars)

	For the Year Ended January 31					
	1981	**1982**	**1983**	**1984**	**1985**	**1986**
Recreational and utility products	$216.0	$215.4	$234.4	$260.2	$198.4	$252.3
Mass-transit products	34.0	67.6	178.4	134.2	202.3	296.4
Rail and diesel products	144.4	165.8	138.3	96.6	114.8	107.9
Total	$394.4	$448.8	$551.1	$491.0	$515.5	$656.6

Source: Bombardier annual reports.

E X H I B I T 5   **Bombardier's Profit from Operations by Class of Business, 1981–1986**
                      (In millions of Canadian dollars)

	For the Year Ended January 31					
	1981	**1982**	**1983**	**1984**	**1985**	**1986**
Recreational and utility products	($5.5)	($24.2)	$ 0.1	$ 7.5	$16.2	$12.1
Mass-transit products	5.0	1.4	17.4	17.6	9.3	3.6
Rail and diesel products	4.2	8.6	7.6	(13.7)	(13.1)	5.7
Total	$3.7	($14.2)	$25.1	$11.4	$12.4	$21.4

Source: Bombardier annual reports.

E X H I B I T 6   **Bombardier's Capital Expenditures by Class of Business, 1981–1986**
                      (In millions of Canadian dollars)

	For the Year Ended January 31					
	1981	**1982**	**1983**	**1984**	**1985**	**1986**
Recreational and utility products	$11.2	$14.3	$ 4.0	$ 9.0	$13.0	$ 8.4
Mass-transit products	5.5	8.0	4.4	8.7	5.4	1.0
Rail and diesel products	2.2	4.3	5.5	3.8	1.0	2.0
Total	$18.9	$26.6	$13.9	$21.5	$19.4	$11.4

Source: Financial Post Corporation Service.

EXHIBIT 7   **Bombardier's Capital Expenditures by Geographic Area 1981–1986**
             (In millions of Canadian dollars)

	For the Year Ended January 31					
	1981	1982	1983	1984	1985	1986
Canada	$15.4	$18.6	$11.2	$17.9	$13.9	$ 4.1
United States	0.2	4.7	0.7	1.3	1.7	2.8
Europe	3.3	3.3	2.0	2.3	3.8	4.5
Total	$18.9	$26.6	$13.9	$21.5	$19.4	$11.4

Source: Financial Post Corporation Service.

EXHIBIT 8   **Bombardier's Consolidated Balance Sheets, 1981–1986**
             (In millions of Canadian dollars)

	For the Year Ended January 31					
	1981	1982	1983	1984	1985	1986
Assets						
Current assets						
Cash	—	—	—	—	—	$ 6.9
Accounts receivable	$ 67.8	$ 73.2	$ 56.9	$ 77.3	$ 90.6	103.3
Inventories	158.6	121.4	149.0	117.2	167.5	152.3
Deficient income taxes	—	18.7	15.9	13.5	10.3	8.0
Prepaid expense	3.0	4.3	4.9	4.1	6.2	7.4
Investments	6.4	13.1	19.0	17.8	18.6	19.5
Fixed assets						
Buildings and equipment	153.6	177.8	171.7	186.9	234.6	234.9
Accumulated depreciation	81.0	87.8	84.0	88.1	110.3	123.1
Other assets	5.0	5.7	4.7	8.6	9.7	10.8
	$313.4	$326.4	$338.1	$337.3	$427.2	$420.0
Liabilities and Shareholders' Equity						
Current liabilities						
Bank loans	$ 19.5	$ 39.5	$ 13.7	$ 1.6	—	—
Accounts payable	80.6	91.1	95.9	73.3	$107.4	$134.7
Advances due	—	—	—	—	—	26.3
Income taxes	0.3	2.8	0.3	0.7	2.4	4.3
Mature long-term debt	11.0	4.4	6.1	6.0	4.6	5.3
Contract advances	—	—	32.6	77.0	132.5	39.5
Long-term debt	65.7	73.0	66.9	49.0	39.8	35.2
Provision for pensions	7.3	5.3	5.8	6.2	6.6	7.4
Shareholders' equity						
Capital stock	93.6	93.4	93.7	94.2	95.6	119.9
Retained earnings	35.4	16.9	23.1	29.3	38.3	47.4
	$313.4	$326.4	$338.1	$337.3	$427.2	$420.0

Source: Bombardier annual reports.

EXHIBIT 9   **Sources of Bombardier's Mass-Transit Technology Capability**

Heavy Rail
Rubber-tired subway cars	License from CIMT France
Steel-wheeled subway cars	License from Kawasaki

Conventional Rail
Commuter cars	License from Pullman
LRC cars	Developed with Alcan & Dofasco

Light Rail
Light-rail vehicles	License from BN Belgium
Monorail	License from Disney
PeopleMover	License from Disney

Source: Tony Hine, McLeod Young Weir Equity Research, 1986.

In order to adjust to these lower levels of sales, the company sold the various firms that were producing parts and accessories for snowmobiles. The result was that, apart from assembling the snowmobiles, Bombardier's actual manufacture of the vehicle was limited to the engine, which was made by the Rotax division in Gunskirchen, Austria.

Bombardier was among the five remaining competitors in snowmobiles. Its share of the market had recently risen to as much as 35 percent (see Exhibit 1). But this position was under attack from Yamaha, a Japanese competitor with strong technological and manufacturing advantages. Other firms in the industry posed less of a threat since they were struggling with the downturn in snowmobile sales. In fact, Bombardier had at one point expressed interest in the purchase of Polaris, a U.S.-based firm that was experiencing some financial difficulties. But the negotiations were dropped when the U.S. Justice Department threatened to block the sale on antitrust grounds.

Apart from snowmobiles, the company had experienced limited success with its other recreational products. Its only other notable offering was its line of Can-Am off-road racing bikes. These appealed to specialized sectors of the market because of their technical performance attributes. Bombardier had received several orders for military versions of these motorcycles from certain NATO countries, such as Britain and Belgium. In 1981 a license was purchased from an Austrian company for the assembly and distribution of moped bicycles in Canada. "Our long term strategy is to develop other recreational products," said Beaudoin.[15]

Mass-Transit Products

The greatest push for sales was being given to mass-transit products. Bombardier was able to offer a wide variety of heavy-, conventional-, and light-rail vehicles as a result of licensing to gain access to the different technologies (see Exhibit 9). Beaudoin was confident that this wide range of products placed his

[15]"Snowmobiles to Subways."

E X H I B I T 10   **Mass-Transit Cars Currently in Use in North America**

Type of Car	Units in Operation	Exceeding Normal Useful Life
Steel-wheeled subway cars	10,200	2,324
Rubber-tired subway cars	792	
Commuter cars	1,282	487
Light-rail vehicles	4,502	568
Intercity rail cars	2,589	837
Total	19,365	4,216

Source: Fred Schilling, Nesbitt Research, 1986.

company in the best possible position to exploit the mass-transit business. He also felt that an energy-conserving society would in the future rely more heavily on mass transit:

> We're forcing a North American mass-transit market of $1 billion annually . . . and we aim to get a good part of it.[16]

Such a strong and sustained demand for mass-transit products did appear to be likely. It had recently been estimated that of the close to 20,000 cars currently in operation all over North America, over 20 percent had already exceeded their normal useful life (see Exhibit 10). These cars would have to be replaced or refurbished. Refurbishing is usually cheaper, costing only about a third or a half of the $1 million purchase price of a new car.

In 1982 Bombardier was able to win a large and prestigious order worth about $1 billion for subway cars from the Metropolitan Transportation Authority of New York (see Exhibit 3). The company had recently started to make its first deliveries to maintain sufficient production activity after the deliveries to New York were completed in 1987.

Bombardier was experiencing severe difficulties in trying to break into large Canadian markets outside of Quebec because of the declared commitment of various provincial governments to award mass-transit jobs to companies that were locally based. For example, Bombardier had just experienced a major setback when it lost out on a bid to acquire UDTC, a significant competitor located in Toronto with a $1.3 billion backlog of orders from the city.

It was also feared that cuts in mass-transit funding by the federal government would make future sales in the United States even harder to come by. In fact, several large U.S. firms, such as Pullman, Rohr, and General Electric, had recently pulled out of the mass-transit business because of uncertainty of orders and problems with contracts. Furthermore, competition for mass-transit orders in the United States and in other export markets was coming from large firms that included Budd in the United States, Kawasaki in Japan, FrancoRail of France, Breda Ferroviaria of Italy, and Siemens-Duwag of West Germany.

---

[16]Ibid.

Since 1981 Bombardier had begun to put much more emphasis on light-rail vehicles due to their cheaper construction and maintenance costs. Toward this end, the company had acquired the rights to build, market, and operate its own versions of elevated and automated monorail systems from the Disney organization. It had also just completed a $13.5 million acquisition of a 45 percent interest in a Belgian mass-transit company that had supplied the technology to develop and build the streetcars it had already delivered to Portland, Oregon. Nevertheless, Vice President Poitras stated: "We don't want to depend completely on mass transit, because transit could also have cycles of good and bad years."[17]

Rail and Diesel Products

Bombardier had made substantial investments to upgrade the MLW facilities for the production of diesel locomotives. Besides manufacturing the locomotives, the plant also produced diesel engines that were used in locomotives, ships, and turbines. In 1984 the company attempted to expand its capacity and to obtain new customers through the $30 million acquisition of Alco Power, located in Auburn, New York. Alco produced diesel locomotives and diesel engines similar to those offered by MLW.

But sales of locomotives had begun to drop in recent years, primarily due to a decline in orders from the various developing countries. Furthermore, the company began to increasingly believe there was little likelihood of substantial improvement in sales unless it coud become more competitive in the development and production of locomotives with greater horsepower, such as those presently produced by General Electric and General Motors.

Bombardier did manage to secure orders for as many as 30 higher-powered diesel locomotives from Canadian National, but serious problems with their performance after production resulted in the eventual delivery of only four of the locomotives. Efforts were made to convince Canadian National to increase the size of its order in order to justify further development work on a higher-powered locomotive. The company also explored the possibility of linking up with existing large competitors such as General Electric or Kawasaki in order to gain better access to technology as well as markets.

Ultimately, Bombardier was forced to terminate the production of new locomotives in 1985 and to focus primarily upon the manufacturing of diesel engines and the servicing of existing locomotives. Most of this work was subsequently channeled into the Alco facility in New York state. Raymond Royer, soon to become the company's president, stated: "It has been very painful to us. It's a major decision to take, but if we can't make a profit, we have to act as good managers."[18]

At the same time, Bombardier was also being forced to reevaluate its potential orders for passenger locomotives that would result from the sales of its LRC train. The company had believed it would eventually make worldwide sales of 150 locomotives and 750 coaches. But by 1986, after the sale of only 31 locomotives and 100 coaches to Canadian-based Via Rail, there were no more

---

[17]"Bombardier's Formula for Growth," *Financial Times of Canada*, November 28, 1983.
[18]"Locomotives to Be Dropped," *Globe & Mail*, July 13, 1985.

orders on hand. Even Via Rail had declined to exercise its options for further orders because of mechanical and electrical problems it had experienced with equipment it had already received. Company officials had recently been trying to generate sales of the LRC outside North America. Said Poitras: "We've had discussions on the LRC in other countries, but it takes time. Up to now, we have not succeeded."[19]

Utility Products

The industrial products of the company were constantly being expanded to include new kinds of vehicles for different types of markets. In recent years, Bombardier had introduced a new hydrostatic-drive vehicle for ski slope maintenance. It had also started to offer wheeled carriers and skidders aimed at the forestry industry. These were being manufactured under license from companies in the United States and Finland.

Industrial products were currently experiencing a period of slow demand. In part, this was attributed by the company to poor snow conditions that had affected demand for vehicles designed for snow removal as well as for ski and snowmobile trail grooming. At the same time, depressed conditions in the construction and forestry industry were being blamed for decline in sales of other industrial products.

But this decline in demand for industrial products was then offset by Bombardier's push into the area of logistic support equipment for the military. The company had already been adapting some of its snowmobiles, motorcycles, and industrial-tracked vehicles to the needs of the military. In 1981 this activity was given a considerable boost when Bombardier was awarded a $150 million contract to build 2,700 trucks for the Canadian Armed Forces. These two-and-a-half ton trucks were built using a design of AM General Corporation, a subsidiary of American Motors.

In 1982 Bombardier also acquired worldwide rights for the production of the Iltis, a four-wheel-drive military vehicle designed by Volkswagenwerk of West Germany. The license led to an initial order of 1,900 Iltis vehicles for the Canadian Armed Forces. This was followed by the sale of 2,500 vehicles to Belgium and 350 vehicles to West Germany. A senior official in the logistics division explained:

> Our principle in developing the logistic division is pretty similar to Bombardier's thinking with any other product—first sell into Canada, build a base in Canada, then go offshore.[20]

Bombardier counted on the worldwide shift away from traditional Jeeps as army vehicles to create a major potential market for the Iltis. More orders for these vehicles were expected not only from Canada, but also from the Netherlands, Turkey, and Saudi Arabia.

Finally, the company signed an agreement with Oshkosh Truck Corporation of Wisconsin to produce and sell an 8.5-ton military truck known as the Oshkosh. The Oshkosh was a six-wheel-drive vehicle designed to carry heavy

---

[19]"Bombardier's Formula for Growth."
[20]"Bombardier Has High Hopes in Military Vehicle Market," *Globe & Mail*, November 12, 1983.

EXHIBIT 11   Businesses Acquired and Divested by Bombardier, 1957–1984

Year of Acquisition	Name and Location of Company	Type of Business	Status as of 1984
1957	Rockland Industries Kingsbury, Quebec	Rubber parts	Divested in 1983
1968	La Salle Plastic Richmond, Quebec	Plastic parts	Divested in 1983
1969	Roski Roxton Falls, Quebec	Fiberglass products	Divested in 1983
1970	Lohnerwerke Vienna, Austria	Streetcars	Still a part of Bombardier
1970	Rotax-Werk Gunskirchen, Austria	Engines	Still a part of Bombardier
1970	Walker Manufacturing Company Montreal, Quebec	Sportswear	Divested in 1983
1970	Drummond Automatic Plating Drummondville, Quebec	Chrome plating	Divested in 1976
1970	Jarry Precision Montreal, Quebec	Transmissions	Closed in 1973
1971	Moto-Ski La Pocatiere, Quebec	Snowmobiles	Merged into Ski-Doo in 1975
1972	Ville Marie Upholstering Beauport, Quebec	Foam seats	Divested in 1979
1976	Montreal Locomotive Works Montreal, Quebec	Locomotives Diesel engines	Still a part of Bombardier
1980	Heroux Longueuil, Quebec	Aeronautical parts	Divested in 1985
1984	Alco Power Auburn, N.Y.	Locomotives Diesel engines	Still a part of Bombardier

Source: Financial Post Corporation Service.

equipment and ammunition in rough terrain and was already in use with the U.S. Army. Bombardier hoped to sell 500 to 1,000 of these trucks to the Canadian Armed Forces. It also obtained the rights to sell the vehicle in 28 countries aside from Canada.

Exhibit 11 presents a list of Bombardier's acquisitions and divestitures during the 1957–1984 period.

PROFILE OF OPERATIONS

Organization

Bombardier's rapid growth and diversification forced top management to seek a more formal and structured approach to running the business. Toward this end, the company had been engaged in a series of moves designed to better integrate its operations with those of its various acquisitions. Beaudoin had anticipated the need for this restructuring in the early 1970s:

EXHIBIT 12   **Organization of Bombardier's Business Divisions**

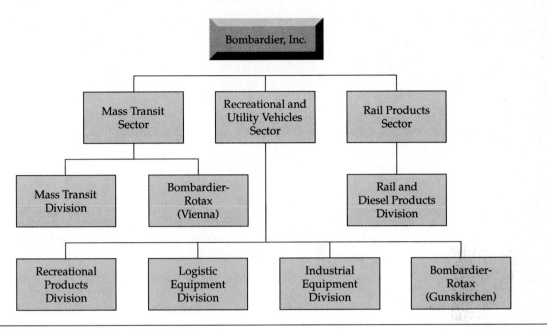

Source: Bombardier annual reports.

As we diversify more and more, we shall need to ensure central control of the overall operation. . . . Our management structure isn't finalized yet and will change with the needs of the business.[21]

By 1986 Bombardier was organized into seven different divisions or subsidiaries. These fell into three different sectors (see Exhibit 12). Total employment stood at between 5,000 and 6,000 employees. The largest number of divisions or subsidiaries was associated with the recreational and utility vehicles sector, which produced recreational products such as snowmobiles as well as certain types of industrial and logistic equipment. However, the main thrust of the company was oriented toward the mass-transit sector that manufactured several forms of subway cars, train cars, and streetcars. Finally, the rail and diesel products sector had concentrated on the production of locomotives, but was now relying mainly upon diesel engines for various industrial uses.

Although Bombardier moved to bring its various divisions and subsidiaries under centralized control, they remained separate administrative and financial entities. Each division or subsidiary was headed by a chief executive who possessed a considerable degree of autonomy. These chief executives were expected to submit on an annual basis a formal draft of a three-to-five-year plan for their own divisions.

---

[21]"Bombardier Skids to Success."

R&D

Bombardier's ability to produce and market such a diverse range of products hinged upon a policy of exploiting proven and tested technologies that were acquired through licensing agreements. As Vice President Poitras explained, it was a policy that made a virtue of necessity:

> The risk that has been taken on the various contracts we've bid for has been minimal. It takes years to develop a technology. It takes years to prove the technology. Bombardier can't afford to do that. What we are trying to find is new products just before they reach the market. Then we would be an ideal manufacturer and marketing organization for those products.[22]

The reliance on licensing was particularly heavy in mass transit (see Exhibit 9). For Beaudoin, product reliability was crucial to success in mass transit. He felt that this reliability could be enhanced through the purchase of proven technology:

> Mass-transit technology may not be as sophisticated as aerospace, but it has to be very, very reliable. It has to be in operation for at least five years before you know that you have a good product. Technology in mass transit has been developed for many years in Europe and Japan, and it's available.[23]

The recent push into logistic equipment was also dependent upon the use of various licensing agreements with U.S. and European firms. But the company's moves in rail products were based upon working in partnership with other companies. The LRC project had been undertaken as a joint venture with Alcan and Dofasco, in which Bombardier invested more than $30 million.

The only products Bombardier had developed through its own extensive research and development were its original recreational products and industrial equipment. The company's primary research facilities had been established in Valcourt for the development of its early snowmobiles and all-terrain vehicles. They included various kinds of laboratories and several different test tracks and chambers. These facilities had been expanded and renovated in 1979 and continued to be used for the early testing of most of the company's extensive range of products.

Production

Bombardier's diverse production activities were carried out in 3 million square feet of plants and warehouses scattered over Canada, the United States, and Austria. All of the company's recreational and utility products were manufactured in a large facility in Valcourt where the company started. An assembly line was designed that was capable of producing several hundred snowmobiles and motorcycles daily. Snowmobiles were manufactured for eight months of the year, from April to November. Facilities had been expanded or adapted for the manufacturing of industrial and logistic equipment, with rates of production that could vary from three to six units per day.

The mass-transit products were primarily constructed at La Pocatiere, in what had formerly been a Moto-Ski plant. The facilities, originally used for the manufacturing of snowmobiles, were converted in 1974 for the construction of subway cars. The complexity of a subway car is several orders of magnitude greater than that of a snowmobile. A subway car has 8,000 parts and 14 kilometers of electric wiring, compared to only 2,000 parts in a snowmobile. The shift to subway cars required considerable retraining of the labor force. It was also costly in terms of physical facilities. The estimated cost of conversion was about $5 million, of which $1 million was provided by a grant from the Canadian government.

The converted facility was then geared toward production of a variety of mass-transit vehicles, and contained about 65 work stations. The plant was capable of producing two to five cars per week based on a single daily eight-hour shift. Bombardier had also recently completed an assembly plant in Barre, Vermont, to handle U.S. orders. Partly assembled transit cars were shipped from La Pocatiere to this facility, where U.S.-made components were added.

Production of the diesel-electric locomotives and diesel engines was spread out over the old MLW facility in Montreal and the Alco plant in Auburn, New York. However, the MLW facility had not been utilizing its capacity for producing 100 locomotives and 50 diesel engines per year since the decision was made to withdraw from the manufacturing of locomotives.

Sales

Each of the categories of products offered by Bombardier represented a different type of sale and required its own marketing effort. Most of the company's products, with the exception of its recreational line, were typically sold in bulk orders to industrial or governmental clients.

Mass-transit equipment tended to require the most complex and extensive marketing effort. The average price for mass-transit vehicles was about $1 million per unit. Sales were generated through the company's submission of competitive bids as it vied for each potential order (see the Appendix concerning the bidding process). In order to be successful, a bid must be low in price, yet fulfill stringent technical requirements. In many cases, orders for mass-transit equipment are accompanied by allegations that the choice was made on the basis of political and regional favoritism. The Montreal and New York orders were both legally contested by the companies that lost out to Bombardier.

Sales of logistic equipment and diesel products are similarly developed through competitive bidding based upon price, specifications, and performance. Most of the military vehicles offered by Bombardier ranged in price from $20,000 to $30,000 per unit. Export sales to the military also depended upon the ability of Bombardier to collaborate with a local firm.

Finally, sales of the company's original lines of recreational products and industrial equipment were separately developed. Its snowmobiles and motorcycles were sold through a network of about 2,000 distributors and dealers throughout North America, as well as in select foreign markets. The list price of snowmobiles typically ranged from $1,500 to $7,000, with a good basic machine selling for about $3,000.

On the other hand, most industrial equipment was marketed directly by the company through its service centers. The various types of all-terrain tracked or wheeled vehicles usually cost between $125,000 and $150,000 per unit. The bulk of sales continued to be made in North America, but the company was concentrating on building sales in overseas markets through its Rotax division in Austria.

Contracts

The sale and delivery of most of Bombardier's product lines, with the exclusion of snowmobiles, was highly dependent on the specific terms as laid out in carefully negotiated contracts. Though contracts tend to be very elaborate, they cannot anticipate all contingencies. Disputes tend to arise over technical specifications associated with the design, unforeseen developments that may contribute to escalation of costs, and the rights of the customer to withdraw from the deal. These disputes are costly in the short run, but more importantly they can damage the reputation of the manufacturer in the long run.

Consequently, Beaudoin frequently emphasized that care must be taken to avoid the problems that forced other companies to drop out of the mass-transit business. To start with, Bombardier tried to avoid technical problems with its designs by obtaining licenses on tried and tested technologies. This policy reduced the likelihood of expensive delays and repairs as well as the possibility of the customer moving to cancel a contract in midstream.

Additionally, Bombardier sought to negotiate contracts that stipulated precise conditions under which the customer could terminate a contract. In the event of disputes over quality or performance, the company attempted to avoid costly litigation by including provisions for specific arbitration procedures. The most serious problems were encountered with the early deliveries of subway cars to New York. Various mechanical and electrical problems led to the temporary suspension of production while the cars were tested. It was speculated that failure on these tests could have led to cancellation of the contract.

Finally, all contracts typically included a schedule for prepayments and progress payments to ensure sufficient financing for carrying out the order. Additional protection was provided through the specification of limits on penalties for delay in deliveries as well as through escalator clauses that index the price to the inflation rate. However, as Vice President Pointras pointed out: "There is no protection against cost overruns. That is our risk."[24]

Labor

Most of Bombardier's products were fairly labor intensive because of the company's dependence upon manual assembly lines. When the company was essentially engaged in the production of snowmobiles and all-terrain vehicles at its facilities in Valcourt, the employees were administered to by committees that set salary levels based upon the average levels that prevailed in the area. Since then, the majority of the company's employees had become unionized and were covered by as many as 10 agreements.

---

[24]"Bombardier's Formula for Growth."

Furthermore, some of the agreements with labor were concluded only after long strikes that disrupted production in various plants. Bombardier had to deal with its first strike in 1975. The strike occurred at the La Pocatiere plant during the conversion to mass-transit production. It lasted almost five months and resulted in considerable delays in the final delivery of subway cars to the city of Montreal. Recurrent and crippling strikes were also encountered at the MLW plant, which underwent a five-month lockout in 1977 and a six-month strike in 1979.

However, Beaudoin felt that the relationship between management and labor had improved considerably over the past few years. This was due to changes in management personnel within the divisions and the introduction of new working arrangements. At the end of 1979, Bombardier also offered to all of its Quebec employees the opportunity to subscribe to a share purchasing plan. This plan was designed to allow employees to benefit from tax advantages recently introduced by the Quebec government, as well as to participate more directly in the growth of the company.

Top Management

Bombardier shifted its headquarters from Valcourt to Montreal in 1975. The move brought together in one location the chairman and chief executive officer of the company and seven vice presidents responsible for different areas of the company's operations. Except for a brief period, the position of chairman and chief executive officer has been occupied by Laurent Beaudoin. Joseph-Armand's son, André Bombardier, and son-in-law, Jean-Louis Fontaine, are among the most senior of the group of vice presidents.

In 1975 Beaudoin tried to bring in an outsider to help with running the company. Sixty-one-year-old Jean-Claude Hébert was appointed chairman and chief executive officer, with Beaudoin keeping the post of president. Beaudoin stated the reasons behind this move: "We really needed someone on the management end to guide the organization going into diversification."[25] It was under Hébert's direction that Bombardier mounted its aggressive search for possible acquisitions. But the poor performance of MLW subsequent to its acquisition led the family to question Hébert's plans for other major acquisitions. He was subsequently forced out in 1978, with the position returning to Beaudoin.

In 1979 Beaudoin appointed Louis Hollander as the president and chief operating officer of the company. Hollander, who had previously been in charge of recreational and industrial products, remained in this position until the end of 1981. The position was then filled by Raymond Royer, who had been responsible for the company's mass-transit products.

Financing

In 1986 the capital stock of Bombardier stood at 6.9 million class A and 5.9 million class B shares. The shares represented close to $120 million of equity on the balance sheets of the company (see Exhibit 8). At the same time, long-term

---

[25]"Why Bombardier Is Trying Out Mass Transit."

debt had dropped to $35 million, most of which was in the form of bonds, notes, and debentures.

Bombardier became a publicly owned organization in 1969. Its initial issue consisted of 2 million class A voting shares, representing about 15 percent of the company's equity. All of the 13 million class B nonvoting shares were kept by Les Enterprises de J. Armand Bombardier, a family-owned holding company. No dividends could be paid on the class B shares unless a dividend of similar nature had been paid during the same fiscal year on the class A shares. But the class B shares were convertible at any time on a share-for-share basis into class A shares.

During 1976 all outstanding class A and B shares were exchanged for a total of 3.9 million class A shares. Starting in 1981, newly created class B shares were again issued to the public. They have fewer voting rights but entitle their holders to dividends. As of early 1986, Les Enterprises de J. Armand Bombardier still held 71.9 percent of the class A shares, which gave it a 66.2 percent voting interest. Another 3 percent of the class A shares were held by directors, managers, and employees of the company.

DEVELOPING PROSPECTS

In the summer of 1986, Bombardier was taking steps to enter into two new areas of activity. One of these would move the company into aerospace, while the other would lead it into automobiles. Each of these would represent a major shift for the company, the first since its entry into mass transit. However, Laurent Beaudoin believed the company had the financial, technical, and management capability to handle both of these moves.

Aerospace

Bombardier was considering making a serious bid to acquire Canadair, an aerospace company located in Montreal. Canadair employed more than 4,000 people and had reported a profit of $19.6 million on sales of $430 million in the previous year. However, the company had only recently begun to show profitability, and this had been largely based upon sales of its newly developed Challenger business jet.

The Challenger executive jet had earned a reputation for being spacious, quiet, and fuel efficient. It was conceived and developed by Canadair following the acquisition of the company from General Dynamics by the Canadian government in 1975. But the design of the aircraft had taken longer than anticipated, resulting in development costs in excess of $1 billion. As a result, the company found itself unable to sell enough of these jets to cover its expenses until the government absorbed the development costs.

Although it was now free of its debt, Canadair still had to contend with the inherent uncertainty of the business jet market. The total market for such aircraft was believed to be between 75 and 100 units per year. Canadair had already sold about 140 of its Challenger jets since it was introduced in 1980, but the company had not yet found buyers midway into the year for the 15 aircraft it needed to build in 1986 in order to break even. In fact, there were no outstanding orders for the Challenger business jet on the books of the company.

Apart from the business jet, the only other substantial Canadair product was a recent version of the CL-215 water bomber. The CL-215 had been the main drawing card for the company through the 1970s while the Challenger was being developed. The water bomber continued to offer excellent fire-fighting capabilities and could also be adapted to other uses. Although annual production stood at only 10 units, demand for this type of aircraft was expected to pick up.

The recent decision to sell Canadair had been made by the newly elected Conservative government, which was determined to privatize many of its business holdings. The book value of the company was estimated to be between $225 million and $250 million, but it was considered quite likely that the government would settle for a lower price in exchange for some assurance that the company would remain intact and continue its operations.

Beaudoin was optimistic about Bombardier's chances of winning the bid to acquire Canadair. He also felt that if successful, the acquisition would provide Bombardier with a complementary business with a strong cash flow. At the same time, Bombardier would have to continue to make investments in Canadair's business jets and water bombers in the face of increasing competition from other U.S. and European firms. A greater push might also be needed to develop more subcontracting work with other aerospace companies and maintenance work for military aircraft.

Automobiles

Bombardier was also actively exploring the possibility of introducing into the North American market a small car designed to carry two people. The car would use a three-cylinder engine and would offer a maximum speed of about 55 to 65 miles per hour. It would be targeted as a second car to be used mainly for city driving.

The company had already concluded an agreement with Daihatsu Motor Company of Japan to obtain the technology that would be used in the design of the car. It was now negotiating a joint venture agreement with the Japanese company under which these cars would be produced. Daihatsu, which was partly owned by Toyota, was the smallest producer of cars in Japan.

The joint venture agreement could lead to the production of a new version of a Daihatsu three-cylinder car that was already being sold in Asia and Europe. Production on these could start as early as 1987 or early 1988. A new front-wheel-drive version of this car being designed by Bombardier could not be ready for production before 1991.

The cars would be produced by Bombardier at Valcourt, where the company had spare factory space. The facilities were initially expected to be able to produce about 200,000 cars annually. It was believed that about 350 of Bombardier's snowmobile dealers in Canada and the United States could handle sales and service. The car was expected to retail for about $7,000.

The company was spending about $15 million, most of which was provided by various levels of government, to undertake feasibility studies. Testing of four prototype cars had been going well, leading to speculation that a positive decision was forthcoming. Beaudoin had recently provided his own assessment about the possible move into the production of small cars: "We have the technical experience and the management depth to handle the job."[26] At the same time, it was widely speculated that Bombardier would take the final plunge only if it were able to develop a joint venture to get strong technical and financial backing for the move.

APPENDIX   THE BIDDING PROCESS*

Bids are very expensive to prepare. The cost of preparing a complex bid often reaches six figures. Each component of the order must be analyzed and costed, and labor overhead and tooling costs must also be evaluated. Working capital, maintenance, and warranty costs must all be factored in.

The process is further complicated by the customized nature of the work. Municipal transit authorities tend to retain consultants to define system and vehicle specifications in great detail. There are variations in tunnel construction and gauge that determine the width of the cars. Furthermore, there are differences in electrical voltages on which the different systems run.

The number of cars ordered is usually a key variable in costing, as there are economies of scale and learning curve developments that must be correctly calculated. Frequently, however, scale economies are impeded by the tendency of the customers to require a certain amount of parts that have been locally manufactured.

Parts usually make up 50 to 60 percent of the final cost, while direct labor accounts for around 10 percent. There is greater profit potential on repeat orders because tooling and start-up expenses are substantially reduced.

---

[26]"Bombardier Plans Mini-Car, Eyes Canadair," *Globe & Mail*, June 17, 1986.
* Adapted from Tony Hine, McLeod Young Weir Equity Research, 1986.

PHILIP MORRIS COMPANIES, INC.*

Tracy R. Kramer, The University of Alabama
Arthur A. Thompson, Jr., The University of Alabama

The business makeup of the Philip Morris Companies (PM) in 1991 was markedly different than its long-time heritage in cigarettes might suggest. In the early 1950s, Philip Morris's business centered entirely on cigarettes, and the company had only a 9.2 percent market share—fourth among the six U.S. manufacturers and far behind R.J. Reynolds (the leader with a 34 percent market share) and second-place American Brands (with a 25.6 percent market share). But the company's management resolved to strengthen PM's position in cigarettes and, beginning in 1956, management launched a major diversification program—the first such move among the U.S. cigarette firms. Philip Morris's basic strategy was to use surplus cash flows from cigarette operations to acquire companies with potential to become market leaders in their industry. Most of the acquired companies represented opportunities to grow the sales of previously undermarketed consumer products with the aid of PM's considerable marketing know-how in cigarettes.

Between 1957 and 1990, Philip Morris made 26 acquisitions (see Exhibit 1). The early acquisitions were small packaging companies whose products were used in cigarette manufacturing. During the 1960s, the company began diversifying into consumer products with the purchase of companies such as American Safety Razor, Clark Chewing Gum, Miller Brewing Company, and Seven-Up. Not all the acquisitions met Philip Morris's growth expectations and 12 were subsequently divested, often for substantially more than their acquisition prices.

Under the guidance of Joseph F. Cullman III, who became chief executive officer in 1957, Philip Morris's sales grew from $400 million in 1957 to $14.1 billion in 1984, a compound annual growth rate of over 14 percent. Cullman took the company from 170th on *Fortune's* list of the 500 largest industrial corporations in the U.S. in 1957 to 32nd in 1984, engineering 16 acquisitions and creating an international cigarette division. Of the company's $13.7 billion growth in revenues between 1957 and 1984, $6 billion came from gains in domestic cigarette sales, $3.8 billion from the new international cigarette division, $2.9 billion from beer sales, and $1 billion from the remaining acquisitions, including Seven-Up and the packaging firms.

Hamish Maxwell replaced Cullman as CEO in 1985. The son of a third-generation tobacco leaf dealer in London, Maxwell took a position with PM in 1954 as a cigarette salesperson in Richmond, Virginia. He headed the development of PM's international operations in the 1960s, and his first major move as CEO was the $5.6 billion purchase of General Foods Corporation in 1985. By 1988 PM, under Maxwell's direction, had purchased Kraft Foods and merged the two companies into a $23 billion food processing company, the second largest in the world. In 1989 and 1990, PM acquired Jacobs Suchard, the second-largest European chocolatier, and five smaller food companies whose products

EXHIBIT 1   **Philip Morris Acquisitions and Divestitures**

Acquisition Date		Divestiture Date
1957	Acquired Milprint, Inc., a flexible packaging plant, and its subsidiary, Nicolet Paper Company, which manufactured greaseproof paper used by the packaging industry	1985
1958	Acquired Polymer Industries, Inc., a manufacturer of industrial adhesives and textile chemicals	1982
1960	Acquired American Safety Razor Products Corporation	1977
1963	Acquired Burma-Nita Company	1973
	Acquired Clark Bros. Chewing Gum Company	1973
1969	Acquired 53 percent ownership of Miller Brewing Company from W.R. Grace & Company at a price of $130 million	
1970	Acquired control of Mission Viejo Company, a California community development and home-building firm	
	Acquired remaining 47 percent of stock of Miller Brewing Company from De Rance Foundation in Milwaukee	
	Acquired Plainwell Paper Company	1985
1971	Acquired Armstrong Coated Products	1982
	Acquired Lindeman (Holdings) Ltd., an Australian wine company	
1972	Completed 100 percent acquisition of Mission Viejo Company for maximum total price of $48 million	
	Acquired Wikolin Werk Willi E. Kohlmeyer G.M.B.H., a West German specialty chemical manufacturer	1982
1973	Formed Surtech Coating Company	1978
1977	Acquired Wisconsin Tissue Mills, Inc., for 314,984 shares of common stock	1985
1978	Acquired 97 percent of the Seven-Up Company for $520 million	1986
1980	Acquired a 31 percent ownership interest of British-based Rothmans International, Ltd., the world's third-largest cigarette producer; also obtained the rights to market major Rothmans brands in the United States and South America	1989
1985	Acquired General Foods for $5.7 billion in a hostile takeover	
1988	Acquired Kraft Foods for $12.9 billion in a hostile takeover	
1989	Acquired Oroweat Baked Goods, Anderson Clayton, Catelli Magic Moments and Light Touch Desserts, DiGiorno Pasta, and Louis Kemp Seafood to fill gaps in its food segment	
1990	Acquired Jacobs Suchard, a Swiss-based coffee and chocolate manufacturer and distributor of the Toblerone brand of chocolates	
1990	Agreed to acquire Dresden Cigarette Company, the largest cigarette-manufacturing operation in Eastern Europe	

filled gaps in the Kraft General Foods product line. Under Maxwell's management, PM's revenues grew from $16.3 billion in 1985 to $44.8 billion in 1989 (a 29 percent annual growth), making PM the 7th largest company on the *Fortune 500* list. Domestic and international tobacco products accounted for 40 percent of sales; beer was 8 percent and food was 51 percent.

Going into 1991, Philip Morris had leading businesses in three industries—cigarettes, beer, and food processing. Philip Morris's business portfolio consisted of:

- The largest cigarette company in the U.S. market, with a 41.9 percent market share (up from 30.8 percent in 1980 and 16.7 percent in 1970).
- The world's second-largest international cigarette company, selling 160 brands in more than 170 countries and territories.
- The nation's second-largest brewer of beer—Miller Brewing Company.
- The world's second-largest food-processing company—Kraft General Foods Group.
- A capital division that included credit financing for PM subsidiaries, customers, and suppliers; leveraged leasing of major equipment; and Mission Viejo, a land planning, development, and sales division.

Exhibit 2 shows PM's diversified structure and business portfolio makeup as of 1990. Exhibit 3 provides sales and operating profit breakdowns by business unit, and Exhibit 4 provides a 10-year financial summary.

PM'S DOMESTIC TOBACCO SBU

During the past 30 years, Philip Morris had been the most successful of all the U.S. cigarette manufacturers, boosting domestic cigarette sales from approximately 46 billion units in 1960 to 220 billion in 1989 and domestic cigarette profits from $47 million in 1960 to $3.6 billion by 1989, to become the largest cigarette producer in the United States. During this period, PM increased its share of U.S. sales from 10 percent to an industry-leading 42 percent. With an operating profit margin of 38 percent in 1989, PM's domestic cigarette business was its primary source of cash surpluses. This segment contributed only 21 percent of PM's total revenues, but 50 percent of total operating profits.

U.S. Cigarette Industry Trends

Ever since the Surgeon General's 1964 report citing cigarette smoking as a health hazard, the cigarette industry in the United States had been struggling to protect its sales and customer base. Rising cigarette taxes, the attempted passage of many no-smoking ordinances, antismoking campaigns, and a slight downturn in per capita cigarette consumption had made cigarettes a declining business in terms of unit volume:

Billions of Units Produced per Year				
	1980	1985	1987	1989
Philip Morris	192	214	216	220
R.J. Reynolds	202	188	185	150
Brown & Williamson	85	71	63	59
Lorillard	60	48	47	42
American Brands	66	45	39	37
Liggett Group	14	30	20	17
U.S. industry total	619	596	570	525

Source: Compiled from *Business Week*'s annual cigarette reports, 1981, 1986, 1988, and 1990.

The Organizational Structure of Philip Morris, 1990 *(Operating revenues and operating profits in millions of dollars)*

Philip Morris Companies, Inc.

Cigarettes

Philip Morris U.S.A.

Revenues: $9,489

Profits: $3,606

Brands: Marlboro, Virginia Slims, Bucks, Benson & Hedges, Merit Cambridge, Parliament and Alpine

Philip Morris International

Revenues: $8,375

Profits: $1,007

Brands: Marlboro, Philip Morris, Lark, Chesterfield, Galaxy, Peter Jackson, Merit, Parliament, Muratti

Beer

Miller Brewing Company

Revenues: $3,435

Profits: $226

Brands: Miller Lite, Miller High Life, Miller Genuine Draft, Milwaukee's Best, Lowenbrau, and Sharp's

Food

Kraft General Foods

Revenues: $22,933

Profits: $2,138

Brands: Kraft cheeses, Maxwell House coffees, Louis Rich turkey, Oscar Mayer luncheon meats, hot dogs, and bacon, Louis Kemp seafood products, Post cereals, Jell-O, Kool-aid, Sealtest, Breyers and Light 'n Lively dairy products, Kraft salad dressings and box dinners

Financial

Philip Morris Capital Corporation

Revenues: $193

Profits: $82

Products: Major equipment leasing financial programs for customers and suppliers

Mission Viejo

Revenues: $334

Profits: $91

Products: Land planning, developing, and sales

E X H I B I T   3   Selected Financial Highlights of Philip Morris, 1987–1989

	Data by Segment for the Years Ended December 31 (In millions of dollars)		
	1989	1988	1987
Operating revenues			
Tobacco	$17,864	$16,586	$14,644
Food	22,933	11,265	9,946
Beer	3,435	3,262	3,105
Financial services and real estate	527	629	488
Total operating revenues	$44,759	$31,742	$28,183
Operating profit			
Tobacco	$ 5,063	$ 3,846	$ 3,290
Food	1,580	392	605
Beer	226	190	170
Financial services and real estate	172	162	68
Other	—	—	19
Total operating profit	7,041	4,590	4,152
Unallocated corporate expenses	252	193	162
Operating income	$ 6,789	$ 4,397	$ 3,990
Identifiable assets			
Tobacco	$ 6,780	$ 6,001	$ 6,467
Food	25,983	24,870	9.125
Beer	1,556	1,623	1,680
Financial services and real estate	3,440	3,169	2,890
	37,759	35,663	20,162
Corporate assets	769	1,297	1,275
Total assets	$38,528	$36,960	$21,437
Depreciation expense			
Tobacco	$ 246	$ 237	$ 214
Food	356	221	201
Beer	137	136	137
Financial services and real estate	2	4	4
Capital additions			
Tobacco	$ 422	$ 467	$ 246
Food	733	466	402
Beer	80	86	57
Financial services and real estate	—	—	2

Source: 1989 Annual Report.

Demographics   Per capita smoking in the United States had been declining for three decades (see Exhibit 5), and in 1990 only about 30 percent of those over 18 smoked, versus about 50 percent in the mid-1950s. The smoking population was increasingly comprised of lower-income and less-educated groups. Thirty-four percent of smokers had less than a high school education, while only 16 percent were college graduates. Smoking demographics had also changed significantly along gender and racial lines, with more women and blacks smoking and more white males quitting.

E X H I B I T   4   Selected Financial Data for Philip Morris Companies, Inc., 1979–1989
(In millions of dollars, except per-share data)

Summary of Operations

	1989	1988	1987	1986	1985	1984	1983	1982	1981	1980	1979
Operating revenues	$44,759	$31,742	$28,183	$25,883	$16,267	$14,102	$13,256	$11,720	$10,886	$9,822	$8,303
United States export sales	2,288	1,863	1,592	1,193	923	925	970	978	834	702	521
Cost of sales	21,829	13,538	12,183	11,901	6,709	5,840	5,665	5,532	5,253	4,675	3,857
Federal excise taxes on products sold	2,140	2,127	2,085	2,075	2,049	2,041	1,983	1,180	1,169	1,105	1,037
Foreign excise taxes on products sold	3,608	3,755	3,331	2,653	1,766	1,635	1,527	1,435	1,411	1,389	1,122
Operating income	6,789	4,397	3,990	3,537	2,664	1,908	1,840	1,547	1,312	1,144	1,096
Interest and other debt expense, net (consumer products)	1,731	670	646	772	311	276	230	244	232	205	190
Earnings before income taxes and cumulative effect of accounting change	5,058	3,727	3,344	2,765	2,353	1,632	1,610	1,303	1,080	939	906
Pretax profit margin	11.3%	11.7%	11.9%	10.7%	14.5%	11.6%	12.1%	11.1%	9.9%	9.6%	10.9%
Provision for income taxes	$2,112	$1,663	$1,502	$1,287	$1,098	$743	$706	$521	$420	$390	$398
Earnings before cumulative effect of accounting change	2,946	2,064	1,842	1,478	1,255	889	904	782	660	549	508
Cumulative effect of accounting change		273									
Net earnings	2,946	2,337	1,842	1,478	1,255	889	904	782	660	549	508
Earnings per share before cumulative effect of accounting change	3.18	2.22	1.94	1.55	1.31	.91	.90	.78	.66	.55	.51
Per share cumulative effect of accounting change		.29									
Net earnings per share	3.18	2.51	1.94	1.55	1.31	.91	.90	.78	.66	.55	.51
Dividends declared per share	1.25	1.01	.79	.62	.50	.43	.36	.30	.25	.20	.16
Weighted average shares	927	932	951	954	959	981	1,008	1,005	999	997	996

Capital expenditures (consumer products)	$ 1,246	$ 1,024	$ 718	$ 678	$ 347	$ 298	$ 566	$ 918	$ 1,019	$ 751	$ 629
Annual depreciation (consumer products)	755	608	564	514	367	341	294	250	211	178	133
Property, plant, and equipment, net (consumer products)	8,457	8,648	6,582	6,237	5,684	4,014	4,381	4,178	3,583	2,806	2,214
Inventories (consumer products)	5,751	5,384	4,154	3,836	3,827	2,653	2,599	2,834	2,922	2,499	2,235
Total assets	38,528	36,960	21,437	19,482	18,712	9,880	9,908	9,756	9,180	7,362	6,379
Total long-term debt	14,861	17,122	6,293	6,887	8,035	2,239	2,549	3,776	3,499	2,598	2,448
Total debt—consumer products	14,887	16,442	6,355	6,889	7,887	2,566	3,054	3,728	3,804	2,800	2,507
Total debt—financial services and real estate	1,538	1,504	1,378	1,141	944	436	141	83	3	1	9
Total deferred income taxes	1,732	1,559	2,044	1,519	1,233	907	825	627	455	327	234
Stockholders' equity	9,571	7,679	6,823	5,655	4,737	4,093	4,034	3,663	3,234	2,837	2,471
Common dividends declared as a percentage of net earnings	39.3%	40.3%	40.6%	39.9%	38.1%	46.8%	40.5%	38.6%	37.9%	36.3%	30.6%
Book value per common share	$10.31	$8.31	$7.21	$5.94	$4.96	$4.21	$4.03	$3.64	$3.22	$2.84	$2.48
Market price of common share—high/low	$45\frac{1}{2}$–25	$25\frac{1}{2}$–$20\frac{1}{8}$	$31\frac{1}{8}$–$18\frac{1}{8}$	$19\frac{1}{2}$–11	$11\frac{7}{8}$–9	$10\frac{3}{8}$–$7\frac{3}{4}$	9–$6\frac{3}{4}$	$8\frac{1}{2}$–$5\frac{1}{2}$	$6\frac{7}{8}$–$5\frac{1}{4}$	$6\frac{1}{8}$–$3\frac{5}{8}$	$4\frac{7}{8}$–$3\frac{7}{8}$
Closing price of common share at year-end	$41\frac{5}{8}$	$25\frac{1}{2}$	$21\frac{3}{8}$	18	11	$10\frac{1}{8}$	9	$7\frac{1}{2}$	$6\frac{1}{8}$	$5\frac{3}{8}$	$4\frac{1}{2}$
Price-earnings ratio at year-end	13	10	11	11	8	11	10	9	9	9	8
Number of common shares outstanding at year-end	929	924	947	951	955	971	1,000	1,007	1,003	998	996
Number of employees	157,000	155,000	113,000	111,000	114,000	68,000	68,000	72,000	72,000	72,000	65,000

Operating income is income before interest and other debt expense, net.

Share data have been adjusted to reflect the 1989 four-for-one stock split.

Certain prior years' amounts have been reclassified to conform with the current year's presentation.

Kraft, Inc. became a wholly owned subsidiary on December 7, 1988. General Foods Corporation was acquired in November 1985. Accordingly, consolidated results of the company include the operating results of these companies since the dates of their acquisition.

Source: 1989 Annual Report

EXHIBIT 5   **Production and Consumption of and Expenditures for
                 Tobacco Products, 1970–1988**

Item	1970	1980	1988
Production			
Cigarettes (in billions)	583.0	714.0	695.0
Cigars (in billions)	8.4	4.0	2.0
All tobacco products (in millions of pounds)	165.0	163.0	N/A
Per Capita Consumption			
Cigarettes (in thousands of units)	4.0	3.9	3.1
Number of cigars	60.0	24.0	14.0
All products (in pounds)	9.7	7.9	6.2
Consumer Expenditures (in billions of $)			
Cigarettes	$10.4	$19.4	$35.9
Cigars	0.7	0.7	0.6
Other	0.4	0.9	1.4

N/A = Not Available.

Sources: U.S. Centers for Disease Control, Office of Smoking and Health, and U.S. Department of Agriculture, Tobacco Situation, quarterly.

Market Segmentation   Quick to recognize the changing demographics, the tobacco companies used market segmentation strategies to attempt to increase market share. The companies segmented on the basis of gender, race, age, income, and type of cigarette. Lorillard's Newport focused on young, urban blacks. PM's Dunhill and RJR's Ritz targeted upscale smokers. PM's Virginia Slims and Brown & Williamson's Capri were aimed at women, and American Brand's filtered Pall Mall was aimed at the price conscious. Kool and Salem shared the majority of the menthol segment, although most popular brands, such as Marlboro and Winston, offered a menthol version.

Antismoking Concerns   In addition to a shrinking smoking population, social, political, and legal pressures against cigarette smoking were increasing. Once cancer researchers announced that nonsmokers subjected to the ambient smoke emitted by cigarette smokers stood an increased probability of contracting lung cancer, the intolerance and hostility toward cigarette smoking increased dramatically. In response, the U.S. Surgeon General was campaigning for a ban on smoking in all public places by the year 2000. By 1990, the U.S. government had banned smoking in most federal work places and 42 states had prohibited smoking in public places, and additional antismoking legislation was pending before Congress. The industry was plagued with lawsuits from lung cancer victims (but had not lost a suit, to date). There was also the threat of declining volumes as a result of a federal excise tax increase. The industry had historically been able to absorb periodic tax increases through increased prices; however, recent studies showed a tendency in older smokers to switch to lower-priced brands. Finally, in California in 1990, a 25 cent-per-package excise tax funded an advertising campaign designed to reduce and eventually eliminate the use of tobacco products. The ads, via radio and television commercials and billboards, portrayed smoking as a nasty habit and tobacco industry officials as merchants of death.

Pricing In 1970, the average price per 20-unit pack was 41 cents; by 1988, that price had escalated to an average of $1.37 per pack. Historically, cigarette demand had been price inelastic, such that cigarette consumption levels were not substantially altered by price changes, which allowed cigarette producers to pass along cost increases and rising excise taxes, as well as widen profit margins, through price increases. In the 1980s, cigarette price increases were as much as 16 cents per pack greater than the standard price increases caused by inflation. However, by 1990 consumers were becoming more price sensitive, forcing cigarette manufacturers to trim the size of further price increases.

Buyer resistance to the prices of major cigarette brands was said to be a prime reason that sales of lower-priced generic and discount brands were growing rapidly. The fastest-growing new brands were those that sold for less. Price-value brands claimed 14.7 percent of the total cigarette market in 1989, up from 11 percent in 1988. However, manufacturers' profit margins on the cut-rate brands were only about one third of their full-priced counterparts, since manufacturers still paid high packaging and promotion costs. Liggett Group used its price-value brand, Pyramid, to stay in the market. It sold the brand for up to $2.50 less per carton and subsequently increased its market share to 3.2 percent. William Campbell, the CEO of Philip Morris U.S.A. (named in 1990), said of the pricing trends: "This was a dream business historically, but it has become like every other consumer business in America. Price competition is a reality."[1]

Innovations Shrinking sales, compounded by higher tobacco-leaf costs, slowed the pace of profit growth. The tobacco industry countered with increasing efficiency of production, increased prices, marketing, and new product development. Tobacco companies tried to grab market share from their competitors by launching new products or recasting existing brands. The levels of tar and nicotine in cigarettes were varied to differentiate products. The manufacturers also experimented with the size and shape of cigarettes. Capri, a Brown & Williamson brand, was very successful in marketing an ultra-slim cigarette to women, and PM had also entered this market with a Virginia Superslims brand. One innovation, RJR Nabisco's smokeless cigarette, was said to look and taste like any other cigarette and to emit much less tar and ambient smoke. However, this product met with limited success.

Diversification Firms in the tobacco industry had diversified for two main reasons: (1) their tobacco businesses were "cash cows" and produced very sizable cash flow surpluses year after year and (2) cigarettes were increasingly seen as a health hazard and cigarette sales were drifting in a slow, long-term decline. The eventual decline in cigarette sales, anticipated by industry executives for many years, had prompted other cigarette manufacturers besides Philip Morris to diversify their business portfolios during the 1960s and 1970s.

[1]As quoted in *The Wall Street Journal*, November 13, 1990, p. 1.

EXHIBIT 6   **Degree of Diversification and Range of Business Interests of Major Tobacco Manufacturers**

American Brands	RJR Nabisco, Inc.	B.A.T. Industries (Parent of Brown & Williamson)	Loews Corp. (Parent of Lorillard)	Liggett Group
American Tobacco Co.	R.J. Reynolds Tobacco Co. (cigarettes, pipe and chewing tobacco)	Tobacco products	Tobacco	Cigarettes
American Cigar Co.		Retailing	CNA Financial (insurance)	NFL trading cards
Gallaher Ltd. (international cigarette operation)	Nabisco Brands, Inc.	Paper	Loews Hotels	Confectionery licensing
James B. Beam Distilling Co.	Planters Lifesavers Co. (nuts, popcorn, candy, gum)	Packaging and printing	Loews Theaters	
Swingline, Inc.	Biscuits: cookies, crackers (Oreo, Chips Ahoy)	Cosmetics	Bulova Watch Co.	
Acushnet Co. (golf products, Titlist)	Grocery products: cereals (Shredded Wheat),	Home furnishings	Residential development	
Franklin Life Insurance Co.	margarine, A-1 steak			
Master Lock Co.	sauce, Milkbone dog			
Wilson Jones Co. (office supplies)	biscuits, Grey Poupon			
ACCO World (fasteners)	mustards, and Royal			
Day-timers	desserts			
Waterloo Industries (tool storage products)	Del Monte Tropical Fruit Co. (canned fruits, vege-			
Twentieth Century (do-it-yourself plumbing)	tables, fruit juices, desserts)			
Aristokraft (kitchen and bath cabinets)	Sports Marketing			
Polland & Atchison (optical goods and services)	Containerized Ocean Freight Shipping			
Forbuoy's (UK candy, tobacco, and news agent chain)	Sea-Land Service, Inc.			
T.M. Group (UK vending machine company)	Signal Petroleum Aminoil Packaging products			

Source: Compiled from 1989 annual reports for each company.

Philip Morris had been moderately successful in reducing its dependence on tobacco revenues. In 1970, tobacco contributed 85 percent of sales and 90 percent of income, in 1980 it was down to 65 percent of sales and 86 percent of income, and in 1990 tobacco products contributed only 40 percent of PM's sales and roughly 65 percent of operating income. But while Philip Morris moved mainly into consumer goods businesses where its cigarette marketing skills could be transferred into a major competitive asset, other tobacco manufacturers chose to diversify more broadly (see Exhibit 6).

Industry Profitability   In 1990, the tobacco producers, despite diversification, still derived a large fraction of their sales and earnings from cigarettes. Combined sales of 524 billion cigarettes in 1989 produced industrywide revenues of $68.6 billion and profits of $7.2 billion. The strong sales and profit performance of the cigarette producers was principally due to hefty price increases over the years (averaging 7 percent annually from 1970 through 1989), rather than increased sales volume; industry volume peaked in 1982 at 640 billion units and had declined about 3 percent annually since then.

Cigarette production required low capital investments, which, combined with the large profit margins, generated substantial cash flows. Exhibit 7 pre-

EXHIBIT 7   **Comparative Financial Data for Selected Tobacco Companies, 1980–1989**
*(In millions of dollars)**

	1980		1985		1989	
	Tobacco Sales	Operating Income	Tobacco Sales	Operating Income	Tobacco Sales	Operating Income
Philip Morris	$6,047	$1,083	$10,602	$2,460	$17,864	$5,062
R.J. Reynolds	5,604	978	5,422	1,483	6,981	2,016
B.A.T. Industries	N/A	N/A	9,321	959	13,395	1,299
American Brands	4,299	439	4.390	520	7,009	909
Loews Corporation	1,053	159	1,501	137	1,771	355
Liggett Group	291	27	N/A	6	573	53

*Figures are for tobacco revenues and operating income only, not total sales of conglomerate companies.
Source: Compiled by the casewriter from annual reports and S&P's Valueline.

sents the size and profitability of the tobacco segments of Philip Morris and the five other U.S. cigarette competitors (R.J. Reynolds, B.A.T. Industries, American Brands, Loews Corporation, and Liggett).

Competition in the Domestic Cigarette Industry

The market shares of the six competitors in the U.S. cigarette industry in 1990 are listed below:

Manufacturer	1952	1961	1970	1980	1985	1989
R.J. Reynolds	26.2%	34.0%	31.7%	2.8 %	31.6%	28.5%
Philip Morris	9.7	9.2	16.7	30.8	35.9	41.9
Brown & Williamson	5.9	9.3	16.7	13.7	11.9	11.4
American Brands	32.3	25.6	19.7	10.7	8.1	8.0
Lorillard	5.6	10.5	8.5	9.8	7.5	7.0
Liggett Group	17.8	10.8	6.5	2.2	5.0	3.2
All others	2.5	0.6	0.2	0.0	0.0	0.0

Philip Morris had 6 of the 20 best-selling brands, including the No. 1 brand, Marlboro. R.J. Reynolds had 7 brands in the top 20, but had experienced a steady decline in market share over the past two decades. Like PM, RJR had diversified primarily into consumer goods—R.J. Reynolds acquired Nabisco Company in 1985 for $4.9 billion and changed its name to RJR Nabisco to reflect the change in direction. RJR Nabisco was subsequently acquired by RJR Nabisco Holdings, a wholly owned subsidiary of Kohlberg Kravis & Roberts, which took the company private in 1988.

American Brands diversified through unrelated acquisitions, such as golf products, office products, insurance companies, optical services, and retailing. Brown and Williamson was owned by B.A.T. Industries, a British company and the world's largest cigarette producer. Lorillard was a subsidiary of Loews

EXHIBIT 8   **Rank, Unit Sales, Market Share, and Advertising Expenditures by Cigarette Brands, 1980–1989**

		1989			
Brand	**Company**	**Rank**	**Billions of Units**	**Market Share**	**Advertising Expenditures**
Marlboro	PM	1	138.0	26.3%	$100,751,000
Winston	RJR	2	47.4	9.0	22,374,000
Salem	RJR	3	32.3	6.2	29,606,000
Kool	B & W	4	31.2	6.0	19,655,000
Newport	Lorillard	5	24.7	4.7	48,759,000
Camel	RJR	6	20.4	3.9	27,222,000
Benson & Hedges	PM	7	20.3	3.9	37,616,000
Merit	PM	8	20.1	3.8	54,223,000
Doral	RJR	9	19.2	3.7	4,692,000
Virginia Slims	PM	10	16.5	3.2	44,361,000
Pall Mall	AB	11	14.0	2.7	8,671,000
Vantage	RJR	12	13.2	2.5	24,981,000
Cambridge	PM	13	11.9	2.3	3,668,000
Kent	Lorillard	14	10.8	2.1	6,102,000
Carlton	AB	15	9.0	1.7	32,862,000
Viceroy	B & W	16	6.8	1.3	13,355,000
More	RJR	17	5.4	1.0	17,825,000
Now	RJR	18	5.1	1.0	18,396,000
Parliament	PM	19	4.6	0.9	6,706,000
True	Lorillard	20	4.5	0.9	7,901,000
Raleigh	B & W	NA	NA	NA	NA
Lucky Strike	AB	NR	NR	NR	2,476,000

NA = Not applicable.
NR = Not reported.
Compiled by the casewriter from several sources, including *Business Week*, Leading Ad Dollar Summary, 1989, 1987, 1985, and 1980.

Corporation, an $11.4 billion conglomerate with businesses in hotels, theaters, and watches. The Newport brand represented 60 percent of Lorillard's sales.

The Liggett Group had experienced several ownership turnovers in the last decade. In 1980, Liggett Group was acquired by the British conglomerate, Grand Metropolitan. By 1986, the group was sold in a private buyout and operated independently. The company had four full-price brands (Chesterfield, Eve, L&M, and Lark), two price-value brands (Chesterfield Filter Lights and Savvy), and one extra-low-price brand (Pyramid), none in the top 20. Liggett Group's only diversification moves were two licensing rights: one for confectionery products and one for National Football League trading cards.

Competitive Weapons   There were three primary competitive weapons used by cigarette manufacturers—advertising, new product innovations, and pricing. Since all cigarette advertising was banned from TV and radio in 1971, print, billboard, and promotional advertising were used extensively by all six domestic manufacturers to create and reinforce brand images and personali-

	1985				1980		
Rank	**Billions of Units**	**Market Share**	**Advertising Expenditures**	**Rank**	**Billions of Units**	**Market Share**	**Advertising Expenditures**
1	133.5	22.46%	$87,446,000	1	108.8	17.8%	$31,349,000
2	68.4	11.51	48,808,000	2	81.1	13.3	36,846,000
3	47.5	7.99	36,093,000	4	54.4	8.9	36,978,000
4	40.2	6.77	29,013,000	3	54.7	8.9	28,285,000
9	20.7	3.48	31,862,000	13	11.7	1.9	9,205,000
6	25.9	4.36	34,319,000	7	26.3	4.3	21,422,000
5	27.8	4.68	37,464,000	6	28.1	4.6	24,177,000
7	24.4	4.10	51,066,000	8	26.0	4.2	26,500,000
16	7.3	1.23	NR	NR	NR	NR	10,002,000
13	16.2	2.72	41,716,000	12	14.0	2.3	17,638,000
8	21.3	3.58	102,000	5	31.8	5.2	7,822,000
10	19.9	3.35	38,706,000	9	23.9	3.9	32,493,000
NA	NA	NA	NA	NA	NR	NR	15,400,000
12	17.9	3.02	14,779,000	10	20.4	3.3	29,565,000
14	11.1	1.87	24,042,000	11	15.4	2.6	19,741,000
NR	NR	NR	268,000	17	10.8	1.8	13,805,000
15	8.6	1.45	23,858,000	NR	NR	NR	12,698,000
NR	NR	NR	21,418,000	NR	NR	NR	26,129,000
NR	5.8	0.98	6,156,000	19	7.5	1.2	1,969,000
18	6.8	1.14	24,257,000	16	11.1	1.8	11,975,000
19	NR	NR	6,456,000	15	11.1	1.8	8,078,000
20	5.8	0.98	7,126,000	NR	NR	NR	NR

ties—in 1989 the six manufacturers spent a combined $674 million on advertising in nine media. Exhibit 8 presents sales and advertising data for the top 20 brands from 1980 through 1989.

New variations of a successful brand, such as different filters, lengths, and packaging, were commonly used to expand a brand's appeal—in 1989 PM marketed 17 versions of Marlboro, and R.J. Reynolds offered 6 versions of its Winston brand. Other innovations included smoke-free or nicotine-free cigarettes, but these had met with little market success so far. In general, attempts to create brand appeal and build brand loyalty paid off, because smokers' brand loyalties were among the strongest relative to other consumer goods products.

As mentioned previously, price-value cigarette brands were the fastest-growing segment. Each manufacturer had developed new products to offer at a lower price to compete in this market. The Liggett Group was aggressively competing in this segment and was the first to offer an extra-low-price brand, Pyramid. PM introduced Bristol and Alpine in the discount category in 1989, following them with the Buck brand in 1990. RJR and PM had invested heavily in the price-value segment in recent years, and in 1990 held 31.3 percent and 24.8 percent of this segment, respectively. Tobacco analysts said the companies were forced to compete in this segment or watch their rivals steal away the "penny-pinching" smokers and drive down prices. The downside of being a major player in this segment was that the advertising promotions for the price-value brands encouraged smokers to trade down, which cannibalized sales from full-priced brands.

Performance of the Philip Morris U.S.A. Division

In the 1970s and 1980s, Philip Morris U.S.A. led all U.S. tobacco manufacturers in growth in both unit cigarette sales and market share. During the 1970s, Philip Morris U.S.A.'s cigarette unit sales grew at an average annual compound rate of 8.5 percent—five times the industrywide rate of 1.7 percent. During the 1980s, PM's unit sales of cigarettes rose from 191 billion units to 220 billion units, a compound annual growth rate of 1.6 percent, even though industry-wide unit sales dropped from 619 to 525 billion units. The division's market share went from 16.7 percent in 1970 to an all-time company high of 41.9 percent in 1989. This ability to take market share away from rivals made the Philip Morris U.S.A. division a growth business in a declining industry. William Campbell, CEO of PM U.S.A., voiced PM's outlook for the division: "We have always viewed PM U.S.A. as a growth company, and, basically, I continue to believe that's a relevant vision. . . . The charge I have from senior management is that we continue to deliver superior income performance in the context of continued share and volume gains."[2]

In 1990, PM's Marlboro brand was the world's best-known brand and best-selling cigarette. Marlboro's national lead had been widening every year since 1975, when Marlboro sales overtook Winston for the No. 1 position. U.S. sales of Marlboro were 138 billion units, 63 percent of PM's total domestic sales of 220 billion units, and had a market share of over 26 percent. PM's Benson & Hedges brand held 3.9 percent of the market; Merit, 3.8 percent; Virginia Slims, 3.2 percent; Cambridge, a price-value brand, 2.3 percent; and Parliament, 0.9 percent.

Cigarette Marketing at PM

Philip Morris had achieved industry leadership by consistently implementing a precise sequence of marketing strategies. As the industry matured and sales declined, PM sought to exploit market niches. The company was alert to demographic trends that signaled the emergence of a new market segment opportunity. When a new segment of ample size was identified, PM would offer a newly developed brand or alter an existing brand and try to grow it into a segment leader. PM developed products and tailored advertising to identify with a particular segment of the market. PM offered cigarettes targeted at women, blacks, and the upper-, middle-, and lower-income levels. Philip Morris followed up on its market segmentation and product positioning strategies by first defining and communicating a brand's individual image and personality, and second tenaciously reinforcing and enhancing the brand's personality via colors, imagery, packaging, consistent advertising, and point-of-sale displays.

---

[2]As quoted in *The Wall Street Journal*, November 13, 1990.

Each brand was given the attention and advertising support necessary to become a segment leader. PM rarely changed its basic advertising theme and image for a brand, although it was common to add new wrinkles and variations.

Top management in the cigarette division was composed almost exclusively of marketing specialists and people with strong marketing experience and backgrounds. The key skills were shrewd market segmentation, imaginative marketing, trend awareness and trend anticipation, and translating perceptions of the "moods of the time" and what was happening in the marketplace into bold actions to exploit new market niches. Because of its large advertising budgets per brand, PM marketing specialists were able to exercise considerable buying power, which enabled PM to capture advertising economies of scale.

Marlboro   Marlboro was initially introduced in 1924 in two varieties: an ivory tip and a red tip (which was targeted primarily at women). In 1954, the company saw the opportunity to capitalize on the changing consumer preference for filtered cigarettes. PM repackaged the brand with a red-and-white geometric-designed box and the Marlboro man was born. The cowboy—in Stetson hat and leather chaps, often on horseback, always silent and always serious—conveyed the image of American independence and frontier spirit. R. W. Murray, president and CEO of PM International, described the Marlboro Man: "The cowboy has appeal to people as a personality. There are elements of adventure, freedom, being in charge of your destiny."[3] PM had changed neither the package nor the image for over 35 years.

The Marlboro man was perhaps PM's greatest asset. Although all cigarette advertising was banned from television in 1971, Marlboro ads appeared extensively in magazines, on billboards, and at point-of-purchase displays. Hollywood westerns paved the way for the Marlboro man internationally, where foreigners were eager to associate themselves with the American image. One Munich-born-and-raised immigrant said, "If Americans want to be chic like a European, they have to buy a Mercedes or BMW. For us it is easier; all we have to do is smoke Marlboros and wear jeans."[4]

PM kept the Marlboro image alive through the use of line extensions, rather than changing the image. The company responded to changing customer preferences by adding Marlboro 100s, a longer cigarette, in 1967; Marlboro Lights, a low-tar-and-nicotine option, in 1972; and Marlboro 25s, which had 25 cigarettes per pack, in 1985. In 1989, the company was test marketing a Marlboro Ultra Light. Marlboro products accounted for 28 percent of PM's $25 billion in revenues in 1989 and brought in more than one half of its operating profits. Since 1980, this brand averaged more than three percent growth in a declining market, selling nearly one pack in four in a field of more than 250 brands.

Other Brands   In 1968, PM introduced Virginia Slims to appeal to the increasing number of women smokers. Using the same logic that was successful with the Marlboro brand, PM linked the brand to the image of the modern woman.

---

[3]As quoted in *Forbes*, February 9, 1987.
[4]As quoted in *Forbes*, February 9, 1987.

The Virginia Slims woman was attractive, fashionable, carefree, and very liberated. The ads always contrasted the Virginia Slims woman with the subjugated woman of the past, accompanied with the tag line, "You've come a long way, baby." Susan Jannetta, Virginia Slims's brand manager, said, "[Virginia Slims] ads have historically tried to convey fun, fashion, and flattery. . . . The Virginia Slims woman is confident, yet approachable." Virginia Slims was the cigarette most preferred by women and held 3.2 percent of the total U.S. market in 1989.

The Benson & Hedges brand cultivated an image designed to appeal to the "yuppie" generation. The ads featured young adults in leisure or relaxing situations, sometimes alone, sometimes in groups. This brand was also popular with the black smoking population and ads often featured black jazz musicians. Benson & Hedges held 3.9 percent of the total market in 1989.

PM introduced the Bucks brand in 1990 to appeal to the growing numbers of price-conscious smokers. Arthur Goldfarb, brand manager, said, "Bucks is positioned to capture price-sensitive male smokers who are looking for an alternative brand choice." This brand was associated with a fully antlered stag on a red or white background for regular or light cigarettes, respectively. Magazines and billboards pictured the buck with engaging tag lines such as "The Buck stops here," "Buck the system," "The almighty Buck," or "Herd of Bucks?" The company pitched the brand to retailers through trade magazine advertisements that exclaimed "There's more than one way to make a Buck." These ads claimed to help retailers "rack up sales to price-sensitive smokers" by offering consumers full, rich flavor for a money-saving low price, with handsome packaging and "off-beat promotions" and "catchy advertising" to capture attention.

Production Efficiencies

In addition to marketing competencies, Philip Morris also had competitive strength in production efficiency. PM's management made conscious efforts to learn how all the bits and pieces of the cigarette business fit together and how they could be better integrated into a smoothly functioning manufacturing, distribution, and sales promotion process. PM strived to keep margins up by stringently controlling costs and producing at maximum efficiency.

The demand generated by advertising allowed PM to achieve manufacturing economies of scale. The company had 10 tobacco manufacturing and processing facilities in the United States: 7 in or near Richmond, Virginia, 1 in North Carolina, and 2 in Kentucky. These facilities produced 300 billion units in 1989, 78 billion of which were purchased by PM's international division for export.

PM had invested over $5.3 billion since 1978 in plants, equipment, and facilities (a figure that was less than 10 percent of total domestic tobacco revenues). Two new state-of-the-art facilities were built—one opened in 1983 in North Carolina and the other opened in 1986 in Kentucky. The company also made capital expenditures to expand or modernize its eight existing plants, with a goal of achieving maximum production efficiencies. State-of-the-art equipment increased capacity to as much as 500 million cigarettes per day per plant. These technologies, combined with rigid cost controls, helped PM position itself as a low-cost producer with an average total cost, including marketing and administrative overhead, of 2.2 cents per unit sold.

Future Prospects for Tobacco

In April 1989, in response to concerns expressed by certain stockholders that the company was "dealing in death" by promoting sales of its cigarettes to consumers, PM's board of directors added a resolution to the agenda at the annual stockholders' meeting proposing that the company discontinue all production and distribution of cigarettes by the year 2000. Management was opposed to this proposal and the resolution was soundly defeated by the stockholders.

Management was bullish about PM's future in domestic tobacco. According to PM U.S.A.'s Vice Chairman William Murray:

> As we look to the future, there is every reason to believe that we can continue to grow our global tobacco business. We have vitality and momentum. We have a unique portfolio of trademarks. Our modern, state-of-the-art factories manufacture low cost, high quality products in ever increasing quantities. And we are investing in research and development in order to have a constant stream of new products available to meet changing consumer needs.
>
> Together, these factors bring us cash flows matched by few companies in any industry anywhere in the world, and give us confidence in the future of our tobacco business.

PM's International Tobacco Strategic Business Unit

All cigarette production and sales outside of the United States were handled by Philip Morris International. In 1989 this segment represented 18.7 percent of PM's total revenues, 47 percent of total tobacco revenues, and 14 percent of total operating income. From 1985 through 1989, PM International's revenues grew at a compound rate of 20.4 percent and operating income grew at 25 percent (as compared with 9.5 percent and 15 percent, respectively, for PM U.S.A.). PM executives saw the greatest opportunities for the company's cigarette business in international markets and were rapidly increasing PM's presence through acquisitions and exports.

Conditions in the International Tobacco Market

Worldwide, tobacco consumption was growing approximately 2 to 2.5 percent per year. This combined with the downward pressure on prices in the U.S. market made the overseas market more attractive, despite the lower profit margins associated with international sales. Of the 5 trillion cigarettes sold worldwide in 1989, U.S. manufacturers held less than a 20 percent share. PM and RJR were expanding their international volumes by 5 to 6 percent per year. Unlike the U.S. market, the international cigarette market was highly fragmented in terms of producers. Many of the foreign producers restricted their operations to a single country or small group of countries.

In 1990, several political and economic conditions offered challenges and opportunities for tobacco manufacturers. The demise of communism, the reunification of Germany, and improved trade relations between the United States and the Soviet Union resulted in new markets for the 1990s. Cigarette consumption was rising most strongly in socialist bloc countries. Eastern Germany represented a market of approximately 31 billion units, half of which were international brands. Both PM and RJR had entered this market through acquisitions of local tobacco companies. In 1989 RJR acquired the third-largest East German cigarette manufacturer, and PM acquired the largest manufacturer in East Germany in 1990.

Although tobacco consumption was relatively flat in Japan, a large percentage of the population smoked, trade barriers were lowered in 1986, and consumers were agreeable to switch or upgrade to U.S. brands. These circumstances made the Japanese markets very attractive to U.S. manufacturers. Finally, the development of a unified European community (EC 1992) offered the opportunity to decrease the market fragmentation in Europe. PM was the leading foreign cigarette manufacturer in terms of volume and market share in the European region (Belgium, France, Germany, Greece, Italy, Luxembourg, Malta, the Netherlands, Portugal, and Spain). Within this area, PM brands held 20 percent of the market. Every cigarette sold by PM in the EC area was manufactured in one of PM's four EC-located facilities: Bergen op Zoom, Netherlands; Brussels, Belgium; and Munich and Berlin, Germany.

Major Competitors

In the international arena, Philip Morris competed against 13 major companies (Exhibit 9). Philip Morris's largest rival was B.A.T. Industries Ltd. (formerly British-American Tobacco Co.), which was the world's largest tobacco company, with unit sales outside the United States of roughly 500 billion units (a 10 percent worldwide market share)—nearly 40 percent greater than second-place PM's 1989 volume of 361 billion units. B.A.T. Industries was represented in over 160 countries, and the British-based company's 1989 tobacco revenues were over $13.4 billion. B.A.T. divided its portfolio of businesses into a financial services group and a tobacco group. The financial services group had three large insurance companies as its principal operating companies. The tobacco group consisted of Brown & Williamson in the United States; British-American Tobacco in over 40 countries in Europe, Australia, Latin America, Asia, and Africa; BAT Cigarettenfabriken in West Germany; Souza Cruz in Brazil; Imperial Tobacco in Canada; Skandinavisk in Denmark; and ITC in India. Brown & Williamson, with brands such as Kool, Viceroy, Kent, Capri, Richland, Belair, and Lucky Strike, held 11 percent of the U.S. market; Imperial held nearly 58 percent of the Canadian market.

Rothmans, formerly in partnership with PM, was a major competitor in the United Kingdom, the European countries, Australia, and Greece. In France, the nationally owned SEITA held 51 percent of the market. Likewise, Greece's state-owned cigarette manufacturers held 66 percent of its domestic market. R.J. Reynolds, the fourth-largest tobacco company worldwide, was the only other U.S.-based manufacturer with a global presence. RJR's Winston brand accounted for most of its international sales.

In 1989, Philip Morris had a 7 percent share of an estimated total 5 trillion-unit worldwide cigarette market and was the leading U.S. cigarette exporter. PM International distributed products to more than 170 countries or territories.

PM's International Cigarette Strategy

PM's basic strategy for building critical mass in the international markets was a combination global/multicountry approach. Philip Morris International

Sales (in billions of units) and Market Share Data for Leading International Tobacco Companies, 1989

Company (Country)	West Germany		France		Belgium		Netherlands		Greece		Portugal		Spain		United Kingdom	
	Sales	Share	Sales	Share	Sales	Share	Sales	Share	Sales	Share	Sales	Share	Sales	Share	Sales	Share
Philip Morris (USA)	35.6	30.3%	21.6	22.8%	3.5	20.4%	3.0	18.6%	4.2	14.7%	0.1	0.5%	8.3	10.5%	4.4	5.0%
RJ Reynolds (USA)	10.4	8.8	7.4	7.8	1.3	7.2	2.1	13.3	1.9	6.6	0.9	0.2	7.6	9.6	3.1	3.5
B.A.T. Industries (UK)	24.6	21.0	1.5	1.6	2.3	8.6	3.7	22.8	9.9	3.2	—	—	—	—	31.2	34.9
Rothmans (UK)	11.7	9.9	13.6	14.3	6.4	36.8	6.3	39.3	1.4	5.1	—	—	—	—	8.3	6.5
Reecotsma (W. Germany)	26.7	33.7	—	—	—	—	—	—	9.5	1.8	—	—	2.9	2.5	—	—
SEITA (France)	—	—	48.7	51.3	1.1	6.4	—	—	—	—	0.9	0.1	—	—	—	—
American Tobacco (USA)	—	—	1.2	1.2	—	—	—	—	—	—	—	—	—	—	—	—
Van Landewyck (Lux.)	—	—	—	—	9.9	5.3	—	—	—	—	—	—	—	—	—	—
Niemeyer (W. Germany)	—	—	—	—	—	—	0.4	2.4	—	—	—	—	—	—	—	—
State-owned companies	—	—	—	—	—	—	—	—	18.5	66.2	—	—	—	—	6.2	6.9
Austria Tabak (Switz.)	—	—	—	—	—	—	—	—	0.5	1.6	—	—	—	—	—	—
Tabaqueira (Spain)	—	—	—	—	—	—	—	—	—	—	14.2	99.2	—	—	—	—
Tabacalera (Spain)	—	—	—	—	—	—	—	—	—	—	—	—	55.8	70.3	—	—
Gallaher (Spain)	—	—	—	—	—	—	—	—	—	—	—	—	—	—	35.6	40.1

Sources: Compiled from issues of *Globe*, a Philip Morris publication.

followed a production strategy that was primarily a multicountry approach—PMI produced cigarettes in facilities located throughout the world and offered brands or products that were tailored for a particular market or region. However, there were also some global aspects to PM's international strategy. The plants and facilities owned and leased by PMI were by no means autonomous; PM headquarters maintained a network of control and coordination among the various overseas facilities. Additionally, PM followed a global approach to producing and marketing some brands internationally, particularly its Marlboro brand. PMI purchased 78 billion units (primarily Marlboros), approximately 22 percent of all international sales, from PM U.S.A., and transferred the brand image it had built in the United States to foreign markets.

Acquisitions   PM acquired local cigarette manufacturers as a way of gaining entry to foreign markets. PM's primary interest in local companies was in acquiring rights to market their brands and to serve as a vehicle for introducing other PMI brands into the local markets. As of 1990, PM had acquired 21 plants located throughout the world. Philip Morris had a 100 percent controlling interest in plants in the following locations:

Australia	1 plant
Belgium	2 plants
Brazil	2 plants
Germany	3 plants
Italy	1 plant
Netherlands	1 plant
Switzerland	2 plants

PM International had an average market share of over 20 percent in each of these countries.

In 1978, PM International acquired the overseas rights to all of the cigarette brands of Liggett, a move that further strengthened PM's international market position. Liggett brands covered by the purchase included Lark, L&M, Chesterfield, Eve, and Decade. The Lark brand was the leading imported brand in Japan in 1989. In 1981, Philip Morris and Rothmans International announced a $350 million deal whereby PM acquired an immediate 22 percent ownership interest in Rothmans along with the U.S. marketing rights for Rothmans brands (Dunhill, Peter Stuyvesant, and Rothmans). Rothmans specialized in top-of-the-line brands and British-style, Virginia-blend cigarettes, which had a deluxe or super-premium image. In April 1989, PM and Rothmans agreed to combine their cigarette sales and distribution in Britain in an effort to revive profits and market share and achieve production and marketing synergies. The combined operations would have resulted in 14 percent of the British market and generated $256 million in cigarette revenues annually. In November 1989, however, PM sold its stake in Rothmans to Switzerland's Compagnie Financiere Richemont AG. Industry analysts said the move was made because PMI management had concluded that the Rothmans venture did not deliver the market penetration potential that PM had initially hoped for.

In 1991, PM acquired Dresden Cigarette Manufacturing Company, the largest cigarette manufacturing operation in Eastern Germany. This purchase added four additional brands to PMI's product line, one of which accounted for about 25 percent of all cigarettes sold in Eastern Germany. Dresden's combined share was approximately 35 percent of the market. This purchase followed a pact in which PM agreed to supply more than 20 billion cigarettes to the Russian Republic—the largest republic in the Soviet Union. In return for providing technical assistance to improve tobacco manufacturing in the Soviet Union, PMI secured an agreement in principle to supply cigarettes to the Russian Republic from 1992 to 1995. Industry analysts noted that Soviet smokers on average spent 8 to 10 percent of their income on cigarettes. During the height of the Soviet cigarette shortage in the late 1980s (analysts predicted the supply was approximately 50 billion units short of the 400 billion demand), packs of Marlboro were sold on the black market for as much as 25 rubles each, or approximately $40 at the official exchange rate.

Capacity   PM's strategy was to renovate the newly acquired facilities, install state-of-the-art equipment, and bring the manufacturing process up to PM's production and efficiency standards. Generally, production continued status quo at the newly acquired facilities, while PM imported Marlboros and other brands until the plant upgrades were complete. At that point, PM ceased most of its imports and began production of both its major brands and the newly acquired brands in the newly renovated facilities. This strategy increased the length of the production run at the upgraded plants and reduced costs in that facility by allowing PM to allocate fixed costs over a greater number of units and lowering the distribution costs of its major brands in that area. However, this also meant that the length of the production runs at the plants that were originally supplying the imports were reduced; hence, the net cost advantage was less than the plant-level advantage.

Brands   Brand marketing and advertising was primarily global, with adjustments for country-level market conditions. PM used the Marlboro cowboy image, with very few exceptions, uniformly in each of the 170 countries and territories to which it distributed. The Marlboro brand, which had been the world's largest-selling cigarette brand since 1972, represented over 50 percent of PM's international volume. Total international sales of the Marlboro brand family in 1989 were 182 billion units. Marlboro was the No. 1 cigarette in France, Greece, West Germany, and the Netherlands in 1989.

As in the United States, the company followed a market segmentation strategy and relied heavily on media advertising to create a brand image and to build customer loyalty. PM transferred its marketing skills and competencies into developing new brands designed to meet the needs of a specific country, such as the Muratti brand in Italy and Peter Jackson in Australia. PM also used its marketing know-how to increase the market share of the newly acquired brands.

Future Prospects for International Tobacco

The management at PM saw great potential in its international tobacco strategic business unit. Worldwide, cigarette consumption was still a growing industry, while domestic consumption was slowly declining. Additionally, international politics, such as *glasnost*, trade agreements with Japan and China, and the emergence of a unified European Community, were opening doors to markets that had previously been closed to PM International. These markets were characteristically dominated by government-run monopolies that had little incentive to offer consumers a wide variety of cigarette types and brands. Too often, these monopolies were poorly managed and consumers were faced with severe cigarette shortages. PMI anticipated using its global brand images and strategic plant locations to capitalize on the unmet consumer demand, offer smokers a wider brand selection, and rapidly increase its worldwide share.

PM's MILLER BREWING STRATEGIC BUSINESS UNIT

Philip Morris's acquisition of Miller Brewing Company in 1969 was motivated largely by PM's desire to use the excess cash flows from its profitable cigarette business to exploit the company's cigarette marketing expertise in other consumer product categories. Following the acquisition, PM spent several years sizing up Miller's situation, replacing Miller's management with some of PM's top-flight cigarette personnel, and giving the newly installed management team time to learn and understand the beer business. Then PM began to put strategic changes at Miller into high gear.

Essentially, Miller's new management relied upon the same classic consumer marketing techniques that had lifted PM from fourth to first place in the tobacco business and that had made Marlboro the leading cigarette brand: it looked on the beer market as being divided into segments, brought out new products and packaging for those segments, and then spent heavily on advertising and merchandising to reach the targeted segments. PM's approach to marketing strategy was a radical departure from the beer industry's traditional approach to treating the beer market as a homogeneous entity that could be served by one product in one type of package. "Philip Morris changed the ground rules by introducing consumer marketing to the popular price segment," said John Bissell, senior vice president of Stroh's Brewery.[5]

In 1970, the first year of operation under PM, Miller Brewing contributed $199 million in revenues and held only a 4.3 percent share of the domestic beer market. In 1990, Miller Brewing Company had 23 percent of the domestic market, with four brands in the top 10 ranked beers (Miller Lite, Miller High Life, Miller Genuine Draft, and Milwaukee's Best), and was selling 43.5 million barrels. In 1989, 8 percent of Philip Morris's revenues and 3 percent of its profits were contributed by the Miller Brewing division.

U.S. Beer Industry Trends

Demographics   Demographic trends in the 1980s tended to have an adverse effect on the levels of beer consumption. The 1980s heralded the maturity of the so-called baby boomers and was referred to as the fitness decade—a period during which physical fitness and nutrition awareness were significantly heightened. As a result, domestic drinking habits had changed. Exhibit 10 indicates the changing composition of beverage consumption. Almost all beverages lost market share to soft drinks and bottled water during the 1980s, an indication of marketing skill of the soft drink manufacturers and the increased health consciousness of the decade. Consumption levels of beer per

---

[5]*Marketing and Media Decisions*, May 1985.

capita had been declining and the levels of beer production in barrels were relatively flat throughout most of the 1980s, with a slight increase in volume in 1990:

Year	Consumption (Millions of barrels)	Per-Capita Consumption (Gallons)
1980	178.0	24.5
1981	181.9	24.7
1982	182.4	24.3
1983	183.8	24.3
1984	182.7	24.0
1985	183.0	23.8
1986	187.5	24.1
1987	187.3	23.9
1988	187.9	23.7
1989	186.9	23.3
1990	191.6	23.6

Source: *Beverage Industry*, January 1990 and January 1991.

Beer drinkers also changed their preferences of beer types. Exhibit 11 shows that from 1981 to 1990 the light beer segment grew from 25.2 million barrels, 13.8 percent of the beer consumed in the United States, to 53.6 million barrels and 28 percent of the market. The only other product category to experience growth was imports, which grew from 2.9 percent to 4.5 percent of the total market.

In addition to competition from other beer brands, brewers faced competition from beer substitutes and small, regional brewers. Microbreweries gained popularity in the 1980s. These breweries were small, often locally owned, and produced a draft beer that was served in-house only. Often these breweries were combined with a restaurant to create a pub-like atmosphere that appealed to young professionals. The no-alcohol segment was advertised as a substitute beer for either the designated driver on evenings out or as a low-calorie option for the health conscious. This segment grew between 10 and 15 percent annually between 1985 and 1990. Heileman's Kingsbury brand was the no-alcohol industry leader, but Anheuser-Busch's O'Doul's brand and Miller's Sharp's brand were gaining share.

Anti-Alcohol Movement   Beer consumption was also affected by government regulations and social issues. In 1984, Congress directed states to raise their legal drinking age to 21 or lose federal highway funds. This move eliminated the 18-to-20-year-old youth market, the segment that traditionally consumed more gallons per capita than any other segment. In addition to the rise in the legal drinking age, some states banned happy hours in bars and imposed stiffer penalties on drunk drivers, to the detriment of away-from-home consumption.

In 1988, Congress mandated that, beginning in October 1990, warning labels appear on alcoholic beverage packages. The labels read: "Government Warning: According to the Surgeon General, women should not drink alcohol during pregnancy because of risk of birth defects. Consumption of alcoholic beverages impairs your ability to drive a car or operate machinery and may

EXHIBIT 10   Comparative Market Shares of Beverages, 1980–1989

	1980	1983	1985	1987	1989
Soft drinks	18.7%	20.3%	22.4%	24.2%	25.5%
Coffee	15.0	14.6	14.1	13.9	13.5
Beer	13.3	13.3	13.0	13.1	12.8
Milk	11.4	11.0	11.1	11.2	11.5
Tea	4.0	3.9	4.0	4.0	4.0
Bottled water	1.5	1.9	2.5	3.1	3.9
Juices	3.7	4.3	3.8	3.7	3.7
Powdered drinks	3.3	3.6	3.4	3.0	2.7
Wine	1.2	1.2	1.3	1.3	1.2
Distilled spirits	1.1	1.0	1.0	0.9	0.8
Subtotal	73.2%	75.1%	76.6%	78.3%	79.6%
Imputed water consumption*	26.8%	24.9%	23.4%	21.7%	20.4%
Total	100.0%	100.0%	100.0%	100.0%	100.0%

*Includes all other beverages.
Source: Beverage Industry, February 1990.

cause other health problems." This regulation represented a potential for increased product liability lawsuits for the industry. Campaigning by groups such as Mothers Against Drunk Driving (MADD) kept anti-alcohol sentiments high, but the industry responded with advertising campaigns that stressed moderation and introduced low-alcohol or no-alcohol products. Other groups sought to ban all beer advertising on the premise that the advertisements unduly influenced young drinkers. However, the brewers countered that their advertising was designed to differentiate among brands, not increase consumption.

Competition in the Beer Industry

Throughout most of the 1970s the beer industry experienced substantial contraction in terms of the number of breweries in operation, and by 1980 had fallen to nearly half the levels in 1970:

Year	Number of Brewing Facilities
1970	154
1980	86
1982	82
1984	96
1986	103
1988	183

Throughout the first half of the 1980s, the number of facilities remained below 100. By the late 1980s, the number of brewing facilities had increased,

EXHIBIT 11   **Malt Beverage Market Breakdown by Product Category, 1981–1990**
(In millions of barrels and market share)

Year	Super Premium Barrels	Super Premium Share	Premium Barrels	Premium Share	Light Barrels	Light Share	Popular Barrels	Popular Share	Malt Liquor Barrels	Malt Liquor Share	Imported Barrels	Imported Share
1981	12.7	6.9%	93.9	51.6%	25.2	13.8%	39.0	21.4%	5.9	3.2%	5.2	2.9%
1982	12.8	7.0	88.4	48.5	32.3	17.7	36.7	20.1	6.4	3.5	5.8	3.2
1983	11.5	6.3	86.3	47.0	34.0	18.5	39.2	21.3	6.5	3.5	6.3	3.4
1984	9.1	5.0	82.2	45.0	36.4	19.9	42.0	23.0	5.8	3.2	7.2	3.9
1985	7.9	4.3	80.1	43.6	37.6	20.5	44.4	24.2	5.7	3.1	7.9	4.3
1986	7.1	3.6	80.6	43.0	41.4	22.1	44.0	23.4	5.6	3.0	6.6	4.7
1987	6.7	3.6	77.6	41.5	44.9	24.0	42.7	22.3	5.8	3.1	9.4	5.0
1988	6.0	2.6	76.6	40.8	48.0	25.6	42.1	23.2	5.5	2.6	9.4	5.0
1989	5.2	2.8	75.8	40.3	50.5	26.9	42.2	22.4	5.6	3.0	8.7	4.6
1990	4.7	2.4	71.4	37.3	53.6	28.0	41.9	21.9	5.7	3.0	8.6	4.5

Source: *Beverage Industry*, January 1991.

but the new facilities were built primarily to accommodate the volume gains experienced by Anheuser-Busch, Miller, and Coors and the growing popularity of microbreweries that sprang up in the late 1980s. Per-capita consumption increased by 5.9 million barrels (3.1 percent) in 1990, the first rise since 1986. However, the top three brewers' (A-B, Miller, and Coors) combined gains exceeded the 5.9-million-barrel industry gain. This meant that the "big three" tightened their hold on the market at the expense of the smaller brewers. Stroh Brewing, with only one beer in the top 10, lost 12 percent of its volume and Heileman Brewing, with no beers ranked in the top 10, lost 6.1 percent in 1990. Exhibit 12 indicates the market share trends of the major brewers from 1962 to 1989.

Competitive Weapons

Advertising was a principal competitive weapon in the beer industry. Brewers relied heavily on media ads to create brand loyalty, establish brand image, and introduce new brands to the public. The total advertising expenditures, in millions of dollars, for the brewers during the 1980s were:

Company	Annual Advertising Expenditures (In millions of dollars) 1980	1985	1989
Anheuser-Busch	$120.0	$250.0	$299.1
Miller Brewing (PM)	95.7	164.4	150.7
Stroh Brewing	68.2	54.5	22.8
Adolph Coors	25.5	56.6	105.3
G. Heileman	15.9	8.7	8.9

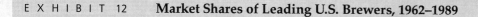

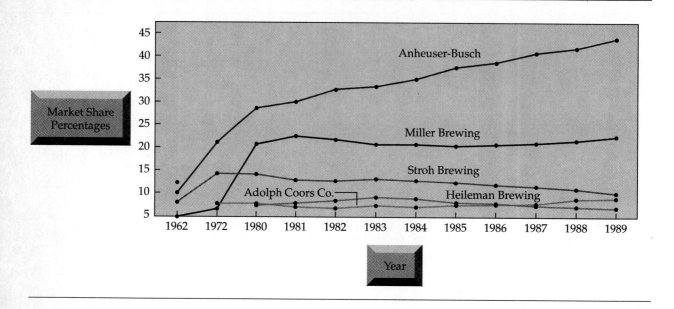

Additionally, Exhibit 13 indicates advertising expenditures and market share data by brand. New products developed for market niches were also important. Miller was attempting to create a market for bottled draft beer with its Miller Genuine Draft brand; A-B was trying to establish a segment for dry beers via introduction of Michelob Dry and Bud Dry; and A-B had entered the light-alcohol segment with its L.A. brand, but had little success.

Pricing was another competitive weapon. Flat consumption rates and the growing buyer sensitivity to price forced brewers to hold price increases to a minimum and try to boost profits through cost reduction. The larger brewers, A-B, Miller, and Coors, benefited from high capacity utilization and economies of scale because of larger volumes.

Additionally, the increase in the federal excise taxes on beer that went into effect January 1, 1991, was predicted to decrease annual consumption by two percent. This in turn was expected to increase the level of competitive rivalry. The "big three" breweries were expected to continue to dominate the domestic beer industry at the expense of the smaller breweries throughout the 1990s.

The Competitors

Anheuser-Busch was the industry leader in 1990 with nearly 45 percent of the total market and six brands in the top 10 ranked beer brands. The market share for its flagship brand, Budweiser, was greater in 1990 (25.7 percent) than all of Miller's brands combined (22.7 percent). A-B was also adept at using advertising to create brand image and loyalty and in developing new products. A-B attempted to replicate Miller's success with Lite and

Advertising Expenditures and Market Share for Selected Beer Brands, 1970–1989
(In thousands of dollars)

Brand	Company	1970		1980		1985		1989	
		Ad Dollars	Market Share	Ad Dollars	Market Share	Ad Dollars	Market Share	Ad Dollars	Market Share
Budweiser	A-B	$8,446	29.8%	$32,091	19.5%	$75,620	24.8%	$90,346	27.6%
Miller Lite	Miller	—	—	32,516	7.4	69,556	10.1	64,615	10.7
Coors Light	Coors	—	—	7,037	1.4	19,142	3.2	51,708	5.5
Bud Light	A-B	—	—	—	—	47,406	3.1	50,114	5.2
Busch	A-B	1,008	—	10,294	1.6	22,434	3.3	27,766	5.0
Miller High Life	Miller	9,294	8.2	36,618	12.7	61,267	6.6	28,278	4.1
Milwaukee's Best	Miller	—	—	—	—	74	1.6	67	3.9
Old Milwaukee	Stroh	2,083	3.9	5,509	2.4	6,407	4.1	5,095	3.7
Coors	Coors	2,107	11.4	13,462	6.4	33,204	4.7	21,608	2.7
Genuine Draft	Miller	—	—	—	—	—	—	46,343	2.4
Old Style	Heileman	—	—	1,677	2.7	3,140	2.7	2,970	2.3
Michelob	A-B	2,496	—	13,323	4.5	37,091	3.3	25,644	2.2
Schaefer	Stroh	—	—	3,634	2.0	405	2.2	46	1.9
Stroh	Stroh	2,735	5.2	8,780	3.2	20,970	2.7	7,272	1.3
Michelob Light	A-B	—	—	16,876	1.3	24,973	1.5	1,930	1.2
A-B Natural Light	A-B	—	—	18,507	1.3	2,349	0.7	1,956	1.1
Old Milwaukee Light	Stroh	—	—	—	—	6,407	1.0	2,633	1.1

Source: Compiled by the casewriter from *Beverage Industry*'s annual beer report, 1985 and 1989, and Leading Ad Dollar Summary.

Genuine Draft by creating a niche for dry beers. Michelob Dry was introduced in 1988 and Bud Dry in 1989. In 1990, the dry beer segment represented 3 percent of the domestic market. Bud Dry held 53 percent and Michelob Dry held 20 percent of the dry beer segment, comparable to 1.6 percent and 0.6 percent, respectively, of the total beer market. A-B was pricing aggressively to gain market share. It sacrificed profits for volume by reducing prices 15 to 40 cents per 12-pack of Budweiser on a market-by-market basis in order to achieve its stated objective of 50 percent market share by 1995. Additionally, A-B was diversified outside of beer production with business interests in breads and bakery products, theme parks (Busch Gardens and Sea World), Eagle Brand snack foods, and major league baseball (the St. Louis Cardinals).

The Adolph Coors Company was a privately held company that competed in the premium, super-premium and light beer segments. The company held 9.9 percent of the domestic market and its Coors Light and Coors brands were ranked second and tenth, respectively, in the top 10 ranked beers. Coors's advertising focused on the quality of the product (as concerns ingredients, the water, the manufacturing process, etc.) rather than the "good times" theme of other brewers' advertisements.

The Stroh Brewing Company, the fourth-ranked brewery, with 8.6 percent of the market, had experienced steady and dramatic losses in market share during the 1980s. The company responded to the decline by reducing the number of brands it offered and concentrating advertising and distribution on the remaining offerings. Conversely, Heileman's strategy was to acquire smaller, declining brands; decrease capital expenditures and advertising to the bare minimum; and ride out the life of the brand. This strategy was relatively successful, but future success depended on the availability of declining brands. Heileman was purchased in a leveraged buy-out by Bond Holding Corporation in 1989 and in 1991 was struggling under the tremendous debt load incurred as a result of the takeover. The company announced plans to sell two breweries and eight brands in March 1990. Heileman President and COO Murray Cutbush said the divestiture was prompted for strategic fit reasons, but industry analysts said Heileman was unloading unused capacity. In 1990, Heileman Brewing filed a Chapter 11 bankruptcy claim and Cutbush resigned as president of Heileman in early 1991; the resignation was apparently prompted by Cutbush's inability to maneuver the company with its declining volume and its heavy debt load.

The Performance of Miller Brewing Company

Throughout the 1970–1975 period when the strategic changes were first initiated and implemented, Miller gained dramatically in market share but not in profitability. Miller spent heavily for advertising—roughly $3 per barrel compared with an industry average of just more than $1 per barrel. Miller's operating profits in the five-year period 1971–1975 averaged less than $7 million per year—a 3.1 percent annual return on the $227 million that Philip Morris had spent in purchasing Miller, a figure that did not take into account either interest expenses or the expenditures for capital additions undertaken by PM during this same period. In the next five years Miller's operating profits rose sharply, and its market share also continued to climb. But by 1980, return on sales and market share had flattened out:

Year	Miller's Operating Revenues (In millions of dollars)	Miller's Operating Profits (In millions of dollars)	Miller's Share of Beer Sales
1970	$ 198.5	$ 11.4	4.3%
1975	658.3	28.6	8.6
1980	2,542.3	144.7	21.1
1985	2,914.0	132.0	20.8
1986	3,054.0	154.0	21.3
1987	3,105.0	170.0	21.6
1988	3,262.0	190.0	21.4
1989	3,435.0	226.0	22.4

Source: PM Annual Reports.

Miller High Life Upon acquisition, Miller's first move was to reposition the Miller High Life brand, the flagship brand Miller had when PM made the acquisition. The new ads touted "Miller Time" and " If you have the time, we have the beer." This repositioning of High Life's identity and image was a resounding success—by 1978 Miller High Life had become the second-largest selling beer in the U.S.; Anheuser-Busch's Budweiser brand ranked first.

However, Miller High Life reached an all-time high of 18.6 percent in 1979. By 1989, the brand's share had fallen to 4.1 percent. The company had to rely on new products to keep capacity utilization at an acceptable level. Reflecting on Miller's performance of the previous decade, Maxwell said:

> I think the steam went out of Miller in the 1980s, partly because the competition, especially Anheuser-Busch, became more determined. And maybe because of some other things. Perhaps we overreached on pricing. So the business trailed off. We built a brewery too many [the inactive Trenton, Ohio, facility was built for $450 million].[6]

By the end of the decade the company had come full circle and was again repositioning the High Life brand. A new advertising campaign, "Buy that man a Miller," was introduced in 1989 and PM had hopes of regaining share in the premium beer segment.

Miller Lite In January 1975 Miller introduced Lite on a national basis with a blitz advertising campaign costing an estimated $10 million. The campaign for Lite stressed the "less filling" advantage of a reduced-calorie beer that "tastes great" like other premium beers. To dramatize the theme, Miller used sports personalities (Whitey Ford, Wilt Chamberlain, Dick Butkus, Joe Frazier) to tout the message. The response to Lite exceeded Miller's expectations, and demand quickly matched Miller's capacity to brew and distribute the Lite brand. More than a few rival brewers belittled Miller's attempt "to enter a market that did not exist," but the success of Lite was so dramatic that within a short time 30 other brands of low-calories beers were rushed onto the market by other brewers. Nonetheless, Miller's Lite brand remained the leading low-calorie brand by a wide margin and became the most successful new beer brand introduced in the century (a record previously held by Anheuser-

---

[6]As quoted in *Fortune*, May 8, 1989.

Busch's Michelob brand). By 1983, Lite was the second best-selling brand of beer. In 1989 sales of Lite totaled 20 million barrels out of Miller's total sales of 44 million barrels and market share had increased to 10.7 percent.

Other Brands In 1974 Miller moved to challenge Michelob—Anheuser-Busch's most profitable product—which dominated the super-premium segment. Miller was attracted to this segment by both the higher margins and the 30-plus percent annual growth in Michelob sales. Miller acquired exclusive import rights for the world-famous Lowenbrau brand of German beer. Anheuser-Busch's reaction to the entry of Lowenbrau was summed up neatly by August A. Busch III: "This is Lowenbrau made in the United States, not the beer imported from Europe, and the consumers are not going to be fooled by that little game." Miller did not achieve the success in the super-premium category that it had enjoyed in the premium and light categories. By 1989, Michelob's market share had risen to 2.2 percent while Lowenbrau was still less than 1 percent.

Miller's recent performance was aided by the introduction of three new brands—Meister Brau, Milwaukee's Best, and Genuine Draft. Meister Brau was introduced in 1983 and Milwaukee's Best in 1984 in attempts to gain share in the popular segment. These brands put Miller Brewing in head-on competition with Anheuser-Busch's Busch brand, which was the popular-beer segment leader. However, Miller was more successful with this endeavor and by 1990 Milwaukee's Best held 4.2 percent of the market, closely behind Busch's 5 percent share.

With the introduction of the Miller Genuine Draft brand, Miller Brewing hoped to create and dominate a new beer category the way Miller Lite did for light beers. Noting that packaged draft beer represented one third of Japanese beer consumption, the company acquired the technology from Sapporo Brewery in Japan for using ceramic filters to remove impurities. The product was introduced in the spring of 1986 and by year-end had achieved sales of more than 1.5 million barrels. By 1990, volume had risen to 5.7 million barrels, a 3.0 percent market share. This volume boost encouraged Miller to refit its inactive Trenton plant for production of Genuine Draft. In 1990, Miller was test marketing a light version of Genuine Draft that industry analysts predicted would steal share away from the Genuine Draft brand. Hamish Maxwell's response to these concerns was: "Every new product you ever bring out takes business away. The issue is, if you have a good idea, do it yourself. Because if you don't and somebody else does it, you're a total loser."[7]

Future Prospects for the Beer Segment

Leonard J. Goldstein, president and CEO of Miller Brewing, discussed Miller's future prospects:

> We are responding to our changing customer and consumer base with major marketing initiatives. Localized marketing programs boosted our volume and share in key markets, such as Texas, while new product tests and introductions expanded our presence in growing segments.
>
> 1989 saw Miller's largest revenue, income, and volume percentage gains in the past three years. We intend to build on this volume.

---

[7]As quoted in *Business Week*, August 8, 1988.

PM'S FOOD STRATEGIC BUSINESS UNIT

PM's entry into the food-processing industry was its latest, and largest, diversification effort. This segment contributed 51 percent of the company's revenues and 30 percent of the operating profits in 1989. PM entered this segment via two major acquisitions—General Foods (GF) in 1985 and Kraft, Inc. in 1988, both hostile takeovers.

General Foods

In 1985, shortly after Hamish Maxwell took over as CEO, Philip Morris made a tender offer for General Foods. Maxwell saw in GF another opportunity to use PM's cumulative knowledge of marketing in a huge consumer market. The offer was initially rejected, but Maxwell's tenacity and PM's cash offer of $5.7 billion won out.

Prior to acquisition by PM, General Foods had sales of $9 billion in 1985. The company operated in four worldwide product groupings:

Segment	Percentage of Net Sales	Brands
Packaged grocery products	42%	Entenmanns Pastries, Crystal Light, Kool-Aid, Grape Nuts, Log Cabin, Jell-O, Stove-Top Stuffing, Shake 'n Bake, Birds Eye, and Hostess Cakes
Grocery coffee	28	Maxwell House, Sanka, and Brim
Processed meats	18	Oscar Mayer and Louis Rich Turkey Products
Food service products	12	Jell-O, Crystal Light, and Oscar Mayer

At the time of the acquisition, GF labored under a stifling bureaucracy that Philip Morris worked to reduce to make the company more responsive to marketing and market trends. Although GF had well-known brands, significant market share in some areas, and strategic positioning in others, the operating earnings indicated that only the processed meats division had experienced consecutive years of growth from 1980 through 1985. Oscar Mayer was GF's best performer and had shown the ability to spot and exploit market opportunities, such as the acquisition of Louis Rich in 1979. Exhibit 14 provides financial highlights for the two-year period prior to GF's acquisition. The division operated independently of PM for the first two years after acquisition while PM executives learned the food-processing business.

In 1987, General Foods contributed approximately 36 percent to PM's operating revenues. This represented a major step in Hamish Maxwell's plan to restructure Philip Morris as a consumer-products company and substantially reduce dependence on tobacco. GF was just beginning to move out from under the bureaucracy when GF Chairman Smith left PM to lead Pillsbury, leaving a restructuring project unfinished. Maxwell needed a leader at GF who would instill some of PM's marketing values, and began looking around for someone that fit the bill.

EXHIBIT 14   **Pre-Acquisition Performance Highlights for General Foods, 1984 and 1985**
(Dollar figures in millions, except for per-share data)

	1984	1985
Net Sales		
Packaged grocery products	$3,788	$3,798
Grocery coffee	2,300	2,536
Processed meats	1,533	2,608
Food service and other	979	2,081
Total Net Sales	$8,600	$9,023
Operating earnings		
Packaged grocery products	$471	$419
Grocery coffee	108	127
Processed meats	97	104
Food service and other	40	51
Total Operating Earnings	$716	$701
Net earnings	$317	$325
Working capital	1,102	975
Capital expenditures	267	303
Stockholders' equity	2,040	1,940
Total debt to equity	47.2%	57.7%
Long-term debt to equity	36.6%	37.4%
Return on Invested Capital	13.7%	14.1%
Per common share		
Net earnings from operations	$6.10	$6.20
Net earnings	6.10	6.61
Dividends	2.40	2.50
Stockholders' equity	39.15	40.92

Source: General Foods 1985 Annual Report.

Kraft Foods

Maxwell targeted Kraft Foods for takeover to fill in the gaps at General Foods, broaden its product line in foods, and increase its share in the food-processing industry, in addition to providing potential leadership for the entire food segment. The company had a portfolio of well-known brands that, when combined with General Foods' brands, translated into more shelf space and increased pricing power for PM. Like PM, Kraft focused on brand building, brand extension, and new product development.

Kraft also brought with it capable managers and superior profit margins. Under the direction of Chairman John Richman and President Michael Miles, Kraft Foods had recently completed a restructuring program aimed at increasing market focus, decreasing costs, and, ironically, avoiding a takeover attempt. In 1987, the company's net sales were $9.9 billion with operating profits of $910 million (see Exhibit 15). The company had sold its profitable Duracell battery division as part of a campaign to return to being an "all-food" company and was aggressively acquiring new food businesses.

E X H I B I T   15   **Kraft Foods Inc. Pre-Acquisition Highlights, 1983–1987**
(Dollar figures in millions except for per-share data)

	1983	1985	1987
Net Sales			
U.S. consumer food	$3,718	$3,911	$4,519
U.S. commercial food	1,173	1,421	3,022
International food	1,770	1,733	2,335
Total Net Sales	$6,661	$7,065	$9,876
Operating earnings			
U.S. consumer food	$ 361	$ 527	$ 593
U.S. commercial food	58	62	86
International food	166	146	230
Total Operating Earnings	$ 585	$ 735	$ 909
Net earnings	$ 435	$ 466	$ 489
Working capital	1,104	723	79
Capital expenditures	104	113	256
Stockholders' equity	2,923	2,880	1,898
Long-term Debt to Equity	18.8%	15.6%	47.2%
Return on Average Equity	15.3%	17.0%	26.5%
Per Common Share			
Net earnings from operations	$ 1.83	$ 2.50	$ 3.20
Net earnings	2.64	3.22	3.60
Dividends	1.28	1.52	1.84
Stockholders' equity	17.77	19.95	14.47

Source: Kraft Foods Inc. 1988 Annual Report.

Kraft was divided into three business units:

Segment	Percentage of Net Sales	Brands
U.S. consumer food	46%	
Refrigerated products		Kraft cheeses: Philadelphia Brand Cream Cheese, Velveeta, and Cheez Whiz
Grocery products		Miracle Whip, Kraft mayonnaise, Seven Seas salad dressings, Kraft macaroni and cheese dinners, and Parkay margarine
Frozen foods		Tombstone Pizza, Lender's Bagels, and Budget Gourmet dinners
Dairy		Breyers ice cream and Frusen Gladji; Light n' Lively, and Breakstone yogurt, sour cream, and cottage cheese
International food	23	All Kraft brands sold internationally
U.S. commercial food	31	
Food service		
Food ingredients		

Philip Morris acquired Kraft in October 1988 for $12.9 billion in a hostile takeover. Industry analysts said that the Kraft acquisition was smoother than that of General Foods because the management at Kraft, after the initial resistance, was committed to making the merger work.

Trends in the Food Industry

In 1989, U.S. consumers spent over $350 billion on retail food products, of which about $250 billion was spent in supermarkets and convenience stores. The food products market was fragmented in terms of the number of product groups, the number of categories within groups, and the number of competitors within each category. The major product groups were baked goods, dairy, frozen foods, fresh and cured meat, fish and poultry, produce, and dry and canned goods. Exhibit 16 indicates the product groups and the major categories with the total food expenditures for each category.

The U.S. food industry was a mature market with an average annual growth of 1 to 2 percent. Including the small, independent, single-product food producers, there were hundreds of participants in this market. New competitors in the industry tended to be large, diversified organizations. Companies such as Philip Morris and R.J. Reynolds, which owned subsidiaries in several industries, were entering the food segment to further diversify their portfolio.

New Product Innovations   There were several growth opportunities for food companies that could come up with new products or reformulated products to meet changing customer needs. First, consumers' eating habits had changed during the last decade. In the 1990s, people wanted products that were lower in calories, lower in cholesterol, more nutritious, and lower in salt. Additionally, the increased number of working mothers, the smaller households, and the decline in the traditional family household created a demand for products that were quick and easy to prepare, serve, and clean up. There was an emphasis on new products throughout the industry, either through extensions of existing products or entirely new offerings. Food producers also met the changing demands by offering specialty products that had particular value to a portion of the consumers, such as low-fat foods for the weight and health conscious. These products generally had higher profit margins than average and companies found that new product innovations could create new niches as well as enable them to establish leadership within the niche by being first in the segment.

Entry Barriers   In recent years, barriers to entry had been increasing due to the volume of sales necessary to obtain production economies and gain shelf space. Most new competitors were entering via acquisition, since distribution channels, shelving, and brand recognition were already in place. Substitution was also a problem for food processors. Every company faced competition not only from brand substitutes within a category but substitution from other categories as well—all under one roof. For instance, a consumer interested in purchasing peas could choose fresh, frozen, or canned peas; then choose between Birdseye, Green Giant, or some other brand of frozen peas.

EXHIBIT 16   **Consumer Food Expenditures by Product Group, 1989**
(In millions of dollars)

	Total Retail Sales	Amount Spent in Grocery Stores	Percentage of Total Sales by Category
Perishables	$220,843	$150,818	61.0%
Baked goods	19,495	12,510	5.4
In-store bakery	6,640	6,640	1.8
Dairy	40,263	22,486	11.1
Frozen foods	21,382	15,907	5.9
Fresh cured meat, fish and poultry	78,529	53,114	21.7
Service deli	11,130	11,130	3.1
Produce	43,405	29,032	12.0
Dry Grocery (food)	$141,474	$ 94,092	39.0%
Baby foods	2,683	2,343	0.7
Baking needs	2,852	2,571	0.8
Beer, wine, liquor	39,458	18,757	10.9
Breakfast foods	7,797	7,652	2.2
Candy and gum	10,432	3,595	2.9
Canned seafood	2,300	2,050	0.6
Canned fruit	2,010	1,741	0.6
Canned bottled juices and drinks	4,960	4,238	1.4
Canned meat and specialty foods	1,831	1,413	0.5
Canned milk	416	375	0.1
Canned prepared food	2,104	1,961	0.6
Canned dry soups	2,876	2,745	0.8
Canned vegetables	3,750	3,323	1.0
Condiments, dressings, spreads, and relishes	7,909	6,366	2.2
Desserts	661	580	0.2
Dried foods	3,896	3,162	1.1
Fats and shortenings	1,904	1,581	0.5
Jams, jellies, and preserves	2,684	2,180	0.7
Pasta	1,817	1,309	0.5
Prepared drinks	9,361	7,394	2.6
Snacks	9,369	6,065	2.6
Soft drinks	17,531	10,331	4.8
Sweeteners and flavors	2,872	2,360	0.8
Total Foods	$362,317	$244,910	100%

Source: *Progressive Grocer,* July 1990.

Competition in the Food Industry

Throughout the 1980s, larger companies acquired or merged with smaller food producers to broaden their product lines, consolidate market share, or, as in PM's and RJR's cases, to diversify. Pillsbury, Inc. was acquired in 1988 for $5.7 billion in a hostile takeover by Grand Metropolitan (a previous owner of the

Liggett Group cigarette company). Companies such as Grand Metropolitan, Philip Morris, and R.J. Reynolds brought strong financial positions and considerable cash reserves to the food-processing industry. In 1990, the industry was dominated by the major players listed in Exhibit 17. Exhibit 17 also indicates the advertising expenditures and relevant financial information per company.

Marketing   Market leadership was crucial because volume sales were necessary to reduce per-unit costs, share advertising and distribution costs, and wield bargaining power with chain grocers. Food companies competed for shelf space in grocery stores. Position in the store, placement on the shelf, the number of facings on the shelf, and end-of-aisle displays were important in obtaining and maintaining volume. A company's ability to gain shelf space for its products was a function of brand recognition, brand loyalty, and breadth of product line. Companies with broad product lines were in a better position to negotiate shelf space than single-product producers, because brand recognition tended to have a cumulative effect so that as the product line increased, the leverage that the food processors wielded over grocers also increased.

Brand recognition and brand loyalty were created primarily through advertising. In addition to access to shelf space, brand strength was critical to generating volume sales, achieving pricing leverage, and facilitating new product innovations. Brand loyalty gave producers some latitude to increase prices without severely affecting volume. Greater volume translated directly into lower per-unit costs. These cost savings either generated surplus cash for the producers or were used to lower prices to further increase volume. Additionally, brand recognition facilitated new product introductions. Food producers were often able to capitalize on brand success through shared advertising and distribution costs. The major players spent over $3.6 billion on advertising in 1989 to generate brand loyalty and carve out a competitive position.

The Performance of the Kraft General Foods Strategic Business Unit

Kraft Foods and General Foods were merged into the Kraft General Foods (KGF) Group in 1989 under the direction of Michael Miles. The combined companies represented the second-largest food company worldwide, behind Nestlé, and sold 14 of the top 50 U.S. food brands. Altogether the KGF Group had a 10 percent share of the American packaged-food market. In fiscal 1989, the group represented 51 percent of PM's operating revenues. The merger increased PM's total advertising and promotional spending in 1989 to approximately $2 billion, making the company the world's largest advertiser. Philip Morris had not merged the advertising expenditures of KGF, Miller, and PM's tobacco business because of divergent audience interests. While KGF was primarily a broadcast-oriented advertiser, PM's cigarette companies were banned from the airwaves. And while Miller was a significant broadcast buyer, its sport/male viewer orientation was not very compatible with that of KGF's family/prime-time audience.

Michael Miles commented in the 1989 annual report on his expectations of the merger:

> The combination of Kraft and General Foods created more than the second-largest food company in the world. It created an organization determined to be the leader in its industry.

Comparative Financial Data for Selected Food-Processing Companies, 1985–1989
(In millions of dollars)

Company	Example Brands	1985			1989		
		Sales	Net Profits	Ad Expenditures	Sales	Net Profits	Ad Expenditures
Beatrice	Tropicana, Wesson	$12,595	$ 479	$ 218	NA [a]	NA [a]	$ 74[a]
Borden	Bama, Cracker Jack	4,716	185	16	$ 7,593	$ 344	22
CPC International	Pastas, Mazola, Skippy	4,210	219	40	5,103	328	61
Campbell Soup	Prego, Pepperidge Farm	3,989	198	124	5,672	131	125
Dean Foods	Dairy products, Calypso	1,034	32	2	1,684	32	2
Flowers Industries	Cobblestone Mill, Sunbeam	626	26	3	783	30	2
General Mills	Cheerios, Betty Crocker	4,285	159	278	5,621	315	353
H.J. Heinz	Ketchup, StarKist tuna	4,366	302	101	6,086	505	147
Hershey Foods	Chocolate candies	1,996	121	67	2,421	171	90
Hormel	Chili, beef stew	1,502	39	31	2,341	70	34
Kellogg Co.	Cereals, Mrs. Smith's	2,930	281	213	4,652	422	428
Kraft General Foods	Maxwell House, cheeses	6,697[b]	582[b]	1,928[b]	22,933[c]	1,580[c]	1,082[c]
Nabisco	Planters, Del-Monte	6,200[d]	549[d]	574[e]	5,783[d]	543[d]	408[e]
Nestlé	Stouffers, Carnation	25,134	2,568	161	30,596	1,436	309
Pillsbury	Green Giant, Häagen-dazs	4,843	417	235	2,872[f]	245[f]	346[g]
Quaker Oats	Van Camp's, Gatorade	3,520	157	106	5,724	203	176
Ralston Purina	Hostess Twinkies	5,864	256	189	6,658	351	152
Sara Lee	Pastries, Bryan Foods	8,117	206	123	11,718	399	168
Unilever	Lipton teas, Ragu	2,405	1,376	233	34,434	1,687	376

[a] Beatrice was purchased in a leveraged buyout in 1988 by BCI Holdings and several divisions were divested.

[b] These figures are a sum of the following:
Kraft Foods 1985: revenues—$7,065; profits—$466; advertising—$215.
General Foods 1985 (a subsidiary of Philip Morris): revenues—$1,632; operating income—$116.
Philip Morris total advertising—$813.

[c] These figures represent the total operating revenues and income for the food segment of Philip Morris. The advertising figure is for all Philip Morris companies combined.

[d] These figures represent the total operating revenues and income for the RJR Nabisco's food segment.

[e] These figures are for all RJR Nabisco companies combined.

[f] These figures represent the total operating revenues and income for the food segment of Grand Metropolitan.

[g] This figure is the advertising for all Grand Metropolitan companies combined.

Source: Compiled by the casewriter from a variety of sources including S&P's *Valueline*, annual reports, and *Leading Ad $ Summary*.

> To lead the industry we must rank first in quality, with products and services that consistently meet all our customers' and consumers' needs and expectations, setting the standards for taste, nutrition, convenience, variety, and value.
>
> We intend to lead in productivity as well as quality. In 1989, Kraft General Foods people achieved more than $425 million in savings by operating more efficiently. These are permanent cost reductions, providing ongoing benefits for our company.
>
> The real opportunity now is synergy—working together so that the Kraft General Foods of the future adds up to more than the sum of its parts in the past.
>
> With our family of brands, and the support of Philip Morris, we have immense strengths and even more potential. We are going to use them to grow still more.

PM's high expectations hinged on building brand loyalty through advertising while ruthlessly cutting costs and improving overall productivity. A consultant to Kraft told *Adweek*, "Kraft believes General Foods is an overstuffed manicotti. They're going to make it a much leaner, tougher company. That's going to mean a lot of changes."[8] Miles began with demands for improved productivity and an intensive search for ways to milk more from existing assets. One executive recruiter who had "outplaced" several executives from both Kraft and General Foods said of Miles: "He's famous for trimming to the bone."[9] Miles consolidated some of KGF's 200 domestic plants and 70 distribution centers. By 1990, KGF had 132 domestic manufacturing and processing facilities and 56 major distribution centers.

Purchasing   Following the merger of GF and Kraft, management moved to reduce raw materials costs by combining GF and Kraft purchasing functions and thereby gain greater leverage with suppliers. KGF realized $36 million in savings by jointly negotiating purchasing contracts on behalf of various KGF companies. The KGF Group formed an executive purchasing council, including PM U.S.A. and Miller Brewing, to provide guidance and policy direction for purchasing decisions. Rick Studemann, vice president for purchasing at KGF, said, "We set goals and instituted an aggressive program to deliver the savings. All prospective suppliers are evaluated first in terms of quality, technology, cost, and service—we don't just run after the low-cost supplier. The benefits of scale follow from this assessment."

Combined Marketing Efforts   KGF was able to achieve cost savings by grouping the Kraft and GF brands into product lines (such as refrigerated foods, frozen foods, and packaged dinners) and by combining its sales forces along product categories (such as cheeses, coffees, and cereals). Previously, a particular territory required two salespersons per product category—one for GF and one for Kraft. With the combined sales force, one salesperson could service the entire territory, which substantially reduced KGF's sales force costs. Grouping the Kraft and GF brands together increased the number of brands that each sales person had to offer, thus giving salespersons more clout with retailers in bargaining over the shelf space allocated to KGF brands. KGF also derived synergies by advertising several products together, such as the "Great American Breakfasts" campaign that featured 10 key brands: Post Raisin Bran,

---

[8] *Adweek*, January 27, 1989.
[9] *Marketing Week*, January 27, 1989.

Post Bran Flakes, Lender's Bagels, Maxwell House coffee, Parkay margarine, Oscar Mayer bacon, Philadelphia Brand cream cheese, Velveeta, Log Cabin syrup, and Kraft cheeses. KGF realized advertising savings with this promotion as well, since the cost of one large promotion was still less than the sum of 10 individual promotions. Ron Toyama, promotion manager of Kraft USA, said, "This is another example of how Kraft and General Foods brands can combine forces to create a program that's bigger than the sum of its parts."

Product Innovations   In addition to marketing and distribution economies of scale, Philip Morris anticipated combining Kraft and General Foods products to create new product offerings, such as the Oscar Mayer Lunchables. Lunchables combined GF crackers, Kraft cheeses, and Oscar Mayer luncheon meats in convenient, single-serving containers. The KGF Group introduced a total of 300 new products in 1989, including those jointly developed, winning the 1990 New Products Company of the Year award presented by *Prepared Foods* magazine. KGF introduced a large number of line extensions, such as Philadelphia Brand neufchatel cheese, Cholesterol-Free Miracle Whip, Kraft Cholesterol-Free Mayonnaise, and Breyers Light ice milk. In light of growing interest in health and nutrition, fat replacement technologies represented a major growth opportunity. In 1989, KGF successfully adapted a variety of proprietary fat replacement technologies to a host of products, from Sealtest Free nonfat ice cream to Kraft pourable salad dressings and Entenmann's reduced-calorie, fat-free, and cholesterol-free cakes. The company also attempted to attract health-conscious consumers with products such as Post Honey Bunches of Oats, Lender's Oat Bran Bagels, Oroweat Oat Nut Bread, Freihofer's Hearthstone Breads, Louis Kemp seafood products, and Light n' Lively products.

In 1989 72 percent of the homes in the United States had microwave ovens, and convenient meal preparation was essential. In response, the company introduced Kraft microwave entrees, Oscar Mayer Zappetites snacks, Minute microwave meals, and Jell-O microwave pudding. Growth in sales of ready-to-eat desserts led KGF to acquire the Catelli Magic Moments and Light Touch mini-desserts lines, increasing market share in Canada to 65 percent. In addition, Oscar Mayer bolstered its U.S. convenience-store presence through contracts with Circle K and Emro Marketing Co., and continued to expand Oscar Mayer Lunchables lunch combinations nationally. The company also supplied Boboli breads for on-site supermarket pizza preparation, and increased capacity in the food service operation helped to keep growth apace with the expanding restaurant food market.

KGF International   In 1989, 17 percent of KGF's revenues and profits were contributed by the KGF International operating unit. This division marketed KGF's strong U.S. brands, such as Kraft cheeses and Maxwell House coffees, as well as products with regional appeal, in Europe, Asia/Pacific Rim, and Latin America. KGF Canada, another KGF operating unit, was Canada's largest packaged food company. This division contributed six percent of KGF's revenues and 9 percent of profits. KGF had 78 plants, facilities, and warehouses in 18 foreign countries and was very interested in acquiring more companies or brands overseas. PM's strategy was to replicate its success in international cigarettes by acquiring established brands and using their distribution channels to market KGF brands in foreign markets.

Jacobs Suchard AG

In 1990, Philip Morris made a takeover bid to acquire 80 percent of Swiss coffee and chocolate maker Jacobs Suchard for $3.8 billion. Jacobs Suchard had 12 percent of the European chocolate market, behind Mars (with 17 percent) and Nestlé (23 percent).

As recently as 1981, Jacobs Suchard had been a single-product company. Under the direction of Klaus Jacobs, the company grew from the largest coffee supplier in West Germany to a worldwide food distributor primarily through acquisitions. In 1982, Jacobs Coffee, a German-based privately held firm, merged with Swiss-based Suchard and Tobler chocolate companies to form Jacobs Suchard. In 1986, Jacobs Suchard acquired the Van Houten Company, a Dutch producer of chocolate and cocoa goods. In 1987, the company entered the Belgium chocolate-manufacturing market by acquiring Cote d'Or, the last remaining independent Belgium chocolate manufacturer. Jacobs moved into the U.S. and Canadian markets with the purchase of Andes Candies and in 1987 acquired U.S.-based E.J. Brach. In 1988, it attempted to enter the British market by acquiring Roundtree chocolates, but lost a takeover battle to Nestlé.

At the time of PM's acquisition, Jacobs Suchard had ambitious plans to use Brach's distribution network of 400 salespeople to win share in the U.S. and Canadian markets. The strategy was to introduce brands with an established international appeal into the U.S. market. Jacobs Suchard hoped to have 100 salespeople in the Tokyo area by the end of 1990 to push the six varieties of its Milka brand in the growing Japanese market. During 1990, the company streamlined European operations by reducing the number of plants in Europe from 22 to 6.

Philip Morris kept the European coffee and chocolate operations and sold back the other businesses, including E.J. Brach, to Mr. Jacobs. The move gave PM market leadership in coffee in West Germany and France and 12 percent of the European chocolate market, plus access to European distribution channels for food products. PM management saw the Jacobs Suchard acquisition as a vehicle through which it could compete as a major player in the European market for food products.

THE FINANCIAL SERVICES AND REAL ESTATE SEGMENT

This segment of Philip Morris operated as a separate corporate division, not as a wholly owned subsidiary. It contributed one percent of PM's revenues and two percent of operating profits. The division operated as Philip Morris Capital Corp. (PMCC), with a primary subsidiary, Mission Viejo. The recent revenues and operating profit performance suggested that while revenues were relatively flat, margins were increasing:

Year	Revenues (In millions of dollars)	Operating Income (In millions of dollars)
1985	$303	$ 66
1986	474	32
1987	488	68
1988	629	163
1989	527	173

Philip Morris Capital Corporation

PMCC was formed in 1982 primarily to provide credit financing for customers of PM's operating companies. The financial activities of PMCC also included leveraged lease transactions for major equipment. PMCC contributed $193 million in revenues and $82 million in operating income to PM's total operations in 1989.

Mission Viejo

PM completed its acquisition of Mission Viejo in 1972 at a price of approximately $48.5 million, and it was organized as a subsidiary of PMCC in 1983. The company was initially engaged in community and residential development and the development of and investment in commercial properties. Its main base of activity was the development of a completely preplanned community named Mission Viejo on approximately 11,000 acres in Orange County, California. Mission Viejo was a major factor in homebuilding in California throughout the 1970s, but by the late 1980s, the company began a planned withdrawal from homebuilding. This move was partly a reaction to the "soft" residential housing market that characterized the 1980s and partly a desire to concentrate on financial activities that had a greater strategic fit. In 1989, Mission Viejo contributed $334 million in revenues and $91 million in operating profits to PM's total operations.

COMPANIES ACQUIRED AND LATER DIVESTED

All of Philip Morris's acquisitions were not success stories. Its diversification moves into chewing gum, shaving products, and soft drinks had not lived up to expectations.

American Safety Razor

Acquired in 1960 in a transaction valued at about $22.5 million, American Safety Razor (1959 sales of $32.1 million and profits of $1.7 million) was PM's first acquisition in nontobacco consumer products and was touted by Philip Morris as being "a nucleus for the addition of new lines of consumer products." ASR's main business was nonelectric (or wet) shaving products—mainly razors and razor blades (its brands were Gem, Pal, and Silver Star); but because of erratic earnings, ASR (through a subsidiary) had recently diversified into electric home-haircutting kits, power tool accessories, missile components (this unit was in the process of liquidation at the time of acquisition), and electronic controls. PM was attracted to the razor blade and shaving supplies market because, just as in selling cigarettes, market success depended upon an effective mass-distribution system and heavy advertising.

As was to become its familiar pattern, Philip Morris began to increase ASR's advertising efforts and to bring out new products. By 1964 ASR's share of the double-edge-blade market was estimated at 25 percent, with the company's share of the total blade market estimated to be 17.5 percent. But the upturn was shortlived; Gillette countered with a new double-edge stainless blade of its own (including a giveaway promotion of 25 million free samples); Wilkinson Sword, Ltd. (a British firm) entered the U.S. market and stepped up its European efforts; and both Eversharp (with its Schick brand) and Gillette built new, efficient blade plants in the United States and Europe. ASR found it hard to match the pace of new products, increased ad budgets, and manufacturing efficiency. Gillette dominated the shaving products industry with a 60 percent market share; ASR and Eversharp (Schick) vied for second place with shares of about 10 percent.

PM came to the conclusion that it would be very difficult to make major inroads against Gillette and Schick. In 1974 PM management opted for divestiture and began efforts to sell ASR. An agreement was reached in 1976 to sell the ASR division to BIC Pen Corp. for $20 million, but the agreement was abandoned when the Federal Trade Commission voiced objections to the anticompetitive potential of BIC's acquisition (BIC was already initiating entry into razors and razor blades on its own). Shortly thereafter, in 1977, the unit was sold to nine top management officials of ASR for $16 million; at the time ASR's sales totaled about $42 million per year.

Clark Bros. Chewing Gum Company

In 1963 when Philip Morris acquired Clark Bros. Chewing Gum Company, Clark's sales were just over $3 million, in a market with total domestic sales at the manufacturing level of $190 million. There were 17 gum manufacturers in the U.S. market, the largest of which was Wm. Wrigley, Jr., Company, with sales of $110 million (57 percent market share). The second-largest manufacturer was American Chicle Company, a division of Warner Lambert Pharmaceutical Inc., with a 25 percent market share. In third place was Beech-Nut, with a 15 percent market share. None of the other firms had as much as a 5 percent share of the U.S. market. These same U.S. firms were also the leaders in most world markets, and many of the smaller U.S. firms sold their gum internationally—Philadelphia Gum, for instance, sold its products in 43 countries.

As before, the strategy employed by Philip Morris entailed increasing marketing efforts—bright new packaging, increased advertising exposure, greater sales efforts, and new products. The capacity of the company's new Belgian plant was tripled. PM's efforts were only marginally successful. Market share rose no higher than the 4 percent level. When sugarless gums were introduced in the mid-1960s, Clark's entry Diet Smile never caught on.

In 1973 Philip Morris sold most of the assets of Clark Gum to Reed Candy Company, a subsidiary of H.P. Hood, Inc. At the time of the sale, Clark's annual sales in the United States and Canada were about $12 million; total factory sales of gum in the United States and Canada in 1973 were in the $350–$400 million range.

The Seven-Up Company

In June 1978 Philip Morris purchased the Seven-Up Company for $520 million in cash. Seven-Up's performance prior to the acquisition is listed below:

Year	Sales Revenues (In millions of dollars)	Net Earnings (In millions of dollars)	Market Shares
1970	$111.6	$ 9.8	7.2%
1975	213.6	20.3	7.8
1976	233.2	24.8	7.7
1977	251.4	25.8	7.4

The 7UP brand was the third-largest-selling soft drink in the world as of 1979, trailing Coca-Cola and Pepsi-Cola by a wide margin and running barely ahead of fourth-place Dr Pepper. Diet 7UP was a leading soft drink in the diet category.

From a strategic perspective, PM believed it had the management skills and marketing know-how to turn Seven-Up into the Miller of soft drinks. PM's turnaround strategy for Seven-Up was virtually a carbon copy of the one employed at Miller Brewing. Family management at Seven-Up was replaced by experienced senior managers from PM. Substantial investments were made in expanding and upgrading Seven-Up's marketing, research, and personnel programs. Other moves included dropping the "Uncola" campaign, which PM felt positioned 7UP too narrowly; boosting advertising expenditures substantially; tripling the field sales force and creating a new distribution planning department to assist bottlers; substantially upgrading product research activities; redesigning 7UP's trademark and packaging; and raising the price of concentrate supplied to franchised bottlers.

However, the turnaround effort at Seven-Up ran into tougher challenges than existed at Miller. First, Seven-Up was unable to steal a march on Coca-Cola and Pepsi with new packaging, product variations, catchy commercials, and market segmentation tactics, since both Coca-Cola and Pepsi were highly skilled and sophisticated at marketing. Second, manufacturing, packaging, and distribution of soft drinks were in the hands of franchised bottlers rather than under the full control of Seven-Up headquarters. Third, Seven-Up confronted a strong, traditional preference of soft drink consumers for cola products. Cola brands accounted for 60 to 65 percent of total soft drink sales, compared with 17 percent for such lemon-lime flavors as 7UP, Sprite, and Teem.

Hamish Maxwell made the following observation:

> With the benefit of hindsight, I don't think Seven-Up was an appropriate acquisition. It had a fine product, and we had the idea that we could make it a major player in the carbonated soft drink market. After all, Pepsi wasn't all that big in the 1930s and has come close to Coke. We found that to do that sort of catch-up in the 1970s and 1980s with Seven-Up was a hell of a lot harder. We were faced with several alternatives: go on beating our heads against such worldwide competition, at great expense, or take Seven-Up back to what it was when we bought it, a small company that made nice profits without getting too entangled in competitive battles. But earnings of $30 million after tax wouldn't stand out on our income statement. It was too small to make strategic sense. So we sold it.[10]

FUTURE PROSPECTS FOR PHILIP MORRIS COMPANIES

PM's top management was confidently optimistic about the corporation's future. They believed that the acquisitions and divestitures of the 1980s had resulted in the "right" business and the "critical mass" necessary for successful operations and growth. Hamish Maxwell, chairman of the board and chief executive officer, summarized the company's outlook for the 1990s in the company's 1989 annual report:

---

[10]As quoted from *Fortune*, October 23, 1989.

Over the past year, we have worked to ensure that the acquisition of Kraft, Inc. not only made us the largest consumer packaged goods company in the world, but also brought us closer to being the best. The acquisition has strengthened the entire company, giving all our product lines new opportunities for increased efficiency and growth. Our greater size and scope are helping us do everything better.

Our operating companies coordinate purchasing, processing, and marketing activities. These common business elements increase our opportunity for more effective and profitable operations.

We have already begun to exploit some of the technology, research, distribution, and packaging skills we now have. These synergies make our operations more effective in many ways, whether through joint purchases of raw materials and advertising media, shared data and technologies, or cross-promotions featuring the extended family of Philip Morris food brands.

Synergies lead not only to savings, but also to new products, packagings, and distribution channels that create sustainable competitive advantages. These business-building benefits are even more important than our cost savings.

We are accumulating greater resources than ever to prepare for the major changes coming to North American, European, and Pacific Rim markets. We are constantly examining options to build further on our international strengths for effective competition in the emerging global marketplace.

Wherever possible, we are using our free cash flow to maximize production consistency and efficiency in our core businesses. We are investing in new plants and equipment, and acquiring advanced manufacturing technologies.

These investments help us maintain our positions as both low cost and high quality producers. Our low cost manufacturing position is the cornerstone of our marketing flexibility. Consistent quality at every step, from purchasing to packaging to distribution, is the key to product quality and consumer loyalty to our brands.

Maxwell anticipated a decade of constant improvement and refinement of the existing businesses. Although Maxwell said he was always interested in acquiring any small, profitable food businesses or parts of a larger food company if it fit with the KGF product lines, PM's immediate plans called for tightening the existing businesses:

I always say I want everyone to be ambitious for the business. People really have got to be conditioned never to be satisfied. If they have a good year, I don't want them saying: "Please pin a medal on my jacket." I want them to say: "How could we have done better? What did we miss?" I certainly don't want to be bitching all the time. But you really have to keep pushing, getting people to feel constructively discontented. I just want people to feel there's always a way to have done something better.[11]

---

[11] As quoted in *Fortune*, May 8, 1989.

GROUPE SCHNEIDER

Tracy Kramer, The University of Alabama*

At approximately 6:00 P.M. on Monday, February 18, 1991, Mr. Jerre Stead, president and CEO of Square D Company, received a telephone call from Mr. Didier Pineau-Valencienne, the CEO of the French conglomerate Groupe Schneider. Mr. Pineau-Valencienne informed Mr. Stead that he would be receiving a letter the next morning, the contents of which were too complex to explain over the telephone. In the letter, Pineau-Valencienne informed Stead that Groupe Schneider (GS) was initiating an unsolicited takeover bid for Square D, and should Square D reject the offer, GS was not adverse to a hostile takeover battle.

From 1988 through 1990, the two companies had met and corresponded on a wide range of possible joint venture opportunities with the intention of mutually increasing the global scope of both companies. Groupe Schneider, founded in 1863, was a European holding company of manufacturers of electrical and electronic equipment. Headquartered in Paris, the company's 1990 sales were $9.93 billion and it employed 80,000 people. Square D was a leading manufacturer of electrical products, systems, and services within the United States, with approximately 25 percent of the distribution equipment market, 35 percent of the lighting transformer market, and 25 percent of the panelboard and switchboard market. Square D's 1990 sales were $1.65 billion and the company had 19,000 employees. In September 1990, Square D's board of directors decided not to pursue an alliance with GS and advised Schneider of their intentions. The two companies could not come to an agreement, according to Mr. Stead, because Schneider wanted an equity interest in Square D and Square D wished to remain independent. In Mr. Pineau-Valencienne's February letter to Stead, he said, "I am now convinced, after two years of unsuccessful discussions, that the only way to achieve the full benefits of this business fit is through a full merger."

THE ELECTRICAL EQUIPMENT INDUSTRY

The electrical industry was one of the most important and pervasive industries in the industrialized world, since virtually nothing happened without using or being dependent upon some form of electricity. The electrical industry of the 1990s consisted of thousands of corporations, companies, and organizations engaged in interrelated activities that provided a wide range of electrical power products and services—from the generation of electricity to applications such as heating, lighting, and powering motors. Once generated, electricity was transmitted from the power plant to end-users (such as industrial manufacturers and residential houses) via power lines and transformers. Exhibit 1 is a generalized diagram of this process.

Public and private utility companies generated, transmitted, and distributed electrical power to industrial, commercial, and residential customers.

*The cooperation and assistance of the Square D Company is acknowledged and appreciated.

831

EXHIBIT 1   **The Electricity Generation and Transmission Process**

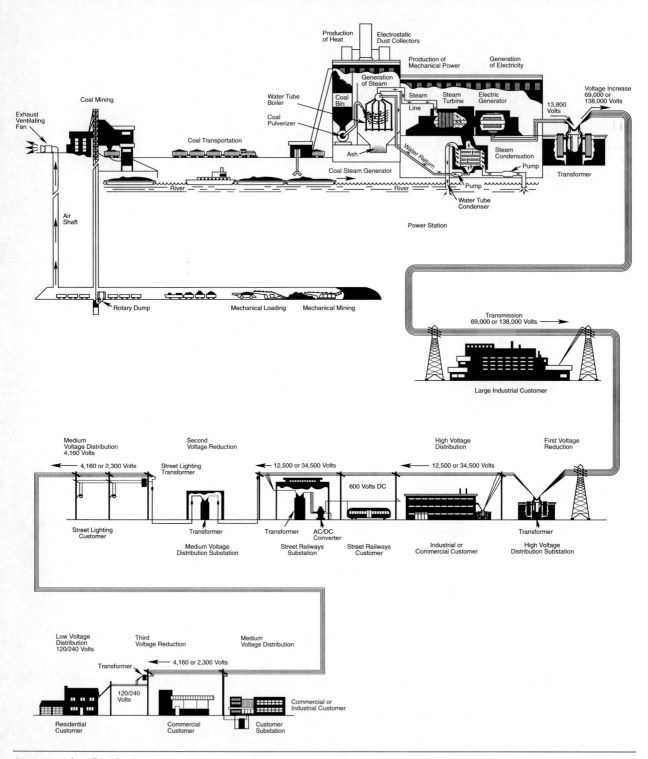

Source: Kentucky Utilities Co.

Electrical equipment manufacturers produced the many thousands of motors, parts, and components that were used in every aspect of the process from generation to end-use consumption.

The Electrical Manufacturing Segment   Only a few electrical manufacturers had the capability to make the sophisticated power generation equipment needed by electric utilities to produce electricity. The vast majority of electrical equipment manufacturers had broad product lines that included power, distribution, and control equipment. Power equipment products included substations, enclosures, controllers, switchgears, metering equipment, transformers, uninterruptible power systems, and power conditioners. Distribution equipment products included panelboards, switchboards, circuit breakers, busways, raceways, and cable trays. Control products included input devices, starters, contactors, and specialized automation products such as programmable controllers, cell controllers, communications networks, and operator interfaces.

Some equipment manufacturers made only a very narrow range of products, such as industrial controls, while others, among them General Electric and Westinghouse, attempted to manufacture products for the entire process from electricity generation to all kinds of end-use applications. The number of possible product-line combinations that equipment manufacturers could build their businesses around were practically infinite. Most manufacturers had in-house sales forces and marketed both to electric utilities and distributors of electrical equipment. The supply side of the electrical products industry was even more fragmented in international markets where the lack of uniform product standards resulted in greater numbers of competitors. For example, in the European market for fuses, Great Britain, France, and Germany all manufactured fuses according to different safety, performance, and dimensions standards. This situation made it difficult for one company to dominate the European market.

Industry Trends

Sales of electrical equipment were driven by two factors: (1) new construction, and (2) maintenance. New construction of any sort, whether it was a new power plant, an industrial manufacturing plant, a commercial project, or a residential home, required substantial electrical equipment. The electrical equipment industry in the United States had been in a decline since 1982 due to an extended slump in construction. However, some economic analysts, citing the upturn in the housing market in early 1991, predicted a somewhat brighter future for the electrical equipment industry. Obsolete or inefficient equipment, worn-out or damaged equipment, and equipment that no longer met current needs represented opportunities for the sale of new electrical equipment. Overall, the growth rate for the electrical equipment industry was between 1 and 2 percent, as indicated in Exhibit 2.

By far the most significant trend in the electrical equipment industry was globalization. Most companies were convinced that the electrical equipment industry was rapidly turning into a global market. GS's main competitors, such as Siemens A.G., ASEA Brown-Boveri, General Electric, and Westinghouse, were all rapidly expanding internationally. The economic unification of Europe in 1992 and the growth and industrialization among the Pacific Rim nations

EXHIBIT 2   **Trends and Forecasts: Electrical Equipment, 1987–1991**
(In millions of dollars)

	1987	1988	1989	1990†	1991‡
Value of Shipments*	$21,051	$22,645	$22,798	$22,555	$22,027
Transformers	3,290	3,571	3,577	3,528	3,562
Switchgear and apparatus	4,907	5,323	5,294	5,334	5,412
Motors and generators	6,753	7,290	7,293	7,074	6,633
Relays and controls	6,101	6,461	6,634	6,619	6,420

*In constant 1987 dollars for purposes of comparison.
†Estimated figures.
‡Forecasted figures.
Source: *U.S. Industrial Outlook*, compiled from U.S. Department of Commerce, Bureau of the Census, and International Trade Administration.

were expected to provide great opportunities. Joint ventures and strategic alliances were common because they represented a way to obtain market access with fewer capital requirements than acquisition. However, the world market was increasingly dominated by a few large competitors; these large competitors were acquiring smaller, specialty manufacturers to broaden their product lines. Such moves were driven by the belief that size, referred to in the industry as "critical mass," was necessary to compete. Access to all the major country markets was critical since the attempts of foreign competitors to build a global position were causing major cracks in the profit sanctuaries of domestic producers.

Besides moving to establish more global market positions, producers were trying to develop products that could be sold worldwide, which required a much greater need for investment and research to design, retool, and produce a more standardized product. Most electrical products in the United States were built according to standards established by the National Electrical Manufacturers Association (NEMA), which stressed uniformity and compatibility of design as well as meeting minimum acceptable safety standards. As a result, U.S. manufacturers tended to offer commodity-type products and attempted to differentiate on the basis of safety, quality control, or service. Electrical equipment buyers supported NEMA guidelines since the uniform standards resulted in parts or components manufactured by different companies that the buyer could use almost interchangeably. This decreased the switching costs to the buyers, thereby increasing their leverage against the equipment manufacturers by forcing them to compete on price. Additionally, altering designs was an expensive procedure, since companies had made substantial capital investments to produce a particular product at a particular level of quality. U.S. manufacturers' facilities were often equipped with old tooling.

Competing products made in Europe were gaining share in the United States, largely because they were smaller, cheaper, and more varied. These products met the standards established by the International Electrotechnical Commission (IEC), based in Geneva. It was widely believed, both in the United States and internationally, that IEC standards would gain strength as an international standard after EC 1992. Mr. Pineau-Valencienne supported this opinion: "All of the new generation of products coming up now are going to be worldwide products, not national or local products."[1]

A final trend in the industry was a decreasing tendency to produce electrical equipment in lower-cost, developing countries. As broader penetration of country markets became increasingly important, global competitors established large, state-of-the-art production facilities in countries where costs were low. Mr. Pineau-Valencienne clearly explained the situation: "Delocalization is no longer the answer; the answer is the concentration of production with wide markets to amortize costs."[2] A multinational base of operations would increase a company's market access, since the company was positioned to capture local markets by producing according to the various regional standards. However, the greatest long-term advantage of globalization was the ability to share expertise and technologies across geographic boundaries with the goal of producing a standardized product that would serve all international markets.

GROUPE SCHNEIDER

Groupe Schneider was ranked 184th on *Fortune*'s Global 500 list of companies. Exhibit 3 provides highlights of GS's financial history. Approximately three quarters of Groupe Schneider's activities involved electrical power in some form—either in the construction of power plants; equipment used in the generation, transmission, and distribution of electricity; or automation products. Groupe Schneider had four core businesses, each operating as an independent subsidiary. Spie Batignolles provided contracting and civil engineering services and accounted for 49 percent of GS's 1990 sales. Telemecanique manufactured industrial automation components. Jeumont-Schneider produced electrical generation and power-drive equipment (in 1989 this subsidiary was merged into Merlin Gerin). Merlin Gerin manufactured electrical distribution equipment; some of its products competed directly with Square D products.

GS made and supplied equipment, systems, and services at all stages of power plant construction, with equipment systems and installations from Jeumont-Schneider and Merlin Gerin and project management and construction from Spie Batignolles. Merlin Gerin manufactured equipment and components for power transmission substations and high-technology protective devices. It had also acquired interest in local companies specialized in the production and installation of distribution panels to meet the broad variety of domestic market needs. Jeumont-Schneider was one of the world's largest manufacturers of power transformers, and GS was also a major supplier of medium-voltage transformers made by France-Transfo, a joint subsidiary of Merlin Gerin and Jeumont-Schneider. Spie Batignolles specialized in power-line installation and in the design and construction of network control and monitoring centers. GS had established technological and market leadership positions in the fast-growing automation components industry—Telemecanique was the world's third-ranking automation component manufacturer, and France's leading and Europe's second-ranked programmable controller

---

[1]*Chicago Tribune*, February 20, 1991.
[2]*Financial Times*, February 21, 1991.

EXHIBIT 3   **Financial Highlights of Groupe Schneider, 1986–1990**
                   (In millions of dollars)

	1986	1987	1988	1989	1990
Sales*	$3,828	$4,133	$5,058	$8,900	$9,930
Net income	39	42	70	176	185
Return on sales	1.0%	1.0%	1.4%	2.0%	1.9%
Percentage of Sales					
Telemecanique			20%	19%	19%
Merlin Gerin	28%	30%	28	31	32
Jeumont-Schneider	18	14	9		
Spie Batignolles	60	62	46	49	49

*Based on Schneider SA share. All sales and income from every subsidiary are not included in these figures.
Source: Standard & Poor's Corporate Reports; analysts' reports.

manufacturer (Telemecanique and Merlin Gerin together ranked as the world's seventh-largest supplier). Both Jeumont-Schneider and Telemecanique manufactured electronic variable speed controllers and certain types of specialized motors. Telemecanique also produced pneumatic valves, while Jeumont-Schneider made architectural components for industrial process-control systems.

Strategic Focus

GS's primary strategic thrust was expansion into global markets. Seventy-five percent of the company's sales came from Europe and 9 percent from North America in 1989. However, the North American market represented 30 to 40 percent of the worldwide markets in which GS was competing, so the company was aggressively searching for ways to enter this market. In 1990, GS's U.S. operations consisted of an electrical contracting firm in Danbury, Connecticut (Spie Batignolles), two industrial control plants in Westminster, Maryland (Telemecanique), and an uninterruptible power supply plant in Costa Mesa, California (EPE, a subsidiary of Merlin Gerin). GS was also strongly interested in entering the Asian markets. Examples of GS's efforts to globalize were acquisitions by Merlin Gerin during 1988—majority interests in Yorkshire Switchgear, a British-based manufacturer of switchgear and transformers; Wickman Energic Technik, a West German manufacturer of transformers and switchgear; and Ometrco, an Indonesian switchgear manufacturer with which Merlin Gerin had had a joint venture since 1979.

In March 1990, GS acquired controlling interest in Federal Pioneer for $300 million (Canadian). Federal Pioneer was Canada's leading electrical equipment manufacturer, with a 30 percent share of the Canadian market and strong U.S. connections. The company operated in manufacturing, wholesaling, and servicing electrical power distribution equipment, transformers, circuit breakers, and switchgears. This acquisition followed a search by Federal Pioneer to find either an alliance or joint-venture partner that would help the company improve its quality and breadth of product range. Federal Pioneer was subsequently incorporated into GS's Merlin Gerin group.

GS's second strategic focus was capitalizing on the growing electronics content of its business and technologies. The company was aware that electronic components were growing in use and decreasing in costs. Also, electronic components were increasingly interconnected in computer networks and becoming essential elements in process control and electrical distribution applications—two of GS's core businesses. Since 1988, GS had conducted an aggressive acquisition campaign in Europe, including a bitter and eventually successful battle to acquire Telemecanique Electrique. Schneider's third strategic focus was its commitment to innovation and energy technologies. The company committed over 7 percent of total revenues to research and development expenditures. All of GS's operating companies had modern research and development centers.

Doctor Attila

Didier Pineau-Valencienne, a confessed lover of American culture and an MBA graduate from Dartmouth College, was nicknamed "Doctor Attila" and "DPV the Destroyer" for his slash-and-burn managerial tactics. In 1981, Baron Empain, a principal owner of Schneider, hired Pineau-Valencienne to save the troubled Schneider conglomerate, which at that time built locomotives, clocks, cannons, and ski boots. Baron Empain described Pineau-Valencienne as a manager who wouldn't hesitate to make a company bleed and cry in order to put it back on its feet. He aggressively streamlined operations, divesting those businesses that did fit his plan to recenter Schneider on the electrical equipment industry. In 1984, Pineau-Valencienne closed Creusot-Loire S.A., a major steel-making subsidiary, despite pressures by the French government not to do so—a move that resulted in 1,000 layoffs. Then he built Groupe Schneider through a series of well-timed, but not always friendly, acquisitions.

Groupe Schneider, led by Pineau-Valencienne, initiated and won the first hostile takeover in France. In 1988, GS made a bid for Telemecanique, France's leading industrial automation company. This bid resulted in one of the most bitter and fiercely contested battles the Paris stock market had ever seen. In fact, an effigy in Pineau-Valencienne's likeness was burned on the steps outside the Paris Stock Exchange and its coffin was carried through the streets, followed by thousands of revelers. GS was forced to outbid Framatome, the state-controlled nuclear power plant builder and a would-be white knight, to successfully acquire Telemecanique.

Telemecanique

Telemecanique contributed 19 percent of GS's 1990 sales, 81 percent of which came from France and other European countries and 5.4 percent of which came from the United States. Exhibit 4 provides financial highlights for this subsidiary. Telemecanique's vision was to "free people throughout the world from tedious or dangerous tasks." It hoped to accomplish this vision by responding to all of industry's automation requirements worldwide. The company described its competitive position in its annual report: "Designer of components and automated systems, Telemecanique provides industry with the building blocks of the factory of the future: a flexible automated production tool, within which machines communicate with each other through processes designed for continuous quality and inventory control."

EXHIBIT 4   **Financial Highlights of Telemecanique, 1986–1990**   *(In millions of dollars)*

	1986	1987	1988	1989	1990
Sales*	$773	$884	$1,003	$1,125	$1,296
Net income*	29	40	50	60	72
Return on sales	3.8%	4.5%	4.9%	5.3%	5.5%

*Translated from French francs.
Source: Telemecanique Annual Reports.

EXHIBIT 5   **Financial Highlights of Merlin Gerin, 1986–1990**   *(In millions of dollars)*

	1986	1987	1988	1989	1990
Sales*	$1,074	$1,283	$1,422	$1,838	$2,136
Net income*	35	42	56	81	108
Return on sales	3.3%	3.2%	4.0%	4.4%	5.0%

*Translated from French francs.
Source: Paribus analyst report.

Telemecanique developed an expansion strategy that allowed it to meet the specific needs of its customers in the 110 countries in which it operated. The company formed subsidiaries through partnerships with local firms or through granting licensing or authorizing representatives while using local distribution networks.

Merlin Gerin

Merlin Gerin, contributing 32 percent of GS's total revenues, often used the tag line, "Mastering electrical power is our specialty." The breakdown of Merlin Gerin's 1989 sales by product line was:

Contracting services	10.3%
Automation and security	18.5
High-voltage transformers and distribution	32.9
Low-voltage distribution	36.4
Other	1.9

GS used this subsidiary as a vehicle for its expansion goals. It acquired companies or formed joint ventures or strategic alliances with companies that would enable GS to market Merlin Gerin products in local markets. In the case of the Square D company, GS hoped to add Merlin Gerin products to Square D's portfolio of products with the goal of increasing overall sales for both companies through Square D's distributor network. The financial highlights for this division are provided in Exhibit 5.

EXHIBIT 6   **Financial Highlights of Square D Company, 1985–1990**
(In thousands of dollars, except per share)

	Year Ended December 31					
	1985	**1986**	**1987**	**1988**	**1989**	**1990**
Net sales	$1,223,193	$1,274,932	$1,330,784	$1,497,772	$1,598,688	$1,653,319
Earnings from continuing operations	101,923	103,911	115,612	111,082	101,106	116,646
Net earnings	87,188	98,928	110,001	118,934	101,904	120,725
Per Common Share Data						
Primary						
Earnings from continuing operations	$ 3.53	$ 3.59	$ 4.01	$ 4.15	$ 3.95	$ 4.76
Net earnings	3.02	3.42	3.82	4.44	3.98	4.94
Fully diluted						
Earnings from continuing operations	3.50	3.56	3.98	4.13	3.88	4.57
Net earnings	3.00	3.39	3.79	4.42	3.91	4.73
Dividends paid	1.84	1.84	1.84	1.92	2.00	2.15
Common shareholders' equity	21.00	23.16	24.57	24.76	23.68	26.37
Stock price range—high	$43^5/8$	50	$65^1/2$	$55^3/4$	$62^3/4$	$60^1/4$
Stock price range—low	$35^1/8$	$39^1/4$	43	$45^3/8$	$47^1/2$	$33^7/8$

Source: 1990 Annual Report.

SQUARE D COMPANY

Square D was a leading manufacturer of electrical distribution and control equipment, and a major supplier of electronic materials, components, products, and systems. Its more than 18,000 products were marketed nationally and internationally to the construction industry, industrial customers, utilities, governmental agencies, individual consumers, and to other manufacturers for use in their products and equipment. Square D operated more than 70 manufacturing and distribution facilities and 160 sales offices across the United States and around the world, employing approximately 19,000 people. Square D had recorded a profit every year for the past 50 years. Exhibit 6 provides financial highlights.

Square D had a tradition of introducing new and innovative products in the industry. These included the Arkless enclosed fuse (1905); Iron Clad fused switches (1909); Saflex power panelboards (1925); the first residential circuit breaker—the multibreaker (1936); the first plug-on circuit breaker distribution panelboard, merchandising off-the-shelf components (1951); the I-LINE panelboard (1966); the industry's first two-pole ground fault interrupter breaker (1973); the world's first microprocessor-based welder control system, the SY/MAX-20 programmable controller (1978); and the WATCHDOG energy management system. Exhibit 7 indicates Square D's businesses, major product lines, and other market data.

Square D had become a stronger, more profitable company since 1987 as a result of an ongoing corporate revitalization program that had improved operating efficiencies. Exhibit 8 explains the vision, mission, principles, goals, and objectives by which the company operated since they were approved by the board of directors in 1987. By divesting marginal businesses, hiring more

EXHIBIT 7   Square D Company Products and Strategic Focus

Business	Major Product Lines	Major Customers
Electrical Distribution Sector		
Distribution equipment	Load centers and circuit breakers, safety switches, molded case circuit breakers, multimetering equipment, home wiring systems	Electrical contractors, commercial and industrial users, and OEMs served primarily through electrical distributors. Emphasis on residential, light commercial, and other nonresidential construction markets
Power equipment	Panelboards, switchboards, raceway, busway, motor control centers, power circuit breakers	Electrical contractors, and commercial and industrial users served primarily through electrical distributors. Emphasis on industrial, commercial, and other nonresidential construction markets
	Stationbreakers, low- and medium-voltage switchgear	Utilities, commercial and industrial users
Transformer	Dry-type lighting transformers, cast resin transformers, pad-mounted small power distribution transformers, oil-filled instrument transformers, control transformers, uninterruptible power systems (UPS), power conditioners, and isolation transformers	Utilities, commercial and industrial users, OEMs and users of computers, process controls, instrumentation, and communications
Connectors	Transmission, distribution, and substation connectors	Utilities, commercial and industrial users, OEMs
Consumer products division	Load centers and breakers, safety switches, water and air compressor switches, voltage testers and surge suppressers	Hardware, home center and do-it-yourself retailers
Industrial Control Sector		
Control and automation products	Pushbuttons, sensors, relays, control switches, pressure switches, crane and mill controls, medium-voltage control	Industrial users and OEMs
	Water pump switches, voltage testers	Industrial users, OEMs, and contractors
	Contactors, motor starters, AC drives	Industrial users, OEMs, and contractors
	Programmable controllers, cell controllers, data communication networks and systems (hardware and software), resistance welding controllers, stamping press controls	Industrial users and OEMs (automotive utility petroleum, chemical, food and beverage, fabricated metals)
Infrared measurement division	Infrared thermometers, line scanners and systems for noncontact temperature measurement and control	Industrial users in steel processing, glass, plastics, metal fabrication, and semiconductor industries, OEMs
Engineered systems division	Computerized control and data gathering systems	Petroleum industry, municipalities, consumers
Technical services division	Service agreements; start-up, training, testing, and emergency services	Existing Square D consumer base
International Sector		
Canada	Distribution and power equipment, transformers, control and automation products	Electrical contractors serving industrial and construction markets, industrial and natural resource industry users, and OEMs
Latin America	Electrical distribution and control and automation products	Electrical contractors serving industrial and construction markets, industrial users, and OEMs
Europe	Control and automation products, distribution and power equipment	Industrial users, panel builders, and OEMs, electrical contractors serving industrial and construction markets
Asia/Pacific, Australia, New Zealand	Circuit breakers, load centers, panelboards, switchboards, busway, control and automation products	Electrical contractors, industrial users, commercial developers, and machine-tool OEMs

Source: 1990 Annual Report

Major Competitors	Economic and Other Variables	Market Position
GE, Siemens, Westinghouse	New construction and renovation of residential and nonresidential structures, capital equipment spending	Leader in North America for low-voltage distribution equipment used in residential, commercial, and industrial building construction
Allen-Bradley, Eaton (Cutler Hammer), GE, Siemens, Westinghouse	New construction and renovation of nonresidential structures	Leader in North America for low-voltage power equipment used in commercial and industrial building construction
Asea Brown Boveri (ABB), GE, Siemens, Westinghouse	Utility capital spending, new construction and renovation of nonresidential structures	Growing position in a broad market
ABB, Acme, American Power Conversion, Balteau, Best Products, Cooper Industries (McGraw & RTE), Emerson Electric, GE, General Signal (Sola), Magne-Tek, Trench, Westinghouse	Utility capital spending, new construction and renovation of nonresidential structures, electronic capital equipment spending	Growing position in a broad transformer market
Bethea (Reliable Products), Blackburn (FL Industries), Burndy (Framatome), Penn Union (Teledyne)	Utility transmission and distribution construction	Leading supplier of electrical connectors to utilities
Cooper Industries (Crouse-Hinds), GE, General Switch, Siemens, Westinghouse	New construction and remodeling, renovation and modernization of residential and nonresidential structures	Leading share in a rapidly expanding market
Allen-Bradley, GE, Westinghouse	Industrial capital equipment spending	Co-leader
Furnas, Telemecanique	Industrial capital equipment spending, residential construction	Leader
Allen-Bradley, GE, Westinghouse	Industrial capital equipment spending, nonresidential construction	Co-leader
AEG (Modicon), Allen-Bradley, GE-Fanuc, Mitsubishi, Omron, Siemens, Texas Instruments	Industrial capital equipment spending	Strong growth potential
Chino, Land, Williamson	Industrial capital equipment spending	Global market leader, dominant in United States
Daniel, Diamond, E-Mark, Petrovend, Spectratek, Veeder Root, William Wilson Co.	Petroleum industry capital spending, fuel cost and accountability, EPA regulations	Dominant in petroleum terminal automation, growing share of fuel management and underground storage tank monitoring markets
Allen-Bradley, GE, Westinghouse	Manufacturers moving from in-house technical service capabilities to contract service by equipment manufacturers	Increasing share of large and expanding market
Allen-Bradley, Eaton (Cutler Hammer), Federal Pioneer, Klockner Moeller, Siemens, Telemecanique, Westinghouse	Residential and nonresidential construction, industrial capital equipment spending	Significant share in many electrical distribution and industrial control product segments
AEG, Allen-Bradley, GE, Merlin Gerin, Siemens, Telemecanique	Residential and nonresidential construction, industrial capital equipment spending	Leader in Mexico for low-voltage distribution equipment and industrial control products
ABB, AEG, GEC, Klockner Moeller, Merlin Gerin, Siemens, Telemecanique	Industrial capital equipment spending, residential and nonresidential construction	Leading share in specific product lines in the U.K., Germany, and Italy and growing share in Spain and other continental markets
Allen-Bradley, Fuji, Furukawa, GE, Merlin Gerin, Mitsubishi, Omron, Siemens, Telemecanique, Terasaki	Residential and nonresidential construction, infrastructure development	Increasing share of markets, varies widely by country and product, leading share for circuit breakers in Thailand and busway in Hong Kong, partnership with IDEC Izumi Corp. for control and automation products in Japan

EXHIBIT 8   Square D Company Vision, Mission, Principles, and Objectives

Our Vision
Dedicated to growth—committed to quality

Our Mission
We are dedicated to growth for our customers, shareholders, and employees through quality, innovation, and profitable reinvestment.

Our Principles
As a company responsible to our customers, shareholders, and employees, we will:

• Provide our customers with innovative, functional, and reliable products and services at a cost and quality level consistent with their needs.

• Concentrate on enhancing long-term shareholder value.

• Actively pursue equal opportunity for all individuals and provide an environment that encourages open communications, personal growth, and creativity.

• Expect integrity and professional conduct from our employees in every aspect of our business.

• Conduct our operations ethically and well within the framework of the law.

• Actively contribute to the communities and industries in which we participate.

Our Financial Goals
We are committed to providing our shareholders with an attractive return on their investment, and our specific goals for doing so are to:

• Achieve a minimum after-tax return on capital of 14 percent.

• Leverage return on shareholders' equity through a capital structure that includes 25 to 35 percent debt.

• Achieve a minimum return on equity of 18 percent.

• Pay dividends equal to approximately 40 percent of earnings.

• Achieve average annual growth in earnings of at least 10 percent.

Our Operating Objectives
The following objectives underlie our performance and guide our actions.

Market leadership
• Have a leading market share position in our major markets.

• Be recognized as a leader in the application of technology to meet customer requirements.

• Be a "best-value" supplier throughout the world.

• Expand our international business to a level equaling 20 to 25 percent of company sales.

• Invest in research and development at a rate of 4 percent of sales as a means of achieving our market leadership objectives.

Employee development
• Encourage initiative, innovation, and productivity by appropriately recognizing and rewarding employee performance.

• Invest in employee training and development at a rate of 2 percent of payroll.

• Honestly and accurately appraise and evaluate the performance of each employee on at least an annual basis.

• Provide for the orderly succession of management.

• Maintain a positive affirmative action program and provide employees with the opportunity for advancement commensurate with their abilities.

Social/community responsibility
• Maintain a safe, clean, and healthy environment for our employees and the communities in which we operate.

• Invest 1.5 percent of net income in social, cultural, educational, and charitable activities.

• Encourage appropriate employee involvement in community activities.

aggressive managers, and streamlining operations, Square D improved productivity. The company also initiated a new marketing program, backed by a new incentives system, that was designed to target large industrial and construction customers with the company's full line of products. The improved productivity significantly enhanced the company's ability to generate cash, and as a result, Square D had purchased over 15 percent of its own shares since the end of 1987. By shrinking its equity base, per-share earnings increased at a faster rate whenever net income increased, improving the company's standing on the stock market.

A key ingredient in Square D's strategy was its desire to expand its international presence. When Jerre Stead took over as CEO of Square D in January 1989, he was determined to transform the company into a global player. In his first letter to shareholders he stated, "Worldwide, our industry is going through a period of consolidation. . . . Square D will come out a winner." In the following 18 months, Mr. Stead talked to over two dozen small and mid-sized candidates for acquisition or joint ventures. Over the past several years, Square D had forgone new product development on certain products in favor of the more immediate results possible through brand label agreements with foreign manufacturers. Square D had negotiated agreements with companies such that Square D purchased certain products designed and produced by foreign companies but labeled with Square D's logo and sold in the United States by Square D. The company was looking for a company that it could acquire or with which it could form a merger or strategic alliance that was strong in the electrical distribution market in Europe, making circuit breakers and other equipment, so that Square D could take advantage of its established distribution channels. In 1990, 20 percent of the company's revenues came from international sales (see Exhibit 9).

One of the main reasons GS was drawn to Square D was its unparalleled distributor network. Over 90 percent of Square D's products were sold through electrical distributors. These electrical distributors purchased electrical equipment for resale to electrical contractors, original equipment manufacturers, and commercial and industrial users. Over the years, Square D had carefully selected its distributors and cultivated relationships designed to ensure that a Square D distributor, and therefore Square D, was the strongest and most competitive in the local market. Additionally, Square D's 170 field offices were staffed primarily with engineers whose primary responsibility was to assist its electrical distributors in project sales. Furthermore, Square D was the clear leader in sales of electrical products for the single-family and multifamily residential markets. Square D enjoyed nationally recognized brand preference in the following product categories: load centers, safety switches, circuit breakers, panelboards, switchboards, busway, and lighting transformers. Overall, Square D's strengths against its competitors were its quality image, high product reliability, complete line of products, knowledgeable sales force, product safety, strong distribution channels, and technological leadership in certain segments.

MAJOR INTERNATIONAL COMPETITORS IN THE ELECTRICAL MANUFACTURING SEGMENT

Both Square D and Groupe Schneider faced global competition from six major companies: Allen-Bradley (A-B), ASEA Brown-Boveri (ABB), Cutler-Hammer (C-H), General Electric (GE), Siemens, and Westinghouse. Exhibit 10 provides financial data for each of these companies.

Allen-Bradley   Allen-Bradley was a leading manufacturer of industrial automation controls. A-B had been acquired by Rockwell International Corp. in 1985. Since the acquisition, Rockwell International had continued to invest in A-B in order to expand its position and build for growth in the industrial automation business. In 1987, A-B expanded its line of photoelectric sensors and

EXHIBIT 9   **Square D Company Financial Information by Geographic Area,**
               1988–1990   *(Dollars in thousands, except per share)*

Geographic Areas	1988	1989	1990
Sales			
United States			
Unaffiliated customers	$1,256,009	$1,321,769	$1,332,390
Intercompany	47,479	62,253	73,646
	1,303,488	1,384,022	1,406,036
Europe			
Unaffiliated customers	105,471	115,678	138,836
Intercompany	25,207	23,691	22,617
	130,678	139,369	161,453
Latin America			
Unaffiliated customers	53,242	68,178	78,867
Intercompany	1,761	1,217	1,300
	55,003	69,395	80,167
Other international			
Unaffiliated customers	83,050	93,063	103,226
Intercompany	620	256	447
	83,670	93,319	103,673
Eliminations	(75,067)	(87,417)	(98,010)
Consolidated	$1,497,772	$1,598,688	$1,653,319
Operating Earnings			
United States	$ 156,791	$ 163,202	$ 164,155
Europe	4,098	212	3,555
Latin America	11,212	12,547	10,445
Other international	3,942	(463)	650
Eliminations	3,176	(204)	(366)
Consolidated	$ 179,219	$ 175,294	$ 178,439
Identifiable Assets			
United States	$ 883,334	$ 952,865	$1,131,085
Europe	109,297	120,483	158,637
Latin America	62,924	62,171	65,847
Other international	64,886	69,357	70,203
Eliminations	(1,056)	(2,356)	(2,704)
Identifiable assets of continuing operations	1,119,385	1,202,520	1,423,068
Net assets of discontinued operations	181,338	170,065	36,681
Consolidated	$1,300,723	$1,372,585	$1,459,749

Source: 1990 Annual Report.

switches with the acquisition of Electronics Corporation of America. Then
Data Myte Corp. was acquired to enhance A-B's quality management product
lines that provided factory equipment operators with information on how to
improve manufacturing productivity. A-B's major markets included domestic
and international automotive manufacturers; the food-processing industry;
chemical, mining, and metals industries; forest products industries; and original equipment manufacturers (OEMs) in the motor control market.

EXHIBIT 10   **Financial Highlights of Selected Global Electric Equipment Manufacturers, 1988–1990**   (*In millions of dollars*)

	1988		1989		1990	
	Sales	**Net Profit**	**Sales**	**Net Profit**	**Sales**	**Net Profit**
Rockwell (A-B)	$11,946	$ 614	$12,518	$ 631	$12,379	$ 624
ASEA*	9,495	239	10,926	316	16,000	405
Eaton (C-H)	3,469	228	3,671	210	3,671	169
General Electric	38,824	3,386	41,019	3,939	43,017	4,303
Siemens†	24,556	558	26,007	611	NA	NA
Westinghouse	12,499	823	12,844	922	12,915	1,001

*These figures represent the income from ASEA, 87% of which comes from ABB.
†Translated from deutsche marks.
NA = not available
Source: Value Line and S&P's Registers.

Allen-Bradley's strengths included a strong sales coverage and distribution channels with high levels of local stock and a reputation of good delivery. It had a long-standing reputation as a quality manufacturer, and it offered automation packages that helped pull through sales of control merchandise. Additionally, A-B had strong joint ventures and product line breadth in programmable controllers and cell controllers.

ASEA Brown-Boveri   Brown-Boveri was established in Germany in 1900 and engaged in the construction of plants and production of machinery, appliances, and components for the generation, conversion, distribution, and use of electricity. On January 1, 1988, Brown-Boveri (BB) and ASEA of Sweden merged their worldwide electrical engineering activities to become the largest energy engineering company in the world. Following the merger, ABB consolidated and rationalized its operations to improve coordination and productivity—a strategy said to have triggered a "wholesale restructuring" of Europe's electrical power industry.

ABB was one of the first electrical equipment manufacturers to begin widespread globalization. In 1989, ABB acquired Westinghouse's transmission and distribution operation (25 factories and businesses with revenues in excess of $1 billion) and Combustion Engineering (a power-generation and process-automation equipment manufacturer) to secure its position in the North American market. By 1991, ABB had acquired or held a minority interest in 60 companies, employed over 240,000 people worldwide, and generated more than $25 billion in revenues annually. ABB's management considered the company "a federation of national companies with a global coordination center."[3] ABB's CEO Percy Barnevik discussed the company's globalization strategy:

---

[3]William Taylor, "The Logic of Global Business: An Interview with ABB's Percy Barnevik," *Harvard Business Review,* March-April 1991, p. 92.

"You want to be able to optimize a business globally—to specialize in the production of components, to drive economies of scale as far as you can, to rotate managers and technologists around the world to share expertise and to solve problems."[4]

Cutler-Hammer   Cutler-Hammer was a subsidiary of the Eaton Corp., whose presence in the controls market was created by a series of acquisitions. In the 1960s, Eaton acquired a series of companies to form a foundation in automotive and appliance controls. During the 1970s, the company used acquisitions to increase its range of control products to include electrical equipment and aerospace and defense projects. C-H, through Eaton, was attempting to provide superior technology and cost-effective manufacturing on a global scale. C-H's primary markets were residential, commercial, and industrial construction; industrial users; utilities; OEMs; and crane assemblers. C-H's strengths included good product features, new product innovations within its product lines, overall company image, perceived quality, sales coverage, and broad control product lines.

General Electric   General Electric was one of the largest and most diversified industrial corporations in the world and was ranked seventh on *Fortune*'s Global 500. General Electric's numerous businesses were organized along three classifications: technology, services, and core manufacturing. Included in the technology group were the production of aircraft engines, aerospace, plastics, medical systems, and factory automation. Financial services, broadcasting (including the NBC network), and communications were grouped into the services classification. The core manufacturing group produced appliances, lighting, industrial and power systems, electrical equipment, electric motors, and transportation systems.

GE's major markets in the electrical equipment manufacturing segment were electrical distributors, commercial and industrial construction, industrial users, OEMs, utilities, and governments. GE's strengths included technological leadership, a strong company image, strong product lines, a good distribution system, broad sales coverage, and customer service. The company spent 3.4 percent of its 1990 revenues on research and development and employed 298,000 people worldwide. GE's cumbersome size restricted its ability to react in some instances and the company suffered limited availability of some of its electrical products. GE believed large transnational alliances were the key to success throughout the world and was attempting to improve its world market shares through acquisitions, cross-sourcing partners, and asset exchanges with Asian and European companies (which called for an exchange of manufacturing and engineering technology with the target of developing global electrical distribution and control products). In 1990, 35 percent of GE's total revenues were from international sales.

Siemens   Siemens A.G. and its subsidiaries constituted the largest electrical company in Germany. It was engaged in the entire field of electrical engineering and electronics, manufacturing products that regulated, controlled, and distributed electrical power; generated electricity; and produced mechanical

----
[4]Ibid.

power from electricity. Corporate policy was aimed at two primary objectives: (1) to strengthen its position in growth sectors with great future potential, including factory and office automation, automotive electronics, microelectronics, telecommunications networks, and medical engineering; and (2) to increase its penetration in the key world markets, especially in Europe and the United States, and in the rapidly growing segments of the electrical equipment industry. Siemens considered the United States its most important foreign market, and its U.S. subsidiaries operated 47 plants and more than 300 sales and service locations. Only about 20 percent of the products Siemens sold in the United States were imported from Germany.

Siemens's primary markets were commercial, residential, and industrial construction; industrial users; and utilities. Siemens had an aggressive pricing strategy and an acceptable product line. However, Siemens was technologically weak in the United States, had a perceived quality problem, and had a weak distributor and field organization.

Westinghouse Westinghouse Electric Corp. was a diversified, global corporation that provided electrical and electronic products and services for industrial, construction, and electric utility applications. It had major operations in radio and television broadcasting, financial services, transport refrigeration, factory automation systems, franchised beverage bottling and distribution, materials for electronic and electrical applications, land and community development, and waste-to-energy and co-generation projects. Westinghouse also operated government-owned facilities under contracts with the federal government. The company was committed to a worldwide effort to improve quality and customer satisfaction, and 10 percent of total revenues came from international sales. In 1989, Westinghouse sold its transmission and distribution operations to ASEA Brown-Boveri. The strategic alliance formed between these two companies led some industry analysts to predict that a full merger between the two was imminent, which would cement ABB's position as the world's largest electrical equipment manufacturer.

Westinghouse was targeting commercial and industrial construction, electrical utilities, electrical utility power generation, municipal waste-to-energy, and government markets. The company's strengths were technological leadership, sales coverage, customer service, ability to compete on price, and a nationwide distribution system. However, the company had quality problems in some product lines and limited product availability in others.

THE HOSTILE TAKEOVER BATTLE

Square D's Previous Dealings with Groupe Schneider

From time to time, Square D had engaged in negotiations with foreign companies concerning possible joint ventures, cross-licensing, and other cooperative strategic arrangements. Such was the case with Square D and Merlin Gerin on January 29, 1988, when the companies entered into a six-year patent and know-how license and distribution agreement providing Square D with certain rights to manufacture and distribute within the United States certain products designed and developed by Merlin Gerin. Beginning in the summer of 1988, Square D and Schneider engaged in extensive discussions concerning possible additional joint business opportunities between the two companies.

On September 14, 1988, Mr. Stead met with GS representatives, including Mr. Pineau-Valencienne, at Square D's headquarters in Palatine, Illinois. During the meeting, Mr. Pineau-Valencienne stated that it would be in the interest of both companies to explore possible joint ventures because of the demand in the global marketplace for products such as those that Square D and GS manufactured and because of the "synergistic opportunities that would flow from an alliance between the companies." Following the meeting, both companies set up teams to study possible joint-venture opportunities. The teams were divided along product lines with managers from Square D and the GS counterparts at Merlin Gerin and Telemecanique meeting to share information and discuss possibilities. At the time, GS's management stated that it intended to proceed on a nonhostile basis. In a letter dated September 23, 1988, Mr. Pineau-Valencienne wrote:

> I would also like to emphasize that we are convinced that a cooperation of both strategic and operational nature between our two Groups will have mutually beneficial consequences. Thus we are quite open to all mutually agreeable solutions, ranging from technical cooperation to cross shareholding, including any other form of alliance such as licensing or joint development work. Any friendly approach, as envisaged, would suit us perfectly.

Square D believed that it could gain substantial strategic and financial advantages from strategic joint ventures with GS. Discussions between the two companies continued until October 1989, when it became apparent that the parties would be unable to resolve the structural issues surrounding the formation of a joint venture. These structural issues pertained to the leadership and management of the projects, financial consequences, and problems with ownership. Therefore, joint venture discussions were terminated in October.

However, after GS purchased Federal Pioneer, Mr. Pineau-Valencienne called Mr. Stead in early 1990 to say that the possibility of a joint venture between GS and Square D was "more compelling than ever" and suggested that the companies renew negotiations. Since the structural issues could not be resolved, Mr. Pineau-Valencienne suggested that Square D might acquire Merlin Gerin in return for a "significant," but noncontrolling, equity stake in Square D. Square D's board of directors and financial advisors considered the offer, but expressed "strong reservations" about the terms being put forth by Schneider. On the evenings of September 11 and 12, 1990, Mr. Pineau-Valencienne attended dinner meetings with Square D's board to discuss the transaction. At both meetings, Mr. Pineau-Valencienne repeatedly assured Square D that if they did not approve a potential transaction, Schneider would honor their wishes and not pursue any takeover on a hostile basis. Later, Mr. Stead received a letter from Mr. Pineau-Valencienne stating, "It appears to me that probably the simplest and most effective way to achieve all of our important goals is through a friendly cash merger transaction." The board responded by confirming its strong support for the continued implementation of the company's strategic plan and concluded that it would not be in the stockholders' best interest to sell at the present time. The board unanimously decided that the interests of Square D and its stockholders would be best served by terminating discussions with GS.

In late 1990, Mr. Pineau-Valencienne called Mr. Stead to inquire about the rumors in the market of a possible takeover of Square D. During the call, DPV informed Stead that GS had not bought any Square D shares and would not do so without Square D's knowledge, but was willing to serve as a "white knight" should Square D wish it. However, by February 1991, GS had changed its approach and was pursuing Square D in a hostile takeover and had acquired over 300,000 shares of Square D stock.

Groupe Schneider's Viewpoint

Groupe Schneider's management felt the need to build a significant presence in the key world markets in order to compete in the global marketplace. The company had identified three large "geographies" that it considered key: the European segment, the Asian/Pacific segment, and the North and South American segment. GS was attempting to build this critical mass by acquiring strong players in all world markets. GS saw Square D as a way to access the U.S. distribution channels; Merlin Gerin's and Telemecanique's products dovetailed nicely with Square D's product line and could be marketed to the same distributors. Mr. Pineau-Valencienne remarked, "The two are very complementary, they are what you call in English a tremendous combination."[5] GS hoped to use Square D's established relationships with electrical distributors to push its product line of low- and high-tension electrical products, including relays, contact breakers, conductors, and products targeted for utility companies. In a letter to Square D shareholders, GS stated: "We can achieve a strong competitive status worldwide without overlaps. From this base, we should have sufficient resources to move into the Far East and the Pacific Rim on a combined basis." Square D was strong in the U.S. markets but weak in European markets, with only a 2 percent share. GS was strong in Europe, but had only a 2 percent share of the U.S. markets. The merger would make GS the world leader in electromechanical industrial controls and low- and medium-voltage distribution. A successful bid would create a group twice as large as the nearest competitor in the world market for electrical distribution equipment.

If successful in the acquisition, GS said it would leave Square D's management primarily intact and have Square D manage all of GS's and Square D's combined North American operations. "We would have Square D run all our operations in North America, in Canada and Mexico where we have 20 to 30 percent of the market, and we would bring into Square D all our American interests," said Mr. Pineau-Valencienne.[6] Additionally, GS management planned to substantially increase Square D's research and development spending. According to DPV, "We don't think the company [Square D] spends enough on research. We spend a lot on research. We have worldwide products, and we could fuel technology to where we are convinced we could help Square D develop presence in the U.S. and abroad."[7] GS envisioned substantial transfer of manufacturing know-how from GS to Square D, particularly as concerned IEC standards.

Groupe Schneider planned to finance the acquisition with 5 billion francs available in short-term securities, and the balance financed with bank loans. This acquisition would increase GS's debt-to-equity ratio by 10 percent and would dilute GS's 1991 earnings between 10 and 20 percent. Standard & Poor's,

---

[5]*The Wall Street Journal*, February 20, 1991.

[6]*Palatine Herald*, February 21, 1991.

[7]Ibid.

a major bond rating agency, reported it was unlikely the capital structure of the combined companies would have the strength and flexibility to warrant Square D's current AA bond ratings. It said the acquisition would reduce GS's financial flexibility by consuming internal cash and raising debt levels. GS contracted Lazard Freres, an international investment bank, to handle the financing—it was not coincidental that Lazard Freres owned an 8.5 percent interest in Square D.

Mr. Pineau-Valencienne, now dubbed "the Shark" by Square D personnel, was tenacious in his efforts to acquire Square D. "We are ready to play the world game. I think Square D would find it very, very hard to stay independent. Underplaying the world game has had a consequence on their profits," said DPV.[8] In March 1991, GS hoped to gain sufficient shares of Square D's stock to elect its own representatives to Square D's board of directors. Said Pineau-Valencienne, "There is a race on for globalization. I regret that Square D isn't as convinced of this as we are."[9]

Square D's Response

In recent years, Square D had invested substantial resources in research and development (R&D) and product and market development to strengthen its prospects for growth and improved profitability. Additionally, the company had restructured and implemented major programs designed to boost productivity through improved manufacturing, marketing plans, and cost-control programs. Square D had just begun to realize the benefits of its efforts in 1990 when financial performance exceeded its long-term targets, achieving a return on average capital of 14.1 percent and a return on equity of 19.3 percent. Square D believed it was poised for even greater success in the future when the economy recovered and when the company could reap the benefits of experience in its strategic programs. After reviewing its businesses, financial condition, and future prospects, Square D's board of directors reaffirmed its conviction that the stockholders would be best served by Square D remaining independent and pursuing its long-term business strategy.

In addition to the desire to pursue its long-term goals, the company was opposed to the merger for a couple of reasons. First, Square D felt that Groupe Schneider was trying to take advantage of the recession in the U.S. economy and the depressed U.S. dollar by buying the company at a time that was most advantageous for GS and least advantageous for Square D. Mr. Pineau-Valencienne commented on this concern: "When the dollar was strong, Americans came over and bought [art]. Now, it's our turn to buy."[10] Additionally, Square D was distrustful of GS's promises. The company felt DPV had reneged on past promises to pursue only friendly mergers and in its assurances that GS had not acquired Square D stock. "Didier would start every conversation by saying that he didn't own a single share of Square D stock and wouldn't take any action without the approval of our board," said Mr. Stead.[11]

---

[8]*The Wall Street Journal*, February 19, 1991.
[9]*The Wall Street Journal*, February 21, 1991.
[10]*Business Week*, March 18, 1991, p. 36.
[11]Ibid.

The following points were made in a letter to Mr. Pineau-Valencienne, signed by all of Square D's board members, formally rejecting the tender offer:

1. We ultimately concluded that the type of transaction between the two organizations that you preferred, as contrasted to the joint venture we were suggesting, benefited Schneider immensely and added nothing to the prospects of Square D which would be beneficial to its shareholders or its other constituencies. We today have reiterated our belief that Square D's strategy to remain independent and to pursue internationalization through partnerships, joint ventures or other strategic initiatives best serves Square D's shareholders and its other constituencies.

2. The proposed acquisition would encounter significant antitrust problems. Square D and Schneider compete in the U.S., Canada, Mexico and Europe in the electrical distribution and industrial controls areas. Schneider's proposed acquisition raises substantial questions regarding the legality of the proposal under the U.S. antitrust laws and the competition laws of Canada and of various countries of Western Europe, including the United Kingdom.

3. We were surprised to learn of Schneider's accumulation of over 300,000 shares of Square D stock. This is contrary to a specific representation made specifically by you last summer that Schneider owned no Square D shares and would not purchase any shares without Square D's knowledge.

4. We are extremely troubled by the unreliability of your commitments and representations. . . . Last week, after receiving your unsolicited "friendly" merger proposal, we received a notice from you that in order to "preserve [your] options and flexibility," Schneider was proposing to nominate directors at the Square D annual meeting of shareholders, presumably in opposition to our slate of nominees in a proxy fight. . . . In addition, just today, we received Schneider's demand for Square D's shareholders list. That act further demonstrates to us your intention to circumvent the Square D Board of Directors and to go directly to Square D's shareholders in direct contradiction to your word. And you also appear to have breached commitments with respect to the use of confidential information.

Square D's Defenses   Square D had several weapons to use against Schneider. First, Square D had a shareholder rights plan, a poison pill designed to make a hostile takeover prohibitively expensive. This plan would require an acquiring company to give each Square D shareholder the right to buy shares of the acquiring company's stock at a discount price once the acquiring company had bought more than a certain percentage of Square D's stock. Square D also filed a claim with the Securities Exchange Commission stating that the takeover, if successful, would constitute a violation of Section 7 of the Clayton Antitrust Act. Square D claimed the merger of two of the world's leading producers of electrical distribution equipment and industrial controls would have immediate and significant adverse competitive effects on a number of equipment product markets within the United States by substantially lessening competition and/or creating a monopoly in these markets. Square D also filed a claim in the state of New York stating that GS was wrongfully using information about Square D, gleaned from confidential meetings in the past, to discuss potential joint ventures. A New York state court issued a temporary injunction blocking GS from "using or disclosing any confidential, non-public business information." Additionally, 7 percent of Square D's stock was in an employee stock ownership plan, a block of shares less likely to be tendered for monetary gain.

By late April 1991, 78 percent of Square D's outstanding shares had been proffered to Groupe Schneider; that is, the shares were offered, but GS had not yet purchased them. As a Delaware corporation, Square D was protected by state-imposed requirements that hostile takeovers acquire 85 percent of the shares; so until 85 percent were tendered, GS could not buy any. In addition to the legal challenges Square D raised, the company disclosed that it was also considering third parties as possible white knights or for possible joint ventures. A leveraged buy-out or reorganization were also possibilities to escape acquisition. Square D announced on April 17, 1991, that it had agreed to pay fees to several banks to have them arrange financing for a transaction that could help the company elude a hostile buyer. Additionally, Square D had postponed its annual meetings three times—a delaying tactic that the investment community interpreted as a signal that Square D believed Groupe Schneider could win control over Square D's board of directors if the meeting were held immediately.

THE POMERLEAU GROUP*

Louis Hébert, University of Western Ontario
J. Michael Geringer, University of Western Ontario

On March 13, 1989, Hervé Pomerleau, CEO and sole owner of the Pomerleau Group, was assessing his company's recent financial performance. The largest construction company in Québec and the ninth largest in Canada, the Pomerleau Group had been following a vertical integration strategy that had enabled the company to double its size since 1984 and its 1988 sales to reach $212 million. However, results from Hyalin International Inc., the group's largest manufacturing subsidiary with sales of $29 million, were less encouraging. Since its acquisition in 1985, this subsidiary specializing in the manufacture of insulated glass and the installation of glazing and curtain walls had experienced continuous financial problems. In 1988, Hyalin was showing its third loss in a row of over $1 million. On his desk Hervé Pomerleau had a report from consultants hired to propose a strategy for Hyalin. Hervé Pomerleau wondered about what decision he should make regarding the consultants' report and Hyalin's future within the group.

THE CANADIAN CONSTRUCTION INDUSTRY

The Canadian construction industry was composed of the firms engaged in the building, renovation, repair, and demolition of immobile structures and in the alteration of natural topography. In 1988, the industry consisted of approximately 130,000 firms, represented more than 680,000 jobs, and accounted for about 51 percent of the $87 billion of construction undertaken in Canada that year. Governments, utility companies, and other firms not primarily involved in construction accounted for the remaining 49 percent. The industry was composed primarily of firms of small size; only 5 percent of the firms had billings of $1 million or more but they accounted for 59 percent of the work. The small firms tended to operate at the local level, while larger firms had a regional or provincial focus. Fewer than 20 firms had operations in all provinces and outside Canada, primarily in the United States and in developing countries. Entry into the industry was perceived as easy since it did not require extensive investments in plant and equipment.

Construction companies were classified as either general contractors, engineering contractors, or trade contractors. General contractors were engaged in the construction of buildings for residential, industrial, commercial, and institutional purposes. Engineering contractors were involved in nonbuilding construction, such as marine construction, roads and highways, waterworks, dams, electric power plants, railways, and oil and gas facilities. Trade contractors were essentially subcontractors performing specialized services for both engineering and general contractors. Such services included electrical and mechanical works, construction of walls and ceilings, roofing and sheet metal, excavation and foundation, steel erection, concrete, glazing and curtain walls, demolition, and painting. Trade contractors accounted for 83 percent of the industry's firms, compared to 14 percent and 3 percent for general and engineering contractors, respectively. They were also of smaller size, with average 1986 revenues estimated at $550,000 versus $2.4 million for engineering contractors and $1 million for general contractors. Nevertheless, their pretax return on sales, at 4.3 percent, was above the overall industry average of 3.6 percent.

Construction contracts were awarded to general and engineering contractors through an open bid process. It was then their responsibility to divide the projects into specific tasks and to distribute them to subcontractors, either through an open bid process or not. Contracts and subcontracts were mostly awarded on the basis of price. However, reputation as a reliable and quality-conscious builder could also heavily influence decisions. Technology, engineering, and project management capabilities were also critical in engineering construction.

Contractors varied in their relative reliance on subcontractors. Many were composed of only a small nucleus of people that assumed supervision of the construction site, while all remaining work was subcontracted and the work force hired on a project-by-project basis. Some other firms relied on internal resources for major parts of a contract and resorted to subcontractors only for specific tasks. All participants to a project were responsible for the on-time completion of their task and the quality of their work. Generally, 10 percent to 15 percent of their individual contract's value was withheld either by the general contractor or the project's owners. That guarantee was returned to contractors and subcontractors 90 days after completion of the job, if their task had been completed on time and with good workmanship.

With variations greater than those of the Gross Domestic Product (GDP), construction activity was volatile and cyclical in nature, in addition to being vulnerable to business cycle fluctuations. Pressures to bid competitively during periods of reduced economic activity, and labor and material shortages during boom times, constrained profitability. Canadian contractors also had to cope with sharp seasonal fluctuations due to Canadian climatic conditions. Furthermore, because construction was a labor-intensive industry, labor represented approximately 30 percent of total costs. As a result, labor–management relations had a significant influence on firms' performances.

Since 1984, construction output had increased by more than 50 percent. Building construction, fueled by a boom in housing, had been the fastest-growing construction market in Canada, especially in Ontario and, to a smaller extent, in Québec (see Exhibits 1 and 2). However, having reached its peak in 1988, the construction market was forecasted to stabilize at around $80 billion until 1992. Furthermore, industry observers were concerned by Canadian firms' limited competitiveness in international markets. The common explanations of this situation were the absence of firms with diversified technological capabilities and integration of engineering and general construction, productivity problems, insufficient or nonexistent research and development (R&D), and shortage of skilled labor. Moreover, Canadian construction performed abroad was estimated at only $900 million in a market evaluated at over $1 trillion. Canada was among the few industrialized countries without integrated construction companies having the size and resources required to compete effectively with international firms such as Bechtel (USA), Fluor (USA), Bourguyes (France), Holzman (FRG), or Shimizu (Japan). This was

Value of Construction Work Performed in Canada, 1976–1988 and Forecast to 1991
(In millions of current dollars)

Actual	Building Construction		Engineering Construction					Total
	Residential	Non-Residential	Roads, Highways, Runways	Marine, Dam, Sewage	Electric Power, Railway, Phone	Oil and Gas Facilities	Other Engineering	
1976	$12,669	$ 7,803	$2,394	$1,756	$4,176	$2,154	$2,178	$33,131
1977	13,126	8,181	2,691	2,065	4,757	2,724	2,259	35,803
1978	13,780	8,454	3,035	2,175	5,298	3,336	2,113	38,190
1979	14,267	10,439	3,380	2,272	5,900	4,643	2,122	43,023
1980	13,762	12,668	3,731	2,467	6,148	6,709	2,731	48,327
1981	16,365	15,173	4,092	2,829	6,943	8,780	2,704	56,884
1982	13,581	15,262	4,310	3,038	7,255	9,706	2,912	56,065
1983	16,851	13,901	4,326	2,946	6,866	8,128	2,930	55,948
1984	16,647	14,765	4,276	2,916	6,387	8,552	3,031	56,574
1985	24,145	17,314	5,179	3,143	6,101	9,207	2,893	67,983
1986	28,885	18,542	5,193	2,955	6,123	6,728	3,275	71,701
1987*	36,003	21,225	5,065	2,903	6,579	5,917	3,164	80,856
1988†	35,651	22,626	5,284	3,329	7,467	7,490	3,432	85,279
Forecasts‡								
1989	$33,000	$21,000	$5,900	$3,400	$7,800	$8,100	$3,500	$82,700
1990	31,000	19,000	6,400	3,700	8,000	8,700	3,600	80,400
1991	30,000	19,000	6,600	3,800	8,900	8,800	3,700	80,800

*Preliminary.

†Intentions.

‡Maclean Hunter Research Bureau estimates in association with Construction Forecast Company.

Source: Maclean Hunter Research Bureau (1988), *Construction Canada*.

E X H I B I T 2   **Value of Construction Performed as a Percentage of Total Construction Activity in Canada, by Region, 1984–1988**

Region	1984	1985	1986	1987	1988
Atlantic provinces	9.0%	8.5%	8.0%	7.3%	7.2%
Québec	20.8	21.2	21.7	22.4	21.9
Ontario	29.6	31.1	35.3	37.4	36.7
Manitoba	3.3	3.6	3.9	3.6	3.7
Saskatchewan	4.6	4.8	4.1	4.1	4.1
Alberta	16.8	16.6	14.4	12.9	14.0
British Columbia	15.7	14.3	12.5	12.3	12.4
Canada, total	100.0%	100.0%	100.0%	100.0%	100.0%
Canada, total (in billions of dollars)	$56.5	$67.9	$71.7	$80.8	$85.2

Source: Maclean Hunter Research Bureau.

happening at the same time that the construction industry was becoming increasingly global and giant Japanese construction companies were moving in force into the North American market.

GLASS AND THE CONSTRUCTION INDUSTRY

The construction industry was the largest user of flat glass, with 50 percent of the Canadian consumption, compared to 33 percent for the transportation industry. Used mainly for windows, doors, and glazings, flat glass's percentage of material costs in building construction had risen from 2 percent to 15 percent in the last 25 years and had thus become one of the main materials used in this type of construction. Flat glass was used for single-glazed applications as well as for the manufacture of processed glass, such as insulated, tempered, and laminated glass.

Insulated glass was made by bonding two or three layers of glass separated by a spacer and sealed around their perimeters. This process was of limited technological complexity and could be done manually. However, automation of facilities was becoming necessary for insulated glass manufacturers wanting to reduce labor costs in the face of intensifying price competition and to meet the increasingly stringent delivery and quality requirements of insulated glass users. Typically, automation of insulated glass manufacturing represented investments of $2 million and required an annual production volume of about 4 million square feet of insulated glass to be cost effective.

Tempering and laminating glass were technologically complex processes. In tempering, glass was toughened by being heated above its strain point and then quickly cooled. In laminating, two or more layers of glass were bonded together with an elastomer interlayer. Laminated and tempered glass were used for insulated or noninsulated windows, and glazing designed principally for nonresidential usage. Compared to tempered glass, laminated glass was less resistant to failure, did not implode, and could be transformed, cut, or machined once laminated. Both processes required investments of at least $1.5 million and a production volume greater than 3 million square feet.

In Canada, unprocessed and processed flat glass was marketed directly from flat glass producers to large glaziers and window and door manufacturers. In this segment, demand consisted mostly of large volumes of standard sizes of glass used for mass production of windows. Customers were highly price-sensitive and requested rapid delivery. Some glazing/curtain wall contractors were also supplied directly from the glass-making plants. These contractors specialized in the installation of glass, windows, and curtain wall systems on construction sites. Curtain wall systems were a lightweight exterior cladding, hung on a building structure, and used for almost all office and nonresidential buildings. These systems were an economic and time-saving construction technique and could provide a variety of finished exterior appearances with glass as well as metal. Flat glass producers also provided their large customers with glazing/curtain wall contracting services.

Unprocessed and processed glass was also marketed through distributors to small glaziers, glazing/curtain wall contractors, and window manufacturers whose demand was usually too small to be supplied directly from flat glass producers. Some distributors were involved in the manufacture of insulated, tempered, and laminated glass for the same clientele. Typically, they served a segment requiring custom sizes of glass and emphasized quality and service in addition to price. However, these firms were often competing directly with flat glass producers for larger supply contracts, and resorted to price cuts to obtain them. In 1986, 35 firms were manufacturing insulated glass in Canada, compared to 18 and 7 for tempered and laminated glass, respectively. In these numbers were included PPG Industries and AFG Inc., both subsidiaries of U.S. companies with facilities in the Toronto area, and Canada's only flat glass producers. These large firms also produced other processed glass such as colored, coated, and stained glass. The typical insulated glass manufacturer had fewer than 20 employees and production below 3 million square feet annually. Furthermore, over 1,800 glazing contractors were in operation, but only the 20 largest were involved in curtain walls.

Demand for glass was directly related to the construction market. As a result of the construction boom, demand had risen sharply since 1982. Consumption of insulated glass reached $108 million in 1986 compared to $57 million in 1983, while demand for tempered glass increased from $29 million to $57 million. However, the market for laminated glass grew from $20 million in 1983 to $30 million in 1985 before dropping to $20 million in 1986. Imports of flat glass were evaluated at $150 million in 1986 and consisted mainly of specialty glass, such as reflecting or wired glass, which was uneconomical to produce locally for markets as small as Canada's. With the exception of tempered glass, where imports accounted for roughly 20 percent of the Canadian market, imports and exports were negligible in the laminated and insulated glass segments, mainly because of transportation costs.

Transportation costs for glass could account for 25 percent of total costs and, consequently, shipment over more than 500 to 700 kilometers was often uneconomical. These costs as well as users' requirements for rapid delivery explained why the Canadian insulated glass market was divided among a small number of regional producers. With many large users switching to just-in-time (JIT) procurement systems requiring more responsiveness, proximity, and service, the regionalization of the industry was expected to further increase in the near future.

With construction plateauing until 1992, industry observers anticipated some difficult years, especially for producers of insulated glass since this type of glass was now present in close to 80 percent of residential and nonresidential buildings. However, demand for tempered and laminated glass was expected to grow with the increasing use of skylights, solariums, greenhouses, sloped glazings, bent glass, and other applications that required these types of glass; indeed, regulations enforcing their use in most nonresidential applications were soon expected.

Low-emissivity (Low-E) and heat-mirror glass were also major emerging products in North America. With a coating or a polymer layer that reduced heat loss in winter and heat gain in summer, these types of glass had the potential to conserve more energy than traditional insulated glass, a characteristic considered ideal for the Canadian market. In 1988 they were used in less than 10 percent of insulated windows in Canada, but this percentage was forecasted to reach at least 30 percent by 1995.

Because of a growing trend to renovate and upgrade existing structures, insulated glass, like many construction materials, was increasingly perceived as a consumer product rather than a mere industrial one. This trend was expected to transform the business strategies of many construction material suppliers. As the industry became more marketing-intensive, producers had to give more emphasis to branding, product recognition, and pull marketing, as well as to the quality and image of the product.

THE POMERLEAU GROUP

In 1964, when the construction company employing him went bankrupt and could not finish a project in Saint-Georges-de Beauce, Hervé Pomerleau went to see the owner and proposed that he complete the project. At age 32, with more than 10 years' experience as a construction worker, no high school degree, and speaking no English, he had decided to start his own construction company in this small town located 100 kilometers southeast of Québec City and 350 kilometers northeast of Montreal. Hervé Pomerleau cited self-confidence and ambition resulting from Québec's "Quiet Revolution," as well as the necessity to contribute to his native region's development, as drivers of his decision. Twenty-five years later, Hervé Pomerleau was CEO and still sole owner of the Pomerleau Group, the largest construction company in Québec (see Exhibits 3 and 4). With 1988 revenues of $213 million, almost totally from Québec, the group ranked ninth-largest among Canada's largest contractors and fourth-largest among builders (see Exhibits 5 and 6). Its profitability was also well above the industry's average. Hervé Pomerleau and his company had become one of the main success stories of Beauce, this remote region of Québec, historically dominated by farming and forestry, that had produced "more free-enterprisers than any other region of the country."[1]

Management often referred to tenacity and perseverance to explain the company's achievements. These characteristics permeated the entire organization and were reflected in the company's policies. For instance, hiring and promotion policies emphasized determination and unremitting efforts in

---

[1]M. Fraser, *Quebec Inc.* (Toronto: Key Porter Books, 1987), p. 43.

EXHIBIT 3   Québec's 10 Largest Contractors, 1988   *(In millions of dollars)*

Rank			Sales		Assets		Employees	
1988	**1987**		**1988**	**1987**	**1988**	**1987**	**1988**	**1987**
1	1	Groupe Pomerleau	$212.9	$181.9	$299.2	$223.9	1,235	1,390
2	2	Sintra	152.4	145.4	59.8	64.7	1,055	1,177
3	3	BG Checo International	113.2	98.8	57.8	42.9	1,170	1,137
4	5	Simard-Beaudry	97.1	89.0	48.6	39.3	550	300
5	4	Groupe Vibec	90.8	90.0	70.0	45.0	660	650
6	—	Laurent Gagnon	80.0	30.0	125.0	75.0	1,000	325
7	7	Pavage Beaver	69.0	62.0	36.0	34.0	600	800
8	8	C. de Const. Nat.	56.0	52.0	3.0	2.5	700	600
9	9	Lambert Somec	43.3	46.5	24.9	28.1	980	940
10	—	Plibrico	42.0	38.5	10.0	10.0	625	625

Source: *Les Affaires*, June 11, 1988, and June 17, 1989.

EXHIBIT 4   Selected Data on the Pomerleau Group, 1979–1988

Year	Sales (In millions of dollars)	Assets (In millions of dollars)	Number of Employees
1979	$ 53.4	$ 42.0	675
1980	60.6	54.2	714
1981	66.4	45.8	737
1982	64.0	68.8	887
1983	89.8	85.4	1,028
1984	122.8	140.9	1,647
1985	166.4	192.3	1,283
1986	184.2	176.4	1,283
1987	181.9	223.9	1,390
1988	212.9	299.2	1,235

addition to superior abilities in the evaluation of potential or existing employees. The company and its management had the reputation of being hard negotiators, and if they required significant concessions from subcontractors, they also allowed them fair returns. As a result, the company was well known for succeeding in projects in which others would have been doomed for failure, or for executing projects within specifications and deadlines that other contractors would avoid or refuse.

The group's goal was straightforward: to provide jobs to workers and ensure the pride of a whole population by becoming the leading construction company in Québec first and in Canada second. In addition, the group took great pride in its entrepreneurship and its capacity to seize opportunities when they occurred. Despite its size, the firm wanted to preserve a familial atmosphere and the respect of the community in which it had grown.

E X H I B I T 5   Canada's 10 Largest Contractors (1988)   *(In millions of dollars)*

Rank		Company	Location	Sales		Main Activities
1988	1987			1988	1987	
1	1	PCL Construction Group	Edmonton, AB	$1,184.5	$1,259.9	Building construction, roadbuilding, industrial construction, heavy civil engineering
2	2	Ellis-Don	London, ON	811.0	756.0	Building construction, excavation and foundation
3	6	Banister Continental	Edmonton, AB	365.8	204.4	Heavy civil engineering, building construction, excavation and foundation, sewer
4	3	Georges Wimpey Canada	Toronto, ON	349.0	351.0	Roadbuilding, heavy civil engineering, excavation and foundation, sewer
5	—	Fluor Daniel Canada	Calgary, AB	314.1	—	Industrial construction
6	8	Commonwealth Construction	Burnaby, BC	290.4	183.0	Heavy construction, industrial construction
7	4	Dominion-Bridge-AMCA	Rexdale, ON	260.0	260.0	Building construction, structural work
8	5	Comstock	Scarborough, ON	232.0	218.8	Mechanical and electrical work, utilities
9	9	Pomerleau Group	St-Georges, QC	212.9	181.9	Building construction, excavation and foundation
10	11	Eastern Construction	Toronto, ON	201.0	173.9	Building construction

Source: Canadian Construction Record, June 1989.

E X H I B I T   6 **Canada's 10 Largest Builders, 1988**
(In millions of dollars)

Rank				Sales	
1988	**1987**	**Company**	**Location**	**1988**	**1987**
1	1	PCL Construction Group	Edmonton, AB	$1,184.5	$1,259.9
2	2	Ellis-Don	London, ON	811.0	756.0
3	3	Dominion-Bridge-AMCA	Rexdale, ON	260.0	260.0
4	5	Pomerleau Group	St-Georges, QC	212.9	181.9
5	7	Eastern Construction	Toronto, ON	201.0	173.9
6	—	Menkes Developments	North York, ON	200.0	NA
7	10	Dilligham Construction	Vancouver, BC	199.6	161.0
8	4	Canron, Inc.	Toronto, ON	181.5	195.2
9	6	Stuart Olson Construction	Edmonton, AB	180.9	175.1
10	—	CANA Ltd.	Calgary, AB	168.7	142.7

NA = not available.
Source: *Canadian Construction Record*, June 1989.

The Structure of the Company

Among the Pomerleau Group's six business units, the construction subsidiary, Hervé Pomerleau Inc., was the core of the company and accounted for 65 percent of the group's revenues. At the beginning, Hervé Pomerleau was especially good at obtaining contracts for government buildings and his company built over 150 public buildings such as schools, prisons, and office blocks in Québec. Later, the company gradually specialized in commercial, industrial, and institutional construction, particularly in larger and more complex projects. This led to the construction of many office buildings, shopping malls, large manufacturing plants, dams, and electricity stations. In periods of slowdown, the company pursued smaller projects that would not be considered at other times, but that enabled it to maintain the volume of its activities. In fact, the company was even profitable throughout the 1978–1982 recession, when it was forced to take possession of many buildings and shopping malls because their owners were unable to continue making payments. During the same period, the company became involved in a couple of small construction projects in Algeria. Nevertheless, for the future the company wanted to maintain its focus on large-scale projects and to expand its geographical scope, mainly toward Ontario and the United States. It also sought to increase its penetration of the industrial construction market and to participate actively in the second phase of the James Bay hydroelectric projects.

Since the 1970s, the firm had been following a vertical integration strategy designed to achieve greater control over those activities critical to the quality of appearance and on-time completion of construction projects. This vertical integration strategy had resulted in the internalization of many activities usually distributed to specialty trade contractors. Compared to its competitors, the Pomerleau Group relied to a significantly smaller extent on subcontractors for critical sections of construction projects. Through the years, the company also developed skills considered unique in Québec in excavation/foundation and concrete work. In areas requiring extensive specialization, such as electrical and mechanical work, the group had built lasting relationships with specific subcontractors. The group had helped to create electrical and mechanical contractors, sometimes even guaranteeing the first bank loans, and had ensured their development by continuously providing them with contracts. In return, these subcontractors provided the group with better prices and conditions for their services.

More importantly, however, the group's vertical integration strategy led to the creation and acquisition of four subsidiaries whose operations were directly related to the visible parts of buildings and the critical path of construction projects. In 1988, these subsidiaries accounted for 25 percent of the group's sales. Ciments et Tuiles de Beauce (CTB) was created in 1970 and specialized in the finishing of concrete floors and the covering of floors, walls, and fronts of buildings with different materials such as ceramics, granite, marble, and terrazzo. Seven years later, Hervé Pomerleau founded Ebénisterie Beaubois (EB), a carpentry and architectural millwork firm. This subsidiary manufactured customized and built-in furniture for offices and public buildings and offered finishing services for malls, stores, restaurants, and offices. After a substantial deficit in 1986, changes in management and implementation of a costing system and a bonus system for employees based on productivity increases quickly returned the subsidiary to profitability. In 1982, the group bought a majority position in Béton Bolduc Inc., which produced different concrete products such as plain and decorative blocks, bricks, paving, and prefabricated concrete architectural elements for exterior facings. The company was on the verge of bankruptcy when the owners came to the group for help. Financial and management support from the group enabled the firm to show its highest profits ever in 1988.

Hyalin International Inc., a manufacturer of insulated glass and a glazing/ curtain wall subcontractor, had been the last firm to become part of the Pomerleau Group. The largest of the group's manufacturing subsidiaries, it was also the only one located outside Beauce. For some years, this firm had been experiencing serious financial problems. Since its acquisition by the group in 1985, turnaround attempts had been unsuccessful and the subsidiary had failed to show any profits yet.

In 1974, the group became involved in real estate through HLP Inc. This subsidiary owned and managed numerous shopping malls, office buildings, warehouses, and hotels throughout Québec, Ontario, and the Maritimes. It helped the group to capitalize, as sole owner or with partners, on its knowledge of the construction industry. Among the $500 million in projects already in the group's order book for the next two years, $60 million were for HLP's projects. Accounting for 10 percent of the group's revenues in 1988, HLP's importance within the company was expected to increase significantly in the future.

The real estate subsidiary, the manufacturing and construction companies, and in-house engineering and architecture resources enabled the group to provide its customers with a wide range of products and services. With its 27 engineers and its own team of architects, the group offered turnkey projects, a capability seldom found among Québec contractors. Such projects included everything from selection of sites and preparation of drawings to suggestion of potential tenants and advice on the management of the buildings, rather than the mere construction of buildings based on drawings and specifications done by another firm. The group also had sometimes obtained contracts because it could rely on internal sources of construction products through its manufacturing subsidiaries. In turn, these subsidiaries participated in the group's projects as often as was possible and economical. In this way, more than 50 percent of CTB's and EB's sales were directly related to the group's projects. Béton Bolduc and Hyalin were much more autonomous and depended on the group for only 15 percent and 25 percent of their sales, respectively.

The Organization

The group was directed by a seven-member executive committee composed of Hervé Pomerleau, three vice presidents (VPs) for construction, and the VPs for finance, administration, and real estate development. Since the 1987 departure of the VP for the subsidiaries, this position's responsibilities had been assumed by the CEO. The executive committee usually met every second Saturday morning for two to four hours. The responsibility for setting the meetings' agendas was rotated among participants at each meeting.

Construction VPs and the CEO devoted a large portion of their time to the research and negotiation of contracts. Construction VPs also supervised the preparation of tender offers and the work of project managers and supervisors. Project managers and supervisors were key elements in the profit ability and on-time completion of projects, as they assumed direct responsibility for each project's execution. These positions had similar functions. Both oversaw construction site superintendents, although managers were more experienced and enjoyed significantly more autonomy. Good project managers and supervisors were difficult to find and their training, under a construction VP or a senior project manager, lasted for up to five years. Sometimes a construction VP assumed direct responsibility for especially large and important projects.

Although the basic functioning of the construction subsidiary was similar to the industry norm, its organization differed in three very significant ways. First, the typical construction VP in the industry was more than 50 years old and, while gaining experience, had passed through the positions of manager and supervisor after having started as superintendent at 25 years of age. Consequently, managers and supervisors were generally around 40 years old. However, at Hervé Pomerleau Inc., the average age of superintendents was somewhat less than 28 years, the average age of managers was less than 35, and VPs averaged less than 40 years. According to management, this allowed the company to benefit from the aggressiveness and dynamism of younger individuals within its organization, while drawing from the experience of older superintendents at individual sites.

Second, in contrast to competitors who typically hired all construction workers on the basis of contracts or individual projects and whose only permanent employees were project managers, Hervé Pomerleau Inc. offered permanency to a large number of employees. In fact, all construction site supervisors and foremen, about 300 individuals, as well as a core of more than 400 skilled construction workers, were assured of work for 12 months a year. The remaining labor was hired according to the size and type of projects the group was executing.

Third, these permanent employees were eligible for a companywide profit-sharing system based on the employee's position in the organization, the profitability of the projects with which he or she had been directly involved, and the company's overall results. As employees moved up in the company's hierarchy, bonuses were increasingly based on the company's overall results. The vice presidents' bonuses depended solely on the group's profits. The manufacturing subsidiaries also had profit-sharing systems, but these bonuses were based strictly on the units' performance. As a result, total remuneration for any position in the group was superior to the industry's average, even though basic wages were below those offered by competitors. Coexistence of permanency and profit-sharing was identified as an important factor in the company's exceptional performance. One vice president affirmed: "This permanency allows us to offer profit-sharing that stimulates our employees and makes them feel more involved in the company. However, it creates substantial pressure on us [the managers] to have so many permanent employees. We have to keep them on the job and always find more projects to keep them working. We don't want to lose people we have trained."

HYALIN INTERNATIONAL INC.

In 1988, Hyalin International Inc. had sales of $28 million and 200 employees, compared to $13 million and 180 employees in 1986 (see Exhibit 7). Despite this growth and continuous efforts to cut costs at all levels of the organization, the firm's deficit was in the range of $1 million for the third consecutive year. The Pomerleau Group had acquired Hyalin, then called Cayouette-Superseal, after that firm went bankrupt in August 1985. Hyalin had been supplying glazing and curtain walls for three of the group's projects and especially for the construction of the Laurentian Group's 32-story, class A office building in downtown Montreal. This was not only the group's largest project ever, but also its first major office tower project in Montreal, a market segment the company had tried to enter decisively for many years. Hyalin's bankruptcy jeopardized the on-time completion of the project, and also threatened the group's reputation as a reliable builder, possibly causing this to be its first and last major project in Montreal. The acquisition was completed when Hyalin's suppliers accepted the group's proposal to receive 25 percent of the $4 million Hyalin owed them.

Problems of the Cayouette Group, a manufacturer of wood windows, kitchen cabinets, and steel and patio doors as well as a glazing/curtain walls contractor, had begun with the 1983 acquisition of Superseal, a major supplier of glass and windows. Following this merger, sales plummeted as Superseal customers that also competed with Cayouette began sourcing from other firms. When the Pomerleau Group took over management of the firm, it was in terrible shape. In the previous two years the firm's headquarters had been moved three times, with the result that most files were still in boxes. The firm was also still in the middle of a troublesome implementation of a new computer system and, consequently, no accurate cost estimates or financial data were available. Furthermore, most young and skilled personnel had deserted the company. Finally, there were concerns among the local community, the personnel, and particularly suppliers and customers that the Pomerleau Group would operate Hyalin until the Laurentian building was finished and then

EXHIBIT 7   Selected Data on Hyalin International, 1985–1988

	1985	1986	1987	1988
Sales (in millions of dollars)	$15.7	$12.9	$17.9	$27.7
Gross margin	11.61%	3.4%	7.7%	10.3%
Assets (in millions of dollars)	$ 7.1	$10.6	$12.9	$17.6

would close down the company. In an assembly of Hyalin's personnel, Hervé Pomerleau made the personal commitment to keep Hyalin in operation. Concerned with the social costs of layoffs, he also promised to protect existing jobs and even to create some more.

With the temporary assistance of the group's VP of finance and an accountant, the VP for subsidiaries took over as Hyalin's general manager, although with some reluctance. Within a few months, Cayouette's window and cabinet businesses and their related plants were sold. Equipment and personnel involved in the door and curtain wall/glazing businesses were concentrated in Superseal's insulated glass facilities in Saint-Hyacinthe. This was accomplished with some difficulties since it required relocation into a single site of personnel from different plants, businesses, and organizational cultures. Nevertheless, the VP for subsidiaries left both Hyalin and the group shortly after an expected $200,000 profit for 1987 was transformed into a $1 million loss by the discovery of an accounting error. Hyalin's marketing manager, hired in April 1987, replaced him as general manager of the troublesome subsidiary.

Hyalin's Operations

Hyalin specialized in the distribution of glass and the manufacture of insulated glass destined for manufacturers and distributors of windows and doors, and for small- and medium-sized glaziers. Despite intense competition, aggressive pricing and rapid delivery (three days rather than the industry's five-day average) resulted in sales of insulated glass reaching $8.5 million in 1988, compared to $3.5 million in 1986. With a 1988 production of 2 million square feet of insulated glass, Hyalin's share of the Québec market was estimated at 20 percent. This growth had been fueled particularly by sales of standard-size insulated glass to residential window manufacturers. Hyalin's strategy of territorial expansion also led the firm to enter the Ontario and Maritimes markets.

In the Québec insulated glass market, Hyalin was competing against single-product firms whose size and scope were similar to or smaller than its insulated glass business. Price competition had traditionally been intense in this market. It had reached new heights in recent months since one competitor, Cover, had automated its facilities and had reduced its debt and interest load by going public. Hyalin and other producers, with their labor-intensive and manual production lines, had encountered difficulties competing effectively in a market where insulated glass prices were lower in 1988 than in 1985. In fact, rumors were that Hyalin's two other competitors had financial difficulties despite their close relationships with large window manufacturers. PPG Industries had even exited the market, but Cover was still showing strong and growing profits.

Hyalin's steel and patio doors were sold to manufacturers and distributors of doors and windows, as well as to manufacturers of prefabricated houses. A steel door was made from two steel sheets, bought from large steel companies and mounted on a wood frame that was injected with foam for insulation. Patio doors were made of tempered glass mounted on a wood and vinyl frame. This product line, after extensive modifications to make it more competitive, had seen its sales grow from $3.5 million to $6.5 million between 1986 and 1988. With 50,000 steel doors worth about $4.5 million, Hyalin was still a small player in this market compared to Stanley, the leader with more than 300,000 doors. Further expansion in this market was perceived as difficult since it would require investment in expensive new equipment. In the patio door market, Hyalin was in direct competition with its supplier of vinyl moulding, a firm that was also one of Québec's major manufacturers of patio doors. In both cases, competition was intense and essentially price-based.

Finally, Hyalin was a glazing/curtain wall contractor for the construction industry. This had been Hyalin's fastest-growing business, with sales rising from $5 million in 1986 to $13 million in 1988. Part of this performance was attributed to contracts with the Pomerleau Group, which accounted for 50 percent of glazing and curtain wall contracts. In spite of reluctance by other contractors to do business with one of Pomerleau's subsidiaries, Hyalin had been able to establish good relationships with many of them, while others worked only with Hyalin's two competitors.

One of these competitors, LBL, was a publicly owned company that focused on the installation of glazing and curtain walls and outsourced all materials. Having doubled in size in the last two years, this firm's sales had reached $30 million in 1988. In contrast, the other competitor, Zimmcor, was a private company more than three times Hyalin's size. It fabricated the metal structure and had the equipment for painting and anodization (electrically coating), but outsourced its glass. Hyalin was somewhat in the middle, buying the metallic structure but using its own insulated glass. However, half the contracts used tempered glass that had to be outsourced. To improve its market position, Hyalin recently hired an individual with 30 years of experience with one of its competitors. Hyalin's management believed this individual would substantially improve the firm's credibility and technological knowledge in the curtain wall market.

Nevertheless, management believed Hyalin's competitiveness was also undermined by high raw materials costs. According to them, suppliers were charging Hyalin a 5 to 7 percent premium on their products to recover the losses encountered at Hyalin's acquisition. A supplier of steel even required the Pomerleau Group to pay a guarantee on behalf of Hyalin in order to deliver the goods ordered by the subsidiary. Moreover, despite efforts in this direction and because of the complexities associated with the number of products and the different sizes and types of glass-related products, Hyalin did not yet have reliable data on its product lines' profitability. Finally, years of deficits and attempts to reduce costs were perceived as limiting Hyalin's potential for long-term development. Indeed, for many years the firm had made few investments in R&D, new product development, and new equipment.

THE CONSULTANT'S REPORT

In an attempt to find solutions to Hyalin's problems, Hervé Pomerleau asked a group of consultants to propose a turnaround strategy for Hyalin. The report was presented to the group and Hyalin management in March 1989. A section of the report's executive summary follows:

> We recommend that Hyalin implement the following strategies for its 3 product lines:
>
> a) for the insulated glass line: Hyalin should try to further increase its penetration in the Québec "non-standard" segment with a product and customer service of superior quality. Furthermore, Hyalin should stop trying to expand the geographical market of its standard insulated glass, at least until accurate profitability data is available.
> b) for the steel and patio doors line: Hyalin should expand its penetration in the fast-growing segment of renovation. Hyalin should also offer a differentiated product, at higher price and to a large array of customers.
> c) for the glazing/curtain wall contracting business: Hyalin should emphasize the development of that business which represents a unique opportunity to build on that market's profitability as well as on the synergies resulting from Hyalin's association with the Pomerleau Group. Hyalin should also continue trying to diversify its customer base in this business.

In their report, the consultants also stressed that Hyalin lacked the elements required to compete effectively on low price. Furthermore, they did not recommend any major changes in the firm's basic product/market focus. According to them, in the absence of a reliable costing system and, thus, of accurate profitability estimates, they could not suggest dropping any of the existing product lines.

The consultants' report was received by the group's managers with mixed reactions. They did not fundamentally disagree with its recommendations. However, it did not provide the short-term solutions to Hyalin's problems that they were looking for. In fact, Hyalin's successive operating deficits had cost the senior managers more than $200,000 in bonuses in the last three years. A decision had to be made regarding Hyalin in order to stop the hemorrhaging. Furthermore, options offered to the group were limited. Attempts to sell the subsidiary as a whole or in part had been unsuccessful, while closing Hyalin was simply out of the question. According to one manager: "This company's culture stresses tenacity. We never abandon and we particularly hate seeing our competitors doing better than ourselves. Moreover, too much pride and personal commitment are involved in this situation for us to quit."

Corporate management believed that implementing the consultants' report would be difficult. Automation of insulated glass production appeared necessary for Hyalin to be competitive, but because of recent losses, management showed little interest in investing more millions in the subsidiary for automation or for tempering or laminating. However, corporate management was dismayed by Hyalin's problems. Being essentially "construction people," they knew little about manufacturing and especially about the insulated glass and door business. According to one of the managers: "This business is a sales and marketing one, involving advertising, public relations, and R&D, about which we know little." Indeed, Hyalin was the group's only manufacturing subsidiary whose operations were not totally related to the commercial and industrial construction industries.

For these reasons, many managers believed Hyalin had to focus on glazing and curtain wall contracting. This business and construction shared many similar traits. Indeed, preparing and presenting projects, negotiating with owners, suppliers, and subcontractors, and supervising construction sites were activities involved in this business for which the group had the required resources and competences to support Hyalin. Because glazing and curtain walls were omnipresent in nonresidential building construction, remaining in this business was consistent with the group's objective to be a major player in this segment. However, turmoil was expected for glazing/curtain wall contractors. Already in the United States, many firms, including PPG, had exited because of their inability to cope with this business' high risk and volatility. According to one contractor, the business had become very complex as developers "asked for Mercedes design and then tried to build at Chevrolet prices." Furthermore, as a result of well-publicized unreliability and leakage problems for many curtain wall systems, project owners required long-term liability from curtain wall contractors and often pressured them to make good on broken glass and other defects for up to 20 years after the job's completion.

Hyalin's general manager did not like the idea of dropping product lines and she was a little annoyed by corporate managers' reactions and comments. She believed that Hyalin first needed some time to allow the organization to adjust to its rapid growth of the last two years. Almost half of Hyalin's personnel were new employees who had required training, since little skilled labor was available. They now needed to gain experience. The new computer system also required a breaking-in period before it could provide the financial information for which everybody had been waiting for years. Furthermore, focusing on glazing/curtain wall contracting involved some risks, since insulated glass and doors provided the firm with some stability. It also meant laying off close to 50 percent of Hyalin's personnel. Manufacturing of insulated glass also increased Hyalin's purchase volume of flat glass, enabling it to benefit from better prices from suppliers. In brief, according to its general manager, Hyalin needed more time as well as more support and attention from corporate management: ". . . Everyone has to recognize that we have come a long way since 1986 and that we changed a lot of things. However, we have not yet shown any profits. This situation is rather difficult to handle in a company as successful as the Pomerleau Group. . . ."

CONCLUSION

A few days after that meeting, Hervé Pomerleau was re-examining the consultants' report. He understood his managers' concerns regarding Hyalin and the report; however, he also remembered his commitment regarding Hyalin and his decision to take that into account. Furthermore, he knew that Hyalin's general manager had been upset by his managers' reactions and that she was thinking about resigning. He wondered what he should do regarding Hyalin.

SECTION

D

STRATEGY IMPLEMENTATION AND ADMINISTRATION

ROBIN HOOD*

Joseph Lampel, New York University

It was in the spring of the second year of his insurrection against the High Sheriff of Nottingham that Robin Hood took a walk in Sherwood forest. As he walked he pondered the progress of the campaign, the disposition of his forces, the Sheriff's recent moves, and the options that confronted him.

The revolt against the Sheriff had begun as a personal crusade. It erupted out of Robin's conflict with the Sheriff and his administration. However, alone Robin Hood could do little. He therefore sought allies, men with grievances and a deep sense of justice. Later he welcomed all who came, asking few questions, and only demanding a willingness to serve. Strength, he believed, lay in numbers.

He spent the first year forging the group into a disciplined band, united in enmity against the Sheriff, and willing to live outside the law. The band's organization was simple. Robin ruled supreme, making all important decisions. He delegated specific tasks to his lieutenants. Will Scarlett was in charge of intelligence and scouting. His main job was to shadow the Sheriff and his men, always alert to their next move. He also collected information on the travel plans of rich merchants and tax collectors. Little John kept discipline among the men, and saw to it that their archery was at the high peak that their profession demanded. Scarlock took care of the finances, converting loot to cash, paying shares of the take, and finding suitable hiding places for the surplus. Finally, Much the Miller's son had the difficult task of provisioning the ever-increasing band of Merrymen.

The increasing size of the band was a source of satisfaction for Robin, but also a source of concern. The fame of his Merrymen was spreading, and new recruits poured in from every corner of England. As the band grew larger, their small bivouac became a major encampment. Between raids the men milled about, talking and playing games. Vigilance was in decline, and discipline was becoming harder to enforce. "Why," Robin reflected, "I don't know half the men I run into these days."

The growing band was also beginning to exceed the food capacity of the forest. Game was becoming scarce, and supplies had to be obtained from outlying villages. The cost of buying food was beginning to drain the band's financial reserves at the very moment when revenues were in decline. Travelers, especially those with the most to lose, were now giving the forest a wide berth. This was costly and inconvenient to them, but it was preferable to having all their goods confiscated.

Robin believed that the time had come for the Merrymen to change their policy of outright confiscation of goods to one of a fixed transit tax. His lieutenants strongly resisted this idea. They were proud of the Merrymen's famous motto: "Rob from the rich and give to the poor." "The farmers and the townspeople," they argued, "are our most important allies." "How can we tax them, and still hope for their help in our fight against the Sheriff?"

---

*Copyright © 1991, by Joseph Lampel.

Robin wondered how long the Merrymen could keep to the ways and methods of their early days. The Sheriff was growing stronger and becoming better organized. He now had the money and the men, and was beginning to harass the band, probing for its weaknesses. The tide of events was beginning to turn against the Merrymen. Robin felt that the campaign must be decisively concluded before the Sheriff had a chance to deliver a mortal blow. "But how," he wondered, "could this be done?"

Robin had often entertained the possibility of killing the Sheriff, but the chances for this seemed increasingly remote. Besides, killing the Sheriff might satisfy his personal thirst for revenge, but it would not improve the situation. Robin had hoped that the perpetual state of unrest, and the Sheriff's failure to collect taxes, would lead to his removal from office. Instead, the Sheriff used his political connections to obtain reinforcement. He had powerful friends at court, and was well regarded by the regent, Prince John.

Prince John was vicious and volatile. He was consumed by his unpopularity among the people, who wanted the imprisoned King Richard back. He also lived in constant fear of the barons, who had first given him the regency, but were now beginning to dispute his claim to the throne. Several of these barons had set out to collect the ransom that would release King Richard the Lionheart from his jail in Austria. Robin was invited to join the conspiracy in return for future amnesty. It was a dangerous proposition. Provincial banditry was one thing, court intrigue another. Prince John had spies everywhere and he was known for his vindictiveness. If the conspirators' plan failed, the pursuit would be relentless, and retribution swift.

The sound of the supper horn startled Robin from his thoughts. There was the smell of roasting venison in the air. Nothing was resolved or settled. Robin headed for camp promising himself that he would give these problems his utmost attention after tomorrow's raid.

TWILL ENTERPRISES, LIMITED*

William R. Killeen, University of Western Ontario
Joseph N. Fry, University of Western Ontario

Ken Shelstad leaned forward in his chair, flashed a great smile, and said, "Look, I love what I'm doing! I'm at it 70 hours a week—but that's the limit, after that I feel fuzzy and I can't concentrate. I enjoy every minute! Hell, I own half this company and we're making money. Lots of it! Profits, I love 'em!"

Shelstad, 51, was president of Twill Enterprises Limited, a growing and prosperous company in the printing and packaging industry. He was clearly in his element, but he expressed some misgivings about the future as he pushed the company into one of its most aggressive expansion projects. The issues, he thought, were not so much in the market opportunity as in his and his people's ability to handle the anticipated growth. "What concerns me," he said, "is that the company may be outgrowing me. I used to know exactly what was going on in every department. Lately, I feel like I've lost some of that control. The consultants have been telling me for years that I should change the way I run things. Maybe they are finally right."

COMPANY BACKGROUND

In 1945, Barry Shelstad, Ken's father, purchased a small Toronto-based producer of business forms and labels and started Twill Enterprises. Over the next 20 years Barry Shelstad built the business by internal growth and the careful acquisition of similar small companies in Canada and the United States. Barry Shelstad also brought his two sons John and Ken into the business. By 1965 John, the eldest, was the president, and in 1974 he became chairman. Ken began in the company as a salesperson, moved up through the ranks to become vice president of manufacturing, and in 1974 became president. When Barry Shelstad passed away in 1975, he left the ownership of the company in equal shares to the two brothers.

By 1988 Twill revenues were over $150 million and the company's product range encompassed blister and flexible packaging, labels, and business forms. The company operated seven packaging, ten business form, and seven label plants at various locations in North America. In recent years Twill's growth had been somewhat higher than the 5 to 7 percent rates experienced by the industry, and profitability had been consistently higher than the 2 to 3 percent after-tax return on sales and the 4 to 7 percent return on average assets of comparable firms.

Twill's new venture was in the rigid plastic container business. Ken Shelstad had acquired the rights to European technology that promised greater design flexibility and lower cost production in some lines of jars and bottles than was currently in place in North America. His projections showed that the new lines would add over $40 million to Twill's revenues within three years of start-up.

*Copyright © 1988, The University of Western Ontario. The financial assistance of the Young Presidents' Organization is gratefully acknowledged. This is a disguised case.

The capital investment implications of the venture were sizeable, however, and for the first time ever Shelstad had run into difficulty working out financial arrangements with Twill's long-time bank. "They wanted to know who the project manager was going to be," said Shelstad, "and when I told them first, that it was none of their business and second, that it was going to be me, they wanted to have a consultant hired to monitor the operation. Well, there was no way I was going to operate with some jerk looking over my shoulder, so we got financing elsewhere." At the time of this case Twill had made commitments for land in Toronto and for the purchase of the major items of equipment.

INDUSTRY CHARACTERISTICS

The markets in which Twill operated were fiercely competitive. Typically, a few large competitors would account for about 70 percent of the sales in a region and the balance would be filled by literally hundreds of small companies. Most products were made to customer specifications, so operations took on job-shop characteristics. Profitability was a reflection of efficient manufacturing operations and local pricing, customer, and product mix decisions. Raw materials usually represented over 60 percent of direct product costs.

Local producers were often quite evenly matched in terms of price, delivery, quality, and service. Often a competitive edge was decided by the reputation of the producer for especially good service and the personal relations between the supplier firm personnel and their customers. The larger suppliers had somewhat more of an advantage with larger accounts because the scope of their operations allowed them to meet the national requirements of their customers.

Twill was fortunate to have focused its operations in Toronto, one of the two largest centers for printing concentration in North America (Chicago being the other). On the downside, this created a fiercely competitive environment in which suppliers had to offer a high degree of sophistication, technical capability, and a range of production options. The challenge was to make more-complicated products with faster response times *and* lower costs.

Industry demand in Twill's market areas had been generally positive. Demand tended to follow the fortunes of the economy as a whole and in recent years had been outpacing this indicator. Existing competitors had reacted by expanding their capacity, and new entrants had been attracted to the industry. Competition would continue to be intense and there was some concern that an economic downturn would leave suppliers in a state of serious overcapacity.

TWILL'S STRATEGY

Goals   The Shelstads' goals for Twill were for it to continue to operate as a large, successful, growing, family firm. Twill had been owned and run by the Shelstad family for nearly 45 years. Ken had three sons working for the firm, and while they were still in their early 20s, he hoped they would provide for family succession.

The Shelstads were known as prudent, successful businesspeople. They had built Twill with a conservative growth strategy. Typically, whether acquisition or internal expansion was involved, Twill started new projects and fol-

EXHIBIT 1   **Twill's Market Position**

	Blister and Flexible Packaging	Labels	Business Forms
Expected overall market growth*	4 to 6%	1 to 3%	3 to 4%
Industry key success factors	Product development	Personal relationships	Personal relationships
	Range of technical capabilities	Service reputation	Service reputation
	Quality and service	Cost control	Cost control
	Cost control		
Twill's share of served market†	12%	19%	10%
Percentage of Twill revenues	Over 50%	About 15%	About 35%
Number of plants‡	7	7	10

*Management estimate.
†Twill did not compete in all product formats or geographic regions in North America. The market share estimates are based on Twill's sales in its served markets.
‡Some of Twill's plants occupied the same site and even the same building. They had distinct plant managers, however.

lowed them to completion before progressing to a new venture. Twill's recent plastic container expansion represented a more aggressive step than had been typical for the company.

Product Market Strategy   Twill had always chosen to expand into markets in which it could be profitable by exploiting its competitive strengths—in particular, high service levels, low-cost production, and in-house capabilities. When a market opportunity was uncovered (usually in the form of a neglected niche with high prices and low customer satisfaction), Twill was quick to respond. Exhibit 1 provides a general review of Twill's market position.

In recent years, Twill had experimented with a variety of plastic container products. Their strategy had been to test the waters with product entries based on subcontracted production. Over time the company had developed its understanding of the market. In 1989, Twill planned to start up its own production facilities in Toronto. The new facility represented a major step by Twill into a highly competitive market. The Shelstads were confident, however, that their current competitive advantages would transfer readily into the new market.

Competitive Strategy   Twill aimed to be competitive in price and distinctive in service. The company had always endeavored to ensure that customers got the product they wanted, when they wanted it. To this end, Twill offered their own in-house design and typesetting service and employed a large direct sales organization and delivery fleet.

The Shelstads ran a no-nonsense, low-cost operation. Money was spent where it was necessary—on equipment modernization and maintenance. Otherwise there were few frills at a Twill plant. Parking lots were not paved and offices were not carpeted. Salespeople shared spartan office space, which kept costs to a minimum and "forced" them to stay on the road. Expediting and cost control were inbred habits throughout the organization.

Recently Twill had been attempting to supplement its low-cost emphasis with a greater concern for quality. The aim was to eliminate situations in which substandard, but usable, products would be sent to customers. Under the current program, such a client would be informed of quality problems, given a sample, and asked for approval prior to shipment.

TWILL'S ORGANIZATION

Management practices at Twill had remained relatively unchanged for 20 years. Growth had added to the complexity of the business, but to this point had not forced any significant change in basic management structures or systems and style. There were, however, continuing questions about how best to handle the inherently and increasingly complicated operations of the company, as will be illustrated in the following description of the way in which the organization worked.

Management Structure

Twill had a functional management structure, as outlined in the partial organizational chart in Exhibit 2. The senior managers—John and Ken Shelstad; Larry Dixon, vice president of sales and marketing; and Doug Burgess, vice president of production—had been in their current positions since 1974. These senior managers frequently stepped outside of their strict functional responsibilities to handle specific projects, and, often, day-to-day activities. Together they nurtured an intense, hands-on approach to the management of Twill.

Top-level coordination was handled through a management committee. The committee consisted of six members—the Shelstads, Doug Burgess, Larry Dixon, Tim O'Dowda (packaging sales manager), and Jeff Bak (vice president of finance). The group attempted to meet weekly (schedules limited this number to about 30 meetings annually) for two to four hours. John Shelstad set an agenda but new topics could be informally introduced. No minutes were taken. The group's role was to develop strategy; day-to-day operations were not discussed. While it was clear that final decisions rested with the Shelstads, the other members of the committee were active in providing assistance and opinions.

John and Ken Shelstad's roles in the management structure were vastly different. The older brother, John, had a number of outside interests and limited his involvement to strategic issues. Ken, on the other hand, was highly involved in all of the company's activities—from the management committee to daily decision making and operations. As one manager observed: "Twill gets its pulse from Ken. He commands respect and he gets it. He's very dynamic. He drives this company. But there is a problem—I think people are losing contact with him."

Another added an ominous note: "Ken is going to kill himself. He pushes himself too hard. He recently delegated the monthly check signing. Umpteen hundred a month and he used to sign (and check) every one. That's 15 hours minimum right there."

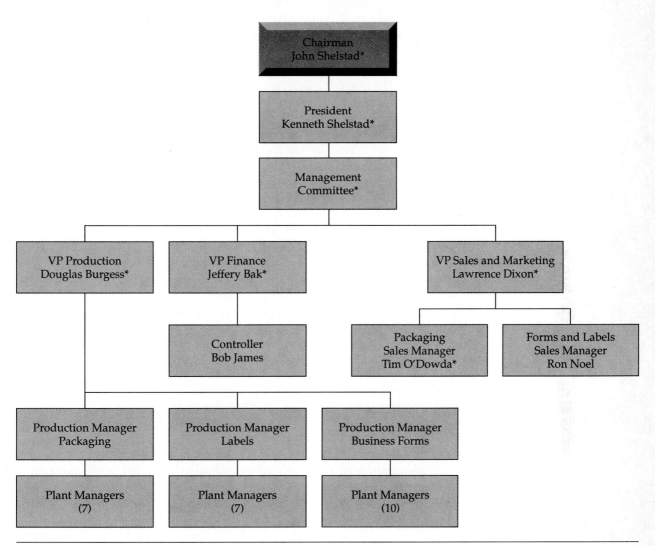

*Member of the Management Committee.

From time to time Twill had attempted to modify its structure and decentralize its operations through the use of general management positions. These attempts had been unsuccessful, however, for a variety of reasons that ranged from incapable personnel to corporate culture to head office interference. Twill's experience with its Denver plant was a prime example.

In 1986, Twill had purchased a profitable business in Denver and had put a general manager in charge. Within one year, however, the revenues and profits of the Denver operation had declined to the point where consideration was being given to shutting it down. The cause of the problem was not clear. The manager may not have been competent, the head office might have stifled him—whatever, the head office did take over, the manager was fired, and another notch was marked against a general manager concept.

Management Systems

Twill's job-shop operations were inherently complex and worked under the pressure of tight delivery schedules and cost containment. The following description of order processing gives some idea of the nature of these operating problems and the way they were handled by the company.

Order Processing   In 1971, Twill had implemented an on-line electronic data interchange (EDI) system. Orders were either brought, phoned, or mailed in, and then keyed into a terminal at the order department. By 1987, three separate systems were in use, reflecting the differing information needs of the major product lines—packaging, labels, and business forms.

An EDI file was created for each client. After entering an order, a delivery slip was created and sent to shipping. Stock items were shipped immediately. Made-to-order product delivery dates were confirmed by the order department representative who acted as an interface between manufacturing and the salesperson or client.

Each salesperson at Twill (over 100 in all) had a corresponding representative in the order department. The order department people served as the vital link between sales and production and helped to maintain the excellent relations between these two departments. This was a significant accomplishment since the processing of a job was very complex.

When a new product order was received, it passed through some or all of the order, graphics, art, typesetting, scheduling, plant, and shipping departments. There was no set pattern within these departments because of the iterative steps required to process each order. The graphics people, for example, could theoretically handle one order dozens of times.

Each department at this level of the organization had its own hierarchy. The order and art departments reported to the sales vice president, while graphics, typesetting, and scheduling reported to the production vice president. Budget authority did not necessarily follow these lines: the graphics budget, for example, was set by sales, yet that manager reported to production personnel.

The complex nature of Twill's structure was also apparent in the sales organization. It was separated as two distinct entities, but in fact operated as a single sales force. The sales force for the packaging division was arranged geographically, while the labels and forms sales force was arranged along product lines. In both cases, large single accounts were handled by a few national salespeople. In spite of these formal differences, the salespeople tended to be generalists, selling all products to their individual customers.

Control   Budgets and standards were the way of life at Twill. In production, for example, standard objectives included waste, productivity, safety, and cost. These standards were set by discussion with everyone, right down to the machine operators who were paid piecework rates related to the standards. Meeting standards was both a corporate goal and an individual goal at Twill. The value system created by the Shelstads dictated that meeting standards would result in a reward and security.

In larger scope, Twill's planning and accounting system was based on 18 separate profit centers, representing individual products, product ranges, or plant/product combinations. Monthly reports were prepared that identified the contribution of each product at each profit center. There was, however, no specific assignment of profit centers to particular managers. Instead, Ken Shelstad and Doug Burgess followed all the monthly reports. They did so very carefully and were quick to pick up on any problems that they observed.

But the pursuit of control at Twill went much deeper. Both Ken and Doug personally reviewed the monthly general ledger, in which every transaction of the company was entered and allocated to the profit centers. They examined activities down to the level of specific orders, customers, and purchases. It was a common occurrence for either Ken or Doug to question a plant manager, for example, about costs that were only slightly off standard or about a specific purchase transaction.

Ken explained the ledger reviews as a type of policing: "You can cross-check the allocations and make sure costs are being charged against the right profit center and you can identify potential problems right at the start. Just the other day I picked off a check for $300 that had been issued to one of our competitors—I had to go down and ask why the hell we were doing business with them." Doug Burgess was proud of the fact that: "We ask more questions and discover more horror stories than any other company. That is what has led to our success." Despite his claims, Burgess admitted that he had been unable to review his ledger, which was literally hundreds of pages deep, for two months. Time was a problem.

Staffing

Twill had always strived to take care of its employees through internal promotion, job security, and profit sharing. Twill encouraged employees to move up through the ranks. In addition, as Doug Burgess explained: "No one has ever been laid off. Jobs have been eliminated but we've always been able to shift people around." Pay was above industry averages and a pension plan was currently under consideration. Every six months, all staff above and including the supervisory level received a bonus based on company profits. This system was highly reliant on the Shelstads' creditability, since actual profit figures were not revealed.

In 1986, Twill had initiated a Management Assistant Program. "We've got to increase our management team," said Larry Dixon, "and our recent management assistant hirees are a step in this direction." In 1987, two young men were hired to assume various roles in the organization with the goal of assuming management (and ultimately, executive) positions within a few years. Slow development from within was essential. Twill's culture dictated that managers ask questions, be nitpickers, work long hours, and get involved in everything. Only by having moved up through the ranks could one develop the essential experience and attitudes. Initiative was the trait most often looked for in personnel and the trait that most often led to promotions.

KEY MANAGER VIEWS

The following comments are excerpts from conversations with Twill's senior managers. It is worth noting that these discussions were frequently interrupted. The diversity of roles and the informal nature of management meant that senior people were inextricably involved in the problems of the day. For example, during an interview with Larry Dixon, Ken Shelstad and Jeff Bak stopped by the office, unannounced, seeking pricing information for Denver. Three hours later, Ken interrupted a meeting with Doug Burgess, this time to discuss a fire wall at one of the new plants under construction. Within 30 minutes, Ken was back for an answer to a shipping problem—no space was available for a loaded truck in the yard.

Doug Burgess

Doug Burgess had been vice president of production since 1969. He was an extremely hard worker, a detail man, a man with a lot of authority.

> I'm very cognizant of my authority, and sure, I like power. I really enjoy it when Ken is away. Don't misunderstand me, because I respect Ken a lot. I think he is Twill's biggest asset. But he's also our biggest drawback.
>
> I don't like detail! It's the culture of the company though. Things have to get done and I'm the one who does it. What I like is solving problems and developing people. [Doug then continued, citing a number of people under him who have progressed to assume various plant manager positions.]
>
> I usually work 8 to 8, with a little weekend work. It ends up being a 70-hour work week and it's been steady like this for the last 10 years. I'm definitely at my limit and I've been actively trying to cut back by delegating a fair bit. I'm tied to my desk too much right now. I get bored with the paperwork.
>
> I see a couple of things occurring within 10 years. Personally, I believe that I'll be managing more generalities, rather than specifics. We must manage toward growth. This may require us to also move toward general managers, with much more sales involvement. I realize that our strength has been in production but there has been a shift in recent years toward sales.
>
> Twill has had difficulties with general managers. A real general manager wants autonomy and we haven't provided it. At Excelon, our Canadian poster plant, we tried a general manager and he delegated too much. He basically abdicated his office. I fired him. The new guy starts next week—with much less authority. In our plastic container start-ups, one guy was given a general manager title but he never grabbed all the reins. He still has the title, but he certainly doesn't run the area.
>
> It's been difficult to change things because the people have been here for too long. We were here when you could check on everything. Now we can't. Another justification for our structure is our results. Both our space utilization and inventory turnover are excellent. We're making money in areas other companies are not.
>
> I acknowledge that we've done little to develop managers here but we're now at a juncture in our history where something has to be done. I believe we'll have to develop from within. Jeff Bak is an exception because he's such a nitpicker that he fits right into the Twill culture.

Larry Dixon

Larry Dixon was vice president of sales and marketing and nominally had profit and loss responsibility for 17 (of 18) profit centers. He worked 60-hour weeks with the majority of his time spent in meetings. When he started at Twill in 1959 he worked 80- and 90-hour weeks.

> I enjoy what I'm doing so I don't mind the long hours. I get my kicks from the diversity—of the job and the organization. The success of the company has also

been an incentive. Many people work hard and don't get the rewards. To use a cliché, at Twill we've seen our hard work bear fruit.

In the early 1960s I was general manager of business forms, but over the years I've grown from a generalist to a specialist. We all have. Twenty years ago the four of us did everything. We can't anymore. The day-to-day work is diminishing because it *has* to diminish. Likewise, we've got to increase the size of our management team. The recent management assistant hirees are an admission of this.

Managing is getting things done through people. We're getting more people to get more done. Perhaps general managers will be that way in the future, but we have not been successful with this concept. The main reason is that we're all hands-on managers and we can't let go. After 30 years of experience, I've seen situations that allow me to understand things better than others. So I get involved to make things happen right.

We've also discussed creating the positions of senior VPs for sales and production and bringing in more VPs (or some other title). I don't know what will happen. We do recognize that we must pass on authority and give people responsibilities for areas.

Each year the six of us [on the committee] go down to a management retreat in Florida for four days in September. This year we are each assuming another's role and providing recommendations to achieve given goals. I want to do a bang-up job on my production role, so I'm putting in 40 hours on the task. I'm sure the others will do the same. Sure it's a challenge, but it's supposed to give each of us a better base of knowledge at Twill.

Jeff Bak

Jeff Bak, the vice president of finance, was responsible for all accounting functions including payables, cost accounting, payroll, and credit.

I've only been here for four and a half years. I guess that makes me the new kid on the block. I've had to adjust somewhat to fit in with these guys, but it hasn't been difficult.

My role here is mainly administrative. The finance title is really a misnomer. When I arrived here the payables were screwed up so I spent half my time fixing them. Last year, half my time was spent in Denver. I still spend one day a week there. Ken thought this was too much time away but it had to be done. We had purchased this plant and the operations were not in good shape. Doug Burgess was already on another plant project so I was given this one.

I like getting responsibilities for these projects. I get a kick out of finding something that's not right, making it right, and then backing off. Denver is a prime example. It's at a point now where production is all set—all we need are sales. I'm a hired hand here. They gave me Denver, so I turned it around.

Another role of mine at Twill is to sit on the management committee. Ken and John are very good at getting the opinions of other people, so that is the ultimate purpose of the meetings. They end up deciding things, because we can't have decision by committee. After all, it is *their* company!

John and Ken have proven they are knowledgeable businessmen. Twill has been successful and I don't foresee any problems with the new plastic container expansion. That is what keeps things exciting around here—growth. I don't want to get bored and as long as we keep growing I won't get bored.

As for general managers, well, it seems that all of our attempts with them have been mistakes. I don't foresee a change in our organizational structure for just that reason. I also believe that a reorganization is generally done to wake people up. We don't need to be woken up at Twill.

Tim O'Dowda

Tim O'Dowda, the packaging sales manager, had been with Twill for 16 years. He oversaw the sales of packaging products, one of Twill's core product lines, representing one half of the company's annual sales. Eighty percent of his time was spent in his office, and seven sales managers reported directly to him.

> Twill has always been a strong manufacturing company. It's been dominated by four individuals for 20 years—John and Ken Shelstad, Larry Dixon, and Doug Burgess. I think the major strength of this company is the dominance of these four individuals. I also think it's our major weakness.
>
> Inside the management committee, Ken and Doug are the two major players and they haven't got a sales bone in their bodies! In my opinion Ken is the autocratic king at Twill, but he's on overload now. He's the best internal auditor I've ever seen. He's always reading. It's amazing. I thought he was at his limit 10 years ago but he keeps on going. He really isn't a good delegator, either of tasks or authority. If someone makes a decision he'll end up questioning it.
>
> Doug Burgess. I've never met anyone who works harder than Doug. His detail is incredible. He's on overload too. He's got no social life. He's also a real taskmaster—I sure wouldn't want to work for him. This has led to quite a turnover in production. In sales, I've lost one person in 10 years, so I know they don't have the depth of quality that we have.
>
> Twill is unique because of the domination of these two men. They're always involved in new plants and construction. Ken really gets his jollies there. They get involved in all the materials purchasing—and I mean *all*. They are tough buyers. I couldn't sell to them.
>
> We've had growing pains. An example right now is a salary problem we're having with our salesmen. Hay Associates have been in here to try and fix things up. Some of the salesmen are pulling in a lot more than their managers. One 24-year-old made $48,000 last year. That's obscene and he knows it. This is one control system that I've got to get a hold on.
>
> One thing we've done in the last year is install Crosby's QYS culture at Twill. The management committee took Crosby's three-day course in Florida. Doug Burgess actually took it first and got hooked. If someone else had brought it back—say Larry—I'm sure it wouldn't have caught on. Anyways, it's certainly helped. Errors in the sales department alone have been reduced 75 percent. We're at the "confrontation stage," as Crosby describes it. We're policing everybody and some people don't like it. This will only last another three months, though.
>
> Twill has to expand. There are too many opportunities out there. I want to double my sales force. I also believe that we'll have to go divisional and "general-managerized" within 10 years. But we're too people-poor now. There's also a low level of trust. General managers have only stepped on the toes, especially Doug's and Larry's, so it's been difficult to change the organizational chart. I started in production and I would love the opportunity to be general manager of packaging and oversee everything in that area. We'll see. I think that Ken's kids are going to end up running the company eventually, so they'll probably be the ones forced to change the structure around here.

Bruce Roberts

In 1987, Twill began a new hiring program to enhance its managerial staff. The new, so-called management assistants were to complete a rotation with each member of the management committee during the first two years with Twill. Bruce Roberts, 27, was the first of two assistants hired.

I remember going through the interview process last year. There I was, sitting in this board room with eight guys that ran Twill. That's the way things work around here. Everyone seems to get involved in everything. "Hands on" is a very appropriate term here, especially when applied to Ken and Doug.

We were hired with the impression that John and Ken Shelstad were looking for people to step into the upper management at Twill within 10 years. They're not going to last forever and they're trying to develop people that can assume their roles. Seeing firsthand how hard these guys work makes me question whether that's where I want to end up.

It has been quite a learning experience thus far. At times it gets frustrating, though. I'm currently trying to solve a problem we have with our branch dealers. Twill bought them years ago and they represent about $20 million in annual sales. But they are losing money, very little mind you, but at Twill any loss is a shock. I've been on this for six months now but my project boss, Tim O'Dowda, had been on it for two years. I can't find a solution. It's really a no-win proposition. I've suggested two alternatives, sell or franchise, and boy, was I shot down by Ken! No way, he said, find an answer that I want to hear. Ever since then he has been checking on me weekly. He's interested but he's really provided no help.

CROSSROADS

Ken Shelstad was quite aware of the pressures and cross-currents in Twill. In fact, some flipcharts in his office summarized his position. One sheet identified the "Corporate Success Factors" as (1) low-cost production, (2) maintaining account relationships, and (3) broad service. However, in small print at the bottom of the sheet, the following words jumped out: *get competent people at all levels.*

A second sheet, entitled "Power Thinking," provided a laundry list of the major personal concerns facing Ken Shelstad. These included questions about himself, his brother, his family, and the business. These sheets had been on Shelstad's wall for over a year and he acknowledged their importance. He, and the others, had to give considerable thought to all of these issues. Management could tire and they would find themselves short of suitable replacements. People could limit the growth. And an economic downturn could severely impact the performance of both the new and existing products. Ken Shelstad and Twill faced an interesting future.

"I know what you are thinking," said Shelstad, smiling again. "I've had smart guys tell me to change our management structure before. And in general I agree—we must free up our time. Why, general managers would allow this simply by taking the phone calls we currently get! But it's not that simple. Our plant and sales set-up makes the general management concept difficult. We have a tough time finding good people—the general management pool is small and most of the prospects don't even know how to spell 'profit'. And we are smarter than they will ever be. I do have an answer though, when people get pushy. I say, 'Look, let's compare tax returns.'"

LARIMER HALL AND THE MAIL-ORDER CATALOG INDUSTRY*

Dave Robinson, University of North Carolina at Chapel Hill

The week before Thanksgiving 1990, as the snow began to fall outside her Denver office, Alice Hall pressed the [Calc] button and watched as the figures on her Lotus 1–2–3® spreadsheet rippled across the screen. As president of Larimer Hall, a specialty mail-order company, Alice worried that a year of record revenue was going to end up with a loss of more than $100,000. Alice chuckled as she recalled Chapter 7 of her favorite management textbook and asked herself: "If things are this good, how come we never have any cash?"

Larimer Hall was founded on a similar snowy evening in 1983. Alice and two friends were trudging home from the Denver Union Train Station with their skis over their shoulders after a joyful but exhausting day skiing at Winter Park, Colorado. Complaining about their discomfort, the three women shared their dislike of synthetic fiber underwear and bemoaned the fact that there didn't seem any place in town where women could buy clothing that wasn't 50 percent this or 25 percent that. Nothing felt as good next to the skin as 100 percent cotton—why wasn't anyone appealing to consumers such as themselves? Later that evening, over mugs of steaming cocoa, Larimer Hall was born on Alice's kitchen table. Alice, Violet Larimer, and Geraldine Dunelm decided to start a mail-order business selling natural-fiber clothes to women.

The three partners coined the company's name from two of their last names (Dunelm never seemed to fit). A mail-order business was an easy way to get started in retailing while still keeping their regular jobs. Alice worked for the University Medical Center as a computer specialist on an international medical project and Geraldine taught Business Communications at a nearby college. A few years after the company was founded, Violet received a scholarship to study in New York and soon became removed from the day-to-day operation of the company, but all three remained owners. They were proud of running a women-owned business and planned to do business with other women-owned companies whenever they could.

COMPANY HISTORY

Alice, Violet, and Geraldine systematically examined the clothes available in the local retail stores and confirmed that all-natural clothes were hard to find and expensive. They studied every book they could find on the mail-order business and with great excitement prepared to visit the merchandise mart in Dallas to place their first orders. Each partner contributed $800 from personal savings to fund their initial inventory and printing costs. The first catalog

*This case was prepared under the direction of Professor Richard I. Levin, with funds provided by the Philip Hettleman Chair of Business Administration. Names have been altered to protect the company's proprietary interest and some figures have been slightly altered. Copyright © 1991, UNC School of Business at Chapel Hill.

was a simple black-and-white flier mailed to everyone they could think of: friends, friends of friends, anyone for whom they could generate an address. Although the partners were interested in any comfortable natural fiber clothes, there seemed to be a particular opportunity for good quality underwear. Geraldine explained: "Contrary to what people think, women don't all like to shop. Certainly not for underwear. You go back to this tiny dressing room with a bra and just as you're getting everything tucked in, a saleswoman . . . "

"Who looks just like your mother!" interjected Alice.

"Flings open the curtain," Geraldine continued, "and says: 'Now, how are we doing, dear?' There are an enormous number of women who would prefer to try things on in their own home."

"Briefs can't be returned," Alice added, "but most people know their size. Bras can be sent back for exchange and once a customer chooses a line that is comfortable and gives a good fit, you've got a steady repeat customer for life."

Although women's underwear remained an important part of the catalog, Larimer Hall also featured comfortable all-cotton clothing for casual and business wear. "Our goal is to provide the basic foundations for a wardrobe, more than just underwear," explained Geraldine, marketing manager for the firm. The 1990 line included 102 different items maintained in nearly 1,000 SKUs,[1] with retail prices ranging from $4 to $50. "We want clothes that are practical and versatile: turtlenecks, tights, shorts, and T-shirts. We expect our customers to dress up our basics with their own accessories. We do try to stay away from items that are easy to find in retail stores, like a simple denim dress. But, on the other hand, we've had great success selling Jockey for Women briefs and tank tops that you can get just about anywhere."

The target customer: "Has an appreciation for natural fibers, health, and the environment. She's 25 to 55 years old—well off, we hope—and isn't especially fashion conscious. We hope that she would never dream of ordering anything from the Victoria's Secret Catalog," Geraldine dissolved in laughter. "We've had one or two requests that we carry men's items that people could buy for their husbands and boyfriends; it'd be more volume, but it would completely ruin the look of our 'book.' We do rely on customers for suggestions, though. Right now, we're trying to come up with a good, comfortable line of plain white, 100 percent cotton clothes for health-care providers. We have had many letters asking for that."

Some of the items (such as basic bras) appeared in every catalog, but others (such as a T-shirt with a special printed pattern) were not expected to become permanent parts of the collection. Larimer Hall had experimented with private labeling. On receipt of a sufficiently large order, a manufacturer would stitch in a label identifying the product as being a member of the Larimer Hall of Fame. The hope was to develop the Hall of Fame name as a house brand for basic items but the idea hadn't gone very far. "We've always had difficulty in ordering in a large enough quantity to convince the supplier to private label," Geraldine explained. "We do think that it might help us build repeat orders, especially on the regular items like underwear."

The company expanded by asking customers to send in the names of friends who might be interested in receiving a catalog, placing occasional

---

[1]SKU means *stock keeping unit*. An item that is kept in three sizes and four colors has 12 (i.e., 3 × 4) SKUs.

EXHIBIT 1   **Larimer Hall's Income Statement, 1985–1990**

	1985	1986	1987	1988	1989	1990 (Estimate)
Sales						
Gross revenues[a]	$ 50,896	$160,128	$329,077	$662,363	$1,249,612	$1,653,044
Lost sales		5,521	9,996	16,589	45,357	36,612
Returns and allowances	869	3,242	4,835	9,270	34,935	50,746
Net revenue	50,027	151,365	314,246	636,504	1,169,320	1,565,686
Cost of goods sold	27,553	71,466	144,725	351,351	568,751	750,691
Gross margin	$ 22,474	$ 79,899	$169,521	$285,153	$ 600,569	$ 814,995
Expenses						
Postage on goods sold	$ 1,346	$ 8,244	$ 14,879	$ 39,359	$ 69,500	$ 87,099
Wages and benefits	3,535	16,631	44,952	77,380	185,851	385,822
Supplies	2,059	4,340	3,862	14,002	22,550	19,589
Professional services	1,175	697	7,738	9,204	10,198	21,814
Catalog expenses						
Printing	6,415	18,424	41,498	43,088	99,868	133,852
Postage	2,253	13,190	24,909	39,679	56,583	94,112
Advertising	2,701	649	2,808	1,203	1,714	3,872
Mailing list, processing	9,225	7,048	7,033	5,055	17,138	34,879
Insurance	501	374	1,275	2,936	2,047	1,345
Occupancy[b]	795	1,497	4,835	7,375	11,330	24,028
Telephone	445	1,045	2,808	3,296	5,113	8,972
Depreciation	398	3,028	2,713	2,870	7,261	
Travel and entertainment[c]	1,025	1,245	943	3,063	6,291	7,807
Taxes	492	2,942	6,252	10,239	15,294	9,132
Bank charges[d]	340	3,790	5,962	13,786	20,616	24,010
Interest	2,304	3,161	6,385	8,048	15,540	33,921
Miscellaneous[e]	331	374	1,508	1,983	17,258	4,915
Total expenses	$ 35,330	$ 84,053	$180,360	$282,566	$ 564,152	$ 925,953
Net profit	$(12,586)	$ (4,154)	$ (10,839)	$ 2,587	$ 36,417	$ (110,958)

[a] Includes postage and handling fees collected, and discounted sale of damaged goods.
[b] Rent and utilities until 1989; for 1990 mortgage PIT of $24,440 and utilities of $6,344.
[c] Includes travel to market.
[d] Includes Visa and MasterCard discount on charge orders.
[e] Includes dues, subscriptions, and donations and cost of sample merchandise.

space advertisements in periodicals, and trading other companies for their lists. By 1990, there were two editions of the catalog being sent each year to a list of about 75,000 people. "Not all of those are good names," Alice allowed. "Our computer systems keep track of whether people who are on the list actually go ahead and place an order and we should tidy up our list. There's never been time to do that—we're always running from one crisis to another." In a recent staff meeting, one of the order clerks suggested that there were at least two types of Larimer Hall customers. Some customers only bought underwear whereas other customers bought from the full line, but they all received the same mailings.

After sales of $700 and $14,000 in 1983 and 1984, respectively, sales more than doubled in succeeding years, reaching a volume of approximately $1.25 million in 1989 (Exhibit 1). The company had no employees until 1985 and Alice did not give up her university job until 1987. "Up until then, I don't think I'd received more than $2,000 for all the work I'd put into the company." By 1990, 25 people were employed by the company, and if Larimer Hall could double its revenues again they would achieve nearly $2.5 million in sales.

THE INDUSTRY

Mail-order has a long history in the United States. The provision of universal mail delivery enabled every farm in America to receive the latest in fashions, appliances, and equipment from the Sears, Roebuck catalog. But the customer of the 1980s and 1990s was no frontier pioneer. Although most mail-order companies operated without the expenses of a retail store, the merchandise was often more expensive (with gross margins as high as 60 percent) than comparable goods available in local stores. Clearly catalog shoppers, many of them from dual-professional families, enjoyed the convenience of shopping by mail and the industry volume reached $35 billion in sales in 1989 from 16.4 billion catalogs mailed.

The mail-order clothing industry included general catalog suppliers (Spiegel); mail-order branches of stores (Talbots, J. C. Penney) and those, like Larimer Hall, which sold only clothing only through the mail. In this group there were a few very large firms:

Firm	1989 Sales (In millions of dollars)
L.L. Bean	$600
Lands' End	$545
J. Crew	$150

There were also several hundred small companies with annual sales ranging from less than $5 million down to a few hundred dollars made on a single product.

As the Larimer Hall partners found, the start-up costs in this business were modest, and hence the barriers to entry for new competitors in the low-volume end were almost nonexistent. In general, mail-order clothing firms did not own production facilities but instead bought all their goods from manufacturers. The same manufacturer might well have made a comparable item for two or more catalogs. There were very few clothing items that were truly "ours alone," as the catalogs touted.

The mail-order business was well organized with trade journals that supplied information on competitors and industry conditions. Mailing-list brokers conducted a large secondary market to trade lists among catalog firms and periodicals. Usually the list was rented rather than sold outright. (Each firm's list contained some decoy names so the firm that owned the list could check how many times it had been used.) The prices for lists varied according to the quality of the names and addresses, from as low as $40 per thousand names and addresses to more than $1 per name. The lowest prices were for compilations from published directories, and the most expensive lists were of recent buyers from high-end catalogs. Most companies would not lease their lists to direct competitors. Mail-order houses rented others' mailing lists to gain new customer prospects and rented out their own lists as a source of additional income, with brokers usually charging a 20 percent commission.

Apparel manufacture and wholesale distribution was a fragmented, low-technology business. Upon order, fabric was cut into pieces and sewed, one garment at a time, by a sewing machine. Because the garments had to be handled individually, there were few economies of scale and few parts of the process where automation could improve production. Much of the industry was fragmented into small workshops that worked on contract for large manufacturers. Because the capital equipment requirements were modest, much of the manufacturing took place overseas, with U.S. companies acting as middlemen.

Traditionally, department and clothing stores operated with four distinct seasons for clothing. Manufacturers displayed samples for an upcoming season at trade shows and merchandise marts and then solicited orders. Once orders were in hand, fabric was ordered and a run of each particular model was done to satisfy those orders. The entire order for a season was shipped to each retailer at one time. Although retailers have attempted to create more flexibility within the business, the industry is still dominated by a seasonal approach. This means that a retailer who runs out of size medium in a green sweater cannot replenish that SKU once the initial order has sold out. Similarly, overstocks in odd sizes and colors must be discounted to clear the shelves at the end of each season. The catalog clothing business was more of a year-round, continuing operation, but some of the relationships with suppliers were still dominated by a seasonal ordering and shipping schedule. When items were produced at only certain times of the year, the mail-order seller had to anticipate demand, order in large quantities, and have large warehouse facilities. Two distinct seasons for summer and winter clothes were still apparent in mail-order clothing catalogs.

OPERATIONS

By 1990, Larimer Hall had achieved some stability in operations. Clothing for the line was selected from twice-a-year buying trips to the merchandise marts in Dallas and Chicago. Goods were ordered from about 50 suppliers, some of them large national companies, some of them small entrepreneurs. The partners liked to give business to women-owned companies where they could. Terms were usually 8/10, net 30[2] but Larimer Hall was rarely able to take advantage of the discount for prompt payment. In fact, funding inventory was a perpetual problem. With the lead time needed to produce and mail a catalog, there was little chance that customers' cash could be received in time to pay suppliers' invoices. New suppliers often insisted on cash upfront

---

[2]Suppliers would give a discount of 8 percent of the invoice total if it were paid within 10 days of the billing date.

and as much as 30 percent of a season's clothing had to be paid for before shipping. Factoring (the practice of manufacturers selling receivables at a discount for cash) was not common in the mail-order business as it was with retail stores.

Alice described the ideal supplier as: "One who'll give us a volume discount on an order of, say, 500 pieces and who'll send one third of the order right when the catalog drops, one third a month later, and one third in mid-season. We'd really like some flexibility, too. If the item isn't selling, we'd like to cancel the last part of the order. In practice, the big suppliers try to make us take everything at once. That means we have to find warehouse space for it, have to find the money for the whole order, and we have the risk if the item doesn't sell." A few of the large manufacturers made some items offshore, and these were the most difficult to order more than once per season. Larimer Hall had not tried to deal directly with foreign suppliers.

Two 32-page catalogs were produced each year. "We want something that people will sit down and read right through," said Geraldine. About two thirds of the catalog's pages were in color and the rest of the pages featured black and white photographs and line drawings. The catalogs included letters from customers, a witty advice column, and stories about the Larimer Hall staff members. Descriptions of clothing were extensive and included comments about sizing ("These tend to run a little large"). An innovation suggested by a customer was to include the color and size that models in the photographs were wearing. The models in the catalogs were everyday people, often Larimer Hall staff members. Each catalog had a theme: one season sported a rustic look at Alice's log cabin ski retreat in Crested Butte, and another shot at the Denver Zoo with the headline "Goin' Bananas!"

The spring/summer "book" was delivered to the post office in March, April, and May; mailings of the fall/winter book began in August and continued through Thanksgiving. Simple fliers and postcards were occasionally used for promotions, but two regular newspaper-style sale catalogs (see Exhibit 2) were used to announce sales. Reductions of 10 to 20 percent usually moved overstocks, but discounts as deep as 33 percent were sometimes offered. Mailings were sent to all 75,000 on the mailing list and occasional trials were made of brokered lists. Larimer Hall rented lists from magazine subscription offices and traded their own list with other catalog companies with noncompeting lines, such as craft supplies. Catalogs were sent to as many as 200,000 prospects from these lists each year. A contractor would match up lists for duplicates, but his fees had risen (more than $12,000 of the processing costs in 1989) to the point where one staffer declared: "With all the computers we have around here, we could just hire one person and do the job ourselves." The catalog printer had a production line that would label catalogs and prepare them for presorted shipment. Unlike most printers, they gave Larimer Hall generous terms for payment of at least net 30 days.

Pricing was by markup on cost. Initially a rule of thumb was to take the wholesale cost and multiply it by 2.0, but recent catalogs used 2.15, which gave a gross margin of 53 percent. Some items, such as briefs, were sold three to a pack. There was some discussion about offering lower prices on underwear packed in sixes. Some staff members felt that this would increase sales volume, others pointed out that the same people who order two three-packs would order one six-pack and the firm would lose profit by discounting.

Supplies Limited ORDER EARLY

Heavyweight champion . . .

The robe that won, hands down, in this catalog round. The matchless successor to our shorter spring version from Monarch Towel–a 100% cotton double wrap terry robe with a shawl collar. It will keep you warm and dry for many moons and has long sleeves (approx. 19¹/₂" from dropped shoulder seam) and a belt with loops. 48" length. Two large patch pockets. Made in Brazil. Machine wash cool, dark colors separately. Rich Colors: Purple, Peach, One Roomy Size.

#0MROBE. $42

FOR FASTER ORDERING, CHARGE BY PHONE

9am-5pm Mon-Sat

Carrie's skirt . . .

Dress it up or down, but wear it year-round. Hand-dyed and pre-shrunk. Already generously sized, and now we've added more material for the X (56" across at the hips)! Made from 100% cotton interlock, medium weight jersey knit fabric, with 2 side seam pockets, and an elasticized waist. Easy to wear. Belt it (see matching "Flash and sash" belts below) or wear it plain with your favorite tops. Machine wash separately cool. Length of Medium approximately 34". Width around lower hem 54". Colors: Black, Aquamarine, Plum, Charcoal. Sizes: S(6-8) M(10-12) L(14-16) X(18-20).

#5DRNDL. $32

NOW ONLY $27
NOT AVAILABLE IN X CHARCOAL

Flash and sash . . .

Choose a matching or coordinating sash/belt to go with "Carrie's skirt" or the "Easy pant." It's a cinch at the waist, around the head as a turban, or at the neck like a scarf. The same garment-dyed 100% cotton interlock fabric as Carrie's skirt or the easy pant. Overstitched finished edges make the ends ruffle when tied loosely. From Spectrum in New Mexico. Size: 6" X 88". Colors: Black, Aquamarine, Plum, Charcoal

#5BELTS. $9.50 ea, 2 for $18.

NOW ONLY $7.50
21% OFF

Suit your space . . .

Our space suit coordinates of choice. Homegrown leggings, paired here with our new Homegrown vest! Both pieces are made of luxurious, smooth 100% cotton double knit. The oversized, deep V-neck cardigan vest has 1 x 1 fine ribbed trim around neck, armholes and lower edge. Very generously cut. Five unusual, futuristic buttons. Vest length: 27".

Vest colors: Black, Olive.
Vest sizes: S(6-8) M(10-12) L(14-16).

#4MVEST. $29 **NOW ONLY $19**
34 % OFF

5MLEGG

The leggings are resized from last season, cut full at the hips and tapered gradually to the ankle. Covered ³/₄" elastic waistband. Pants don't get much more comfortable than this. Inseam on Large measures 32". Made in USA. Machine wash cool, line dry. Expect 5% shrinkage, more if machine dried.

Leggings Colors: Black, Plum, Olive, Purplish Blue.
Hip Sizes: S(34") M(36") L(38-40") X(42-44") XX(46-50").

#5MLEGG. S,M,L. $19.50 ea, 2 for $38.
X,XX. $21 ea, 2 for $40.

NOW ONLY $17
AVAILABLE IN:
Black: XX Only
Blue: S, XX Only
Olive: XX Only
Plum: S, M, L, X, XX

CHARGE YOUR ORDER BY PHONE:

Waist band

Sash & flash →

5DRNDL

9SWANS

Supplies Limited ORDER EARLY

4MVEST

Wing it . . .

Still flying, now into its third edition of BRIEFS, here's the scoop neck tunic with the long dolman sleeves. Nearly as hefty as a lightweight sweatshirt, but dressier and super soft. Paired with our leggings or layered for cold weather, its unflappable. 100% cotton interlock knit. Ribbed cuffs. Straight hem. Imported from China. Machine wash cold. Medium approx. 26" in length. Sizes: S(8-10) M(12-14) L(16-18). Colors: Black, Red, Periwinkle Blue, Peach, White.

#9SWANS. $16.50 ea, 2 for $32.

5SPANT

The easy pant . . .

And that's what these pants (pictured on the right) are–easy to wear, easy to fit, easy to move in. And they have pockets, as so many of you requested in a Homegrown™ pant. The same wonderfully soft 100% cotton knit as "Carrie's skirt." This pant has a 1 ¹/₂" elastic waist, and ample room to fit loosely at the hips. A walloping wide cut that tapers to 7" across at the ankle. Inseam on medium measures approx. 28 1/2". Garment dyed to mix and match with sashes. Made in New Mexico by Spectrum. Machine wash cool, hang dry. Colors: Black, Marine Blue, Plum, Charcoal. Hip Sizes: M(44-46") L(48-50") X(52").

#5SPANT. S, M, L $40
X $43

NOW ONLY $32.
20% OFF

AVAILABLE IN:
Black: X Only
Blue: M, L Only
Charcoal: M Only
Plum: M, L Only

Two thirds of orders came in by mail, using the order form in the catalog. The average order was for $51 of merchandise although the typical order was a little smaller in the summer months ($40) and higher ($60–$65) close to Christmas. The remaining orders were taken by telephone. Four phone lines were monitored Monday to Saturday 9 A.M. to 5 P.M., and a telephone answering machine was available for customers who wanted to dictate an order after hours. Few took advantage of this and there were only a handful of calls to transcribe each Monday morning. Installing an 800-number for toll-free customer calls was a topic of frequent debate among the Larimer Hall staffers. On the one hand, some felt: "If I was getting ready to order, there's no way I'd pay for the call—we must be losing all kinds of business." Others felt that it wouldn't increase volume: "We'd just end up paying for the calls we get anyway. Some of our customers really like to chat, and that's on *their* phone bill. Imagine what it'll be like when we're paying for the call. Also, a toll-free line will switch orders from mail to phone and we'd have to handle more operators and put in more lines." The market for toll-free calling was competitive; typical charges were $0.20 per minute, with an initial fee of about $1,000 per line. One of the long-distance carriers had been wooing Larimer Hall by suggesting that the fee might be substantially discounted if the firm made all four incoming lines 800-numbers.

Customers paid shipping and handling on each order:

Order Size	Shipping Fee
$20 and under	$3.00
$21–$40	$4.00
$41–$75	$5.00
$75 and over	$6.00

The actual costs of outbound postage (Larimer Hall used UPS almost exclusively) were less than the fees collected, and so the shipping fee was a source of revenue that covered the costs of packaging supplies and staff time to process the order. The company aimed to spend no more than 50 percent of the shipping fee on UPS charges, but at times when back-orders required multiple shipments the UPS charges equalled the fees collected.

Customers paid by check or charged to Visa or MasterCard; Larimer Hall's bank charged 2 percent for processing the charged sales. American Express was not accepted because the processing charge offered was 5 percent. Check orders were delayed for 10 days to make sure that the check had cleared, although returned checks were a rare problem for the company and they always cleared on a second presentation for payment. A check-guarantee company had recently offered to process all checks for a 2 percent payment (the same as the cost of bank card charges) in return for guaranteed payment to Larimer Hall.

Order entry, inventory control, and the production of packing lists and UPS manifests were done on a network of nine microcomputers. Alice used her computer expertise to give the company a level of sophistication that was well above other catalog firms of similar size. In fact, there was more information available than there was time to analyze it: "We know a lot about our customers and products—who orders what, what sells, and what doesn't. But it's difficult to spend the time to sort it out when there are more important things to do, like getting our new accounting package working." The computer network would support on-line order entry but without enough terminals for peak times, order-processing employees wrote down customer orders. It was possible to check whether an item was in stock for a telephone customer if a terminal was available.

Returns and exchanges could run as high as 15 percent in the catalog clothing business, including those transactions where a customer just wanted a different size. Larimer Hall did not track these simple exchanges (which did not affect gross revenue), but returns (where the customer was unsatisfied with the product and wanted money back) were easy to monitor because the refund checks written showed up on the accounting statements as about 3.6 percent of sales in 1989. Returned merchandise was repaired (in the case of an unravelled seam), cleaned, and placed on sale racks for walk-in customers. Some staff members were enthusiastic about the retail business and viewed it as an avenue for further expansion. Others saw it as a necessary evil and one that took staff time away from the primary business. In rare instances where there was a problem with a whole shipment of clothing Larimer Hall sought an adjustment from the manufacturer, but the firm tolerated one or two bad items from each shipment as the staff costs in pursuing a refund from the supplier never seemed to be worth the effort.

More important than returns and allowances were "lost sales," which occurred when Larimer Hall received an order for an item that was out of stock. Some items were expected to be seasonal (for example, swimsuits) and it was a goal to be sold out by the end of the season. Other items were part of the catalog's basic line, and out-of-stocks were a problem. Not only was that sale lost, but a repeat customer might search for an alternate supplier and thus be lost for future sales. Total inventory of goods available for sale varied considerably, with the year-end inventory being a low point. Highest inventories (about 2.5 times the year-end level) occurred in June and November. Because of the Larimer Hall focus on basic lines, seasonality of orders was not as pronounced as in gift catalogs. April and May together had 25 percent of the sales volume, as did November and December, with the remaining 50 percent distributed evenly over the remaining eight months of the year.

This moderate seasonality enabled Larimer Hall to operate with mainly full-time, permanent staff (in contrast with Lands' End, for example, which had to add more than 1,000 temporary workers to its order staff of 2,200 to handle the Christmas rush). The warehouse and packing area was configured to handle five packing stations but there were typically only four packers (Exhibit 3). Customer service and packing jobs were low-paid, but there was no difficulty in quickly filling the positions from newspaper help-wanted advertisements when vacancies occurred. A friendly working environment was important to Geraldine and Alice. They knew each of the staff personally and couldn't imagine running a company where people were hired and fired just to meet business goals.

EXHIBIT 3   **Larimer Hall's Organizational Chart, November 1990**

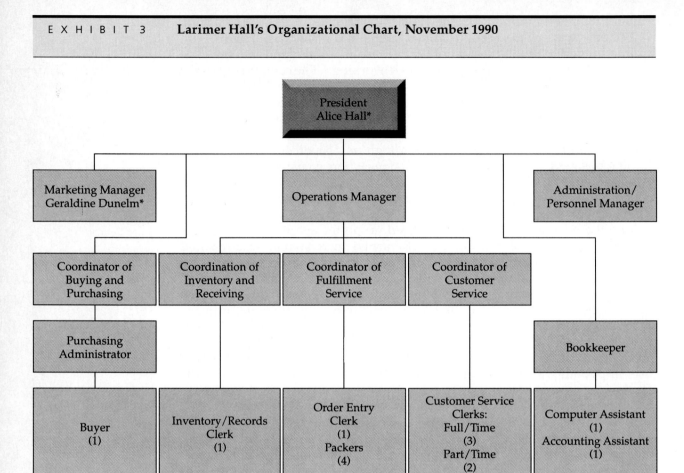

*Alice Hall and Geraldine Dunelm were owners as was Violet Larimer, who was no longer active in the daily activities of the firm.

FINANCES

Larimer Hall became a Subchapter S corporation (a firm legally organized as a corporation but taxed as a partnership) during the first year of operation and Alice, Violet, and Geraldine began as owners of equal shares. By 1990 Alice and Geraldine had contributed more sweat equity and together owned 90 percent of the stock and had received salaries for their work since 1987. The initial partnership contributions of $2,400 appeared on the balance sheet (Exhibit 4) as "additional paid-in capital" and the three women received stock in return for a total of $13,000 at the formation of the corporation. The corporation generated a loss for each year before 1988 (and then turned a scant $2,600 profit); the accumulation of these losses led to negative equity shown on the books. The owners felt that the corner was turned in 1989 when a profit of almost 3 percent on sales brought the net worth of the corporation into the black.

With such modest equity capital, Larimer Hall relied heavily on bank financing to grow and fund current assets (chiefly inventory, as there were

EXHIBIT 4   **Larimer Hall's Balance Sheet, 1985–1990**

	1985	1986	1987	1988	1989	1990 (Estimate)
Assets						
Cash and equivalents	$ 4,085	$ 9,985	$ 6,027	$ 8,127	$ 9,319	$ 45,538
Inventory	9,046	26,988	38,093	59,662	92,023	93,000
Prepaid expense	794	700		1,000	482	41,550
Land					147,000	147,000
Building					80,000	80,000
Accumulated depreciation					0	2,900
Net					80,000	77,100
Equipment	2,652	3,200	11,080	17,578	45,539	60,395
Accumulated depreciation	398	800	3,513	7,219	14,480	29,916
Net	2,254	2,400	7,567	10,359	31,059	30,479
Mailing list			17,000	25,000	36,000	75,000
Other assets	6,250	6,240	76	312	312	0
Total assets	$22,419	$46,313	$68,763	$104,420	$396,195	$509,667
Liabilities and Owner's Equity						
Customer deposits	$ 781	$ 300	$ 1,328	$ 1,528	$ 5,488	$ 374
Accounts payable	4,413	25,802	31,192	47,857	44,272	130,333
Taxes payable					12,145	3,104
Notes payable: line of credit	7,572	6,288	21,551	39,546	76,502	147,679
Notes payable: long term	11,627	20,051	31,659	27,519	53,000	135,000
Mortgage payable					180,000	179,347
Total liabilities	$24,393	$52,441	$85,730	$116,450	$371,407	$595,837
Common stock	$10,600	$10,600	$10,600	$ 12,950	$ 12,950	$ 12,950
Additional paid-in capital	2,400	2,400	2,400	2,400	2,400	2,400
Retained earnings	(14,974)	(19,128)	(29,967)	(27,380)	9,438	(101,520)
Total shareholders' equity	(1,974)	(6,128)	(16,967)	(12,030)	24,788	(86,170)
Liabilities and equity	$22,419	$46,313	$68,763	$104,420	$396,195	$509,667

no accounts receivable in the catalog business). Based on annual cash flow projections, the firm's bank set up a line of credit facility to enable Larimer Hall to order and pay for merchandise while waiting for orders to come in from customers each season. In 1988, at the end of December after the Christmas season, the line of credit was at $40,000 and a year later the firm had borrowed the full $75,000 of its line and owed interest. The interest rate varied but was about 12 percent in 1989 and 1990. The bank had offered the firm a five-year interest-only note (at 12 percent fixed) to purchase computers and office furniture and this had been rolled over and extended as the business grew and needed additional equipment. The long-term debt had risen to $27,000 at the end of 1988 and $50,000 plus accrued interest in 1989.

Space was a constant problem for Larimer Hall as it grew. The seasonal shipments of merchandise demanded large warehouse facilities. The firm had moved twice and in 1989 was cramped into 1,500 square feet of garage space: "Just to have a staff meeting, we had to make coffee, put on our coats, and sit on the wall outside!" During the rush of the 1989 Christmas season, Alice and Geraldine were looking around for new premises to rent and mentioned their search while they were renegotiating their bank loans with Roger Smith, the bank officer who handled their accounts. As it happened, the bank had just repossessed a building that had been used by a cable TV operator and was anxious to find a buyer. Set a few blocks away from the gleaming high-rises of downtown Denver, the building was the last outpost of civilization before a row of temperance missions, flop houses, and pawn shops. The simple flat-roofed warehouse building was about 20 years old and had excellent front offices. It stood in the middle of a cleared city block (about half an acre, or 20,000 square feet) and a high barbed-wire fence surrounded what used to be the parking lot for the cable TV trucks. Alice and Geraldine had been looking for a 5,000-square-foot building and this was just the right size, although they would have no use for the parking lot. They had planned to spend no more than $5.00 per square foot for rent, so their budget was $25,000 per annum. Roger pointed out that the bank would be happy to loan 80 percent of the $225,000 asking price and the payments (principal, interest, taxes, and insurance) would be about $2,000 per month.

Motivated by the chance to finally build up some equity in the business and encouraged by initial projections that showed a profit of more than $35,000 for the year, Geraldine and Alice purchased the building in the name of the firm, tapping cash flow for the $47,000 down payment. All the staff were delighted with their new home and there was a sense that Larimer Hall had come of age.

The realities of owning a building were a little less joyous. The expenses of repairing the long-empty building to meet their needs were more than they thought. With the bank's urging they began 1990 with a complete overhaul of their computerized accounting systems and although the partners knew the work needed to be done, the professional fees from the new accounting firm were daunting.

Afterward, Alice jokingly referred to the spring of 1990 as "the season from hell." Some of the large number of small suppliers whom Larimer Hall had tried to support failed to deliver at all or delivered unsalable merchandise. "We had one group that made some pants for us and the samples looked great. But they decided to go for garment dyeing (dyeing the pants after they were sewn for a more uniform color) and the very hot temperatures used shrank the cloth. The first batch were 12 inches too short—we weren't selling matador pants! We went back and forth with them. Eventually we stopped ordering from them and took a loss on selling them cheap on our retail racks to walk-in customers."

In addition, the expenses of the move caused some difficulties in making prompt payments to suppliers. As Larimer Hall stretched its terms, suppliers neglected them. When advertised goods didn't arrive on time, customer back-orders had to be shipped separately. The staff worked hard to keep customers informed (and hence loyal), but shipping costs rose and additional staff time was needed to process the same order two or three times. The bank was supportive and impressed by Larimer Hall's ability to grow sales volume, and after a series of temporary arrangements Alice's spreadsheet suggested that they would end the year with almost $150,000 out on their line of credit in addition to the long-term debt, which now stood at $135,000.

The Future

Alice was confident that Larimer Hall could achieve profitability without the one-time expenses of early 1990. Growth in sales revenue always seemed easy to achieve and all the mechanisms were in place to handle a large sales volume. But there was no point in increasing sales unless more could be brought to the bottom line. Alice pondered what actions to take.

PUBLIC SERVICE COMPANY OF NEW MEXICO (A)*

Arthur A. Thompson, Jr., The University of Alabama

John Bundrant, president of Public Service Company of New Mexico's electric utility division, walked into his office shortly after 7 A.M. on a Friday in February 1986, sat down in his chair, and swung around to the computer terminal adjacent to his desk. He flipped on the switch, hit a few keys to "log on" to the system, hit another key to bring up the "PROFS" menu, and chose the "Open the Mail" option. Just over a year earlier, the company's ESBU (electric strategic business unit) had embarked on a program to install IBM's Professional Office Systems (PROFS) for 80 percent of its white-collar work force. The project had involved providing each of some 900 "knowledge workers" with a computer terminal connected to the company's mainframe computer. The PROFS software gave each user instant capability to (1) send notes and messages to other users (using the electronic mail option), (2) maintain daily calendars and schedule meetings (using the electronic calendaring and scheduling option), (3) create and process documents of all kinds (using the document and text processing features), (4) create and maintain files (via the electronic filing option), (5) arrange for automatic reminder messages, and (6) do a variety of other functions. Once the basic PROFS framework had been installed, the company had quickly followed up with an expanded menu, including spreadsheet analysis, graphing, daily operating reports, and access to other databases on the mainframe.

Bundrant was pleased with the ESBU's foray into office technology. Acceptance of the new office information system (OIS) had been enthusiastic. White-collar productivity had risen an estimated 11 percent, almost twice the original 6 percent projection. Virtually all of the OIS project's goals had been achieved. The previous week, Bundrant had gotten a status report on PROFS/OIS, outlining what had been done and achieved so far; a copy of the report is reproduced in Exhibit 1.

When Bundrant pressed the "Open the Mail" key, a short note from Jerry Geist, Public Service Company of New Mexico's chairman and chief executive officer, popped up on his screen. The message was terse: "John, if PNM is to make its corporate profit target for 1986, it looks like we are going to have to cut $27–$36 million out of the electric division's budgets for 1986 through 1988. Can you generate a proposed cutback plan for the corporate office to consider by the end of the month?" The note was not a big surprise; Bundrant and several other officers of the ESBU had concluded weeks ago that cutbacks were just a matter of time. The only question had been how much. Now he knew. Bundrant hit a few more keystrokes, automatically forwarding Geist's note to members of the electric division's top policy-making committee—a group known internally as USET (company shorthand for Utility Sector Executive Team).

*The author gratefully acknowledges the assistance, cooperation, and sponsorship of IBM Corporation and Public Service Company of New Mexico in preparing this material as a basis for analysis and discussion in an educational setting.

E X H I B I T   1   **Status Report: OIS Value/Benefit Impact in PNM's ESBU, February 1986**

1. *What is OIS?*
   - OIS is PNM's Office Information System. The backbone of OIS is IBM's Professional Office System (PROFS), which provides most of the functions of our system, plus a platform upon which our numerous enhancements and additions have been made.
   - Major non-PROFS OIS capabilities include Megacalc (a mainframe spreadsheet), Information Center/1, DisplayWrite/370.
   - OIS serves more than 900 internal users, a number which represents over 40% of the employees within the ESBU and Corporate Office. OIS also serves a number of employees in Meadows, Sunbelt, and SDCW.

2. *Justification*
   - Original justification assumed 6% productivity gain; follow-up survey conducted at year-end 1985 showed 11% improvement.
   - Bulk of original justification based on productivity to be achieved from electronic mail, text processing, and calendar functions. Since that time many additional features have been added to OIS, without raising cost to the end-customer, Megacalc, InfoCenter/1, DisplayWrite/370, Easygraph, and many other customized features.
   - Also assumed 9% reduction in Word Processing Center (WPC) traffic. Statistics show WPC production (number of lines) decreased by roughly 45% between 1983 and 1986. There have been several factors contributing to that decrease, and it is not possible to tell how much is directly attributable to OIS, but it is safe to assume that OIS has been a major factor.

3. *Cost—$140/month/user*
   - Flat fee has not increased since day 1, even though system is constantly being upgraded, enhanced, and includes extended features like Megacalc and IC/1 in addition to the original basic PROFS.
   - Operational cost of OIS is covered by monthly OIS charges; OIS is not being subsidized by other computer billings.

4. *Intangibles*
   - We are in the midst of the "information age," wherein information is an increasingly valuable corporate asset that not only allows us to do our jobs properly, but may actually impact the financial bottom line. In many respects, accurate and timely information is a necessity in today's business world, not a luxury. . . . OIS helps us collect, process, format, and disseminate that information.
   - Automation in general, and OIS specifically, helps us be more responsive to each other as employees, and by extension, to our customers.

   - OIS has put hundreds of computer terminals on admin/clerical/prof/exec desks . . . helped make hundreds of PNM employees more computer literate, aware of the power and productivity of automated systems . . . resulted in more use of the computer in general, not just OIS, for department/company productivity.
   - Value-added products on OIS (in addition to PROFS) such as Megacalc and IC/1 promote departmental computing and control over certain amount of information processing that would otherwise have to be analyzed, programmed, and maintained by our software group (or possibly not done at all). Existence of such tools may help reduce application backlog or provide information that otherwise would not exist.
   - Availability of text editor, spreadsheet, graphics, IC/1, etc., has reduced the number of personal computers required by individuals and/or departments.
   - Improved communication; impossible to put $ benefit on; can communicate with nearly half of the company within seconds, without paper expense of mailroom impact; greatly reduces "telephone tag"; has improved the timelines of communication since notes, documents, and messages can be sent, received, forwarded, replied to, all in a matter of minutes without waiting for copies, mail lag, etc.; great potential for making decisions more timely, based on the availability of timely info.

5. *Survey of other utilities with PROFS*
   - Per information supplied by IBM, approximately 50% of large utilities have office automation systems in place.

6. *Triggers for other automation*
   - Many OIS terminals are used for other applications as well.
   - Widespread availability of terminals as a result of OIS has made possible the development of certain applications dependent upon that availability, such as events reporting and on-line budget input. Such widespread availability of terminals also provides a foundation or basic level of equipment, already in place, that will benefit and support other on-line applications in the future.

7. *Reduced clerical support/word processing capacity*
   - Downsizing of word processing staff would have been very difficult without OIS in place. Example: clerical assistants were reduced from 5 to 2 in the Information Systems Department, an improbable accomplishment in the absence of OIS. Number of clericals now in place probably could not handle the work if OIS were to go away.

Bundrant quickly read through three other short messages on his mail list, then flipped through the calendar on his desk to see what next week's schedule looked like, pressed another key to reaccess the PROFS menu, and chose the "Schedule a Meeting" function from the options. He keyed in next Monday's date, then indicated he wanted a one-hour time slot. When the screen prompted him for names of the meeting participants, Bundrant typed in USET. A few seconds later the screen displayed two times when the other USET members could meet with Bundrant. He keyed in his preference for 10 A.M.; next the screen prompted him with the message "Send a notice of a meeting." He responded by typing in information on the location—eighth-floor conference room, along with the comment, "Let's bounce around our ideas on Jerry's note Monday at 10." Bundrant hit a key, automatically forwarding his message to all USET members.

Bundrant made a mental note of the fact that all of this had been done in less than five minutes and that without OIS it probably would have taken his secretary 30 to 45 minutes to make copies of Jerry's note, distribute them to the others, and then go through the ritual of setting up a meeting—calling everybody on the telephone, catching the other people or their secretaries at their desks, communicating the purpose of the meeting, checking the calendars of everyone involved, calling back and forth to arrive at a mutually open time slot, typing a meeting notice, running off copies, and sending them out through the interoffice mail.

Had Bundrant's secretary been at her desk at the time, he would not have gone through the "Schedule a Meeting" routine himself. His usual practice was to let her handle such details; his personal use of the system was pretty much restricted to "Open the Mail," a feature he found convenient and efficient. Despite his engineering background, Bundrant did not use his computer terminal personally to the same degree that most other officers and managers did. While he suspected that some people thought this was because he was from "the old school" and wasn't comfortable with all the gadgetry of computers, the truth was that he thought the time-saving benefits applied more to managers without a secretary and to clerical workers whose normal tasks could be done more quickly and easily using the capabilities built into PROFS. His secretary sometimes spent as much as four hours a day using various PROFS functions, and he had heard her praise the system. Bundrant saw the value of OIS to him personally as being faster, better communication between his office and the rest of the organization.

COMPANY BACKGROUND

With sales of $690 million and assets of $3 billion in 1985, Public Service Company of New Mexico (PNM) ranked among the 100 largest utility companies in the United States. Headquartered in Albuquerque, PNM's main business consisted of providing electric and gas service to about 65 percent of the state's population; the electric division served about 267,000 customers, and the gas division served over 322,000 customers. In addition to its electric and gas utility operations, PNM had several other business interests:

EXHIBIT 2   **Corporate Structure of Public Service of New Mexico**

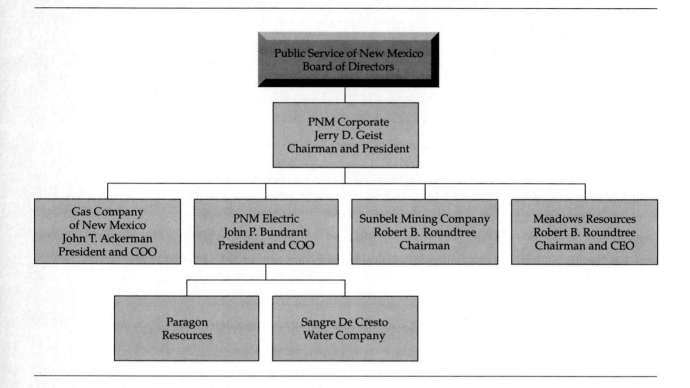

- Sangre de Cristo Water Co., which provided water utility services to the city of Santa Fe.
- Sunbelt Mining Co., which owned and operated coal and other mineral mining interests in New Mexico and Oklahoma and supplied coal to PNM's San Juan Generating Station and other electric utilities.
- Meadows Resources Inc., which had made a portfolio of financial investments in companies unrelated to utilities and had strategic goals of trying to attract new companies to locate in New Mexico, provide job opportunities to New Mexicans, enhance New Mexico's economic growth prospects, and broaden PNM's earnings base.
- Paragon Resources, which acquired water rights and property for future power plant projects and utility-related activities.

Exhibit 2 depicts PNM's corporate structure.

Electric and gas operations were PNM's principal revenue and profit producers. In 1985, 59 percent of PNM's revenues and 88 percent of its operating income came from electric operations. Gas operations accounted for 40 percent of operating revenues and 11 percent of operating earnings. About 1 percent of corporate revenues and operating income came from the other activities (however, Sunbelt Mining's sales of coal to the San Juan plant were included as a cost to the electric division and were recovered in the rates PNM charged its electric customers). Exhibit 3 shows a financial breakdown for 1985 by business segment.

EXHIBIT 3   **Public Service Company of New Mexico's Financial Summary, by Business Segment, 1985** *(Thousands of dollars)*

	Electric	Gas	Other	Total
Operating revenues	$ 408,101	$273,737	$ 8,144	$ 689,982
Operating expenses excluding income taxes	227,228	250,899	4,891	483,018
Pretax operating income	180,873	22,838	3,253	206,964
Operating income tax	17,931	2,965	954	21,850
Operating income	$ 162,942	$ 19,873	$ 2,299	$ 185,114
Depreciation expense	$ 47,113	$ 7,515	$ 738	$ 55,366
Utility construction expenditure	$ 242,559	$ 17,675	$ 1,697	$ 261,931
Identifiable assets				
Net utility plant	$1,923,939	$216,178	$ 31,340	$2,171,457
Other	460,514	92,352	285,915	838,781
Total assets	$2,384,453	$308,530	$317,255	$3,010,238

Source: 1985 Annual Report.

The gas utility operations were a new business for PNM. The company had acquired the New Mexico natural gas utility assets of Southern Union Company in 1985 as part of a settlement of antitrust litigation brought against Southern Union by PNM and others. Falling natural gas prices, deregulation of the natural gas industry, and increased competition from the wellhead all the way to end-use customers were forcing PNM to find ways to protect the gas division's profitability and at the same time initiate the transition from being a traditional regulated gas utility to being a more price competitive, service-oriented operation. Going into 1986, it looked as though soft natural gas prices and depressed profitability from natural gas operations would continue to affect the whole natural gas industry until the early 1990s.

PNM's electric business hit difficult times soon after the 1980s began. During the 1970s, New Mexico appeared to be on the threshold of sustained economic growth. The state's oil and gas business was booming. Natural resource deposits, principally uranium and coal, were attracting investors, and new mining ventures were being launched. Electronics firms were locating new plants in the Albuquerque area, boosting job opportunities significantly. Because it took 8 to 12 years to bring new electric generating capacity on stream, PNM responded to the projected upturn in New Mexico's economy by initiating construction of several new power plants in the mid-1970s, so as to be in position to meet New Mexico's electricity needs in the mid-1980s and beyond.

By the early 1980s, just as PNM's program to complete the new electric generating stations entered its final phase, the New Mexico economy and electric energy demand flattened. A worldwide slide in oil and natural gas prices caught both end-users and producers by surprise. The resulting slowdown in drilling and exploration produced a depression in New Mexico's oil and gas fields. Meanwhile, the state's uranium and coal mining industries were also hit hard by slack demand and falling prices. Production cutbacks were so severe that, in early 1986, PNM's uranium mining customers were using only 14 percent as much electricity as they used in 1979, and the peak load they placed on PNM's electric system was 97 percent below what had been projected; coal mining customers were using only 40 percent of the projected peak loads.

In Albuquerque, the electronics industry, hit hard by international competition, had not expanded to the expected degree. In fact, the largest electricity-using industrial facility to locate in PNM's service area during the 1980s was a small fiberboard plant that had been financed by PNM's Meadows Resources subsidiary.

As a consequence, PNM found itself with more electric generating capacity than its customers could use. In 1986 PNM had reserve generating capacity nearly 70 percent above that needed to meet its annual peak load requirement (the industry norm was a reserve margin about 20 percent above the annual peak). Completion of Unit 3 of the Palo Verde nuclear plant in 1987 would increase PNM's reserve margin by an additional 8 percent.

While PNM had been and still was trying to market its extra generating capacity to other electric utilities, the regional wholesale power market was temporarily glutted and buyers could bargain on price. Consequently, while 35 to 45 percent of PNM's total electric energy sales were coming from "off-system" sales to other electric utilities, the profit contributions on these sales were low. This threw the financial burden of PNM's construction program and the high fixed costs of underused plant capacity back on New Mexico ratepayers and the company's stockholders. The company's need to raise its retail electric rates to earn a decent return on its new construction investments had attracted much attention in the media and was emerging as an issue in New Mexico's gubernatorial campaign. With no turnaround in sight for the New Mexico economy, the company was projecting it would be deep into the 1990s before customers would need all the generating capacity available at the new Palo Verde and San Juan plants. All of this meant the electric division's sales were likely to be flat for the next five years and, in the absence of budget cuts and streamlining, the company return on investment was in jeopardy.

In addition, adverse regulatory developments were brewing. PNM was using an innovative accounting treatment that kept the costs of PNM's Palo Verde nuclear generating plants out of the rate base (using an "inventorying of capacity" rate-making method) until the 1990s when higher rates would be phased in to cover the plant investment. However, proposed changes in national accounting standards would disallow the use of this rate-making methodology and require PNM to use accounting treatments that would severely dampen the company's reported earnings.

To make matters worse, the chances were good that the New Mexico Public Service Commission would soon decide to investigate the prudency of the costs incurred by PNM to construct the Palo Verde nuclear plant; hearings could be long. Any costs determined by the New Mexico PSC to be imprudent could end up being excluded from the rate base, effectively preventing PNM from recovering its investment through electric rates and forcing the company to incur writeoffs against earnings. To ease the financial burden to its ownership interest in Palo Verde, in 1985 PNM initiated a sale and lease-back transaction for its part of Units 1 and 2; this was the first such sale and lease-back transaction involving a nuclear plant.

THE OFFICE INFORMATION SYSTEMS PROJECT

Interest in considering office automation applications at PNM was sparked when an information systems manager saw PROFS demonstrated at a data processing conference in 1982. Soon after, David Bedford, then-vice president for corporate services and considered something of a visionary by his peers, began to look into whether the company could benefit from "office of the future" technology. His first step was to call in a consultant to assess PNM's information systems needs; the consultant concluded the company needed to do something "regardless." Bedford recalled how the OIS project at PNM evolved in its formative stages:

> Our project really started as a way to reduce costs. I had heard pitches from IBM as to what their office systems would do. And because we had an IBM mainframe and a multitude of computer terminals already installed, I was interested in doing something that was compatible with the equipment investments we had already made.
>
> I asked our IBM representatives for information on PROFS and they got it for me. The more I learned, the more willing I became to try it. Of course, it wasn't a new product at that time, but it was new to us. We were among the first companies that IBM marketed PROFS to outside of their own organization.
>
> In 1983, we put together a joint company-IBM study team [known internally as the Application Transfer Team (ATT)] to evaluate the benefits and costs of going to office automation. My interest grew as the team dug out more facts about PROFS's capabilities and what the cost of installing it would be for different user levels. We looked very hard at the numbers and decided that the cost of office automation was in the range of something we could afford to experiment with. But it was the communications improvements, none of which were measurable directly, that convinced us to keep going ahead with our preliminary investigation. The communications features really turned me on.
>
> When the team made its report, they concluded we could realize a 6 percent gain in productivity. Not long thereafter, IBM came in and offered to bring in enough equipment for a 90-day pilot test for 32 users—it was all essentially free to the company except for the shipping cost. We decided that the pilot should be done in the offices of some of the executives and in the corporate services departments reporting to me. I got a terminal on my desk, my secretary got one, and all of the managers who reported directly to me got one. Then there were several managers one level down and some other staff members who participated. We created a pilot study team to evaluate the test and determine the technical feasibility and cost/benefit of implementing PROFS on a wider scale.

Exhibit 4 shows excerpts from the ATT study and pilot study reports. The supporting documentation for these two studies was over 3 inches thick. When questioned about why the benefit-cost studies and documentation were so extensive, Terry Othick, one of the key project managers, said:

> I think if it were redone today it wouldn't necessarily be as thick. The style of the senior vice president was very analytical, and people that went to him requesting to spend corporate funds expected to have to answer a lot of questions. Therefore, this document went into a significant amount of detail in anticipation of Mr. Bedford's probing questions.
>
> In this particular instance, he really wanted to know what type of return the investment was going to get, what productivity gains from individuals we might expect, and what equipment costs and software costs would be incurred. He was

EXHIBIT 4   **Excerpts from the Reports of the Office Automation Study Teams**

ATT Study—Summary Conclusions

- Presently, the automated office functions which contribute most to potential dollar and time savings are text processing and electronic mail. Additional savings can be achieved through electronic calendaring.

- The estimated dollar value of time saved per year through installment of an office automation system ranges from $1.858 million (low estimate of time savings, 500 terminals) to $7.073 million (high estimate of time savings, 900 terminals).

- The dollar value of savings associated with reducing the work load of word processing, convenience copying, corporate manuals, internal mail, filing, and micrographics is approximately $124,000 per year.

- There is a general willingness within PNM to accept office automation. This conclusion is based on the following factors:

  A generally high level of interest throughout the company in the topic of OA.

  The high response rate (approximately 55 percent) of people who responded to the invitation to participate in the questionnaire.

  The relatively high degree of familiarity with computer terminals and products of automated systems, which suggests an already existing degree of competence with and a willingness to use additional automated tools.

The main benefits projected are:

- A minimum weekly average reduction of 6.4% in administrative and management work hours. This represents a 3.1 hour per week reduction from 49.8 to 46.7 hours per person.

- A minimum weekly average reduction of 5.9% in administrative support work hours. This represents a 2.6 hour per week reduction from 45.5 to 42.9 hours per person.

- An approximate Word Processing Center volume reduction of 9%, or about 10,000 pages per month, which relates to a 15% labor reduction, or an annual savings of $79,000.

- An approximate monthly copying reduction of 149,000 pages from both the Reproduction Center and satellite copiers, representing an annual savings of $45,000.

OA Pilot Study—Summary Conclusions

The on-site in-depth evaluation of the IBM/PROFS system as a solution to the office automation question produced the following conclusions:

- The PROFS system provides the basic as well as many advanced functions of an automated office and can technically support PNM's transition from a "manual" to an integrated office systems concept.

- IBM offers a complete solution to the OA question in terms of hardware, software, and necessary data communications technology.

- A full range of end user terminals is available to meet user requirements. These terminals range from relatively inexpensive "dumb" terminals to high resolution color graphics terminals and fully functional personal computers, all of which can access and use the Professional Office System (PROFS).

- A major commitment to the office automation concept has been made by IBM.

- Each user of PROFS needs his/her own terminal to maximize utilization and benefit.

- The IBM/PROFS system is not perfect. The basic functions of the system are easy to learn and use; however, the advanced functions are basically data processing oriented and require the user to understand some basic data processing concepts.

- Implementation of Office Automation implies that roughly one-third of all PNM's employees will adopt and use tools to accomplish their daily jobs. This will require a major shift in PNM's office work culture.

- A continuing user training and technical support program will be required to bring 900 non-data processing users up to a proficiency level adequate to achieve OA benefits. Computer operations, user training, and user support will require a permanent trained staff of 8 to 12 people (included in projected costs).

- The low benefit level cannot be achieved without an actual net reduction of ~55 jobs.

also very concerned about what an OIS would do to the time and effort it took to process all the other computing jobs we had on the mainframe on a regular basis.

To get a handle on the productivity and other benefits, we did a survey of about 1,000 employees who dealt with documents, spreadsheets, and the like. We asked them all kinds of questions about what they could do with an office automation system, how long they would use it daily, how much time they thought it might save—really, we asked just about everything we could think of. The survey was five pages long. Our estimates of potential productivity came pretty much directly out of the survey responses.

Othick saw Dave Bedford as the right person to champion OIS at the company:

> He got turned on to this particular type of technology. He continued to push and prod and keep his hands more in this project than in many other projects. I think the reason was that he wanted very much to make it succeed. He kept asking questions dealing with security, training, use of the tools—everything he could think of. The questions were very hard and made us keep fine-tuning our approach.

Bill Wygant, who succeeded Dave Bedford as vice president for administrative services in early 1986 and who was heavily involved in the OIS project all along, echoed Othick's observation:

> Dave was a young senior executive—single, very bright, technically competent. One of the things that he did was use systems. He discovered that most all systems except office systems were interconnected, and he felt that office systems would be more productive if connected through the mainframe. Our OIS proposal represented an opportunity to begin to do this. At the time, there were very few people who would approach office automation with a mainframe and dumb terminals. This was a very unusual route.
>
> Dave normally built support for his decisions on very, very firm numbers. There were some soft spots in our benefit estimates, so Dave did the personal research necessary to convince himself that going to OIS was the proper thing to do. One of the major elements in that research was the ATT study, which he had me work through the IBM. That formed the basic justification for going ahead with the pilot. Then during the pilot, he was a very active user himself and he spent a lot of time listening to the reactions and opinions of the other trial users.

APPROVAL FOR THE OIS PROJECT

As the pilot project progressed, top management discussions about taking PROFS companywide began in earnest. Dave Bedford became convinced during the first 30 days of the pilot that PROFS delivered some very positive benefits and that the actual costs would be in line with the estimates. However, several senior executives were skeptical whether OIS was really cost justified. Bedford recalled the discussions:

> At the time, I was pushing all the other executives to hold the budgets in their areas down, yet here I was advocating that the company spend extra money installing PROFS. They argued that if an engineer or a surveyor became more productive using PROFS, the company would never see the cost-saving dollars because such people would just have more time to do their jobs thoroughly. They didn't deny that PROFS would be a plus. They just said they would never be able to capture the dollar savings in their budgets except in the case of clerical personnel—where it might be possible to get by with fewer people.
>
> To counter their arguments, I guaranteed enough actual dollar savings in the administrative services departments reporting to me to pay for installing the equipment companywide. In my service departments—about 700 people total—I could see that we could make enough reductions in bodies to recover the added costs of PROFS dollar for dollar from my own budget. Our forecasted benefits were two to three times the projected costs. My guarantee was what sold Jerry Geist, our CEO. There really wasn't any risk; it was all upside potential. I always had very good budget relations with Jerry. I never promised him something I couldn't deliver.
>
> But the hardest part of the process was getting my peers to install it in their own offices and getting agreement that we senior officers would pioneer the use

of PROFS in our respective areas of responsibility. Some of them didn't want to be bothered because it was pretty much a break-even proposition in their departments. They didn't see where they could get the bucks back and they didn't want their budgets to go up. Jerry was the one who influenced the decision for all the senior executives and their direct reports to be the first ones to go on PROFS. He maintained that all the officers should give it a try since it wasn't going to be a drag on the bottom line and since no one's overall budget costs were at risk.

THE OIS IMPLEMENTATION PLAN

In February 1984 a top-level PNM policy group approved a full-scale OIS project to roll out PROFS companywide to 900 users by year-end 1985. The estimated payback period for the project was just under three years. The schedule called for new users to be brought onto the PROFS network at the rate of 40 per month. An IBM 4381 computer was installed to replace the company's 4341 model. A training program was put together to introduce new users to the functions available through PROFS; four training classes were offered—one that introduced the features of PROFS and how to use them and three advanced classes to enhance user proficiency in document creation, ad hoc tools, and expanded OIS applications.

When the capacity of the IBM 4381 model was fully taken up at the 500-user level, an IBM 3084 mainframe was installed, giving PNM not only enough computing power to handle all the foreseeable PROFS users but also enough to permit major enhancements to the basic PROFS functions and to handle most of PNM's other data processing needs as well.

Although the number of users brought onto the system ran slightly behind schedule for the first nine months, by fall 1984 users were being put on the system at rates above the scheduled 40 users per month. The OIS project reached its goal of 900 users in October 1985, approximately 10 weeks ahead of schedule and $350,000 under budget.

Almost immediately, efforts began to add enhancement functions and major non-PROFS OIS capabilities to the system, including Megacalc (a mainframe spreadsheet system with business graphics capability), Information Center/1 (for use in filing and reporting), DisplayWrite/370 (a more sophisticated document composition software package), and Easygraph. An OIS user support program was established to provide several services on an ongoing basis:

- A telephone hotline available from 8 A.M. to 5 P.M. five days a week to give users quick problem resolution (the hotline was averaging 625 calls monthly)
- A consulting service that gave users one-on-one assistance to handle problems not able to be resolved over the phone
- Training classes in using the new tools/functions
- Periodic refresher courses in the use of PROFS and of the enhancements that had been added (for occasional users who might have forgotten or felt the need for more instructions and for users new to the system)
- A menu option on PROFS that provided "new bulletins" about upgrades to PROFS, dates for new classes, instructions for the newly introduced enhancements, and other information of value to users

Terry Othick, one of the managers deeply involved in implementing the project companywide, commented on some of the factors that contributed to the OIS project being completed ahead of schedule and under budget:

Doing the pilot was extremely important. It allowed us to gain knowledge and experience of how the operating system worked and get comfortable with running the system on a day-to-day basis. We were able to work out all of the bugs with a small, controlled, supportive audience.

Another big thing was that the pilot project included the offices of the folks on USET. We saw them as a key group because they needed to see firsthand what PROFS could do and they, of course, in the end would either support the project or not. The pilot helped sell them. Then when USET approved full-scale implementation, the senior officers agreed among themselves that they would be the first group to adopt OIS, to go through training, and to begin to use the system. Their taking the lead on this sent a signal to all the managers below them that this was something they had better look at too.

When we launched into marketing PROFS to the rest of the organization below USET, we did some things that surprised people. My I/S counterparts in other companies told me that their office automation implementation strategy was to offer OIS to managers and departments "free"—that is, the costs of OIS would either be added to their budgets automatically or else covered entirely in the I/S budget. What we did was go to each manager and ask if they wanted to try the system. If the answer was "yes," we would say "great, but, by the way, we're going to hit you with a $140 per month per user charge for it on your existing budget." That was the tough part of it. Many folks felt we shouldn't charge them for it. We explained that the way to absorb it was to do all those wonderful things that they said they could do in the ATT survey when we asked them about all of the benefits and savings they could generate in their areas if they had OIS to work with. A number of managers said "OK, let's go ahead." This was surprising to some people, but we never pressured any manager to put in OIS and we never told them how many terminals they could have in their areas. We felt since they would be paying for it out of their budgets, they would not opt to put in any more terminals than they could really justify.

Our marketing plan worked. Almost from the start, we had a waiting list to go on the system and get employees into the next training class.

Exhibit 5 shows the distribution of PROFS/OIS users across the company.

INTERVIEWS WITH USERS

The reactions of users of the PROFS/OIS network at PNM were generally favorable. Below are excerpts of interviews conducted by the case researcher. The first interview was with Ernie C. de Baca, staff analyst.

Q: Could you tell us how enthusiastic a user of OIS you are?
A: I'm a real fan. In fact, one of the things that I would miss most if I left this company would be not having OIS. It is a very good communication tool. The best part of it is the way it holds notes for you until you can respond to them. It gives a good trail.
Q: How easy is the system to use?
A: OIS is scary at first to someone who has never seen it because it's so big, but it's really simple if you devote the time to it.

EXHIBIT 5 **Distribution of Users of PNM's Office Information System, December 31, 1985**

Area of Company	Officials and Managers	Professionals	Technicians	Office and Clerical	Totals
Chairman and president (corporate office)	1	1	1		3
Meadows and Sunbelt	1			2	3
Corporate affairs	10	5		8	23
Corporate finance	27	16	1	13	57
Electric utility	297	360	55	112	824
Gas Company of New Mexico*	1			1	2
Totals	337	382	57	136	912†

*GCNM figures do *not* include approximately 75 PROFS IDs maintained on its own internal system.
†Total does *not* include 82 miscellaneous IDs (i.e., group-user IDs, lawyers, consultants, contractors, a doctor, etc.).

Q: How long did it take for you to become proficient with the system?
A: About a week of trying to make sure I really knew it.
Q: Tell us a little bit about how PROFS fits into your job.
A: I check every morning to see if there is any type of communication that I need to respond to. Our department needs to communicate with some of the higher management people who aren't readily available when you want them. Use of this tool provides access to them.
Q: What about the noncommunication aspects of PROFS and OIS?
A: I mostly use electronic mail, calendaring, document creation, and the spreadsheet functions. I have to look at a lot of data and work on many different reports. The OIS features help me gather data from other departments on a spreadsheet and not have to redo my spreadsheet every time I have a monthly report to turn out. It gives me quick access to that information without having to start over from scratch every time.
Q: How much time do you think that saves you?
A: It's just more efficient. It provides me a better way of doing my job.
Q: Do you think it allows you to get more done during the work day?
A: Yes. It provides a great amount of flexibility in my time.
Q: Does this system let you be your own secretary rather efficiently?
A: It can if you allow it to by doing all your own work. It also provides you with a way to let your secretary clean up things for you.
Q: Does your terminal stay on all day?
A: Yes.
Q: How long are you sitting at the terminal in a given day?
A: Three to four hours.
Q: Do you see your use going up, down, or staying about the same?
A: When you first become associated with OIS and its capabilities, usage goes up quite a bit. Then you plateau at a comfortable point for you.

The interview with Don Tidwell, design supervisor, generating engineering group, follows:

Q: How enthusiastic a user of PROFS are you?

A: Probably more so than the average user.

Q: What are your favorite features?

A: Notes, messages, scheduling, and electronic mail. Our particular group is a matrix organization. We, in turn, support several different projects. Our people are assigned to four or five projects at a time. In trying to support all of these projects, there are many meetings that have to be attended and decisions made, and it turns into a lot of communicating. Many of the people we deal with work at our San Juan station 180 miles away. Prior to OIS, we mostly used the telephone. You'd have to call, leave a message, call back, and go through the telephone tag game. With OIS, I can send them a quick note that is concise, and they can easily respond. Scheduling is now a breeze. I used to have to go around and match up schedules, but now I can just send out a note and find out where everyone stands. I don't have a lot of secretarial support; one girl in my area covers 17 people, so I can't just turn over tasks like that to a secretary.

Q: Are there any other aspects of the PROFS system that you use frequently?

A: I take advantage of the fact that we do a lot of correspondence on PROFS. If I send out a particular question over the network to several people and I need their concurrence on some issue, when they respond, I stick it in Notes and file it for documentation. I would be doing it by hand otherwise. I do that 10 or 15 times a day.

Q: What about some of the add-on features like Megacalc?

A: We have used Megacalc. I used it for setting up a work-load schedule for the people on my staff. One guy has five or six projects, and he has 20 or 30 hours a month committed to each, but they build up and taper off. I'd like to know three or four months ahead of time when he'll be free to take on another project. A spreadsheet does that and we used Megacalc for that purpose.

Q: What I've heard you saying is that OIS saves you a good bit of time, and it's low-quality time that you've been saving. What have you done with the extra time now that you have PROFS?

A: It just means that I'm able to work on other things sooner. I can focus on the long-term needs of a project.

Q: So it allows you to spend more time managing instead of doing the administrative support things?

A: It does speed things up. That's just as big a benefit as the time saved. Things happen sooner because of the OIS user connections.

Q: Do you have any rough estimates of about how much time you spend on the system?

A: A couple of hours.

Q: What's the first thing you do when you come to work?

A: Log on.

Q: What's next?

A: I open the Mail.

Q: Then what?

A: I check the Schedule.

Q: Do you turn off the system or leave it on during the day when you're working?

A: I leave it on till I go to lunch, turn it off during lunch, then turn it back on for the afternoon.

Q: Do you use the Reminder feature?

A: Yes.

Q: If we were to go to the people that you supervise and ask them if you are a more impersonal manager than you used to be because you use this computer to talk to them, what do you think they would say?

A: That's tough. Probably they would say that there are times when they would rather talk to me face to face. On the other hand, they might say they'd rather get a note than have me barge in every 20 minutes interrupting them. I don't know, but that isn't a concern that I've heard expressed. A lot of my people prefer this to a personal confrontation. I try to utilize it when it's proper and speak in person when I should.

Q: Do you find it pretty easy to pick out the issues that need eyeball-to-eyeball communication as opposed to those that can be handled on this system?

A: Yes, because you know the people and how they communicate; you can read into their writing style and see what their concerns are.

The casewriter's interview with Sherry Rice, clerical assistant, follows:

Q: How enthusiastic are you about the PROFS/OIS system?

A: I use it about four hours a day. My favorite features are Mail, Document Creation, Notes, Calendar, Phone Directory, and Stock. I like this system of doing things; it saves a lot of time.

Q: Has PROFS changed the way you do your job?

A: Yes. I don't use the typewriter or shorthand like I used to.

Q: Has OIS changed the relationship you have with the person you're secretary to?

A: No, I don't think so. The thing that PROFS helps a lot is when they're out of the office you can still send them notes. That cuts down on phone calls.

Q: How has it changed filing?

A: There's a lot less physical filing because it's all right there in the PROFS system.

Q: Do you like using OIS for opening the Mail?

A: Yes, I think it's a lot quicker.

Q: Why do you use Stock?

A: I like to know what our stock price is doing. I have a few shares.

Q: What do you call your machine?

A: The tube or the terminal. Mostly the tube.

Q: Is that a complimentary term?

A: Just a term.

Q: What are your complaints about PROFS?

A: When the system goes down, we lose a lot of documents.

Q: Does that happen very often?

A: Not really, but it's very frustrating when it does.

Q: Do you think you've been given enough training in the use of OIS?

A: They've offered enough, but I don't think I've taken enough.

Q: Why?

A: I don't know; I schedule it and then just don't go. I think that's true of a lot of people.

The casewriter found Ellen Wilson, manager of administrative services, San Juan plant, to be a real fan of the PROFS system:

Q: How enthusiastic a user of PROFS are you?

A: Quite enthusiastic. I couldn't get by without it.

Q: Can you tell us how you use it? What do you like?

A: I use Calendar. My secretary is quite comfortable and knowledgeable in the use of OIS because when I'm not there she checks all the Mail and the Calendar; we communicate that way rather than on the telephone. When I'm in Albuquerque, and I am quite a lot, we communicate via OIS. I use the basic memo- and letter-writing in Document Creation. I use the reminders on the calendar as well. I really believe that if my colleagues in Albuquerque and I didn't communicate a lot via this system, that we would find it very difficult to catch each other.

Q: Do you think this OIS communication saves you very much time?

A: Definitely. It's not more effective than the phone, but it is quicker and I utilize it to ask quick questions. It's not a substitute for the phone. I like face-to-face encounters, but it makes sure that when we talk, we're talking about something that we both need to have a discussion about.

Q: Does it change the way you communicate with your staff?

A: Yes. At my job in Albuquerque, I communicated with my staff on OIS a lot. We were all used to it and very comfortable with it. When I moved up to my present job at the San Juan plant, my staff was not used to it. I think it really changed the way they communicated with me. I use OIS for informal-type things. Often I write a note to someone who has been on vacation saying I hope they've had a good time, and I usually use OIS to send holiday wishes to everyone. When I first came here I would send messages just to say hello and get marvelous messages back.

Q: When you went to San Juan and discovered that your staff members weren't using OIS, how did you handle introduction of it to them?

A: I started out incorrectly. I made the assumption that if I let them know that I was a strong OIS user that they would begin using it; that didn't work at all. After a short while I realized that they were not even opening the Mail and reading the messages I sent to them on OIS. I then explained why I liked OIS, why and how I used it, and how it could help them. I ended up asking them to check their mail twice a day and just try that much. There was quite a bit of resistance to that. It was a machine to them. So I went back and explained again how it helped me to save time. They pointed out that it was too impersonal, so I agreed not to use OIS in place of a real need to talk to them personally. After about six months, I began to get responses. We're now doing more of our business together on OIS, though not as much as I'd like.

Q: Have you noticed any impact of OIS on your personal productivity?

A: When I first got to the plant, I wasn't very certain of the scope of the job and I found myself not using OIS all that much. I was returning a lot of the phone calls instead of answering back on OIS. Slowly I realized that I couldn't possibly return all the calls and still do my job. Most of my time saving is in being able to communicate with a lot of people faster and quicker. I also can do the short drafts on memos and letters quicker than I could writing them out and going through my secretary.

Ed Kist, manager of system planning, was more tempered in his enthusiasm for PROFS:

Q: How enthusiastic a user of OIS are you?
A: I'm enthusiastic about some uses of it. The parts that I like very much are Notes and the Calendar (which my secretary mostly uses for me). Things that I don't like about it are that it's frustratingly slow to me, the system seems to go down frequently, and there are functions that I don't feel are necessary to me as a manager that I'm probably paying for. It's expensive, too.
Q: How many people use this system in your group?
A: About 35.
Q: So that's a nice cut into your budget?
A: It makes a difference.
Q: About how much time is OIS saving you?
A: At least one half-hour a day, I think. I used to run down the halls and try to leave messages. OIS stops that.
Q: Has OIS changed the way you communicate with your staff?
A: Not a lot. I believe in personal contact, but it leverages the current style that I have.
Q: Has OIS made your style better?
A: I think it has made it more efficient. Sometimes I'll get a message from someone that I want to pass along to my staff. It's very easy to do that.
Q: How many people report to you in your group?
A: About five.
Q: Do you think with your improved ability to communicate using OIS that you could handle seven direct reports rather than just five?
A: I don't think that the number of people who report to me would be a function of the machine. The choice of how I allocate my half-hour average of time savings a day isn't going to be affected in a major way by the number of people that I have reporting to me. If I could handle seven, then it would be because of what those seven were doing and what my capabilities are and not necessarily because I'm 5 percent more productive using OIS.

Exhibit 6 shows use statistics for PNM's office automation system for a typical month.

EXHIBIT 6   **Use Statistics for PNM's OIS/PROFS Network for a Typical Month**

OIS/PROFS Functions	Times Accessed This Month	Total Elapsed Time (In seconds)	Average Number of Times Accessed per User	Average Elapsed Time per Use (In seconds)
(Total number of users = 985)				
Open the mail	87,080	36,578,531	88.4	420.06
Process notes and messages	33,247	10,369,303	32.7	311.89
Process schedules	14,900	3,927,451	15.3	263.59
Look at phone list	14,027	7,709,381	14.2	549.61
Prepare documents	7,784	9,497,960	7.9	1220.19
Look at current stock quote	7,430	1,183,067	7.5	159.23
Process postponed documents	6,294	7,776,956	6.4	1235.61
Facts	4,256	586,176	4.3	137.73
Megacalc	3,582	4,674,171	3.6	1304.91
Process the mail log	3,325	1,272,231	3.4	382.63
Add an automatic reminder	2,472	194	2.5	0.08
Job openings in PNM	2,019	323,710	2.0	160.33
Search for documents	945	133,040	1.0	140.78
IC/1 spreadsheet	730	941,251	.7	1289.38
List available commands	544	53,907	.6	99.09
Create author profile	530	65,907	.6	107.28
List note files	434	115,724	.4	266.65
Process distribution lists	420	98,666	.4	234.92
Process to-do lists	346	125,518	.35	362.77
List all PROFS users	334	24,387	.34	73.01
Look at financial/operating statements	321	143,868	.33	448.19
Change nicknames	294	45,465	.30	154.64
Check status of outgoing mail	264	5,640	.27	21.36
Select individual printer list	215	14,487	.22	67.38
Change user password	205	6,272	.21	30.60
List news	90	3,162	.09	35.13
Easygraf	70	19,335	.07	276.21
Look at PNM OIS guidelines	51	7,827	.05	153.47
Process documents from other source	47	1	.05	0.02
Budget	21	552	.02	26.29
Forms	14	3,408	.01	243.43
Issues	11	2,873	.01	261.18
Invest	4	11	.004	2.75
Look at new PROFS functions	2	3	.002	1.50
All others combined	1,498	916,493	1.5	611.81

Source: Company records.

MARY KAY COSMETICS, INC.*

Robin Romblad, The University of Alabama
Arthur A. Thompson, Jr., The University of Alabama

In spring 1983 Mary Kay Cosmetics, Inc. (MKC), the second-largest direct-sales distributor of skin care products in the United States, encountered its first big slowdown in recruiting women to function as Mary Kay beauty consultants and market the Mary Kay cosmetic lines. As of April, MKC's sales force of about 195,000 beauty consultants was increasing at only a 13 percent annual rate, down from a 65 percent rate of increase in 1980. The dropoff in the percentage of new recruits jeopardized MKC's ability to sustain its reputation as a fast-growing company. MKC's strategy was predicated on getting even larger numbers of beauty consultants to arrange "skin care classes" at the home of a hostess and her three to five guests; at the classes consultants demonstrated the Mary Kay Cosmetics line and usually sold anywhere from $50 to $200 worth of Mary Kay products. MKC's historically successful efforts to build up the size of its force of beauty consultants had given the company reliable access to a growing number of showings annually.

Even though MKC's annual turnover rate for salespeople was lower than that of several major competitors (including Avon Products), some 120,000 Mary Kay beauty consultants had quit or been terminated in 1982, making the task of recruiting a growing sales force of consultants a major, ongoing effort at MKC. Recruiting success was seen by management as strategically important. New recruits were encouraged to spend between $500 and $3,000 for sales kits and start-up inventories; the initial orders of new recruits accounted for over one third of MKC's annual sales. The newest recruits were also instrumental in helping identify and attract others to become Mary Kay beauty consultants.

Richard Rogers, MKC's cofounder and president, promptly reacted to the recruiting slowdown by announcing five changes in the company's sales force program:

- The financial incentives offered to active beauty consultants for bringing new recruits into the Mary Kay fold were increased by as much as 50 percent.
- A new program was instituted whereby beauty consultants who (1) placed $600 a month in wholesale orders with the company for three consecutive months and (2) recruited five new consultants who together placed $3,000 in wholesale orders a month for three straight months would win the free use of a cream-colored Oldsmobile Firenza for a year (this program supplemented the existing programs whereby top-performing beauty consultants could win the use of a pink Cadillac or pink Buick Regal).
- The minimum order size required of beauty consultants was increased from $400 to $600.

*The assistance and cooperation provided by many people in the Mary Kay organization are gratefully acknowledged. Copyright © 1986 by Arthur A. Thompson, Jr.

- The prices at which MKC wholesaled its products to consultants were raised by 4 percent.
- The requirements for attaining sales director status and heading up a sales unit were raised 25 percent; a sales director had to recruit 15 new consultants (instead of 12), and her sales unit was expected to maintain a monthly minimum of $4,000 in wholesale orders (up from $3,200).

In addition, MKC's 1984 corporate budget for recruiting was more than quadrupled and, as a special recruiting effort, the company staged a National Guest Night in September 1984 that consisted of a live closed-circuit telecast to 78 cities aired from Dallas, Texas, where MKC's corporate headquarters was located. Mary Kay salespeople all over the United States were urged to invite prospective recruits and go to one of the 78 simulcast sites.

NATIONAL GUEST NIGHT IN BIRMINGHAM

Jan Currier, senior sales director for MKC in the Tuscaloosa, Alabama, area, invited two other women and one of the casewriters to drive to Birmingham in her pink Buick Regal to attend what was billed as "The Salute to the Stars." On the way, Jan explained that as well as being entertaining, the evening's event would give everyone a chance to see firsthand just how exciting and rewarding the career opportunities were with MKC; she noted with pride that Mary Kay Cosmetics was one of the companies featured in the recent book *The 100 Best Companies to Work for in America*. As the Tuscaloosa entourage neared the auditorium in Birmingham, the casewriter observed numerous pink Cadillacs and pink Buick Regals in the flow of traffic and in the parking lot. Mary Kay sales directors were stationed at each door to the lobby, enthusiastically greeting each person and presenting a gift of Mary Kay cosmetics. Guests were directed to a table to register for prizes to be awarded later in the evening.

Inside the auditorium over 1,500 people awaited the beginning of the evening's program. A large theater screen was located at center stage. The lights dimmed promptly at 7 P.M. and the show began. The casewriter used her tape recorder and took extensive notes to capture what went on:

> **Mark Dixon** [*national sales administrator for the South Central division, appears on stage in Birmingham*]: Welcome, ladies and gentlemen, to National Guest Night, Mary Kay's Salute to the Stars. Tonight, you're going to be a part of the largest teleconference ever held by a U.S. corporation.
>
> Now please help me welcome someone all of us at Mary Kay love very dearly, National Sales Director from Houston, Texas, Lovie Quinn.
> [*The crowd stands and greets Lovie with cheers and applause.*]
> **Lovie Quinn** [*comes out on stage in Birmingham to join Mark Dixon. Lovie is wearing this year's Mary Kay national sales director suit of red suede with black mink trim.*]: Good evening, ladies and gentlemen, and welcome to one of the most exciting events in the history of Mary Kay. An evening with Mary Kay as she salutes the stars. . . . During the evening you'll learn about career opportunities. There will be recognition of our stars. We'll see the salute to them with gifts and prizes you hear about at Mary Kay. You'll hear about . . . pink Cadillacs . . . pink Buick Regals, and Firenza Oldsmobiles.
>
> You're going to hear about and see diamond rings and beautiful full-length mink coats. And of course we'll talk about MONEY.

If you've never attended a Mary Kay function you might very easily get the impression that we brag a lot. We like to think of it as recognition. . . . But we would not be able to give this recognition of success if you, the hostesses, our special guests, did not open up your homes so we may share with you and some of your selected friends the Mary Kay skin care program. For that reason we would like to show our appreciation at this time. Will all the special guests please stand up.

[*About 40 percent of the audience stands up and the remainder applaud the guests.*]

Lovie Quinn: Now I need to have all our directors line up on stage. [*Each one is dressed in a navy blue suit with either a red, green, or white blouse—the color of the blouse signifies director, senior director, or future director status.*] Enthusiasm and excitement are at the root of the Mary Kay philosophy. This is why we always start a meeting like this with a song. We invite all of you to join with the directors and sing the theme song, "That Mary Kay Enthusiasm." [*Lovie motions for the audience to stand; the choir of directors begins to clap and leads out in singing. The audience joins in quickly.*]

> I've got that Mary Kay enthusiasm up in my head, up in my head, up in my head.
> I've got that Mary Kay enthusiasm up in my head, up in my head to stay.
> I've got that Mary Kay enthusiasm down in my heart, down in my heart, down in my heart.
> I've got that Mary Kay enthusiasm down in my heart, down in my heart to stay.
> I've got that Mary Kay enthusiasm down in my feet, down in my feet, down in my feet.
> I've got that Mary Kay enthusiasm down in my feet, down in my feet to stay.
> I've got that Mary Kay enthusiasm up in my head, down in my heart, down in my feet.
> I've got that Mary Kay enthusiasm all over me, all over me to stay.

[*The song concludes to a round of applause. The crowd is spirited.*]

Lovie Quinn: Now we'd like to recognize a group of very special consultants. These ladies have accepted a challenge from Mary Kay and have held 10 beauty shows in one week. This is something really terrific. It demonstrates the successful achievement of a goal. We have found when you want to do something for our chairman of the board, Mary Kay Ash . . . you don't have to give furs. The most special gift you can give to Mary Kay is your own success. . . .

[*All of those recognized are seated in the first 10 rows with their guests; seating in the front rows is a special reward for meeting the challenge. The crowd applauds.*]

Lovie Quinn: It is almost time for the countdown to begin, but before it does one more special group must be recognized. These ladies are Mary Kay's Gold Medal winners. In one month they recruited *five* new consultants.

[*A number of ladies stand; they beam with pride and each has been awarded a medal resembling an Olympic gold medal. The audience gives them a nice round of applause.*]

Lovie Quinn [*Lovie continues to fill the crowd with excitement and anticipation.*]:   The countdown is going to be in just a few moments. It will be a treat for those of you that have not met Mary Kay before. Please help me count down the final 10 seconds before the broadcast.

[*But the crowd is so excited it starts the countdown when one minute appears on the screen. As the seconds wind down, the crowd gets louder with anticipation and then gets in sync chanting: 10, 9, 8, 7, 6, 5, 4, 3, 2, 1. More screams and applause.*

On the screen a Gold Mary Kay medallion appears, then the production lines at the plant are shown, and then trucks shipping the products. The audience claps as they see these on the screen. Headquarters is shown. Now a number of the Mary Kay sales directors are shown framed in stars on the screen. People clap when they recognize someone from their district. Loud applause fills the auditorium when Mary Kay Ash, MKC's chairman of the board and company cofounder, is shown in a star.

The Dallas-based part of the simulcast opens with female dancers dressed in pink and male dancers dressed in gray tuxedos. They perform the "Mary Kay Star Song," which includes a salute to various regions in the United States. The Birmingham crowd cheers when the South is highlighted.

A woman is chosen out of the audience in Dallas. Her name is Susan; the audience is told that at various intervals in the broadcast we will see her evolution into a successful Mary Kay Beauty consultant. Initially we see her get a feeling that maybe she can be a Mary Kay star. The message is that personal dreams of success can come true. Will she be successful? The answer comes back, "Yes, She Can Do It."

Mary Kay Ash is escorted on stage by her son Richard Rogers. She is elegantly dressed with accents of diamonds and feathers. The applause, the loudest so far, is genuinely enthusiastic and many in both the Dallas and Birmingham audiences are cheering loudly.]

Mary Kay Ash: Welcome everyone to our very first Salute to the Stars, National Guest Night. How exciting it is to think that right now over 100,000 people are watching this broadcast all over the United States. . . . Even though I can't see all of you, I can feel your warmth all the way to Dallas.

During the program this evening one expression you're going to hear over and over again is YOU CAN DO IT. . . . This is something we really believe in. What we have discovered is the seeds of greatness are planted in every human being. . . . Tonight we hope to inspire you, to get you to reach within yourself, to bring out some of those star qualities that I know you have. And no matter who you are and no matter where you live, I believe you can take those talents and go farther than you ever thought possible and we have a special place waiting just for you.

Now I would like to introduce someone who has a special place in my heart. Someone who has been beside me from the very beginning. Without him Mary Kay Cosmetics would not be what it is today. Please welcome your president and cofounder of our company, my son, Richard Rogers.

Richard Rogers [*steps to the microphone, accompanied by respectful applause.*]: When we started this company over 20 years ago my mother and I never dreamed we would be standing here talking live to over 100,000 of you all across the country. . . . Tonight we've planned a memorable evening just for you. A program that conveys the spirit of Mary Kay. Going back 21 years ago, Mary Kay saw a void in the cosmetics industry. The observation she made was that others were just selling products. No one was teaching women about their skin and how to care for it. . . . This is the concept on which she based her company. So on September 13, 1963, Mary Kay Cosmetics opened its doors in Dallas, Texas.

Throughout the decade Mary Kay's concepts continued to flourish. . . .

By the end of the 60s, Mary Kay Cosmetics had become a fully integrated manufacturer and distributor of skin care products. In 1970 the sales force had grown to 7,000 consultants in Texas and four surrounding states.

California was the first state MKC designated for expansion. When we first went there, no one had ever heard of Mary Kay Cosmetics. Within three years California had more consultants selling Mary Kay Cosmetics than the state of Texas. . . . With this success, expansion continued throughout the United States. . . . By 1975 MKC had grown to 700 sales directors, 34,000 consultants, and $35 million in sales.

International expansion was initiated in 1978 by selling skin care products in Canada. In just 36 months MKC became the fourth-largest Canadian cosmetic company. . . . Since that time, Mary Kay has expanded to South America, Australia, and in September we opened for business in the United Kingdom.

At the end of 1983, MKC had over 195,000 consultants. Sales had reached over $600 million around the world. . . . With total commitment to excellence setting the pace, MKC is still working towards achieving the goal of being the finest teaching-oriented skin care organization in the world. . . . Mary Kay is proud to have the human resources necessary to meet this goal. At Mary Kay P&L means more than profit and loss. It also stands for People and Love. People have helped MKC reach where it is today, and they will play a big part in where it will be tomorrow.

Tonight we're proud to announce the arrival of a book that expresses the Mary Kay philosophy of Golden Rule management, a book that outlines the management style that has contributed to the success of Mary Kay Cosmetics. The new book is *Mary Kay on People Management*. [*The crowd applauds at this announcement.*]

Mary Kay Ash [*reappears on stage.*]: We're so excited about the new book. I am pleased to have the opportunity to talk with you about it tonight. Actually, I started to write that book over 20 years ago. I had just retired from 25 years of direct sales. I wanted to share my experiences, so I wrote down my thoughts about the companies I had worked for. What had worked and what had not. . . . After expressing my ideas, I thought how wonderful it would be to put out these ideas of a company designed to meet women's needs into action. That is when Mary Kay Cosmetics was born. . . . The company helps women meet the goals they set for themselves. . . . I feel that is what has contributed to the success of the organization. Everyone at MKC starts at the same place, as a consultant, and everyone has the same opportunities for success.

[*The broadcast returns to the scenario of Susan as she becomes a new Mary Kay consultant. Susan sings about the doubts people have about her joining Mary Kay.*

She disregards this and decides to climb to success. At the end of the scene, she projects a positive, successful image that her friends and family recognize. The audience responds favorably.]

Dale Alexander [*national sales administrator for Mary Kay Cosmetics appears on stage in Dallas.*]: It is a great honor to be with you tonight and I want to add my most sincere welcome. . . . Recognition is one of the original principles on which our company is based. It's an essential ingredient in the Mary Kay formula for success. . . . I want to start out by recognizing the largest group. The group of independent businesswomen who are out there every day holding beauty shows, teaching skin care, selling our products, and sharing the Mary Kay opportunity. At this time will all of the Mary Kay beauty consultants across the nation stand to be recognized? [*In Birmingham the lights go up and the crowd applauds the consultants in the audience.*] Next we want to recognize the Star Consultants. . . . Will these ladies stand?

Many of our people are wearing small golden ladders. This is our Ladder of Success. Each ladder has a number of different jewels awarded for specific accomplishments during a calendar quarter. Star consultants earn rubies, sapphires, and diamonds to go on their ladders. The higher they climb, the more dazzling their ladders become. A consultant with all diamonds is known at Mary Kay as a top Star Performer. It is like wearing a straight-A report card on your lapel.

In addition to Ladders, consultants have an opportunity to earn great prizes each quarter. . . . This quarter's theme is Salute to the Stars. . . . and these prizes are out of this world.

[*The scene shifts to a description of the fall 1984 sales program; it utilizes a "Star Trek" theme, and across the screen is emblazoned "Starship Mary Kay in Search of the Prize Zone." Captain Mary Kay appears with members of her crew on Starship Mary Kay. She remarks their mission is to seek out prizes to honor those that reach for the sky. They are approaching the prize zone. The awards and prizes are flashed onto the screen.*]

The Prize Zone
Bonus Prizes Available
Based on Fourth-Quarter Sales

$1,800 wholesale sales	Cubic zirconia necklace and earrings or travel set with hair dryer
$2,400 wholesale sales	Leather briefcase with matching umbrella
$3,000 wholesale sales	Diamond earrings with 14K gold teardrops
$3,600 wholesale sales	Telephone answering machine
$4,200 wholesale sales	Sapphire ring
$4,800 wholesale sales	Electronic printer by Brother—fits in a briefcase
$6,000 wholesale sales	Diamond pendant—nine diamonds—.5 karat on a 18K gold chain

[*Even though this "space" presentation of prizes is humorous, the ladies know that the rewards are real; they respond as the scene ends with a round of applause and a buzz of excitement. The scene concludes with the message, "When you reach for the sky you bring home a star."*]

Mary Kay [*returns to the stage.*]: You can climb that ladder of success at Mary Kay. It is up to you to take that very first step. . . . There are so many rewards for being a Mary Kay consultant. There are top earnings, prizes, and lots of recognition. But there is even more to a Mary Kay career and that is the fulfillment of bringing beauty into the lives of others. . . .

When a woman joins our company she knows she can do it. But not alone. She'll receive support from many people. A big sister relationship will form between a new consultant and her recruiter. . . . Whoever invited you tonight thought you were a special person. She wanted to share this evening and introduce you to our company and let you see for yourself the excitement and enthusiasm Mary Kay people have when they are together. . . . The enthusiasm of our consultants and directors is responsible for our success.

[*The vignette about Susan returns to the screen. This time she is thinking about concentrating her efforts on recruiting. After five recruits, she will become a team leader. A good goal to strive for, she thinks. A woman that had doubted Susan's career earlier is the first one recruited. Then four more ladies are recruited: a waitress, a teacher, a stewardess, and a nurse. All kinds of people can be Mary Kay consultants. Susan has reached her goal—she is a team leader. The crowd applauds her success.*]

Dale Alexander [*returns to the microphone in Dallas.*]: There is the perfect goal of a Mary Kay career. And now it is time to recognize a very special group of individuals who are proof of this point. Will all the team leaders please stand and remain standing for a few moments? [*The lights go up and team leaders stand. All are wearing red jackets.*]

To qualify for a team leader, each consultant must recruit five new consultants. . . . And now will you please recognize these ladies' achievements with a round of applause? [*The audience applauds.*] Now it is time to draw for the prizes. In each of the 75 locations, two names will be drawn. These lucky people will both win this exquisite 14K diamond earring and pendant set. [*The crowd oohs and aahs when the jewelry is shown on the screen.*] These two winners will also be eligible for the prize to be given by Mary Kay when the broadcast resumes.

[*The lights go up in the Birmingham auditorium. Lovie draws two tickets from a big box. When she calls out the names, the winners scream and run on stage to accept their gifts. The crowd applauds the winners.*]

Lovie Quinn [*on the stage in Birmingham*]: Please join me in counting down the final seconds left before we rejoin the broadcast.

[*Everyone stands and enthusiastically counts off "11, 10, 9, 8, 7, 6, 5, 4, 3, 2, 1." The crowd applauds and cheers.*]

Mary Kay [*appears on the screen as the broadcast from Dallas is rejoined.*]: I wish I could be there to congratulate each winner. . . . The two lucky winners in each of the 75 cities are eligible to win the grand prize. . . . It used to be you just drew a number out of a hat. Now that is considered old-fashioned. Tonight, we'll use a computer. All I have to do is push a button and a city will be randomly selected. The local winners in that city will also win this .75 carat diamond ring. [*The crowd buzzes as a close-up of the ring is shown on the giant screen.*] Are you ready? OK. Here goes. [*Mary Kay presses a button.*] The lucky city is Philadelphia. [*The crowd applauds.*]

Congratulations, Philadelphia, and we will be sending each of you a ring real soon.

By the way, while we are talking about prizes, would you happen to have a spare finger for a diamond ring? [*The crowd cheers.*] Or could you squeeze into your closet room for a full-length mink coat? [*The crowd is really excited.*] Or is there by any chance a space in your driveway for a car? [*The crowd cheers and applauds. One member of the audience remarks how she would be glad to get rid of that old blue thing she is driving.*] Well, all you have to do is set your Mary Kay career goals high enough to achieve the recognition and rewards available just for you. . . .

I remember the first sales competition I set my goals to win. I worked so hard and all I won was a flounder light. [*The audience laughs.*] Does anyone know what you do with it? It is something you use when you put on waders and gig fish. [*The audience laughs again.*] I thought the prize was awful . . . but my manager was a fisherman and he thought it was great.

Winning that flounder light taught me a lesson. I decided if I was ever in a position to give awards, they would be things women appreciate, *not* flounder lights. . . . things women would love to have. Absolutely no washing machines and certainly no ironing boards. [*The audience shows their approval by cheers and applause.*] At MKC, you are rewarded for consistent sales and recruiting performance. . . . This past spring, a new program was added. . . . We call it our VIP program. It stands for Very Important Performer. . . . This program allows a person to win a cream-colored Oldsmobile Firenza with rich brown interior. . . . A consultant is eligible for this prize only three months after joining MKC.

Mary Kay Cosmetics can offer several unique career opportunities:

- A 50 percent commission on everything you sell.
- Earnings of a 12 percent commission on your recruit's sales.
- You work your own hours.
- After three months, you can be eligible for a car. The car is free. MKC pays the insurance.
- When you do well, you get a lot of recognition. Not dumb old things like turkeys and hams. We're talking diamonds and furs.
- You work up to management because of your own efforts and merit.

Other companies would think these things are part of a dream world. At Mary Kay, we do live in a dream world and our dreams do come true. [*The audience applauds loudly. The broadcast then returns to the scenario about Susan. She sets a goal to be a VIP. Through song and dance, her group illustrates setting goals and receiving recognition. Step by step they climb the ladder of recognition. The audience applauds this short scene on success.*]

Dale Alexander [*comes back to the Dallas stage.*]: We have some VIPs among us tonight. . . . Mary Kay's Very Important Performers. Will all the VIPs now stand? [*The lights go up in Birmingham; the VIPs stand and the audience applauds.*] Through her enthusiasm and hard work, each VIP has worked hard to achieve this status. And to recognize her accomplishments, she was awarded an Oldsmobile Firenza to show off her achievement and success. Now let's give all our VIPs a round of applause. [*The Birmingham and Dallas audiences respond with more applause.*]

Mary Kay Ash [*comes onto the stage in Dallas and the crowd in Birmingham turns its attention to the screen.*]: With Mary Kay you can achieve success. . . . All you have to do is break down your goals into small manageable steps. . . . You are able to move on to bigger accomplishments as you gain confidence in yourself.

Let's look at some of the provisions of the Mary Kay career plan and see how it works:

- Your products are purchased directly from the company.
- Generous discounts are offered on large orders.
- There are no territories. You can sell and recruit wherever you want.
- We provide our customers the best possible way to buy cosmetics. They can try the products in their own home before they buy.
- All Mary Kay products are backed by a full 100 percent money-back guarantee.

Mary Kay is a good opportunity to go into business for yourself. . . .

There are many benefits of running your own business. . . . You meet new people and at the same time you enjoy the support of the Mary Kay sisterhood. . . . Plus you earn financial rewards as well as prizes. . . .

Now we need to talk about the position of Mary Kay sales director. Directors receive income not only from shows, facials, and reorders but also from recruit commissions. . . . In addition they earn unit and recruiting bonuses from Mary Kay. . . . Some earn the privilege to drive pink Regals and Cadillacs. . . . Each year, hundreds of sales directors earn over $30,000 a year. And today in our company we have more women earning over $50,000 a year than any other company in America. [*The audience applauds.*] At the very top are our national sales directors. . . . Their average is about $150,000 a year in commissions. How about that? [*The audience applauds.*] Everyone at Mary Kay starts at the same place with the same beauty showcase. I've always said you can have anything in this world if you want it badly enough and are willing to pay the price. With that kind of attitude anyone can succeed at Mary Kay.

[*The vignette about Susan comes back onto the screen. Susan sets a goal to achieve sales director. She sings about how invigorating her new career is and how she now wants to be a coach, a teacher, a counselor, and a friend to others. Everyone around her recognizes how her success has positively affected her whole life. The scene ends and the audience applauds.*]

Dale Alexander [*comes onto the screen from Dallas.*]: Those individuals that advance on to directorship lead our organizations. They set the pace for their units. Will all our sales directors please stand? [*The sales directors stand as the lights go up in Birmingham and the audience applauds.*] Among all our directors there are some that have reached a very special level. They have earned the privilege of driving one of Mary Kay's famous pink cars. . . . One thing is guaranteed. Whenever you see one of those pink cars on the road, you know there is a top achiever behind the wheel. At this time, we want to honor all these ladies. [*First the Regal drivers stand and then the Cadillac drivers. The audience recognizes each group with applause.*] Finally, there is one last group we want to recognize. A group whose members have already committed to a future with Mary Kay. . . . They are our DIQs or directors in qualification. They are working towards meeting the goals to qualify for directorship. . . . Will all the DIQs stand for a round of applause?

[*The lights go up and the DIQs stand. They are recognized with applause from the audience. The lights fade and the scene shifts back to Dallas.*]

Mary Kay: I want to congratulate these ladies. Next week I'll have the pleasure of hostessing our traditional tea for the DIQs at my home. [*The audience applauds.*] Our DIQs are a perfect example of one of the points we have tried to make this evening. . . . You can set your goals and achieve them if you want them badly enough.

I've always felt our most valuable asset is not our product but our people. . . . I wish I could tell you all the success stories of consultants at MKC. . . . We have chosen a few stories we think best represent Mary Kay consultants. The first person you'll meet is Rena.

[*The audience applauds; Rena is recognized by the Mary Kay people present. The narrator of the film clip tells us that Rena has been with MKC for 17 years. She has been Queen of Unit Sales four consecutive years, an honor that was earned when the sales unit she managed exceeded $1 million in sales in one year. Her reward was four $5,000 shopping sprees at Neiman-Marcus Co. in Dallas. When she started, she was living on $300 a month in government housing with her husband and three small children. One day a friend offered to buy her dinner and pay for a babysitter if she would attend a meeting. She couldn't pass up this offer so she went to the Mary Kay meeting. The meeting inspired her and she joined MKC. At the end, we learn that Rena has had cancer for the last eight years, a fact that is not well known; the point is made that it has never affected her ability to succeed with Mary Kay Cosmetics. The crowd applauds her success story.*

Next comes a film clip about Ruel; the audience is told that Ruel was raised in Arkansas, a daughter of a sharecropper. She joined Mary Kay in 1971. By 1976 she was a national sales director. A career with Mary Kay has given her confidence. She has two children in medical school and one of her sons just won a national honor, the Medal of Valor. All of this she attributes to Mary Kay. Her children saw her achieve and they knew they could too. Her career with Mary Kay has allowed her to climb up the scale from a poor sharecropper's daughter to become financially independent. Along the way, she has had the opportunity to meet many wonderful people. As her success story ends, the audience applauds.

The third story is about Arlene. Arlene has been a national sales director since 1976. She achieved this just five years after joining MKC. She had been at home for 13 years and wanted to have her own business, set her own hours, and write her own checks. She found she could achieve these goals in a career with Mary Kay. Arlene, we are told, has been able to reach inside herself and achieve great success. Arlene testifies that one of her biggest rewards at Mary Kay has been helping other women achieve the goals they set. The audience loudly applauds the last of the success stories.]

Mary Kay: I am so proud of these ladies. . . . It makes me feel good to be able to offer all these wonderful opportunities to so many women.

Every journey begins with a single step. All you have to do is make up your mind that YOU can do it! Isn't it exciting. You CAN do it.

All you need to start a Mary Kay career is a beauty case. It carries everything: vanity trays, mirrors, products, and product literature.

Tonight it becomes easier. . . . If you join us as a beauty consultant tonight, we will give you your beauty showcase. [*The audience interrupts with a round of applause.*] When you submit your Beauty Consultant agreement along with your first wholesale order, you will receive the beauty case free, an $85 value.

At Mary Kay you'll make lasting friends and you'll achieve a feeling of growth. . . . Tonight we wanted to give you a feel for Mary Kay Cosmetics. We have a place for you to shine. . . . Believe in yourself and you can do anything.

[*The broadcast from Dallas concludes; the audience stands and applauds the program.*]

Lovie Quinn [*comes on stage in Birmingham.*]: I started at Mary Kay just to earn money for Christmas. I told Mary Kay I could only work four hours a week. Believe it or not Mary Kay welcomed me into the organization.

Things were different then. There were no manuals or guides. I was given my first cosmetics in a shoe box. Mary Kay Cosmetics has come a long way. Each consultant has her own beauty case and is trained in skin care.

Last year I earned over $112,000. This does not include my personal sales. . . . I am now driving my 13th pink Cadillac. . . . For three years I have been in the half-million dollar club. The prizes for this honor include either a black mink, a white mink, or a diamond ring, all worth $10,000 each. I have all three.

Mary Kay Cosmetics offers many opportunities to women. . . . Tonight, if you join MKC, I would be honored to sign your agreement. This will let Mary Kay know you made your commitment tonight.

[*Lovie invites the new consultants to meet her up front. The audience applauds her. Many of the women eagerly go up to meet Lovie and have their agreements signed.*]

THE DIRECT-SALES INDUSTRY

In 1984 Avon was the acknowledged leader among the handful of companies that chose to market cosmetics to U.S. consumers using direct-sales techniques; Avon, with its door-to-door sales force of 400,000 representatives, had worldwide sales of about $2 billion. Mary Kay Cosmetics was the second-leading firm (see Exhibit 1). Other well-known companies whose salespeople went either door-to-door with their product or else held "parties" in the homes of prospective customers included Amway Corp. (home cleaning products), Shaklee Corp. (vitamins and health foods), Encyclopedia Britannica, Tupperware (plastic dishes and food containers), Consolidated Foods' Electrolux division (vacuum cleaners), and StanHome (parent of Fuller Brush). The direct-sales industry also included scores of lesser known firms selling about every product imaginable—clothing, houseplants, toys, and financial services. Although Stanley Home Products invented the idea, Mary Kay and Tupperware were the best-known national companies using the "party plan" approach to direct selling.

The success enjoyed by Avon and Mary Kay was heavily dependent upon constantly replenishing and expanding their sales forces. New salespeople not

| E X H I B I T   1 | **Estimated Sales of Leading Direct-Selling Cosmetic Companies, 1983** |

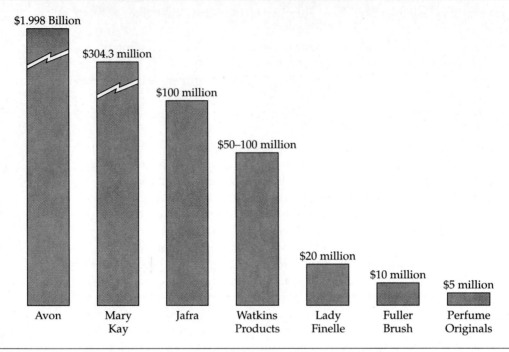

Source: "Reopening the Door to Door-to-Door Selling," *Chemical Business*, February 1984.

only placed large initial orders for products but they also recruited new people into the organization. Revenues and revenue growth thus were a function of the number of representatives as well as the sales productivity of each salesperson. Market size was not seen as a limiting factor for growth because direct-sales companies typically reached fewer than half the potential customer base.

Direct selling was grounded in capitalizing on networking relationships. Salespeople usually got their starts by selling first to relatives, friends, and neighbors, all the while looking for leads to new prospects. Direct-sales specialists often believed that party-plan selling was most successful among working class, ethnic, and small-town population groups where relationships were closer knit and where the social lives of women had a high carryover effect with work and high school. However, industry analysts saw several trends working against the networking approach and party plan type of direct selling—rising divorce rates, the scattering of relatives and families across wider geographic areas, weakening ties to ethnic neighborhoods, declines in the number and strength of the "old girls" networks in many towns and neighborhoods, increased social mobility, the growing popularity of apartment and condominium living where acquaintances and relationships were more transient, and the springing up of bedroom communities and subdivisions populated by commuters and/or by families that stayed only a few years.

In the 1980s, direct-selling companies began to have problems recruiting and retaining salespeople. During the two most recent recessionary periods in the United States, it was thought that the pool of potential sales-women available for recruitment into direct-sales careers would expand owing to above-normal unemployment rates. It didn't happen. As it turned out, many women became the sole family support and even greater numbers sought steady, better-paying jobs in other fields. Part-time job opportunities mushroomed outside the direct-sales field as many service and retailing firms started hiring part-time permanent workers rather than full-time permanent staffs because part-time workers did not have to be paid the same extensive fringe benefits that full-time employees normally got. When the economy experienced upturns, the pool for direct-sales recruits shrank even more as people sought security in jobs offering regular hours and a salary; in 1983 all direct-sales companies reported increased difficulty in getting people to accept their part-time, sales-oriented, commission-only offers of employment.

Avon and Mary Kay were both caught offguard by these unpredicted events. Staffing plans at Avon had originally called for expansion in the number of sales force representatives from 400,000 in 1983 to 650,000 by 1987; in 1984 the company revised the 1987 goal down to 500,000 representatives. Four straight years of declining earnings convinced Avon that the traditional approach of depending on increasing the number of representatives for growth was not feasible any longer.

Sarah Coventry, a home-party jewelry firm, decided in 1984 that relying solely upon direct-selling approaches would not only be a continuing problem but also a growing problem. The company began to look for ways to supplement its direct-sales methods and shortly announced a plan to begin to sell Sarah Coventry products in retail stores. Fuller Brush, a long-standing door-to-door seller, began to distribute mail-order catalogs displaying a wider line of "househelper" products.

As of 1984, virtually every company in the direct-sales industry was critically evaluating the extent to which changes in the economy and in employment demographics would affect the success of direct selling. Many firms, including Avon and Mary Kay, were reviewing their incentive programs and sales organization methods. A number of industry observers as well as company officials believed some major changes would have to be made in the way the direct-sales industry did business.

MARY KAY ASH

Before she reached the age of 10, Mary Kay had the responsibility of cleaning, cooking, and caring for her invalid father while her mother worked to support the family. During these years, Mary Kay's mother encouraged her daughter to excel. Whether at school or home, Mary Kay was urged to put forth her best efforts. By the time she was a teenager, Mary Kay had become a classic over-achiever, intent on getting good grades and winning school contests. Over and over again, she heard her mother say "you can do it." Years later, Mary Kay noted on many occasions, "The confidence my mother instilled in me has been a tremendous help."[1]

---

[1]Mary Kay Ash, *Mary Kay* (New York: Harper & Row, 1981), p. 3.

Deserted by her husband of 11 years during the Great Depression, Mary Kay found herself with the responsibility of raising and supporting three children under the age of eight. Needing a job with flexible hours, she opted to try a career in direct sales with Stanley Home Products, a home-party housewares firm. One of the first goals Mary Kay set at Stanley was to win Stanley's Miss Dallas Award, a ribbon honoring the employee who recruited the most new people in one week; she won the award during her first year with Stanley. After 13 years with Stanley, Mary Kay joined World Gift, a direct-sales company involved in decorative accessories; a few years later she was promoted to national training director. Her career and life were threatened in 1962 by a rare paralysis of one side of the face.

After recovery from surgery, she decided to retire from World Gift; by then she had remarried and lived in a comfortable Dallas neighborhood. She got so bored with retirement she decided to write a book on her direct-sales experiences. The more she wrote, the more she came to realize just how many problems women faced in the business world. Writing on a yellow legal pad at her kitchen table, Mary Kay listed everything she thought was wrong with male-run companies; on a second sheet she detailed how these wrongs could be righted, how a company could operate in ways that were responsive to the problems of working women and especially working mothers, and how women could reach their top potential in the business world. Being restless with retirement, she decided to do something about what she had written on the yellow pad and began immediately to plan how she might form a direct-sales company that had no sales quotas, few rules, flexible work hours, and plenty of autonomy for salespeople.

Finding a product to market was not a problem. In 1953, when she was conducting a Stanley home party at a house "on the wrong side of Dallas," she had noticed that all the ladies present had terrific-looking skin. It turned out that the hostess was a cosmetologist who was experimenting with a skin care product and all the guests were her guinea pigs. After the party, everyone gathered in the hostess's kitchen to get samples of her latest batch. The product was based on a formula that the woman's father, a hide tanner, developed when he accidentally discovered that some tanning lotions he made and used regularly had caused his hands to look much younger than his face. The tanner decided to apply these solutions to his face regularly, and after a short time his facial skin began looking more youthful too. The woman had since worked with her father's discovery for 17 years, making up batches that had the chemical smell of tanning solutions, putting portions in empty jars and bottles, and selling them as a sideline; she gave out instructions for use written in longhand on notebook paper. Mary Kay offered to try some of the hostess's latest batch and, despite the fact that it was smelly and messy, soon concluded that it was so good she wouldn't use anything else. Later, she became convinced that the only reason the woman hadn't made the product a commercial success was because she lacked marketing skills.

In 1963, using $5,000 in savings as working capital, she bought the formulas and proceeded to organize a beauty products company that integrated skin care instruction into its direct-sales approach. The company was named Beauty by Mary Kay; the plan was for Mary Kay to take responsibility for the sales part of the company and for her second husband to serve as chief administrator. One month before operations were to start, he died from a heart attack. Her children persuaded her to go ahead with her plans, and Mary Kay's 20-year-old son, Richard Rogers, agreed to take on the job of administration of the new company. In September 1963, they opened a small store in Dallas with one shelf of inventory and nine of Mary Kay's friends as saleswomen. Mary Kay herself had limited expectations for the company and never dreamed that its sphere of operations would extend beyond Dallas.

All of Mary Kay's lifelong philosophies and experiences were incorporated into how the company operated. The importance of encouragement became deeply ingrained in what was said and done. "You Can Do It" was expanded from a technique used by her mother to a daily theme at MKC. Mary Kay's style was to "praise people to success." She put into practice again the motivating role that positive encouragement had played in her own career; recognition and awards were made a highlight of the sales incentive programs that emerged. By 1984, recognition at MKC ranged from a single ribbon awarded for a consultant's first $100 show to a $5,000 shopping spree given to million-dollar producers.

The second important philosophy Mary Kay stressed concerned personal priorities: "Over the years, I have found that if you have your life in the proper perspective, with God first, your family second, and your career third, everything seems to work out."[2] She reiterated this belief again and again, regularly urging employees to take stock of their personal priorities and citing her own experience and belief as a positive example. She insisted on an all-out, firmwide effort to accommodate the plight of working mothers. Mary Kay particularly stressed giving beauty consultants enough control over how their selling efforts were scheduled so that problems with family matters and sick children were not incompatible with a Mary Kay career. A structure based on no sales quotas, few rules, and flexible hours was essential, Mary Kay believed, because working mothers from time to time needed the freedom to let work demands take a backseat to pressing problems at home.

Fairness and personal ethics were put in the forefront, too. The Golden Rule (treating others as you would have them treat you) was high on Mary Kay's list of management guidelines:

> I believe in the Golden Rule and try to run the company on those principles. I believe that all you send into the lives of others will come back into your own. I like to see women reaching into themselves and coming out of their shells as the beautiful person that God intended them to be. In my company women do not have to claw their way to the top. They can get ahead based on the virtue of their own ethics because there's enough for everyone.[3]

To discourage interpersonal rivalry and jealousy, all rewards and incentives were pegged to reaching plateaus of achievements; everybody who reached the target level of performance became a winner. Sales contests based on declaring first place, second place, and third place winners were avoided.

---

[2]Ibid., p. 56.

[3]As quoted in "The Beauty of Being Mary Kay," *Marketing and Media Decisions*, December 1982, pp. 150, 152.

MKC, Inc.

The company succeeded from the start. First-year wholesale sales were $198,000; in the second year, sales reached $800,000. At year-end 1983, wholesale revenues exceeded $320 million. Major geographical expansion was initiated during the 1970s. Distribution centers were opened in California, Georgia, New Jersey, and Illinois, and the company expanded its selling efforts internationally to Canada, Argentina, Australia, and the United Kingdom.

Early on, Mary Kay and Richard decided to consult a psychologist to learn more about their personalities. Testing revealed that Mary Kay was the type who, when encountering a person bleeding all over a fine carpet, would think of the person's plight while Richard would think first of the carpet. This solidified their decision for Mary Kay to be the company's inspirational leader and for Richard to concentrate on overseeing all the business details.

In 1968 the company name was changed to Mary Kay Cosmetics, Inc. Also during 1968 the company went public and its stock was traded in the over-the-counter market; in 1976 MKC's stock was listed on the New York Stock Exchange. Income per common share jumped from $0.16 in 1976 to $1.22 in 1983. An 11-year financial summary is presented in Exhibit 2; Exhibits 3 and 4 provide additional company data.

Richard Rogers, president, gave two basic reasons for the success of MKC:

> We were filling a void in the industry when we began to teach skin care and makeup artistry and we're still doing that today. And second, our marketing system, through which proficient customers achieve success by recruiting and building their own sales organization, was a stroke of genius because the by-product has been management. In other words, we didn't buy a full management team, they've been trained one by one.[4]

One of the biggest challenges MKC had to tackle during the 1970s was how to adapt its strategy and operating style in response to the influx of women into the labor force. Full- and part-time jobs interfered with attending beauty shows during normal working hours, and many working women with children at home had a hard time fitting beauty shows on weeknights and weekends into their schedules. To make the beauty show sales approach more appealing to working women, the company began to supplement its standard "try before you buy" and "on-the-spot delivery" sales pitch themes. Consultants were trained to tout the ease with which MKC's scientifically formulated skin care system could be followed, the value of investing in good makeup and attractive appearance, the up-to-date glamour and wide selection associated with MKC's product line, the flexibility of deciding what and when to buy, and the time-saving convenience of having refills and "specials" delivered to their door instead of having to go out shopping. Mary Kay consultants quickly picked up on the growing popularity of having beauty shows on Tuesday, Wednesday, and Thursday nights; a lesser proportion of weekday hours were used for morning and afternoon showings, and a greater proportion came to be used for seeking and delivering reorders from ongoing users.

MKC's corporate sales goal was to reach $500 million in revenues by 1990. As of 1984, about 65 percent of total sales were made to customers at beauty

---

[4]Mary Kay Cosmetics, Inc. "A Company and a Way of Life," company literature.

Selected Financial Data, Mary Kay Cosmetics, Inc., 1973–1983
(In thousands, except per-share data)

	1973	1974	1975	1976	1977	1978	1979	1980	1981	1982	1983
Net sales	$22,199	$30,215	$34,947	$44,871	$47,856	$53,746	$91,400	$166,938	$235,296	$304,275	$323,758
Cost of sales	6,414	9,054	10,509	14,139	14,562	17,517	27,584	52,484	71,100	87,807	88,960
Selling, general, and administrative expenses	9,674	13,128	15,050	19,192	21,394	27,402	45,522	86,998	120,880	154,104	168,757
Operating income	6,111	8,033	9,388	11,540	11,900	8,827	18,304	27,456	43,316	62,364	66,041
Interest and other income, net	377	443	202	501	175	660	493	712	1,485	2,763	3,734
Interest expense	58	54	60	43	212	504	958	635	1,014	1,284	2,886
Income before income taxes	6,430	8,422	9,530	11,998	11,863	8,983	17,839	27,533	43,787	63,843	66,889
Provision for income taxes	3,035	3,973	4,480	5,854	5,711	4,110	8,207	12,398	19,632	28,471	30,235
Net income	$ 3,395	$ 4,449	$ 5,050	$ 6,144	$ 6,152	$ 4,873	$ 9,632	$ 15,135	$ 23,155	$ 35,372	$ 36,654
Net income per common share	$.09	$.11	$.13	$.16	$.17	$.15	$.33	$.52	$.82	$1.18	$1.22
Cash dividends per share	$.01	$.03	$.03	$.05	$.05	$.06	$.06	$.09	$.10	$.11	$.12
Average common shares	38,800	38,864	38,982	39,120	35,480	33,408	29,440	28,884	29,324	29,894	30,138
Total assets	$19,600	$24,743	$27,996	$34,331	$35,144	$36,305	$50,916	$ 74,431	$100,976	$152,457	$180,683
Long-term debt	$ 756	$ 87	$ 42	—	$ 5,592	$ 3,558	$ 4,000	$ 3,000	$ 2,366	$ 4,669	$ 3,915
Return on average stockholders' equity			21%	23%	24%	20%	38%	48%	48%	45%	32%
Stock prices											
Year high			2³/₄	2⁷/₈	2⁵/₈	1⁷/₈	3⁷/₈	8³/₄	18³/₄	28¹/₂	47¹/₈
Year low			1⁷/₈	1³/₄	1¹/₂	1¹/₄	1¹/₄	3	6¹/₈	8³/₈	13¹/₈

Source: Mary Kay Cosmetics, Inc., 1983 Annual Report.

EXHIBIT 3   **Growth in the Number of MKC Sales Directors
and Beauty Consultants, 1973–1983**

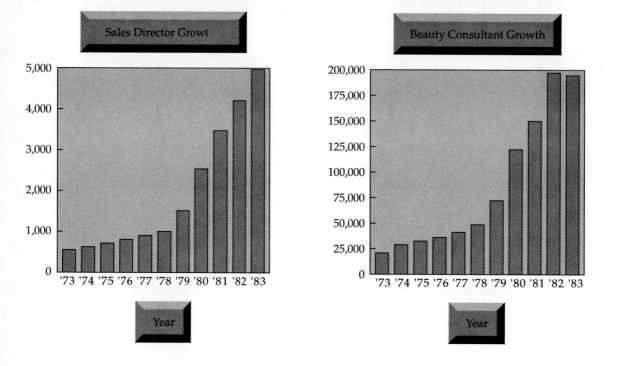

	Average Number of Consultants	**Net Sales ($000)**	**Average Annual Sales Productivity per Consultant**
1983	195,671	$323,758	$1,655
1982	173,137	304,275	1,757
1981	134,831	235,296	1,745
1980	94,983	166,938	1,758
1979	57,989	91,400	1,576

Source: 1983 Annual Report.

shows. However, it was expected that as the size of the company's customer base grew, the percentage of orders from repeat buyers would rise well above the present 35 percent level. MKC estimated that the average client spent over $200 a year on cosmetics. The company saw its target clientele as middle-class women in the 18–34 age group primarily and in the 35–44 age group secondarily and believed that a big percentage of its customers consisted of suburban housewives and white-collar clerical workers. The company's literature always pictured upscale women, dressed in a classy and elegant yet understated way, in either the role of a Mary Kay beauty consultant or the role of a user of Mary Kay cosmetics. As company figurehead, Mary Kay Ash personally made a point of being fashionably and expensively dressed, with perfect makeup and hairstyle—a walking showcase for the company's products and a symbol of the professionally successful businesswoman (Exhibit 5).

E X H I B I T 4   **Percentage Breakdown of Product Sales at Mary Kay Cosmetics, 1979–1983**

	1979	1980	1981	1982	1983
Skin care products for women	49%	52%	49%	46%	44%
Skin care products for men	1	2	1	1	1
Makeup items	26	22	26	26	30
Toiletry items for women	10	10	10	12	11
Toiletry items for men	2	2	2	2	2
Hair care	2	2	2	2	2
Accessories	10	10	10	11	10
Total	100%	100%	100%	100%	100%

Source: 1983 Annual Report.

E X H I B I T 5   **Mary Kay Ash in 1983**

Source: 1983 Annual Report (picture on front cover).

MANUFACTURING

When Mary Kay Cosmetics commenced operations in 1963, the task of making the products was contracted out to a private Dallas-based manufacturing company. Mary Kay explained why:

> In 1963 I had no previous experience in the cosmetics industry; my forte was recruiting and training salespeople. After I acquired the formulas for the skin-care products, the first thing I did was seek out the most reputable cosmetics manufacturer I could find. Specifically I wanted a firm that not only made quality products, but observed the Food and Drug Administration's regulatory requirements to the letter. I knew it would be a fatal mistake to attempt to cut corners. With the right people in charge, we would never have to concern ourselves with that aspect of the business.[5]

In 1969, MKC built a 300,000-square-foot manufacturing and packaging facility adjacent to corporate headquarters. Packaging, warehousing, purchasing, and research labs were all housed in this location. Also included was a printing setup that created Mary Kay labels in English, Spanish, and French. Many of the operations were automated.

The company's scientific research approach to skin care was supported by a staff of laboratory technicians skilled in cosmetic chemistry, dermatology, physiology, microbiology, and package engineering. Ongoing tests were conducted to refine existing items and to develop new products. Laboratory staffs were provided with the comments and reactions about the products that came in from the beauty consultants and their customers. Consultants were strongly encouraged to report on their experiences with items and to relay any problems directly to the laboratory staff. About 80 percent of the R&D budget was earmarked for improving existing products.

MKC believed that it was an industry leader in researching the properties of the skin (as concerned skin elasticity and moisture) and the anatomy of skin structure. Much of the research at MKC was performed in cooperation with academic institutions, particularly the University of Pennsylvania and the University of Texas Health Science Center.

PRODUCT LINE AND DISTRIBUTION POLICIES

As of 1984, the Mary Kay product line consisted of the Basic Skin Care Program for various skin types, the glamour collection, the body care products line, and a line of men's products called Mr. K. Most of the women's products were packaged in pink boxes and jars. When the company first began operations, Mary Kay personally put a lot of thought into packaging and appearance:

> Since people do leave their toiletries out, I wanted to package our cosmetics so beautifully that women would *want* to leave them out. So I was looking for a color that would make a beautiful display in all those white bathrooms. There were some shades of blue that were attractive, but the prettiest complementary color seemed to be a delicate pink. It also occurred to me that pink is considered a more feminine color. But my main reason for choosing it was that delicate pink seemed

---

[5]Mary Kay Ash, *Mary Kay on People Management* (New York: Warner Books, 1984), p. 13.

to look prettier than anything else in those white tile bathrooms. And from that I gained a *pink* reputation.[6]

Mr. K, the men's line, was introduced in the 1960s in response to a number of confessions from men who used their wives' Mary Kay products. A rich chocolate brown package accented with silver was chosen for Mr. K. The men's line included a Basic Skin Care Program as well as lotions and colognes. The majority of Mr. K purchases were made by women for their husbands and boyfriends.

Consultants bought their supplies of products directly from MKC at wholesale prices and sold them at a 100 percent markup over wholesale. To make it more feasible for consultants to keep an adequate inventory on hand, the product line at MKC was kept streamlined, about 50 products. Mary Kay consultants were encouraged to carry enough products in their personal inventories that orders could be filled on the spot at the beauty shows. As an incentive to support this practice, MKC offered special awards and prizes when consultants placed orders of $1,500 or more.

A consultant could order as many or as few of the company's products as she chose to inventory. Most consultants stockpiled those items that sold especially well with their own individual clientele, and consultants also had the freedom to offer special promotions or discounts to customers. Nearly 50 percent of sales were for the skin care products that had evolved from the hide tanner's discovery. Consultants were required to pay for all orders with cashier's checks or money orders prior to delivery. MKC dealt only on a cash basis to minimize accounts receivables problems; according to Mary Kay, "Bad debts are a major reason for failure in other direct-sales companies." In 1984, the average initial order of new consultants for inventory was about $1,000 ($2,000 in retail value). Consultants who decided to get out of the business could resell their inventories to MKC at 90 percent of cost.

During the company's early years, consultants were supplied only with an inventory of items to sell; shipments arrived in plain boxes. There were no sales kits and no instruction manuals to assist in sales presentations. However, by the 1970s, each new recruit received training in skin care techniques and was furnished with a number of sales aids. Later, new consultants were required to buy a beauty showcase containing everything needed to conduct a beauty show (samples, pink mirrors, pink trays used to distribute the samples, and a step-by-step sales manual that included suggested dialogue. In 1984 the showcase was sold to new consultants for $85. Along with the showcase came a supply of beauty profile forms to use at showings; guests filled out the form at the beginning of the show, and from the information supplied a consultant could readily prescribe which of the several product formulas was best suited for the individual's skin type.

In addition to the income earned from product sales, consultants earned bonuses or commissions on the sales made by all of the recruits they brought in. MKC paid consultants with one to four recruits a bonus commission equal to 4 percent on the wholesale orders of the recruits. A consultant with five or

---

[6]Ash, *Mary Kay*, pp. 150–51.

more recruits earned an 8 percent commission on the orders placed by recruits, or 12 percent if she also placed $600 a month in wholesale orders herself. MKC consultants who were entitled to a 12 percent commission and who had as many as 24 recruits were averaging about $950 monthly in bonuses and recruitment commissions as of 1984.

MKC's Sales Organization

The basic field organization unit for MKC's 195,000-person force of beauty consultants was the sales unit. Each sales unit was headed by a sales director who provided leadership and training for her group of beauty consultants. The top-performing sales directors were designated as national sales directors, a title that signified the ultimate achievement in the Mary Kay career sales ladder. A corporate staff of seven national sales administrators oversaw the activities of the sales directors in the field and their units of beauty consultants.

The sales units were not organized along strict geographical lines, and sales directors were free to recruit consultants anywhere; Mary Kay explained the logic for this approach:

> One of the first things I wanted my dream company to eliminate was assigned territories. I had worked for several direct-sales organizations in the past, and I knew how unfairly I had been treated when I had to move from Houston to St. Louis because of my husband's new job. I had been making $1,000 a month in commissions from the Houston sales unit that I had built over a period of eight years and I lost it all when I moved. I felt that it wasn't fair for someone else to inherit those Houston salespeople whom I had worked so hard to recruit and train.
>
> Because we don't have territories at Mary Kay Cosmetics, a director who lives in Chicago can be vacationing in Florida or visiting a friend in Pittsburgh and recruit someone while there. It doesn't matter where she lives in the United States; she will always draw a commission from the company on the wholesale purchases made by that recruit as long as they both remain with the company. The director in Pittsburgh will take the visiting director's new recruit under her wing and train her; the recruit will attend the Pittsburgh sales meetings and participate in the local sales contests. Although the Pittsburgh director will devote a lot of time and effort to the new recruit, the Chicago director will be paid the commissions. We call this our "adoptee" program.
>
> The Pittsburgh recruit may go on to recruit new people on her own. No matter where she lives, she becomes the nucleus for bringing in additional people for the director who brought her into the business. As long as they're both active in the company, she will receive commissions from the company on her recruit's sales activity.
>
> Today we have more than 5,000 sales directors, and most of them train and motivate people in their units who live outside their home states. Some have beauty consultants in a dozen or more states. Outsiders look at our company and say, "Your adoptee program can't possibly work!" But it does work. Each director reaps the benefits from her recruits in other cities and helps other recruits in return.[7]

---

[7] Ash, *People Management*, pp. 2–3.

THE BEAUTY CONSULTANT

Nearly all of MKC's beauty consultants had their first contact with the company as a guest at a beauty show. A discussion of career opportunities with Mary Kay was a standard part of the presentation at each beauty show. As many as 10 percent of the attendees at beauty shows were serious prospects as new recruits.

All beauty consultants were self-employed and worked on a commission basis. Everyone in the entire MKC sales organization started at the consultant level. The progression of each consultant up the "ladder of success" within the MKC sales organization was tightly linked to (1) the amount of wholesale orders the consultant placed with MKC, (2) her abilities to bring in new sales recruits, and (3) the size of the wholesale orders placed by these recruits. There were five rungs on the ladder of success for consultants, with qualifications and rewards as follows:

1. *New Beauty Consultant* (member of "Perfect Start Club").
   "Perfect Start Club" qualifications:

   Study and complete Perfect Start workbook.

   Observe three beauty shows.

   Book a minimum of eight shows within two weeks of receiving beauty showcase.

   Awards and recognition:

   Receives "Perfect Start" pin.

   Earns 50 percent commission on retail sales (less any discounts given to customers on special promotions).

   Becomes eligible for a 4 percent recruiting commission on wholesale orders placed by active personal recruits (to be considered active, a consultant had to place at least a $600 minimum wholesale order during the current quarter).

2. *Star Consultant.*
   Qualifications:

   Must have three active recruits.

   Be an active beauty consultant (place a minimum wholesale order of $600 within the current calendar quarter).

   Awards and recognition:

   Earns a red blazer.

   Earns a star pin.

   Earns "Ladder of Success" status by placing $1,800 in wholesale orders in a three-month period.

   Earns 50 percent commission on personal sales at beauty shows.

   Earns 4 percent recruiting commissions on wholesale orders placed by active personal recruits.

   Is eligible for special prizes and awards offered during quarterly contest.

Receives a Star of Excellence ladder pin by qualifying as a star consultant for 8 quarters (or a Double Star of Excellence pin for 16 quarters).

3. *Team Leader.*
   Qualifications:

   Must have five or more active recruits.
   Be an active beauty consultant.

   Awards and recognition:

   Earns 50 percent commission on sales at own beauty shows.
   Earns a "Tender Loving Care" emblem for red blazer.
   Earns an 8 percent personal recruiting commission on wholesale orders of active personal recruits.
   Earns a 12 percent personal recruiting commission if (*a*) five or more active personal recruits place minimum $600 wholesale orders during the current month and (*b*) the team leader herself places a $600 wholesale order during the current month.
   Receives Team Leader pin in ladder of success program.
   Is eligible for quarterly contest prizes and bonuses.

4. *VIP (Very Important Performer).*
   Qualifications:

   Must have obtained Team Leader status.
   Must place wholesale orders of at least $600 for three consecutive months.
   Team must place wholesale orders of at least $3,000 each month for three consecutive months.

   Awards and recognition:

   Earns the use of an Oldsmobile Firenza.
   Earns 50 percent commission on sales at own beauty shows.
   Earns a 12 percent personal recruiting commission.
   Receives VIP pin in Ladder of Success program.
   Is eligible for quarterly contest prizes and bonuses.

5. *Future Director.*
   Qualifications:

   Must have qualified for Team Leader status.
   Must have 12 active recruits at time of application.
   Must make a commitment to Mary Kay to become a sales director by actually giving her letter of intent date.

   Awards and recognition:

   Earns a future director crest for red jacket.
   Plus all the benefits accorded team leaders and VIPs, as appropriate, for monthly and quarterly sales and recruiting performance.

New recruits were required to submit a signed Beauty Consultant Agreement, observe three beauty shows conducted by an experienced consultant, book a minimum of eight beauty shows, and hold at least five beauty shows within their first two weeks. Each consultant was asked to appear in attractive dress and makeup when in public and to project an image of knowledge and confidence about herself and the MKC product line. Mary Kay felt the stress on personal appearance was justified: "What we are selling is beauty. A woman is not going to buy from someone who is wearing jeans and has her hair up in curlers. We want our consultants to be the type of woman others will want to emulate."[8]

Consultants spent most of their work hours scheduling and giving beauty shows. A showing took about two hours (plus about an hour for travel time), and many times the hostess and one or more of the guests turned out to be prospective recruits. New consultants were coached to start off by booking showings with friends, neighbors, and relatives and then network these into showings for friends of friends and relatives of relatives.

Consultants were instructed to follow up each beauty show by scheduling a second facial for each guest at the showing. Many times a customer would invite friends to her second facial and the result would be another beauty show. After the follow-up facial, consultants would call customers periodically to check on whether the customer was satisfied, to see if refills were needed, and to let the customer know about new products and special promotions. Under MKC's "dovetailing" plan, a consultant with an unexpected emergency at home could sell her prearranged beauty show to another consultant and the two would split the commissions generated by the show.

THE SALES DIRECTOR

Consultants who had climbed to the fifth rung of the consultants' Ladder of Success were eligible to become sales directors and head up a sales unit. In addition to conducting her own beauty shows, a sales director's responsibilities included training new recruits, leading weekly sales meetings, and providing assistance and advice to the members of her unit. Sales directors, besides receiving the commission on sales made at their own showings, were paid a commission on the total sales of the unit they headed and a commission on the number of new sales recruits. In June 1984, the top 100 recruiting commissions paid to sales directors ranged from approximately $660 to $1,900. It was not uncommon for sales directors to have total annual earnings in the $50,000 to $100,000 range; in 1983, the average income of the 4,500 sales directors was between $25,000 and $30,000.

There were six achievement categories for sales directors, with qualifications and awards as shown below:

1. *Director in Qualification (DIQ).*
   Qualifications:

   Must have 15 active personal recruits.

---

[8]Rebecca Fannin, "The Beauty of Being Mary Kay," *Marketing & Media Decisions* 17 (December 1982), pp. 59–61.

Submits a Letter of Intent to obtain Directorship.

Gets the director of her sales unit to submit a letter of recommendation.

Within three consecutive months:

- Must recruit an additional 15 consultants for a total of 30 personal active recruits.
- The unit of 30 personal active recruits must place combined wholesale orders of $4,000, $4,500, and $5,000 for months one, two, and three, respectively.

Awards and recognition:

Earns personal sales and personal recruiting commissions (as per schedules for at least team leader status).

Eligible for prizes and bonuses in quarterly contests.

2. *Sales Director.*
Qualifications:

Sales unit must maintain a minimum of $4,000 in wholesale orders each month for the sales director to remain as head of her unit.

Awards and recognition:

Receives commissions of 9 percent to 13 percent on unit's wholesale orders.

Receives monthly sales production bonuses.

- A $300 monthly bonus if unit places monthly wholesale orders of $3,000–$4,999.
- A $500 monthly bonus if unit places monthly wholesale orders of $5,000 and up.

Receives a monthly recruiting bonus (for personal recruits or for recruits of other consultants in the sales unit).

- $100 bonus if three to four new recruits come into unit.
- $200 bonus if five to seven new recruits come into unit.
- $300 bonus if 8 to 11 new recruits come into unit.
- $400 bonus for 12 or more recruits.

Is given a designer director suit.

Is entitled to all commission schedules and incentives of future sales directors.

3. *Regal Director.*
Qualifications:

Members of sales unit must place wholesale orders of at least $24,000 for two consecutive quarters.

Must qualify every two years.

Awards and recognition:

Earns the use of a pink Buick Regal.

Is entitled to all the commission percentages, bonuses, and other incentives of a sales director.

4. *Cadillac Director.*
   Qualifications:

   Sales unit members must place at least $36,000 in wholesale orders for two consecutive quarters.

   Must qualify every two years.

   Awards and recognition:

   Earns the use of a pink Cadillac.

   Is entitled to all the commission percentages, bonuses, and other incentives of a sales director.

5. *Senior Sales Director.*
   Qualifications:

   One to four sales directors emerge from her unit.

   Awards and recognition:

   Earns a 4 percent commission on offspring directors' consultants.

   Is entitled to all the commission percentages, bonuses, and other incentives of at least a sales director.

6. *Future National Director.*
   Qualifications:

   Five or more active directors emerge from her unit.

   Awards and recognition:

   Is entitled to all the commission percentages, bonuses, and other incentives of a senior sales director.

As of late 1983, the company had about 700 Regal directors and about 700 Cadillac directors; in one recent quarter, 81 sales directors had met the qualifications for driving a new pink Cadillac.

THE NATIONAL SALES DIRECTOR

Top-performing sales directors became eligible for designation as a national sales director, the highest recognition bestowed on field sales personnel. NSDs were inspirational leaders and managers of a group of sales directors and received commissions on the total dollar sales of the group of sales units they headed. In 1984, MKC's 50 national sales directors had total sales incomes averaging over $150,000 per year. A 1985 *Fortune* article featured Helen McVoy, a MKC national sales director since 1971, as one of the most successful salespeople in the United States; in 1984 she earned $375,000. McVoy began her career with Mary Kay in 1965 at the age of 45. Her family was on a tight budget, having lost all of their savings in a bad mining investment. To support her plant-collecting hobby, Helen started selling Mary Kay products on a part-time basis—two hours a week. Her original investment was for a beauty case; by the end of her first year she had made $17,000. From 1970 through 1984, she was the company's top volume producer.

TRAINING

Before holding a beauty show, a new consultant had to observe three beauty shows, attend orientation classes conducted by a sales director, and complete a self-study set of MKC training materials. This training covered the fundamentals of conducting skin care shows, booking future beauty shows, recruiting new Mary Kay consultants, personal appearance, and managing a small business. Active consultants were strongly encouraged to continue to improve their sales skills and product knowledge. In addition to weekly sales meetings and frequent one-on-one contact with other consultants and sales directors, each salesperson had access to a variety of company-prepared support materials—videotapes, films, slide shows, and brochures.

In 1983, a new educational curriculum was introduced to support each phase of a Mary Kay career. A back-to-basics orientation package provided a foundation for the first stage of career development. A recruitment notebook provided dialogue of mock recruiting conversations, and sales directors were provided with an organizational kit to help them make a smooth transition from being purely a consultant to being a sales manager as well as a consultant.

Additional learning opportunities were provided in the form of special product knowledge classes, regional workshops, and annual corporate-sponsored seminars.

MOTIVATION AND INCENTIVES

New sales contests were introduced every three months. Prizes and recognition awards were always tied to achievement plateaus rather than declaring first-, second-, and third-place winners. Top performers were spotlighted in the company's full-color monthly magazine, *Applause* (which had a circulation of several hundred thousand).

Mary Kay Ash described why MKC paid so much attention to recognition and praise:

> I believe praise is the best way for a manager to motivate people. At Mary Kay Cosmetics we think praise is so important that our entire marketing plan is based upon it.[9]
>
> Praise is an incredibly effective motivator; unfortunately, many managers are reluctant to employ it. Yet I can't help feeling that they know how much praise means, not only to others, but to themselves. . . . I believe that you should praise people whenever you can; it causes them to respond as a thirsty plant responds to water.[10]
>
> The power of positive motivation in a goal-oriented structure such as ours cannot be overstated. This is what inspires our consultants to maximize their true potentials.[11]

---

[9]Ash, *People Management*, p. 21.
[10]Ibid., p. 23.
[11]Ibid., p. 26

As a manager you must recognize that everyone needs praise. But it must be given sincerely. You'll find numerous occasions for genuine praise if you'll only look for them.[12]

Because we recognize the need for people to be praised, we make a concentrated effort to give as much recognition as possible. Of course with an organization as large as ours, not everyone can make a speech at our Seminars, but we do attempt to have many people appear on stage, if only for a few moments. During the Directors' March, for example, hundreds of directors parade on stage before thousands of their peers. In order to appear in the Directors' March, a director must purchase a special designer suit. Likewise we have a Red Jacket March, in which only star recruiters, team leaders, and future directors participate. Again, a special uniform is required for participation.[13]

How important are these brief stage appearances? Frankly I think it means more for a woman to be recognized by her peers than to receive an expensive present in the mail that nobody knows about! And once she gets a taste of this recognition, she wants to come back next year for more![14]

SEMINAR

MKC staged an annual "Seminar" as a salute to the company and to the salespeople who contributed to its success. The first Seminar was held on September 13, 1964 (the company's first anniversary); the banquet menu consisted of chicken, jello salad, and an anniversary cake while a three-piece band provided entertainment. By 1984, Seminar had grown into a three-day spectacular repeated four consecutive times with a budget of $4 million and attended by 24,000 beauty consultants and sales directors who paid their own way to attend the event. The setting, the Convention Center in Dallas (see Exhibit 6), was decorated in red, white, and blue in order to emphasize the theme, "Share the Spirit." The climactic highlight of Seminar was Awards Night, when the biggest prizes were awarded to the people with the biggest sales. The company went to elaborate efforts to ensure the Awards Night was charged with excitement and emotion; as one observer of the 1984 Awards Night in Dallas described it, "The atmosphere there is electric, a cross between a Las Vegas revue and a revival meeting. Hands reach up to touch Mary Kay; a pink Cadillac revolves on a mist-shrouded pedestal; a 50-piece band plays; and women sob."

Mary Kay Ash customarily made personal appearances throughout the Seminar period. In addition to Awards Night, the Seminar featured sessions consisting of informational and training workshops, motivational presentations by leading sales directors, and star entertainment (Paul Anka performed in 1984, and in previous years there had been performances by Tennessee Ernie Ford, John Davidson, and Johnny Mathis). Over the three days, Cadillacs, diamonds, mink coats, a $5,000 shopping spree at Neiman-Marcus for any director whose team sold $1 million worth of Mary Kay products, and lesser assorted prizes were awarded to the outstanding achievers of the past year. Gold-and-diamond bumblebee pins, each containing 21 diamonds and retailing for over $3,600, were presented to the Queen of Sales on Pageant Night;

[12]Ibid., p. 27.
[13]Ibid., p. 25.
[14]Ibid., p. 26.

EXHIBIT 6	**Share the Spirit, 1984 Annual Seminar, Mary Kay Cosmetics**

Source: Mary Kay Cosmetics, Inc., Interim Report, 1984.

these pins were not only the company's ultimate badge of success, but Mary Kay felt they also had special symbolism:

> It's a beautiful pin, but that isn't the whole story. We think the bumblebee is a marvelous symbol of woman. Because, as aerodynamic engineers found a long time ago, the bumblebee cannot fly! Its wings are too weak and its body is too heavy to fly, but fortunately, the bumblebee doesn't know that, and it goes right on flying. The bee has become the symbol of women who didn't know they could fly but they DID! I think the women who own these diamond bumblebees think of them in their own personal ways. For most of us, it's true that we refused to believe we couldn't do it. Maybe somebody else told us, "You can do it!" So we did.[15]

CORPORATE ENVIRONMENT

The company's eight-story, gold-glass corporate headquarters building in Dallas was occupied solely by Mary Kay executives. An open-door philosophy was present at MKC. Everyone from the mailroom clerk to the chairman of the

---

[15]Ash, *Mary Kay*, p. 9.

board was treated with respect. The door to Mary Kay Ash's office was rarely closed. Often people touring the building peeked in her office to get a glimpse of the pink and white decor. Mary Kay and all other corporate managers took the time to talk with any employee.

First names were always used at MKC. Mary Kay herself insisted on being addressed as Mary Kay; she felt people who called her Mrs. Ash were either angry at her or didn't know her. In keeping with this informal atmosphere, offices didn't have titles on the doors, executive restrooms didn't exist, and the company cafeteria was used by the executives (there was no executive dining room).

To further enhance the informal atmosphere and enthusiasm at MKC, all sales functions began with a group sing-along. Mary Kay offered several reasons for this policy:

> Nothing great is ever achieved without enthusiasm. . . . We have many of our own songs, and they're sung at all Mary Kay get-togethers, ranging from small weekly meetings to our annual Seminars. Our salespeople enjoy this activity, and I believe the singing creates a wonderful esprit de corps. Yet outsiders, especially men, often criticize our singing as being " strictly for women." I disagree. Singing unites people. It's like those "rah-rah-rah for our team" cheers. If someone is depressed, singing will often bring her out of it.[16]

The company sent Christmas cards, birthday cards, and anniversary cards to every single employee each year. Mary Kay personally designed the birthday cards for consultants. In addition, all the sales directors received Christmas and birthday presents from the company.

THE PEOPLE MANAGEMENT PHILOSOPHY AT MKC

Mary Kay Ash had some very definite ideas about how people ought to be managed, and she willingly shared them with employees and, through her books, with the public at large. Some excerpts from her book on *People Management* reveal the approach taken at Mary Kay Cosmetics:

> People come first at Mary Kay Cosmetics—our beauty consultants, sales directors, and employees, our customers, and our suppliers. We pride ourselves as a "company known for the people it keeps." Our belief in caring for people, however, does not conflict with our need as a corporation to generate a profit. Yes, we keep our eye on the bottom line, but it's not an overriding obsession.[17]
>
> Ours is an organization with few middle management positions. In order to grow and progress, you don't move upward; you expand outward. This gives our independent sales organization a deep sense of personal worth. They know that they are not competing with one another for a spot in the company's managerial "pecking order." Therefore the contributions of each individual are of equal value. No one is fearful that his or her idea will be "stolen" by someone with more ability on the corporate ladder. And when someone—anyone—proposes a new thought, we all analyze it, improve upon it, and ultimately support it with the enthusiasm of a team.[18]

---

[16]Ash, *People Management*, p. 59.

[17]Ibid., p. xix.

[18]Ibid., pp. 11–12.

Every person is special! I sincerely believe this. Each of us wants to feel good about himself or herself, but to me it is just as important to make others feel the same way. Whenever I meet someone, I try to imagine him wearing an invisible sign that says: MAKE ME FEEL IMPORTANT! I respond to this sign immediately and it works wonders.[19]

At Mary Kay Cosmetics we believe in putting our beauty consultants and sales directors on a pedestal. Of all people, I most identify with them because I spent many years as a salesperson. My attitude of appreciation for them permeates the company. When our salespeople visit the home office, for example, we go out of our way to give them the red-carpet treatment. Every person in the company treats them royally.[20]

We go first class across the board, and although it's expensive, it's worth it because our people are made to feel important. For example, each year we take our top sales directors and their spouses on deluxe trips to Hong Kong, Bangkok, London, Paris, Geneva, and Athens to mention a few. We spare no expense, and although it costs a lot extra per person to fly the Concorde, cruise on the Love Boat, or book suites at the elegant Georges V in Paris, it is our way of telling them how important they are to our company.[21]

My experience with people is that they generally do what you expect them to do! If you expect them to perform well, they will; conversely, if you expect them to perform poorly, they'll probably oblige. I believe that average employees who try their hardest to live up to your high expectations of them will do better than above-average people with low self-esteem. Motivate your people to draw on that untapped 90 percent of their ability and their level of performance will soar![22]

A good people manager will never put someone down; not only is it nonproductive—it's counterproductive. You must remember that your job is to play the role of problem solver and that by taking this approach of criticizing people you'll accomplish considerably more.

While some managers try to forget problems they encountered early in their careers, I make a conscious effort to remember the difficulties I've had along the way. I think it's vital for a manager to empathize with the other people's problem, and the best way to have a clear understanding is to have been there yourself![23]

Interviews with Mary Kay consultants gave credibility to the company's approach and methods. One consultant described her experience:

I had a lot of ragged edges when I started. The first time I went to a Mary Kay seminar, I signed up for classes in diction and deportment; believe me, I needed them. I didn't even have the right clothes. You can only wear dresses and skirts to beauty shows, so I sank everything I had into one nice dress. I washed it out every night in Woolite and let it drip dry in the shower.

But I was determined to follow all the rules, even the ones I didn't understand—*especially* the ones I didn't understand. At times, it all seemed foolish, especially when you consider that all my clients were mill workers and didn't exactly appreciate my new grammar. But I kept telling myself to hang in there, that Mary Kay knew what was good for me.

[19]Ibid., p. 15.
[20]Ibid., p. 19.
[21]Ibid., p. 20.
[22]Ibid., p. 27.
[23]Ibid., p. 6.

When I first started, I won a pearl and ruby ring. A man or a man's company may say I'd have been better off with the cash, but I'm not so convinced. Mary Kay is on to something there. From the moment I won that ring, I began thinking of myself as a person who deserved a better standard of living. I built a new life to go with the ring.[24]

Another consultant observed:

The essential thing about Mary Kay is the quality of the company. When you go to Dallas, the food, the hotel, and the entertainment are all top notch. Nothing gaudy is allowed in Mary Kay.[25]

When asked if she didn't think pink Cadillacs were a tad gaudy, she responded in a low, level tone: "When people say that, I just ask them what color car their company gave them last year."

On the morning following Awards Night 1984, a group of Florida consultants was in the hotel lobby getting ready to go to the airport for the flight home.[26] One member had by chance met Mary Kay Ash in the ladies' room a bit earlier and had managed to get a maid to snap a Polaroid photograph of them together. She proudly was showing her friends the snapshot and was the only one of the group who had actually met Mary Kay. The consultant said to her friends, "She told me she was sure I'd be up there on stage with her next year. She said she'd see me there." Her sales director, in noting the scene, observed, "She's got the vision now. She really did meet her. And you've got to understand that in Mary Kaydom that's a very big deal."

THE BEAUTY SHOW

It was a few minutes past 7 P.M. on a weeknight in Tuscaloosa, Alabama. Debbie Sessoms and three of her friends (including the casewriter) were seated around the dining room table in Debbie's house. In front of each woman was a pink tray, a mirror, a pencil, and a blank personal Beauty Profile form. Jan Currier stood at the head of the table. She welcomed each of the ladies and asked them to fill out the personal Beauty Profile form in front of them.

When they were finished, Jan started her formal presentation, leading off with how MKC's products were developed by a tanner. She used a large display board to illustrate the topics she discussed. Next Jan told the group about the company and the founder, Mary Kay Ash. She showed a picture of Mary Kay and explained she was believed to be in her 70s—though no one knew for sure because Mary Kay maintained that "A woman who will tell her age will tell anything." Jerri, one of the guests, remarked that she couldn't believe how good Mary Kay looks for her age. Jan told her that Mary Kay had been using her basic skin care formulas since the 1950s.

Jan went on to talk about the growth of the sales force from 9 consultants to over 195,000 in 1984. She explained how the career opportunities at MKC could be adapted to each consultant's ambitions. A consultant, she said, determined her own work hours and could choose either a full-time or part-time

---

[24]As quoted in Kim Wright Wiley, "Cold Cream and Hard Cash," *Savvy,* June 1985, p. 39.
[25]Ibid., p. 41.
[26]Ibid.

career. Advancement was based on sales and recruiting abilities. The possible rewards included diamonds, minks, and Cadillacs.

Before explaining the basic skin care program, Jan told the women that with the Mary Kay money-back guarantee, products could be returned for any reason for a full refund. Jan distributed samples to each of the guests based on the information provided in the personal Beauty Profiles. Under Jan's guidance, the ladies proceeded through the complete facial process, learning each of the five basic skin care steps advocated by Mary Kay. There was a lot of discussion about the products and how they felt on everyone's skin.

When the presentation reached the glamour segment, each guest was asked her preference of makeup colors. Jan encouraged everyone to try as many of the products and colors as they wanted. Jan helped the guests experiment with different combinations and worked with each one personally, trying to make sure that everyone would end up satisfied with her own finished appearance.

After admiring each other's new looks, three of the women placed orders. Jan collected their payments and filled the orders on the spot. No one had to wait for delivery.

When she finished with the orders, Jan talked with Debbie's three guests about hostessing their own shows and receiving hostess gifts. Chris agreed to book a show the next week. Debbie was then given her choice of gifts based on the evening's sales and bookings. To close the show, Jan again highlighted the benefits of a Mary Kay career—being your own boss, setting your own hours—and invited anyone interested to talk with her about these opportunities. Debbie then served some refreshments. Shortly after 9 P.M., Jan and Debbie's three guests departed.

Walking to Jan's car, the casewriter asked Jan if the evening was a success. Jan replied that it had been "a pretty good night. Sales totaled $150, I got a booking for next Wednesday, I made $75 in commission in a little over two hours, the guests learned about skin care and have some products they are going to like, and Debbie got a nice hostess gift."

THE WEEKLY SALES MEETING

Jan Currier, senior sales director, welcomed the consultants to the weekly Monday night meeting of the members of her sales unit.[27] After calling everyone's attention to a mimeographed handout on everybody's chair, she introduced the casewriter to the group and then invited everyone to stand and join in singing the Mary Kay enthusiasm song. As soon as the song was over, Jan started "the Crow Period" by asking Barbara, team leader, to stand and tell about her achievement of VIP (Very Important Performer) status. Barbara told of setting and achieving the goals necessary to win the use of an Oldsmobile Firenza. Her new goal was to assist and motivate everyone on her team to do the same. Jan recognized Barbara again for being both the Queen of Sales and the Queen of Recruiting for the previous month.

---

[27]Most sales directors had their sales meeting on Monday night, a practice urged upon them by Mary Kay Ash. Mary Kay saw the Monday night meeting as a good way to start the week. "If you had a bad week—you need the sales meeting. If you had a good week, the sales meeting needs you! When a consultant leaves a Monday meeting excited, she has an entire week to let excitement work for her." Ash, *Mary Kay,* p. 40.

Jan began the educational segment by instructing the consultants on color analysis and how it related to glamour. She continued the instruction by explaining the proper techniques of a man's facial.

Next everyone who had at least a $100 week in sales was asked to stand. Jan began the countdown "110, 120, 130 . . . 190." Barbara sat down to a round of applause for her $190 week in sales. "200, 220 . . . 270." Melissa sat down. The ladies applauded her efforts. Mary was the only one left standing. There was anticipation of how high her sales reached as the countdown resumed. "280, 290, 300 . . . 335." Mary sat down. Everyone applauded this accomplishment of a consultant who had only been with MKC for four months and who held a 40-hour-a-week full-time job in addition to her Mary Kay sales effort.

At this time Jan asked Linda and Susan to join her up front. She pinned each lady and congratulated them on joining her team. The Mary Kay pin was placed upside down on the new consultant's lapels. Jan explained this was so people would notice and ask about it. When they did, a consultant was to respond by saying: "My pin is upside down to remind me to ask you if you've had a Mary Kay facial." The pin would be turned right side up when the consultant got her first recruit. Each of the new consultants also received a pink ribbon. This marked their membership in the Jan's Beautiful People sales unit. Both Linda and Susan were given some material Jan had prepared (Exhibit 7); Jan said she would go over it with them after the meeting.

Next a new competition was announced. This contest focused on recruiting. For each new recruit, a consultant would receive one stem of Romanian crystal. So everyone could see how beautiful the rewards were, Jan showed a sample of the crystal.

A final reminder was made for attendance at the upcoming workshop on motivation. Jan sweetened the pot by providing a prize to the first one in her unit to register and pay for the seminar. Next week she would announce the winner.

The meeting was adjourned until next Monday evening.

An Interview with Jan Currier

One night shortly after attending the meeting of Jan's Beautiful People sales unit, the casewriter met with Jan to ask some questions.

Casewriter: How many are in your unit?

Jan: We're down right now. I had a small unit to start with. I only had 56. . . . A decent unit has got a hundred, 75 to 100 at least.

Casewriter: Is it the size of the town that hampers you?

Jan: No, no it's me who hampers me. The speed of the leader is the speed of the unit. If I'm not out there doing it, then they're not going to be doing it. If I'm recruiting, they're recruiting.

Casewriter: What about your leader, is your leader not fast?

Jan: No, it's me; see when you point a finger, three come back.

Casewriter: How do you handle a situation where a consultant would like to do well, but she doesn't put in the time necessary to do well?

Jan: You have to go back to that premise, that whole philosophy that you're in business for yourself but not by yourself. So if a girl comes in and says

EXHIBIT 7   **Example of Material Provided to New Beauty Consultants at Weekly Sales Meeting**

The Mary Kay Opportunity	Yearly Total
3 Shows per week with $150.00 sales per show	
Less 15 percent hostess credit = $191.25 profit (per week)	
Three persons buying per show, three shows per week	$9,945
468 prospective customers per year	
Average selling to 7 out of 10	
327 new customers per year	
Call each customer at least six times per year	
Average $15.00 in sales per call	
Yearly reorder profits will be	14,715
1 Facial per week—52 prospective customers per year	
Average selling to 7 of 10, 36 new customers	
If each buys a basic, your facial profits will be	702
36 New customers from facials	
Call each customer six times per year	
Average $15.00 in sales per call	
Your yearly *reorder* profit will be	1,620
Recruit one person each month	
Each with at least a $1,500 initial order (wholesale)	
Ordering only $500.00 every month thereafter	
Your 4 percent–8 percent commission checks from these 12 recruits	3,490
Your yearly profits will be approximately	$30,472

This is a simple guideline designed to show you, in figures, approximately how much you can benefit from your Mary Kay career. These figures may vary a little, due to price changes. These totals are based on orders placed at our maximum discount level and do not include referrals, dovetail fees, and prizes.

Working hours per week for the above should not exceed 20 hours, if your work is well planned. Attitude and consistency are the keys to your success.

                            Jan Currier
                            Senior Sales Director

I want to make X number of dollars, then I will work with her and we will do it. I try to get them to set goals and really look at them every week and work for it. One gal comes in and wants to make $25 a week and another says, "I have to support my family." There's a big difference.

Casewriter: How do you handle those that only want to make $25 a week?

Jan: If you get rid of the piddlers, you wouldn't have a company. It's the piddlers that make up the company. There are only going to be one or two superstars.

Casewriter: How do you motivate the people in your unit?

Jan: The only way you can really motivate is to call, encourage, write notes, and encourage recognition at the sales meetings and recognition in the newsletter. If they're not doing anything, they usually won't come to the sales meeting, but once in a while maybe, they'll find excuses.

Casewriter: What do you do when a person hits that stage?

Jan: Everybody has to go through that phase. . . . If you're smart, you'll go to your director, read your book, and go back to start where you were before—with what was working to begin with and you'll pull out of it. There are a lot of them who never pull out of it. They came in to have fun.

Casewriter: And the fun wears out.

Jan: Let's face it. This is a job. It's work, it's the best-paying hard work around, but it's work. I just finished with one gal last week who ended up saying, "Well, I just thought it would be fun. I thought it was just supposed to be fun." And I said, "Yes, but it's a job."

Casewriter: Can you tell before a person starts if she'll be successful?

Jan: There's no way to predict who's going to make it; the one you think is going to be absolutely a superstar isn't. You give everybody a chance. I measure my time with their interest and I tell them that. I'll encourage them, but they are going to pretty much do what they want to do. I learned that the hard way. There is no point laying guilt trips, no point pestering them to death, and pressure doesn't work.

Casewriter: Do you feel recognition is the best motivator?

Jan: Absolutely, recognition and appreciation. I think appreciation more than anything else. Little notes, I'm finally learning that too. Some of us are slow learners. . . . So I'll write little notes telling someone, I really appreciate your doing this, or I'm really proud of you for being a star consultant this quarter, or I'm so glad you went with us to Birmingham to the workshop.

Casewriter: Does it upset you when people don't come to the sales meetings?

Jan: I used to grieve when they wouldn't come to sales meetings. I'd ask what am I doing wrong. . . . Finally I realized that no matter how many people aren't there, the people who are there care and they are worth doing anything for. It's strange we seem to get a different batch every meeting.

Casewriter: I get the impression that you are always looking for new recruits.

Jan: Yes, I've gotten more picky. I'm looking more for directors. I'm looking for people who really want to work. I look for someone who is older, not just the 18-year-olds because they don't want to work. They want to make money, but they don't want to work. . . . I'd like to build more offspring directors.

Casewriter: What kind of people do you look for?

Jan: Not everybody's right for Mary Kay. It takes somebody who genuinely cares about other people.

Casewriter: Is there a common scenario that fits most new recruits?

Jan: Mary Kay attracts a lot of insecure women who are often married to insecure men. And that woman is told over and over by Mary Kay how wonderful she is and how terrific she is and how she can do anything with God's help. She can achieve anything. And like me she is dumb enough to believe it and go along with it.

Casewriter: What do you feel is the reason for the slowdown in recruiting at Mary Kay?

Jan: The key to this drop has been partly the economy, but partly a lot of people are weeding out. That's OK because the cream is going to rise to the top. I really believe that. We're going to have a stronger, much better company. I could see it at leadership (conference). The quality of people was much higher. It gets higher every year.

MKC'S FUTURE

MKC's sales in 1984 fell 14 percent to $278 million (down from $324 million in fiscal year 1983). The company's stock price, after a two for one split at about $44, tumbled from $22 in late 1983 to the $9–$12 range in 1984. Profits were down 8 percent to $33.8 million. The declines were blamed on a dropoff in recruiting and retention (owing to reduced attractiveness of part-time employment) and to the expense of starting up the European division. As of December 31, 1984, the company had about 152,000 beauty consultants and 4,500 sales directors as compared to 195,000 beauty consultants and 5,000 sales directors at year-end 1983. Average sales per consultant in 1984 amounted to $1,603, versus $1,655 in 1983 and a 1980–1982 average of $1,753; only 60,000 of the 152,000 consultants were thought to be significantly productive. A cosmetic analyst for one Wall Street securities firm, in talking about the company's prospects, said, "Brokers loved this stock because it had such a great story. But the glory days, for the time being, are certainly over."[28]

The company's mystique was upbeat, however. Mary Kay Ash was on the UPI list of the most interviewed women in America. And when the Republicans chose Dallas for its 1984 convention, the Chamber of Commerce had to persuade Mary Kay to change the date of the 1984 Seminar, which was slated for the same week in the same convention center. Positive anecdotes about Mary Kay Ash and how MKC was operated were cited in numerous books and articles.

Mary Kay Ash indicated that the company had no plans for changing the main thrust of the company's sales and recruiting strategies:

> This is an excellent primary career for women, not just a way to get pin money. We see no need to alter our basic approach. It's taken us this far.[29]
>
> We have only 4 percent of the total retail cosmetics market. The way I see it 96 percent of the people in the United States are using the wrong product. There's no reason why we can't become the number one cosmetics company in the United States.[30]

---

[28]As quoted in Wiley, "Cold Cream and Hard Cash," p. 40.

[29]Ibid.

[30]As quoted in *Business Week*, March 28, 1983, p. 130.

WAL-MART STORES, INC.*

Arthur A. Thompson, Jr., The University of Alabama
Kem Pinegar, Birmingham–Southern College
Tracy Kramer, The University of Alabama

"Give me a W!" shouted Sam Walton, the founder of Wal-Mart Stores, Inc., to associates at the weekly Saturday morning headquarters meeting in Bentonville, Arkansas (population approximately 9,000). "W!" the crowd of several hundred roared back. "Give me an A!" Walton then exhorted. And so it went down to the last T. Then everyone joined in a final ringing chorus: "Wal-Mart, We're Number 1!" This rah-rah style set the tone for all Wal-Mart gatherings, and the upbeat spirit permeated Wal-Mart's drive to overtake Sears as the largest national discount department store chain. Wal-Mart was already poised to move past Kmart into second place, and surpassing Sears appeared within reach (see Exhibit 1).

The 1980s had been an era of spectacular growth and expansion for Wal-Mart. No other retailer in U.S. history could come even close to matching the growth Wal-Mart had achieved over the past 10 years. Sales revenues had risen from $1.6 billion in 1980 to $25.8 billion in 1990, a compound average growth rate of 35 percent. Net income over the same period grew at an even faster 38 percent annual rate—from $56 million to $1.08 billion (see Exhibit 2 for a 10-year financial summary). Wal-Mart had made *Fortune*'s list of "Most Admired Corporations" several times and, most recently, had been named "Retailer of the Decade" by *Discount Store News*. The market value of Wal-Mart's common stock (current stock price × the number of shares outstanding) was the sixth highest of all U.S. companies. A $10,000 investment in Wal-Mart stock in 1980 was worth $800,000 in January 1991. Sam Walton and members of his immediate family owned about 35 percent of Wal-Mart's stock (about 380 million shares), worth about $18 billion.

Company Background

Sam Walton, Wal-Mart's founder, graduated from the University of Missouri in 1940 with a degree in economics and began his retail career as a management trainee with the J. C. Penney Co., an experience that began to shape his thinking about department store retailing. His career with Penney's was ended by a call to military duty in World War II. When the war was over, Walton decided to open a Ben Franklin retail variety store in Newport, Arkansas, rather than return to Penney's. Five years later, when the lease on the Newport building was lost, Walton relocated his Ben Franklin in Bentonville, Arkansas, where he bought a building and opened Walton's 5 & 10 as a Ben Franklin-affiliated store. By 1960 Walton was the largest Ben Franklin franchisee, with over a dozen stores.

In 1961 Walton became very concerned about the long-term competitive threat to variety stores posed by the emerging popularity of giant supermarkets and discounters. Walton, an avid pilot, took off in his plane on a

---

*Copyright © 1991 by Arthur A. Thompson, Jr.

EXHIBIT 1   **Comparative Financial Performance of Sears, Kmart, and Wal-Mart, 1980–1989**

	Sales (In millions of dollars)			Net Income (In millions of dollars)			Net Income as a Percentage of Sales		
Year	Sears	Kmart	Wal-Mart*	Sears	Kmart	Wal-Mart*	Sears	Kmart	Wal-Mart*
1980	$25,161	$14,118	$ 1,643	$ 610	$ 429	$ 56	2.4%	3.0%	3.4%
1981	27,357	16,394	2,445	650	311	83	2.4	1.9	3.4
1982	30,020	16,611	3,376	861	408	124	2.9	2.5	3.7
1983	35,883	18,380	4,667	1,342	859	196	3.7	4.7	4.2
1984	38,828	20,762	6,401	1,455	835	271	2.7	4.0	4.2
1985	39,349	22,035	8,451	1,294	757	327	3.3	3.4	3.9
1986	42,303	23,812	11,909	1,339	1,028	450	3.2	4.3	3.8
1987	45,904	25,627	15,959	1,633	1,171	627	3.6	4.6	3.9
1988	50,251	27,301	20,649	1,454	1,244	837	2.9	4.6	4.1
1989	53,794	29,533	25,811	1,509	1,155†	1,076	2.8	3.9	4.2

*Wal-Mart's fiscal year ends January 31 of each year; data for the period January 31, 1980 through January 31, 1981 are reported in Wal-Mart's annual report as 1981 results. Because Wal-Mart's fiscal year results really cover 11 months of the previous calendar year, this exhibit shows Wal-Mart's 1981 fiscal results in the 1980 row, its 1982 fiscal results in the 1981 row, and so on. This adjustment makes Wal-Mart's figures correspond more to the same time frame as the calendar year data for Sears and Kmart.

† Before a pretax provision of $640 million for restructuring.

Source: Company annual reports, 1980–1990.

cross-country tour studying the changes in stores and retailing trends and then put together a plan for a discount store of his own. He went to Chicago to try to interest Ben Franklin executives in expanding into this growing segment; they turned him down. However, Walton decided to go forward on his own.

The first Wal-Mart Discount City was opened July 2, 1962, in Rogers, Arkansas. By 1970 Wal-Mart was a 38-store operation with revenues of $44.3 million. By 1980 Wal-Mart had 276 stores and sales revenues of $1.6 billion. By 1990, Wal-Mart was a $25.8 billion company with 1,402 Wal-Mart Discount City stores and 123 Sam's Wholesale Club warehouses.

Walton's insights into successful discount retailing were evident from the start. Although he began as a seat-of-the-pants merchant, he had great instincts, was quick to learn from other retailers' successes and failures, and was adept at soliciting ideas for improvements from employees and promptly trying them out. As the company grew, Sam Walton proved an effective and visionary leader. Despite great wealth, he was a man of simple tastes and had a genuine affection for people. His folksy demeanor, and his talent for motivating people combined with a very hands-on management style, produced a culture and a set of values and beliefs that kept Wal-Mart on a path of continuous improvement and rapid expansion. Moreover, Wal-Mart's success and Walton's personable style of leadership generated numerous stories in the media that cast the company and its founder in a positive light. During the period that Wal-Mart was emerging as the premier discount retailer in the country, an unusually large segment of the American public came to know who Sam Walton was and to associate his name with Wal-Mart.

Ten-Year Financial Summary, Wal-Mart Stores, and Subsidiaries
(Dollar amounts in thousands, except per-share data)

	1990	1989	1988	1987	1986	1985	1984	1983	1982	1981
Earnings										
Net sales	$25,810,656	$20,649,001	$15,959,255	$11,909,076	$8,451,489	$6,400,861	$4,666,909	$3,376,252	$2,444,997	$1,643,199
Licensed department rentals and other income—net	174,644	136,867	104,783	84,623	55,127	52,167	36,031	22,435	17,650	12,063
Cost of sales	20,070,034	16,056,856	12,281,744	9,053,219	6,361,271	4,722,440	3,418,025	2,458,235	1,787,496	1,207,802
Operating, selling, and general administrative expenses	4,069,695	3,267,864	2,599,367	2,007,645	1,485,210	1,181,455	892,887	677,029	495,010	331,524
Interest costs										
Debt	20,346	36,286	25,262	10,442	1,903	5,207	4,935	20,297	16,053	5,808
Capital leases	117,725	99,395	88,995	76,367	54,640	42,506	29,946	18,570	15,351	10,849
Taxes on income	631,600	488,246	441,027	395,940	276,119	230,653	160,903	100,416	65,943	43,597
Net income	$ 1,075,900	$ 837,221	$ 627,643	$ 450,086	$ 327,473	$ 270,767	$ 196,244	$ 124,140	$ 82,794	$ 55,682
Per share of common stock										
Net income	$ 1.90	$ 1.48	$ 1.11	$ .79	$ .58	$ .48	$ .35	$ .23	$ .16	$ .11
Dividends	.22	.16	.12	.085	.07	.0525	.035	.0225	.0163	.0125
Stores in operation at the end of the period										
Wal-Mart Stores	1,402	1,259	1,114	980	859	745	642	551	491	330
Sam's Wholesale Clubs	123	105	84	49	23	11	3			
Financial Position										
Current assets	$ 4,712,616	$ 3,630,987	$ 2,905,145	$ 2,353,271	$1,784,275	$1,303,254	$1,005,567	$ 720,537	$ 589,161	$ 345,204
Net property, plant, equipment, and capital leases	3,430,059	2,661,954	2,144,852	1,676,282	1,303,450	870,309	628,151	457,509	333,026	245,942
Total assets	8,198,484	6,359,668	5,131,809	4,049,092	3,103,645	2,205,229	1,652,254	1,187,448	937,513	592,345
Current liabilities	2,845,315	2,065,909	1,743,763	1,340,291	992,683	688,968	502,763	347,318	339,961	177,601
Long-term debt	185,152	184,439	185,672	179,234	180,682	41,237	40,866	106,465	104,581	30,184
Long-term obligations under capital leases	1,087,403	1,009,046	866,972	764,128	595,205	449,886	339,930	222,610	154,196	134,896
Preferred stock with mandatory redemption provisions	—	—	—	—	4,902	5,874	6,411	6,861	7,438	—
Shareholders' equity	3,965,561	3,007,909	2,257,267	1,690,493	1,277,659	984,672	737,503	488,109	323,942	248,309
Financial Ratios										
Current ratio	1.7	1.8	1.7	1.8	1.8	1.9	2.0	2.1	1.7	1.9
Inventories/working capital	2.4	2.1	2.3	2.0	1.8	1.8	1.5	1.5	2.0	1.7
Return on assets*	16.9	16.3	15.5	14.5	14.8	16.4	16.5	13.2	14.0	12.2
Return on shareholders' equity*	35.8	37.1	37.1	35.2	33.3	36.7	40.2	38.3	33.3	33.8

*On beginning-of-year balances.

Source: 1990 Annual Report.

WAL-MART'S STRATEGY

Wal-Mart's long-term strategic objective was to become the largest U.S. discounter and retailer via continued, controlled, profitable growth. The hallmarks of Wal-Mart's strategy were low everyday prices, wide selection, a heavy percentage of name-brand merchandise, a customer-friendly store environment, low operating costs, disciplined expansion into new geographic markets, and extensive use of merchandising innovations. Exhibits 3 and 4 show typical scenes from Wal-Mart's two types of stores—Wal-Mart Discount City stores and Sam's Wholesale Clubs. On the outside of every Discount City store was the message "We Sell for Less." The company's advertising tag line reinforced the low-price, brand-name merchandise strategy: "Always the low price on the brands you trust. Always." The major merchandise lines included housewares, consumer electronics, sporting goods, lawn and garden items, health and beauty aids, apparel, home fashions, paint, bed and bath goods, hardware, automotive repair and maintenance items, toys and games, and nonperishable supermarket items (paper products, laundry detergents and soaps, snack foods). Store sizes averaged about 75,000 square feet, with a range of 40,000 to 110,000 square feet. In-store fixtures were basic, but the atmosphere was bright, cheery, and fresh, with ample aisle space and attractively presented merchandise displays. Store personnel were friendly and helpful; the aim was to make each shopper's experience pleasant and satisfying.

A low-cost theme pervaded every part of Wal-Mart's operations—from store construction to pressuring vendors and suppliers for low prices on every item Wal-Mart stocked to supplying stores via an efficient distribution system to keeping corporate overhead costs down. The cost-savings that Wal-Mart achieved were passed on to customers in the form of lower retail prices.

Wal-Mart's Geographic Expansion Strategy

One of the most distinctive features of Wal-Mart's strategy was the manner in which it expanded outward into new geographic areas. Whereas some chain retailers achieved regional and national coverage quickly by locating stores as much as several hundred miles apart and entering the largest metropolitan centers before trying to penetrate less-populated markets, Wal-Mart always expanded into *adjoining* geographic areas, saturating each area with stores before moving into new territory. The areas Wal-Mart chose to expand into next were usually within 200 miles of one of the company's existing distribution centers so that deliveries to newly opened stores could be made cost-effectively on a daily basis; new distribution centers were added as needed to support store expansion into additional states. Wal-Mart's strategy for penetrating a new geographic area involved opening stores in small towns surrounding a targeted metropolitan area *before* moving into the metropolitan area itself—an approach that Sam Walton termed "backward expansion." The target area was gradually saturated by opening Discount City stores in 20 to 40 towns clustered around the area's largest trade center. Wal-Mart management believed that any town with a shopping-area population of 15,000 or more persons was big enough to support a Discount City store. Once stores were opened in many of the targeted towns around the most populous city, Wal-Mart would locate one or more stores in the metropolitan area and begin major market advertising.

E X H I B I T   3   **Sample Layouts and Scenes at Wal-Mart Discount City Stores**

By clustering new stores in a relatively small geographic area, the company's advertising budget for breaking into a new market could be shared across all the area stores, thus helping to keep Wal-Mart's total advertising spending under 1 percent of sales (compared to 2 or 3 percent for other discount chains). When the targeted geographic area approached its store saturation level, the expansion effort shifted to penetrating adjoining market areas. Don Soderquist, vice chairman of Wal-Mart, explained why the company preferred its backward expansion strategy:

> Our strategy is to go into smaller markets first before we hit major metro areas because you've got a smaller population base to convince over. So you begin to get the acceptance in smaller markets and the word begins to travel around and people begin to travel further and further to get to your stores.[1]

Exhibit 5 shows the pattern of Wal-Mart's geographic expansion during the 1980s.

In the small towns Wal-Mart entered, it was not unusual for a number of businesses that carried merchandise similar to Wal-Mart's lines to fail within a year or two of Wal-Mart's arrival. Wal-Mart's low prices tended to attract customers away from apparel shops, general stores, pharmacies, sporting goods stores, shoe stores, and hardware stores operated by local merchants. The "Wal-Mart effect" in small communities was so big that it spawned the formation of consulting firms specializing in advising local retailers on how to survive the opening of a Wal-Mart. One small-town Chamber of Commerce official observed:

> Wal-Mart is responsible for changing downtown America more than any business in the 20th Century. Sam Walton built his empire on going into small communities. As he went into a small community, overnight, buying patterns went from downtown to . . . Wal-Mart.[2]

In many small towns, the Wal-Mart store was a landmark and social center; one local official in a small town (population 5,600) said, "Anybody who is anybody goes to Wal-Mart."

Experimentation with New Store Formats

A second element of Wal-Mart's growth strategy involved the development of different store formats. Sam's Wholesale Club marked Wal-Mart's first major venture to expand its merchandising reach. The company saw excellent strategic fit between its Wal-Mart discount operations and the concept of wholesale club merchandising.

Sam's Wholesale Club   Sam's Wholesale Clubs were a membership-only, cash-and-carry warehouse, approximately 100,000 square feet in size, which carried mostly best-selling brands in bulk quantities. In effect, it was a Wal-Mart Discount City operating in a different merchandising dimension. To qualify for membership, one had to be the owner of a business, self-employed, a government employee (federal, state, or local), Wal-Mart stockholder, or be

---

[1]*Discount Store News*, December 18, 1989, p. 162.
[2]As quoted in *USA Today*, October 11, 1990, p. 3A.

EXHIBIT 5   **Number and Location of Wal-Mart Discount City Stores and Sam's Wholesale Clubs, by State, 1980, 1985, and 1990**

Legend: Circled numbers indicate the number of Sam's Wholesale Clubs in the state; uncircled numbers represent the number of Wal-Mart Discount City stores.

Source: Annual Reports.

buying on behalf of a civic or community service organization; a federal tax I.D. or a business license was often used to establish an applicant's membership eligibility. The annual membership fee was $25. Sam's was aimed primarily at serving the needs of small businesses for general merchandise and supplies for internal use. The advertising tag line for Sam's was "Our business is your business."

The shopping environment at Sam's was a warehouse-type atmosphere where most goods were displayed in the original cartons stacked in wooden racks and bins or on wooden pallets. Where feasible, goods sent to Sam's were premarked and palletized, allowing the merchandise to be moved from delivery trucks into the selling/display area by mechanized means rather than by hand. In the greatly downscaled apparel department, merchandise was displayed on tables, in boxes, and from metal hanging racks. The major lines paralleled those of Discount City stores, but the selection was narrower and the emphasis was on either big-ticket items (tires, appliances, consumer electronics) or items that shoppers used frequently enough to buy in quantity. Many items stocked were sold in bulk quantity (five-gallon containers, bundles of a dozen or more, and economy-size boxes). Prices tended to be 10 to 15 percent below the prices of Discount City stores since merchandising costs and store operation costs were substantially lower.

The first Sam's was opened in 1983, and by 1990 there were 123 wholesale warehouses open in 25 states. Sales in fiscal year 1990 exceeded $5.1 billion, averaging just over $40 million per unit. In recent years, revenues from the Sam's Wholesale Club units had grown faster than those from Wal-Mart's other discount stores. The club's share of total Wal-Mart revenues had increased from 14 percent in 1986 to almost 20 percent in 1990. Wal-Mart was experimenting with several modifications of the Sam's Wholesale Club format, including increasing the size from 100,000 to 130,000 square feet and offering such service and merchandise enhancements as an on-premise bakery, a butcher shop, a produce department, an optical facility, and an express shipping service.

Hypermart*USA and SuperCenters   A second variation of the discount store format were the Hypermart*USA stores and SuperCenters that Wal-Mart began testing in 1987. Both were experiments to determine if Wal-Mart could profitably merchandise groceries, fresh produce, and frozen foods jointly with general merchandise to create an even more appealing one-stop shopping environment. Wal-Mart's management described the Hypermart*USA store format as a "blend of the best of a Wal-Mart store, a combination supermarket/ general merchandise store and a Sam's Wholesale Club." The format of Super-Centers combined a typical Wal-Mart Discount City and a supermarket to offer traditional selections in general merchandise and food. Hypermarts covered 225,000 square feet and were targeted toward medium- and large-population centers where sales per store could reasonably be expected to reach $100 million annually. SuperCenters were about 125,000 to 150,000 square feet in size and were targeted for smaller locations where sales per store of $30 to $50 million annually were thought feasible. Scenes from these two stores are displayed in Exhibit 6.

As of 1990, Wal-Mart was not satisfied with the Hypermart format; the store size was so large that many customers were overwhelmed and found it took

E X H I B I T 6   Sample Scenes and Layouts at Hypermart∗USA and SuperCenters

too much time to find all the items they were shopping for. Although Wal-Mart planned to continue to experiment with the three Hypermart∗USA stores that it had opened, only one new Hypermart∗USA was planned until the format was refined and better results were achieved. However, the Super-Center format was deemed quite promising; numerous experiments were underway in the three SuperCenters already open and the company was planning to further market test the SuperCenter concept by opening three additional stores of this type in 1990. In testing the SuperCenter concept the company was focusing on improving merchandise layouts and displays and on learning all it could about grocery marketing and grocery distribution. Industry observers felt that Wal-Mart would step up the opening of Super-Centers as soon as management was confident it had the skills and the organizational ability in place to execute the concept with a high degree of proficiency. In addition, Wal-Mart in 1989 had opened six convenience store prototypes adjacent to SuperCenter, Hypermart, Sam's, or Wal-Mart Discount City locations and was experimenting with a concept called "vendor stores," which featured goods of selected brand name merchandisers.

Merchandising Innovations

Wal-Mart was unusually active in testing and experimenting with new merchandising techniques. From the beginning, Sam Walton had been quick to adopt good ideas developed first by other retailers. Wal-Mart prided itself on its "low threshold for change" and much of management's time was spent talking to vendors, employees, and customers to get ideas for how Wal-Mart could improve. Suggestions were actively solicited from employees. Almost any reasonable idea was tried; if it worked well in stores where it was first tested, then it was quickly implemented in other stores. Experiments in store layout, merchandise displays, store color schemes, merchandise selection (whether to add more upscale lines or shift to a different mix of items), and sales promotion techniques were always underway. Wal-Mart was regarded as an industry leader in testing, adapting, and applying a wide range of cutting-edge merchandising approaches. Innovation and continuous improvement were a fundamental part of Wal-Mart's strategy.

THE COMPETITIVE ENVIRONMENT

Discount retailing was an intensely competitive business. Exhibit 7 presents comparative data for the leading discount retailers in the United States in 1989. Wal-Mart's closest competitor was Kmart. Both firms had comparable strategies and store formats, but throughout the 1980s Wal-Mart had grown far faster than Kmart (see Exhibit 1). In 1989 Sears, concerned with lagging sales and Wal-Mart's rapid climb toward industry leadership, switched to an everyday low-price strategy and started stocking leading brand-name merchandise to complement its own private-label goods. In 1990, nearly all discounters were using some form of everyday low pricing.

Competition among discount retailers centered around pricing, store location, variations in store format and merchandise mix, store size, shopping atmosphere, and image with shoppers. Wal-Mart was the only major discount

EXHIBIT 7   **Comparative Financial and Operating Statistics for Leading Discount Retailers, 1989**

Store	Revenues (In millions of dollars)	Net Income (In millions of dollars)	Number of Stores	Total Square Feet of Retail Sales Space (In millions of dollars)	Number of Employees (In thousands)	Average Store Size (In square feet)	Retail Sales per Square Foot of Store Space
Kmart	$29,533	$1,155	2,105	124.4	350	59,097	$237.40
Wal-Mart	25,810	1,076	1,525	107.0	275	70,164	241.21
Sears	53,794	1,509	1,649	126.0	343	76,410	257.94‡
Target	7,519	449*	399	40.0	NA	100,251	187.98
Montgomery Ward	5,374	130†	324	25.9	49	79,938	207.49
Ames	3,271	47	850	52.6	61	61,882	62.19
Bradlees	2,117	84*	131	9.4	NA	71,756	225.21
Hills	2,076	108	167	13.4	25	80,240	154.93
Roses Stores	1,439	26	250	10.5	21	42,000	137.05
Venture	1,339	81	75	6.1	NA	81,333	219.51

*Data are operating income for the subsidiary. Target is owned by Dayton-Hudson Corp. and Bradlees is a wholly owned subsidiary of SSC Holdings.

†1988 net income. 1989 data not available because Montgomery Ward became a privately owned company in 1989.

‡Based on retail store sales of approximately $32.5 billion; Sears' total revenues of $53.8 billion include sales from other subsidiaries not associated with its retail store operations.

NA = not available.

Sources: Company annual reports and Standard & Poor's Corporate Records.

retailer that located a majority of its stores in rural areas. Surveys of households comparing Wal-Mart with Kmart and Target indicated that Wal-Mart had a strong competitive advantage. According to *Discount Store News*:

> When asked to compare Wal-Mart with Kmart and Target, the consensus of households is that Wal-Mart is as good or better. For example, of the households with a Wal-Mart in the area, 59 percent said that Wal-Mart is better than Kmart and Target; 33 percent said it was the same. Only 4 percent rated Wal-Mart worse than Kmart and Target. . . . When asked why Wal-Mart was better, 55 percent of the respondents with a Wal-Mart in their area said lower/better prices. . . . Variety/selection and good quality were the other top reasons cited by consumers when asked why Wal-Mart is better. Thirty percent said variety; 18 percent said good quality.[3]

Going into 1990, 90 percent of U.S. households with a Wal-Mart in their area also had a Kmart nearby; however, since Wal-Mart's coverage did not extend nationwide, as did Kmart's, only 39 percent of Kmart's stores faced competition from Wal-Mart. Wal-Mart had a favorable reputation in areas where it did not have stores, making it less of a problem to push the company's geographic perimeters outward. Numerous stories in the media about Sam Walton and the company he had founded had given Wal-Mart a high recognition factor among the public. According to a Wal-Mart executive:

---

[3]*Discount Store News*, December 18, 1989, p. 168.

EXHIBIT 8 **Comparative Financial and Operating Statistics for Leading Membership Warehouse Clubs, 1989**

Chain	Revenues (In millions of dollars)	Earnings (In millions of dollars)	Number of Stores	Average Store Size (In thousands square feet)
Price Club	$4,901	$191.1	47	100
Sam's	4,841	131.0	123	110
Costco Wholesale	2,943	55.5	62	110
Pace*	1,710	NA	47	100
BJ's Wholesale Club	985	18.6	23	105
Price Savers	685	NA	14	105
The Wholesale Club	570	8.6	23	105
Makro*	270	NA	9	100
Warehouse Club	267	2.2	12	100
Club Wholesale	70	NA	5	82
Wholesale Depot	6	NA	2	60

NA = not applicable.
*Both Pace and Makro are subsidiaries of Kmart.
Source: *Discount Store News*, July 2, 1990.

The acceptance is incredible. In Arizona there's a lot of retired people who shop Wal-Mart. In Florida, we are known by a lot of people. People who travel to Arizona or Florida for vacation or part of the winter go back to Pennsylvania, New York, Michigan, Ohio and say, "When are we going to get a Wal-Mart up here?" They've already been preconditioned a bit.[4]

The Warehouse Club Segment The two largest competitors in the warehouse club segment were Price Club and Sam's Wholesale Clubs. These two accounted for a combined total of 58 percent of total sales among wholesale clubs and had 46 percent of the number of store outlets (see Exhibit 8). Sam's expected to pass Price Club in sales in 1990.

There was an industrywide effort among the club competitors to differentiate themselves on the basis of service. The drive to enhance the services offered to qualifying members was intended to make club membership appealing to a broader segment of the market. Prior to the late 1980s, none of the six major warehouse clubs operated in the same geographic markets. However, the success of the club concept had fueled geographic expansion by all competitors. As competitors saturated the geographic areas surrounding their initial stores, they were expanding outward to increase market coverage and were trying to beat rival clubs to the most attractive market areas. By 1990, several warehouse club competitors had moved into their rivals' markets and were competing head-on for the first time.

---

[4]*Discount Store News*, December 18, 1989, p. 162.

WAL-MART'S APPROACHES TO STRATEGY IMPLEMENTATION

To implement its strategy, Wal-Mart put heavy emphasis on forging solid working relationships with both suppliers and employees, paying attention to even the tiniest details in store layouts and merchandising, capitalizing on every cost-saving opportunity, and creating a high-performance spirit. The characteristics that often stalled the growth and success of large companies— too many layers of management, lack of internal communication, and an unwillingness or inability to change—were absent at Wal-Mart.

The Everyday Low-Price Theme

While Wal-Mart did not invent the everyday low-price strategy, it had done a better job than any other discount retailer in executing the concept. The company had the reputation of being the everyday lowest-priced general merchandise retailer in its market. In areas where Wal-Mart had a store, consumer surveys showed 55 percent of the households considered Wal-Mart's prices as lower or better than competitors; an impressive 33 percent of the households not having a Wal-Mart store in their area had the same opinion.[5] Wal-Mart touted its low prices on its storefronts ("We Sell for Less"), in advertising, on signs inside its stores, and on the logos of its shopping bags.

Advertising

Wal-Mart made limited use of advertising as compared to other retailers. Using only one or two circulars per month (versus an average of one per week at Kmart), the company relied primarily on word-of-mouth to communicate its marketing message. As a percentage of sales, Wal-Mart's advertising expenditures were the lowest in the discount industry, several percentage points below what Kmart spent. The company's spending for radio and TV advertising was so low that it didn't register on national ratings scales. Most Wal-Mart broadcast ads appeared on local TV and local cable channels. Wal-Mart's low ad expenditures were sometimes compensated for by the publicity the company got from programs it had put in place. Sam Walton's announcement that Wal-Mart would give preferential treatment to products made in the United States generated thousands of local newspaper articles, nearly all of which quoted Wal-Mart statistics that its Buy American plan had saved or created thousands of American jobs. More recently, Wal-Mart had gotten free media publicity with its program to spotlight products with environmentally safe packaging. Wal-Mart often allowed charities to use its parking lots for their fundraising activities.

Distribution

Over the years, Wal-Mart management had turned the company's centralized distribution systems into a competitive edge. David Glass, Wal-Mart's president, said, "Our distribution facilities are one of the keys to our success. If we do anything better than other folks that's it."[6] Wal-Mart got an early jump on competitors in distribution efficiency because of its rural store locations.

---

[5]*Discount Store News*, December 18, 1989, p. 168.
[6]*Discount Store News*, December 18, 1989, p. 54.

Whereas other discount retailers relied upon manufacturers and distributors to ship directly to their mostly metropolitan-area stores, Wal-Mart found that its rapid growth during the 1970s was straining suppliers' ability to use independent trucking firms to make frequent and timely deliveries to its growing number of rural store locations. To improve the delivery of merchandise to its stores, in 1980 the company began to build its own centralized distribution centers and to supply stores from these centers with its own truck fleet. Wal-Mart added new distribution centers when new, outlying stores could no longer be reliably and economically supported from an existing center. In 1989, the company had 16 distribution centers covering 11.5 million square feet. Together the centers employed 10,000 workers who handled 300 million cases of merchandise annually, with a 99 percent accuracy rate on filling orders. Wal-Mart's distribution centers made extensive use of automated systems:

> The conveyor system starts with walk-pick modules where order selection occurs. The cartons move on a conveyor to a central merge where an operator releases cartons onto a sortation system. A laser scanner reads a bar code and tells the automatic sorter where to divert cartons at rates in excess of 120 per minute. The cartons are diverted to various shipping doors.[7]

Wal-Mart's distribution cost advantage over Sears and Kmart was significant:

	1988 Sales (In millions of dollars)	Distribution Costs (In millions of dollars)	Distribution Costs as a Percentage of Sales
Sears	$50,251	$2,513	5.0%
Kmart	27,301	956	3.5
Wal-Mart	20,649	263	1.3

Source: *Discount Store News*, December 18, 1989, p. 201.

Whereas Wal-Mart had the capability to make daily deliveries to nearly all its stores, Kmart delivered to its stores about once every four or five days and Target delivered every three to four days. As a consequence, Wal-Mart's stores stayed amply stocked, rarely losing a sale due to a stock-out.

The Use of Cutting-Edge Technology

Wal-Mart was aggressive in applying the latest technological advances to increase productivity and drive costs down. Wal-Mart's use of technology had one overriding goal: to provide employees with the tools to do their jobs more efficiently and to make better decisions. Technology was not used as a means to replace people. Moreover, Wal-Mart's approach to technology was to be on the offense—probing, testing, and then deploying the newest equipment, retailing techniques, and computer software programs ahead of most, if not all, other discount retailers.

In 1974 the company began using computers to maintain inventory control on an item basis in distribution centers and in its stores. In 1981 Wal-Mart

---

[7]*Discount Store News*, December 18, 1989, p. 54.

began testing point-of-sale scanners, and in 1983 it committed to chainwide use of scanning bar codes—a move that resulted in 25 to 30 percent faster checkouts of customers. In 1984 Wal-Mart developed a computer-assisted merchandising system that allowed the product mix in each store to be tailored to its own market circumstances and sales patterns.

Between 1985 and 1987 Wal-Mart installed the nation's largest private satellite communication network, which allowed two-way voice and data transmission between headquarters, the distribution centers, and the stores, and one-way video transmission from Bentonville's corporate offices to distribution centers and to the stores. The system was less expensive than the previously used telephone network. The video system was used regularly by company officials to speak directly to all employees at once.

In 1989 Wal-Mart established direct satellite linkage with about 1,700 vendors who supplied close to 80 percent of the goods sold by Wal-Mart; this linkup allowed the use of electronic purchase orders and instant data exchanges. Wal-Mart had also used the satellite system's capabilities to develop a credit card authorization procedure that took five seconds, on average, to authorize a purchase, thus speeding up credit checkout by 25 percent compared to the prior manual system. The company had exemplary data processing and information systems. Not only had the company developed computer systems to provide management with detailed figures on nearly any aspect of Wal-Mart's operations, but the company was also regarded as having one of the most low-cost, efficient data processing operations of any company its size in the world. The company's rapid adoption of cutting-edge retailing technologies across many areas of its business had given Wal-Mart a technology advantage over most other discounters.

Construction Policies

Wal-Mart management worked at getting more mileage out of its capital expenditures for new stores, store renovations, and store fixtures. Ideas and suggestions were solicited from vendors regarding store layout, the design of fixtures, and space needed for effective displays. Wal-Mart's store designs had open-air offices for management personnel that could be furnished economically and featured a maximum of display space that could be rearranged and refurbished easily. Because Wal-Mart insisted on a high degree of uniformity in the new stores it built, the architectural firm Wal-Mart employed was able to use computer modeling techniques to turn out complete specifications for up to 12 new stores a week. Moreover, the stores were designed to permit quick, inexpensive construction as well as to allow for low-cost maintenance and renovation. All stores were renovated and redecorated at least once every seven years. If a given store location was rendered obsolete by the construction of new roads and highways and the opening of new shopping locations, then the old store was abandoned in favor of a new store at a more desirable site.

In keeping with the low-cost theme for facilities, Wal-Mart's distribution centers and corporate offices were also built economically and furnished simply. The offices of top executives were modest and unpretentious. The lighting, heating, and air-conditioning controls at all Wal-Mart stores were connected via computer to Bentonville headquarters, allowing cost-saving energy management practices to be implemented centrally and freeing store managers from the time and worry of trying to hold down utility costs. Wal-Mart mass-produced a lot of its displays in-house, not only saving money but also cutting the time to roll out a new display concept to as little as 30 days.

Relationships with Suppliers

While the company was noted for harmonious vendor relations, Wal-Mart drove a hard bargain with its suppliers, bringing all of its considerable buying power to bear. The company's purchasing department was austere and utilitarian. Purchasing agents were dedicated to getting the lowest prices they could, and they did not accept invitations to be wined or dined by suppliers. The marketing vice president of a major vendor told *Fortune* magazine:

> They are very, very focused people, and they use their buying power more forcefully than anybody else in America. All the normal mating rituals are verboten. Their highest priority is making sure everybody at all times in all cases knows who's in charge, and it's Wal-Mart. They talk softly, but they have piranha hearts, and if you aren't totally prepared when you go in there, you'll have your ass handed to you.[8]

Despite Wal-Mart's reputation for buying merchandise at an absolute rock-bottom price, the company worked closely with suppliers to develop mutual respect and to forge a long-term partnership relationship that benefited both parties. Vendors were invited to tour Wal-Mart's distribution centers to see firsthand how things operated and to learn what kinds of problems Wal-Mart might be having in achieving greater efficiency. Vendors were also encouraged to voice any problems in their relationship with Wal-Mart and to become involved in Wal-Mart's future plans. For example, Procter & Gamble (P&G) had a team of people stationed near Wal-Mart headquarters to work with Wal-Mart on a continuing basis. One top-priority project involved working to supply more P&G items in recyclable packaging to meet Wal-Mart's publicly stated goal of selling products that were environmentally safe. Another concerned helping to set up a just-in-time ordering and delivery system for P&G disposable diapers in all Wal-Mart stores; when diaper stocks reached the reorder point, a computer automatically sent a resupply order by satellite to the nearest P&G factory, which then shipped more diapers directly to the store. P&G and Wal-Mart saw the arrangement on diapers as a win-win proposition because both ended up with lower costs.

Wal-Mart looked for suppliers who were dominant in their category (thus providing strong brand-name recognition), could grow with the company, had full product lines (so that Wal-Mart buyers and merchandise managers could both cherry-pick and get some sort of limited exclusivity on the products the company chose to carry), had the long-term commitment to R&D to bring new and better products to retail shelves, and had the ability to become more efficient in producing and delivering what it supplied. As one supplier remarked, "Wal-Mart wants suppliers who can keep up." Several suppliers described Wal-Mart's approaches to doing business with them:

---

[8]*Fortune*, January 30, 1989, p. 53.

They challenge us constantly. Can we do this? How about if we tried that? They're constantly on the lookout for ways to improve themselves. . . .

They approach problems as opportunities, not as complaints. They're completely genuine in meetings . . . all cards are on the table.

No matter how good your products are, if they don't tell the story on the shelf, they won't do well at Wal-Mart. They're looking for dynamic, creative packaging that will act as a sales[person].

They know their stores, their products, and their markets, and they have an uncanny ability to predict what their customer wants. Their advice about products is valuable to us.

We have to do what we say we're going to do. . . . Wal-Mart's demands can be staggering, like when they need many thousands of VCRs for a promotion. If we can't be sure that we can have the stock *in their warehouses* on a given day, we let them know that, [and] suggest moving the promotion back a month.

They honor their commitments and they expect the same in return. If we gear up for a promotion, and the circular gets cancelled, they'll still take the goods. That's how they do business.[9]

The Vendor Store Concept   An outgrowth of Wal-Mart's commitment to working with its suppliers was the testing of a new store concept, the vendor store. Vendor stores involved selecting a key supplier in a major category and giving the supplier wide latitude in merchandising their products. Suppliers participating in the vendor store test included Rubbermaid, Black & Decker, Gitano, Cannon, Pioneer, Toshiba, and Wrangler. Wal-Mart saw the vendor store not only as a way to secure even more involvement from recognized brand-name suppliers but also as a way to offer greater value to upscale consumers.

The "Buy American" and "Environmentally Safe" Policies

Wal-Mart had implemented two policies for which it received much media attention. In a March 1985 letter sent to about 3,000 domestic suppliers, Sam Walton discussed the serious threat of the nation's balance of trade deficit and conveyed the company's intention to carry U.S.-made goods in Wal-Mart's stores:

> Our Wal-Mart company is firmly committed to the philosophy of buying everything possible from suppliers who manufacture their products in the United States. We are convinced that with proper planning and cooperation between retailers and manufacturers many products can be supplied to us that are comparable, or better, in value and quality to those we have been buying offshore. . . . Wal-Mart believes our American workers can make the difference if management provides the leadership.

Walton then sent a now-famous edict to Wal-Mart buyers and merchandise managers: "Find products that American manufacturers have stopped producing because they couldn't compete with foreign imports." Wal-Mart kicked off its Buy American program publicly with newspaper and TV ads featuring the slogans "We Buy American Whenever We Can So You Can, Too" and

---

[9]*Discount Store News*, December 18, 1989, pp. 109 and 156.

"Wal-Mart—Keeping Americans Working and Strong." As of 1990, Wal-Mart claimed that the policy had created or saved over 43,000 American jobs. The use of imported goods had been cut 5 percent, reducing the total to between 25 to 30 percent of everything Wal-Mart sold. Wal-Mart stores had "Bring It Home to the USA" signs hanging from store ceilings, and display shelves that held American-made goods had special posters citing job-creating statistics (see Exhibit 9). However, Wal-Mart was generally unwilling to substitute U.S.-made products for foreign imports if it meant higher prices to customers. According to industry analysts, Wal-Mart imported about twice as much as Kmart. Yet, because of the manner in which Wal-Mart had implemented and communicated its Buy American policy, consumer awareness of Wal-Mart's efforts were high in comparison with other companies that had followed Wal-Mart's lead in promoting American-made products.

In 1989 Wal-Mart embarked on a program urging suppliers to develop products and packaging that would not harm the environment. It was the first major retailer to exhibit environmental concerns by taking concrete actions as opposed to giving lip service. The campaign was kicked off with full-page ads in *USA Today* and *The Wall Street Journal*, using the theme "We're Looking for Quality Products That Are Guaranteed Not to Last." The policy was implemented because Wal-Mart's top management saw the environment as a top priority national issue; Wal-Mart's president David Glass told an audience:

> I believe that retailers and suppliers must now be socially conscious in a way that we haven't before. Those of you who don't believe that we have a terrible problem with the environment are naive. We are running out of land to bury things. We are quickly spoiling our drinking water and eroding the ozone layer. . . .
>
> We need to take a responsibility for the role we play and for our own actions. What we will do is identify these products in our showrooms and ask our customers to buy those rather than other products that are not safe for the environment. . . . We believe we can bring [environmentally safe products] to market at the same kind of price.[10]

Despite some cynical observations that Wal-Mart's policy was a publicity and marketing ploy, Wal-Mart began efforts to influence its suppliers to spend more on R&D to develop products with more environmentally safe ingredients and to find ways to use recyclable packaging materials. Wal-Mart committed to highlighting vendor improvements with special store signs alongside the products. Procter & Gamble was among the first suppliers to be responsive to Wal-Mart's environmental program; by year-end 1989 all of P&G's soap and detergent packages had been converted to 100 percent recycled cartons and its plastic containers were being coded so they could be efficiently separated for recycling. The head of P&G's team servicing the Wal-Mart account commented, "They're trying to do the right thing and to educate the consumer." Wal-Mart was negotiating with suppliers of its signs, shopping bags, and other such items to convert them to environmentally safe products; for years, the company had used paper bags made from recycled paper while competitors had switched to nonbiodegradable plastic bags.

---

[10]*Discount Store News*, December 18, 1989, pp. 214 and 235.

EXHIBIT 9   **Examples of Wal-Mart's Signs and Ads Advocating American-Made Products and Environmental Consciousness**

Bring It Home To The U.S.A.

At Wal-Mart, we are committed to forming partnerships with American manufacturers to produce products we are currently buying from foreign markets.

PREVIOUSLY IMPORTED
NOW PURCHASED IN THE USA

Girls Flannel Shirts
Hampton Girl - Greenville, NC.
26 Jobs Created

.6 Cubic Foot Microwave
Magic Chef Inc. - Anniston, AL.
633 Jobs Created

JOBS FOR AMERICANS!

With your support, since 1985, we have created or retained over...

43,000
Manufacturing Jobs
for Americans

Our Commitment To Land, Air, & Water

You Can Make A Difference

- **Run washing machine and dishwasher only when full.**

- **Plant trees.**

- **Put in a toilet dam and reduce water use by 50%.**

- **Start a compost pile in your backyard.**

- **Keep a coffee mug at work.**

- **Water lawns and plants in the morning to minimize evaporation.**

- **Don't litter.**

- **Request a low-cost home energy audit from your utility company.**

- **Take glass, aluminum, paper to recycling centers. Each U.S. citizen produces 4 to 6 pounds of waste per day, 80% of which ends up in land fills.**

- **Look for the three-arrow recycling symbol on packages.**

RECYCLE

Wal-Mart's Approach to Providing Superior Customer Service

Wal-Mart placed extraordinary emphasis on making sure that customers enjoyed their shopping experience at Wal-Mart and were satisfied with their purchases. A "greeter" was stationed at the entrance to Wal-Mart stores and Sam's Wholesale Clubs to welcome customers with a smile, thank them for shopping at the store, assist them in getting a shopping cart, and answer questions about where items were located. Clerks and checkout workers were trained to be courteous and helpful and to exhibit a "friendly, folksy attitude." All store personnel took an oath of friendliness: "I solemnly promise and declare that every customer that comes within 10 feet of me, I will smile, look them in the eye, and greet them, so help me Sam." Wal-Mart's management stressed to store personnel that they needed to do five things to be successful:

1. Think like a customer.
2. Sell the customers what they wanted to buy.
3. Provide a genuine value to the customer.
4. Make sure the customer had a good time.
5. Exceed the customer's expectations.

One of the standard Wal-Mart chants drilled into all employees was:

Who's No. 1? The customer.
The customer is the boss.

Wal-Mart's newest stores had wider aisles and significantly more customer space. In all stores, efforts were under way to present merchandise in "easier-to-shop" shelving and displays. Floors in the apparel section were carpeted to make the department feel homier and to make shopping seem easier on customers' feet. Store layouts were constantly scrutinized to improve shopping convenience and make it easier for customers to find items. Store employees wore blue vests to make it easier for customers to pick them out from a distance. Fluorescent lighting was recessed into the ceiling, creating a softer impression than the exposed fluorescent lighting strips used at Kmart stores. The decor of Wal-Mart's stores conveyed feelings of warmth and freshness, the objective being to signal customers that Wal-Mart was a bit more upscale and carried merchandise of a little better quality than rivals. Yet nothing about the decor conflicted with Wal-Mart's low-price image; retailing consultants considered Wal-Mart as being very adept at sending out an effective mix of vibes and signals concerning customer service, low prices, quality merchandise, and friendly shopping environment.

Wal-Mart's management believed that the attention paid to all the details of making the stores more user-friendly and inviting caused shoppers to view Wal-Mart in a more positive light. A reporter for *Discount Store News* observed:

The fact is that everything Wal-Mart does from store design to bar coding to lighting to greeters—regardless of how simple or complex—is implemented only after carefully considering the impact on the customer. Virtually nothing is done without the guarantee that it benefits the customer in some way. . . . As a result Wal-Mart has been able to build loyalty and trust among its customers that is unparalleled among other retail giants.[11]

---

[11]*Discount Store News*, December 18, 1989, p. 161.

Sam Walton's Leadership Style and Approaches

"Sam Walton is the warmest, most genuine human being who's ever
walked the face of the earth."
Bill Avery,
Wal-Mart management recruiter

Mr. Sam, as he was often called, was not only Wal-Mart's founder but also the company patriarch. His outgoing personality, unpretentious manner, and genuine regard for people and their feelings caused Wal-Mart employees to hold him in the highest esteem. Despite his enormous wealth, he lived in a modest house in Bentonville, Arkansas, and drove a pickup truck. The comments of several Wal-Mart associates indicated their feelings for him:

He's a beautiful man. I met him when this store opened. He came back two and one half years later and still remembered me. He walked over to this department and said, "Grace, you and I have been around a long time, I'm gonna hug your neck." That's just the type of guy he is. He's just a wonderful person.

I was just . . . I was thrilled [to meet him]. He's a very special person. He is a very outgoing person, and it kind of motivates you just to sit and listen to him talk. He listens—that's another thing.

I think he's a fine person. He's just an everyday person like one of us. When you meet him he's just like one of us. You can talk to him. Anything you want to ask him—you can just go right up and ask.

He's really down-to-earth. He'll put his arm around you, hug you, and tell you you're doing a good job.

Mr. Walton cares about his employees. You get the feeling that you're working for him instead of Wal-Mart. And although he may not need the money, he's good to us and we try to be good to him.

His business philosophy underpinned the company's culture and could be summarized in four key core values and beliefs:

- Treat employees as partners, sharing both the good and bad about the company so they will strive to excel and participate in the rewards.
- Build for the future, rather than just immediate gains, by continuing to study the changing concepts that are a mark of the retailing industry and be ready to test and experiment with new ideas.
- Recognize that the road to success includes failing, which is part of the learning process rather than a personal or corporate defect. Always challenge the obvious.
- Involve employees at all levels in the total decision-making process.[12]

Sam Walton practiced these principles diligently in his own actions and he insisted other Wal-Mart managers do the same. His own direct, hands-on approach involved visiting the stores, listening to employees discuss what was on their minds, learning what was or was not selling, gathering ideas about how things could be done better, and complimenting them on their works. Charles Cates, a former manager of the second store Wal-Mart opened, described what happened on a typical visit by Sam to a Wal-Mart store:

---

[12]*Discount Store News*, December 18, 1989, p. 29.

First, you get a telephone call from Sam. He says, "Charlie, can you pick me up at the airport?" Then, in the car, he wants to know who your assistant managers are . . . the names of their children, wives, and what's happening in their lives. So you brief him on your assistants and their families.

When he gets to the store, he wants to take a tour. He goes to each department manager. He'll say, "The department looks good," and ask, "Why are we out of merchandise? What are your sales this year? What's your markup? What's your best-selling item?"

He pats them on the back, shakes their hands, and thanks them for doing a good job. He's always motivating people. The associates feel like they're working directly for Sam Walton.

After the tour, he'll meet with the associates in the store lounge. He commends them for the store's sales increases and he talks about merchandise. He has contests with merchandise. He'll tell a department manager: "You all find an item and I'll find an item and we'll see which item sells better."

He's always challenging us. He'll look at another item and ask, "It's priced at $5. How many more can we sell at $4?"[13]

Following Walton's lead, it became established practice for Wal-Mart managers at all levels to spend much time and effort motivating employees to achieve excellence, offer ideas, get involved, and function as partners. A theme iterated over and over was that every cost counted and every worker had a responsibility; the slogan that every employee heard repeatedly was "The customer is boss and the future depends on you." David Glass explained the philosophy underlying this approach:

> Wal-Mart is unique because we require involvement. There's a pressure to get involved. Whatever level you're at, you'll perform far better if you're involved and believe that you can make a difference.[14]

Wal-Mart fostered the concept of involvement by referring to all employees as "associates," a term Sam Walton had insisted on from the company's beginnings because it denoted a partnerlike relationship.

Soliciting Ideas from Associates

Associates at all levels of the company were encouraged to come up with ideas and suggestions to make the company better. An assistant store manager explained:

> We are encouraged to be merchants. If a sales clerk, a checker, or a stockman believes he can sell an item and wants to promote it, he is encouraged to go for it. That associate can buy the merchandise, feature it, and maintain it as long as he can sell it.[15]

That same assistant store manager, when he accidentally ordered four times as many Moon Pies for an in-store promotion as intended, was challenged by the store manager to be creative and figure out a way to sell the extra inventory. The assistant manager's solution was to create the first World Championship Moon Pie Eating Contest, held in the store's parking lot in the small town of

---

[13]*Discount Store News*, December 18, 1989, p. 235.

[14]*Discount Store News*, December 18, 1989, p. 235.

[15]*Discount Store News*, December 18, 1989, p. 83.

Oneonta, Alabama. The promotion and contest drew thousands of spectators and was so successful that it became an annual store event.

Wal-Mart's Participatory Management Techniques

Wal-Mart stressed participatory management from the top to the bottom, and listening was a very important part of each manager's job. All Wal-Mart executives relied on MBWA (management by walking around); they visited stores, distribution centers, and support facilities regularly, staying on top of what was happening and listening to what employees had to say about how things were going.

David Glass, Wal-Mart's president and successor to Sam Walton as chief executive officer, commented on the store visitation effort:

> Our focus is spending two, three days out of the week talking to our people, going to the stores, relating to them. . . . Yesterday I went to a store and spoke to all the department managers in the back and asked them what's going on. We take the hourly people out to lunch or eat in the back room with them. . . .
>
> People want to know deep down inside that they're doing a good job. They want to be able to go home and say, "Guess what? The manager came by today and recognized that I did something well, and he told the other people in the store meeting about it. . . . " You have to catch people when they're doing something right, not always when they're doing something wrong. Don't hold to the belief they're sluggards, always goofing off and that you have to be on their tail every minute. . . . Presume these people are hardworking people. . . .[16]

One manager told a casewriter that up to 90 percent of his day was spent walking around the store communicating with the associates—praising them for a job well done, discussing how improvements could be made, listening to their comments, and soliciting suggestions. A steady stream of ideas from associates on how to improve performance was the rule rather than the exception. Moreover, Wal-Mart associates were encouraged to put their ideas into action. According to Sam Walton:

> Our philosophy is that management's role is to get the right people in the right places to do a job and then to encourage them to use their own inventiveness to accomplish the task at hand.

Task forces to evaluate ideas and plan out future actions to implement them were common, and it was not unusual for the person who developed the idea to be appointed the leader of the group.

The task of involving employees in the management process at Wal-Mart began with store management asking each associate what he or she could do individually or what could be done to improve store operations. If anyone believed a policy or procedure detracted from operations, associates at all levels were encouraged to challenge and change it.

The Work Atmosphere at Wal-Mart   Throughout company literature, comments could be found referring to Wal-Mart's "concern for the individual." Such expressions as "Our people make the difference," "We care about people," and "People helping People" were used repeatedly by Wal-Mart executives. "It's a lot of hard work, but it's so much fun," one Wal-Mart executive told

---

[16]*Discount Store News*, December 18, 1989, pp. 83 and 231.

a casewriter concerning his job with Wal-Mart. He indicated that he enjoyed working for a company that promoted a concerned feeling toward its associates. He also stated that work at Wal-Mart was never dull. New challenges were always cropping up in the form of new products to be marketed or new merchandising techniques to be tested or implemented. In interviewing a number of Wal-Mart management associates, one of the casewriters was told several times that Wal-Mart was a wonderful place to work because of all the human resource practices carried out by the company. One of the company's management recruiters said:

> It's a special feeling you get when you walk in a Wal-Mart store. And when you're working there is when you really notice it because the people care about each other. It's like being with a successful football team, that feeling of togetherness, and everyone is willing to sacrifice in order to stay together.

In questioning Wal-Mart associates about how they liked working at Wal-Mart, a number of comments were made to a casewriter about the family-oriented atmosphere that was fostered among store associates:

> There is no comparison between Wal-Mart and other places I've worked. Wal-Mart is far above. They just treat customers and associates really nice.
>
> It's more of a family-oriented place than anywhere I've worked. They seem to really care about their employees. It's not just the money they're making, but a true concern for the people working here.
>
> We're just like a family. Everybody cares for each other. The management is fantastic. You can go to them for anything and feel free to contradict them if you want to.
>
> They select such nice people to work with. We get along well.
>
> I care about my responsibilities. You're just more proud of it. You're more apt to care about it. You'll want people to come in and see what you've done. I guess the pats on the back let you know what you've done is appreciated. And when they show their appreciation you're going to care more and do better.
>
> We're a united group. We may be from different walks of life but once we get here we're a group. You may leave them at the door, but when you're in here you're part of a family. You help each other; you try to be everybody's friend. It's a united feeling.

Yet, Wal-Mart still had vestiges of some old-fashioned beliefs and employment practices that in 1990 seemed out of step in an otherwise progressive company. Restrictions on hiring persons over 65 were not formally lifted until Sam Walton himself approached the mandatory retirement age of 65. There were relatively few women in store management positions even though the majority of the employees in many stores were female. Only two of the company's top 80 executives were women. Associates were not allowed to date one another without authorization from the executive committee.

At the close of interviews with Wal-Mart associates at two Alabama stores, the casewriters asked associates to relate what made Wal-Mart special from their perspective:

> They tell us that we are the best.
>
> I like working at Wal-Mart better than any other place. I'm freer to handle the work better. . . . I can go at my own speed and do the work the way I want to do it.
>
> I enjoy Wal-Mart; I've been here eight years. Of course, we work, but that's what we're here for. You've got potential with Wal-Mart.

I think Wal-Mart is one of the best companies there is. I wouldn't want to work for anyone else.

The editors of the trade publication *Mass Market Retailers* paid tribute to the some 275,000 Wal-Mart associates by recognizing them collectively as the 1989 Mass Market Retailers of the Year. They summed up the contributions and efforts of Wal-Mart's employees:

The Wal-Mart Associate. In this decade that term has come to symbolize all that is right with the American worker, particularly in the retailing environment and most particularly at Wal-Mart. . . .

Compensation and Incentives

Wal-Mart had installed an extensive system of incentives that allowed associates to share monetarily in the rewards of their achievements. In fiscal year 1990, Wal-Mart's incentive payouts of all kinds amounted to $190 million.

Profit-Sharing Plan   In 1990 the company contributed over $90 million to profit sharing; there were over 147,000 associates participating in the company's $800 million profit-sharing trust fund. Associates were eligible to participate in profit sharing the month following one year of continuous full-time service in which the individual had worked 1,000 hours or more. At the end of an associate's second year of service, the company began contributing to the plan, in the associate's name, a certain percentage of its profits. The money, contributed solely by the company, became vested at the rate of 20 percent per year beginning the third year of participation in the plan. After seven years of continuous employment the associate became fully vested; however, if the associate left the company prior to that time, the unvested portions were redirected into a company fund and redistributed to all remaining employees. A significant portion of the profit-sharing contributions were invested in Wal-Mart's common stock, with the remainder put into other investments. Associates could begin withdrawals from their account upon retirement or disability, with the balance paid to family members upon death.

Stock Purchase Plan   A stock purchase plan was adopted in 1972 to allow eligible employees a means of purchasing shares of Wal-Mart's common stock on the NYSE through regular payroll deduction or annual lump-sum contribution. Prior to 1990, the yearly maximum under this program was $1,500 per eligible employee; starting in 1990 the maximum was increased to $1,800 annually. The company contributed an amount equal to 15 percent of each participating associate's contribution. About 92,000 of the 275,000 associates were participating in the plan; in 1990 alone almost 1.2 million shares were purchased. Long-time employees who had started participating in the early years of the program had accumulated quite substantial sums—a $10,000 investment in Wal-Mart stock in 1980 was worth $800,000 as of January 1991.

Base Compensation and Benefits   Although only full-time associates were allowed to participate in Wal-Mart's benefits programs, Wal-Mart did not go out of its way to hire a large ratio of part-time employees to avoid having to pay benefits. In one store, there was approximately a five-to-one full-time to part-time associate ratio.

Associates at Wal-Mart were hired at higher than minimum wage and could expect to receive a raise within the first year at one or both of the semi- annual job evaluations. An associate told a casewriter that at least one raise was guaranteed in the first year if Wal-Mart planned to keep the individual on the staff. The other raise depended on how well the associate worked and improved during the year. At Wal-Mart only the store managers were salaried. All other associates, including the department managers, were considered hourly employees.

Sales Contest and Other Incentive Programs   One of Wal-Mart's most successful incentive programs was its VPI (volume-producing item) contests. In this contest, departments within the store were able to do a special promotion and pricing on items they themselves wanted to feature. Management believed the VPI contests boosted sales, breathed new life into an otherwise slow-selling item, and helped keep associates thinking about how to help bolster sales; two sales associates commented on the VPI incentive scheme:

> We have contests. You feature an item in your department and see how well it sells each week. If your feature wins, you get a half-day off.
>
> They have a lot of contests. If you're the top seller in the store you can win money. For four weeks in a row I've won money. That gives you a little incentive to do the very best you can. You kind of compete with other departments even though we're a big family in the long run. You like a little competition, but not too much.

Associate incentive plans were in place in every store, club, distribution center, and support facility. Associates received bonuses for good ideas, such as how to reduce shoplifting or how to improve merchandising. Walton instituted a shrinkage bonus in 1980. If a store held losses from theft and damage below the corporate goal, every associate in that store was eligible to receive up to $200. As a result, Wal-Mart's shrinkage in 1989 was just above one percent compared to an industry average of two percent. Wal-Mart's incentive plans, along with store management bonuses and compensation programs, resulted in Wal-Mart associates earning more than $100 million over and above their wages and base compensation in 1989.

Another motivational tactic that Wal-Mart employed involved dress-up days on which associates dressed according to a theme (for instance, Western days or Halloween); these added fun and excitement for associates and the festive mood carried over to the customer.

Training

> *"At Wal-Mart we guarantee two things: opportunity and hard work."*
> Bill Avery,
> Wal-Mart management recruiter

Management Training   Wal-Mart managers were hired in one of three ways. Hourly associates could move up through the ranks from sales to department manager to manager of the check lanes into store management training. Second, people with outstanding merchandising skills at other retail companies were recruited to join the ranks of Wal-Mart managers. And third, Wal-Mart recruited college graduates to enter the company's training program. Exhibit 10 shows a letter sent by Sam Walton to a University of Alabama student who had just finished a summer internship at Wal-Mart.

Casewriter interviews with Wal-Mart associates revealed a positive attitude concerning advancement opportunities and the company's work climate:

> You have the option to go as far as you want to go if you do a good job.
>
> It's up to you; if you do the work, you'll get the raises. I think it's a good place to work. There's a lot here [as far as advancement] if you want to work for it. It's a good open relationship with management. The benefits are good and the pay is above average for most discount stores.

The management training program involved two phases. In the first phase the trainee completed a 16-week on-the-job training program.

Week 1	Checkouts/service desk
Week 2	Cash office
Weeks 3 and 4	Receiving
Week 5	Invoicing
Weeks 6, 7, and 8	Hardlines merchandising
Weeks 9 and 10	Merchandise office
Weeks 11, 12, and 13	Home and seasonal merchandising
Weeks 14, 15, and 16	Apparel merchandising

At designated times during Phase I, trainees were tested and evaluated by the store managers. During this time, the individual was encouraged to complete a self-critique of his/her own progress and the caliber of guidance being received from the training effort. At the end of Phase I, the trainee moved at once into Phase II.

The initial three weeks of Phase II were structured to cover such management topics as internal/external theft, scheduling, store staffing, retail math, merchandise replenishment, and the Wal-Mart "Keys to Supervision" series, which dealt with interpersonal skills and personnel responsibilities. After completion of the first three weeks of Phase II, the trainee was given responsibility for an area of the store. The length of time during the remainder of Phase II varied according to the rate at which each trainee progressed. After showing good job performance, demonstrated leadership, and job knowledge, the trainee was promoted to an assistant manager. As an assistant manager training continued with the Retail Management Training Seminar, which was designed to complement the in-store training with other vital management fundamentals. With the quickly paced growth rate of Wal-Mart stores, the above-average trainee could progress to store manager within five years. Through bonuses for sales increases above projected amounts and company stock options, the highest-performing store managers earned around $70,000 to $100,000 annually.

E X H I B I T 10   **Sam Walton's Letter to a Summer Intern at Wal-Mart**

WAL-MART

WAL-MART STORES INC.
CORPORATE OFFICES
BENTONVILLE, ARKANSAS 72716-00001

Sam M. Walton
Chairman of the Board
(501)273-4210

August 9, 1990

Mr. Lee Hood
Wal-Mart Stores, Inc.
P. O. Box 116
Bentonville, AR 72712

Dear Lee:

Congratulations on completing your summer internship with us here at the General Office! We're awfully proud of your contribution and the assistance you've given us during this introductory period that you've just completed. We hope you learned something in the retail business which will be of value to you when you continue your education at the University of Alabama. I know our folks in Hardlines Merchandising gained much from your participation in their efforts and your sharing with them the knowledge you've gained from your past experience.

I hope you will consider a career in retailing and that you will select our Wal-Mart Company. As an effective Wal-Mart associate and partner on our team, your opportunities couldn't be greater. We believe we have an outstanding program to offer and that you can become a positive force in helping us reach our objectives.

Gook luck in all that you pursue and the activities you will be involved in when you return to campus. May you always enjoy the blessings of health and success. Please give your family my personal regards and best wishes. Thanks, my friend, for your interest in Wal-Mart and your support.

Very truly yours,

Sam Walton

SW/jbc/0809/02/A-3

To further promote management training, in November 1985 the Walton Institute of Retailing was opened in affiliation with the University of Arkansas. Within a year of its inception every Wal-Mart manager from the stores, the distribution facilities, and the general office were expected to take part in special programs at the Walton Institute to strengthen and develop the company's managerial capabilities.

Associate Training   Wal-Mart did not provide a specialized training course for its hourly associates. Upon hiring, an associate was immediately placed in a position for on-the-job training. From time to time, training films were shown in the Friday morning associates' meetings, but no other formalized training aids were provided by Wal-Mart headquarters. Store managers and department managers were expected to train and supervise the associates under them in whatever ways were needed.

A number of associates commented on the Wal-Mart training programs:

> Mostly you learn by doing. They tell you a lot, but you learn your job every day.
>
> They show you how to do your books. They show you how to order and help you get adjusted to your department.
>
> We have tapes we watch that give us pointers on different things. They give you some training to start off—what you are and are not supposed to do.
>
> The training program is not up to par. They bring new people in so fast—they try to show films, but it's just so hard in this kind of business. In my opinion you learn better just by experience. The training program itself is just not adequate. There's just not enough time.
>
> We have all kinds of films and guidelines to go by, department managers' meetings every Monday, and sometimes we have quizzes to make sure we're learning what we need to know.
>
> The most training you get is on the job—especially if you work with someone who has been around awhile.

Meetings

The company used meetings both as a communication device and as a culture-building exercise. Wal-Mart claimed to hold the largest annual stockholders' meeting in the world. The 1989 shareholders' meeting, held in the University of Arkansas Razorback basketball arena, was attended by over 7,000 people, including associates and vendors. The meeting began with a dimming of the lights and the audience saying the Pledge of Allegiance while patriotic scenes flashed on three large screens. Then, as the lights came back up, Sam Walton on bended knee led the group in prayer. The necessary formalities of the meeting were conducted in minutes, at which point Sam Walton orchestrated a two-hour corporate pep rally featuring company cheers, skits, and a parade of vendors and associates who were cited for special accomplishments. Vendors were singled out for having met tight delivery deadlines, lowered prices, or cooperated extensively. Associates who had exceeded goals, helped people in distress, or written new cheers or songs were brought up and recognized on stage, with scenes of their accomplishments appearing on the screens behind them.

The Year-End Managers' Meetings   Held in February in a convention hall set up like a Wal-Mart store, with new displays and product lines, these three-day meetings brought together Wal-Mart managers from the store department level on up. Geography and numbers had recently forced Wal-Mart to have four meeting sessions held at two different sites. Everyone, including spouses, wore Wal-Mart name tags with first names in big letters and last names in fine print. Sam and Helen Walton, wearing "Sam" and "Helen" name tags, mingled with attendees. The meetings included presentations by managers and vendors, discussions of expansion plans and company goals, training videos, achievement awards, Wal-Mart cheers (often led by Sam Walton), a banquet, and entertainment. Wal-Mart's senior executives viewed these meetings as a way to reinforce the bonds of teamwork within the management ranks.

The Saturday Morning Headquarters Meeting   At 7:30 A. M. every Saturday morning since 1961, the top officers, the merchandising staff, the regional managers who oversaw the store districts, and the Bentonville headquarters' staff—over 100 people in all—gathered to discuss Wal-Mart issues (see Exhibit 11). Topics covered might include the week's sales, store payroll percentages, special promotion items, and any unusual problems. Reports on store construction, distribution centers, transportation, loss prevention, information systems, and so on were also given to keep everyone up to date.

The meetings were deliberately very informal and relaxed. Those attending might show up in tennis or hunting clothes so that when the meeting was over they could go on to their Saturday activities. The meetings were always upbeat and sometimes began by Walton "calling the hogs" (a practice common in Arkansas razorback country) or with several Wal-Mart cheers. Walton used his cheerleading and hog-calling tactics to loosen everyone up, inject some fun and enthusiasm, and get things started on a stimulating note.

The Friday Morning Store Meetings   On Friday morning, general store meetings were held in each Discount City store and wholesale club. Associates at every level could ask questions and expect to get straightforward answers from management concerning departmental and store sales and cost figures, along with other pertinent store figures or information. The meeting might also include information on new company initiatives, policy change announcements, and perhaps video training films (the use of video films was a popular Wal-Mart training technique). More often than not, the meeting would end with one or more Wal-Mart cheers.

As David Glass, Wal-Mart's president, said, "Most of us wear a button that says, 'Our People Make the Difference'—that is not a slogan at Wal-Mart, it is a way of life. Our people really do make a difference." Believing in this and encouraging superior performance was ingrained in all Wal-Mart staffers. Each week, department and store figures were posted on the back wall of each store. That way associates could see how their departments ranked against other departments and how the store was doing overall. If the figures were better than average, associates were praised verbally and given pats on the back; associates in departments that regularly outperformed the averages could

E X H I B I T 11 **A Scene from a Wal-Mart Saturday Morning Meeting at Headquarters in Bentonville**

expect annual bonuses and raises. When departmental performances came out lower than average, then the store manager would talk with department associates to explore ways to improve.

WAL-MART'S FUTURE

In 1988 Sam Walton, at the age of 70, reduced his role in active day-to-day management by relinquishing the title of chief executive officer to David Glass, but retained the title of chairman of Wal-Mart's board of directors. Walton continued to make appearances at major company events and to serve as company patriarch, but the task of leading the company into the 1990s was turned over to Glass and his next-in-command, Donald Soderquist, who functioned as chief operating officer. Both were highly regarded inside and outside the company, and both were seen as having the full complement of retailing savvy and management skills to follow in Walton's footsteps. The management team underneath Glass and Soderquist was believed by retailing experts to be very talented and very deep in the skills needed to move Wal-Mart to the top of the retailing industry during the 1990s. At the 1990 annual stockholders' meeting, Sam Walton expressed his belief that by the year 2000 Wal-Mart should be able to double the number of stores to about 3,000 and to reach sales of $125 billion annually. Some retailing industry experts were even more bullish on Wal-Mart's long-term prospects, predicting that the number of stores, clubs, and SuperCenters could number over 4,300 and could generate nearly $200 billion in sales by the turn of the century. Wal-Mart's two biggest sources of growth potential were seen as (1) expanding its present store formats to the remaining states to become a true national chain and (2) perfecting the SuperCenter format to expand Wal-Mart's retailing reach into the whole grocery and supermarket arena—a market with annual sales of about $300 billion.

Most recently, Wal-Mart had purchased a Texas-based food distributor to gain increased knowledge about the economics and operating characteristics of the food distribution business. Numerous experiments involving store size, layout, and merchandise mix were underway in the Hypermarts and Super-Centers already open to try to learn more about how best to combine the Discount City and supermarket formats into a shopping experience that could be effectively executed. In November 1990 Wal-Mart acquired Wholesale Club in a $172 million transaction, a move that increased the size of the Sam's chain to 168 stores by adding 27 stores in six Midwestern states. The per-store cost of the acquisition was just over $6 million, compared to $5.5 million to build and open a new Sam's. Analysts said the acquisition cut a year off the time it would have taken to enter these states and, at the same time, provided an established customer base. With the acquisition Sam's became the undisputed leader of the warehouse club segment, surpassing Price Club.

In the company's 1990 annual report, Glass and Soderquist stated:

> We are confident and optimistic about our prospects because we have what we believe to be the best group of Associates in retailing today.
>
> We have aggressive plans for new store and club growth in the 1990s. In calendar 1990, we anticipate retail square footage expansion approaching 18 to 20 percent by adding 165 to 175 Wal-Mart stores, 25 to 30 Sam's Clubs, two SuperCenters and one Hypermart*USA. We will enter seven new states with Wal-Mart stores and four with Sam's Clubs. In moving even closer to our objective of not having a single operating unit that has not been updated in the past seven years, we plan 75 relocations or expansions, and 88 refurbishings and remodels. In support of this expansion we will open three new one-million-square-foot-plus distribution centers in calendar 1990.
>
> We approach this new exciting decade of the 90s much as we did the 80s—focused on only two main objectives, (1) providing the customers with what they want, when they want it, all at a value, and (2) treating each other as we would hope to be treated, acknowledging our total dependency on our Associate-partners to sustain our success.

VILLAGE INN

Diana Johnston, The University of South Florida
Russ King, The University of South Florida
Jay T. Knippen, The University of South Florida

The Village Inn, located on Bermuda Boulevard in San Diego, was only a few blocks away from San Diego State University and was within several miles of some of California's largest tourist attractions. Visiting lecturers, speakers, professors interviewing for jobs, and people attending conferences at the university resulted in a considerable amount of business for Village Inn.

The inn was also near a concentrated area of light and heavy industry. The largest shopping mall in San Diego was under construction across the street from the inn. A relatively new Veterans Administration hospital and the University Community Hospital were both located within one mile. The inn's very favorable location, together with the fact that it was a franchise of a major national chain, had made it a profitable investment. During the past 12 months, the inn had an average occupancy rate of between 65 and 70 percent, some 15 or more percentage points above the break-even occupancy rate of 50 percent.

Although the Village Inn had only modest competition from other hotel or motel facilities in the immediate vicinity, a new Travelodge Inn was under construction next door. The other closest competitors were nearly three miles away at the intersection of Bermuda Boulevard and Interstate 8. Village Inn offered a full range of services to its guests, including a restaurant and bar. The new Travelodge next door was going to have just a coffee shop. Insofar as its restaurant/bar business was concerned, the Village Inn's strongest competitor was the popular-priced University Restaurant, two blocks away. Village Inn did not consider its own food service operations to be in close competition with the area's fast-food franchises or with higher-priced restaurants.

OWNERSHIP OF VILLAGE INN

Mr. Johnson, a native of Oregon, opened the first Village Inn in San Diego in 1958. Since that time he had shared ownership in 15 other Village Inns, several in the San Diego area. He opened the Bermuda Boulevard Inn in October 1966. Prior to his focusing on the motel and restaurant business, Johnson had owned and operated a furniture store and a casket manufacturing plant. A suggestion from a business associate in Oregon influenced his decision to seek Village Inn franchises and get into the motel business. In some of his Village Inn locations, Johnson leased the restaurant operations; however, the restaurant and bar at the Bermuda Boulevard Village Inn were not leased. Johnson felt that because the occupancy rate at his location was so favorable, it was more profitable to own and operate these facilities himself.

MANAGEMENT OF THE INN

Johnson had employed Mrs. Deeks as the innkeeper and manager of the entire operation. She had worked at Village Inn for the past seven and one-half years. Previously, Deeks had done administrative work for San Diego General Hospital and before that had been employed as a photo lab technician for two years. Her experience in the motel/restaurant business included working for several restaurants and lounges for five years as a cocktail waitress just before joining Village Inns.

Deeks stated that her main reason for first going to work for Village Inn was because she felt there was more money to be made as a waitress than anything else she had tried. Her formal education for her present position of innkeeper consisted of a three-week training course at the Home Office Training Center in Louisville, Kentucky, and one-week refresher courses each year at the center.

Recently the assistant innkeeper had been promoted and transferred to another location. Both Johnson and Deeks agreed that there was a pressing need to fill the vacancy quickly. It was the assistant innkeeper's function to supervise the restaurant/bar area, and this was the area that always presented the toughest problems to management. Unless the food was well prepared and the service was prompt, guests were quick to complain. Poor food service caused many of the frequent visitors to the area to prefer to stay at other motels. Moreover, it was hard to attract and maintain a sizable lunchtime clientele without having well-run restaurant facilities. With so many restaurant employees to supervise, menus to prepare, and food supplies to order, it was a constant day-to-day struggle to keep the restaurant operating smoothly and, equally important, to see that it made a profit. Deeks, with all of her other duties and responsibilities, simply did not have adequate time to give the restaurant/bar enough close supervision by herself.

While searching for a replacement, Johnson by chance happened to see a feature article in the *Village Inn Magazine*, a monthly publication of the Village Inns of America chain—copies of which were placed in all of the guest rooms of the inns. The article caught Johnson's attention because it described how a successful Village Inn in San Bernardino had gained popularity and acclaim from guests because of the good food and fast service provided by the head chef of the restaurant operations. After showing the article to Deeks, Johnson wasted no time in getting in touch with the head chef of that inn, Mr. Bernie, and persuading him to assume the new role of restaurant/bar manager for the Bermuda Boulevard Village Inn in San Diego.

FOOD SERVICE FACILITIES AND LAYOUT

Exhibit 1 depicts the arrangement of the lobby area and food service facilities at the inn. A brief description of the restaurant/bar area follows.

Restaurant The restaurant itself consisted of a dining room that seated 74 people, a coffee shop that seated 62 persons, and a bar that seated 35 people. The inn's banquet facilities were just behind the main dining room and could seat 125 people.

EXHIBIT 1   **Partial Layout of Village Inn**

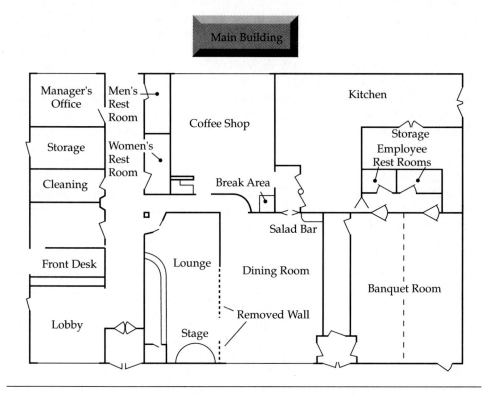

The essential role of the restaurant and bar area was to provide pleasant and convenient facilities for the inn's guests. The contractual franchise agreements with the national chain required all owners to provide these services in conjunction with the overnight accommodations. There were periodic inspections of the facilities by a representative from Village Inn's corporate office. Village Inn required each franchisee to comply with minimum standards for its food service facilities in an effort to promote comparability and ensure attractiveness. Restaurant services were to be available to guests from 6:30 A.M. until 11 P.M.

Coffee Shop   The coffee shop was open from 6:30 A.M. to 11 A.M. to serve breakfast to motel guests. At 11 A.M., these facilities were closed and the main dining area was opened. The coffee shop was occasionally used beyond scheduled hours to serve customers for lunch and dinner when there was an overflow from the dining area. Tables in both the coffee shop and the dining room were decorated and set uniformly.

Dining Room   The dining area was open from 11 A.M. until 11 P.M. It was located next to the lounge and was physically separated from the coffee shop by a wall. The lunch and dinner offerings featured a salad bar with menu items that were somewhat uniform with other Village Inns and were prescribed by the franchise agreement. However, menu deviations were allowed if approved by corporate representatives from Village Inn's central office.

Bar   The bar, separated from the dining room by a partition, was open for business from 10 A.M. until 1 A.M. It had tables and booths, and customers who preferred to do so could have their food served to them in the bar area. A small dance floor was located in front of the entertainer stage near the front window; a jukebox furnished music when there was no live entertainment. A small bar stockroom was located at one end of the bar counter. The cash register area was centrally located to receive payments from customers in all three areas—dining room, coffee shop, and bar.

Kitchen   The kitchen facilities, located beside the coffee shop and dining room, had a stainless steel counter at the entrance door from the restaurant area. It was here that waitresses turned orders in to the cooks and that the cooks served the orders up to the waitresses. The cooking area was located in the center of the room and sinks were located along the sides of the kitchen.

RESTAURANT OPERATIONS

As was to be expected, customer traffic in the restaurant fluctuated widely. Busy periods were generally at the traditional meal hours, but the peak load at any given mealtime period often varied by as much as an hour from one day to the next. At lunchtime, for example, customers sometimes seemed to come all at once, while on other days the arrival times were more evenly distributed throughout the 11:30 A.M. to 1:30 P.M. interval. Experience had shown that these peaks were hard to anticipate and that the staff had to be prepared for whatever occurred. Moreover, on Monday, Tuesday, Wednesday, and Thursday evenings, the customers were mostly businesspeople, sales representatives, and university visitors, whereas on weekends there were more family travelers. Because of the inn's location, its clientele consisted somewhat more of the former than the latter.

   The inn's restaurant business was also subject to some seasonal fluctuations. There were always a certain number of people who spent the winter in Southern California to escape the harsh northern and Canadian winters; these included not only winter tourists but also the "Canadian Snow Birds" who came to Southern California to work in the late fall and returned to Canada in March or April. In addition, the inn's business picked up noticeably during the June graduation exercises at San Diego State University and during the week when the fall term opened. By and large, the daily fluctuations were harder to predict than the seasonal fluctuations.

RESTAURANT STAFFING

Because of the alternating between peak periods and slack periods, the employees in the food service area tended to work together, take breaks together, and eat their meals together. In commenting on the kind of people who tended to work in hotel-motel operations, Deeks indicated that employees were typically gregarious and were there because they wanted to be. They had to contend with an uneven work pace, a low-wage scale (often no more than the minimum wage), and irregular working hours. Since waitresses earned only a token wage and relied mainly on tips for their income, they could not afford many "slow days" or "bad days" at work. Their livelihood and degree of service was dependent upon how well they greeted customers, a friendly smile, prompt service, and, in general, an ability to make customers feel satisfied with the attention they received. When the food was cold or ill-prepared or the service poorer than expected, customers left smaller tips and the waitresses' disgruntlement carried over to the kitchen staff, the hostess, and the busboys. But even more disruptive than the loss of tips were the customers who complained directly to the inn's management; if this occurred frequently, then the pressure and anxiety felt by the restaurant staff increased noticeably. Deeks noted that people who could not adjust to the tempo and temperament of the restaurant business usually did not stay in it long. She noted further that it was extremely difficult to "standardize" the human service aspects of the restaurant business and that trying to attract and keep a good, experienced food service staff was a challenging task.

Deeks supplied the following job descriptions of the restaurant staff. These descriptions, however, came from her thoughts and perceptions and had never been formally set forth in writing to the inn's employees:

Bartender Cut up fruit for drinks, wash glasses, serve counter drinks, clean behind bar, stock liquor and mixes, stock beer, fill room service orders, ring up checks, balance register, and help with inventory.

Hostess/Cashier Take room service orders, seat guests, deliver menu, direct seating, supervise waitresses and busboys, perform any functions within his/her prescribed area that speeds service, check out customers from dining area, check out register, file cash register receipts, and assign stations.

Waitresses Take food orders, deliver orders to kitchen, pick up and serve food orders, serve beverages, and perform any function that speeds service as directed by the hostess.

Busboys Bus tables, put clean place settings on tables, clean dining rooms, stock supplies, take ice to all areas, get supplies for cooks, help set up banquets, deliver room service orders, help with maintenance, and perform any function that will speed service as directed by the hostess and manager.

Dishwasher Wash dishes, pots, and pans. Sweep and mop floors.

Cook Prepare meals, schedule meals for prep cook, assist management in ordering supplies, receive food supplies, supervise and direct kitchen help, and assist management in menu changes. Report to management any changes or problems that occur.

Prep Cook Prepare all food that the cook needs for the dinner and evening meals; assist cook in any meal preparation that is necessary to expedite service to guests; inform cook of any problems that need attention, and help cook see that facilities are clean at all times.

Breakfast Cook Open the kitchen in the morning; prepare breakfast food for motel guests; and provide information necessary to maintain in-stock supplies.

E X H I B I T 2   **Memo Number One from Mr. Bernie to Food Service Staff**

> People,
> Please help keep the floor clean.
> If you drop something, pick it up.
> Wipe table off into a trash can.
> If you spill something, the mops and brooms are outside.
> It's no fun scrubbing the floor Saturday, and if you don't
> believe it, be here Saturday night at 11:00 P.M.
>   Mr. "B"

MR. BERNIE

When Mr. Bernie arrived to assume his new duties as restaurant/bar manager, he wasted no time in demanding and receiving total obedience from the personnel under his direction. He made it clear that he would not tolerate insubordination and that the consequences would be immediate discharge. Although Bernie stayed in his new job less than three months (from January to March), he nonetheless created an almost instantaneous climate of ill will and hatred with his subordinates. The intense dislike for Bernie was voiced by nearly every employee. One example of this was a statement by Elaine, the day hostess/cashier who had been employed in this capacity for the past two and one half years: "I enjoy my job because I like people. But Mr. Bernie was something else! I generally do not use this term in my vocabulary, but Mr. Bernie was a bastard from the day he arrived until the day he left."

Bernie's unpopularity was further brought out by a busboy's impromptu comment. Elaine was trying to possibly justify Bernie's temperament by pointing out that he was not of American nationality. Unable to recall his nationality she inquired of a nearby busboy if he could remember. The busboy immediately and sincerely replied, "He crawled out from under a rock."

Bernie spent considerable time trying to impress upon his staff the "right way" (his way) of accomplishing tasks (see Exhibits 2 and 3). Most of the employees resented Bernie's close supervision. Ann, a veteran employee and waitress, describing her resentment, said, "No one really needs to supervise us, especially the way Mr. Bernie stood over us. Usually the hostess is the supervisor, but all the old girls know what they are doing and everyone does their job."

Although an intense dislike for Bernie was foremost in the minds of the employees, he did make a number of improvements and innovations. Physical changes became obvious within all departments under his authority. In the kitchen, a general cleanup campaign was instituted, an order spindle was added, and new oven equipment installed. In the coffee shop and restaurant, new silverware, china, and glasses were purchased, and the menu was improved and complemented by the use of a salad bar. Explicit work duties were written and verbally defined to all employees under Bernie.

Bernie separated the cashier/hostess function into two distinct jobs. The cashier was confined to the cash register station and given instructions as to the duties she was to perform in that area. The hostess was given instructions

E X H I B I T 3   **Memo Number Two from Mr. Bernie to Food Service Staff**

March 11

TO ALL FOOD AND BEVERAGE EMPLOYEES:

I wish to thank each and every one of you for the very good job you have done in the past two weeks. The service has greatly improved on both shifts. There has been a better customer-employee relationship, but there is a long way to go yet. We are nearing the end of our winter season so it is most important to all of us that we concentrate on more service in order to obtain a local year-round business. Appearance, neatness, and good conduct on the floor will obtain this, along with good food.

A waitress and busboy are like salesmen. The hostess-cashier can determine the quality of service in this organization.

I expect my waitresses while on duty to be on the dining room cafe floor at all times. I should find waitresses and busboys at the cashier stand only when getting a ticket or paying a check.

I smoke myself—probably more than the rest of you put together. Your service area is beginning to look like a cigarette factory. I do not expect people to give up their smoking habits, but I do expect them to conform to the rules and regulations of Village Inn, Inc., and those of the health department, "No Smoking on Premises." I would not like to enforce the law.

In the last two weeks I have walked into the operation after a busy breakfast or dinner and found everyone sitting around the first three booths of the cafe. I do not say it cannot be used, but when I find no waitresses on either floor day or night and customers have to call for service because waitresses are off the floor, I believe each waitress and busboy on all shifts should ask themselves one thing: what kind of service would I like if I were a guest? There is only one thing I know, in this part of California when the tourist is gone, half of the employees work on a part-time basis, which is not good on anyone's pocketbook. Therefore, I say let's not be second best but let's be first.

With regard to employees taking their meal breaks, I do not wish to schedule them but I cannot have everyone eating at once. Busboys will eat one at a time.

Thank you once again for your good performance.

Mr. "B"

to greet people, seat them, and supply menus. When Bernie was absent, he instructed the hostess to see that the waitresses and busboys carried out their jobs efficiently and effectively. According to Gay, one of the two day hostesses:

> When Mr. Bernie was here I never had any employee problems. Waitresses and busboys did what I asked. But now if we have a busboy absent or we are crowded, some of the waitresses inform me they will not bus tables. Today there's no one in charge of anything. We need more employees here. It is always better to have more help than not enough. That's one thing Mr. Bernie did, he doubled the help the day he came.

The changes that Bernie instituted regarding the waitresses were significant in several aspects. All waitresses were required to wear fitted uniforms. This necessitated them driving across town for a uniform fitting. Bernie's detailed scrutinizing consisted of specific instructions on how to serve customers and which station locations each waitress would serve. He even went as far as to show them how to wrap the silverware and the napkins and gave explicit instructions to veteran waitresses on how to fill out the order tickets.

Bernie had the wall between the dining room and bar taken down. He then brought in an entertainer who supplied dinner music for both the restaurant and bar guests. Today the waitresses are getting some dysfunctional effects from this innovation; according to one:

> Mr. Bernie brought in an organ player. While this was conducive to a more pleasant dining atmosphere, the organist was not good enough to keep the people beyond their meal. But now that Mr. Bernie is gone our new entertainer is causing

some serious problems. For example, last night I had a family of five sit at a table in my station for two and a half hours after their dinner. If people won't leave and they won't buy drinks, I can't make tips.

Bernie instilled an atmosphere of insecurity and day-to-day doubt in the minds of the employees as to how long they could weather the barrage of innovation and directives. To some, just remaining on the job became a challenge in itself. Elaine (the day hostess) phrased it in this manner:

> I have been employed with the Village Inn for almost two and one half years. I have worked most of my life and have never felt insecure in any of my jobs. The last job I held was a swimming instructor for 10 years with the Academy of Holy Names in San Diego. The reason I had to leave there was because of the change in the educational background requirement, which called for a college degree.
>
> My children are all college graduates with highly responsible positions. They achieved this by hard work. I instilled this in their minds because I am a hard worker. But when Mr. Bernie was here, I experienced for the first time in my life the feeling of not knowing from one day to the next if my job would be there when I came to work. What few personnel he failed to drive away, he fired.

Linda, who was a bartender in the lounge area, commented further on Bernie's supervisory tactics:

> Bernie was a rover. When he walked into an area, including my area, he could not stand to see someone not involved with busy work. He even made me clean under the bar on the customer's side. I'm not a maid and I often wanted to tell him so. But the way he was hiring and firing employees, I just kept my mouth closed and did as he told me. My experiences with Mr. Bernie were nothing compared to the relationship he had with the busboys. From the bar he would sneak around and watch them in the dining area. If they did anything the least bit out of line, he would call them aside and give them lectures that could last for half an hour. He really treated the busboys like the scum of the earth. When the boys did get a break, they would come over to the bar and get a coke and ice. You know, he even started charging them 25 cents for that!

Sam, a cook hired by Bernie, offered a slightly different perspective of Bernie:

> My wife was working here as a hostess and I used to bring her to work every day. One day I came in with her and for some reason they were short of help in the kitchen. They needed a dishwasher. I was sitting in the coffee shop and Mr. Bernie walked over and asked me if I could use a job. I had been interested in cooking ever since I was in the Navy. There are two things you can do in your spare time in the Navy . . . drink and chase women or find a hobby. I found a hobby, which was cooking. On my two days off, I used to go down in the galley and help the cooks. There I learned everything I know today. When I got out of the service I worked as a prep cook in a restaurant in Pennsylvania for a year or so. My real specialty is soups, though. Anyway, I had been a dishwasher here for about two days when the cook walked off the job after three years of service here. Mr. Bernie came in and asked how I'd like to be the new cook and here I am today. Mr. Bernie really taught me a lot. He taught me that a restaurant has three things it must give a customer: service, good food, and a pleasing environment to dine. If you have these three, customers will return.
>
> I've spent most of my working career in the automotive business doing such things as driving trucks. But I'm really into this cooking thing. Mr. Bernie taught

me that about 50 percent of the customers who come in and order from the menu have no idea what they are ordering. The menu is too complicated. The customer doesn't know what he thinks he ordered and what you think he ordered. Another thing that fascinates me is trying to think like the customer. His definition of rare, medium, and well done is altogether different from my idea of how it should be. One addition by Mr. Bernie was the salad bar. This is a tremendous help to my job. If the waitress can get to the customer before they go to the salad bar and take their order, this gives me plenty of lead time to be sure the meal will be cooked right and served in the attractive manner that Mr. Bernie was so particular about. This lead time is especially important on those days that we are unusually busy. For example, I have prepared as many as 250 meals on some days and as few as 40 on others.

The employees who left or were dismissed by Bernie included two hostesses, two waitresses (one had an employment record at the inn that dated back five years), and two busboys. Two of the personnel that Bernie fired have since returned to their old jobs. One of the waitresses that subsequently was rehired described her reason for leaving as follows:

I really enjoy being a waitress and have been here for about five years. The work isn't really too hard and the pay is good. I took all the "directives" I could take from Mr. Bernie! A week before he left, I gave my resignation and took a vacation. When I returned, I learned of his departure and here I am again. I'm really glad things have worked out as they did.

Deeks's opinion of Bernie's performance was one of general dissatisfaction with the way he handled his dealings with employees.

Mr. Bernie was highly trained, but he was an introvert who stood over his subordinates and supervised everything they did. Cooks are a rare breed of people all to themselves. The help situation has changed greatly in the past few years. It used to be that you could give orders and tell people what they were supposed to do. Now, you have to treat them with "kid gloves" or they'll just quit and get a job down the street. This problem is particularly true with cooks. They are very temperamental and introverted and they expect to be treated like prima donnas.

Mr. Johnson and I really tried to work with Mr. Bernie during his 90-day trial period. We knew that terminating him without a replacement would be hard on us, but we had no choice. We are now without a restaurant/bar manager or assistant innkeeper. We have been looking for a replacement, but finding a person that is knowledgeable in both the hotel and restaurant management is something of a chore.

CONDITIONS AFTER MR. BERNIE'S DEPARTURE

Since Bernie had departed, the restaurant personnel were in general agreement that their operation was understaffed. Often guests were seated in both the dining area and coffee shop waiting to be served; even though the waitresses were apparently busy, many customers experienced waits of 20 to 30 minutes. Elaine, one of the two hostesses, explained the lack of prompt service as follows:

The coffee shop is supposed to take care of the guests until 11 A.M. and then the restaurant part is to be opened. Mr. Bernie handled the situation differently than we do now. When he was here, he would not open the dining hall in the morning no matter how crowded the coffee shop was. I can remember mornings when people were lined into the hallway and all the way outside the front door. I guess he knew two girls and two busboys could not handle two rooms.

But today we handle the situations differently. If the coffee shop gets crowded or we have many dirty tables, we open up both rooms. This really makes it hard on the girls trying to serve both rooms. What we generally have when this happens is poor service to all concerned and consequently some guests leave unhappy and without tipping the waitresses.

Ralph, a busboy, indicated the problem was not exclusively felt in the restaurant only. He seemed to feel the lack or absence of a manager was the primary problem:

Mrs. Deeks just can't run this operation by herself. It is physically impossible for her to be here seven days a week from 6:30 A.M. until 11 P.M. and manage the kitchen, restaurant, bar, coffee shop, front desk, maid service, and maintenance crew all at the same time.

Some of the employees perceived their duties and functions differently. For instance, the restaurant's two day hostesses alternated work shifts. Elaine would seat customers, give them their menu, take beverages to customers to help out the waitresses, help out busing tables when it was very busy, and had very little to say in supervising the waitresses and busboys. On the other hand, the other day hostess, Gay, would seat customers and give them menus but would not do what she perceived to be the duties of waitresses and busboys. Instead, she exercised supervisory authority over these personnel and when they were not able to get everything done, she would try to find out why not, rather than doing them herself.

There were similar discrepancies in the ways the waitresses and busboys performed their duties. In some cases, waitresses would help busboys clear tables during overcrowded periods and busboys would also help out the waitresses by bringing water and coffee to the people who were waiting to be served. The other side of the coin occurred also. Some of the waitresses, particularly those who had been employed for some time, felt that it was the busboys' responsibility to clear tables and would not lift a finger to help them. In these instances, the busboys did not go out of their way to help the waitresses.

Gene, the other bartender, offered yet another view of the inn's problems:

You know, I could tell management a few things about the restaurant business if they asked me. I knew from the first day Mr. Bernie arrived that he wouldn't work out. But Mr. Bernie is not the only problem they had. One of the biggest problems they have with this restaurant is in the banquets they have. We have a luncheon here every week with such clubs as the Sertoma, Kiwanis, and the like. Their luncheons start at noon and last until 1:30 or so. Have you ever noticed how they park outside? Well, I'll tell you they park all over the front parking lot and when local people drive by they assume our restaurant is full and go on down the street. These businessmen tie up most of our help and yet the dining room may be empty. These banquet people don't buy drinks with lunch like the local businessmen do who take clients out to lunch and often have a bigger bar bill than their restaurant checks. There's only one successful way to have a banquet business and that's not next to your dining room. If the banquet room was on the opposite side of the restaurant, then it would be OK.

EMPLOYEE TRAINING

The Village Inn provided a minimal amount of job training for employees with the exception of the management staff. The contractual agreement between franchise owners and Village Inns of America required all innkeepers, assistant innkeepers, and restaurant managers to attend the Home Office Training Center within a year of being hired. They also had to attend refresher courses on a yearly basis.

The restaurant personnel, in contrast, were given little job training. Instead, efforts were made to hire cooks, waitresses, and bartenders who had previous experience in the field. But in practice, this policy was not always adhered to—as was exemplified by the way Linda became a bartender:

> My training on the job was really short and sweet. Mr. Bernie came in one day and inquired, "How would you like to be a bartender?" At the same time he handed me a book on mixing drinks. I went home and studied it and "poof" I was a bartender.
>
> Within a short time on the job, I began getting a lot of help and advice from the waitresses who came over to the bar for drink orders. Sometimes when we do get a drink mixup they are very nice about it. I've even had people from other departments in the inn to help me when the situation called for it. One night I had two ladies in here, one from the "crazy house" and the other her bodyguard. After a few "shooters," as they referred to the drinks, they asked for their check. They wanted to use a credit card instead of paying cash. This was not a problem, but so I would get my tip I offered to carry the check and credit card to the front desk. Then they said I would cheat them on their bill once I was out of their sight. The front desk man heard the hassle and came in and escorted the ladies to the desk. This type of working together happens here all the time. Mrs. Deeks, my boss, is really a nice person to work for. She doesn't come around very much, except if she needs information or to advise me about something.

PAY SCALES

Management indicated that there was a shortage of good employees and that a low pay scale was characteristic of the restaurant business. Some of the employees expressed their awareness of this also.

(Bartender) Linda: The pay scale is really low compared to other areas. My first job as a cocktail waitress in San Diego was in a dive downtown. They paid us $2 an hour plus tips, but the tips were lousy. Here they're paying $3 an hour plus tips, which is somewhat better, but it's still way below the wages elsewhere. I really don't feel like I'm suited for this work, but I make more money at the bar than I did as a cocktail waitress.

(Hostess) Gay: I make $4 an hour here. With all the responsibility and experience I've had, the pay scale here compared to other parts of the country is deplorable. The busboys make almost as much as I do. They make $3.50 an hour plus 15 percent of the waitress's tips. Even though the pay scale is low, there is always overtime available to most of all of the employees who want it. My husband who is a cook here has worked 145 hours so far in this two-week pay period and he still has five more days to go.

Barb, one of the waitresses, further substantiated the availability of overtime by saying she got at least one hour overtime each day. She attributed the extra hours of overtime to the fact that the inn's restaurant staff always seemed to have at least one person unexpectedly absent each day.

The problem in the restaurant was apparently compounded by the fact that it was operating with a minimum number of employees. Timmy, a busboy, indicated the wide range of activities that were expected of him and the other busboys:

> We do everything; I clean and bus tables, sweep floors, and do janitorial work. I don't mean in just my area either. If the front desk needs a porter or runner or if some type of room service is needed, I do that too. Mr. Bernie was really hard to work under, but he always confined us to restaurant duties. When he was here, we didn't do all those jobs outside our area. Those duties were handled by a front-desk porter. But I'd still rather have to do things all over the place than have to put up with Mr. Bernie.

SEARCHING FOR MR. BERNIE'S REPLACEMENT

In outlining her thoughts on trying to replace Bernie, Deeks stated:

> I really had a good track record with personnel before Mr. Bernie came along. I strongly objected to his dictatorial supervision. In my experience I have learned employees perform their jobs better when left alone most of the time. I once tried to set up off-job activities for my employees. I reserved a room at the hotel for employees to meet together after working hours to play cards and drink coffee. Unfortunately, the room was not used enough to merit keeping it on reserve. However, I still support functions that the employees suggest. We are presently sponsoring a bowling team that two of my waitresses belong to.
>
> Most of the waitresses would rather work night shifts if they have their choice. Some of the girls have children and husbands that require them to be home at night. This balances the shifts real well. One reason I prefer to schedule the waitresses is because of peculiar problems which occur. For example, I have two extremely good waitresses that will not work on Saturdays and Sundays. The other waitresses do not know this, and I feel if I were to allow the hostess to do the scheduling I would have some immediate personnel problems. To further complicate any benefits that might be derived by allowing the hostesses to make out schedules, it would be necessary to reveal my awareness of the slower waitresses we have which I schedule on Saturday and Sunday—our slower business days.
>
> I am really more active in management and day-to-day problems than most of the employees realize. Any significant changes in rules or policies are usually passed in the form of a written memo. I prefer to handle communication in this way for two reasons: first, there is no room for distortion, and second, it does not give the employees a feeling that they are being closely supervised. However, I do need an assistant to help me manage this place. I have verbally put the word out to other inns and motels. I'm really not concerned whether I get a restaurant manager or an assistant innkeeper so long as he has a knowledge of the food and beverage service. I'm really going to be cautious in the selection of this person as I don't want to jump out of the frying pan into the fire.

KENTUCKY FRIED CHICKEN IN CHINA (B)*

Allen J. Morrison, University of Western Ontario

In early February 1987, Tony Wang, vice president of Kentucky Fried Chicken's (KFC) Southeast Asia region, was feeling a growing sense of anxiety over the company's prospects of establishing its first restaurant in China. Although KFC had just recently signed a joint-venture partnership in Beijing, Wang had serious reservations about proceeding further with the project. Much of this concern was a function of the extreme difficulty in getting things done in a city governed by a bureaucracy that seemed impossible to either understand or work with. The timing of the new restaurant seemed in disarray as endless delays in finding a location and winning approval from a myriad of government regulatory agencies began to mount. Furthermore, Wang had clear doubts whether Chinese workers could be motivated to provide the type of quality, service, and cleanliness demanded by the restaurant chain around the world. The time had come for a go/no-go decision on the project. And while Wang was intrigued by the enormous potential of the Chinese market, he knew that many others had failed in similar ventures.

BACKGROUND

In accepting the challenge of bringing KFC to the Chinese market, Wang also took on the responsibilities for the company's entire Southeast Asia operations. As in other areas of the world, KFC had expanded in the region by relying extensively on franchisees. Locally managed franchises had a clear advantage in penetrating the widely diverse national markets of the region. The downside was that local franchisees often lacked a commitment to KFC's QSC (quality, service, cleanliness) standards. Another problem was that managerial capabilities in the regional office remained largely undeveloped. Recognizing that strong managerial backing would be required for a move into China, Wang insisted that corporate financial support increase in the region. This request was strongly supported by KFC executives responsible for international markets; they saw a need for more KFC-owned stores, not only in Southeast Asia, but throughout other international regions. During the same period, KFC announced its intention of buying out its Singapore franchisee's 29 stores.

With a strengthened regional structure and a mandate to take KFC into China, Wang began the process of examining alternative locations in the country. Options were examined on a city-by-city basis. Complicating the decision-making process was the lack of any reliable market information governing demand or pricing considerations. With no indigenous industry as a guide, the decision was made to pursue the option that provided the greatest long-term leverage in penetrating the larger Chinese market. Beijing, with its Western

*This case was prepared with assistance from Professor Paul Beamish. Funding was provided by The Federation of Canadian Municipalities' Open City Project through a grant from the Canadian International Development Agency (C.I.D.A.), and by the University of Western Ontario. Copyright © 1990 by C.I.D.A. and the University of Western Ontario.

hotels, relatively affluent and liberal populations, and national profile, was tentatively chosen as a starting point. Beijing also had the advantage of being one of only three cities in China in which the municipal government had been granted the authority typically vested only in provincial governments. This meant the avoidance of one level of bureaucracy within the vast Chinese governmental system.

FINDING A PARTNER

After settling on Beijing as a tentative site for KFC's first Chinese store, the process of locating potential local partners was begun. The establishment of a joint venture with a local partner was viewed as essential. Chinese investment regulations were a complex set of policies that Wang described as "completely impossible for us to understand. In fact, trying to do so is a total waste of time." Not only was it impossible to understand investment regulations, but winning approval for operating licenses, leases, and employment contracts could be a nightmare given the disorganized and disinterested Chinese bureaucracy. Evidence available to KFC in the fall of 1986 was indicating a growing disillusionment by Western businesspeople with the Chinese market. Wang realized that although local equity participation was not a technical requirement of Chinese law, finding the right local partner would help in not only setting up the operation but in ensuring its ongoing viability.

The first lead in identifying a potential local partner came through the corporate offices of R.J. Reynolds, which had established ties with the Ministry of Light Industry in Beijing. At the recommendation of the Ministry, KFC was encouraged to contact the Beijing Corporation of Animal Production, a Beijing city government-controlled producer of chickens. Upon further investigation, it was learned that indeed the Beijing Corporation of Animal Production could be useful as a possible supplier of grain-fed chickens for the venture. In fact, of KFC's six approved chicken breeds, Animal Production was already producing three. These breeds had been introduced by European and American breeders in the early 1980s and had flourished in the suburban Beijing farms operated by Animal Production.

Negotiations with Animal Production were carried out primarily with Mr. Jue Xia, a senior manager in the Beijing corporation. According to Xia:

> The company had some trade and technology transfers with Western companies in the past. Most of this involved the introduction of new feed products and breeds. KFC was our first experience with food processing. We were not really interested at first. KFC was looking for a major supplier when our supply was already limited. The major problem was our limited ability to expand capacity because we just couldn't get our hands on enough feed grain. We were also concerned about KFC's quality standards. They would only accept chickens that had been raised for seven weeks. We knew that far more money could be made by keeping the chickens for another week. So we thought, this is a not a really good deal for us.

Still, Xia thought that as a partner and not simply a supplier the venture could make sense for Animal Production. The main appeal would be the exposure to foreign business practices that the venture would provide. Also, Xia felt that Tony Wang, unlike most American managers, was a man he could deal with.

From the perspective of Tony Wang, he had little choice but to find a local partner who could provide access to a secure supply of KFC- approved chickens. Animal Production seemed like a sure bet. Yet, even this came with the realization that the company had little exposure to Western business or fast food, did not itself have much money to put into the venture, and had no close contacts with the Beijing city agencies that would be essential to setting up operations. There was also concern that although Animal Production could supply 400 or 500 chickens per day, this would be nowhere near enough to meet eventual demand at a large single store or a series of smaller stores in Beijing. In fact, Animal Production might even block future expansion by restricting the partnership to one location in the city. Still, Wang realized that he had little choice but to proceed.

After considerable negotiations, tentative agreement was won with Animal Production to form a partnership with KFC. Until a third partner could be found and an official agreement signed, both Animal Production and KFC would proceed on faith. Animal Production accepted the lead in finding an appropriate local partner.

One agency both partners agreed would be an ideal partner was the Beijing Tourist Bureau. This was a city government organization that was established to supervise the construction and operation of all hotels and restaurants in Beijing. The Tourist Bureau had been deeply involved in expediting the construction of a score of new Western hotels and had frequently participated as a joint-venture partner in their operation. Said Tony Wang of their initial contact with the Tourist Bureau:

> When we first contacted the Tourist Bureau, they were very skeptical. They had been involved in very big projects—typically averaging well over a million dollars in equity participation. They were controlling 100 hotels at the time. Many people thought that we wanted them as a partner because of their connection with tourists, but this was never the case. (All along we were anticipating tourist or FEC [Chinese Foreign Exchange Certificate] sales of between two and five percent of total sales.) We wanted the Tourist Bureau because they were very well connected, they knew how to work with Western business, and because Beijing has a high degree of autonomy in tourist matters. It also didn't hurt that the chief of the Tourist Bureau is a son of a member of the Politbureau.

KFC Is Sold to Pepsico

It was during the ongoing negotiations to link up with Animal Production and the Beijing Tourist Bureau that it was announced that KFC would be sold to Pepsico for $850 million in cash. The deal was completed on October 1, 1986. By this time, KFC was the second-largest restaurant chain in the world, with over 6,500 stores and sales of almost $3.5 billion.

Pepsico had itself entered the fast-food restaurant business in 1977 with the purchase of Pizza Hut. The next year the company purchased Taco Bell. Fast food represented the fastest-growing segment of the food industry. With the KFC acquisition, Pepsico would be in three of the four fastest-growing segments of the industry (chicken, pizza, and Mexican food). The acquisition would also facilitate the conversion of thousands of fast-food stores from offering Coca-Cola to Pepsi soft drinks and would move the company past McDonalds as the leading fast-food vendor in the industry. According to

Wayne Calloway, Pepsico chairman, "KFC is a great strategic fit and a logical extension of our existing business."

The transfer of KFC to Pepsico had a positive effect on KFC's worldwide operations. Pepsico was clearly interested in KFC because of its strong international position. Shortly after the acquisition, Pepsico announced a goal of even more rapid growth for KFC through a strengthening of its franchise network and a greater reliance on international joint-venture partnerships.

In China, the concern was that perhaps Animal Production had come on board because of pressure from the Ministry of Light Industry, itself interested in winning points with Reynolds, and that the acquisition had not come at a good time. However, Pepsi's contacts with top Chinese officials were seemingly better than those of R.J. Reynolds, leading to a renewal in the negotiations. In fact Pepsico had considerable experience and interest in operating in the communist world. In 1973, Pepsico entered an agreement with the Soviet government to establish a bottling plant in Novorossiysk. By 1976, five bottling plants were either in operation or had been announced for the Soviet market. Under the arrangements, Pepsico equipped and supplied concentrate for the Soviet-owned and operated plants in exchange for the export of Russian vodka for sale by Pepsico in the United States. Buoyed by the success and publicity generated by this experience, Pepsico opened its first bottling plant in the Chinese city of Shenzhen in 1982. In January 1986, Wayne Calloway announced Pepsico's plan to invest an additional $100 million in China by the mid-1990s.

Formalizing the Partnership

With potential partners selected, Tony Wang began a series of meetings designed to both establish closer personal ties among the principals and negotiate the details of the venture. Wang was aided in these meetings by KFC's top international lawyer from Louisville and a group of assistants from KFC's Hong Kong and Singapore offices. To convince the partners to become part of the venture, Wang offered a guarantee of five percent return on their equity— much better than they were able to get domestically. This was a turning point in winning the cooperation of both partners.

The mayor's office in Beijing controlled the Foreign Economic Development Commission and the City Planning Commission, agencies from which KFC would need approval over the details of any partnership arranged and registered in Beijing. Although the mayor was interested in developing the city's food service industry, he also needed to balance impressions of being too close to Western business. His own political career would be hurt if he took a high-profile position in the project. It also became evident that even a powerful mayor was often powerless in dealing with the vast city bureaucracy.

In early December 1986, the partners signed an agreement giving KFC a 60 percent equity position in the new venture, Beijing Kentucky Fried Chicken Corporation, Ltd. (B-KFC). The Tourist Bureau's position represented a 27 percent stake in the partnership, and Beijing Animal Production assumed a 13 percent interest. These percentages represented portions of the actual assets contributed to the venture (total assets to be invested represented approximately 3.7 million renminbi[1]) and were privately preapproved as acceptable in

---

[1]In December 1986, 1 renminbi (RMB) was fixed at $0.27. The RMB was set at a par value equal to the Chinese Foreign Exchange Certificate (FEC). FECs were hard currency-equivalent notes in China.

negotiations with the Foreign Economic Development and City Planning Commissions. The approval of the partnership was also contingent on a sharing of directors of the corporation, with one half of the directors supplied by KFC and one half supplied by the Chinese partners. The arrangements also stipulated that the chairman of B-KFC would be an appointee from Animal Production—Mr. Jue Xia—while the vice chairman would be selected by the Tourist Bureau—Mrs. Chun Fang Gao. These were major concessions by KFC, which was particularly concerned about the distribution of control in such a precedent-setting agreement.

In an interesting move, however, Wang was able to establish B-KFC as a franchisee, with the franchiser being KFC's regional office in Singapore. This move shifted much of the power over the operation to KFC. Under this contract, royalty payments to KFC of three percent were specified. These payments as well as payments for the imported KFC seasoning mixes were to be made using hard currency. Wang also insisted on moving control over the day-to-day operations to a Beijing general manager, who would necessarily be a KFC appointee. It was argued by Wang that KFC's real strength was in managing its own restaurants and that such a move would be essential for profitable operations. Formal approval by the Foreign Economic Development and City Planning Commissions came one week after the agreement was signed.

NEW CHALLENGES

With the partnership formalized, Tony Wang was hoping the hard part was over. It wasn't. In fact, the approval of the joint-venture agreement did not provide any operating authority for B-KFC in the city. What was needed for this was a "License to Execute a Business Activity." Approval for this required the signatures of the district government, the Commerce Department, the Taxation Department, the Health Department, and the Food Supply and Logistics Department. None of these agencies was coordinated, meaning that approval could take months or years as the document was signed by each organization. Getting these signatures would require the concerted efforts and resources of all three partners. Everywhere they went they met opposition from within the government. Tony Wang commented:

> We are pioneers in China, but so are the Chinese. However, whether they want to learn or not is another story. Many Westerners make the same big mistake in China: they assume that they can just pay to have the required work done or at least expedited. This just doesn't work in China. The Chinese are not motivated by a desire to do things right simply for the sake of doing things right. They don't want your help in speeding up the process. They just want to avoid problems. And unless we can convince them otherwise, we are their biggest problem.

What clearly troubled Wang was the uncertainty that hung over the entire situation. Even with a license, which was necessary before a lease could be signed, there was no guarantee that a satisfactory location for a store could ever be found. Indeed, virtually every building in Beijing was currently being occupied. Furthermore, Chinese regulations stipulated that new tenants would have to guarantee the employment of any workers left jobless when the

---

While RMB could not be legally converted into FEC, FEC could be readily and legally converted into hard currency.

new tenant took over. Almost undoubtedly this would force B-KFC to maintain a small contingent of unskilled Chinese laborers. What impact would this have on controlling the precarious working environment of the venture?

The concern over finding a location had other dimensions as well. Ideally, the first store would be the company's flagship store. This was inherent in the decision to invest in Beijing. According to Wang, "We all decided from the outset that we wanted a big, flashy, visible store. The image created by this first store would go a long way in determining our success or failure in China." Yet, while this made strategic sense, it seemed to run counter to China's history of hostility toward Western culture.

Issuing a License

In February 1987, a license was issued by the city, enabling B-KFC to operate legally within Beijing. The role of the Tourist Bureau in speeding the application process was invaluable. Under terms of the agreement, B-KFC was given a tax remission for two years; profits in years three, four, and five would be taxed at 16.5 percent, with profits thereafter taxed at 33 percent.

By this time, the number of possible locations for the premier Beijing store had been reduced to a handful. Topping the list were three locations: one near the zoo and Beijing's Exhibition Hall in the northwest part of Beijing; the second near the university area, also in the northwest part of the city but further out than the zoo; and the third was just off Tiananmen Square in the heart of the city.

Each of these locations seemed to have advantages and disadvantages. The zoo location would provide ready access to tourists—both Chinese and foreign. Although the zoo closed by 6:00 P.M., the nearby Exhibition Hall and Cinema remained open most evenings, drawing a more sophisticated crowd of potential customers. The site was also close to the Xizhimen train station, which brought travelers from northwest China into Beijing. According to Wang, the particular facility that was being made available seemed to "lack visibility and was not big enough." Similarly, the university location had the appeal of meeting the likely demand of more liberal students. Students placed considerable status on wearing Western clothes and it was thought that eating American-style fast food would be similarly attractive. However, in discussing the possible facilities being made available, Wang commented "the trade area here was good but the location was again too small with restricted access." The third site, off Tiananmen Square, was currently vacant, large—it occupied three stories—and had perhaps the most prominent location in the city.

Without a doubt, securing the Tiananmen Square location would require the mayor's personal approval. Such a prominent location, just off the southwest corner of the square, presented a full view of Mao's mausoleum. From the third-story windows a view of the Great Hall of the People was clearly visible. Hundreds of thousands, if not millions, of Chinese would pass the store each day in the busy city center. Almost certainly, China's top leaders would also pass by the restaurant on a regular basis. There was considerable discussion over the potential reaction of top city and national leaders to Colonel Sanders in the heart of Communist China. No one was sure whether the location would invite customers or provoke negative government reaction. And although in principle only city permission was required in negotiating the lease, the high profile of a Tiananmen Square location would clearly open the project to Central Government censure.

Irrespective of which location was selected, B-KFC would still need a building permit, as well as hookups of electricity, water, gas, and heating, before the store could open. Wang had learned that many of these services were very difficult to get in Beijing. Indeed, it was not uncommon for applications for service to go unanswered for extended periods of time. There were also concerns over the company's ability to secure import licenses needed for bringing equipment into the country—pressure frying machines, cash registers, and blending and cutting equipment for the kitchen. Each of these could be imported by permit only and could take months to secure.

Growing Concerns

The timing of these considerations was becoming critical. Ideally, the application for permits and licenses would proceed in a sequential manner so that all would be received at the appropriate time. It was becoming clear, however, that everything was hinging on a lease being signed—this would determine the size and location of the store, critical issues as yet unresolved. Yet, once a lease was signed, there would be no turning back.

It was with considerable trepidation that Tony Wang faced the spring of 1987. Even if the venture could somehow pass all of the seemingly insurmountable hurdles being thrown up, there was still no guarantee that the venture would work. Even with the signing of the joint venture, it had occurred to him that no one had thought to test market Kentucky Fried Chicken in China: "I had a gut-feel it would sell since chicken is a desirable food in China, yet we were all too busy to test this assumption." No one had any information, other than very mixed results coming from Hong Kong, that the Chinese would like the product. It was also becoming clear that the venture would be unable to find a reliable supplier of quality potatoes for french fries, suggesting the possibility of introducing not only fried chicken but mashed potatoes to the Chinese. What would they think? Clearly, no one knew.

Perhaps the greatest concern Tony Wang was facing was whether or not the operation could work from a quality, service, and cleanliness perspective. The problem here was with the employees that the venture would necessarily hire. With the exception of possibly a few managers, none of the employees would have ever seen a fast-food restaurant. Employees would have little appreciation for KFC's international standards of cleanliness or product quality. In many Chinese organizations, lacking *any* incentive systems, work was regarded by some as something to be avoided, service shunned. These attitudes were seen everywhere in China. And yet quality, service, and cleanliness were standards that corporate inspectors would rightfully expect before the franchise could open. There would be no compromising here. What was ironic was that customers would likely settle for far less than the company would accept. This would surely bring friction to the partnership and could ensure an acrimonious relationship with employees.

Even as Tony Wang sat back in the chair of his Singapore office his voice expressed mixed emotions. A lease would represent a symbolic point of no return for KFC. With it would come a commitment of significant hard currency funds. Should they push for a Tiananmen Square-type location or a lower-profile site? He wondered whether he had even made the right decision in selecting Beijing in the first place. Perhaps the uncertainty would be less in Guangzhou or Shanghai where the government would almost certainly be more accommodating. Perhaps partners with more restaurant experience could be found—surely they would be supportive of KFC's QSC efforts.

Tony Wang felt that the world was watching and waiting. KFC corporate headquarters had given him a mandate, one that Wang realized would likely capture the public's attention. Whether or not the venture was successful, the company and Wang himself would earn a certain notoriety throughout the industry over what was happening in China. Yet, there was so much uncertainty, so much that was beyond his control. Even the wildest thoughts of success could provide little real consolation as the company had yet to figure out what to do with the soft currency profits the venture would generate. He even wondered if there would be any profits. Recent discussions with Animal Production indicated that the local partner was prepared to charge B-KFC 8,500 RMB per ton of cleaned chicken. These chicken prices were somewhat higher than those charged in the United States. Could profits be supported at these costs—particularly given that demand would be tempered by average Chinese wages of about 100–120 RMB per month? No precise calculations could be made.

Yet, what should be done? In analyzing his options, three came to mind. He could pull out and cut his losses. This would result in minimizing negative publicity for both himself and KFC given the assumption that the venture was unworkable. It would also permit a more thorough examination of both the Chinese market and potential partners at a later, more opportune time. A second alternative would be to adopt a go-slow approach. Rather than pull out, a commitment on a location could wait until KFC was better acquainted with the partners, markets, locations, and potential employees. It would also permit KFC—either with or without its partners—to proceed with government negotiations, thus possibly shortening the time gap between the signing of a lease and the opening of the restaurant. A third option was to proceed with all haste. KFC had shown that it could be successful in the region. And China, with its 1.1 billion people, was a market being primed for fast food. To delay would only invite competitor response.

As Wang considered his alternatives, he reflected upon the recent discussion he had with KFC's president on the go-ahead decision. The KFC chief responded, "We have complete confidence in you. You clearly know the situation better than we do."

KENTUCKY FRIED CHICKEN IN CHINA (C)*

Allen J. Morrison, University of Western Ontario

In early March 1988, Tony Wang stared out the third-story window of Kentucky Fried Chicken's (KFC) Beijing restaurant as the crowds gathering on the street below. It was barely 10:00 on a Sunday morning and already people were lining up to purchase a meal that for most would cost over one-quarter of their weekly salary. To Wang, vice president for KFC for Southeast Asia and China, the crowds came as no surprise. In fact, in only four short months since opening, the Beijing restaurant had become the highest-selling single KFC store in the world. What was surprising to Tony Wang were his growing reservations about proceeding further in the Chinese market.

Wang was particularly worried about the mounting uncertainty of the entire venture. Although the restaurant had been successful in capturing the interests of Chinese consumers, conflicts with the company's two local partners were frequent and showed no signs of immediate resolution. Most of these disputes revolved around the imposition of KFC's management practices, which Wang regarded as essential to the operation's profitability. KFC's control mechanisms were designed to ensure standard levels of quality, service, and cleanliness (QSC) at all of the restaurant's chain stores around the world. Yet, the strictness with which these standards were enforced angered the local partners, who felt left out of the decision-making and believed lower requirements would be equally acceptable to customers.

In spite of these concerns, sales continued to climb to the point where chicken supplies were running out. Adding to the confusion were the requests of both local partners for more rapid expansion into other Beijing locations. Should KFC feel compelled to spearhead further expansion at this point in time? Tony Wang wondered how and when to respond to his partners, his employees, and the burgeoning Chinese market.

CHOOSING THE TIANANMEN SQUARE LOCATION

With the partners in place, Beijing KFC (B-KFC) in early 1987 had decided to pursue the location just off Tiananmen Square. The site featured a vacant three-story facility in excellent condition. The location in the heart of the city would provide unsurpassed visibility.

However, with the benefits of visibility came the possibility that the location would be difficult to obtain. Much time could be wasted in negotiations that could be publicly encouraged by government officials eager to seek political gain from the West. The fear was that in the end the site would be silently vetoed by Communist party leaders troubled by the cultural imagery of Colonel Sanders in the shadow of Mao's tomb.

*This case was prepared with assistance from Professor Paul W. Beamish. Funding was provided by The Federation of Canadian Municipalities' Open City Project through a grant from the Canadian International Development Agency (C.I.D.A.), and by the University of Western Ontario. © 1989 C.I.D.A. and the University of Western Ontario.

In winning the site, it was becoming ever more apparent that the imagery battle would be critical. According to Wang, their key strategy was "to convince the government that the restaurant would represent a symbol and statement of the People's Republic of China's commitment to an open policy with the West. Just as our image was important, we tried to play on the Chinese concern that they present a positive image with the outside world."

While this strategy was supported in principle by the two local partners, Animal Production and the Tourist Bureau knew they had far more to lose than their American partner by pushing the government too hard. According to Mr. Jue Xia, Chairman of B-KFC and a senior manager for Animal Productions, "We had several disagreements. Our position was that we shouldn't push too much. Government backlash was always possible."

Through sensitive negotiations, a government backlash was avoided and a lease was finally approved in April 1987 for the Tiananmen Square location. The lease represented a 10-year commitment from B-KFC. The store's facilities would represent KFC's largest restaurant in the world, with 1,400 square meters of space allowing for a capacity of 500 seats and considerable office space for B-KFC staff.

Still lacking was a building permit (to make renovations to the site) and hookups for water, gas, and heating. Many times in Beijing applications for service would get "misplaced" or service would be "unavailable" for no apparent reason. Heating was a particular problem—all facilities in the city were heated by common pipes from central Beijing heating plants. In these matters, KFC relied on the local partners for assistance but often found them reluctant to press for timely and adequate service.

KFC'S ORGANIZATION IN CHINA

By contractual arrangement, KFC was to provide a general manager responsible for the day-to-day operations of B-KFC. The man who held this position was Sim Kay Soon, a 30-year-old Singaporean. Sim joined the KFC system in 1980, and was selected for this position by Wang in the spring of 1987. In the interim period he had held area manager and more recently training officer positions. As general manager, Sim reported to Daniel Lam, KFC's newly appointed Area Director for China. Lam was based in Hong Kong and spoke fluent English, Mandarin, and Cantonese.

As events in China progressed, Wang began relying more and more on Lam for management support. Wang's attention was increasingly being split with his other duties in Southeast Asia. Estimates were that by the end of 1988 KFC would have 155 units established in the region, an increase of 45 units in the last two years. Exhibit 1 presents a breakdown of sales, by country, for Southeast Asia.

For Sim, the move to Beijing represented an 18-month appointment out of the booming regional office. It also represented a significant promotion. Nevertheless, the position was somewhat of a hardship posting as few of the conveniences found in Singapore were available in Beijing. Sim expected that a combination of stress and monotony would characterize his stay. His intended residence for 18 months was a Chinese hotel room negotiated by the Tourist Bureau.

EXHIBIT 1   **KFC Regional Sales Estimates for 1988**

	Number of Units	Sales (In millions of U.S. dollars)
Malaysia	66	$33.9
Indonesia	34	11.3
Hong Kong	13	12.3
Thailand	7	2.8
Singapore	33	27.0
Total	155	$64.1

HIRING LOCAL WORKERS

When initial announcements were made in the local papers that B-KFC would soon begin hiring, the joint venture was flooded with applicants. The decision to hire any particular applicant was made by Sim as the general manager of B-KFC. From the outset, KFC insisted on a policy that treated all applicants equally. No referrals would be accepted under any circumstance. This was a unique move in China, where family contacts were often used to land highly sought-after jobs. This was also a move that was initially opposed by the two local partners.

Working for a foreign joint venture was an attractive opportunity for many Chinese, because foreign partners often paid considerably above local wage levels. In Beijing, for example, it had been reported that English-speaking doormen at the joint-venture Sheraton Great Wall Hotel could earn up to three times as much as the top brain surgeon in the country. At KFC, the base salary promised to applicants was set at 140 RMB per month. This level was about 40 percent more than could be received at typical industrial facilities and up to 10 percent more than the remuneration received by associate professors at the country's universities. As was common among foreign joint ventures, B-KFC also devised an additional incentive scheme to encourage worker productivity. Incentive pay for conscientious employees could amount to another 150 RMB per month. For the Chinese worker it was a bonanza. So attractive was the compensation package that 20 people applied for every opening available.

The example of Mrs. Liu is indicative of the type of employees hired by B-KFC. Before coming to work for B-KFC, Liu was employed as an English teacher at a local Beijing public school. According to Liu:

> As an English teacher I was not well paid. The job was very dull, although most of my students enjoyed learning English. Still, I wasn't getting ahead. I was teaching English, but I wasn't learning English—I had no one to speak to. At KFC you have more chances to use and learn English. We are paid more here but we also work harder.

CONCERNS ABOUT EMPLOYEES

While employees were attracted to B-KFC because of the opportunities for high pay and training, KFC was concerned about the abilities of employees to provide the levels of quality, service, and cleanliness demanded by corporate standards. Employees seemed to have little understanding of these principles. The Chinese had limited exposure to quality products, long (and reluctantly) accepting goods of substandard quality as normal. The attitude was one of making do, of lowering expectations. Because employment was guaranteed in Chinese society, hard work was also viewed by some as something to be avoided. Some workers were apathetic toward their jobs and found little incentive to overcome the challenges inherent in most work. This could potentially impact on the Western norms for cleanliness and service.

Control over workers was exercised through three primary mechanisms: hiring, training, and incentive pay. Under Chinese joint-venture law, B-KFC was given the power to hire and fire workers according to its own criteria. Hiring at B-KFC was based on five key qualifications: acceptable applicants must be high school graduates, must speak some English, must be presentable in grooming and dress, must demonstrate a willingness to work hard, and cannot have had previous restaurant work experience. The typical applicant was in his or her early 20s, and had taken some English in school.

With almost 120 of the most promising applicants hired by early August, B-KFC set out on the arduous task of acculturating employees and training them in the fine art of American fast food. Under previous arrangements, all training expenses were borne by the franchiser—KFC. Training began with the extensive playing of a videotape of KFC's operations in both Hong Kong and Singapore. According to Tony Wang, "We customized the training videotape that we had used elsewhere in Southeast Asia to meet particular Chinese needs. Our main objective was to show the employees what fast food was like."

Beyond this, the company imported cooking equipment, blending machinery, heating racks, cash registers, etc., to begin hands-on training of the employees. Concurrent with these efforts, four new assistant managers—all Chinese nationals—were sent to Singapore for intensive training at local restaurants. According to Anthony Leung, a senior manager in KFC's Singapore office who helped supervise the training and who was later transferred to Beijing as B-KFC General Manager, "These new employees were bright, hard working, and eager to take in all that there was to learn. It was a very positive experience."

Incentive pay played a major role in improving employee attitudes toward QSC. Every job was assigned an index of 100 points. Unsatisfactory work meant a reduction of points, with a corresponding cut in bonus pay. According to Mrs. Liu:

> All employees get bonuses, unless they miss work, then they only get a percentage of their bonuses. Each job has standards set; if the standards are not met, we get points taken off. This also means a smaller bonus. The average bonus each month is from 50 to 150 RMB. The best I could ever expect in a factory would be about 120 renminbi per month. . . . So we work harder, but we get paid more. I like this.

STARTUP OPERATIONS

To add real-life experiences to the training, B-KFC began experimenting with sales to the public in September. Chicken was purchased from Beijing Animal Production, while potatoes, cabbage, and carrots were all purchased locally. Cases of Pepsi and 7Up were shipped in from southern China. A small dry-goods warehouse was leased in the city and uniforms were ordered. According to Anthony Leung: "We opened on a trial basis in the fall of 1987. We were only open seven hours a day—from 10 A.M. to 2 P.M. and from 5 P.M. to 8 P.M. The times we were closed in the morning and afternoon we spent reviewing and training."

By this time, the store had been connected to electricity and gas, but was lacking heat. As the fall weather approached, the lack of heat was becoming increasingly problematic. With the start-up of operations, the restaurant was drawing between 2,000 and 3,000 customers per day and the fear was that with the onset of colder weather many of these customers would be scared off if there was no heat. To make matters worse, a visit by corporate QSC inspectors resulted in the fledgling start-up receiving failing grades. Much more work was clearly needed.

After testing various menu options, a decision was made to limit the number of items offered to the bare requirements of KFC. Attempts at producing quality french fries had ended in failure—adequate frying potatoes could not be found in China. Mashed potatoes and gravy were offered instead. Chicken was regular flavor only. The restaurant was decorated with two life-size statues of Colonel Sanders and posters of American cities.

Setting prices for the store was a unique challenge. With no other fast food available in the city, prices were set to meet expectations of operating efficiencies, raw material costs, and "market pressures" for restaurant meals in the city. Prices for a three-piece dinner including potatoes, gravy, and a bun were set at 9.40 RMB. FEC (Chinese Foreign Exchange Certificate) prices were set at the same rates. While this seemed high compared to street food in Beijing, it was comparable with prices charged at many city restaurants. When asked about price, one teenaged customer observed: "The prices are really very good. When you consider the food as a treat, it is very affordable. Besides, where in Beijing can you find such a nice atmosphere? This is a perfect place to take a girl on a date."

After months of training and trial meals, operations had reached a point when corporate inspectors could recommend an official opening. A gala affair was planned for November 12, 1987, and included speeches by the U.S. ambassador, the mayor, the chairman of KFC, and other dignitaries. The international and domestic news media were also invited. The opening was covered by local newspapers and the national press and was watched with great interest by tens if not hundreds of millions of Chinese.

From the outset, sales were brisk. The restaurant opened with eight cashiers on duty—seven for local RMB sales, one for FEC sales. The crowds were so large that it was not unusual for local customers to wait up to 45 minutes in line to be served during peak times. Rarely were there more than a few people in line at the FEC counter. A separate window was also opened for take-out orders. Average daily sales during the winter of 1988 were about 25,000 RMB per day, equal to about 750 chickens. However, the trend was upwards, with demand rising on many days in March to well over 1,000 chickens per day.

With sales booming, discussion among the partners centered around the feasibility of adding an additional restaurant in Beijing. Clearly, existing capacity was being overstretched. B-KFC was overwhelmed by customer interest. The operation was also generating huge cash flows. There were early predictions that the initial investment of the three partners would be repaid within the first year of operation. Also, it seemed that the city was pleased with the way the venture was being run. Even the heat had finally been turned on, indicating that patience and tenacity were qualities that eventually would pay off in China.

UNRESOLVED PROBLEMS

Still, many doubts were lingering in Tony Wang's mind and he wondered if the venture should adopt more of a go-slow approach. His first concern lay with challenges in imposing Western management practices on the employees. Even though incentive pay had played an important part in improving employee productivity, the employees still required constant supervision. According to Anthony Leung:

> There are major differences which separate American management practices from the Chinese perspective. In America, managers try to be objective—they assess people's performance. In China, they judge employees by other criteria. What is their personality like? Are they friendly? How well can they talk? Let me give you an example. I recently asked one of our employees to mop the floor. He told me that it had just been mopped. When I pushed him on this he admitted that he really didn't know when it had been mopped. Finally, after some arguing he agreed to mop it "again." However, when I returned later I saw that the job had still not been done. Again, he used the same argument that "it was mopped earlier." What can you do?
>
> In fact, we have a very mixed group of employees here. It is a constant challenge to get employees to follow QSC procedures. Probably the biggest problem is that they feel very insulted when you try to tell them how to do a particular job. They may agree in principle, but this is seldom enough.

The need to supervise employees placed a particular strain on local management. Most of this team had been imported on term assignment from Singapore or Hong Kong. For these managers, Beijing was regarded as somewhat of a hardship post; most were eager to leave at the earliest possible time. A serious challenge facing Tony Wang was in replacing these managers with competent and motivated KFC managers who spoke Mandarin Chinese and preferably some English. Even in Singapore and Hong Kong these people were hard to find.

Personnel problems were also having an effect on the relationship among the partners. These problems often stemmed from Chinese partner resentment of the imposition of Western management practices. With offices located within B-KFC's Tiananmen Square store, Chun Fang Gao and Jue Xia both received salaries from the company and selected and employed their own small personal staffs. The restaurant's operations were clearly observable, as were conflicts between the KFC-appointed managers and the local employees. Not infrequently, disagreements erupted over the handling of employee disputes. Furthermore, employees had a tendency to turn to the local partners for support in dealing with the KFC-appointed managers. The frequency of disputes increased the concern among both local partners that perhaps KFC's rigid QSC expectations were unnecessary for Chinese employees or customers. In fact, the belief among employees was that sales would not suffer and morale would improve with a slackening of company standards.

From KFC's perspective, the local partners were overstepping their authority. Tony Wang viewed the primary role of the Tourist Bureau as one of facilitating a smooth relationship with the government. Yet, with operations booming, good public relations were coming more naturally, thus diminishing the importance of the partner. As for Animal Production, its responsibility was to provide a constant supply of quality chickens. However, with skyrocketing sales, Animal Production had reached its capacity and it appeared that a second supplier would be necessary. From KFC's perspective, the partners were becoming more of a bother than a necessity. This was particularly true the more they delved into the day-to-day operations of the company. This perspective was echoed by Anthony Leung: "It seemed that the partners were overly enthusiastic. They wanted to get involved in everything. The KFC people were pushing very hard for them to back off."

Not surprisingly, the partners had different perspectives of their roles. Their belief was that they understood Chinese customers much better than KFC and they could and should participate in improving operations. From the Tourist Bureau's perspective, Gao maintained that just as their active involvement had been essential for the project to get off the ground, it would be required to ensure its smooth operation in the future. The only obstacle to expansion was KFC. The position of Animal Production was in many ways similar. According to Xia:

> I think that we all would agree that our biggest problem is interpersonal. Each partner controls who it will send as its representative. Just as I cannot control who KFC brings in as general manager, KFC cannot control who Animal Production brings in. With Chinese and American partners, we are bound to have conflicts. My personal belief is that profits are helping to diminish the inherent conflict between partners.
>
> Our major concern with KFC doesn't revolve around operating matters, but around their quality standards. They only accept chickens from us that have been raised for seven weeks. Yet, far more money can be made by keeping the chickens for another week when weight gain is most rapid. But KFC refuses to go along with this. We have other places that can provide more money for our chickens than B-KFC. So we thought "this is not a really good deal for us." Yet, we are strong supporters of more rapid growth. Problems with chicken supply can be overcome. We have no problem with using outside suppliers.

Problems with employees and partners and the difficulty finding an adequate supply of chicken raised important questions in Tony Wang's mind about the long-term desirability of operating in China through B-KFC. Clearly customer demand had been great, suggesting many opportunities outside Beijing. Indeed, letters had begun pouring in from enterprises throughout China eager to explore joint-venture opportunities. Yet, what had been learned from the B-KFC experience? Other than a greater appreciation of the difficulties of working in China, Tony Wang wasn't sure what he would do differently the next time around—if there was to be a next time.

Even though the Tiananmen Square store was generating attractive profits, it remained uncertain what the money could be used for. It appeared that hard currency generated from the operation would amount to about $50,000 per year. This was a respectable sum, but hardly seemed commensurate with the efforts put into setting up and running the venture. Hard currency profits would likely represent an even lower percentage of sales at alternate locations in the country. Expansion costs for a new store would also be high. It was estimated that KFC spent about $250,000 in U.S. dollars in training and materials costs for the Tiananmen Square location alone. Tony Wang wondered if this one store would ever be worth it from a hard currency profit perspective. What good was soft currency to KFC, when there were ultimately few things to buy in China?

The challenge of setting up an American-style fast-food restaurant in China had been met with phenomenal success. Tony Wang felt that he had made a significant positive impact on Chinese perceptions of Americans in general and American food more specifically. He had appeared on national television and had been quoted in newspapers around China. Yet, the future remained uncertain. Clearly, much more needed to be done to improve existing operations. However, cleaning up disputes was not something that Tony Wang found personally compelling. He was beginning to wonder whether the personal challenge of China was beginning to wane. He had made perhaps too many trips to Beijing as it was. In fact, he suffered regular flare-ups of gout brought on by his constant travels. He wondered if he could assign others to do the job. Furthermore, it was uncertain what sort of timetable the expansion plans should follow. To delay would result in more friction among the partners and might foreclose on future expansion possibilities. What was not clear at all was whether the time was right for expansion. Perhaps instead of placating the partners, expansion would exacerbate existing problems. Furthermore, why these partners; why not others, in other cities? Why China at all? Indeed, corporate resources might be better directed at other emerging markets throughout Southeast Asia—Thailand, Malaysia, Indonesia, and the Philippines. Time was running out for some sort of response.

VIDEO COMPUTER TECHNOLOGIES INC.*

Rebecca L. Kaufman, Stanford University
L. A. Snedeker, Stanford University

It was mid-October of 1989, the same month that the Loma Prieta earthquake shook the San Francisco Bay Area, and a crisis of a different nature was threatening to shut down the European office of San Jose-based Video Computer Technologies Inc. (VCT). Julian Breashers, general manager of VCT's European operations, had quit unexpectedly. Don Edlinger, the president of VCT, had hoped that Julian would bring organization and stability to the European arm after the previous European general manager, Brian Erikson, had been asked to resign. Brian had had serious differences with one of the two founders, Bill Bacher, a situation compounded by a serious lack of communication between the San Jose headquarters and the European office.

Yet, this crisis situation abroad was only the most immediate problem facing VCT; the domestic house was not in order either. No single person had majority control of VCT or the European arm, rendering decision-making nearly impossible. (See Exhibit 1 for a list of the players and their stock ownership). Even worse, the two original founders (Bill Bacher and Dick Kauk) had entirely different philosophies about the business; communication between them took place only at infrequent board meetings. Furthermore, delayed product development, a lack of internal control systems, and an unclear vision and strategy for the future were additional challenges facing Don, as he began his eighth month as president of VCT.

COMPANY ORIGINS

Video Computer Technologies Inc. was born out of the related circumstances of two Silicon Valley entrepreneurs. Dick Kauk ran an Akai video equipment distribution business in San Jose, while Bill Bacher ran a service center for Akai in Los Gatos. Together, they were a full-service center. The two shared many deals over time and eventually began arguing over how to divide revenues. To solve the problem they decided to merge in 1974, forming Video Computer Technologies Inc. (VCT). Each took exactly 50 percent ownership. Bill described the decision to join their separate companies: "Dick would have died without [me], [I] would have died without him, so it seemed like a natural thing to merge." They solidified the deal with a handshake.

Dick Kauk was the salesperson of the two, with an affinity for video recording; he assumed the title and responsibilities of marketing manager. Bill was more of a tinkerer, with a strong interest in improving video technology. Bringing both engineering and manufacturing experience to VCT, he became engineering manager. Each respected the other's talents, but even at the beginning

---

*This case was prepared under the supervision of James C. Collins, Lecturer in Business, Stanford University Graduate School of Business. Revised by L. A. Snedeker, August 1990. The case was made possible by a grant from John W. and Nancy R. Sasser, M.B.A.s 1976 and Jon D. Tompkins, M.B.A. 1964.

E X H I B I T 1   **Owners and Key Players in VCTI and VCTE**

Name	Role	Percentage of Stock Ownership	Year Joined the Company
Video Computer Technologies Inc. (VCTI)			
Richard Kauk	Founding partner; division manager for retail/rental	50%	1974
William Bacher	Founding partner; division manager for products	50%	1974
Arthur Yaniro	Outside board member; insurance broker	None*	1979
Donald Edlinger	President	None*	1989
Video Computer Technologies Europe (VCTE)			
Brian Erikson	Founding partner; managing director	50%	1984
VCTI	Founding partner	50%	1984
Steve Ferguson	Head engineer (partner-to-be)†	None (Some percentage when appointed partner)	1984
Julian Breashers	Engineer (general manager-to-be)	None	1987

*Future stock options were to be made available.

†Steve and Brian had worked together at Zoom and had started at VCTE as a team with the plan that Steve would acquire stock at some future date, but Brian never worked this out with Steve.

was aware of the differences in the other's personality and motivations for being in the business. Dick summed it up: "I'm not motivated to go out and make enough money to buy a yacht—I'd rather putz around. Bill's strength is his energy and drive to want to do everything." Bill stated his life philosophy simply as: "I don't believe there is anything such as a wrong decision—there is only indecision. You just take a path and you do it!" Art Yaniro, an outside board member of 10 years, characterized the two: "Bill likes to do everything. Dick doesn't want to do anything. Together they are a great team."

Evolution of the Company

VCT started off as just a video equipment dealership and service center, but both Dick and Bill were opportunistic in their approach to the business. If an interesting proposal or deal came their way, they often took it. As a result, they felt little need to chart a proactive strategy. For instance, early in VCT's history they started building video studios for schools. They were so good at it that every school district in the Bay Area soon hired them. Next they acquired the JVC video line, and finally, in 1976, they attained Dick's ultimate dealership goal: the right to be a Sony dealership. According to Dick, a Sony dealership was like a "license to print money." At the same time, Bill convinced Dick of the need to create a marketing and sales force.

By 1978, the company had grown to 14 people. Despite the company's growth, Dick and Bill never articulated what business they were in, nor where they wanted the company's growth to lead. They also did not discuss their personal expectations or goals for the business. Rather, they worked day to day, traveling down any path that appeared in front of them.

Entry into Manufacturing

Because video sales were rocky and cyclical, Bill and Dick constantly sought ways to diversify their business. According to Dick, "Video sales were easily undercut by price-slashing competitors, because a certain manufacturer's lens was . . . basically a commodity." To differentiate themselves, Dick and Bill began to customize standard products by adding convenience and style features. Once they did this, VCT found their customers were sole-sourcing them for many products. VCT was thus in the business of "making things," not just distributing other manufacturers' equipment. Diversifying into manufacturing turned out to be profitable and fun, particularly for Bill who was able to put his engineering and inventing skills to work. Their products were, in effect, low-cost video recorder lines that looked and acted like the professional Japanese models.

Then, in 1978, without warning, the supplier of their video editors cut them off. VCT had to move fast, for video editor machines were a central part of the video editing system that VCT advertised and sold. Fortunately, Bill and Dick knew a programmer across town who was losing money on his computer-run editor. VCT bought his design in 1978 and began making its own version of computer-run editors. Thus, in 1978, VCT was fully engaged in low-volume, high-value editing systems design and manufacturing.

PRODUCTS AND MARKETS

VCT was divided into two major divisions: *products* (headed up by Bill Bacher) and *dealership/rental* (headed up by Dick Kauk). The products division designed, manufactured, and sold products invented by Bill. The dealership/rental division sold and rented other vendors' products. In 1988, the products division contributed roughly 25 percent to VCT's total revenues. However, due to the higher margins in products, the products division contributed a significantly higher percentage to the corporation's overall profitability. The products division produced two types of products: editor systems and V-LAN interface boxes.

Editor Systems

VCT currently offered two products in this category: the Mickey and the VLC-32. In April 1989, the VLC-32 had replaced the Eagle model, which had been discontinued in September 1988 because of unreliability under heavy field use. The VLC-32 retailed for $10,000 (see Exhibit 2). The low-end Mickey took input via a mouse-click mechanism, similar to that found on a Macintosh computer, and retailed for $5,000 (see Exhibit 3).

The ease of use of these products allowed them to be used in "professional" (broadcast studio videos), "nonprofessional" (corporate promotional or

**EXHIBIT 2   Content of Company Promotional Literature Describing the
VLC-32 Editing System**

Today's computerized editing systems are designed to give you greater control over the tools in your work environment. They are expected to take care of routine mechanical details, so you can focus on what you do best—creative decision-making. VLC-32 was developed to fulfill all of your post-production needs—today as well as tomorrow. By offering all the power you need at a price you can afford, VLC-32 allows you to fulfill your basic needs and expand as they grow. It is a fully modular approach to all pre- and post-production functions—the most advanced concept in production technology ever created

VLC-32 Expands As Your Needs Grow

VLC-32 lets you start with exactly the features you require today. Tomorrow, as your needs grow, VLC-32 expands to the most powerful Production Control Environment ever created. Utilizing the industry-standard V-LAN^{TM} Universal Control Network, VLC-32 is 100% expandable. VLC-32 can function as a 2-machine cuts editor or expand control up to 31 different devices on the same network at one time. Since each VLC-32 module builds on your existing system, there is absolutely no wasted investment.

VLC-32 reliability is built in. Each module uses the highest quality state-of-the- art components. When you look inside a V-LAN module, you can see why this is so. There are no wiring harnesses, and all ICs are fully socketed for ease of service.

VLC-32 is marketed by qualified dealers throughout the world. If you have any techni-

cal or operational questions regarding VLC-32 that cannot be answered by your local dealer, the factory is there to support you. Factory installation and training packages are available.

VLC-32 Performance Makes You More Productive

VLC-32 delivers unprecedented performance at an exceptionally reasonable price. Even the most basic configuration of VLC-32 provides integrated high-end features like these:

- Uses industry standard V-Lan protocol
- Automatic match-frame effects into and/ or out of an event
- 500-event, dynamically allocated, non-volatile memory
- Multilevel transitions with active buss assignment
- Sync roll up to 6 source transports
- Slave up to 4 record transports
- Up to 16 transports on line
- Control up to 8 GPSI (General Purpose Switcher Interface) or switcher memory functions per event
- AUTO-EDIT
- Animation
- Slow-motion control of applicable transports
- INSERT, DELETE, SUSPEND, COPY and RIPPLE list management features.
- Disk storage and retrieval via standard PC
- Insert and Assemble editing
- Park and Perform editing
- Scratch Pad memory

EXHIBIT 3   **Promotional Literature for the Mickey Editing System**

The most technically advanced editing system in the industry.

Low-Cost A/B Roll Editing.

- Frame accurate A/B roll editing.
- User-friendly mouse control.
- *V-LAN™* distributed intelligence.
- Auto-match and extend.
- Automatic monitor switching.
- Assignable VTRs.
- Programmable sync rolls.
- Printer output.
- Built-in video dissolve.
- Built-in 2-channel audio follow video mixer.
- 50-event nonvolatile internal memory.
- GPI interface for external devices.
- User programmable functions.
- Wide variety of options, including PC-LINK.

training videos), and computer graphics environments alike. In the United States, 85 percent of the products were sold to nonprofessional institutions, while only 15 percent were sold to professional customers. Internationally, these products were sold 50 percent to each market. (Institutions included corporations, military agencies, government offices, and school systems. Professional customers included post-production houses and broadcasters.) The market for the VLC-32 and the Mickey, although traditionally the bread and butter of the manufacturing division, were not expected to show much growth over the next five years.

V-LAN Controller Interface Box

If the Mickey and the VLC-32 were thought of as "cash cows" for VCT, then the V-LAN controller interface box was a potential "star." A huge market was

EXHIBIT 4   **VCTI Products Diagram**

Price	Input	Mainframe	V-LAN	
$10,000	Keyboard	VLC-32	V-LAN	vtr
			V-LAN	vtr
			V-LAN	vtr
$5,000	Mouse	MICKEY	V-LAN	vtr
			V-LAN	vtr
			V-LAN	vtr
$1,000 (for each V-LAN)	NA	Any Computer	Transmitter	
			V-LAN	vtr
	Receivers		V-LAN	vtr
			V-LAN	vtr

NA = not applicable.

projected for the device, which was a universal controller for the computer with two functions: it could act as either a transmitter or a receiver to the computer controlling the editing function. Bill Bacher had invented the V-LAN product, which was perceived as a revolutionary though relatively unknown product. As one customer remarked, "I can't believe the universal controller hasn't caught on yet." (See Exhibit 4 for a descriptive diagram of VCT's products.)

VCT management felt that the potential for the V-LAN product was enormous. Currently, computer graphics customers (the primary target for the V-LAN) composed 20 percent of VCT's 1989 manufacturing division revenues. However, VCT expected this market to grow over *one hundredfold* by 1995 due to the growth in the number of computer software applications (i.e., desktop video, multimedia, and animation packages).

V-LAN retailed for $1,000, and VCT made over 50 percent margin on them. V-LAN was becoming an industry standard, although it was competing against well-known manufacturers. At National Association of Broadcasters' conferences, Bill Bacher noted that people often asked if other manufacturers' products were "V-LAN compatible." VCT was currently the only company to manufacture such a product as the V-LAN interface box.

SELLING IN EUROPE

A European Distributor

Video Computer Technologies' manufacturing division began selling its products in Europe in 1981. Bill had made contacts with European distributors and dealers at National Association of Broadcasters (NAB) conferences. The Europeans liked VCT products and felt there was a market for them abroad; Bill decided to give Europe a try by signing with London-based Zoom Television. He commented: "Europe is a necessary market for us. The competition had PAL[1] products. Either you get in the pool or you don't play. If we didn't have PAL products we wouldn't be recognized, we wouldn't even be in the game."

For two years Zoom acted as a distributor of VCT products until it decided to discontinue this line of business. Then one of Zoom's most active editor salespeople, Brian Erikson, approached VCT with a proposal to set up a European distribution center for VCT products. It seemed like an excellent opportunity to get a stronger foothold in Europe, and, as one of the founding partners noted, "It was a real ego boost to have our own European office."

Video Computer Technologies Europe

Brian's proposal for Video Computer Technologies Europe included another partner, who later dropped out. The final proposal was hammered out during verbal negotiations with Bill Bacher, Dick Kauk, Art Yaniro, and Brian. The deal originated in Switzerland, where Dick was attending a video products show. When talks began to get serious, Dick told Brian that he could not negotiate further without majority board presence. Coincidentally, Art—who was there on vacation with his family—was standing behind Dick in the hotel in Switzerland as he spoke these words. Hence, two out of the three board members were present, and they went ahead with negotiations to create a European office. Video Computer Technologies Europe was established as a 50/50 partnership: Brian owned 50 percent of the shares and VCT owned the other 50 percent. Like Bill and Dick's original agreement to form VCT, the agreement to form a European operation was a handshake, not a written, deal. Brian Erikson put up the initial working capital, while VCT supplied the products and support materials.

Transfer Pricing for European Operations

The first two years produced losses. But by the third year, European operations' sales exceeded expectations, and then was profitable for two consecutive years (see Exhibit 5 for financial information). However, the pricing structure made it unclear whether the European arm was actually profitable: VCT had structured its transfer pricing such that Europe was shipped product at full manufacturing cost plus 10 percent, a substantially lower amount than a

---

[1]In Europe, PAL, Phrase Alternate Line, was the equivalent of NTSC, National Television Standards Commission, in the United States.

EXHIBIT 5   **Financial Information for VCT, Selected Years**

Profit and Loss Summary for VCT's European Operations
Year Ended December 31 (In dollars, unless otherwise noted)

	FY 1986(£)	FY 1987	FY 1988	FY 1989	FY 1990 (E)
Sales	$294,000	$396,800	$716,800	$548,800	$400,000
Cost of sales	164,000	200,800	391,200	288,000	200,000
Gross margin	130,000	196,000	325,600	260,800	200,000
Gross margin percentage	44%	49%	45%	48%	50%
Expenses	138,400	176,800	261,600	315,200	224,000
Pre-tax profit (loss)	$ (8,400)	$ 19,200	$ 64,000	$ (54,000)	$ (24,000)

Profit and Loss Summary for VCT's Consolidated Operations
Year Ended December 31 (In dollars, unless otherwise noted)

	FY 1986	FY 1987	FY 1988	FY 1989 (E)
Sales	$5,748,800	$5,844,000	$7,016,800	$8,800,000
Cost of sales	4,015,200	4,052,800	4,483,200	6,160,000
Gross margin	1,705,600	1,791,200	2,533,600	2,640,000
Gross margin percentage	30%	31%	36%	30%
Expenses	1,580,800	1,504,000	1,961,600	2,160,000
Pre-tax profit (loss)	$ 124,800	$ 287,200	$ 572,000	$ 480,000

VCT's Consolidated Balance Sheets
December 31, 1987 and 1988

	1987	1988
Assets		
Current assets		
Cash	$ 287,200	$ 122,400
Accounts receivable	665,600	976,800
Inventory	297,600	524,000
Prepaid expenses	45,600	64,000
Total current assets	$1,296,000	$1,687,200
Fixed assets less accumulated depreciation	107,200	283,200
Total assets	$1,403,200	$1,970,400
Liabilities and Stockholders' Equity		
Current liabilities		
Accounts payable	$ 190,400	$ 265,600
Accrued taxes	59,200	91,200
Other accrued	72,000	133,600
Total current liabilities	$ 321,600	$ 490,400
Stockholders' equity		
Capital stock	$ 32,000	$ 32,000
Retained earnings	1,049,600	1,448,000
Total shareholders' equity	$1,081,600	$1,480,000
Total liabilities and shareholders' equity	$1,403,200	$1,970,400

Note: The inconsistency in the fiscal years and discrepancy in currency are a true reflection of the information available from the company. These financial statements are disguised.

EXHIBIT 6   **Distributor, Dealer, and Transfer Pricing: An Example**

	Pricing to U.S. Channel	VCTI Pricing to VCTE
Unit cost (i.e., parts, labor)	$ 100	$ 100
Full manufactured cost (i.e., parts, labor, overhead—not including marketing, etc.)	200	200
Distributor cost (wholesale)	500	280
Dealer cost	700	700
Consumer cost (i.e., list price)	1,000	1,250*

*Includes freight and duty.

Note: This pricing structure reflects the inconsistency in the relationship between VCTI and VCTE with regard to other distributors.

domestic distributor would have to pay. (See Exhibit 6 for breakdown of the transfer pricing mechanism.) According to Don Edlinger, "A major part of the deal was that the transfer price from VCT to European operations was based on manufacturing cost only, and that profits would be shared equally. In other words, the European operations shared in [an equal amount of] the profits without making any contribution to R&D, marketing, or any other corporate expenses."

Erikson's Spending Spree

After two years of profitability (FY 1987 and FY 1988—see Exhibit 5), Brian Erikson's confidence began to grow—as did his hopes for Europe. Brian geared up for increased sales, despite the historical trend of cyclical sales in the video editor market. He hired three new employees, expanding the U.K. staff to seven. He bought himself a Lotus company car (Value = £25,000, or $40,000), and put his wife on the payroll, claiming that this was an "acceptable" tax avoidance practice in the United Kingdom. The San Jose-based management was unfamiliar with British cultural norms, and felt at a disadvantage in evaluating these expenditures. Brian furthermore started his own European R&D division to improve Video Computer Technologies' products and to create animation packages. Since VCT also made animation software to work on OEM's hardware, these packages were essentially competing with VCT's. This was particularly threatening to Bill Bacher, who ran VCT's R&D effort back in San Jose. As a result, tension between Bill Bacher and Brian Erikson ran high.

One member of VCT management described this period as pure craziness:

> Brian began living in a fantasy world. He did not talk with us about his gearing up. He felt the sky was his limit. He was working very hard and felt that what he was doing was the right thing despite the fact that his animation hardware product was in direct conflict with VCT's corporate goals and in direct conflict with our customers' products.

Further Problems with European Operations

Meanwhile, there was no communication between San Jose and London regarding corporate direction, planning, or budgeting. Brian was given free rein. There was a conflict in San Jose in how Brian's actions were perceived.

Some, like Bill Bacher, thought Brian was entirely out of line and should be fired. Others felt more sympathetic toward him. Art noted, "When things were going well, everyone was happy. But, when things were slow, Brian was the bad guy, the irresponsible manager. Brian was never told what his budget was—in fact, he didn't have one." Indeed, Brian Erikson was not asked to cut costs until April 1989. According to Dick Kauk, "We told Brian to 'go ahead, set it up' without any controls—everything we did was sloppy except for the effort. In effect, we gave the keys to the candy store to the kids, and now we were complaining that they took too much. That's backwards."

Things began to sour in 1987. As more and more customers were disappointed by the Eagle, Brian promised his long-time customers that a replacement product for the Eagle would be out soon (the VLC-32) and that customers who bought the Eagle would get a 40 percent discount off the replacement product's list price. Meanwhile, the VLC-32 was late in coming on the market; in fact, VCT was a year and a half late in getting the VLC-32 to the market worldwide.

Meanwhile, Steve Ferguson, an engineer in Europe who was highly respected (by Bill Bacher in particular) and one of the original players in setting up the European operations, began calling Bill at home. Steve told Bill that Brian was preparing business plans outside of his original charter (i.e., business plans that included non-VCT products) and spending huge amounts of discretionary funds (e.g., on hospitality suites at shows). Steve's calls raised doubts in San Jose about Brian's ethics and ability to run a sound operation, but according to Dick, "We should have squashed this overriding of the chain of command right away. Brian became a sacrificial lamb." According to Art, "Brian was bucking Bill by pointing the finger at him and saying if he didn't have product he couldn't have sales. Once you buck Bill, he fights back." The problems overseas exacerbated the problems between the two founders, who now communicated with each other very little. Bill Bacher, in fact, threatened to quit more than once because of problems with Dick Kauk; Art always convinced him to return.

Then, in late 1987, Art himself threatened to quit after 10 years of service as an outside board member if Dick and Bill did not hire a professional manager. He said, "I didn't want to have the fiduciary responsibility if one day one of the owners died and his estate decided to look into VCT's books and found out that we never really kept any books worth using. We needed professional management and leadership. Everyone was burnt out. VCT needed new blood." As a result, VCT started a search for a president to whom both Bill and Dick would report. The president, in turn, would report to the board. Through its search, VCT found Don Edlinger.

DON EDLINGER

Don Edlinger graduated from high school in California, whereupon he joined the U.S. Navy. After leaving the Navy, he continued on at the University of California—Davis in electrical engineering. Graduating in 1966, he then went to work for IBM as a design computer engineer. However, after three years of back-room experience, Don decided he wanted more interaction with the customers and more applications work. He tried to transfer internally to a marketing arm, yet no one in IBM's marketing area thought he fit. After exploring other ways to enter the customer side of high-tech business, he decided to get an advanced degree. At 29, he entered the MBA program at Stanford's Graduate School of Business. After graduation, Don went to work for the light-emitting diode (LED) marketing arm of Hewlett-Packard (HP). He felt good about HP, since many of his colleagues had EE/MBA double degrees. Don noted, "I also really enjoyed selling visual display products."

After Don was at HP a few years, the LED division changed directions, so he decided to leave. He joined Coherent Incorporated as a product manager and moved up to a top management position during the 12 years he spent with the company (1975–1987). By 1985, Don was president of Coherent's industrial division (later renamed Coherent General), of which 40 percent was owned by General Electric. At Coherent, Don had to deal frequently with international issues. In 1986, he decided to close down the California operations of Coherent General and move it east—closer to GE's laser technology research center. He moved with the company to help during the transition year and then returned to the Bay Area to start his own business. He actually participated in the start-up of four companies—all high-tech and all related to software, computer, and visual display products. However, after a year or so of this, his family was too uncomfortable with the insecurity of start-ups, so Don decided to put his resumé on the market.

Don described his decision to join VCT: "I like small groups, I like team building, I want to be close to the customer and applications, I like networking, and I am a good administrator. Visual display and computer software products are my interest." Don joined VCT as president in February 1989. (See Exhibit 7 for an organization chart after Don Edlinger's arrival.)

DON'S FIRST SEVEN MONTHS—A WORSENING INTERNATIONAL SITUATION

Resentment Builds

Video Computer Technologies Europe was top priority for Don when he started at VCT. By the time Don arrived, all communication had broken down between Bill Bacher and Brian Erikson. Not only was Brian doing R&D in direct conflict with Bill's R&D, but he was also blaming the European operation's poor sales on Bill's year-and-a-half delay in releasing the VLC-32. Moreover, Brian had geared up to such an extent that each employee had a company car. According to Don, "Brian did not respond by cutting costs, as most owner/managers would do; instead he continued to give himself a six-month pay raise and produce flashy brochures."

Furthermore, the negativity surrounding the whole European experience was a drain on everyone at home in San Jose. Said Don, "It was a big pain, a big hassle, all for a small amount of sales and no profit contribution to VCT. Something had to give." Don hired a personnel consultant in London to determine which of Brian Erikson's expenses were truly the British norm and which were symptomatic of Brian's excessive spending. The result: Don determined that the number and value of the cars were out of line and that Brian's salary was about 30 percent above standard for a company of this size.

EXHIBIT 7   **Video Computer Technologies' Organization Chart**

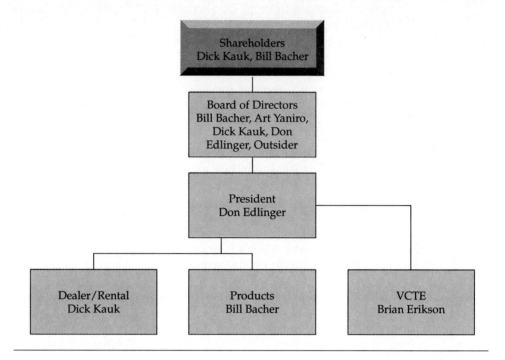

Brian had plans to come to San Jose in February, so Don asked him to bring a proposal for cutting the European operations' costs. Brian arrived with a simple plan to cut his staff from seven to five. His plan specifically called for dismissing Steve (the engineer who had been calling Bill) and a support staff secretary. Unfortunately, Steve was one of the European engineers in whom Bill had the highest technical confidence, so feelings between Bill and Brian went from bad to worse. Don asked Brian to reevaluate additional expenditure cuts, including his salary and benefits (his Lotus, his wife's car, and his wife's salary). In addition, European operations owed VCT $270,000, which Don was uncertain of how to collect.

The situation was complicated by the fact that Brian brought both strengths and weaknesses to the European operation. His strengths included excellent sales skills, a clear understanding of video products, good relations with customers, devotion to his work, and a strong drive to succeed. His weaknesses included poor communication skills, plans for Europe outside the realm of VCT's plans, poor management skills, and an aversion to learning about new products and new markets. According to Don Edlinger, Brian Erikson was weak in financial management and, because he was so sales-driven, appeared incapable of profit and loss responsibility. He did not adapt to the professional mode of operations that declining sales and new product introductions required.

Planning for Brian's Departure

In June, Don went to London. The tension between Bill and Brian had reached monumental proportions, so during his June visit, Don asked Brian to start looking for another job. "I told him there was no future for him in running the European branch. I told him we would be friendly, give him good recommendations, and buy him out—but that the situation had reached a point where someone had to go and it wasn't going to be Bill." Don and Brian agreed that Brian would send a severance proposal before the August 17, 1989 board meeting in order to have his input into the final severance agreement.

In the final agreement, it was determined that Brian had indeed created value for the European operation—it had a customer base, some level of goodwill, and a foothold in Europe, Eurasia, and Africa. Don devised a plan in which Brian would be phased out over six months while training Julian Breashers to take over as general manager of European operations. The proposal called for giving Brian the Lotus car lease, his salary in severance pay, and half of fiscal year 1990 profits, if there were any. Don felt the severance package was fair and said Brian did also. Art felt the severance package was the least VCT could do: "We never managed Brian. We didn't give him product. We didn't give him direction, and now we are kicking him out because he didn't put in the controls that we never asked him to, nor have we ever even implemented domestically. We owe him a good parachute."

From Brian Erikson's standpoint, there were four major problem areas in VCT's European operation. First, he felt the most dominant problem was the complete breakdown of communications. He and the management at VCT never clearly communicated about goals and aspirations for Europe, nor about problems as they arose. Second, he believed that "inexperience on both sides of the ocean led to miscommunication, misplanning, and lack of understanding about what the VCT/Brian partnership meant." Third, Brian noted, "Products have been developed by people who love engineering without checking into market need and market demand first—this needs to change for operations in Europe to be successful." And finally, Brian believed the timing of the introduction of new products in the European/international marketplace had been off.

In addition, trust had broken down over the cultural misunderstandings. Brian believed that once communication and trust were established both in San Jose and in London, VCT could be a great success in Europe. According to Brian, the product was top-notch and market demand was growing, so only the organization itself needed improvement.

THE SITUATION IN OCTOBER 1989

Brian Erikson had verbally accepted the severance package proposed on August 17, with the agreement that VCT would send a final, legal copy to him in London. But VCT was slow in getting it to Brian, and in the meantime, Julian Breashers quit. According to Don Edlinger, Julian's departure rendered the whole severance agreement with Brian Erikson null and void. "It was based on European operations having ongoing value, goodwill, and an established customer base. Without Julian and Brian, the European operation was furniture only."

Yet VCT did not necessarily want to do away with the division. The future in Europe looked very promising. With the introduction of satellite television and with the increasing use of videotapes for training in corporations, there would be an increase in production companies and a growing need for both editors and V-LAN products. Moreover, the PAL marketplace was already half the world marketplace and growing. It consisted of China, Hong Kong, India, Africa, Saudi Arabia, and many other Middle Eastern and Asian countries. The "PAL world" was *the* place for sales growth, according to Brian. In 1989, 50 percent of VCT's manufacturing sales was in the PAL market. Within the PAL market, 35 percent was in the United Kingdom and 65 percent was in the 18 other PAL countries. According to Don, "We have actually done better in Europe than here in terms of percent market share."

But to successfully negotiate this market, Don Edlinger needed to straighten out several issues with VCT's European operation. During September and the beginning of October, Don worked continually with his London personnel consultant to straighten out the employee termination legal issues. He also explored the possibilities for taking over the European operation's $270,000 in receivables. Brian Erikson was the only signatory with the British banks and the only signatory on the European operation's checks. Brian was out of the country and it was unclear whether he would repay the European operation's $270,000 receivables debt to VCT. Don looked into having agents act as receivers. He also checked out what legal action was necessary for VCT to go into receivership of the European operations' receivables. Meanwhile, Bill Bacher went to London in early October to look for possible distributors for VCT's products, and to hire two of the European operation's engineers for product support.

Don wondered if he should also travel to London to consolidate Bill's efforts and to deal with the other tasks necessary to keep the European arm of VCT in operation. He worried that his lack of experience with European culture had put the San Jose management at a disadvantage, and wondered how he could overcome this. He was also concerned with the overriding issue: should VCT be involved in international operations at all? And if so, was the current European arm the proper vehicle? What other options might there be? Don also wondered if indeed this was *his* decision to make, or if the board of directors should make it.

The international issues were only a segment of Don's responsibilities as president of VCT. He also had several considerations requiring his attention at home in the San Jose office. He was hired to make VCT an ongoing business that would survive the departure of any key players. At an off-site meeting in 1989, Dick Kauk had in fact stated that he would like to build the company to the point where it would run itself. (A summary of the motivations of each board member is shown in Exhibit 8.) Video Computer Technologies had had one outside board member for 10 years, Art Yaniro, which Don considered a positive, but they had never instituted a buy-out agreement among Bill, Dick, and the company, nor a means by which anyone else could attain stock. This was a problem in light of the 50/50 split between the two founders, who didn't talk to each other. The lack of a buy-out agreement had become such a point of contention for Art, and partially for Dick, that Don was told this must be high on his priority list as well. Yet, writing a buy-out agreement would be no

E X H I B I T 8   **Personal Goals and Motivations of VCT's Board Members**

Bill Bacher
- To help others get what they want out of the business.
- To have fun at whatever we do.
- To win.
- To have something challenging and interesting to do.
- To have personal flexibility in my life.

Dick Kauk
- To be responsible to the people who work here.
- To have something challenging and interesting to do.
- To get out of routine—to have a project to do.
- To do something significant—so that I can say "We did that."
- To have fun.
- To meet the financial needs of my family.
- To have pride in the products we sell.
- To build the company to a point where it runs itself.

Don Edlinger
- To be the person who carries the company on.
- To make a contribution.
- To meet the financial needs of my family (put my kids through college).
- To put value in the company stock.

Art Yaniro
- To help Bill and Dick.
- To have something challenging and interesting to do.
- To put value in the company stock.
- To have pride in being part of this company.
- To have fun.

small feat for Don, since one founder's attitude was clear: "I don't believe all the paperwork in the world can replace a handshake with the right people. If we're not the right people, we shouldn't be in business together."

Both Don and Art were told they would receive stock, but hadn't yet. In fact, a final employment agreement between VCT and Don had yet to be finalized in writing. Don was additionally promised a seat on the board. Then, a fifth seat for an outsider would be added to avoid stalemates in voting decisions.

Aside from the urgent situation in Europe and these pressing domestic issues, Don needed to develop a vision for VCT. He had been hired to, among other things, spearhead VCT's efforts to make V-LAN the industry standard. Don noted: "I view my role as president as one in which I must take the company somewhere—make a difference—establish manufacturing and proprietary technology as a major part of the company—i.e., V-LAN."

Don also had to set up domestic accounting controls, including budgeting and cost accounting. Historically, VCT had done no cost accounting and never even knew whether some of its products were profitable. Don intended to set up a marketing department, put aside funds for R&D, work with lawyers to draft a buy-out agreement between Bill and Dick, create an employee stock option and profit-sharing plan, and institute internal systems that would go forward year to year (e.g., business plans, cash flow forecasts, employee reviews, etc.). In other words, Don wanted to provide professional management in an environment that had been running for over 15 years by the seat of its pants.

As he struggled to prioritize these challenges, he thought about his own awkward situation. As president, both Bill Bacher and Dick Kauk reported to him. But as president, Don reported to the board, which included the two founders. As he thought about how to handle the future, Don Edlinger knew he needed to proceed delicately.

STRATEGY, ETHICS, AND CORPORATE SOCIAL RESPONSIBILITY

TDK de Mexico

Manab Thakur, California State University—Fresno

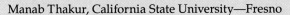

"I want to be the main supplier base of magnets for South and North America," proclaimed Fumio Inouye, general manager of TDK de Mexico, located in Cd. Juarez, a border city of millions close to El Paso, Texas. He continued:

> To help gain this status, our operating targets need to be met, and that might include expansion of present plant facilities and more automation. Increasingly I feel, though, that people here don't want to see expansion. . . .They seem to enjoy excuses! Whether you call it Japanese or American management, I cannot accept delays, wastes, and excuses! Culture to me is important only when the process of production and the importance of work are clearly understood. Make no mistake, my parent company (TDK of Japan) wouldn't stand for anything other than making acceptable margins. I am having difficulty in putting reasons for all the problems on culture. . . . I refuse to take it as a dumping ground.

PRODUCTION METHODS AND TECHNOLOGY

TDK de Mexico produced ceramic ferrite magnets of various shapes and sizes that were used for speakers, generators, and motors. It was one of the few plants in its area that produced a final product from the raw material. Production was based on job orders—in other words, production was scheduled as TDK de Mexico received orders for a given number of a given type of magnet. Exhibit 1 shows TDK's plant layout and production process. The raw material used to make the final product was a black powder called ferrite powder. The ferrite powder, a critical raw material, was imported, although it was available in the Mexican market. But to ensure quality, TDK of Japan insisted on using ferrite powder from Japan. The manufacturing process started by wetting and mixing the powder in large containers. The mixture was dried and then was fed into the press machines that gave the shape to the magnets. The shape was determined by the mold inserted into the press machine (Exhibit 2). All of the molds used also came from Japan. The various molds for the different shapes and sizes were stored at the plant and used as needed.

Two distinct methods were used during the press stage of the production process, the dry method and the wet method. The basic difference between the two was that the wet method, installed at TDK de Mexico in 1983 after Fumio Inouye took charge, utilized water during the pressing of the raw material. It made stronger magnets, but it took more time. With the wet method, the worker collected the magnets just pressed and placed them in a temporary drying area before they were baked in the ovens. With the dry method, the worker collected the magnets just pressed, and they were sent straight to the ovens for baking. While collecting the magnets, the worker visually checked each magnet for cracks or other defects. Defective ones were thrown out for scrap. It was important to spot defective magnets at this stage because it was much harder to convert them into scrap after they were baked. All scrap materials were broken down and used again in the raw material mixture.

EXHIBIT 1   **Plant Layout and Production Process**

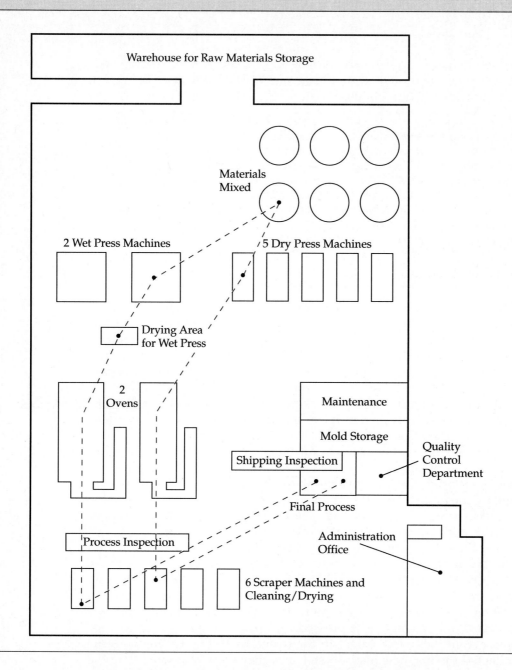

After pressing, the magnets were mechanically moved through a series of ovens (Exhibit 3). One set of pressed magnets was placed in the oven every 12 hours. The magnets were baked at progressively higher temperatures from entrance to exit. After their exit from the ovens, the magnets continued moving to a temporary storage area to cool. The ovens presently in use were electrically powered, but there was a plan to convert them to gas ovens to take advantage of the lower cost of gas. Once cooled, each magnet was subject to process

EXHIBIT 2 Production Technology

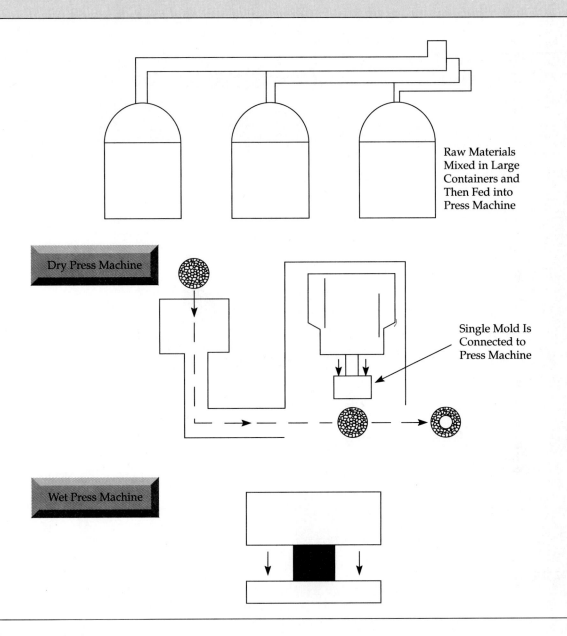

Raw Materials Mixed in Large Containers and Then Fed into Press Machine

Dry Press Machine

Single Mold Is Connected to Press Machine

Wet Press Machine

inspection by workers. This was one of two main quality control checkpoints in the production process.

Cooled magnets were taken to the scraper machine. The scraper machine smoothed the rough edges and surface of the magnets. The scrapings were collected and used again in the raw material mixture. From the scraper machine, the workers placed the magnets in water to be cleaned. After cleaning, the magnets were sent through the drying machine. At the exit point of the drying machine, the magnets were collected by workers and placed in boxes. The boxes of magnets were taken to the final process department where each

EXHIBIT 3   Production Technology and Magnets Made

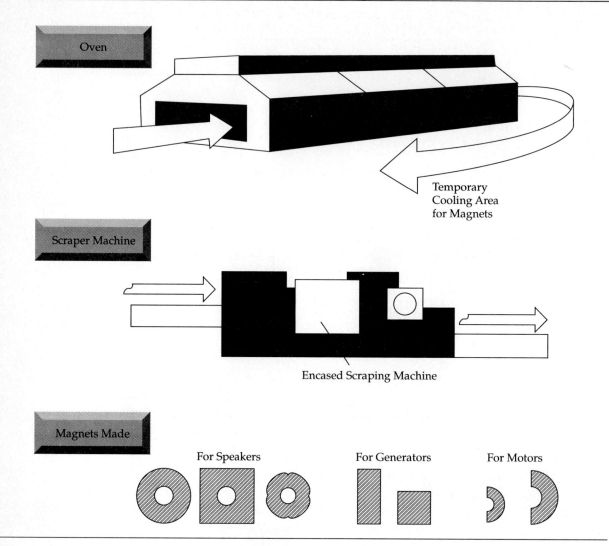

Oven

Temporary
Cooling Area
for Magnets

Scraper Machine

Encased Scraping Machine

Magnets Made

For Speakers   For Generators   For Motors

magnet was given a final check. This stage was called the shipping inspection, and it represented the second main quality control checkpoint. Quality control and specification requirements adhered to at this stage included measurement of weight, length, and appearance of magnets.

About 85 percent of production was exported to the United States—to TDK of America facilities in Chicago, Los Angeles, New York, and Indiana. The remaining 15 percent was exported to Hong Kong. The sales offices and warehouse facilities in these cities were in charge of all selling, shipping, and billing functions. TDK of America sold most of its products to Briggs and Stratton of Milwaukee, Wisconsin, and to Buehler Products of Kingston, North Carolina.

TDK de Mexico had encountered no bureaucratic delays or customs problems in shipping out final products, even though other companies in the area were having difficulties arranging for timely shipment of their merchandise out of Mexico. Inouye was proud that he had been able to secure the necessary clearances and paperwork for getting the product out of the country without much hassle. His explanation was, "You don't create systems when you simply need some people who can do things for you. You need to get out and find them. You create systems where systems are accepted. . . . It is not here!"

Hiratzuka, TDK's production manager, commented: "We hear that the Mexican government may change the rules of the game. There are rumors that we may have to buy 20 to 25 percent of our raw materials from Mexican suppliers." He went on, "Other than what the government will and will not do, I think you also need to understand that our primary concern is to attract quality labor, since our production process demands it. . . . We can't just hire anyone who walks in."

TDK de Mexico had not looked into possible changes in the Mexican government's local procurement rules to any extent, but had expressed its apprehension to Mexican officials if the firm was forced to buy ferrite powder locally. On another issue, Hiratzuka stated, "As you know, border plants in Mexico like ours have a 'no sale' rule where all goods produced must be exported. But the government is considering a compulsory selling rule whereby 20 percent of a border plant's goods must be sold locally." Such a rule was potentially more troublesome to TDK de Mexico because it was not clear that there was much of a market in Mexico for TDK's products.

The Mexican Maquiladoras

In 1965 the United States, working in conjunction with the Mexican government, set up the *maquiladora* program to create jobs for unemployed and underemployed Mexican workers. The idea was to get U.S. companies to open light assembly plants just across the Mexican border and to use cheap Mexican labor to assemble American-made parts into finished goods. In many cases, the components were manufactured in plants located on the U.S. side of the border; this allowed the components to be easily and quickly transported to the Mexican side for final assembly. The effect was to create twin plants a few miles apart—the U.S. plant being used for capital-intensive/skilled-labor operations and the Mexican plant being used for labor-intensive, assembly operations.

When the finished products were shipped back into the United States, U.S. companies were taxed only on the value added in Mexico (mostly labor costs) rather than on the total value of the goods being imported. When the Mexican government experienced a debt crisis in 1982 and the value of the Mexican peso collapsed against the dollar, cheap Mexican wages triggered a *maquiladora* explosion. By early 1987, there were over 630 plants employing over 178,000 people along the Mexican side of the U.S. border. These plants, known as *maquiladoras* (or "in-bond" or twin plants), were all engaged in assembling components in Mexico for reexport in the United States and elsewhere and had become an important economic force along the U.S.-Mexican border. Juarez, where TDK de Mexico's plant was located, had a big concentration of *maquiladoras*. Exhibit 4 presents some of the features of the *maquiladoras* program.

EXHIBIT 4   **The *Maquiladora* Program: Legal and Regulatory Requirements Imposed by the Mexican Government**

A. Foreign investment

As a rule, a foreign company may subscribe and own only up to 49 percent of the stock in Mexican corporations with the exception of *maquilas*, which may be totally owned by foreigners. Except wearing apparel, all items may be produced by in-bond assembly enterprises. Wearing apparel, due to the restriction of textile imports into the United States, is subject to a quota.

B. Import duties

In-bond plants are not required to pay import duties, but the product assembled or manufactured may not be sold in Mexico. Bonds are generally posted by bonding companies and are renewed yearly.

C. Taxes

The maximum income tax on corporate profits is 42 percent on taxable income of P$$500,000 or more in a fiscal year, and employees' share in profits before taxes is at the rate of 8 percent. There are other taxes such as the Social Security Tax based on salaries earned and state taxes.

D. Maquiladora versus joint venture

A comparison of the different rules and practices for joint ventures between Mexican and foreign companies is summarized below:

Concept	*Maquiladora*	Joint Venture
1. Doing business in Mexico	To operate in Mexico under a *maquila* program, a company must be incorporated under Mexican laws.	To carry out industrial or commercial activities for the Mexican market, a corporation or other recognized corporate entity must be organized.
2. Equity ownership	100% foreign ownership is allowed.	The general rule is that foreigners may not hold more than 49% of the stock of a corporation doing business in the Mexican market. Exceptions to allow higher percentages of foreign owner-ship, up to 100%, may be authorized by the Mexican government under special circumstances.
3. Special operating authorizations	To operate under *maquila* (in-bond) status, the Ministry of Commerce must authorize a *maquila* program, setting forth the products or activities the company may manufacture/assem-ble or carry out. Certain commitments must be made, the compliance with which shall be reviewed periodically.	Unless the company intends to work within a branch of regulated industry, a joint-venture company may freely operate without the need to obtain any special operating permits.
4. Importation of equipment	All production equipment may be imported free of duties, under bond, subject to it being exported once the company ceases to operate under the *maquila* program.	The importation of equipment for the production of items that are to be sold in the Mexican market requires an import permit to be obtained and normal duties to be paid thereon.
5. Importation of raw materials	All raw materials and supplies may be imported free of duties under bond, subject to it being exported within an extendable six-month period, shrinkage and wastage excepted. Under special circumstances, *maquiladoras* may be authorized to sell up to 20% of a specific product within the Mexican market.	The importation of raw materials and supplies for the production of items that are to be sold in the Mexican market re-quires an import permit to be obtained and normal duties to be paid thereon. In all cases, import permits are granted on an absolutely discretionary basis. Cur-rently such permits are quite restricted. Under certain conditions, the negotia-tion of a manufacturing or integration program with the government may be required.

E X H I B I T 4   *(Concluded)*

Concept	Maquiladora	Joint Venture
6. Currency exchange controls	Any operating expense, including rent, payroll, taxes, etc., must be paid in Mexican pesos that must be obtained from a Mexican bank by selling dollars thereto at the controlled rate of exchange. Fixed assets may be paid for in dollars at the free rate of exchange.	There are no specific exchange controls on domestic transactions. If the company exports, it will, in general, be required to sell foreign currencies received to a Mexican bank at the controlled rate of exchange.
7. Labor law requirements	Subject to the Federal Labor Law.	Equally subject to the Federal Labor Law.
8. Acquisition of real estate	Real estate to establish a production facility may be freely bought in the interior of the country. In the border areas or coasts, it may be acquired through a trust.	Same as a *maquiladora*.
9. Leasing of real estate	Real estate may be leased under freely negotiated terms, up to a maximum of 10 years.	Same as a *maquiladora*, although the term may be longer.
10. Immigration requirements	Foreign technical or management personnel are readily granted work visas, subject to very lenient requirements.	Work visas for foreign technical or management personnel are granted on a very limited basis. Requirements for the obtainment thereof are significantly more stringent.
11. Transfer of technology	For tax purposes it is advisable that a Technical and/or Management Assistance Agreement be executed between the *maquiladora* and its parent. Such agreement would need to be registered with the National Transfer of Technology Registry (NTTR).	If technical or management assistance is granted to a domestic company from a foreign source and royalties or fees are to be paid therefor, an agreement must be registered with the NTTR. To obtain such registration the agreement must meet certain criteria and the amounts which may be charged are limited.
12. Taxes	A *maquiladora* is in principle subject to the payment of all Mexican taxes. However, since such operations are intended to be cost centers rather than profit centers, the income taxes to be paid are limited. Also, any value added tax paid by the *maquiladora* shall be refunded to it upon its request.	A domestic company is subject to all normal taxes such as income tax and value added tax (maximum corporate income tax rate = 42%).

Maquiladoras operated within a highly volatile political environment, one that affected every aspect of their existence. They were dependent upon the Mexican government continuing to permit raw materials and components to enter duty free and the U.S. government simultaneously permitting finished products to return with duty paid only on the value added in Mexico. Any major change in these policies by either company could shut down most *maquiladoras* overnight by making assembly operations on the Mexican side of the border uneconomical. Both countries had strong political groups opposed to the *maquiladora* concept. Opponents labeled such operations as sweatshops and claimed that workers were being exploited by capitalistic interests.

The average age of the *maquiladora* workers was 24, with a relative dearth of workers over 30. Seventy percent were young women and teenage girls.

Workers lived under crowded conditions—the mean household size of *maquiladora* workers was 7.8 persons. Their wages averaged about $0.80 per hour, barely more than half the 1987 Mexican manufacturing wage of $1.57 an hour (including benefits). The low wages made it very attractive for mass-assembly operations requiring low-skill labor to be located on the Mexican side of the U.S. border. Managers of the *maquiladoras* expressed a preference for hiring "fresh or unspoiled" workers that had not acquired "bad habits" in other organizations. The work was so low-skilled that workers received very little training. The turnover rate ran 50 percent to 100 percent a year in many plants.

However, many of the large multinational companies with *maquiladoras* paid more than the wage minimums, and their overall compensation package was more attractive than the lowest-paying operations. Some of the multinationals also spent substantial amounts in training and employee development.

The location of twin (or *maquiladora*) plants along the northern border of Mexico was increasing at a phenomenal speed, and unemployed Mexicans were flocking to northern border towns to fill the rapidly expanding number of job openings. By the end of 1988, it was predicted that *maquiladoras* would employ 350,000 workers, one tenth of Mexico's industrial work force, and that the plants would import $8 billion in U.S. components, add $2 billion in value (mostly labor), and ship $10 billion in finished goods back to the United States for sale in the United States and other world markets. A number of Japanese-based companies had begun to set up *maquila* operations to handle the production and sale of their products in U.S. markets—TDK de Mexico was one of these companies.

Despite concerns over the *maquiladoras*, the program was central to the Mexican government's economic revival plans. Mexican leaders were most enthusiastic about a new kind of *maquiladora*. These were plants built in the interior of Mexico that were geared to exports, like the border plants, but unlike the border operations, they undertook in-house manufacture of many of the components used in the final assembly process. These plants used higher-skilled employees and paid wages much closer to the average manufacturing wage in Mexico, and they did not rely so heavily on the use of female labor. They also relied more heavily on Mexican companies for raw material supplies and services.

TDK's INTERNAL MANAGEMENT

TDK de Mexico had 183 employees (158 women and 25 men). Inouye, before he came to TDK de Mexico, operated machines in a Taiwan plant to help gain a better understanding of workers at that level. After his move to Mexico in 1983, Inouye organized the work force into teams consisting of workers, subleaders, and leaders. Leaders were not entrusted with the job of supervision: all supervisory responsibilities remained with individuals having a title of supervisor. It took an average of two years for a worker to become a subleader. All subleaders at TDK de Mexico were Mexican; they had a median age of 28.2 years. Only three were women.

There were 11 leaders. The specifics of their job were dependent upon their department. Generally, they oversaw workers and machines in their respective departments but were given little authority and were not accountable for achieving set objectives. They were also in charge of training new workers. The leaders at TDK de Mexico had been at the company for an average of

6.4 years. The average time it took to become a leader was about three years. All of the leaders at TDK de Mexico were Mexican. Very few had ever been promoted to the supervisory level.

Five Japanese filled the 12 positions of supervisors and assistant supervisors (Exhibit 5). Like the leaders, their jobs varied based on the department they supervised. Primarily their duties included supervision of the leaders as well as the teams under the leaders. They determined production plans for their respective departments. Although there were Mexican nationals in higher positions, all Japanese employees, irrespective of their job titles, reported directly to Inouye. Because most of the Japanese could not speak Spanish, Inouye thought it was wise to have this direct reporting relationship. However, some of the managers of Mexican origin did not accept this line of reasoning (one manager called it "clannish behavior"); their protests to Inouye had not met with much success.

WAGE POLICIES

TDK de Mexico paid higher wages than most other companies located in the Juarez industrial park plants. TDK de Mexico had several pay incentives available to the workers. They received a bonus after 30 days on the job. There was extra pay for overtime, night shifts, weekend work, and also generous incentives for attendance. Yet, Alfred Gomez, personnel manager of TDK de Mexico, stated, "Absenteeism and lateness are becoming problems. In some cases, when a worker decides to leave her job, she just stops coming to work without any notice. One reason for this problem is that Juarez public health hospital gives out medical excuses to workers to miss work for the slightest illness. . . . There is very little we can do about it."

TRAINING

TDK had invested a lot of resources in training its employees; most of its training, however, had been confined to leaders and subleaders. Gomez, the head of personnel, did not go through any systematic training need analysis but professed to know "who needed training and who did not by sight." Inouye's position was, "We will spend money on training, of course, but only with those who show promise." Asked how did he see promise, he replied, "I have been working for 25 years. . . . I know!" A leader who had just finished an in-house training program on motivation commented, "Whenever we face a major crisis, the six Japanese managers get together with Mr. Inouye and decide what course of action to take. It seems like the only decisions I am allowed to participate in are of routine nature that are easily solved. What do I do with what I learned from the training sessions?"

FUMIO INOUYE'S CONCERNS

In March 1988, Inouye met with all the managers (Mexican and Japanese) and presented the plant's most recent operating statistics (Exhibit 6). He was clearly unhappy with the data. A senior manager from Japanese headquarters also attended the meeting along with two other managers from TDK of America. Inouye laid out several options that could be pursued:

EXHIBIT 5

TDK de Mexico Organization Chart

Japan

President
T. Kamata*

Mexico

General Manager
F. Inouye*

Production Manager
N. Hiratzuka*

Planning Administration Manager
T. Takahasi*

Operations Manager
S. Ishida*

Technical Department Manager
K. Mtyagishima*

Maintenance Manager
J. Davalos†

Personnel Manager
A. Gomez†

Accounting Manager
I. Morales†

Purchasing Manager
J. Jaquez†

Exportation/Importation Manager
R. Robles†

Design/Sample Leader
D. Martinez†

Quality Control Leader
J. Hernandez†

Maintenance Leader
R. Romero†

Production Control Leader
M. DeLaCruz†

Final Process Leader
H. Gonsales†
B. Cameras†

Ovens Leader
P. Lopez†

Molds Leader
N. Delgado†

Materials Leader
H. Pena†

Supervision

Department	Chief	Assistant
Materials	S. Ishida*	N. Nakazawa*
Press	S. Ishida*	H. Nitta*
Ovens	K. Mtyagishima*	N. Hiratzuka*
Final Process	N. Nakazawa*	S. Ishida*
Molds	S. Ishida*	H. Nitta*
Maintenance	H. Nitta*	H. Hiratzuka*

*Japanese National
†Mexican National

EXHIBIT 6   Statistics of TDK de Mexico, 1984–87

	1984	1985	1986	1987
Total sales (U.S. dollars)	$4,168,000	$3,774,000	$3,837,000	$3,168,000*
Employees	112	128	140	183
Sales per person	$ 29,000	$ 22,000	$ 20,000	$ 23,000
Efficiency rate	82%	81%	80%	80%
Labor turnover rate	16%	47%	46%	39%†
Selling/administrative expenses	$1,623,000	$1,529,000	$1,698,000	$1,878,000
Cost of raw materials	$1,052,000	$1,071,000	$1,099,000	$1,181,000

Shipping cost = .01¢ per gram or 2–10% of total costs.
Price of magnets = .05¢ per gram.
Average production for a year = 5,100,000 grams.
Production figure for 1987 = 6,900,000 grams.
Plant is presently at full capacity.

*Based on the then exchange rate.
†Other *maquilas* in the park ranged from 35 to 170 percent per year.

1. Downsize the labor force, to correct for the decline in sales and the increase in expenses.
2. Try to avoid downsizing and try to reduce operating costs by buying ferrite powder locally. Since it was not known where and how ferrite powder could be obtained from Mexican sources, Inouye suggested that immediate consideration be given to making the material locally or acquiring a native company.
3. Send some senior managers (Inouye emphasized Mexican nationals) to Japan for further training.

The Mexican managers thought the concerns expressed in the meeting were addressed specifically to them. One Mexican manager said after the meeting, "If these people would live in Mexico and not run to their comfortable homes on the other side of the border after 5:00 o'clock, maybe they would understand us a little better!"

Several Mexican managers again suggested to Inouye that the Japanese managers learn the language and work closely with the workers. Inouye was sympathetic to the suggestion but questioned whether learning the language was essential. He advised them to examine "the pockets of inefficiency" and lectured them about the value of hard work.

The manager from TDK Japan left with a stern warning for imminent improvement or else. He explained to the casewriter:

> You see, I came over here in late 1983, after spending years in Singapore, Taiwan, and Hong Kong. I don't know how useful it is to have a grand strategy or any plan per se for an operation like this. . . . What it boils down to is *shooten* (focus), *shitsu* (quality), and *bunai* (distribution). . . . I'm not about to give up because of cultural differences here; you do what you have to do to earn more money! And if the answer is anything but work harder, I have problem!

Inouye began to contemplate what actions he should take.

E. & J. GALLO WINERY

Daniel C. Thurman, U.S. Air Force Academy
A. J. Strickland III, The University of Alabama

In the mid-1980s, alcohol consumption in the United States had been declining in virtually every category except low-priced wines. A number of producers in the wine industry did not believe they should be producing what they called skid-row wines (wines fortified with additional alcohol and sweetener and sold in screw-top, half-pint bottles). Richard Maher, president of Christian Brothers Winery in St. Helena, California, who once was with E. & J. Gallo Winery, said he didn't think Christian Brothers should market a product to people, including many alcoholics, who were down on their luck. "Fortified wines lack any socially redeeming values," he said.

Major producers of the low-end category of wines, called "dessert" or "fortified" (sweet wines with at least 14 percent alcohol), saw their customers otherwise. Robert Hunington, vice president of strategic planning at Canandaigua (a national wine producer whose product, Wild Irish Rose, was the number one low-end wine), said 60 percent to 75 percent of its "pure grape" Wild Irish Rose was sold in primarily black, inner-city markets. Hunington described Wild Irish Rose's customer in this $500 million market as "not super-sophisticated," lower-middle-class, low-income blue-collar workers, and mostly men. However, Canandaigua also estimated the annual national market for dessert category wine to be 55 million gallons; low-end brands accounted for 43 million gallons, with as much as 50 percent sold in pints (typically the purchase choice of alcoholics with a dependency on wine). Daniel Solomon, a Gallo spokesperson, said Gallo's Thunderbird had lost its former popularity in the black and skid-row areas and was consumed mainly by retired and older people who didn't like the taste of hard distilled products or beer.[1]

Tony Mayes, area sales representative for Montgomery Beverage Company, Montgomery, Alabama, said one-third of the total revenue from wine sales in the state of Alabama was from the sale of one wine product—Gallo's Thunderbird. Sales crossed all demographic lines. According to Mayes, a consumer developed a taste for wine through an education process that usually began with the purchase of sweet wines from the dessert category. He attributed the high sales of Thunderbird to the fact that the typical wine drinker in Alabama was generally not the sophisticated wine drinker found in California or New York.

COMPANY HISTORY AND BACKGROUND

The E. & J. Gallo Winery, America's biggest winery, was founded by Ernest and Julio Gallo in 1933. More than 55 years later, the Gallo Winery was still

---

[1]Alix M. Freedman, "Misery Market—Winos & Thunderbird Are a Subject Gallo Doesn't Like to Discuss," *The Wall Street Journal*, February 25, 1988, pp. 1, 18.

a privately owned and family-operated corporation actively managed by the two brothers. The Gallo family had been dedicated to both building their brands and the California wine industry.

The Gallos started in the wine business working during their spare time in the vineyard for their father, Joseph Gallo. Joseph Gallo, an immigrant from the Piedmont region in northwest Italy, was a small-time grape grower and shipper. He survived Prohibition because the government permitted wine for medicinal and religious purposes, but his company almost went under during the Depression. During the spring of 1933, Joseph Gallo killed his wife and chased Ernest and Julio with a shotgun. He killed himself following their escape. Prohibition ended that same year, and the Gallos, both in their early 20s and neither knowing how to make wine, decided to switch from growing grapes to making wine. With $5,900 to their names, Ernest and Julio found two thin pamphlets on wine-making in the Modesto Public Library and began making wine.[2]

The Gallos had always been interested in quality and began researching varietal grapes in 1946. They planted more than 400 varieties in experimental vineyards during the 1950s and 1960s, testing each variety in the different growing regions of California for its ability to produce fine table wines. Their greatest difficulty was to persuade growers to convert from common grape varieties to the delicate, thin-skinned varietals because it took at least four years for a vine to begin bearing and perhaps two more years to develop typical, varietal characteristics. As an incentive, in 1967, Gallo offered long-term contracts to growers, guaranteeing the prices for their grapes every year, provided they met Gallo quality standards. With a guaranteed long-term "home" for their crops, growers could borrow the needed capital to finance the costly replanting, and the winery was assured a long-term supply of fine wine grapes. In 1965, Julio established a grower relations staff of skilled viticulturists to aid contract growers. This staff still counsels growers on the latest viticultural techniques.[3]

Private ownership and mass-production were the major competitive advantages contributing to Gallo's success. Gallo could get market share from paper-thin margins and absorb occasional losses that stockholders of publicly held companies would not tolerate. Gallo was vertically integrated, and wine was its only business. While Gallo bought about 95 percent of its grapes, it virtually controlled its 1,500 growers through long-term contracts. Gallo's 200 trucks and 500 trailers constantly hauled wine out of Modesto and raw materials in. Gallo was the only winery to make its own bottles (2 million a day) and screw-top caps. Also, while most of the competition concentrated on production, Gallo participated in every aspect of selling its product. Julio was president and oversaw production, while Ernest was chairman and ruled over marketing, sales, and distribution. Gallo owned its distributors in about a dozen markets and probably would have bought many of the more than 300 independents handling its wines if laws in most states had not prohibited it.

Gallo's major competitive weakness over the years had been an image associated with screw tops and bottles in paper bags that developed

---

[2]Jaclyn Fierman, "How Gallo Crushes the Competition," *Fortune*, September 1, 1986, pp. 24–31.

[3]"The Wine Cellars of Ernest & Julio Gallo, a Brief History," a pamphlet produced by Ernest & Julio Gallo, Modesto, Calif.

because of its low-end dessert wine, Thunderbird.[4] There were stories, which Gallo denied, that Gallo got the idea for citrus-flavored Thunderbird from reports that liquor stores in Oakland, California, were catering to the tastes of certain customers by attaching packages of lemon Kool-Aid to bottles of white wine to be mixed at home.[5]

Thunderbird became Gallo's first phenomenal success. It was a high-alcohol, lemon-flavored beverage introduced in the late 1950s. A radio jingle sent Thunderbird sales to the top of the charts on skid rows across the country. "What's the word? Thunderbird. How's it sold? Good and cold. What's the jive? Bird's alive. What's the price? Thirty twice." Thunderbird had remained a brand leader in its category every since. In 1986, Ernest Gallo poured $40 million into advertising aimed at changing Gallo's image to one associated with quality wines.

Information on Gallo's finances were not publicly available, and the brothers maintained a tight lid on financial details. In a 1986 article, *Fortune* estimated that Gallo earned at least $50 million a year on sales of $1 billion. By comparison, the second leading winery, Seagram's (also the nation's largest distillery), had approximately $350 million in 1985 wine revenues and lost money on its best-selling table wines. *Fortune* stated that several of the other major Gallo competitors made money, but not much.[6]

Gallo produced the top-selling red and white table wines in the country. Its Blush Chablis became the best-selling blush-style wine within the first year of its national introduction. Gallo's award-winning varietal wines were among the top sellers in their classification. The company's Carlo Rossi brand outsold all other popular-priced wines. Gallo's André Champagne was by far the country's best-selling champagne, and E & J Brandy had outsold the number two and three brands combined. Gallo's Bartles & Jaymes brand was one of the leaders in the new wine cooler market.[7]

THE U.S. WINE INDUSTRY

Wine sales in the United States grew from about 72 million gallons in 1940 to nearly 600 million gallons by 1986, accounting for retail sales in excess of $9 billion (see Exhibit 1). This retail sales volume had exceeded such major established grocery categories as detergents, pet foods, paper products, and canned vegetables. While wine consumption had grown at an astonishing rate, trends toward moderation and alcohol-free life-styles made this growth rate impossible to maintain. Nevertheless, annual growth was projected to be 3.2 percent through 1995.

Per-capita consumption of wine was low in the late 1950s and early 1960s because wine drinking was perceived as either the domain of the very wealthy or the extreme opposite. "Fortified" dessert wines were the top-selling wines of the period. The first surge in consumption in the late 1960s was the result of the introduction of "pop" wines, such as Boones Farm, Cold Duck, and Sangrias. These wines were bought by baby boomers, who

---

[4]Jaclyn Fierman, "How Gallo Crushes the Competition."
[5]Alix M. Freedman, "Misery Market."
[6]Jaclyn Fierman, "How Gallo Crushes the Competition."
[7]"Gallo Sales Development Program," a pamphlet produced by Ernest & Julio Gallo, Modesto, Calif.

E X H I B I T 1   **The National Wine Market, 1977–1986**

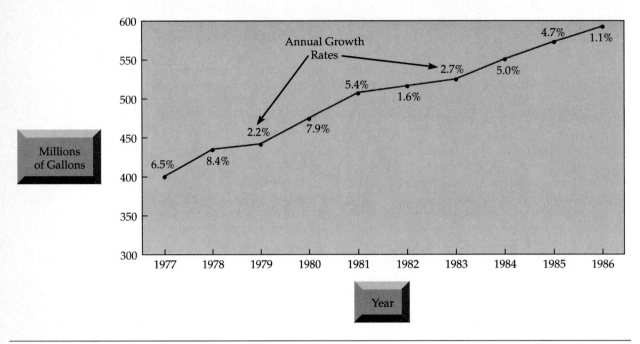

Source: *National Beverage Marketing Directory*, 10th ed., 1988.

were now young adults. Their palates were unaccustomed to wine drinking and these wines were suited to them. By the mid-1970s, the pop wine drinkers were ready to move up to Lambruscos and white wine "cocktails," and per-capita consumption increased (see Exhibit 2). The wine spritzer became the trend, still the alternative to more serious wines for immature palates. Just as this surge began to wane, wine coolers were introduced in 1982 and exploded on the market in 1983. Wine coolers were responsible for a 5 percent market surge in 1984 and experienced four consecutive years of very high growth rates, rising 6 percent in 1987 to 72.6 million nine-liter cases.

The imported wines category enjoyed an upward growth rate from 6.6 percent of the market in 1960 to a high of 27.6 percent in 1985 (see Exhibits 3 and 4). The category lost market share to 23.1 percent in 1986 primarily because of the shift from Lambruscos to wine coolers. Additional factors were the weakening dollar and an overall improved reputation for domestic wines.

There were about 1,300 wineries in the United States. *Fortune* identified the major market-share holders in the U.S. market in a September 1986 article. It showed Gallo as the clear leader, nearly outdistancing the next five competitors combined (see Exhibit 5).

A number of threats had faced the wine industry, not the least of which had been the national obsession with fitness and the crackdown on drunken driving. Americans drank 6.5 percent less table wine in 1985 than

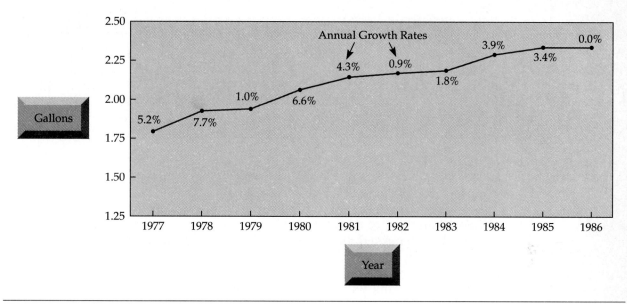

EXHIBIT 2 Per-Capita Consumption of Wine in the United States

Annual Growth Rates

Gallons

1977	5.2%	
1978	7.7%	
1979	1.0%	
1980	6.6%	
1981	4.3%	
1982	0.9%	
1983	1.8%	
1984	3.9%	
1985	3.4%	
1986	0.0%	

Year

Source: *National Beverage Marketing Directory*, 10th ed., 1988.

EXHIBIT 3 Wine Production by Place of Origin *(Millions of nine-liter cases)*

						Average Annual Compound Growth Rate			Percent Change
Origin	1970	1975	1980	1985	1986	1970–1975	1975–1980	1980–1985	1985–1986
California	82	115	139.5	133.2	133.3	7.0%	3.9%	−0.9%	0.1%
Other states*	18	19	18.7	16.9	17.3	1.4	−0.3	−2.0	2.4
United States	100	134	158.2	150.1	150.6	6.1	3.3	−1.0	0.3
Imports	13	21	43.1	57.2	45.3	10.5	15.8	5.8	−20.8
Total†	113	115	201.3	207.3	195.9	6.6%	5.4%	0.6%	−5.5%

*Includes bulk table wine shipped from California and blended with other state wines.
†Addition of columns may not agree because of rounding.
Source: *Impact* 17, no. 11 (June 1, 1987), p. 4.

in 1983 (see Exhibits 6 and 7), and consumption was projected to be down another 5 percent in 1986. The industry answer to this problem had been the introduction of wine coolers—Gallo's Bartles and Jaymes coolers were number one until they lost the lead by only a slight margin to a Seagram's brand in 1987.

Another trend had been a shift toward a demand for quality premium wines made from the finest grapes. Premium wines increased market share from 8 percent in 1980 to 20 percent in 1986. Again, Gallo had sold more

EXHIBIT 4   **Market Share Trends in Wine Production**

Place Produced	1970	1975	1980	1985	1986	Share Point Change		
						1970–1980*	1980–1985	1985–1986
California	73%	74%	69.3%	64.2%	68.0%	3.7	−5.0	3.8
Other states	15	12	9.3	8.2	8.9	−6.7	1.1	0.7
United States	88	86	78.6	72.4	76.9	−9.4	6.2	4.5
Imports	12	14	21.4	27.6	23.1	9.4	−6.2	−4.5
Total	100%	100%	100.0%	100.0%	100.0%	—	—	—

*1980 based on unrounded data.
Source: *Impact* 17, no. 11 (June 11, 1987), p. 4.

premium wine than any other producer, but Gallo's growth had been limited by its lack of snob appeal.[8]

Although more than 80 percent of the U.S. adult population enjoyed wine occasionally, Gallo's research indicated that by global standards most Americans were still infrequent wine drinkers. Only about one in four Americans drank wine as often as once a week. Per-capita consumption in the United States was less than 2.5 gallons per year, compared to about 20 gallons in some Western European countries.[9]

Though the health-consciousness and alcohol-awareness of the 1980s had a moderating influence on wine growth patterns as consumers traded up in quality and drank less, long-term growth was expected to be steady but slower than that of the 1970s and early 1980s. Exhibit 8 provides drinking patterns for 1986. Personal disposable income was expected to grow in the United States through 1995, busy life-styles contributed to more dining out, and sale of wine in restaurants was expected to increase. As the aging baby boomers grew in number and importance, their wine purchases were expected to increase. All these factors contributed to the projected average yearly increase in growth rate of 3.2 percent through 1995.[10]

THE DESSERT WINE INDUSTRY

Dessert wine represented a 55 million gallon, $500 million industry. As mentioned earlier, the dessert wine category, also called fortified wines, included wines that contained more than 14 percent alcohol, usually 18 to 21 percent. They were called fortified because they usually contained added alcohol and additional sugar or sweetener. This category included a group of low-end-priced brands that had been the brunt of significant controversy. Canandaigua's Wild Irish Rose had been the leading seller in this category, with Gallo's Thunderbird claiming second place, followed by Mogen David Wine's MD 20/20.[11]

---

[8]Jaclyn Fierman, "How Gallo Crushes the Competition."
[9]"Gallo Sales Development Program."
[10]"Coolers Providing Stable Growth," *Beverage Industry Annual Manual*, 1987.
[11]Alix M. Freedman, "Misery Market."

EXHIBIT 5   1985 Share of U.S. Wine Market

Company	Percent
E. & J. Gallo Winery	26.1%
Seagram & Sons	8.3
Canandaigua Wine	5.4
Brown-Forman	5.1
National Distillers	4.0
Heublein	3.7
Imports	23.4
All others	24.0
Total	100.0%

Source: Jaclyn Fierman, "How Gallo Crushes the Competition," *Fortune*, September 1, 1986, p. 27.

Dessert wines had shown a decreasing trend both in amount of wine consumed and in market share from 1970 through 1985. However, the trend changed in 1986 when dessert wine's market share rose six-tenths of a share point to 7.5 percent of the total wine market (see Exhibit 7). The rise was attributed in large measure to the 19 percent federal excise tax increase on distilled spirits. An additional factor in the increase in the dessert wine category was the shift to fruit-flavored drinks, which also affected the soft drink industry and wine coolers.[12]

A number of factors indicated that the growth trend would continue for the $500 million dessert wine category. The desire to consume beverages that contained less alcohol than distilled spirits and were less expensive than distilled spirits, the desire for fruit flavor, and the American trend toward eating out at restaurants more often contributed to the trend toward increased consumption of dessert wines. Additionally, the dessert wine category had survived relatively well with virtually no promotion or advertising. This had been possible because, of the category's 55 million gallons, low-end brands accounted for 43 million gallons, approximately 50 percent of which was sold in half pints; and this market had not been accessible by traditional advertising or promotion.

The dessert wine category had been a profitable venture because many of the wines in this category were made with less expensive ingredients, packaged in less expensive containers, and had usually been sold without promotion. Canandaigua estimated that profit margins in this category were as much as 10 percent higher than those of ordinary table wines. Gallo said this was not true for its products, but it would not reveal the figures.

The low-end dessert wines were a solid business. *The Wall Street Journal* reported that, of all the wine brands sold in America, Wild Irish Rose was the number 6 best seller, Thunderbird was 10th, and MD 20/20 was 16th. In contrast to the growth expectations of other brands and categories, sales of these low-end brands were expected to be up almost 10 percent. Yet the

[12]"U.S. News and Research for the Wine, Spirits and Beer, Executive," *Impact*, 17, no. 11 (June 1, 1987); and *Impact* 17, no. 18 (September 15, 1987).

EXHIBIT 6 **Shipments of Wine Entering U.S. Trade Channels, by Type**
(Millions of nine-liter cases)

Type	1970	1975	1980	1984	1985	1986	Average Annual Compound Growth Rate 1970–1975	1975–1980	1980–1985	Percent Change* 1985–1986
Table	55.9	88.9	150.8	170.9	159.2	147.1	9.9%	11.2%	1.1%	−7.4%
Dessert	31.1	28.2	19.1	15.5	14.3	14.7	−2.0	−7.5	−5.7	3.2
Vermouth	4.2	4.2	3.7	3.0	2.9	2.7	—	−2.5	−4.8	−6.9
Sparkling	9.3	8.4	12.7	19.7	19.4	18.7	−1.9	8.6	8.6	−4.5
Special natural	11.8	24.0	13.6	10.9	10.7	10.9	15.3	−10.7	−4.7	1.9
Imported specialty†	0.3	1.0	1.5	1.0	0.9	1.8	25.4	8.1	−9.7	104.7
Total‡	112.6	154.7	201.3	220.1	207.3	195.9	6.6%	5.4%	0.6%	−5.5%

*Based on unrounded data.
†Imported fruit wines and wine specialties (includes sangria and fruit-flavored wines).
‡Addition of columns may not agree because of rounding.
Source: *Impact* 17, no. 11 (June 11, 1987), p. 3.

EXHIBIT 7 **Share of Market Trends in Shipments of Wine Entering U.S. Trade Channels, by Type**

Type	1970	1975	1980	1984	1985	1986	Share Point Change 1970–1980*	1980–1985	1985–1986
Table	50%	57%	74.9%	77.2%	76.8%	75.1%	25	1.9	−1.7
Dessert	28	18	9.5	7.0	6.9	7.5	−18	−2.6	0.6
Vermouth	4	3	1.8	1.4	1.4	1.4	−2	−0.4	†
Sparkling	8	5	6.3	9.0	9.4	9.5	−2	3.0	0.2
Special natural	10	16	6.8	5.0	5.2	5.6	−3	−1.6	0.4
Imported specialty	‡	1	0.7	0.5	0.4	0.9	+	−0.3	0.5
Total	100%	100%	100.0%	100.0%	100.0%	100.0%	—	—	—

*1980 based on unrounded data.
†Addition of columns may not agree because of rounding.
‡Less than 0.05%.
Source: *Impact* 17, no. 11 (June 11, 1987), p. 3.

producers of these top-selling wines distanced themselves from their products by leaving their corporate names off the labels, obscuring any link to their products. Paul Gillette, publisher of the *Wine Investor,* was quoted in a discussion of this unsavory market as saying: "Makers of skid-row wines are the dope pushers of the wine industry."[13]

---

[13]Alix Freedman, "Misery Market."

EXHIBIT 8   **Beverage Consumption Patterns, 1986**

1986 National Beverage Consumption, by Gender (Percentage of volume)

Gender	Malt Beverages	Wine	Distilled Spirits	Coolers	Total Nonalcoholic Beverages	Total Beverages
Male	80.8%	51.6%	62.6%	44.9%	51.1%	52.7%
Female	19.2	48.4	37.4	55.1	48.9	47.3
Total	100.0%	100.0%	100.0%	100.0%	100.0%	100.0%

1986 National Alcoholic Beverage Consumption, by Household Income (Percentage of volume)

Household Income	Malt Beverages	Wine	Distilled Spirits	Coolers	Total Alcoholic Beverages
Under $15,000	26.1%	11.7%	19.7%	22.3%	26.5%
$15,000–$24,999	19.1	13.9	18.1	19.5	21.3
$25,000–$29,999	10.8	14.2	6.6	10.9	12.1
$30,000–$34,999	11.7	9.9	14.7	7.9	10.3
$35,000 & over	32.3	50.3	40.9	39.4	29.8
Total	100.0%	100.0%	100.0%	100.0%	100.0%

1986 National Beverage Consumption, by Time of Day (Percentage of volume)

Time of Day	Malt Beverages	Wine	Distilled Spirits	Coolers	Total Nonalcoholic Beverages	Total Beverages
Breakfast/morning	2.7%	2.1%	4.6%	1.5%	32.7%	30.6%
Lunch	6.8	5.8	4.2	4.4	20.8	19.8
Snack	27.5	19.0	31.9	27.0	10.9	12.0
Dinner	14.2	45.8	15.5	13.7	22.9	22.6
Evening	48.8	27.3	43.8	53.4	12.7	15.0
Total	100.0%	100.0%	100.0%	100.0%	100.0%	100.0%

1986 National Beverage Consumption, by Location of Consumption (Percentage of volume)

Location	Malt Beverages	Wine	Distilled Spirits	Coolers	Total Nonalcoholic Beverages	Total Beverages
Total home	64.6%	75.8%	61.4%	76.9%	76.1%	75.5%
Total away from home	35.4%	24.2%	38.6%	23.1%	23.9%	24.5%

Source: *Impact* 17, no. 18 (September 15, 1987), pp. 3–4.

UNION CAMP CORPORATION*

William R. Boulton, Auburn University

On February 1, 1988, Raymond E. Cartledge, chairman, president, and chief executive officer of Union Camp Corporation (UCC), wanted a decision on the proposed Savannah mill modernization project. Before presenting the project to his board of directors, however, he wanted the $375 million request reviewed and approved by his senior management team. Jerry H. Ballengee, senior vice president, and his staff were asked to present their proposal to the senior management committee. Cartledge's memorandum informed all those involved:

> I would like you to attend with me on Thursday, February 11, a review of the proposed presentation to the Board of Directors, requesting approval of the PDQ Modernization Project for the Savannah Mill.

As the largest of its four pulp and paper mills, the Savannah mill produced 2,900 tons per day (TPD) of kraft paper and linerboard. With expansion of the Prattville, Alabama linerboard mill nearing completion, it was now time to consider modernization of the Savannah mill.

UNION CAMP OVERVIEW

Union Camp Corporation, with headquarters in Wayne, New Jersey, was a forest product company whose principal products included paper, packaging, chemicals, and building materials. UCC ranked among the top 200 industrial companies in America with about 18,000 employees worldwide. This Virginia corporation resulted from a merger in 1956 of Union Bag and Paper Corporation (a New York corporation) and Camp Manufacturing Company, Inc. (a Virginia corporation). These companies had been in business since 1861 and 1887, respectively. Union Bag had patented the first paper bag machine. Camp, located in Franklin, Virginia, manufactured lumber and began paper production in 1938.

UCC's 1987 performance had been admirable, with revenue growth of 15 percent to $2.3 billion and operating income growth of 54 percent to $374 million. The company had achieved new highs in sales, net income, and volume of paper products shipped. The company's fourth quarter earnings in 1987 marked the ninth consecutive quarter of earnings growth. Growing worldwide demand for corrugated containers had created demand for kraft linerboard. UCC's linerboard mills at Savannah, Georgia and Prattville, Alabama had been running at full capacity. The company's container business had increased its production of finished products. The shipment of fine paper had also continued to grow over the past five years, with industry shipments of uncoated free sheet up 5.5 percent to a record 11 million tons in 1987. UCC's Eastover, South Carolina mill had set new production records in the last four months of 1987.

*© 1991 by William R. Boulton, Olan Mills Professor of Strategic Management, Auburn University, for The Pulp and Paper Executive Development Institute and the North American Case Research Association. All rights reserved. Reproduced by permission of the author.

Regarding the company's objectives, Cartledge commented:

Looking ahead, we believe we have products of the highest quality in the right markets, with the most efficient plants to produce them and the best people in our industry to make it all work. We intend to continue to be a leader in quality and service to our customers and to be among the top of our industry in the returns we achieve on the capital invested in our business.

We have also taken aggressive steps to provide for the highest levels of safety in our plants and mills. I'm proud of the fact that even as we ran our operations "flat-out," we continued to improve our safety performance. Union Camp's accident rate in 1987 dropped to its lowest level in this decade and was significantly below the average for our industry. We have made safe working conditions, throughout Union Camp, a major focus of management attention and we can see the results.

Union Camp's financial condition continues to be strong, enabling the company to move forward with aggressive plans for growth. Over the next five years we anticipate capital expenditures in excess of $2 billion, of which a significant portion will be provided by internally generated funds.

Union Camp's financial performance from 1983 to 1987 is shown in Exhibit 1.

UCC was organized by major product lines, including packaging, fine papers, chemicals, and building products. The packaging group operated the company's kraft paper and linerboard division and all packaging divisions whose raw materials were primarily kraft paper and linerboard. Continued emphasis on the development of unique products for special applications, as well as higher performance across the container line, had created a strong customer preference for Union Camp packaging. The fine paper division produced white paper and coated and uncoated bleached board used primarily for promotional literature, and printed communications, envelopes, and business forms. The chemical group consisted of the chemical products division and the Bush Boake Allen division—a producer of flavors and fragrances acquired in 1982. The building products division supplied home improvement and construction products. Group performance is summarized in Exhibit 2.

As shown in Exhibits 1 and 2, UCC was capital intensive with assets of $2.9 billion on sales of $2.3 billion. The company had invested nearly $182 million in 1987, with $116 million going to paper and paperboard operations, and $40 million going to packaging products. The chemical business received $18.6 million.

Packaging Group

UCC's paper and paperboard operations were centered at four major mills. Savannah, Georgia produced various grades of kraft paper and paperboard. Prattville, Alabama manufactured 2,000 TPD of kraft linerboard. The Franklin, Virginia and Eastover, South Carolina mills produced white paper and board. The group's product line included forms, bond, envelope paper, tablet paper, copy paper, uncoated offset printing paper, coated and uncoated bristols, kraft paper, linerboard, and saturating kraft. Shipments by major product area are shown in Exhibit 3.

The kraft paper and board division operated the mills in Savannah and Prattville. Their combined capacity was almost 5,000 tons per day. Nearly two-thirds of their output supplied the company's own packaging plants,

EXHIBIT 1   **Financial Review, Union Camp Corporation, 1983–1987**
(Dollar figures in millions, except per share amounts)

Selected Income Data	1983	1984	1985	1986	1987
Net sales	$1,973,781	$1,973,781	$1,865,871	$2,045,215	$2,307,599
Cost and other charges	1,689,252	1,689,252	1,697,109	1,803,918	1,935,052
Income from operations	284,529	284,529	168,762	241,297	372,547
Interest expense	27,583	27,583	63,771	58,482	60,140
Other (income)—net	(29,601)	(18,355)	(17,701)	(18,919)	(26,526)
Income before income taxes	161,236	275,301	122,692	201,734	338,933
Income taxes	28,500	93,850	27,600	71,800	131,450
Net income	$ 132,736	$ 181,451	$ 95,092	$ 129,934	$ 207,483
Net income per share	$ 1.81	$ 2.48	$ 1.30	$ 1.77	$ 2.83
Dividends per share	1.00	1.09	1.09	1.09	1.14
Balance Sheet Items					
Current assets	$ 480,943	$ 493,128	$ 514,534	$ 578,063	$ 729,992
Current liabilities	286,244	295,757	344,996	262,070	277,163
Working capital	194,699	197,371	169,538	315,993	452,829
Total assets	2,381,204	2,566,880	2,660,609	2,751,482	2,896,895
Long-term debt	620,344	608,180	592,464	641,539	632,706
Deferred income taxes	277,427	371,562	408,057	477,304	535,009
Stockholders' equity	1,197,189	1,291,381	1,315,092	1,370,569	1,452,017
Other Information					
Percentage of long-term debt to total capital	29.6%	26.8%	25.6%	25.8%	24.2%
Cash provided by operations	$ 263,962	$ 354,261	$ 279,184	$ 334,518	$ 434,571
Capital expenditures	$ 411,487	$ 315,993	$ 240,133	$ 209,045	$ 181,817
Depreciation and cost of company timber harvested	$ 117,875	$ 125,909	$ 152,064	$ 166,384	$ 177,767
Tons sold—paper and paperboard products	2,193,041	2,421,459	2,328,558	2,656,920	2,675,541
Average shares of common stock outstanding	73,096,215	73,210,921	73,328,341	73,533,126	73,391,106

with the remainder being sold to domestic and overseas customers. Savannah was the largest pulp and paper mill complex in the world. The output from its seven machines ranged from the lightest weight, unbleached paper to heavy-duty linerboard used in the manufacture of corrugated containers. One machine also produced saturating kraft, the base material for decorative laminates used in kitchen and bath cabinets and counter tops. The Savannah mill produced over 1 million tons of paper and board in 1980 and was cited in *The Guinness Book of World Records*. The Prattville mill had two linerboard machines. Both mills had easy access to major ports—Mobile and Savannah—making them ideal for serving export markets.

With a 5 percent growth in domestic demand for corrugated containers, industry shipments reached nearly 300 billion square feet in 1987. An

EXHIBIT 2   **Financial Data by Business Segment, Union Camp Corporation, 1987**
             (In thousands of dollars)

	Paper and Paperboard	Packaging Products	Building Products	Chemicals	Corporate Items	Total
Sales to customers	$ 917,061	$875,500	$166,065	$348,183	$ 790	$2,307,599
Intersegment sales	399,969	4,025	548	4,868	(409,620)	—
Total revenue	1,317,030	879,525	166,613	353,051	(408,620)	2,307,599
Operating profit	355,212	24,002	21,022	20,887	(48,576)	371,547
Identifiable assets	1,869,695	441,873	79,094	279,144	227,089	2,896,895
Depreciation/timber harvest costs	125,363	23,583	9,529	12,677	6,615	177,767
Capital expenditures	115,915	39,741	5,293	18,636	2,232	181,817

improved economy coupled with a more competitive posture in export markets, helped by a weaker U.S. dollar, pushed linerboard mills in Savannah and Prattville to their upper limits of capacity. A rebuilding of the number one linerboard machine in Prattville, started in 1987, was intended to add 145,000 tons of annual linerboard capacity with improved quality and productivity.

The container division operated a network of 24 container plants in 19 states. The division's primary product was corrugated containers, a form of packaging used for almost 95 percent of all consumer goods. The division was also the country's largest producer of heavy-duty solid-fibre containers produced from laminated layers of linerboard. The division had developed containers for specialized packaging needs of plastics, tobacco, produce, dairy, and poultry and meat packaging industries. The division also operated three "Tri-Supply" packaging distribution centers in Alabama, Georgia, and Mississippi, which targeted the poultry industry, and "Packaging Distributors" in the Rio Grande Valley of Texas, which supplied the produce industry. Overseas, UCC had four corrugated container operations including one in Gandia, two in the Canary Islands, and one near Dublin.

The bag division, with 13 manufacturing plants, included multiwall packaging, retail packaging, and plastic packaging. Multiwall bags, with a reputation for high-quality printing, were produced at seven plants and were used to package commodities such as cement, chemicals, lawn products, feed, pet food, charcoal, flour, and cookies. Retail packaging, with its mix of two paper and two plastic bag plants, offered one of the most diverse lines available from a single supplier. Local paper merchants were the primary customers along with national and regional retail chains. Two plastic packaging plants extruded plastic films and converted them into flexible polyethylene shipping sacks and bags for ice cubes, foods, pallet covers, sheeting tubing, shrink wrap, and stretch wrap.

The folding division, known for its high-quality graphics, manufactured consumer product packaging for cosmetics, pharmaceuticals, and food industries, at three locations. The school supply division produced school, home, and office products at three locations.

EXHIBIT 3   Shipments of Forest Products, Union Camp Corporation, 1983–1987

	1983	1984	1985	1986	1987
Paper and Board Products (tons)					
Kraft paper and board	541,859	635,123	467,489	693,004	658,032
Fine paper	658,315	681,482	775,060	827,174	873,905
Total primary	1,200,174	1,316,605	1,242,549	1,520,178	1,531,937
Converted kraft	16,722	18,055	16,223	16,778	16,315
Converted fine	27,503	28,052	30,931	30,765	38,258
Bags	237,328	247,335	236,985	240,518	222,791
Containers	711,314	811,412	801,870	848,681	860,240
Total converted	992,867	1,104,854	1,086,009	1,136,742	1,143,604
Total paper and board products	2,193,041	2,421,459	2,328,558	2,656,920	2,675,541
Non–Paper Products					
Lumber (thousands of board feet)	396,273	416,853	386,050	374,575	392,508
Plywood (thousands of square feet)	200,025	190,656	177,497	197,148	201,967
Particleboard (thousands of square feet)	81,978	86,087	83,722	84,956	89,023

The Fine Paper Division

The fine paper division included the Franklin, Virginia and Eastover, South Carolina mills that produced printing, writing, converting papers, and bleached board. The Franklin mill, the largest fine paper mill in the world, had six paper machines with capacity of about 1,850 tons per day. A $200 million modernization program at Franklin had been completed in 1987. Eastover had one machine with a 600 ton-per-day capacity. These mills accounted for seven of the 30 U.S. fine paper machines. Plants in Franklin and Normal, Illinois also converted roll stock into sheets. About 60 percent of the division's products were sold to converters for the manufacture of envelopes, computer paper, business forms, greeting cards, and folding cartons. The remainder was sold as printing papers for commercial printing, book publishing, and in-house publishing. Bond, xerographic, duplicator, and mimeo papers were sold under UCC's Jamestown and Yorktown brand names.

The industry demand for fine paper grades had grown by 40 percent over the past five years. Shipments of uncoated free sheet were up 5.5 percent to a record 11 million tons. UCC's shipments were up nearly 6 percent as output from the Eastover mill reached record levels. Weak prices had firmed up by mid-1987 and price increases had been announced for January 1988.

Chemicals

The largest part of UCC's chemical operations involved by-products of the kraft pulping process. These raw materials underwent processing at distillation plants in Savannah, Georgia; Jacksonville, Florida; and Chester-le-Street, England. In addition, upgraded products from papermaking, as well as other raw materials, were processed at distillation plants in Dover, Ohio, and Widnes, England. Additional chemical facilities included Valdosta, Georgia; Long Medford, England; and numerous other sites worldwide. Savannah produced tall oil products including fatty acids, rosins and rosin derivatives, high performance resins, and resinates. Valdosta converted rosin into synthetic resins for inks, coatings, and adhesives industries. The Dover plant produced tallow and castor oil for use in fatty acids and esters for the cosmetics, plastics, lubricants, and detergent industries. Lower oil costs had improved results in oil-based activities. Profits were $21 million in 1987, up from $15 million in 1986.

Building Products

UCC facilities engaged in the production of building products were located in four Southeastern states. Six plants produced dimensional lumber. Two plants in Alabama specialized in the production of plywood products and veneer, while one Virginia facility manufactured particleboard. Despite a decline in housing starts in 1987, lower Canadian imports allowed the division to post a 70 percent improvement in profits for the year to $21 million.

Wood and Land Resources

UCC owned or controlled 1.74 million acres of woodlands located in Alabama (337,000), Florida (107,000), Georgia (837,000), North Carolina (148,000), South Carolina (97,000), and Virginia (213,000). Seedling nurseries in Belleville, Georgia; Capron, Virginia; and Union Springs, Alabama; plus, a forestry research center in Rincon, Georgia provided support for these operations. In 1987, the woodlands division supplied over 13.5 million tons of wood to paper and building product operations from company and privately owned woodlands. During the year, UCC reforested nearly 63,000 acres of land with superior seedlings grown in the company's nurseries. UCC had also donated land in every state in which it maintained woodlands, including 16,600 acres in Georgia on the perimeter of the Okefenokee Swamp.

PROJECT PDQ CAPITAL EXPENDITURE REQUEST

Jerry Ballengee, manager of Union Camp's kraft paper and board division, had proposed a major modernization of the Savannah mill. Ballengee had joined Union Camp in 1981 with 19 years of paper industry experience. In 1984 he moved from engineering to take over as general manager of the kraft paper and board division, which included the mills in Prattville and Savannah. Ballengee described the situation:

> I had three years of exposure to the Savannah mill before I came over to run the division. I knew that my predecessor had been struggling with a mill that was approaching 50 years old. First, there were age and obsolescence problems involved. The early 1980s were not profitable years in the linerboard business, but

there was a recognized need that something had to be done prior to my becoming the division's general manager.

Second, we had community relations problems that had focused during the early 1980s on odor. Those who were most concerned about it were getting play from the media. More importantly, it was inevitable that odor control regulations would soon be promulgated by the state and those regulations would have to be dealt with.

Third, we had a marketplace issue. We have a fairly significant output here of unbleached paper that goes into grocery bags and sacks and industrial bag packaging applications. We have been in the business, though, for years, making multiwall bags for the packaging of everything from cement to pet food and kitty litter. We know the business well and we are good at it. We have a good reputation as well in grocery bags and grocery sacks. But the grocery bag and sack market is declining. Plastic checkout sacks are cheaper than paper and paper is simply being displaced.

So we had problems of age and obsolescence, pending environmental regulations, and some declining markets to face at this mill. We went back to square one. We looked at making everything from tissue, a business that we are not in, to newsprint, another business we are not in, to corrugated medium. We are a big consumer of corrugated medium but we are not a producer of corrugated medium. We looked at printing and writing papers, a business we are in.

We thought there might be some opportunity to put in bleaching capacity here, but it made more sense to add such capacity at our Eastover printing and writing paper mill. That mill was designed to be tripled in capacity. It made little sense to install it in Savannah. Making linerboard made the most sense. We had a high-cost machine that had limited capability as presently configured. With the evolving quality demands for linerboard, this machine was not competitive. We were going to have to spend a lot of money on that machine just to meet the quality demands.

In commenting on the proposed modernization, Stuart Howell, director of strategic planning, explained:

We had a huge site in Savannah making kraft linerboard, bags, and saturating kraft, and we needed a vision and an understanding as to where each of those three markets were headed and why. First of all, we had economic expectations that drive everything. We made five-year projections for each of the three markets. We had a set of expectations for the economy. We projected an average annual growth of about 3 percent between the years 1985 and 1991. We projected growth in industry production over that with climbing rates of interest. We projected housing starts in the 7 million range. The dollar we expected to weaken.

We looked at alternative scenarios. The reason is that we needed to model this and these are very key determinants for the demand of these products in the future. First, fibre boxes are the principal consumer of our linerboard. We projected its growth at about $2\frac{1}{2}$ percent annually through 1991.

The Review of Project PDQ

On February 11, Union Camp's chairman, along with his three executive vice presidents, assistant comptroller, and director of planning, assembled in the main conference room of the corporate engineering building at the Savannah mill, awaiting Ballengee's presentation. Ballengee began:

My purpose today is to win your approval of what we call Project PDQ. By the way, the project got its title through an employee competition at the Savannah mill in January 1987. The winning entry, Project PDQ, standing for:

P—**P**roductivity improvement.

D—**D**ependability in plant operations, and

Q—**Q**uality excellence,

was submitted by one of our outside machinists, and he won a VCR for his effort.

I know that you have all received a copy of the capital job request and I expect that you may have some questions. I hope that my presentation this morning will answer any questions that you may have. However, interrupt at any time if a point needs clarification. I will be covering the following items in the next few minutes:

1. *Economic and market assumptions*—Our projections and assumptions about general economic factors and those specific to the unbleached paper and board business.

2. *Key issues*—The key issues that must be dealt with at the Savannah Mill. These issues are the driving force behind PDQ.

3. *Project main elements*—A review of the main elements of the project—that is, what we are proposing to build.

4. *Base case/PDQ comparison*—Then we'll go into a brief definition of the base case to which PDQ will be compared, identifying the primary differences.

5. *Financials*—And, finally, a review of the financials connected with the project.

Future Market Assumptions

Ballengee continued:

I'm not going to spend a great deal of time on this because you have all been through this information last November as part of the review of the five-year strategic plan for each of the operating divisions. Briefly then:

1. *Moderate economic growth, recession probable*—We have assumed continuing moderate economic growth over the next five years. We expect a recession sometime in 1989 or 1990. Even so, real GNP and industrial production growth are predicted to average 2.5 percent, while inflation will average 4 percent to 5 percent.

The economic outlook from 1986 through 1992 was for an average growth rate of below 3 percent. The average growth in GNP had declined from the 3.8 percent of the 1960s to 2.8 percent in the 1970s. It was projected to average only 2.5 percent from 1980 through 1992. UCC's forecasting panel, Wharton Econometrics, Merrill Lynch Economics, and Data Resources, Inc. (DRI) forecasted real GNP growth rates at between 2.1 percent and 2.7 percent from 1986 through 1992. Wharton assumed a mild two-quarter recession beginning at the end of 1989 and ending in early 1990. Merrill Lynch assumed only a one-quarter recession beginning the same time. They all saw the problem of limited growth being caused from a large federal budget deficit and trade imbalance. The strongest factor was seen as a growth in exports.

Consumer spending, which accounted for almost two-thirds of GNP, was expected to slow from a growth of 4.5 to 2.3 percent over the next five years. Housing starts were expected to fall from a 1987 high of 1.8 million to an average 1.6 million due to saturated demand and higher interest rates. Auto sales were forecasted to average 10.6 million per year as foreign car sales grew from 29 percent in 1986 to 31 percent by 1992. During this period, populations were expected to decline in the Northeast and Midwest as they grew in the South and West. Inflation was expected to be modest at an average 4.5 percent through 1992.

Ballengee went on:

> **2.** *Dollar stabilizes and remains low*—We expect the dollar to retreat a little bit more this year. But more importantly, we believe the dollar will remain, within the limits of normal fluctuations, stable and low.

The depreciation of the dollar in 1985 by 33 percent began to improve the trade deficit. Further depreciation was forecasted over the next five years. An improvement in the trade imbalance was expected, but slowly. Europe, Japan, and Third-World countries were potential customers, but were linked to the global economy. Third-World countries were also strapped with debt.

Ballengee continued with his presentation:

> **3.** *Demand for domestic linerboard and fibre boxes will grow with the economy*— Domestic linerboard and fibre box volumes should grow at about 2 percent per year, basically in line with the economy. Fibre boxes should average over 4 BSF (billions of square feet) of annual growth, pushing linerboard growth to about 220 million tons annually.

After growing at 6.1 percent in the 1960s and 3.4 percent in the 1970s, fibre box volumes were projected to average 2.3 percent growth between 1980 and 1992. Given the projected recession, fibre box shipments were projected to grow 1.9 percent annually. The projected growth in shipments was 34 billion square feet (BSF) between 1986 and 1992, which represented more than 2½ million tons of containerboard.

While fibre box volumes followed industrial production, it was also affected by changes in the import/export balances, since exports were "box"-intensive activities and outsourcing reduced the demand for boxes. The change in various business sectors also affected demand for boxes. However, over time, the correlation between fibre boxes and economic activity was high. Shipments from the Northeast, Midwest, and North Central regions were projected to be flat, while the Southeast, South Central, and Western regions increased their market value.

Domestic production of unbleached kraft board was projected to grow at a rate of 1.5 percent through 1992, less than fibre box growth, due to the growth in recycled linerboard and bleached grades, and the slight reduction in fibre box consumption of liner board due to performance packaging advancements. This put the overall growth of kraft board at 2.2 percent for the 1980–1992 period, as compared to 3 percent during the decade of the 1970s.

A 1987 study by Resource Information Systems, Inc. of the world demand for containerboard projected growth of 3.4 percent to the year 2000, a total increase of 32 million metric tons (Exhibit 4). Kraftliner exports by major producing country were projected as shown in Exhibit 5. Projected sales by containerboard grades are shown in Exhibit 6.

> **4.** *Linerboard export growth assisted by favorable dollar*—Near term, exports of linerboard are expected to continue to be constrained by capacity. By 1992, however, linerboard exports are expected to approach 2.6 million tons, about 12 percent higher than they were in 1987.

Unbleached kraft board production was projected to grow at 2 percent between 1986 and 1992. Exports would grow by 300,000 tons aided by expected

EXHIBIT 4   **Regional World Containerboard Demand**   *(In millions of metric tons)*

	1986	2000	Average Change
North America	20.8	27.5	2.0%
Western Europe	11.5	14.9	1.9
Eastern Europe	4.2	7.3	4.0
Asia	13.0	28.1	5.7
Latin America	3.1	6.2	5.1
Africa	0.8	1.4	4.1
Oceania	0.4	0.6	2.9
Total world	53.5	86.1	3.4%

EXHIBIT 5   **World Kraftliner Exports by Major Producing Country**
(In millions of metric tons)

	1986	2000	Average Change
United States	2.0	2.6	1.9%
Sweden	1.0	1.2	1.3
Western Europe	0.4	0.6	2.9
Eastern Europe	0.4	0.7	4.1
Latin America	0.2	0.9	11.3
Africa	0.1	0.2	5.1
Oceania	0.0	0.5	n.m.
Asia	0.2	0.3	8.2
Total world	4.8	7.6	3.3%

n.m.—not meaningful

EXHIBIT 6   **World Containerboard Grade Summary—World Share, by Type**

	1970	1986	2000
Kraft liner	48%	45%	40%
Recycled liner	18	20	24
Semi-chemical medium	22	19	15
Recycled medium	12	16	20
Total	100%	100%	100%

EXHIBIT 7   **U.S. Liner Exports to Major Geographical Areas**
(In thousands of short tons)

Area	1986	1992 (Estimated)	Average Change
Europe	632 (28%)	695 (27%)	1.6%
Latin America	493 (22)	550 (22)	1.8
Asia	789 (35)	915 (36)	2.5
Other	350 (15)	390 (15)	1.8
Total	2,264 (100%)	2,550 (100%)	2.0%

decline in the value of the U.S. dollar. Since the dollar's high in 1984, foreign converters had seen a dramatic renewal of the cost competitiveness of U.S.-produced linerboard. Since the recent low of $315 in August 1985, U.S. prices had increased 54 percent to $485 per metric ton in April 1987. However, due to the increase in foreign buyers' purchasing power, the actual increase to foreign buyers was considerably less: France saw a 12 percent increase, Germany a 2 percent increase, the United Kingdom a 33 percent increase, and Japan a 5 percent decrease. In fact, Japan was paying only 12 percent more for U.S. linerboard in 1987 than in 1977. However, high linerboard operating rates had constrained liner supply to the export market. As a result of price and demand, relative U.S. export shares had shifted slightly toward Asian markets by 1 percent, while European markets had declined by 1 percent as shown in Exhibit 7.

   5. *Modest capacity additions expected*—The capacity assumptions project growth of a little less than 3 percent per year. This is very close to the rate of growth over the past decade.

Capacity projections are shown in Exhibit 8. Ballengee continued:

These projections include the two new linerboard machines that have been announced: a 1,000 TPD machine for the Bogalusa, Louisiana mill of Gaylord and about the same size machine for Mead at their Marht, Alabama mill.
   Gaylord Container has announced the only dedicated linerboard machine for the industry. They plan to invest over $100 million to install the 1,000 TPD machine, giving them a 2,500 TPD capacity by late 1989. Mead announced a 1,200 TPD machine for early 1990. The Mead machine will be equipped with clay coaters for the production of, primarily, carrier stock. Their intention is to sell the machine out on clay coated. Until this is accomplished, they will produce linerboard to the extent that machine hours are available.

New industry capacity in kraft board was expected to increase 2.8 million tons between 1987 and 1992, in contrast with an increase of only 1.6 million tons in the period 1982 to 1986. Union Camp's increase in linerboard capacity was expected to come from the Savannah modernization program (125,000 tons) and the "Prattville Stretch" project (140,000 tons). The restart of the Jacksonville, Florida mill by Stone Container would add 350,000 tons. Temple-Inland planned 88,000 ton and 180,000 ton modernizations at Orange, Texas and Rome, Georgia, respectively. Most other additions involved small projects to boost the output capability of existing plants by a few thousand tons annually. Ballengee continued:

EXHIBIT 8   **Union Camp's Projected Changes in Unbleached Kraft Paper Board Capacity, Base Case** *(In thousands of tons)*

	Annual Capacity						
	1986	**1987**	**1988**	**1989**	**1990**	**1991**	**1992**
Arkansas Kraft	342	0	0	0	0	0	0
Boise Cascade	374	26	0	0	0	0	0
Champion International	253	0	0	0	0	0	0
Chesapeake	347	−135		48	52	46	0
Gaylord Container	419	27	0	50	170	60	70
Georgia Pacific	1,054	32	64	124	21	0	0
Great Southern	807	0	12	0	0	0	0
International Paper	1,664	0	0	0	0	0	0
Interstate	251	32	21	9	9	0	0
Jacksonville/Seminole	0	220	130	0	0	0	0
Jefferson Smurfit	1,307	89	18	0	80	0	0
Longview Fibre	474	45	0	0	0	0	0
Louisiana Pacific	172	0	0	0	0	0	0
MacMillan Bloedel	415	0	0	0	0	0	0
Manville	504	40	42	0	0	0	0
Mead	795	−395	0	0	0	245	64
Owens-Illinois	340	11	8	18	28	0	0
Packaging Corp.	666	33	0	36	0	0	0
Pratt Holdings	0	565	0	0	0	0	0
St. Joe	463	0	0	0	0	0	0
Simpson	197	0	0	0	0	0	0
Southwest Forest (Stone)	448	11	0	0	0	0	0
Stone Container	1,876	18	30	32	0	0	0
Temple-Inland	1,210	−170		0	268	0	0
Union Camp	1,266	35	35	110	63	68	73
Westvaco	855	0	0	0	0	0	0
Weyerhaeuser	1,368	63	30	74	0	0	0
Willamette	656	69	64	22	9	0	0
Capacity change	—	616	502	795	671	192	207
Balance	—					230	225
Total capacity	18,523	19,139	19,641	20,436	21,107	21,529	21,961
Percent change	2.9%	3.3%	2.6%	4.0%	3.3%	2.0%	2.0%

6. *Linerboard operating rates will be favorable*—Operating rates will remain very high prior to the next recession. Depending on the recession scenario you choose, you can cause operating rates to look about any way you want to after the recession—good or bad.

Over the period 1974–1986 operating rates averaged 93 percent, in spite of sharp drops during recessions in 1975 (82 percent) and 1985 (91 percent). Exhibit 9 shows Union Camp's outlook for fibre box/linerboard production assuming a recession in 1990. Union Camp saw an opportunity in light-weight kraft linerboard. Ballengee explained:

EXHIBIT 9   **Fibre Box/Linerboard Outlook (1987–1992)—1990 Recession Scenario**

	1987	1988	1989	1990	1991	1992	Average Change
Industrial production	128.9	134.1	136.6	134.2	141.4	44.7	2.5%
Fibre box production (BSF)	296.5	304.5	307.0	300.0	313.0	318.0	1.9%
Liner consumption (thousands of tons)	15,410	15,835	15,965	15,540	16,180	16,380	1.5%
Liner/BSF	52.0	52.0	52.0	51.8	51.7	51.5	—
Bleached recycled liner (thousands of tons)	480	490	515	460	485	490	2.6%
Bleached liner (thousands of tons)	135	140	145	130	145	150	2.2%
Unbleached kraft liner (thousands of tons)	14,795	15,205	15,305	14,950	15,550	15,740	1.5%
Other unbleached kraft board (thousands of tons)	1,350	1,410	1,435	1,540	1,575	1,600	3.7%
Unbleached kraft board exports (thousands of tons)	2,300	2,350	2,400	2,500	2,450	2,550	2.1%
Inventory change	218	100	150	145	—	80	—
Unbleached kraft board production (thousands of tons)	18,663	19,065	19,290	19,135	19,575	19,970	2.0%
Kraft board capacity (thousands of tons)	19,139	19,641	20,436	21,107	21,529	21,961	2.9%
Kraft board operating rate	98%	97%	94%	91%	91%	91%	—

We determined from interviewing offshore that there was a need for light-weight kraft linerboard that was not being satisfied by U.S. producers. We were configured for heavier weights of linerboard. Forty-two pound linerboard is the predominant grade in the United States and represented 55 percent of the consumption of linerboard, with higher-basis weights representing another 30 percent, and with the remaining 20 percent in 38, 33, and 26 pound product. Since we were in a good export city and we had been selling into the export markets around the world for nearly 40 years, we were well known and had a good selling network set up through some high-class people in the form of exclusive agents. If we could build this facility into a world-class operation and have some part of the output committed to light-weight linerboard, then we might have a strategic formula that would make sense for this mill.

Ballengee continued his presentation:

7. *Plastics continue to penetrate kraft paper markets*—Lastly, we have assumed continued penetration of the paper retail bag markets by plastic. Plastic will have more than 60 percent of this market by 1992, up from 35 percent last year. In total, we expect unbleached kraft paper demand to decline 5 percent per year over the next several years.

Unbleached kraft paper volumes, excluding saturating kraft, had declined by over 750,000 tons since 1974 (an average decline of 2 percent annually). Grocers' bag and sack grades had fallen by 11 percent, almost 250,000 tons, between 1984 and 1986 as plastics gained share of the market. Multiwall paper

EXHIBIT 10   **Retail Paper Bag Market, 1986–1992**   *(In thousands of tons)*

	1986	1992	Average Change	Total Decline
Sacks	1,074	648	(8)%	(426)
Bags	442	234	(10)	(208)
Variety	102	86	(3)	(16)
Total retail	1,618	968	(8)%	(650)

sack usage had dropped 37 percent since 1974, for an average decline of 4 percent, as converters used less expensive grocer grades. Union Camp used grocer grades for over 25 percent of its unbleached kraft paper consumption. Wrapping paper volume had dropped nearly half since 1974, and had stabilized at less than 100,000 tons. Other converting paper had declined 3 percent annually due to plastic penetration but still represented about 10 percent of industry volume. Exhibit 10 shows the market outlook for retail paper bags.

UCC had carried out extensive research on the impact of plastic bags on the retail bag market. According to Stuart Howell, director of strategic planning:

> We saw a significant structural change taking place in the retail bag business. The demand for grocery bags was shifting from paper to plastic. Our projection of the penetration of plastic into the retail bag markets was expressed in terms of the industry's total equivalent market in paper tons. We saw an acceleration of penetration of plastic into our traditional paper markets. One of our guys named it the "Jaws of Death"; plastic bags just kept eating up market share as it penetrated the retail bag market. We were guestimating that the market was almost a quarter plastic and, in five years, would have about 40 percent of the market.

Plastic retail bags were following the classic "S curve" substitution pattern, which meant an acceleration in the rate of penetration through 1992. Merchandise bags had the longest history of substitution and plastic bags had exceeded two-thirds share of that market. Other retail bag/sack segments were expected to see increased penetration over the next five years. According to Howell:

> We had underestimated the rates of penetration for plastic, so we remodeled these major products in 1987. Grocery sacks differ according to grocery store. Small bags from half a pound to 25 pounds are used in smaller retail outlets. McDonald's uses a 12 pound bag. Merchandise bags are used by firms like Kmart and Sears. When we used the "S" curve to model the rate of substitution, our computer model allowed us to predict the rate of penetration. The good news is that our model is quite accurate. The bad news is that we are predicting faster penetration than before.

While the market for retail bags was expected to grow at 1.7 percent between 1986 and 1992, the market for retail paper bags was projected to decline by 650,000 tons. Plastic bag volumes were projected to grow 15 percent annually and gain increased penetration (Exhibit 11). By 1992, plastic was projected to replace an equivalent of 1.5 million tons of retail paper bags. Imports were estimated at over 25 percent of the plastic bag market and accounted for 9 percent of the total paper bag market. The number of paper bag manufacturing plants had fallen from 115 in 1979 to 90 in 1987, while plastic bag plants

EXHIBIT 11   **Plastic Bag Penetration—Retail Bag Market**

	1983	1987	1992
Sacks	10%	34%	60%
Bags	NA	17	55
Variety	36	68	75
Total retail	11%	35%	61%

NA = not available.

had increased from 24 in 1979 to 60 in 1987. Sonoco had just added a new plastic bag plant with 2 billion bag capacity.

The only potential slowdown in plastic bag penetration came from problems with waste disposal. Plastic represented 7 percent of municipal waste. Of the 49 billion pounds of plastic consumed in the U.S. in 1986, 7 billion pounds were polyethylene films. Retail bags were under 600 million pounds. Paper and paperboard represented 37 percent of municipal waste. The 9,300 landfills remaining in the United States were being overwhelmed with 133 million tons of garbage each year. Incineration and recycling were alternatives available to both plastic and paper products.

In addition, consumer preference and economics were in favor of plastic over paper bags and sacks. Howell continued:

> We had tested the consumer preference for grocery bags. We interviewed 1,800 people in Brooklyn, in California, in Georgia, in Chicago, and in parts of the Midwest. Half the people we interviewed preferred plastic, about 30 percent preferred paper, and the rest didn't care. We interpreted that to mean that 70 percent preferred plastic or didn't care, and only 30 percent preferred paper.
>
> The second nail in the coffin was the economics. We made cost comparisons between plastic and paper. We had operations in Kentucky for plastic so we had good cost data. It cost 42 cents per pound for resin to make plastic bags. At that raw material cost, it would cost $14.11 per 1,000 plastic sacks. Paper cost $422 per ton for 70 pound paper. That would cost $32.86 per 1,000 bags. There is no way that paper could be cost competitive with plastic. You would have to double your resin costs and half your paper costs to make them competitive. This was grim news since we are in this business with both feet.
>
> We also had to get a handle on movable bags, those large bags used for pet foods, fertilizers, and other commodities. It's an important market for us, but we saw it as declining over time. The question was, at what rate of decline? We began testing various levels of plastic penetration in the future and realized we had to get out of this business. While there was no new capacity, no one [was] announcing their exit either. That meant that operating rates would deteriorate. It was certainly not an area in which to increase your capacity. So, as a part of the Savannah rebuilding and expansion review, it made sense to shed part of that operation.

The increased use of bulk containers, bulk transportation, heavy-duty plastic sacks, and a weak agricultural sector had combined to lower multiwall bag volumes about 3.6 percent annually since 1979. The projection of a 1990 recession was expected to lower volumes 6 percent, with only 1 percent growth by 1991. The only positive signs in the multiwall bag business were a weaker dollar and the potential for agricultural exports. There was also a growth in bag variety, which offered some opportunity for more printable bags. However, no one foresaw a turnaround in the competitive position of multiwall bags. Union Camp and Stone Container were both committed to the multiwall business. They produced high-performance, specialty grades with improved surfaces for printing, and were considered a steady source of supply.

Unbleached kraft paper capacity, excluding saturating kraft, had declined by 745,000 tons between 1982 and 1986, down from 4,150,000 tons to 3,405,000 tons. Capacity conversions to other grades accounted for the majority of the decline. Georgia Pacific converted its Crossett, Arizona mill to bleached products and its Monticello, Mississippi mill to linerboard, for a reduction of 260,000 tons of kraft paper capacity. International Paper converted its Mobile, Alabama mill to uncoated free sheet, for a 140,000 ton reduction in kraft paper capacity. Champion converted its Pensacola, Florida mill to uncoated free sheet and idled some capacity, cutting unbleached kraft paper output by 315,000 tons since 1984. Gilman and Temple-Inland were planning to withdraw from the segment. Union Camp moved its Savannah number 2 machine to linerboard. Only Seminole Kraft had restarted its Jacksonville kraft paper machine. By 1992, capacity was projected at 3,105,000 tons.

Additional withdrawals were required from this segment as declines continued. Potential candidates to withdraw capacity from unbleached kraft paper production are shown in Exhibit 12. Union Camp's studies showed that there were 24 machines that could swing their production between paper and linerboard, accounting for 40 percent of the unbleached kraft paper in 1986. They produced over 1.4 million tons of unbleached kraft paper in 1986. In addition, these machines produced an additional 3 million tons of linerboard. In spite of the projected 4.5 percent decline in 1988 in unbleached kraft paper shipments, swing producers could easily accommodate the decline by shifting production to linerboard. With just six shifts, kraft paper operating rates would be pushed above 100 percent but would only boost linerboard capacity by 2 percent. These swing machines on average were 23 years old. The average machine had 405 TPD capacity on paper and 565 TPD on linerboard. About 25 percent of the machines were already predominantly producing linerboard in 1987. In fact, linerboard operating rates were above 100 percent. Excluding saturating kraft, about 40 percent of 1986's unbleached kraft paper production, or 1.3 million tons, was produced on swing machines. The remaining 1.9 million tons were produced on dedicated machines.

Key Issues

In considering Project PDQ, Ballengee's team had identified the issues that were considered key to the decision facing the Savannah mill. He explained:

1. *Age and obsolescence*—First, we are running batch digesters, brown stock washing lines, lime kilns, and other equipment that is over 30 years old and is simply reaching the end of its useful life.

2. *Environmental regulations*—Second, the regulation of total reduced sulfur (TRS) emissions, the primary source of odor in a kraft mill, is soon to be upon us. The regulations have been written by the Georgia Environmental Protection Division and approved by the Federal Environmental Protection Agency (EPA). Georgia is waiting only on 10 other states to impose EPA- approved TRS control plans. Seven have already done that and four more states have plans submitted to EPA for approval.

EXHIBIT 12   **Unbleached Kraft Paper—Potential Capacity Withdrawals** *(In tons)*

Company/Mill Location	Potential Capacity Withdrawal	Comments
Arkansas Kraft, Morrilton, AR	30,000	Swing to linerboard
Gaylord Container, Bogalusa, LA	120,000	New linerboard machine
Georgia Pacific, Palatka, FL	180,000	May convert to bleached kraft
Gilman, St. Mary's, GA	150,000	Convert to printing/writing grades
Great Southern, Cedar Springs, GA	70,000	Swing to linerboard
International Paper, Camden, AR	260,000	May close down
Manville, W. Monroe, LA	55,000	May close down
Pratt Group, Macon, GA	60,000	May shift to containerboard
Port Townsend, Pt. Townsend, WA	115,000	May convert to bleached kraft
Stone Container, Florence, SC	130,000	Restart, may swing to linerboard
Temple-Inland, Orange, TX	55,000	Eliminate paper via upgrade
Union Camp, Savannah, GA	190,000	May swing to linerboard and shut down
Weyerhaeuser, Valliant, OK	15,000	Swing to linerboard
Total tonnage	1,430,000	

Ballengee commented on the environmental issue:

The state of Georgia, in the late 1970s or early 1980s, had taken steps to promulgate TRS control regulations. They had backed away from that on the appeal of the industry. We argued that it was a problem that we were all going to have to deal with, but that it was an expensive problem to deal with. We argued that total reduced sulphur emissions, as demonstrated by the scientific and medical community and the EPA, were a welfare pollutant, so it was not anything that represented a health hazard to anyone. We argued further that, in the state of Georgia, we were the biggest industry and that they were putting us at a competitive disadvantage because no other state in the country had promulgated such regulations at the time.

So the state backed away and said, "You are probably right. So what we will do is trigger our regulations once 25 percent of the kraft pulp capacity in this country is under regulation or once 10 states having kraft pulping operations have instituted such regulations."

To deal with TRS emissions prior to this proposal would not have been the brightest move to make because a lot of the equipment back in the pulp mill was either technologically obsolete or just worn out. It was going to be [an] extraordinarily high cost just to keep it running. To try to control odor emissions from that equipment would have been extremely difficult and terribly expensive. We would have had four or five times the amount of money in TRS emission collection equipment than the value of the assets from which we were collecting the emissions. It just didn't make any economic sense.

3. *Cost effectiveness*—Next, the Savannah mill, we believe, is not today one of the highest-cost producers, but over time it is drifting inexorably in that direction. This is simply not acceptable if we are to stay in the highly competitive packaging business.

4. *Quality effectiveness*—Fourth, the quality required by the buyers of corrugated containers is changing. Many are demanding boxes with higher stacking strength and practically all are demanding better graphics and overall appearance. We view this as an opportunity to differentiate ourselves from much of the competition, and we set about doing this three years ago. Although much progress has been made, the product quality goals we must achieve to fully implement our "Performance Packaging" program cannot be met without the PDQ Project.

5. *Declining unbleached paper demand*—And finally, you have heard much about the declining demand for unbleached kraft paper and it is real. We must reduce our dependence on the need to make and sell kraft paper. We believe the solution for Savannah, after studying many other possibilities, is to replace paper capacity with linerboard capacity.

To summarize then, we have five key issues that must be addressed, and PDQ addresses them all.

1. It will resolve the most critical of our worn-out equipment problems.
2. PDQ will bring the Savannah mill into compliance with the TRS regulations, which will be promulgated by the state of Georgia very soon.
3. The project will also address manufacturing cost, quality improvement, and declining paper demand issues. There is one vital point, though, that needs to be said at this early stage in the presentation. To do nothing is not an option that is open to us at Savannah. If the mill is to run, if the income stream is to be preserved, then, if for no other reason, TRS regulations preclude a "maintain the status quo" option.

Main Elements

Ballengee highlighted the main elements of Project PDQ's investment:

1. *Woodyard.*

    Conversion of chippers to bottom discharge—In the woodyard, we have two blowing chippers. These will be converted to bottom discharge units, which will reduce their horsepower requirements, produce more uniform chips, and reduce the generaton of fines.

2. *Lime kiln and causticizing area.*

    New lime kiln and appurtenances—The project includes a new energy-efficient lime kiln plus a major upgrade of the causticizing area. The three old kilns will be shut down.

3. *Pulp mill.*

    Upgrade K-1 system—In the pulp mill, the existing K-1 continuous digester system will be upgraded and converted to top sheet/paper grade pine.

    Convert number 8 wash line to hardwood—The number 8 wash line will be converted to hardwood.

    Install a new 1,850 TPD pulping line—A new 1,850 TPD pulping line will be installed to produce all the high-yield pine required for linerboard production and the remainder of the top sheet pine that will be needed. All the old wash lines—numbers 2 through 7—will be shut down along with their supporting batch digesters, blow tanks, and other ancillary equipment.

4. *Paper mill.*

    Install a new 333" trim lightweight linerboard machine—In the paper mill, we are proposing to install a new linerboard machine designed specifically to produce 42 pound and lighter basis weight products. This will give us the ability to exploit the fast-growing export demand as well as to better serve the domestic lightweight market.

EXHIBIT 13   **Capital Cost Summary**

Woodyard/improvements	$ 13,429,000
Lime kiln/causticizing area upgrade	48,837,000
Pulp mill	
Modifications to existing equipment	22,094,000
New pulping line	92,549,000
Paper mill	
New linerboard machine	184,735,000
Power distribution system modifications	13,356,000
Total capital cost	$375,000,000

Our focus on the export market deserves some special emphasis. At Savannah, we are located at one of the best break-bulk and container shipping ports in the country. Because we have no inland freight, we can put our product on board ship at a $15 to $30 per ton advantage over all but three other East Coast U.S. linerboard mills. And none of the three is a cost- or quality-effective producer of lightweights.

The number 1 kraft paper machine will be shut down, removing over 90,000 TPY of paper capacity. The number 4 linerboard machine will also be shut down. Its capacity is about 215,000 TPY. These two machines are being shut down because they are both high-cost producers and are approaching a condition where substantial capital will be required if they are to continue in service. And in the case of the number 1 paper machine, there will not be sufficient paper demand to keep the machine running.

The new machine, with a nominal capacity of 1,300 TPD, not only provides 120,000 TPY of incremental capacity, it replaces over 300,000 TPY of the highest-cost production in the Savannah mill.

Capital Cost Summary

The cost of Project PDQ was estimated to be $375 million (Exhibit 13). Ballengee described the cost breakdown:

> You should be aware that our original intention was to rebuild the two existing linerboard machines and increase their output levels to 1,000 TPD each. However, after considerable study, the estimated cost to do this was more than the cost of a new machine. And with the new machine, a work force reduction is possible; the machine can be designed specifically for cost-effective production of highest-quality lightweight liner; and, most importantly, the machine can be built with virtually no interruption to ongoing operations. With an absolute minimum of 40 days of downtime per machine to rebuild, a loss of profit contribution in excess of $7.5 million can be avoided.

PDQ versus the Base Case

Ballengee noted that the Savannah mill did not have a "do-nothing" option. As a result, the trade-off related to the cost of meeting environmental regulations and keeping the equipment in operation versus the proposed upgrade. Ballengee presented Exhibit 14 and continued:

E X H I B I T   14   **PDQ versus Base Case**

	Base Case	PDQ	Difference
Mill operating configuration	7 machines	6 machines	−1 machine
Capital required (in millions of dollars)	$110	$375	$26
Production (thousands of tons)			
Paper	298	298	—
Saturating	157	157	—
Liner	603	722	119
Total	1,058	1,177	119
Wood required (in thousands of tons)			
Pine	3,004	3,036	32
Hardwood	1,014	998	(16)
Hardwood whole-tree chips	—	204	204
Total	4,018	4,238	220

Let me review with you quickly what we are using as our base case in the left-hand column. We have assumed for the base case that the mill would be maintained in its present configuration with all seven paper and board machines running. However, because of the declining demand for kraft paper, single-ply liner would be run on [the] number 2 paper machine for 291 days per year. As mentioned before, we have no choice to do nothing. It is, therefore, our best estimate that $110 million will have to be spent during the next several years if the mill is to be run at full capacity. I will show you a breakdown of where the $110 million is required in a minute.

On the production side, we expect to produce and sell:

298,000 TPY of paper.

157,000 TPY of saturating kraft.

603,000 TPY of linerboard.

This will require the fibre mix indicated—a total of 4,018,000 tons of wood annually.

The base case is optimistic. It specifies an output level of salable tons that is higher than has ever been achieved. This is due primarily to the heavier mix resulting from running single-ply liner on [the] number 2 machine 80 percent of the time. Therefore, we believe our rate of return calculations, which you will see shortly, are very conservative since they are premised on a most ambitious base case.

PDQ is in the next column. Six machines running with 1,177,000 total tons of production per year requiring 4,238,000 tons of wood. This represents only a modest increase in wood consumption, and, as discussed, this increase is accommodated from our existing land base. The capital requirement is $375 million.

The right-hand column simply indicates the differences between PDQ and the base case for this set of data. PDQ requires $265 million more in capital. It will provide for another 119,000 tons of linerboard to be produced and at only a modest increase in wood demand. However, as important or maybe more so, PDQ addressses the several other key issues described earlier, that is, age and obsolescence, TRS regulation, cost effectiveness, and the need for quality improvement.

Ballengee went on to show the breakdown in expenditures of the $110 million required for the base case.

Paper mill	$ 38,600,000
Finishing and shipping	200,000
Woodyard	2,300,000
Lime kiln/causticizing	6,800,000
Number 8 wash line	1,700,000
Old wash plant	4,700,000
Environmental	43,900,000
Power distribution	11,800,000
Total	$110,000,000

As you see, the big hits are in the paper mill—and that's essentially money required to put numbers 1 and 4 machines in good condition—environmental, and power distribution. The environmental expenditure is essentially all required to collect and destroy TRS gases. The high-voltage power distribution upgrade is an absolute necessity and the money to do this is included in PDQ as well.

Project PDQ's Economic Analysis

As shown in Exhibit 15, Ballengee then presented the forecasted rates of return on the project's investment:

The minimum capital required is $110 million to accomplish the base case and it has no return. For $265 million more, you can do Project PDQ. And the return on that incremental capital is 17 percent. The return on the entire $375 million is 13 percent, very respectable for a major project. At the bottom of this chart, please note that over half of the combination comes from cost reductions. This is fairly unusual for this kind of project where, more normally, the project's success is much more heavily tied to incremental tons.

After PDQ, the cost of all liner produced at Savannah will be reduced $43 per ton, paper $19 per ton, and saturating kraft $6 per ton. Overall, then, we will have reduced costs 12 percent, or $35 per ton, at Savannah through PDQ. This is significant. It represents over $22.6 million in cost savings every year. Some cost savings examples are:

Water consumption will be reduced from 12,000 gallons per ton to 7,500 gallons per ton, a 38 percent reduction.

Energy costs will be reduced 10 percent or $3.00 per ton.

[Labor] hours per ton will drop from a record low 3.79 in 1987 to 2.95, a 22 percent reduction.

As mentioned earlier, this project, unlike most major paper industry revitalization projects, is not totally dependent on incremental tons. And the cost savings will accrue during the bad times as well as the good.

We believe that the number 1 paper machine in Prattville will be one of the lowest-cost and highest-quality producers of linerboard in the world after it is rebuilt. We have tried to take a look at how the new Savannah linerboard machine would stack up against it. The one grade that is common to both machines is 42 pound linerboard. We estimate that the Prattville machine will still have a 4

E X H I B I T 15   **PDQ Economic Return**

	Capital Cost	DCF Rate of Return (5 percent inflation)
Minimum capital	$110 million	0
Incremental capital	265 million	17%
Total project	375 million	13%
Return results from cost reductions	22.6 million	
Incremental volume (119,000 tons)	20.2 million	
Total	$42.8 million	

E X H I B I T 16   **PDQ Cash Flow Projection Assuming a 5 Percent Inflation Rate**
(In millions of dollars)

	Cash Flow
1988	$ (17)
1989	(152)
1990	(182)
1991	12
1992	61
1993	54
1994	50
1995	49
1996	51
1997	51
1998–2007	550

percent cost advantage, but this is only a marginal difference. Both will be manufacturing the highest-quality board at some of the lowest costs of any machines in the world.

In considering the cash flow projections, the design and construction period would take three years, 1988, 1989, 1990, and into the first quarter of 1991. All new equipment would be in place and running by April 1991 and net cash flow would be positive that year. The project would pay back in 7.4 years. Over 20 years, the net positive cash flow would be $527 million based on the project delivering operating profits totalling over $1.25 billion.

Ballengee provided the cash flow projections shown in Exhibit 16.

CITIZENS FOR CLEAN AIR (A)*

William R. Boulton, Auburn University

The Citizens for Clean Air (CCA) was organized in 1982 by a small number of concerned professionals whose goal was to take the stink out of Savannah's air. They had spent years trying to get the support of federal, state, and local government, but without much success. Sam Adler, an officer of the Citizens for Clean Air in 1985, said, "I'm fed up with it; I've lived with it in this town for 30 years and it is disgraceful and it is ridiculous. It has no right to be." WSTV news reporter Kevin Dooley reported: "It's that attitude which has prompted Citizens for Clean Air to build a strong grassroots coalition of local citizens to convince Union Camp and other industry officials that it is in their best interest to install the necessary equipment to cut down on the waste discharge into the air."

The Citizens for Clean Air had approached federal, state, and local authorities to do something to make industries in Savannah clean up the air. They flew to the corporate headquarters of Union Camp in New Jersey to talk to the corporate president about the problem, but were stonewalled. They were now starting a local campaign to get citizens in Savannah to back their cause and they were asking for media support. They had approached the management of WSTV television to help launch a major campaign to bring the issue before the public. According to Dooley:

> What Adler and other members want is a commitment from a news organization that will cover the odor and pollution problem in Savannah with unbiased reports and not back down in the face of political or corporate pressures. A local television station in Jacksonville produced a number of reports and a documentary detailing similar problems there and within six months managed to get the public behind them and clean up the air by pressuring local politicians to tighten local ordinances and make Jacksonville's air easier to breathe and smell.
>
> What causes the rotten-egg smell in Savannah is hydrogen sulfide gas, which is a by-product of paper mills like Union Camp. The Citizens for Clean Air say that they have secured nearly 200 names of citizens from in and around Savannah who say their health has been affected by the gas.

According to Dr. William Dickinson, a member of CCA, "Union Camp and other polluters will indicate that there is no evidence of permanent health effects, but what about being sick? What about having headaches and nausea?" Kevin Dooley, on a WSTV news program, said to viewers:

> Union Camp officials claim that they are within the legal guidelines for waste discharge under EPA laws, and EPA agrees. But Citizens for Clean Air say those guidelines are too slack. They believe in the old saying that there is strength in numbers, and if citizens join together and insist that things be changed, maybe local industries will heed their advice.

UNION CAMP AND SAVANNAH

To celebrate its 50th anniversary, Union Camp published the company's history in Savannah to highlight the long-standing relationship it had had with the community. The history was titled *50 Years of Friendship and Growth*, and the introduction stated:

> This is a story of a company, of a city, and of people who, 50 years ago, discovered that they shared the same dream and who worked together to bring the dream to life.
>
> The story begins in the 1930s, amid the greatest Depression in our nation's history. Throughout the country, the economic troubles of the time caused many Americans to lose hope. The people of Union Bag and Paper Corporation and the city of Savannah, however, still continued to believe in the "American dream." They believed that the promise of a better future still depended upon the action they took then.
>
> In 1935, the people of Union Bag and Savannah formed an alliance which held the promise of growth for both the company and the city. In order to bring this promise to reality, each made a commitment to the other to work together for greater economic opportunity.
>
> It wasn't always easy . . . no new relationship is . . . yet, over the years, trust began to form and friendship began to grow. Today, as we look back over the past half century, we can see that the working alliance between Union Bag and Savannah has resulted in substantial progress for both. It brought more jobs, more opportunities for growth, and the promise of a more secure future.
>
> This book traces the history of the relationship between Union Camp and the city of Savannah from its beginning to the present day, through the eyes of a few who were a witness to its development. In a greater sense, however, it is also a tribute to all the people of Savannah and Union Camp who dared to dream and worked so hard to bring the dream to life.

In the height of the Depression, negotiations were completed between Alexander "Sandy" Calder, president of Union Bag and the Savannah Industrial Committee, to construct a $4 million pulp and paper mill. Union Bag of New York city was the world's largest manufacturer of bags and wrapping papers, and other commodities produced from wood pulp. When the process of converting Southern pine into paper was developed by Dr. Charles Herty, a Savannah chemist, Union Bag took the lead in commercializing the process. Calder explained, "It was plain from the outset that we needed Savannah and Savannah needed us. That is why this project cannot help but be a success if we continue to pull together." The mill employed approximately 875 persons with an annual payroll of $1 million, in addition to 500 people working in the woods supplying logs to the mill. Even before initial construction was completed, the company had formulated plans to triple the mill's production capacity. The second and third paper machines were operating within two years.

Fourteen other paper companies followed Union Bag's lead and announced plans for paper mills in the South, with investments of $40 million. With the new influx of business, private landowners of pine forests discovered that their trees were a valuable cash crop: money, indeed, was beginning to grow on trees. Union Bag paid over $300,000 a year for pine wood upon starting its pulping operations.

E X H I B I T   1   **Union Bag's Cost of Making Kraft Paper (1936)**

	Industry Standards in the South, 1926–1936	Union Bag's Mill in Savannah, 1936
Cost of making kraft paper	$65.00 per ton	$33.00 per ton
Paper machine speed	550 feet per minute	1,400 feet per minute
Energy generated from bark burning	0	1,000 lbs. per ton of pulp
Steam regeneration of pulp	0	10,000 lbs. per ton of pulp

In reflecting on Union Bag's decision, Alexander Calder, Jr., president between 1956 and 1980, explained:

> Union Bag's survival depended upon coming down to the Southeast. That was something my father realized during the Depression. He was a fierce competitor and he was determined to get the company turned around. I know that other places were interested in attracting the company but, ultimately, he selected Savannah. Savannah had a lot to do with our success . . . and we had a lot to do with the turnaround of Savannah. It's a two-way street, which is the best kind. They work better. Everyone wins.

The design of Union Bag's mill represented the latest in paper-making technology. The result was a significant cost advantage for Union Bag, as shown in Exhibit 1.

During World War II, the heavy-duty linerboard and multiwall bags produced by the Savannah mill were used nearly 75 percent for the war effort. By the 1950s, the Savannah mill had six of the nine largest machines of their kind in the world. By 1953, employment had grown from 600 to 5,400, daily production from 130 to 1,700 tons, and annual payroll from $1 million to $18 million. In 1956, Union Bag and Camp Manufacturing of Franklin, Virginia merged.

In 1965, the port of Savannah was developed into one of the finest, and largest, deep water facilities in the South Atlantic. These improvements helped Union Camp expand its export program and enabled the mill to grow into a world leader in the export of paper products and chemicals. President Lyndon Johnson recognized the company as a leading exporter of paper products and chemicals.

According to Malcolm Bell, a retired banker and former president of the Savannah Chamber of Commerce:

> In the economic life of Savannah, our rebirth stems from the day the Savannah plant began. It was Union Bag that carried us out of the financial doldrums of the early Thirties. Every businessman in Savannah, and many from beyond our city and country lines, knows the value of Union Bag to the area's economy.
>
> But it is not in our economic life alone that Union Bag looms large. It is in every worthwhile community endeavor that you will find Union Bag or Union Baggers. . . . So, something that we all know and realize is that in our midst is a fine corporate citizen. A big company with a big heart and a wonderful way of instilling in its people the desire to work for a better community.

E X H I B I T 2   **Economic Impact of Union Camp Corporation's Savannah Complex, 1984**

Total Wages	
Savannah complex	$100,400,000
Construction	6,600,000
Savannah trucking	500,000
Total	107,500,000
Goods and Services	
Savannah complex	199,000,000
Pulp wood purchases	76,000,000
Total	275,000,000
Exports–Georgia Ports	
Savannah plant (275,000 tons)	69,800,000
Chemical division—Savannah (54,000 tons)	12,700,000
	$ 82,500,000

The company's involvement in community activities had been well known. The company's employees were ongoing supporters of the Scouts, Red Cross, and other community organizations. Union Camp had donated company lands for use as parks, schools, and recreational areas. In 1977, the company's Land Legacy Program included donation of the company's entire holdings in the Okeefenokee swamp. Nick Mamalakis, a local insurance and real estate broker, had served as president of both the Lion's Club and Jaycees. He noted:

> The company's philosophy was to be a part of the town, to be involved. When new technologies, for example, came along to protect the environment, Union Camp was in the forefront of all our industry to introduce these technologies for both their benefit and the benefit of the entire community. . . . I think the end result of their involvement is that you can say, over the years, Union Camp has made a lot of friends in this town.

In 1974, Union Camp's total investment on the air and water improvement program at Savannah represented the largest environmental investment at any one single manufacturing facility. Union Camp's willingness to adapt its facilities to the latest in technology kept the complex at the leading edge of the industry. Between 1960 and 1985, nearly $600 million was invested in the mill complex. Exhibit 2 shows the estimated economic impact of Union Camp mill on the Savannah area in 1984.

THE 1979 GEORGIA CONSERVANCY REPORT

A 1979 report by the environmental group, Georgia Conservancy, detailed the odor problem and the steps to get rid of it. The 75-page report began by saying that residents of Chatham County recognized that air pollution existed there. The State Environmental Protection Division was quoted as saying "that the county is the most industrialized area of Georgia." Out of more than

100 industries around Savannah, the report claimed that at least 30 were classified as major air polluters, primarily Union Camp Corporation's paper mill, built in 1936. The document recognized a number of factors that contributed to the air pollution problem, but put the primary blame on inadequate government regulations. According to Georgia Conservancy's Hans Neuhauser: "We thought that there were some serious deficiencies in how the state of Georgia looked at and supervised air pollution in Savannah."

Ogden Doremus, an environmental lawyer from Metter, Georgia explained:

> I was contacted in 1970 by Richard Ayers just before the Federal Clean Air Act was about to be passed. Dick was with the Natural Resources Defense Council and was chairman of the Clean Air Coalition. He asked if I would make a comparison of the Georgia Clean Air Act. Georgia's Clean Air Act was a "Dirty Air Act" that allowed any kind of pollution that you wanted. You could pollute anything under this Georgia law.
>
> I told Dick that the provisions of the Federal Clean Air Act had to be put into Georgia's Clean Air Act. After some lobbying, we passed all the necessary provisions to conform the Georgia law to the federal law. All through that period we were experiencing intense lobbying efforts in the Georgia General Assembly and in the governor's office, against doing anything to improve the environment.

According to Hans Neuhauser, Savannah had had no resident inspector to check environmental compliance at Union Camp's mill or other area plants since 1979, and major corporations were notified up to 48 hours in advance of a state inspection. The report said that state officials had been lenient in regulating odor. Out of the report came a new set of odor-control regulations ordering all 12 paper mills in Georgia to clean up by installing more effective equipment.

Six months later, the state modified the regulations to take effect only after 10 other states made their plants do the same. As of 1985, just eight other states had adopted similar odor-control programs.

PAPER MILL EMISSIONS AND CONTROL REGULATIONS

In the kraft or sulfate process, wood chips are cooked in a water solution containing sodium sulfide (Na_2S) and sodium hydroxide ($NaOH$). The cooking process dissolves the lignin that binds wood fibers together. These fibers subsequently are washed and further processed for papermaking.

Reclaiming, recycling, and reprocessing are integral parts of kraft mill operations. In the various stages, vapors containing total reduced sulphur (TRS), which contribute to the characteristic paper mill odor, are released. The result is a variable mixture of hydrogen sulfide and other gases that contain sulphur.

Under the Clean Air Act, the U.S. Environmental Protection Agency is responsible for determining which pollutants adversely affect human health and which pollutants do not. Certain pollutants from kraft pulp mills have been found to affect health—sulphur dioxide and particulates. According to Union Camp: "Union Camp has spent over $70 million at Savannah to control these health-related air pollutants to the safety levels established by the U.S. Environmental Protection Agency and Georgia Environmental Protection Division (EPD)."

Union Camp's Response

In response to media attention beginning on April 17, 1985, Union Camp Corporation's Savannah mill issued a fact sheet relating to paper mill odor-control issues. It stated:

> Due to public interest and some misconceptions about paper mill emissions, Union Camp Corporation wishes to clarify three important points:
>
> 1. Paper mill odor does not endanger human health, according to the Environmental Protection Agency (EPA).
> 2. During the last 20 years, Union Camp's capital improvements have helped reduce its Savannah mill odor emissions by almost 70 percent.
> 3. Union Camp, since 1979, has been engineering and evaluating a series of capital improvements necessary to reduce further the paper mill odor emanating from its Savannah plant. Estimated capital cost is in excess of $25 million.
>
> The odor-reduction program, which will take three to five years when begun, will be related to other major capital improvements. These improvements are designed to keep the Savannah plant competitive with other kraft mills in Georgia and surrounding states, thus enhancing job security for its some 3,500 employees.

In describing previous action that the company had taken, Union Camp officials reported:

> In 1962, an oxidation system was installed. This system oxidized reduced sulphur gases in residual pulping liquid. As a result, Union Camp achieved at that time a 70 percent reduction in the emission of total reduced sulphur gases from recovery boilers.
>
> In 1965, the company replaced many of its batch digesters with a continuous digester that employs a pulping process with considerably less TRS emissions.
>
> In the mid-70s, a new state-of-the-art recovery boiler was completed. It replaced four old recovery boilers and further reduced the level of odor.
>
> Simultaneously, technology had moved forward; and an improved, high-efficiency oxidation system replaced the earlier system. This upgrading of control equipment further reduced odors from the residual pulping liquid, increasing the 70 percent odor reduction of 1962 to more than 90 percent.

The company argued that odor-control activities had reduced odor emission by 70 percent over the past 20 years. In 1979, the federal agency published the document on kraft pulping that provided an outline of retrofit guidelines for various states as they formulated their respective state regulations for existing mills. These EPA guidelines were followed closely by the state of Georgia in setting state standards on TRS. The regulations were written on a source-by-source basis in terms of 5 to 40 parts per million, measured at the source. Even so, the areas around paper mills would not be odor free.

The Georgia plan first called for individual mills to submit compliance plans by March 1, 1981. The deadline was postponed after companies appealed that they would not be competitive since other papermaking states were not moving as fast toward implementing their retrofit plans. The Georgia mills argued that capital expenditures to meet the plan would cost over $150 million, while the competitor mills in other states would not be affected. Before EPA action was taken on the Georgia plan, it was recalled and amended. The Georgia plan was postponed for implementation until 10 other states, representing at least 25 percent of kraft mills, had plans with similar provisions approved by the U.S. Environmental Protection Agency. Louisiana, Kentucky California, Maryland, and South Carolina had filed their plans with the EPA. These five states represented about 19 percent of the nation's kraft mills.

Once this condition was met, each mill would be required to submit a compliance schedule for controlling TRS emission at five major sources within each mill. The sources included digesters, evaporators, lime kilns, recovery boilers, and smelt-dissolving tanks. This required a massive collection and incineration system, plus improved scrubbing and washing at various points. Capital costs for Union Camp were expected to be over $25 million, with operating costs of some $12 million annually.

ENVIRONMENTAL REGULATION

Stone Container Corporation, a smaller paper mill in Georgia, was not in compliance with government odor-control standards. Bob Column of the Environmental Protection Division said Stone had not been in compliance for several years but it was no one's fault. Stone had installed a new boiler that had unforeseen technical problems. Column said that the plant should come into compliance in 1985. The odor would never be completely gone, just reduced, to current technical levels. Column said that special boilers were needed to burn odorous sulfur gases and reduce the odor at a cost of $50 to $300 million depending on the size and age of the plant.

Column said Union Camp officials had already spent quite a few dollars to reduce the odor with chemical treatment. He said the stacks were putting out about half the odor that they once did. EPD officials said the odor could be reduced even further, but paper mills hadn't voluntarily taken that step because of the costs. Column expected 10 states to adopt odor-control laws in a year, which would put Georgia's law into effect. Then Union Camp would be forced, under Georgia law, to install the new odor-control equipment within three years.

According to Dooley, the Savannah Chamber of Commerce had studied potential distracting factors to the tourism industry and the city's image and they concluded that Savannah's bad odor was a major problem. Local leaders said it was up to the state and federal government to enact odor-control regulations and that if any change was to come, it would have to be negotiated through those channels.

TEKTRONIX, INC. ETHICS PROGRAM (A)*

Steven N. Brenner, Portland State University
Patricia Bishop, Portland State University
Colleen Mullery, Portland State University

Earl Wantland, President and CEO of Tektronix, Inc. (Tek), a Beaverton, Oregon-based electronic instrument manufacturing company, sat at his desk looking at the September 14, 1987, *Wall Street Journal* article reporting improprieties and possible fraud in the company's West German subsidiary, Tektronix GmbH. This was just the latest problem facing the company that had grown from an eight-person operation to a world leader in oscilloscope manufacturing in just over 30 years. In the 1980s Tek faced a recession in high-technology industries, intensified global competition, and shortened product life cycles, all of which put severe profit pressures on the company (see Exhibit 1).

The company's financial difficulties resulted in several expense reduction decisions, which tended to change the atmosphere within the company. Tek's management tried to avoid work force size reduction by implementing shortened work schedules, unpaid shutdowns, mandatory vacation usage, voluntary leaves of absence, hiring and pay freezes, upper management pay cuts, and the combining of redundant functions. Unfortunately, revenue growth slowed and the company undertook three major layoffs, which trimmed its size from 24,000 to 17,000 employees.

Employees at all levels questioned the cutback decision, believing that management had violated the values and morality inherent in the "Tek Culture." Tek's corporate strategist felt so strongly that the personnel-level reductions should have been avoided that he resigned from his position, noting, "I'm not sure that because business conditions change, the ethics on which you operate a business ha[ve] to change."

Historically, ethical issues had not been a concern for Tektronix. The company's founders, Jack Murdock and Howard Vollum, had a strong belief in the honesty and integrity of the individual employee. When the company was small there were open cash drawers, free coffee, and a tacit no-layoff policy. As the company grew larger and more divisionalized, it became more difficult to continue these policies. With growth there also came a diminution of commitment to the company. Examples of a change in atmosphere were numerous, including employees working for their divisions at the expense of the entire company; defections to competitors or to new start-up companies; and moonlighting ventures (some of which were carried out on Tek premises).

In partial response to these issues, the electronic industry's ethical standards, and the overall climate at Tektronix in 1987, Earl Wantland decided to hold a business ethics seminar for upper-level managers. The intent of the seminar was to identify corporate values and the pressures that make it hard to live up to those values and to develop an action plan for managing ethical issues.

*The help of present and former Tektronix employees is acknowledged. This research was supported in part through a grant from the Chiles Foundation, Portland, Oregon. Copyright © 1988 by Steven N. Brenner.

Summary of Tektronix's Consolidated Financial Performance, 1979–1987

	1979	1980	1981	1982	1983	1984	1985	1986	1987
Net sales (in thousands of dollars)	$786,936	$971,306	$1,061,834	$1,195,748	$1,191,485	$1,332,958	$1,438,082	$1,352,212	$1,395,885
Earnings (in thousands of dollars)	$ 77,151	$ 85,072	$ 80,167	$ 9,290	$ 46,807	$ 112,054	$ 90,181	$ 39,327	$ 51,188
Gross margin	54.3%	52.8%	51.7%	49.6%	47.6%	48.8%	50.9%	50.9%	54.2%
Operating margin	15.4%	15.2%	13.0%	12.2%	9.4%	9.8%	8.9%	5.1%	7.3%
Return on equity	21.3%	19.4%	15.5%	13.4%	7.2%	16.1%	11.1%	4.7%	5.9%
Return on capital	18.7%	15.8%	12.3%	11.0%	6.4%	13.5%	10.2%	4.7%	5.7%
Earnings per share	$2.14	$2.33	$2.17	$2.12	$1.22	$2.87	$2.20	$0.98	$1.33
Total assets (in thousands of dollars)	$642,907	$841,693	$ 953,753	$1,044,188	$1,092,446	$1,222,168	$1,224,372	$1,196,947	$1,159,413
Inventory turns	4.19X	4.02X	3.66X	4.04X	3.91X	4.60X	5.97X	6.94X	8.68X
Asset turns	1.44X	1.34X	1.19X	1.20X	1.12X	1.18X	1.22X	1.15X	1.16X
Debt/total assets	18.5%	27.4%	26.1%	23.9%	21.9%	20.3%	11.5%	10.3%	6.0%
Employees	21,291	23,890	24,028	23,241	21,121	20,816	20,525	19,251	17,099
Year-end price of common stock	$24.63	$24.88	$30.38	$26.32	$37.00	$28.25	$29.00	$30.75	$34.88

Note: Returns, ratios, and turnover are based on average assets and capital.

The Germany subsidiary's fraud disclosure, coming only a few weeks after the initial ethics seminar, made Wantland wonder if his decision to initiate an ethics program had come too late or had been too limited in scope. Was this the best method of reinforcing the Tek culture and values given the problems and pressures of the past decade? Should Tek pursue further ethics-related steps and, if so, what should be the action's focus?

HISTORY AND BACKGROUND OF TEKTRONIX

The principal founders, Jack Murdock and Howard Vollum, started Tektronix in 1946. Their goal was to manufacture the finest oscilloscope in the world. (Note: The function of an oscilloscope is to visually display the electrical signals of electronic devices.)

The 1950s were a time of dramatic innovation in the electronics industry. Tek introduced numerous innovations in its products and began to develop a reputation for producing the highest-quality, most technologically advanced oscilloscopes in the world. To ensure that its customers were well served, Tek established its own sales force of technically knowledgeable "field engineers" rather than depend on independent electronics distributors (which was the normal industry marketing approach). This sales technique was consistent with the founders' view of Tek's responsibility to its customers. Tek continued to grow and in 1956 purchased 313 acres in Beaverton, Oregon for a new Tektronix "campus" (a term purposefully used to denote the collegiality and intellectual rigor of the work environment).

A new executive vice president was appointed in 1959 to deal with the management problems that followed the company's rapid growth. At the same time both Murdock and Vollum sought to reduce their responsibility for day-to-day operations. The early years of the 1960s were among the most technologically challenging yet faced, and Tek funded virtually any research and development project that might meet the new marketplace demands. While such scientific freedom was important at Tek, it was a relatively expensive, duplicative approach to product development. Concerns about lack of direction and unsatisfactory financial results caused Vollum to resume direct leadership of Tek in 1962. In the next nine years Tek increased international sales, restructured into a functional organization, had its first public stock offering, and formed a joint venture with Sony Corporation.

Tektronix suffered its first downturn in 1971. Net sales dropped 11.6 percent to $146 million from the 1970 high of $162 million, while earnings fell from $14.3 million to $9.3 million in the same period. Tek's problems at this time were not just caused by the general economic climate; explosive expansion, high profits, and inattention to management processes during the initial growth years had resulted in a poorly coordinated, complex organization. Informal communications channels that were effective in the old days were no longer adequate. As a result of the downturn Tek was forced to have its first layoff (350 manufacturing employees). A significant proportion of these workers were rehired within 90 days, but for many old-timers the level of trust in management never returned.

While Tek had expanded its product line during its early years, it still concentrated on oscilloscope manufacturing. In an effort to increase revenue, R&D efforts were expanded and by the end of 1971 Tek had introduced over

100 new products. In December 1971 sales, orders, and earnings were at a record rate. Real diversification came as Tek moved into the information display business, which became 20.0 percent of company sales by 1987.

In 1972 Howard Vollum stepped down as president. The new president, Earl Wantland, retained the Boston Consulting Group and Stanford Research Institute to help Tek deal with its organizational problems. An insider described the company at that time as "a strong vertical organization centered around the oscilloscope." The informal leadership styles of both Jack Murdock and Howard Vollum had fostered an intensely competitive atmosphere within Tek. Efforts to diversify suffered from this situation. Ideas that were brought up within one part of Tek would not get support from the others. The organizational challenge was to improve efficiency and control without stifling creativity and innovation while preserving major managers' influence and status. The proposed solution was a divisionalized structure composed of two business groups and eight divisions.

The 1980s were marked by a recession in high-technology industries and increased competition. By 1984 Tek's core business (oscilloscopes) was under pressure from competitors both at home and abroad. Tek missed the emerging market for color display terminals (even though it was a leader in all aspects of the technology required to produce the devices) and it was slow to move into the new generation of digital test equipment known as computer- aided work stations. As a result Tek experienced flat sales and declining profits and responded with a series of layoffs that reduced the work force from 24,000 to 17,000 (see Exhibit 1). The layoffs further reduced the morale and loyalty of many long-term employees who still believed in the unwritten "no-layoff" policy.

Between 1985 and 1987 Tek repurchased over 10 million shares of its stock at a cost of over $400 million. The company indicated that the goal of this use of funds was to increase shareholder return and to reduce the company's cost of capital. Observers questioned whether share repurchase was the best use of these resources given the competitive trends and conditions existing in the industry during these years.

Despite its recent economic problems, Tektronix finished the 1987 fiscal year as Oregon's largest private employer and was ranked 249th on the *Fortune* 500. Within the United States there were six manufacturing facilities, eight manufacturing subsidiaries, and 44 field offices. International operations included manufacturing in Japan (joint venture with Sony), the Channel Islands, the Netherlands, and the United Kingdom, and 62 field offices in 23 countries. (For a more complete chronology, see Exhibit 2.)

The Tektronix Culture

The Tek Culture is, in many ways, a direct reflection of the personalities, motivations, and values of Tek's two founders, Jack Murdock and Howard Vollum. The corporate motto, "Tektronix: Committed to Excellence," expressed their belief that customer service and quality products were the key ingredients to a successful enterprise. Success was not defined as acquiring great wealth, but rather as occupying honorably a financially secure market niche. An equally important guiding principle was the founders' innate respect for, and belief in, the dignity of the individual. They believed that the goals of the enterprise and of the employee should be complementary, not contradictory.

In the early days of the company there was no organization chart and no specific personnel policies. The founders wanted a small, friendly, family atmosphere. Early management practices and values such as open cash drawers, free coffee, use of first names, company-sponsored Friday afternoon birthday parties, and no reserved parking evolved out of the founders' personal views about the integrity of people and the climate in which they felt creativity and excellence could be fostered.

A Tektronix annual report put into words the elements that seemed to make up this culture:

- Respect for the individual human being.
- Profit sharing as part of the pay system.
- Open communications.
- Trust as evidenced by the honor system.
- Informal atmosphere.
- Little built-in awe of management.
- High tolerance for criticism.
- Absence of formal organizational charts.
- Preference for nonauthoritarian behavior.
- Promotion from within the company.
- Respect for technical expertise.
- Absence of labor unions.
- Passion for quality.

While actual practices and procedures did not always follow the ideal (e.g., organizational charts did exist and open communication was not always present), there were many examples of these values in action. Tek's commitment to quality and service was expressed in its policy of providing replacement parts virtually at cost. This policy was based on the assumption that the need to replace a component was caused by a design error and therefore the resulting costs should not be borne by the customer. Murdock and Vollum, the company's founders, believed that a successful enterprise could only be built through the close cooperation of all employees. Consequently, they instituted a policy of sharing a substantial portion (targeted at 35 percent) of the company's pretax earnings with employees as a way of instilling pride, creating a sense of ownership, and providing above- average compensation. This profit-sharing system was begun in 1949 and, at the time, was considered as a very enlightened management practice.

The egalitarian attitude of the Tek founders led to other innovative management and employee relations programs, including:

A retirement trust fund was established in 1953 and two employee stock plans, TEKEM and TEKEY, were set up to establish employee ownership in the company.

Workers were regarded as individuals with lifelong tenure; consequently, extreme care was taken in hiring.

Some employees were kept on the payroll even when their performance was not up to Tek's standards.

Direct effort was exerted, long before it became fashionable, to hire minorities and handicapped persons.

E X H I B I T   2   Tektronix Chronological History, 1946–1987

Date	Operations	Technology
1946	Tektronix, Inc., an Oregon corporation, certified on February 2, 1946.	
1947	Moved to new location on Hawthorne Blvd., Portland, Oregon.	511 Series: first "triggered scope."
1948	"Production sharing" bonus instituted.	
1949	Profit sharing introduced—25 percent of pretax income.	Transformers and inductors produced in-house.
1950	Tek's own sales force created.	
1951	Moved to Sunset Highway location, Beaverton, Oregon.	Cathode ray tubes (CRT) produced in-house.
1952	Tektronix Foundation established.	
1953	Profit-sharing retirement trust established.	530 Series: first plug-in scope.
1954	Stock split (2,000 for 1), creating 266,000 shares @ $1.00 par value.	315D: first portable scope.
1955	10th anniversary bonus—15 percent pretax income	540 Series: fast-rising plug-in scope with vertical amplifier.
1956	Purchase of 313 acres in Beaverton for Tek campus.	
1957	Completion of first building on Beaverton campus.	First transistor curve tracer.
1958	Foreign operation established on island of Guernsey.	
	First TEKEM shares issued in June.	
	TEKEY program instituted for rewarding employees.	
1959	Davis replaced Murdock as EVP.	525 Series: first vectorscope.
1960	Profit share revised to 35 percent of pretax income.	321 Series: first solid scope.
	Expansion into the Common Market.	
1961		Ceramic CRT envelope developed.
		Series 661: first sampling scope.
1962	Vollum replaced Davis; retained presidency and assumed EVP duties.	
1963	Tektronix's first public stock offering (540,000 shares).	
1964	Listed on New York Stock Exchange.	547 Series; first all-transistorized scope.
	Acquires Pentrix Corp. (manufacturer of spectrum analyzers).	
1965	Sony/Tektronix established.	
1966	Employee share purchase plan instituted.	
1968		Decision made to produce information display products (IDP).
1969	Corporate Group created.	7000 Series introduced.

Employees had access to an in-house counseling staff of psychologists and the company retained the Menningers, nationally known industrial psychologists.

Employee participation in management was encouraged and formalized through the "Advisory Group" in the 1950s.

Plant facilities were designed to be bright and airy with the physical surroundings as natural as possible. Corporate signs were understated.

The Founders' Management Style and Leadership

Howard Vollum's and Jack Murdock's talents complemented one another as if they had been preordained to start a company together. Murdock, general manager and personnel director until 1958, represented the company in the business community and was influential in the development of many of Tek's

EXHIBIT 2   *(Concluded)*

Date	Operations	Technology
1970	Began reorganization into functional groups.	Development of Gilbert gain cell.
1971	Death of Jack Murdock—May 16, 1971.	
	First employee layoff.	
	110 new products announced or introduced.	
1972	Wantland replaced Vollum as president.	326 Series: Dual trace miniaturized scope.
	Stanford Research Institute and the Boston Consulting Group created formal planning system for Tek.	
1973	Operational planning led to formation of business units.	
	First dividend paid—$.20 share.	
1974	Statement of Corporate Intent developed.	200 Series: ultra-miniaturized scope.
	Pension plan established.	
	Grass Valley Group, Inc. (CA) acquired.	
1975	Formation of business units led to divisionalization.	
1976	Formal corporate objectives published.	
1977	Walker Road plant opened.	
	100 percent stock dividend paid.	
1978	First executive incentive plan begun.	
1979		7104 Series: first gigahertz scope (fastest writing scope in world).
1981	Functional division structure in place:	
	Instruments Division.	
	Communications Division.	
	Design Automation Division.	
	Information Display Division.	
1983	Downsizing began (early retirement package offered).	2400 Series: state-of-the-art small portable scope.
1984	Employee layoffs occurred (severance pay provided).	Entered computer-aided engineering market.
1986	Death of Howard Vollum.	
1987	Fraud discovered in West German subsidiary.	

innovative personnel policies and practices. In the early years at Tek he personally knew every employee and assumed the role of "corporate father figure." As the company grew he was intimately involved in instituting humanistic policies aimed at imparting self-worth to every employee. He was particularly identified with maintaining the informal atmosphere throughout the company, encouraging participative management, and promoting company-sponsored social and recreational activities. These practices are credited by many in the company with creating high morale and increasing productivity.

Under Murdock's leadership Tek implemented a carefully designed profit-sharing program. Recognizing the cyclical nature of the electronics industry, Murdock sought a way to provide a soft landing to profits when volume declined and to share profits with employees when times were good. The program ultimately adopted combined a salary (which averaged about 90 percent of the industry norm) and a profit-share payment (which generally ranged from 10 to 15 percent of the individual's salary). In most years the total of salary and profit share resulted in a rate of pay above the industry average. When demand diminished, the profit-share percentage was reduced, thus trimming expenses.

Vollum, the engineer, pioneered the development of the oscilloscope and guided product development until 1971, when he resigned as president of Tek. His first love was the engineering lab and technical world. His leadership was marked by an "active interest in many aspects of the company: The design of the buildings, the landscaping, the tone and wording of ads . . . and the annual report to shareholders. Howard," someone said, "added value to everything."

The 1986 Tektronix annual report quoted Vollum as saying that he "disagreed with the concept of 'managing' and believed that a company should develop leaders rather than managers." To encourage creativity in product development he promoted an unstructured work environment. Neither Murdock nor Vollum were comfortable with confrontation. Their management style, and thus the style of the company, was one of consensus and careful decision making.

Generosity was the hallmark of both founders and this was mirrored in the large-scale philanthropic actions of the company. The Tektronix Foundation was established in 1952 with 5 percent of the company's net profits. Since Tek was a closely held company at that time, a substantial share of these monies came directly out of Vollum's and Murdock's pockets, as did the profit share that routinely exceeded 50 percent of pretax profits in the 1950s. Social responsibility and corporate generosity were values practiced by Tektronix as it became one of Oregon's major philanthropic donors.

Both founders believed in leadership by example and the provision of unconditional support to their employees. A Tek executive described Murdock and Vollum as having an "impeccable personal code of conduct." Honesty, humility, egalitarianism, and straightforward dealings with people characterized their management style. Their belief that human nature was basically good was expressed in Vollum's words, "Every individual wants to do the best job he or she can." This attitude permeated the company. One former employee indicated that for many years there were no strong controls to ensure honesty—it was expected.

ETHICAL PROBLEMS, THE GERMAN SUBSIDIARY, AND TEKTRONIX'S ETHICS PROGRAM

Ethical values had a special place at Tektronix. The founders' basic beliefs about the inherent integrity of the individual employee and the importance of an open and trusting environment set a clear behavioral tone for the organization.

Conversations with current and former employees indicated that Tektronix management believed its policies and controls were sufficient to eliminate significant unethical behavior. While this may have been true during the early years when the organization was small and top management knew each worker by name, some observers questioned the ethical correctness of a number of employee actions, including:

- Going to work for a competitor.
- Conducting a small outside business on Tek premises.

- Killing a project proposed by another division, even though it would be good for the company as a whole.
- Circumventing the resource allocation approval system by acquiring capital equipment in component parts.
- Laying off workers during downturns (even though the benefits provided were considered generous) without seeking to take other possible steps, including living with reduced profits.

Beyond these activities, the most significant ethical problem in Tektronix history came to light on September 14, 1987. On that day *The Wall Street Journal* reported that:

> Tektronix, Inc. said "improprieties and possible fraud" in its West German unit forced it to take a charge of $3.4 million, or 10 cents a share for its fiscal quarter. . . .
>
> For the quarter, ended Aug. 22, the maker of scientific instruments posted an 88 percent drop in net income to $1.8 million, or five cents a share, from $14.6 million or 38 cents a share, in the year earlier period. . . . Sales fell 1.8 percent to $299.5 million from $309.4 million. . . .
>
> A Tektronix spokesman said the company's finance manager in West Germany and his assistant loaned money, without the company's knowledge, to Rhein Neckar, a West German leasing concern. The leasing concern went into bankruptcy-law proceedings in August, he said. . . . The finance manager and his assistant have been fired . . . no legal action had been taken against the pair so far, but [the spokesman] declined to say whether any would be pursued. . . .

A few days later at Tektronix's annual stockholders meeting, Larry Choruby, senior vice president and chief financial officer, reported that the fraud was not just a singular type of action, but instead involved a number of different "scams." While Tektronix indicated in public documents that its review of the matter showed that all prudent precautions had been taken to prevent criminal conduct, some observers felt that pressures for results and lack of attention to the accuracy of reports may have contributed to the problem.

The announcement of the German subsidiary problem came more than six months after Tek took the first steps toward implementing a more formal ethics program. Larry Choruby directed a memo on January 13, 1987, to Earl Wantland indicating that more than five years had passed since the senior management group had reviewed the company's written statements of business ethics. The memo further proposed that Tek's Policy Council meet to review existing ethics policies, discuss and document proposed changes and verify the process of communicating these policies throughout the company.

The idea of reviewing Tektronix's ethics-related policies and taking steps to refine and renew them seemed very appropriate to Earl Wantland, especially at a time when the entire corporation was looking to him for direction and leadership. After some thought he recalled that Kirk Hanson of the Stanford Graduate School of Business had presented some interesting ethics materials to Tek's Manager of Managers internal management education program. He contacted Professor Hanson to explore the development of an ethics-focused corporate values workshop for Tek's senior management. At the conclusion of the discussions, Earl was convinced that Hanson's approach would result in greater ethical awareness at Tek.

Following some initial discussion between Tektronix and Professor Hanson, it was decided to modify and use a one-day business ethics seminar that Hanson had previously developed. After senior managers had gone through the seminar a decision would be made about extending it to lower levels of management. The seminar was aimed at an "examination of the operating principles and values of the firm, the strains on those values, and techniques for managing the risks when those values are under pressure." The initial seminar was held for the Policy Council on June 9, 1987, and it was repeated for one Tek divisional management team on September 16, 1987 (which, by coincidence, was two days after the *WSJ* story appeared).

The workshop's morning session explained the importance of the role that values and ethics play in an organization and used two case studies to involve participants and to communicate concepts. The afternoon session focused on identifying Tektronix's stakeholders, the organization's values, pressures on these values, and an action plan to deal with these pressures.

Earl Wantland decided to initiate a more active ethical program at this time, because he perceived a need to raise consciousness on ethical issues and bring ethics discussions "to the table." He explained "It's important that ethics be a legitimate thing to talk about with your subordinates, especially due to the number of unresolvable dilemmas present in the business world today."

Responses to the ethics workshop were mixed. Some people were quite positive, indicating that it was taken very seriously and was found to be useful. One participant said that "it raised a lot of issues, which is good. . . . It made it an OK thing to talk about." Another attendee said that some participants were disappointed with the lack of concrete guidelines: "We were hoping to have some very clear-cut guidelines that you could pull out of your pocket and use to know what to do in any circumstance. . . . I'm not sure what we really got out of it . . . but it made people aware that there were shades of grey and there were behaviors that some thought acceptable and others unacceptable." Some insiders expressed frustration over the timing of the seminars and felt it was a "diversion from working on the things that we really needed to make decisions on. . . . There were too many other pressing, critical business priorities and tremendous business pressures at that time."

At the same time the ethics workshops were being developed and presented, two other components of Tek's ethics program were moving forward. Alan Leedy, vice president, secretary, and general counsel at Tektronix, was given the task of updating the company's Code of Conduct. During the summer of 1987 a number of meetings were held and redrafts of the Code of Conduct written. A revised Code of Conduct was formally adopted in 1988 (see Exhibit 3). Tek's corporate controller and director of internal auditing were working on an Internal Controls Seminar, which was tentatively scheduled for early November 1987.

EARL WANTLAND'S DILEMMA

Earl Wantland realized that he was expected to improve Tektronix's profitability and to deal with the German subsidiary situation. Wantland was concerned whether recent external competitive and internal organizational pressures had simply overwhelmed both the company's traditional ethical values and its newly implemented ethics program.

Earl realized that his personal situation was a factor that had to be taken into consideration. It was common knowledge that Tek's Board of Directors was in

EXHIBIT 3   **Tektronix's Code of Conduct**

Business conduct that meets the highest ethical standards is fundamental to our success as a company. These standards were not acquired by accident at Tektronix. They grew out of the basic beliefs and values on which our company was founded and has operated since 1946. Today, Tektronix is a large and complex organization, operating in an increasingly complex world. Our traditional management and communication practices, based on individual initiative, judgment, and responsibility, are the "active ingredients." Preserving the advantages of this traditional Tek environment requires that we periodically revisit and reacquaint ourselves with the values on which it is based. That is what this brief statement is designed to do.

The basic standards of ethics and conduct that apply to Tektronix are simply stated. They are:

1. *Respect for the individual.*
   To base our business actions on a fundamental respect for the dignity and rights of each individual—including both those within our company and those outside it.

   Examples include the way we deal with our fellow employees and with our suppliers', customers', and competitors' representatives, and what we say about people, wherever they may work.

2. *Loyalty to Tektronix.*
   To bring to Tektronix our undivided business loyalty.

   Examples include avoiding both actual and apparent conflicts of interest. (A conflict of interest exists when someone at Tektronix has an advantage from a position, or has a duty to take a position, that is opposed to the position of Tektronix.)Further examples include avoiding situations involving favors offered, given, or received, or any appearance of favoritism.

3. *Compliance with the law.*
   To know, and conform our action to, the requirements of all applicable laws.

4. *Observance of other ethical standards.*
   To conduct the company's business in accordance with the highest standards of ethics and integrity.

   Examples of those ethical standards, in addition to those listed above, include honesty, candor, and integrity, which are the essential bases for our relationships with customers, suppliers, fellow employees, shareholders, and the communities of which we are a part.

There is one further guidepost that belongs on this list: our primary, fundamental, and continuing commitment to give unmatched value to our customer. Customers keep us in business. They pay for our facilities and raw materials; our labor; our research and development efforts; our taxes; and the profits that go to our employees as profit share and to our shareholders as dividends and capital appreciation.

Much of what is included here is also reflected in our Statement of Corporate Intent, which underscores the importance to us as a company of these basic values. Whenever we depart from the basic standards set out in this brief list, we only diminish our ability to keep this central promise to our customers.

October 11, 1988.

the process of searching for a new president for the company. In fact, Earl himself had been quietly encouraging the board to find a successor so that he could move out of direct, day-to-day responsibility for operations.

As he sat and considered his alternatives, he was aware that there was a certain tension between increasing company profitability and improving the ethical behavior of its employees. By putting more emphasis on an ethics program, time and money that might be devoted to improved results would be allocated instead to ensuring more "proper" behavior.

Some Tek employees and stockholders were urging Earl Wantland to expand Tek's ethical programs. Suggestions for additional steps came from many differing sources. Earl hoped that he could gather information about the ethics programs of other firms and thereby not have to "reinvent the wheel." (Note: In February 1988, the Business Roundtable, a Washington, D.C.-based group of major United States companies, published a study of the corporate

EXHIBIT 4   **Corporate Ethics Program Components**

In February 1988, the Business Roundtable of Washington, D.C. published *Corporate Ethics: A Prime Business Asset.* It contains descriptions of the ethics programs in 10 major international corporations: The Boeing Company, Champion International Corporation, Chemical Bank, General Mills, GTE Corporation, Hewlett-Packard Company, Johnson and Johnson, The McDonnell Douglas Corporation, The Norton Company, and Xerox. Six of these companies' ethics programs are summarized below.

The Boeing Company

1. All Boeing ethics policies are printed in one booklet entitled *Business Conduct Guidelines.*
2. Operating divisions conduct ethics training programs that are presented by divisional top management and roll down to lower levels in each division.
3. An "ethics advisor" is designated for the entire company. The advisor's role is to interpret ethics policies and provide advice and clarification.
4. Some of Boeing's subsidiary companies organize "ethics focal points," which serve as ethics advisors.
5. An Office of Business Practices handles employee calls relating to misuse of funds.
6. The Ethics and Business Conduct Committee, composed of Boeing's vice chairman and senior corporate executives from the legal, controller, and human resources functions, oversees all company ethics programs.

Chemical Bank

1. The Code of Ethics is the keystone of the bank's standards of conduct. It is revised approximately every 18 months.
2. Specific functional areas have drafted behavioral guidelines and standards of conduct (e.g., the Purchasing Department has its Standards and Ethics of Buying).
3. The chairman reinforces the code and guidelines in speeches, meetings, articles, and letters to employees.
4. Employee ethics education begins with new-employee orientation. A video features the bank's chairman discussing corporate values, and employees agree in writing to abide by the Code of Ethics.
5. Outside consultants conduct a two-day, off-site management seminar (Decision Making and Corporate Values). This seminar uses 12 case studies of actual ethical dilemmas faced by Chemical Bank managers.
6. A variety of special programs and procedures are used to head off unethical conduct (e.g., the Reporting and Compliance Department and a hotline for employees with personal financial problems).
7. Various committees and units monitor enforcement of bank standards (e.g., the Board of Directors Audit Committee does ethics reviews).
8. Chemical Bank maintains a long-standing reputation for corporate responsibility through a variety of community outreach programs.

General Mills

1. A strong, continuous, clearly communicated ethics leadership stance is taken by the company's CEO.
2. The company tradition of ethical behavior is based on actual management action.
3. Explicit statements of belief and policy were developed, including a Statement of Corporate Values and a Statement of Business Ethics and Conduct.
4. Compensation and performance evaluation are closely linked to individual social responsibility objectives.
5. High value is placed on open decision making and honesty.
6. A strong internal control network is maintained to supplement trust with awareness of actual behavior.
7. Violations of law or policy are punished.
8. The General Mills Foundation's gifts show support for community needs.

ethics programs of 10 major United States firms.[1] See Exhibit 4 for a selected look at corporate ethics program components.)

As Earl thought about his situation his eyes glanced across the room at the plaque containing Tektronix's Statement of Corporate Intent, which served as a reminder of what Tek stood for:

---

[1]The Business Roundtable, *Corporate Ethics: A Prime Business Asset* (New York: The Business Roundtable, 1988).

EXHIBIT 4   *(Concluded)*

Hewlett–Packard Company
1. Three documents summarize HP values and ethics: "The HP Way" describes how employees are expected to act; "The Corporate Objectives" outlines the objectives and principles that govern behavior of managers and employees at HP; and "Standards of Business Conduct" spells out an employee's ethical obligations to HP, to customers, to competitors, and to suppliers.
2. The core HP values include confidence in and respect for people, open communications, honesty, integrity, concern for the individual, and sharing benefits and responsibilities.
3. The Internal Audit Department reviews compliance with the standards (e.g., the auditing team interviews the top managers of each entity, asking a series of detailed questions related to ethical behavior and training of subordinates).
4. HP educational programs dedicate a major portion of their time to ethics.
5. A bimonthly magazine and videotape featuring company news items communicate HP values directly to all employees.

Johnson & Johnson
1. Our Credo is the ethical framework for all business decisions of the 150 J&J companies. It describes J&J's relationships with customers, employees, communities, and stockholders. The credo is revised every three years.
2. The Credo Survey provides employee feedback on company performance in relation to Credo principles.
3. Management willingness to take stands on ethical matters reflects its commitment to the Credo.
4. Compliance procedures include:
    a. The Executive Committee meets twice a year and goes over consumer complaints, surveys, audits, and safety records.
    b. Internal audits include safety, quality, and financial areas.
    c. Manager performance assessments cover Credo-related factors.

Xerox
1. An Understanding states the basic code of ethics in straightforward, informal, understandable language.
2. The Xerox Policy on Business Ethics outlines how managers should deal with customers, government officials, political contributions, and conflicts of interest.
3. The manager's handbook, "Managing in Xerox," discusses traditions, beliefs, values, policies, and practices in employee relations.
4. A large number of policy statements focus on specific issues or functional areas (e.g., the Statements of Corporate Policy deal with antitrust laws, the ethics of selling, and the ethics of buying).
5. An annual letter from the chairman and periodic letters from the president emphasize ethics and compliance.
6. Articles about ethics often appear in corporate publications like the *Agenda* or *Xerox World*.
7. Numerous training, development, and education programs focus on values and standards of conduct.
8. Strong internal control systems and an active Audit Committee of the Board of Directors monitor and enforce ethics.
9. Corporate responsibility is manifested in a number of company actions (e.g., the Xerox Foundation disburses over $10 million annually).

- To provide unmatched value in the product and service we offer customers.
- To recognize the one limitless resource: the individual and collective potential of the human being.
- To provide employees with maximum opportunity to exceed their own expectations.
- To achieve continued improvement in the use of company resources.
- To grow as a means of maintaining and renewing vitality.
- To insure that corporate objectives, wherever possible, enhance the goals of the immediate and larger communities of which we are a part.

Earl wondered whether this document, which he had helped develop in the early 1970s, would help him sort out just what to do about Tek's ethics program.

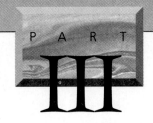

INSTRUCTIONS
FOR USING THE
STRAT-ANALYST™
SOFTWARE PACKAGE

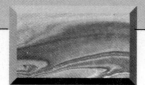

Instructions for Using
STRAT-ANALYST™

STRAT-ANALYST™ is user-friendly. Even if you are a novice on the personal computer, you can learn to use STRAT-ANALYST successfully in an hour or two. STRAT-ANALYST gives you the capability to *quickly* and *easily*:

1. Obtain calculations showing financial ratios, profit margins and rates of return, the percentage composition of income statements and balance sheets, annual compound growth rates, and Altman's bankruptcy index (a predictor of impending financial crisis).
2. Construct line graphs, bar graphs, pie charts, and scatter diagrams using any of the case data or calculations on file.
3. Make five-year financial projections of a company's performance.
4. Do "what-if" scenarios and compare the projected outcomes for one strategic option versus another.
5. Get report-ready printouts of all these calculations and graphs.
6. Go through an easy-to-use procedure for doing:

   - Industry and competitive situation analysis (as described in Chapter 3).
   - Company situation analysis (as described in Chapter 4).
   - Business portfolio analysis (as described in Chapter 8).

   Then get report-ready printouts of all your work.
7. Develop a set of action recommendations for:

   - Revising/improving a company's strategy and competitive position (a particularly useful option for Cases 1–20).
   - Improving strategy implementation and addressing internal problems/issues (a particularly useful option for Cases 1–6 and 26–37).

   Again, the software will generate report-ready printouts of your recommended action plan.

Complete step-by-step instructions for using all of these capabilities are provided on the STRAT-ANALYST screens as needed. You will find that the STRAT-ANALYST software package will give you a major assist in doing higher-caliber strategic analysis, and it will significantly cut the time it takes to do the number-crunching needed for first-rate preparation of a case assignment.

HARDWARE REQUIREMENTS

To successfully run STRAT-ANALYST, the computer set-up you use must meet the following requirements:

- IBM or 100% IBM compatible.
- 640k of RAM with at least 550k of RAM available for program execution after DOS and any other memory-resident programming has been loaded. (The program will recognize expanded memory but not extended memory.)
- At least one normal or high density removable disk drive ($3\frac{1}{2}$ or $5\frac{1}{4}$ inch).
- Printer access: IBM or Epson compatible dot-matrix printer, or HP LaserJet or compatible laser printer.
- DOS version 2.1 or later.

GETTING STARTED

Due to the variety of personal computer disk drive configurations that are available, we have provided separate start-up instructions for each of the three basic types of disk drive set-ups that will run STRAT-ANALYST.

A. INSTRUCTIONS FOR SYSTEMS WITH TWO $5\frac{1}{4}$ INCH REMOVABLE (FLOPPY) DISK DRIVES

1. To begin, you will need a DOS disk of version 2.1 or later (DOS stands for Disk Operating System) and your STRAT-ANALYST disks.
2. Insert the DOS disk (label side up) into Drive A of the personal computer and close the drive door. Turn the computer on and wait for it to start. The drive light is the signal that the disk drive is running. DO NOT OPEN THE DRIVE DOOR, INSERT OR REMOVE A DISK, OR STRIKE ANY KEY ON THE KEYBOARD WHEN THE DRIVE LIGHT IS ON.
3. You may be prompted to enter the date and the time. Type the date and the time if necessary—you may be able to get around this by simply pressing [Return] when prompted to enter the date and time.
4. At this point, the A prompt (A>) will appear somewhere on the left side of the screen. A> is your signal that the computer is ready for a command.
5. Remove the DOS disk from Drive A, insert in its place Disk 1 of STRAT-ANALYST (label side up), and close the door to Drive A. Be sure the write protect notch on Disk 1 is uncovered—otherwise you will get a disk error.

6. Insert Disk 2 of STRAT-ANALYST into the B drive and close the drive door. Be sure the write protect notch on Disk 2 is uncovered—otherwise you will get a disk error.

7. At the A prompt (A>), type:

RUN SA

and press [Return]. The drive light will come on again, signalling that Disk 1 is being loaded into the computer. After a few seconds the STRAT-ANALYST title screen will appear on the screen.

8. You are now "in" and you are ready to begin. Read the opening screens and follow the instructions as they come up.

B. **INSTRUCTIONS FOR SYSTEMS WITH ONE 5$\frac{1}{4}$ INCH REMOVABLE (FLOPPY) DISK DRIVE AND A FIXED DISK**

1. Turn on the computer and wait a few seconds for it to come on.

2. Enter the time and date if required. The C prompt (C>) will appear on the screen. C> is your signal that the computer is ready for a command.

3. Insert Disk 1 of STRAT-ANALYST into the A drive. (If the 5$\frac{1}{4}$ inch disk drive on your computer is drive B, insert Disk 1 into the B drive.) Be sure the write protect notch on the STRAT-ANALYST disk is uncovered—otherwise you will get a disk error.

4. Assuming you are using the A drive, type:

A:

and press [Return]. The A> will appear on the left side of the screen. (If the 5$\frac{1}{4}$ inch disk drive on your computer is drive B, type B: and press [Return].)

5. At the A> (or the B>), type:

RUN SA

and press [Return]. The drive light will come on and the STRAT-ANALYST title screen will appear soon thereafter. DO NOT OPEN THE DRIVE DOOR, INSERT OR REMOVE A DISK, OR PRESS ANY KEY ON THE KEYBOARD WHEN THE DRIVE LIGHT IS ON.

6. You are now "in" and you are ready to begin. Read the opening screens and follow the instructions as they come up. The computer will prompt you to insert Disk 2 as needed. When you use Disk 2, be sure the write protect notch is uncovered—otherwise you will get a disk error.

C. **INSTRUCTIONS FOR SYSTEMS WITH AT LEAST ONE 3$\frac{1}{2}$ INCH REMOVABLE DISK DRIVE**

1. Turn on the computer and wait a few seconds for it to come on (if the computer does not have a fixed disk you will need to put a DOS disk into the A drive).

2. Enter the time and date if required. The C prompt (C>) will appear on the screen. C> is your signal that the computer is ready for a command. (If the computer does not have a fixed disk an A> will appear on the screen.)

3. Insert your STRAT-ANALYST disk into the A drive. (If the $3\frac{1}{2}$ inch disk drive on your computer is drive B, insert your Company Disk into the B drive.) Be sure the write protect window (the square hole on the STRAT-ANALYST disk) is closed—otherwise you will get a disk error.

4. Assuming you are using the A drive, type:

$$\text{A:}$$

and press [Return]. the A> will appear on the left side of the screen. (If the $3\frac{1}{2}$ inch disk drive on your computer is drive B, type B: and press [Return]).

5. Type the following command:

$$\text{RUN SA}$$

and press [Return]. The drive light will come on indicating that your STRAT-ANALYST disk is being loaded into the computer, and the STRAT-ANALYST title screen will appear soon thereafter. DO NOT OPEN THE DRIVE DOOR, INSERT OR REMOVE A DISK, OR PRESS ANY KEY ON THE KEYBOARD WHEN THE DRIVE LIGHT IS ON.

6. You are now "in" and you are ready to begin. Read the opening screens and follow the instructions as they come up.

STRAT-ANALYST MENUS

Moving from file to file from screen to screen is easy with STRAT-ANALYST menus. STRAT-ANALYST menus appear in two forms: (1) in a column on the screen or (2) in a line at the top of the screen. To make a menu selection from either of these types of menus, simply press the letter corresponding to your menu selection.

Some STRAT-ANALYST screens will have no menu. These screens will always present instructions as to how to proceed (the usual procedure is to press [Return]).

Unless otherwise indicated, the [Esc] key will send you to the first screen (usually the main menu) for the particular file you are in. Use the [Esc] key to "escape" from any screen you have accessed; it will return you to the Main Menu of the current file. [Esc] will NOT cause you to leave the STRAT-ANALYST file you are currently using.

When accessing files with the STRAT-ANALYST Main Menu, you will (if you have $5\frac{1}{4}$ inch disks) occasionally be prompted by STRAT-ANALYST to replace Disk 1 with Disk 2 or vice versa. This occurs when the computer needs to access a file stored on the other STRAT-ANALYST disk—i.e., the one NOT currently in the machine. When you encounter this screen, instructions for proceeding will appear.

> FIXED DISK USERS: If you have loaded all of the STRAT-ANALYST disks onto your hard disk and the program prompts you to exchange disks, simply press [Return] to continue the execution of your menu selection.

Important Notice. All other instructions you will need to use STRAT-ANALYST's capabilities successfully are self-contained on STRAT-ANALYST and will appear on the screen as needed.

MAKING A BACKUP COPY OF STRAT-ANALYST

It is always good practice to make backup copies of your working disks. In the event that your original STRAT-ANALYST disks are lost or damaged, your backup copies will serve as replacements. To make backup copies, simply use the normal procedure for whatever type of computer system you work with.

Needless to say, you should always observe safe disk-handling procedures.

SUBJECT INDEX